FOR REFERENCE

Do Not Take From This Room

Twentieth-Century Literary Criticism

Guide to Gale Literary Criticism Series

For criticism on	Consult these Gale series
Authors now living or who died after December 31, 1959	*CONTEMPORARY LITERARY CRITICISM (CLC)*
Authors who died between 1900 and 1959	*TWENTIETH-CENTURY LITERARY CRITICISM (TCLC)*
Authors who died between 1800 and 1899	*NINETEENTH-CENTURY LITERATURE CRITICISM (NCLC)*
Authors who died between 1400 and 1799	*LITERATURE CRITICISM FROM 1400 TO 1800 (LC)* *SHAKESPEAREAN CRITICISM (SC)*
Authors who died before 1400	*CLASSICAL AND MEDIEVAL LITERATURE CRITICISM (CMLC)*
Black writers of the past two hundred years	*BLACK LITERATURE CRITICISM (BLC)*
Authors of books for children and young adults	*CHILDREN'S LITERATURE REVIEW (CLR)*
Dramatists	*DRAMA CRITICISM (DC)*
Hispanic writers of the late nineteenth and twentieth centuries	*HISPANIC LITERATURE CRITICISM (HLC)*
Native North American writers and orators of the eighteenth, nineteenth, and twentieth centuries	*NATIVE NORTH AMERICAN LITERATURE (NNAL)*
Poets	*POETRY CRITICISM (PC)*
Short story writers	*SHORT STORY CRITICISM (SSC)*
Major authors from the Renaissance to the present	*WORLD LITERATURE CRITICISM, 1500 TO THE PRESENT (WLC)*

ISSN 0276-8178

Volume 61

Twentieth-Century Literary Criticism

**Excerpts from Criticism of the
Works of Novelists, Poets, Playwrights,
Short Story Writers, and Other Creative Writers
Who Lived between 1900 and 1960,
from the First Published Critical
Appraisals to Current Evaluations**

Jennifer Gariepy
Editor

Laurie Di Mauro
Nancy Dziedzic
David M. Galens
Thomas Ligotti
Scot Peacock
Associate Editors

GALE

An International Thomson Publishing company I(T)P®

STAFF

Jennifer Gariepy, *Editor*

Laurie Di Mauro, Nancy G. Dziedzic, David M. Galens,
Thomas Ligotti, Scot Peacock, *Associate Editors*

Marlene S. Hurst, *Permissions Manager*
Margaret A. Chamberlain, Maria Franklin, *Permissions Specialists*
Susan Brohman, Diane Cooper, Michele Lonoconus, Maureen Puhl, Shalice Shah, Kimberly F. Smilay,
Barbara A. Wallace, *Permissions Associates*
Sarah Chesney, Edna Hedblad, Margaret McAvoy-Amato, Tyra Y. Phillips, Lori Schoenenberger, Rita Velazquez,
Permissions Assistants

Victoria B. Cariappa, *Research Manager*
Mary Beth McElmeel, Tamara C. Nott, Michele P. Pica, Tracie A. Richardson,
Norma Sawaya, *Research Associates*
Alicia Noel Biggers, Julia C. Daniel, *Research Assistants*

Mary Beth Trimper, *Production Director*
Deborah Milliken, *Production Assistant*

Sherrell Hobbs, *Macintosh Artist*
Randy Bassett, *Image Database Supervisor*
Robert Duncan, *Scanner Operator*
Pamela A. Hayes, *Photography Coordinator*

Library of Congress Catalog Card Number 76-46132
ISBN 0-8103-9306-9
ISSN 0276-8178

Printed in the United States of America

10 9 8 7 6 5 4 3 2 1

I(T)P™   Gale Research, an ITP Information/Reference Group Company.
ITP logo is a trademark under license.

Contents

Preface vii

Acknowledgments xi

Preface

Since its inception more than fifteen years ago, *Twentieth-Century Literary Criticism* has been purchased and used by nearly 10,000 school, public, and college or university libraries. *TCLC* has covered more than 500 authors, representing 58 nationalities, and over 25,000 titles. No other reference source has surveyed the critical response to twentieth-century authors and literature as thoroughly as *TCLC*. In the words of one reviewer, "there is nothing comparable available." *TCLC* "is a gold mine of information—dates, pseudonyms, biographical information, and criticism from books and periodicals—which many libraries would have difficulty assembling on their own."

Scope of the Series

TCLC is designed to serve as an introduction to authors who died between 1900 and 1960 and to the most significant interpretations of these author's works. The great poets, novelists, short story writers, playwrights, and philosophers of this period are frequently studied in high school and college literature courses. In organizing and excerpting the vast amount of critical material written on these authors, *TCLC* helps students develop valuable insight into literary history, promotes a better understanding of the texts, and sparks ideas for papers and assignments. Each entry in *TCLC* presents a comprehensive survey of an author's career or an individual work of literature and provides the user with a multiplicity of interpretations and assessments. Such variety allows students to pursue their own interests; furthermore, it fosters an awareness that literature is dynamic and responsive to many different opinions.

Every fourth volume of *TCLC* is devoted to literary topics. These topic entries widen the focus of the series from individual authors to such broader subjects as literary movements, prominent themes in twentieth-century literature, literary reaction to political and historical events, significant eras in literary history, prominent literary anniversaries, and the literatures of cultures that are often overlooked by English-speaking readers.

TCLC is designed as a companion series to Gale's *Contemporary Literary Criticism,* which reprints commentary on authors now living or who have died since 1960. Because of the different periods under consideration, there is no duplication of material between *CLC* and *TCLC*. For additional information about *CLC* and Gale's other criticism titles, users should consult the Guide to Gale Literary Criticism Series preceding the title page in this volume.

Coverage

Each volume of *TCLC* is carefully compiled to present:

- criticism of authors, or literary topics, representing a variety of genres and nationalities

- both major and lesser-known writers and literary works of the period

- 8-15 authors or 4-6 topics per volume

- individual entries that survey critical response to each author's work or each topic in literary history, including early criticism to reflect initial reactions; later criticism to represent any rise or decline in reputation; and current retrospective analyses.

Organization of This Book

An author entry consists of the following elements: author heading, biographical and critical introduction, list of principal works, excerpts of criticism (each preceded by an annotation and a bibliographic citation), and a bibliography of further reading.

- The **Author Heading** consists of the name under which the author most commonly wrote, followed by birth and death dates. If an author wrote consistently under a pseudonym, the pseudonym will be listed in the author heading and the real name given in parentheses on the first line of the biographical and critical introduction. Also located at the beginning of the introduction to the author entry are any name variations under which an author wrote, including transliterated forms for authors whose languages use nonroman alphabets.

- The **Biographical and Critical Introduction** outlines the author's life and career, as well as the critical issues surrounding his or her work. References to past volumes of *TCLC* are provided at the beginning of the introduction. Additional sources of information in other biographical and critical reference series published by Gale, including *Short Story Criticism, Children's Literature Review, Contemporary Authors, Dictionary of Literary Biography,* and *Something about the Author,* are listed in a box at the end of the entry.

- Most *TCLC* entries include **Portraits** of the author. Many entries also contain reproductions of materials pertinent to an author's career, including manuscript pages, title pages, dust jackets, letters, and drawings, as well as photographs of important people, places, and events in an author's life.

- The **List of Principal Works** is chronological by date of first book publication and identifies the genre of each work. In the case of foreign authors with both foreign-language publications and English translations, the title and date of the first English-language edition are given in brackets. Unless otherwise indicated, dramas are dated by first performance, not first publication.

- Critical excerpts are prefaced by **Annotations** providing the reader with information about both the critic and the criticism that follows. Included are the critic's reputation, individual approach to literary criticism, and particular expertise in an author's works. Also noted are the relative importance of a work of criticism, the scope of the excerpt, and the growth of critical controversy or changes in critical trends regarding an author. In some cases, these annotations cross-reference excerpts by critics who discuss each other's commentary.

- A complete **Bibliographic Citation** designed to facilitate location of the original essay or book precedes each piece of criticism.

- **Criticism** is arranged chronologically in each author entry to provide a perspective on changes in critical evaluation over the years. All titles of works by the author featured in the entry are printed in boldface type to enable the user to easily locate discussion of particular works. Also for purposes of easier identification, the critic's name and the publication date of the essay are given at the beginning of each piece of criticism. Unsigned criticism is preceded by the title of the journal in which it appeared. Some of the excerpts in *TCLC* also contain translated material. Unless otherwise noted, translations in brackets are by the editors; translations in parentheses or continuous with the text are by the critic. Publication information (such as footnotes or page and line references to specific editions of works) have been deleted at the editor's discretion to provide smoother reading of the text.

■ An annotated list of **Further Reading** appearing at the end of each author entry suggests secondary sources on the author. In some cases it includes essays for which the editors could not obtain reprint rights.

Cumulative Indexes

■ Each volume of *TCLC* contains a cumulative **Author Index** listing all authors who have appeared in Gale's Literary Criticism Series, along with cross references to such biographical series as *Contemporary Authors* and *Dictionary of Literary Biography*. For readers' convenience, a complete list of Gale titles included appears on the first page of the author index. Useful for locating authors within the various series, this index is particularly valuable for those authors who are identified by a certain period but who, because of their death dates, are placed in another, or for those authors whose careers span two periods. For example, F. Scott Fitzgerald is found in *TCLC,* yet a writer often associated with him, Ernest Hemingway, is found in *CLC*.

■ Each *TCLC* volume includes a cumulative **Nationality Index** which lists all authors who have appeared in *TCLC* volumes, arranged alphabetically under their respective nationalities, as well as Topics volume entries devoted to particular national literatures.

■ Each new volume in Gale's Literary Criticism Series includes a cumulative **Topic Index,** which lists all literary topics treated in *NCLC, TCLC, LC 1400-1800,* and the *CLC* yearbook.

■ Each new volume of *TCLC,* with the exception of the Topics volumes, includes a **Title Index** listing the titles of all literary works discussed in the volume. In response to numerous suggestions from librarians, Gale has also produced a **Special Paperbound Edition** of the *TCLC* title index. This annual cumulation lists all titles discussed in the series since its inception and is issued with the first volume of *TCLC* published each year. Additional copies of the index are available on request. Librarians and patrons will welcome this separate index; it saves shelf space, is easy to use, and is recyclable upon receipt of the following year's cumulation. Titles discussed in the Topics volume entries are not included *TCLC* cumulative index.

Citing *Twentieth-Century Literary Criticism*

When writing papers, students who quote directly from any volume in Gale's literary Criticism Series may use the following general forms to footnote reprinted criticism. The first example pertains to materials drawn from periodicals, the second to material reprinted from books.

[1]William H. Slavick, "Going to School to DuBose Heyward," *The Harlem Renaissance Re-examined,* (AMS Press, 1987); excerpted and reprinted in *Twentieth-Century Literary Criticism,* Vol. 59, ed. Jennifer Gariepy (Detroit: Gale Research, 1995), pp. 94-105.

[2]George Orwell, "Reflections on Gandhi," *Partisan Review,* 6 (Winter 1949), pp. 85-92; excerpted and reprinted in *Twentieth-Century Literary Criticism,* Vol. 59, ed. Jennifer Gariepy (Detroit: Gale Research, 1995), pp. 40-3.

Suggestions Are Welcome

In response to suggestions, several features have been added to *TCLC* since the series began, including annotations to excerpted criticism, a cumulative index to authors in all Gale literary criticism series, entries devoted to criticism on a single work by a major author, more extensive illustrations, and a title index listing all literary works discussed in the series since its inception.

Readers who wish to suggest authors or topics to appear in future volumes, or who have other suggestions, are cordially invited to write the editors.

Acknowledgments

The editors wish to thank the copyright holders of the excerpted criticism included in this volume and the permissions managers of many book and magazine publishing companies for assisting us in securing reprint rights. We are also grateful to the staffs of the Detroit Public Library, the Library of Congress, the University of Detroit Mercy Library, Wayne State University Purdy/Kresge Library Complex, and the University of Michigan Libraries for making their resources available to us. The following is a list of the copyright holders who have granted us permission to reprint material in this volume of *TCLC*. Every effort has been made to trace copyright, but if omissions have been made, please let us know.

COPYRIGHTED EXCERPTS IN *TCLC*, VOLUME 61, WERE PRINTED FROM THE FOLLOWING PERIODICALS:

Ariel: A Review of International English Literature, v. 11, July, 1980 for "Lawrence's Quest in 'The Rainbow'" by Daniel R. Schwarz. Copyright © 1980 The Board of Govenors, The University of Calgary. Reprinted by permission of the publisher and the author.—*Contemporary Literature*, v. 17, Winter, 1976. © 1976 by the Board of Regents of the University of Wisconsin System. Reprinted by permission of The University of Wisconsin Press.—*Critical Quarterly,* v. 20, Autumn, 1978 for a review of "The Rainbow" by R. P. Draper. Reprinted by permission of the author.—*Criticism*, v. XXV, Summer, 1983 for "Thinking Cassirer" by Hazard Adams. Copyright, 1983, Wayne State University Press. Reprinted by permission of the publisher and the author.—*English Studies*, Netherlands, v. 63, 1982. © The English Association 1982. All rights reserved. Reprinted by permission of the publisher.—*ETC.: A Review of General Semantics*, v. 33, December, 1976. Copyright © 1976 by the International Society for General Semantics. Reprinted by permission of the publisher.—*ETC.: A Review of General Semantics,* v. 46, Fall, 1989. Copyright © 1989 by the International Society for General Semantics. Reprinted by permission of the publisher.—*Journal of the History of the Behavioral Sciences,* v. IX, April, 1973. Reprinted by permission of the publisher.—*Man and World*, v. 6, September, 1973. Reprinted by permission of the publisher.—*Modern Fiction Studies*, v. XIII, Winter, 1967-68. Copyright © 1968 by Purdue Research Foundation, West Lafayette, IN 47907. All rights reserved. Reprinted by permission of The Johns Hopkins University Press.—*Mosaic: A Journal for the Comparative Study of Literature and Ideas*, v. XII, Autumn, 1978. © Mosaic 1978. Acknowledgment of previous publication is herewith made.—*PMLA*, v. 89, January, 1974. Copyright © 1974 by the Modern Language Association of America. Reprinted by permission of the Modern Language Association of America./ v. LXXVIII, March, 1963. Copyright © 1963, renewed 1991 by the Modern Language Association of America. Reprinted by permission of the Modern Language Association of America.—*Social Forces*, v. 16, December, 1937. Copyright 1937, renewed 1965 Social Forces. Reprinted by permission of the publisher.—*The D. H. Lawrence Review*, v. 7, Fall, 1974; v. 8, Fall, 1975; v. 13, Summer, 1980. © James C. Cowan. All reprinted with the permission of *The D. H. Lawrence Review.*—*The Explicator*, v. XVIII, November, 1959. Copyright 1959, renewed 1987 by Helen Dwight Reid Educational Foundation. Reprinted with permission of the Helen Dwight Reid Educational Foundation, published by Heldref Publications, 1319 18th Street NW, Washington, DC 20036-1802.—*The Hudson Review*, v. VII, Summer, 1954. Copyright © 1954, renewed 1982 by The Hudson Review, Inc. Reprinted by permission of the publisher.—*The Journal of Religion*, v. XXXV, July, 1955. © 1955, renewed 1983 by The University of Chicago. All rights reserved. Reprinted by permission of The University of Chicago Press.—*The Monist*, v. XLVI, July, 1936. Copyright © 1936, renewed 1964 *The Monist,* LaSalle, IL 61301. Reprinted by permission of the publisher.—*The Nation*, New York, v. CXV, December 20, 1922. Copyright 1922, renewed 1950 *The Nation* magazine/ The Nation Company, Inc. Reprinted by permission from *The Nation* magazine. © The Nation Company, L.P.—*The New Republic*, v. 137, November 25, 1957. © 1957 The New Republic, Inc. Reprinted by permission of *The New Republic.*—*The New Scholasticism*, v. XLII, Winter, 1968. © copyright 1968 by American Catholic Philosophical Association. Reprinted by permission of the publisher.—*The New Yorker*, v. 4, March 9, 1935. Copyright 1935, renewed 1963 by *The New Yorker* magazine. Reprinted by permission of the publisher.—*The Papers of the Bibliographical Society of America*, v. 64, 1970 for " 'Of Time and the River': The Final Editing" by Francis E. Skipp. Copyright 1970 by the Bibliographical Society of America.

Reprinted by permission of the author.—*The Review of Politics*, v. 29, April, 1967. Copyright, 1967, by the University of Notre Dame. Reprinted by permission of the publisher.—*The Thomas Wolfe Review*, v. 9, Fall, 1985; v. 11, Spring, 1987. Both reprinted by permission of the publisher.—*The Thomist*, v. XXXIII, October, 1969. Reprinted by permission of the publisher.—*The Yale Review*, v. XI, January, 1922. Copyright 1922, renewed 1950, by Yale University. Reprinted by permission of the editors.

COPYRIGHTED EXCERPTS IN *TCLC*, VOLUME 61, WERE REPRINTED FROM THE FOLLOWING BOOKS:

Beecher, Willard, and Marguerite Beecher. From "Memorial to Dr. Alfred Adler," in *Alfred Adler: His Influence on Psychology Today*. Edited by Harold H. Mosak. Noyes Press, 1973. Copyright © 1973 by American Society of Adlerian Psychology. Reprinted by permission of the publisher.—Black, Max. From *Language and Philosophy: Studies in Method*. Cornell, 1949. Copyright 1949, renewed 1977 by Cornell University. Reprinted by permission of Naomi Black.—Brachfeld, Oliver. From *Inferiority Feelings in the Individual and the Group*. Translated by Marjorie Gabain. Routledge & Kegan Paul, 1951. All rights reserved. Reprinted by permission of the publisher.—Canby, Henry Seidel. From *Seven Years' Harvest: Notes on Contemporary Literature*. Farrar & Rinehart, 1936. Copyright, 1936, by Henry Seidel Canby. Renewed 1963 by Marion Ponsonby Gause Canby. All rights reserved. Reprinted by permission of Henry Holt and Company, Inc.—Chase, Stuart with Marian Tyler Chase. From *Power of Words*. Harcourt Brace & Company, 1954. Copyright, 1953, 1954, renewed 1982 by Stuart Chase. Reprinted by permission of Harcourt Brace & Company.—Eggers, Walter F., Jr. From "From Language to the Art of Language: Cassirer's Aesthetic" in *The Quest for Imagination: Essays in Twentieth-Century Aesthetic Criticism*. O. B. Hardison, Jr. Press of Case Western Reserve University, 1971. Copyright © 1971 by The Press of Case Western Reserve University. All rights reserved. Reprinted by permission of the publisher.—Gardner, Martin. From *In the Name of Science*. Putnam-, 1952. Copyright 1952 by Martin Gardner. Copyright © 1957, renewed 1985 by Martin Gardner. All rights reserved. Reprinted by permission of Dover Publications, Inc.—Hagan, John. From "Thomas Wolfe's 'Of Time and the River': The Quest for Transcendence," in *Thomas Wolfe: A Harvard Perspective*. Edited by Richard S. Kennedy. Croissant, 1983. Copyright © 1983 by Croissant & Company. All rights reserved. Reprinted by permission of the publisher.—Hoffman, Edward. From *The Drive for Self: Alfred Adler and the Founding of Individual Psychology*. Addison-Wesley Publishing Company, 1994. Text © 1994 by Edward Hoffman. Foreword © 1994 by Kurt Adler. All rights reserved. Reprinted by permission of the publisher.—Karier, Clarence J. From *Scientists of the Mind: Intellectual Founders of Modern Psychology*. University of Illinois Press, 1986. © 1986 by the Board of Trustees of the University of Illinois. All rights reserved. Reprinted by permission of the publisher and the author.—Langer, Susanne K. From "On Cassirer's Theory of Language and Myth" in *The Philosophy of Ernst Cassirer*. Edited by Paul Arthur Schilpp. Library of Living Philosophers, 1949. Copyright, 1949, renewed 1977 by The Library of Living Philosophers, Inc. Reprinted by permission of the publisher.—Lipton, David R. From *Ernst Cassirer: The Dilemma of a Liberal Intellectual in Germany, 1914-1933*. University of Toronto Press, 1978. © University of Toronto Press 1978. Reprinted by permission of University of Toronto Press Incorporated.—McCullen, Maurice L. From *E. M. Delafield*. Twayne, 1985. Copyright © 1985 by G. K. Hall & Company. All rights reserved. Excerpted with the permission of Twayne Publishers, an imprint of Simon & Schuster Macmillan.—Montagu, M. F. Ashley. From "Cassirer on Mythological Thinking" in *The Philosophy of Ernst Cassirer*. Edited by Paul Arthur Schilpp. Library of Living Philosophers, Inc., 1949. Copyright, 1949, renewed 1977 by The Library of Living Philosophers, Inc. Reprinted by permission of the publisher.—Muller, Herbert J. From *Thomas Wolfe*. New Directions Books, 1947. Copyright 1947, renewed 1975 by New Directions Publishing Corporation. Reprinted by permission of the publisher.—Murry, John Middleton. From *Son of Woman: The Story of D. H. Lawrence*. Jonathan Cape & Harrison Smith, 1931. Copyright, 1931, renewed 1959 by John Middleton Murry. Reprinted by permission of Society of Authors as literary representive of the Estate of John Middleton Murry.—Priestley, J. B. From *English Humour*, Stein and Day, 1976. Copyright © 1976 by J. B. Priestly. All rights reserved. Reprinted with permission of Stein and Day Publishers.—Reichardt, Konstantin. From "Ernst Cassirer's Contribution to Literary Criticism" in *The Philosophy of Ernst Cassirer*. Edited by Paul Arthur Schilpp. Library of Living Philosophers, 1949. Copyright, 1949, renewed 1977 by The Library of Living Philosophers, Inc. Reprinted by permission of the publisher.—Rubin, Louis D., Jr.

PHOTOGRAPHS AND ILLUSTRATIONS APPEARING IN *TCLC*, VOLUME 61, WERE RECEIVED FROM THE FOLLOWING SOURCES.

Alfred Adler

1870-1937

Austrian psychologist.

INTRODUCTION

Adler is remembered both for his role in the early development of psychoanalysis and for his theories relating to "individual psychology," which stresses the essential unity and uniqueness of every individual and his or her "life-pattern." Many of the tenets of Adler's individual psychology, such as the importance of the "inferiority feeling" in character development, have become conventional psychological principles.

Biographical Information

Adler was born in a suburb of Vienna, Austria, to a prosperous middle-class Jewish family. As a young child he suffered from rickets and pneumonia, which spurred both his interest in the medical profession and his psychological insights into "organ inferiority" and the "inferiority feeling." After graduating from the Medical School of the University of Vienna in 1895, Adler began his career as a private practitioner, developing from the start a conception of the relationship of medical to psychological dysfunction, and in turn of psychological to social problems. In 1902 Adler joined and became a prominent member of Sigmund Freud's Vienna circle of psychoanalysts. Adler, however, was never a patient or a disciple of Freud, and fundamentally disagreed with him about the centrality of sexual trauma in the development of mental illness. In 1911, Adler broke away from Freud and founded the "Society for Free Psychoanalysis." He also began advocating his own system of "individual psychology." Adler's *Über den nervösen Charakter* (*The Neurotic Constitution*) was rejected as a post-doctoral dissertation by the medical faculty at the University of Vienna, which left Adler to lecture on psychology at continuing-education institutions for adults. Such appointments, however, were consistent with Adler's lifelong concern over social issues, as was his founding in 1919 of a pioneering "child-guidance" clinic in Vienna. In 1926 Adler accepted a visiting professorship at Columbia University in New York, thereby beginning an international career as a popular teacher, lecturer, and writer. In 1935, due to the rise of nazism, Adler moved his family to the United States. He died in 1937, during the course of a European lecture tour.

Major Works

Adler's first major work was *Studie über die Minderwertigkeit von Organen* (*Study of Organ Inferiority and Its Psychical Compensation*), which stressed the role that real and perceived physical inferiority played in spurring the child, as a form of compensation, to self-assertion and a quest for superiority. Adler's subsequent *The Neurotic Constitution* defines neurosis as the unsatisfactory, anti-social, or delusional enactment of this psychic self-assertion. In 1912 Adler founded the *Zeitschrift für Individualpsychologie* (*Journal for Individual Psychology*), which has continued publication under various forms. In *Menschenkenntnis* (*Understanding Human Nature*), which was written for a more popular audience, Adler focused on work, community, and sex as the primary components of human experience. Adler's concern with child-rearing and early education—the stages, according to Adlerian theory, in which individual psychology is molded—was reflected in publications such as *The Education of Children*. In later writings such as *What Life Should Mean to You* and *Der Sinn des Lebens* (*Social Interest*), Adler increasingly stressed the role that social and communal instincts play in tempering self-assertion and securing mental health.

PRINCIPAL WORKS

Studie über die Minderwertigkeit von Organen [*Study of Organ Inferiority and Its Psychical Compensation*] (nonfiction) 1907

Über den nervösen Charakter: Grundzuge einer vergleichenden Individual-Psychologie und Psychotherapie [*The Neurotic Constitution: Outline of a Comparative Individualistic Psychology and Psychotherapy*] (nonfiction) 1912

Die andere Seite: Eine massenpsychologische Studie über die Schuld des Volkes 1919

Praxis und Theorie der Individualpsychologie [*The Practice and Theory of Individual Psychology*] (nonfiction) 1920

Menschenkenntnis [*Understanding Human Nature*] (nonfiction) 1927

Die Technik der Individualpsychologie: Volume 1, *Die Kunst eine Krankengeschichte zu lesen*; Volume 2, *Die Seele schwererziehbaren Schulkinder* [*The Problem Child: The Life Style of the Difficult Child Analyzed in Specific Cases*] (nonfiction) 1928-29

The Case of Miss R. (nonfiction) 1929

Individualpsychologie in der Schule: Vorlesungen fur Lehrer und Erzieher [*Individual Psychology in the School: Lectures for Teachers and Educators*] (nonfiction) 1929

Problems of Neurosis: A Book of Case-Histories (nonfiction) 1929

The Science of Living (nonfiction) 1929

The Education of Children (nonfiction) 1930

The Pattern of Life (nonfiction) 1930

Das Problem des Homosexualitat [*The Problem of Homo-sexuality*] (nonfiction) 1930
The Case of Mrs. A. (nonfiction) 1931
What Life Should Mean to You (nonfiction) 1931
Religion und Individualpsychologie [*Religion and Individual Psychology*] (with Ernst Jahn) (nonfiction) 1933
Der Sinn des Lebens [*Social Interest: A Challenge to Mankind*] (nonfiction) 1933
The Individual Psychology of Alfred Adler: A Systematic Presentation in Selections from His Writings (nonfiction) 1956
Superiority and Social Interest: A Collection of Later Writings (nonfiction) 1965
Cooperation Between the Sexes (nonfiction) 1978

CRITICISM

H. M. Kallen   (essay date 1925)

SOURCE: "Psychology without Compromise," in *The Dial,* Vol. LXXVIII, March, 1925, pp. 236-39.

[*In the following review, Kallen offers a skeptical summary of Adler's system of individual psychology.*]

Nowadays, when people talk of the "new psychology," they mean prevailingly the ideas about the human mind deriving from the work of Freud and his associates. Although the custom is to lump this work in a single, solid, homogeneous mass, it is, in fact, still nebular, with three definite heads distinguishable in it. At the centre is the system of human nature constructed and stated, more or less architecturally, by Freud himself and accepted as the incontrovertible orthodoxy by the congregation of the faithful. To the right and to the left are the heterodoxies of Jung, the Swiss, and Adler, the Austrian. Both heterodoxies consist primarily in a rejection or deprecation of the cardinal orthodox dogma regarding the supreme *rôle* of sexuality in the life of man from birth to death. Jung absorbs this sexuality in a prior and wider stream of activity which turns his speculations regarding human nature into a metaphysical sentimentalism of the type of Eucken or Bergson. Adler subordinates this sexuality to a prior and wider "will-to-power" which allies his speculations concerning human nature with a metaphysical voluntarism of the type of Schopenhauer, Nietzsche, and Vaihinger. Both philosophers of mind differ from their metaphysical relatives in that they generate their speculative dogmas out of the material provided by means of the technique of psychoanalysis, of which both are practitioners. This technique is the common denominator of the three sects. The rest may be considered what Alder would call "arrangements" of the material drawn out by the technique.

[*The Practice and Theory of Individual Psychology*] is a redundant compilation of Adlerian "arrangements." It consists of a collection of twenty-eight occasional pieces, the earliest dating from 1911. Their sequence has been made, as nearly as it could be, logical rather than temporal, and the themes mount in technicality and range as the essays proceed. There are subjects as varied as the psychic treatment of trigeminal neuralgia and Dostoevsky; myelodysplasia and the individual-psychology of prostitution. Nevertheless, the essays do not avoid being boresomely repetitious. Dr Radin, in his work of translation, seems not to have succeeded so well as he might have in reducing the unnecessarily technical, involved, and pontificating style of the originals to a direct and readable English. Those who are familiar with Dr Adler's German will, however, not too greatly blame him. They will remember how much worse that is than even the bad German most of the German-speaking psychoanalysts seem to have fallen into.

Adler calls his system of human nature the system of "individual psychology." He intends by this phrase that the psyche of each man is always to be considered an organic and indissoluble unity. It is a whole, as the Hegelians used to say, with a capital W. In every single act or aspect of a life, no matter how contradictory any may be to any other, this whole is present as the effective agent. Its essence is to be a goal, generating the means of its attainment by its reactions upon its environment; its quality is of drive or will aiming at power, at superiority over its settings. The specific conditions it reacts to will provide the instruments with which it establishes its superiority *in feeling,* and the moulds of character in terms of which this superiority is pursued and maintained. The process begins in earliest infancy. Indeed, the first cry of the new-born is a sign of felt insecurity; an insecurity extended and intensified by its manifold relations to the adult world on which it depends. The child early begins to feel inferior, often because of some sensed or perceived inferiority of organ in itself. The whole of its life soon becomes a persistent effort to overcome this *feeling* of inferiority, and to replace it by a *feeling* of superiority and security. Such a feeling need not, and hardly ever does, register a real superiority and security. It is not a recognition of reality and an adjustment thereto; it is an aversion from reality, an evasion of it, a compensation for it. The *feeling* of superiority is attained by means of autogenous fictions and in the pursuit of a "fictitious goal." Sometimes it is created by bullying, aggression, self-assertion; sometimes by submission, weakness, all the frailties and perversions, many sorts of disease. Sexuality and sex-relations are often its instruments, and merely instruments.

The feeling of superiority, centred in the fictitious goal, is striven for universally. Everybody is doing it, but doing it without knowing, hiddenly. Everybody has a "secret lifeplan" that dominates and directs every phase of his conduct and evinces itself in his carriage, his postures, his fantasies, his dreams, his dogmatisms, his intolerances, his envies, his pleasure in the misfortunes of others, and so on. These are all substitutes for the struggle with reality, short-cuts to security; as a rule their intensity exceeds the requirements of self-preservation in the struggle. All the relationships they designate are reducible to the basic one of superior-inferior and this is especially symbolized in terms of the relationships of the sexes. The superior is always masculine, the inferior always feminine; Alder designates the demand for superiority as "the masculine protest." It stands out in neurotics.

The urge to superiority is not, however, the all of the Adlerian system of human nature. Over against the will-to-power is set "the eternal, real, physiologically-rooted community feeling." This Adler signalizes as the source of tenderness, love of neighbour, friendship, and love. His system of psychology, in fact, is described as seeking to make the "community-feeling" dominant—"to gain a reinforced sense of reality, the development of a feeling of mutual goodwill, all of which can be gained only by the conscious evolution of a feeling of the common weal and the conscious destruction of the will-to-power."

Well. . . .

In the matter of systems of psychology, you can pay your money and take your choice. The limen at which observation drops out and speculation sweeps in is very low. The body of observed and verifiable data is not too large and is neutral to the inferential systems which abut upon it. It will set at the same time with equal indifference and equal ease into the mutually contradictory elaborations of Freud, of Jung, of Adler, of the behaviourists, and all the other schools. Its neutrality carries a warning for those observers to whom correctness is more important than systematization, and accuracy more desirable than cure or reform. For my taste, Dr Adler is too ardent. He says in the preface:

> Individual psychology is now a definite science with a limited subject-matter and no compromise can be admitted. This intransigence arises . . . from the inexorable logic of a treatment of phenomena as mutually related. We shall never agree to change the fundamentals of human psychology which it has established and to adopt others in their stead. And we shall also never be under the necessity of undertaking a special enquiry into sexual factors long after the other aspects of psychic life have been investigated. Individual psychology covers the whole range of psychology in one survey, and as a result it is able to mirror the indivisible unity of the personality.

Maybe so. Unhappily the history of science, and of psychology no less, is a history of compromises. "Fundamentals" change very often in it, and "never" is a word not written in its painful lexicon.

Wayland F. Vaughan   (essay date 1927)

SOURCE: "The Psychology of Alfred Adler," in *Journal of Abnormal and Social Psychology*, Vol. XXI, No. 4, January-March, 1927, pp. 358-71.

[*In the following essay, Vaughan provides a survey of the tenets of Adler's psychological system.*]

The heterodox nature of the Freudian psychology and the authoritative, dogmatic manner of its presentation, both favored the rise of spirited opposition in its train. Prominent among the secessionists are Jung and Adler. Jung has gained a wide audience for his theories through the attrac-

tive literary form in which they have been advanced. Adler has been less fortunate in a literary way, for his heavy, involved style has obscured a system of psychology which, on its merits, deserves a larger public than it has reached. Convinced of the value of Adler's contribution, I believe it worthwhile to survey the principal tenets of his system in such a lucid manner as to awaken the interest of the general psychologist. I have selected those aspects of his theory that bear particularly upon the understanding of normal personality.

THE INDIVIDUAL-PSYCHOLOGICAL METHOD

Adler approaches the problems of psychopathology through what he calls the "Individual-Psychological" method. The task of psychoanalysis is to look for the life purpose of the individual, since it is in the service of this ideal that the symptoms assume their meaning. The individual psychological phenomena can be traced historically and genetically with reference to the person's plan of life about which all his activities are centered. Inasmuch as personal idiosyncrasies are related to the fiction of superiority peculiar to each person, traits of character can only be understood in the light of the goal of masculinity that constitutes the basis of that fiction. Conclusions should be drawn only when all the evidence is in and never from a single fact. Intimate knowledge of the individual's entire life, therefore, is essential to the legitimate interpretation of any one event in his career. Each case is to be judged only in its own peculiar setting. It is important to guard against over-generalization, to avoid "approaching the psychic life of the individual with a dry formula, as the Freudian school attempt" [*The Practice and Theory of Individual Psychology*].

Adler's psychology is thoroughly purposive. Every psychic phenomenon is a preparation for the attainment of some end. "We cannot think, feel, will, or act without the perception of some goal." Every one, healthy or diseased, lives to achieve his peculiar ideal of superiority in his own particular way.

"Every marked attitude of a man can be traced back to an origin in childhood." It is the purpose of the Individual-Psychological method to lay bare the sources of the feeling of inferiority, especially those associated with childhood, and to follow out the compensatory career of the masculine protest with its accentuated fictions,—and thus to disclose the aim toward which the particular person is working and the means he employs to arrive at his ideal.

THE NEUROTIC INDIVIDUAL

Although the neurotic "shows no single trait which cannot likewise be demonstrated in the healthy individual" [*The Neurotic Constitution*], there are certain traits that appear in exaggerated prominence, such as egotism and anxiety, which express themselves in intense modes of self-assertion that are peculiarly characteristic of this type of person. A few illustrations will show how Adler has worked out his study of the neurotic personality.

The neurotic goes out of his way to assert his independence. Most of his strange ways can be traced to a background of unsatisfied wants, predominantly sexual in nature. Thus a woman, to avoid the assumption of the feminine rôle in coition, will evince obstinacy, wildness, and unruliness in order to escape the shame of submission. A female patient will display an open hostility for her male physician, refusing to submit to his authority. Another person will be habitually cruel in his treatment of others and his friends will be at a loss to understand such behavior in one whose nature is fundamentally gentle. If his motives are analyzed, it may be found that he has set his mind on dominating others and for the sake of his masculine guiding line he has determined to shut out all tenderness as effeminate. The peculiarities of the neurotic center about sex as it is related to the attainment and the exercise of power. The man who is sexually impotent strives to exercise authority in other fields: With the underlying concept of power in view, the traits of the neurotic fall into line, taking on a new meaning in a consistent whole.

It is natural that the neurotic, with his deficiencies, should be unusually sensitive to the estimate others place upon his dignity. Cursed with the "sentiment d'incomplétude", and suffering under every slight injury to his self-respect, he grows over-insistent in his demands upon the respect of his associates. He looks for insults and he finds them, satisfying his suspicions but at the same time irritating the tender spots of his ego. To recover his lost dignity he may take an unjustifiable pride in his ancestry. He may develop a loud voice with which he noisily interrupts those who are conversing with him. He may become silent to impress others with the importance of his cogitations or loquacious to convince any listeners who may be dubious of his erudition. Or his self-esteem may be fostered by dreaming that he is dead and that all his relatives are mourning at the funeral. Though the means may vary in different cases, the end in view is always the enhancement of self-respect.

A prominent trait of the neurotic is his childlike timidity. Conscious of his vulnerable points, he lacks the confidence one needs for competition. His policy is dilatory in all matters, ever anticipating the disagreeable consequences which ensue upon action. He may even bring about minor defeats to justify his caution. If he is inveigled into a test of strength and is defeated, he is ready with an alibi to excuse his failure. In the fear of defeat, insomnia may suddenly develop to furnish a reason to pardon his losses. "I didn't do well to-day. I didn't sleep much last night." His fearfulness precludes any peace of mind. At times the neurotic may conjure up small tests to give him confidence for bigger ones but when the bigger trials face him, he finds an excuse to withdraw. In his dread of the uncertainties of life, he may even resort to suicide to obtain security from humiliation.

The neurotic is obsessed with a persistent craving for power. His highest happiness lies in the domination of others. This goal is reached by several approaches—actively (compensation), by appropriating instruments of power, and passively (decompensation), by developing neurotic symptoms which attract attention to the individual's importance. The goal and the achievement may both remain in the unconscious as the subject, in ignorance of the real drift of affairs, believes he is working for other ends than those he actually is contemplating.

One of the active roads to power is that of greediness. Money is power. The accumulation of wealth is consequently the amassing of influence. In his greed for gain, the individual grows more and more avaricious, eagerly sacrificing the good-will of his friends while he hoards the funds upon which he intends to base his authority. His unconscious will to power encourages stinginess. Adler tells of a patient who made a bequest to a certain institution and who for the rest of the day suffered from an attack of depression. His generosity pained him because it meant disloyalty to his miserly ideal. Another was bitter in his contempt for women. In uncovering the motive behind his antipathy, it was learned that he wanted to avoid marriage, not believing that two can live cheaper than one.

Another of the active modes of compensation is the exercise of superiority through the derogatory critique. The neurotic disparages others to elevate his own self-esteem. He is apt to shed his faults by projecting them on to others and then to pour upon them a deluge of disdain. The neurotic is always willing to "run down" anybody so that he may call attention to his own superior worth. By lowering the standing of others he renders easier the task of surpassing them.

When the direct paths to domination have failed, the neurotic resorts to decompensation—he develops symptoms by which he imposes his authority upon those around him. A neurosis indicates the failure of the guiding fiction. The individual covers up his unsuccess by a smoke-screen of handicaps. He exaggerates his suffering until the family is all attentive to him. He weeps loudly enough to be heard. He excels others in pain. The neurosis serves to head off the humiliation of defeat. Everybody is obliged to make allowances for "the poor fellow", as he is sick and nervous. "Think of what I might have been, had I not been so seriously handicapped." Neurotic devices are likely to crop out in a time of stress when a crisis imposes a strain on the personal resources. Artificial deficiencies excuse the patient from taking a chance in the ring of competitive life. It is easier for him to lord it over others by being sick than by staking his ability upon an actual test of strength.

Decompensation is an unfortunate device for him who falls back on it, since it forestalls constructive measures. The power gained through the enlistment of sympathy does not bring the enduring satisfaction that comes through winning the respect of competitors on the ground of actual merit. The construction of symptoms reduces the chances for the correction of the inferiorities since the individual glories in a false prowess that blinds him to his faults. Decompensation stands in marked contrast to that mode of compensation by which the realization of deficiency leads to the actual conversion of the weakness into strength or to the compensatory development of another source of power.

THE ORIGIN OF THE FEELING OF INFERIORITY

Adler, in his treatment of neuroses, was convinced that the seat of disorder invariably lies in an inferior organ. The organic deficiency is the weak link that debilitates the whole personality through the psychic disturbances involved. Somatic anomalies have been overlooked in the past because physicians have failed to see the defect behind the compensatory blinds. Adler found that specific bodily weaknesses are very common in the neuroses and he observed that a feeling of inferiority, an inferiority complex, is a complicating factor. As an analyst Adler was interested in organic inferiorities only as they form a basis for the psychical disorders to which they give rise. The ***Studie ueber Minderwertigkeit von Organen [Study of Organ Inferiority and Its Psychical Compensation]*** was published in 1907 and on this work as a physiological foundation he developed the psychological theory propounded in his **"Ueber Neurotische Disposition"** of 1909, in which he traces the wide derangements of the psyche that flourish on the soil of the neurotic constitution. [W. A. White, in an introduction to Adler's ***The Neurotic Constitution***, writes]: "The distinctive feature of Adler's approach to the problem of the neurotic character traits is that it approaches from the organic rather than from the functional side and in this way, I think, affords a very valuable viewpoint because it tends to bring together the organicist and the functionalist, who have too long been separated by the misconception of irreconcilable differences between mind and body."

There are five aspects in which one should examine organic imperfection. (1) Heredity plays a significant rôle in inferiority. Since the mechanism of transmission is sexual, Adler argues that an hereditary weakness must exist in the spermatozoa and the ovule. "There exist no organ-inferiorities without an accompanying defect in the sexual apparatus,"—an observation that he reiterates time and again under the principle of "manifold organ inferiorities". Heredity, according to Adler, must be considered in analyzing neurotic disorders, since "the accentuated traits of character are to be found already in the neurotic disposition where they give rise to peculiarities and perversions of conduct".

(2) Disease is another factor to be taken into account in the study of inferiority. Disease picks on the inferior organ as the weakest spot in the defense of the organism. In renal pathology, it is helpful to remember that most renal diseases are due to a fundamental inferiority of the urine-excreting apparatus. Inferior organs invite disease.

(3) There are certain definite stigmata that should be diagnosed as peripheral traces of an underlying organ-inferiority. Very often these outward signs, such as abnormal eyelids, are believed to be the whole thing and the physician fails to discover the fundamental disability of which the peripheral evidences are only indicators. Where stigmata are found, further search will reveal a deep-seated organic blemish at the root of the trouble.

(4) Childish defects also point to underlying somatic imperfections. Wet garments should not be laid to wilful neglect but to organic inferiority. A child, following the pleasure principle, takes the line of least resistance and certain organs of the body which are the source of pleasure-giving sensations cannot be trained, on account of their inherent deficiency, to conform to cultural requirements. Lack of control of the bowels, for instance, indicates a basic organic deficiency. "The limitation of organic sensory pleasure for the benefit of cultural progress becomes the test of organic normality."

(5) Reflex anomalies stand as indications of organ-inferiority. Both the deficiency and exaggeration of reflexes mark the presence of a defective physiological mechanism.

Inferiorities fall into two categories, the morphological and the functional. Morphological inferiority dates from the period of embryonic growth. "The organ inferiority usually enforces itself genetically in the individual and hinders embryonic or functionally related parts from fully developing. . . . The inferior organ bears with it in morphology and function, its embryonic characteristics." Causes of deformity lie in a primitive lack of formative material, inflammatory processes during embryonic development, or the disturbing influence of a neighboring organ during the fetal period. If the faulty organ proves ineffective, regression occurs.

Functional inferiorities make up the chief group, since morphological defects manifest themselves through some disorder of function. The organism has to adapt itself in one way if it fails in another. Compensation through the central nervous system passes the burden on from the incapacitated to the healthy organs. It is a case of the strong helping the weak organs where environmental necessity calls for adequate performance.

The inferior organ is a handicap which nourishes a feeling of inferiority. Adler even goes so far as "to refer all phenomena of neuroses and psychoneuroses back to organ inferiority". Organic deficiency is very significant for personality through the range of serious psychological consequences to which it gives rise. One consequence is the attempt at compensation. "The realization of somatic inferiority by the individual becomes for him a permanent impelling force for the development of his psyche."

COMPENSATION

In each of us there is a persistent craving for security, a "Sicherungstendenz". The realization of a failing, by undermining the sense of certainty, exaggerates the determination to over-come the handicap. There is a tendency to do too much rather than not enough towards building up strength and we find the inferior organ may actually become supernormal (overcompensation). In the blind, for example, the touch organs grow supersensitive. It is possible, therefore, that the inferior organ may develop a functional capacity exceeding that of the normal. "The cause lies in the compulsion of a constant training in the capacity for adaptation and variability often adhering to inferior organs and surely also in the development of the related nervous and psychical complexes heightened by inner attention and mental concentration upon the weaker organ."

A special interest seeks to protect the vulnerable point from excessive strain and to give it a chance to grow strong enough to withstand its adversaries successfully, for it is especially the infirm structures that fall a prey to any dangers which beset the organism. When there is a call for reinforcements, the surplus energy is drawn from the central nervous system. Organic defect may thus be compensated by an excess of nervous activity. If the compensation requires too much effort and the central nervous system is overtaxed, there is a drain on the bodily resources and neurosis results. Where any part of the organism is unduly feeble, the constitution must be strong to endure the stresses involved in protecting its vulnerable spot. Some organ has to double up on its performance, as it were, to take care of the extra load left uncarried by the defective organ. The neurotic constitution, being unable to effect an adequate compensation for an inferiority, amounts to a predisposition towards breakdown or neurosis. Compensation, in any case, is a difficult task.

There are various types of compensatory activity, each appropriate to the need which it is fulfilling. (1) There may be vicarious replacement of function by a symmetrically situated organ, such as we find in the cerebrum, lungs, kidneys, and thyroids. (2) Compensatory aid may be rendered by a portion of an organ related to the defective organ, in the case of asymmetrical structures. (3) There may be the employment of another organ, such as we observe in the cardiac hypertrophy by which a deficiency of the kidney or lung is compensated. (4) Or, lastly, we may see the heightened use of the inferior organ itself.

Compensation tends to carry over into overcompensation. Beethoven and Mozart both had deformed ears. The fact that the same organ is apt to be inferior in the different members of a family helps to explain why they often suffer from the same disease or repeatedly follow the same, usually artistic, profession. Adler relates the case of one family in which three children suffered from otosclerosis. The other two children displayed marked musical ability, one of them afflicted with herpes of the auricle and both of them showing indications of organ-inferiorities in the mouth, nose, and sexual apparatus. Palatal reflex anomalies are found often in cooks, speakers, and singers. One patient with a deformed palatal cleft and pulmonary weaknesses, is an excellent singer. Says Adler, "I should only like to emphasize that to me the impression of the connection between a beautiful singing voice and the organ inferiority which I have outlined is a definite one, and that I have considerable material to support it."

THE ACCENTUATION OF THE FICTION

Under the impulse from his feelings of inferiority the neurotic seeks salvation for his self-regard in the elaboration of a fiction, a false ideal, after which he strives, in order to redeem his good standing. Unable to assert himself as a man of power, he acts "as-if" he were strong. In fancy he confers upon himself the glory withheld by reality.

The fiction comes into being to save his self-esteem. The fictitious ideal is a grandiose conception by means of which the individual bestows a symbolic style upon himself. The dream is never related to reality because it is beyond the possibility of achievement. Burdened with his handicaps the neurotic can only win success in the realms of fancy to which his ideal is accommodated.

The fiction, aiming as it does, at the maximation of the ego-consciousness, draws all the psychic forces into its service. No energy is left for actual accomplishment. All the

neurotic's strength is dissipated in daydreams in which he appears in the rôle of hero. "All psychological powers are under the control of a directive idea, and all expressions of emotion, feeling, thinking, willing, acting, dreaming, as well as all psychopathological phenomena are permeated by one unified life-plan"—the goal of converting failure (inferiority) into success.

The concentration of energy upon one goal makes for efficiency in that one line. It is a wise move where the end is discreetly chosen. It is in the selection of his ideal that the neurotic plots his own doom. The plan he outlines for himself not only remains unrelated to reality but also beyond the bounds of realization for one of limited capacities. A "distance" remains between the dreams of the neurotic and their fulfillment, between his ideals and their accomplishment. He grows more unsure of himself—of his ideals and of his ability to attain them. A strain is imposed upon the personality as he tries to do justice to both the real and imaginary requirements facing him. The result is neurosis. Fancy dubs him a hero—but the glory fades as a dream, for the achievement is only fictitious.

THE MASCULINE PROTEST

The "Sicherungstendenz" is especially strong where self-respect is jeopardized by the presence of inferiority. Assurance mechanisms are plentiful. A man who is drawn away from his ideal of chastity by lustful desires rears up in his mind, as an assurance process, the syphilophobia syndrome and behind this wall he feels safe. Bjerre has put the theory succinctly when he states that the neurosis is the negation of life; the assurance mechanism is the passive side of this negation; the active side is the masculine protest.

The masculine protest is a form of the will to power, under the impulsion of which a weak person aims to become strong—strong like a man. Manliness is the symbol of forcefulness and superiority. "The wish to be a complete man" is the heart of the protest against the limitations of inferiority.

Adler bases his theory of the masculine protest on psychical hermaphroditism. Every personality holds within its psyche both masculine and feminine tendencies. The conflict of these two elements can be resolved only by an adequate synthesis of the feminine with the masculine, with the latter side in authority. The neurotic denies his feminine trends instead of applying himself to synthesize them with the masculine. The result is a split personality.

The masculine constellation includes power, strength, greatness, riches, knowledge, violence, and victory. The feminine traits, not so brilliant an array, comprise the craving of a child for nestling, weakness, submissiveness, despair, helplessness, timidity, shyness, and fear of punishment. In short, masculinity means dominating power, femininity, cringing submission.

It will be easy now to see what the masculine protest signifies in psychological terms. Adler assumes that the feminine sex is inferior and that the superiority of the male is generally recognized. To be a complete man, therefore, is to succeed well in the art of self-assertion. The neurotic makes the next best move, in acting as if he were a complete man.

The attitude toward the contrasting trends, the feminine and the masculine, makes up the antithetical perspective. The mind tends to classify experience into high-low, above-beneath, strong-weak. It is the contrast between the opposing forces that exaggerates the masculine protest. The neurotic views everything in the light of his ideal of manliness. "This formula: 'I wish to be a complete man' is the guiding fiction in every neurosis."

In woman the protest is to act like a man. The little girl who sees the large male genitals and wonders why she has no such organs, is seized with feelings of inferiority. Later in life she has to humiliate herself before man in sexual intercourse. It is she who has to submit to man and it is she who must bear the children. As a protest against her inferior rôle she assumes a defiant front. She becomes a "tomboy", a "heart-breaker", or a nagging wife, or she refuses to participate in coition. In man the protest is the aspiration toward completeness, toward the fullest development of masculinity.

The will to power, the masculine protest, is a force that drives us on to the perfection of our capacities. The aggressive impulse fed by the ideal of manliness refuses to acknowledge inferiority and clings steadfastly to the cultivation of strength.

ADLER AND FREUD

Let us first consider two points on which Adler diverges from Freud. In the first place, Adler attacks the view that the libido is the force behind the symptoms of the neurosis. Adler contends that the force, on the contrary, is derived from the adoption of an ideal end (a complete man) for the attainment of which the neurotic's powers are mobilized. In other words, the important thing is not the force behind the neurosis but the goal toward which the force is directed. The libido works in normal as well as abnormal individuals. It is not the libido, therefore, that is the critical cause of psychic disturbance. It is, rather, the fictitious nature of the goal upon which the neurotic is bent. The perversion of the libido is due to the abnormality of the ideal. Compensation, not sex, furnishes the motive force.

Secondly, sexual feeling is not the hub of the psychic universe. The sex-content of neuroses originates in the hermaphroditic antithesis of masculine-feminine. The sexual fantasy is a compulsion toward the masculine goal. Sex is symbolically represented in the neurosis by the end upon which all strivings are concentrated. Freud failed to recognize the symbolic character of the process, overlooking the fact that sex merely offers the most convenient terms in which to posit the antithetical scheme of the masculine protest. The Oedipus complex thus symbolizes the desire of the son to dominate his mother. Infantile sex wishes represent the struggle to outgrow the limitations of childhood. The sexual evidences are manifestations of a deeper tendency of human nature, the desire for power.

Though divergent in the details of their theories, Adler and Freud still remain in fundamental agreement, their denials to the contrary notwithstanding. Adler bases his

whole theory on organ inferiority and psychical compensation. He approaches Freud when he admits that the inferior organ is most frequently sexual. Sex, for both then, plays a main rôle, though playing that rôle, to be true, from apparently different motives—the one out of sexual desire, the other out of the wish to dominate the opposite sex. It might be suggested that the domination of the opposite sex is actually an integral element in the satisfaction of desire, so that the apparent divergence, upon more thorough examination, dissolves into virtual agreement. The neurotic, in following out his masculine protest, resorts, to certain safety-devices, often infantile and regressive tendencies, that afford him a refuge from uncertainty. Why do we have these devices! A feeling of uncertainty threatens the integrity of the individual's self-esteem. The neurotic must posit a goal to make life bearable. "The entire picture of the neurosis as well as all its symptoms are influenced by, nay, even wholly provoked by an imaginary fictitious goal." Such is the service of fictions in thought, action, and volition. The motivation is sexual perhaps in its origin, but more specifically, the conviction of inferiority within the sex life.

CONCLUSION

Without going much into detail, I am going to select a few weaknesses in Adler's theory for criticism. Let us first examine the proposition that neuroses are most frequent among women during pregnancy, parturition, and climacteric, because these feminine periods impress upon the female a feeling of inferiority. Adler here has taken a contributing factor and elevated it to the position of sole cause. It seems to me that another account of the etiology is more sound. [in C. Mercier *Sanity and Insanity*] attributes the breakdown to what he calls the "indirect stress of internal origin". During puberty the development of the reproductive organs adds a new complication to the physical and psychical life. The beginning of love is beset with trials that were never known before. The presence of a new physiological structure aggravates the coenesthesis. During the menses, pregnancy, and parturition vast organic changes are taking place which are bound to have their effect on the psyche, exclusive of any feeling of inferiority that might be involved. At the climacteric, the reproductive organs again alter their structure and the change exerts another stress upon the nervous system. Painful menstrual periods, the dreaded "change of life", various female troubles with pregnancies scattered in between, lead the female to believe she pays a heavy penalty for being a woman. She envies man, not for his power alone, but the mere freedom from feminine ills which he enjoys. It seems more sane to place the responsibility for the neurosis primarily upon the strain which organic vicissitudes impose upon the nervous system and the psyche. Of course the feeling of inferiority may be one of the psychical effects, but it need not be the principal effect, much less the one eminent cause of the neurosis.

Next arises the question as to whether all women want to be men. Masculinity is symbolic of domination and femininity of submission, but how many of us use this symbolism in dealing with experience! The masculine protest, for most of us, is not the longing to be a complete man, but less symbolically the craving for power. There is no necessity that compels us to take the circuitous path through symbolism. We want power primarily and we want to be men secondarily, if that means power. Take the case of a girl, mentioned by Adler, who suffered from attacks of migraine. The headache was a neurotic symptom by means of which she hoped to rule her family. It was a part of her wish to be a man. But headaches are not especially manly. Neurotic symptoms savor more of childishness than of virility. If the dominant wish was to be a man, masculine hardiness would be a more suitable trait to develop. Migraine cannot represent masculinity, even symbolically. It is more honestly sensible to say frankly that what the girl wants is not a headache, or manliness, but power. The desire for domination is the crucial motive.

Strange to say, Adler is at his worst in his treatment of sex problems. Consider, for instance, his account of exhibitionism. A girl is seized with shame because she does not posses the large external genitals that belong to the male. She feels she has been slighted by her Creator. Thereupon, she conceives a plan to assert herself. She exposes her genitals "as-if" she were a man, satisfying herself by this procedure that she has convinced her audience that she must no longer endure the disgrace of being labeled a woman. What an absurd picture! Exhibitionism is motivated by sex desire. There is no pleasure in exposing one's genitals to the view of one's own sex. The exposure of the sex organs before the opposite sex, however, gives rise to the agreeable sensations of lust. Adler strains his theory to cover facts more simply and more adequately explained on other bases.

Adler has called attention to a point of view that is valuable for medicine and for psychology. The scheme of motivation embodied in compensation for inferiority can be legitimately extended to account for many of the mysteries that surround the strange ways of man. The work of Adler has given us a deeper insight into human nature.

Herbert Blumer   (essay date 1928)

SOURCE: A review of *Understanding Human Nature*, in *American Journal of Sociology*, Vol. XXXIV, No. 2, September, 1928, pp. 391-93.

[*In the following review, Blumer provides an assessment of three Adlerian themes: the inferiority feeling, the life-pattern, and the nature of character.*]

Of all psychiatrists Dr. Adler seems to be most akin to sociologists in spirit and perspective. In earlier works he has shown a keen appreciation of the rôle of social relations in personal development; in [**Understanding Human Nature**], which is constructed out of a series of popular lectures, we have the simplest and clearest picture of these views.

Amid a wealth of varied and valuable discussion his central theses are easily isolated. They are essentially three: the basic importance of the inferiority feeling, the presence in each of us of a life-pattern, and the appearance of character traits as expressions of the life-pattern. The conception of the inferiority relation scarcely needs any stating.

Every child acquires a feeling of inferiority because of "his inability to cope single-handed with the challenges of his existence." From this feeling of inferiority arises the life-pattern. The feeling of inferiority "determines the very goal of his existence and prepares the path along which this goal may be reached." "It is this goal which gives value to our sensations, which links and co-ordinates our sentiments, which shapes our imagination and directs our creative powers, determines what we shall remember and what we must forget;. . . . our very perceptions are prejudiced by it, and are chosen, so to speak, with a secret hint at the final goal toward which the personality is striving." It results that the individual shows an enduring behavior pattern throughout life, even though the situations encountered vary greatly. The medical implication of this view is apparent. The neurotic is one who has an unsatisfactory and unsocial life-pattern; he is cured by revealing to him this unconscious life-pattern and by aiding him to construct a new goal or pattern. Traits of character—such as vanity, hate, anxiety, cheerfulness, joy, anger, and disgust—are "only the external manifestation of the style of life, of the behavior pattern of any individual." These traits are not inborn but are forced into being by the secret goal of the personality.

This short presentation scarcely does justice to the discriminating and thorough treatment given these views by Dr. Adler, but it will suffice to indicate the general tenor of the work. Dr. Adler's view of the inferiority complex is well known; it has run the gauntlet of criticism, but alas, has emerged untested. What truth it contains is still a matter of controversy. It seems to the reviewer that Dr. Adler errs in attributing the appearance of the inferiority feeling to the helplessness of the infant. To feel one's self inferior presupposes that one views one's inadequacies through the eyes of others. This identification with another marks the birth of personality and is scarcely to be found in the infant. To assign the inferiority feeling to personal experience is sound; to base it on mere physical helplessness is to make it a phenomenon essentially of mammalian life, and not merely human life.

The critical point, as well as the pivot, of the discussion which Dr. Adler gives in this book is constituted by the conception of a life-pattern. The contention that the life of each of us falls into a definite pattern which is formed early and endures unchanged amid great variety in experience is as important as it is startling. Here is a view built out of Dr. Adler's vast clinical experience which cannot be passed over lightly. Unfortunately little concrete material is given to its support in this volume, due, likely, to lack of space. What constitutes the nature of this life-pattern? Is it as unchanging as Dr. Adler tells us? To the reviewer it seems that constancy in personal behavior depends upon the maintenance of a certain conception of one's self, whatever be the complex of psychological factors which is implied by this amorphous concept. To change this pattern one must change one's conception of one's self. Indeed, this seems to be exactly the aim and means involved in the scheme of therapeutics advocated by Dr. Adler for the cure of neuroses. If, however, to change one's conception of one's self is to change one's life-pattern, personal life-patterns presumably are not as crystallized as Dr. Adler thinks.

One is forced to recognize that however amiss his interpretations, Dr. Adler understands human nature in a most intimate way. Probably no other living writer shows a shrewder insight into its character nor a more comprehensive grasp of its elements. His book is replete with keen observations and revealing judgments. The social psychologist who reads this work in a sympathetic mood will garner a rich income.

E. L. Grant Watson (essay date 1932)

SOURCE: A review of *What Life Should Mean to You,* in *The Criterion,* Vol. XI, No. XLV, July, 1932, pp. 733-35.

[*In the following review, Watson contrasts Adler's stress on social cooperation to the sexual theories of Freud and the metaphysics of Jung.*]

No statement on the meaning of life from Dr. Adler can avoid comparison with the statements of Freud and Jung, yet it seems strange that these writers should so consistently neglect each other's conclusions, and should follow exclusively, with what seems an almost compulsive energy, their own lines of thought. Dr. Jung has more than either of the others made allowance for his rivals, and, in relegating them to different types, has admitted their use and function. Dr. Adler in this last of his numerous publications [*What Life Should Mean to You*] seems completely satisfied with his own view, which has the undeniable advantage of standing firm and four-square on the ground of common sense. There is much kindly wisdom and a well-nigh convincing assurance in the way in which he answers his own categorical statement: *What Life Should Mean to You.* Co-operation is his panacea, and in every chapter he emphasizes the importance of co-operation in curing all human ills. Yet in judging of his book we cannot forget the emphasis with which Freud or Jung would stress other means to the satisfying of man's nature; each portrays a different aspect, each offers a solution for the satisfying of his need. To make the simplest comparison. Adler is the wise family physician—Freud the scientific psychologist, and Jung is the metaphysician who wishes to see all metaphysics in terms of psychology. In their differences they mark the stage of our modern development; and we must seek back to the wisdom of the past to find these differences resolved into harmony. There is an ancient Indian fable which tells how the gods and demi-gods brought their offerings to Man on his first birthday. The last and the greatest of these gifts, which the high gods concealed under many lesser blessings, are as follows: first, the power to express will in action, second the power to find sensual gratification, third the power to find fame through service to his kind, and fourth and last, peace. Dr. Adler lays his emphasis so heavily upon the first and third, chiefly on the third, that he seems scarcely aware of the second and fourth. He speaks of other schools of psychology with an impatience, which bordering on contempt, does little to enhance his own wisdom. He would find in co-operation an escape from all ills; through co-operation

alone can happiness and fame come to the individual; it is the flowering of the third gift. Dr. Adler does not tire of urging the expediency of such action. He is full of good advice and sound maxims. So too was Polonius, and indeed Dr. Adler might be considered a Polonius amongst psychologists. He can give advice not only to the children but to the parents—and very good advice too. All parents and educators should read this book, and few readers will find themselves proof against the home-thrusts of his analysis. Yet excellent as these precepts may be, it would seem unlikely that such simple confidence and such homely moralizings would ever rescue Hamlet from his doubt, or save Ophelia from drowning.

Modern psychology is as yet exploring the ways of self-realization. Freud has delved to the roots of sensual gratification, has glimpsed also the need of the fourth way, told of in the Indian story, but seeing the fourth, last and perhaps greatest of the gifts from the angle of modern, mechanistic science, has described it as Death. The great religions of the world have known it in its life-expressing reality, and Dr. Jung in his commentary on *The Secret of the Golden Flower,* has seen it from a very different angle from that which defines the Freudian death-principle. Yet the old fable is not resolved, only very partially stated in modern terms. It is doubtful whether it can ever be so stated; the images by which we speak of these things remain indistinct, and ancient symbols still serve our vague concepts. The genius of Freud has led his followers deep under the surface of human nature; from a purely psychological approach, he has discovered a spiritual and complementary opposite of sensual gratification, and by so doing has rendered simple, moralistic solutions, such as that offered by Dr. Adler, no longer completely adequate. Dr. Adler remains limited in his view of *one* aspect of human nature, and, for this very limitation, it may well be that he is the most practically useful of all modern phychologists. He is unembarrassed by speculation, and with cheerful confidence defines the meaning of life, the relation of mind to body, the meaning of memories and dreams, the significance of family and other environmental influences. He resolves the problems of adolescence, of criminality, of love and marriage. All this no doubt is very useful as far as it goes, but to many readers it will give the impression of falling short of all but a superficial view of human nature. Co-operation is a good word, never to be despised, but Dr. Adler's essentially unpoetic approach to life, which prevents him from recognizing the genius of Freud, marks his limitation. Yet this is no reason why we should not be grateful for the sincere and kindly presentation of one aspect of man's fourfold destiny.

Oliver Brachfeld (essay date 1936)

SOURCE: "Alfred Adler and His Comparative Psychology of Individuals," in *Inferiority Feelings in the Individual and the Group,* Routledge & Kegan Paul, 1951, pp. 73-93.

[*In the following excerpt, which was originally published in Spanish in 1936, Brachfeld situates Adler's conception of human nature within the context of a social and philosophical debate over degeneracy.*]

In Levin D. Schucking's work *The Sociology of Literary Taste* we possess an able, if incomplete, study of the changes of fashion in the domain of literature. But no one so far has attempted to give an account of the formation and development of taste in psychological matters. And yet psychology is a popular science nowadays, especially in America, and, by ricochet, throughout the world. The cult has had its repercussion on literary fashion. Hence the vogue for Kafka and Proust in the United States, with the result that these authors' works, somewhat neglected during the last twenty years, are now being displayed in all the European bookstalls. The psychology of Adler has undergone a similar revival, all the more salutary as it was still far from being appreciated at its true worth.

The conception of 'feelings of inferiority' is now inseparably connected with the name of Alfred Adler, and we shall have, therefore, to deal at some length with the body of his theories. His contribution to sociology will be the subject of a later work, which will also touch upon his 'personal equation' and the social factors which contributed to the formation of his ideas. We shall follow in this the lines laid down by the late Professor Karl Mannheim in his theory of the sociology of knowledge.

In this volume sociological factors will only be lightly touched upon, but we must nevertheless attempt to throw some light upon the scientific background against which Adler's ideas on the feelings of inferiority took shape.

At the beginning of the present century these ideas were already, so to speak, in the air. If we look through any Central European review on psychology or sex we shall find at this period 'a great fear' on every page. Everywhere the same lament is raised—'Humanity is *degenerating!*' The idea of degeneracy was, no doubt, derived from the ideas of Darwin and Spencer on evolution, but it also gave an echo to the dissatisfaction felt at this period in an ultra-urbanised civilisation. Everywhere 'degenerates' began to crop up—*Minderwertige,* as the Germans called them, i.e. persons of *minus* biological value. This minus-value gave the medical men food for thought, and their concern was being increasingly shared by the general public.

At the same time, the university professors were turning their attention not only to pathological psychology but to the minor defects of ordinary thought called 'inhibitions'. The studies of the Hungarian writer, Paul Ranschburg, on this subject created a sensation, and where to-day we speak of the 'inferiority complex', the talk then was all of 'inhibition' and 'inhibited persons'.

This period also witnessed a revolt against the psychological atomism which was superseded by the psychology of Acts leading to the more complex psychology of Function. In his *Gestaltqualität,* Ehrenfels discovered a whole new psychology of Form. In German-speaking countries, the *Ganzheitsbetrachtung* of William Stern broke fresh ground and found brilliant confirmation in the Vitalism of Hans Driesch. The study of sex inevitably led to a deeper appreciation of the psychic factors involved, partly through the influence of Freud, but also independently of him. Thus Näcke, though he contributes to the *Jahrbücher für sexuelle Zwischenstufen* edited by the materialist Magnus Hirschfeld, came to the conclusion that human sexuality cannot be understood without taking account of psychic factors. Adler himself started from a naturalistic standpoint in his studies of the Organic Inferiority in 1907, since this conception was already present in medical science. Independently of this, Professor Carl Pelmann's sensational work *Die Psychischen Grenzzustände,* Bonn, was already in its second edition in 1910. In it, he wrote of conditions which he regarded as taking place at the borderline between body and mind. Like Adler he can, therefore, be regarded as one of the forgotten forerunners of the psychosomatic therapy of to-day. He circumscribes with great eloquence the term 'mental minus-value' (*geistige Minderwertigkeit*). The term 'mental' need not mislead us, for in the technical vocabulary of this period the word is equivalent to 'moral' or 'psychological'; to-day we should say 'psycho-genetic'. The notion of mental degenerates was adopted by the psychology of this time, and psychogenetic factors began to be taken into consideration in addition to those of a purely hereditary, biological, or somatic character. In *Sexual-Probleme,* 1910, one of Pelmann's critics, the sexologist Max Marcuse, noted the preponderant influence exercised on our civilisation by the French *Minderwertige, les dégénérés supérieurs.* This was the same path along which Lombroso was travelling, and it led to the present *Pathography* [*The Problem of Genius*] of Lange-Eichbaum.

The final stage had yet to be reached. Once Freud had crossed the Rubicon with the help of his idea of psychological determinism, it only needed a thinker of courage and genius to take the decisive step forward. It was at this point that Alfred Adler appeared on the scene and rescued the idea of *Minderwertigkeit* by incorporating it into a new theory of striking simplicity. Thus Adler's ideas are in no way a *creatio ex nihilo* (such a thing does not exist in the evolution of ideas). He is the author of a new and creative synthesis gathering the many converging rivulets into one mighty stream. Adler's ideas on *Minderwertigkeit* and on mental degeneracy (wrongly so-called) combine logically, naturally, one might almost say organically, in the formation of a new and extremely original theory.

The war of 1914 was a severe setback to the diffusion of Adler's ideas, which for the time being merely followed in the wake of the Freudian theories.

In spite of the marked hostility of Professor McDougall, England was, however, one of the countries where from the start Adler's ideas met with a certain success. The novelist Phyllis Bottome was one of his best-known sponsors, and contributed an interesting biography, *Alfred Adler, the Man and his Work* (Putnam), which very usefully supplements that of Hertha Orgler. We may mention in passing that Adler came into contract with General Smuts, who contributed to his review *Internationale Zeitschrift für Individualpsychologie.* The great South African discovered a close affinity between his philosophy of *Holism* and Adler's psychology. In America, Morton Prince helped appreciably to spread the Adlerian teaching. Adler made his first visit to the United States in 1926, where his daily lectures at Columbia University were heard by over three thousand persons. He then went to Long Island

Medical College, of which he was professor till his untimely death in 1937 at Aberdeen, where he was delivering a course of summer lectures. During his sojourn in America he edited the *International Journal of Individual Psychology* (1934-37) in Chicago, where a large group of his disciples is still in existence.

In France, on the other hand, where the term alone *sentiment d'infériorité* (translated from *Minderwertigkeitsgefühl*) ought to have aroused echoes of Montaigne, Vauvenargues, Stendhal, and the contemporary Pierre Janet, the reception of Adler's ideas was less than mediocre. The result is that his theories are in the main unknown in France. The two lectures he gave in Paris in 1926 and again in 1937, barely ten days before his death, attracted only the specialists. The only work of his that has been translated into French is **Über den nervösen Charakter,** and then under the completely erroneous title of *Le Tempérament nerveux,* which in a sense contradicts the fundamental thesis of the book. The psycho-analysts were the first to speak of him; among the psychologists, Pierre Janet, among the writers, Paul Morand, spoke of an 'inferiority complex imported from America', but without knowing the name of Adler. Professor Wallon would quote him sometimes in his lectures on Vocational Guidance. Dr. Gilbert-Robin spread his ideas in a more popular field. I myself with the collaboration of Mlle. Rose Pfeiffer conducted, from 1929 to 1930, a circle of Adlerian studies in Paris which organised lectures among the various groups of students at the Sorbonne; I also published a number of articles and tried to interest publishers in my master's work. Berthold Friedl continued the good work in student circles, and the name of Adler and his ideas appeared more and more frequently in reviews and newspapers. André Maurois seems to have met Adler in America and read his books, as may be seen from some of his novels; when an enquiry was conducted as to 'what books to translate', he recommended all the works of the Viennese master. Intelligent specialists like Dr. Ombredanne have taken careful note of Adlerian results, not to mention the man who has done most to introduce modern ideas on psychology in France, Dr. René Allendy, the indefatigable and inspiring director of the Groupe d'Études Philosophiques et Scientifiques pour l'Examen des Tendances Nouvelles. For a long time this was the only place where foreign specialists could establish contact with the educated public in Paris. In 1933 Manes Sperber began to present the Adlerian ideas in Paris, but in an expanded form of his own, against a background of a distinctly political character. A few years later a pupil and friend whom Adler valued very highly, perhaps beyond his deserts, Dr. Alexandre Neuer, organised a feminine association of Adlerian 'initiates'. Another personal friend, Herr Schlesinger, proved a zealous and skilful propagandist in the paper *Vendredi,* while Mr. Paul Plottke, a young German professor in exile, who later served in H.M. Forces in Africa and Italy as psychologist and is now established in England, brought out roneographed bulletins on Adlerian psychology in German and in French.

Thus Adler's ideas have not penetrated into France to anything like the same extent as have Freud's. There has never been a real Adlerian movement comparable to the Freudian movement. The latter was enormously helped by the interest aroused by psycho-analytical ideas in certain artistic and literary circles, especially those of Surrealism, and one can safely say that without the moral and financial support of a princess of the blood royal Freud's ideas would certainly have met with far more resistance. The Adlerian psychology, handicapped by an ill-chosen name and by the unwillingness on the part of its followers to use it as an artistic and literary stimulus, was therefore infinitely less of a social and literary success in France than in Germany, Austria, Hungary, Spain or America.

In Hungary I was one of the founders of the Magyar Individual-psychologiai Tárasàg, with Professor Stephen de Màday as president. This society survived the disasters of the political reaction caused by Hitler's influence, and thanks to the ability of Professor de Màday it continued its good work even throughout the last war.

In 1929 I lectured in Madrid and Barcelona on 'Post-Freudian Psychology: Alfred Adler'. As Ortega y Gasset was interested in Adlerian ideas, **Menschenkenntnis (Understanding Human Nature)** was immediately translated into Spanish and is now in its third edition. In 1931 I took up my residence in Spain, lecturing and publishing many papers on Adlerian psychology. In 1934 I translated **What Life Should Mean to You,** which became the psychological best-seller in Spain, running to four editions. Then **The Problem of Homosexuality:** the first edition of the present book was published in 1936; two 'private' editions appeared in Chile (1937) and in the Argentine (1942); and the second legal edition (1944) has been out of print for a few years. Dr. Ramón Sarró, author of the preface to that edition, remarked in his preface to the third edition of **What Life Should Mean to You** that of the big three—Freud, Adler and Jung—Adler's psychology seemed to him the best suited to the Spanish character. When, in 1936, Adler was planning a lecture tour in Spain, the Madrid teachers wanted to invite him to a banquet at which 10,000 guests were to be present.

Individualpsychologie in der Schule was the first of his books to be translated into Spanish; it is now in its third edition, in Buenos Aires, as the publisher emigrated to Argentina. A book called *Guiando el Nino* (Guiding the Child) has also appeared recently in Buenos Aires. It contains a selection of articles originally published in Adlerian reviews. The editor, Señor Bernstein, is occasionally at fault in his method of introducing Adler's ideas to Spanish-speaking countries.

In general, Adler's idea met with varied and contradictory fortunes. Sometimes it was held up as a kind of revelation, sometimes dismissed as a commonplace, a 'psychology for schoolmasters'—which is true enough, but in no derogatory sense. Some writers, such as E. Utitz in his *Charakterologie,* look upon Adler as a modern Christian Wolff, Freud being the corresponding Leibnitz. Others regard it as Adler's merit to have made it possible for the first time to discuss openly the results of psycho-analysis by freeing these of their somewhat stifling pansexualist aura. Some again saw in Adlerism a useful complement to the economic theories of Karl Marx, while others were to find in it the first attempt to free man from the network of scientific determinism, thus restoring his freedom of will in spite of an inexorable biological heredity. As a matter of fact, none of these views is completely false. They are due to the many-sided character of Adler's work, where psycho-therapy, pedagogy, medicine, social improvement mingle with 'hints for the conquest of happiness' and 'a quick and infallible method for the Conquest of Health'. Nearest the truth are those who see in it a way of interpreting the problems of the modern world regarded as family conflicts on a gigantic scale. Like Freud, Adler starts from the analysis of neuroses rooted in family life, in *libido* and *destrudo,* in Eros and Thanatos; but he is the first to offer a psychology that will enable one to evaluate oneself and others. 'Among all the schools and trends of modern psychology,' says Sperber, 'Adler's was the only one to give to the purely psychological problems of power and valence (*Geltung*) the position they deserve, i.e. one of cardinal importance.' The Americans speak of 'feeling important', and this is also one aspect of the German *Geltung*.

But the circumstances in which this psychology first arose were peculiarly unfavourable, and were to lead to errors and confusions from which neither Adler nor his followers remained exempt. From the start their pitch was queered by factors of purely social and historic order, and for a long time their teaching appeared in a wrong perspective.

It is a hard fate to live in the shadow of a great personality possessed of powerful ideas, and yet it is by no means certain that Adler ever harboured this as a grudge against Freud, as the latter maintains in his autobiography, *My Life in Psycho-Analysis*. What is certain is that in 1907 Adler discovered the precious vein from which he was laboriously to quarry all his theories during the next twenty years, and that although he did not realise it himself, his work was thwarted by the presence of Freud in Vienna. Freud was fifteen years his senior, exercised a powerful influence in intellectual circles, and enjoyed the reputation of being the creator of psycho-analysis. Adler himself felt his personal charm; he was his collaborator, but he was not his pupil. It may be that without Freud Adler would not have carried his ideas in the direction he chose, but it is no less certain that his thought was something very different from a mere 'imitation by opposition' (Tarde) of psycho-analysis. And yet that is what the world believed, and what it still believes, thus placing Adler on the same footing as men like Jung, Stekel, Rank or Bjerre. Thus, in his work as in his life, he is over-shadowed by the mighty figure of Freud.

The influence of a master from whom one wants to liberate oneself can sometimes be fatal. Had it not been for Hegel's idealism, Marx might have christened his own philosophy historical realism, instead of materialism, a term which has completely misrepresented his true thought and even more so that of his votaries.

It has been thought that the Adlerian and the Freudian systems resemble each other like two brothers; it has been thought that both have sprung from the same *social need*—collective nervosity, disproportionate neglect of the science of man as compared to the technical and natural sciences—which is true. But it has also been claimed that both arise from, or are part of the same spiritual tendency,

the same mental approach, the same historical line in the development of ideas—which is not true at all. 'The Comparative Psychology of Individuals', i.e. of the individual as an undivided unity (*in-dividuum*) is not a form of psycho-analysis. True, it may have regarded itself as such at one time, and this error arose because the Adlerians themselves thought that the necessity of their historic 'moment' should make them offer dialectical battle to the ideas of Freud. The results achieved by Adler and his school are something of a different order from that attaching to the 'Psycho-analytical Revolution'. And this is true in spite of all appearances, in spite of the mutual imprecations of both sides, in spite of the hatred which continues after both the masters are dead.

Far too much importance has been given to the various differences between Adler and Freud. It has been said that the latter wanted merely to be the 'retrospective historian' of the psychic development of the individual, while the former was 'turned towards the future'; that Psychoanalysis looked for the *causes* of nervous symptoms, while Individual Psychology attributed them to *goals,* to characteristic pieces in a teleological puzzle. Actually this argument is merely 'popular' since the idea of *final cause* bridges the gap in question. That Freud sees in the dream the *via regia* leading to the heart of the unconscious, whereas for Adler it is merely *auch ein Symptom*, one more symptom amongst so many others. It has also been said that Freud atomises the personality with his conception of partial and more or less autonomous impulses, whereas for Adler only the integral man, only the 'psycho-physical unit' exists; that Freud is a 'pansexualist' whereas for Adler the sexual problem is at the most a *primus inter pares*. I know all these arguments, because for years I have myself repeated them *ad nauseam*. They are not false, certainly not; but to repeat them indefinitely, to elaborate them, to add to them is—futile. The real difference is elsewhere; it lies much deeper. It is axiomatic, for it resides in a difference of fundamental inspiration, of *Weltanschauung*. Here again we have been met with a host of arguments: Adler, at any rate to begin with, was a moderate Socialist, in the opposite camp to Freud, a 'bloated bourgeois'; again, the psycho-analyst has his patient lying on a sofa in a darkened room and takes up his position behind him, as though he wanted to shove himself into his unconscious, whereas the Adlerian engages in a talk as between equals, expressing by this attitude a complete difference of conceptions. We may add that Freud was an *Ausläufer*, a last representative of the liberal epoch marked by disorder and anarchy, in which the liberty of all was to create a general harmony, even *in sexualibus,* whereas Adler is the herald of a new era of Order, since according to him 'sexuality cannot be regarded as a private matter'. His supreme postulate was the Community (*Gemeinschaft*), and he regarded events in the lives of individuals as having no meaning except as participating in a collective whole.

But the differences spring from a deeper source. All the points we have mentioned are only symptoms, only derivative results. In reality Freud's system is a physiology that does not dare to call itself so. The master himself admitted that he was only dealing with a 'provisional science, pending the advent of a more perfect physiology'. This important point has, with the exception of Gerö, been ignored or forgotten by all the writers on the subject, especially by the new brand of Catholic psycho-analyst, headed by Mme. Maryse Choisy. Freud's system is the final consequence of the Darwinian Theory of Evolution (the Jungian version being pure mythology and the starting-point of the curious literary psycho-analysis very much in fashion in France—witness the curious Gaston Bachelard). Adler was the first to revive the true concrete *Characterology,* which had been castigated by Humboldt almost as soon as it appeared, and then committed to oblivion. The Adlerian psychology is not a science, it is not even a psychology in the usual sense of the word. It is more than that, it is a 'science', only with certain reservations and in a new sense. At the most it is an *ideographic* and not a *nomothetic* science, for the luminous phrase which Pierre Abraham wrote as a heading in his book, *Figures,* could also be made to serve here—'Apart from the general, no science; apart from the individual, no truth.'

Adler was always very much concerned to retain the strictly scientific character of his 'Psychology of the Individual'. But at the same time he always maintained that his Individual Psychology was an art, and on his lips the word assumed the same meaning as when one speaks, for example, of the Hippocratic *art.* The Greek $\tau\epsilon\chi\nu\eta$ means art; just as medicine is a technique based on science, or on several sciences, without being itself a science, so much the same could be said of the Adlerian method. Psychoanalysis, on the other hand, though born under the impulse of certain results in the field of psycho-therapy, is a theory, whereas the Adlerian system is merely a corollary to practice. The Adlerian 'discoveries' can be 'theorised' after the event, as it were, and that is the task which we have set ourselves at the moment. But is it not significant that Adler was never able to construct a 'theory'? That was the task which, from the first, fell to his disciples, and one of which, let us admit it, they have not acquitted themselves too well. One cannot accept Freud's ideas without *ipso facto* adopting a definitely materialistic and mechanistic ideology. But one can be an Adlerian and remain what one was, go on thinking what one thought before, just as one can be a doctor and still be either a Catholic or a Communist. And when men like Rühle or Sperber have to 'enlarge' the Adlerian theory till it has become a Marxist tool, they have been no more successful than a writer like Rudolf Allers, Professor at the Catholic University of Washington, who claims to have incorporated the whole Adlerian system into his own Thomistic system of thought. (*The Psychology of Character,* 1939, and *The Successful Error, a Critical Study of Freudian Psychoanalysis,* 1943.)

Freud was a man of science, Adler an educator. The fact that both were doctors was an accident due to their 'moment', to their 'milieu,' and not to their 'dominant faculty' (Taine's *faculté maîtresse*). They do not speak the same language. The words may often be the same, but they are used in a totally different sense. There is neither identity nor opposition. Not only are their points of view utterly different, but the two men are not, in spite of appearances, talking of the same thing. With the tenacity of a Sherlock Holmes and the searching eye of a Public Prosecutor, Freud has brought forward a gigantic indictment of humanity. Whatever is obvious, whatever is clearly there, is only façade (as he says in connection with our 'earliest memories'), a façade designed to cover something hidden. Whatever is manifest is only the symbol of what is latent. The descriptive geography of the human psyche does not satisfy him, he wants to write its geology, its geodesy. His psychology therefore becomes a *Tiefenpsychologie,* a 'depth psychology'. For a very long time this term was used to denote both systems, the Freudian and the Adlerian. This was a mistake. Regarded as 'depth psychology' the Adlerian method would appear very superficial. Jung's is the only system that really deserves the name.

Oceanography is certainly a noble science, but woe to the sailor who relies on it alone to cross the ocean! Adler never wanted to give men more than a practical treatise on how to sail most successfully, given the means at his disposal, through the troubled waters of life. If he does plumb the depths of the unconscious—which he does not at all regard as an inferno to which all the worst in man has been relegated—he does so only the better to find the course which the ship must steer.

Adler took as his starting-point a paradox of biology, viz. the faculty of compensation for defective or inadequate organs. From this he travelled step by step towards the ambitious aim of creating with psychology a Scientific Knowledge of Man. For him, psychology was not the research carried on in laboratories designed to impress us with a bewildering array of figures; he distrusted tests as heartily as he distrusted the 'infinitesimal analysis of the ego' which Freud carried to such lengths. A knowledge of the soul and of human conduct, worked out on a human scale, inspired simply by good sense and accessible to the man in the street—such was his aim. A doctor of sick souls, his chief concern was to heal. And since to heal is not so much a science as an art, Adler, whose penetrating spirit was devoid of all philosophical or metaphysical preoccupation, dreamed of a psychology which would be at once a science and an art. He gave intuition its due, although this inevitably shocked those who rather stupidly regarded the empirical data of natural science as alone of any positive value. He has been reproached with his distrust for psychological apparatus, his scorn for the battery of tests, his general dislike of psycho-technique or psychometry. But since in experimental psychology practically everything can become a test, so Adler's 'test' was a *determinate situation in life.* He could open a 'human document' at any page; the least fragment of autobiography was enough for him to tell us with almost unerring vision the essential points of the subject's *style of life.* His enormous practical knowledge of men enabled him to skip the earlier stages of interpretation and to dispense with 'profiles' and 'psychological batteries'. Where there was only one in 1929 there are no less than five professors teaching the statistical method at the *Institut de Psychologie* at the Sorbonne to-day, and yet we know how frail is this method of tests, based as it is on a misconception of social facts and involving a veritable *petitio principii.*

Adler, who at the outset would eagerly embrace any idea

or tendency faintly resembling his own, was fortunately preserved from following the methods then in vogue—psycho-analysis and psycho-technique. He was prevented from doing so by the discovery of the physiological and psychological relativity residing in the law of compensation and over-compensation. His thought was not 'evolved'; it was contained in embryo in his first work, the ***Studie über Minderwertigkeit der Organen,*** first published in 1907 and reprinted twenty years later without the author having to change a single word in it. It is in this book, moreover, that we shall find the starting-point of his theories and of all our present knowledge on the subject of the feelings of inferiority.

Inferiority, a term long used in medicine and in jurisprudence, is a notion that has come to us from Darwinism. In human beings the existence of organic inferiorities can really only be noted at the moment of birth or during childhood. All the organs may suffer from a complete or partial deficiency, or inferiority; the sensory organs, the digestive system, the organs of respiration, the circulation of the blood, the glandular, urinary or genital systems, the nervous system. The fate of an 'inferior' organ will always vary according to the individual. Under the impact of external stimuli the instinct of self-preservation will drive the individual afflicted with a deficiency to level things up, to compensate for his inferiority. From an extensive study of persons and families showing organic deficiencies of all kinds, Adler concludes that the levelling process generally goes through the following stages: vital incapacity, morphological or functional anomalies; inability to resist and predisposition to certain definite illnesses; compensation through the organ itself; compensation through another organ; compensation by 'psychic superstructure'; organic or, alternatively, psychological over-compensation. The central nervous system takes part in a general way in any partial compensation, beginning with an increase of growth or of function (e.g. the one-armed man's arm which assumes athletic proportions). The inferior organ takes longer to function properly than the perfect organ. Adler was therefore able to state that to overcome an inferiority presupposes increased cerebral activity, a cerebral compensation. The next step seemed to be the assumption that every defective organ called forth the creation of a 'psychic superstructure', and that the individual in question will be 'more gifted' than if his organ had been perfectly constituted from the first. Thus it might well be, thought Adler, that an inadequate digestive system might acquire higher working capacity than a normal one. But at the same time, since the starting point of the compensation is in the digestive organs, the psychic superstructure founded on the deficiency would logically be stronger than anything else and attract all the other psychic complexes around it. In such a case anything connected with digestion or nutrition will have a special psychic 'value' or 'accent'. The nutritive instinct will therefore predominate in the subject, with greediness and avidity in its wake; but it may also produce greed, avarice, covetousness and possessiveness generally on the moral plane. Such a process (which is only one example, for compensations take place analogously in the case of inferiority of any organ) would seem to favour the formation in the individual of *psychic axes* closely dependent upon *one* or *several* inferior organs.

These 'psychic axes' manifest themselves in the subject's whole psychological set-up, in his dreams, in the choice of his profession, etc. The defective organ then indulges in regular exercises—rather like an athlete training for a contest, and having overcome its difficulties, it is rewarded by the pleasure that henceforth accompanies its activity. Hence the special attitude of the subject towards this functional pleasure brought with such effort, as indeed towards all pleasure and towards sexual pleasure in particular. In a word, Adler has found the concrete point where purely physical or physiological facts are transformed into psychic facts. The discovery is of capital importance and was not exploited as it should have been. For very soon Adler was to discover that it was not so much the organic inferiority as its psychic superstructure which released the compensation. Similarly the compensations vary qualitatively and quantitatively in response to an imponderable element—a vague, confused and ill-defined feeling of insufficiency. Having started from purely biological work on the heredity of certain organs, especially those of the visual organ, in which he was a specialist, Adler now turned to the study of inferiorities *in natura vili,* i.e. in children without, however, going into the problem of *Kinderfehler.* Thus, from being a child doctor he became, in pursuing the paradoxical destiny of organic inferiorities, a nerve doctor and a psychiatrist. The *psychic axes,* which were the result of the compensation or over-compensation for inadequate organs, had thus been discovered. But the word 'psychic' presupposes an opposition to 'somatic'. Adler, however, had gradually become convinced that body and soul were so closely connected as to constitute a single undivided unity and that even purely imaginary inferiorities, or such as existed only in virtue of some social convention (such as being left-handed, having red hair, etc.), would call forth compensations without the presence of any organic inferiority properly so called. Thus the *psychic axes,* which at first were landmarks for the exploration of the personality, became directing lines of behaviour—the meridians, as it were, of the subject's life.

But man does not live in a vacuum. Organism presupposes environment, the one cannot exist without the other. The human person receives a host of stimuli from the external world and this amorphous mass becomes ordered along certain 'axes' or 'directing lines' which we may call tendencies. But Adler was not content with what the manuals of psychology called 'directed attention'. He saw at once that memory itself did not escape from this *law of tendencies.* Memories are in a sense like metal filings lying on a piece of cardboard. If a magnet is placed above them they will dispose themselves along symmetrical magnetic lines. The magnetic pole which determines the directing lines of character is the *ideal aim* pursued by the subject; its opposite pole is the *earliest childhood recollection.* Man's whole being tends, whether he knows it or not (and more often he does not know it), towards a fictitious goal of superiority. We are set in motion, not by our innate dispositions, but by the position in which we stand in relation to this goal. Each of our actions indicates our position in this continual voyage which starts from inferiority and moves towards superiority—a position of struggle or an attitude of hesitation and indecision. There is a whole 'dialect of the organs', including a 'sexual jargon' which, to the astute observer, will indicate the kinetic law of each. For in Adler's view there was nothing static in man, everything was in motion, and no one psychic process could be taken as expressing the whole human being. What does it matter what we bring with us into the world at birth? What we do with it, that alone is important. It would therefore be useless to make out a list of our innate dispositions— (*Besitzespsychologie*—the psychology of possession). The Adlerian psychology aims quite consciously at the utilisation of what we have—(*Gebrauchspsychologie*the psychology of use). Hence the *heuristic* principle which is of primary importance in the Adlerian psychology. It tells us not to lose ourselves in questions of detail, such as how the eye or the ear functions, how dreams are produced, etc. These theoretical matters can be left to the academic psychologists. What matters to the Adlerian psychologists is what the eye wants to see, what the ear wants to hear, the *tendency* which the dream reveals, the function of the dream—whether it encourages or discourages.

Later on, a new term replaced the 'directing lines', which had themselves replaced the 'psychic axes'. Not that the facts observed by Adler had changed, nor his methods of interpretation and cure; only the theoretical conception had altered. The new term was *style of life*. The importance of this change in terminology must not be overestimated. It certainly marks a new stage in the emancipation of Adler's thought from the ultra-naturalistic ideas in which he had been educated and which had gone to form his first terminology. But it should be noted that this emancipation was never complete. Nevertheless, to talk of a 'style of life' expresses a definitely *personalist* point of view and an approach to the idea of life as being man's continual creation.

According to Adler, the *style of life* is established in early childhood, generally between the third and fifth year. In his analyses of **'The Neurotic's Conception of the World'** or of the **'Soul of the Criminal'** in the *Internationale Zeitschrift für Individual Psychologie* of Vienna and in the *International Journal of Individual Psychology* of Chicago, he claimed that the neurosis or delinquency *invariably* mirrored a situation in childhood when the neurotic or the criminal was taking his first steps in life. This is particularly true of criminals. 'It is sufficient', he writes, 'to ask them for their earliest memory, the oldest impressions which have lasted since their childhood. They will answer something like this. "I was helping to clean some clothes: and it was then I noticed a coin and I took it. I was six." Or else, "When I was five I saw a railway carriage catch fire. It was full of children's balloons that were being thrown out: I took as many as I could." Or again, "My mother was in the habit of leaving money lying about; every week I used to take a little." '

It would seem, then, that in affirming that the style of life is established in early childhood, Adler is basing his deduction on such early memories, or mirrors of the adult's style of life. But in this I am of the opinion that Adler is guilty of a *petitio principii*, or that he has been the victim at any rate of an error in perspective. The idea that our subsequent fate is cast in childhood 'between the third and fifth year' is nothing but a legacy from Freud, in spite of the fact that Adler understood the supposed Oedipus Complex in a completely different sense from Freud's. The Freudian idea that with the establishment of the Oedipus Complex the fate of our *libido* and consequently of the whole of our life is cast, was the logical outcome of the author's belief in Evolution. But such an idea appears out of place in the Adlerian system and does not conform to its general spirit. Had not Adler himself shown us that the earliest memory, far from being a manifest façade hiding an older and latent memory, was most often germane to the present situation, or simply expressed that same *style of life*, of which, like the dream, it was only a consequence? It was he, too, who had shown us that these earliest memories were very often not authentic, that they were often 'arranged' in favour of the subject's preoccupations at the time, that they were 'false recognitions' purely in function of the *present* goal. I have studied this question myself in several hundred subjects, and I can state that very often a change in the style of life will automatically arouse a fresh 'earliest recollection' which will be in conformity with the new situation.

Very often, too, a number of earliest memories subsist without our being able to say which of them is the oldest. We shall therefore name sometimes one, sometimes another as such, and this not by a chance caprice but in virtue of the magnetic attraction exercised by the *present situation* on the confused mass of mnemonic material. But, it will be asked, if according to Adler's own results the earliest memory is 'arranged' in virtue of the existing style of life or of the present situation, how can it be claimed that these same memories point to the precocious but definitive establishment of this very style of life? Adler used to say that to cure a patient consisted in changing his style of life. But could one change it if it dated from early childhood? It was all very well for the psycho-analysts to say that even in the case of an unfavourable Oedipus constellation (e.g. fixation on the parent of the same sex, leading to homosexuality in the adult) the normal form of the complex could always be 'diluted'. The Adlerian psychology (except in the case of the dissident Künkel) did not recognise the idea of affective transference. So all Adler could do was to appeal to commonsense, to the 'community feeling' which he believed to exist *a priori* in the depths of every human soul. He attacked the psycho-analysts' assumption that the child is a fundamentally selfish little creature; this he regarded as an error in perspective. Since man, from the dawn of his existence on this globe, has always lived and always will live in a society, it is impossible that this fact should not have made a deep mark upon the species and implanted in it a profound sense of community which is expressed in the mother-child relationship. The baby's relationship to its mother is not at all, as some have dared to maintain, a 'parasitical' one. The mother with her breasts full of milk, and the functional changes brought about in her organism by motherhood, needs the child just as much as the child needs her.

Let us try to sum up the Adlerian theory very briefly in its final form and with its ultimate implications. Every human being lives in accordance with a certain style of life which is peculiar to him. This style of life is marked through and through with the goal of superiority, real or fictitious, towards which tend all the great directing lines of the subject's behaviour. Everyone tends to assert his own worth (*Geltung*) to avoid situations of inferiority, and aspires to situations of superiority.

The stupid assertion has been made, and how often repeated, that Adler 'defied Nietzsche's Will to Power', that he proclaimed and extolled Hobbes' *libido dominandi* (cf. Ernest Seillière). Some of Adler's early writings lend a certain colour to this erroneous interpretation. In them he speaks of a *Streben nach Macht* and lays undue stress on the importance of the 'aggressive impulses' in neurosis and in life in general. But the more he deepened and elaborated the results he drew from the analysis of thousands of subjects, the further he moved from this terminology. 'People confuse my psychology with that of my patients', he would say jokingly. For in his view the most powerful motive in every human action was not, as Nietzsche claimed, *power,* but *superiority,* whether fictitious or real. That superiority which lurks even in the soul of the masochist, for he is seeking it in the very extremity of the humiliation to which he subjects himself. To show one's worth, to feel important—that is the secret of the human soul. And here we can borrow a term from chemistry, that of *valence,* so as to distinguish clearly between real and objective worth (the German *Wert*), and this *Geltung* or *Geltungsstreben,* which is a deeply implanted and purely subjective tendency to show or display our worth. Thus the Will to Power would be only one form among a thousand others of this tendency towards valency; one of a theoretically infinite number of variants of the same theme.

But according to Adler this tendency to show our worth is not a primordial factor in human nature. It arises as compensation for a painful and sometimes burning feeling of a *lack,* of a *minus,* the Feeling of Inferiority, the *Minderwertigkeitsgefühl.* Man, owing to his greater differentiation as compared to the higher mammals and even to his cousin, the ape, has become, in a sense, an inferior species. He is an animal whose birth is premature. According to biologists he ought not to see the light until he has reached the weaning stage. This is what has forced him to live in society, for only union makes for strength. Society or, in Adlerian terminology, the Community (*Gemeinschaft*) is the primordial fact. It is prior to the individual, and in the latter there exists from the first a strong impulse towards communal solidarity. In this view, man, is fundamentally altruistic and not, as so many psychologists seem to think, fundamentally egoistic. The sense of community is as natural to him as breathing. But alas, the feeling of his own insufficiency breaks in upon his spirit of solidarity and collaboration, and at each blow suffered by his self-esteem this spirit will lose strength. Hence all the many deviations from the 'straight' path. Here we have a man or woman showing nervous symptoms, another will succumb to psychosis, another to crime; yet another will compensate his feelings of insufficiency by a definite sexual perversion, while another will seek for a return to community by the path (somewhat problematic in Adler's view) of art. Mental hygiene would therefore require that the patient should adapt himself to the community. But what is this community? What is this mysterious entity? Adler has refused to define it. Every psychic deviation is an error which brings about inevitable retribution; it is a diseased state of our feeling of community, of our *common sense.* In **What Life Should Mean to You,** in the important chapter that bears the title of the book, we read, 'The Community Feeling means above all the urge towards a form of community conceived as eternal, such as one might imagine humanity to be if it had already achieved perfection. I am not thinking of any *existing* community or society, nor of any religious or political group. I am simply pointing out that the most suitable human ideal is the perfect community, which would contain the whole of humanity and thus mark the final stage of Evolution.'

At this point Adler ventures into Utopian regions which are far removed from the field of serious sociological observation. We do not wish to follow him in these metaphysical speculations, though he is the first to recognise that they do not admit of proof. In his view, 'Community' is to be regarded as 'absolute truth', as the 'absolute imperative'; but the notion has unfortunately remained completely vague and undefined. Religion is a community, and so is a political group, the relationship between mother and child, between the members of the same family or of the same nation. All these are 'communities', but Adler has neglected to set them out in any kind of hierarchy. He does not argue about the notion, just as a Christian does not argue about his God, and it is not difficult to see in Adler's work the mark of a religious and metaphysical mind, though expressed in purely secular form. The community takes the place of the divinity; the feeling of inferiority that of evil or sin, and altruism or solidarity that of virtue. The scheme is that of all Christian moralists and recalls in a curious way the doctrine of Mandeville, which we expounded in an earlier chapter.

Thus, in the Adlerian system, the feeling of inferiority seems to acquire the role of prime mover. It is the pivot around which all psychic movement revolves, the force that conditions all our actions, even our thoughts, our talent, our happiness or our unhappiness. And just as Mandeville admitted that, paradoxical as it may seem, the vices of individuals tended to the public advantage, so Adler drew attention mainly to the useful, the *socially* useful side of many feelings of insufficiency and minus-value.

The Times Literary Supplement   (essay date 1958)

SOURCE: "Individual Psychologist," in *The Times Literary Supplement,* No. 2960, November 21, 1958, pp. 665-66.

[*In the following review, the critic provides an overview of Adler's life, career, and writings.*]

Since Freud's death in 1939 psycho-analysis has certainly not remained stationary. Although the basic method has changed little, several of the major Freudian ideas have undergone considerable revision. In particular, serious attempts have been made to shake off the doctrine of instinct and to replace it by new conceptions of inter-personal relationship. There has also been a shift of interest from the unconscious mechanisms supposed to underlie neurosis to the defences evolved by the personality in counteracting them. In Freudian parlance, the focus of attention is no longer the id but the ego.

The changing outlook in psychoanalysis has led to a revival of interest in the work of one of its long-rejected pioneers—Alfred Adler. This is clearly appreciated by Dr. H. L. and Dr. R. R. Ansbacher, the editors of a carefully chosen and thoughtfully presented selection of Adler's works. As they rightly point out, the modern emphasis upon social rather than biological issues, upon character rather than instinct and upon self-expression rather than sex, has brought many neo-Freudians close to the Adlerian position. Although this suggestion will be indignantly repudiated by many who have been conditioned to regard Adlerian theory as a major heresy, one may agree that a *prima facie* case exists for the revaluation of Adler and his place in psychology. Even should Adler not prove to have been right in his dissension from Freud, at least he may not now appear so far wrong as to have deserved excommunication.

Alfred Adler, the self-styled "legitimate father of the inferiority complex," was born in Vienna in 1870. Of Hungarian-Jewish parentage, he became a Christian early in life but never appears to have been much troubled by matters of religious belief. His family was well-to-do and his home life by all accounts easy-going and cultured. Yet Adler's childhood was by no means wholly happy. He was delicate in health and consumed by an altogether excessive envy of his older brother's prowess. This sense of inferiority *vis-à-vis* his brother appears to have remained with Adler all his life and had doubtless a good deal to do with the birth of his legitimate brain-child. Indeed, Adler himself spoke of the accord existing between the facts of his childhood and the views which he had expressed in his psychological writings. But he seems never to have suspected the origin of these views in the accident of his own psychological history.

Adler qualified in medicine at the University of Vienna and practised for many years as a general physician. Unlike Freud, he was at no time engaged in pure scientific research and hence had little opportunity to acquire firm standards of scientific evidence. Nonetheless, he won considerable respect as a general practitioner and, indeed, remained in practice through all the years in which he was close to Freud. Yet even before he met Freud Adler appears to have had a keen eye for the psychological aspect of physical illness. In this respect he was undoubtedly ahead of his time.

The circumstances of Adler's adherence to Freud are still far from clear. According to his biographer Phyllis Bottome (*Alfred Adler: Apostle of Freedom*. Faber and Faber, 1939), their association grew out of a newspaper article by Adler strongly defending Freud's much maligned work on the *Interpretation of Dreams*. On the other hand, the late Ernest Jones claims in his biography of Freud to have been quite unable to trace the existence of any such article. Nor was he able to confirm the report that Adler had once been Freud's family doctor. Nonetheless, there can be no doubt that Freud invited Adler to join his circle—almost certainly in 1902—and that Adler thereafter played a most im-

portant part in the early growth of the psycho-analytical movement.

Freud's acceptance of Adler as a close colleague is all the more remarkable when it is borne in mind that Adler never underwent an analysis with Freud and never really committed himself to the Freudian position. Indeed, he advanced a theory of neurosis very different from that of Freud as early as 1908, while still a trusted member of Freud's entourage. It cannot, therefore, be said that Adler's defection involved the abandonment of a position which he had formerly accepted. Adler never repudiated Freud. Strictly speaking, he had never been a Freudian at all.

The formal break with Freud took place in 1911. Part of the discussion at the Vienna Psycho-analytical Society which preceded it is reproduced by the Ansbachers and will be of lively interest to the psychological historian. As has been said, Adler's conception of neurosis at this time was very different from Freud's and had been so for some years. This difference had long been tacitly acknowledged within the Society. The critical issue was whether adherence to the Adlerian view was compatible with psychoanalysis as understood by Freud. This issue was closely and evenly fought, at least as many members of the society speaking for Adler as against him. Yet, in the end, Freud prevailed and Adler resigned, along with nine of his sympathizers—about a quarter of the total membership. These formed themselves into a "Society for Free Psycho-Analysis," acknowledging Adler's leadership. Adler later renamed his school "Individual Psychology," by which name it has since been generally known.

Adler's later career was active and in its way distinguished, though he made no further theoretical contribution of real importance. In Vienna he organized a pioneer child guidance service, the full story of which has more recently been told (in *The Psychology of Alfred Adler and the Development of the Child,* by Madeleine Ganz, 1953). He lectured widely not only to doctors but to educationists and the general public. Indeed, he cast himself as a missionary in the cause of psychological enlightenment. In his later years Adler spent long periods in the United States, though his transatlantic reception does not appear to have been particularly happy and he had little impact upon American psychiatry. Yet he influenced many by his psychological teachings and his courageous and positive attitude to life. He died suddenly in 1936, in Aberdeen, while on a lecture tour of Great Britain.

Not even Adler's death mollified Freud. "The world," he wrote to Arnold Zweig, "rewarded him richly for his service in having contradicted psycho-analysis."

Adler's best-known work was published in 1907, in the period of his close association with Freud. Yet the **Studie über die Minderwertigkeit von Organen** (later translated as **Study of Organ Inferiority and its Psychical Compensation**) owed surprisingly little to the work of the older man. In this study Adler put forward a theory of disease based upon the supposed inborn weakness or inferiority of particular bodily organs or systems. To weakness of a particular organ, he argued, the body responds by a widespread effort of compensation. This process may involve organs other than the one directly affected and is to be viewed as a compensatory reaction of the whole organism. Thus the central nervous system—and through it the mind—may have an important part to play in compensating the inherent weaknesses of the body.

This hypothesis of compensation has found broad acceptance in modern medicine. Indeed, it has since reappeared in a variety of special forms, not always with the acknowledgment it deserves. But Adler was not content with a statement of his theory in purely biological terms. It had, he supposed, important application to psychology. Thus the awareness of any physical weakness may be presumed to provoke strong psychological counter-reaction. Often, indeed, compensation becomes over-compensation, as with Demosthenes, the stutterer, who became the greatest orator of Greece. Physiological defect, in short, provides an important spur to psychological achievement.

This general idea was soon extended by Adler to embrace inferiorities other than those directly due to physical deficiency. He supposed that any inadequacy, real or imagined, might become the focus of a feeling of inferiority and thereby provoke effort directed to its conquest. Thus the ubiquitous "inferiority complex" was born. Adler's next task was to classify the main sources of psychological inferiority and to analyse the principal traits of character to which they gave rise. The outcome of this endeavour was *The Neurotic Character* (1912), which still perhaps remains as Adler's best book.

As is well known, Adler placed much emphasis upon the inferiority commonly felt by a child towards its older siblings, in which he doubtless drew heavily on his own childhood experience. He also laid stress on the inferiority commonly felt by women towards the superior position of the male—the so-called "masculine protest." But he soon went beyond the concept of compensation and adduced the craving for superiority as a basic human motive. This he related to a primary instinct of aggression—a concept accepted only very much later by Freud. At the same time, Adler never doubted the reality of human cooperation. As early as 1908 he wrote a paper on the need for affection in children—a need which he believed to lie at the root of all fellow-feeling. To this need and its derivatives he later gave the name of "social interest."

Adler's theory of neurosis is at bottom very simple. The basis of neurosis is aggression—but neurosis results from aggression only under circumstances in which "social interest" is deficient. In the neurotic, the striving for superiority operates without due regard to social reality and is consequently expressed in a variety of autistic or psychopathic forms. Neither sexual nor infantile processes need be implicated to any real extent. The unconscious, moreover, exists but in name and is for the most part an unnecessary assumption. Psychotherapy is less a process of analysis than a matter of re-education. Its aim is the rebirth of social responsibility.

With some justice, Adler reproached Freud for his neglect of the power-motive and its undeniable significance in some cases of nervous illness. Although Freud rejected Adler's views there is good evidence that he took his work extremely seriously. It is doubtful whether the same may be said of Adler. One may wonder, indeed, if Adler ever really understood Freud's position. And he certainly repudiated the most important outcome of psychoanalysis, namely, the evidence which it had provided of infantile sexuality and unconscious motivation as basic causal factors in neurosis. To anyone who accepts this evidence, it is easy to agree with Freud that the Adlerian theory just will not do.

After his break with Freud, Adler published much work but little of it broke new ground. *The Practice and Theory of Individual Psychology* (1924) was a collection of papers, many of which had previously appeared elsewhere. This book represents Adler's most convincing attempt to apply his ideas to the clinical problems of neurosis. But it was only partially successful.

In his later work Adler tended increasingly to address himself to the educator and the layman rather than to the medical world. *The Pattern of Life* (1930), *What Life Should Mean to You* (1931) and *Social Interest: A Challenge to Mankind* (1933) were books aimed at the new post-war public avid for psychological enlightenment. They presented their author as an effective popularizer of his own brand of psychological self-help. No doubt they had influence in their time. To-day they are virtually forgotten.

What, then, is the significance of Adler for present-day thought? At first glance, one would be tempted to say that little remains of his psychological edifice. True, the "inferiority complex" has been accepted as a useful name for a very prevalent source of human unhappiness. Yet there is no good reason to believe that feelings of inferiority, in the absence of deeper disturbances, are of much significance in psychological medicine. Similarly, few people can nowadays accept the sense of inferiority as the principal goad to human achievement. In some cases this may be so—but hardly in all. As so often in psychology, Adler spoiled a good case by facile over-generalization.

And what of the Adlerian "will to power"? This highly Teutonic notion, which goes back at least to Nietzsche, has never really established itself as a valid psychological conception. Needless to say, the advent of Hitler constrained psychologists to inquire closely into the origins of the impulse to dominate and of what has recently been called the authoritarian personality. But few have found it possible to accept a solution in terms of a unique and irreducible human faculty. The striving for superiority has a complex origin in which constitution, upbringing and social convention play their respective parts. Adler's view of dominance in terms of a single psychological variable is both too vague and too all-embracing to possess real explanatory value.

Nonetheless, a more careful glance at contemporary psychology does reveal some parallels between Adler's outlook and more recent lines of thought. First, there has been a marked tendency to distrust the more analytical approach to problems of personality and to stress once again the unitary, coherent and purposeful character of human conduct. This outlook, well represented in the writings of Gordon Allport and Gardner Murphy, undoubtedly owes something to Adler's insistence upon the study of the whole individual and his characteristic "life-style." To this extent at least. Adler anticipated an influential standpoint in present-day psychology.

Secondly, we have witnessed since the war a tremendous upsurge of interest in social issues, which has even penetrated to psychiatry. Freud, it will be remembered, conceived the individual as in fundamental opposition to the claims of society. For him, social forces appeared as almost entirely restrictive and as basically hostile to individual self-expression. In his well-known phrase, neurosis is the price paid for civilization.

Psycho-analysis to-day takes a less gloomy view of organized society. To some neo-Freudians, indeed, mental health is virtually synonymous with social adjustment. And so it was with Adler. His "social interest" was conceived as a basic human capacity and its lack as a *sine qua non* of neurosis. No treatment of neurosis that evades the re-connexion of the patient with his society stands a chance of lasting success.

This more optimistic view of organized society is undoubtedly the real reason for the present revival of interest in Adler. Both he and our modern neo-Freudians share a belief not only in the therapeutic function of the group but in the ultimate betterment of society itself. Neurosis, they seem to say, is the price paid not for civilization but for its lack.

Yet when all is said, it remains true that Adler was never analysed, never really understood Freud and contributed hardly anything to the theoretical development of psychoanalysis. He expounded a view of neurosis that was both exaggerated and over-simple; a generalization from a few cases without adequate control or possibility of proof. In presenting his argument, moreover, Adler relied almost wholly on personal authority with scant regard to the evidence upon which his system was based. Present-day psychology has little use for prophets and pamphleteers. It seeks its foundations in the decent obscurity of the laboratory, the clinic and the statistician's office.

The most that can be said for Adler is that he stood up to Freud at a time when psycho-analysis showed signs of hardening into a quasi-religious sect. Courage, indeed, he never lacked. And, significantly, this was the trait which he most admired in others and which he spent the greater part of his life in trying to instill into his patients. "Courage," he was wont to say, "is the health of the soul."

Alfred Adler will remain as a figure of real—if minor—importance in the history of modern psychology. A man of complex nature, he was not without internal contradictions. Alongside his aggressiveness was a strong feeling for democracy and socialism. His philosophy of ruthless self-interest was tempered with a deep compassion for the sick and the unhappy. In his slightly ludicrous way he strove earnestly to bring psychological insight within the compass of the ordinary man and woman. Behind the fictive mask of the Superman lay concealed the face of one whom Israel Zangwill might have called a Dreamer of the Ghetto.

Willard Beecher and Marguerite Beecher (essay date 1973)

SOURCE: "Memorial to Dr. Alfred Adler," in *Alfred Adler: His Influence on Psychology Today,* edited by Harold H. Mosak, Noyes Press, 1973, pp. 1-5.

[*In the following essay, Beecher and Beecher outline the insights into human nature gained from their association with Adler.*]

The tallest measure of a man is the effect that he has on the lives of others. And the deepest measure of his value lies in what they learn from him in terms of enduring wisdom—the kind that helps them when critical forks-in-the-road confront them. In the few years that we were fortunate enough to share with Alfred Adler before he died he revealed some monumental truths to us. He gave us a give of the comprehensive as well as the particular aspects of human behavior. The greatest honor we can pay him at this time is to share with others that which he helped us to see through his vision. It is our hope that it will not die with us and that it may be of some help to others.

We learned from him essentially:

> 1. That the individual's approach to life is a result of early self-training due to his interpretation of his situation. He can change it in later years only if he realizes that his disturbing, conditioned responses are nothing more than inappropriate, inadequate holdovers from childhood. The adult is expected to replace such behavior with more useful responses to be a help and not a burden. He should realize it is useful to try to escape the pain he creates for himself trying to solve adult problems with a child's tricks and evasions, since problems are only situations for which we have not trained ourselves.

> 2. That the problems of behavior, which make us feel and act like inferior second-class passengers in life, are no more than the results of our failure to develop the habit of both emotional and physical self-reliance. We retain from childhood the mistaken expectation that others should "hold up our pants" for us emotionally and physically and be interested in as well as responsible for our welfare.

> 3. That leaning on others emotionally or physically is a child's way of life. We should not permit this habit to follow us into adult life, *since dependency is the root of all feelings of inferiority.* Dependency generates the feeling of second-class citizenship. Out of this grows the habit of competition, envy, making comparisons and similar mistaken compensatory strivings we create in our effort to assuage the pain of feeling second class in relation to others. Humiliating feelings of inferiority produce the gnawing, distracting, disruptive, destructive craving for personal recognition and prestige, with its inescapable fear of failure.

4. That unhappiness, loneliness, neurotic symptoms, crime and similar distresses arise directly from this unresolved process of leaning and depending on others whom we try to control, rule, dominate or exploit for our own benefit, since we cannot otherwise support ourselves physically and emotionally.

5. That only those who are self-reliant emotionally and physically can function as *adult* human beings able to cooperate with other adults, because life demands that we be useful and productive or, as Adler said, to "be a help and not a burden."

6. That the inadequate responses of envy, greed, competition and sabotage—with which we try to solve confronting problems of life—are only reactions *which would not arise in the first place* if we were in the habit of standing on our own feet and were not always trying to find someone on whom to lean and exploit; whom we demand prop us up and hold us there.

7. That defects of self-reliance and the *inescapable pain* that accompanies them can be changed only when we *fully realize* that the pain we suffer is but the other-end-of-the-stick of our leaning, dependent, subaltern habits of mind. Our problems do not have mysterious, hidden sources in some hypothetical "Id." We do not have to look far or deep to find the source; we keep stumbling, tripping and falling over it all day long, even though *we refuse to identify it as our own childishness.*

8. That all human beings are the product of evolution, and that we share the inheritance of all human potentialities and are each equally based in evolution. Each can evoke his store of potentialities to shape them into his *own creation* and discover his own reality. Each is his own architect. Whatever one human being has done can be done by others. Creation is a built-in attribute of each of us. It waits, however, for the awakening touch of self-reliance to shape its parts and aspects. [from Beecher and Beecher, *Beyond Success and Failure,* 1966.]

In addition to the comprehensive view of human behavior pictured above, he gave us the most specific and particular way of seeing things directly as they unfold before us. He encouraged us to TRUST ONLY MOVEMENT! He revealed that each of us puts the whole meaning we are presently giving to life in whatever we happen to be doing at any current moment. He made us look at the immediate confrontation and blocked escape into alibis, self-pity or recriminations about the situation.

Adler taught us that living is a process which takes place in the *here-and-now* and that any relationship one makes is a process of self-revelation. In other words, an individual reveals himself in everything he does. From Adler we learned that behavior is not some dead thing which is a mere result of inner or outside compulsions from the self, the environment, or the past. He urged us to watch not only the relationships a person makes but to avoid getting trapped into some imputed or hypothetical "why" of

things. He stressed that the unfolding behavior in a situation reveals its own explicit dynamics.

Adler made clear that the way an individual can alter the mistakes of his own personality—his own behavior—is to see with the impartial, uncritical eye of a camera. He must see himself to discover his own "law of movement" when coping with confronting situations. He must view this approach non-judgmentally without evasion or aversion so that he does not shift blame on anyone or anything outside himself. He must be able to see that no one is destroyed from "causes" outside himself. And, when he has learned to see himself in his law of movement, he can see others through their eyes and help them to a similar self-discovery. Thus no one needs to live indefinitely blinded by his own mistaken certainties, illusions or wishful thinking.

If we confine ourselves to watching the behavior of individuals in coping with situations, we can understand the challenging and exciting phenomenon we call behavior. Contrary to common belief, our behavior does not have a cause which is reaching out of our past, driving us to do what we do. Behavior is a response to a challenge arising in the here-and-now. It is something we create to achieve security in the confronting present. We alone select our behavior and are responsible for what we are doing at any moment. Each chooses whatever he estimates will resolve the encounter or get him out of it. Or, as in neurosis, bring someone to his side to solve the problem for him.

Much of our behavior is made up of old habits which are only conditioning-with-a-purpose. Habit never rests and it persists until we choose to alter it to serve another purpose. Habits are forms of behavior we have invented and tested repeatedly in the past. We like our habits, *both those we label good and especially those we label bad.* The habits we retain for current use are like old friends on whom we lean for our comfort and security—as the alcoholic lovingly hugs his bottle! We hide our admiration of our vices—a fact we quickly discover when someone brings pressure on us to get rid of them; we defend them against all opposition.

Habits operate much like a satellite in orbit. As long as a person finds them useful to his way of life, he keeps them in orbit. (Certainly, he is not the helpless victim of habits, although it might be flattering to believe this.) Once we launch habits in orbit, they remain of their own momentum until we alter the purpose they serve for us or use them to serve a different goal. Habits do not rule an individual at any time in any way as he would like to pretend they do. They are his obedient servants all the way.

It is not necessary to know or investigate the past of an individual to change his behavior. It makes no difference how he got the way he is. All that it is important to know is that he is holding on to his present behavior because it suits his purpose. He may wish to escape the side effects of some of his old habits but these penalties are unavoidable unless he gives up the habit itself that is at the root of his pain. The pain lies in resisting pain. A problem is only a situation for which a person has not trained himself and he *resists the situation* instead of facing it. Thus, he remains in pain.

Pain, then, is not the result of something in the past. It lies in our present refusal to meet a confronting situation on its own demands. We are trying to face it with old habits, traditions, attitudes and prejudices; in short, with wishful thinking!

Analysis of the past does not recondition behavior or change our goals and is not essential for anyone who wants to get rid of his own disturbing behavior. An individual may like to believe that behavior has causes rising out of the past and that he is a blameless victim so that he can escape personal responsibility for what he is doing now (by blaming it on the past). This explains the popularity of psychoanalysis which allows the individual to continue his old behavior without feeling responsible for it in the present.

Emotional difficulties arise only in those areas of life in which one still leans and depends on people or things outside himself rather than on the innate power of his own mind. The mind is a product of evolution and is millions of years old. It works properly only when it is free of all outside dependence. Under such conditions, it works spontaneously; it is on constant alert and sees directly into situations without any dithering, anxieties or confusion. When dependency exists, the Wishful Mind grasps for something outside itself such as authority figures, traditions, deals, habits and beliefs in which to wrap itself for support. But the mind is not able to function when caught in such a bind as it cannot serve the self and an outside authority *at the same time*. The wish to do both simultaneously becomes a double bind—or "chasing two rabbits at once," thus catching neither. Such an hesitating attitude (a step forward and a step backward) results in a dither so that, actually, one stands still in fear.

One does not achieve freedom of the mind by any form of discipline, effort or mind-developing, mind-expanding exercises or drugs. Nothing can be added to the mind in any way; one can only liberate it from clinging dependencies that thwart its spontaneity. When the last crutch has been eliminated and an individual stands alone, the mind is no longer under any outside pressures of conformity. At that moment it assumes its natural contours.

The solution of emotional problems, as Adler said, is to increase self-reliance in areas where an individual is dependent and thus in pain. When he becomes non-attached, the mind can "let go and walk on." The center of gravity is no longer placed on those around him and on crutches outside himself on which he has leaned. He brings the center of gravity back into the self and stands on his own two feet. Only under such conditions may he function as a wholly adequate and self-reliant being. This is the natural heritage granted to each of us who claims his heritage.

This, then, is Alfred Adler as we experienced him. Others will see him differently. And that is as it ought to be as there are multiple facets to his great genius. He needs no adulation since his work speaks for him to each of us differently in a language of its own.

Clarence J. Karier   (essay date 1986)

SOURCE: "Alfred Adler: Social Interest as Religion," in *Scientists of the Mind: Intellectual Founders of Modern Psychology,* University of Illinois Press, 1986, pp. 226-54.

[*In the following excerpt, Karier offers a study of Adler's life and intellectual legacy.*]

In the early morning hours of a day in late May 1937, Alfred Adler lay prostrate on a cobblestone street in Aberdeen, Scotland, stricken by a fatal heart attack. When, very much moved by the news, Arnold Zweig reported Adler's death to Sigmund Freud, the latter is said to have replied: "I don't understand your sympathy for Adler. For a Jew boy out of a Viennese suburb a death in Aberdeen is an unheard-of career in itself and a proof of how far he had got on. The world really rewarded him richly for his service in having contradicted psychoanalysis." For twenty-six years, Freud had nurtured a bitter hatred for Alfred Adler, cringing with each report of his former pupil's success. Why this was so is a complicated issue, owing to the existential circumstances and the characters and personalities of the people involved.

Adler was noteworthy on Freud's long list of friends who became his enemies. He was the first to break ranks from the Wednesday Society (later the Vienna Psychoanalytic Society) and the first to create a counter-movement. From 1902, when the Wednesday Society was formed, until 1911, when the final break with Freud came, Adler was an active, regular participant in Freud's inner circle. In the context of those weekly discussions, however, he gradually tested and shaped his own views about psychology. Particularly distressing for Freud was his belief that Adler not only was creating a complete system of character formation, something Freud thought impossible at the time, but that he seemed to be "creating" his system from many of Freud's constructs, loosely altering the terminology and simply watering down some of his teacher's most important ideas. The latter deceit moved Freud to write the "History of the Psychoanalytic Movement," and in it to proclaim to the world that "psychoanalysis is my creation." Freud never rested easy with what his students did with his "creation." Likening them to dogs, he complained, "They take a bone from the table, and chew it independently in a corner. But it is my bone!"

Adler's deviations were bitterly resented by Freud, who repeatedly referred to his once highly respected student as a "malicious paranoiac." As time went on, Freud described Adler as a shallow thinker who constantly reduced psychoanalysis to the "commonsense" simplicity of the man in the street. Although Adler would not have been insulted by such a remark, Freud meant it disparagingly. Reflecting on nine years of association with Adler, Freud regretfully concluded, "I have made a pygmy great." The intensity of his reaction is reminiscent of earlier conflicts with Josef Breuer and Wilhelm Fliess. In fact, Freud himself made the association. Shortly before Adler's final break, he wrote to Carl Jung: "It is getting really bad with Adler. You see a resemblance to Bleuler; in me he awakens the memory of Fliess, but an octave lower. The same paranoia." And a few days later: "I am very glad that you see Adler as I do. The only reason the affair upsets me so much is that it has opened up the wounds of the Fliess affair. It was the same feeling that disturbed the peace I otherwise enjoyed during my work on paranoia; this time I am not sure to what extent I have been able to exclude my own complexes, and shall be glad to accept criticism."

At this point one cannot help but be reminded of the nature of Freud's "own complexes" and of his analysis as to how his own childhood problems ultimately affected his adult relationships. Freud had clearly described how his death wish for his brother Julius, as well as his struggle for dominance with his nephew, John, would be reenacted over and over again with respect to any future close friends, turning them into enemies. They would all become ghostly figures, or *revenants,* out of his past. As Freud put it, "In a certain sense all my friends are incarnations of this first figure, 'which early appeared to my blurred sight'; they are all *revenants.*" Breuer had become a *revenant,* while Fliess was just about to become one. The time when Adler and then Jung would join Freud's menagerie of ghostly figures remained in the not-too-distant future. While Freud's analysis of his attitude toward friends and foes is helpful in explaining the intensity of the break with Adler, it is so only in a partial sense. The other aspects of this dynamic situation are to be found in Adler's own personal history, in his character, and in the vast differences in fundamental ideas, values, and beliefs that existed between the two men. Alfred Adler's personality, life history, life-style, and fundamental values were all the near opposite of Freud's.

The very style of cognition to which Freud and Adler each adhered was quite different. Adler rejected the significance of dreams and the unconscious, calling dreams "the adversary of common sense." Common sense, on the other hand, was the key to cooperation and, in turn, the key to solving most of the world's problems. People who dream a lot, Adler insisted, are simply people who like to practice a form of self-hypnosis, deluding themselves into thinking they have found answers to their problems when they really have not. Adler disliked metaphors and symbols, complaining that they were too often used to hide the real meaning of our thinking because we lacked the courage to be forthright. He was a literalist, distrustful and unhappy with the playful world of the poet. As such, he attempted to destroy the significance that Freud attached to both the dream and the unconscious. Little wonder that Freud was angry. Adler argued that the poetic world of Freudian analysis was nothing more than the imaginary world of those spoiled and pampered children who lack the courage to speak in commonsensical terms: "If we speak plainly, without metaphors or symbols, we cannot escape common sense." In cognitive style as well as personality, character, life history, and fundamental social values, both men were near opposites. It is understandable why Adler's individual psychology turned out to be so very different from Freud's psychoanalysis.

In certain respects, however, Freud and Adler were similar. Both men looked deeply into their own troubled souls and found problems that also afflicted their patients and all of humanity. Both men created quasi-religious movements in an attempt to conquer the world: Freud, the Jew, wanted to lead the children of Israel and Rome out of their irrational bondage (by overcoming through sublimation his own obsessional neurosis, which he universalized to the world); Adler, the Jew turned Christian, wanted to overcome his own inferiority complex, which he also universalized to the world, by practicing the virtue of courage and preaching the gospel of social interest.

Alfred Adler was born of prosperous Jewish middle-class parents in 1870, in Penzing, a suburb of Vienna. His parents hailed from Burgenland, the home of composers Haydn and Liszt and a somewhat unique area of the Austro-Hungarian Empire, in that Jews there enjoyed a most liberal social status, relatively untouched by anti-Semitism. Perhaps, as Henri Ellenberger suggests, that is why Adler never complained about anti-Semitism. Whatever the case, it is clear that his father's occupation as a prosperous corn dealer led Alfred into personal contact with both the rural, predominantly gentile, peasant population and the urban, modern, religiously diverse Viennese. Adler grew up in a suburb of Vienna in which there were few Jews, and most of his playmates were of the lower class. His family was musically inclined, affluent, and non-Orthodox, leaning in the direction of assimilation into a gentile world. Unlike Freud, Adler grew up in an environment that was conducive to crossing cultural as well as religious and social-economic class lines.

In contrast to Freud, who wrote of the "happy child of Frieberg," Adler often spoke of his childhood as having been most unhappy. Part of his suffering he attributed to the misfortunes of being a second-born son. He saw himself in the undesirable position of forever, either literally or symbolically, having to compete with his older, always successful brother. Toward the end of his life, Adler reported to Phyllis Bottome, "My eldest brother . . . is a good industrious fellow—he was always ahead of me—and for the matter of that, he is *still* ahead of me." From early childhood on, Alfred was no match for sibling competition. Suffering from a severe case of rickets, he could only watch his healthy older brother run and jump freely, with no pain and little effort. Adler also suffered from spasms of the glottis, which brought him near suffocation when he cried.

During Alfred's early years, a younger brother, Rudolph, drew the family's attention, especially his mother's, away from him. Then, when Alfred was almost four years old, his one-and-a-half-year-old brother died in the bed next to him. At that same age "he decided" to cure himself of spasms by refusing to cry or scream anymore. The traumatic experience of his brother's death seemed to have affected him deeply. Recall that Freud's brother's death in early childhood also deeply affected him. However, it affected Adler in a significantly different way than it had affected Freud. Whereas Freud took on the heavy burden of guilt associated with having wished his brother's death, Adler focused his feelings of resentment onto his mother, whom he believed had failed to give him the kind of pampered attention he had become accustomed to receiving before his younger brother's birth, and who now smiled too readily after his brother's death. Bottome notes [in her

Alfred Adler: A Portait from Life]: "Alfred had always been much less attached to his mother than to his father. She was colder in her nature, and it is probable that she preferred her first-born to Alfred. Alfred did not understand, and never quite forgave her for smiling soon—he thought far too soon—after the sudden death of a little brother." Such a mother was not to be trusted, especially by a youngster who faced the daily competition of a more-favored brother, and who just as often faced the danger of suffocation whenever he cried.

No sooner had Adler decided to cure himself of his glottal spasms—by refusing to cry or scream ever again—than he, himself, faced imminent death. Suffering from a severe case of pneumonia, the five-year-old accidentally overheard the doctor advise his father that there was "no point in going to the trouble of looking after [him] as there was no hope of [his] living." Adler recalled: "At once a frightful terror came over me and a few days later when I was well I decided definitely to become a doctor so that I should have a better defence against the danger of death and weapons to combat it superior to my doctor's." Thus, at an early age, Adler chose an occupation that would help him in adult life to overcompensate for the insecurities of his childhood. In Adlerian terms he chose a life-style that would overcome his "organ inferiority." This kind of childhood experience later led him to write his first major book, **Studies of Organ Inferiority** (1907). Few would disagree with his professional claim, "I am the legitimate father of the Inferiority Complex."

As an adult, Adler admitted that his feelings toward his mother were mistaken, although this was the error upon which he had creatively built his own inferiority complex. Throughout his life, he identified most closely with his father, whom he thought was plentifully supplied with ego strength. In contrast to Freud's father, who meekly picked his new hat out of the gutter when an anti-Semite flicked it into the street with his cane, it is reported that Adler's father, "when he saw people with their legs crossed on a tram, . . . would push one foot down with his walking stick, saying politely, with a charming smile: 'I do not like to clean my trousers on your shoes as I pass!' " In later years, Adler would write a good deal about the necessity of "courage" in overcoming one's feelings of inferiority. Throughout his childhood, his father symbolized for him a courageous man who did everything he could to overcome his own physical and psychical defects. He made a lasting impression on his young son, especially when he took him on early morning strolls, during which time he taught him a variety of life's lessons. One such lesson, often repeated, was, "Never believe what anyone tells you!" Skepticism thus became a necessary trait for the young rebel.

Alfred Adler was a complex person whose childhood history was in many ways transparently related to the course of his adult life. Feeling a lack of support and warmth in his home, the youthful Adler took to the streets and found the needed support in the camaraderie of the street gang. It became for him an important window to the world, one that allowed him to study the diversity of human character and satisfy his psychic need for security. When Adler later developed individual psychology as a movement, he did so in the cafes of Vienna, not in the relative cloister of the academic community. He insisted throughout, even at the cost of some followers, that individual psychology must be kept free of the unnecessary abstract trappings of intellectuals and be clearly understandable to the people on the streets.

Some years after Freud graduated at the top of his class at the Sperl Gymnasium, Adler flunked mathematics there and had to repeat his form. "His teacher advised his father to take him out of school and apprentice him to a shoemaker because he was not fit enough to do anything else" [Hertha Orgler in *Alfred Adler: The Man and His Work*]. His father left him in school, however, and the next year young Alfred conquered his problem and became, by his own description, one of the best mathematics students in his class. He went on to pass all his examinations and entered the University of Vienna to study medicine, where his academic record was average. In 1895 he passed the university examinations without distinction and went to work in the Vienna hospital. At this point in his career he seemed to drift from being an eye specialist to becoming a general practitioner, although in the latter role he was uncomfortable, suffering a sinking feeling of helplessness every time a young patient died. In a sense, each terminal case was a special failing of a calling that had its roots in his childhood. Gradually, he shifted his attention to psychology and philosophy, and later he became a practicing psychiatric therapist. Aside from attending a few Kraft-Ebing lectures, Adler did not have any formal training in psychiatry. He was successful as a therapist, however; his personal characteristics allowed people to relate easily to him.

From the time Adler received his medical degree in 1895 until 1902, when he joined the Freudian circle, he served a short term in the Hungarian army, shifted careers into psychotherapy, became interested in the social causes of disease, and wrote a monograph entitled **A Health Book for the Tailoring Trade,** in which he outlined the social conditions leading to the particular diseases afflicting tailors. During this same period, Adler wrote a series of short articles dealing with a variety of human ailments and their possible social causes and cures. One such article, **"The Physician as Educator"** (1904), written shortly after joining the Freudian circle, clearly reveals the direction he would take later, after breaking with Freud in 1911. Adler's concern for courage in overcoming feelings of inferiority, and the need he felt to educate children so as to build their self-confidence, are themes he explicitly developed.

During his student days at the University of Vienna, Adler became interested in socialism and attended socialist meetings. At one such meeting he met Raissa Timofeyevna Epstein, whom he married in 1897. Raissa came from a wealthy Jewish merchant family of Moscow; she had studied in Switzerland and now was a student in Vienna (females were not permitted to formally register, although they were permitted to attend lectures). Raissa was a strong-willed, beautiful young girl, notable for her fanatic honesty as much as for her neglected interest in formal dress. She knew that the world needed changing, and she was interested in changing it. An active, liberated woman, Raissa's social beliefs lay considerably to the left of her young doctor-husband. When the Leon Trotzkys lived in Vienna from 1907 to 1914, they frequently visited the Adlers, and Trotzky's wife became a close friend of Raissa's. During this period Adler accepted Yoffe, a Russian revolutionary, as one of his patients.

Early on, the Adler marriage seemed most happy and stable, blessed by the births of Valentine in 1898 and Alexandra in 1901. However, as the years passed, and with the births of Kurt in 1905 and Nelly in 1909, the marriage seemed to falter. Small conflicts surfaced, and Alfred and Raissa became increasingly estranged. Although their specific problems remain obscure, we can postulate a number of possible reasons for their difficulties. Obviously, considerable cultural differences existed between the middleclass Austrian concerned with liberal social reform and the upperclass Russian interested in radical revolution. Also, while Adler espoused equality for women, there were many practical differences between his theory and his life with a liberated woman. There is reason to believe that Adler had some difficulty making the transition between theory and practice.

Throughout his career, Adler insisted that women were not only equal but in many respects were superior to men. He perceptively analyzed the repressed role of women and the psychic consequences for both sexes. Nevertheless, his values with respect to the ideal family remained structurally typical, idealized, and middle-class. Nowhere in his work did Adler ever propose a radical restructuring of the family unit or the functional roles of husbands and wives. It is interesting to note that when he finally broke with Freud, Adler was giving a paper before the Vienna Psychoanalytic Society that dealt with what he called the "Masculine Protest." In it he suggested that sex-role competition, behind which could be found deep feelings of inferiority and superiority, was more important in explaining one's character development than Freud's Oedipus complex. Adler's life with Raissa, a very strong-willed person, no doubt made him aware of the importance of this concept.

The Adlers seemed destined to be on opposite sides. When, for example, Alfred was baptized in 1904 into the Protestant faith, along with his two daughters, Valentine and Alexandra, Raissa refused to join them. When World War I broke out, Raissa supported the cause of the Allies against the Austro-Hungarian Empire; once the war was over, Raissa supported the Russian revolution. Alfred, however, came out against the violence of the communists and predicted the ultimate failure of the revolution. Serious grounds thus existed for the estrangement between Alfred and Raissa that would last throughout most of the remaining years of their marriage. Not until late in life, when Adler took ill in America, did he and Raissa seem to reconcile their differences.

As Adler formulated his views about individual psychology within the Freudian circle, he found the Jewish faith too limiting and wished to "share a common deity with the universal faith of man." He gradually developed his own psychology and his own faith, both of which not only separated him from Raissa but clearly enabled him to become the most serious competitor of Freud's psychoanalytic movement.

The years (1902-11) that Adler spent within the Freudian circle were important developmental ones for him. During this time he published the *Studies of Organ Inferiority* (1907), which Freud believed supported his own ideas, and he also put together his unique ideas about neurosis. Thus, only a year after resigning from the Vienna Psychoanalytic Society, Adler was able to publish his most important work, *The Nervous Character* (1912), which laid the groundwork for the individual psychology movement.

While many Freudian psychoanalysts have insisted that Adler was one of Freud's students, Adlerian psychologists have insisted that he was not. The issue ultimately depends on one's conception of the teacher-student relationship. If that relationship is such that the student learns and incorporates the teacher's ideas, then Adler was, indeed, not a student of Freud—or he was a very poor one. If, however, the proper teacher role is to act as a catalytic agent, spurring the student to develop his or her own ideas, then the Freud-Adler relationship was that of teacher-student, albeit, from Freud's standpoint, unintentional. Freud and his inner circle did serve as a counterfoil against which Adler could test his ideas. Clearly, many of his ideas had already germinated, having been expressed in a variety of forms before he actually joined the group in 1902. However, in the smoke-filled crucible of those heated Wednesday night discussions, Adler tested and sharpened his ideas against some of the very best critics.

Out of this experience Adler proposed a psychology that was the opposite of Freud's on virtually every issue. Freud believed that dreams were "wish fulfillments" which could be decoded in understanding the unconscious; Adler believed that dreams were little more than unnecessary distortions of the more important conscious world. Freud emphasized the role of the unconscious in determining behavior; Adler emphasized the role of consciousness. Freud looked for the causes of neurosis in the libido; Adler looked to the ego. Freud universalized his idea about the Oedipus complex to all humankind; Adler universalized his own inferiority complex to all humanity—"to be a human being means to feel oneself inferior." Freud's movement was to be theoretical and abstract, given to a heavy use of metaphor and poetic, symbolic interpretations; Adler's movement was common-sensical, concrete, and given to simple, practical interpretations. Freud saw the neurotic individual as divided against himself; Adler saw that same individual as a unity. Freud's psychoanalytic movement sought a causal explanation for neurosis; Adler's individual psychology sought a teleological explanation. And so on.

Although shortly after their break, Freud complained that "Adler's system is founded entirely upon the impulse of aggression. It leaves no room at all for love," later in life Freud himself wrote more about aggression, suggesting that there was, in fact, a "beast" in men and women to whom sparing their own kind was something alien. Adler, by contrast, eventually emphasized cooperation, insisting that human nature, if not innately good, carried the urge for perfection which was valued as good. To Freud, women occupied an inferior position in society for biological reasons; whereas Adler assumed that women were by nature superior, but because of faulty social reason, men dominated. Both men and women suffer, Adler insisted, from the masculine protest. While the woman errs in wanting to be a man, the man errs in his fear of not being manly enough. Striving for superiority, as a reflection of their drive for perfection, men become mixed up in the competition of the sexes and this symbolically affects all of their sexual behavior, even to the extent of their insistence on being on top during intercourse. The masculine versus feminine problem was not sexual, Adler insisted, but social, an issue of inferiority versus superiority within society's framework.

Adler's relationship with his wife no doubt helped him clarify his theory of masculine protest, just as his relationship with his mother initially helped understand his own inferiority complex. His will to power grew from his sense of inferiority, which resulted not only from his own organ inferiority, but also from his mother's withdrawal of her pampering support for him at the birth of his younger brother. He grew up distrusting his mother, and later came to believe that this was the error upon which he created the notion of an inferiority complex, which in turn set into motion his own life-style. It is notable that his adult relationship with his mother was characterized by overprotectiveness. Friends were very surprised at the extent to which Adler would interrupt his routine work to accompany his mother whenever she left the house. When asked why,

> He answered gravely, "But I cannot let my mother go out alone; she is not used to that." He was especially careful in helping his mother to cross the street. He noticed later that though he crossed the street quietly when he was alone, he was always very careful about the person he was accompanying, and directed them right and left. Finally he found out that he wanted to overcompensate an old insecurity in this way. He had been run over twice when he was a child; that is to say, had had bad experiences, and wanted to demonstrate that he was the only one who could lead others across the street correctly. This insight enabled him to rid himself of this disagreeable habit [Orgler, *Alfred Adler: The Man and His Work*].

While this incident reflects Adler's insecurity stemming from his childhood accidents, it also very much reflects the insecurity he felt toward his mother. Although she had deserted him in those crucial childhood years, he was not going to desert her! Significantly, when it came time to select a mate, he chose someone he perceived in most respects to be the opposite of his mother, someone he felt he could trust. In Raissa he found an honest, forthright person. Still, she did not readily give him the mothering he had missed as a child.

A significant portion of individual psychology clearly grew out of Adler's personal problems. He saw in himself and in his patients a deep-seated feeling of inferiority, and he observed that both he and his patients attempted to overcompensate, playing tricks on themselves and the community through a variety of devices. He found his way out through a process of extending his "social interest." Like Freud, Adler expressed in his final work a religious-like faith. Freud's bore the mark of a stoic, fundamentally Hebraic kind of moral system, while Adler's led to a kind of humanized Christian dictum of "love thy neighbor as thyself." Freud, in *Civilization and Its Discontents,* had ridiculed this dictum as an impossible ideal, just as Friedrich Nietzsche once portrayed the same notion as the groveling weakness of spineless Christians. Clearly, Freud and Adler drew on vastly different ethical codes.

As opposed to Freud, who saw neurosis as the almost inevitable price we pay for civilization, Adler thought neurosis was a correctable error. Adler would sit facing his patients, and his brand of therapy led to a much quicker assessment of the patient's life-style, the errors made in its development, and the practical steps necessary for remediation. Errors in life-style were to be determined by the therapist's personal experiences, knowledge of individual psychology, and "a guess." This added method of guessing was viewed by Adler's followers as a distinctive contribution to the "science" of individual psychological therapy. One such follower, Rudolf Dreikurs, noted: "Adler frankly admitted that he used guessing in this procedure, thereby introducing into science a technique which up to then was considered the most 'unscientific' approach to a problem. But Adler demonstrated that we can learn to 'guess in the right direction.' " While a "guess in the right direction" may or may not enhance the "scientific" validity of a diagnosis, it is clear from the standpoint of most observers that it did increase the speed with which any diagnosis could be made.

In comparison to Freudian therapy, Adlerian therapy was a "quick fix." In this regard Freud could say of Adler's therapy what he once had said of Otto Rank's therapy: it was designed to suit an American clientele. Americans, Freud believed, were not prepared to accept lengthy, drawn-out, expensive therapeutic practices. The issue here, however, is not so much one of European versus American as one of social and economic class differences. The upper classes Freud serviced could afford the cost of protracted analysis, while the middle and lower classes Adler—and later Otto Rank—serviced could ill afford such a lengthy process. Isidor Wassermann, of the Psychiatric Clinic of the Medical Academy, in Wroclaw, Poland, did a comparative study of the socioeconomic class differences of Freud's and Adler's patients and concluded that not only was the ability to pay significantly different in the two therapies, but also the very content appeared to be class-determined. In general, Adlerian concerns involving inferiority and the desire for power are typically lower- and middle-class problems; those involving sexual sublimation for cultural purposes are of more central concern to the upper classes, who have already overcome an inferior social position. The great bulk of Adler's patients were situated within or very near to the middle class. The middle-class values that permeated Adler's psychology clearly fit the class he was serving, while the upper-class elite values that permeated Freud's psychology were similarly appropriate for the class he served.

Although Freud evidently created a movement designed to serve the elite groups in society, and built this movement with a select priesthood of analysts possessing esoteric knowledge, he repeatedly argued for a "lay" movement. However, Freud did not want a movement that was simple and easily understood by all concerned, which might include the lower classes; rather, he wished to keep psychoanalysis out of the controlling hands of medical doctors. Freud lectured to medical students at the university, but that served his personal status needs more than anything else. He wanted to create a new lay cadre of analysts unencumbered by established medical practice. Had the rise of fascism not occurred and the holocaust not wiped out Freud's "lay" movement in Europe, that thrust of psychoanalysis might well still exist. Very much to the dislike of Freud, psychoanalysis in America developed as the special domain of medical doctors. Thus, as a consequence of World War II, America became the stronghold of psychoanalysis and the field became dominated by the medical profession.

While Freud failed to develop a lay movement free of medical practitioners in America, he did develop a select group of lay elite expert analysts in Europe. Adler, on the other hand, created a lay movement on both sides of the Atlantic that was clearly geared away from the notion of a select priesthood possessing expert, esoteric knowledge. While he would have liked to lecture to medical students, as Freud did, he purposely designed and championed a movement that would be easily and clearly understood by all concerned. Indeed, when his individual psychology movement was well underway, there were several among his followers who pushed hard to create a more esoteric knowledge and thus a functional role for a new priesthood. At the price of some defectors, Adler insisted on keeping his analysis simple, unabstract, practical, and guided by common sense. He intended to create a truly lay movement, to spread his gospel among the people as far as possible. While Freud lectured to medical students at the university, Adler lectured in cafes and eventually to larger groups at the Pedagogical Institute of Vienna, as well as the city's schools and guidance clinics. His audiences were composed primarily of teachers, teacher trainees, parents, child guidance counselors, and rank-and-file mental health workers from the growing therapeutic community.

Given the remarkable, vast differences between Alfred Adler and Sigmund Freud, we might seriously wonder what was in Adler's mind during the nine years he was a member of Freud's Psychoanalytic Society. Ernest Jones's impression of him during those days was that he was argumentative, "a morose and cantankerous person, whose behavior oscillated between contentiousness and sulkiness. He was evidently very ambitious and constantly quarreling with the others over points of priority in his ideas." Inasmuch as Adler used the group to clarify his own contrasting ideas, then this view seems reasonable. Many years after their initial encounters, Jones noticed a change in Adler: "I observed that success had brought him a cer-

tain benignity of which there had been little sign in his earlier years." Success no doubt helped Adler overcome his inferiority complex and thus bring under control the inordinate drive for superiority that was so much a part of his personal character. Competitive from childhood, hating to stand in the shadow of his older brother, Sigmund, Adler reportedly told Freud at the end, "Do you believe that it is such a great pleasure for me to stand in your shadow my whole life?" We can only speculate as to which Sigmund's shadow Adler felt most heavily.

The break with Freud was not a clean one. As it dragged on people took sides, and when Adler finally resigned from the Psychoanalytic Society, he and those who left with him created a competing organization with the unfortunate name "Society for Free Psychoanalysis" (rather quickly changed to "Society for Individual Psychology"). There were some who wished to remain active in both organizations, which Adler permitted; Freud, however, moved his organization to exclude any member who attended Adler's group, with the exception of a very special friend, Lou Andreas-Salomé. She kept Freud informed as to what the renegade group was doing, while at the same time pursuing her own course of psychological inquiry.

Shortly after Adler published *The Nervous Character* in 1912, he wrote to Hertha Orgler, "With this book, . . . I have founded the school of Individual Psychology." In it he described what he believed to be the origin of neurosis, the development of feelings of inferiority, the development of psychic compensations to overcome that inferiority, as well as the fictions individual neurotics choose to create, around which they build a life-style. Throughout this and other works, Adler attempted to create distance between himself and Freud, suggesting that while Freud sought causal factors for neurosis, he (Adler) was more concerned with the life-style the individual created as a consequence of some early childhood problematic experience.

Adler argued that early experiences were so laced with fictions that precise causal factors could not be determined. Furthermore, even if we could know the exact causal factor or factors, we could not change the original experience, only evaluate our present life-style, constructed over time, and its supporting operational fictions. In this stance, Adler aligned himself with typical twentieth-century ahistorical thinking. He treated the patient's life-style as the cause of his or her current ailment, and usually traced the creation of that life-style back to the age of three to five years, where, in the context of too much or too little pampering by father, mother, sister, or brother, a certain life-style was chosen. For the neurotic personality the choice was an error, but one that could ultimately be corrected by therapy.

While Adler claimed he did not deal with exact causal factors, whenever he spoke about the "correct" or the "best" child-rearing practices, he implicitly assumed that certain causal factors were productive of the neurotic personality. Even so, he repeatedly turned away from what he considered to be the fictitious history of the patient, stressing instead the current fictions and possible pragmatic consequences for the future of the patient. Thus Adler insisted that the teleological purposes or "fictitious goals" of the individual could tell us more about the individual's problems than any lengthy inquiry into the unconscious, itself laced with imaginative creations.

Throughout this work and his later exposition of individual psychology, Adler relied on H. Vaihinger's *The Philosophy of "As If"* for the key to interpreting neurotic behavior. Adler saw the individual almost as a monad, always situated in a social environment in which he or she acted and reacted. In this life process the individual creates ideas and self-conceptions that collectively reflect his or her overall life-style. Within this life-style, purposes emerge that serve as teleological goals, which become so when the individual acts upon them as if they were, in fact, real. Thus individual "fictions" are created about self and world, and by acting "as if" these fictions were true, individuals create their own meaningful, unified world. Whether neurotic or normal, the world of the individual is always unified.

The individual was thus never completely determined by the environment but was actively shaping that environment. Paraphrasing Johann Pestalozzi to that effect, Adler said, "The environment molds man, but man molds the environment." Heinz and Rowena Ansbacher point out that Adler's position here is similar to the one taken by Marx and Engels: "The circumstances make men just as men make the circumstances." Like Marx, Adler saw individuals as creative actors who shaped not only their physical but also their psychical and spiritual worlds. Neurosis occurs when individuals err in their psychic creations and generate a sense of self that leads them away from legitimate social interest. The issue is not so much whether a particular idea about one's self is true or false, but more importantly, where that particular idea may lead. The neurotic's ideas about self usually lead toward an increasingly alienated state, until insanity and death ultimately ensue. Neurosis can be cured, Adler believed, if the individual can be taught to see and understand the error of these "fictions," be encouraged to create new, more socially desirable fictions, and to act on *those* ideas "as if" they were true—in effect, to be reeducated to an entirely new life-style.

Adler's psychology was a holistic one which combined both material and spiritual concerns. It was a total way of life. His psychology touched upon all aspects of human character formation: avarice, sloth, and envy, as well as spiritual virtue and the meaning of God. *The Nervous Character* began Adler's movement, which he preached throughout Europe and America from 1912 to 1937. He was bent on replacing psychoanalysis with a total psychology, created from a theory about character formation that was based on a view of aggression as involving the struggle for superiority, especially in terms of the sexes. Freud's key concept of a universal Oedipal complex, around which all psychosexual repression occurs, was, from Adler's standpoint, nothing more than his own notion of the masculine protest dressed up in mother's clothing: "A proper insight for instance into the 'Oedipus complex' shows us that it is nothing more nor less than a figurative, sexually clothed conception of what constitutes masculine self-

consciousness, superiority over woman. . . ." Adler described these neurotics, like Freud, who suffered from an Oedipus complex, as nothing more than "pampered children," spoiled by a doting mother who ill prepared them for the world of cooperation and social interest. Thus Adler not only attempted to replace Freud's psychology, but he thereby attempted to explain away Freud's own neurosis as well.

Once the individual psychology movement was underway, Adler applied for the title of *Privat Dozent* at the University of Vienna, so that he also might lecture to medical students. He submitted ***The Nervous Character*** as evidence of his scholarship, but in 1915 a faculty of twenty-five voted unanimously against his appointment. Although they found his ideas imaginative, facile, and ingenious, they also found them totally lacking in any kind of rigorous, scientific, disciplined methodology: ". . . it is dangerous for research when it is only ingenious. The products of imagination must undergo the refining process of criticism, which Adler's writings show themselves not even to have begun." The door to the medical students of Vienna was closed to Adler from the beginning of his movement.

The bitterness of this rejection faded from Adler's immediate consciousness as he faced more pressing problems. As war clouds gathered, Raissa took their four children for a visit to Russia. When the Archduke was shot, Adler telegraphed Raissa to return home at once. At first she refused; then she became entrapped, and it took five months to arrange return passage for her and the children. Raissa returned from Russia a pro-ally; Alfred left for the Russian front to do his duty for Austria-Hungary. Their strained marriage was not helped when Russia sued for a separate peace and slid into the communist revolution which Raissa supported. When Adler returned to his beloved Vienna after the war, he became actively involved in the Social Democratic party and the reform committees which swept political radicals into office. Raissa took up the cause of the Trotzky revolutionaries; Alfred argued against their violent methods. Pitting himself against his wife, as well as many of his radical friends, Adler argued in the cafes and in print that violence would breed violence, and in the end, the communist revolution would fail, unable to achieve its dreamed-of goals. Adler slowly but clearly steered his individual psychology movement away from the choppy waters of radical revolution and toward the calmer waters of liberal reform, where it eventually took anchor.

As the old group congregated at the Cafe Central, after the war, to hear and discuss with Adler his ideas about psychology and philosophy, it became apparent that they all had passed through the portals of the twentieth century. Each person was different; the world they faced was different. Adler himself sounded different, insisting that what the world needed and wanted was *Gemeinschaftsgefühl*, "community feeling." Over the next twenty years he would develop the meaning of that term, teaching and preaching his gospel of social interest, the new religious faith of Alfred Adler. While some thought it to be a bland oversimplification, and walked away in disgust, others stayed and listened. His new faith was interpreted by one of his critical followers in this way:

> there was a law binding man to the universe, moving always in the same direction, and towards a goal that could never be reached, but which never varied; and as man obeyed this law and co-operated with it, he would develop in a direction that furthered universal welfare—but his co-operation with others was the price he must pay for this development. The egocentric goal must be broken up. Social Interest *was* the only goal for mankind; and every human being must be trained towards it in childhood, until it became as natural to him "as breathing or the upright gait" [Bottome, *Alfred Adler: A Portrait from Life*].

Although both Marx and Adler dreamed the impossible dream of a perfect social order, Marx saw the road to his vision paved with class conflict, while Adler insisted that it must be paved with cooperation. Unlike Marx, who turned to revolutionary praxis to change his world, Adler turned to educational praxis. He and his followers now became actively engaged in educational reform in Vienna. Through the influence of a close friend and follower, Carl Furtmüller, Adler was introduced to the new minister of education, Otto Glöckel. Glöckel was impressed with Adler and his small band of followers and thus gave them entrance to the school system, where they fostered ongoing educational reforms. They helped make the Vienna school system the educational showplace of Europe in the 1920s. Adler's group was directly involved in creating experimental schools, which attracted international attention, and in developing institutes and workshops for teacher training, on a regular basis. They formed and supervised over thirty child guidance clinics, attached to the Vienna schools. Through his forthright lectures to both parents and teachers, Adler helped to develop a strong attitude toward the use and acceptance of therapeutic practices in educating children in both the school and the home. Adler assumed the post of lecturer at the Institute of Pedagogical Studies in Vienna, clearly reaching the high-water mark of his career. All Vienna seemed to react positively to his ideas. His fame spread from Vienna to Germany, England, France, and America, and in 1930 his beloved city awarded him the title "Citizen of Vienna."

From 1926 to 1934, Adler divided his time between American and Viennese audiences. New Adlerian groups were forming in America, and he was rapidly finding a second home there. He talked to overflowing, appreciative audiences in some of the major academic centers, lecturing in extension courses at Columbia University from 1929 to 1931. His friends there prematurely put him up for a chair, for which he was rejected. By 1932 he was teaching as a regular member of the faculty at Long Island Medical College. Although his individual psychology, especially its "born-again-of-the-spirit" message, did not set well with the established Freudians in the United States, Adler made an impact on social workers, penal institution officers, guidance counselors, mental health workers, family therapists, and parents and teachers. While his American lectures received limited coverage in the more-established psychotherapeutic journals, they received extensive coverage in the *Police Journal, Good Housekeeping,* and *Parents Magazine.*

By 1934, Adler's divided home life between America and Vienna came to a close. The national socialists had taken power in Vienna, and all his reform work was halted. In that same year he became seriously ill with an untreated carbuncle and was hospitalized. Raissa, hearing of his illness, immediately joined him, and the results were therapeutic for both his physical health and their marriage. "His illness and Raissa's instant response to his need of her changed both their lives. For the first time, Adler realized how deep his wife's devotion to him really was; and his whole nature responded to it, and to her care for him." [Bottome, *Alfred Adler: A Portrait From Life*]. Recall that illness had played an important role in Adler's own early childhood character formation. His inferiority feelings, as he had analyzed them, lay in his response to his mother's inability to satisfy his need for attention when ill. He had married someone he thought was different, but through the years her emancipated outlook tended to undercut his overwhelming need for security. Yet when Raissa quickly responded to his need for attention during his first and only illness as an adult, their marriage was at last reconciled, and they remained together until Adler's death three years later.

The three great problems of life, or so Adler argued, were community feeling, work and occupation, love and marriage. *Gemeinschaftsgefühl,* "community feeling," must permeate all activities of life. We must turn away from our selfish ways, not through self-sacrifice so much as through self-development—indeed, through the continuing expansion of social interest. The key word in all this was "cooperation": men and women must learn to cooperate, for their own individual good and for the good of humanity. Problems with friends, work, or family always could be solved by increasing cooperation, or social interest. Individual problems of crime, delinquency, drug addiction, alcoholism, and sexual perversion were all similar, in the sense that each showed a lack of social responsibility and each erred against any true social interest. In response to a critic who had accused him of making a religion out of his notion of social interest, Adler said, "I have propounded religion as a constructive step towards the advancement of co-operation so much that I was frequently suspected of being a Philistine. . . . I refuse to teach religion being not qualified for it, and leave it to others. I only represent the viewpoint of science which, in its application in fact often corresponds with the commandments of religion. We do not demand anything, however, we merely explain."

Adler was doing something much more than explaining, however; he was, in fact, preaching a particular way of life, a kind of middle-class, liberal, religious humanism. In **Understanding Human Nature** (1927), **What Life Should Mean to You** (1931), **Religion and Individual Psychologie** (with Ernest Jahn, 1933), and **Social Interest: A Challenge to Mankind** (1936), Adler detailed the values that "ought" to be taught in the home, the school, the workplace, and the general community. All of this led Freud, late in his life, to refer to the Adlerians as "buffoons . . .

publishing books about the meaning of life(!)" Buffoons or not, Adler and his followers were preaching a religious faith laced with conventional middle-class values: the ideal family was based on a monogamous marriage in which the role of motherhood was exhorted; masculine and feminine social roles remained separate and distinct, by nature. "The bisexuality of the human race conditions another division of labor. Woman, by virtue of her physical construction, is excluded from certain activities, while on the other hand, there are certain labors which are not given to man, because man could better be employed at other tasks."

Although the term "individual" in Adler's individual psychology placed emphasis on the individual as a choosing being, Adler did not see individuals as an end in themselves; rather, their very value or worth was to be determined by a communal measure: "Any man's value . . . is determined by his attitude toward his fellow men, and by the degree in which he partakes of the division of labor which communal life demands." A productive system requiring ever-greater divisions of labor reflected, to Adler, a system that was evolutionary, advancing, and progressing; it reflected increasing degrees of cooperation and therefore was viewed in a positive way. The problem facing the individual was simply to find a place within this vast system of work in which to satisfy his or her need to contribute to the social interest. All occupations, Adler argued, were equally useful, and therefore the wishes of the child must be honored in the selection of an occupation. "We must let him value as he chooses; since we ourselves have no means of saying which occupation is higher and which is lower. If he really does his work and occupies himself in a contribution to others, he is on the same level of usefulness as any one else. His only task is to train himself, try to support himself, and set his interest in the framework of the division of labor."

Repeatedly, Adler treated the productive system as a positive "given" that was socially desirable and fundamentally sound. In 1931, Adler viewed the unemployment situation with "alarm." Dangerous, antisocial interests lurked in the large army of unemployed persons who did not fit into the existing division of labor. One of the worst effects of unemployment was that it impeded those who were "trying to improve cooperation." When Adler himself considered what should be done, he did not advocate changing the means of production or the economic system of distributing wealth; rather, he called for training the unemployed to improve their skills and their social interest, so that they might better fit into the prevailing division of labor. In his analysis of work, he escaped reality through a process of idealization. For example, Adler felt that if we all do our jobs, then somehow we are all equal, because we are all contributing to the commonweal. This may be true in an ideal society but not in the real world of sharply differentiated pay scales. To suggest, as Adler did, that we have "no means of saying which occupation is higher or lower" is pure idealization. A similar kind of false consciousness emerged when Adler blamed unemployment on the unemployed, rather than on the economic system and its failure to provide work opportunities. This displacement of blame occurred when he sought solutions to

the unemployment problem in education rather than the economic system. This same false consciousness has served repeatedly to protect our current economic system from critical scrutiny.

Significantly, this therapy, which presumes to be so heavily oriented toward practical, ongoing life, repeatedly returns at critical junctures to a benign idealization of that social existence. The net consequence was an obfuscation of social reality. In the midst of severe economic dislocation in the monopoly-capitalist system of the West, Adler called for group cooperation in place of class struggle. "What we must disagree with is the view of life in which people are looking only for what is given them, looking only for a personal advantage. This is the greatest conceivable obstacle to individual and common progress. It is only through our interest in our fellows that any of our human capacities develop." The solution, then, to all problems was to expand one's social interest. Neurosis itself would thus be overcome. Adler said, "As soon as he can connect himself with his fellow men on an equal and cooperative footing, he is cured." He urged teachers, psychological counselors, and mental health workers to teach the values of cooperation: "All that we demand of a human being, and the highest praise that we can give him, is that he should be a good fellow worker, a friend to all other men, and a true partner in love and marriage. If we are to put it in a word, we may say that he should prove himself a fellow man."

As Adler's audiences increased in size and he received more support, it was almost possible to sense in him a growing confusion between the world as he thought it ought to be and the way it actually was. With the dark clouds of fascism gathering on the near horizon, Freud wrote about human nature "as a savage beast to whom consideration towards his own kind is something alien," while Adler insisted that human nature was basically good:

> Thus the long-standing dispute as to whether man is good or evil by nature is settled. The growing, irresistible evolutionary advance of social feeling warrants us in assuming that the existence of humanity is inseparably bound up with "goodness". Anything that seems to contradict this is to be considered as a failure in evolution; it can be traced back to mistakes that have been made—just as in the vast experiments of nature there has always been material in the bodies of animals that could not be used.

Adler often quoted Christ's command, "Thou shalt love thy neighbor as thyself," which Freud had concluded was a false expectation that ran counter to human nature itself. Given man's beastly aggressiveness, Freud suggested, Heinrich Heine's dictum, "One must, it is true, forgive one's enemies—but not before they have been hanged," was perhaps more appropriate. Adler, of course, charged that Freud's psychology was derived from a "pampered child," and that it was fundamentally unethical and immoral.

At times, however, Adler seemed to waver regarding his conception of human nature. For example, he said, "Man is not born good or evil, but he can be trained in either direction. Whose fault is greater? That of the erring community or that of the erring child?" In general, however, he returned to his normative ideal of social interest, which he found implanted in the evolutionary progress of humankind. Just as individuals carried with them a goal for perfection, so did the collective community carry within its evolution a guiding normative goal of perfection. For Adler, this idealized goal lay beyond immediate experience; it rested in a new, yet-unborn, ultimate synthesizing of ideas. He said, "I must admit that those who find a piece of metaphysics in Individual Psychology are right." His faith was total, resting on a metaphysics of his own creation; the very purpose of life was perfection. Adler continued: "We conceive the idea of social interest, social feeling, as the ultimate form of mankind, a condition in which we imagine all questions of life, all relationship to the external world as solved. It is a normative ideal, a direction-giving goal. This goal of perfection must contain the goal of an ideal community, because everything we find valuable in life, what exists and what will remain, is forever a product of this social feeling."

Thus, for Adler, humankind's quest for superiority was in reality an evolutionary quest for perfection, directed at "mastering the environment." However, it errs—indeed, fails—when it is directed at people.

> Individual Psychology has uncovered the fact that the deviations and failures of the human character—neurosis, psychosis, crime, drug addiction etc.—are nothing but forms of expression and symptoms of the striving for superiority directed against fellowmanship, which presents itself in one case as striving for power, in another case as an evasion of accomplishments by which another might benefit. Such erroneous striving leads to the psychological decline and fall of the individual, as any biological erroneous striving has led to the physical decline and fall of entire species and races.

Errors on the part of the individual in creating his or her guiding fictions lead to psychological decline just as errors in biological development lead to the disappearance of the species. Under Adler's leadership, individual psychology had discovered a special formula for overcoming the errors that would lead to the decline of human civilization: "Individual Psychology has found a special formula for the correct striving for perfection of man: The goal which the individual must pursue must lie in the direction which leads to the perfection of *all of mankind sub specie aeternitatis*." Virtue was defined as the advancement toward the common goal of the cooperating community, not as in the existing community, but in the yet-unborn ideal community where all people would be striving for perfection. "This is how the Individual Psychology concept of social interest (*Gemeinschaftsgefühl*) is to be understood."

God could be found in this individual and collective quest for perfection, in this final and ultimate goal which sheds grace on humankind in its continual upward striving on the path of life. "Whether one calls the highest effective goal deity, or socialism, or, as we do, the pure idea of social interest, or as others call it in obvious connection with

social interest, ego ideal, it always reflects the same ruling, perfection-promising, grace-giving goal of overcoming." Adler's individual psychology would light the path to the "sanctification of human relations." While the true *Gemeinschaftsgefühl* had not yet arrived, it was on its way. The psychology advanced by Adler would replace traditional religion when its most profound insights were acted upon and lived, as if true. He wrote: ". . . profound recognition of interconnectedness, which closes all doors to error and proves that virtue is teachable, has not as yet become realized by many. Religious faith is alive and will continue to live until it is replaced by *this* most profound insight and the religious feeling which stems from it. It will not be enough only to taste from this insight; mankind will have to devour and digest it completely" [critic's italics].

Adler perceived the promised land as a place where "error" was no more and "virtue" abounded. For him and his followers, individual psychology was the holistic faith that would lead men and women out of the bondage of antisocial errors. In Adler's world, sin had disappeared and was replaced by error. His social message was well within that eighteenth-century Enlightenment tradition which saw human nature as "good, but susceptible to error." Ignorance would eventually be banished and all evil thus would be overcome. In Adler's quasi-religious-therapeutic world, we would no longer suffer from the Christian sense of guilt but from the anxiety of having erred. Adler believed people were trying to escape the responsibility of those errors in the life-styles they had created for themselves, just as Cain had attempted to escape the error of his sin by asking, "Am I my brother's keeper?" Adler's answer would have been "Yes!"

In the unified but insulated world that neurotics tend to create, Adler saw their escape from responsibility as an escape from community, one that would lead them away from humanity and toward individual isolation, insanity, and ultimately death, for both themselves and the community. In the real, alienating world of industrial capitalism, where "competition," not "cooperation," reigns supreme and we are each pitted against the other for our very physical existence, the path we tread is clearly not one of Adlerian neighborly love, but that of a sickly, alienating society where the term *Gemeinschaftsgefühl* is difficult, if not impossible, to comprehend. This loss of community is clearly reflected in much of the literature of the Western world—in Marx's radical utopian vision, in Dewey's liberal view of community, or in Adler's *Gemeinschaftsgefühl*.

In Adler's beloved Vienna, the "City of Dreams," where Martin Buber studied philosophy and art and discovered the communal values of Hasidism, and where Theodor Herzel cultivated his liberal philosophy and discovered Zionism as a way toward a Jewish community, Adolf Hitler, during his Viennese years, cultivated his early hatred of the Jewish people. As Hitler's anti-Semitism gradually bore its bitter fruit, Adler's voice could still be heard urging his fellow citizens to "love thy neighbor as thyself." It was much like listening to Norman Vincent Peale's varied claims for the power of positive thinking during the time of the holocaust. As Adler lectured in cafes about "loving thy neighbor," the violent sounds of the fascists taking over the streets of Vienna were clear enough for all to hear. His benign, nonrevolutionary, nonviolent social gospel of cooperation might have been harmlessly incongruous, except that Adler's faith created for him a social cocoon, one that in the end insulated him from the noise of the streets. Early on, Raissa had sensed the problem— by ignoring the political and economic roots of the pending disaster and ministering to the psychological needs of the victims, and by ignoring the social roots of the disease and preaching an idealized metaphysical future, Adler was creating a consciousness which, in the end, can and often does easily lead one to blame the victims. It also creates the necessary social blindness that allows one to preach brotherly love during the very birth of Austrian fascism.

While we are struck by the distance between Adler's benign cooperative world and the actual competitive world of the streets he thought he understood, we are also struck by the fact that the psychologist who prided himself on his "commonsense" philosophy and his psychology of "practical solutions" in the end propounded a faith for humanity that was far afield from where men and women actually lived and died. In the modern world of alienated existence, a one-eyed psychology of praxis, blind in the other eye to the social-economic vested interests of power, is a psychology that can be expected to create a world of false security by creating a world of false consciousness. The philosophy of "as if," as applied in Adlerian psychology, thus easily slips into a kind of consciousness which, through its idealization of the cooperative way, actually protects the nihilistic competitiveness it abhors.

The legacy left by Alfred Adler is a strange one. While, on the one hand, there are today relatively few Adlerians—or at least people who admit to being Adlerians—on the other hand, his ideas heavily permeate the modern therapeutic community as well as the general public. Adler was clearly an important forerunner in the field of psychosomatic medicine, thanks to his original work on the psychic effects of organ inferiority, but in general, his most lasting impact can be found in the Adlerian concepts and terms that have become commonplace. In psychiatric hospitals or on the streets, we hear about "inferiority complex," "overcompensation," "life-style," "masculine versus feminine psychosexual roles," "ego psychology," "the child's place in the family," the psychology of "as if," and "organ inferiority." It is ironic that the term Adler believed to be most important—*Gemeinschaftsgefühl*—the key to his therapy, did not take hold.

In many ways the religion that Adler ended up preaching in the cafes of Vienna and the lecture halls of America was, in the end, just another failed religion—a "quick fix," an opiate to help people produce an "as if " fiction, an optimistic euphoria that momentarily overcame the "soulless conditions" of a "heartless world." Nevertheless, those who continue to struggle to overcome the crippling effects of alienation in American society, with its growing signs of fascism, by preaching a gospel of practical "social relatedness," "interpersonal relations," and "communica-tion," devoid of any serious social critique, do not appear to be far afield.

Edward Hoffman   (essay date 1994)

SOURCE: " 'Books Like Firecrackers' and Mass Politics" and "The Trap of Personality," in *The Drive for Self: Alfred Adler and the Founding of Individual Psychology,* Addison-Wesley Publishing Company, 1994, pp. 248-70, 325-30.

[*In the following excerpt, Hoffman discusses a number of Adler's later publications in terms of their political context.*]

The spring of 1930 saw the release of [Adler's] three new books, all aimed at a relatively popular audience. These were *The Pattern of Life, Guiding the Child,* and *The Education of Children*. Their nearly simultaneous publication in the United States clearly reflected Adler's own shift in professional emphasis from Europe to his present base of activity.

Based on his demonstration lectures at the New School two years before, *The Pattern of Life* presented twelve cases of schoolchildren with differing types of emotional difficulty, such as conduct disorders or extreme shyness. Many of the youngsters came from immigrant families (Italian, Jewish, or Slavic) populous in New York City during the 1920s and were of decidedly lower socioeconomic background. Yet, similar to Adler's other writings during this period, *The Pattern of Life* had little to say about cultural or economic factors that might be affecting such pupils. It was edited by the young psychiatrist Walter Beran Wolfe, who also provided a lucid overview of individual psychology.

The Pattern of Life presented transcribed accounts of Adler's comments about each case and his brief interviews with family members brought to the New School class. While it illuminated Adler's mode of interpreting specific kinds of childhood maladjustment, *The Pattern of Life* would have been a far stronger work for professionals had it contained a more detailed exposition of how he viewed each type of emotional disorder. Too often, his interesting comments appeared telegraphed, undoubtedly due to the book's transcribed lecture format.

Major reviewers generally found *The Pattern of Life* worth recommending. "Usually on the basis of the circumstantial evidence of the case," descriptively noted the *New York Times,* "[Adler] was able correctly to reconstruct the family situation to which he attributed the child's conduct. Afterward, the child's parents were brought in for questioning and advice, and finally, the child himself. The too docile, the rebellious, the neurotic, the feeble-minded and the maternally dominant child are some of the types analyzed."

More critical was the weekly *Outlook and Independent,* which regarded Adler's intense therapeutic optimism as unrealistic. "Dr. Wolfe's preface reveals the aspects of Adler's philosophy which have made some academicians place it in the realm of religion rather than science," its reviewer sarcastically remarked. "Essentially free will appears in a new dress. For the underlying idea of Individual

Psychology is that 'Every human being can do everything.' The determinism of heredity, the limitations of environment, the stupidities of society are not, it is declared, insuperable obstacles to one who is facing forward to a goal of social usefulness. The [individual's] job is to understand his pattern of life and if his conduct is unworthy, and his goal useless and selfish, master his fate by turning in the right direction."

In the ensuing years of the Great Depression, many American intellectuals would likewise find Adler's buoyant confidence in individual self-determination as overly simplistic. In this sense, his strong socialistic outlook after World War I gradually shifted to a far vaguer perspective on how people are affected by wider social forces. Even during the heyday of President Franklin Roosevelt's New Deal legislation, rarely did Adler ever provide concrete proposals for actually improving America's social conditions. He instead seemed content in late middle age to offer what many perceived as moralisms instead of empirical findings. Thus, the *Outlook and Independent* archly suggested that Adlerian psychology had begun to acquire the trappings of a religion. "Perhaps that is why [he] is hailed by his followers as a prophet rather than a psychologist. A well known Jesuit priest in Germany has said that if Adler continues to expound his social ideals, although a Jew he will establish the first Christian psychology."

Less moralistic in tone was Adler's second new book issued that same spring of 1930, *Guiding the Child: On the Principles of Individual Psychology*. Published by Greenberg, it was an anthology of twenty-one articles written by Vienna's chief Adlerian practitioners. The translator was physician Benjamin Ginzburg, who had organized and edited Adler's *The Science of Living,* published the year before. Adler himself contributed only one essay, "A Case from Guidance Practice," although his daughter Alexandra (Ali), now a fledgling Viennese psychiatrist committed to individual psychology, provided two. Other contributors included Ferdinand Birnbaum, Alice Friedmann, Arthur and Martha Holub, Olga Knopf, Alexander Müller, Alexander Neuer, Regine Seidler, Lydia Sicher, Oskar Spiel, and Erwin Wexberg. Together with Ali, these men and women had become the most important Viennese clinicians to practice and promulgate Adlerian psychology.

Certainly, *Guiding the Child* was aimed at a professional rather than popular American audience. Its well-integrated chapters had originally appeared as articles in Adler's journal during the preceding year. Most were descriptive rather than theoretical, and showed concretely how Adlerian therapists diagnosed and treated maladjusted schoolchildren. The majority of cases were drawn from either child-guidance or teacher-training sessions that Adler's associates had led for Vienna's public schools in the late 1920s.

Guiding the Child predominantly featured children of lower- or workingclass Austrian families. Many of the youngsters had lost a parent to death or desertion, and their health was often poor. With little parental supervision, teenage youths were sexually active and several cases involved prostitution or pregnancy. Yet curiously, not a single contributor to *Guiding the Child* even discussed tangentially how socioeconomic factors like poverty or overcrowding might be relevant to such students' lives.

Nevertheless, Adler's associates offered a progressive view of early maladjustment. They decisively rejected the notion, still advocated by many at the time, that these youngsters represented "genetically inferior stock" associated with specific ethnic groups. Rather, the Adlerians optimistically emphasized that virtually all such cases could be treated successfully through the modern principles of psychology. Emphasizing esteem building rather than coercive forms of discipline, they specifically condemned corporal punishment as an outmoded way of treating children. Generally, though, Adler's collaborators expressed satisfaction with the growing enlightenment of Austria's parents and schoolteachers.

With its sober style and sharp focus, *Guiding the Child* received positive comments from most American reviewers. Typical of these was the *New York Times,* observing approvingly that the book "shows how children are readjusted to school work and home conditions through the application of [Adler's] principles in the Vienna free guidance clinics which now exist in every school district. Initially, some ten years ago, partly by the public school teachers themselves, they have been largely fostered by parents' and teachers' associations."

In what may have set an American publishing record for the time, Adler authored yet another new book that same spring. *The Education of Children* marked his fourth work for Greenberg Publisher, and his sixth for the English-speaking world, in just three years. As was true for all his other volumes appearing in this brief period, *The Education of Children* mainly represented lecture material edited extensively for organization and readability. Combining this challenging task with translation from the German were Friedrich and Eleanor Jensen, a husband-and-wife team of Adler's Austrian associates. They performed their task well, for the book was probably Adler's most lucid since *Understanding Human Nature*. Unlike *Problems of Neurosis, The Pattern of Life,* and even *Guiding the Child,* this volume presented in detail Adler's insights on personality development. *The Education of Children* was too specialized for most parents, and had its widest appeal among those professionals already acquainted with Adler's name.

Arguing that all children suffer from feelings of inferiority, Adler attributed early behavioral problems to their intense desire to gain esteem and power. As he had long argued before, most childhood disorders are rooted not in sexuality but in the drive for mastery. Adler saw many problem behaviors as essentially strategies that youngsters unconsciously use to assert their will against much bigger and more powerful family members. In this sense, parents can start feeling helpless or enraged by a peevish child who will not sleep, who seems to eat nothing, or who continually soils the bedsheets.

"These weapons may be compared to [those] which nature has given animals for their protection—claws and horns. It is easy to see how they [originate] in the child's weakness, and his despair of being able to cope with life without such extraneous equipment. And it is remarkable how many things may serve for such weapons. There are some children who have [none] but their lack of control of stools and urine."

Adler advised parents to be gentle and understanding, rather than harsh, when faced with such problems. To threaten or actually carry out punishments is ultimately useless, and only exacerbates the difficulty. "What is essential is for us to see the child's situation with the eyes of the child himself, and interpret it with his own mistaken judgment. We must not suppose that the child behaves logically—that is to say, according to adult common sense—but we must be ready to recognize that children make mistakes in interpreting their own positions." Thus, for example, a five-year-old girl whose mother works a night shift may begin to develop a sleeping disorder. Its origin might lie in the youngster's fear of abandonment, and her intense desire, therefore, to actually witness her mother walk through the front door.

The Education of Children also offered Adler's rather detailed comments on [parental] sex education for children. Adopting a cautious viewpoint, he commented that, "There are many persons who are . . . insane on the subject . . . want [it] at any and all ages, and play up the dangers of sexual ignorance. But if we look into our own past and into the past of others, we do not see such great difficulties nor such great dangers as they imagine." As in previous writings, Adler stressed that parents should explain sexuality to children according to their degree of interest and intellectual capability.

Typical for Adler's earlier books, he highlighted the important role of schooling in aiding a child's emotional development. "An educator's most important task—one might almost say his holy duty—is to see to it that no child is discouraged at school, and that a child who enters school already discouraged regains his confidence through his school and his teacher. This goes hand in hand with the vocation of the educator, for no education is possible except with children who look hopefully and joyfully upon the future." In keeping with his optimistic faith in psychological progress as the key to social improvement, Adler ended his book by triumphantly declaring, "We are entering a period which is bringing with it new ideas, new methods, and new understanding in the education of children. Science is doing away with old worn out customs and traditions."

Despite its insights, *The Education of Children* offered little that was really new to Americans familiar with individual psychology. It covered ground that Adler himself had fully mapped in numerous earlier works, and to many reviewers who had initially been quite receptive to his writing, he was clearly rushing too many books into print. Rather harshly, the *New York Times* related that, "One finds much good sense in this book, much that is suggestive, and borne out by individual experience, but its form detracts from its value. The style is rambling, and the subject matter essentially unorganized. Juggling the titles of the chapters would not matter much. The book is descriptive and interpretative rather than explanatory in the sci-

entific sense or practical in its effort to teach those responsible for children."

Although its tone was more cheerful, even the sympathetic *Outlook and Independent* could no longer shrug off the repetitive quality of Adler's recent writing. Conveying a backhanded compliment mixed with an unmistakable touch of sarcasm, its reviewer remarked that, "Alfred Adler's new books come off the presses with the rapidity of exploding firecrackers. *The Education of Children* is a third arrival within as many months. But we are not with those who suggest that Dr. Adler should be persuaded to practice Book Control. Even if he does say the same thing over and over, repetition is a well known educational device."

During that same year, the influential William Alanson White, former president of the American Psychiatric Association, scathingly wrote: "While it has slowly been growing in [my] mind that Adler's other books are becoming stereotyped, [I am] now becoming convinced that they are deteriorating. . . . [I have] tried therefore to be tolerant and considerate and to see the good that was in the works of this author, but it is becoming painfully evident that an adverse note must be struck, and [I] therefore with this last work [cry] 'Enough!'

Why was Adler at the age of sixty inviting such unnecessary criticism at the risk of his formidable reputation? The answer is not altogether clear. Certainly, he had little to gain financially from authorizing the release of these "firecrackers" into the American zeitgeist. Greenberg Publisher's advances were not large, and none of his books since *Understanding Human Nature* had enjoyed sizable sales. Nor was Adler at this stage in his long career in need of professional recognition; his ideas were well known to colleagues throughout the world. From the almost casual manner that he entrusted free-lance editors to organize— even embellish—his books, it hardly seems likely that these works were important sources of ego gratification.

It may be that Adler decided that launching quickly done popularizations would be the most effective way to propel individual psychology into wider public awareness. From this perspective, he may have viewed books like *The Education of Children* as merely extending the seemingly successful approach he had initiated more than a decade before in postwar Vienna. By offering countless lectures to nonprofessionals at the People's Institute and by opening his society meetings to all comers, hadn't he greatly expanded the sphere of influence of individual psychology? Most of Adler's career had developed outside academia's groves, and as a social democrat at heart, he had always taken pride in rejecting the intellectual elitism that the University of Vienna medical faculty had long symbolized for him.

Nevertheless, Adler probably understimated the extent to which he began to alienate once-sympathetic American colleagues by his unbending effort to democratize his psychological system. . . .

Although Adler's work in the late 1920s had clearly blossomed in both Austria and the United States, matters were proving very different in England. There his nascent movement of individual psychology had become increasingly embroiled in extraneous social-political causes and factionalism. To restrengthen appropriate developments, Adler decided to make a special visit in January 1931.

Adler, of course, was aware that mental-health services in the British Isles still lagged behind those in the United States as well as in his native Austria. It had only been as recently as 1927 that British professional interest in child treatment had become organized. That year, the newly formed Child Guidance Council, based in London, had dispatched a fact-finding team to the United States to learn the latest interdisciplinary methods. Two years later, the first mental-health course for English social workers was offered at the London School of Economics. Likewise, the country's first child-guidance clinic and child study center was founded in the late 1920s.

Perhaps deciding that his approach might therefore be relatively unfamiliar to English practitioners, Adler offered a fairly rudimentary lecture to psychiatrists of the Royal Academy of Physicians. Published soon after in the British medical journal *Lancet,* **"The Structure of Neurosis"** was a formal presentation that emphasized a combination of social interest and co-operativeness as a key aspect of mental health. Summarizing his longtime perspective on personality development, Adler recounted how during our preschool years we each create a unique style of life designed to help us cope best with our powerful surrounding environment. "No two individuals are identical in their conceptions, perceptions, feelings, actions, and thoughts," he declared. "Each of these belongs to the style of life created by the child."

Adler explained that with repeated experiences of failure, children develop feelings of inferiority and subsequent difficulties in relating well to others. While conceding that the trait of cooperativeness probably had a hereditary component, he stressed that it was "not very deep and must be taught like history or geography . . . from the kindergarten onwards." Similar to Adler's prior remarks in books like *Understanding Human Nature,* he urged that mental-health prevention "be started at school [where] teachers look out for faulty styles of life and shrinking social interest."

In the brief question-and-answer period that followed, Adler addressed such topics as criminal behavior and its possible link to poverty, suicide as a form of revenge, and the value of traditional English education. The final questioner somewhat humorously challenged: "At what stage does the semisanity of us all become neurosis?"

"No general rules can be laid down," Adler gently replied, "for all individuals differ. The degree of social interest is the best guide to [our] amount of neurosis."

Two days later, Adler offered his next major lecture before the London branch of the International Society for Individual Psychology. This was the lay group founded at Gower Street four years earlier by Dimitrije Mitrinovic and his fellow intellectuals, artists, and writers. Although initially focused clearly on Adlerian psychology, they had become steadily immersed in Mitrinovic's eccentric mixture of occult study and the advocacy of pan-European

guild socialism. It must have been somewhat uneasily, therefore, that Adler addressed this audience with a formal lecture entitled **"The Meaning of Life."** It was published shortly thereafter in the journal *Lancet,* and later formed the nucleus for Adler's well-acclaimed book, **What Life Should Mean to You**.

Unlike his presentation before the Royal Academy of Physicians, Adler's talk was both more philosophical and eloquent. "The problem I want to discuss tonight is a very old one. Probably human beings have always asked such questions as: 'What is life for? What is the *meaning* of life? Perhaps they have said that life has no meaning at all. You hear it still in our own time."

Adler specifically attached Freud's gloomy assessment of human nature. Without mentioning his former mentor or *Civilization and its Discontents* even once by name, Adler nevertheless declared, "It is often said that human beings are governed by the 'pleasure principle.' Many psychologists and psychiatrists, however, are sure that this is not true." All emotionally healthy people, Adler insisted, "strive for the *happiness* of others; this is the true pleasure principle of the socially interested person." In contrast, to search for physical gratification is "the striving of a person who is only interested in himself and not others."

Adler went on to highlight the difference between the emotionally secure and the neurotic. He identified the latter as tending toward pessimism rather than optimism, seeking transient pleasure rather than enduring happiness, and living selfishly for themselves rather than cooperating with others. Those who grow up with such a negative outlook, Adler emphasized, are "not rightly prepared for life. . . . They always feel irritated and are always irritable, because they are not living [fully] in the world."

How can more people acquire true social feeling? The earlier this emphasis begins in life, the better. "We say that the ability to cooperate can be and must be trained. . . . On all points, we can prove that that meaning of life must be, for the greatest part, cooperation. And now we have to make it [alive]."

The following evening, Adler offered a third and quite different public lecture. It was sponsored by the Medical Society of Individual Psychology and was soon excerpted by the *British Medical Journal.* Later in the year, Adler's medical supporters in England published his presentation as a complete monograph entitled *The Case of Mrs. A.*

In order to demonstrate vividly his particular approach to personality diagnosis, Adler created an unusual and almost theatrical format. He pre-arranged with a few medical colleagues, that a completely unfamiliar psychiatric case history be given to him on the lecture platform. Then sentence by sentence, he read the notes aloud while immediately voicing specific deductions about the woman's life, attitudes, and relationships—all based solely on his thirty years of clinical experience.

In a way, this format resembled that of Adler's book *The Case of Miss R.,* published in 1929. He was now, however, interpreting case material extemporaneously as a teaching device. More broadly, Adler's predilection for a Sherlock

Holmes-style analysis of small clues to unmask one's basic personality had long been part of his professional repertoire. Indeed, in later years Adler confessed to greatly admiring Arthur Conan Doyle's most famous literary creation.

"Mrs A." was a thirty-one-year-old married woman with two young children. She had been raised in a working-class family with an alcoholic, physically abusive father. Mrs. A's husband had been vocationally ambitious, but due to a war injury was relegated to menial shop labor. Frustrated and embittered, he had expressed his urge for dominance by the continual bullying of family members. Mrs. A. felt little sympathy for him; in fact, for the past eighteen months, she herself had been suffering from a variety of phobias, anxieties, and violent compulsive thoughts, including suicide and the murder of their two small children. As a result, Mr. A. was forced to be at home constantly with never-ending vigilance, lest his wife or offspring come to physical harm.

In Adler's remarkably contemporary viewpoint, the case could best be understood in terms of family dynamics revolving around the vital axis of power. He declared Mrs. A's life-style a "masterpiece" of creativity, for she had developed a complex of seemingly debilitating symptoms whose end result actually gave her true power in the family. "By her neurosis," explained Adler, "she had given [her spouse] rules which he must obey. He became a husband under command. He was required to assume responsibility for her, and she utilized and exploited him. . . . By this strange route," Adler pointedly concluded, "she had conquered and subjected her husband."

Adler's audience was delighted with his artful demonstration of case analysis. . . .

Today, Adlerian institutes and therapeutic training centers are growing modestly throughout the United States, Central Europe, and elsewhere. Although he surely would be dissatisfied with Freud's unquestionably greater impact upon Western civilization, it seems likely that Adler would be content to see how much of his impassioned life's work has proven beneficial to the world.

FURTHER READING

Biography

Bottome, Phyllis. *Alfred Adler: A Biography*. New York: Putnam, 1939, 324 p.
    Popular biography written by a novelist who became a student and patient of Adler.

Dennis, Nigel. "Alfred Adler and the Style of Life." *Encounter* 35, No. 2 (August 1970): 5-11.
    Includes personal reminiscences of Adler by the author and an evaluation of his psychological theories.

Hoffman, Edward. *The Drive for Self: Alfred Adler and the Founding of Individual Psychology*. Reading, Mass.: Addison-Wesley, 1994, 390 p.

A complete account of Adler's life, including his later career in the United States.

Orgler, Hertha. *Alfred Adler: The Man and His Work*. London: Sidgwick and Jackson, 1973, 270 p.
    General study of Adler's life and career written by a prominent member of his Vienna circle.

Criticism

Ansbacher, Heinz L., and Ansbacher, Rowena R., eds. *Cooperation Between the Sexes*, by Alfred Adler. Translated by Heinz L. Ansbacher and Rowena R. Ansbacher. Garden City, N.Y.: Anchor, 1978, 468 p.
    Contains an essay by Heinz L. Ansbacher, a prominent Adler scholar and editor, on Adler's theories about human sexuality.

Bagby, English. Review of *The Practice and Theory of Individual Psychology*, by Alfred Adler. *Yale Review* XIV, No. 2 (January 1925): 392-94.
    Discusses Adler's conceptions of the inferiority complex, the will to power, and the distinction between normal and neurotic psychological functioning.

Crandall, James E. *Theory and Measurement of Social Interest: Empirical Tests of Adler's Concept*. New York: Columbia University Press, 1981, 181 p.
    Presents empirical research to support Adler's theories on the relationship between social instincts and mental health.

Denver, James. Review of *The Practice and Theory of Individual Psychology*, by Alfred Adler. *Mind* XXXIV, No. 133 (January 1925): 111-12.
    Briefly characterizes the relationship of Adler's theories to Freud's and argues that Adler's book is of uneven quality, while finding that the sections on child psychology are of some value.

Farnsworth, Paul R. "Further Data on the Adlerian Theory of Artistry." *The Journal of General Psychology* 24, No. 2 (April 1941): 447-50.
    Reports on empirical research to refute Adler's assertion that artistic creativity reflects an "overcompensation" for below-average physical abilities (low auditory acuity for musicians, poor color perception for painters, and so forth).

Porter, Alan. Review of *Understanding Human Nature*, by Alfred Adler. *The Criterion* VIII, No. XXX (September 1928): 146-49.
    Suggests a parallel between Adler's theory of "individual psychology," whereby the will to power is tempered by a sense of inferiority, and classical Roman Stoicism, with its dialectic of desire and fear.

Ruggles, Arthur H. Review of *Understanding Human Nature*, by Alfred Adler. *Yale Review* XVIII, No. 1 (September 1928): 181-83.
    Brief treatment of Adler's book notes its focus on the spoiled child.

Stepansky, Paul E. *In Freud's Shadow: Adler in Context*. Hillsdale, N.J.: The Analytic Press, 1983, 325 p.
    Stresses the basis of Adler's psychological concepts in his early career as a general practitioner of medicine.

Additional coverage of Adler's life and career is available in the following source published by Gale Research: *Contemporary Authors*, Volume 119.

Ernst Cassirer

1874-1945

German philosopher.

INTRODUCTION

While frequently identified with the neo-Kantian school of modern philosophy, Cassirer wrote on many different subjects, his works ranging from a book about the Enlightenment to an attempt to reconcile Albert Einstein's theory of relativity with the work of Immanuel Kant. With his best-known and most highly regarded work, *Philosophie der symbolischen Formen* (*The Philosophy of Symbolic Forms*), Cassirer advanced the idea that symbols and myths are the basis of all cultural activity and the foundation of philosophy.

Biographical Information

Born into a wealthy and cultured Jewish family in Breslau, Silesia, Cassirer began studying jurisprudence at his family's insistence, only to change his focus to philosophy after attending a course on Kant taught by Georg Simmel. Simmel also introduced Cassirer to the work of Hermann Cohen, a principal figure in the neo-Kantian school of philosophy. Cassirer sought out Cohen and wrote his doctoral dissertation under him at the University of Marburg, where Cassirer was profoundly influenced by the "back-to-Kant" movement and its emphasis on the philosophy of science. From 1919 to 1933 Cassirer taught as a professor at the University of Hamburg. There he had access to the Warburg Library and its vast collection of books on primitive culture and folklore, allowing him to begin research on his magnum opus—*The Philosophy of Symbolic Forms*—which he labored over for more than a decade. Cassirer's later works reflect the changing political climate in Germany between World War I and World War II. In one of the more famous philosophical confrontations of the twentieth century, Cassirer met Martin Heidegger at an academic conference held in Davos, Switzerland, in 1929; the two clashed when Cassirer voiced doubts about the possibility of human freedom in Heidegger's philosophy. Cassirer further criticized Heidegger in *The Myth of the State*. When the Nazi party was elected to power in 1933, Cassirer resigned his position at the University of Hamburg and left Europe. In exile Cassirer taught himself English and lectured at Oxford, Yale, and Columbia University, where he was teaching at the time of his death in 1945.

Major Works

Cassirer's first published works were primarily concerned with the development of modern philosophy and with the works of such philosophers as Gottfried Wilhelm Leibniz, Immanuel Kant, René Descartes, and Jean-Jacques Rousseau. Cassirer demonstrated his interest in the philosophy of science with his first original philosophical work—*Substanzbegriff und Funktionsbegriff* (*Substance and Function*). Although he is widely regarded as the most distinguished member of the neo-Kantian school of philosophy, Cassirer began to write about ideas outside the neo-Kantian realm after World War I. In his most ambitious and well-known work, *The Philosophy of Symbolic Forms*, he contends that human beings understand the world with the help of symbolic forms, which include language, myth, art, religion, and science. Symbols, according to Cassirer, express, represent, and ultimately create their own worlds of meaning. Cassirer believed that his three-volume investigation of language, myth, and the phenomenology of knowledge laid the groundwork for any future philosophy of culture. One of Cassirer's later works—*Essay on Man*—is an extension of his views on the ways in which individuals use symbols to give form to their perceptual experience. Some critics believe that the rise of the Weimar Republic in Germany spurred Cassirer to rethink and revise some of his earlier ideas. Cassirer's last work, *The Myth of the State*, is also his most overtly political and argues that human beings often mythologize their political existence rather than embracing a rational basis for the state. Although *The Myth of the State* represents a departure for Cassirer in terms of subject matter, it confirms that throughout his career, Cassirer viewed symbols and myths as the foundation of all knowledge.

PRINCIPAL WORKS

Descartes' Kritik der mathematischen und naturwissenschaftlichen Erkenntnis (philosophy) 1899

Leibniz' System in seinen wissenschaftlichen Grundlagen (philosophy) 1902

Das Erkenntnisproblem in der Philosophie und Wissenschaft der neueren Zeit. 3 vols. [*The Problem of Knowledge*] (philosophy) 1906-1920

Substanzbegriff und Funktionsbegriff: Untersuchungen über die Grundfragen der Erkenntniskritik [*Substance and Function*] (philosophy) 1910

Freiheit und Form: Studien zur deutschen Geistesgeschichte (philosophy) 1916

Kants Leben und Lehre [*Kant's Life and Thought*] (philosophy) 1918

Idee und Gestalt: Fünf Aufsätze (essays) 1921

Zur Kritik der Einsteinschen Relativitätstheorie [*Einstein's Theory of Relativity*] (philosophy) 1921

Die Begriffsform im mythischen Denken (philosophy) 1922

Philosophie der symbolischen Formen. 3 vols. [*The Philosophy of Symbolic Forms*] (philosophy) 1923-1929

Die Philosophie der Greichen von den Anfangen bis Platon (philosophy) 1925

Sprache und Mythos: Ein Beitrag zum Problem der Götternamen [*Language and Myth*] (philosophy) 1925

Individuum und Kosmos in der Philosophie der Renaissance [*The Individual and the Cosmos in Renaissance Philosophy*] (philosophy) 1927

Goethe und die geschichtliche Welt: Drei Aufsätze (criticism) 1932

Die Philosophie der Aufklärung [*The Philosophy of the Enlightenment*] (philosophy) 1932

Die Platonische Renaissance in England und die Schule von Cambridge [*The Platonic Renaissance in England*] (philosophy) 1932

Determinismus und Indeterminismus in der modernen Physik [*Determinism and Indeterminism in Modern Physics: Historical and Systematic Studies of the Problem of Causality*] (philosophy) 1936

Axel Hägerström: Eine Studie zur schwedischen Philosophie der Gegenwart (philosophy) 1939

Descartes: Lehre—Persönlichkeit—Wirkung (philosophy) 1939

Zur Logik der Kulturwissenschaften: Fünf Studien [*The Logic of the Humanities*] (philosophy) 1942

Essay on Man: An Introduction to a Philosophy of Human Culture (philosophy) 1944

Rousseau, Kant, Goethe: Two Essays (criticism) 1945

The Myth of the State (philosophy) 1946

The Problem of Knowledge: Philosophy, Science, and History since Hegel (philosophy) 1950

Symbol, Myth and Culture: Essays and Lectures of Ernst Cassirer, 1935-1945 (essays) 1979

CRITICISM

M. F. Ashley Montagu   (essay date 1949)

SOURCE: "Cassirer on Mythological Thinking," in *The Philosophy of Ernst Cassirer*, edited by Paul Arthur Schlipp, The Library of Living Philosophers, Inc., 1949, pp. 359-77.

[*In the following essay, Montagu explains Cassirer's views on mythological thinking, especially as it relates to preliterate societies.*]

In **Substanzbegriff und Funktionsbegriff** (1910) we learn that the study arose out of the attempt to comprehend the fundamental conceptions of mathematics from the point of view of logic. Cassirer found that it became necessary to analyze and trace back the fundamental presuppositions of the nature of a concept itself. This led to a renewed analysis of the principles of concepts in general.

In the course of his analysis of the special sciences it became evident that the systematic structure of the exact sciences assumes different forms according to the different logical perspectives in which they are regarded. Hence the necessity of the analysis of the forms of conceptual con-

struction and of the general function of concepts; for it is obvious that the conception which is formed of the fundamental nature of the concept is directly significant in judging the questions of fact in any criticism of knowledge or metaphysics.

From such considerations with respect to the processes of knowing, and the conceptual formalization of that knowing as related to the pure sciences, Cassirer was led to a consideration of the more fundamental problem of the primitive origins of these processes and their development. The first fruits of his studies in this field he published in 1923, as the first instalment of a large work entitled **Philosophie der symbolischen Formen**; this first volume was devoted to *"Die Sprache,"* in which the nature and function of language was considered. A second volume devoted to *"Das mythische Denken"* . . . was published in 1925; and the third and last volume, entitled *"Phänomenologie der Erkenntnis,"* made its appearance in 1929. Of these volumes I think it is no exaggeration to say that they constitute perhaps the most important and certainly the most brilliant work in this field which has yet been published.

Before entering upon a presentation of Cassirer's treatment of the nature of mythological thinking it is necessary to present something of his views with respect to the nature of language as propaedeutic to the former.

Cassirer insists on the fact that in consciousness, whether theoretical, artistic, or linguistic, we see a kind of mirror, the image falling upon which reflects not only the nature of the object existing externally but also the nature of consciousness itself. All forms brought into being by the mind are due to a creative force, to a spontaneous act in the Kantian sense, thanks to which that which is realized is something quite other than a simple reception or registration of facts exterior or foreign to the mind. We are now dealing not only with an entering into the possession of facts, but with the lending to them of a certain character, with an integration of them in a determinate physical order. Thus, the act of consciousness which gives birth to one or the other of these forms, to science, to art, and to language, does not simply discover and reproduce an ensemble of pre-existent objects. This act, the processes which give birth to it, lead rather to this objective universe, and contribute towards constituting its being and structure. The essential function of language is not arbitrarily to assign designations to objects already formed and achieved; language is rather a means indispensable to that formation, even of objects. Similarly, in the plastic arts, the creative act consists in the construction of space, in conquering it, in opening a path of access to it, which each of these arts makes according to the manner that is specific to it. Similarly, in respect of language it is necessary to return to the theory of Wilhelm von Humboldt according to which the diversity of languages expresses the diversity of aspects from which the world is seen and conceived by the different linguistic groups, and which consequently contribute to the formation of the different representations of the world. But one cannot observe the intimate operations of the mind which are at work in the formation of language. Psychology, even after having abandoned the concepts of apperception and of association—

concepts which during the nineteenth century stood in the way of the realization of Humboldt's ideas—does not provide a method which permits direct access to the specific process of the mind which ends by leading to the production of the verbal. What experimentation and introspection renders perceptible are the facts impregnated by language and by them, not the manner of formation, but the achieved state.

If one wishes to go back to the origin of language and, instead of being content with the linguistic facts and findings, one seeks to discover the creative principle, one can be satisfied only with those regions in which the formation of the language is known, in all its particulars, and to attempt by an analysis of the structure of the languages of these regions, by a regressive method, to arrive at the genetic factors of language.

Cassirer's study deals with the languages of a number of regions of this kind, inquiring into their mode of arriving at *an objective representation of the world*. According to Cassirer the lower animals are incapable of such objective representations; they find themselves enclosed in an environment, in which they live, move, and have their being, but which they are unable to oppose, and which they are incapable of viewing objectively, since they cannot transcend it, consider or conceive it. The impressions they receive do not pass beyond the level of urges to action, and between these they fail to develop those specific relations which result in a true notion of that objectivity which is essentially defined by the constancy and identity of the object. This transition from a world of action and effectiveness to the world of objective representation only begins to manifest itself, in mankind, at a stage which coincides with a certain phase in the development of language; viz., at that stage which the child exhibits when it grows to understand that a whole thing corresponds to a particular value or denomination, and at which it is constantly demanding of those about it the names of things. But it does not occur to the child to attach these designations to the representation of things already stabilized and consolidated. The child's questions bear rather more on the things themselves. For in the eyes of the child, as in the eyes of primitive peoples, the name is not an extrinsic denomination of the thing which one arbitrarily attaches to it, but it is rather an essential quality of the object of which it forms an integral part. The principal value of this denominative phase is that it tends to stabilize and to consolidate the objective representation of things and permits the child to conquer the objective world in which it is henceforth to live. For this task he needs some name. If, for a multiplicity of impressions one sets apart the same name, these different impressions will no longer remain strange to one another; in this way they will come to represent simply aspects of the modes of appearance of the same thing. The loss of this conceptual and symbolic function of the word leads to such effects as one may observe in those suffering from aphasia. That which language renders possible on the plane of objects, viz., a separation or distinction between *subjects* and *things,* it permits *equally in the domain of sentiment and volition*. In this domain also language is more than a simple means of expression and of communication; this it is only at the beginning of

human life, when the infant gives expression without any reserve to the states of pleasure and of pain which it experiences; and it is language which provides the infant with a means of getting into contact with the outside world. Language prolongs these affective states, but it does not in any way alter them. Things, however, present another aspect as soon as the child acquires representational language. Henceforth, his vocal expressions will no longer be simple exclamations, nor of pure expansiveness apart from these emotional states. That which the child expresses is now informed by the fact that his expressions have taken the form of intelligible words, the child hears and understands what he himself says. He thus becomes capable of knowing his own states in a representative and objective manner, of apperceiving and looking at them as he does at external things. He thus becomes capable of reflecting upon his own affective life, and of adopting in relation to that life an attitude of contemplation. In this way his affective energies gradually lose that power of brutal constraint which it exercises, during early infancy, upon the "self." The fact that emotion attains to a consciousness of itself, renders man to some extent free of it. To the pure emotion are henceforth opposed those intellectual forces which support representational language. Emotion will now be held in constraint by these forces, it will no longer obtain an immediate and direct expression, but will have to justify itself before language, which now assumes the position of an instrument of the mind. In this connection we may recall the Greek idea that man must not abandon his passions, that these rather must be submitted to the judgment of the *Logos,* to that reason which is incorporated in language.

Thanks to its regulative powers, language transforms sentiments and volitions, and organizes them into a conscious will, *and thus contributes to the constitution of the moral self*. There is still another domain into which one can gain entry only through the medium of language, it is the *social* world. Up to a certain point in the moral evolution of humanity, all moral and intellectual community is bound to the linguistic community, in much the same way as men speaking a foreign language are excluded from the protection and advantages which are alone enjoyed by members of the community considered as equals. And in the development of the individual, language constitutes for the child, who is beginning to learn, a more important and a more direct experience than that of the social and normative bond. But when for his characteristic infantile state he commences to substitute representational language, and experiences the need of being understood by his environment, he discovers the necessity of adapting his own efforts without reservation to the customs characteristic of the community to which he belongs. Without losing anything of his own individuality, he must adapt himself to those among whom he is destined to live. It is thus through the medium of a particular language that the child becomes aware of the bond which ties it to a particular community. This social bond becomes closer and more spiritualized during the course of its development. When the child commences to pose the questions—*What it is?* and *Why?*—not only is he going to penetrate into the world of knowledge, but also into a conquest of that world and a collective possession of it. Not only does the tendency to possess a thing begin to give way before the desire to acquire knowledge, but what is still more important, the relations which hold him to his environment are going to be reorganized. The desire for physical assistance begins to transform itself into a desire for intellectual assistance; the contact of the child with the members of its environment is going to become a spiritual contact. Little by little, the constraint, the commands and prohibitions, the obediences and resistances, which up to now have characterized the relations between the child and the adult gives way to that reciprocity which exists between the one who asks and waits for a reply, and the one who takes an interest in the question asked and replies. Thus arise the bases of spiritual liberty and of that free collaboration which is the characteristic mark of society in so far as it is human.

Cassirer's approach to mythology is that of the neo-Kantian phenomenologist; he is not interested in mythology as such, but in the processes of consciousness which lead to the creation of myths.

—M. F. Ashley Montagu

Finally, Cassirer assigns a capital importance to language in the *construction of the world of pure imagination,* above all to that state of conscious development wherein the decisive distinction between the real and the imagined is not made. The question that has so much occupied psychologists, whether the play of the child represents for it a veritable reality or merely a conscious occupation with fictions, this question, asserts Cassirer, is malposed, since the play of the child, like the Myth, belongs to a phase of consciousness which does not yet understand the distinction between that which is real and that which merely is simply imagined. In the eyes of the child the world is not composed of pure objects, of real forms, it is, on the contrary, peopled by beings who are his equals; and the character of the living and the animate is not limited for him, to that which is specifically human. The world, for him, has the form of *Thou* and not of *That.* This anthropomorphism of the child arises out of the fact that the child speaks to the things which surround him, and the things speak to him. It is no accident that there is no substitute for dumb play; when playing the child does not cease to speak of and to the things with which he is playing. It is not that this activity is an accessory commentary of play, but rather it is an indispensable element of it. The child views every object, all beings, as an interlocutor of whom he asks questions and who reply to him. His relation to the world is above all else a verbal relation, and Cassirer asserts that *the child does not speak to things because he regards them as animate, but on the contrary, he regards them as animate because he speaks with them.* It is much later that the distinction is made between that which is pure thing and that which is animate and living. The most developed of languages still retain traces of this original state. The lack of

such distinctions is strikingly evident when we study the languages, the mental instruments, of the simpler peoples, a study which is obviously necessary for any true understanding of mythological thinking.

Cassirer's approach to mythology is that of the neo-Kantian phenomenologist; he is not interested in mythology as such, but in the processes of consciousness which lead to the creation of myths. It will be recalled that he was originally concerned with inquiring into the bases of empirical knowledge, but since a knowledge of a world of empirical things or properties was preceded by a world characterized by mythical powers and forces, and since early philosophy drew its spiritual powers from and created its perspective upon the bases of these mythical factors, a consideration of them is clearly of importance. The relation between myth and philosophy is a close one; for if the myth is taken to be an indirect expression of reality, it can be understood only as an attempt to point the way, it is a preparation for philosophy. The form and content of myth impede the realization of a rational content of knowledge, which reflection alone reveals, and of which it discovers the kernel. An illustration of this effect of myth upon knowledge may be seen in the attempts of the sophists of the Fifth Century to work from myth to empirical knowledge, in their newly founded scientific wisdom. Myth was by them understood and explained, and translated into the language of popular philosophy, as an all embracing speculative science of nature or of ethical truth.

It is no accident, remarks Cassirer, that just that Greek thinker in whom the characteristic power of creating the mythical was so outstanding should reject the whole world of mythical images, namely, Plato. For it was Plato who was opposed to the attempts at myth-analysis in the manner of the Sophists and rhetoricians; for him these attempts represented a play of wit in a difficult, though not very refined, subject (*Phaedrus*).

Plato failed to see the significance of the mythical world, seeing it only as something opposed to pure knowledge. The myth must be separated from science, and appearance be distinguished from reality. The myth however transcends all material meaning; and here it occupies a definite place and plays a necessary part for our understanding of the world, and according to the philosophy of the Platonic school it can work as a true creative and formative motive. The profounder view which has conquered here has, in the continuity of Greek thought, not always been carried through nor had quite the same meaning. The Stoics as well as the neo-Platonists returned to the Platonic view—as did the Middle Ages and the Renaissance.

In the newer philosophy the myth becomes the problem of philosophy when it is recognized that there exists a primordial directive of the spirit, an intrinsic way of forming knowledge. The spirit (Geist) forges the conditions necessary to itself. In this connection Giambattista Vico may be regarded as the founder of the new philosophy of language and of mythology. The real and true knowledge of the unitary idea of the spirit is shown in the triad of Language, Art, and Myth.

The critical problem of the origin of the aesthetic and ethical judgment, which Kant inquired into, was transferred by Schelling to the field of myth. For Kant the problem does not ask for psychological origins or beginnings—but for pure existence and content. Myth does not make its appearance, like morality or art, as a self-contained world in itself, which may be measured by objective values and reality measurements, but it must be understood through its own immanent laws of structure and of being. Every attempt to make this world understandable by simple direct means only reveals the reflection of something else.

In the empirical comparisons of myths a distinct trend was noticeable to measure not only the range of mythical thinking but also to describe the unitary forms of consciousness and its characteristics. Just as in physics the concept of the unit of the physical world led to a deepening of its principles, so in folklore the problem of a general mythology instead of special research gained for it a new lease on life. Out of the conflicting schools there appeared no other way than to think in terms of a single source of myth and of a distinct form of orientation. From this way of treating myth arose the conception of a fundamental mythical view of the world. Fundamental and characteristic motives were found for the whole world, even where space and time relations could not be demonstrated. As soon as the attempt was made to separate these motives, to distinguish between them, and to discover which were the truly primitive ones, conflicting views were again brought to the fore more sharply than ever. It was the task of folklore in association with folk psychology to determine the order of the appearances and to uncover the general laws and principles with respect to the formation of myths. But the unity of these principles disappeared even before one had assured oneself of the existence of the necessary fullness and variety of myths.

Besides the mythology of nature, there is the mythology of the soul. In the first there are involved a large variety of myths which have a definite object of nature for their kernel. One always asked of each single myth whether it bore a distinct relation to some natural thing or event. One had to approach the matter in this way because only in this way could phantasy be distinguished, and a strictly objective position arrived at. But the arbitrary power of building hypotheses, seen in a strictly objective way, showed that it was nearly as great as the creation of phantasy. The older form of the storm and thunder mythology was the opposite of the astral mythology which itelf, again, took different forms, sun mythology, lunar mythology, and stellar mythology.

Another approach to the ultimate unity of myth creation attempted to see it not as a natural but more as a spiritual unity, expressing this unity not in the field of the object but as in the historical field of culture. Were it possible to find such a field of culture for the general origin of the great fundamental mythical motives and themes, as a center from which they eventually spread over the whole world, it would be a simple matter to explain the inner relation and systematic consequences of these themes and motives. If any such relation in a known form is obscure, it must appear at once, if one but refers to the best historical source for it. When the older theorists, e.g., Benfey,

looked to India for the most important motives, there seemed to be certain striking evidences for the historical unity and association of myth forming; this became even more so when Babylonian culture became better known. With the finding of this homeland of culture the answer was also found to the question as to the home of myth and its unitary structure. The answer to Pan-Babylonianism is that myth could never have developed a consistent world viewpoint if it had been constituted out of a primitive magic, idea, dream, emotion or superstition. The path to such a *Weltanschauung* was much more likely to be there where there was in existence a distinct proof of a conception of the world as an ordered whole—a condition which was fulfilled in the beginning of Babylonian astronomy and cosmogony. From this spiritual and historical viewpoint the possibility is opened up that myth is not only a form of pure phantasy but is in itself a finished and comprehensive system. What, remarks Cassirer, is so interesting about this theory in the methodological sense is that not only does it attempt the empirical proof of the real historical origin of myth, but it also attempts to give a sort of *a priori* substantiation to the proper direction and goal of mythological research. That all myths have an astral origin and should in the end prove to be calendric, is stated by the students of the Pan-Babylonian school to be the basic principle of the method. It is a sort of Ariadne's thread, which is alone able to lead through the labyrinth of mythology. By this means it was not very difficult to fill in the various lacunae which the empiric tradition had somehow failed to make good,—but this very means showed ever more clearly that the fundamental problem of the unit of the mythological consciousness could not really be explained in the manner of the historical objective empirical school.

It becomes more and more certain that the simple statement of unity of the fundamental mythical ideas cannot really give any insight into the structure of the forms of mythical phantasy and of mythical thinking. To define the structure of this form, when one does not desert the basis of pure descriptive considerations, requires no more elaborate conception than Bastian's concept of *"Völkergedanken."* Bastian maintained that the varieties of the objective approach do not simply consider the content and objects of mythology, but start off from the question as to the function of myth. The fundamental principle of this function should remain to be proved; in this way various resemblances are discovered and relations demonstrated. From the beginning the sought-for unity is both from the inside and the outside transferred from the phenomena of reality to those of the spirit. But this idealism, as long as it is received psychologically and determined through the categories of psychology, is not characterized by a single meaning. When we speak of mythology as the collective expression of mankind, this unity must finally be explained out of the unity of the human soul and out of the homogeneity of its behaviour. But the unity of the soul expresses itself in a great variety of potencies and forms. As soon as the question is asked which of these potencies play the respective rôles in the building up of the mythical world, there immediately arise conflicting and contradictory controversial explanations. Is the myth ultimately derived from the play of subjective phantasy, or does it in some cases rest upon a real view of things, upon which it is based? Is it a primitive form of knowledge (*Erkenntnis*) and in this connection is it a form of intellection, or does it belong rather to the sphere of affection and conation? To this question scientific myth-analysis has returned different answers. Just as formerly the theories differed with respect to the objects which were considered necessary to the creation of myths, in the same way they now differed in respect of the fundamental psychic processes to which these are considered to lead back. The conception of a pure intellectual mythology made its reappearance, the idea that the essence of the myth was to be sought in the intellectual analysis of experience.

In opposition to Schelling's demand for a tautegorical (expressing the same thing in different words, opposed to allegorical) analysis of myth an allegorical explanation was sought for (See Fritz Langer, *Intellektualmythologie*).

In all this is evident the danger to which the myth is exposed, the danger of becoming lost in the depths of a particular theory. In all these theories the sought-for unity is transferred in error to the particular elements instead of being looked for in that spiritual whole, the symbolic world of meaning, out of which these elements are created. We must, on the other hand, says Cassirer, look for the fundamental laws of the spirit to which the myth goes back. Just as in the process of arriving at knowledge The Rhapsody of Perceptions (*Rhapsodie der Wahrnehmungen*) is, by means of certain laws and forms of thinking, transmuted into knowledge, so we can and must ask for the creation of that form unity, the unending and manifold world of the myth, which is not a conglomerate of arbitrary ideas and meaningless notions, a characteristic spiritual genitor. We must look at the myth from a genetic-causal, teleological standpoint; in this way we shall find that what is presented to us is something which as a complete form possesses a self-sufficient being and an autochthonous sense.

The myth represents in itself the first attempts at a knowledge of the world, and since it furthermore possibly represents the earliest form of aesthetic phantasy, we see in it that particular unity of the spirit of which all separate forms are but a single manifestation. We see too, here, that instead of an original unity in which the opposites lose themselves, and seem to combine with one another, that the critical-transcendental idea-unit seeks the clear definition and delimitation of the separate forms in order to preserve them. The principle of this separation becomes clear when one compares here the problem of meaning with that of characterization—that is, when one reflects upon the way in which the various spiritual forms of expression, such as "Object" with "Idea or Image," and "Content" with "Sign," are related to one another.

In this we see the fundamental element of the parallelism, namely, the creative power of the "sign" in myth as in language, and in art, as well as in the process of forming a theoretical idea in a word, and in relation to the world. What Humboldt said of language, that man places it between himself and the internal and external world that is acting upon him, that he surrounds himself with a world of sounds with which to take up and to work up the world

of objects, holds true also for the myth and for the aesthetic fancy. They are not so much reactions to impressions, which are exercised from the outside upon the spirit, but they are much more real spiritual activities. At the outset, in the definite sense of the primitive expression of the myth it is clear that we do not have to deal with a mere reflection or mirage of Reality (*Sein*), but with a characteristic treatment and presentation of it. Also here one can observe how in the beginning the tension between "Subject" and "Object," "Internal" and "External," gradually diminishes, a richer and multiform new middle state stepping in between both worlds. To the material world which it embraces and governs the spirit opposes its own independent world of images—the power of *Impression* gradually becomes more distinct and more conscious than the active power of *Expression*. But this creation does not yet in itself possess the character of an act of free will, but still bears the character of a natural necessity, the character of a certain psychic "mechanism." Since at this level there does not yet exist an independent and self-conscious free living "I," but because we here stand upon the thereshold of the spiritual processes which are bound to react against each other, the "I" and the "World," the new world of the "Sign" must appear to the conciousness as a thoroughly objective reality. Every beginning of the myth, especially every magical conception of the world, is permeated by this belief in the existence of the objective power of the sign. Word magic, picture-magic, and script-magic provide the fundaments of magical practices and the magical view of the world. When one examines the complete structure of the mythical consciousness one can detect in this a characteristic paradox. For if the generally prevailing conception, that the fundamental urge of the myth is to vivify, is true, that is that it tends to take a concrete view in the statement and representation of all the elements of existence, how does it happen, then, that these urges point most intensely to the most unreal and non-vital; how is it that the shadow-empire of words, of images, and signs gains such a substantial ascendancy and power over the mythical consciousness? How is it that it possesses this belief in the abstract, in this cult of symbols in a world in which the general idea is nothing, the sensation (*Empfindung*), the direct urge, the (sensible) psychic perception and outlook seem to be everything? The answer to this question, says Cassirer, can be found only when one is aware of the fact that it is improperly stated. The mythical world is not so concrete that it deals only with psychically 'objective' contents, or simply 'abstract' considerations, but both the thing and its meaning form one distinct and direct concrete unity, they are not differentiated from one another. The myth raises itself spiritually above the world of things, but it exchanges for the forms and images which it puts in their place only another form of restrictive existence. What the spirit appears to rescue from the shackles now becomes but a new shackle, which is so much more unyielding because it is not only a psychical power but a spiritual one. Nevertheless, such a state already contains in itself the immanent condition of its future release. It already contains the incipient possibility of a spiritual liberation which in the progress of the magical-mythical world-idea will eventually arrive at a characteristic religious world-idea. During this transition it becomes necessary for the spirit to place itself in a new and free relation to the world of images and signs, but, at the same time, in a different way than formerly, sees through this relationship, and in this way raises itself above it, though living it still and needing it.

And in still further measure and in greater distinctness stands for us the dialectic of these fundamental relations, their analysis and synthesis, which the spirit through its own self-made world of images experiences, when we here compare the myth with all other forms of symbolic expression. In the case of language also there is at first no sharp line of separation by means of which the word and its meaning, the thing content of "idea" and the simple content are distinguished from one another. The nominalist viewpoint, for which words are conventional signs, simply *flatus vocis,* is the result of later reflection but not the direct expression of the direct natural language consciousness. For this the existence of things in words is not only indicated as indirect, but is contained and present in it anyway. In the language consciousness of the primitive and in that of the child one can demonstrate this concrescence of names and things in very pregnant examples—one has only to think of the different varieties of the taboo names. But in the progression of the spiritual development of language there is also here achieved a sharper and ever more conscious separation between the Word and Being or Existence, between the Meaning and the Meant. Opposed to all other physical being and all physical activity the word appears as autonomous and characteristic, in its purely ideal and significative function.

A new stage of the separation is next witnessed in art. Here, too, there is in the beginning no clear distinction between the "Ideal" and the "Real." The beginning of the formation and of the cultivation of art reaches back to a sphere in which the act of cultivation itself is strongly rooted in the magical idea, and is directed to a definite magical end, of which the picture (*Bild*) is yet in no way independent, and has no pure aesthetic meaning. Nevertheless already in the first impulse of characteristic artistic configurations, in the stages of spiritual forms of expression, quite a new principle is attained. The view of the world which the spirit opposes to the simple world of matter and of things subsequently attains here to a pure immanent value and truth. It does not attach itself or refer to another; but it simply is, and consists in itself. Out of the sphere of activity (*Wirksamkeit*), in which the mythical consciousness, and out of the sphere of meaning, in which the marks of language remain, we are now transferred to a sphere, in which so to say, only the pure essence (*Sein*), only its own innermost nature (*Wesenheit*) of the image (*Bildes*) is seized as such. Thus, the world of images forms in itself a Kosmos which is complete in itself, and which rests within its own centre of gravity. And to it the spirit is now first able to find a free relation. The aesthetic world is measured according to the measure of things, the realistic outlook according to a world of appearance:—but since in just this appearance the *relation* to direct reality, to the world of being and action (*Wirken*), in which also the magical-mythical outlook has its being, is now left behind, there is thus made a completely new step towards truth. Thus there present themselves in relation to Myth, Lan-

guage, and to Art, configurations which are linked directly together in a certain historical series, by means of a certain systematic progression (*Stufengang*), and ideal progress (*Fortschritt*), as the object of which it can be said the spirit in its own creations, in its self-made symbols, not only exists and lives, but gains its significance. There is a certain pertinence, in this connection, in that dominant theme of Hegel's *Phenomenology of the Spirit,* namely, that the object of development lies in the comprehension and expression of the fact that the spiritual being is not only "Substance" but just as much "Subject." In this respect the problems which grow out of a "Philosophy of Mythology" resolve themselves once more to such as arise from the philosophy of pure logic. Then also science separates itself from the other stages of spiritual life, not because it stands in need of any kind of mediation or intervention through signs and symbols, seeking naked truth, the truth of "things-in-themselves," but because it uses the symbols differently and more profoundly than the former is able to do, and recognizes and understands them as such, i.e., as symbols. Furthermore, this is not accomplished at one stroke; rather there is here also repeated, at a new stage, the typical fundamental relation of the spirit to its own creation. Here also must the freedom of this creation be gained and secured in continuous critical work. The utilization of hypotheses, and its characteristic function to advance the foundations of knowledge, determines that, so long as this knowledge is not secured, the principles of science are unable to express themselves in other than *dinglicher,* i.e., material, or in half mythical form.

Every student of primitive peoples and of mythology would recognize in Cassirer's views on mythological thinking, which have here been presented only partially, a valuable contribution towards the clarification of a difficult problem. In a brilliant chapter in which Cassirer discusses "the dialectic of the mythical consciousness," he shows how interrelated and interdependent the mythical and religious consciousness are, and that there can really be no distinction between them; there is a difference in form, but not in substance. An admirable discussion of the relation of "speech" to "language" and of "sound" to "meaning" (already dealt with at length in the first volume of the **Symbolischen Formen**) leads to a brief discussion of writing.

Cassirer points out that all writing begins as picture-signs which do not in themselves embrace any meaning or communicative characters. The picture-sign takes the place rather of the object itself, replaces it, and stands for it.

This statement is perfectly true of all forms of primitive writing. One of the most primitive forms of writing, for example, with which we are acquainted is that invented and practiced by certain Australian tribes. On the message sticks which they send from one tribe to another the signs which they make fulfill all the specifications stated by Cassirer.

Cassirer also states that at first writing forms a part of the sphere of magic. The sign which is stamped on the object draws it into the circle of its own effect and keeps away strange influences.

The anthropological data lend full support to this idea. It may even be that the magicians were the first to invent writing, though it would at present be impossible to prove such a suggestion or even to prove that the magicians were among the first to use picture signs. The evidence does, however, suggest that this is highly probable.

I can only have succeeded in giving a faint indication of the value and quality of Cassirer's contribution to our understanding of mythological thinking in general and that of pre-literate peoples in particular. To appreciate Cassirer's great work at its full value the reader is recommended to go to the original work. This essay must be regarded as but a footnote to it.

Susanne K. Langer   (essay date 1949)

SOURCE: "On Cassirer's Theory of Language and Myth," in *The Philosophy of Ernst Cassier,* edited by Paul Arthur Schlipp, The Library of Living Philosophers, Inc., 1949, pp. 381-400.

[*In the following essay, Langer explores the relationship between myth and language in Cassirer's work.*]

Every philosopher has his tradition. His thought has developed amid certain problems, certain basic alternatives of opinion, that embody the key concepts which dominate his time and his environment and which will always be reflected, positively or by negation, in his own work. They are the forms of thought he has inherited, wherein he naturally thinks, or from which his maturer conceptions depart.

The continuity of culture lies in this handing down of usable forms. Any campaign to discard tradition for the sake of novelty as such, without specific reason in each case to break through a certain convention of thought, leads to dilettantism, whether it be in philosophy, in art, or in social and moral institutions. As every person has his mother tongue in terms of which he cannot help thinking his earliest thoughts, so every scholar has a philosophical mother tongue, which colors his natural *Weltanschauung.* He may have been nurtured in a particular school of thought, or his heritage may be the less conscious one of "common sense," the popular metaphysic of his generation; but he speaks some intellectual language that has been bestowed on him, with its whole cargo of preconceptions, distinctions, and evaluations, by his official and unofficial teachers.

A great philosopher, however, has something new and vital to present in whatever philosophical mold he may have been given. The tenor of his thought stems from the past; but his specific problems take shape in the face of a living present, and his dealing with them reflects the entire, ever-nascent activity of his own day. In all the great periods of philosophy, the leading minds of the time have carried their traditional learning lightly, and felt most deeply the challenge of things which were new in their age. It is the new that calls urgently for interpretation; and a true philosopher is a person to whom something in the weary old world always appears new and uncomprehended.

There are certain "dead periods" in the history of philosophy, when the whole subject seems to shrink into a hard, small shell, treasured only by scholars in large universities. The common man knows little about it and cares less. What marks such a purely academic phase of philosophical thought is that its substance as well as its form is furnished by a scholastic tradition; not only the categories, but the problems of debate are familiar. Precisely in the most eventful epochs, when intellectual activity in other fields is brilliant and exciting, there is quite apt to be a lapse in philosophy; the greatest minds are engaged elsewhere; reflection and interpretation are in abeyance when the tempo of life is at its highest. New ideas are too kaleidoscopic to be systematically construed or to suggest general propositions. Professional philosophers, therefore, continue to argue matters which their predecessors have brought to no conclusion, and to argue them from the same standpoints that yielded no insight before.

We have only recently passed through an "academic" phase of philosophy, a phase of stale problems and deadlocked "isms." But today we are on the threshold of a new creative period. The most telling sign of this is the tendency of great minds to see philosophical implications in facts and problems belonging to other fields of learning—mathematics, anthropology, psychology, physics, history, and the arts. Familiar things like language or dream, or the mensurability of time, appear in new universal connections which involve highly interesting abstract issues. Even the layman lends his ear to "semantics" or to new excitements about "relativity."

Cassirer had all the marks of a great thinker in a new philosophical period. His standpoint was a tradition which he inherited—the Kantian "critical" philosophy seen in the light of its later developments, which raised the doctrine of transcendental forms to the level of a transcendental theory of Being. His writings bear witness that he often reviewed and pondered the foundations of this position. There was nothing accidental or sentimental in his adherence to it; he maintained it throughout his life, because he found it fruitful, suggestive of new interpretations. In his greatest works this basic idealism is implicit rather than under direct discussion; and the turn it gives to his treatment of the most baffling questions removes it utterly from that treadmill of purely partisan reiteration and defense which is the fate of decadent metaphysical convictions. There is little of polemic or apologetic in Cassirer's writings; he was too enthusiastic about solving definite problems to spend his time vindicating his method or discussing what to him was only a starting-point.

One of the venerable puzzles which he treated with entirely new insight from his peculiarly free and yet scholarly point of view is the relation of language and myth. Here we find at the outset the surprising, unorthodox working of his mind: for what originally led him to this problem was not the contemplation of poetry, but of science. For generations the advocates of scientific thinking bemoaned the difficulties which nature seems to plant in its path—the misconceptions bred by "ignorance" and even by language itself. It took Cassirer to see that those difficulties themselves were worth investigating. Ignorance is a negative condition; why should the mere absence of correct conceptions lead to misconceptions? And why should language, supposedly a practical instrument for conveying thought, serve to resist and distort scientific thought? The misconceptions interested him.

If the logical and factual type of thought which science demands is hard to maintain, there must be some other mode of thinking which constantly interferes with it. Language, the expression of thought, could not possibly be a hindrance to thought as such; if it distorts scientific conception, it must do so merely by giving preference and support to such another mode.

Now, all thinking is "realistic" in the sense that it deals with phenomena as they present themselves in immediate experience. There cannot be a way of thinking that is not true to the reports of sense. If there are two modes of thinking, there must be two different modes of perceiving things, of apprehending the very data of thought. To *observe* the wind, for instance, as a purely physical atmospheric disturbance, and *think* of it as a divine power or an angry creature would be purely capricious, playful, irresponsible. But thinking is serious business, and probably always has been; and it is not likely that language, the physical image of thought, portrays a pattern of mere fancies and vagaries. In so far as language is incompatible with scientific reasoning, it must reflect a system of thought that is soberly true to a *mode of experiencing,* of seeing and feeling, different from our accepted mode of experiencing "facts."

This idea, first suggested by the difficulties of scientific conception, opened up a new realm of epistemological research to its author; for it made the *forms of misunderstanding* take on a positive rather than a negative importance as *archaic forms of understanding.* The hypostatic and poetic tinge of language which makes it so often recalcitrant to scientific purposes is a record not only of a different way of thinking, but of seeing, feeling, conceiving experience—a way that was probably paramount in the ages when language itself came into being. The whole problem of mind and its relation to "reality" took a new turn with the hypothesis that former civilizations may actually have dealt with a "real world" differently constituted from our own world of things with their universal qualities and causal relationships. But how can that older "reality" be recaptured and demonstrated? And how can the change from one way of apprehending nature to another be accounted for?

The answer to this methodological question came to him as a suggestion from metaphysics. *"Es ist der Geist der sich den Körper baut,"* said Goethe. And the post-Kantian idealists, from Fichte to Hermann Cohen, had gone even beyond that tenet; so they might well have said, *"Es ist der Geist der sich das Weltall baut."* To a romanticist that would have been little more than a figure of speech, expressing the relative importance of mind and matter. But in Cassirer's bold and uncomplacent mind such a belief—which he held as a basic intellectual postulate, not as a value-judgment—immediately raised the question: How? By what process and what means does the human spirit *construct* its physical world?

Kant had already proposed the answer: By supplying the transcendental constituent of *form.* Kant regarded this form as a fixed pattern, the same in all human experience; the categories of thought which find their clearest expression in science, seemed to him to govern all empirical experience, and to be reflected in the structure of language. But the structure of language is just what modern scientific thought finds uncongenial. It embodies a metaphysic of substance and attribute; whereas science operates more and more with the concept of *function,* which is articulated in mathematics. There is good reason why mathematicians have abandoned verbal propositions almost entirely and resorted to a symbolism which expresses different metaphysical assumptions, different categories of thought altogether.

At this point Cassirer, reflecting on the shift from substantive to functional thinking, found the key to the methodological problem: two different symbolisms revealed two radically different forms of thought; does not every form of *Anschauung* have its symbolic mode? Might not an exhaustive study of symbolic forms reveal just how the human mind, in its various stages, has variously construed the "reality" with which it dealt? To *construe* the equivocally "given" is to *construct* the phenomenon for experience. And so the Kantian principle, fructified by a wholly new problem of science, led beyond the Kantian doctrine to the Philosophy of Symbolic Forms.

The very plan of this work departs from all previous approaches to epistemology by not assuming either that the mind is concerned essentially with facts, or that its prime talent is discursive reason. A careful study of the scientific misconceptions which language begets revealed the fact that its subject-predicate structure, which reflects a "natural" ontology of substance and attribute, is not its only metaphysical trait. Language is born of the need for emotional expression. Yet it is not exclamatory. It is essentially hypostatic, seeking to distinguish, emphasize, and hold the object of feeling rather than to communicate the feeling itself. To fix the object as a permanent focus point in experience is the function of the *name.* Whatever evokes emotion may therefore receive a name; and, if this object is not a thing—if it is an act, or a phenomenon like lightning, or a sound, or some other intangible item—, the name nevertheless gives it the unity, permanence, and apparent substantiality of a "thing."

This hypostasis, entailed by the primitive office of language, really lies deeper even than nomenclature, which merely reflects it: for it is a fundamental trait of all *imagination.* The very word "imagination" denotes a process of image-making. An image is only an aspect of the actual thing it represents. It may be not even a completely or carefully abstracted aspect. Its importance lies in the fact that it symbolizes the whole—the thing, person, occasion, or what-not—from which it is an abstract. A thing has a history, an event passes irrevocably away, actual experience is transient and would exhaust itself in a series of unique occasions, were it not for the permanence of the symbol whereby it may be recalled and possessed. Imagination is a free and continual production of images to "mean" experience—past or present or even merely possible experience.

Imagination is the primary talent of the human mind, the activity in whose service language was evolved. The imaginative mode of ideation is not "logical" after the manner of discursive reason. It has a logic of its own, a definite pattern of identifications and concentrations which bring a very deluge of ideas, all charged with intense and often widely diverse feelings, together in one symbol.

Symbols are the indispensable instruments of conception. To undergo an experience, to react to immediate or conditional stimuli (as animals react to warning or guiding signs), is not to "have" experience in the characteristically human sense, which is to conceive it, hold it in the mind as a so-called "content of consciousness," and consequently be able to think *about* it. To a human mind, every experience—a sensation of light or color, a fright, a fall, a continuous noise like the roar of breakers on the beach—exhibits, in retrospect, a unity and self-identify that make it almost as static and tangible as a solid object. By virtue of this hypostatization it may be *referred to*, much as an object may be *pointed at*; and therefore the mind can think about it without its actual recurrence. In its symbolic image the experience is *conceived*, instead of just physiologically remembered.

Cassirer's greatest epistemological contribution is his approach to the problem of mind through a study of the primitive forms of conception. His reflections on science had taught him that all conception is intimately bound to expression; and the forms of expression, which determine those of conception, are symbolic forms. So he was led to his central problem, the diversity of symbolic forms and their interrelation in the edifice of human culture.

He distinguished, as so many autonomous forms, language, myth, art, and science. In examining their respective patterns he made his first startling discovery: myth and language appeared as genuine twin creatures, born of the same phase of human mentality, exhibiting analogous formal traits, despite their obvious diversities of content. Language, on the one hand, seems to have articulated and established mythological concepts, whereas, on the other hand, its own meanings are essentially images functioning mythically. The two modes of thought have grown up together, as conception and expression, respectively, of the primitive human world.

The earliest products of mythic thinking are not permanent, self-identical, and clearly distinguished "gods"; neither are they immaterial spirits. They are like dream elements—objects endowed with daemonic import, haunted places, accidental shapes in nature resembling something ominous—all manner of shifting, fantastic images which speak of Good and Evil, of Life and Death, to the impressionable and creative mind of man. Their common trait is a quality that characterizes everything in the sphere of myth, magic, and religion, and also the earliest ethical conceptions—the quality of *holiness*. Holiness may appertain to almost anything; it is the mystery that appears as magic, as taboo, as daemonic power, as miracle, and as divinity. The first dichotomy in the emotive or mythic phase

of mentality is not, as for discursive reason, the opposition of "yes" and "no," of "a" and "non-a," or truth and falsity; the basic dichotomy here is between the sacred and the profane. Human beings actually apprehend *values* and expressions of values *before* they formulate and entertain *facts*.

All mythic constructions are symbols of value—of life and power, or of violence, evil, and death. They are charged with feeling, and have a way of absorbing into themselves more and more intensive meanings, sometimes even logically conflicting imports. Therefore mythic symbols do not give rise to discursive understanding; they do beget a kind of understanding, but not by sorting out concepts and relating them in a distinct pattern; they tend, on the contrary, merely to bring together great complexes of cognate ideas, in which all distinctive features are merged and swallowed. "Here we find in operation a law which might actually be called the law of the levelling and extinction of specific differences," says Cassirer, in *Language and Myth*. "Every part of a whole is the whole itself, every specimen is equivalent to the entire species." The significance of mythic structures is not formally and arbitrarily assigned to them, as convention assigns one exact meaning to a recognized symbol; rather, their meaning seems to dwell in them as life dwells in a body; they are animated by it, it is of their essence, and the naïve, awe-struck mind *finds* it, as the quality of "holiness." Therefore mythic symbols do not even appear to be symbols; they appear as holy objects or places or beings, and their import is felt as an inherent *power*.

This really amounts to another "law" of imaginative conception. Just as specific differences of meaning are obliterated in nondiscursive symbolization, the very distinction between form and content, between the entity (thing, image, gesture, or natural event) which is the symbol, and the idea or feeling which is its meaning, is lost, or rather: is not yet found. This is a momentous fact, for it is the basis of all superstition and strange cosmogony, as well as of religious belief. To believe in the existence of improbable or quite fantastic things and beings would be inexplicable folly if beliefs were dictated essentially by practical experience. But the mythic interpretation of reality rests on the principle that the veneration appropriate to the meaning of a symbol is focussed on the symbol itself, which is simply identified with its import. This creates a world punctuated by pre-eminent objects, mystic centers of power and holiness, to which more and more emotive meanings accrue as "properties." An intuitive recognition of their *import* takes the form of ardent, apparently irrational belief in the physical reality and power of the significant forms. This is the hypostatic mechanism of the mind by which the world is filled with magical things—fetishes and talismans, sacred trees, rocks, caves, and the vague, protean ghosts that inhabit them—and finally the world is peopled with a pantheon of permanent, more or less anthropomorphic gods. In these presences "reality" is concentrated for the mythic imagination; this is not "make-believe," not a willful or playful distortion of a radically different "given fact," but is *the way phenomena are given* to naïve apprehension.

Certainly the pattern of that world is altogether different from the pattern of the "material" world which confronts our sober common sense, follows the laws of causality, and exhibits a logical order of classes and subclasses, with their defining properties and relations, whereby each individual object either does or does not belong to any given class. Cassirer has summed up the logical contrast between the mode of mythic intuition and that of "factual" or "scientific" apprehension in very telling phrase:

> In the realm of discursive conception there reigns a sort of diffuse light—and the further logical analysis proceeds, the further does this even clarity and luminosity extend. But in the ideational realm of myth and language there are always, besides those locations from which the strongest light proceeds, others that appear wrapped in profoundest darkness. While certain contents of perception become verbal-mythical centers of force, centers of significance, there are others which remain, one might say, beneath the threshold of meaning. [*Language and Myth*]

His coupling of myth and language in this passage brings us back to the intimate connection between these two great symbolic forms which he traces to a common origin. The dawn of language was the dawn of the truly human mind, which meets us first of all as a rather highly developed organ of practical response *and of imagination*, or symbolic rendering of impressions. The first "holy objects" seem to be born of momentary emotional experiences—fright centering on a place or a thing, concentrated desire that manifests itself in a dreamlike image or a repeated gesture, triumph that issues naturally in festive dance and song, directed toward a symbol of power. Somewhere in the course of this high emotional life primitive man took to using his instinctive vocal talent as a source of such "holy objects," *sounds* with imaginative import: such vocal symbols are *names*.

In savage societies, names are treated not as conventional appellations, but as though they were physical proxies for their bearers. To call an object by an inappropriate name is to confound its very nature. In some cultures practically all language serves mystic purposes and is subject to the most impractical taboos and regulations. It is clearly of a piece with magic, religion and the whole pattern of intensive emotional symbolism which governs the pre-scientific mind. Names are the very essence of mythic symbols; nothing on earth is a more concentrated point of sheer meaning than the little, transient, invisible breath that constitutes a spoken word. Physically it is almost nothing. Yet it carries more definite and momentous import than any permanent holy object. It can be invoked at will, anywhere and at any time, by a mere act of speech; merely *knowing* a word gives a person the power of using it; thus it is invisibly "had," carried about by its possessors.

It is characteristic of mythic "powers" that they are completely contained in every fragment of matter, every sound, and every gesture which partakes of them. This fact betrays their real nature, which is not that of physical forces, but of meanings; a meaning is indeed completely given by every symbol to which it attaches. The greater the "power" in proportion to its bearer, the more awe-inspiring will the latter be. So, as long as meaning is felt as an indwelling potency of certain physical objects, *words* must certainly rank high in the order of holy things.

But language has more than a purely denotative function. Its symbols are so manifold, so manageable, and so economical that a considerable number of them may be held in one "specious present," though each one physically passes away before the next is given; each has left its *meaning* to be apprehended in the same span of attention that takes in the whole series. Of course, the length of the span varies greatly with different mentalities. But as soon as two or more words are thus taken together in the mind of an interpretant, language has acquired its second function: it has engendered *discursive thought*.

The discursive mode of thinking is what we usually call "reason." It is not as primitive as the imaginative mode, because it arises from the syntactical nature of language; mythic envisagement and verbal expression are its fore-runners. Yet it is a natural development from the earlier symbolic mode, which is pre-discursive, and thus in a strict and narrow sense "pre-rational."

Henceforth, the history of thought consists chiefly in the gradual achievement of factual, literal, and logical conception and expression. Obviously the only means to this end is language. But this instrument, it must be remembered, has a double nature. Its syntactical tendencies bestow the laws of logic on us; yet the primacy of *names* in its make-up holds it to the hypostatic way of thinking which belongs to its twin-phenomenon, myth. Consequently it leads us beyond the sphere of mythic and emotive thought, yet always pulls us back into it again; it is both the diffuse and tempered light that shows us the external world of "fact," and the array of spiritual lamps, light-centers of intensive meaning, that throw the gleams and shadows of the dream world wherein our earliest experiences lay.

We have come so far along the difficult road of discursive thinking that the laws of logic seem to be the very frame of the mind, and rationality its essence. Kant regarded the categories of pure understanding as universal transcendental forms, imposed by the most naïve untutored mind on all its perceptions, so that self-identity, the dichotomy of "*a*" and "non-*a*," the relation of part and whole, and other axiomatic general concepts inhered in phenomena as their necessary conditions. Yet, from primitive apprehension to even the simplest rational construction is probably a far cry. It is interesting to see how Cassirer, who followed Kant in his "Copernican revolution," i.e., in the transcendental analysis of phenomena which traces their form to a non-phenomenal, subjective element, broadened the Kantian concept of form to make it a variable and anthropologically valid principle, without compromising the "critical" standpoint at all. Instead of accepting one categorial scheme—that of discursive thought—as the absolute way of experiencing reality, he finds it relative to a form of symbolic presentation; and as there are alternative symbolic forms, there are also alternative phenomenal "worlds." Mythic conception is categorially different from scientific conception; therefore it meets a different world of perceptions. Its objects are not self-identical, consistent, universally related; they condense many characters in one, have conflicting attributes and intermittent existence, the whole is contained in its parts, and the parts in each other. The world they constitute is a world of values, things "holy" against a vague background of commonplaces, or "profane" events, instead of a world of neutral physical facts. By this departure, the Kantian doctrine that identified all conception with discursive reason, making reason appear as an aboriginal human gift, is saved from its most serious fallacy, an unhistorical view of mind.

Cassirer called his **Essay on Man,** which briefly summarizes the **Philosophie der symbolischen Formen,** "An Introduction to a Philosophy of Human Culture." The subtitle is appropriate indeed; for the most striking thing about this philosophy viewed as a whole is the way the actual evolution of human customs, arts, ideas, and languages is not merely fitted into an idealistic interpretation of the world (as it may be fitted into almost any metaphysical picture), but is illumined and made accessible to serious study by working principles taken from Kantian epistemology. His emphasis on the constitutive character of symbolic renderings in the making of "experience" is the masterstroke that turns the purely speculative "critical" theory into an anthropological hypothesis, a key to several linguistic problems, a source of psychological understanding, and a guidepost in the maze of *Geistesgeschichte*.

It is, as I pointed out before, characteristic of Cassirer's thought that, although its basic principles stem from a philosophical tradition, its living material and immediate inspiration come from contemporary sources, from fields of research beyond his own. For many years the metaphysic of mind has been entirely divorced from the scientific study of mental phenomena; whether mind be an eternal essence or a transient epiphenomenon, a world substance or a biological instrument, makes little difference to our understanding of observed human or animal behavior. But Cassirer breaks this isolation of speculative thought; he uses the Kantian doctrine, that mind is constitutive of the "external world," to explain the *way* this world is experienced as well as the mere fact *that* it is experienced; and in so doing, of course, he makes his metaphysic meet the test of factual findings at every turn. His most interesting exhibits are psychological phenomena revealed in the psychiatric clinic and in ethnologists' reports. The baffling incapacities of impaired brains, the language of childhood, the savage's peculiar practices, the prevalence of myth in early cultures and its persistence in religious thought—these and other widely scattered facts receive new significance in the light of his philosophy. And that is the pragmatic measure of any speculative approach. A really cogent doctrine of mind cannot be irrelevant to psychology, any more than a good cosmological system can be meaningless for physics, or a theory of ethics inapplicable to jurisprudence and law.

The psychiatric phenomena which illustrate the existence of a mythic mode of thought, and point to its ancient and primitive nature, are striking and persuasive. Among these is the fact that in certain pathological conditions of the brain the power of abstraction is lost, and the patient falls back on picturesque metaphorical language. In more aggravated cases the imagination, too, is impaired; and

here we have a reversion almost to animal mentality. One symptom of this state which is significant for the philosophy of symbolism is that the sufferer is unable to tell a lie, feign any action, or do anything his actual situation does not dictate, though he may still find his way with immediate realities. If he is thirsty, he can recognize and take a glass of water, and drink; but he cannot pick up an empty glass and demonstrate the act of drinking *as though* there were water in it, or even lift a full glass to his lips, if he is not thirsty. Such incapacities have been classified as "apractic" disorders; but Cassirer pointed out that they are not so much practical failures, as loss of the basic symbolic function, *envisagement of things not given.* This is borne out by a still more serious disturbance which occurs with the destruction of certain brain areas, inability to recognize "things," such as chairs and brooms and pieces of clothing, directly and instantly as objects denoted by their names. At this point, pathology furnishes a striking testimony of the real nature of language: for here, names lose their hypostatic office, the creation of permanent and particular *items* out of the flux of impressions. To a person thus afflicted, words have connotation, but experience does not readily correspond to the conceptual scheme of language, which makes *names* the preeminent points of rest, and requires *things* as the fundamental relata in reality. The connoted concepts are apt to be adjectival rather than substantive. Consequently the world confronting the patient is not composed of objects immediately "given" in experience; it is composed of sense data, which he must "associate" to form "things," much as Hume supposed the normal mind to do.

Most of the psychological phenomena that caught Cassirer's interest arose from the psychiatric work of Kurt Goldstein, who has dealt chiefly with cases of cerebral damage caused by physical accident. But the range of psychological researches which bear out Cassirer's theory of mind is much wider; it includes the whole field of so-called "dynamic psychology," the somewhat chaotic store of new ideas and disconcerting facts with which Sigmund Freud alarmed his generation. Cassirer himself never explored this fund of corroborative evidence; he found himself in such fundamental disagreement with Freud on the nature of the dynamic motive—which the psychologist regarded as not only derived from the sex impulse, but forever bound to it, and which the philosopher saw liberated in science, art, religion, and everything that constitutes the "self-realization of the spirit"—that there seemed to be simply no point of contact between their respective doctrines. Cassirer felt that to Freud all those cultural achievements were mere by-products of the unchanging animalian "libido," symptoms of its blind activity and continual frustration; whereas to him they were the consummation of a spiritual process which merely took its rise from the blind excitement of the animal "libido," but received its importance and meanings from the phenomena of awareness and creativity, the envisagement, reason, and cognition it produced. This basic difference of *evaluations* of the life process made Cassirer hesitate to make any part of Freud's doctrine his own; at the end of his life he had, apparently, just begun to study the important relationship between "dynamic psychology" and the philosophy of symbolic forms.

It is, indeed, only in regard to the *forms* of thought that a parallel obtains between these systems; but that parallel is Freud's "unconscious" mental mechanism is almost exactly the "mythic mode" which Cassirer describes as the primitive form of ideation, wherein an intense feeling is spontaneously expressed in a symbol, an image seen in something or formed for the mind's eye by the excited imagination. Such expression is effortless and therefore unexhausting; its products are images charged with meanings, but the meanings remain implicit, so that the emotions they command seem to be centered on the image rather than on anything it merely conveys; in the image, which may be a vision, a gesture, a sound-form (musical image) or a word as readily as an external object, many meanings may be concentrated, many ideas telescoped and interfused, and incompatible emotions simultaneously expressed.

> The mythic mind never perceives passively, never merely contemplates things; all its observations spring from some act of participation, some act of emotion and will. Even as mythic imagination materializes in permanent forms, and presents us with definite outlines of an 'objective' world of beings, the significance of this world becomes clear to us only if we can still detect, underneath it all, that dynamic sense of life from which it originally arose. Only where this vital feeling is stirred from within, where it expresses itself as love or hate, fear or hope, joy or sorrow, mythic imagination is roused to the pitch of excitement at which it begets a definite world of representations. (*Philosophie der symbolischen Formen*.)

> For a person whose apprehension is under the spell of this mythico-religious attitude, it is as though the whole world were simply annihilated; the immediate content, whatever it be, that commands his religious interest so completely fills his consciousness that nothing else can exist beside and apart from it. The ego is spending all its energy on this single object, lives in it, loses itself in it. Instead of a widening of intuitive experience, we find here its extreme limitation; instead of expansion . . . we have here an impulse toward concentration; instead of extensive distribution, intensive compression. This focussing of all forces on a single point is the prerequisite for all mythical thinking and mythical formulation. When, on the one hand, the entire self is given up to a single impression, is 'possessed' by it and, on the other hand, there is the utmost tension between the subject and its object, the outer world; when external reality is not merely viewed and contemplated, but overcomes a man in sheer immediacy, with emotions of fear or hope, terror or wish fulfillment: then the spark jumps somehow across, the tension finds release, as the subjective excitement becomes objectified and confronts the mind as a god or a daemon.

> . . . this peculiar genesis determines the type of intellectual content that is common to language and myth . . . present reality, as mythic or linguistic conception stresses and shapes it, fills the entire subjective realm. . . . At this point, the word which denotes that thought content is not a mere conventional symbol, but is merged with its object in an indissoluble unity. . . . The potential between 'symbol' and 'meaning' is resolved; in place of a more or less adequate 'expression,' we find a relation of identity, of complete congruence between 'image' and 'object,' between the name and the thing.

> . . . the same sort of hypostatization or transubstantiation occurs in other realms of mental creativity; indeed, it seems to be the typical process in all unconscious ideation . . . . . [*Language and Myth*]

> Mythology presents us with a world which is not, indeed, devoid of structure and internal organization, but which, none the less, is not divided according to the categories of reality, into 'things' and 'properties.' Here all forms of Being exhibit, as yet, a peculiar 'fluidity'; they are distinct without being really separate. Every form is capable of changing, on the spur of the moment, even into its very opposite. . . . One and the same entity may not only undergo constant change into successive guises, but it combines within itself, at one and the same instant of its existence, a wealth of different and even incompatible natures. . . . .

> Above all, there is a complete lack of any clear division between mere 'imagining' and 'real' perception, between wish and fulfilment, between image and object. This is most clearly revealed by the decisive rôle which dream experiences play in the development of mythic consciousness. . . . It is beyond doubt that certain mythic concepts can be understood, in all their peculiar complexity, only in so far as one realizes that for mythic thought and 'experience' there is but a continuous and fluid transition from the world of dream to objective 'reality.' [*Philosophie der Symbolischen Formen*]

> The world of myth is a dramatic world—a world of actions, of forces, of conflicting powers. In every phenomenon of nature it [mythic consciousness] sees the collision of these powers. Mythical perception is always impregnated with these emotional qualities. Whatever is seen or felt is surrounded by a special atmosphere—an atmosphere of joy or grief, of anguish, of excitement, of exultation or depression. . . . All objects are benignant or malignant, friendly or inimical, familiar or uncanny, alluring and fascinating or repellent and threatening . . . .

> The real substratum of myth is not a substratum of thought but of feeling. . . . Its view of life is a synthetic, not an analytical one. . . . There is no specific difference between the various realms of life. . . . To mythical and religious feeling nature becomes one great society, the *society of life*. Man is not endowed with outstanding rank in this society. . . . Men and animals, animals and plants are all on the same level. [*Essay on Man*]

To all these passages Freud could subscribe wholeheartedly; the *morphology* of the "mythic mode" is essentially that of dream, phantasy, infantile thinking, and "unconscious" ideation which he himself discovered and described. And it is the recognition of this non-discursive mode of thought, rather than his clinical hypothesis of an all-pervading disguised sexuality, that makes Freud's psychology important for philosophy. Not the theory of "libido," which is another theory of "animal drives," but the conception of the unconscious mechanism through which the "libido," operates, the dream work, the myth-making process—that is the new generative idea which psychoanalysis contributed to psychological thinking, the notion that has put modern psychology so completely out of gear with traditional epistemology that the science of mind and the philosophy of mind threatened to lose contact altogether. So it is of the utmost significance for the unity of our advancing thought that pure speculative philosophy should recognize and understand the primary forms of conception which underlie the achievement of discursive reason.

> The broadening of the philosophical outlook achieved by Cassirer's theory of language and myth affects not only the philosophical sciences, the *Geisteswissenschaften,* but also the most crucial present difficulty in philosophy itself—the ever increasing pendulum arc between theories of reason and theories of irrational motivation.
>
> —*Susanne K. Langer*

Cassirer's profound antipathy to Freud's teaching rests on another aspect of that psychological system, which springs from the fact that Freud's doctrine was determined by practical interests: that is the tendency of the psychoanalyst to range all human aims, all ideals on the same ethical level. Since he deals entirely with the evils of social maladjustment, his measure of good is simply adjustment; religion and learning and social reform, art and discovery and philosophical reflection, to him are just so many avenues of personal gratification—sublimation of passions, emotional self-expression. From his standpoint they cannot be viewed as objective values. Just as good poetry and bad poetry are of equal interest and importance to the psychoanalyst, so the various social systems are all equally good, all religions equally true (or rather, equally false, but salutary), and all abstract systems of thought, scientific or philosophical or mathematical, just self-dramatizations in disguise. To a philosopher who was also a historian of culture, such a point of view seemed simply devastating. It colored his vision of Freud's work so deeply that it really obscured for him the constructive aspect, the analysis of non-discursive ideation, which this essentially clinical psychology contains. Yet the relationship between the new psychiatry and his own new epistemology is deep and close; *"der Mythos als Denkform"* is the theme that rounds out the modern philosophical picture of human mentality

to embrace psychology and anthropology and linguistics, which had broken the narrow limits of rationalist theory, in a more adequate conceptual frame.

The broadening of the philosophical outlook achieved by Cassirer's theory of language and myth affects not only the philosophical sciences, the *Geisteswissenschaften*, but also the most crucial present difficulty in philosophy itself—the ever increasing pendulum arc between theories of reason and theories of irrational motivation. The discovery that emotive, intuitive, "blind" forces govern human behavior more effectively than motives of pure reason naturally gave rise to an anti-rationalist movement in epistemology and ethics, typified by Nietzsche, William James, and Bergson, which finally made the truth-seeking attitude of science a pure phantasmagoria, a quixotic manifestation of the will. Ultimately the rôle of reason came to appear (as it does in Bergson's writings) as something entirely secondary and essentially unnatural. But at this point the existence of reason becomes an enigma: for how could instinctive life ever give rise to such a product? How can sheer imagination and volition and passion beget the "artificial" picture of the world which seems natural to scientists?

Cassirer found the answer in the structure of *language*; for language stems from the intuitive "drive" to symbolic expression that also produces dream and myth and ritual, but it is a pre-eminent form in that it embodies not only self-contained, complex meanings, but a *principle of concatenation* whereby the complexes are unravelled and articulated. It is the *discursive* character of language, its inner tendency to grammatical development, which gives rise to logic in the strict sense, i.e., to the procedure we call "reasoning." Language is "of imagination all compact," yet it is the cradle of abstract thought; and the achievement of *Vernunft*, as Cassirer traces it from the dawn of human mentality through the evolution of speech forms, is just as natural as the complicated patterns of instinctive behavior and emotional abreaction.

Here the most serious antinomy in the philosophical thought of our time is resolved. This is a sort of touchstone for the philosophy of symbolic forms, whereby we may judge its capacity to fulfill the great demand its author did not hesitate to make on it, when he wrote in his ***Essay on Man***:

> In the boundless multiplicity and variety of mythical images, of religious dogmas, of linguistic forms, of works of art, philosophic thought reveals the unity of a general function by which all these creations are held together. Myth, religion, art, language, even science, are now looked upon as so many variations on a common theme—and it is the task of philosophy to make this theme audible and understandable.

Konstantin Reichardt   (essay date 1949)

SOURCE: "Ernst Cassirer's Contribution to Literary Criticism," in *The Philosophy of Ernst Cassirer,* edited by Paul Arthur Schlipp, The Library of Living Philosophers, Inc., 1949, pp. 663-88.

[In the following essay, Reichardt explores the implications of Cassirer's writings for literary criticism.]

In his **Essay on Man,** Cassirer—in the form of a paradox—defines the historian's aspiration as "objective anthropomorphism." Whereas the process of scientific thought shows a constant effort to eliminate "anthropological" elements, history appears not as a knowledge of external facts or events, but as a form of self-knowledge: man constantly returns to himself attempting to recollect and actualize the whole of his past experience. The historical self, however, aspires to objectivity and is not satisfied with egocentricity. In his discussion of the various methods of historical research Cassirer expresses greatest warmth when speaking of the work of Ranke, who once voiced the desire to extinguish his own self and to make himself the pure mirror of things. This wish, clearly recognized both by Ranke and Cassirer as the deepest problem of the historian, remains at the same time the historian's highest ideal. His feeling of responsibility and his ethical standing will determine the value of his results according to the definition of "objective anthropomorphism." Cassirer reveals Ranke's ethical conception and his universal sympathy for all ages and all nations as his principal merits and he contrasts Ranke's basic attitude with that of Treitschke's Prussian school.

According to Cassirer, history belongs not to the field of natural science, but to that of hermeneutics. Our historical knowledge is a branch of semantics, not of physics. Cassirer stands closer to Dilthey than to Taine. Submitting the "scientific," statistical and psychological methods of Taine, Buckle, and Lamprecht to criticism he maintains that history, not being an exact science, will always keep its place and its inherent nature in the organization of human knowledge, and the speeches in Thucydides' work will retain their historical value, because they are objective and possess ideal, if not empirical truth. Cassirer asks for greater susceptibility in exactly this sense: "In modern times we have become much more susceptible to the demands of empirical truth, but we are perhaps frequently in danger of losing sight of the ideal truth of things and personalities. The just balance between these two moments depends upon the individual tact of the historian. . . . " In order to achieve the high task, the last and decisive act is "always an act of the productive imagination." "It is the keen sense for the empirical reality of things combined with the free gift of imagination upon which the true historical synthesis or synopsis depends."

In other words, the just balance in historical research postulated by Cassirer will depend upon two basic elements: on the historian's ethical conception of his duties and on the disciplined greatness of his productive imagination,—the full knowledge of the material being self-understood. Thus conceived, history becomes a sister of art. Art turns our empirical life into the dynamic of pure form; history molds the empirical reality of things and events into a new shape and gives it the ideality of recollection.

> We could make psychological experiments or collect statistical facts. But in spite of this our picture of man would remain inert and colorless. We should only find the "average" man—the man of our daily practical and social intercourse. In the great works of history and art we begin to see, behind the mask of the conventional man, the features of the real, individual man. [**Essay on Man**]

In August 1943 I had the opportunity to read a—then unpublished—manuscript by Cassirer on Thomas Mann's Goethe novel *Lotte in Weimar.* I began to read the manuscript with a special kind of expectation. Knowing Cassirer's stern demand for the highest degree of objectivity in historical research, including literary criticism, and the complete absence of humor, irony, or any lighter tone in general in his writings, I was eager to see if Cassirer would make an exception in this case, which—as I thought—would tempt even the most serious and objective critic to some application of Thomas Mann's own and possibly most characteristic style element, his "loving irony." However, Cassirer had written his critical essay in the Cassirer mood: sympathetically and without one deviation from full seriousness. This consistency throughout all his publications shows how deeply his general demand for ethics and tact in historical research are rooted in his personality, and it also explains the almost complete absence of polemics in his contributions to the field of literature. Compared with many of his German contemporaries Cassirer distinguishes himself by the objective spirit of his work. He seems to be urged to write whenever he feels able to improve or to elucidate, and not because he would like to correct or to attack. Thus, his own discussions appear usually as an investigation of a point without an edge. "Man cannot live his life without constant efforts to express it," this would be Cassirer's general answer to a question about the value of literary documents in the past or present. Every document requires, from a historian, a sympathetic and expert reading, and the true historian will remain sympathetic, since every document will be a contribution to his "self-knowledge" and the knowledge of man. How he himself will express his own attitude and beliefs will be a matter of ethics and tact. It is highly revealing how gently and without a trace of irony or impatience Cassirer treats far-fetched theories in aesthetics or the immature statements on art by the young Schiller. They receive his serious attention as historically logical efforts of man to express the fact that he is living. And without sympathy significant interpretation is impossible.

Cassirer considered himself a philosopher, not a literary critic. With the exception of one article, all his publications in the field of literature appeared either in independent form or in strictly philosophical periodicals. The scope of his contributions is wide: the German enlightenment period and German classicism and romanticism stand in the foreground; however, there are many valuable chapters, passages, or remarks on Classical, French, English, Swedish, etc., literature in his work. They all deal with literary-philosophical questions and they are all directed toward an understanding of the relation between certain literary personalities and certain philosophers or systems of philosophy; however, Cassirer's ideal problem seems never to be merely that. His investigations always exceed the concrete question of influences or individual works of art, and his deepest interest seems to lie elsewhere. Although Cassirer, as far as I can see, nowhere makes a statement to this end, his publications concerned with literature are of greater interest for the aesthetician than for either the philosopher or for the literary critic in general. Whenever Cassirer writes about a writer X in relation to a philosopher Y, he seems to be—in spite of all his attention to X and Y—more interested in Z, and Z is the individual essential poetic element (*dichterisches Wesenselement*) of X.

In the introductory part to his essay on Hölderlin Cassirer expresses the aim of his investigation most significantly. I translate the passage:

> It [the investigation] will have to try to draw from Hölderlin's poetic essence, as it belongs to him originally and as it precedes all abstract reflection, the interpretative conclusion in regard also to those trends which manifest themselves more and more distinctly in the totality of his theoretical attitude toward the world and life.
> (*Idee und Gestalt*)

This means clearly that Cassirer considers it the first duty of his investigation to clarify the character of Hölderlin's "poetic essence" which he regards as Hölderlin's "original property," before any possible statement about the development of his theoretical attitude can be made. Cassirer's wording looks like a sanctification of deductive method; however, the essay itself gives clear proof of the opposite and his other publications on literature support it. An inductive analysis is always made—as far as such an analysis can go. The final evaluation of the material, however, is no longer a matter of scientific method.

Thus, Cassirer's task here and elsewhere is a two-sided one. He does not limit himself to the never quite satisfactory investigation of certain philosophical influences on certain elements or periods of an artist's work, but tries to find a concrete picture of the artist's essence *qua* artist before the question of the artist's reflective world is raised. As a matter of fact, Cassirer—without mentioning it—has the tendency to protect the artist both from literature and from philosophy as these fields are usually represented in criticism. Cassirer, the philosopher, shows his greatest sympathy for the world of creative art and its individual rights.

The essay on Hölderlin may serve as an example for Cassirer's general attitude and method in the realm of literary-philosophical problems. The ideal subject for this purpose would be Cassirer's intensive occupation with his master, Goethe. However, this latter would greatly exceed the scope of our contribution.

Before Cassirer wrote his Hölderlin essay, three modern and important works on Hölderlin had appeared,—Dilthey's famous essay, Zinkernagel's book, and Gundolf's deep analysis of Hölderlin's *Archipelagus*. The result of Cassirer's essay shows, besides important additions, intensification of Dilthey's views, agreement with Gundolf, and a sharp contrast to Zinkernagel's method.

One of the foremost questions in regard to Hölderlin had been the exact determination of his position within the philosophy of German idealism. That Hölderlin had been

greatly and constructively influenced by Platonic reflections, Kantian criticism, and Spinoza's system was known. However, Hölderlin's relation to Fichte, Schelling, and particularly to Hegel had not been clarified. In this respect, Professor Zinkernagel had tried to reach results by an analysis of Hölderlin's foremost work *Hyperion* and had offered a very thorough appearing list of "influences" which seemed to make Hölderlin a receptive organon of all kinds of stimulations. A reader of Zinkernagel's book, in spite of all possible admiration for the author's knowledge and minute scholarship, would ask in vain why Hölderlin, as both poet and philosopher, shows such remarkable and generally acknowledged unity, and proved at the same time to be able to survive all these "influences" as an individual and to maintain his artistic personality to such an extent that today he is considered one of the most consistent and full grown lyric poets in world literature. It is in connection with Zinkernagel's book that Cassirer made his statement that Hölderlin's artistic personality was to be the *res prior* of his investigation and all other questions were to be regarded as *res posteriores*. The reciprocity between Hölderlin's imaginative and rational world was to be investigated.

Since Hölderlin's poetry as a whole is an expression of his personal conception—or philosophy—of nature, Cassirer chooses at first to characterize Hölderlin's peculiarity in contrast to Fichte and Schelling. Hölderlin, seeing in Kant's Critical philosophy a propaedeutic step towards a "system" and finding the ideal form of a system represented in Spinoza, tried—as did Fichte and Schelling—to establish an idealistic counterpart of Spinoza's construction. However he distinguished himself from Fichte and Schelling by regarding the One not as the supreme principle of deduction but as a $\epsilon\nu$ $\delta\iota\alpha\phi\epsilon\rho\omega\mu\epsilon\nuo\nu$ $\epsilon\alpha\upsilon\tau\omega\sigma\sigma$ conceived in direct relation to his conception of nature. The study of Plato contributed greatly to Hölderlin's peculiar mythical imagination; however, myth never was and to Hölderlin never became a mere symbol or a poetic ornament; but it was a necessary organon to apprehend reality. Myth and mythical phenomena appear in all of Hölderlin's works, including his letters and philosophical fragments, as sensuous-spiritual realities in which he believed without any noticeable sense of dualism. Hölderlin's conception of nature manifests an intertwinement of the reflective and perceptive elements without any break or inconsistency, and what Schiller tried to evoke sentimentally (*sentimentalisch*) in his poem "Die Götter Griechenlands," Hölderlin achieved naïvely and faithfully: to him the gods of Greece were not welcome poetical elements, but realities and therefore means towards the cognition of truth. The contact with Fichte's writings stimulated the depth of Hölderlin's reflective thinking, however—again—he reached his independent conclusion: nature, for him, was not matter but form.

Zinkernagel's belief that Schelling's influence was telling for Hölderlin's repudiation of Fichte's doctrine is denied by Cassirer. Moreover, Cassirer is able to provide almost irrefutable proof for the opposite. Disregarding the fact that Schelling had been Fichte's follower until 1796,—the year in which the "influence" was supposed to have taken place,—we have (with Cassirer) to take into consideration that Schelling's later philosophy of nature reminds one of Hölderlin's earlier general attitude. A document made available in 1913 seems to correct all former interpretations of the Schelling-Hölderlin relation. In 1913, the Royal Library at Berlin acquired a folio-sheet which shows Hegel's hand and contains a brief outline of a philosophical system. The editor called it "the oldest systematic program of German idealism" and was able to prove that the manuscript is a Hegelian copy of a Schelling text. The text expresses a demand for a system of philosophy that would combine "the monotheism of reason" with "the polytheism of imagination," in order to develop a "mythology of reason." This is exactly what Hölderlin in his more imaginative rather than rational way of thinking had felt and fought for. Cassirer's conclusion seems good enough: the widely discussed meeting between Hölderlin and Schelling in 1795 had not brought about a Schelling influence on Hölderlin, but had given Schelling an opportunity to find stimulation from the side of Hölderlin and to formulate rationally what had already been in Hölderlin's mind.

The result is the historically significant fact that Hölderlin had been the responsible agent implanting the thoughts into the man who was to become the most Romantic representative of German idealism. Cassirer was able to supply the proof for this contention because of his correct basic presumption that Hölderlin's imaginative world was clearly outlined before any outside influences came upon his reflective world. What follows in the last part of Cassirer's essay is an intensively compressed description of Hölderlin's pantheism. After giving one of his masterly surveys of the dialectic method in Kantian and Romantic philosophy, Cassirer shows that Hölderlin, who used the categories and terms of philosophical idealism, transformed them gradually but consistently into a dialectic of feeling—the simultaneously consistent and antithetic essence of every lyric poet. Hölderlin did not try to solve the dialectical problem concerning the relation of the general and the particular; he only expressed the depth of the problem as an artist.

I do not find sufficient reason for divergence from Cassirer's interpretation and, in particular, from his discussion of Hölderlin's "artistic essence." Newer and fuller investigations, carried through with greater ambition in regard to completeness, have enlarged on the material; however, they have not improved our understanding in general. Yet, I should like to take up one specific statement in Cassirer's essay, a statement which makes me uneasy.

In the introduction to his brilliant last section Cassirer expresses himself rather apodictically about the general character of a lyric poet. According to him the peculiarity of a lyric poet is to be found in two elements: his individual conception of nature (*Naturgefühl*), and his individual feeling for form and development (*Ablauf*) of spiritual occurrences (*seelisches Geschehen*). When these two elements meet and determine each other reciprocally, the peculiar lyric form of expression arises. In other words, the individual conception of nature and of the human soul is the basic condition for a meeting which—in the world of an artist—makes lyric art. The important attribute here

seems to be "individual," since all art shows the interrelationship of nature (all manifestations of nature, from a flower to a slum dwelling) and man (the life of soul in all possible aspects). Therefore, what does "individual" mean? In the following passages Cassirer speaks lucidly of Hölderlin's tragic efforts to find objectivity, and he manages, very methodically, to leave the impression that Hölderlin as an individual was one of the unusual artistic phenomena who were both influencing and being influenced in regard to their philosophical or cognitive achievements. However, this did not make Hölderlin a lyric poet, and his individuality as such—if we accept Cassirer's two conditions—does not differ in principle from other artists who were not lyric poets, but, for instance, dramatists.

I do not believe that Cassirer, in his statement about the lyric poet, and speaking of his "individual" conceptions, was entangled in the still rather common belief that subjectivity is one of the foremost elements of lyrics. Many years after he wrote his Hölderlin essay Cassirer expressed himself clearly in this respect. After a discussion of Croce's aesthetic theories, he says:

> It is of course true that the great lyrical poets are capable of the deepest emotions and that an artist who is not endowed with powerful feelings will never produce anything except shallow and frivolous art. But from this fact we cannot conclude that the function of lyrical poetry and of art in general can be adequately described as the artist's ability "to make a clean breast of his feelings." . . . The lyric poet is not just a man who indulges in displays of feeling. . . . An artist who is absorbed not in the contemplation and creation of forms but rather in his own pleasure or in his enjoyment of "the joy of grief " becomes a sentimentalist. Hence we can hardly ascribe to lyric art a more subjective character than to all the other forms of art. For it contains the same sort of embodiment, and the same process of objectification. . . . It is written with images, sounds, and rhythms which, just as in the case of dramatic poetry and dramatic representation, coalesce into an indivisible whole. In every great lyrical poem we find this concrete and indivisible unity. [*Essay on Man*]

There is an interval of twenty-six years between the Hölderlin essay and the *Essay on Man*. Yet I cannot find any basic inconsistency between the quoted passages from the latter and Cassirer's general attitude in the former. However, the statement about the principal elements of a lyric poet still remains unexplained. Perhaps, Cassirer used a cliché—an unusual process in his writings—in order better to express the content of the directly following statement about the peculiarity of the German lyric poets in the period of Idealism, their desire to become conscious of their actions as creative artists, and their further desire to verify these actions philosophically. This is, to be sure, not a singular incident in the history of lyrics—the French symbolists and their successors show a more than general parallel—, but it is true.

There are many relations between philosophy and literature which have been noticed surprisingly late or have not as yet found a satisfactory explanation. Those cases appear most puzzling in which there exists a deep similarity between a philosophical system and the expression of a poet without permitting the assumption of a "physical" influence. In the case of Hölderlin the existing material is such that his development simply could not be understood after eliminating the surrounding philosophical situation. In the case of Corneille, however, and his position in relation to the Cartesian system, the problem is much more involved. In consideration of the methodically different approach, Cassirer's attitude seems to be significant.

G. Lanson expressed the situation very well in a few words: *"Il y a non seulement analogie, mais identité d'esprit dans le Traité des passions et dans la tragédie cornélienne."* The curious facts are that Descartes and Corneille were contemporaries—Descartes' *Discours de la Méthode* appeared in 1637, immediately after the first performance of the *Cid* at the Théatre du Marais in Paris—, that they represented a school of thought which was new and individual, and that yet a direct relation between them cannot be established. G. Krantz tried to show Descartes' constructive influence on the aesthetic theories of French classicism, and Faguet made the attempt to establish reasons for a possible influence on Descartes by Corneille,—both in vain. Lanson, who is certainly right in not trusting either theory, explains the similarity between Descartes' and Corneille's psychological and ethical aspects from their physical environment and tries to ascertain that the spiritual-moral reality in French seventeenth century life was reason enough to stimulate both the philosopher and the poet toward the same end; that the active-intellectual type of man, then representative in France, gave both of them an object of experience which contributed to the results in their respective attitudes.

In his book on Descartes, Cassirer devotes a chapter to the discussion of Descartes and Corneille.

Cassirer does not assume any direct influence. A Cartesian influence on Corneille is impossible chronologically, and a Corneillean influence on Descartes highly improbable because of Descartes' well-known attitude toward literature in general and modern literature in particular. Since Lanson's explanation does not appeal to Cassirer, he directs his efforts towards finding reasons which may have brought about something like a preestablished harmony between Descartes and Corneille. His method is *geisteswissenschaftlich,*—the essence in Descartes' reflective and in Corneille's poetic psychology and ethics is to be defined and explained in their connection with the historically preceding or simultaneous philosophical development.

According to Cassirer, both Descartes and Corneille were dealing with an object of thought which had been one of the foremost topics since the early Renaissance: the relation between Ego and World. They both express the "pathos of subjectivity," theoretically-ethically or poetically, and—a striking parallel—they have the same theory of freedom in contrast to their contemporaries.

Essential for both Descartes and Corneille was their occupation with the world of passions. Descartes tried to investigate his object as a physicist (*en Physicien*); only through

cognition of the passions can we master them and use them to our ethical advantage. In Descartes' scale of values the highest ideal is represented by the combination of full energy of will and perfect judgment, although Descartes does not deny the existence of a relative ideal besides the absolute one, which ideal would consist of a combination of full energy of will and not perfect judgment. Corneille, in his plays, shows an exactly equivalent attitude and was attacked by his contemporary critics as immoral because of his opinion that the application of great will power, no matter whether the aim is good or not, has its own value.

Furthermore, Cassirer shows clearly that the Stoicism, as it appears both in Descartes' and in Corneille's work, experienced a significant transformation, losing its passive attitude (*sustine et abstine!*) and its moral characteristic as a doctrine for "bodiless beings." Descartes' psychophysical interpretation of the passions and Corneille's similar attitude distinguish them both from the classical and the Christian conception.

Cassirer succeeds very well in pointing out sharply the general parallels which, without any doubt, are essential. In addition to it, his literary discussion of Corneille's tragedies is of high value because of its historical objectivity. Corneille's *dramatis personae* will seem unreal or psychologically improbable to anyone who has not been initiated into the essence and the laws of the poet's individual world; yet they regain their ideal truth as soon as the doors to this world have been opened. Then, and then only, is it not a question of liking or immediate appreciation any more, but a case of following a creative poet on his excursions through his imaginative world.

All this granted, we are still waiting for an answer to the original question. There can be no doubt that certain lines of development can be traced down to Descartes and Corneille which will make them appear as historically "logical" personalities; yet their peculiar conformity in reaching the same conclusions in regard to such specific objects as human passions and the scale of values has not been explained by Cassirer. In his interpretation, Descartes and Corneille still remain lonesome giants, having many clear connections with the past and, at the same time, with modern views, yet lacking any significant connection with their own time. The clarification of their philosophical or poetic systems is helpful for our understanding of them; however not sufficient for the understanding of their positions in their time.

Lanson's idea that Descartes and Corneille were basically influenced by the peculiarity of their time is enticing in its methodical aspect. Cassirer finds the connection between them in the past; Lanson stresses their immediate relations as not resulting from any direct physical influence but from the source of life surrounding them. And Cassirer himself, in a different chapter of his Descartes book, offers new material which seems to give Lanson substantial support.

In the chapter about Descartes and Queen Christina of Sweden, Cassirer discusses the question whether Christina might have been acquainted with Corneille's writings.

There is no conclusive answer; yet Christina's interest in contemporary thought and art is established so well that her ignorance of the first great French dramatist would seem unbelievable. Cassirer goes farther; he not only shows that Christina in her reactions and actions resembles greatly the heroines in Corneille's plays, but also gives a highly interesting, concrete example which manifests a deep affinity between one historical reaction of the Queen of Sweden and a poetic one in Corneille's *Pulchérie*: Christina's decision to dissolve her engagement to Karl Gustaf and the parallel Pulchérie—Léon. Corneille wrote his play twenty-five years after Christina had made her famous decision. Therefore, no fantastic hypothesis about the influence of poetry on life can be offered in this case.

Queen Christina, after Cassirer's very valuable interpretation, appears as an addition to the list of seventeenth century personalities who, according to Lanson, showed Corneillean character *in concreto*. It is surprising that Cassirer, in spite of this, reacts so indifferently to Lanson's theory in his Descartes-Corneille chapter. Descartes and Corneille would become fully comprehensible, if not only their common roots in the past but also in their own time could be shown. Great philosophers and artists, I think, never stand apart from their own time, no matter whether they act as friends, enemies, or prophets. The sociological aspect of both philosophy and literature should never be forgotten, and in the case of Descartes' and Corneille's "strange" affinity it should be applied in full. Therefore, Lanson's treatment of the question, although deplorably incomplete, shows the way to future research. I am not at all in favor of giving the sociological method a prominent position in literary research; however, I think that the physician should know which medicine to use in each specific case.

A completely different problem appears in connection with the most controversial German romanticist, Heinrich von Kleist.

Kleist's relatively small artistic output stands in no quantitative relation to the amount of work dedicated to him in literary criticism. The Kleist-specialization in Germany has resulted in research conditions which have made every element in Kleist's life and work an object of passionate discussion. The phenomenon Kleist represents an in many respects interesting riddle which, in order to be solved, seems to require a co-operative effort on the part of rather broadminded literary critics, historians, and psychiatrists. The limitations of critics manifest themselves almost necessarily in regard to Kleist. To make things worse, Kleist has some national importance for his country, and we need hardly enlarge upon the almost inevitable results in criticism. The most significant example of misunderstandings in regard to Kleist, however, is in my eyes the *Kätchen von Heilbronn* interpretation in F. Gundolf's book on Kleist, in which this truly exceptional and far-sighted critic manifests a complete lack of hermeneutic ability in this particular respect. All the difficulties of interpretation *in re* Kleist arise from Kleist's own super-nervous and chaotic personality more than from his artistic work. He is one of the best examples both of the inability of the soul of man to master absolute ideal demands and also of a psycho-pathic condition together with a capacity for exceptionally creative and lucid artistry.

Kantian philosophy, as generally acknowledged, had a great influence on Kleist as a man and as a writer. Obvious records, among them his letters, give a solid basis for this contention; and his artistic works show Kleist's symbolical transformations of philosophical (and other) problems. However, the exact significance of Kant's philosophy for Kleist as an artist has not been clarified as yet, and certain gaps of understanding prevailed when Cassirer enlivened the Kleist research by his daring essay on Kleist and the Kantian philosophy. Among other contributions to the point, Cassirer advanced a new hypothesis which—if accepted—would, even though it would not change our general attitude toward Kleist, compel us to take new data into consideration.

In his letters to his sister Ulrike and his fiancée Wilhelmine von Zenge, young Kleist gave an intimate account of his state of mind and his general views. The letters are sometimes so expressive and self-interpreting that many a statement in them has been taken for granted without due regard to Kleist's general characteristic of being very inconsistent and versatile in his moods, predilections, and self-expression. In his plays and short stories Kleist offers a magnificent example of his creative ability to transform a moment into a life. However, his letters suffer from the dualism between his creative, and therefore practically not always reliable imagination, and the attempt of giving an empirically realistic account of his life. This is likely to be a rather general situation in an artist's letters. Yet in this case it is more prominent than in others, perhaps because of the constant efforts in the Kleist research to establish the empirical truth instead of pursuing the wiser way towards the ideal truth.

In a much discussed letter of March 22, 1801, Kleist, in utter despair, describes to his fiancée the annihilating effect of his occupation with the Kantian philosophy and gives a vivid picture of his total apathy after learning that "We cannot decide, whether what we call truth is really the truth or only appears to us as such." Kleist's world of ideals, for which he had lived and from which he had received his strength, seemed to be destroyed. This letter is a masterpiece of writing and could, without a change, fill the place of a monologue in any suitable tragedy.

At least three specific questions arise directly from this letter. First, Kleist gives the impression that he had begun his occupation with Kant's philosophy "a short time ago" (*"vor kurzem"*), although we know that he had already studied Kant in 1800. Secondly, speaking of Kant, Kleist uses the strange expression "the more recent so-called Kantian philosophy" (*neuere sogenannte Kantische Philosophie*). Thirdly, Kant's Critical method and philosophy seem to have been misunderstood by Kleist.

The discussion of these three points is the backbone of Cassirer's hypothesis in the first part of his essay: that Kleist in this letter had in his mind not Kant's transcendental idealism but Fichte's *Bestimmung des Menschen*.

The question is not of great importance outside the circle of the professional Kleist experts. However it has methodical significance. We know that in 1800 Kleist had occupied himself with Kant without experiencing any disastrous results. On the other hand, it is easy for Cassirer to show that Kant's Critical method did not imply the denial of the objectivity of man's cognitive efforts. These two facts, in connection with the strange formula "so-called Kantian philosophy," leads Cassirer to the possibility that Kleist, in 1801, had read Fichte's *Bestimmung des Menschen,* which had been published in 1800 in Berlin—where Kleist lived—under circumstances which made this book immediately one of the most widely discussed in Prussia's capital. Kleist must have known the book; and it contained ideas which would make his reaction very plausible.

Cassirer's hypothesis may be correct. However, I think that it represents one of the very few instances in his writings on literature where he presses a point less from necessity than from his own status as a Kant expert. It is certainly strange to observe that Kleist, who in November 1800 had written his sister that he would like to go to France in order to spread there the new (i.e., Kantian) philosophy, would have had such a shocking experience on account of this same philosophy less than half a year later. The explanation that Kleist was shocked after reading the *Critique of Pure Reason* is not sufficient, since this work does not express an attitude that would have been basically different from Kant's earlier works. On the other hand, Fichte had become such a well-known personality in Germany, after his "atheism controversy" and his leaving Jena for Berlin, that it is hardly comprehensible that Kleist should have hidden Fichte's name in his letter, if it was Fichte and not Kant whom he had in mind. Cassirer sees that the acquaintance with Fichte's *Bestimmung des Menschen* would have been—without any misunderstanding—a sufficient cause for Kleist's despair; however, he does not sufficiently take into consideration a possible misunderstanding by Kleist as to the meaning of Kant's philosophy. Strong inconsistencies and quick impulsive reactions were characteristic of the violently emotional Kleist, and these two letters of 1800 and 1801 may be just other examples of this sort of conduct. If Fichte, a "Kantian" philosopher, misunderstood Kant, why should not Kleist, certainly not a professional philosopher, have made a similar mistake? And his desire to spread Kantian philosophy in France is no proof by itself that Kleist, in 1800, had an intimate knowledge of Kant's transcendental idealism.

To prove either opinion is, of course, impossible; and it was to be expected that critics of Cassirer's hypothesis were split into two camps. Oskar Walzel, one of the foremost experts in the field of German romanticism, remarked: "Among the numberous discussions of Kleist's 'Kant experience,' only . . . [Cassirer's essay] needs to be emphasized." Eugen Kühnemann, in his lecture on "Kleist und Kant," took the stand against Cassirer.

The discussion of Kleist's confusing letter is only a part of Cassirer's essay. Its second half deals with the significance of transcendental idealism for Kleist as a creative artist, and shows in an exemplary manner how Kleist's artistic work received a constructive impetus from Kantian thoughts. Kleist's personal tragedy, experienced by him consciously in continuous philosophic reflections, ex-

pressed itself in his art. Cassirer may be right in stating that Kleist is perhaps the only example of a great poet whose creative power had been awakened by a reflective experience (*gedankliches Erlebnis*); at least I do not find any striking parallels. In this connection Cassirer, after his adventure into the realm of empirical truth, is again searching for the ideal truth and is, consequently, at his best.

I do not want to leave the Kleist essay without calling attention to a brief passage in it which is very characteristic of Cassirer as a historian. In the history of German literature there is one of those rather common little events which, *sub specie aeternitatis,* would appear as mere trifles but which come up again and again and are discussed with much satisfaction: I am speaking of those numerous examples of apparent pettiness in great men. Our example concerns Goethe and his relation to Kleist and refers to the simple fact that Goethe had no understanding for the tragic genius of his younger colleague. We know some examples of Goethe's not exactly admirable reactions in similar cases; but we do not think their discussion particularly valuable. However, if a discussion were necessary, the only possibly fruitful method is that used by Cassirer in his essay. His brief analysis appears to me to be a perfect example of the ideal method of procedure. Showing Goethe's individual views and his certainly broad, but naturally limited, i.e., defined, personal requirements for what he would have considered great art, Cassirer puts Goethe's lack of understanding for Kleist in the light in which it needs to be seen. There are worlds of thought and of art where friendship is not possible, and that is all. Another sober interpretation of one of Goethe's peculiar reactions was given by Cassirer in his essay, **"Goethe and the 18th Century."** Goethe astonished Mr. Soret, Prince Karl Alexander's educator at Weimar, in August 1830, by his total indifference to the fact of the July revolution in Paris and at the same time by his very strong interest in the fact that his, Goethe's, synthetic method in scientific research had just been accepted by Geoffroy St. Hilaire. In this context Cassirer is able to give an objective and, to me, doubtlessly correct interpretation. Goethe believed in "representative moments" in history. To him the July revolution was less representative than the victory of his synthetic method. As we know today, Goethe was right.

In the history of literary criticism Cassirer is one of the representatives of the field and methods of *Geisteswissenschaft*—the study of the development of ideas. Usually the work of the individual in this line of endeavor shows individual concentration, since what is investigated is not ideas *par excellence* but ideas in their relation to something else. Our survey of a few of Cassirer's contributions shows that his main concern is to be found in the investigation of the relation between the reflective and the imaginative world of the artist. Cassirer is most explicit and most eloquent when recreating the life of the artist's imaginative conceptions which manifest themselves as transformations of his reflective life. His most significant contribution seems to me to be in the neighborhood of this particular point. I find it in the gap which Cassirer leaves unexplained, because he does not want to make a pretentious statement without offering the scale of processes which would solidify it. In spite of everything, Cassirer's apparent interest in the clarification of historical items—Kleist and Fichte or Kant—, or in the truer understanding of a poet's philosophical contribution—Hölderlin and Schelling—, or a better psychological interpretation of a great individual's momentous reactions—Goethe and Soret—, he dedicates his greatest effort to re-telling the story of artistic imagination in those individual lives which caught his fancy. There is no doubt that Goethe is for Cassirer the most significant phenomenon since he is the broadest; a phenomenon which, in the rare combination of pure artistry, profound understanding of the sciences, and peculiarly unacademic philosophizing, represents an object of investigation beyond the usual scope. In his writings on Goethe Cassirer has the opportunity to apply his own wholly constructive, positive, and synthetic mind better than anywhere else. But here also a lacuna remains. Cassirer expresses with great penetration his conception of Goethe's artistic essence as he sees it, and the discipline of his knowledge and thought restrains him from overstepping the limits of the material at his disposal. However, here also a point appears again and again where I would ask for further objective penetration; Cassirer would probably reply that the remaining part is a matter of experience, tact, and taste. The demand for more becomes consequently so urgent that,—if the demand is followed by a new investigation,—Cassirer surely would have stimulated it. The investigation ought to be directed toward a more objective foundation of our conception of the artist's creative world.

To be sure, Cassirer has never published a statement referring to what I shall try to express. He knew, however, that such a demand is a logical consequence of his writings on literature; and in conversations he liked to dwell on this point. Fortunately, Cassirer has published a comprehensive chapter on "Art" and there has given a clear picture of his aesthetic views. There is no inconsistency between his general theoretical discussion and the method used in his more practical contributions.

We must mention a few of Cassirer's statements, in order to clear the ground.

Cassirer conceives art in general as a reality of the same value as, for example, science. *"Rerum videre formas* is a no less important and indispensable task than *rerum cognoscere causas."* Art has its own rationality, the rationality of form.

> Art is not fettered to the rationality of things or events. It may infringe all those laws of probability which classical aestheticians declared to be the constitutional laws of art. It may give us the most bizarre and grotesque vision, and yet retain a rationality of its own—the rationality of form. [**Essay on Man**]

The artist who discovers the form of nature is philosophically equal to the scientist who discovers nature's laws. Moreover, "language and science are abbreviations of reality; art is intensification of reality. Language and science depend upon one and the same process of abstraction; art may be described as a continuous process of concretion." "Science gives us order in thoughts; morality gives us

order in actions, and art gives us order in the apprehension of visible, tangible, and audible appearances." And—"We cannot speak of art as 'extrahuman' or 'superhuman' without overlooking one of its fundamental features, its constructive power in the framing of the human universe."

These incomplete quotations help us to summarize Cassirer's attitude. Cassirer believes in a creative world of art as a fundamentally independent world of human behavior, with its own conditions and laws. The essence of the artist's mind is different from the reflective mind of the scientist or philosopher. The scientist deals with phenomena and makes the intellectual attempt to bring order into them, renouncing to the highest possible extent an interference of anthropomorphic elements. The artist offers the principal human example of free creative action. The scientist's work comprises a reciprocity of the phenomenal and his intellectual world; his reflective activity has the form of conquest: he becomes master of the phenomena by fully conscious induction, trying (never quite successfully) to reduce the exciting but dangerous combination by means of an always threatening semi-conscious deduction. The artist, on the contrary, uses his intellect rather as a function than as a condition, in order to express the results of his creative imagination.

The transformation of the "real" world which takes place in every great work of art shows something else which may be called intensification or concretion, a something which otherwise does not make an unhindered appearance in the regions of human behavior. In art, and only in art, a decade can be made an hour, and a life made a mere moment.

The intellect's interference manifests itself most clearly in literature, because literature is a linguistic art. However, the total work of literary art does not always have any, and sometimes has very little, direct relation to the world of reflection. The main characteristic of art, in contrast to philosophy and science, is its inherent particularity not to be basically dependent upon the laws of scientific reflection. Since form is the only common rational factor of every art, and the form of each art manifests a specific order, the order and form of the arts are to be investigated, if we want to examine the artist's imagination at work and the architecture of the world of art.

This has certainly been done again and again; however from a different methodical point of view. Since, in this context, we are not interested in the biographical, psychological, or general historical implications of an artist, nor in a more or less casual or accidental investigation of certain elements in the work peculiar to a certain artist, our task should be a complete investigation of the artist's formative tendencies which result in the total of his artistic creation. Art's main element is not the content; it is the creation of a form which—in all its dimensions—offers us the cognition of a content. The formative tendencies may vary in one or in all artists.

When Cassirer speaks of poetic essence (*dichterisches Wesenselement*), he does not use simply a general term for an unclear conception, but thinks of the full essence of the artist's creative and created world. The method of finding it remains undiscussed. Aesthetic judgment, experience, taste, and tact combined in a mind of methodical strength and constructive imagination reach,—as we know and as Cassirer himself shows,—remarkable results. However, the stimulation to a "more" is given at the same time, since the road toward subjectivity is wide open and the question arises whether among the aesthetic opinions of several experts some may not approach the "ideal truth" more closely than others. As long as the object of investigation is not the function of pleasure but the formative conditions of a work of art, an objective method should, at least, be visualized. That such a method can never consist of the traditional formidable computations of, for instance, rhymes, influences, or new words, is obvious.

In literary research we find some of the finest examples of hermeneutic ability. The changes and the continuous development of evaluation do not necessarily make the quality of the preceding or following critical opinions appear weak, because the liking of individuals, groups, and generations may differ. This will remain so forever. However, we are not dealing with a sociology of art or with a history of taste. We may not "like" a certain artistic creation. However we ought to find a method of discovering whether our dislike is simply a dislike or whether it is based on the fact that the work in question is not a work of art. We ought to have the methodical means of finding the characteristics of the numerous "essences" or "worlds" of art as objectively as possible. Acknowledging that form and order in art are a *conditio sine qua non,* we certainly should be able to reach a better understanding of all the forms and orders appearing in the history of art. This has been achieved quite admirably in one of the non-linguistic arts—painting.

An ideal work of art may be compared with a sphere, every external and internal point of which stands in a meaningful connection with every other point. To determine the connections and the necessity of their full reciprocity is the aim of an investigation in regard to the form of art. Obviously, such an ideal example may be found best in an artistic genre which by necessity lends itself to a relatively easy analytical approach, for example in music and also in painting. Linguistic art is far more complex. A lyric poem or a drama can be approached much more easily than for instance a novel, a widely changing and only superficially definable object which, because of the lack of formal limitation, appears as the most difficult possible problem in this respect.

The enervating element in literary research, as in all arts, is the difficulty of determining why an apparently good work of art is good. Here Cassirer says: "It is the task of the aesthetic judgment or of artistic taste to distinguish between a genuine work of art and those other spurious products which are indeed playthings, or at most 'the response to the demand of entertainment'." I believe that more concrete results can be reached. A novel may be good, because it manifests profound psychological insight in spite of bad style; and another novel may be bad, because it shows superficiality of content in spite of a very good style. But it is not psychology or style or content which make a novel good or bad; it is something else. We

should try to find this "something else." We should find the conditions under which art manifests itself in literature. We should, in every work of real or presumed art, investigate and define those elements which make it art.

Experience shows that certain results can be achieved very quickly, for instance in the field of the novel. An initial two-sided attempt usually clarifies the ground. A novel combines, under normal circumstances, the description of man with the description of man's environment—nature in any kind of variation. A minute investigation of the formative elements pertaining to the representation of man is the foremost aim. What literary research has done so far is only a part of the whole task. In discussions of paintings we are accustomed to point out every detail of a depicted being's characteristics; in literary research we are usually satisfied with less. It is not a question of physical colors,—an artist's language transforms ideas and feelings into its own colors; "it is written with images, sounds, and rhythms . . . which coalesce into an indivisible whole." The character of a person in a novel as concerns his actions, feelings, and thoughts is the most obvious, although not the artistically most important part of it. A look at the formative tendencies of a novelist shows numerous, but not innumerable, peculiarities in making a person come, go, think, speak, impress, yawn, weep, live, and die. A thorough examination of these peculiarities will tell us something rather important about, not the mere technique, but the creative activity of the artist. A complete analysis of a novel will give us a fairly objective comprehension of his formative action. The literary critic should become a neighbor of the fine arts, since literature, in its greatest performances, manifests the same purity of form and order as does great painting. The reason why a complete analytical investigation of a novel or even of a short story has never yet been made lies in the apparent enormity of the task. The task is great. However, considering the immense amount of time spent on other—and sometimes hardly worthwhile—types of literary research, one may be permitted to think this and similar objects worthwhile.

Remaining with our subject, the novel, we may say that an investigation of nature as a formative element is much easier than is that of man. In literary criticism we are accustomed to find statements about the particular tendency or ability of certain artists to describe nature. Very little has been said of the various types of nature descriptions in prose works and still less about the part which descriptions of nature play as a constructive power, necessary for the understanding of the total essence of the work, or as a mere embellishment with no other reason than that of serving the pleasure of the reader. In the first, artistically significant, case there are various patterns or types of form, and in each individual example an objective picture of the artist's aim and creative ability can be found. The results may sometimes be surprising; here I am able to offer a small but concrete example, since a concrete analysis has been published.

In the history of the German novel, Theodor Fontane holds an eminent place. Fontane's descriptions of North German landscape, an inherent and distinct element in his best novels, were praised by critics as creative achievements of high quality. An analysis of these descriptions, however, showed that Fontane used a superficial pattern, introducing the descriptions without necessary inner connection, phrasing them rather monotonously, and using them as a kind of background music. Fontane was clever, but not a creative artist in his descriptions of nature. His quality in other respects has thus far not been investigated. In his technical dealing with nature he shows a tendency toward ornament or embellishment. In the history of human taste, in regard to literature, fine arts, and music—technical ornamentation has been one of the safest steps to popularity and has often been mistaken for true art.

"So long as we live in the world of sense impressions alone we merely touch the surface of reality. Awareness of the depth of things always requires an effort on the part of our active and constructive energies." The active and constructive energies have not yet been used sufficiently for our better understanding of the means which make it possible for a creative artist to show, in a symbol, a concretion of his poetic world. Better understanding does not mean destructive analysis or hair-splitting. I believe with Cassirer that creative art is the noblest activity of man. The investigation of the formative elements of poetic creation is a noble task.

Northrop Frye   (essay date 1954)

SOURCE: "Myth as Information," in *The Hudson Review,* Vol. VII, No. 2, Summer, 1954, pp. 228-35.

[*In the following essay, Frye discusses the implications of Cassirer's use of the word "myth" for the study of logic and of literature.*]

The first volume of the English translation of Ernst Cassirer's **Philosophy of Symbolic Forms** has just appeared. As the German edition of this volume was published in 1923, the translation is very belated, and by now will chiefly interest students of philosophy who are not sufficiently concerned with Cassirer or acquainted with German to have consulted the original. This is a restricted range of usefulness, not enlarged by the fact that the real contemporary importance of Cassirer's thought is displayed not in this book but in the later **Essay on Man,** written in English and now available in a pocket edition. The **Essay on Man** is crisper, more concise, more conclusive in the direction of its arguments, and, as befits its American setting, more evangelical. Cassirer's work as a whole has been pretty thoroughly assimilated since his death in 1945, and the first volume of his *magnum opus* has now a largely historical importance for anyone who, like the present writer, cannot claim to be a technically competent philosopher.

That historical importance is, of course, very considerable. It is hardly too much to say that the bulk of what is distinctive in twentieth-century thought, in the non-mathematical division, has been constructed around the word "myth". The major political philosophies of today, whether democratic, communist or fascist, are still firmly rooted in their nineteenth-century formulations. But when the century opened the study of myth in psychology by Freud, and in anthropology by Frazer and others, had

started a radically new departure in social thinking, and in 1922, the year that Proust died with his great mythical *Recherche* complete, the appearance of *The Waste Land, Ulysses* and the more ectoplasmic *Fantasia of the Unconscious* startled the literary public also into realizing the importance of myth. It was the next year that Cassirer began to bring the problem into systematic philosophy, and in the thirty years since then the word *myth* has continued to produce that uninterrupted flow of talk which is generally called, and sometimes accompanies, a steady advance in thinking.

Cassirer appears to have done a good deal to break down the provincialism of the discursive reason in philosophy. Logic is based on language, and is a specialized development of language, but it is by no means the final cause of language. Not only is language itself prelogical, but there is no evidence whatever that man learned to speak primarily because he wanted to speak rationally. The simultaneous and parallel development of the languages of myth and literature show that there are other kinds of structures to be made out of words. Thinking is one of many things that man does; hence it is a part of a whole, the whole being the "functional unity" of human work in the world. To put logical thought in its place as one of a number of human operations is more realistic than to consult it as an oracle which reveals to man the existence of a systematic and rational order in the objective world. For when reason in the mind discovers rational order in the universe outside it, this discovery is largely a matter of falling in love with its own reflection, like Narcissus.

The "philosophy of symbolic forms," then, is a philosophy which starts by looking at the variety of mental constructions in human life. These include science, mathematics, philosophy, language, myth and the arts, and in the aggregate are called culture. Each of these constructions is built out of units called symbols, which are usually words or numbers, and which, approximately, owe their content to the objective world and their form to the categories of human consciousness. For further details see Professor Hendel's lucid introduction, which traces Cassirer's conception back to the "schema" of Kant. We may also divide these constructions into a logical group and another group which is either pre- or extra-logical, and which consists mainly of language, myth and the arts. Folke Leander, writing in the volume of the Library of Living Philosophers devoted to Cassirer, remarks that Cassirer has not established the relation among these three, any more than he has established that there are in fact three of them, because there is no adequate treatment of aesthetics in his work. (The chapter on art in the **Essay on Man** is largely amiable burble.) It is perhaps worth while trying to follow up this suggestion, and to see if we can discover what, on the basis of Cassirer's general conception of symbolic form, the relation of myth actually is to language on the one hand, and to literature (the only one of the arts which seems to have a *direct* connection with myth) on the other.

The relation of grammar to logic may provide us with a useful analogy. Logic grows out of grammar, the unconscious or potential logic inherent in language, and we often find that the containing forms of conceptual thought are of grammatical origin, the stock example being the subject and predicate of Aristotelian logic. It would be interesting to develop John Stuart Mill's suggestions about the relations of grammar and logic, which are referred to by Cassirer, and are perhaps not as indefensible as he thinks, though they may need restating. One wonders, for instance, about the parallelism between the parts of speech and the elements of thought in our Classical-Western tradition, where nearly all the important languages belong to the Aryan group. There is surely some connection between the noun and the conception of a material world, the verb and the conceptions of spirit, energy and will, the adjective and universals, the adverb and value, the conjunction and relation, and so forth, that would bear investigating.

It is disappointing to find that not even in the **Essay on Man** is there any reference to the *contemporary* problems involved in the relation of grammar and logic. Cassirer shows how language begins in spatial mythopoeia and the projection into the outer world of images derived from the human body. He does not show how these metaphors organize our writing and thinking as much as ever today: nearly every time we use a preposition we are using a spatial myth or an unconscious diagram. If a writer says: "But on the other hand there is an additional consideration to be brought forward in support of the opposing argument," he may be writing normal (if wordy) English, but he is also drawing elaborate geometrical doodles, like an armchair strategist scrawling plans of battle on a tablecloth. Again, the fluid primitive conceptions dealt with by Cassirer, the Polynesian *mana,* the Iroquois *orenda,* and the like, are participal or gerundive conceptions: they belong in a world where energy and matter have not been clearly separated, either in thought or into the verbs and nouns of our own less flexible language-structures. As energy and matter are not clearly separated in nuclear physics either, we might do well to return to such "primitive" words ourselves. The words "atom" and "light", for example, being nouns, are too material and static to be adequate symbols for what they now mean, and when they pass from the equations of a physicist into the linguistic apparatus of contemporary social consciousness, the grammatical difficulties in the translation show up clearly.

Of course one would have to avoid the scholar's mate in this kind of argument: the fallacy of thinking that we have explained the nature of something by accounting for its origin in something else. Logic may have grown out of grammar, but to grow out of something is in part to outgrow it, and to try to reduce logic to grammar would be as futile as a good many earlier attempts to reduce grammar to logic. For grammar may also be a hampering force in the development of logic, and a major source of logical confusions and pseudo-problems. These confusions extend much further than even the enormous brood of fallacies spawned by paronomasia, or the use of words in a double or manifold sense, which make up the greatest number of such booby traps. Even Cassirer's major effort in thought illustrates a grammatical problem: he abandoned the search for a systematic or rational unity in human consciousness in favor of recognizing a "functional unity" of a number of various activities that obviously do exist. This

had the effect of transferring his conception of reason from the definite to the indefinite article, of saying that reason is *a* phenomenon of human consciousness, which is indisputably true, instead of saying that human consciousness is rational (or *the* reason), which involves one in a wholly unnecessary struggle for the exclusive possession of an essence. The other day two students came to me and one said: "I say art is expression; Jim here says it's communication: which is it?" I said that if he would admit that art may communicate, Jim would probably admit that it may also express, and they could divide the essence peaceably between them. It was the same grammatical *pons asinorum* on a small scale. It is no wonder, then, that many logicians tend to think of grammar as something of a logical disease. Some of them have maintained that mathematics is the real source of coherence in logic. I have no opinion on this, but as a literary critic I know that as long as logic continues to make a functional use of words, it will continue to be involved in all the problems of words, including grammar and rhetoric.

When people speaking different languages come into contact an *ideogrammatic* structure is built up out of the efforts at communication. The figure 5 is an ideogram, because it means the same number to people who call it five, cinq, cinque, fünf and a dozen other things. Similarly, the purely linguistic associations of English "time" and French "temps" are perceptibly different, as a comparison of the phrases "good time" and "beau temps" shows. But it is quite practicable to translate Proust or Bergson on time into English without serious risk of misunderstanding the meaning. When two languages are in different cultural orbits, like English and Zulu, the ideogrammatic structure is more difficult to build up, but it always seems to be more or less possible. The problems of communication between two people speaking the same language may be at least equally great, because more difficult to become aware of, but even they can be surmounted.

This ideogrammatic middle ground between two languages must itself be a symbolic structure, not simply a bilingual dictionary. When we learn a closely related language like French we discover French equivalents for all English words and constructions. But obviously one cannot walk into a Polynesian or Iroquois society and ask: "What are *your* words for God, soul, reality, knowledge?" They may have no such words or concepts, nor can we give them our equivalents for mana and orenda. Yet it is equally obvious, after examining the evidence in Cassirer's book, that it is possible, with patient and sympathetic study, to find out what is going on in a Polynesian or Iroquois mind, and thereby do something to disentangle one's own mental processes from the swaddling clothes of their native syntax. But we can only do so by trying to get the "feel," the sense of a comprehensible and communicable inner structure, in the other language which can be identified with another inner structure growing out of our own language, even if its syntactic setup is entirely different. It is out of such ideogrammatic inner structures, whether produced linguistically between two languages, or psychologically between two people speaking the same language, that the capacity to assimilate language to rational thought develops. The humanist theory of education has always, and rightly, stressed the importance of the conflict of different habits of linguistic expression, specifically of the modern and Classical languages, in the training of the mind. In his ***Essay on Man*** Cassirer suggests that the historical origin of scientific and mathematical thought may have been a similar linguistic conflict in Mesopotamia between the Sumerian and the Semitic Akkadian languages.

It is not so often realized that the relation between grammar and literature is closely parallel to the relation between grammar and logic. Poetry seems to be much more deeply involved in verbalism, because so much of it is untranslatable, and because ambiguity and paronomasia are as much virtues in poetry as they are vices in discursive thought. Yet in reading a poem we make an effort to comprehend the meanings of the words employed in it which is quite separate from the understanding of their dictionary meanings. The question of what a word conventionally means is always qualified, sometimes contradicted, by the other question of what it means in the poem, and the poet, like the philosopher, may protest against a merely conventional understanding of his more precise meaning, his "sens plus pur," in Mallarmé's phrase. Poetry, as much as discursive or rational writing, grows out of language, yet remains in a state of tension against language. Hence the development of an understanding of literature, as of rational thought, involves the building up of ideogrammatic inner structures like those above mentioned, though the inner structures in this case would not be structures of ideas but of something else.

Cassirer's "symbolic form" is neither subjective nor objective: it is intermediate, taking its structure from the mind and its content from the phenomenal world. In the symbolic forms of all the arts this inseparable unity of a mental constructive principle and a reproductive natural content reappears.

—*Northrop Frye*

The content or sense of poetry, its aspect as an imitation of nature, is always more or less translatable into another language, or another aspect of the same language. But to render the sense of a poem only is not full communication. What cannot be translated is a complex of elements, of which one is a quality that we may vaguely call word-magic, and which seems to depend on the characteristics of the language employed. Yet one feels that poetry is more communicable than this. Surely the languages of Europe have co-operated to produce a great literary culture in a way that goes far beyond such a mixture of exchangeable sense and competing tintinnabulations. We seem to have missed something. The content of a poem, we say, is translatable. What about the form, which is usually the complementary term to content? Nobody would call

word-magic or anything dependent on linguistic factors the form.

Cassirer's "symbolic form" is neither subjective nor objective: it is intermediate, taking its structure from the mind and its content from the phenomenal world. In the symbolic forms of all the arts this inseparable unity of a mental constructive principle and a reproductive natural content reappears. Painting, for instance, has the imitation of nature as one of its elements, and design, the symmetry and balancing of outlines and masses, as the other. Abstract, or more strictly non-representational, painting (which is still imitating nature in the Aristotelian sense) is about as close to the formal pole as we can get; *trompe l'oeil* puzzles are nearest the imitative pole. For some reason the main emphasis has been well over towards the imitative end in nearly all the theory and most of the practice of Western painting. Music, on the contrary, has always been primarily formal in our tradition, and imitative or "programme" music kept within strict bounds. Literature, like painting, has, at least in its criticism, tended to give more attention to its extroverted, nature-imitating aspect. Its formal or constructive principles are still so little understood that there is no adequate terminology to describe them.

The word myth means different things in different fields: in literary criticism it is gradually settling down to mean the formal or constructive principle of literature. Where there is a fiction, the shaping form, to which every detail in the writing has to be assimilated, is the story or plot, which Aristotle called *mythos* and declared to be the "soul" of the fiction. In primitive periods such fictions are myths in the sense of anonymous stories about gods; in later ages they become legends and folk tales, then they gradually become more "realistic", i.e., adapted to a popular demand for plausibility, though they retain the same structural outlines. Profound or "classic" works of art are frequently, almost regularly, marked by a tendency to revert or allude to the archaic and explicit form of the myth in the god-story. When there is no story, or when a theme (Aristotle's *dianoia*) is the center of the action instead of a mythos, the formal principle is a conceptual myth, a structure of ambiguous and emotionally charged ideas or sense data. Myths in this sense are readily translatable: they are, in fact, the communicable ideogrammatic structures of literature.

Literature resembles mathematics, and differs from other structures in words, in that its data are hypothetical: mathematician and poet alike say, not "this is so," but "let this be". Mathematics appears to be a kind of informing or constructive principle in the natural sciences: it continually gives shape and coherence to them without being itself involved in any kind of external proof or evidence. One wonders whether, in future, when we shall know so much more about what literature says and how it hangs together than we do now, we shall come to see literary myth as similarly a constructive principle in the social or qualitative sciences, giving shape and coherence to psychology, anthropology, theology, history and political theory without losing in any one of them its own autonomy of hypothesis. Thus it looks now as though Freud's doctrine of an Oedipus complex were an explanation for the dramatic effectiveness of *Oedipus Tyrannnos*. Perhaps in another few years we shall decide that we have got it the wrong way round: that the dramatic myth of Oedipus informed and gave coherence to Freud's psychology at this point. Such a reversal of perspective would bring us close to Plato, for whom the purest formulation of dialectic was either mathematical or mythical. The basic structure of myth is the metaphor, which is very similar in form to the equation, being a statement of identity of the "A is B" type. I imagine that the third quarter of the century will see Cassirer's principles developed in some such direction as this.

Willard E. Arnett   (essay date 1955)

SOURCE: "Ernst Cassirer and the Epistemological Values of Religion," in *The Journal of Religion,* Vol. XXXV, No. 3, July, 1955, pp. 160-67.

[*In the following essay, Arnett discusses Cassirer's philosophy of symbolic forms, especially as it relates to the study of religion.*]

The struggles of religions with the truth—their efforts, their claims, and their contradictions—are such as to baffle and frustrate all but the most persistent students of religions. Various religions have, on occasion, claimed to be, if not the only road, then certainly the high and privileged road to truth, while seekers of the truth in other areas, especially in recent years, have frequently denied that religion is a way to the truth at all. Thus philosophers interested in religion and in truth or knowledge of the truth find themselves confronted with a number of problems: What is the function of religion in regard to knowledge of the truth? Does religion, as the positivists claim, have no epistemological value? Are religious propositions and the religious experience simply expressions of emotion and subjective contortions of the human organism? Is there no existential reality, objective or relational, in the religious experience that is comparable to the so-called "objective" world that science claims to know?

Ernst Cassirer, in his philosophy of symbolic forms, has perhaps provided the religious epistemologist (if the label is not a contradiction in terms) with a new and potent weapon in the struggle for a share of the claim to knowledge, though, indeed, traditional religious claims may have to be reinterpreted in a manner not altogether satisfactory to many religious orthodoxies.

Actually, there is a great deal of ambiguity in Cassirer's attitude toward religion. By faith he was ostensibly a Jew, though this was perhaps largely a matter of respect and sympathy for a cultural and intellectual tradition rather than any ritualistic, theological, or cosmological orientation. He was possibly a Jew in the sense that Santayana was a Christian. Cassirer consistently included religion and myth—which he never clearly distinguished—among the symbolic forms out of which human reality is created; yet, time and again and especially in his latest work, ***The Myth of the State***, he suggested that the myth-making propensity of man—and consequently most religious orientations—must somehow be outgrown or brought under the control of the cognitive symbols of science. That this final emphasis was a result of the despair and terror he experienced as a witness of the contemporary and deliberate German myths is surely a matter for speculation only. That he did not exploit the implications of his symbolic philosophy as fully in religion as in either science or art, however, or with the same cool objectivity is fairly evident to the student of his writings. Perhaps this was not a matter of bias, but one of perspective and interest only. At any rate, he has done the spring plowing in a field which epistemologists with a flair for religion might prepare for the harvest by religionists with a bent for epistemology. By temperament Cassirer was a humanist, and in method a scientist; and in these two things he should prove himself interesting and perhaps congenial to a wide variety of philosophical seekers who might find little or nothing to admire in one another.

Cassirer, following the anthropologists, has presented striking evidence that it is not—at least not fundamentally—the rhythms and vicissitudes or the order and disorder of an external world or inner rational considerations which produce mythical and religious activities. Myth and religion, according to Cassirer, grow out of the internal, spontaneous, nonconceptual nature of man. The mythical and religious are *forms of experience*—which, of course, may be influenced and modified according to environmental conditions but which remain essentially the same in all the varied expressions.

Indeed, the fundamental theme of Cassirer's philosophy of symbolic forms, in the remodeled framework of epistemological idealism, is that reality is determined by the nature of the experiencing organism. He suggests that it simply does not make sense to talk of a sea-urchin environment if one is concerned to understand flies. Likewise, it is nonsense to attempt to talk of an objective world of things for man apart from the symbolic forms through which the human world is constructed and seen. The real world for man, then, is a spiritual world—a world of linguistic sounds, mythic activity, artistic images, religious rites, and scientific concepts. These are the spiritual forms through which the dynamic human self is expressed and created. The world in which man lives, according to Cassirer, is not a world of hard, irreducible data or matters of fact; it is rather a world of meaning, a world interpreted or, perhaps more accurately, constructed; it is a world which, strictly speaking, would not exist apart from the forms which experience takes. But this is not a subjective world: The worlds produced by symbolic forms "are image-worlds whose principle and origin are to be sought in an autonomous creation of the spirit. Through them alone we see what we call 'reality,' and in them alone we possess it. . . . In this sense each new 'symbolic form'— not only the conceptual world of scientific cognition but also the intuitive world of art, myth, and language— constitutes, as Goethe said, a revelation sent outward from within, a 'synthesis of world and spirit,' which truly assures us that the two are originally one." Subject and object are inextricable parts of a whole, and the history of human culture is the story of man's continuous attempt further to humanize the cosmos—a dynamic, spontaneous, necessary humanization—through the creation of instances of symbolic forms. Language, myth, religion, art, and science are thus fundamentally autonomous ways of humanizing the universe or, it might be said more correctly, ways of constructing human universes: "Cognition, language, myth, and art: none of them is a mere mirror, simply reflecting images of inward or outward data; they are not indifferent media, but rather the true sources of light, the prerequisite of vision, and the wellsprings of all formation." Man, beginning with what might be called the "miracle" of language, goes on to ever more diverse and complex modes of creation and expression; the world in which he lives becomes richer; and the world symbolized becomes a part of man's spiritual self, even as food eaten and digested becomes a vital part of the body. "It is symbolic thought which overcomes the natural inertia of man and endows him with a new ability, the ability constantly to reshape his human universe."

The world in which man lives, according to Cassirer, is not a world of hard, irreducible data or matters of fact; it is rather a world of meaning, a world interpreted or, perhaps more accurately, constructed; it is a world which, strictly speaking, would not exist apart from the forms which experience takes.

—*Willard E. Arnett*

There is, then, no apparent theoretical justification in Cassirer's philosophy for any hierarchy of the forms of experience. At least, there is no adequate indication that the later symbolic forms are superior to the earlier forms either in complexity or in function; indeed, each symbolic form undergoes a constant and internal evolution, possibly providing a foundation for new developments but never becoming synonymous with, or being superseded by, another form. Language, apparently one of the earliest symbolic forms, is thus a necessary step toward scientific symbols and concepts; but scientific symbols and concepts can never arrogate to themselves the functions that belong to ordinary discursive symbols. Each symbolic form, being spontaneous and necessary, takes its place in the development of human culture. Each symbolic form represents an irreducible and peculiar approach to the unity that is the world and the human self. Therefore: "Instead of measuring the content, meaning, and truth of intellectual forms by something extraneous which is supposed to be reproduced in them, we must find in these forms themselves the measure and criterion for their truth and intrinsic meaning." Yet, methodologically, Cassirer was a scientist, and, with or without justification, he applied to science such phrases as, "the highest and most characteristic attainment of human culture" and neglected what he called the "nonconceptual" symbols. However, in his latest writings he gave considerably more attention to the arts than to myth and religion, so far as epistemological elements are concerned. But that art and religion are quite

closely related is indicated. He suggests: "Religion and art are so close to one another in their purely historical development, and so permeate one another, that sometimes the two seem indistinguishable in content and in their inner formative principle. It has been said that the Gods of Greece owed their origin to Homer and Hesiod." And art, to Cassirer as to Santayana, is fundamentally an intensification or restoration of the dynamic fulness of reality, which science must deny by its process of abstraction. The reality with which art is concerned, however, is not that of causes and consequences, but the reality of forms. "The artist is just as much a discoverer of the forms of nature as the scientist is a discoverer of facts or natural laws." Consequently, two painters who are concerned to paint the very same landscape may paint two very different pictures, but nevertheless both present reality. What each presents "is the individual and momentary physiognomy of the landscape." However, "the imagination of the artist does not arbitrarily invent the forms of things. It shows us these forms in their true shape, making them visible and recognizable. The artist chooses a certain aspect of reality, but this process of selection is at the same time a process of objectification. Once we have entered into his perspective we are forced to look on the world with his eyes. It would seem as if we had never before seen the world in this peculiar light. Yet we are convinced that this light is not merely a momentary flash. By virtue of the work of art it has become durable and permanent. Once reality has been disclosed to us in this particular way, we continue to see it in this shape." In some sense, then, art, no less than physics, is an "interpretation of reality—not by concepts but by intuitions; not through the medium of thought but through that of sensuous forms." Indeed, Cassirer's chief emphasis in his philosophy of art, as in the entire philosophy of symbolic forms, is this: "The artistic eye is not a passive eye that receives and registers the impression of things. It is a constructive eye, and it is only by constructive acts that we can discover the beauty of natural things." Art is an independent universe of discourse, and "a great painter or musician is not characterized by his sensitiveness to color or sounds but by his power to elicit from his static materials a dynamic life of forms." Art may be called knowledge, then, in that it gives man "a richer, more vivid and colorful image of reality, and a more profound insight into its formal structure." "Art discloses a new breadth and depth of life. It conveys an awareness of human things and human destinies, of human greatness and misery, in comparison to which our ordinary experience appears poor and trivial." If this is truly the function of art, surely the arts may be excluded from epistemological considerations only at the risk of a too narrow theory of knowledge.

The affinity between religion and the arts is further suggested in ***The Problem of Knowledge***: "By its very nature religion can never escape from the sphere of the 'image,' the sphere of intuition and fantasy. From them it derives its peculiar power; it would wither away and die were it not continuously nourished from this soil." Paradoxically, however, religion is always attempting to escape from the confines of the image, to destroy the icon and approach reality immediately. Thus religion and art are apparently distinguished, in part at least, by the fact that the religious "image can never be treated as merely a picture, as an arbitrary play of the powers of imagination. The image has a meaning, in that it not only represents the truth but is the truth itself." In other words, art may on occasion be content with the sensuous surface, with the image out of context, with isolated events and patterns—or, like the individual sciences, with one aspect of reality; but religion demands, though perhaps in vain, that its symbols be somehow indicative of, or even identical with, total reality.

With the affinity between art and religion in mind and in the light of Cassirer's suggestion that "it is characteristic of the nature of man that he is not limited to one specific and single approach to reality but can choose his point of view and so pass from one aspect of things to another," an attempt will now be made to develop, as explicitly as possible, some implications of the philosophy of symbolic forms for the problems of religious knowledge. Cassirer himself, I am suggesting, never faced frankly the problems of religious knowledge, although he did observe that "religion claims to be in possession of an absolute truth; but its history is a history of errors and heresies. It gives us the promise and prospect of a transcendent world—far beyond the limits of our human experience—and it remains human, all too human." And, indeed, this is apparently the only instance in which Cassirer suggests that to be human is a vice rather than a virtue. To summarize briefly Cassirer's philosophy of myth and religion, he disagrees with those who maintain that myth is simply make-believe and with those who suppose myth can be fully interpreted by a process of intellectual reduction—to sex, to economics, or to some other obvious or dominant need or characteristic of man. Neither is myth, according to Cassirer, simply a nonreasonable or pseudo-scientific attempt at theoretical explanation. Myth, he suggests, must be understood in terms of action—a formative action that has its genesis in the nature of man, even as singing has its genesis in the nature of the bird. He accepts the conclusion of the anthropologists that "ritual is prior to dogma, both in a historical and in a psychological sense," and he makes the inference that myth is the concrete, active creation and expression of feelings and emotions. Thus he quotes Malinowski, apparently with approval: "Supernaturally founded ceremonial grows out of life, but it never stultifies the practical efforts of man. In his rituals of magic and religion, man attempts to enact miracles, not because he ignores the limitations of his mental powers, but on the contrary, because he is fully cognizant of them." (This is not less interesting because it is so directly opposed to Dewey's pragmatic denunciation of the supernatural.) Myth and religion are quite different, then, from science and logic. "The real substratum of myth is not a substratum of thought but of feeling. . . . Its view of life is a sympathetic attitude"—an attitude that recognizes "a fundamental and indelible *solidarity of life*," and in this attitude, "nature becomes one great society, the *society of life*." Cassirer sees primitive religion as one of the greatest affirmations of this thesis, and he regards ancestor worship, in so far as it emphasizes the continuity and indestructibleness of life, as "a really universal, an irreducible and essential characteristic of primitive religion." This, he suggests, belies the hypothesis that religion begins in fear, although fear is obviously a powerful and persuasive element of

human life. In their origin, then, myth and religion are not, Cassirer suggests, separable from the feeling that all life is one; in the development of religion, this feeling of oneness remains and is expressed in the highest ethical perceptions and commandments. In his earlier writings Cassirer separated myth from religion by noting that whereas in myth there is no distinction between existence and meaning, between the image and the deity, in religion this distinction is crucial, and the sensuous images and signs must be recognized for what they are: as inadequate attempts to express meanings. But he also notes that myth and religion are so interwoven that it is impossible ever to make a definite separation. In his later writings, if he distinguishes between myth and religion at all, it is largely in terms of the predominant concern by religion with moral issues, with the problem of good and evil. In the ethical religions, nature is no longer simply the source and locus of all life and processes; it is rather "the sphere of law and lawfulness," the sanction of goodness and righteousness. In the monotheistic religions a universal ethical sympathy, emphasizing the importance of individuals, replaces the feeling of a natural or magical continuity of all life. According to Cassirer, then, the fundamental religious fact—expressed in the rites of magic, myth, and religion—is the sympathy of the individual with the whole, with his community, with man, and ultimately with the universe of life. Religion, says Cassirer, is distinguished by its preoccupation with the moral relationship of man to man in a universe that is characterized by oneness.

But Cassirer's philosophy of religion ends rather abruptly at this point. He suggested in one of his earlier works:

> Myth, art, language, and science appear as symbols; not in the sense of mere figures which refer to some given reality by means of suggestion and allegorical renderings, but in the sense of forces each of which produces and posits a world of its own. In these realms the spirit exhibits itself in that inwardly determined dialectic by virtue of which alone there is any reality, any organized and definite Being at all. Thus the special symbolic forms are not imitations, but organs of reality since it is solely by their agency that anything real becomes an object for intellectual apprehension, and as such is made visible to us. . . . Once language, myth, art, and science are recognized as such ideational forms, the basic philosophical question is no longer that of their relation to an absolute reality which forms, so to speak, their solid and substantial substratum; the central problem now is that of their mutual limitation and supplementation. Though they all function organically together in the construction of spiritual reality, yet each of these organs has its individual assignment.

Yet he does not proceed to develop the implications in regard to the religious "supplementation," and it is in view of this lacuna that I turn now to the most fascinating, but also the most dangerous, task of philosophical criticism—i.e., to suggesting what Cassirer should have said.

Cassirer should have pointed out that, in the philosophy of symbolic forms, questions about the relevance of scientific fact to the dogmas of religion and in regard to the intra and mutual contradictions of the various religions are actually meaningless questions. He has no theoretical justification, apparently, for the suggestion that the history of religion "is a history of errors and heresies," unless he applies the criterion of some particular religion, or a nonreligious criterion, to the history of religion. For each individual religion, being in some measure symbolically unique, must develop its own criterion; it cannot be judged by the criterion of science or by that of another religion. He might have observed, too, that often the denial of epistemological value to religion is simply a consequence of defining knowledge so narrowly that nothing is knowledge except that which can be predicted or achieved through the conceptual symbols of science. Further, he might have suggested even more explicitly that science itself, by reflecting in symbolic terms the structure and processes of physical reality, should recognize that its own understanding of the world is selective, hypothetical, pragmatic, and functional—not true, certainly, in being a complete and accurate account of the actual physical events. And he should have added that, though the myths, the poetic visions, and the parables of the religions are not literally true, if a search is made into the meaning of these, there is discovered a human world that is served as pragmatically and functionally by the religious experience as are other human interests by the sciences. For surely the human mind and personality, with the capacity for love, beauty, and goodness, with the power of aspiration and vision, and with a perennial predilection to metaphor as well as to formulas, are no less a part of "reality" than the processes and structure of matter. Thus it is, I believe, an implication of Cassirer's philosophy that there is a dimension of human experience—a human reality—to which the conceptual symbols of physics, chemistry, biology, psychology, and even the social sciences and philosophy are inappropriate and useless instruments. There is, in other words, a dimension of human experience which, if known at all, is known only as the individual participates in the communal experience that gives an enduring meaning to "goodness," "holiness," "sacred," "divine," and other religious terms. For these are symbols of community values, of experiences that nurture and are nurtured by the common life of kindred minds. This is a reality—an area of knowledge, if you will—that cannot be exhausted by the formal and experimental approach of the scientist in his laboratory or the thinker at his desk; it is a reality that exists and is known only in being generated by a congress of congenial spirits. The ritualistic, poetic, metaphorical, and ethical elements of religion are the creation and revelation of a reality latent in the dynamic and intricate recesses of the human soul. It is a reality actually created by the activity that is indicative of it and without which the soul may be stunted and solitary.

If Cassirer had said something of this sort, he would most probably have gone on to say—and rightfully, I think—that religion is not the only approach to this reality, that in the best of poetry, in the communion of dedicated souls in any human association, something of this flamelike reality is kindled. But he might have observed that for a large segment of humankind the various religions are presently the chief avenues to this dimension of existence. And, indeed, the diversity of religions is perhaps in no way

better justified than in the view that religion is an autonomous approach to a certain dimension of human existence; for the symbols which a people can understand and appreciate depend apparently on culture, training, and temperament, so that it is foolish to expect all men to respond to the symbols of each and all religions. Each religion, like each poet, speaks about the affairs of the human heart, about human relations and the pursuit of happiness, on a specific cultural, intellectual, and emotional level. If one does not understand the comfort and the meaning which a person derives from his religious symbols and activities, it is not that there is no comfort or meaning there; it is rather that he is tuned, in terms of his mental and cultural heritage, to a different frequency.

Cassirer would perhaps be apalled by what has been suggested here as the implications of his philosophy in the area of religion. Yet I can see no other consistent interpretation, in spite of the fact that it is suggested in the final chapter of *The Myth of the State* that man must abandon, or subject to control by his conceptual symbols, the mythical and religious approach to reality. And, indeed, I intend a tribute to a very humane and learned man. For apparently it is only in some such theory as Professor Cassirer's that the poet and the logician, the priest and the philosopher, the physicist and the prophet, may all feel at home and equally useful in the human community; it is only in some such system as his that one may accept and proceed to understand the whole of human experience—religion, art, science, and social institutions. If the religious is truly a form of human experience, like unto science and art, then surely it cannot be safely obliterated or thwarted. If man learns by experience, religion and art no less than science are inseparable from the potential expanse of man's knowledge of man. Scientists, then, as well as the philosophers and priests might well join in the task of unraveling that frayed and entangled web which religious epistemology presently is.

There are, indeed, serious limitations in Cassirer's philosophy of symbolic forms. From time to time suggestions creep in that there is a certain formal necessity or determinism in the development of any given symbolic system and a consequent circumscription of man's ability to deal with both the physical and the human world. "In language, in religion, in art, in science," Cassirer has suggested, "man can do no more than to build up his own universe—a symbolic universe that enables him to understand and interpret, to articulate and organize, to synthesize and universalize his human experience." Thus there is a very definite limit to the nature and extent of possible progress in the solution of the most critical human problems. The philosophy of symbolic forms, then, may be inadequate to enable man to deal at all confidently with the present human crisis. As Cassirer himself realized all too keenly, human symbols may be turned to nonhuman ends. And this seems to suggest, if one wants to steer clear of the morass of contemporary existentialism and neoorthodoxy, that somehow the human mind must either penetrate beneath the forms of experience to the powers and resources of experience or transcend the forms to offer a valid and efficacious criticism of them in terms of a metasymbolic system. For a symbolic or methodological determinism is no less fatal to human confidence and hopes than metaphysical or physical determinism. But perhaps both alternatives are actual possibilities within the framework of the philosophy of symbolic forms. At least, this limitation by no means invalidates the value of Cassirer's suggestions in regard to the possibilities open to artistic and religious epistemology.

John J. Schrems (essay date 1967)

SOURCE: "Ernst Cassirer and Political Thought," in *The Review of Politics,* Vol. 29, No. 2, April, 1967, pp. 180-203.

[*In the following essay, Schrems discusses the political aspect of Cassirer's work by exploring Cassirer's ideas about culture and freedom.*]

Ernst Cassirer's renown is the fame of a philosopher, not of a political theorist. Amongst his voluminous writings only **The Myth of the State** is regarded as a political treatise and its precise political character is problematic. Nevertheless, the rudiments of a Cassirer political philosophy may be derived from an exposition of his understanding of culture and from an examination of his views of freedom, myth, and the state. Cassirer extolled freedom, and he sought to "combat" myth. His own fulfillment of man's "progressive self-liberation," however, presents difficulties which are the subject matter of this essay.

THE CRISIS OF "SELF-KNOWLEDGE"

In the first chapter of the **Essay on Man** Cassirer sketched the history of man's knowledge of himself—"the highest aim of philosophical inquiry." The path traces man's gradual approach to freedom, but ends in what Cassirer calls the crisis of our age: the "loss of intellectual center." We have achieved a complete anarchy of thought in which each individual thinker gives his own picture of human nature and of culture. In our "materialization of culture" there is lost "a general orientation, a frame of reference, to which all individual differences might be referred." There is no "central power capable of directing all individual efforts." It is critical in that for Cassirer himself, as he said of Pico, "the problem of freedom is closely allied to the problem of knowledge." With the modern crisis freedom itself is endangered.

For Cassirer there is an answer, a "common center," which, despite "multiplicity and disparateness," finds "harmony in contrariety, as in the case of the bow and the lyre." This center is found and determined by a philosophy of culture. The **Essay on Man** subtitled "An Introduction to a Philosophy of Culture" takes its significance from this. To appreciate Cassirer's proposed solution it is necessary to investigate his understanding of the development of human freedom and its role in human life.

FREEDOM AND THE SOCIAL ORDER

The history of man's knowledge of himself, culture, is a history of man's progressive self-liberation. A decisive step is taken in the modern age when the study of man parallels the development of the modern (Copernican) cosmology and takes as its postulate "the removal of all the artificial barriers that had hitherto separated the human world

from the rest of nature." Presuppositions such as the hierarchic order of man in the universe, the concept of man as the end of the universe, the belief that there is a general providence ruling over the world and the destiny of man were no longer relevant to understand the "true nature and essence of man." Now the "imaginary boundaries . . . erected by a false metaphysics and cosmology" are eliminated and man achieves an independence and autonomy in his own consciousness and his own existence.

For Cassirer, Machiavelli is one of the great contributors to freedom. With him "we stand at the gateway of the modern world," for he is "the founder of a new science of politics." Like Galileo, he was a revolutionary: he set his science along a new path by cutting the political world off from all the strings that tied it to the past. But in this blow for freedom Cassirer does not overlook the "dangerous consequences." Not only does the sharp knife of Machiavelli's thought cut the religious and metaphysical strings from the past, but the political world is severed from "*all* the . . . forms of man's ethical and cultural life." It is "completely isolated." That is, the state is even isolated by Machiavelli from a morality based on the reason which is nature itself, considered as the original formative and sufficient principle. That is, it is even cut off from a morality which man gives himself—as the natural right theorists were to do—by a method which is, as Cassirer says, "analytical and deductive"; it is cut off from a method which derives "political principles from the nature of man and the nature of the state."

It is through this latter source of morality in the reason of nature that the political thinkers of the seventeenth and eighteenth centuries "counterbalanced," as Cassirer put it, Machiavelli's splendid wickedness and prevented Machiavellism from coming to its full maturity. The partisans of the "Natural Right theory of the state," Grotius, Pufendorf, Rousseau, and Locke, who looked upon the state "as a means, not as an end in itself," regarded the state as bound by certain limits and hence restricted, theoretically at least, from certain actions. These thinkers who counterbalanced the influence of Machiavellism also took their inspiration for political theory, Cassirer explains, from the "great historical example of Galileo." Through mathematical language Galileo exposed the reason of nature which gave man a knowledge of the universe and its law that is not inferior to that of God. The thinkers of the seventeenth century sought to create a theory of the body politic "equal to the Galilean theory of physical bodies— equal in clarity, in scientific method, and in certainty." They sought "to demonstrate truth." What was needed in this endeavor was for political theory to find out and formulate certain axioms and postulates that are incontrovertible and infallible. The needed *"principle"* was found in a rejuvenated Stoicism.

The reason for turning to Stoicism was its neutrality in disputes between creeds, sects, and nations. Stoicism provided a natural foundation for a restoration of man's ethical dignity resting exclusively on "the moral will—on the worth that man attributes to himself." In the **Essay on Man** Cassirer explained that Stoic human dignity "does not depend on external circumstances; it depends exclusively on the value he gives to himself." With no dependence on external help the philosophic thinkers of the seventeenth century rely on the autonomous and self-dependent human reason. This very reliance finds expression and fruition, politically, in the "doctrine of the state-contract."

This doctrine becomes a "self-evident axiom of political thought." Here the state is explained wholly from *within*. There is no external natural law that imposes law from without. The state and its laws are founded in, and explained by, a "natural law," expressed "in a classical way" by Grotius, which the moral subjects give entirely to themselves. The doctrine of the social contract becomes, according to Cassirer, the legal basis of the state, the foundation for "the *validity* of the social and political order." This is the decisive step. The legal and social order is reduced to a voluntary human contract, perfectly clear to all. What is present in the state-contract is "the principle of the state—its *raison d'être*," not its historical origin. Thus the contract-thinkers seek to explain the state by an inner principle and not from without as happens in the "empirical origin" accounts. In this way the new political theories come to parallel even more closely the example of the physical sciences, which, as indicated above, it was their intention to do.

Speaking of "Nature and Natural Science," in his treatment of *The Philosophy of the Enlightenment,* Cassirer explained that here the scientist proceeds on the premise: "The law which governs individual entities is not prescribed by a foreign lawgiver, nor thrust upon them by force; it is founded in, and completely knowable through, their own nature." Likewise the seventeenth-century philosophers of natural right proceed on the identical premise:

> Just as the mind is capable of constructing the realm of quantity and number entirely from within itself by virtue of its "innate ideas," so it has the same constructive ability in the field of law. Here too the intellect can and should begin with fundamental norms, which it creates from within itself. . . . [*Philosophy of the Enlightenment*]

This notion of a principle entirely "from within" rather than "from without," Cassirer has treated in abstract general application in his " 'Spirit' and 'Life' in Contemporary Philosophy." He applied the notion more concretely to the social and political order when he wrote that the political thinkers of the Enlightenment were convinced: "The ability to overcome the evils of the state and of society can only arise from a real 'enlightenment,' from clear insight into the grounds and origins of abuses."

"Rational insight" overcomes the evils of the state and society, and in line with this view Cassirer finds that Rousseau especially contrary to the views of many, qualifies as a rationalist. Rousseau, according to Cassirer, "did not overthrow the world of the Enlightenment; he only transferred its center of gravity to another position. By this intellectual accomplishment he prepared the way for Kant as did no other thinker of the eighteenth century." What

Rousseau possessed was the clear insight of a "firm law within himself before he [sought] the laws of external objects." With this insight Rousseau undertook his peculiar reform of the social and political order.

The character of the reform does not matter—"the whole political and social edifice is razed"—what is important is that he provided Kant with the clue to the "real man": "Man should seek the real law of his being and his conduct neither below nor above himself; he should derive it from himself, and should fashion himself in accordance with the determination of his own free will." Kant's argument according to Cassirer, was that in order to derive this real law man "requires life in society as well as inner freedom from social standards and an independent judgment of conventional social values." Cassirer's own humanism, James Gutmann concluded, derives from this Kantian humanistic ideal; indeed, from his understanding of Kantian humanism Cassirer develops his philosophy of culture.

Many scholars have supported this conclusion about Kant's influence on Cassirer. Robert S. Hartmann stated that "Cassirer's philosophy . . . completes and substantiates empirically Kant's 'Copernican revolution.' " David Bidney believed that with Cassirer there is a transformation of the Kantian *Critique* into the critique of culture. William H. Werkmeister appears to agree with Bidney; he regards Cassirer's Philosophy of Culture as an "expansion of Kant's 'Copernican revolution,' " which, incidentally, involves "a step beyond orthodox neo-Kantianism" that "leaves many questions unanswered."

From all these witnesses and from the evidence assembled it becomes quite clear that this tracing of Rousseau's contribution to Kant is of singular importance to this study for it is a contribution, through Kant, to Cassirer and the development of his own philosophy. Rousseau's insight as expressed by Kant is reflected by Cassirer in this statement:

> Man's social consciousness depends upon a double act, of identification and discrimination. Man cannot find himself, he cannot become aware of his individuality, save through the medium of social life. But to him this medium signifies more than an external determining force. Man, like the animals, submits to the rules of society but, in addition, he has an active share in bringing about, and an active power to change, the forms of social life. [*Essay on Man*]

Cassirer, like Rousseau and Kant, requires for man a life in society and yet requires a distinction and independence from society. This line of thought, then, finally contributes to an understanding of the conception of freedom in the philosophy of culture and its role in social life. It does so by investigating what Cassirer calls Rousseau's insight into the "true nature of the 'social bond.' "

Rousseau regards his own conception of the social bond, and indeed of natural law to which the social compact is tied, as superior to the theories of men such as Hobbes and Grotius. The latter theorists, to follow Cassirer, fail because they derive the "social contract" from a contract involving subjection—in Hobbes from an agreement between rulers and ruled, in Grotius from an actual enslavement in the course of conquest. For Rousseau the social bond "cannot be something imposed on the wills of [freely acting] persons from without; they must constitute and create it themselves." Thus, Rousseau's notion of law as a "universal voice" is a law from within, a "heavenly voice that dictates to each citizen the precepts of public reason, and teaches him to act in accordance with the maxims of his own judgment, and not to be in contradiction to himself." The basic principle of individual freedom contained in this, Rousseau's conception of law and society, finds expression, freed of its "various ambiguities" and its lack of precise statement, in Kant's "categorical imperative."

With respect to the central thought of the social contract Cassirer pointed out that

> in the *Metaphysical Basis of the Theory of Law* [Kant] declares that "the act through which a people constitutes itself a state, or to speak more properly the *idea* of such an act, in terms of which alone its legitimacy can be conceived, is the original contract by which all (*omnes et singuli*) the people surrender their outward freedom in order to resume it at once as members of a common entity, that is the people regarded as the state (*universe*). [*Rousseau, Kant, and Goethe*]

It was, however, only in this "one sense" that Kant could grasp and elaborate clearly and unequivocally Rousseau's central thought. Only in their "great common task" "to establish and validate in an objective sense . . . the pure idea of right" are Kant and Rousseau united, otherwise in the fulfillment of this task "there fell to their lot quite different missions." Kant was to go on to achieve "a new and distinctive attitude toward life" in which civilization "is not the source of happiness, . . . it is rather the setting in which man is to test and prove his freedom." Thus, Cassirer related, freedom advances beyond the eudaemonism to which it is tied in Rousseau to where in Kant it constitutes man's "distinctive dignity." In this way "life achieves that meaning with which man alone can endow it. . . ."

Kant's new and distinctive attitude toward life is one in which man achieves his distinctive dignity by "creating" freedom. Freedom, for him, is "a special kind of determinism" according to which "the law which we obey in our actions is not imposed from without but . . . the moral subject gives this law to itself." Freedom is given by the subject to himself. It is like the truth of autonomous and self-dependent reason which Cassirer has described as the "principle" and "cornerstone" of all the systems of natural right. Autonomous natural reason is the "source of all truth"; likewise, it is equivalent to freedom. But as man must "discover" truth, so freedom must be produced. "It is no datum, but a demand; an ethical imperative." Kant's "new . . . attitude toward life" views freedom as a task which must be constantly achieved in order to be maintained.

It is the doctrine that "freedom is equivalent to autonomy" and the whole doctrine of natural rights which Cassirer credits with "counterbalancing" the influence of Machiavellism in the seventeenth and eighteenth centu-

ries. The "fertile seeds . . . of Kant's social philosophy" are found by Cassirer to have influence in the development of socialistic theories of the nineteenth century. However, he finds that the "immanent ideal force" behind the principles of freedom of these theories was "superior" to the varying historical developments and interpretations. Hence, for an understanding of the essence of freedom it is sufficient to recognize it in its formulation in the "language and systematic relations of critical philosophy." In other words, the Kantian formulation appears sufficient for an understanding of the principle of freedom in its modern role. According to the Kantian "idea of freedom," we see that

> the greatest problem for the human race and the greatest concrete task placed before it become the attainment of a universal law administering civil society; i.e., a society which is not founded on a mere relationship of might, a relationship of rulers and ruled, but which considers every one of its members as an end in itself, as a free agent who participates in the constitution and administration of the whole and who to that extent heeds the laws only because he has given them to himself.

In the statement just quoted we meet Kant's "idea of freedom," and that of Cassirer as well. Incorporated in this proposition are these ingredients: Stoic autarky, the "social bond" of Rousseau, and Kant's arduous task. According to Cassirer, after Machiavelli's revolutionary but liberating blow only two paths are possible for men to follow: either the enslavement of totalitarianism which is the logical term of splendid wickedness, or the freedom of natural right which counterbalanced Machiavellism. For Cassirer the first alternative is unthinkable; it is contrary to the highest aim of philosophy and human culture, that is, self-knowledge and self-liberation through self-realization. In the "great and decisive" step of the natural right and the state contract theory the "wickedness" of the Machiavellian tyrant is avoided. For Cassirer, then, man achieves freedom with the natural right theory counterbalancing the dangerous consequences of Machiavelli's liberating efforts; man himself in his voluntary activity is accountable for his freedom and for the (legal) origin of civil society. With this new development the founding of the state depends "exclusively on . . . himself" and the man achieves ethical dignity.

The contract theory, however, avoids only the wickedness which is determined by "on one but the prince himself." Since the contract state has no limits other than those which it itself sets, then any common good of which the contract theory might speak is easily reducible, like the common good of Machiavelli, to the common evil. Here again "self-interest" will dictate what is "good," but now as a principle. Now there is no limit, not even a moral one, on what self-interest might desire. Even the Kantian categorical imperative is no real limit, for there is no ultimate restriction on *what* it may universalize. Moreover, the counterbalance that Cassirer here envisaged allows a greater wickedness. Indeed, it was the ground for his rejection of the myth of the state in favor of a philosophy of culture.

MYTH AND THE VALIDITY OF THE SOCIAL AND POLITICAL ORDER

For Cassirer "the most important and most alarming feature in . . . modern political thought" is the appearance of myth. This phenomenon, while understandable in ancient thought, is incongruous in a scientific and technical age. *The Myth of the State* is designed to explain myth and trace its history. The development parallels the process of self-knowledge and self-liberation: man is increasingly freed of myth and correspondingly his life comes more under rational direction and control. Why, then, does myth appear in the twentieth century, and especially in the "secular sphere" from which even ancient thought had precluded it? Cassirer makes it clear that the glorification of myth and the preparation found elsewhere in the nineteenth century, while instrumental to its development, are not the principal cause for the twentieth-century myth. Instead, he relates, the technical and scientific abilities of our age combine the skills of *"homo magus"* and *"homo faber"* and these effect the return of myth on its grand scale. Myth has gained a position beyond its due proportion because the forces ("intellectual, ethical, and artistic") responsible for holding it in check have not maintained their strength. Thus, myth will always have its place, but it is, Cassirer tells us, a limited place. It might for a time achieve "great triumphs," and extend its bounds, nonetheless its success will be ephemeral. "For there is, after all, a logic of the social world just as there is a logic of the physical world. There are certain laws that cannot be violated with impunity."

It is the power of philosophy which helps man to understand and contain myth. Particularly a philosophy of culture, that is, the philosophy of symbolic forms, can maintain the cosmic order, like, Cassirer suggested, Marduk of Babylonian mythology. The philosophy of culture has a proper but limited place and function for myth. Myth is one of the symbolic forms (along with art, science, religion, language) of man who is, according to Cassirer, a symbol-making animal. Further, the philosophy of culture provides a "broader basis" for understanding man, a broader basis in which the whole of human nature is seen in an ethical and nonmythical light. This view of man is made possible through a "new and positive power of 'self-knowledge.' "

The central portion of *The Myth of the State* is precisely a tracing of "the struggle against myth in the history of political thought" culminating in the ethical light of a revived Stoic attitude toward man. This is the climactic point of the historical process: the social-contract theory of the seventeenth and eighteenth centuries restoring man to his ethical dignity. Plato's postulate of a "rational theory of the State," replacing the earlier, and mythical, theories, is finally achieved in the "perfectly clear and understandable fact" of voluntary contractual submission—the social contract. The right of personality, of the autonomous self-dependent individual reasoning being—consonant with the "enlightened" philosophies of the natural right theories of Rousseau and Kant which attain autonomy and achieve an understanding of law as a "universal voice"—establishes the "validity of the social and political order." Where in the beginning with Plato man was explained in terms of the state, we have progressed through the medieval period and Machiavelli to the point where now "all mystery is gone" and the state is explained in terms of man. The process has culminated in the "clear and understandable fact" of "free individual acts."

With this understanding we are in a position to appreciate what, for Cassirer, are the "laws of the social world." Most certainly they cannot be laws related to religion or metaphysics. Rather they would be laws, eschewing myth, related to the doctrine which insists that the dignity of man "rests exclusively on the worth that man attributes to himself," that reason "recognizes completely only that which it can produce according to its own design," and that reason makes only those judgments that "depend upon a free act which creates a world of its own." In brief, they will be laws in keeping with the autarky of human reason and the autonomy of nature. The rules of the social world are designed in the "new science" by Galileo and his successors who perceived that "reason has insight into that only which she herself produces on her own plan." The "contract-natural right theory" fulfills all requirements. But, with the state reduced to the clear fact of human personality, the further, and ancient, question remains as to the nature or character of man. This Cassirer provided in his philosophy of symbolic forms.

THE PHILOSOPHY OF CULTURE

Cassirer intended a philosophy of culture which, while aware of the "various powers of man," does not lose sight of "humanity." In the philosophy of symbolic forms the various powers of man, seen in language, art, religion, science, are "looked upon as so many variations of a common theme." This common theme of "symbolic expression" is the "common denominator of all [of man's] cultural activities: in myth and poetry, in language, in art, in religion, and in science." Such a philosophy of humanity looks not at the results of the various human activities but at the "unity of action." What is sought is "not a unity of products but a unity of the *creative process*." Man in his activities "creates" myth, religious rites or creeds, works of art, scientific theories. It is in the light of this notion of human, creative, symbolic activity that Casirer can say: "It is this work, it is the system of human activities, which defines and determines the circle of 'humanity.' " For Cassirer, man is characterized and distinguished by his work: the work of creation through symbolic expression. Through this understanding of man's work Cassirer comes to a different application of the philosophical adage, man is what man does, whereby in the past man was defined as an *animal rationale*. Reason "is a very inadequate term with which to comprehend the forms of man's cultural life in all their richness and variety." For him the old definition was the expression of a "moral imperative" not a designation of man's "specific difference." In order to arrive at the specific difference it must be observed that all forms of man's cultural life are "symbolic forms." The clue to the nature of man is "the symbol." "Hence, instead of defining man as an *animal rationale,* we should define him as an *animal symbolicum.*" Here we have a profoundly new conception of man. He is an animal *symbolicum* who builds upon his own world. "Symbolic thought . . . overcomes the natural inertia of man and endows him with a new ability, the ability constantly to reshape his human universe."

With this understanding there is found a "clue of Ariadne," the philosophy of symbolic forms, which can lead us out of the labyrinth of our "mass of disconnected and disintegrated data" concerning human nature. Myth and religion, language and art, science and history, previously considered "disparate and heterogenous" are, with a philosophy of symbolic forms, "*one* subject. They are different roads leading to a common center." The way to overcome "the myth of the twentieth century" and "the loss of intellectual center" is revealed in a philosophy of culture. Cassirer's statement that "myth ends where philosophy begins" can now be read as "myth of the State" ends where philosophy of culture—philosophy of symbolic forms—begins.

The process of man's progressive self-liberation culminates in the notion of man creating culture in the notion that man "builds up a world of his own, an 'ideal' world." This is the liberal, that is, liberating, conclusion of the philosophy which begins with the maxim that "self-knowledge is the highest aim of philosophical inquiry." Here in the philosophy of culture eudaemonism is abandoned; any notion of a goal or an end is, as with Aristotle's final causes, now characterized as a mere "*asylum ignorantiae*." In the philosophy of culture we are even free of happiness as a goal. Now it is held that "true worth does not lie in that which man receives from nature and Providence; it resides only in his own act and in what he creates through these acts." It might be further argued that the new "true worth" amounts to self-glorification in culture without happiness even as a result.

Thus Cassirer's resolution of the paradox of our age gives way to an unnoticed dilemma. He began his ***Essay on Man*** and ***The Myth of the State*** by lamenting the crisis of our age and the presence of the totalitarian mythical state where every thinker gives his own "conception and evaluation of human life" and where human life falls prey to the twentieth-century myth. In Cassirer man is set free: set free to "reshape his human universe," "to build up his own universe . . . and universalize his human experience." But this self-liberating activity is done in such a way that not only is an intellectual center lost but now man himself is lost.

Man himself is lost in that: "The artist, the scientist, the founder of a religion, are able to perform truly great achievements only if they abandon themselves completely to their work, if they neglect their own being for it." This loss of self is what Cassirer, using George Simmel's *Philosophische Kultur,* identifies as the "tragedy of culture." The dilemma of the advancement of culture and the abandonment of self is resolved, for Cassirer, in the realization that "a work of culture" is "only a *point of passage*" in the "*living process* of culture." This "living process of culture" Cassirer has elsewhere referred to as a development of the forms of social life into a state of social consciousness, "a society of thought and feeling." Here, it is said, man "has

discovered a new way to stabilize and propagate his works." Thus we are told that, "Language, myth, art, religion, science are the elements and the constitutive conditions of this higher form of society," but what is more important is that these "expressions of life" "have a life of their own, a sort of eternity by which they survive a man's individual and ephemeral existence."

Cassirer's statement that for man the medium of social life "signifies more than an external determining force," and that man "has an active share in bringing about, and an active power to change, the forms of social life" is nonetheless to be understood in terms of man defining himself *only* in "the living process of culture." For we must note that even with the active ingredients man "cannot find himself save through the medium of social life." This is the same theme of the individual found in the creation of culture and yet lost in his own "ephemeral existence." This situation, according to Cassirer, is justified in terms of what is proper to the "spirit" and "life," what is proper to the "spirit" of culture and what is denied to the species of "life." And "spirit" of course consists of the "symbolic forms," the expressions of life that survive man's individual and ephemeral existence:

> "Spirit" has accomplished what was denied to "life." Here the coming-to-be and the activity of individuals are linked to that of the species in a very different and profoundly formative manner. What the individual feels, wills, and thinks does not remain enclosed within himself; it is objectified in his work. These works of language, poetry, plastic art, and religion, become the "monuments," the symbols, of recognition and remembrance of human kind. They are "more lasting than bronze"; for within them there remains not only something material; in addition, they are the manifestation of a spirit—manifestation which can be freed from its material covering and awakened to new power whenever a sympathetic and sensitive soul encounters it. [***Logic of Humanities***]

This notion of the "sort of eternity" of the individual objectified in his work through the "manifestation of a spirit" as opposed to the notion of "man's individual and ephemeral existence," is also found in the "objectified humanity" of Cassirer's conception of historical knowledge. And thus in history is also revealed the loss of individual man in Cassirer's notion of humanity. For Cassirer history is an essential link in the evolution of "the organism of human civilization"; it is "an indispensable instrument for building up our human universe." Thus it is that Cassirer says that "in the great works of history . . . we begin to see . . . the features of the *real* individual man." But it must be carefully noted that this real, individual man found in history is not "a *mere* individual self." The self found in history "is anthropomorphic but it is not egocentric." The historian, it is true, "looks for a human and real cultural life—a life of actions and passions, of questions and answers, of tensions and solutions." But this life and culture must be understood as one that, for Cassirer, "may be described as . . . protest against the fact of death, . . . challenge [to] the power of time, . . . striving to eternize and immortalize life." Culture is viewed as the product of man's striving, through his work, "to break the chain of his individual and ephemeral existence." Thus the life and culture which the historian is concerned with is the life which is short-lived and the culture which, so to speak, survives. In this way real life is effaced for culture; individual real man is effaced for the "historical self." "The enrichment and enlargement . . . of the self, of our knowing and feeling ego, which is the aim of historical knowledge" is achieved in the "real man" of objectified humanity, the man "eternized and immortalized" through culture. The traditionally individual self, Cassirer's "mere" man of ephemeral existence, is replaced by the "real" man of universal culture, the amorphous man who creates culture and the historical self.

This understanding marks the full development of self-knowledge: the definition of man in terms of human culture. For Cassirer, as with Alexander Pope, the title of whose poem he borrowed for his **Essay on Man,** "the proper study of mankind is man." However, as James Gutmann put it, Cassirer, following Pico, went farther than this maxim of Pope, holding that "for man to know himself . . . is to recognize the rich and varied potentialities of his nature." This richness and this variety are found in culture and thus "Cassirer seeks to understand human nature by exploring culture, . . . he seeks to understand man in terms of culture." But the important thing to note is that "this understanding," as Gutmann added, "is rooted in the rich soil of humanism." It is based on what Gutmann calls "Cassirer's Humanism." In this humanism man is conceived of as a functional developer of cultural forms: "Man is no longer considered as a simple substance which exists in itself and is to be known by itself. His unity is conceived as a functional unity." Gutmann commented: "The common focus of all cultural forms is man—and man, in turn, must be conceived in terms of his functional unity in the development of these forms." Robert Hartman described this blend of man and culture as "the horizontal-vertical integration of man's soul and culture—a symbolic cross, to which man will not be fixed in agony, but in which he will live." And in Hartman's view the ethical era to come must be built to a large extent on Cassirer's "symbolic cross" of culture.

It is this new cross in which man will live and on which is founded the new morality of "the comprehensive love of life and of all its forms." What is so new about this de-

velopment is that it is the fulfillment of the self-liberation of man through symbolism, it is, in other words, man made. With this the cross of agony is replaced by the symbol of culture. This latter is by no means an impossible proposition for, as Fritz Kaufmann related,

> according to Cassirer man learns to recognize his own capacities as a free agent by projecting them into the figure of his God. In this way it is *man* who is understood in the symbol of his God, instead of God's being approached, however inadequately, through the human symbols. The God-man relationship in which man is confronted by another, infinitely superior (if not altogether different) being is re-absorbed by one of the forms of the cultural process, one of the modes of objectification.

Kaufmann further related that with Cassirer, "the inadequacy of the religious *symbol* is emphasized . . . almost to the point of neglecting the insufficiency of the human *being*. The gap between the human and the divine is said to be 'created' by consciousness." On this point, however, it should be noted that the insufficiency of human beings appears, in Cassirer's philosophy, to be completely neglected in favor of man's creative life. It is precisely the point of Cassirer's philosophy that man should be liberated from "all the imaginary boundaries" which have been erected by earlier religious as well as metaphysical and cosmological thought. Man is set free from the "primitive" symbolic creations in order that he "might build up a world of his own."

With respect to creation, Cassirer appears to agree with Boccaccio in his *Genealogia deorum* in distinguishing between two creations: "the one called man into existence, and the other conferred upon this existence an intellectual content. . . . The first gave him his physical reality; the second gave his specific form." It is this second creation which, according to Cassirer, man gives to himself and thereby achieves autonomy. Cassirer, however, is also in close agreement with Giordano Bruno in the belief that "the ideal of humanity includes the ideal of *autonomy;* but as the ideal of autonomy becomes stronger, it dissociates itself more and more from the realm of religion." This would explain the emphasis on the inadequacy of the religious symbol and the neglect of human insufficiency noted by Kaufmann. In the process of man's progressive self-liberation in the creation of culture, religion becomes less and less important.

What must be noticed, and this is a primary point, is that despite man's enhanced position in the creation of culture it is culture alone that survives. Only through culture does the "comprehensive love of life and of all its forms" surmount man's "individual and ephemeral existence." It might appear likely that the fact of death—individual personal destruction—might disrupt the serenity of the cultural challenge to the power of time. In Cassirer's philosophy, however, death is no disturbing factor.

Cassirer explained that mythical thought sought to answer the problem of death by having "the mystery of death . . . 'turned into an image'—and by this transformation death . . . becomes understandable and supportable." Thus it is taught, he said, that, "death . . . means no extinction of man's life; it means only a change in the form of life. One form of existence is simply exchanged for another." For Cassirer this answer, intended for the "primitive" mind, is not satisfactory because in this homily myth and religion—which is but the *metamorphosis* of the fear of death—attempt to "deny" or "explain away" the fact of death and its inevitable natural destruction of personal existence. According to Cassirer, "myth could not give a rational answer to the problem of death." The only rational answer is apparently for man to "be reconciled with the fact of death," to "be persuaded to accept the destruction of his personal existence as an inevitable natural phenomenon." This answer is, of course, found in the Philosophy of Culture's notion of man's individual and ephemeral existence. Of the Philosophy of Culture's rational answer to the fact of death it can be said, as Cassirer himself said of the victory of death in the dramatic dialogue between the peasant and death described by Johannes von Saaz, that

> the destruction of life, the fact that God makes it subject to death, no longer signifies the nullity of life. For though it be destroyed in its being, life nevertheless retains an indestructible value: the value that the free man gives to himself and to the world. The faith of humanity in itself guarantees the re-birth of humanity. [*Individual and Cosmos*]

The victory in death, then, is not for man; it is not even for death pictured as in conflict with life; the victory in death is for humanity.

Cassirer so facilely accepted personal destruction, and found the "simple fact of death" not "painful" and not tragic in the sense that with death man is "knowingly losing the greatest goods" in a goal or happiness which he sought. In the "Philosophy of Culture" such a painful loss is not possible, for man seeks no goal inasmuch as "true worth" resides only in action. Further, Cassirer stated:

> Not happiness but the condition of being worthy of happiness ["*Glückswürdigkeit*"] is what culture [and civilization] promises to man; it cannot give him more. Its goal is not the realization of happiness in this life, but the realization of freedom—that genuine autonomy which consists . . . [in] man's moral mastery of himself. [*Logic of Humanities*]

Therefore man loses nothing, for there never was anything that he could gain. Man simply accepts the destruction of his personal existence as an inevitable natural phenomenon and finds fulfillment in "the condition of being worthy of happiness" in the "living process of culture" wherein he is given "a sort of eternity." There is, consequently, in Cassirer's formula for culture a hidden tragedy which Helmut Kuhn touched upon when he commented:

> . . . the timeless validity of symbolic structures is not enough to forestall tragedy, because the old imperious desire for "world without end" is not entirely put to sleep. The individual is not wholly banished. His ghostlike presence suffuses the great unconcern of the philosophy of Symbolic Forms with an elegiac mood.

Kuhn's comment need suggest no more than, as already proposed, that in Cassirer's philosophy the individual real man, who, as even Cassirer tacitly acknowledged, seeks a sort of eternity, is lost in the concern with culture. In the comments of Kuhn, Hartmann, Gutmann, in Cassirer's own explanations of culture, of history, of death, we find the same recurring point: the individual is lost. Despite Cassirer's great attempt to provide an insight into the general character of human culture through a rediscovery of an intellectual center, he did so at the expense of making man a slave to a cultural process in which the individual is a mere point in passage.

Why has this occurred? Why has the myth of the state been replaced with a new philosophy, read *myth*, of culture in which the individual is once again lost? Cassirer's understanding of the science of politics as seen in his comparison of Machiavelli with Galileo removes from man's social life any natural element which in the past had served as a barrier to the impingement of human freedom. Further, the very liberating process which Cassirer traces can have no other result than the development of a new and most capable and ruthless *homo faber* who will, using his modern techniques and magic, rise to the top by the very logic of his freedom. Cassirer's *homo faber* (he may be the majority in a democracy) can, so to speak, with social contract in hand, without hindrance from "artificial barriers," proceed to the making and remaking of society according to his own plan. As all previous "barriers"— like metaphysical and religious principles—are exorcised from man's life there are no limits—not even that of the contrast between *homo faber* and *homo magus*—to the designs of the modern politician. Indeed, Cassirer very explicitly pointed out that the modern politician very methodically and deliberately plans and produces as an artisan the new political myths. Myth is manufactured like any other weapon in our great technical age. This new "creative" power combined with the enhanced sense of freedom explains why the twentieth-century totalitarian myth came about: the modern "mythical monsters" are the result of the very development which allows nothing except that which "reason can produce according to its own design."

It is now possible for myth to pervade the whole of man's life. In finding a "clue of Ariadne" to remedy the anarchy of thought of our age Cassirer fashioned a philosophy which in its rational explanations, and rational organization of society, loses sight of, and abandons the individual man who, for Cassirer, first started out to "know himself." And not only is the individual lost, but, in order to guarantee the rational constructs of the Philosophy of Culture it is necessary to "combat" and "subdue" all that is mythical, which is all that is outside of the rational and scientific, or, more correctly, all that reason has not produced according to its own design. Furthermore, this very intolerant rationalism seems to point to, and culminate in, though unwittingly, a scientifically devised return of myth.

Cassirer suggested that the way to overcome the "myth of the twentieth century" and to recover "the loss of intellectual center" is revealed in a "philosophy of culture." The reason the solution is sought in a philosophy of culture is because it alone can make room for myth as one of the symbolic forms of man who is, according to Cassirer, a symbol-making animal. The place of myth, we will recall, is seen as a symbolic expression of the desire for the "unity of life"; it is an expression of the nonrational, interpreted as all that lies outside the competence of human reason. Hence, there is a place and function for myth. But, the place for myth is not in, what Cassirer called, the "secular sphere." The "secular sphere" is the sphere of "rational theory" and is expressed by the symbols of science. Cassirer's very understanding of science, however, seems to point to myth as the highest form of knowledge.

Cassirer stated that for scientific thought to describe and explain reality,

> it is bound to use its general method, which is that of classification and systematization. Life is divided into separate provinces that are sharply distinguished from each other. The boundaries between the kingdoms of plants, of animals, of man—the differences between species, families, genera—are fundamental and ineffaceable. [***Essay on Man***]

What Cassirer considered to be Darwin's contribution to science, however, appears to run counter to what Cassirer described as the "scientific method": "The theory of evolution had destroyed the arbitrary limits between the different forms of organic life. There are no separate species; there is just one continuous and uninterrupted stream of life." Indeed, it should be noticed that this Darwinian biological principle appears exactly to express the approach and method of the primitive mind (whose characteristic use of symbols is in myth):

> But the primitive mind ignores and rejects [the boundaries between species, families, genera]. Life is not divided into classes and subclasses. It is felt as an unbroken continuous whole which does not admit of any clean-cut and trenchant distinctions. . . . There is no specific difference between the various realms of life. Nothing has a definite, invariable, static shape. [***Essay on Man***]

Finally, it must be noticed, Cassirer gave approval to this primitive view as containing a deep insight into reality. Speaking immediately of the naturalist's desire to classify things, and of the division of sciences into theoretic and practical, he wrote:

> In this division of sciences [into theoretic and practical] we are prone to forget that there is a lower stratum beneath them both. Primitive man is not liable to such forgetfulness. . . . [In] his conception of nature and life all these differences are obliterated by a stronger feeling: the deep conviction of a fundamental and indelible *solidarity of life* that bridges over the multiplicity and variety of its single forms. [***Essay on Man***]

This same admiration of the primitive insight over the scientific stratification appears, once again, in an entirely separate writing by Cassirer where he says: "Aristotle's logic is unexcelled in the precise working out of contradictions,

in setting up the categories by which the classes of being are distinguished. But it is unable to overcome this opposition between the various classes of being; it does *not press on to their real point of unification*." For Cassirer then, it seems, that science reaches its ultimate stage when it presses on to the "real point of unification" of all things; and this is the "chaos" of the primitive mind given "classification" in mythical symbols (this real point of unification of all things is the Darwinian type unity given in scientific classification and systematization). Consequently, if the production of myth is one function of the symbol-making animal and the production of science is another, and if science itself points to myth as the expression of the "real point of unification" of all things, there is nothing to keep the man of science from converting his own "secular sphere" into, what Cassirer called, that "new, entirely irrational and mysterious religion" of the twentieth-century political myths. Myth will, as Cassirer himself says, have a different *quality*—it will be "manufactured," "technically produced." And now it will do so of necessity according to the "rational" and "scientific" bases of the philosophy of culture.

Cassirer, to be sure, did not intend these results. But that is beside the point. The subsumption of the individual in culture rests soundly on the reduction of the state to the clear fact of human personality expressed in freedom. It appears once again that before the laws of the social world are discovered, the question "What is Man?" (and further, "What is the State?") must be re-examined.

J. Ralph Lindgren   (essay date 1968)

SOURCE: "Cassirer's Theory of Concept Formation," in *The New Scholasticism,* Vol. XLII, No. 1, Winter, 1968, pp. 91-102.

[*In the following essay, Lindgren explores the formal logic that undergirds Cassirer's theory on how concepts are formed.*]

In English speaking countries we have always been inclined to jump to the conclusion that the feature of Cassirer's thought which catches our notice must be the central and unifying theme of his work. In 1941, when he first came to America, his work was characterized as a philosophy of science and in 1943 it was thought to be a type of language philosophy. The only book-length interpretation of his work [Carl H. Hamburg, *Symbol and Reality*] considers it as a type of semantic philosophy. The discouragement which follows the discovery that none of these themes adequately organizes his theories into a coherent whole is amply witnessed by the few studies of his work which have appeared since his death in 1945.

Adequate understanding of the meaning of any one of Cassirer's doctrines awaits a grasp of the unity of his thought. This paper is intended to contribute to that understanding by clarifying the precise nature of his method. Both his statement and his demonstration of his central methodological principles will be indicated. It will also be contended that although these principles are stated in many contexts, their demonstration is available only in the opening chapter of ***Substance and Function***. There it becomes clear that what characterizes the work of Cassirer most essentially is a new logic of the concept which, when applied to the various subjects of inquiry, yields awe-inspiring transformations which have always captured the fancy of his readers.

Perhaps the most widely read of Cassirer's books is his *Essay on Man*. In it the author focused attention upon the implications of his philosophical position for the study of myth, art, language, history, religion and science. The most widely quoted sentence of this work, however, does not bear upon any of these fields of inquiry. Instead, it is the remark which captures the peculiar vantage point from which each of these particular areas is considered and illumined. "Hence, instead of defining man as an *animal rationale*, we should define him as an *animal symbolicum*."

Cassirer attempted to demonstrate few of the points mentioned in the *Essay*. He did not indicate the basis of his proposed definition of man. He advised those of his readers who were interested in discovering the demonstrations of this and other of the points merely posited in the *Essay* to turn to the more detailed discussions of the *PSF* [*Philosophy of Symbolic Forms*]. Indeed, any thoughtful attempt to understand any of his later thought must include this one at a very early stage.

Cassirer began the *PSF* by stating his purpose and his methodological assumption. The purpose was to continue the work which he began in *S&F* [*Substance and Function*] in which he laid bare the logical structure of the natural sciences by mounting a similar critique of the cultural sciences. "It seemed to me that the theory of scientific concepts and judgments which defines the natural 'object' by its constitutive traits, and apprehends the 'object' of cognition as contingent on the function of cognition must be amplified by an analogous specification of pure subjectivity."

Having stated his purpose he indicated his methodological assumption and then proceeded to the task of rejuvenating the cultural sciences by a general critique of all forms of human consciousness, concentrating mainly upon language, and myth and conceptual thinking, to which he devoted one volume each. Like the *Essay*, however, the *PSF* consists in the elaboration of the broad ramifications of a single principle, methodological in character, which is stated but not given explicit justification in that context. In the *Essay* that principle was the definition of man as a symbolical animal. In the *PSF* it is the basic epistemological postulate that relation holds primacy over substance or that function-concepts are logically prior to substance-concepts. The passage which is usually cited in this regard reads: ". . . [T]he fundamental principle of critical thinking [is] the principle of the 'primacy' of the function over the objects. . . . " This same principle was asserted with slightly greater precision in an earlier remark: "This postulate of a purely functional unity replaces the postulate of a unity of substance and origin, which lay at the core of the ancient concept of being."

Just as we were obliged to have reference to an earlier work in order to discover the demonstration of the funda-

mental principle of the *Essay,* so too we must look to an earlier work in order to discover the justification of the methodological principle of the *PSF*. Since the *PSF* was proposed as a continuation of the work begun in *S&F* it is not surprising that Cassirer's demonstration of the 'primacy of function' and so of the definition of man is to be found in the opening chapter of his first systematic work. That chapter develops his theory of the formation of concepts, which theory constitutes the continuing philosophical perspective from which he approached the remainder of his work. In what follows this theory will be shown to be the immediate basis of the 'primacy of function' doctrine as well as that of the definition of man. The theory of concept formation is the ultimate ground of Cassirer's definition of man just as it had been that of the rational-animal definition which he proposed to replace.

Cassirer's purpose in *S&F* was to assist in the transformation of formal logic by issuing a critique of the general doctrine of the construction of concepts. This project first occurred to him when he discovered traditional logic to be inadequate to account for some of the more advanced concepts of modern mathematics. He was quick to observe, however, that these concepts were not in any way limited to mathematics. The exact sciences are also founded upon them. Thus, while the task at hand was a purely logical one, it was conceived from the onset as pertinent to mathematics and the exact sciences as well.

At the heart of the traditional theory of concept formation lies the doctrine of the generic concept. This doctrine presupposes only the inexhaustible multiplicity of existing things and the power of the mind to select from that multiplicity those features which are common to several of them. Thought, by a process of comparison and differentiation, gathers objects characterized by common features into classes. As this same process is repeated upon the classes themselves, a determinate and hierarchical order begins to arise and finally achieves a classification of things which approaches completeness. The guiding principles of the generic concept follow from these foundations. The generic concept or class comprehends within itself all the determinations in which these objects agree. The species or subclasses which divide the genus at various levels are distinguished by features which are common to only a portion of those objects. The rule of inverse ratio of comprehension and extension follows immediately from this description.

An immediate difficulty with this account of concept formation would seem to be that in organizing the multiplicity of objects by similar features it clearly calls for the substitution of a portion of that multiplicity for the whole. Such an objection, however, would miss the whole point of concept formation. The negation of objects characterized by dissimilarity, it is held, is simply the reverse side of the act of discerning the essential moment of the whole. True, a part is substituted in thought for the sensuous whole, but this part is no random section. Rather, it is the ground, reason, or cause according to which that whole is determined. There is no difficulty here. But one soon appears, for the rule of "inverse ratio" contains in itself no guarantee that this end will actually be achieved. It is at this point that the metaphysical presupposition of Aristotle's logic becomes clear.

The only way to justify the employment of the generic concept is to assert that what is common in knowledge is at the same time ". . . the real *Form* which guarantees the causal and teleological connection of particular things." By achieving a generic knowledge of things, thought isolates the specific type which, as the active factor in individual things, gives the general pattern to the manifold of special forms. "The determination of the concept according to its next higher genus and its specific difference reproduces the process by which the real substance successively unfolds itself in its special forms of being. Thus it is this basic conception of *substance* to which the purely logical theories of Aristotle constantly have reference." Accordingly, Aristotle constantly proposes the primacy of the category of substance over all other categories, especially that of relation.

Modern empiricists have developed Aristotle's logical theory of concept formation by inquiring into the manner in which abstract objects arise. Of particular note in this regard is their "psychology of abstraction." Cassirer singled out the work of Mill for specific consideration. According to Mill the mind is possessed of the power of selecting common features from the sensuous manifold in virtue of its ability of reproducing any given content of presentation. In the course of time, sense determinations leave behind certain traces of themselves in the form of memory residues. These contents of past presentations are again aroused by newly occurring sense stimuli of a similar sort. On such an occasion the association of the past contents with the present one is established. As this process continues, a firm connection is established between the similar contents of successive presentations while the traces or residues of dissimilar ones—not being freshly aroused—tend to recede from explicit consciousness until they finally form only a shadowy background against which the similar features stand out more clearly. This progressive solidification of those features which agree into a unitary and indivisible whole constitutes the whole psychological nature of the concept.

By considering the empiricists and the realists as being within the same tradition Cassirer did not intend to gloss over their real metaphysical differences, but only to emphasize that in matters of logic they are at one. Both claim that the common feature captured in the concept is identical with the essential feature of the series of objects which confront the formative process, whether that is thought to be a series of things or their presentations. As regards the presupposition of a metaphysics of substance and the resultant logical doctrine of the primacy of the category of substance over relation there is no conflict between these traditions. Yet, it is precisely here, where there is no conflict within traditional logic, that the modern mathematical concept occasions profound difficulties.

The concepts employed in modern mathematics and the exact sciences cannot be adequately comprehended within the traditional doctrine of the generic concept. The crucial difficulty lies in the fact that the object of such a concept cannot be given either as a thing or as a presentation. On the one hand, such an object is not given at all but is posited by a progressive synthesis as a systematic connection of thought-construction (*Denkgebilder*). The object of such a concept is the product rather than the starting point of concept formation. On the other hand, such an object cannot even be represented in a presentation with accuracy. Not even a straight line is susceptible of sensuous representation. On both counts, then, the traditional doctrine of the generic concept along with the theory of concept formation which is founded upon it fails to account for the concepts of modern mathematics and the exact sciences.

That the traditional logical doctrine fails to admit of sufficient scope to accommodate mathematical and scientific concepts constitutes a limitation but not of itself a fundamental failure. There is still the possibility that it may be developed sufficiently to allow of such procedures. In order to show that this difficulty is more than a mere shortcoming, that it is symptomatic of a profound failure and so requires a radical transformation of the very foundations of logic itself, Cassirer proceeded to indicate the source of the inadequacy of the traditional doctrine of the concept.

Mill's doctrine of abstraction requires that concepts arise for us by the gradual predominance of the similarities of things over their differences. Memory residues are aroused when similar presentations occur. "The similarity of things, however, can manifestly only be effective and fruitful, if it is understood and judged *as such*." A presentation can trigger the arousal of memory residues only on the condition that this presentation is seen to be similar to those residues and vice versa, i.e., only on the condition that they are *recognized* as similar. The doctrine of abstraction glosses over this by allowing that the similarities between the contents of the several presentations are apprehended as themselves members of the presentational sequence. Once this is exposed to the light of day it falls by the wayside. "And yet even the most simply *psychological* reflection shows that the 'likeness' between any contents is not itself given as a further content; that similarity or dissimilarity does not appear as a special element of sensation side by side with colors and tones, with sensations of pressure and touch."

The generic concept is formed according to Aristotle's theory by progressive negation or neglect of objects characterized by dissimilarity. Accordingly, as thought proceeds concepts become more and more emptied of content. The whole idea of the generic concept thus stated seems to fly in the face of scientific thought, for the whole purpose of taking thought in the first place is to resolve an original indefiniteness and ambiguity and to achieve in its stead sharp lines of distinction. Aristotle's generic concept, on the contrary, works in exactly the reverse order. The further thought proceeds along generic lines the more effaced become the lines of distinction and so the greater become the confusion and ambiguity. This difficulty is fatal. The very law of generic concepts—the inverse ratio rule—spells the doom of thought. Universality can be achieved only at the expense of content and at that price the project is self-defeating.

Cassirer proceeded from the two objections just stated to formulate a more adequate theory of concept formation. From the observation that abstraction, of necessity, involves recognition he went on to show that the act of identification is the very foundation of abstraction. Objects in the sensuous manifold which are to be recognized as similar and so grouped together must first be identified as like one another. In order to do so some principle of comparison must be employed. By allowing that "likeness" and "difference" are themselves members of the presentational sequence Mill insisted that the principle of identification is obvious from mere inspection of that manifold. In fact, however, the sensuous manifold may be ordered according to any number of the most divergent principles, e.g., according to equality, inequality, number, magnitude, spatial or temporal relation, causal dependence, etc. There are a variety of ways in which the sensuous manifold may be ordered. Accordingly, it must be admitted that the sensuous manifold is indeterminate in respect of its order and that the principle by which the manifold is ordered is independent of sensation. The sensuous manifold as an ordered series must, therefore, be considered to be a composite. On the one hand, there is the manifold of members which is indeterminate in respect of its order, and on the other, there is the principle, function, or law of arrangement according to which that manifold is determined in respect of its order.

By thus defining the concept as a propositional function f(x), Cassirer indicated with utmost clarity the failures of both Aristotle and Mill. The latter attempted to seize the propositional function as if in his hands, while the former assigned it to a suprasensory abode while still regarding it as something substantial. On the contrary, the propositional function can neither be reduced to one of its own variables, a mere "x," nor be intelligible apart from all variables; it is always a function of *some* variable. Mill viewed it as one of the variables, while Aristotle made it into one of the absolute separate substances. Both erred in the same sense, however, by failing to distinguish between the members of an ordered series and the general law of arrangement by which this serial order is determined.

The advent of the concretely universal mathematical concept signals the collapse of the Aristotelian doctrine of substance, which had previously formed the implicit basis of formal logic. Both empiricists and realists agree that the common feature captured in the concept is identical with the essential feature of the series of objects which confront the formative process. The determination of the order of the members of the series is, according to that scheme, fixed independently of thought. Nature is here conceived as an already ordered series of substances which thought can only accept, achieving universality in its concepts by systematic forgetfulness. But when it is seen that the determination of the order of the members of the series is deduced from the concept itself, it must be concluded on the one hand that thought is the source of the ordering of the sensuous manifold, and on the other that the common feature achieved in the concept is the law of arrangement according to which that manifold is thus determined. "In opposition to the logic of the generic concept, which, as

we saw, represents the point of view and influence of the concept of substance, there now appears the *logic of the mathematical concept of function*."

The transformation of formal logic is now all but complete. The primacy of function-concepts over substance-concepts is established. The primacy of function over object is clearly demonstrated. Still Cassirer had yet to draw his most original conclusion. All that had been said does not differ widely from the position of Kant. Indeed, Cassirer, correctly or not, everywhere attributes the doctrine of the primacy of function to Kant. It remained for him to break with his master and show that: "Instead of saying that the human intellect is an intellect which is 'in need of images' we should rather say that it is in need of symbols."

So far, in the argument of **S&F**, Cassirer had confined his argument to showing that the manifold in sensation is ordered by thought under its own laws. Yet even this will not suffice for the concepts of modern mathematics or even those of the natural sciences, for the objects of these concepts can not be given in sensation. Later in the **PSF** he indicated that non-Euclidean geometries make it necessary to depart from Kant on this point. It can no longer be required that mathematical concepts be grounded in sensuous intuition in order to assure their validity. Rather, all that is necessary is that they be represented in a set of marks which as variables substitute for the sensuous manifold.

This is usually the discussion cited when reference is made to Cassirer's departure from Kant. Yet, as was seen to be the case with the other cardinal methodological principles of Cassirer's synthesis, it was demonstrated only in the opening chapter of **S&F**. Lotze had criticized the traditional doctrine of abstraction on the score that in actual practice the universality of the concept is never advanced by neglecting the particular properties of objects without retaining an equivalent for them. Thus, when forming a concept of metal we may not ascribe to that abstract object the color of gold or the weight of copper, but the positive thought must be added that it is colored in *some* way and that it have *some* weight. It is not, as the traditional rule of abstraction would have it, that the peculiar "marks" p_1p_2, q_1q_2 are neglected, but that the general terms P and Q are substituted in their place, of which the particular "marks" are one of their values. "We represent this systematic totality (*Inbegriff*) when we substitute for the *constant* particular 'marks,' *variable* terms, such as stand for the total group of possible values which the different 'marks' can assume." What had seemed to be a falling aside of the peculiar "marks" of particular objects is only the substitution of another type of mark in their stead. Thus, concept formation proceeds according as variable terms, one value of which are the particular "marks," are substituted for them as the members ordered under a law. It is only in this way that thought may proceed, i.e., by the substitution of symbols for images.

In the opening chapter of **S&F** Cassirer accomplished a considerable transformation of formal logic. Such a change always has profound repercussions in all ranges of our knowledge of reality, whether of objectivity or subjectivity. "Whenever, in the history of philosophy, the question as to the relation of thought and being, of knowledge and reality, has been raised, it has been dominated from the first by certain *logical* presuppositions, by certain views about the nature of the concept and judgment. Every change in this fundamental view indirectly produces a complete change in the way in which the general question is stated. The *system* of knowledge tolerates no isolated 'formal' determination without consequences in all the problems and solutions of knowledge. The conception, therefore, that is formed of the fundamental nature of the concept is directly significant in judging the questions of fact which are generally considered under 'Critique of Knowledge,' (*Erkenntniskritik*) or 'Metaphysics.' "

In this paper we have been content to explore the changes in logical presuppositions which announced themselves to Cassirer at the onset of his professional career. It is no exaggeration to suggest that the remainder of that career was devoted to completing the cycle which he began in this early work by showing how reality must appear when viewed from this more profound logical perspective.

Harry M. Campbell   (essay date 1969)

SOURCE: "The Philosophy of Ernst Cassirer and Fictional Religion," in *The Thomist,* Vol. XXXIII, No. 4, October, 1969, pp. 737-54.

[*In the following excerpt, Campbell explores the limitations of Cassirer's philosophy of symbolic forms when the forms are applied to religion.*]

Anyone familiar with the history of philosophy in this century will know that some of the most influential philosophers have been those who have considered that the right knowledge and use of language will solve world problems; in fact, some even believe language to be the only reality, which "creates" the world which we think we see as "given." Even the logical (sometimes called mathematical) positivists may be included in this group, if we consider mathematical symbols as a kind of language: it is their conviction that ordinary language, though very important, is somewhat ambiguous and in need of extended supplementation by the more exact symbols of mathematics. The ontological status of mathematics and the other sciences as well as language has been argued at great length, but an important group of philosophers of this century has decided that such an argument is futile, since the important thing for all such symbols is not their reference to an objective truth (if indeed such exists) but their function. In other words, do they enable us more efficiently and satisfactorily to live our lives? Perhaps the most learned philosopher in this century to emphasize the problem of linguistic and other symbols was Ernst Cassirer, a German refugee who spent the last four years of his life (after two years in England and six in Sweden) lecturing and writing in America until his death in 1945. Cassirer vigorously denounced the positivists, and, though he never mentioned Vaihinger, he would surely have denounced Vaihinger's "idealistic positivism" as it is expressed in the theory of fictions. This failure to mention Vaihinger is a little hard to understand, since both men were important modern professors and philosophers in Germany (their careers to some extent overlapping, though Vaihinger was much older) and since both wrote extensively on Kant. Their views, furthermore, as it shall be the purpose of this essay to demonstrate, were basically very similar, in spite of Cassirer's repeated denial that his system of idealism should be construed as mental fictions.

The discussion of Cassirer's philosophy in this essay will be based on three of his works: *Language and Myth, An Essay on Man,* and *The Philosophy of Symbolic Forms,* the first two of these being popular and condensed versions of the last, which is his magnum opus in three volumes. His system is usually called a kind of modified philosophical idealism, but, as I shall demonstrate later, the modification is little more than an occasional brief and unemphatic reference to an objectivity that is soon forgotten in the all-embracing creative activity attributed to the human spirit and expressed through language. Perhaps it might be said that he always recognizes a certain amount of objective reality in the material world, but the noumenal world exists only as the creation (or "objectification") of the human spirit (always expressed through some form of language).

In the beginning one may wonder why he lists language as parallel with myth, art, and science, sometimes adding religion as a fifth "cultural form." It would seem, one might suppose, more logical to subordinate language as the instrument through which most aspects of the other "cultural forms" are expressed. It is soon clear, however, that he wishes to exalt language as a creative force equivalent, as an expression of the human spirit (in modern terms, of course), to the Greek Logos and the Christian Word. Indeed, in some respects, language is supreme among the forms, because myth (which includes religion) and science are types of language, as, from one point of view, is art. Language, furthermore, is the source of what we call reasoning, as Mrs. Susanne Langer, one of Cassirer's most ardent disciples and interpreters in America, explains: "It is the discursive character of language," says Mrs. Langer, interpreting Cassirer, "its inner tendency to grammatical development, which gives rise to logic in the strict sense, i.e., to the procedure we call 'reasoning.' " But in his definition (in *Language and Myth,* hereafter referred to as *LM*) of the symbolic forms Cassirer prefers to consider language as parallel with the others:

> Myth, art, language, and science appear as symbols; not in the sense of mere figures which refer to some given reality by means of suggestion and allegorical renderings, but in the sense of forces each of which produces and posits a world of its own. In these realms the spirit exhibits itself in that inwardly determined dialectic by virtue of which alone there is any reality, any organized and definite Being at all. Thus the special symbolic forms are not imitations, but *organs* of reality, since it is solely by their agency that anything real becomes an object for intellectual apprehension, and as such is made visible for us. The question as to what reality is apart from these forms, and what are its independent attributes, becomes irrelevant here. (*LM*)

Cassirer is here emphasizing what he elsewhere (*The Philosophy of Symbolic Forms,* hereafter referred to as *PSF*) calls "the modern, 'subjective' trend in speculation" which does not worry about reality or truth apart from these forms, "each of which produces and posits a world of its own." In his Introduction to *PSF* Professor Hendel explains and approves of Cassirer's appeal to Kant as the authority for this kind of idealism. Cassirer, according to Hendel, used the authority of Kant for the idea that "whatever reality we know is precisely such as 'conforms to' our human ways of knowing" (Introduction, *PSF*) and that, "instead of human knowledge being shaped to reality, it is our human judgment which determines whatever is to have the character of reality for us" (Introduction) or, to put it another way, "the world is 'constituted' in accordance with the forms of man's intuition and understanding" (Introduction). Kant, of course, believed that "the principle of formal purposiveness" is an *a priori* principle necessary for the knowledge of nature, but it is still only "regulative" for the knowing, and not essentially "constitutive of the known, the appearances, or the phenomena." Cassirer went beyond this, believing, as does Hendel, that he is still faithful to the Kantian orientation and method when he obliterates the distinction between "regulative" and "constitutive" principles and makes all of them constitutive. There is, however, some ambiguity (not mentioned by Hendel) in Cassirer's use of the adjective "constitutive." The question is whether purposive form is "constitutive of" nature in the sense of existing in nature and being discovered by the human mind or whether the human mind (or spirit, for Cassirer a synonymous term) contributes the purposive form which does not exist independently in nature. As a good idealist Cassirer would like to escape from this difficulty by treating the elements of form and matter in what he calls a "functional" as distinguished from a "substantive" manner, and yet he cannot deny that in the realm of biology any organism reveals substantive form. Hendel can see no contradiction in Cassirer's system here or anything contradicting Kant in Cassirer's belief that "the character of 'whole-forming' or 'system-forming' pertains to the world itself of living nature" (Introduction). In other words, as Cassirer says elsewhere, "Developing organisms are, in substance, self-contained complexes of activities that are determining and productive of form" (Introduction, quoting Cassirer's *Problem of Knowledge*). But this kind of objective reality is hardly compatible with the prevailing emphasis on the creative activity of the human spirit, "by virtue of which alone there is any reality, any organized and definite Being at all." And in neither of these contradictory views is Cassirer being, as Hendel believes he is, "faithful to the Kantian orientation and method." Kant certainly did not believe that the human spirit created all the cultural forms, including religion and metaphysics in general. The phenomenal world may be "constituted" in accordance with the forms of man's intuition and understanding, but, in Kant's opinion, this was not true of the noumenal realm, which Kant said (again and again, even in the *Critique of Pure Reason*) man cannot cognize, but in the objective reality of which he had faith to believe. Nor did Kant believe in the other (contradictory) view that nature itself was the source of purposive form in organisms. Again, though this

point could not be settled cognitively for what Kant called the "determinant judgment," certainly for the "reflective judgment" behind any organized being there must be a design with its "root origin" in a supreme Being: "It is absolutely impossible for us," says Kant, "to obtain any explanation at the hand of nature itself to account for any synthesis displaying finality," by which he means complexity of organization. The proximate source lies in what Kant calls the "supersensible substrate of nature," and the ultimate source in a transcendent God.

In explaining the development of this wonderful creative power which he attributes to the human spirit, Cassirer begins with the primitive belief in the "physico-magical power of the Word," meaning language, and traces the history of it until its "spiritual power" was finally recognized. This "spiritual power" is the ability to create all the cultural forms, including religion, concerning the nature of which the unenlightened man is in error, for with him, "as in the case of tools and instruments, all creativity is felt as being, and every product of subjectivity as so much substantiality" (*LM*). This naive interpretation, however, says Cassirer, is necessary before the correct one can develop: "The Word has to be conceived in the mythic mode, as a substantive being and power, before it can be comprehended as an ideal instrument . . . in the construction and development of spiritual reality" (*LM*). And when Cassirer refers to the Word he means language, the great creative or "spiritual" power of which he proclaims in no uncertain terms as a "form-creating power, which at the same time has to be really a form-breaking, form-destroying one." But Cassirer forgets that for orthodox theology the Word is still conceived as a substantial being, identified in the prologue to the Fourth Gospel and in later writings with Jesus Christ, not in the sense of attributing physico-magical power to language, but, as Webster's puts it, as "the actively expressed, creative, and revelatory thought and will of God, at once distinguished from and identified with him." For both Cassirer and for the believer in a transcendent God the physico-magical use of language is superseded gradually in the development of the human race by its use to refer to a higher spiritual reality, but for Cassirer this spiritual reality is the human mind or "spirit" and for the believer in a transcendent God this spiritual reality is that God.

Cassirer, like so many other moderns, has served the metaphysical part of the Great Chain of Being and believes that the truncated remainder will stand on its own. This truncation, though without reference to Cassirer, has been well explained by Professor William York Tindall in his book entitled *The Literary Symbol*. Most of us in the modern world, says Tindall,

> do not use allegory, for on the whole, lacking certainty, we prefer indefinite analogies. Definite analogies, such as the allegory and metaphor of the Middle Ages and the Renaissance, were designed to present not abstractions alone but the nature of things. If we are to distinguish these limited instruments more plainly from the romantic symbol which we prefer, we must consider two worlds. The first, organic, lasted from the time of Pythagoras to the late seventeenth centu-

ry. The second, which replaced it, is mechanical in one of its aspects and developmental in another. What we call the romantic movement is the endeavor to make the world organic again . . . to recover the upper half of the broken chain. . . . The upper half of this restoration, however, acquired new meanings. Not only the place of spirit, it came to mean the imaginative, the subjective, the unconscious, or sensibility, separated by that famous dissociation from fact and reason, which continued to occupy the lower half of the chain. . . . The French symbolists . . . mark the second stage of the romantic movement. These poets used symbol not so much to unite worlds as to create them. . . . [Baudelaire called] "The visible universe . . . a kind of fodder that the imagination must digest and transform." In the second place, moving beyond existing analogies, the queenly faculty the imagination [or what Cassirer would call the human "spirit"] has power to create new ones, "la plus haute fiction," or what Stevens called a "supreme fiction." As seer Baudelaire belongs with the earlier transcendentalists and as artist with those who, finding aesthetic construction a substitute for cosmic reconstruction, made something like autonomous worlds.

Not all of this description, of course, would apply to Cassirer, who does not make much of the unconscious. However, he is trying to make the world organic again, trying to recover the upper half of the broken chain in the manner of the French symbolists, only by "using symbol not so much to unite worlds as to create them." But the French symbolists, and Wallace Stevens following them, were more aware than Cassirer of the limitation of their creation since they called it "la plus haute fiction" or a "supreme fiction," which, of course, takes us back where (philosophically) all of this belongs, to Vaihinger's As-If theory of fictions. Cassirer always evaded this point by talking about meaning rather than truth, or about function rather than substance. He did, however, in one memorable passage at the end of *PSF* and in another at the end of *LM*, praise the "aesthetically liberated life," in which "language becomes an avenue of artistic expression." The statement in *PSF* is more eloquent and more revealing:

> In the image myth sees a fragment of substantial reality, a part of the material world itself, endowed with equal or higher powers than this world. From this first magical view religion strives toward a progressively purer spiritualization. And yet, again and again, it is carried back to a point at which the question of its truth and meaning content shifts into the question of the reality of its objects, at which it faces the problem of "existence" in all its harshness. It is only the aesthetic consciousness that leaves this problem truly behind it. Since from the outset it gives itself to pure "contemplation," developing the form of vision in contrast to all forms of action, the images fashioned in this frame of consciousness gain for the first time a truly immanent significance. They confess themselves to be illusion as opposed to the empirical reality of things; but this illusion has its own truth because it possesses its own law. In the return to this law there

arises a new freedom of consciousness: the image no longer reacts upon the spirit as an independent material thing but becomes for the spirit a pure expression of its own creative power.

Cassirer does not realize that he has here given an excellent description of what (in spite of his great devotion to learning) is implied by his whole philosophy when he faces the unvarnished truth: like the French Symbolists and the English decadents of the "Yellow Nineties," he is really an aesthete (a kind of epicurean of the intellect, substituting philosophy for belles lettres) who rests in the supremacy of the aesthetic consciousness with its images which "confess themselves to be illusion as opposed to the empirical reality of things," and which thus avoid "the problem of 'existence' in all its harshness." We can see behind the mask here, and what we see is a world-weary thinker who, like Santayana, recognizes that he cannot change the "harshness" (and it is to be noted that he does not put "harshness" in quotation marks) of reality with all its disappointments and therefore leaves it for the realm of art, where, as Santayana says, "what is good is altogether and finally good, and what is bad is at least not treacherous." Cassirer still refers to this kind of illusion as one that "becomes for the spirit a pure expression of its own creative power," but the term "creation" has far less force when, instead of transforming or transcending existence, it "confesses" itself to be only illusion and "leaves behind . . . the problem of 'existence' in all its harshness." What, then, becomes of Hendel's claim that for Cassirer, as for Goethe and Hegel, "the Ideal is Actual and the Actual is Ideal" (Introduction, *PSF*)?

Of course, even in the above passage on the aesthetic consciousness, Cassirer puts "existence" in quotation marks and thus leaves some room for his idealism, though the power of this idealism is definitely threatened when he "confesses" that it is only illusion. Most of the time, however, Cassirer does sound like Hegel in maintaining the identity of "idea" and "phenomenon." But Hendel, after contending for this similarity between Hegel and Cassirer in the passage quoted above, reverses himself and argues that the two are unlike in this respect. "Hegel," says Hendel, "advances from the engagement of spirit with life to the ultimate resolution of the dialectic where Spirit has 'absolute knowledge' of itself. But Cassirer keeps the twain ever twain, spirit and its other. . . . There is always the added phrase 'and reality,' the reality of the phenomenal world" (Introduction). In the unguarded "illusion" passages quoted and discussed above this is true, but very seldom is he this frank or (one might add) perceptive in analyzing the realistic implications of his philosophy. His whole philosophy, on the contrary, is based on the grandiose claims which he makes for the creation by the human spirit of the "cultural forms," including "the highest objective truth." Cassirer says:

> The highest truth that is accessible to the spirit is ultimately the form of its own activity. . . . The illusion of an original division between the intelligible and the sensuous, between "idea" and "phenomenon," vanishes . . . each new "symbolic form"—not only the conceptual world of scientific cognition but also the intu-

itive world of art, myth, and language—constitutes, as Goethe said, a revelation sent outward from within, a "synthesis of world and spirit," which truly assures us that the two are originally one. (**PSF**)

This certainly does not seem as if Hendel is correct in saying that Cassirer "keeps the twain ever twain, spirit and its other." The "and reality," which Hendel quotes out of context to prove that Cassirer keeps spirit separate from the reality of the phenomenal world, is taken from this very paragraph arguing the oneness of world and spirit. Here is the sentence: "In the totality of its [the spirit's] own achievements, in the knowledge of the specific rule by which each of them is determined and in the consciousness of context which reunites all these special rules into *one* problem and one solution: in all this, the human spirit perceives itself and reality." It is clear here that "reality" is perceived in, and owes its existence to, the totality of the spirit's "own achievements."

Elsewhere [in ***Substance and Function***] Cassirer elaborates on the advantage of this idealism:

> The "thing" is thus no longer something unknown, lying before us as a bare material, but is an expression of the form and manner of conceiving. What metaphysics ascribes as a *property* to things in themselves now proves to be a necessary element in the process of objectification [the process, that is, by which the spirit "achieves" what he calls "reality"]. While in metaphysics the permanence and continuous existence of objects is spoken of as distinguishing them from the changeableness and discontinuity of sense perceptions, here identity and continuity appear as *postulates,* which serve as general lines of direction for the progressive unification of laws. They signify not so much the known properties of things, but rather the logical instrument, by which we know.

Reality, then, being an "achievement" of the human spirit, must also be spiritual, in Cassirer's sense of this word. . . .

Professor Fritz Kauffman has well expressed the existential inadequacy of Cassirer's system:

> . . . Cassirer's pre-occupation with the boundless objectifying process almost blinds him to the essential limitations of human life. This applies, above all, to the life of the individual. Cassirer's main concern is, like Kant's, with the "intelligible substrate of humanity," not with human existence. The problems of individual birth and death—personal problems rather than merely creatural ones—are scarcely handled at all (death only in a negative way) . . . he recognized in man's knowledge of his finiteness the very dawn of the infinite. . . .

> Cassirer did not and could not proceed the way Kierkegaard, Jaspers and, within their sphere, the great tragedians and also such novelists as Joseph Conrad and Franz Kafka did: he could not "define" man with a view to the extreme situations (*Grenzsituationen*) in which man's true being, his greatness and weakness come out—

most eloquently in the very moments of his growing silent and succumbing to destiny. (Personal "destiny" is not a category that fits into a dialectical schema of the objective mind.)

Professor Kauffman goes on to say that Cassirer's philosophy "neglects man's inability to express certain experiences in an adequate way as well as his unique capacity for going into hiding by the very means of communication." Indeed, Cassirer has essentially gone into hiding by overemphasizing the creative power of language in calling it "a form-creating power, which at the same time has to be really a form-breaking, form-destroying one." Here language, usually one of the "cultural forms" created by the human spirit, seems to usurp the place of its creator, but this is no doubt a kind of synecdoche, as is doubtless his idea in his derivation of reason from language, explained thus by Mrs. Langer: "It is the *discursive* character of language, its inner tendency to grammatical development, which gives rise to logic in the strict sense, i.e., to the procedure we call 'reasoning.'" For Cassirer, says Mrs. Langer approvingly (and she does not call it synecdoche), language "embodies not only self-contained, complex meanings, but a principle of concatenation whereby the complexes are unravelled and articulated."

> In Cassirer's opinion, it would be highly illogical to consider the human spirit as derived either from matter or from a spirit higher than itself. Apparently Cassirer would agree with Poe, who said, "I cannot imagine any being in or outside the universe superior to myself."
>
> —*Harry M. Campbell*

But, even if we assume that the above exaltation of language is really, by synecdoche, to be construed as referring to the human spirit (of which language in Cassirer's system is in one way a part and in another a product), there is still in Cassirer's central argument a logical inadequacy quite as serious as the existential defect referred to by Professor Kauffman. Cassirer is attempting to supply an explanation of the origin of reason and knowledge that avoids the faulty logic of both materialism and traditional religious revelation. In Cassirer's opinion, it would be highly illogical to consider the human spirit as derived either from matter or from a spirit higher than itself. Apparently Cassirer would agree with Poe, who said, "I cannot imagine any being in or outside the universe superior to myself." But is there not even more difficulty in imagining the human spirit to be self-originating? Such an assumption would involve what M. F. Ashley Montagu, in explaining Cassirer's system (which he accepts), calls "a primordial directive of the spirit, an intrinsic way of forming knowledge." Presumably this "primordial directive" was contained in the primordial protoplasm that first evolved in the ocean slime, or if it was later added, how was it added—and by what or by whom? The only answer that Cassirer gives to this question is that "the spirit (*Geist*) forges the conditions necessary to itself." The human spirit, according to Cassirer, created, as part of its religious "cultural form," the myth of a transcendent God who created the world and all that dwell therein. Was the human spirit, then, self-creating? Of course, Cassirer would say that to consider such a question as this would be to consider the human spirit "substantively" rather than, as he prefers, "functionally." But is he not speaking "substantively" when he says that the human spirit "created" the culture forms? And can he really avoid the question of the origin of the human vessel in which this spirit is "contained," or in which it "functions"? Mrs. Langer has worked out her "new key" to philosophy in the spirit of her master, Cassirer, when she simply "rejects" such a question as this by saying, "If we have new knowledge, we must get us a whole world of new questions" (*Philosophy in a New Key*, hereafter referred to as *PNK*). But both she and Cassirer are really often giving old answers to old questions. When Mrs. Langer says that the answer to the question "How did the world become as it is?" is "It has not 'become' at all" (*PNK*), she is not, as she says she is, "repudiating the very framework" (*PNK*) of traditional logic. She is simply, by implication, giving to this very old question one very old answer, namely, that the world, in some form or other, has always existed. She does this more openly in another instance when she says, "If we ask how physical objects, chemically analyzable, can be conscious, how ideas can occur to them, we are talking ambiguously; for the conception of 'physical object' is a conception of chemical substance *not* biologically organized" (*PNK*). But presumably it would not be ambiguous to ask how a biological organism can be conscious or have ideas, nor would it be ambiguous to consider how the biological organism became organized. She is referring to the human organism and how it evolved out of "physical objects," as her next sentence shows: "What causes this tremendous organization of substances, is one of the things the tremendous organisms do not know; but with their organization, suffering and impulse and awareness arise" (*PNK*). Again she is giving another very old answer to another very old question when she says in the next sentence: "It is really no harder to imagine that a chemically active body wills, knows, thinks, and feels, than that an invisible, intangible, something does so, 'animates' the body without physical agency, and 'inhabits' without being in any *place*" (*PNK*). The old answer is that what Cassirer would call the human spirit, "creator" of all the "culture forms" (including, under the heading of myth, the account of its own origin), simply "arises" when the "organization of substances" becomes sufficiently "tremendous." In Mrs. Langer's and Cassirer's opinion, it is naive to imagine that a transcendent God creates the human spirit, as well as the world in which it functions, but it is sophisticated to assume that it simply, at the appropriate time in evolution, "arises."

Nor is Cassirer's "synthesis" of all the various culture forms a new one. It is certainly as old as Protagoras's attempt to make "man the measure of all things." Protagoras indeed would not have objected to the essential meaning of the following statement by Cassirer:

The various products of culture—language, scientific knowledge, myth, art, religion—become parts of a single great problem-complex: they become multiple efforts, all directed toward the one goal of transforming the passive world of mere impressions, in which the spirit seems at first imprisoned, into a world that is pure expression of the human spirit. (*PSF*)

But such a synthesis is by the very nature of what would be its parts unattainable when traditional religion, at least, claims to be derived from a source which cannot be defined as "pure expression of the human spirit," but which transcends, and is the ultimate Creator of, the world and all (including the human spirit) that dwells therein. Cassirer admits that the different cultural forms are often in conflict with one another, but, in his opinion, philosophical thought can "find a standpoint situated above all these forms and yet not merely outside them" and can understand "particular aspects of cultured life and the concrete totality of its forms" (*PSF*). But Cassirer's position is not "above all these forms"; he is simply adopting as his own one aspect of one of these forms, the interpretation (in the romantic tradition) of religion as man-made. The nineteenth century "higher critic" Feuerbach expressed this view as follows: "We have reduced the supermundane, supernatural, and superhuman nature of God to the elements of human nature as its fundamental elements. . . . The beginning, middle, and end of Religion is Man." Many poets could be cited with the same view: for example, Swinburne, who said:

> Glory to Man in the highest! for Man is the master of things. . . .
> There is no God, O son,
> If thou be none.

Professor Wilbur M. Urban . . . wonders why Cassirer never discusses the language of metaphysics except in his brief refutation of Bergson's purely intuitive metaphysics which seeks to dispense with symbols.

> . . . if it is true, as we are told by Cassirer, that science as symbolic form has no exclusive value, but is only one way of constructing reality, and has value only from the standpoint of science, then it would appear that a metaphysics, to be adequate, must be a metaphysics of art and religion also and must have a language and symbolic form which includes these forms also—in which case it could no longer be a symbolism of relations merely, but must be a symbolism of things also.

Of course, by "things" Professor Urban does not mean either "material" or "anthropomorphic" existence, but rather, for example, a transcendent Being superior to the human spirit, the latter being really Cassirer's God. Professor Urban answers his own question, though he is not sure—one wonders why—that his answer is correct. "It may be, after all," he says, "that it is merely a phenomenology and not a metaphysics with which Cassirer presents us." This is most certainly the answer. The ultimate for Cassirer is the human spirit, beyond which for him there is no metaphysical reality (Cf. *PSF*, quoted shortly above). Of course, it might be argued that Cassirer's belief in "spirit," even though only the human spirit, would take him out of the realm of phenomenology, "the science dealing with phenomena as distinct from the science of being," into that of metaphysics, but this objection would be quibbling, for it is clear enough that for Cassirer the problem of the human spirit is no more than a phenomenological one to be explained in such terms as "expression," "function," and "meaning." A good illustration of Cassirer's avoidance of the metaphysical is his chapter entitled "The Expressive Function and the Problem of Body and Soul" in *PSF*. The nexus between body and soul, says Cassirer, is not a causal one, but is one of those "basic forms of combination, which can only be understood if we resist the temptation to dissolve them into causal relations, if we leave them as they are and consider them as structures *sui generis*" (*PSF*). He thinks it unfortunate that this "phenomenological question" has too often been "transformed into an ontological question. . . . The history of metaphysics shows us clearly that every attempt to describe the body-soul relationship by transforming it into a relation of the conditioning and the conditioned, cause and effect, has culminated in inextricable difficulties" (*PSF*).

One may well wonder whether the combination of body and soul is really "understood" by considering it as a "structure *sui generis*" or as an "authentically original phenomenon," and one may also wonder whether Cassirer's whole system, at least in the realm of religion (which for him is actually no different from myth when it believes in the reality or truth of its object), does not find itself in a self-imposed dilemma. "The problem," says Cassirer, "is not the material content of mythology [and for him when religion believes in the reality or truth of its object it is synonymous with mythology], but the intensity with which it is experienced, with which it is *believed*—as only something endowed with objective reality can be believed." This intensity of belief in the reality of its object is what gives myth "the incomparable force it has demonstrated over and over again in the history of the human spirit." If this force depends on belief, then the force must be lost when the sophisticated approach of Cassirer's "religion" is substituted for the belief in the reality or truth of its object. This was the same dilemma in which Vaihinger found himself with his "law of ideational shifts" in the history of religion, the shift being from dogma to hypothesis to fiction. He says:

> At first all religion consists of general dogmas. . . . Then doubt appears and the idea becomes an hypothesis. As doubt grows stronger, there are some who reject the idea entirely, while others maintain it either as a public or a private fiction. This last condition is typical of every religion so far known when it has reached a certain age. It can be seen to great advantage in Greek religion, where the Greek folk-deities were at first general dogmas . . . Subsequently they became fictions for the educated classes, who adhered tenaciously to the worship of God, or rather of the gods, although convinced that the ideas represented nothing real.

Vaihinger considered that the approach through a consideration of religion as fiction would bring mighty spiritual benefits, but at the same time he associated the "law of ide-

ational shifts" with the "decline and break-up" of religion. Cassirer, of course, would deny that his "spiritual" approach would make of religion a fiction, but it is really no different. The dogma stage for him would be myth, which would become truly "spiritual" when it ceased to believe in the reality or truth of its object, and then what the spirit "created" in the metaphysical realm would really be a fiction. (A fiction, etymologically a variant of the past participle of *facere, to make,* is something "made.") This is no different from Cassirer's "created." Vaihinger starts with what he calls the human psyche, Cassirer with what he calls the human spirit. Vaihinger says that the psyche uses fictional hypotheses, including religion, to produce spiritual benefits; Cassirer says that all the culture forms, including religion, are "function" of the human spirit. The idea of God is a fiction of the human psyche, says, Vaihinger; the idea of God is a "creation" of the human spirit, says Cassirer. There is absolutely no difference. Both originate in the human mind and deny any kind of metaphysical reality superior to the human mind. To be sure, Cassirer constantly uses the word "spirit," as if to give his philosophy some lofty connotation, while Vaihinger, more frankly, calls himself basically a materialist and at times an "idealistic positivist." Urban argues that Cassirer is superior to the positivists because he insists upon "the autonomy of the speech notion" and the great gap between animal expressions and human speech. For Cassirer, says Urban, "Language is not limited to the 'practical' functions for which it was primarily made, but in its development has achieved a freedom which makes it, in the words of Von Humboldt, 'a vehicle for traversing the manifold and the highest and deepest of the entire world'." But Vaihinger claims that his fictions, too, accomplish all these wonders: "Thus, before our very eyes does a small psychical artifice not only develop into a mighty source of the whole theoretical explanation of the world—for all categories arise from it—but it also becomes the origin of all the idealistic belief and behaviour of mankind."

One can only conclude that neither of these learned philosophers has solved what Cassirer, in an unguarded moment calls, in reference to the combination of body and soul, "the mystery of efficacy" (*PSF*). If he had grasped the full import of this unguarded admission, he might have been led, by a logic at least as convincing as his, to the conclusion that there may be, existentially and metaphysically in very truth, more things in heaven and earth than are dreamt of in his "journey round the world, the *globus intellectualis.*"

Walter F. Eggers, Jr.   (essay date 1971)

SOURCE: "From Language to the Art of Language: Cassirer's Aesthetic," in *The Quest for Imagination*, edited by O. B. Hardison, Jr., The Press of Case Western Reserve University, 1971, pp. 87-112.

[*In the following essay, Eggers compares Cassirer's views on language with those of other aesthetic philosophers.*]

Ernst Cassirer's interest in the symbolic form called language arises directly out of his allegiance to the long tradition of idealist philosophy. The history of attitudes toward language which comprises the introductory chapter of his *Phenomenology of Linguistic Form* (the first volume of *The Philosophy of Symbolic Forms*) reaches from Plato to Croce, and whatever impedes the gradual revelation of Kantian epistemology in the realm of language analysis gets short shrift. For example, he dismisses the dull mechanics of modern descriptive linguistics as an evasion of that same, fundamental problem of language which empiricism in all its historical shapes could never solve. A psychology of simple associations, whether strictly rationalist or "psychophysical," offers no explanation for language in its creative aspect. For this we need an image of man which frees him to create, a philosophy which grounds a "universal principle of form" in the originality of human action. Such has been the basic tenet of idealism throughout its history:

> This desire and capacity for giving form to experience is what Herder and Humboldt show to be the essence of language, what Schiller points to as the essential nature of play and art, and what Kant shows us to be true of the structure of theoretical knowledge. For them, all of this would not be possible as outgrowth, as sheer product, if unique modes of formal construction [spheres of possibility] did not underlie [the working out of] these creations. The very fact that man is capable of this type of productivity is precisely what stands out as the unique and distinguishing characteristic of human nature. [*The Logic of the Humanities*]

That the actions of man are essentially problematic, that the modes themselves through which he perceives his world are finally irreducible, *sui generis*—it is here that Plato, Kant, and Croce all begin.

To Croce goes the credit for turning the tide against linguistic positivism by equating language with spiritual expression and viewing the analysis of language as ultimately a problem in applied aesthetics. But Crocean "expression" is too reductive a concept for a systematic philosophy of the scope which Cassirer proposes. Aesthetics has its place within the full range of symbolic forms; but each of these forms, each of the "sciences of expression," must be kept in place if only for methodological reasons. Unless first we recognize their independence one from another, we cannot go on to describe the generic humanity which underlies them all: "Despite any systematic *combination* into which [language] may enter with logic and aesthetics, we must assign to it a *specific* and autonomous position within the whole." It is true that there is "no break in the life of the spirit" between the various symbolic forms; they are functionally identical as modes of symbolization, and the symbol-systems they produce lie on a continuum. Indeed, it is this argument which ties the three volumes of *The Philosophy of Symbolic Forms* together. But this is the argument to be proved, and we can proceed only analytically. In fact what Cassirer discovers when he surveys the full range of languages and possible languages is that although the impulse which lies behind the perpetual recreation of language is spiritually free, its evolution seems inevitably to be away from the metaphorical and the concrete toward "the expression of pure relation." His demonstration is a complex one, and we will return to this point later in this essay.

Cassirer attacks Croce's notion of expression on more strictly aesthetic grounds as well. For Croce, all of the human domain is divided into two parts, the artistic and the scientific, the intuitive and the logical:

> Knowledge has two forms: it is either *intuitive* knowledge or logical knowledge; knowledge obtained through the *imagination* or knowledge obtained through the *intellect;* knowledge of the *individual* or knowledge of the *universal;* of *individual things* or of the *relations* between them; it is, in fact, productive either of *images* or *concepts.* [Croce, *Aesthetic*]

Not only are these two realms independent of each other, they are fundamentally antagonistic—the artistic image is "pure intuition," simple and singular in its expression, revealing no trace of the abstract, the logical, the universal. Moreover, expression itself is bound immediately to intuition—to isolate the phenomenon of expression is only to view the process of intuition the other way around, from object to subject, from image to artist. It is on this basis that Croce is able to condemn as "the greatest triumph of the intellectualist error" the concept of "genre," the "theory of artistic and literary kinds." We cannot, he argues, apply a canon of normative values to a work of art which, by the nature of its inception in the imagination of the artist, posits its own rules. The logical mind is unable to penetrate artistic intuition: it can with its abstract schemes manipulate the art-object, but it cannot apprehend the object of expression because the object manifests a unity of its own.

Cassirer too is suspicious of normative aesthetics. What he disputes is Croce's apparent disregard of artistic medium. In Crocean terms, the distinctions between material modes of artistic construction are simply accidental; intuition will out in one form or another, and the very individuality of the expression becomes an argument against considering material form: "one painting is as different from another as it is from a poem; and painting and poetry have value, not because of the sounds filling the air or the color refractions in the light, but because of what they are able . . . to convey to the mind." Cassirer's complaint is that to regard distinctions in material form as "mere 'physical' differences in means of presentation" is to destroy that same unity of intuition and expression which Croce insists upon:

> As I see it, such a view does not do justice to the artistic process; for it would break the work of art into two halves, which would then stand in no necessary relation to each other. In actuality, however, the particular manner in which the work of art is expressed belongs not only to the *technique* of the construction of the work but also to its very *conception.* Beethoven's intuition is musical, Phidias' intuition is plastic, Milton's intuition is epic, Goethe's intuition is lyric. In each case this fact involves not only the surface but the very heart of their creative work. It is only with this reflection that we strike the bedrock, the true meaning and profound justifica-

tion for the classification of the arts into various "species." [*Aesthetic*]

What may here appear to be little more than an assertion on Cassirer's part takes on the weight of argument when we regard it as an integral element of his complex system: significantly it is by generalizing on this subject of genre that he concludes his ***Logic of the Humanities***. The chapter from which it is drawn, "The 'Tragedy of Culture,'" is perhaps Cassirer's most expansive and most eloquent statement of his broad humanistic concerns. Like Croce with whom he takes issue, he uses the art-construct as a paradigm of human freedom. Their vocabularies here are identical: "By elaborating his impressions, man *frees* himself from them. By objectifying them, he removes them from him and makes himself their superior." In all, there could be no better summation of Cassirer's own humanistic thrust than these words of Croce.

But we have concluded before we have begun. One specific purpose of this essay is to elucidate the concept of "genre" in Cassirer's terms, to provide in some detail the defense which he only hinted at for an aesthetics of artistic kinds. For this purpose we must keep Cassirer's dispute with Croce clearly in mind. Yet even in reviewing Cassirer's own terminology we are susceptible to two extremes. On one hand, in order to remain faithful to the spirit of the man, we cannot avoid generalizing as in the paragraph above on some of the broader issues involved. On the other—because this too is a part of Cassirer's philosophic spirit—we must proceed step by step, utilizing the scattered bits of aesthetic theory throughout Cassirer's works for what they reveal. Still, Cassirer does provide a general methodological framework for an investigation of this sort in the three volumes of ***The Philosophy of Symbolic Forms***. The attempt in this essay will be to extend his analysis of language as a symbolic form in Volume I to the particular problem of poetic language, language turned to the special purposes of the symbolic form called art. We should expect of the art of language what we find in each of the symbolic forms, a "specific structural principle," a "modality" which is "specific to it and in a sense lends a common tonality to all its individual structures."

Of all the theorists of language who have had the courage to deal with the problem of its evolution historically and logically, Cassirer is indebted primarily to two—to Herder for his concept of "reflection" and to Wilhelm von Humboldt for solving the objective-subjective crux of communication by incorporating the concept of "subjective universality" in the domain of language analysis. Together these two philosophers provide a firm foundation for an idealist's approach to language, and thus it is here that we should begin.

> Even if all language is rooted in feeling and its immediate instinctive manifestations, even if it originates not in the need for communication but in cries, tones, and wild, articulated sounds—even so, such an aggregate of sounds can never constitute the specific "form" of language. [***The Philosophy of Symbolic Forms,*** I]

Cassirer's insistence upon the radical distinction between man and beast, his identification of the symbolic forms as specifically and exclusively human—this is the axiom upon which his entire systematic philosophy rests, and it is this which accounts for his scientific preoccupation with "threshold experiences," with so-called animal languages, with aphasia and amusia, with Helen Keller and Laura Bridgman, and with as many primitive languages as were available to him. But if the materials he draws upon for demonstration most often take on an historical shape, and if his emphasis falls continually on the rudimentary or the primitive, still, the importance of his historical speculations lies in the models or patterns they offer for the philosophic analysis of linguistic conceptualization. So it is that he is willing to accept a metaphorical explanation where an historical illustration cannot be found.

On "reflection," which he designates as the specifically "human function" in the process of language formation, he quotes Herder at length:

> Man demonstrates reflection when the force of his soul works so freely that in the ocean of sensations that flows into it from all the senses, he can, in a manner of speaking, isolate and stop One wave, and direct his attention toward this wave, conscious that he is doing so. He demonstrates reflection when, emerging from the nebulous dream of images flitting past his senses, he can concentrate upon a point of wakefulness, dwell voluntarily on One image, observe it calmly and lucidly, and distinguish characteristics proving that this and no other is the object. He demonstrates reflection when he not only knows all attributes vividly and clearly, but can *recognize* one or more distinguishing attributes: the first act of this recognition yields a clear concept; it is the soul's First judgment—and what made this recognition possible? A characteristic which he had to isolate and which came to him clearly as a characteristic of reflection. Forward! Let us cry eureka! The first characteristic of reflection was the word of the soul. With it human speech was invented! [Herder, "Über den Ursprung der Sprache"]

The general Kantian orientation is apparent here, but the discovery which accounts for Herder's enthusiasm lies beyond the strict domain of Kantian epistemology, beyond the simple mechanics of cognition. An application of the Kantian "organic form"—the form which a voluntarist epistemology recognizes as the unfilled content of perception—to the cultural phenomenon of language is an extension of the Kantian model of perception to the domain of the *understanding*. It makes legitimate an analysis of *culture* in terms of the "new science" and thus is the necessary first step in the establishment of that "morphology of the human spirit" which Cassirer took as his own life's work.

More specifically, Herder's concept of reflection affirms as irreducible the unit-elements of the understanding. Such an assertion is, as we have already noted, characteristic of the whole tradition of idealist philosophy. But what is more important in terms strictly of language analysis is that it offers a new perspective on that tendency toward the general (or abstract, or universal) which seems inherent in the very process of language formation. Locke saw in the mechanics of language a model example of the sensation combined and separated: the universal is abstracted from the independent particles of empirical data. But with Herder no longer do we have "an artificial system of signs" hung onto our perceptions, the natural stuff of our experience; rather, "here perception itself, by virtue of its spiritual character, contains a specific factor of form which, when fully developed, is represented in the form of words and language." The essence of language could now no longer be sought in "abstraction from differentiation" but only in the "totality of differentiations," since it was this totality which for Herder determined the formal nature of abstraction in language.

The thrust of Herder's argument was of course directed against empiricist skepticism: having forsworn the rationalist faith in a pre-existent harmony between the ideal and the real, the universal and the particular, Berkeley for one could only conclude that if language is a mirror, the mirror of language falsifies and distorts. Humboldt followed Herder in attempting to affirm the truth value of language in general and poetic language in particular. But before we proceed to consider Humboldt's contribution to the idealist philosophy of language, we need to examine further the implications of "reflection" for Cassirer's own system in the *Language* volume.

Cassirer devotes an entire chapter to the problem of "concept and class formation in language" and opens it with his own attack on the nominalist view of abstraction. Language, it is argued, provides not only the perfect paradigm for concept formation in general; in fact, says the nominalist, language is the functional basis for conceptualization. And the means through which the concept arises is linguistic abstraction: common characteristics are abstracted from similar things, and these characteristics are identified by *names*. But the question is, how do we get the concepts by which we judge "common characteristics"? The nominalist argument on this point is simply circular: "any attempt to form a concept by abstraction is tantamount to looking for the spectacles which are on your nose, with the help of these same spectacles."

To solve this problem, Cassirer attempts to discover the conditions of that first intuition or "primary formation" effected in language which provides the foundation for later complex syntheses. The "secret of predication" is discoverable in the factors of synthesis and analysis which determine the formation of individual words, and as he builds his examination of the verbal concept from rudimentary to the complex, Cassirer explicates the term "reflection" more precisely.

The first step in concept formation is not to raise our perceptions to a higher degree of universality but rather to make them more determinate. In order for contents of perception to be classed according to similarities, they first must be identified *as* contents, they must be objectified. The content is recognized as objectively real—and yet this reality is not independent of the content. Rather, the content is determined for knowledge, "identical with itself and recurrent amid the flux of impressions." This act of "objectivization" (reflexive in the sense that it posits its own phenomenal reality) is designated a "naming": a

"whatness" is conferred upon specific content as it is individuated, and this "whatness" is its form. Thus the formal nature of the primary intuition is irreducible; but as we shall see, what logically are secondary elaborations of this process of objectivization, complex "namings," retain this same quality of irreducibleness.

The next step in the formation of the concept is the articulation of various relationships between "named" contents. The relationships are not arbitrary since they themselves disclose objective forms; yet neither can they be abstracted from their contents and considered apart from them. Now for there to exist objective and yet not substantial relationships between perceptual contents, we must conclude that the giving of a name, the logically original formation, has been a qualifying formation—the thing is named on the basis of some particular property:

> The work of the spirit does not consist in the subordinating the content to another content, but in distinguishing it as a concrete, undifferentiated whole by stressing a specific, characteristic factor in it and focusing attention on this factor. The possibility of "giving a name" rests on this concentration of the mind's eye: the new imprint of thinking upon the content is the necessary condition for its designation in language. [*The Philosophy of Symbolic Forms*, I]

All of this is rather difficult, but we need to follow the intricacies of Cassirer's argument on this one point in order to appreciate fully the impact of the general argument which lies behind it. And we are here at the heart of the one issue which will most concern us throughout this essay. Once again, the process of linguistic conceptualization is functionally identical with "objectivization" in any and each of the symbolic forms. When we turn to the specific problem of artistic genre—the designation in artistic symbols of relationships between contents of perception—there too will we see that the complex "naming" is irreducible, that the relationships are objective and yet not substantial, and that the intuition of relationships may be viewed as simultaneous with the "naming" of simple contents since this "naming" itself is a qualifying formation. For now, what we need to recognize about the nature of reflection in each of the symbolic forms is that as an intuitive transformation of impressions into representations and representations into concepts it does not abstract but *particularize* and that in its particularity it determines the whole before the part. By now it should be clear that for Cassirer reflection designates man's symbol-making function itself: the paradox of a concept which in its particularity expresses the whole is the familiar paradox of the symbol.

The final elaboration or complication of concept formation in language manifests itself in that whole which is an entire language. And here we return to Humboldt, for it is at this point that Cassirer introduces Humboldt's concept of "inner form":

> That each particular language has specific inner form meant for [Humboldt] primarily that in the choice of its designations it never simply expressed the objects perceived in themselves, but that this choice was eminently determined by a

whole spiritual attitude, by the orientation of man's subjective view of objects. [*The Philosophy of Symbolic Forms,* I]

It is this general orientation which man brings to the formation of his language—to the very process of naming—which is determinate. The example Cassirer draws here he repeats later in the *Essay on Man*: that the moon in Greek is named "the measurer" and in Latin "the glittering" indicates that words in different languages cannot be fully synonymous, for here the same sensory impression is "assigned to very different notions of meaning and made determinate by them." And the inner form of a language determines its larger structural features, not simply its vocabulary. With the help of Humboldt, Cassirer has extended the scope of the reflective process to include among the undifferentiated and irreducible unities of expression languages themselves. But here two difficulties arise. If we cannot grasp the special subjectiveness of various languages, how do we attain the objectivity in language which makes communication possible? And how can we rise from the perspectives of various languages to the perspective of language itself, since it is with language as a unique symbolic form that we are primarily concerned? These questions are, of course, directly related, and it is Humboldt again who provides the basis for an answer to them both.

With Humboldt, the subjective-objective dualism of language is almost completely resolved. Each individual language is an individual world view, and objectivity is attainable only within the community of world views:

> . . . language is subjective in relation to the knowable, and objective in relation to man as an empirical-psychological subject. Each language is a note in the harmony of man's universal nature: "once again, the subjectivity of all mankind becomes intrinsically objective." [Cassirer quotes Humboldt, "Über das Vergleichende Sprach-studium"]

We are not far at this point from the Kantian subjective universality in epistemology, but what is more important here is the idea that objectivity is not a given only to be described but "a goal which must be achieved by a process of spiritual formation." Language-making is a function of man's characteristically purposive activity. That objectivization which is an integration of individual world views into the languages by which we communicate constitutes the project of language as symbolic form. Such we should expect is the relationship too between individual artistic intuition and the articulate whole which is art.

We have so far left out of our consideration the second and third chapters of the *Language* volume, and before we can proceed to draw our own conclusions from Cassirer's systematic investigation of this primary symbolic form we need to recognize the distinction he draws between "sensuous" and "intuitive" expression. The plan of the volume as a whole is progressive—Cassirer builds from the simple to the complex, from the mechanics of naming to the "expression of pure relation"—and thus to rearrange its chapters is to violate the essential unity of his argument. Yet the sense we now have of the argument as a whole should

help enforce the point of these central chapters and carry us from language to the art of language. For in Cassirer's terms it is with the radical distinction between sensuous and intuitive expression that we find the moment of the symbolic form called art.

To this point we have reviewed Cassirer's logical demonstration that the genesis of the linguistic concept is unique. In chapters two and three he substantiates his understanding of the genesis of language on other than logical—on anthropological—grounds. At the center of the anthropologist's view of language is the element of "dynamism"—expression viewed as the movement of will and action directed toward one single point—and this concept is sanctioned even by the psychologists. Dynamism as willed action argues against the very basis of sensationalist psychology, however; and its workings are apparent even in the simple gestures of sign languages. The sensationalist would regard the pointing gesture of the human as an attenuation of the grasping or clutching movement of the animal. But this is false anthropology. Rather, Cassirer insists, the very disparity between animal *movement* and human *action* underscores the uniqueness of the human animal: "It is one of the first steps by which the perceiving and desiring I removes a perceived and desired content from himself and so forms it into an 'object,' an 'objective content.' " Since for Cassirer conceptual learning means surpassing "sensory immediacy," the human gesture of indication is a threshold experience in man; it reveals a process of objectivization as dynamic activity.

But besides the deictic or indicative gesture there is the mimetic or imitative, and this second fundamental class seems by its nature to deny that very freedom from the constraint of sensation which we regard as characteristically human: the more accurate the imitation, the more bound the "I" is to outward impression, the less spontaneous. But imitation may be understood in a broader, distinctly Aristotelian sense as something more than mere reproduction. The difference between the inarticulate imitation of animal sounds which express mere sensation and the articulate mimesis of human speech is that mimetic "reproduction never consists in retracing, line for line, a specific content of reality; but in selecting a pregnant motif in that content and so producing a characteristic 'outline' of its form." This is to say that the simplest human mimetic act is implicitly symbolic. With the spoken word, the symbolic possibilities of mimetic gestures are manifest, since the single word not only expresses immediate duration and location in the moment of its utterance but it carries with it as well reference to a systematic whole of which it is the definitive part: "the element exists only insofar as it is constantly regenerated: its content is gathered up into the act of its production." Language is vital precisely in that it is self-perfecting strictly according to its own laws. Cassirer devotes the remainder of his second chapter to this new perspective on the evolution of language through its mimetic, its analogical, and finally its fully "symbolic" phases.

Yet once again what appear to be later and more complex phases of development in the process of language formation prove instead to be aspects of the intuitive whole which is language itself, aspects separated one from another strictly for purposes of explanation. It is difficult here as throughout the *Language* volume to decide upon the logical or chronological priorities involved. Where a phonetic representation breaks the tie with a single sensuous object or sense impression to express *relation,* we have an instance of *analogical* signification. The linguistic phenomenon of reduplication is a good example. At first reduplication seems to be governed by the principle of imitation since phonetic repetition resembles repetition in the sensuous reality or impression. But there is a curious inconsistency which argues against such an interpretation. Reduplication can be an intensifier or an attenuator, and in temporal sequences it can designate past, present, or future: "This is the clearest indication that it is not so much a reproduction of a fixed and limited perceptual content as the expression of a specific *approach,* one might say a certain perceptual movement." Cassirer wants to view the linguistic phenomenon of reduplication as an implicit trope, itself an "unfilled content" which becomes functional in language according to the purpose it takes on. He has reduced what might seem a secondary and mechanical complication of the principle of imitation to a simple and primary intuition in itself. It is the semblance of purpose which this phenomenon reveals—its "content as the expression of a specific approach"—and not its relational character which Cassirer stresses. What he discovers is that in fact his tripartite division of linguistic functions breaks down; for however we wish to describe the character of the individual linguistic phenomenon in its capacity to *designate* (whether the relationship between sign and referent is imitative or analogical), in its capacity to *signify* the individual element of language partakes of the symbolic function of language as an intuitive and undifferentiated whole:

> All these phenomena, to which we might easily add others of like nature, make it evident that even where language starts as purely imitative or "analogical" expression, it constantly strives to extend and finally to surpass its limits. It makes a virtue of necessity, that is, of the ambiguity inevitable in the linguistic sign. For this very ambiguity will not permit the sign to remain a mere individual sign; it compels the spirit to take the decisive step from the concrete function of "designation" to the universal and universally valid function of "signification." In this function language casts off, as it were, the sensuous covering in which it has hitherto appeared; mimetic or analogical expression gives way to purely symbolic expression which, precisely in and by virtue of its otherness, becomes the vehicle of a new and deeper spiritual content. [*The Philosophy of Symbolic Forms,* I]

In this passage too, Cassirer seems to establish a sequence of development in language from designation to signification. But we misapprehend the very basis of his argument if we fail to recognize that language as symbolic action presupposes a fundamental identity between the objective and subjective spheres of intuition, an identity which renders designation and signification simultaneous aspects of a single process. This point should become clearer as we move on to Cassirer's third chapter.

Cassirer's primary concern in this chapter is with the interpenetration of sensuous and spiritual experience in language, and for this purpose he describes the dependence of linguistic conceptualization upon the Kantian intuitions of space, time, and number. For the substance of his argument he draws a full array of illustrations from anthropology and child psychology. But more pertinent to our investigation is the new conclusion he reaches about the relationship between designation and signification. It is true that a part of what language does is to give us new specifications for what we regard as the world of objects; this function (we might call it the "nominal" function of language, the "naming" or "noun-making" function) is expressive in that the objective and subjective spheres are correlative (to confer a name is to objectify the self). But language has another independent means of giving form to subjective existence, for the terms which disclose the reality of the self are not drawn exclusively from those of the external world. The pronoun does not "stand for" a noun: its priority is a necessary inference from the nature of the speaking situation. This new function of language (in the broadest sense "pronominal") is perhaps best exemplified by the modal distinctions in verbs, another implicit trope or system of tropes by which the "I" expresses any of various attitudes toward or relationships with the sphere of objective reality.

And yet, as Cassirer goes on to point out, this subjective "I" continually seeks objective form: the worlds inside and outside must, when language first incorporates the "I," be differentiated on objective grounds. Thus the first personal pronouns are possessive pronouns. Nonetheless, such objectivization is spiritual expression, and once more we discover that any attempt to break down the spiritual unity of expression into its component phases finally must fail:

> . . . the power demonstrated by language . . . lies not in regarding the opposition between subjective and objective as a rigid, abstract opposition between two mutually exclusive spheres, but in conceiving it as dynamically mediated in the most diverse ways. Language does not represent the two spheres in themselves but reveals their reciprocal determination—it creates as it were a middle realm in which the forms of substance and the forms of action are referred to one another and fused into a spiritual unity of expression. [*The Philosophy of Symbolic Forms,* I]

The model here for the relationship between subject and object obtains with reference to all symbolic activity; the concept of symbolic form as mediation is important for Cassirer's aesthetics.

He begins the last chapter of the *Language* volume with another of Humboldt's fundamental insights, that the true and original element in all language formation is not the simple word but the sentence. It was Humboldt who described the conceptualization of the single word as expressive of "inner form," and up to this point it has been with the single word in its formation that Cassirer has dealt almost exclusively. And yet his procedure here is identical with his procedure throughout: what might seem a secondary complication is revealed as logically or chronologically prior. Now Cassirer is able to adopt the principle of "organism" and make it his own. Aristotelian "organism" postulates the whole as prior to its parts, and language proves itself organic in nature as we see "inner form" specifically expressed in the relationship between linguistic elements.

> Here again that relation between "essence" and "form" which is expressed in the old scholastic dictum *forma dat esse rei,* is confirmed also for language. Epistemology cannot analyze the substance and form of knowledge into independent contents which are only outwardly connected with one another; the two factors can only be thought and defined in relation to one another; and likewise in language, pure, naked substance is a mere abstraction—a methodological concept to which no immediate "reality," no empirical fact corresponds. [*The Philosophy of Symbolic Forms,* I]

Thus the "progression" toward the "expression of pure relation" which characterizes the development of language culminates in the expression of pure relation, the *copula* itself, the "is." And thus the culmination of linguistic development is at the same time the threshold of judgment, the expression without which no judgment is possible. Yet even here there is no breakdown in the unity of subject and object, of the spiritual and material, in expression. For even the abstract form of pure relation cannot cast off its materiality or there can be no expression; rather,

> Here again, the spiritual form of relational expression can be represented only in a certain material cloak, which, however, comes ultimately to be so permeated with the relational meaning that it no longer appears as a mere barrier, but as the sensuous vehicle of a purely ideal signification. [*The Philosophy of Symbolic Forms,* I]

In the chapter on art in *An Essay on Man,* his most extended treatment of the subject, Cassirer focuses on two problems: first, he attempts to demonstrate the specifically symbolic character of artistic form, and second—because the danger arises immediately of our granting the domain of symbolic expression *exclusively* to art—he argues that artistic form is only one of the various symbolic realms of expression. It is here then that we should find the distinction Cassirer draws between language and the art of language. And it should be possible to elaborate Cassirer's aesthetics on the basis of our review of the *Language* volume. In particular, his discussion of genre in this chapter is only cursory. Perhaps on the basis of this chapter and the systematic philosophy of symbolic forms we can organize what are scattered arguments in defense of genre into a coherent exposition.

That same "basic division in the interpretation of reality" between objective and subjective which we found in the philosophy of language is apparent in the history of aesthetics. Only, surprisingly, philosophers of art are even more susceptible than philosophers of language of falling to one or the other of the extremes of interpretation and of failing, in either case, to recognize the specifically symbolic function of the artistic form. The chief danger in the realm of language is to regard symbol as sign, to deny linguistic form its special autonomy and its expressive power. We tend not to see the trope in the syntactical element or the word. Although of course we never deny language its practical value as a vehicle of communication, its expressive value is seldom recognized. Aesthetic theorists, on the other hand, especially sensitive to the problem of communication, either defensively assert or radically deny the continuity of art with the rest of man's activities. But there is another alternative. We can dismiss the criterion of communication as inadequate to explain either the motivation or the function of the art symbol and look instead to its expressive value. Beauty, according to Schiller, is "living form"; it is an active, "spontaneous" intuition of the forms of things. And the symbolic function of the articulate whole which is art resolves the possible antinomy between truth and beauty:

> To be sure, it is not the same thing to live in the realm of forms as to live in that of things, of the empirical objects of our surroundings. The forms of art, on the other hand, are not empty forms. They perform a definite task in the construction and organization of human experience. To live in the realm of forms does not signify an evasion of the issues of life; it represents, on the contrary, the realization of one of the highest energies of life itself. We cannot speak of art as "extrahuman" or "superhuman" without overlooking one of its fundamental features, its constructive power in the framing of our human universe. [*Essay on Man*]

But the spontaneous, constructive power of art (as of language) may be called into question by another misconception of its truth-function, the *imitation* theory.

In art as in language there is a sense in which the mimetic impulse is primary: "Language originates in an imitation of sounds, art is an imitation of outward things. Imitation is a fundamental instinct, an irreducible fact of human nature." But in the sense that imitation is constraint, in the sense that it is understood as a mere mechanical reproduction either of external *things* or internal *emotions,* in that sense the symbolic form of art would be denied the very quality of spontaneity which distinguishes it as symbolic. Art is not the shadow of reality but reality itself expressed in a unique mode of symbolization.

The artist does not find creative freedom simply by turning his attention from the external to the internal, from the sensual to the emotional life. It was Croce's mistake to think that freedom is attained for artistic intuition simply by its becoming inner-directed, that it gains its creative strength by withholding itself for the moment of art from sensuous medium. Croce's emphasis upon the spiritual is a healthy one, but as a solution to the problem of freedom in art it is simply inadequate. By denying the function of sensuous medium in the process of artistic intuition, Croce has fallen back upon an essentially imitative concept of art; he has failed to recognize that as a symbolic form art unifies the spiritual and the sensual and only thereby attains freedom:

> Like all the other symbolic forms art is not the mere reproduction of a ready-made, given reality. It is one of the ways leading to an objective

view of things and of human life. It is not an imitation but a discovery of reality. [**Essay on Man**]

The purposive activity of art as symbolic form is the same
process of "objectivization" which characterized "discovery" in language.

But the Crocean construct of the imagination is inadequate on other grounds as well. At this point we need to
explore further the way in which such objectivization
works in the symbolic domains of language and art. Once
again, the "motive for metaphor," the impulse toward the
symbolic use of language is a private one; it does not rise
out of any need to communicate. To Goethe's despair over
the way that language seems finally to be a barrier and not
a bridge between men, Cassirer answers:

> If the function of language and art were only
> that of building bridges between the inner
> worlds of different subjects, the objection that
> this task is utopian would be justified. . . . [But]
> language is *not merely an externalization* of our-
> selves; like art and any of the other symbolic
> forms, it is a *pathway to* [the realization of] our-
> selves. It is productive in that consciousness and
> knowledge of ourselves is first achieved by
> means of it. [**Logic of the Humanities**]

The artist discovers himself in the art which he creates in
that, simply, the artist expresses himself in substantial
form. For such an internal dialogue there is no direct need
for an audience. If art is to be understood as communication, it is communication, as Susanne Langer says, "not
anxious to be understood." On this point there would
seem to be no disagreement with Croce, for what Cassirer
is reminding us of is that the objectivity which we attribute
to our surroundings is a quality which we have given
them, that when the artist identifies what is inside with
what is outside he does so not to get along with the external world but to satisfy an order within. But Cassirer qualifies his argument with his concept of symbolic form as
mediation within that community of "artists" which as a
community represents the possibility for objective value in
art:

> . . . the "I" does not exist as an original and
> given reality which related itself to other
> realities . . . thus entering into communion with
> them. [Rather,] *separation* between "I" and
> "you," and likewise that between "I" and
> "world," constitutes the goal and not the start-
> ing point of the spiritual life. [**Logic of the Hu-
> manities**]

We can see more clearly the tradition in which Cassirer
stands by comparing his concept of symbol as mediation
with what Schiller has to say about the freedom which art
affords in the *Letters on the Aesthetic Education of Man*.
Schiller's starting point too is language, but the myth of
the origin of language which he draws has broader implications:

> Whilst man, in his first physical condition, is
> only passively affected by the world of sense, he
> is still entirely identified with it; and for this rea-
> son the external world, as yet, has no objective
> existence for him. When he begins in his aesthet-
> ic state of mind to regard the world objectively,

then only is his personality severed from it, and
the world appears to him an objective reality, for
the simple reason that he has ceased to form an
identical portion of it.

What art instructs us in is the capacity for reflective contemplation:

> Whereas desire seizes at once its object, reflec-
> tion removes it to a distance and renders it in-
> alienably her own by saving it from the greed of
> passion. The necessity of sense which [man]
> obeyed during the period of mere sensations,
> lessens during the period of reflection; the senses
> are for the time in abeyance; even ever-fleeting
> time stands still whilst the scattered rays of con-
> sciousness are gathering and shape themselves;
> an image of the infinite is reflected upon perish-
> able ground. . . . Nature, which previously
> ruled him as a power, now expands before him
> as an object. What is objective to him can have
> no power over him, for in order to become objec-
> tive it has to experience his own power. [Schiller,
> *Letters on The Aesthetic Education of Man*]

What Schiller describes as the objectivizing power of the
artistic symbol Cassirer would extend to all of man's symbolic forms, which is to say from one point of view that
all of man's symbols are artistic and from another that art
holds no unique sway over the powers of the imagination.
This is a point to which we will return immediately, for
in it lies the crux of Cassirer's dispute with Croce. But
about Schiller we should notice first that he makes no distinction here between artist and audience but rather
speaks of man in his *aesthetic state of mind* and second,
and in this connection, that the criterion of communication between artist and audience plays no part in the
power the symbol has in freeing the human spirit through
objectivization.

The ideal audience, that audience the writer writes for, is
his projection of himself in the realm of freedom; the reader who approximates this ideal realizes that freedom
which for Cassirer separates man from beast. What we
learn from our experience of art is that the artist creates
in a state of freedom; what we do then, because we too
would be free, is to become artists ourselves, to recognize
the manifold symbolic forms which constitute culture as
human creations and strive to make them beautiful. To return to Schiller:

> Does . . . a state of beauty in appearance exist,
> and where? It must be in every finely harmo-
> nized soul; but as a fact it is only in select circles,
> like the pure ideal of the Church and state—in
> circles where manners are not formed by empty
> imitations of the foreign, but by the very beauty
> of nature; where man passes through all sorts of
> complications in all simplicity and innocence,
> neither forced to trench on another's freedom to
> preserve his own, nor to show grace at the cost
> of dignity.

Cassirer and Croce both subscribe to the idea that culture
as a purposive activity is a possible realm of expressive
freedom.

But Croce would subsume all of man's cultural activities

under the broad heading of aesthetics. Cassirer spends a good portion of his chapter on art in the ***Essay on Man*** marking the bounds of the aesthetic domain, marking it off from others of the symbolic forms:

> Language and science are abbreviations of reality; art is an intensification of reality. Language and science depend upon one and the same process of abstraction; art may be described as a continuous process of concretion. . . . [Art] does not inquire into the qualities or causes of things; it gives us the intuition of the form of things.

> What we call "*aesthetic* semblance" is not the same phenomenon that we experience in games of illusion. Play gives us illusive images; art gives us a new kind of truth—a truth not of empirical things but of pure forms.

> Science gives us order in thoughts; morality gives us order in actions, art gives us order in the apprehension of visible, tangible, and audible appearances. . . . Art may be defined as symbolic language. But this leaves us only with the common genus, not with the specific difference. In modern aesthetics the interest in the common genus seems to prevail to such a degree as almost to eclipse and obliterate the specific difference. Croce insists that there is not only a close relation but a complete identity between language and art. . . . There is, however, an unmistakable difference between the symbols of art and the linguistic terms of ordinary speech or writing. These two activities agree neither in character nor purpose; they do not employ the same means, nor do they tend toward the same ends. Neither language nor art gives us mere imitation of things or actions; both are representations. But a representation in the medium of sensuous forms differs widely from a verbal or conceptual representation.

Taken together, these remarks scattered throughout the chapter all point in one direction. The specific difference between art and language is a difference of medium, and so Croce, who would leave out of aesthetics any consideration of material form, misapprehends the very process of artistic creation.

It is precisely this consideration of material form which demands that as critics of art we recognize the function of artistic genre. The principle of Aristotelian "organism" which is evident in language in the priority of the sentence over individual syntactical elements and individual words—a phenomenon in language which Humboldt designates "inner form"—has its parallel application within the realm of art. Artistic intuition is unique and undifferentiated in its logically and temporally primary phase: it is an intuition of the whole which only subsequently (or consequently) becomes differentiated into its parts. Thus Cassirer may speak of the various idioms of art and the architectonic process by which intuition finds material expression.

Such a statement carries its own qualification, for the intuition does not seek out the medium of its expression; rather, characteristically of symbolic activity in general, the medium itself is a part of that intuition:

> The context of a poem cannot be separated from its form—from the verse, the melody, the rhythm. These formal elements are not merely external or technical means to reproduce a given intuition; they are part and parcel of the artistic intuition itself.

Croce argues that to remove from the individual poem a single one of its constituents is to destroy its essential unity, that "the poem is born with [its] words, rhythms, and meters." "From this," says Cassirer,

> it also follows that the aesthetic intuition is born at the same time—i.e., as musical, plastic, lyric, or dramatic—and that these distinctions are, therefore, not mere verbal labels or notations which we fix on works of art, and finally, that true differences of style, divergent directions of artistic intention, correspond to these differences. [***Logic of the Humanities***]

The term "epic" as it applies to an epic poem works in two ways. On one hand it *designates* a certain complex of characteristics which seem derived, seem to be secondary elaborations of individual words or lines or images when those elements of the poem are taken as its simplest constituents—when, that is, we read the poem word by word, line by line, image by image. An epic poem is a complex poem. At the same time, though, the simplest constituent element of an epic poem is that single, comprehensive intuition (or "direction of intention") which is its epicness. And this is what the term epic *signifies*. When does that epic form come into being? Not, of course, until the complex of the poem which it designates is complete. And yet that comprehensive intuition which "epic" signifies exists prior to the individual words, lines, images, etc., which embody it since it determines their relationship one to another. In more simple terms, the form is fulfilled over the course of the poem—fulfilled and discovered simultaneously. In more practical terms, the reader comes to an epic poem with a certain expectation of its major form, and that expectation is satisfied or frustrated.

But our "practical" conclusion begs several very practical questions. Is genre in fact an intuition born of the artistic medium and not a mechanical and academic deduction on the artist's part from a tradition of historical precedents? Can the intuition which is genre ever be perfectly expressed? Is its expression invariable? What specifically is the relationship between one epic poem and another? Cassirer answers questions like these in a convincingly practical way by examining the function of tradition in the history of culture at the conclusion of his ***Logic of the Humanities***.

Clearly the kind of coherence, the unique "rationality of form," which the successful poem or statue or piece of music exhibits is a sufficient guarantee and the only guarantee of its truth, for such coherence is the only criterion for symbolic expression. Yet the symbolic form called art, like the other symbolic forms, is a comprehensive and articulate whole with its own specific modality (representation in the medium of sensual forms) and its own history.

Two opposing factors are continually at work in the historical evaluation of art and the arts, the factor of "constancy of form" and the factor of "modifiability of form." But this evolution, this process, can only be carried on by individual artists. The tradition remains in one sense autonomous, and the individual retains his freedom within that tradition:

> The creative process must always satisfy two different conditions: on the one side, it must tie itself to something existing and enduring, and, on the other, it must be receptive to new use and application. Only in this way does one succeed in doing justice to both the objective and the subjective demands [implicit in the creative act]. . . . The tie to tradition is most readily evident in what we call technique in the various arts. It is subject to rules as fixed as in any other use of tools; for it is dependent upon the nature of the materials in which the artist works. Art and craft, imaginative activity and skill, have disengaged themselves only very slowly; and it is precisely when artistic achievement is highest that we are likely to find a particularly intimate union between these two factors. No artist can really speak his language if he has not previously learned it through the relentless experience of give and take with its materials. And this is by no means restricted merely to the material-technical side of the problem. It also has its exact parallel in the sphere of form as such. For, once created, even the artistic forms become part of the fixed tradition handed down from one generation to another. . . . The language of forms assumes such fixity that specific themes, with their determinate modes of expression, seem so firmly grown together that we encounter them again and again in the same or only slightly modified forms. [*Logic of The Humanities*]

Indeed Cassirer observes of lyric form that "there are, after all, only a few great and fundamental themes to which lyric poetry may apply itself." The reason for this phenomenon lies not so much in the limitations of human experience, of course, as in the restricted nature of that experience which lyric intuition discloses. For Croce, such "restriction" seems a constraint, but only because he persists in regarding form and matter as antagonistic forces in the process of creation. With Cassirer, the opposition of form and matter is resolved in their reciprocal determination:

> From the standpoint of phenomenological inquiry there is no more a "matter in itself " than a "form in itself "; there are only total experiences which can be compared from the standpoint of matter and form and determined and ordered according to this standpoint. [*The Phenomenology of Language*]

The concept of genre is a meaningful one precisely in that the degree of determination which it identifies is the measure of freedom achieved. Such, as Harry Slochower describes it, is the thrust of Cassirer's insistence upon art as mediation.

But there can be no perfect lyric, no perfectly lyrical poem. Nor is the expression of lyric intuition invariable.

We can erect critical paradigms for genres in art—in fact as critics responsive to generic unity within individual works of art we are obliged to—but we will find no single example which perfectly conforms to the paradigms we erect. Does this invalidate the concept of genre as a critical tool? Here we can appropriate Cassirer's defense of Burkhardt's generic "Renaissance man":

> Shall we regard it, in the logical sense, as a null class—as a class containing no single member? That would be necessary only if we were concerned here with one of those generic concepts arrived at through empirical comparison of particular cases, through what we commonly call "induction." [*Logic of the Humanities*]

But neither the historian nor the critic of art works quite this way. What Burkhardt discovered about men of the Renaissance was no common characteristic or set of characteristics but rather a "specific ideal connection," a "unity of *direction,* not a unity of *actualization,*" a "common task," the manifestation of a specific "will."

The historian's apprehension of epochal characterization, because it is a "logico-intellectual activity which is *sui generis,*" is not functionally different from the aesthetic critic's apprehension of genre. The relationship between one epic poem and another is, likewise, an ideal relationship: epic poets cooperate in the task of disclosing epic experience, and the critic who is able conceptually to identify such unity of direction has penetrated into that articulate whole which is the symbolic form of art as it evolves in time. The process of that evolution, the dynamics of innovation in the arts, is, as we should expect, much like that in language itself. To speak of genre as static form with fixed characteristics would be to deny the vitality of culture as an achievement:

> In this process the hardened forms are also ever and again melted down, so that they cannot "clothe themselves in rigid armor"; but on the other hand, only in this process do even the momentary impulse, the creation of the moment, receive their continuity and stability. This creation would, like a bubble, have to dissolve before every breath of air if it did not, in the midst of its originating and becoming, encounter earlier structures—forms already originated and in existence—to which it may cling and hold fast. Thus even this which has already come into being is for language not merely material, against which foreign and ever stranger material is ever pressing; but is the product and attestation of the same formative powers to which even language itself owes it existence. . . . And the same fundamental relationship exhibited here in the realm of language holds true of every genuine "symbolic form." [" 'Spirit' and 'Life' in Contemporary Philosophy"]

We can return in this connection to Schiller's description of the relationship between artist and audience. The critic's activity is finally not much different from that of the artist himself, for in his apprehension of genre the critic engages in the process of objectivization inherent in all symbolic activity. Artist and critic alike are liberated for participation in that culture which is their common task.

Louis Carini   (essay date 1973)

SOURCE: "Ernst Cassirer's Psychology: A Unification of Perception and Language," in *Journal of the History of the Behavioral Sciences,* Vol. IX, No. 2, April, 1973, pp. 148-51.

[*In the following essay, Carini explores the often-neglected implications of Cassirer's language philosophy for the field of modern psychology.*]

While Ernst Cassirer's three volume philosophy of symbolic forms is clearly a philosophy, there is also a psychology presented there that Cassirer assumed would be the forerunner of any modern psychology. But Cassirer's optimism on that score was not borne out, for that psychology has been completely bypassed. And yet, Cassirer was so astute on scientific matters that Margenau, the Yale physicist, in his Preface to Cassirer's **Determinism and Indeterminism in Modern Physics,** concludes that, except for minor details, Cassirer's 1935 views may still be taken as the last word on that issue. The psychology that Cassirer espoused had the novel feature of unifying perception and language; it should prove worthwhile then to examine the psychology that Cassirer outlined in the 1920s.

The psychology that Cassirer provided was related to Gestalt psychology, but there are features in it which also differ from what the Gestaltists presented, and these characteristics have been lost to American psychology. He proposed that even our percepts of things are a way of formulating those things, and thus a symbolic element had to be contained in our most ordinary perceptions of things. He says:

> If perception did not embrace an originally symbolic element, it would offer no support and no starting point for the symbolism of language. [The difficulty in] the skeptical critique of language consists precisely in making the universal begin only in the concept and word of language, whereas perception is taken as something utterly particular, individual, and punctual. When this is done, there remains an unbridgeable gap between the world of language, which is a world of meanings, and the world of perception, which is regarded as an aggregate of simple sensations.

A symbolic moment in perception would take it out of the realm of being ". . . utterly particular, individual, and punctual," and provide a bridge between perception and language. The two would be unified by sharing a symbolic component.

The assumption of an aggregate of simple sensations as comprising perception was also one of the tenets of introspectionist psychology. Gestalt psychologists, of course, objected to the sensationistic view, and proposed instead that all percepts were themselves the fundamental units, and were not decomposable into elementary sensations. But Cassirer goes further than that. He is suggesting that if psychology starts from the proposition that perception must be devoid of even a potential, personal meaning before the labels of language are applied, then words and percepts become arbitrarily separated when they in fact operate together and belong together. Words are not the only containers of meaning with percepts meaningless; there is a symbolic component in percepts which places perception and language in the same realm. The arbitrary, and merely assumed, separation between words and percepts has the tendency of making irreconcilable that which belong together.

Cassirer continues discussing the skeptical critique which allows only to language a symbolic component:

"But the question takes on a different form once we realize that the dividing line that is here drawn between the worlds of perception and language should actually be drawn between the worlds of sensation and perception." Sensations may be meaningless, but percepts are not meaningless and thus the symbolic must already be present in the perceptual world. When we observe the Necker cube it may at first present its nearer face as up, and then with continued viewing it presents its front face as down. Up is one meaning perceptually presented to us; down is a second meaning perceptually presented to us. Language does not give us these different meanings; the meanings inhere directly in the percepts themselves.

From this point of view, and as evidenced in the Necker cube example, perception changes from being a merely passive receiver of stimuli, to being an organizer of stimuli in an active fashion. As Cassirer formulates it:

> Perception is no longer purely passive, but active, no longer receptive, but selective; it is not isolated or isolating, but oriented toward a universal. This perception as such signifies, intends, and 'says' something [just as the Necker cube 'says' that the front face is up, and though we have to use language to express that fact the *upness* is given in the perception]—and language merely takes up this first significatory function to carry it in all directions, toward realization and completion. The word of language makes explicit the representative values and meanings that are embedded in perception. . . .

Cassirer shows just how language does this in a real-life example. He reports on walking through a wood and seeing before him on the path some lime saturating the ground. Then suddenly he realized that it was not lime, but merely the sun shining through the trees onto the ground. Now he saw light on the ground, but he had just seen lime on the ground. Lime is one meaning and it is given directly as a percept; sunshine is a second meaning—also given directly as a percept. Thus even in perception there can be seeings from differing perspective. It is Cassirer's position that differing perspectives would have to arise in a symbolic realm. And though the perspectives of perception are limited, they are there and thus share with a word the symbolic form. Language greatly extends the meanings inherent in perception, but language is not on a different order from perception.

Cassirer has thus proposed a new view of the relations between perception and language. But how can we know that what he says is so? For he intends here no mere abstract proposition, but a proposal grounded in fact. He is not proposing merely an alternate interpretation of the phenomena, but a belief that there can be an empirical determination in the facts. That determination is to be found, according to Cassirer, in the known perceptual facts derived from brain pathology. Indeed, he says:

> . . . the thoroughly individual, singular perception which sensationalism and with it the skeptical critique of language sets up as a supreme norm, an ideal of knowledge, is essentially nothing more than a pathological phenomenon . . . which occurs when perception begins to lose its anchor . . . [Cassirer observed Gelb and Goldstein's brain damaged patients. He says of one of them] . . . his sensations of light and color were intact or so little modified that their impairment could be regarded as irrelevant to optical recognition. [Then he quotes Gelb and Goldstein.] 'The patient sees colored and colorless spots. . . . He also . . . sees whether a certain spot is . . . thin or thick, large or small, short or long . . . altogether, the spots arouse a chaotic impression and not, as in the normal individual, the impression of a specifically formed whole.

The sensationistic impressions that the introspectionist doctrine espoused appear to be found only in the brain damaged individual. His perceptions are spots rather than organized entities whose meaning is directly given: lime, sunlight, face up, etc. The spots do not possess spontaneous meanings, but are empty of meaning and can be used only by making intellectual inferences about them.

And despite the severity of his brain damage, this patient is able to make inferences about what is happening. At one point Cassirer is walking with the patient when there is a man sweeping about 50 paces away. Cassirer reports:

> The patient says spontaneously: 'That man is sweeping, I know it. I see him every day.' (What do you see [Cassirer asks]?) 'A long line, then something down below, sometimes here, sometimes there.' On this occasion he relates spontaneously how he distinguishes people from cars on the street. People are all alike: narrow and long, cars are wide; you notice that at once, much thicker.

Instead of seeing a person, he sees a kind of line and infers that it is a person; instead of seeing a car, he infers that the extended spot is a car.

It is the brain damaged then who fit the picture that a sensationalist and intellectualist psychology provided. The optical picture of their world is one of isolated fragments which have no meaning. And the meaning is then inferred by an intellectual operation. The sensationalistic and intellectualistic doctrine which was ment to describe all normal perception is found to apply only to the brain damaged. As Cassirer says: "In normal perception every particular aspect is always related to a comprehensive context, an ordered and articulated totality of aspects, and draws its interpretation and meaning from this relation." The French-English dictionary before me is certainly particular, but it has a general component. That dictionary has a place among all other dictionaries and 'draws its interpretation and meaning from this relation.' The percept, just as is the concept of language, 'is always related to a comprehensive context.' Cassirer has here united his defi-

nition of the concept with his definition of the percept. The concept is a general term which organizes and relates those items that belong together and separates them from those that do not belong with them. But the percept also, he says, has the quality of relating and separating. The lime seen is related to other white powders—and this is given in the percept—and the lime is separate from the nonpowders—and this too is given in the percept itself.

Cassirer has united percepts and language by showing that the sensationalistic and intellectualistic doctrines that would rob the percept of its own meaning apply only to the brain damaged. He then shows that percepts themselves have, in rudimentary form, the relating and separating qualities that concepts have. And since concepts are linguistic, language and percepts share a symbolic component and function in a like manner. Even today the empirical fields of perception and of the psychology of language have not fully grasped this unification.

Leon Rosenstein   (essay date 1973)

SOURCE: "Some Metaphysical Problems of Cassirer's Symbolic Forms," in *Man and World,* Vol. 6, No. 3, September, 1973, pp. 304-21.

[*In the following essay, Rosenstein explores Cassirer's philosophy of symbolic forms, placing it within the context of works by other philosophers, particularly Immanuel Kant and G. W. F. Hegel.*]

If Cassirer's philosophy of symbolic forms were to be classified in traditional terminology, it could perhaps best be called a critical, functionally-monistic, objectively-relativistic, cultural idealism. The meaning of such a nomenclature as well as its essential inadequacies can only be exposed, however, through an analysis of the structure and purpose of the concept of symbolic forms upon which Cassirer bases his philosophy. It will be seen that these forms are a *function* of the human spirit, since they form the constitutive pre-conditions of all experience, knowledge, and activity.

What kind of function are these forms? Cassirer claims both that (in his early work) it is a *way of seeing* (it "may be said of any symbolic form . . . that in each of these is a particular way of seeing, and carries within itself its particular source of light . . . it is not a question of what we see in a certain perspective, but the perspective itself ") and that (in his later work) it is a *way of acting and becoming,* of expressing and existing. Thus, his philosophy must be both an analysis of the "structures" of human consciousness *per se* and a "re-construction" of all that human history has concretely produced in the form of what may broadly be termed culture. Cassirer himself refers to his philosophy as a *critique of culture,* "an inquiry which will accomplish for the totality of cultural forms what the transcendental critique has done for pure cognition," and as a "phenomenology of human culture," showing how Spirit renders the world intelligible to itself through the symbolic forms, which collectively constitute a unity of particular ways of seeing and acting at different stages of human thought. Thus, "humanity attains its highest insight into objective reality only through the medium of its own activity and the progressive differentation of that activity." Philosophy as comprehending the immanent relations of the symbolic forms to one another will be a systematic philosophy of culture, the meaning, content, and significance of whose forms is dependent upon the nature of those relations. What Cassirer seeks is a unity of "transcendental meditation" in function of the symbolic forms with regard to their "grammar" and "index of refraction." He seeks as well a unity of world and spirit, of the human universe (and not simply "intellectual comprehensiveness" as such), of man and culture as actor in context. Thus, the task of philosophy is the exposition and comprehension of the function of symbolization in establishing the dynamic cultural community of mankind as achieved in the functional unity of the symbolic forms, and, consequently, the comprehension of the significance, content, relation, and meaning of these forms for mankind as maintained by that functional unity.

If the influence of the philosophies of Kant and Hegel seems particularly apparent in the preceding introductory remarks, this is to expected. Indeed, I believe it will be most fruitful if, before going on to a fuller exposition and subsequent criticism of the symbolic forms, we note briefly which difficulties inherent in the philosophies of his two great predecessors Cassirer tries to avoid and why, which of their positions he accepts, which he rejects.

Beginning with Kant, we find the most basic similarity of approach—namely, Kant's conception of epistemology as commencing with the notion of mind "making" experience through constitutive principles, his emphasis upon the necessity of analysing the pre- conditions and limits of knowledge rather than attempting the proof of a correspondence between knowledge and reality. That is, beginning with Kant's thesis that there can be no objectivity without synthesizing forms, Cassirer expands these to include a great variety of syntheses. "Facts" alone are never given and have no meaning, because they are nothing without context, without symbolic form. Cassirer equally maintains Kant's position with regard to the dependence of forms upon intuitions of sense. This mutual dependence is maintained in the Kantian manner through the developed notion of the "schema" (an earlier version of the symbolic form) which is both intellectual (as agreement with categories) and sensuous (as having actuality and significance with regard to objects). "The schema is the unity of concept and intuition, the common achievement of both factors." Again, just as Kant took for granted the objective facts of science due to its success, so Cassirer generalizes and accepts the factual givenness and employment of the many forms of culture. These latter somehow are held to justify, presuppose, postulate, or require the entire philosophical characterization of the formulating principles of mind with which he deals.

What Cassirer rejects in Kant is his rationalism and intellectualism, understood as his lack of historical perspective, his indifference to cultural evolution and its myriad manifestations. Calling for a wider application of the "critical method," he affirms that "cognition . . . is only one of the many forms in which the mind can apprehend and interpret being." Thus,

the Copernican revolution with which Kant began, takes on a new and amplified meaning. It refers no longer to the function of logical judgment but extends with equal justification and right to every principle by which the human spirit gives form to reality . . . The fundamental principle of critical thinking, the principle of the "primacy" of the function over the object, assumes in each special field a new form and demands a new and dependent explanation . . . in such a way as to disclose how in all of them there is attained an entirely determinate formation, not exactly of the world, but rather making for the world, for an objective, meaningful context and an objective unity that can be apprehended as such. [*The Philosophy of Symbolic Forms*]

Likewise, Cassirer drops the distinction between noumenal and phenomenal, for, since symbolization does not permit a real separation of principle and object (of sense and the senses), the dualism of form and content is done away with. Removing, as well, the Kantian distinction between regulative ideals and constitutive principles, we find that purpose also is constitutive of the understanding of Nature with regard to the organic forms of life and that, consequently, the "whole as product" is constitutive of the understanding of culture with regard to human creations (and is therefore historical). Moreover, scientific and/or logical thinking, which Kant takes as his paradigm, is not to be thought of (as Kant believed) as an innate characteristic of all human understanding but itself as an historical achievement.

Despite the usual emphasis upon Kantianism both by Cassirer himself and his interpreters it seems that Hegel had an equal if not greater influence upon Cassirer's philosophy. Perhaps the most pervasive mutual presupposition is that the ultimate subject of philosophy is the development of Spirit in the form of man. Then, too, there is common view of the internal (subjective) as the expression and phenomenal comprehension of the external (objective)—and vice versa. Coupled with the consequent rejection of "things in themselves," the historical evolution of mind is conceived of more as taking place in spirit and life rather than as existing between inquiring subject and fixed object. Again, just as Kant's schema can be seen as the precursor of Cassirer's symbolic forms, so equally can Hegel's concept of the concrete universal and the notion. Thus, Cassirer claims, for example, that symbolic forms are their own criterion—the achievements of each one of which "must be measured by itself, and not by the standards and aims of any other." Then, too, as with Hegel's dialectic of the notion, Cassirer conceives of different symbolic forms as each claiming more than is its "due" in the course of its historical development.

In the course of its development every basic cultural form tends to represent itself not as a part but as the whole, laying claim to an absolute validity, not contenting itself with relative validity, but seeking to imprint its own characteristic stamp on the whole realm of being and the whole life of the spirit. From this striving toward the absolute inherent in each special sphere arise the conflicts of culture and the antinomies within the concept of culture. [*The Philosophy of Symbolic Forms*]

Complementary to this line of thought is the emphasis upon the historical evolution of forms and their possible presence in the present. As he states in his *Essay on Man*:

> Human works . . . are subject to change and decay not only in a material but also in a mental sense . . . they are in constant danger of losing their meaning. Their reality is symbolic . . . and such reality never ceases to require interpretation and reinterpretation . . . a new synthesis—a constructive act . . . Behind these fixed and static shapes, these petrified works of human culture, history detects the original dynamic impulses . . . and this is where the great task of history begins.

Cassirer's conception of history is also parallel to Hegel's insofar as he also conceives of the levels of culture (the growth of the spirit), which are nevertheless historical, as contemporaneously present. Indeed, as we shall see, Cassirer seems to construct a double classification—the modes or dimensions of the growth of spirit (the principles of differentiation or orientation within given symbolic forms) and the formative or constitutive categories or principles inherent in all symbolic forms—not unlike the classification Hegel uses in his philosophy of art, for example, wherein the phases of art (symbolic, classical, romantic) intersect with the various art types or media of embodiment (architecture, sculpture, poetry, etc.). Neither last nor least of Cassirer's borrowings from Hegel is his insistence upon the comprehension of the parts through the whole, for consciousness cannot posit anything without ultimately everything—or at least everything within the complex of a given symbolic form. Yet this whole, he claims, is to be construed as a dynamic whole and a unity which is not a simplicity.

What Cassirer rejects in Hegel is the latter's conception of philosophy as having reached it end in the exhaustive synthesis which he himself had created. Cassirer conceives of his philosophy as a program to progress, a method to discover and understand things as they are in the mode in which they appear. Rather than sweeping them in dialectic to become concrete for the castle of the Absolute, Cassirer opposes in principle philosophy's subsumation of other cultural forms to itself in such a way as to abrogate the autonomy and independent importance of each by allowing finally only the cultural form of "logic" to be autonomous qua form. Although for Cassirer, too, there exists a unity, it is not a substantial "One," but rather a community of function; and the whole is not such as to exclude its parts as integral and valid appearances. To insist upon a dynamic evolution of the symbolic forms in the same manner as did Hegel with his notions would coalesce the independence and unique structure of each, vitiate their peculiar "directions of creativity," and collapse and negate their internal value and truth. That is why, Cassirer claims, this "metaphysical formula must be transformed into a methodological one." (As will be seen, however, it remains questionable whether or not Cassirer himself is successful in his attempt to do this.) In any case, Cassirer implies that Hegel's failure on this account is due, first, to

his being "too subjective" in forgetting that there must always be something besides mind in the form of givenness, and second, to his insistence upon the determinism of a dialectic bringing forth stages of knowledge in such a way as to make culture entirely contingent upon necessary history.

Whatever a fuller exposition of the Kantian and Hegelian influences upon Cassirer's symbolic forms might disclose—and it seems evident that Cassirer's philosophy is essentially and must be viewed essentially as an attempted synthesis of both these great traditions—let us turn now to Cassirer's philosophy itself. We have seen how Cassirer is concerned, on the one hand, to deal with the "critical" and cognitive, to describe and analyse the workings of conception, maintaining the objectivity and logic of the Critique, without its narrowness, and yet, on the other hand, to deal with the evolutionary and cultural, to account for the equal truth of the historical and human, including the relativity of all the cultural forms, without reducing them. What, then, are these symbolic forms, cultural forms, regulative-constitutive concepts whereby Cassirer hopes to achieve this? They collectively comprise a mediating function as organs of reality furnishing the regulative contexts of objectivity, constituting and conditioning what (in the various universes of perception, expression, and communication) is meant by "the thing signified" (the object), and thus exhibit "sense in the senses." And it is through this functional aspect of his philosophy—representing the process of mind in material and material in mind—that Cassirer attempts to avoid both traditional philosophical pitfalls of psychologism and ontologism.

How do these functions function? How is it that "a variety of media will correspond to various structures of the object, to various meanings for 'objective' relation"; that "knowledges frame their questions each from its own particular standpoint and, in accordance with this standpoint, subject the phenomena to a special interpretation and formulation"; that

> every authentic function . . . embodies an original formative power . . . creates its own symbolic forms . . . none reduced to, or derived from others . . . each designating a particular approach in which and through which it constitutes its own aspect of 'reality'? [*The Philosophy of Symbolic Forms*]

To answer this Cassirer sets up various categories or ways of approaching the subject. His prime concept, "symbolic form," covers in its functioning at least three areas. There are, first, the forms of culture proper (myth, art, religion, language, science, etc.). Second, there are what may be alternatively termed "constitutive forms," "categories," "symbolic relations," or "formative principles" (space, time, causality, number, etc.). Then, third, there seem to be the three "modal forms," the historical stages, moments, dimensions, or levels of culture, "orientations" of the cultural forms whereby the latter can be shown to exhibit a continuous growth of spirit—the expressional (affective-emotive), the representational (volitive-teleological-"common"), and the systematically-significatory or intellective-theoretical (scientific).

Through these three general form functions, it is proposed, any phenomenon of nature or creation of culture can in principle be understood—through some formative or constitutive principle by which it is constituted for the mind, on some modal level, and qua some symbolic (cultural) form in whose "world" it will find its definition and "live."

However, to my knowledge Cassirer never in fact systematically takes a phenomenon (material, object, experience, event) through all its possible meanings ("lives") so as to illuminate in a concrete and coherent way both its manifold appearances and the appearance of its manifolds. Let us therefore attempt to choose a phenomenon and, interpreting it by means of two symbolic cultural forms qua one of its characteristics (i.e., "common" or "analogous" relations), at least point out what would seem to be taking place through some of the functions designated above.

Before taking a particular instance, however, let us outline the nature of this process *in general*. We begin with an experience or phenomenon, which, n.b., does not however exist as a "primary datum," and with a world or context which does not exist in itself as a necessary and unique antecedent condition given. Rather, there exists always a function or structure of integration and differentiation operating upon the phenomenon. There is, more precisely, a reciprocity: through the "sensed" (object, experience) a world (manifold, complex) comes into being; by "intending" a world the sensed itself has meaning ("sense"); and by the world intended the object is constituted in its particular objectivity. "What defines each particular is that in it the whole of consciousness is in some form posited." It (the object or experience) has a vectoral character, and "this precisely is the nature of a content of consciousness—it exists only insofar as it immediately goes beyond itself in various directions of synthesis." This "part" expresses the whole of its context; yet the "whole is not obtained from its parts . . . does not originate in its parts, it constitutes them." Thus from the experience there arises one of a variety of points of view, each under the head of some *symbolic form*. This form will have its *formative principles*—or set of categories, "relational forms," "original forms of synthesis," or "universal relations"—each (or the totality) of which, though having its "own self-contained, formal law," will be viewed under the particular *"index of modality"* concerned. These formative or constitutive principles are said to be "indispensable wherever . . . a manifold is to be broken down and articulated according to determinate forms"; whereas the modal forms lend a "common tonality" to the way in which all the "individual structures" are construed in the sphere of the symbolic form in which this articulation is effected. In this way, the index of modality of a relation becomes its "meaning for the whole" and will be involved in the motive of explanation of an experience; for the "quality" of the relation—"the particular type of combination by means of which it creates series within the whole of consciousness, the arrangement of whose members is subject to a special law," as Cassirer calls it—may function in different ways. And through the integrated relations thus posited under the given index of modality there arises in

the constituting intersection of the symbolic form a "world picture."

In particular, let us take as an example the experience or phenomenon of lightning for our illustrated reconstruction of these functions. Let us attempt to apprehend this phenomenon under the two worlds (symbolic cultural forms) of myth and science with regard to the relation (i.e., under the constitutive form) of causality and in accordance with its emergent modal forms. From the point of view of the mythic consciousness (i.e., under the cultural form of myth), one of the constitutive (or relational) forms of the experience "lightning"—namely causality—is conceived (though implicity) as having the quality of "succession" (an inherent character of the relation) under the principle of simple contiguity in time and space where all factors in general are actively present in the integration and expansion of the particular. The value of this unique instance is especially of concern for the mythic consciousness. The relation's "index of modality" (the context of the relation and its meaning for the whole) under this symbolic form thus becomes the concern for a motivated efficacy guided by the implicit concept of an originating potency and will. Since the mythic consciousness perceives the drama of physiognomic characters in and through the relation of causality in this fashion, the cultural level (or dimension) of the modality (the orientation of the form) is the "expressive." The "expression-phenomenon" is "inherently sombre or cheerful, exciting or appeasing, frightening or reassuring." An interpretation of the experience of this particular phenomenon in this mythic view, then, in the relation of causality, could well result in the concept "wrath of god." This in turn could (would, has) led to the world picture "all things are full of gods."

From the point of view of the theoretical consciousness, on the other hand, the relation of causality with regard to the experience "lightning" is conceived (here, presumably explicitly) as having the quality of succession under the principle of differentiation and limitation of particulars (here, diverse and not co-temporal or co-spatial). For the theoretical consciousness of especial concern is a rule, as the condition for the relation of specific factors in general. Thus, the index of modality of the relation here being the requirement of a stipulation of the means through which phenomena are constituted in experience, the theoretical consciousness reduces the phenomenon "to certain universal conditions." Subordinating it "to that universal complex of conditions we call nature . . . assigning a place to it within this complex," the cultural level of this index of modality here is the "systematically-significatory and intellective." In this "conception-phenomenon" the "moments which condition the order and structure of the perceptual world are grasped as such and recognized in their specific significance. The relations which on the former levels were established implicitly are now explicated." An interpretation of the experience in the scientific view, then, in the relation of causality could well result in the concept "electromagnetic charge." And the parallel world picture might be "all things are determined in their becoming according to causal laws of which the laws of electrodynamics are an instance."

Cassirer distinguishes the "different" causalities (or, more properly, the different indices of its modality) as follows:

> Mythical thinking is by no means lacking in the universal category of cause . . . This is evidenced . . . by the mythical cosmogonies and theogonies . . . But mythical causality is distinguished from the scientific principle of causality by the characteristic to which the opposition between the two concepts of the object ultimately reduces itself . . .
>
> . . . In scientific thinking diverse phenomena are grasped as a unity and subjected to one and the same universal *rule*. This isolating abstraction, which singles out a specific factor in a total complex as a "condition," is alien to mythical thinking. Here every simultaneity, every spatial coexistence and contrast, provide a real causal "sequence" . . . whereas empirical thinking is essentially directed to establishing an unequivocal relation between *specific* causes and *specific* effects. [*The Philosophy of Symbolic Forms*]

Apparently, the possible number of formal variations for this phenomenon is indefinite. A similar explication could be made with regard to any formal relation or on any cultural modal level or within any symbolic form complex. So, for example, under the symbolic cultural form of the developed religion of the Greeks, the phenomenon of lightning might be conceived more concretely as "weapon of Zeus." In the aesthetic sphere (another cultural form), in a painting by Ryder, for example, or in the Sixth Symphony of Beethoven, different conceptions, different meanings of this phenomenon arise. And, in parallel order, depending upon the world (complex, cultural symbolic form) in which it occurs, different factors (constitutive and modal forms) become relevant or irrelevant to it. So, the world in which it occurs does not require of Zeus's thunderbolt that it be heard or of Beethoven's programmatic dissonant percussions that they be mapped out in length, of lightning as a geometric configuration of hot gases that it be held sacred, or of an electrostatic charge that it be a symptom of will.

Let us take yet another phenomenon, an artificial thing, a book. We may imagine the book to appear as an object within the world of the mythic consciousness. Among its formative principles we may list "number." Number, though again having its "own self-contained, formal law," will be viewed here under the index of modality called the expressional or affective-emotive. The "meaning" or "quality" of number as a formative principle of the whole will be conceived as having the special characteristic of singularity. It will have the appearance of being a "one and only"; and its especial concern or value for the mythic consciousness will be its holiness, its preeminence. An interpretation of the experience of this particular object phenomenon in the mythic view with regard to its singularity could well result in the notion "the law of the land." This in turn could lead to the world picture "divinity instructs mortals in their daily affairs." From the point of view of the theoretical consciousness, on the other hand, the relation of number with regard to the experience "book" may be conceived as having the quality of diversity. It will have the appearance of being one sample among many such

codifications or concretizations of thought in language and writing. Its especial concern might be the truth value of its contents in comparison with other similar samples. An interpretation of the phenomenon in the scientific view, then, with regard to this formative principle could well result in the notion "man produces books." And the parallel world picture might be "books are manifestations of man's attempt to obtain and preserve truth."

In the above examples I have attempted to imagine or reconstruct how Cassirer's forms could be shown to intersect at their "instantiation" in order to reveal the structure and functional unity of consciousness as the representation of one content in and through another. It is precisely this type of functional analysis which would be consistent with Cassirer's metaphysic. "Metaphysics' should be taken guardedly, however, since (as we noted in the foregoing discussion of Kant and Hegel) it is the traditional monolithic and rationalistic conception of Being as the ground of metaphysics to which Cassirer objects. Employing such notions as symbol rather than ontological structure, vectoral (intentional) content within a relative context rather than objective data, function rather than substance, if Cassirer conceives an ontological ground for his philosophy at all, it is one which is entangled in manifold beings perpetually becoming rather than a fully integrated and articulated Being. Yet Cassirer does seek a functional unity and what seems (or should seem) most crucial to him is precisely this unity of function within a diversity of forms, an identity of phenomenal surd behind differences in its intentional possibilities. The critical question is—Does he (can he) render such an account?

Do the symbolic forms hold together as Cassirer wishes and yet maintain their independence? Does he face the same difficulties of Plato's "mixing of the forms"—the substantial here replaced by the functional? Is he not, in a more comprehensive way, "deducing" (against Kant's own injunction and as Kant himself nevertheless did) contents out of *a priori* conditions—or at least treating that which is empirically distinguished as somehow the consequence of an *a priori* distinction? And, influenced by Hegel's evolutionism of spirit's progressive self-enlightenment, does he not propound a significant and unexplained bias towards certain of the "more developed" symbolic forms? Let us attempt at least partially to answer some of these questions and to account for the relevance of traditional metaphysical problems to Cassirer's philosophy of symbolic forms.

Given the preceding exposition of the functions of cultural forms, constitutive forms, and modal levels, we may now discuss some of the problems inherent in this formulation. How are these functions and the components within them known—directly through empirical investigation, *a priori* as preconditions, qua their position within the total system? What is the essential (or functional) difference between them, since they are, as Cassirer claims, irreducible? Have they a hierarchy? What is its criterion? A history? Then what is its relevance to this hierarchy? What is the number of each? How definite are the ranges of each? Ultimately all these questions must be answered before one can come to understand how their interrelations form a unity or how Cassirer's philosophy forms a unitary system.

Let us begin with the functions of the modal level (the modal forms or dimensions of spiritual growth, as Cassirer calls them)—the expressive, the representational, and the scientific-theoretical. Apparently these are known and dinstinguished, not *a priori,* but directly through empirical investigation and through knowledge of their historical evolution and position within the entire system. Hence, they are not invariant or necessary pre-conditions as such, but, rather, attitudes, modes (moods), possible transfigurations of experience. But Cassirer never goes so far as to say so, much less to say whether or not they are the only possible levels. Further, Cassirer gives no definite number of them (the theoretic, for example, has itself three stages—mimic, analogic, and symbolic). Most important, however, there seems to be a difference and hierarchy between them according to their evolution based on the greater or lesser "objective representation" (the polarity of "sense within the senses") which they exhibit. Yet we are offered no criterion for "objective representation." Further, with the mythic cultural form at one end and the scientific at the other, the cultural forms themselves tend to fall into the various modal levels through the progress of history. But, Cassirer claims, it is more than an historical progression from primitive to modern consciousness which has occurred in and through these modes. It is also psychological (from child to adult) and organic (from animal to human) development, a parallelism of ontogeny and phylogeny. But then it remains to be asked how truly we now can exist as apprehending creatures in the expressive mode, for example. Can we react to myth, can we see in it, as did primitive man? Could one ever know, in principle? Cassirer seems to identify the "a-logical" with the "pre-logical" (particularly in *Language and Myth*); and so, presumably, anyone who functions on the expressive level in the mythic world would have to "grow up" or transverse millenia before he could comprehend Kant's *Critique of Pure Reason.* Such a thesis of historically grounded hierarchy and evolution needs support which is not offered.

The internal problems of the cultural forms and constitutive forms are more acute. First of all, is there really a difference between them and what is it? Are not the cultural forms also constitutive? Charles Hendel, in his introduction to the English translation of Cassirer's *The Philosophy of Symbolic Forms,* claims Cassirer "abolishes the Kantian disparity between the regulative ideas and constitutive forms—all are constitutive." He notes that Susanne Langer agrees with this interpretation, whereas Carl Hamburg disagrees, finding Cassirer "retaining a distinction between constitutive form and cultural form." This contradiction, however, seems to be incorrectly conceived. The cultural forms are constitutive, but that does not make them identical with the constitutive forms or make the latter a subclass of them. As we have already noted with regard to causality, for example, the relational form does constitute an experience with regard to one of its aspects, bringing to it this specific continuity of series. But the kind of constitution of the experience by the cultural form is not of the same sort, for it brings to the experience

a world of meaning valid for all relations thus constituting "this possible" objectivity. Whether one wishes to call either of these functions regulative or constitutive is a matter of indifference—neither is more real or necessary than the other.

But what about these constitutive or relational forms themselves? Unlike the case of the modal forms, Cassirer seems to think of these as being known strictly as preconditions, as the necessary or *a priori* invariants of all possible experience. Thus, though apparently not agreeing with Kant's stipulation of the exact number of nature of these relations (most—time, space, casuality, etc.—are traditional) and though the "qualities" of each may vary with the modal and cultural forms, their function for consciousness remains essentially similar. In consequence they seem to manifest no hierarchy or history in themselves—though of course, they progressively come to be more and more recognized for what they always were and are. They *seem* to be the only set of relations possible. Cassirer refers to them as "ultimate logical invariants which lie at the foundation of every determination," as "constituting the unity of consciousness as such and therefore just as well that of mythic consciousness and that of pure knowledge," and as "the necessary pre-conditions for all meaningful experience." What is supposed to be logically invariant is the "self-contained formal law" of the particular relation. But what precisely happens to this "invariant" under the shiftings and transmutations which occur through the indices of modality? If, for example, the essential quality of causality is, in the mythic consciousness, an amorphous spatiotemporal contiguity and, in the scientific consciousness, a specific and unequivocal condition in accordance with a rule, what then remains invariant *a priori* in this relational form—especially since Cassirer believes that only the latter view of causality is genuinely valid of reality—why are they both "causality"?

The cultural forms, which (it seems) Cassirer conceives of as the symbolic forms proper, raise similar, if more complex, questions. This is to be expected, because they are the combination, or better, the "intersection," of the relational, and morals forms. The first difficulty concerns the knowledge we have of them. Cassirer, on the one hand, thinks of them as historically evolving, empirically discoverable divisions of functions of consciousness, so that, as performing the self-emergence of consciousness, "each new symbolic form . . . signifies a revelation of inner and outer." On the other hand, he understands them as in some sense preconditions and *a priori* classifications. Not "merely empirical," not reducible in any way to one another, they are *"organs* of reality" which is nothing apart from them. Thus, would they be known both (either) by position within the evolved system as found and (or) by that for which they must be necessarily the preconditions? Or, are they merely hypothetical postulates? This ambiguity might in part be explained by their dual aspects of modality and relational-constitutiveness—but not entirely. The history of the cultural forms of language, myth, and art discloses (as Cassirer himself is the first to assert) that they all have a common origin in the mythopoeic consciousness of the primitive mind. Yet Cassirer never explains how the one time unity was as it was or why the forms separated and distinguished themselves, except to state it as a fact (necessary or not we are not told) of the development of the self-realization of spirit. Further, we can well ask whether the cultural form of "art," for example, is the same as it was in (or would be to) the primitive consciousness? Apparently Cassirer believes so. But even after the distinction of the forms of science, myth, religion, and art had been made at some theoretical point in history, I think it difficult to maintain that these forms or worlds of apprehension were the "same" as now, even in so general a way as an attitude or tuning of consciousness. Moreover, granting the evolutionary distinguishment of these forms into more definite areas out of some unity, this does not imply, as I think Cassirer would conceive it, that there is a destiny of progressive differentiation. Indeed, in the modern world there seems to be a reconvergence of cultural forms in many areas.

> The "ultimate" in Cassirer's philosophy is the human spirit, for the human spirit as represented in culture is a variety, a functioning, a meaning, a center, a task, and a unity.
>
> —Leon Rosenstein

Considering, thus, the "mixing" of the cultural forms, the further question of their internal hierarchy arises. That is, if we grant definitive indices of modality for the relational within, say the cultural form of art, what about the internal differences of modality within the cultural form? Is there a difference between the indices of modality in art in general and such particular arts as music and sculpture, between twelve-tone music and baroque music? Or in science, is there a difference index of modality of (say) temporality between "science," and biology and geophysics and quantum mechanics?

But how many forms are there, after all? Is there a symbolic form of love, of baroque, of leisure, of hippydom? Cassirer never makes it clear, though there seems to be a limit. But what is the criterion of this limitation; and what is the criterion for limiting the scope of each? Like Hegel, Cassirer says that the criterion of the truth of a symbolic form is internal. Where, however, without Hegel's Absolute, can Cassirer find the external criterion even for the number of symbolic forms? Shall only the "most important" symbolic forms, the top section of the hierarchy, be considered true symbolic forms? If so, then it must be asked what is meant by "importance," for what and to whom? Cassirer (early) seems to think in terms of importance to cognition for knowledge, and (later) in terms of importance to humanity for the service of mankind. But which of the forms will fulfill either of these requirements? Shall it be language, which is "most pervasive," being basic to all other symbolic forms, as "an all embracing medium in which the most diverse forms meet"? Shall it be art, which is the "richer, more vivid and colorful image of reality,

and a more profound insight into its formal structure," and which in contradistinction to language and science ("abbreviations of reality") is an "intensification of reality . . . a continuous process of concretion"? Shall it be science, which is "the last step in man's mental development . . . may be regarded as the highest and most characteristic attainment of human culture . . . and is the most important subject of a philosophy of man"? Or shall it be some other, say, the one in which most people most of the time are happiest? Cassirer seems clearly to favor science, for this is "the realm of pure meaning; and in it henceforth is grounded all certainty and constancy, all final truth and Knowledge." Yet Cassirer states at the outset that, regarding the symbolic forms in general, "no attempt is made to fit them into a single simply progressing series."

What emerges from all this is that Cassirer's attempt at a unity which is functionally homogeneous, historically cumulative, and substantially heterogeneous, is at least incomplete. Ultimately, this unity is a promise and a task rather than an accomplishment, for there remains a *de facto* multi-dimensionality. The symbolic forms are the ideal unification of that which is both *a priori* and historically contingent, just as in any symbolic instance there exists a polarity of formal and sensuous elements. And yet multi-dimensionality itself appears to be necessarily the unity of Cassirer's philosophy, for "it is characteristic of the nature of man that he is not limited to one specific and single approach to reality but can choose his point of view and so pass from one aspect of things to another." That is why Cassirer seeks in the symbolic "a purely functional unity [which] replaces the postulate of a unity of substance and origin." Nevertheless Cassirer presents us with an historical unity and cannot entirely avoid the substantial. And though Cassirer does attempt to avoid Being, his symbolic function could be seen as "the ideal center" for "the conviction that the varied and seemingly dispersed rays may be gathered together and brought into a common focus." And since the unity is functional it is indeed an activity of creative process, not simply the effect, but the task of culture, its "common project" as the "expression of human spirit." For it is only as the community of mankind that the many "configurations towards Being . . . are ultimately held together by the unity of meaning." In this sense is achieved the

> task of demonstrating the unity of the spirits as opposed to the multiplicity of its manifestations,—for the clearest evidence of this unity is precisely that the diversity of the *products* of the human spirit does not impair the unity of the *productive process,* but rather sustains and confirms it. [*The Philosophy of Symbolic Forms*]

Hence, the "ultimate" in Cassirer's philosophy is the human spirit, for the human spirit as represented in culture is a variety, a functioning, a meaning, a center, a task, and a unity. And now we can better understand Cassirer's reference to the Heraclitean "lyre" at the close of the *Essay on Man*—the unity of function being the harmonious chord plucked as part of a composition in a given musical style as one of many harmonies and created by many tensions, and the musicality of the lyre itself being that through which all harmonies in all styles have become and do become present.

Of course some of the general objections cited above to Cassirer's symbolic forms still hold. Ultimately it may be nothing more than Cassirer's bias towards "science," rationalism, and evolutionism which creates several of the difficulties and contradictions we have found there, causing him to assert that the most abstract and historically advanced form is therefore the most "human"—and not art or myth which are only immediate, implicit, and noncumulative unities. Likewise the existentiality of the individual and personal becomes subsumed in the historico-cultural unity, for as a critique of culture it becomes difficult to include the functions of the personal. Thus, for example, error, preference, and value cannot be discriminated or judged beyond the given symbolic form in which they appear.

In any case, what ultimately is most valuable in Cassirer's philosophy of symbolic forms is the fecundity of the functional notion of the symbolic form itself. Through it—and its appreciation of a "perspectivism" and "relativism" not identical with "subjectivity" and "illusion" (however difficult these may be to specify)—great and necessary breadth is allowed to knowledge and truth. Of no less worth is the continual emphasis upon the humanity of knowledge, the hopeful guarantor of an intelligibility without sterility and perennial progenitor of a creativity without indirection.

David R. Lipton   (essay date 1978)

SOURCE: An introduction to *Ernst Cassirer: The Dilemma of a Liberal Intellectual in Germany, 1914-1933,* University of Toronto Press, 1978, pp. 3-16.

[*In the following excerpt, Lipton provides an overview of the evolution of Cassirer's philosophical thinking against the backdrop of German politics from 1914 to 1933.*]

Ernst Cassirer was born to Jewish parents on 28 July 1874 in Breslau. His was an extended family from the upper middle class with commercial and publishing interests. He lived in Germany until May 1933, when he left his homeland because of the Nazi regime's anti-Semitic policies. Even though for a large part of his life Cassirer confined most of his social and intellectual activities to his family circle and a few select colleagues, the course of his life and work were clearly influenced by the events of the period from 1871 to 1933.

The most striking characteristic of Cassirer's life and work was his commitment to preserving the spiritual autonomy of the individual. Throughout his philosophical career Cassirer never doubted that humanity in general and man in particular were free. This fundamental belief was at once the beginning and the end of his intellectual endeavours. Cassirer's desire to affirm the fact of human freedom as completely and convincingly as possible reflected his deep-seated liberalism and its ethical ideal. In the tradition of Kantian ethics, he believed that each individual should be treated as a rational being and as an end in himself, rather than as a means to an end.

It was the courage to use one's own reason, together with

his belief in human freedom, that Cassirer sought to pass on to his contemporaries. In pursuing this goal he found himself on the horns of a dilemma. The greater his effort to create a rationalist, liberal world view acceptable to himself, the greater his estrangement from the majority of his compatriots. Conversely, the more he tried to accommodate his contemporaries, the greater his infidelity to his rational, liberal ideals. In order to resolve this dilemma he would have had to rethink his fundamental assumptions and constantly expand the scope of his work. While he was prepared to do this to some extent from 1916 to 1926, he refused to doubt the ability of human reason to satisfy humanity's deepest needs. Instead he fell back on a dogmatic rationalism in the critical years of 1927 to 1933. His overly intellectual world outlook undermined his defence of individual autonomy. Few people found his approach to the human condition very palatable or inspiring.

One of the most remarkable features of Cassirer's work was his consistency. Throughout his life he returned to the idea that man as an individual contained within himself the principles underlying the development of all humanity. In his own words, 'in man as a microcosm all lines of the macrocosm run together.' By stressing the universal significance of the individual and by conceiving each man as an agent of all humanity, Cassirer provided his reader with the theme for comprehending his wide-ranging studies. Whether he dealt with a problem in physics, the Renaissance conception of art, the evolution of language and myth, or the German idea of freedom, Cassirer always argued as if the matter under consideration were best understood through the thoughts of various individuals.

Cassirer's projection of the individual into the centre of historical and cultural developments was a reflection not only of his own bias but of that of his profession as well. German academics, particularly from 1890 to 1933, saw themselves as the bearers of German culture, as a chosen, élite group, which was endangered by the rapid industrialization of Germany. The values of the emerging materialistic society were, they felt, antithetical to their own values. German intellectuals, like their counterparts in other countries, believed they owed their positions in German society to their educational qualifications, not to material or monetary considerations. Hence, they exalted the spiritual quality of a man rather than his financial situation. This view of the world was summed up in the concept of *Kultur*, which sought to elevate the individual to a superior level of existence through the cultivation of his ethical, artistic, and intellectual abilities. The individual was trained to form and perfect the world within and around him. The process assumed universal significance because each individual was potentially a single manifestation of humanity's collective activities. It was this attitude towards culture and the cultivated individual that German intellectuals felt they had to protect from a hostile, rapidly industrializing society and to transmit to future generations.

Cassirer entered the German university system in 1892 and completed his doctorate in 1899. His first years in academic life coincided with the university community's heightened awareness of its isolation from the mass society which supported it. Faced with a society increasingly un-interested in the autonomy of the cultivated man, Cassirer too adopted the German academicians' view of the individual. This kind of individualism postulated that the cultured individual could achieve a total understanding of every aspect of human activity yet preserve his identity in the faceless masses of an industrialized society.

During the first two years of his academic career Cassirer wandered from subject to subject and from university to university. However, his vacillation between various subjects abruptly ceased in the summer of 1894, when, while taking a course on Kant given by Georg Simmel, Cassirer was introduced to the work of Hermann Cohen, leader of the Marburg School of neo-Kantianism. During one of his lectures, Simmel announced that 'the best books on Kant are written by Hermann Cohen; but I must confess that I do not understand them.' Cassirer apparently held his teacher in such high regard that a strong recommendation by Simmel was enough to induce him to give Cohen's works serious consideration. He became convinced that Simmel's estimation of Cohen had been correct and went to Marburg in 1896 to study philosophy under Cohen.

Despite his move to Marburg and although he later became a prominent member of the neo-Kantian movement, Cassirer remained influenced by Simmel. The most important theme that Cassirer absorbed from Simmel was the idea of the unavoidable and insoluble conflict between the individual and society. Simmel's view of this conflict was not original in itself. It was a classic expression of the German academicians' anxieties about the future of the cultivated individual in a society which demanded more regimentation and standardization from its members as well as a statement of liberal credo affirming the rights of the individual. Simmel believed that the practical problem of society always revolved around the tension between societal forms (that is, institutions, laws, customs, opinions) and the individual's desire for freedom to create his own life style. Simmel envisioned this tension between freedom and form as an insoluble conflict between 'the whole, which imposes the onesidedness of partial function upon its elements, and the part, which itself strives to be a whole.'

Cassirer sought to place this conflict in a wider philosophical and historical context. By placing the free and rational individual at the centrepoint of his speculations, he connected the history of humanity with each individual's struggle to establish himself as a spiritually autonomous entity. For Cassirer it was important to realize that the perpetual conflict between the individual and his society, a conflict which resulted in the quest for personal freedom, was the essential ingredient of history.

Cassirer's individualism was in effect the intellectual synthesis of three closely related ideas: a specific idea of freedom, a commitment to the use of reason, and a cosmopolitan view of history. Each of these ideas was meaningful only in combination with the other two. A man was free in so far as he used the dictates of reason to guide his own activities and to comprehend his place in the continuous chain of human history. The dictates of reason were those principles that made knowledge and existence intelligible

to all men. On realizing that those principles were the collective, historical creation of humanity, each individual could live in accordance with them and consider himself free. For to live according to one's own rules is to be free. The universal or cosmopolitan view of history was attained once the individual recognized that all peoples participated in the growing awareness of the role of reason in human history, and that this awareness itself was the condition of the possibility of individual freedom. Cassirer's concept of the individual was in effect an imperative: to be free one must have the courage to follow the dictates of reason in one's own life, and thereby to discover the meaning and place of reason and freedom in human history. Cassirer's *Kultur*-oriented vision of history first clearly emerged in his wartime study of German thought (1916) and was to remain a permanent fixture of his philosophical speculations until his death. Significantly, his cosmopolitan humanism later played a very important role in his studies of the philosophies of the Renaissance (1927) and the Enlightenment (1932).

The idea of progress was another cardinal element of Cassirer's historical vision. In the intellectual sense, progress was humanity's increasing realization that all men became free through the use of reason. In political terms, progress was the actual expansion of human freedom through the increasing application of reason to political and social affairs. Ideologically speaking, this position placed Cassirer in the liberal camp. Liberals, especially in the late nineteenth and early twentieth centuries, cherished the belief that the history of mankind was in effect the story of man's achievement of freedom and of the establishment of a political order which would institutionalize and preserve human freedom. A republican parliamentary system of government was considered the best way to guarantee the individual's autonomy by protecting his right to be in opposition to the regime and to other members of society. Generally, Cassirer's view of politics was in the Kantian tradition of political liberalism, where politics was primarily a matter of principles, not of actual ruling. The split between theory and practice, between the formulation of the theoretical basis of a liberal regime and the means of establishing that regime in fact, afflicted Cassirer's politics as it did all other German followers of Kant's idealist conception of liberalism.

When mixed with his own neo-Kantian inclinations, Cassirer's commitment to individual liberty and the *Kultur* ideal resulted in a unique outlook on the world (*Weltanschauung*). While his writings went through different phases, his rationalist liberal world view remained the same. There were three distinct yet closely related levels to Cassirer's *Weltanschauung;* these provide the schematic basis for this analysis of his work. First, on the philosophical level, he remained a neo-Kantian who maintained a relational theory of knowledge. He believed that conceptual relations, that is, a priori ideas, were the basis of any comprehension of reality. Furthermore, knowledge of reality was not something that required the acceptance of immutable facts. On the contrary, such knowledge was an endless task of establishing relations between facts and values, between the particular and the whole. Second, on the cultural and historical level, Cassirer remained a cosmopolitan humanist who included all peoples, from primitive tribes to the inhabitants of industrial urban centres, in humanity's movement towards freedom and enlightenment. Third, on the political or ideological level, Cassirer remained dedicated to liberal values. The development and preservation of free and rational individuals was a task that always absorbed his energies.

Cassirer's *Weltanschauung* evolved through several distinct phases. In the first phase (1899-1914), we see him as a philosopher in Imperial Germany, dealing with the problem of knowledge as discussed in neo-Kantian circles in Germany from 1871 to 1914. The second phase, the years 1914-22, covers the reorientation of his intellectual standpoint in connection with the issues arising in the German academic community and in reaction to the war of 1914-18. In the years 1923-33, his Weimar period, Cassirer tried to unite all his past and contemporary intellectual activities with his liberal political ideas in order to create a lasting and all-encompassing spiritual synthesis—a critique of human culture.

In the first stage of his Weimar period, 1923-26, Cassirer waged a successful fight to maintain the harmony of his *Weltanschauung*. This intellectual equilibrium, which is one of my major considerations, rested on Cassirer's balancing of a specific view of humanity's progressive enlightenment, a commitment to a logical analysis of consciousness, and a respect for and interest in the totality of concrete life forms. In the second stage of the Weimar years, 1927-33, Cassirer's orientation changed, and he returned to his pre-1914 interest in epistemological problems which focused primarily on an analysis of human consciousness. This was because he felt it would be the best way to defend his rationalist outlook on the world. . . .

From 1933 to 1945 [Cassirer] was a political refugee. After being driven from his homeland by the Nazis Cassirer moved to England, then to Sweden, and finally to the United States, where he died on 13 April 1945. In the last twelve years of his life Cassirer gradually re-examined his philosophical assumptions in the light of the events of 1933-45.

LIBERAL VALUES AND PRACTICES: THE LIBERAL DILEMMA

Although no record exists of Cassirer's political preferences prior to the first world war, he probably voted liberal. Since the Napoleonic era liberalism had championed Jewish emancipation. This circumstance and the fact that most Jews were middle class predisposed them to vote overwhelmingly for one of the liberal parties. Apparently, many of them felt that liberalism offered the best way of attaining full political and social equality for all Germans without jeopardizing the freedom of the individual. In any event, Cassirer's politics largely remained a private matter, and he deliberately avoided active party politics.

However much Cassirer side-stepped political issues, he could not escape his Jewish background. He was constantly affected by the anti-Semitic feelings pervading German society in general, and more particularly the government-controlled universities. These sentiments not only delayed his acquisition of a university teaching position until 1906;

they also caused the abrupt termination of his academic career in April 1933. Cassirer's interest in individual freedom and tolerance of human diversity was not only an intellectual response to his times but an emotional one as well.

Cassirer's correspondence with his fiancée in December 1901 clearly showed that his difficulties in securing a university post were due to the anti-Semitism of many university officials. Statistics dealing with the religious composition of the student bodies and teaching staffs of German universities from 1890 to 1910 confirm that German Jews were both over-represented in the universities and subject to discrimination. In Prussia from 1888 to 1890 Jews constituted about 9 per cent of the university student body. From 1890 to 1910 approximately 12 per cent of the university teaching assistants were Jews. So far there seemed to be no evidence of discrimination. On the contrary, the Jews seemed to have more than held their own, since between 1890 to 1910 they never constituted more than 1 per cent of the German population. However, when we examine the percentage of Jews in the higher academic ranks, the bias against them becomes clear, since less than 3 per cent of the full professors were Jews. One would expect that the teaching assistants would in the usual course of events rise in the ranks, so presumably Jews were promoted far less frequently than their Christian counterparts. Most Jews, like Cassirer, were never promoted at all in Imperial Germany. Despite the publication of his work on Leibniz's system in 1902 and his growing reputation as a philosopher and a scholar, Cassirer was not invited to take up a university teaching position. When he was finally appointed a Privatdozent at the University of Berlin in 1906, it was primarily due to the personal intervention of Wilhelm Dilthey, and he remained in that position until 1919. No university in Imperial Germany ever rewarded Ernst Cassirer with the professorial position he deserved.

Cassirer's experiences would probably have embittered most people, but this apparently never happened to him. He was often described by his contemporaries as possessing an imperturbable inner serenity coupled with a gracious bearing towards others. These personal qualities did more than prevent Cassirer from becoming embittered. In his work he transformed the social and cultural disharmony surrounding him into an intellectual vision which sought and often found the deeper unity underlying the discordant world of appearances. His belief that a unity pervaded human affairs and his unrelenting efforts to give all human thoughts and actions a proper place in his philosophical speculations imbued Cassirer's work with a liberal and open-ended quality.

What connected Cassirer to his liberal compatriots in active politics was not so much any participation in political activities, which he abhorred, but his commitment to liberal beliefs. Cassirer's high estimation of the role of freedom in human affairs, his inclination to approach politics through the dictates of reason, and his faith in the inevitability of progress were beliefs held, in varying degrees, by all liberals.

Cassirer's politics displayed the characteristics of one of the two major tendencies of German liberal theory and practice. As with European liberalism generally, the German variant suffered from tension between its idealist and materialist tendencies, but in Germany this clash became acute.

The idealist conception of liberalism gave priority to abstract interpretations of such matters as individualism, the inalienable and natural rights of man, and the necessity of human freedom. Kant became the great philosophical representative of this liberalism. It used the idea of freedom as the means of uniting ethics with politics. Cassirer showed the connection between Kant and liberal values when he said that freedom was the beginning, the centrepoint, and the goal of Kant's entire philosophy.

The materialist conception of liberalism focused on more practical matters. Its position may be summarized in one phrase: laissez faire. A government's best achievements would be those which cleared the way for a free market economy. The abolition of internal tariffs and the suppression of all organizations (for example, guilds) interfering with the free circulation of labour would be good examples of desirable state action from this liberal viewpoint. These liberals were not so much interested in the preservation of individual freedom as in the establishment of a social order that would guarantee the supremacy of the profit motive together with its economic system, the free market economy.

While the materialist-idealist dichotomy split German liberals into two opposing camps, the conflicting demands of freedom and equality further divided them. Generally speaking, liberals extolled the virtues of freedom, be it of the spiritual or free market variety, but feared equality. In social terms this fear was translated into anxiety about the masses, while in political terms it became an aversion to satisfying any substantial number of their demands for equality. This attitude decisively affected the history of modern German liberalism. Since the revolution of 1848 most liberals, except for the radical democrats, had initiated a pattern of political behaviour that effectively isolated them from the majority of the German people. When the crunch came in 1848-9, and the middle classes had to choose between order or democracy, they refused to make common cause with the latter. Subsequently, the liberal movement could not, from 1848 to 1933, collectively decide on and consistently follow one course of action in relation to the radical democrats or, later, the social democrats.

With the readmission of the Social Democratic Party (SPD) into the legal political life of Germany in 1890 the principal elements of the German political spectrum were set until 1918. Those groups on the left wanted reform or revolution; those on the right favoured the status quo or a return to the past. From left to right the political groups were situated as follows: socialists, left (idealist) liberals, Catholic Centre party, right (materialist) liberals, conservatives. After 1890 socialism and democracy became equivalents in the public mind; social democracy was synonymous with the industrial masses' demands for the equalization of social and economic benefits. The rising power of social democracy demanded a response from the liberals as it did from the other political and social groups.

In political terms, liberals had to ask themselves whether they were willing to co-operate with the SPD in parliamentary elections—a problem of party tactics that exacerbated the idealist-materialist tension in liberalism.

The tactical problems of the liberals were aggravated by a lack of cohesion in their supporters. Their electoral support came largely from the industrial upper class, large and small merchants, artisans, white collar workers, civil servants, and farmers. The demands of these groups were bound to conflict and create striking fluctuations in the party programs which limited the liberals' capacity to enter coalitions with other parties. When left (idealist) liberals, like Theodor Barth and Friedrich Naumann, tried from 1893 to 1910 to build bridges from the liberal centre to the SPD to strengthen the forces of political reform, they were rebuffed both at the polls and within their own parties. In 1910 the left liberal parties unified themselves into the Progressive Party. However, this unity was a fragile one. After the leadership of the party decided to cooperate with the socialists in the runoff federal elections of 1912, the bulk of the Progressive Party's voters preferred to cast their ballots for the conservative rather than for the agreed-upon SPD candidates.

The liberals' reaction to social democracy was an important symptom of their larger problem: between 1871 and 1933 German liberalism encountered insuperable difficulties in reconciling theory and practice. In the wake of national unification in 1871, the rapid industrialization of Germany combined with the nationalist and authoritarian tradition produced a society which placed liberalism on the defensive to such an extent that its theoretical principles had little chance of being realized.

While industrialization had produced an economic system where the middle classes became important in the economic life of the nation, this same economic progress undermined the political independence and social cohesion of the middle classes. The industrial revolution in Germany had created an urban working class (mostly represented by the SPD) that had, at least in theory, a unified vision of history and society, which made it the implacable enemy of the middle-class or capitalist economic system. On the other hand, industrialization fragmented the middle class so that it had 'lost most of its homogeneous social character by the end of the nineteenth century.' Thus, while middle-class liberal voters remained identifiable to their opponents, that is, to the socialists on the political left as well as to the anti-capitalist right-wing parties like the conservatives, they lost their own sense of identity.

The growth of nationalism in Germany also aggravated the liberals' dilemma of choosing between two courses of action, one leading to political and social reform, the other to a passive acceptance of the Imperial status quo, neither of which gave much satisfaction to liberal ideals. While the process of industrialization undermined the social basis of liberal unity, nationalism undermined its spiritual component. German liberalism expounded a system of government under law (*Rechtsstaat*). In the *Rechtsstaat* a society would be governed only by those laws which had been approved by the members of the national community. Brute force or dictatorial government had no place in this concept of the state. While this was only an ideal, it was crucial to German liberalism. Once this principle of government under law was violated or abandoned, a good portion of liberal ideology was meaningless. Between 1862 and 1866 Bismarck ruled Prussia without the consent of the Prussian parliament. The liberals led the opposition to Bismarck's policies, but after the Prussian victory over Austria in 1866, many liberals went over to Bismarck's side and voted for a bill in parliament (the indemnity law) to legalize the past four years of his de facto government. In March 1867 the liberals institutionalized this division with the formation of the National Liberal Party, which broke away from the Progressive party.

The significance of this split was clear. The desire to create a unified German nation had become more important to many liberals than the rights of the individual and the rule of law. Henceforth, a large portion of the middle classes favoured the benevolent dictatorship of the Prussian monarchy, which would not hesitate to sacrifice the rule of law for the maintenance of national unity. Bismarck had succeeded between 1867 and 1871 where the liberals failed in 1848-9; Germany had been unified by force of arms and not by the force of law. The National Liberals felt they were realistic in accepting Bismarck's *fait accompli* and that the Progressives were too idealistic in rejecting it. The Progressives sensed that their former political allies were all too willing to disregard the rule of law, the principal safeguard of individual freedom, when it suited their immediate needs. While the National Liberals became enthusiastic supporters of the Bismarckian system, the Progressives acquiesced to the new political realities. They continued to stress the importance of individual freedom within the context of a *Rechtsstaat* and attempted to build political bridges to the left, culminating in their 1912 electoral agreement with the social democrats. After the founding of the Weimar Republic in 1918, the German People's Party (DVP) took the place of the National Liberals in the liberal political spectrum, and the German Democratic Party (DDP) assumed the tasks of the Progressive Party.

The division of German liberalism into two distinct wings not only was a reaction to the pressure of events but also constituted an ideological response to the question of the relation between freedom and equality. The liberal right (the National Liberals and DVP), arguing from materialist premises, extolled the virtues of economic freedom and opposed any movement towards social equality; they tended to co-operate with the more conservative parties. The moderate and liberal democrats (the Progressives and the DDP), starting from idealist premises, tended to see individual freedom and social equality as interrelated issues and hesitantly sought to co-operate with the left. In spite of their different ways of dealing with the issues of freedom and equality, both the materialists and idealists ultimately failed to sustain the liberal's main cause—the autonomy of the individual. In their responses to the events of 1871 - 1933 all German liberals progressively, though not intentionally, undermined the very ideal they sought to preserve. While the materialists were so committed to their society that they readily sacrificed the individual to the demands of the nation and its economic system, the idealists effectively undermined their own ideals by mak-

ing them too abstract and general enough to satisfy everyone. Unfortunately, such programs failed to win massive electoral support (with the exception of the elections of January 1919). Regardless of their actions liberals could not remain true to their ideals and gain widespread popular support. The failure to solve this dilemma became the tragedy of German liberalism.

NEO-KANTIAN LIBERALISM: POLITICS TREATED ABSTRACTLY

It was the idealist component of German liberalism between 1871 and 1933 that influenced Cassirer's outlook on the world and was in turn reflected in his life and work.

Cassirer had in common with the idealist liberals a certain intellectual predisposition which may be called the formalizing tendency—the tendency to conceive concrete problems in abstract terms. Cassirer's formalizing inclination was expressed by his commitment to neo-Kantianism. He felt that this philosophical movement continued the work of Kant, whose ultimate goal had been to dissolve the facts of the natural world into the pure functions of knowledge. For Cassirer these pure functions were none other than human judgments which established relations between the ideas of the mind and the data of the natural world. This 'relational' conception of knowledge and existence transformed every concrete fact into pure relations of facts and values. Thus, when considering legal and political matters, Cassirer shared Leibniz's belief that the study of law focused on definitions and logical proofs, not on historical facts and personal experiences.

The formalizing tendency of neo-Kantianism appealed to many legal and political academicians whose tradition exhibited an inclination for dealing with concrete matters in abstract terms. Throughout the late nineteenth century and until 1933 a substantial part of German legal philosophy was devoted to showing that laws and rights were themselves somehow independent of existing conditions. This tendency was criticized by de Ruggiero in his study of German liberalism:

> The mistake of German legal science is that, wishing to make rights an autonomous reality, it makes them an abstraction, something unreal: the true reality of right [*Recht*] lies in its connexion with the activities of a nation's historical life. Hence, the 'State of Rights' [*Rechtsstaat*] . . . taken by itself is only an empty form. [*The History of European Liberalism*]

However, we are less concerned with exposing the mistakes of German legal philosophy than with stressing the following point: the formalizing inclinations of German legal philosophy made it a willing ally of neo-Kantian philosophy. Beginning with the publication in 1900 of Georg Jellinek's *Allgemeine Staatslehre* (General theory of the state), legal scholars increasingly applied the neo-Kantian theory of knowledge to the study of law and politics. Hans Kelsen, one of the prominent neo-Kantian philosophers of law, expressly noted his intellectual debt to Hermann Cohen and the Marburg neo-Kantian philosophical school. Interestingly, one of the works of Cohen's most famous student, Cassirer, was directly responsible for another legal scholar's critique of law. Siegfried Marck's

Substanz- und Funktionsbegriff in der Rechtsphilosophie (Concepts of substance and function in legal philosophy) published in 1925, explicitly adopted the conceptual framework established by Cassirer in his study of substantial and functional concepts in mathematics and science which appeared in 1910. Legal philosophy was also decisively influenced by the work of Heinrich Rickert, leader of the Baden School of neo-Kantianism.

Starting with Kant's premise that an unbridgeable gulf separated thought from existence, neo-Kantian legal philosophers attempted to establish absolutely valid laws, called pure legal norms, based solely on human reason. In their minds it was not possible to have a law valid for all times and peoples which was also bound to a particular historical or social context. Only a law rooted in the unchangeable realm of thought, with its pure forms, could provide the certainty the neo-Kantians desired. As Cassirer put it, true legal science dealt with definitions and logical proofs, not with experiences and historical facts.

The neo-Kantian preference for the abstract over the concrete had two consequences. One was desirable from their philosophical point of view, the other unacceptable for political reasons. The first consequence was the divorce of the study of law from its political and social environment. Law was confined to the realm of thought and pure forms. This suited the ideals of the neo-Kantian liberal philosophers because the defence of individual freedom and of the *Rechtsstaat* was safest in a realm where the hazards of worldly existence were by definition excluded. The second consequence was disastrous for the liberals because it carried them towards political isolation, which followed from their unwillingness to bring their speculations into the actual political, social, and economic context in which most Germans dwelled. Aside from making general comments about the inalienable rights of man and the equality of all free individuals under the law, the idealists were reluctant to say what ought to be done. This reluctance in dealing with everyday realities infuriated most Germans, particularly after 1919, when decisive government was needed.

Once this idealist predilection for the abstract was transferred to the political arena, an abundance of declarations in favour of the rights of all citizens were made, but no consistent support ever materialized for thorough social and political reform aimed at realizing those rights. Liberal promises remained just promises. For example, from 1918 to 1919 many liberal democrats believed that their party, the DDP, was not a party only of the middle class but of the entire people. However, in February 1919, when Friedrich Naumann, a committed democrat and one of the prominent DDP leaders, had the opportunity to give his party's support to the mine worker's demands for the nationalization of the mining industry, he said: 'Of course we want to maintain capitalist enterprise.' Naumann's statement should be properly understood. His hasty return to the capitalist position was not voluntary; he had previously moved too close to the socialist position, and this had caused a stir in the right wing of the party. In order to assuage their fears Naumann made more conservative public statements. This episode was yet another symptom of the constant tension between the left and right wings of the party, which made it vacillate in both its promises and its policies. This ideological wavering threatened the DDP with either disintegration or loss of electoral support from 1919 to 1930.

The idealists' aversion to initiating any steps that might lead to the implementation of their claim to represent all classes was reflected in Cassirer's own work. His preference for the general statement of intentions over the formulation of steps to effectuate those intentions is understandable. After all, he was a philosopher. Whenever Cassirer did make political statements he relied on the same device as many other liberals sharing his creed. He appealed to his compatriots to be more enthusiastic in their support of the Weimar Republic because it endeavoured to instil in the body politic the liberal commitment to the preservation of human freedom in a society ruled by reason and law. Like his political counterparts, he did not provide a concrete way of achieving his goal.

Even though Cassirer's work covered a wide range of subjects, he did not specifically formulate an ethical position until after his departure from Germany in 1933. This omission was critical because ethics is the application of philosophical principles to common (concrete) life situations. Cassirer's inability to formulate a way of actualizing his political ideals was no accident, but part of a more general flaw in his philosophy, namely, his formalizing tendency. Perhaps Cassirer never specifically formulated an ethics because in his mind ethics, politics, and philosophy were the same thing—the application of pure reason to human affairs. Nevertheless, his failure to say explicitly what was good or bad or right or wrong in a specific situation undoubtedly contributed to the vagueness of his writing. With few exceptions Cassirer avoided the use of specific social and political contexts in his work.

From 1871 to 1933 moderates and democrats in the liberal ranks perpetually hovered between progress and reaction. They vacillated between their commitment to the achievement of freedom for all men and their fear of the masses' demands for equality, which made many liberals retreat into élitism and co-operation with the more conservative elements in German society. The conflict between the idealists' theoretical principles and the practical demands of their middle-class social and economic position had the unfortunate effect of undermining their primary goal: the preservation of human freedom. The interaction between major events in German history since 1871, especially the rising impact of nationalism and industrialization on German society, and the idealists' predilection for making general statements of intention, resulted in the inability to ground their ideal of freedom firmly in the concrete world of everyday life. The pressure of events together with the formalizing tendency inherent in the idealist liberals' philosophy maximized their inability to put their ideals into practice because the rapidly changing economic and social environment in Germany caused many problems requiring specific responses. When these were not forthcoming the idealists naturally lost their attraction to many potential voters.

The more specific the liberal commitment to the status quo, as in the cases of the National Liberals and the German People's Party, the more limited was their appeal to other classes. However, when the more democratic-minded liberals in the Progressive and German Democratic Parties tried to broaden their parties' appeal by relying on general political platforms designed to attract other groups, they still could not permanently expand the social basis of their support. Indeed, the attempted expansion lost them support within the ranks of the middle classes.

While both the materialist and idealist conceptions of liberalism tended to be limited to the industrial and professional middle classes, the latter conception was tied to a particular view of man and the universe with which Cassirer identified himself. Neo-Kantianism was, in a sense, an academic version of the idealist-liberal *Weltanschauung.*

Hazard Adams   (essay date 1983)

SOURCE: "Thinking Cassirer," in *Criticism,* Vol. XXV, No. 3, Summer, 1983, pp. 181-95.

[*In the following essay, Adams reexamines Cassirer's thought in light of recent trends in philosophy, especially the widespread acceptance of Martin Heidegger's philosophy.*]

In the latter part of the nineteenth century, when Ernst Cassirer was a doctoral candidate at Marburg preparing his study of Descartes and Leibniz, there was a movement led by his teachers, the Marburg philosophers Hermann Cohen and Paul Natorp, which had as its rallying cry "Back to Kant." One was not simply to return to Kant to accept all he said, but to start *from* Kant again. Cassirer's thought was formed in this atmosphere, and it proved to be a liberation for him. More recently it has been regarded as a limitation everywhere present in his work. Contemporary phenomenologists have particularly regarded it as so. Cassirer is not any longer in the high style of contemporary literary theory. Ricoeur mentions his theory of the symbol only to declare it too broad for his use, though Foucault, it is said, has shown some liking for him. Even in the earlier days of twentieth-century American theory he was never quite *in,* in spite of his lurking in Susanne Langer's various books, Wilbur M. Urban's *Language and Reality,* some of Philip Wheelwright, Frye's notion of the symbol, Eliseo Vivas' appropriation of him to justify certain procedures roughly associated with the New Criticism, Kenneth Burke's transfer of his concept of the symbolic from its neo-Kantian base into Burkeism, and Charles Feidelson's use of him to study symbolism in American literature.

But it can be said on the whole that in academic literary fashion three things are true that bear on Cassirer's present reputation: 1.) many academic critics are not very happy about commitment to any philosophical position, especially Americans, who would rather use things than embrace them, turning commitment to method; 2.) Cassirer seemed to lose out to Heidegger sometime in the sixties; and 3.) post-structuralism would regard Cassirer as someone who never managed to come to a true appreciation of difference.

Right now we do not have a true appreciation of Cassirer

and what *his* difference from certain contemporary trends may mean to us and possibly lead us to. I do not have in mind a "Back to Cassirer" movement; however, I do want to advocate that we think Cassirer anew, but not by rejecting the Heideggerian opposite. Indeed, my point will be that Cassirer and Heidegger are true contraries in the Blakean sense of prolific use, and I like to think of them in the phrase of Empedocles: "Never shall boundless time be emptied of that pair." Empedocles was thinking of concord and discord, and these terms will serve for my characterization of Cassirer and Heidegger respectively.

Cassirer was a prodigious writer, and his work covers such a vast array of subjects and disciplines that I cannot begin to claim a grasp of a whole that contains writings on Leibniz, Descartes, the Platonic Renaissance, the Enlightenment, Rousseau, Kant, Goethe, Einstein's theory of relativity, concepts of substance and function, freedom and form, the problem of knowledge, myth, language, the phenomenology of science, the myth of the state, and of course the symbolic. But as Blake suggests that fools should, I shall persist in my folly. With a touch of the prudence Blake warns against, I shall try to speak only about the Cassirer that seems important to literary theory and criticism, leaving aside his works in intellectual history and the philosophy of science. But to limit my task in this way is exceedingly difficult, because (as it is with most philosophers) Cassirer's writings on literature and art are not the ones that are most provocative for criticism and theory. In any case, Cassirer's whole way of thinking about any symbolic form such as art was to emphasize its relations (his term for "difference") to other human symbolic activities.

I want to begin with a story that interested him and that he retells and comments on in *An Essay on Man,* one of his last works. It is a story on which he came to base much of what he had to say about the symbol. I want to end by recalling a once well-known story about him. In between I shall endeavor to show what seems to be his specific importance to literary theory through brief consideration of Cassirer on language and his connection with structuralism, Cassirer on mythical thought and myth's connection with art, and Cassirer and phenomenology. My view is that Cassirer stands at a critical point between his romantic forebears and the post-modern. At one time he seemed to me a way into the future *from* the romantic. Now he seems to me an important link to attitudes it would be well to recall though not necessarily call up, for the sake of the future.

The story that interested Cassirer and that he retells in *An Essay on Man* is the well-known one about Helen Keller and her progression from the use of the sign to possession of symbols. The story begins when her teacher, Mrs. Sullivan, one day casually spelled out the word "water" for her. I now read directly from Mrs. Sullivan's account of Helen Keller's life and education, quoted at greater length by Cassirer:

> This morning, while she [Helen] was washing, she wanted to know the name for "water." When she wants to know the name of anything, she points to it and pats my hand. I spelled "w-a-

t-e-r" and thought no more about it until after breakfast . . . [Later on] we went out to the pump house, and I made Helen hold her mug under the spout while I pumped. As the cold water gushed forth, filling the mug, I spelled "w-a-t-e-r" in Helen's free hand. The word coming so close upon the sensation of cold water rushing over her hand seemed to startle her. She dropped the mug and stood as one transfixed.

From this moment, Helen Keller knew that everything had a name, that, to quote Cassirer, "the symbolic function is not restricted to particular cases but is a principle of *universal* applicability." Words had become instruments of thought. This famous case, and that of Laura Bridgman, which Cassirer also mentions, shows that human beings are not dependent entirely on the quality of their sense impressions. The cultural world is not based on materials but on its form and structure, and this form can be expressed in any sense material. Further, form and structure are always seen as function. One of Cassirer's most important early works in the philosophy of science, his *Substance and Function,* concerns itself with the shift in physics from the notion of things to events, substance to function—a function that is the form or structure by which physics constitutes the world. This notion in science Cassirer applies with modifications everywhere in his *Philosophy of Symbolic Forms*. In every case—myth, art, religion, history, science—these symbolic forms show the breakdown of the notion of a substance to be copied or represented and transform that old notion into the mobile, variable, relational, dynamic, reflective, constitutive world made in the symbol. Even the word "form" itself undergoes this change.

In the story I have retold from Cassirer's retelling, Helen Keller came suddenly to understand the symbolism of speech, passing in the process from a more subjective state to an objective state, from an emotional attitude to a theoretical attitude. That was the first step. The second step was recognition that "a symbol is not only universal but extremely variable." This term "variability" is Cassirer's for Saussure's idea of the arbitrary nature of the sign. It is characteristic of Cassirer that this term tends to express positively the power of language as an instrument. The third step was to see the symbol as belonging to a system of "relations," Cassirer's term for the linguistic "difference" of structuralism, again a positive term. (I use the term "positive" not by any means to identify Cassirer with positivism, which he opposed, but to emphasize Cassirer's sense of the cultural potentiality of language.) Now the important thing about Cassirer on this matter is that he reminds us of the constitutive power of language, which maintains some element of referentiality, even as he recognizes difference, though a difference which always belongs to some system or anti-system and is therefore relational. Cassirer holds to a connection to the world even as he sees language as differential (or, as he says, relational). The connection lies in language's power to constitute, in the Kantian sense, culture. And this is what the Helen Keller story illustrates for him. In his short book *Language and Myth* and the later *An Essay on Man*, Cassirer makes reference to the old search for the origins of language and says only that language and myth must have been of a twin

birth. His Helen Keller story begins language in the individual case. Language is already there, of course, but it is *discovered* by the individual in its fullness, and the discovery particularizes the word all over again, rather in the way that Usener's theory posits primitive creation of the "momentary deity," a theory Cassirer mentions in *Language and Myth*. Helen Keller's moment is a Crocean moment where the general term is recognized as general but in a unique context so that its constitutive power momentarily dominates its differential character and forces reference.

On the matter of language and this point in particular Cassirer is quite self-consciously in the debt of the neo-Kantian theorist of language Wilhelm Von Humboldt. Writing in the late forties, Wilbur M. Urban remarked: "Ernst Cassirer is, in my opinion, the first of modern philosophers to see the full significance of the relations of the problems of language to problems of philosophy and, therefore, the first also to develop a philosophy of language in the full sense of the word." It was Cassirer who shifted the epistemological question to the area of language. Cassirer fully embraces the Humboldtian notion that "languages are not really means for representing already known truths but are rather instruments for discovering previously unrecognized ones" and that "no object is possible without [language] for the psyche." Humboldt also wrote:

> The least advantageous influence on any sort of interesting treatment of linguistic studies is exerted by the narrow notion that language originated as a convention and that words are nothing but signs for things or concepts which are independent of them. This view up to a point is surely correct but beyond this point it is deadly because as soon as it begins to predominate it kills all mental activity and exiles all life.

Humboldt's aim here is to emphasize the constitutive element. What Cassirer calls the variability of the symbol allows for constant renewal of this constitutive power, since language in its relationality and variability is dynamic, always on the move, and people gather experience into themselves by means of it.

But both Humboldt and Cassirer recognize that in another sense language is an enclosure. Humboldt says:

> Man thinks, feels, and lives within language alone. . . . But he senses and knows that language is only a means for him; that there is an invisible realm outside it in which he seeks to feel at home and that it is for this reason that he needs the aid of language. The most commonplace observation and the profoundest thought, both lament the inadequacy of language.

Cassirer says:

> Man cannot escape from his own achievement. He cannot but adopt the conditions of his own life. No longer in a merely physical universe, man lives in a symbolic universe. Language, myth, art, and religion are parts of this universe. They are the varied threads which weave the

symbolic net, the tangled web of human experience. [*An Essay on Man*]

Language, you note, is something man-made, not something given by God. There was, then, an origin. Man was not always already in language, as Derrida's differential philosophy implies. But the origin can't be known. A sort of beginning, in Edward Said's sense (as I understand it), might be imagined. One assumes it has the shape of Helen Keller's experience and is tied to personal emergence from a sign world to a symbol world at the moment when one begins the art (and science) of one's life. There are ominous metaphors in Cassirer's statement, as I am sure Paul de Man would be the first to observe—the net and the tangled web—figures that surely a student of Blake like myself cannot let pass. They are, of course, mild compared to those with which de Man himself characterizes language, figures of seduction, aberration, subterfuge, illusion, lies, underhandedness, secretiveness, pretence, deceit, and complicity. And there are others in Cassirer: Man is so "enveloped" in this web that he "cannot see or know anything except by the interposition of this artificial medium." Yet Cassirer is inclined not to emphasize the sense of loss that Edward Said notices in all beginnings, or the element of transgression.

Cassirer is interested in the other side by temperament and ethical stance; and that, today, could be his value to us. He will study language outside the limits that naturalistic assumptions create, and he will see man as the animal potentially liberated by his capacity to symbolize. But he must liberate himself, and the task never ends, for not only is the symbol dynamic itself, but its constitution of the cultural world never ceases to require interpretation and reinterpretation. For Cassirer man is the *animal symbolicum*. Now, as you can see, the symbol as Cassirer understands it is not the miraculous or theological symbol of religious tradition, so much deplored by Walter Benjamin. Cassirer would hold with Croce that the symbol symbolizes nothing on the other side from nature or from us. Rather, it symbolizes relations, functions, differences, which its system constitutes from human experience for the future. The symbolic always has a further potential of meaning, and this idea, though not, I think developed adequately by Cassirer is, nevertheless, an important reflection of his general attitude and ethic, which connects the use of language with spiritual growth.

The notion of reference implicit in the constitutive symbolic system—system as reference—makes it possible, as Cassirer shows in his *Substance and Function,* to evade the necessity of a material object of reference and to constitute the world of physics as one of functions. Helen Keller constituted the idea of water in the word as physics constitutes function as substance or, shall we say, dissolves the idea of substance in function. Helen Keller made possible a life for herself, which she had been shut out from until the age of seven. "What's water but the generated soul?" asks Yeats, whose line might be an epigraph for the Helen Keller story. Cassirer says:

> In the usual logical view, the concept is born only when the signification of the word is sharply delineated and unambiguously fixed through

definition according to *genus proximum* and *differentia specifia*. But to penetrate to the ultimate source of the concept, our thinking must go back to a deeper stratum, must seek those factors of synthesis and analysis which are at work in the process of word formation itself, and which are decisive for the ordering of all our representations according to specific linguistic categories. [*The Philosophy of Symbolic Forms*]

When water generated Helen Keller's spirit or Helen Keller projected her spirit into "water," a polarity also occurred; as Urban remarks, "Without the element of polarity, and therefore of the reference of the presentation to that which is presented, that is without some elements of representation, the entire notion of knowledge collapses." Cassirer displaces the polarity itself into language as a symbolic form—or almost, for I think he was not as radical as he could have been in this matter. By this I mean that the polarity of subject-object regarded as a product of language becomes a category of the symbolic form of science.

That Cassirer employs the term "relation" rather than "difference," for the most part, emphasizes his notion of the synthetic process of language as thought generating wholes from differences, which the wholes then contain. Language, then, is for Cassirer neither closed, nor open, or it is both closed and open. It is referential by means of its relationality and constitutive power. It is "fictive," in the sense of making, a term Cassirer takes over from the mathematician Heinrich Hertz, though he could have gotten it from Vaihinger and elsewhere. However, Cassirer would no doubt have rebelled against Vaihinger's neo-Kantian critical positivism. Language is a vehicle of making; the idea of the made henceforth takes the place, for the most part, of truth.

But Cassirer does not deny that this forming, making language can go wrong. It often does:

> The philosophy of language is here confronted with the same dilemma as appears in the study of every symbolic form. The highest, indeed the only, task of all these forms is to unite men. But none of them can bring about this unity without at the same time dividing and separating men. Thus what was intended to secure the harmony of culture becomes the source of the deepest discords and discussions. This is the great antinomy of the religious life. This same dialectic appears in human speech. Without speech there would be no community of men. Yet there is no more serious obstacle to such community than the diversity of speech. [*An Essay on Man*]

One cannot help noting here the curious remark that language was "intended to secure the harmony of culture." By whom? By a God who gave language to man? Then certainly language cannot be called a human achievement. By man who consciously invented it? Impossible. Man was not man before language. A slip? The ghost of theology? Perhaps. I deliberately resist the temptation of deconstruction for the possibility and the risk of construction: Cassirer must, indeed has to, (at least I want him to) mean that language *embodies the possibility* of attaining a cultural whole of differences. But this whole is imagined not as a fixed substance but as on the move, as function. It should be noted too that Cassirer's notion of language is fundamentally not that of communication, but rather of creation. Still, creation can go as easily wrong as communication, and Cassirer is well aware of this. But for him language is fundamentally all we have, for better or for worse. He hopes it can be for better. Also one notes that when language goes wrong, it ought to be regarded as doing so not *vis à vis* some *truth* independent of function but *vis à vis* making a liveable culture, which suggests that truth is relative to the nature of each form of the symbolic and is a product of those forms rather than something retrieved by them. This, in turn, suggests that symbolic forms generate an ethic of human relations. The ethical world, for Cassirer, is never given. It is always in the making.

"Myth" for Cassirer does not mean "myths" but the dynamic which gives rise to them. He rejects the tradition of allegorical interpretation of myths as of no use in determining the dynamic of myth. He accepts what he regarded as Vico's notion of mythical thought as an independent configuring power of human consciousness.

—Hazard Adams

Cassirer tried to broaden epistemology beyond the boundaries of scientific cognition where the Marburg neo-Kantians left it. He chose this path rather than the rejection of epistemology characteristic of modern phenomenology. He himself began as a student of scientific cognition, but his development was toward consideration of other ways of knowing or making. These ways are themselves systems or symbolic forms. In addition to language, the fundamental or primordial form is mythical thought. On the matter of myth Cassirer's principal forebears are Vico, Herder, and Schelling. From Vico he takes the idea of "poetic logic" and "imaginative universals" as well as the idea of trying to know something from inside itself even while maintaining the polarity necessary to knowledge. In *The New Science,* Vico speaks of the difficulty of such a vantage: "We had to descend from these human and refined natures of ours to those quite wild and savage natures, which we cannot at all imagine and can contemplate only with great effort." Cassirer writes: "We cannot reduce myth to certain fixed static elements; we must strive to grasp it in its inner life, in its mobility and diversity, in its dynamic principle." These words embody description of what Cassirer means by a phenomenological approach. He uses the term in a roughly Hegelian sense of understanding from within and grasping the whole in the form of its internal relations.

"Myth" for Cassirer does not mean "myths" but the dynamic which gives rise to them. He rejects the tradition

of allegorical interpretation of myths as of no use in determining the dynamic of myth. He accepts what he regarded as Vico's notion of mythical thought as an independent configuring power of human consciousness. He emphasizes the creative element in Vico's notion of the poetic and turns the imagistic element into the creative. He thinks that Schelling's characterization of myth as requiring "tautegorical" interpretation expresses a similar attitude, but he is suspicious of Schelling's tendency to blur all difference. Myth is one of the means by which consciousness moves from passive captivity in sense to a world of its own theoretical creations. He would, I think, accept Lévi-Strauss' characterization of myth as a "science of the concrete" only if one were to allow the term "science" to enlarge itself to contain other forms of making from that of normal science. This would have to include the rule of metaphorical relation. In Cassirer's view this means that one tries to grasp myth on its own terms. These matters are discussed at length in volume two of *The Philosophy of Symbolic Forms*. Myth, on the whole, operates with "concrete unifying images" instead of ideal relational forms. In scientific cognition relation comes between elements as an ideal signification, but in myth there is simply a concrescence or coincidence of the members of a relation. The ground here seems to be one of the sort of relation implicit in the tropes of metaphor and synecdoche, freed of their rationalistic, rhetorical definitions. In the cultural world myth eventuates in arts and religion, which are two quite different forms. *The Philosophy of Symbolic Forms* stops just short of a discussion of art or of a systematic, or let us say anti-systematic, discussion of tropes. I say his discussion would have to have an element of anti-system (by way of irony about his predicament) in order to keep trying to see myth from its own point of view—an impossibility, of course, because in myth there is no point of view, no subject or object. Still the effort is the important thing, and has an ethical element and achieves a balance. In *An Essay on Man* the chapter on art leaves us somewhat dissatisfied because of a fundamental ambiguity in Cassirer's approach, not this critical balance which would seem to be necessary between rational and aesthetic constitution. The ambiguity arises because Cassirer's discussion of art and language draws a contrast between art and language even though most of his examples of art are linguistic in nature. Further, he has already treated language and myth, which prefigures art, as a twin birth. This problem has its roots in a scientific positivism that lingers in his vocabulary. In considering language, he tends to assume that language's progressive development is strictly toward the conceptual abstractions of science. Language, in this view, gradually emancipates itself from myth. Art is contrasted to language and science by being shown to perform another function. Language and science abbreviate reality, while art intensifies it:

> Language and science depend upon one and the same process of abstraction; art may be described as a continuous process of concretion. In our scientific description of a given object we begin with a great number of observations which at first sight are only a loose conglomerate of detached facts. But the farther we proceed the more these individual phenomena tend to as-

sume a definite shape and become a systematic whole. What science is searching for is some central feature of a given object from which all its particular qualities may be derived. . . . But art does not admit of this sort of conceptual simplification and deductive generalization. It does not inquire into the qualities or causes of things; it gives us intuition of the form of things. But this too is by no means a mere repetition of something we had before. [*An Essay on Man*]

This statement unfortunately suggests an "actual" world that can be known and that can be abbreviated or intensified. But Cassirer's basic view, to which he comes at the end, is that knowledge is made symbolically, not copied from a previous given. There is a more difficult problem: The distinction between art and language leaves poetry in the void unless Cassirer is prepared to make an addendum that offers a theory of the poetic use of language as somehow special and explains its nature. But his theory of myth as born a twin with language ought to lead him to a notion not of the special nature of the poetic but rather of the scientific. The relation of myth to art awaits development here, for in Cassirer art clearly ought to be regarded as surpassing myth in the direction of the emancipated Viconian "imaginative universal" as science does in the direction of the "abstract universal." Cassirer's last work *The Myth of the State* worries the dangers of a myth not surpassed. It stands, incidentally, as an answer to those who thought Cassirer saw all through rose-colored glasses.

The analogy of literary art and myth would appropriately begin for Cassirer with their common opposition to the subject/object distinction characteristic of science. But art differs from myth in its acceptance of the polarity even as it opposes it. Art is conscious of its making something. Myth is not. Here Cassirer needs a distinction that opposes difference and indifference to *identity*, which includes while at the same time is contrary to both of the others; in other words a true Blakean contrariety with its own logic or (we might say) anti-logic. Cassirer never quite gets this far, and his theory of art remains ambiguous, but provocative.

Cassirer's position, particularly *vis à vis* religion has been strongly opposed by modern phenomenology, sometimes unfairly. The complaint arises out of the difference between a neo-Kantian and a hermeneutic perspective. One of the earliest phenomenological critics of Cassirer was Heidegger himself. This phenomenological criticism is, of course, implicit in Heidegger's *Kant and the Problem of Metaphysics,* and I shall return to their opposition when I tell my concluding story.

Briefly, Cassirer treats religion as a symbolic form that arises in a sophisticated way from mythical thinking. It is never entirely removed from its source, but it is different, too, by virtue of the way it constitutes its knowledge about the signs it employs. For religion, signs are "means of expression which, though reveal a determinate meaning, must necessarily remain inadequate to it, which 'point' to this meaning but never wholly exhaust it." Religious signs are thus allegorical, a term which is not opposed to symbol, as in so much romantic usage, but lies within it, as a

mode of symbolic. It appears that Cassirer, like Walter Benjamin and others, thinks of the romantic and theological symbols as immediately falling from their miraculous power of containing their signified and referents (as in the Eucharist) to the arbitrary relations of allegory. Mysticism, in Cassirer's view, goes farther to reject even the religious allegorical sign as completely inadequate. In religion, the world itself is a world of signs like Baudelaire's dictionary of nature. There is always a something else from which the sign borrows its authority. Cassirer's point is that the process of allegoresis allows religion to remain in the particular while yet not being confined strictly to it, and religion depends on the tension between a hidden reality and a sensuous image standing for it.

It is fair to say, I think, that the contemporary phenomenologists' attitude toward Cassirer, arising in part from his treatment of religion, is fundamentally still that of Fritz Kaufmann's essay of the late forties: "Cassirer's philosophy," he remarks, "suffers from too much light," that is, too much humanism. Where, Kaufmann asks, is love and hatred, fear and trembling, shame and repentance, guilt and sin? The objection is principally against Cassirer's neo-Kantian holding to the unknowability of the *ding an sich* and his apparent reduction of religion simply to another example of human creativity—yet another symbolic form. For the phenomenologist, creativity is not all. It needs to be opposed and finally, I think, triumphed over by recognition of some greater reality that is not symbolically determinable. Cassirer, it is claimed, ignores the spiritual poverty of man, his ultimate need for divine mercy, his radical inability to "express certain experiences in an adequate way as well as his unique capacity for going into hiding by the very means of communication." It is true that Cassirer does not dwell much on this last matter, though he recognizes it; and on the need for divine mercy I do not think he dwells at all. He certainly was in dread much of his life of what man was making. But his early work on the philosophy of science turned him toward the power of the Kantian constitutive understanding to make and the possibility of its making well. When he came to art this positivity remained characteristic of his approach. Art he sees as a positive making rather than a constant prelude to a negative theology.

In this sense, Cassirer's Apollonian attitude seems a deliberate contrary or reprobate approach to what he saw around him and in the dark future he feared. He seems to have believed that God expresses Himself in and through man rather than dispensing punishment or mercy from some position in the sky or hiding there. This Apollonian nature Hendrik J. Pos describes in his essay "Recollections of Ernst Cassirer," which contains the story I borrow to conclude these remarks. In 1929, Cassirer and Heidegger appeared at a symposium at Davos University on the subject of Kant. Cassirer, of course, had written extensively on and edited Kant. Heidegger's book on Kant would be reviewed by Cassirer in *Kant-Studien* two years later. Their differences in approaching Kant were fundamental. Heidegger's view was that the central problem in Kant was that of the "metaphysical comprehension of being"; Kant's philosophy was one of finitude with no access to divinity. Pos remarks:

Heidegger persisted in the *terminus a quo,* in the situation at the point of departure, which for him is the dominating factor in all philosophizing. Cassirer aimed at the *terminus ad quem,* at liberation through the spiritual form, in science, practical activity, and art.

The two views did not meet. About Pos' sensitive recollection one can perhaps say that "terminus" is not quite the right word since for Cassirer the task is endless. If in taking his position Heidegger had not much to say about or in behalf of science, Cassirer in his way tended to diminish religion in its usual sense, locating God in the human spirit and fictionalizing the relation between man and an external deity. In this matter Heidegger and Cassirer seemed to be continuing the nineteenth-century wars of religion and science. With respect to art they clashed in a somewhat different way. Art for Heidegger, it seems to me, is subordinate to religion. For Cassirer it is an independent form, part of cultural making, completely secular, containing possibilities for a secular culture. If Cassirer had carried out the dialectic of symbolic forms at which he hints at the end of **An Essay on Man,** we would have found art and religion contrary in a positive Blakean sense.

In Davos in 1929 the debate went on for some time, with Cassirer admitting that metaphysical expressions are not lacking in Kant's text; but Heidegger refused to grant that the *Critique of Pure Reason* was aimed at the grounding of scientific knowledge of nature. Pos describes Cassirer as representing in this debate the "best in the universalistic traditions of German culture," Apollonian, the master of exposition, as he had so often shown in his writings. Pos describes Heidegger as sending forth "feelings of loneliness, of oppression, and of frustration, such as one has in anxious dreams, but now present in a clear and wakeful mind." Heidegger had the ear of Germany's academic youth. The soil for the reception of his philosophy had been prepared. When the discussion ended, Cassirer offered his hand to Heidegger, who refused it.

The man who offered his hand was forced under Naziism to resign his professorship at Hamburg in 1933 and to emigrate to Sweden, coming finally to the United States where he taught first at Yale, then at Columbia, until his death in exile on April 13, 1945.

Heidegger's connection with or tolerance of or by the Nazi regime has been much debated, and I have no opinion about it or its relation to his thought. Let me say only two things. First, there is something to be pondered on in the offer of that hand and its refusal, and it is not just the anti-Semitism there, though there is an irony, for Vico and, I think, Edward Said would regard Cassirer as what Vico called a "Gentile," that is to say, "secular" philosopher. Cassirer, hounded from Germany, speaks consistently of human cultural possibility, and he builds his ethic on this stance. Heidegger speaks often enough of darkness and loss, and he finds his ethic by negativity in the nothingness there. Cassirer speaks of the future of language, Heidegger of a past from which we and language fell. Second, in that moment of the proffered hand, Cassirer did in my view triumph over Heidegger, though whether there will be an-

other triumph in the future I do not know. In any case, my aim has been not to engineer a second triumph for Cassirer, but to *think* him and to see both Cassirer and Heidegger—concord and discord—a pair never emptied out of time.

Ivan Strenski   (essay date 1987)

SOURCE: "Ernst Cassirer: Political Myths and Primitive Realities," in *Four Theories of Myth in Twentieth-Century History: Cassirer, Eliade, Lévi-Strauss, and Malinowski,* The Macmillan Press, Ltd., 1987, pp. 13-41.

[*In the following essay, Strenski contends that Cassirer's work on myth was an attempt to alert intellectuals to the dangers of irrationalism in Weimar Germany.*]

WHY DID CASSIRER CARE ABOUT MYTH?

Most people have never given more than passing thought to myth. Thus it is strange when in the course of the history of thought we find great outpourings of learned writing on this subject, and on the second-order subject of the philosophy or theoretical study of myth. Now we have a doubly knotted problem: why did a second group of people care about the way the first group had cared about myth in the first place? To collect and edit myths is strange-enough behaviour. How much more unusual to study the literature of myths in a theoretical way.

Ernst Cassirer, who at two distinct times in his life was a philosopher of myth, is one of those unusual persons. I want to elucidate his theory of myth and at the same time try to understand why he took on such a challenging and specialised subject. I am especially drawn to Cassirer because his theory of myth stands as one of the most ambitious and erudite examples of that enterprise. Moreover, by the time he published his first major work in the philosophy of myth—**Mythical Thought** (1925), the second volume of his **Philosophy of Symbolic Forms**—Cassirer had already established himself as a leading authority in epistemology, philosophy of science and Kantian studies. Why should such an illustrious scholar have devoted himself to the theoretical understanding of myth? What could have been so important to Cassirer as to move him to take on this major work? There are, I think, several strong candidate answers to this question.

I think that one can distinguish generally two sorts of reasons why Cassirer took up the philosophy of myth. These are reasons having to do with both the internal and external contexts of his theory; they conform in part to the audiences Cassirer imagined his writing would eventually reach. On the internal side, his prior intellectual interests in language and science and his Kantian and Hegelian philosophising were compatible with his interest in myth. For him, it was a way to deepen his sense of belonging to the traditions of German Idealism, which in Cassirer's day was more than a matter of imagined intellectual affiliation; it was a social matter as well. Specifically, I have here in mind Cassirer's desire to speak as an intellectual heir of Hegel and the first philosopher of myth, Schelling. On the 'external' side, and perhaps more controversially, I want also to argue that Cassirer had strong and even overriding *moral* and *public* reasons for studying myth. He wanted to counteract irrationalist trends among his own intellectual class, and chose the subject of myth with special care as a way of doing this. Interestingly, the trends of thought these German intellectuals found attractive were also more properly characteristic of the broad cultural moods of late-nineteenth- and early-twentieth-century Germany—especially romantic primitivism and what George Mosse has called 'Volkishness'.

I am the first to admit that it will not be easy (or perhaps even possible) to prove, in a way that historians would regard as conclusive, that Cassirer directed his theory of myth at the general run of German intellectuals. There is no 'smoking gun'. But there is much circumstantial evidence, far too interesting to shelve for possible future use. Using this, I hope to make a convincing and honourable case for significance of the 'external' context for understanding Cassirer's theory of myth. I shall make a special point of trying to show how one might defensibly read Cassirer's theory of myth as a public moral document aimed at arguing the general run of German intellectuals of the Weimar period away from their 'Volkish' and irrationalist habits. In Cassirer's philosophy of myth, I think we have a document whose intellectual relatives were Max Weber's *Wissenschaft als Beruf* and Ernst Troeltsch's *Spectator—Briefe* of 1918. Although these are very different pieces, both in explicit content and in style, they share a certain moral tone and sensitivity to the dangers of irrationalism in Weimar Germany, along with a sense that intellectuals should take a firm stand against this corrupting force.

A reader who knew Cassirer only from his posthumously published work *The Myth of the State* (1946), might find my hesitation puzzling. In this work Cassirer clearly admits the connections to which I have alluded. For the Cassirer of *The Myth of the State,* myth ought to be understood theoretically because it had already figured in public life. For Cassirer in 1945, myth had revealed its true meaning in Alfred Rosenberg's *The Myth of the Twentieth Century,* and in the Nazi fulfilment of Gobineau's 'myth' of racism, Carlyle's 'myth' of the political hero, and so on. There can be little doubt that Cassirer wrote *The Myth of the State* with a kind of public purpose, directed at matters external to the strictly academic domain.

In fact, it was *The Myth of the State* which led me to ask whether one could trace the same awareness of the external or public realm in Cassirer's earlier work on myth. Was Cassirer as farsighted in the 1925 *Mythical Thought* as he was wise in the retrospective *The Myth of the State*? Or was *The Myth of the State* perhaps a liberal's public act of contrition for not having been more explicitly critical of mythical thought in 1925, when it might have done some good? Since no explicit criticisms of 'Volkish' mythical thinking are to be found in *Mythical Thought,* one would have to assume that the critique (if present) appears in cryptic or coded form. If this is so, in writing *Mythical Thought* Cassirer felt compelled to restrain himself to some extent. This view credits Cassirer with the same public spirit and awareness of the popular implications of mythical thought as he had in 1945, and sees the differ-ences between the two books as resulting chiefly from the different environments in which they were written: the first in an intimidating environment, and the second in relative freedom from political threats. The alternative view casts the Cassirer of 1925 as a rather introverted and high-born scholar who paid little attention to contemporary cultural trends and thus was virtually oblivious to the possible relation between 'Volkish' mythologising and the specialised philosophical and anthropological term 'myth'. This seems to be what Peter Gay has in mind when he cites Cassirer for a 'failure to do justice to the social dimension of ideas' and labels his thought as 'unpolitical Idealism'. On this view, *The Myth of the State* was written to correct this 'flaw'.

From all we know of Cassirer's inquisitive and thoughtful nature, it is absurd to believe that he was ignorant of the deeper import of the 'Volkish' and primitivist trends on 1925. *The Myth of the State* was not written under the spell of new revelations. Cassirer was a scholar's scholar, but he was also an extraordinarily worldly man. Toni Cassirer tells us that her learned husband read the sports pages of the daily newspaper avidly and followed economic news with as much relish. Whether plotting the fortunes of his favourite professional football teams through an exciting season, or of the stock market during the rampant inflation of the 1920s, Cassirer was, it seems, always on the look-out for reasons why events were taking a particular course. Likewise, he comprehended the anti-semitism and political radicalism of his day as well as anyone. Although he maintained faith in Germany, he harboured no illusions about the Nazis. He led his family into exile shortly after Hitler assumed power in 1933. In her biography of her husband Toni Cassirer explains what led him to this decision. Speaking of the first weeks of the Hitler regime she says,

> The first [official Nazi] publications were not all that alarming. Nothing was mentioned about persecution or laws restricting Jews. But then one day one of Hitler's edicts read, 'Whatever serves the Führer is law.' Ernst said to me, 'If tomorrow every jurist in Germany to a man does not rise and protest these paragraphs, then surely Germany is lost.' Not a single voice spoke out. [Toni Cassrer, *Aus Meinem Leben mit Ernst Cassirer*]

Cassirer also had a historical sense of the political role of myth at this time, although it was not as well developed as it was to become in *The Myth of the State*. In *Mythical Thought,* Cassirer notes with Schelling and the German romantic nationalists that myth lays the basis for nationhood. It is behind the feeling of nationality, and gives it its force. As Schelling says, in a remark Cassirer quotes but whose implications even he could not fully comprehend at the time, 'it is inconceivable that a *nation* should exist without a mythology'. But what a nation and what a mythology, Cassirer would fully realise only many years later.

Yet Cassirer did not brood about this; he thought and acted. He seems to have internalised the moral lessons of his time even as its affairs engulfed him. Dimitri Gawronsky, Kerensky's personal secretary, had recently escaped from Lenin's Russia to the safety of Switzerland. He and Cassirer had known each other as students of Hermann Cohen. Now Gawronsky had taken it upon himself to warn German socialists of the treachery awaiting them at the hands of the Bolsheviks. In his biographical essay on Cassirer, Gawronsky tells us that as early as 1917 Cassirer had conceived *The Philosophy of Symbolic Forms* partly as an attempt to speak of the chaos which fell hard upon the Germans after their defeat in the First World War. In connection with the political concept of 'myth', Gawronsky also offers the opinion that Cassirer had been influenced by Georges Sorel. Gawronsky believed Cassirer shared Sorel's view of myth as a driving irrational force in human affairs. But whether Cassirer took note of Sorel is doubtful. Sorel was influential for Mussolini's religious view of fascism, but much less so in his native France or Germany. Perhaps Gawronsky mentions Sorel because of his relation to Lenin's idea of revolution led by the 'conspiratorial plot' of the small disciplined party.

To his credit, Gawronsky maintains the right sort of balance in talking about Cassirer, noting that, while he was primarily a 'philosopher, not a politician', he 'found his own way of expressing his attitude toward ultimate human values.' To substantiate this, Gawronsky claims that Cassirer wrote *Freiheit und Form* (1916) under the disillusioning influence of duty in the War Press Office. Consider Toni Cassirer's inside account of its writing:

> At first the work in the office interested him [Cassirer] very much. But, in the end, it destroyed every illusion he had about the war, and especially about the 'German Case'. His task was to study all the French newspapers carefully, and to seek out certain places in them which he had to revise (with the help of a pair of scissors) until they suited the purpose of misleading ordinary German opinion. He went through the motions of this reprehensible social game in exemplary fashion. When he came home in the evenings he did not need to violate official secrecy to explain to me what was going on inside him. It was not only the daily work which oppressed him, however. In the office, he felt he was really being changed into a machine, and like every soldier, being robbed of personal responsibility. And now he knew nearly two years before the end of the war that Germany would lose. Yet, he confronted this gloomy realisation in characteristic style: despite his heavy duties in the service, he worked on a new book in his office—*Freiheit und Form*—and then locked up the manuscript in his desk at the office every evening. . . . In this way he salvaged for himself the image of the indestructible and unchangeable Germany which was to become wholly unrecognisable because of the 'rubbish' which was dumped on it.

Thus, turned by his war experiences away from an interest in history of philosophy, epistemology and philosophy of science, Cassirer worked to reaffirm the indigenous liberal-humanist and Idealist traditions of German thought. By 1916, at least, Cassirer had become a spokesman and interpreter for the Germany of Luther, Leibniz, Kant, Goethe, Schiller, Hegel and the other heroes of *Freiheit und Form*.

Cassirer also represented German liberalism in situations where an academic code language was less appropriate and perhaps unnecessary. He never totally abandoned his sense of the role of the scholar, even when he appeared in explicitly political gatherings. Perhaps the most celebrated and typical of such occasions (which, to be sure, were rare for Cassirer) was his Weimar Republic Constitution Day speech of August 1928. Cassirer cut short his won vacation to accept the invitation of the politically beleaguered Social Democratic senate of the city of Hamburg to deliver this public address. They wanted a man of Cassirer's stature to lend his support and personal prestige to an event which in the late 1920s had taken on a rather marked political significance. It was already the practice of German academics conspicuously to ignore the national celebration of the republican constitution and to celebrate instead the old Reich holiday. By enlisting Cassirer's support, the city fathers hoped in some way to help stem the reactionary tide among its youth and intelligentsia. By many accounts, Cassirer performed brilliantly. He argued cleverly that the republican ideal was not ultimately French in origin (and therefore anti-German), despite the precedent of the French Revolution. In fact, this republican upheaval would not have been possible without the intellectual foundations laid for it by a host of German thinkers. Therefore, what could be more German than to be republican! Cassirer's courage is all the more surprising when one considers that as a Jew he was taking considerable personal risks in participating in what he and everyone else knew to be an outright political attempt to rally support for the weak liberal-democratic Weimar regime and its constitution. Cassirer was, in short, neither politically naïve nor uninformed. As a Jew and a scholar, he knew professional politics was both impossible and personally unsuitable for him. Yet, his personal life and scholarship reflect a brave yet prudent public spirit.

THE 'MANDARINS' AND DAS VOLK

But just who were those German intellectuals to whom, in part, Cassirer addressed both his Constitution Day speech and his theory of myth? Why should they have been interested in such exotica as myth?

One can identify this audience as that amorphous elite group Fritz Ringer calls the 'Mandarins', drawing upon the ambivalent associations this term has had at least since Max Weber's *Religions of China*. In their own ways, the Mandarins fused the concerns of the higher and lower strata of German culture. They led the revival of German philosophical Idealism and the great movements of educational reform in the humanities to which we are heirs today. But many also led various movements characterised by 'Volkish' cultural chauvinism and irrationalism, propensities shared with the German masses.

As intellectuals, the Mandarins counted among their number several different sorts of thinkers: the learned leaders of the Idealist Baden School of neo-Kantians, Rickert and Windelband; the pioneers of the method of *Verstehen* and empathetic understanding, Dilthey and his followers; plus the partisans of *Lebensphilosophie,* from Klages to Heidegger.

At the risk of superficial generalisation, one can identify certain concerns common to all these thinkers. If Ringer is to be believed, it would be hard to overestimate the vast influence the Mandarin discontent with modernity had on German academic life. Here originate many of the attitudes against modern mass society still heard today. The Mandarins decried the specialisation and professionalisation a technological society demanded of its educated elites. They felt that these trends narrowed human perspectives to the merely utilitarian or instrumental aspects of life. These in turn aided the mechanisation and bureaucratisation of society, producing in the end a lifeless culture unfit for human beings. Opposition to modern society had to be thorough and fundamental, the Mandarins reasoned. In some way, the intellectualism and positivism grounding technological society had to be undermined, and plausible alternatives constructed. If industrial society 'alienated' mankind across a whole range of activities, a humanised society would have to work to build humankind into a 'whole' again. Thus, for example, knowledge and world-view might be harmonised so that knowledge would become 'relevant' to spiritual concerns. No longer could one hide behind the cloak of neutrality which positivism interposed between knowledge and values. 'Objectivity' and 'critical analysis' had to be moderated by a recognition of the place of subjectivity and speculative synthesis in the agenda of modern knowledge. Especially when it came to the question of the proper study of mankind, the Mandarins insisted that the human sciences or humanities stood on their own independent and autonomous ground, because they were disciplines which sought an inner understanding of human life. This consisted in encouraging empathetic understanding of human experiences as people actually felt they lived them.

These were emphatically not methodological proposals alone. Such methodological points arose out of moral and ideological conviction. Methodological attention was turned to subjectivity, for example, because the Mandarins sought to do right by the dignity of humankind. Thereby they hoped to achieve spiritual revival in the mechanistic age. They sought to nourish both the 'inner man', by paying heed to the inner life of the persons studied, and the imaginative talents of the humanist scholar for empathising with that 'inner' nature.

Finally, by bringing together subject and object with the inner and outer aspects of their study, the Mandarin humanists thought they could achieve a truly rounded view of humanity. This, for them, marked a real breakthrough to synthetic knowledge, a chance to produce work which reflected the 'whole' man. This in turn would bring one closer to the ideal of discovering moral certainties. If one could achieve virtually complete knowledge of humankind, by covering, as it were, all the angles, perhaps one could bridge the fact-value gap and discover how one ought to live.

As intellectual revolutionaries in the humanities, the Mandarins have probably never been equalled. Yet their revolution, like others before, was fraught with ambiguities—

especially at a time when, to scholars such as Ringer, their ideas seemed to play into the hands of the forces associated with the rise of Nazism. In general, Ringer believes that Mandarin ideas fostered softheadedness and escapism, which the romantic propaganda of Nazism readily exploited: their flight from utilitarian and humdrum concerns left these necessary jobs to those perhaps less competent or more opportunistic. Their disenchantment with the ideal of objectivity made public discussion difficult, and their exaltation of subjectivity opened a door for authoritarianism. Their infatuation with the 'inner man' left the 'outer man' in the hands of others all too willing to command. Their craving for wholeness and synthesis at times seemed indulgent and escapist—a grasping for verities at a time when they were not to be found.

The Mandarins' 'Volkish' side was evident in their yearning for the simple, unified, organic agrarian life they saw being broken on the rack of Germany's rapid industrialisation. For them, as for others, nationalism provided a kind of tonic to counter alienation, a sense of 'rootedness' in a time of change. This sense of ethnic belonging also extended to the imagined historical and racial antecedents of modern Germans. Thus, the Mandarins indulged a taste for archaism, if not outright primitivism and, at times, racism. Mandarin primitivism excited the fashion for ancient Teutonic myth, ritual drama, the occult, magic and astrology.

FOR AND AGAINST THE MANDARINS

Cassirer opposed the Mandarins, yet represented what was best in them. Since he traced his philosophical lineage from the 'critical' or Marburg school of neo-Kantianism, he was somewhat at odds with the metaphysical tendency of the Idealist or Baden branch of neo-Kantianism. Although historians are correct to consider Cassirer an *Aufklärer* rationalist and classicist misplaced in the hostile anti-intellectual environment of Weimar German, he was also a great defender of the romantics and nineteenth-century German Idealist philosophers. This much is evident from Cassirer's particular devotion to Hegel, but in **The Myth of the State** it is especially remarkable. Writing in the darkest days of both Jewish and Aryan Germany, Cassirer here launched what was then an extraordinarily unfashionable defence of the German romantic thinkers at whose feet so much of the blame for Nazism had been laid.

Accordingly, some scholars call Cassirer an 'accommodationist' thinker: he leaves himself open to association with the Mandarin Idealists and romantics on a number of fronts. In **Mythical Thought** Cassirer seems wedded to the Mandarin quest for a grand synthesis, putting together ideas from here and there and, by the vocabulary he uses, often creating misleading impressions of agreement with those chiefly associated with it. This certainly blunts his would-be criticisms of Mandarin mythologising. That Cassirer the philosopher of science should have taken up the subject of myth at all in the 1920s—laden as it was with 'Volkish' and primitivist associations—also creates its confusions. This urban, modernist republican was no partisan of the occult or the mystical. Cassirer held science and mathematics in the highest esteem. Yet, with the

Mandarins, Cassirer felt his share of unease about the mechanisation of modern life. Reporting on this, Robert S. Hartman says,

> after showing the entire many-branched labyrinth of man's development to modernity, Cassirer focuses on the hero himself, modern Theseus, who has left the guiding hand of nature and, at the end of his course, encounters a monster, the master of the maze, the Minotaur of Machinery, ready to devour him. . . . ["Cassirer's Philosophy of Symbolic Forms"]

Cassirer was also deeply divided about the need for and nature of 'wholeness':

> Philosophy cannot give up its search for a fundamental unity in this ideal world. But it does not confound this unity with simplicity. It does not overlook the tensions and frictions, the strong contrasts and deep conflicts between the various powers of man. These cannot be reduced to a common denominator. [*Essay on Man*]

Finally, although, like the Mandarins, a critic of positivism, in the 'critical phenomenology' of *Mythical Thought* Cassirer makes a self-conscious attempt to bridge the gap between the newly revived Idealism and positivism. Thus, he argues mightily on behalf of the autonomy, unity and integrity of the human sciences (the Mandarin *Geisteswissenschaften*) as well as the extra-scientific modes of culture, such as myth. Yet all this is done on behalf of an unfavourable comparison to science. Myth embodies a form of primitive thought which, though flawed in comparison to modern knowledge, prepares the way for it.

This picture of Cassirer's accommodationist attitude to myth and other primitivist elements in culture agrees well with the remarkably similar convictions of one of Cassirer's chief intellectual patrons of the Hamburg years: the art historian and benefactor Aby Warburg. The special collections of the Warburg Library encouraged Cassirer to develop his interest in occult and primitive subjects, such as myth. But it is generally overlooked that Warburg's scholarship on the survival of pagan and primitive elements in Western art also roughly paralleled the theories of Cassirer. Even a casual perusal of the monographs sponsored by the Warburg Library during the 1920s and later will show how Warburg sought both to promote an appreciation of 'primitive' subjects and to warn of their potential threat to the fragile structure of rationality which protected liberal-democratic culture. Although Cassirer and Warburg thought along very much the same lines, it is hard to know about specific cases and/or directions of influence. Cassirer claims that *The Philosophy of Symbolic Forms* was already well under way by the time he accepted the chair of philosophy at Hamburg. But it will surprise no one familiar with Warburg's work that Cassirer's first publication of myth, *Die Begriffsform im Mythischen Denken,* should have appeared under the auspices of the Warburg Library in 1922.

With benefit of hindsight, one might be tempted to look uncharitably on the likes of Cassirer and Warburg. One wishes they had spoken more forthrightly against Weimar primitivism, rather than tried to see its best side. Yet it would be absurd to blame them, as accommodationists, for deficiencies in courage or for the errant course history took in their day. Even Ringer's indictment of the Mandarins is perhaps too severe. After all, the Nazis were as good at being 'machine-like' and 'scientific' as they were at tapping the irrationalist and romantic primitivist sentiments of their day. The ability of intellectuals to affect the events of their time is probably more circumscribed than they themselves would care to admit. Perhaps the best one can expect of them is to tell the truth as they see it. Cassirer did this and more in the way he dealt with mythical thinking. Without losing his own bearings, he tried to appeal to the best in the mythically motivated movements of his day. He tried to show them how they might interpret their own mythologising instincts as part of the same human intellectual tendencies as culminated in science and ordinary reason. By arguing that Mandarin mythophiles should see in 'rational' thinking a neutralised yet transcended form of mythical thinking, Cassirer sought to reconcile them to the kind of liberal-rationalist tradition for which he stood. That he failed to sway his irrationalist contemporaries may testify more to the limitations of his time and place than to any deficiency in his own moral courage. He was not in the position to be a Max Weber. As it was, one ought to admire the ingenuity of Cassirer's plan, as well as the risks he took on behalf of liberal values in a period unfriendly to republican (and especially Jewish) intellectuals.

If Cassirer's work on myth can be well located within these interwoven 'internal' professional and 'external' cultural and political contextual networks, it also accords well with the overall logic of *The Philosophy of Symbolic Forms*. *Mythical Thought,* the second volume of this work, fits with the first volume, on language, and with the third and final volume, on knowledge, in a way which is integral to Cassirer's thought. It is to some extent independently intelligible in terms of the arguments of the three volumes, although we should not understand the reason for the existence of this volume, nor of the thrust of its arguments as Cassirer had intended them, without considering the context in which those arguments were conceived. We shall now, therefore, consider how *Mythical Thought* fits the progression of Cassirer's philosophy of symbolic forms and weave our findings this back into the contextual network already elaborated. Cassirer starts with language.

HUMBOLDT AND THE PHILOSOPHY OF LANGUAGE

Language holds a special place in Cassirer's epistemological scheme as the ordinary medium of rational or cognitive discourse. But he was troubled by the discrepancies between the presupposed ontologies of modern physics and ordinary language, which in turn cast doubts on the utility of rational discourse to order human affairs. Cassirer saw that, unlike ordinary language, modern physics dispensed with the old fundamental categories of substance and property. The world it laid bare was devoid of emotion, meaning or human warmth; yet it had immense cognitive prestige. As best one knew, the cosmology of modern physics told one what the world was really like. For Cassirer, this created a double problem: he was inclined to respect science as much as he cared about the integrity of ordinary rational discourse. How could one avoid the inevitable conclusion that ordinary language reflected merely a 'form of misunderstanding', as Suzanne Langer put it? And how, moreover, could one resist the even harsher incipient criticism of the fantastic world-view of myth? Cassirer's answer to this dilemma is first to view myth historically, as an 'archaic mode of understanding' rather than just a 'mode of misunderstanding'. Along with language, myth had to be given a second look in order to evade the damaging consequences of the rise of the 'ideal languages' of modern physics and mathematics.

One way to escape these consequences of an unfavourable comparison with the new ideal languages was to think about ordinary language as an activity rather than a mere counter-sign or picture of reality. Though the ideal languages may represent superior 'pictures' of reality, they are inferior 'agents' in the drama of social life. Ordinary language, by contrast, while representing a poor picture of reality, is an excellent agent force in social life. With this in mind Cassirer could proceed to defend ordinary language and, by extension, myth.

By posing the problem this way, Cassirer was able to draw upon the linguistic thinking of the Kantian Wilhelm von Humboldt. In Humboldt's work one meets a rationalist theory of language similar in some ways to Noam Chomsky's. Humboldt believed that language 'creates' the world, rather than merely reflects it. Language presses certain *a priori* forms onto bare sensations, and orders them into totalities, ideas and world-views. Here, language may be said to 'act' or be an instrument. It is therefore practical, although for Humboldt (and Cassirer) linguistic 'praxis' is what I should call 'Idealist'. For Humboldt and Cassirer, language works spontaneously and creatively for human beings. In fact, the Idealist theory of praxis rests on the belief that human beings create only when free from compulsion. Yes, the causality of linguistic processes differs from that of material processes—but not in a way which diminishes the integrity of language. Although language may not reflect the material world as physics does, it does reflect the spontaneity of the spirit, while also working to build the human realm of culture.

One can thus see how for Humboldt and Cassirer language became a prototype of culture, which they understood similarly to the Mandarin revivers of Idealism. Since culture is produced by the spirit, it bears the trademark of the spirit—freedom. It is therefore incumbent upon us to distinguish the products of the epistemologically quite different worlds of physics and ordinary language. This in turn inspires the quest for an autonomous theory of language, a quest begun by Humboldt and continued by Cassirer as a theory of the autonomous symbolic (cultural) forms. In Humboldt's view, reports Ellen Wood, 'man has the right to fulfil his essential creative nature, the nature that is best exemplified by the spontaneous and creative qualities of language'.

Thus Cassirer's debt to Humboldt is profound: Humboldt allows Cassirer to accept the bifurcation of nature which the new ideal language of physics demands. But this does not force Cassirer to degrade the lived-in world of human culture. Indeed, this becomes a spacious and challenging place in which men can exercise the freedom that is theirs by right. What does it matter if the natural sciences show us a world of strict determinism? Let the natural sciences monopolise the role of picturing reality—if indeed they really do. The symbolic forms of language, myth, art, religion, and so on, apply themselves to the far more interesting task of producing culture.

Built as it is on Humboldt's theory of language, Cassirer's theory of myth should also be seen as pragmatic in the Idealist sense. In myth, Cassirer says, 'word and name do not designate and signify, they are and act'. Myth labours in a 'great spiritual process', a process by which 'consciousness frees itself from the passive captivity in sensory impressions and creates a world of its own in accordance with a spiritual principle'. Thus in mythical stories, as indeed in every aspect of culture, one finds evidence of creative human agency, here operating on the epistemological plane.

HEGEL

If one were to try to isolate the chief Kantian element in Cassirer's theory of myth, it would surely be his *a priori* approach. Although Cassirer differs from Kant in supposing that many *a priori* modes of experience may be isolated, he goes about his investigations with a Kantian eye for the principles of formation which make possible various symbolic forms. But scholars have been particularly troubled by idealistic (particularly Hegelian) elements in Cassirer's thought. Some believe he departed from the strictly 'critical' line of Cohen and Natorp and verged toward the Idealist neo-Kantian position, because he did not *unambiguously* grant mathematics and science pride of place as prototypes of human knowledge. Cassirer's resistance to the positivist monistic scheme of knowledge did not, however, prevent him from thinking of mathematics and the sciences as ideals. Like a true positivist, Cassirer maintained his respect for mathematics and science, but he put them into relation with the symbolic forms of culture. Here, as elsewhere, Cassirer accommodated contrasting positions by synthesis. But no Absolute haunts the scene. Cassirer simply wants to affirm the autonomy of the various symbolic forms: 'all content of culture presupposes and involves a primordial act of mind, an act of creative integration'.

Although he dismissed the Absolute, one must not think that Cassirer could or would do without Hegel. He very much needed and wanted Hegel. Through the theory of *Aufhebung*, linked as it is with an evolutionary progressive theory of the growth of knowledge, Hegel offered Cassirer the classic model of accommodationist synthesising. One will accordingly recognise in **Mythical Thought** that, although myth may itself be a lowly form of consciousness, it develops into the higher forms of knowledge we call science, mathematics, and so forth. Hegel's organic metaphor also entails that primitive forms (like the larval stage of insect growth) die away as the higher forms come to maturity. Thus the theory of *Aufhebung* permits Cassirer *both* to criticise mythical thinking as a 'primitive' form of consciousness (not really as good as the later stages—immature) and at the same time to accept it gratefully as a necessary stage in the birth of higher, more mature forms of knowledge. Referring to the process Cassirer says,

> the same universal forms of intuition and thought . . . constitute the unity of consciousness as such and . . . accordingly constitute the unity of both the mythical consciousness and the consciousness of pure knowledge. In this respect it may be said that each of these forms, before taking on its specific logical form and character, must pass through a preliminary mythical stage. [*Mythical Thought*].

Hegel encouraged a salutary optimism about, and willingness to think the best of, the long-term consequences of modern civilisation—something many of Cassirer's Mandarin contemporaries found impossible. One thinks especially of Spengler's gloomy forecast of the decline of the West and Heidegger's resigned vision of human *Geworfenheit* (man's being thrown into or abandoned in the world). In *The Myth of the State* Cassirer assessed these fashionable philosophies of the 1920s and noted their ill effects on the time:

> the new philosophy did enfeeble and slowly undermine the forces that could have resisted the modern political myths. . . . [It has] given up all hopes on an active share in the construction · and reconstruction of man's cultural life. Such philosophy renounces its own fundamental theoretical and ethical ideas. It can be used then as a pliable instrument in the hands of the political leaders.

Thanks to Hegel, Cassirer could see in the rise of the new physics and the developments of mathematics a marked improvement in what we know. Here were not signs of man's alienation or 'need for roots', as the anti-modernist Mandarin critics of science believed. Moreover, even in the face of less reassuring signs, such as inhumane technological and economic developments, Cassirer's Hegelian faith could keep him going. These bleaker aspects of modernity were transient and would be overcome (*aufgehoben*). As a result, Cassirer could muster a marvellous confidence at a time when many of his compatriots were laid low by the pessimism that followed Germany's defeat in 1918. In this context, Cassirer's Hegelian faith in the future led him to place his hope in the eventual defeat and transmutation of mythical thinking, and the progressive triumph of reason in history.

CATEGORIES OF MYTHICAL THOUGHT AND
'WHOLENESS'

It would be impossible to appreciate this grand vision without some sense of the nature of the mythical *a priori*. What made it for Cassirer at once the source of higher modes of thinking and a level of consciousness which enlightened folk would want to transcend?

One will seek in vain in the rambling details of Cassirer's account of particular categories of mythical thinking for the nature of the mythical *a priori*. Cassirer himself really cares only about the common 'tonality', or dominant integrating idea characteristic of mythical thinking. Like many another Idealist thinker, he is much too concerned

with the central principle to care much about the welter of details. Admitting as much he says,

> This tonality assumed by the particular concepts within the mythical consciousness seems at first glance totally individual, something which can only be felt but in no way known and understood. And yet beneath this individual phenomenon there lies a universal . . . [which] encompasses and determines the particular configurations of this thinking and, as it were, sets its imprint upon them. [*Mythical Thought*]

And what might this 'universal' be? It is nothing less than the Mandarin idea of 'wholeness' or 'unity'. With respect to mythical space Cassirer says, for example,

> All species and varieties of things have their 'home' somewhere in space, and their absolute reciprocal strangeness is thereby annulled: local mediation leads to a spiritual mediation between them, to a *composition of all differences in a great whole,* a fundamental mythical plan of the world. [*Mythical Thought*]

Yet not only are the distinctions presented in the myths more apparent than real, but there is also something bogus about the unity of myth. Although their tasks paralleled each other, Cassirer believed that he and Kant discovered rather different sorts of 'unities' in the fields they investigated. Cassirer believed the unity of myth was essentially 'emotional', while the epistemological investigations of Kant disclosed so-called 'logical' or 'rational' unities or wholes. The world of myth, Cassirer tells us, 'becomes intelligible only if behind it we can feel the dynamic of . . . feeling from which it originally grew'. In this sense, there is something bogus about the unity or wholeness of myth for Cassirer.

This is unfortunately a complicated point, but I should like to try to elucidate it by treating the grounds of Cassirer's viewpoint here. Two items need to be discussed in this connection: (1) the nature and status of the *principle* by which myths are thought to cohere internally; (2) the meaning of the idea of 'emotional' unity.

The 'Principle of Concrescence' and 'das Lebensgefühl'

Cassirer's reading of anthropological literature led him at first to the conclusion, shared by many in his time, that the thinking of primitive man was flatly irrational. This was evidenced by the anarchy of myths, totemic associations and other manifestations of mythical thinking. For one thing, it seemed that anything could happen in myths—any relationships could be posited between elements in a mythical story: 'Whereas scientific cognition can combine elements only by differentiating them in the same basic critical act, myth seems to roll everything it touches into unity without distinction. Or, in particular connection with the notion of class membership, such as in totemism, Cassirer says, 'In mythical thinking, *any* similarity of sensuous manifestation suffices to group the entities n which it appears into a single mythical "genus". Any characteristic . . . is as good as another. . . .'

Thus, if anything could happen in myths, how could one make a case for their logical integrity? How could myth reveal any sort of *a priori* whatsoever? Even if one claimed that myth revealed a unique mode of rationality, one would still need to show what this was. Myths seemed unlikely to be able to do so, since all they showed Cassirer was anarchy.

Yet Cassirer was unwilling to admit that other men could be incorrigibly and consistently irrational. His Enlightenment humanist faith held firm. When it came to the subject of the manifest inconsistencies in mythical thinking, therefore, this faith in universal rationality led Cassirer into the peculiar view that mythical thinking was governed by the 'law of concrescence'. I say 'peculiar' because this so-called 'law' seems really only Cassirer's label for logical anarchy—the law of 'anything goes':

> mythical thinking shows itself to be concrete in the literal sense: whatever things it may seize upon undergo a characteristic concretion: they grow together. Whereas scientific cognition seems a synthesis of distinctly differentiated elements, mythical intuition ultimately brings about a coincidence of whatever elements it combines . . [the] law of concrescence or *coincidence of the members of a relation in mythical thinking*. . . . [**Mythical Thought**]

One is, I think, free to interpret Cassirer here as writing partly tongue-in-cheek. Because he distinguishes this mythical unity from the 'logical' unity of science, he clearly realises a certain difference in meaning. Yet he wants to press on with the concept of the 'law of concrescence', knowing all the while that the regularity of irregularity does not make for any sort of 'law'. Is this just another example of what Peter Gay calls Cassirer's 'rage for coherence', a kind of Kantian polemical habit he could break? Or does Cassirer perhaps have certain reasons—related to the external context of his theory—for wanting to find the prototypes or traces of logical thinking in unlikely places?

The argument of this section, and, indeed, of this chapter, has been that Cassirer had *external* as well as internal contexts in mind when constructing his theory as he did. It seems to me that in coming up against such a notion as the 'law of concrescence' one naturally feels the need to look for signs of extra-textual concerns. The tortuous way Cassirer labours to construct his position here cries out for closer attention. How does it serve his extra-textual arguments—whether internal or external?

To answer this question one needs to attend more closely to the *way* 'grow together', as Cassirer puts it. For him, mythical thinking coheres in an 'emotional' unity. The 'wholeness' of myth is not logical or 'rational'; it is 'emotional'. In his later ***Essay on Man*** Cassirer says, 'Myth and primitive religion are by no means entirely incoherent, they are not bereft of sense or reason. But, their coherence depends much more upon unity of feeling than upon logical rules.'

What is more, Cassirer identifies that particular emotion unifying myth as none other than *das Lebensgefühl*. This feeling of the unity of life connoted an especially sentimental attitude to mindlessness perhaps unknown outside the tradition of German romanticism. In the ideology of the Mandarins, as well as in popular parlance, terms such as

das Leben and *Lebensgefühl* suggested a vague and moody opposition to modernity and all its trappings. *Lebensphilosophie* taught the superiority of immediate experience over reflection, emotion over reason, synthesis over analysis, past over present, and so on. As Fritz Ringer puts it, 'In a very general sense, life philosophy was the doctrine that life in its immediacy is man's primary reality'.

Cassirer well understood this philosophy and its popular manifestations. Yet, unlike strict opponents of *Lebensphilosophie*, Cassirer sought to reconcile *das Leben* with its dialectical opposite, *der Geist*. This he tried to do theoretically in his essay ' "Spirit" and "Life" in Contemporary Philosophy' (1930) and, indirectly, in his work on mythical thinking. Mythical thought demonstrates a unity of spirit (*der Geist*) and feeling (*das Gefühl*). Here Cassirer was undertaking nothing less than a reconciliation of romanticism with rationalism, primitivism with modernism, tribalism with cosmopolitanism—to mention only a few possible meanings of the noble opposition of *Leben* and *Geist*.

The Meaning of 'Emotional' Unity

All this may be well and good, but it still does not explain just how *das Lebensgefühl* spoke to the problem of the coherence of mythical thinking. What precisely did the *feeling* of the unity of life have to do with whether and why a story made sense for traditional folk? How did the feeling of the unity of life perform as any sort of prototype of a Kantian unity? What can Cassirer possibly mean when he tells us that the world of myth 'becomes intelligible only if behind it we can feel the dynamic life feeling from which it originally grew'?

To understand this, one needs to appreciate that Cassirer held a variety of faculty psychological beliefs, treating the 'emotions' and the 'intellect' as if they were subtle internal organs of some sort. Unlike physical organs, which secrete hormones and other physical substances, these subtle organs 'secrete' their own distinctive products—the intellect generates thoughts, the emotions generate feelings, and so on. Thus, for Cassirer to attribute an element of culture to the 'emotions' is virtually for him to say that such an element cannot be judged by rational standards. If mythical thought originates in the emotions, it cannot come from the intellect. It must thus be irrational, a mode of pseudo-thought.

Put differently, when Cassirer attributes a belief to emotional, he is making at least two strong claims: (1) the belief is false; (2) it is held without good reasons—it derives from strong wants or desires on the part of the believer, from coercion or need, impulse, confusion, or the like. In short, Cassirer rejects such beliefs because they fail to meet the normal criteria of rationality: the believer is not able to offer (good) reasons why the belief is held.

Cassirer believed that no good *reasons* could be offered for saying the kinds of things found in myths. No good *reasons* could be given for making the kinds of connections made in myths. Yet myths persisted. And people manifestly believed in myths—and believed that they made a kind of 'sense'. This could only be explained, Cassirer believed, by appealing to the 'emotions'—and in particular the feeling of the unity of life. By evoking this he seems to have meant that myths cohered simply because people wilfully insisted that they did, felt *coerced* to believe that they did, *impulsively* concluded that they did, or the like. In this way, myths represented in some sense the paradigm of an active irrationally constituted cultural form. No autonomous logical force made myths make sense in the way a good valid syllogism would make sense. It was merely human wilfulness which prevented myths from flying apart in a shower of narrative fragments. The mythical 'unity' testified to the stubborn, impulsive, arbitrary and uncritical will of the people devoted to them. Cassirer even dramatises this irrationality by casting myth as an appropriate object of *physical* analysis. In myth the elements are linked together by a 'real force'. In myth 'the relations which it postulates are not logical relations . . . they are a kind of glue which can somehow fasten the most dissimilar things together'.

This talk of physical connection and emotional force may come as a surprise from one who had promised a 'spiritual' analysis of myth. Yet the logic of Cassirer's internal position dictates that he treat myth and emotion in this material way. In Cassirer's Hegelian hierarchy of value, knowledge ranks higher the more abstract and ideal it is. Abstract mathematics, logic and the new physics rank high, while sensory awareness, immediate experience and feelings rest at the bottom. If thought-like entities occupy the highest status, then act-like things take the lowest places. What is more, if Cassirer wanted to neutralise the Mandarin infatuation with irrationalism in his time, he could have done no better than to associate myth, life, emotion, materiality and so on as he did. From both the internal and the external perspective, Cassirer's peculiar argument here makes sense.

That myth is held together by 'real force' also fits nicely with the fact that Cassirer held that it works as a 'real force'. By speaking of myth as an action, and thus as something which can impose its a priori forms onto nature, Cassirer claims the legacy of Humboldt. Humboldt was an Idealist pragmatist with respect to the agency of language; in *Mythical Thought* Cassirer comes very close to being a materialist pragmatist, as he does later in *The Myth of the State*. This he does by likening and logically subordinating myth to ritual activity. Unless one understands ritual, one cannot understand mythical stories:

> It can clearly be shown that a vast number of mythical motifs had their origin in the imitation of a cultic rather than natural process. . . . The action is the beginning; the mythical explanation . . . comes later . . . it is . . . the cult which forms the preliminary stage and objective foundation of myth. [*Mythical Thought*]

It also seems evident that Cassirer had particularly good *external* reasons for casting myth in this ritualist, irrationalist and material light: the 'Volkish' movements not only sought to ground their behaviour in the exemplary images of Teutonic mythology, but also sought to ground these myths in ritual performances which involved the entire community in a ceremonial celebration of the 'Volkish' world-view. Known as *Thinge*, these open-air rituals were first staged in the late nineteenth century under the

direction of Ernst Wachler, and later were taken over by the Nazis as the basis of their mass liturgical spectacles. One ought also to keep in mind here the place of Wagner and his *Ring* cycle and the ritualistic use of theatre to impress the lessons of Germanic mythology on its audiences. It would be surprising indeed if Cassirer had been insensitive to these features of contemporary culture, and if they were not in some way behind his implicit criticism of ritual. Later, in *The Myth of the State,* Cassirer becomes much more explicit in his criticism of ritual, giving it the Freudian sense of 'ritualistic' by linking it with the irrational unconscious and merely motor activity: 'Rites are . . . mere motor manifestations of the psychic life . . . they disclose . . . appetites, needs, desires; not . . . "representations" or "ideas" . . . these tendencies are translated into movements—into rhythmical solemn movements or wild dances. . . . '

In the 'Volkish' view, these rituals, which were staged out in the countryside, served to unite their participants with the spirit of the Volk. One was made 'whole' again by breathing the fresh air and at the same time absorbing the healing lesson these dramas narrated and acted out. In this natural and ritual setting, the 'life force' of the Volk flowed into the participant, healing the ills of modernity and acting as a tonic. From Cassirer's point of view, ritual was also a stiff narcotic which incapacitated human reason.

CASSIRER AND 'PROPHETIC FAITH'

One wonders how Cassirer managed, so remarkably, to keep his balance amid such a tumult of social, political and philosophical conflicts. The faith of a Hegelianised *Aufklärer* can be mighty indeed. Yet Cassirer did not hold this faith in its pure secular form. He synthesised his Enlightenment faith with a universalist prophetic Judaism, which gave added depth and perspective to his critique of mythical thinking.

Although he always thought of himself as a German first and then as a Jew, Cassirer's religious moorings were strong and steady. Unlike many of his Jewish contemporaries, he was repelled by the thought of a conversion of convenience to Christianity. On the other hand, his Judaism was universalistic and cosmopolitan. Until his exile from Nazi Germany, Cassirer found the thought of Zionism and Jewish ethnocentrism 'completely foreign'. One gathers that it was the rise and triumph of anti-semitism in Germany from the 1920s on which pushed him, like Einstein and others, to acknowledge his own Jewishness and then, later, even entertain the thought of emigration to what in 1933 was still Palestine. In her biography of her husband, Toni Cassirer recounts her astonishment at her first personal encounter with blatant anti-semitism. In Hamburg in 1922, a disagreement with a neighbour erupted into a personal verbal attack on the Cassirers, who were told, in precise words, to 'go back to Palestine'. The highborn Cassirers associated Palestine with either narrow orthodoxy or displaced East European Jewry. 'Unser Vaterland was Deutschland—Ernst war ein deutscher Philosoph', Toni Cassirer writes with indignation.

Cassirer's Judaism was not, however, as assimilationist as

this may suggest. Beyond rejecting all thoughts of conversion to Christianity, he deeply admired the Jewish prophetic tradition as interpreted by his teacher at Marburg, Hermann Cohen. With Paul Natorp, an acknowledged leader of the critical branch of the neo-Kantian movement, Cohen was also an inventive and influential thinker in his own right. Although loyal to the special message of the Old Testament prophets, Cohen believed they taught the gospel of universalist humanitarian cosmopolitanism. His belief that to be most Jewish was to be most universal may in part explain his early aloofness to the young Cassirer. Cohen suspected Cassirer was one of those ambitious converts to Christianity who ignorantly threw off their cultural, racial and religious heritage for the sole purpose of conforming to the common culture. Cohen's coldness to him was especially disappointing for Cassirer, both because he did not then know the reason for Cohen's behaviour and because he had come all the way from Berlin especially to study Kant under Cohen's direction. Once, however, Cohen had realised his mistake and recognised Cassirer's sympathy with his own views, the two men became fast friends. They remained so until Cohen's death in 1918.

Cassirer seems to have been particularly affected by Cohen's theory of the distinctive nature of prophetic Judaism. Cohen taught the distinction between 'religion' and 'prophetic faith', his term for Old Testament monotheism as taught by the prophets. 'Religion' here refers to that element in a religion which man contributes. For Cohen, this includes cultural elements such as myth, ritual, feelings and the general tendencies among religious folk to anthropomorphise the deity. 'Prophetic religion' refers to God's contribution to the relationship with man. For Cohen, this consists in monotheism, universalist morality and orientation given to the future development of mankind as a whole. Cohen's preference for the ideal conforms nicely to certain anti-ritualist interpretations of the role of the Old Testament prophets, centred in reform traditions of both Judaism and Christianity. Cohen could not have been unaware either of German 'Volkish' criticisms of Judaism as legalistic and sterile in contrast to the supposed vitality of German national neo-pagan or pseudo-Christian religions. At times, Cohen's formulation of Judaism seems almost a direct reply, to the 'Volkish' detractors of the prophetic faith. True Judaism—the faith of the prophets—is a Judaism of internal and universal moral purity, not the ritual purity of legalistic and parochial orthodoxy. Judaism is indeed a 'living' faith. What is more, unlike the narrow nationalistic and mystically inspired 'Volkish' religions, it had broken free of all parochialism, ritualism and myth. Cassirer puts these sentiments as well as Cohen himself might have done:

> In the prophetic books of the Old Testament we find an entirely new direction of thought and feeling [as compared to primitive myth-laden religions]. The ideal of purity means something quite different from all the former mythical conceptions. To seek for purity or impurity in an object, in a material thing, has become impossible. Even human actions, as such, are no longer regarded as pure or impure. The only purity that

has a religious significance and dignity is the purity of the heart. [*Essay on Man*]

Anticipating Cassirer in other ways, Cohen held that, while religion may be lifeless without myth, myth had to be subordinated to the rule of reason. True religion should complete and perfect theoretical thought. Since myth grew out of human emotions and fantasies, it could never be the basis for a purified religion. Thus, as the prophets in their own time overcame idolatrous mythical and ritual religions, so also modern man could and should learn to overcome the new political and racial mythologies of the twentieth century. This required firm commitment to transcendental elements of religion which, for Cohen and Cassirer, were the universal, moral and intellectual truths found in the immemorial teachings of the prophets. Cohen himself, in addressing the 1913 World Congress for Free Christianity and Religious Progress, says,

> We have to regain the belief in moral regeneration, in the moral future of mankind. We have to regain this belief in the face of, and in spite of the egoism of nations and the materialism of classes. The true living God cannot breathe except in social morality and cosmopolitan humanity. [Quoted in Cassirer, **"Hermann Cohen, 1842-1918"**]

Whether Cohen had German 'Volkish' movements specifically in mind as he spoke I cannot say. In theory, his pointed remarks apply just as well to their tribalistic nationalism as to the egoistic 'nations' and 'classes' actually mentioned.

Cassirer picked up Cohen's tune and played it as Hegelian fugue: to be most profoundly Jewish meant to follow the example of the Hebrew prophets; to follow the example of the prophets meant to be most profoundly universalist and rational. Even the evolution of the spirit one witnesses with the modern triumph of science and mathematics over mythical conceptions of nature was foreshadowed and prepared by the zealous anti-ritualism and demythologising of the Hebrew prophets. Both mark the growing power of abstraction and generality, and man's freedom from his 'lower' nature—the life of the emotions and sensuous experience. In Cassirer's view, of course, emotion and sense experience are the essence of mythical thinking. As the spirit evolves to newer heights, it does the work both of the prophets and of the great thinkers of the modern world.

This again brings us full circle to my earlier characterisation of Cassirer as classicist and rationalist. Both his religious background and his philosophical background in Kant, Hegel and the philosophy of science and knowledge equipped him to do battle with the forces of irrationalism as they displayed themselves in the occult, mythically motivated movements of Weimar Germany. That Cassirer tried to oppose these trends in a conciliatory way shows, I think, his own disciplined sense of fairness and humanity, rather than the weakness of character that seemed to afflict other Weimar intellectuals.

A THEORETICAL AFTERWORD

It would be treacherous indeed to attempt a summary of

Cassirer's views here. Rather, let me conclude by dwelling on some theoretical matters, since they have been better put into perspective by the historical inquiry. It is possible to treat Cassirer's theory outside the context I have argued that it had, and this in fact is what every previous critic has done. Yet to ignore the context is to produce less pertinent understanding. Thus, in raising here certain general theoretical points my aim is to illuminate them within Cassirer's Weimar context. The internal and external aspects of Cassirer's theory intertwine themselves with the systematics of Cassirer's theory; it is not always possible or desirable to keep these aspects of an interesting piece of intellectual work separated.

Cassirer's systematics—his monistic *a priori* approach—typifies a whole style of philosophical and theoretical anthropology. Granted, one *can* deduce ever more abstract common principles in so-called 'myths'—perhaps even a single unifying principle. But what is achieved in the end? What is the logical status of such a mythical *a priori*? Are 'myths' only those stories having essentially to do with that idea of 'unity', and an 'emotional' unity at that? Clearly not. Without saying so explicitly, Cassirer simply stipulates that 'myth' is a story 'held together' by the monistic principle of 'emotional unity'.

Thus Cassirer commits the offence of 'prescribing' what 'myth' is under the guise of simple description; he *assumes* a notion of 'myth' and prescribes its employment, when he should have been persuading us to accept a recommendation. If there is anything the endless wrangling about the nature of myths should have indicated, it is that 'myth' has meant, and is likely to continue to mean, just about whatever one would like it to mean. On the face of it, there is no *one* strong candidate for *the* meaning of the term. 'Myth' means *many* things, and not one thing. In this light, even the good-faith *descriptions* of myth that mythologists of the past have offered must be looked on as *prescriptions*.

It is partly Cassirer's Hegelian inheritance, with its universalist and monist ambitions, that leads him to think he can grasp a *single* coherent essence in 'myth'. But we can also understand his deepened attraction for universalist and monist values in the context of the virulent national tribalism in the Germany of his time. Part of the purpose of assuming a single sense of 'myth' is to reduce the possible meaning of the term to manageable proportions—the better to attack and destroy what it is taken to signify. Cassirer seems never even to have considered a more culturally limited enterprise, say in the manner of Georges Dumézil. In the light of his inheritance and purpose, we can perhaps even admire Cassirer's universalism and sympathise with his hidden prescriptive strategy.

This appreciation of the limits to his intentions should free us from facile conceptual criticism of his theory. For example, Cassirer's theory might be criticised for having left out some particular characteristic of myth which another theorist has picked out. Or one might criticise him for saying that *all* myths manifest an emotional unity, when emotional factors seem to affect the formation of only *some* stories. Such criticisms are fair in so far as Cassirer earnestly and unambiguously sought to avoid prescription,

but their usefulness is diminished by to the degree to which Cassirer confused description and prescription—although his confusion of the two is liable to censure on grounds of logic. It is better, I think, to describe Cassirer's theory of myth as a proposal of the broad agenda of modified evolutionist Enlightenment modernism.

Above all, Cassirer was recommending that we look on mythical thinking (and, of course, the mythical *stories* which we produce by that thinking) as a product of the emotions and as a survival of pre-modern ways of thinking. Cassirer's theory of myth is his way of trying to put to the mythophiles and romantics of his day some very hard questions about the consequences of their infatuation with a broad spectrum of occult, 'Volkish', mystic and irrationalist beliefs: Is the immediacy of the emotional experience of unity with Life really enough on which to ground a way of life? Might not this kind of emotionalism be as unreliable and regrettable as earlier kinds? Is the experience of the unity of the Volk really preferable to wider, perhaps more temperate, feelings of unity with all mankind?

In thus relativising the ideological choices people made, Cassirer tried, it seems, to afford people a perspective on their own moral and ideological positions. Granted, presenting believers with the possibility that their beliefs are at least partly matters of choice may not invariably cause them to abandon beliefs one considers evil, such as the various racist beliefs current in Cassirer's time. It is hard to imagine how any arguments could be guaranteed to dislodge beliefs strongly held. Yet showing people what their beliefs entail and asking them whether they want these consequences would seem at least a way of helping them begin to question beliefs which they may not have fully understood.

Having characterised (or caricatured) myth by associating it with a modernist concept of primitivism, Cassirer the *Aufklärer* could draw on the whole rich tradition of Enlightenment polemic. 'Primitive' not only meant emotional, traditional, rural, organic and 'folksy': it also meant irrational, tradition-bound, underdeveloped and economically backward and superstitious. One could well argue that in his own time Cassirer was justified in sounding the alarm against primitivism. Debate over whether Nazi ideology was primarily romantic and primitivist or mechanistic and modernistic will probably never be resolved. The Nazis succeeded politically probably because they were both possessed by the 'dark gods' and also because they possessed powerful 'machines'. Thus the analyses of Cassirer and the other modernist critics of Nazism were not so much wrong as incomplete. If, in all this, Cassirer has left behind the innocent stories of tribal folk, one will understand that in many ways he had far more serious and urgent matters on his mind.

Thus, although Cassirer's theory has little utility as a general theory of myth, it may well tell us about Nazi political uses of myth and how sensitive thinkers could oppose them. But this perhaps tells us as little about myths in general as Cassirer's critique of Weimar 'primitivism' tells us about all 'primitive' folk. To be sure, we might pick out *formal* resemblances between the modern political myths and those of traditional societies, between Nazi mythology and ancient Teutonic mythology. But talk of *substantial* connections is absurd. The *Volk* would find Bayreuth as puzzling as the Bauhaus, Wagner's *Die Walküre* as modern as Lang's 'Metropolis'. The fact is, we know virtually nothing about ancient Germanic uses and interpretations of special stories; and, even if the opposite were true, they would still need to be translated across the centuries separating us from them. Furthermore, we have no evidence that 'myths' (however described) had any kind of emotional value for the *Volk*. Did the Teutonic ancestors experience the same kind of unity of feeling enjoyed by Nazis in Nuremberg? Who knows? Who *could* know? It is one thing that an alienated *Lumpenproletariat* might be stimulated emotionally by the old narratives; it is quite another thing to be sure that *Volk* felt the same way. Modern people should take responsibility for their own 'primitive' antinomian lusts and furies, without attributing them to a long-ago or faraway *Volk*.

Thus Cassirer's acceptance of the 'Volkish' thesis of a substantial continuity between ancient and modern German mythology causes his general theory of myth considerable grief. It also causes him to cast myth in ways which are at best irrelevant to many instances in which myths occur. The tragedy was that Cassirer had to work out his theory of myth within the framework established by those he opposed.

FURTHER READING

Criticism

Allers, Rudolf. "The Philosophy of Ernst Cassirer." *The New Scholasticism* XXV, No. 2 (April 1951): 184-92.
    Overview of the importance of Cassirer's work.

Carini, Louis. "Ernst Cassirer's Psychology II: The Nature of Thinking." *Journal of the History of the Behavioral Science* IX, No. 3 (July 1973): 266-69.
    Observes that Cassirer proposes a view of thinking that is inferential, suggesting an ability to simultaneously conceive what is possible and what is actual.

Goodman, Nelson. "Words, Works, Worlds." In *Ways of Worldmaking*, pp. 1-22. Indianapolis: Hackett Publishing Company, 1978.
    A discussion of the way in which the variety and function of symbols creates a multiplicity of worlds in Cassirer's philosophy.

Hamburg, Carl H. *Symbol and Reality: Studies in the Philosophy of Ernst Cassirer*. The Hague: Martinus Nijhoff, 1956, 172 p.

Explains and elaborates upon Cassirer's philosophy, focusing on his concept of symbolic forms and how that concept relates to the work of other twentieth-century philosophers.

Heidegger, Martin. A review of Ernst Cassirer's *Mythical Thought*, in his *The Piety of Thinking*, translated by James G. Hart and John C. Maraldo, pp. 32-45. Indiana University Press, 1976.
    Review, which originally appeared in 1928 in a German literary journal, raises some critical questions regarding the second volume of Cassirer's three-volume work *The Philosophy of Symbolic Forms*.

Hendel, Charles W. "Introduction." In *The Philosophy of Symbolic Forms, Volume 1: Language*, by Ernst Cassirer, pp. 1-65. Translated by Ralph Manheim. New Haven, Conn.: Yale University Press, 1953.
    Discusses developments in Cassirer's thought which led to his philosophy of symbolic forms.

Itzkoff, Seymour W. *Ernst Cassirer: Scientific Knowledge and the Concept of Man*. Notre Dame: Notre Dame University Press, 1971, 286 p.
    Examines Cassirer's neo-Kantianism and his views about discursive knowledge in terms of recent developments in the philosophy of science.

———. *Ernst Cassirer: Philosopher of Culture*. Boston: Twayne Publishers, 1977, 198 p.
    Links the historical origins of Cassirer's neo-Kantianism to his later philosophical thinking, focusing primarily on Cassirer's outlook on cultural knowledge, especially as it is set forth in *The Philosophy of Symbolic Forms*.

Lenneberg, Eric H. "A Note on Cassirer's Philosophy of Language." *Phenomenological Research* XV, No. 4 (June 1955): 512-22.
    Examines how Cassirer's philosophy of language evolved and changed between his earlier and later works.

Sundaram, K. *Cassirer's Conception of Causality*. New York: Peter Lang, 1987, 151 p.
    Provides an analysis of Cassirer's concept of causality and questions the consistency of Cassirer's view of causality in light of quantum theory.

Verene, Donald Phillip. "Introduction: Cassirer's Thought 1935-45." *Symbol, Myth, and Culture: Essays and Lectures of Ernst Cassirer, 1935-45*, edited by Donald Phillip Verene, pp. 1-45. New Haven, Conn.: Yale University Press, 1979.
    Contends that Cassirer's late, unpublished essays demonstrate that he should not be considered as simply a neo-Kantian, but should also be viewed as a philosopher of culture who grappled with what it means to be human.

E. M. Delafield

1890-1943

(Full name Edmée Elizabeth Monica de la Pasture Dashwood) English novelist, essayist, playwright, and journalist.

INTRODUCTION

Delafield is best known as the author of satiric fiction and humorous essays, particularly the "Provincial Lady" series of novels, which comprises social commentary in the form of fictionalized diaries. She also wrote historical fiction set in the Victorian and Edwardian periods of English history and produced such crime novels as *Messalina of the Suburbs* (1923), an examination of the motivations of a woman accused of murder. Although Delafield's works fell out of print soon after her death, her reputation has been maintained by such critics as J. B. Priestley, who favorably appraised her ability to reveal common human pretensions through irony, and by feminist critics who have praised her realistic presentation of domestic issues.

Delafield was descended from French nobility who settled in England at the time of the French Revolution. Her mother, Elizabeth Lydia Rosabelle Bonham, was a novelist who specialized in sentimental fiction and Victorian drawing room comedies. Delafield herself published four novels before she married Major Arthur Paul Dashwood, OBE, in 1919. Themes in her early novels seem to have been drawn from her youthful experiences with minor European royalty, as a postulant for Catholic sisterhood, and later in service to the British government during World War I. After her marriage Delafield's literary interests turned towards domestic issues of education, child-rearing, and the emotional dramas of lost romantic love, divorces, and arranged marriages. She died following a brief illness in 1943.

Major Works

Delafield is best remembered for the semiautobiographical series of "Provincial Lady" sketches commissioned by the feminist publication *Time and Tide*. The first of these works, *Diary of a Provincial Lady* (1930), put a comedic spin on the domestic pressures facing rural nobility during the Great Depression. Other titles in the series include *Further Diary of a Provincial Lady* (1932) and *The Provincial Lady in America* (1934). While Delafield often drew inspiration from everyday life, she also pursued an interest in crime fiction, most notably in *Messalina of the Suburbs*, a novelization of a murder case involving a married couple and the wife's lover. In the work Delafield explored the moral and psychological vapidity of the central female character rather than the more sensational aspects of the crime and subsequent execution. Despite such forays into crime fiction, Delafield was better known for amusing anecdotes that she contributed to such periodicals as *Punch*

and for such literary studies as *The Brontës: Their Lives Recorded by Their Contemporaries* (1935) and *Ladies and Gentlemen in Victorian Fiction* (1937). Throughout the 1920s and 1930s Delafield wrote in a variety of genres, exploring her most prominent themes, including issues of child-rearing and complacency in marriage, competition among women in the workplace, fads in education, medicine, and politics, and the mannerisms of life in high society. The last installment of her famous alter-ego, *The Provincial Lady in War-Time* (1940), returned to the civilian follies first depicted in her novel *The War-Workers* (1918). Delafield's final works include the historical novels *No One Now Will Know* (1941) and *Late and Soon* (1943).

Critical Reception

Delafield's works were widely popular among both English and North American audiences during her lifetime. In 1947, Margaret Haig Thomas, Lady Rhondda, the editor of *Time and Tide,* wrote a reconsideration of Delafield's subjects and approach, praising the tone and style of her novels while noting that they address timeless concerns of domestic life. Later commentators have noted a resemblance between her humorous depiction of common human pretensions and that of the nineteenth-century English novelist Jane Austen and have praised Delafield's use of irony in the presentation of everyday life.

PRINCIPAL WORKS

Zella Sees Herself (novel) 1917
The Pelicans (novel) 1918
The War-Workers (novel) 1918
Consequences (novel) 1919
Tension (novel) 1920
The Heel of Achilles (novel) 1921
Humbug (novel) 1921
The Optimist (novel) 1922
Messalina of the Suburbs (novel) 1923
The Chip and the Block (novel) 1925
The Entertainment, and Other Stories (short stories) 1927
The Way Things Are (novel) 1927
Women Are Like That (short stories) 1929
Diary of a Provincial Lady (novel) 1930
To See Ourselves: A Domestic Comedy (drama) 1930
Turn Back the Leaves (novel) 1930
Challenge to Clarissa (novel) 1931
Further Diary of a Provincial Lady (novel) 1932; also published as *The Provincial Lady Goes Further*, 1932, and as *The Provincial Lady in London*, 1933

Thank Heaven Fasting (novel) 1932; also published as
    A Good Man's Love, 1932
General Impressions (journalism) 1933
The Glass Wall (drama) 1933
The Provincial Lady in America (novel) 1934
The Bazalgettes [published anonymously] (novel)
    1935
*The Brontës: Their Lives Recorded by Their Contempo-
    raries* [editor] (biography) 1935
As Others Hear Us: A Miscellany (sketches) 1937
Ladies and Gentlemen in Victorian Fiction (criticism)
    1937
Straw without Bricks: I Visit Soviet Russia (journalism
    and essays) 1937; also published as *I Visit the Sovi-
    ets: The Provincial Lady Looks at Russia,* 1937
When Women Love (short stories) 1938; also pub-
    lished as *Three Marriages,* 1939
Love Has No Resurrection, and Other Stories (short sto-
    ries) 1939
The Provincial Lady in War-Time (novel) 1940
No One Now Will Know (novel) 1941
Late and Soon (novel) 1943

CRITICISM

R. Brimley Johnson (essay date 1920)

SOURCE: "E. M. Delafield," in *Some Contemporary Novelists (Women),* Leonard Parsons, 1920, pp. 177-84.

[*In the following essay, Johnson discusses egoism and the
sense of self portrayed in Delafield's female protagonists.*]

There is a certain competent serenity about Miss Delafield's work which excludes her, perhaps, from the ranks
of those who are—rather aggressively "new" in their manner. Though actually a "war-product" and, in one novel
at least, humourously intent upon the lighter psychology
of war, she does not—like most of her contemporaries—
write with the new subtlety of analysis, from the soul outwards. Like the conventional novelist she relates, while
they speak. Her four stories are observed, composed, and
presented in the normal manner of fiction: where the author permits herself to see inside all her characters—as
one cannot in real life. They are not the actual utterances
of one tortured soul, who can only interpret life through
her own experience: but, on the other hand, she is—like
the others—most frankly feminine: always revealing the
woman's outlook, gently satirical upon the fact that "gentlemen"—as Aunt Marianne so naïvely expresses it—"do
not always think quite as we do about these things"; i.e.
about anything.

It has been noticed already that in women-novelists, the
analysing habit is very frequently devoted to the study of
egoism; and Miss Delafield's Zella affords the most striking example of this tendency: not quite so intense as Miss
Dane's studies, but equally subtle.

"Zella," indeed, "sees herself" clearly at all times; and the
comparative indifference of other people about this fasci-

nating topic constitutes her main grudge against life. For
she *is* fascinating (therein lies the triumph of Miss Delafield) and, in reality, quite astonishingly dependent upon
public opinion. In fact, the type of egoism is very original,
and most exceptionally attractive. Zella is governed—not
only in action but even in thought—by a very passion for
adaptability. She demands always to be in the "centre of
the picture"; but she expects to *find* this position by absolutely conforming to type; doing and thinking just exactly
what people wish, and expect, her to do. The effort leads,
naturally, to failure and confusion, because no two people
expect at all the same thing: and, in her case, the difficulty
is to emerge with emphasis through the dramatically opposed standards and tastes of her nearest relations and her
most intimate friends. It may seem a strange thing to say
of a confirmed egotist: but the real difficulty about Zella
is to discover whether she has any individuality at all,
really her own.

Treating, as many of our contemporary women seem to
prefer, only the beginnings of life; Miss Delafield leaves
Zella "still on the threshold" echoing "the question of
ages: what is Truth?" and yet the girl-heroine has, after
all, a clearly defined, easily recognised character, humourously portrayed. She "gets at" the reader; so that we
utterly sympathise with her childlike eagerness to impose
herself upon her surroundings, to enter into the realities,
to *be* somebody. She possesses one side of the artistic temperament (which is always attractive, if difficult): being a
born actress, an inveterate *poseur,* more or less self-
conscious: and just because, superficially, one can "see
through her" so easily, we cannot avoid loving the real
Zella under the pathos of her most naïve affectations, and
sympathising with every one of her most ridiculous, but
quite serious, attempts at asserting herself. The key of the
position lies here: that whereas most of us are, at least fairly often and at our best moments, content with being what
God made us: she is perpetually engaged in the quite hopeless task of trying to *make herself* into something she was
never intended to be.

All this is, obviously, an extreme case of the romance-
craving common to all young people—an almost inevitable phase in the development of character: but if one can
accept the paradox—Zella charms one because she is always sincere. She has the gift of all true artists, that she
does really enter into the self-imposed mood, actually feels
and is—for the moment—all she appears to be. Only because others are less quick and sensitive—more "set"
along a precise line, they generally deem her affected.
Thus, in the end, Miss Delafield would have us believe, she
may not only see, but find, herself: since she had learnt
that they—who had influenced her—"had one and all,
conviction at the back of them. She, afraid and alone, had
none. Again and again she had tampered with something
real, and to her it had not been real."

Miss Delafield, like the others, believes in Reality—
somewhere. That is what she tries, everywhere, to express.

Again, in ***Consequences,*** and ***The Pelicans,*** she penetrates
into the back of things. The fascinating sisters in ***The Pelicans*** have each their own mystery: their strain towards
what life and "the others" fail to recognise, it would seem:

whence they perpetually divert. To Francie, indeed, comes rest and finality: from serene submission to perfect Faith. For her the convent is peace, death, fulfilment; not easily attained, indeed, but with a strangely gentle determination, which is at once cruel and kind. Never beaten by opposition, always certain of *her* Reality; she dares even to accept Love's Sacrifice: seeing only the Right, she has the courage to hurt.

And Rosamond, her mother-devotion cut through, baffled and for a time at least torn in shreds by the very passion of revolt, learns her lesson at last. Loving that little sister through whom alone life *meant* anything to her, she yet stumbles, hesitating, out of chaos into the Light. "You see, for *Francie* to do or say anything that hurt *me* was the greatest sacrifice that she could ever have offered," and "there is only one thing that counts, and that's loving, and loving is giving."

Thus understanding, she gives herself—to the man who loves her. For Francie, it was an end; for her a Beginning: but it was one and the same gift.

Fate in *Consequences,* indeed, is more freakish. Whether child or woman, Alex could never "fit in" anywhere. She has all Zella's impetuosity for throwing herself into a part, without the artist's enjoyment of the performance. Having a dangerous insight towards her own instability; fully alive to the tragedy of loving, without understanding, other people; always aware of her own baffling "wrongness," and the impossibility to conform: she never escapes "the muddle" of things. Experimenting—as Zella had done—in the haven of Romanism, and (unlike Francie) equally without conviction; she struggles from one failure to another; with that infinite pathos of the unpractical idealist with no fixed ideal, which produces, inevitably, the most deadening of all tragedies: a tragedy without meaning and grandeur: that need never have happened, and leads nowhere. "After all, she had nothing much to live for, poor Alex. She'd got out of touch with all of us—and she had no one of her very own." It was a sister's epitaph!

Such in outline are the central motives, or inspirations, of Miss Delafield's three first novels: but she does not depend, exclusively, upon the central framework. However intense or subtle the main idea; it is always—with her—embroidered, and enriched, by the craft of the normal novelist. She has, to begin with, a rich fund of humour extending beyond the mere phrase to her conception of character. She is as masterly in the painting of an atmosphere as of an individual; because she not only observes, but interprets. She re-creates life in its entirety, not as a mere setting for her heroine, but as it actually moves round every one of us with all its baffling complexities that may stand alone, as it were, for a time and then suddenly (through incidents most trivial or most dramatic) interfere to spur or to depress. The conventions—in Zella—as represented by Mrs. Lloyd-Evans—have little in common with the exasperating "family" who torture Alex: yet both are *true;* while the varied experiences of Zella—from her artist father and the French grandmère—do colour the atmosphere which is drab to Alex. In *The Pelicans,* again, the Family itself is as abnormal as the heroine: blank to her, indeed, but quite amazingly wide-minded and receptive to

youth in general and to many of its imaginings. The minor persons themselves have their own problems, their own pose—mark the very original relations between Nina Severing, song-writer, and her son Morris; linked to Ludovic and his mother, still more closely associated with the incomparable wisdom of cousin Bertie.

There is everywhere, again, the broad foundation of a compact plot, that story-structure which both separates and joins sound fiction to real life: usually regarded as the first test of a good novel; what one may call the mark of the expert.

And in *The War Workers,* where alone the author evokes, what, in fact, overshadowed the period of her productiveness, she seems to depend almost entirely upon such side-issues, the artifice in her form of expression. True that here, again, Miss Vivian certainly occupies the centre of the picture: an egoist of the first water (almost a "study" for Miss Clemence Dane's full-length portrait of the one and only Clare Hartill): but she is, after all, only a "personage" in her own eyes: and the art of the tale comes from its *tout ensemble.* It is not, perhaps, surprising that Miss Delafield, like all her contemporaries, has not attempted the psychology of War. We have here only the fringe: its effect on those who are in it, but not of it: those who met the crisis by different "changes" of viewpoint, largely hysterical; crowding out thought by hustle. Satire prevails, though the picture is not unkindly. Char Vivian, indeed, is a martyr of sorts: her sufferings are real enough—like her efficiency in organisation—but they are self-inflicted and self-centred.

Miss Delafield has attempted no more than a sketch, or "turn" as they say in stageland—wherein the surface of unrest provides atmosphere; and women—at any rate—having lost their bearings, are burying themselves under "doing their bit." There is, of course, adroit sympathy and unsparing satire: the observation is sound and brisk—for the author is an expert: but the work reveals no more than craft, an easily used instinct for competent handling of an attractive episode. It could scarcely, perhaps, have been better done; but does not seem quite worth doing.

J. W. Krutch   (essay date 1922)

SOURCE: "Slaying the Slain," in *The Nation,* New York, Vol. CXV, No. 2998, December 20, 1922, pp. 694-95.

[*Krutch was one of America's most respected literary and drama critics. Noteworthy among his works are* The American Drama since 1918 *(1939), in which he analyzed the most important dramas of the 1920s and 1930s, and "Modernism" in* Modern Drama *(1953), in which he stressed the need for twentieth-century playwrights to infuse their works with traditional humanistic values. In the following review, Krutch compares* The Optimist *to Hamilton Fyfe's* The Fruit of the Tree.]

Neither [Hamilton Fyfe's *The Fruit of the Tree* or E. M. Delafield's *The Optimist*] is initially promising, for both threaten to do what novel after novel does—fight brilliantly a battle which has already been won. *The Fruit of the Tree* tells humorously but with a good deal of stress upon argument the story of two young women who kicked over the restraints formerly supposed to be proper to their sex. *The Optimist* pokes away with the rapier of accomplished irony at a terribly benign old Canon who is ever ready, like Strachey's Dr. Arnold, to rise and explain "the general principles both of his own conduct and that of the Almighty." Both are more seriously concerned than a contemporary writer need be with the education of the reader, and if there remain any Victorians among us they can hardly withstand this twofold attack. It is difficult to believe that anyone could read the first book and remain convinced that marriages are necessarily made in heaven or read the second and fail to realize that the Christian gentleman of the old school was likely to be a prig. The arguments of both seem irrefutable, but direct satire upon the ideas of the eighteen-eighties, though no doubt still a pleasant sport, is but slaying the slain. The best novels are written from a point of view but they do not consist simply in a definition of it, and though it may be that the point of view altered so greatly during the past forty years that there was a period during which definition was the writer's first duty, that time has passed. The outlines of iconoclastic modernism have been laid and the future lies before the novelist who, assuming these as a background, will create character against them.

The greatest enemy to his art which the contemporary novelist has to fight is the too complacent sense of his modernity and the feeling that his principal duty is to demonstrate it. . . .

Though Miss Delafield is still struggling a little with the delusion that it is worth while to demonstrate her superiority to the Victorians, she has, in her latest novel, pretty nearly reached a real maturity, and this maturity lies not in the keenness of her dialectic but in the realization that such keenness is not enough. She is a clever writer but she has achieved what few clever writers achieve; she has created a character. One begins her book with admiration for her finesse but without great enthusiasm, for she seems bent upon a much simpler thing—the analysis of an outworn point of view embodied in a puppet. She lays upon the table her Optimist, the self-righteous old Canon, and begins to work upon him with a terribly keen scalpel of satire, laying bare the pomposity of his thoughts and the devastating character of his benign tyranny over his children. It is skilfully done but it has been done before, and the main thesis "that the normal evolution of self-sacrifice is self-advertisement" is almost banal.

Then gradually a surprising thing happens. The Canon gets up from the table, as it were, and begins to live in his own right. Miss Delafield forgets the superiority of herself and her readers, and the pasteboard embodiment of fatuity becomes a creature of flesh and blood. No less grotesquely wrong than he was before, he becomes understandable, and as he feels and suffers in his own right, as the children, victims of his own personality, drop here and there into their various fates, he takes on a pathetic dignity. The Optimist finishes as he had begun, and when, upon his deathbed even, he repeats in his wilful blindness his favorite phrase, "all things work together for the good of those who love God," even the most skeptical of the characters is compelled to agree with the daughter who has sacrificed her life to him, "He is magnificent." Without any weakening of her contempt and without yielding in her insistence that all was well to the Canon only because he was determined to see it so, Miss Delafield has given the devil his due. She has made her Optimist a real person and not a straw man made to be kicked by the clever, and as a result it becomes a matter of complete indifference that her thesis is not new.

Her book is a lesson to all young novelists, a proof that to be modern does not necessarily mean to leave the real business of fiction in order to argue, but it can be studied again by her with even more profit than by others. She can see how perilously she has stood upon the edge and how from time to time she has stepped over into the region of complacent superiority. Does anyone ever doubt that Flaubert was superior to the provincial ideals of Madam Bovary? Yet he correctly assumes that it is not necessary for him to say so and, similarly, no sophisticated reader needs to have it proved to him again that Victorian optimism was shallow. Yet character, Victorian or Babylonian, is still interesting.

Robert H. Hull   (essay date 1932)

SOURCE: "E. M. Delafield as a Novelist," in *The Bookman,* London, Vol. LXXXII, No. 491, August, 1932, pp. 240-41.

[*In the following essay, Hull surveys Delafield's novels from* Zella Sees Herself *through* Thank Heaven Fasting.]

The publication of Miss E. M. Delafield's latest novel, *Thank Heaven Fasting,* affords a welcome pretext briefly to review a range of achievements placing this author among the most accomplished fiction-writers of our time. Although the present survey is necessarily confined to aspects of Miss Delafield's art as revealed through her novels, readers will recall for themselves the exceptional talent illuminating numerous short stories from her pen, no less than dramatic capabilities ensuring unqualified success for that delightful comedy, *To See Ourselves,* produced at the Ambassadors Theatre in December, 1929.

When *Zella Sees Herself* appeared in 1917, Miss Delafield was immediately acclaimed for those powers of witty and devastating portraiture with which to-day she is extensively associated. It is a misfortune, perhaps, that critics have too often expected her to preserve a similar vein throughout the score of novels written since that date. As a satirist Miss Delafield has eminent gifts, but she may be credited, on the evidence of more recent volumes, with the increasing realisation that among aspects of life meriting discussion, some, at any rate, scarcely invite treatment in satirical terms. She is, for that matter, too fine an artist to acquiesce in infinite repetition of an early success. To dissuade admirers from their irrational clamour for an endless sequence of novels designed simply to reproduce, with slight variations, the entertainment of *Zella,* must have been a delicate task; yet Miss Delafield, while submitting her style and subject-matter to stricter discipline, has contrived not only to retain but vastly to enlarge her public.

Zella, The War-Workers and, to some extent, *The Pelicans* are all illustrative of experiences common to those whose instinct for self-dramatisation, or insincere conformity to type, outruns not only discretion but intellectual honesty. Selecting theses so various as conversion to Roman Catholicism and the exploitation of feminine tendencies to revere personalities above abstract values, Miss Delafield postulates "What is Truth?" as a question to be answered in the light of disasters and exposures inseparable from attempts to shirk this vital (if not always agreeable) issue. She never falsifies conclusions to secure the dubious advantage of a "happy ending," but neither are we vexed with those totally negative findings which can banish so successfully every vestige of interest from the problem discussed. Her most derided characters are, as a rule, less bad than sorely exercised in consistent preservation of their self-appointed pose. Miss Delafield knows them sufficiently to admit cool pity for such foolishness even while stripping, with consummate skill, the masks which they struggle so vainly to retain.

If the caustic ridicule enlivening many pages in these and other early novels seems on occasion too carefully underlined, the apposite nature of Miss Delafield's shrewd commentaries upon human frailties invites little dispute. Her characters, as we are constantly reminded, often represent types to be scarified but, with few exceptions, the author further persuades us to their existence as living people. The reality of Mrs. Lloyd-Evans in *Zella,* of Charmian Vivian in *The War-Workers* and Nina Severing in *The Pelicans* remains with us long after the book is closed. There may be at times excessive anxiety to reinforce dialogue by emphasis upon satirical implications quite evident to the reader; yet Miss Delafield's insight can reach beyond scorn to accurately placed sympathy, and at the great moments her touch is unerring.

Few writers surpass her ability to strike in a sentence the key-note of minor characters. One example, from *The Pelicans,* must suffice:

> Miss Blandflower belonged to that numerous and mistaken class of person which supposes the art of witty conversation to lie in the frequent quotation of well-known tags, and the humorously-intended mispronunciation of the more ordinary words of the English language.

If disproportionate space seems to have been given to discussion of the novels so far mentioned, it is because they epitomise the technical and philosophical address dominating their immediate successors. *Consequences* deals with the perplexities of a Roman Catholic convert who becomes a nun, but renounces her vows after ten years, to meet, in a strangely altered world, bewilderment finally driving her to suicide. Neither this volume nor, one must add, *Tension* and *The Heel of Achilles* show quite the expected advance upon Miss Delafield's brilliant apprenticeship, though *Humbug* and *The Optimist,* each exhibiting the inescapable penalty for an existence ruled by false values, suggest more keenly the intellectual expansion germane to maturer craftsmanship. In *Messalina of the Suburbs* Miss Delafield departs, with conspicuous success, from her accustomed genre, to present a psychological analysis of events culminating in a murder akin to that for which Bywaters and Mrs. Thompson were arraigned. The study is vividly worked out, with finely captured atmosphere and an astonishing perception of motives animating the primary characters of this tragedy.

The close of a period, anticipated by *The Chip and the Block,* is confirmed in *The Way Things Are.* Throughout nearly a dozen novels Miss Delafield had wittily exploited, often with success and always with variety, the limitless manifestations of human nature governed by egotism and unheroic self-deception. *The Chip and the Block* portrays with refreshing irony an author whose uncommon power to misinterpret his innate selfishness and unjustified conceit as subscriptions to a lofty ideal of self-sacrificing parenthood are at first dimly realised, and at the last eminently unshared, by his clearer-sighted children. *The Way Things Are,* more abundant in lighter moments, centers round a woman whose agonised incompetence as a housewife is equalled only by her distraught refusal of opportunity to escape from a husband in whose affections she has long been supplanted by the morning newspaper. Both novels are strong in characteristic touches; but one can sense the author's sharpened ambition for less charted seas; and the departure when it occurs comes suddenly.

Turn Back the Leaves suggests at first reading a complete metamorphosis. We find in these pages a new serenity of style; suppression of emphasis and incidental commentary; and qualities of permanent dignity enhancing portraiture memorable, in any event, for fine perspective and sympathetic vision. True it is that the crucial *motif*—the despair of an old Roman Catholic family at the marriage of their daughter to a Protestant—echoes to some extent the preoccupation of earlier novels; but beyond this point similarity cannot be pressed. The dominant tragedy of Miss Delafield's theme demands that humour, though allowable at moments of relief, shall be strictly disciplined. Here ridicule has no place. Such unaccustomed control has caused one or two critics, looking for wit where none is intended, to speak of this book as "disappointing." Yet to accept Miss Delafield on the terms she proposes—the only terms artistically tolerable for her subject—is to appreciate how immeasurably she has advanced upon her former standards by an achievement of exceptional notability.

Turn Back the Leaves marks a supreme crisis in Miss Delafield's career, establishing her, beyond possible doubt, high among contemporary novelists. She has since proved an ability to enjoy conquests in both her accepted worlds. *Challenge to Clarissa* maintains, in comedy, all the new distinction. *The Diary of a Provincial Lady* is memorable for masterly entertainment too widely known to need comment here. . . . Concerning *Thank Heaven Fasting,* I must not usurp the reviewer's prerogative beyond submitting that, in my own opinion, it enriches yet further the deserved reputation of this distinguished novelist.

Henry Seidel Canby   (essay date 1933)

SOURCE: "Charm with Irony," in *The Saturday Review*

of Literature (New York), Vol. IX, No. 26, January 14, 1933, p. 376.

[*Canby was a professor of English at Yale University and one of the founders of the* Saturday Review of Literature, *where he served as editor in chief from 1924 to 1936. He was the author of many books, including* The Short Story in English *(1909), a history of that genre which was long considered the standard text for college students. In the following review, Canby favorably appraises the* Further Diary of a Provincial Lady.]

Readers of the first *Diary of a Provincial Lady* will not be disappointed in this sequel. These apparently random and artless notes upon the difficulties in being literary in Devonshire with a family on your back, and upon the trials of playing up to a literary reputation amidst the professional sophistry of London, are not so artless and so random as they seem, although their informality is an excellent medium for the witty charm of the book. Miss Delafield has made a self-portrait here, and a family portrait, and a portrait of that strange assemblage which buzzes about a new literary reputation, which are indeed more evidence that she is one of the really skilful novelists of manners in our day. Why has she not had the resounding critical success which so many English women writers less excellent than she have grown great upon? Because, I think, of her unpretentiousness, the unpretentiousness of one who, like Jane Austen, seems to write easily upon her lap, while others talk and clamor about her. She is somewhat too ironic, too unsentimental, to get the reputation (which she deserves) of humorist, too delicate, too unpointed in her satire, to arouse fear or indignation, too much concerned with the humors of everyday manners as the best index of society, to interest the heavy-handed advocates of social changes. She illustrates the difficulties of belonging to the Jane Austen school in the nineteen thirties. Not that she is antiquarian, in spite of her delightful *A Good Man's Love,* which was a tragedy worked out in iced wedding cake, or imitative. She is of our age and no other; belongs to the genteel tradition of which she makes fun, while rather loving it; dips into the milieu of platinum blondes or Bloomsbury sexualists with a delight in new experience, not for an instant losing her head; is aware of all the new ideas and new moralities abroad without ceasing to love her own people who, by turns, make novelties incongruous, and are made incongruous by them. Indeed, if anyone writing fiction is better equipped for the business of comedy, I do not know her name.

I would not overstate the case of Miss Delafield. That would be to commit the precise error of which she is never guilty. She will never be a great novelist. She will never be a serious novelist in terms of that seriousness approved by those whose concern is with the class war, or the sex struggle, or the depicting of new and unlovely types thrown up by democracy. She is an aristocratic writer, which does not mean that she is in love with the aristocracy, but does imply a certain delight in the trials and errors of civilized living quite apart from concern as to its philosophy or sociology. I think that her circle of readers will widen and that those she gets she will keep.

As for the *Further Diary of a Provincial Lady,* here is a

novel exposed in its making; plotless but with the characters all made and well made; themeless, unless the attempts of a lady writer to keep up with her reputation is a theme, but with the incident and personality for which, if the truth were told, we follow themes; informal yet constructed to catch the intellectual whimsies of Emma Hay, the naive sexualism of Parmela Pringle, the attractive stolidity of Robert, and also to express perfectly the business of being both mother and novelist, and the charm with irony which is Miss Delafield's especial forte.

Margaret Lawrence   (essay date 1936)

SOURCE: "Sophisticated Ladies," in *The School of Femininity: A Book for and about Women as They Are Interpreted through Feminine Writers of Yesterday and Today,* 1936. Reprint by Kennikat Press, Inc., 1966, pp. 281-310.

[*In the following excerpt, Lawrence praises simplicity and humor in the* Diary of a Provincial Lady.]

E. M. Delafield has . . . self-sufficiency in her writing. In *The Diary of a Provincial Lady* she set the reading English world smiling about the funny slant of an ordinary woman's existence. She has written other stories which in their way are good pieces of experimental portraiture of women, but none of them has the ingenuous sparkle of the provincial lady's record of her affairs. She has no affairs. She has a husband who hides behind his newspapers when she wants to talk to him, and reaches for his hat when the question of more money for household expenses comes up. He is a nice husband, and does take an interest in the things that go on in his home. He is nice, too, about allowing his wife to write in her spare time, but he is only a man, and a woman has to have some outlet for her thoughts other than a man. The book is significant for all its slightness because it is possibly the first time a woman ever set down the doings of her day-to-day life in all their simplicity, and attached to them her own tentatively philosophical conclusions.

The writing might appear at first glance to be the writing of a helpmeet. Certainly it is the writing of a woman painting the situation of a helpmeet woman. Living in honorable matrimony with a man, rearing his children, attending to his house. But the sophisticated element raises its signs in the fact that she thinks her own thoughts as she goes through her days, and also in the fact that these thoughts happen to be amusing thoughts. She is under no psychological strain about the unfair emotional relationship between men and women. She is under no need to worship her man. But she wants to be entertaining. She must be entertaining. So she in her limited circumstance makes a fine story out of the irritating visits of the rector's wife, and the daily struggle with inadequate help in her own house. It is all a great game to her. The husband is varyingly attentive to the entertainment she provides. He reads his papers. He gives a snort or a grunt as the case may be, and he sees fit to be amused or disgusted, but the show goes on whether he applauds or not. He sticks and that is the main thing. He pays the bills, which is another thing, and it is up, therefore, to any lady to make it all seem extraordinarily interesting. Which is exactly what she does, and while she does it, she draws a picture of the life of an average couple together after the tense emotion of romance has died down and the long business of pulling together in harness has engrossed them to the exclusion of almost every other consideration. It is more to the point that there is enough cream in the house for the tea than that a woman have power to rouse all manner of fine feeling around her. It is more important for a man to be able to pay the coal bills than to have power to drive a woman to distraction over the stray thoughts he may be thinking. The helpmeet woman would be concerned about the subsiding of the feeling. She would be digging and prodding into the reactions of the man—"Are you happy?" "Do I satisfy you?"—the sophisticate is practical. She takes it for granted that the man is happy, and she sees to it that she does her part to satisfy him. This is the example without par of the sophisticated lady handling the prevailing matrimonial situation in complete normality. It is a lady of the ingénue type, playing her simple part with all its funny nuances, easy on the emotions, easy on the mind, gentle yet lively, full of fun, yet full of technical appreciation of every least little movement there is to be taken with it.

Margaret Haig Thomas, Lady Rhondda (essay date 1947)

SOURCE: "E. M. Delafield," in *Time and Tide,* Vol. 28, No. 48, December 13, 1947, pp. 1346-48.

[*Rhondda was the editor of* Time and Tide. *In the following essay, she comments on the lasting appeal of Delafield's semiautobiographical fiction.*]

E. M. Delafield was the perfect provider of good 'lights'. And, as every editor knows, there is nothing so rare. It is as difficult to find the really right 'light' as it used to be in more spacious days, to find the perfect savoury for a good dinner. I doubt whether one should too often use short stories. Occasionally, no doubt, for variety is the most important thing. But the most perfect short story ever written is seldom in its absolutely right place in the pages of a weekly review. Indeed in one sense it may be said that the better the story the less suitable it is. For just as in choosing the savoury, one had to remember the food that went before, the wine, the company, the appetite of the guests, so in choosing the 'light' one must relate it to the mood in which the reader sits down on a Friday or Saturday to his weekly review. In what frame of mind will he come to it? What will his appetite demand? He will come to it to some extent in a work-a-day mood. He will find the 'light' bound up with the notes and the leaders, with the news of the latest books, pictures, plays, films, with the talk of the week in fact. He will not often probably want to make the effort to transport himself completely for the space of two or three columns of print into another world, to move, as the first class story often asks of him, on to a different layer of consciousness. He will prefer probably to stay fairly close to the world in which he finds himself on the other pages. He will expect a variation certainly, a lighter and perhaps more pointed and witty variation of the theme, but he will expect the tune, even in a different key, to fit. There should, in fact, usually be some flavour of topicality about the good 'light.'. It should illustrate

lightly and effortlessly if not topical events then topical moods ("This Column" guided by the inimitable A.P.H. is doing that to perfection in *Punch* at the moment). The theme should be similar, the treatment only different.

Now E. M. Delafield might not be a politician, but she had the most delicate sense for the exact flavour of the mood of the moment. At times of crisis (when the flavour becomes so much keener) she could capture the mood not only of the year or the month, but of the very week, and she salted everything that she wrote with point and wit. That was why she came near to having the perfect touch for the perfect 'light'. She was the answer to all good editors' prayers. Her work, when she wrote in that vein, was not only in *The Provincial Lady* but in all her other 'lights', topical, hot, perfect for the week. But first class topical work is seldom ephemeral. (That is why people who speak as if good journalism were not literature are so profoundly wrong.) Much of the world's enduring literature was in origin topical work.

Take as an example of E.M.D.'s recapture of a mood the very first page of *The Provincial Lady in War Time*:

> Enquire of Robert whether he does not think that, in view of times in which we live, diary of daily events might be of ultimate historical value to posterity . . . Explain that I do not mean events of national importance, which may safely be left to the Press, but only chronicle of ordinary English citizen's reactions to war which now appears inevitable.
>
> Robert's only reply—if reply it can be called—is to enquire whether I am really quite certain that Cook takes a medium size in gas-masks. Personally, he should have thought a large, if not outsize, was indicated . . .
>
> I suggest that Cook had better be asked to clear up the point once and for all . . .
>
> Robert selects frightful-looking appliances, each with a snout projecting below a little talc window, from pile which has stood in corner of the study for some days . . . and tells me that Cook's nose is in quite the wrong place, and he always thought it would be, and that what she needs is a large size. Cook is accordingly extracted from the medium-size, and emerges looking heated, and much inclined to say that she'd rather make do with this one if it's all the same to us, and get back to her fish-cakes before they are spoilt. This total misapprehension as to the importance of the situation is rather sharply dealt with by Robert, as ARP Organizer for the district, and he again inducts Cook into a gas-mask and this time declares the results to be much more satisfactory. . . . .
>
> Cook's gas-mask is put into cardboard box and marked with her name, and a similar provision made for everybody in the house, after which Robert remarks, rather strangely, that that's a good job done.

How that takes one back to an almost forgotten mood. One thought that one had mislaid the feeling of those weeks but as one reads, the very flavour of them comes back. We were not all ARP Wardens or cooks but we all have our memories—sharp memories too—of the gas-mask episodes.

There is one sense in which *The Provincial Lady* has always especially interested me. It is the type of writing that falls halfway between two categories: between fiction and autobiography. It happens that I usually very much prefer fiction to autobiography. I prefer it because it seems to me to be so much more true to life. If one wants to learn something about human beings one should, in my view, seldom trouble over-much about autobiographies, which are apt to tell one little more than an expanded *Who's Who;* one should turn to novels. There, very plain for those who have eyes to read, lie truths about the writers and about all human nature which, often enough, the writers have not the faintest intention of revealing. They are to be found in all good novels but very seldom in autobiographies. For the good novelist is almost always in my experience endowed with one curious faculty. He can hide from himself that anything in his novels reveals anything about anybody. Between himself and the consciousness of those revelations hangs an iron curtain. But about his autobiography he knows better. When a man hands to the public the key of his private rooms you may be very sure that he has tidied them extremely carefully first. He has put away the photographs he prefers they should not see. He has touched up to taste the photographs which are allowed to remain. He has made sure, if he is of a kindly or even discreet disposition, that nothing in the rooms will redound seriously to the discredit of friends and acquaintances whom he may have to meet again—or for that matter to his own. Rooms in fact that are deliberately made available to the public are never private rooms and what is told about them is seldom very much. But a good novelist's inveterate desire to tell the truth, and the necessity that besets him to write what he knows, will lead him in his novels to show from time to time to the perspicacious glimpses of all the private rooms. There, but not in the autobiography, you will find the real man.

The Provincial Lady falling as it does half-way between fiction and autobiography has some of the advantages and some of the disadvantages of each. It may be read for the very revealing attitude towards life of its author as well as for its own sake. The attitude was not just posed for a photograph. It was a genuine one, but we should be making, as Kate O'Brien suggests in her preface, a bad mistake if we supposed it to be the whole of E. M. Delafield's attitude.

The author of *Thank Heaven Fasting* and of *Turn Back the Leaves* could go deep into life and find it very bitter. It did not lie within the formula of *The Provincial Lady* to do that. Once the frame was made the tapestry fitted it, for it was woven with the hand of the artist. The formula was strictly adhered to.

Here in a sense is E. M. Delafield's real life. Robert and Robin and Vicky and the little house in Devonshire and the local Women's Institute Meetings and the flat in Doughty Street to which she sometimes escaped to write, all those in fact existed. So probably, at one time or another, did most of the people whom she meets in the pages

of *The Provincial Lady*. "Dear Rose" may be used as a pseudonym to cover some four or five different friends. In another instance some one person whom she knew may be as conveniently split into several different characters. "Mademoiselle" (whose flavour is more nearly 1900 than 1930) may have existed not as Mademoiselle to Robin and Vicky but as Mademoiselle to Elizabeth herself some thirty years earlier, but she is sketched from, or at least based upon, a real person. It all fitted. But it fitted with discretion. It is unlikely, for example, that "Cook" was exactly as stated. Any cook might have given notice if she had found herself as portrayed in the book (and cooks do read books). No modern mistress (certainly not Elizabeth) would have risked that . . . But some of the minor characters were, I have reason to believe, and am startled to believe, drawn, or rather caricatured, directly from life without any softening whatsoever. That was the artist. That was the truth as she saw it, driving out the discretion proper to a semi-autobiography. And that is why the book is so vividly alive. E. M. Delafield drew always more directly from life than many writers do. She belonged essentially I have always thought to the critical rather than the creative branch of literature and her criticism expressed itself never in the ordinary way but always in that comparatively slight caricature that emphasizes and so reveals to us the oddities and queernesses of the world.

E. M. Delafield has written, as Kate O'Brien rightly tells us, greater books than this. She has written none more likely to endure.

J. B. Priestley   (essay date 1976)

SOURCE: "Feminine Humour," in *English Humour,* Stein and Day Publishers, 1976, pp. 115-38.

[*Priestley was the author of numerous popular novels that depict the world of everyday, middle-class England. His most notable critical work is* Literature and Western Man *(1960), a survey of Western literature from the invention of movable type through the mid-twentieth century. In the following excerpt, Priestley reflects on humor in Delafield's* Provincial Lady *series.*]

[*Diary of a Provincial Lady* (1930) and *The Provincial Lady in War-Time* (1940) (There were two other Provincial Lady diaries between these)] are now so far removed in time that they have acquired a social-historical interest, but they still succeed, it seems to me—and I have just re-read them—as humour. I must admit they are spiced with irony that other readers may miss, simply because I knew E. M. Delafield fairly well as a firm strongh character, whereas her Provincial Lady is presented in terms of very feminine inadequacies, a frequent sense of inferiority, all manner of doubts and dubieties. Here, in 1930, she is at the bank hoping for an overdraft:

> Am never much exhilarated at this prospect, and do not in the least find that it becomes less unpleasant with repetition, but rather the contrary. Experience customary difficulty in getting to the point, and Bank Manager and I discuss weather, political situation, and probable starters for the Grand National with passionate suavity for

some time. Inevitable pause occurs, and we look at one another across immense expanse of pink blotting-paper. Irrelevant impulse rises in me to ask if he has other supply, for use, in writing-table drawer, or if fresh pad is brought in whenever a client calls. (Strange divagations of the human brain under the stress of extreme nervousness presents itself here as interesting topic for speculation. Should like to hear opinion of Professor met last night on this point. Subject far preferable to Molecules.)

. . . Bank Manager reduces me to spiritual pulp by suggesting that we should see how the Account Stands at the Moment. Am naturally compelled to agree to this with air of well-bred and detached amusement, but am in reality well aware that the Account Stands—or, more accurately totters—on a Debit Balance of Thirteen Pounds, two shillings and tenpence. Large sheet of paper, bearing this impressive statement, is presently brought in and laid before us.

Negotiations resumed.

Eventually emerge into the street with purpose accomplished, but feeling completely unstrung for the day. Rose is kindness personified, produces Bovril and an excellent lunch, and agrees with me that it is All Nonsense to say that Wealth wouldn't mean Happiness, because we know quite well that it *would.*

Another and very different scene, also genuinely chosen at random:

Barbara calls. Can she, she says, speak to me in *confidence.* Sit, seething with excitement, in the hope that I am at least going to be told that Barbara is engaged. Try to keep this out of sight, and to maintain expression of earnest and sympathetic attention only, whilst Barbara says that it is sometimes difficult to know which way Duty lies, that she has always thought a true woman's highest vocation is home-making, and that the love of a Good Man is the crown of life. I say Yes, Yes, to all of this. (Discover, on thinking it over, that I do not agree with any of it, and am shocked at my own extraordinary duplicity.)

Barbara at length admits that Crosbie has asked her to marry him—he did it, she says, at the Zoo—and go out with him as his wife to the Himalayas. This, says Barbara, is where all becomes difficult. She may be old-fashioned—no doubt she is—but can she leave her mother alone? No, she cannot. Can she, on the other hand, give up dear Crosbie, who has never loved a girl before, and says that he never will again? No, she cannot.

Barbara weeps. I kiss her. (Tea is brought in.) I sit down in confusion and begin to talk about the Vicarage daffodils being earlier than ours. . . . Atmosphere ruined, and destruction completed by my own necessary enquiries as to Barbara's wishes in the matter of milk, sugar, bread-and-butter, and so on. (*Mem:* Must speak to Cook about sending in minute segment of sponge-cake, remains of one which, to my certain recollection, made its first appearance more than ten

days ago. Also, why perpetual and unappetising procession of small rock-cakes?)

Robert [husband] comes in, he talks of swine-fever, all further confidence becomes impossible. Barbara takes her leave immediately after tea, only asking if I could look in on her mother and have a Little Talk? I reluctantly agree to do so, and she mounts her bicycle and rides off. Robert says, That girl holds herself well, but it's a pity she has those ankles.

Its successor, ten years later, *The Provincial Lady in War-Time,* is not so funny on a personal level, but it offers us a bright satirical picture of the Phoney War period. These were the months when the lucky few Got Into Something and then found they had little or nothing to do, except wear a uniform or a badge, while so many others, especially the middle class, were running round trying to Get Into Something. Now established as a writer, the Provincial Lady penetrates at last the Ministry of Information, arriving at a Mr M. and a young man with a beard. Can she do anything?

All of us can do something, replies Mr. M. There are, for instance, a number of quite false rumours going about. These can be tracked to the source—(how?)—descredited and contradicted.

The man with the beard breaks in, to tell me that in the last War there were innumerable alarms concerning spies in our midst.

(As it is quite evident, notwithstanding the beard, that he was still in his cradle at the time of the last war, whilst I had left mine some twenty years earlier, this information would really come better from me to him.)

The Government wishes to sift these rumours, one and all—(they will have their hands full if they undertake anything of the kind)—and it is possible to assist them in this respect.

Could I, for instance, tell him what is being said in the extreme North of England where I live?

Actually, it is the extreme *West* that I live. Of course, of course. . . . What exactly then, is being said in the extreme West?

Complete blank comes over me. Can remember nothing but that we have told ourselves that even if butter *is* rationed we can get plenty of clotted cream, and that we really needn't bother to take our gas-masks wherever we go. . . . Can see that my chances of getting a job—never very good—are now practically moribund. . . . Mr. M. tells me—evidently in order to get rid of me—that I had better see Captain Skein-Tring. He is—or *was,* two days ago—in Room 4978, on the fourth floor, in the other building. . . .

However, Mr M. takes pity on her and offers to escort her himself:

. . . We meet with a pallid young man carrying hundreds of files, to whom Mr. M. says compassionately, Hallo, Basil, moving again?

Basil says Yes, wearily, and toils on, and Mr. M.

explains that Poor Basil has been moved three times within the last ten days.

Just as he disappears from view Mr. M. recalls him, to ask if he knows whether Capt. Skein-Tring is still in Propaganda, 4978. Basil looks utterly bewildered and replies that he has never heard of anybody called Skein-Tring. Anyhow, the Propaganda people have all been transferred now, and the department has been taken over by the people from National Economy.

Mr. M. groans, but pushes valiantly on, and this bulldog spirit is rewarded by totally unexpected appearance—evidently the very last thing he has expected—of Captain S.-T.'s name on the door of Room 4978. He accordingly takes me in and introduces me, says that I shall be absolutely all right with Jerry, hopes—I think untruthfully—that we may meet again, and goes.

As soon as Jerry understands that she is a writer, he tells her that 'All You People' must go on *exactly as usual,* but keep away from war topics. Not a word about the war:

> I feel obliged to point out to Jerry that the present international situation is what most people, at the moment, wish to know about. Jerry taps on his writing-desk very imperatively indeed and tells me that All You People are the same. All anxious to do something about the war. Well, we mustn't. We must keep right out of it. Forget about it. Go on writing just as though it didn't exist. . . . Authors, poets, artists—(can see that the word he really has in mind is riffraff)—and All You People must really come into line and be content to carry on exactly as usual. Otherwise, simply doing more harm than good. . . .

As I never happened to visit the Ministry of Information looking for a job, I cannot vouch for the truth of this account of it, but I suspect that satire here has not left truth far behind. Meanwhile, the Provincial Lady, just to be Doing Something, has volunteered to take night duty at a large canteen, where various kinds of war-workers, though probably doing nothing all day, have to keep late hours. Here is one out of many glimpses of her there:

> Serena is not on duty when I arrive, and telephone-call to her flat has only produced very long and painstaking reply in indifferent English from one of her refugees, of which I understand scarcely a word, except that Serena is The Angel of Hampstead, is it not? Agree that it is, and exchange cordial farewells with the Refugee who says something that I think refers to the goodness of my heart. (Undeserved.)
>
> Canteen gramophone has altered its repertoire—this a distinct relief—and now we have 'Love Never Grows Old' and 'Run, rabbit, run'. Final chorus to the latter—Run, Hitler, run—I think a great mistake and quote to myself Dr. Dunstan from *The Human Boy:* 'It ill becomes us, sir, to jest at a fallen potentate—and still less before he has fallen.'
>
> Helpers behind the counter now number two very young and rather pretty sisters, who say that they wish to be called Patricia and Juanita.

> Tendency on the part of all the male *clientèle,* to be served by them and nobody else, and they hold immense conversations, in undertones, with youths in leather jackets and brightly-coloured ties.
>
> This leaves Red Cross workers, female ambulance drivers, elderly special constables and stretcher-bearers, to me.
>
> One of these—grey-headed man in spectacles—comes up and scrutinises the menu at great length and then enquires What there is to-night? Suppose his sight has been dimmed by time, and offer to read him the list. He looks offended and says No, no, he has read it. Retrieve this error by asserting that I only made the suggestion because the menu seemed to be so illegibly written.
>
> Instant judgment follows, as Scottish lady leans down from elevation beside the urns and says severely that *she* wrote out those cards and took particular pains to see that they were not illegible.
>
> Decide to abandon the whole question without attempting any explanations whatever.

Social historians, wanting to examine some of the most foolish months in English history, may find some good material in this book. And even if they don't they can enjoy its humour. Finally, as irony is never far away from humour, I offer a last melancholy point. I knew E. M. Delafield (her real maiden name was de la Pasture—a kind of joke here too) for many years, and though I fully recognized and much relished her humorous gifts, she always seemed to me a tragic figure. She died, too soon, in 1943.

Maurice L. McCullen (essay date 1985)

SOURCE: "Perspectives," in *E. M. Delafield,* Twayne Publishers, 1985, pp. 115-29.

[*In the following excerpt, McCullen examines the Victorian influences, feminist viewpoint, and comic strategy evident in Delafield's works.*]

Ladies and Gentlemen in Victorian Fiction ironically enough kept [E.M.] Delafield's name alive in academic circles all the while her fiction was dropping out of print. Its title defines her subject: the "social moralities" of the Victorian upper-middle-class as these were chronicled by a number of minor women writers like Rhoda Broughton, Elizabeth Jewell, and her beloved Charlotte Mary Yonge. These minor Victorians never ceased to give her pleasure. From the beginning to the end of her life, her one hobby of record was reading, and she had literally grown up on the English, American, and French romances which so colored her thinking. She wrote about them, corresponded and traded books with other addicts, and studied them in a scholarly way.

Delafield's interest, as always, resided in people—what the Victorians thought, how they acted, how they dealt with social problems. She found their manners quaintly charming in comparison with the relaxed manners and morals of a postwar world; and she took their minor fiction to be a kind of historical record similar to an album of old photographs. For she assumed that these writers, like herself, tried to present a substantially true record of their times. While this delightful social history grew directly out of a long article Delafield wrote for the *Times* in 1935, its genesis really goes all the way back through the many articles she wrote on Victorians and Victorianism, beginning in the twenties, to her childhood.

Delafield's favorite Victorian, whom she loved even more than Dickens, deserves special mention. She was *the* acknowledged expert on Charlotte Mary Yonge and was primarily responsible for the swell of interest in Yonge's work before World War II. Yonge was the subject for biographical and bibliographical study, lively correspondence, lectures, and numerous articles and citations over the years. Delafield's attitude toward her work may be summed up in one statement: "It is impossible to think of the influences that went into building up the Victorian Age without including Charlotte Mary Yonge." In addition, she empathized tremendously with Yonge's outlook and life, especially her "strange and rigorous upbringing."

Her lifelong involvement with C. M. Yonge would make a fascinating study. Equally fascinating is her Victorian parody, *The Bazalgettes*. Hamish Hamilton published this literary hoax anonymously because Delafield was under contract to Macmillan and Harpers. Word was leaked to London literary and journalistic circles that a prominent writer had written the handsomely bound volume, and a coy "Publisher's Note" attempted to heighten suspense: "This Anonymous novel of the years 1870—76 is something of a literary conundrum and will, we believe cause much discussion. When it came to us the style seemed faintly familiar and we suspected who might have written it. . . ." It would be pleasant to record that the hoax succeeded, but unfortunately no sensation occurred. What remains is a delightful exercise in a minor key.

While Delafield's outrageous romantic plot and her stiffly correct characterizations add to the fun, the chief enjoyment lies in her lighthearted writing. Her sentences radiate the relish she felt for this project, whether, through straight comedy, comic allusion, or reduplication of quaint Victorian phrasing: "Is it an effect of the fading light that her face, when she raises it, is ashy-pale?" Her allusiveness constantly delights: little Fanny Bazalgette, dressed up for church, is coyly conscious of her finery, which "finds expression in many nods and becks and wreathed smiles." In the comic subplot, a meretricious Chaucerian poet's first entrance is announced thus: "Blanden is i-cumen in."

Even without knowledge of her great affection for the Victorians and her childlike delight in literary games, the joy Delafield felt in writing this now rare book transmits itself on every page. The elation of little Fanny at the prospect of a fete stands as well for the author's: "O wonderful, wonderful and most wonderful wonderful! And yet again wonderful, and after that out of all whooping!"

Another charming period piece, *When Women Love,* contains three novellas on the same theme: a woman cannot be sure of herself in love until her passion has been awakened. The three stories are set, respectively, in Victorian, Edwardian, and contemporary times—complete with period title pages for each. Delafield put a high finish on these fine stories. Period atmosphere is well-maintained through dress, manners, talk, and the conceptualization of "love." Through careful reconstruction of period tone, the noble romanticism of the Victorians gives way to the New Woman and the ironic iconoclasm of the 1890s, and the reader is left with the bleak cynicism of the postwar mood in "We meant to be Happy."

Delafield's lifelong love of the Victorians extended almost indefinitely into print. We should mention her book, *The Brontës,* in passing; and stress that Victorian literature was a very large part of the fabric of her life. Books, articles, speeches, letters, games (some of which she printed), and constant allusions all show her knowledge and love. That she was as effective in dealing with the Edwardians can be seen throughout her work, particularly in her comedy of manners, *Thank Heaven Fasting*. Her period sense was exquisite, and it is to be found as well in her short stories.

Delafield's more than one hundred short stories appeared in numerous publications. The best have been reprinted, most of them in three collections: *The Entertainment, Women Are Like That,* and *Love Has No Resurrection*— the best of the three. Even the collected stories vary in quality. At her middle level, the O. Henry formula appears markedly: tight focus, good dialogue and structure, a reversal or epiphany ending in which either the main character or the reader perceives a deeper ironic truth. A handful of her satires of circumstance have real merit, especially because of their perceptive handling of women's concerns.

In her most serious play, *The Glass Wall,* Delafield returned to her convent days and dealt for the last time with her awful religious experience. Markedly similar to *Consequences,* this play takes up again Delafield's main themes: love is necessary for life; love cannot be satisfied by renouncing the world; women who live for and through "personal relations" must remain in the world to find a human object for their loving emotions.

Her title comes from her major metaphor for convent life: "It's like a glass wall, between the people inside the Convent—and the ones outside. They can see in and we can see out—but there's no contact." The view Delafield provided through cloistered convent walls and the action taken by her nun were controversial enough that the Catholic press rumbled against the play and the Church blacklisted it.

Delafield wrote other plays, several of which were produced by BBC radio, but only one adds anything to her reputation. *To See Ourselves,* her most famous play, appeared in the same year Robert so perplexed the Provincial Lady and dealt even more severely with the dull British husband.

The title of this loaded picture of "the average husband and wife" presents yet another instance of her conceptual debt to Robert Burns's "To a Louse." The domestic situation of her average couple, Caroline and Freddie, is devastatingly dull—because Freddie is devastatingly dull. The conflict concerns Caroline's emotional needs: "Life *oughtn't* to be like this—it isn't enough"—and Freddie's utter insensitivity to these needs. Caroline tries repeatedly to arouse her near comatose spouse, but at most succeeds in making him slightly nervous.

> FREDDIE. I don't know what's the matter with you tonight.
>
> CAROLINE. Nothing that hasn't been the matter for years, only you've never noticed it. You— you don't take much notice of me anyway, do you Freddie?
>
> FREDDIE. Why on earth *should* I take any notice of you, dear? You're my wife, aren't you?

Freddie simply does not want to be bothered, especially by anything resembling an emotion. His needs are confined to the simple, the immediate, and the external: his dinner (punctually), his bath water (hot), and his privacy (to fall asleep behind the newspaper). His typical, transparent dullness causes all of the characters to generalize about husbands by basing their observations on him, and a distinction between husbands and men occurs early in the play: men are sensitive; husbands are insensitive. The sensitive male of the subplot reacts against Caroline's sister's attack on male insensitivity with, "I'm afraid you think men are extraordinarily dense!" Jill retorts, "Well, I'm not really talking about men at all—only about husbands."

Both of Delafield's plays owe a debt to the Shavian discussion play, and they suffer by comparison. Talky, static, and theme-ridden—both are tied closely to Delafield's life. But while **The Glass Wall** seems too parochial, **To See Ourselves** might well merit production still. Certainly it was a success in its day. It ran for nearly six months at the Ambassador's Theater in London, with young Maurice Evans in the cast, and, produced and staged by Joshua Logan, enjoyed a shorter run in New York. It was printed in Gollancz's *Famous Plays of 1931* and subsequently in *Burns Mantle's Best Plays of 1934—5*. The reason for its success was Freddie.

Like her historical bias, Delafield's feminism cuts across her writing in any mode. The viewpoint is always women's. But while her readers considered her a spokeswoman for women's concerns, and although the Provincial Lady considered herself a "feminist," those who knew Delafield well deny the applicability of that term to her. They point out that she was too well bred for the shrillness and acrimony associated with feminist writing and that she satirized women more frequently than she did men.

It is true that almost no variety of female phoniness escaped Delafield's observation, and that as she never solved the puzzle of maleness her male characters rank of necessity below her fine female figures, but it is also true that she satirized repeatedly the type of Englishman represented by Freddie. Freddie and his frustrated wife Caroline appeared first in her prototypic short story **"Appreciation,"** are next found in **To See Ourselves,** and reappear in sketches down through the years. Freddie is a blood brother of Robert in the Provincial Lady books, Alfred in

novels, stories, and sketches, and a number of other male characters in other works. As Delafield observed in introducing a book of cartoons by Pont, "It has been well said—by myself, as it chances—that every Englishman is an average Englishman: it's a national characteristic." There was *one* primary male type, she believed, and nearly every Englishman in his domestic role belonged to it.

George symbolizes the type in Delafield's contribution to *Man, Proud Man,* a "Commentary" on the male by eight women novelists of the *Time and Tide* circle (among them, Rebecca West, G. B. Stern, and Storm Jameson). The title for these eight essays comes from *Measure for Measure:* "but man, proud man, / drest in a little brief authority." Delafield's contribution, **"Man and Personal Relations,"** plays with one of her major themes: man's insensitivity in dealing with his wife and children. She illustrates her theme through ironic remarks on four headings: religion, love, friendship, and parenting. After disposing of George as a dull clod, she adds this proviso: "Because George is not romantic, it does not follow that he is not sentimental." He is. Sports, animals, business, "or anything vital of that sort" generally brings out a rash of sentimentality—which just as generally passes as quickly as it came. But as George never gets in touch with his own emotions or those of others, his personal relations with people remain underdeveloped:

> "Women sometimes permit themselves to wonder what George's subconscious mind can be like, in view of the number of emotional considerations which he never admits to the light of day. And the simile that suggests itself, is that of a pawnbroker's shop, on the eve of a stocktaking that never actually takes place."

Delafield never took part in any feminist movement, nor did she ever articulate feminist doctrine. She did espouse a woman's point of view dealing with women's concerns and problems in both her serious and humorous writing. In her continuing attack on male insensitivity to women's emotional needs, she was clearly a forerunner of much that was to come. Her feminism, always rooted in her own experience as daughter, woman, wife, mother, and career-woman, makes labeling unsatisfactory and ultimately unnecessary—even though we should no doubt call her a feminist today. Her genius lay in her witty and perceptive analyses of incongruities inherent in women's roles. That she was able to make these concerns typical and give them general significance made her famous with her audience.

Ellen Moers, in her recent history of the "feminine literary tradition," stresses the importance of women writers to social history. She asserts that theorists dealing historically with women's roles must turn to literature for data, "for the depth that only acquaintance with the thought of other times and places can give." Delafield will need to be ranked among the contributors to this tradition.

J. B. Priestley observed that the "richest mixture" of humor contains wit, irony, absurdity, a certain closeness to life and affection. Priestley also contended that women have "their own kind of humor" and that while their humor, especially prior to their full emancipation, tended to be narrower than men's, it was also quicker, sharper, less self-indulgent, and more social: "The term *sharp* is important here. Women on the whole have sharper eyes and ears, and when not in the grip of strong emotions have sharper minds, quick to notice pretensions, dubious motives, and all manner of social absurdities. They live closer to life, the actual living tissue of it, than we men do, half lost as we are in doubtful abstractions and vanity, so often lacking in self-knowledge." This eminent humorist's observations catch exactly the quality of E. M. Delafield's achievement, the point to which her hard-won development led.

She was simply a first-rate humorist. While her feminist bias and her firm sense of history and tradition led inevitably toward satire, even her critical comedy was tempered always by human affection and understanding. She is that rarity among humorists: a late-flowering talent that continued to bloom in spite of aging and adversity. She never gave up on people and life. We have seen from examples of her humor in novels, plays, and journalism that her irony ranged across the spectrum from light to dark. At either end of the spectrum lie pure humor and invective respectively. Her gentlest irony is nearly pure humor; invective with her took the form of moral earnestness. With some subjects she could not be indirect. Intermediate forms like parody and mock heroic were well within her grasp, and she shows technical facility all across the spectrum.

Her strengths as a humorist argue most strongly for a place in the history of English literature, and this final perspective aims at giving shape and substance to that argument. As the cacophony of critical terms sometimes drowns out communication on this subject, *humor* will be employed here as the general term, with *comedy* and *irony* as subsets. Comedy's connotations include intellectual criticism; humor connotes warm understanding. Delafield, of course, wrote both; but the general term conveys a truer sense of her development and her typical vision.

Delafield's humorous talents did not develop in any unified way until after her thirtieth year; and their development then, as we have seen, occurred in connection with her work in journalism. Although comic characters and some wit may be found in the early novels, this comic light peers in, as it were, from the periphery. The omniscient narrator is almost never humorous. She is from the first ironic.

David Worcester has typed irony as either "the Ally of Comedy" or "the Ally of Tragedy," and in her early work Delafield's irony veers toward the tragic. Alex Clare in *Consequences* desperately needs to establish a loving personal relationship, but her society has scripted her to hide or falsify her emotions. Increment by increment this ironic pattern weaves Alex's destruction. Worcester calls this form of irony "the satire of frustration" and terms it "cosmic." It forms the negative pole in the spectrum of Delafield's irony.

Movement toward the opposite pole of light irony was difficult for her, as we have seen, although characteristically she made a joke of it: " 'What a number of disadvantages there are in having a reputation for being amusing!' I said,

with all that bitterness, gloom and profound pessimism that is so apt to characterize the private life of a humorous writer." An influenza attack, a war scare, "whatever happens people always think that I'm going to be amusing about it."

She fought to gain and then to maintain objectivity throughout her life. The large irony implicit in the title of her first novel is that Zella sees that she does not see. At the end of her situation she wonders if she will ever see "reality." Less than ten years after projecting her own youthful problems ironically through Zella, Delafield's vision had cleared, and her objective eye was sharpening by presenting the British public to themselves in her first journalistic series, *General Impressions*. While friction between the objective and the subjective remained the one great constant in all of her writing, and the dialogue of the mind with itself continued to the end, Delafield's irony by the thirties had become inclusive rather than rejective. Her great sense of fun found a vehicle in her journalism, and informed her novels of manners. Light, lively, and discriminating irony began to justify the comparisons of her work with that of Jane Austen, and although her tone would darken, especially in her late novels, she kept her sense of humor alive to the last.

Her considerable reputation as a humorist survived her death, but postwar critics quickly forgot her, although an occasional bibliographic note recalled her "lively yet cool observation," which yielded "its own kind of irony." The long critical silence which ensued was broken only in 1976 when J. B. Priestley recognized her in his *English Humour* as the equal of the best women humorists—even the incomparable Jane Austen. Priestley knew Delafield and knew also of the comparisons of their work. By putting Delafield in the best company, he intended to "set the record straight" by demonstrating the enduring appeal of her humor.

Priestley's classification of Delafield among the best women humorists to have written in English assumes a high level of technical competence, and her full command of humorous techniques is evident by mid-career. The examples given above show that the bulk of her humor yields readily to analysis through existing incongruity theories: humor arising from poorly suited pairings of ideas or situations. She set herself up as that spirit of comic intelligence which showed people as they really looked and sounded, always acknowledging that she drew her material from closely observed life. Like all great comedy, hers is firmly based in reality.

Principal incongruity theorist Henri Bergson viewed comedy as an instrument of social correction and discussed its forms and mechanisms under three headings: situation, language, and character. Delafield's humorous writing presents a plethora of comic situations all based upon incongruity. The disconcerting reply, the puncturing of vanities, those ironic situations that appear over and over in the human comedy—such incongruities form the basis for her humor.

Bergson finds that the most sophisticated comedy is *created* by language rather than merely expressed by it, and once she developed the necessary objectivity, verbal wit became a Delafield trademark. Her quick wit produced many of the "one-liners" recently in vogue, for example her riposte "to parody Michael Arlen one needs only quote him." As examples of verbal incongruity may be given summarily, here are several that suggest her range: at the Hotel Britannia, "all is red plush, irrelevant gilt mouldings, and literary club members"; a Belgian asks a pretty English tourist, "What is the English for Autobus," to which she responds, "Charabanc"; the Provincial Lady politely urges "our Vicar's wife to come in; she says No, No, it is far too late, really, and comes"; at an early wartime lecture "on the treatment of shock," a character observes that the only shock she anticipates "is the one we shall all experience when we get something to do." Again, the Provincial Lady becomes involved in a comic romantic crisis during which "a period of fearful stress sets in, and Barbara and Crosbie Carruthers say [tearful goodbyes to each other.] They have, says Barbara in tears, parted For Ever, and Life is Over, and will I take the Guides meeting for her tonight—which I agree to do." Finally, two English travelers in France discuss (in French) the desirability of speaking French to the French, only to decide (again, in French) that English is the more expressive language ("C'est le plus expressif langage qui est").

These examples show Delafield running the gamut of verbal incongruity. In order, we find simple incongruity, inversion, reversal, transposition in key (shifting the sense of "shock"), strained expectation come to nothing, and cultural incongruity with reversal. A further comic technique involves sensitive handling of the "time-lag" of irony: frustrating the expectations set up by a simple series, for instance, as in the first example above.

Delafield's keen sense for language and her playfulness appear throughout this study in selected quotation. Her humorous techniques invoke every rhetorical possibility: expressive verbs, the mot juste, orthographic devices, and schemes and tropes humorously intended abound in her writing. One trope noted above appears consistently—the Dickensian metonym. In *The Provincial Lady in Wartime*, a Mr. Weatherby is introduced thus: "Mr. W. very tall and cadaverous, and has a beard which makes me think of Agrippa." Thereafter, of course, he is referred to only as Agrippa. At one point in the conversation, the Provincial Lady praises President Roosevelt: "Agrippa seems surprised and I feel would like to contradict me but politeness forbids—and we pass on to cocker spaniels, do not know how or why."

Delafield's typical self-directed irony peeks through here. Somehow the ball always winds up in the Provincial Lady's court, making her feel that she has, however slightly, mishandled the situation. But while her irony is usually critical to some degree, her way of seeing also resulted quite naturally in the purely humorous vision. When the dowager Lady Frobisher invites the Provincial Lady and Robert to dinner to meet the Blamingtons, the Provincial Lady stalls, forcing Lady Frobisher to press her hard over the telephone: "She has promised to produce me . . . and we *must* come. The Blamingtons are wildly excited (have idle and frivolous vision of the Blamingtons standing

screaming and dancing at her elbow, waiting to hear the decision)."

Exaggeration has long been a basic comic technique, and it fits hand in glove with Bergson's main theoretical insight: a human being invariably becomes comic when there is something mechanical about him. The Blamingtons amuse because we visualize them as puppets responding mechanically like windup toys. Bergsonian mechanism may reside in a physical condition, like crossed eyes; it may be an involuntary gesture, like an inevitable scratching of the chin when under stress; or it may reveal a mechanical habit of mind, like Robert's falling asleep each evening behind his newspaper. Whatever its manifestation, it partakes of the absurd and is often given exaggerated expression through comic logic, as the Provincial Lady's mechanical rigidity and her use of comic logic here: "Frightful conviction that I shall miss the train causes me to sit on extreme edge of seat in taxi, leaning well forward, in extraordinarily uncomfortable position that subsequently leads to acute muscular discomfort. However, either this, or other cause unspecified, leads to Victoria being reached with rather more than twenty minutes to spare."

Bergson's last category, the comic in character, is exemplified by the Provincial Lady above and requires little additional discussion. From the unimportant Dickensian walk-on to the Provincial Lady, Delafield's skill in comic characterization can be seen throughout her writing. All three elements—situation, language, and character—require careful orchestration. To support the final argument for recognition of her talent as a humorist, consider this scene from *The Chip and the Block*.

Charles Ellery arrives in Cornwall after a touch of influenza to visit his three children who are recuperating from more serious cases of the disease. His wife, to whom he has also transmitted the flu, is too weak to leave London, although Charles stirs the ire of his children's nurse by announcing that she is "stronger than she looks."

As his cab pulls up at the hotel, Charles crawls from it "with the help of a large walking-stick." "That's a new stick," pipes Victor, his youngest son. Charles expresses his entire satisfaction with his children's health and ignores Nurse Mordaunt's growing irritation over his complacency: "It's wonderful how children throw these things off," he chirrups, "if only we elders could do as much!"

> He coughed a little and sighed. "Well, this has pulled me down, but I expect [Cornwall] to do wonders for me. It must. We family breadwinners can't afford to be ill for long, you know."
>
> Father looked at Nurse Mordaunt as he said this, but when she didn't answer he looked at Paul. . . .

Paul, the point of view character, betrays his discomfort, and Charles turns to his daughter, exclaiming over the view and planning a walk with her. "Aha," he shouts, "the open road!": "Father drew himself up—he had been standing with his shoulders bowed, leaning on the stick, since he arrived—and seemed to forget about the stick. He waved it briskly in the air." Delafield allows Charles to rattle on for another hundred words before she interrupts him with the dinner gong from the hotel:

> "Come along!" Father shouted gaily, catching Jeannie.
>
> "You're forgetting your stick, Father," said Victor's baby voice. He pointed to the stick that had fallen unnoticed to the ground.
>
> Father looked at Victor, and Victor looked back at his father. Paul could not help noticing them.

Paul views the scene but does not understand it. All he feels is uneasiness.

> It was all over—whatever "it" was—in a moment.
>
> Father stooped, slowly and carefully, and picked up the walking-stick, raising himself with one hand pressed into his back, and groaning slightly under his breath, began to walk very slowly towards the house, once more leaning heavily on the stick.

The discriminating irony in this scene recalls that of Jane Austen. Phoney Charles is carefully set up. His *large* stick, his exclamatory speech, his comic absent-mindedness are lovingly built up. The clues leading to the revelation of his pose are unforced. Nurse Mordaunt's silence and Charles's waving his stick are quite natural. A nice balance and sense of timing are evident, too. Little Victor, whose eyes are only for the walking-stick, speaks twice, each time his father moves; and while Paul's point of view points up the satiric hit, the understated closure of the scene allows it to speak for itself.

Priestley's implicit comparison of E. M. Delafield with Jane Austen is neither wishful nor willful. Both women, for example, were omnivorous readers of novels. Both were ferociously verbal, essentially feminine, similar in temperament and outlook. While the two writers are comparable in many ways, the reason for comparing them is not to attempt to equate them. It is, rather, to demonstrate the validity of E. M. Delafield's credentials as a humorist.

Delafield created memorable characters whose dramatic conflicts with social manners and mores retain their appeal: "Her way led through the world of men and women in their personal relationships." She created art "from the dreary intercourse of daily life," exploring to the full "the possibilities of domestic humor." Her work was "self-limiting," exhibiting a restricted focus, and furthermore marked by clearness and lucidity: she is among "the least recondite" of authors. Yet her work has depth beyond what its mimetic surface suggests, primarily because of her controlled and discriminating irony. She utilizes "humor as a way of criticizing characters and their society; and irony as a means of moral evaluation."

These few critical comments summarize the main headings of modern Jane Austen criticism. They describe Delafield at her best as well: small fictional world, overwhelming concern with personal relationships, dramatic method, witty ironic tone, lucid, readable style. The bases for negative criticism, and in Delafield's case neglect, appear here, too: simplicity, narrowness, feminine subjects and point of view. In the old scale versus stature argument, women writers have in the past often been found wanting: their domestic visions omit too much of life. In the case of Austen, Henry James once wondered if a novel of the future might not begin where Austen's usually end.

An important note here: comparisons with Austen are flattering to Delafield, whether they deal with Austen's strengths or her "feminine weaknesses." But historical differences set a limit to them. Whereas Austen's fictional world is informed by eighteenth-century rationalism, Delafield's fragmented world reflects the chaos of the twentieth century. Her "small square two inches of ivory" was constantly smeared by contaminating outside pressures. That this furiously committed, self-divided woman won a reputation for cool, dry wit testifies again to her strength of character and skill as a writer.

Although James's demurrals find its echoes in Austen criticism, such critical positions have now largely been abandoned as sexist and tunnel-visioned. At least feminist criticism now recognizes a female literary tradition, which while different is not inferior to that of men. James's formalistic aesthetic imperatives, in other words, are not the best measure of Austen's moral comedy.

This is essentially Malcolm Bradbury's position as he argues against a too rigidly aesthetic criticism of Austen's work, using James as his focal point. James presumed that Austen observed rather than composed, that her mimetic method dealt so closely with real life that it could not attain to high art. But all novels which interest the reader, Bradbury feels, bring aesthetic order to raw life. It is only a preoccupation with "symbolist and aesthetic notions of fictional creation" that cause us to forget this fact: "There are novels which appeal to the socially normative or comprehensible more than others: novels of manners rather than romances or existential novels or works of high aesthetic composition."

Such an approach to Delafield's work would help to rescue her reputation from the obscurity into which it has fallen.

Bradbury's argument for a reasonable pluralistic criticism tailored to the specific *kind* of novel under discussion has been made also by Norman Friedman, Robert Langbaum, and others. Considered in the light of a now-recognized feminine literary tradition, in which for example domestic subject from a strictly feminine perspective are to be appreciated for what they are, a pluralist approach would allow for a reassessment of Delafield's achievement in all its facets. And it could stimulate criticism of her work in areas important to the history of English literature: feminist, humorist, journalist, sociocultural critic, and psychological novelist.

Her accomplishment as writer and speaker reveals both breadth and depth. While she spent her talent lavishly rather than concentrating it, specific works of high quality should now be isolated for study from the mass of her prolific output. Although she cannot be ranked as the equal of a towering figure like Jane Austen, as we have seen she can stand comparison with her. Like Browning's Andrea del Sarto, her "forthright artists's hand" produced a body of notable work, especially in humor. And as Virginia

Woolf showed in "Women and Fiction," the extraordinary woman artist's achievement assumes classic proportions only in the context of the art of her peers—women who stuck close to the surface reality of the life most women of their time lived. Such writers provide the cultural glue that fastens together our social and artistic history. Without them, cultural continuities cannot be properly understood or appreciated.

E. M. Delafield, distinguished woman of letters, deserves a place, however small, in the Great Tradition.

FURTHER READING

Biography

Powell, Violet. *The Life of a Provincial Lady: A Study of E. M. Delafield and Her Works.* London: William Heinemann, 1988, 190 p.

Portrays Delafield as worldly and unlimited by the subgenre of comedic fiction.

Criticism

Arrowsmith, J. E. S. Review of *Diary of a Provincial Lady.* *The London Mercury* XXIII, No. 136 (February 1931): 383-85.

> Praises Delafield's humor. According to Arrowsmith, "Delafield's taste and tact are never at fault, she shows a masterly power of selection; over and over again in places where a less wise writer might have gone wrong, she says just the right thing. . . . The result is an exuberantly funny book."

Moran, Helen. Review of *The Provincial Lady Goes Further.* *The London Mercury* XXVII, No. 158 (December 1932): 170-72.

> Favorable assessment that suggests the sequel surpasses the original "Provincial Lady" book.

Review of *Humbug. The Nation* CXIV, No. 2963 (19 April 1922): 472.

> Judges Delafield as too brisk and businesslike to be profound.

Additional coverage of Delafield's life and career is contained in the following source published by Gale Research: *Dictionary of Literary Biography*, Vol. 34.

Alfred Korzybski

1879-1950

(Full name Count Alfred Habdank Skarbek Korzybski) Polish-born American linguist.

INTRODUCTION

Korzybski was a founder of the general semantics movement in the United States, which sought to develop a linguistic system that would lead to a more precise use of language. Taking precepts from linguistics, philosophy, psychology, neurology, and sociology, Korzybski believed that understanding between groups and individuals could be reached by investing words with greater accuracy.

Biographical Information

Korzybski was born in Warsaw, Poland, to Ladislas Habdank Korzybski and Countess Helena Rzewuska. He was educated at the Warsaw Polytechnic Institute, and also studied in Germany, Italy, and the United States. During World War I Korzybski served in the Polish Army and worked in the Russian General Staff Intelligence Department, for whom he travelled to the United States and Canada as an artillery expert. Around 1916 Korzybski emigrated to the United States, marrying the American portrait painter Mira Edgerly in 1919; he became a naturalized citizen in 1940. From 1920 until his death in 1950, Korzybski taught at several American universities. He published his most notable work, *Science and Sanity: An Introduction to Non-Aristotelian Systems and General Semantics*, in 1933. The book quickly became the seminal handbook for the general semantics movement, leading Korzybski to found the Institute of General Semantics in Chicago, Illinois, in 1938. Korzybski and other general semanticists published much of their work in the journal *ETC.: A Review of General Semantics*, edited by Korzybski's close colleague, S. I. Hayakawa. After ideological differences led to a break with Hayakawa, Korzybski moved the Institute to Lakeville, Connecticut, in 1946. He died there four years later.

Major Works

Korzybski's main tenets throughout his work are concerned with fostering communication between conflicting groups. He contended in his first published work, *Manhood of Humanity: The Science and Art of Human Engineering*, that mathematical philosophy can help us to discover the true essence of what human beings are, which can in turn lead to a scientifically sound system of ethics. In *Science and Sanity* Korzybski delineated his "non-Aristotelian" theory of semantics. According to Korzybski, Aristotelian thinking causes people to confuse words with the ideas they represent, fails to recognize differences between individuals and the various groups to which they

may belong, and leads to a dichotomous value system that makes statements either right or wrong, good or bad. His solution was to train individuals to distinguish between the words they use and the idea or thing they mean to talk about. Korzybski believed this system would lead to greater understanding among groups and to the realization that every "fact" has indefinite levels of abstraction—what he called the "etc."—about which we can know very little.

Critical Reception

Despite what many called an arrogant manner, Korzybski had the ability to inspire intellectual enthusiasm among numerous followers, who staunchly defended him and helped promote his theories. Detractors contended that the size and density of *Science and Sanity* were proof of the failure of Korzybski's theories about concision of language. The use of his principles in such varied fields as marital counseling, film-making, and horticulture led some critics to doubt the worth of much of his work. Korzybski's ideas continue to generate debate through the publication *ETC.*

PRINCIPAL WORKS

Manhood of Humanity: The Science and Art of Human Engineering (nonfiction) 1921
Time-Binding: The General Theory (nonfiction) 1926
Science and Sanity: An Introduction to Non-Aristotelian Systems and General Semantics (nonfiction) 1933

CRITICISM

Alexander Petrunkevitch (essay date 1922)

SOURCE: "The Science of Social Engineering," in *The Yale Review,* Vol. XI, No. 2, January, 1922, pp. 431-33.

[*In the following essay, Petrunkevitch praises Korzybski's theory of "time-binding" as discussed in* The Manhood of Humanity.]

Unlike practical discoveries in the field of applied science or industry, new conceptions in pure science and thought have innumerable forerunners whose chief work lies in preparing the human mind for the final reception of the great truth to be formulated by some genius. Neither new religions, nor philosophies, nor theories have ever been called into being without such preliminary work, and whenever a genius put forward some thought too early for the rest of the world to grasp it, such a thought invariably perished and had to be rediscovered centuries later. Yet the time comes when the world finally grasps a new truth, makes it part and parcel of its own method of thinking and wonders how people could have been so blind as not to have seen the plain truth before. Such a truth concerning the nature of human thought is now beginning slowly to dawn on the world and, when once clearly conceived, will profoundly change not only scientific conceptions of energy and its laws of preservation, but human relationships as well.

I do not want to convey the impression that the author of **The Manhood of Humanity** has spoken the word which will reverberate throughout the thinking world. He, too, is only a forerunner, though he brings us considerably nearer the goal. His theories revolve around the idea that man is neither an animal nor a creature endowed with a spirit, but alone belongs to the "time-binding" class. By this he means that man has "the capacity to summarize, digest, and appropriate the labors and experiences of the past . . ."; and he contrasts man with animals as representatives of the "space-binding" class. Now this thought in itself would not be anything new, were it not for the elucidation of its meaning given by Korzybski. For he shows that not only do we learn from the experiences of the past, not only do we make use of things done before us and of wealth accumulated, but that in all our calculations of work done by ourselves, of wealth accumulated by us, of production based on our possession of knowledge, an inalienable element has been persistently overlooked, an element which he terms the "dead men's work." That work represents energy which may be and is being made use of in our daily life, but as yet has not been taken into account by any scientific thinker or student of human affairs. Like a true engineer Korzybski is not interested in discussing the "essence" of the time-binding power of man. That is for him metaphysics. He studies its manifestations and treats it as time-binding energy; and "the science and art of directing the energies and capacities of human beings to the advancement of human weal" he terms "human engineering."

For many years the reviewer has been pondering over the reason for the apparent discrepancy between energy received and energy produced by different individuals. The conditions of life, food, training, the amount of knowledge, the object of study and the time and the energy put into it, may be all approximately the same with different individuals; yet in the one case an important truth is gleaned, in the other materials wasted on results of no interest to anybody. The discovery of calculus makes the construction of modern instruments and engines possible, while the speciously serious production of the average man of science frequently only retards progress by its unwieldy bulk. It is merely a question of "talent," the average man will say. Yes, but the talented man may not have spent so great an amount of measurable energy as the other fellow, and yet may have made possible the production of things undreamt of before. Korzybski's idea of treating the "dead men's work" as time-binding energy, while it does not completely clear the problem, brings us

a step nearer to its solution. We may not know for ages to come how the human brain transforms one kind of energy into another kind; but it is something to know that knowledge itself passed to us by bygone generations is not an accumulation of dead letters on dusty paper, but powerful energy stored up for the use of those among us who know how to transform it. Naturally, according to this conception, accumulated wealth itself "consists of the fruits or products of this time-binding capacity of man." But wealth is of two kinds: "One is material, the other is knowledge. . . . The first kind perishes, . . . the other is permanent in character; it is imperishable." Wealth itself, the "measure and symbol of work," is "in part the work of the living, but in the main the living work of the dead."

Having given a new definition of man and of wealth, Korzybski goes on to the next problem. To whom should wealth rightly belong? Here he is brought face to face with the problems of capital and labor in their broadest sense. The solution that he offers is characteristic of the modern trend—the wealth produced by the use of inventions should after a certain period of years become public property. Perhaps this would be a just method of distribution of wealth, and humanity will possibly some day see its way to achieving it, but the logic of this conclusion is not binding, although Korzybski thinks that it is. For the use of capital for the development of an enterprise also requires knowledge, brains, and talent. A captain of industry may be squandering energy in one field of his enterprise and amassing it in another; Korzybski sees the negative side, but who can justly balance the one against the other?

I think that the book would have been better if Korzybski had left out all that deals with the reconstruction of human society and had limited himself to the analysis of the time-binding capacity of man and the meaning of knowledge and wealth. There will be many who will condemn it for its conclusions and who will discard the basis of the author's theories along with the theories themselves. Yet the main principles are so important that the book not only deserves a wide circle of readers, but should be very carefully studied by all men of science lest the elements of truth contained in it should be overlooked and remain idle instead of being transformed into creative energy.

Cassius J. Keyser   (essay date 1922)

SOURCE: A review of *The Manhood of Humanity*, in *The Monist*, Vol. XXXII, No. 4, October, 1922, pp. 637-40.

[*In the following essay, Keyser quotes from various reviews of Korzybski's* The Manhood of Humanity *and commends Korzybski's analysis of what it is to be human.*]

"In the name of all you hold dear, you must read this book; and then you must re-read it, and after that read it again and again, for it is not brewed in the vat of the soft best-sellers to be gulped down and forgotten, but it is hewn out of the granite, for the building of new eras."

It must not be supposed that those powerful words are an irresponsible utterance of an exited enthusiast. Far from it. They were written by no less a person than Mr. H. L. Haywood, the sober-minded editor of *The Builder,* and may be found in the August number of that official organ of The National Masonic Research Society.

Indeed Haywood's estimate of the book does but confirm the judgment of many other competent critics including educators, engineers, logicians, mathematicians, biologists, psychologists, political philosophers, publicists, and other thinkers.

Let us hear a word from some of them.

"It is," writes Alleyne Ireland, "a contribution of the highest importance to the study of every problem in which human life is one of the factors."

In *The Freeman,* Ordway Tead says: "It is a forthright, earnest book by one who has seen a vision and would share it with his fellows."

Dr. Eric T. Bell, an eminent mathematician, says that "it took a genuine flight of genius" to make "Korzybski's main discovery that plants, animals and men are respectively energy-binders, space-binders, and time-binders." And Dr. Bell adds that "Anyone but a congenital idiot will get out of this book as much entertainment of a lasting kind as is contained in a whole library of romance."

"I consider Count Korzybski's discovery of man's place in the great life movement," writes Robert B. Wolf, Vice-president of the American Society of Mechanical Engineers, "as even more epoch-making than Newton's discovery of the law of gravitation."

Writing in *The Journal of Applied Psychology,* Max Meenes states that "**The Manhood of Humanity** is a truly remarkable contribution toward a scientific study of humanity and should command the attention of all interested in humanity's problems."

Dr. Petrunkevitch, Professor of Zoology at Yale, thinks its "main principles are so important that the book should be carefully studied by all men of science."

Dr. L. O. Howard, eminent entomologist, in his presidential address at the annual meeting of the American Association for the Advancement of Science, Toronto, 1921, said: "Count Korzybski in his remarkable book, **Manhood of Humanity,** gives a new definition of man, . . . and concludes that humanity is set apart from other things that exist on this globe by its time-binding faculty, or power, or capacity." Dr. Howard adds: "It is, indeed, this *time-binding* capacity which is the principal asset of humanity."

And Dr. Walter N. Polakov, well-known engineering counselor and distinguished author of *Mastering Power Production,* says: Korzybski's book "is bound to become our new Organum, interpreting Humanity to itself, and ushering in a new epoch."

It would be easy to swell the chorus of similar testimony to vast proportions, for abundant material is at hand, but it would be superfluous to do so. What has been submitted is enough to arrest the attention of even the dullest minds. For it is perfectly evident that a book that calls forth such words from such men, representing as they do almost every great field of scientific scholarship, is a book that

you and I must read, and re-read till we understand, if we are not to be dumbly ignorant of the most helpful and hopeful thought of our troubled time.

Lest any one reading these words might suspect that my own estimate of the book is but an echo of the opinions above quoted, I may be permitted to say that more than a year ago and shortly after the book came from the press I wrote as follows in *The New York Evening Post*: "We have here a book that is worthy of the times. Physically it is not large, but spiritually it is great and mighty—great in its enterprise, in its achievement, in the implications of its central thought, and mighty in its significance for the future welfare of men, women and children everywhere throughout the world."

What, pray, is that enterprise? What does the book aim at? It aims at turning the world's thought towards establishing the greatest of all conceivable things—the science and art of *human* engineering—the science and art of an engineering statesmanship magnanimous enough to embrace the entire world.

But what, pray, is human engineering? Human engineering—engineering statesmanship—is to be the science and art of coordinating the civilizing energies of the world and directing them to the advancement of the welfare of all mankind including posterity. Nothing conceivable could be nobler than that. In that great good are embraced all possible goods.

We are at once confronted with a great question. What is the science and art of human engineering to be *based* upon? It goes without saying that the basis must be a scientific basis—some kind of scientific knowledge. And the question is: scientific knowledge of *what*? The answer is: scientific knowledge of human nature—scientific understanding of the essential nature of Man.

Here we encounter the most important question that can be asked: What *is* Man? What is that quality or capacity in virtue of which human beings are *human*? What is the *distinctive* place of mankind in the hierarchy of the world's life?

In connection with that question Korzybski has rendered the world an immeasurable service. He has indeed propounded the question to himself but that is not what I mean. He has made it perfectly plain that the question is at once supreme and fundamental but neither is that what I mean. What I mean is that he has given the great question the *best* answer it has received in the history of thought—an answer which, because it is true, is infinitely superior to all its rivals. What is the answer? It is an answer defining our humankind in terms of Man's peculiar relation to what we call *Time*. The words are these: "Humanity is the time-binding class of life."

What do the words mean? It is evident that the burden of the meaning is borne by the term *Time-binding*. For the significance of this really mighty term the reader must be referred to the book itself where, says the mathematician and poet Professor Bell, "the ideas are stated with such admirable clearness in so many different and illuminating ways that any person of average intelligence can grasp the essential meaning at one reading." Should any one desire to examine my own attempt to lay bare in a few words the great term's central nerve, I may refer him to pages 428-431 of my *Mathematical Philosophy* where I have dealt with Korzybski's conception of man in the light of modern advances in logical theory.

Just as soon as readers grasp the meaning of the term *time-binding* and come thus to understand the author's concept of Humanity, then and not before they will understand both why he denies the ages-old mythical idea that humans are hybrids of natural and supernatural and why he also denies and denounces the zoological conception that humans are a *species* of *animals*.

It is instructive to compare the logic of Korzybski's great work with that of Professor Robinson's interesting book, *The Mind in the Making*. The aim of the authors is the same—the welfare of mankind. They are both of them evolutionists. They both believe that man is sprung from Simian stock. Korzybski nevertheless maintained that humans are not animals for animals, says he, are merely *space*-binders while man is a *time*-binder. Robinson, on the other hand, contends that humans are animals and endeavors again and again to rub that belief indelibly into the minds of his readers. *Why* do such thinkers as Robinson regard man as a species of animal? Is it because man has been evolved out of animal ancestry? If *A* has been evolved from *B*, do they really think that *A* is therefore necessarily a species of *B*? If heat be applied to ice there is evolved first water and then steam. Is steam to be rightly regarded as a species of ice? Man has been evolved from Simian mammals, mammals from reptiles, reptiles from fishes, and these probably, through a long course, from "microscopic globules of living matter, not unlike the simplest bacteria of today." Are thinkers like Professor Robinson prepared to follow their own "logic" and say that our humankind may be helpfully regarded as a species of ape, as a species of reptile, as a species of fish, as a species of ancient microscopic globule of living matter, not unlike the simplest bacteria of today? If it should be discovered in Professor Robinson's time that the organic and the living have been evolved from the non-living and inorganic, would the learned historian then argue that the living is a species of the non-living and that the organic is a species of the inorganic? The evolution of the *Novel* is an indubitable fact but it is a ridiculous contention that whatever is new must be a species of all the things from which it has sprung.

Is it contended that humans are species of animal *because* humans have certain animals organs, functions, and propensities? One would be not less foolish to contend that animals are plants because they have many organs and functions that plants have or to contend that solids are surfaces because solids have some properties that surfaces have or to contend that fractions are whole numbers because they have some properties that whole numbers have.

The philosophy of many a historian and many a zoologist would be greatly improved by a solid course in freshman logic.

Korzybski's concept of Man is the core of his book and the organic center of his philosophy. If you will master that concept you will find that it is related to the other ideas in the work as the sun is related to the planets and planetoids of our solar system. And as you continue your meditation you will discover much more.

If you are a historian you will find that the new concept of man demands a new philosophy of history—a philosophy that shall study the evil roles which false concepts of human nature have played from time immemorial.

If you are a student of ethics, you will find that the new concept affords a scientific basis for a moral system infinitely superior alike to the ethics of magic and myth and to the zoological ethics of the righteousness of might—the ethics of tooth and claw, competition, combat, and war.

If you are an educator you will find that the highest obligation of home, school, and press is to teach boys and girls and men and women everywhere to understand and to feel what they as humans really are—not animals nor hybrids of angel and beast but time-binders, civilizers, inheritors of the achievements of the dead, charged to use the inheritance justly and to transmit it with increase to he yet unborn.

If you are an engineer—and we are all of us engineers in some respect—you will find that Korzybski's conception of man is the solid basis for that science and art of *human* engineering—that science and art of engineering statesmanship—whose function it is to study the time-binding energies of the world, the civilization-producing energies of our kind, to coordinate them and to direct them to the welfare of all mankind including posterity.

I will close by repeating what I said elsewhere. "Not to read this book is to miss the best thought of these troubled years."

Sidney Hook   (essay date 1934)

SOURCE: "The Nature of Discourse," in *The Saturday Review of Literature*, Vol. X, No. 34, March 10, 1934, pp. 546-47.

[*In the following review of* Science and Sanity, *Hook commends Korzybski's work in logic and mathematics, but considers the presentation of his material to be overbearing and repetitious.*]

It is interesting to note that although philosophers have discoursed about all things, real and imaginary, the nature of discourse itself has received philosophical attention only during the last generation. It has become increasingly evident, however, that some of the great historic problems of metaphysics and logic have arisen primarily as a result of profound linguistic confusion. Clarification can only be achieved if we take the nature of discourse as the subject matter of discourse and ask under what conditions it is possible for discourse to render what is not discourse with a minimum of ambiguity and indeterminancy. Alfred Korzybski's book [*Science and Sanity*] is an attempt to answer this question with novelty, comprehensiveness, and as far as fundamentals go, with finality.

At the very outset I wish to make it clear that although the large claims which Mr. Korzybski enters in behalf of his work cannot be allowed, he has written one of the most suggestive books in the philosophy and methodology of the sciences which has appeared in recent years. The central problem with which he grapples is one which in different ways every intelligent specialist or layman has run up against in pondering over the difficulties of communication or in trying to adjust his verbal responses to the unceasing flow of new experience and accumulation of new truths. How can our language, which is composed of a finite number of words with fixed meanings, express the manifold distinctions, differentiations, and nuances which flow from the inexhaustible nature of events? For Mr. Korzybski our language or semantic reactions do not involve only our tongues but our entire nervous system. Inability to understand the world and make the proper adjustments to it, therefore, leads to emotional frustration and mental disorder. Where we stubbornly insist upon imposing our elementary language fixations upon the world, our behavior approaches overt insanity. We take the word for the substance and the substance for an independent power and end by letting our own magical abstractions dominate our civilization and destiny. In attempting to reform the foundations of logic and science, Mr. Korzybski claims to be offering a clue to the reform of the whole of our culture and education. The suggestions for a transvaluation of cultural and social values are not indicated, but his program for scientific reorientation has won such acclaim from distinguished savants throughout the world that this alone would entitle the author to a respectful hearing.

The root evil of all false thinking and living, according to Mr. Korzybski, is our tendency to make identifications—of one thing with another, of one time-situation with another, of one personality with another. This not only leads to simplification of thought but to a disregard, and often a violation, of qualitative diversity in experience. Even worse, different meanings of identity are identified; as a consequence the incurable ambiguities of the little word *is* revenge themselves upon us by generating paradoxes and puzzles which have concerned philosophers from Parmenides to Russell. Thinking which is characterized by an adherence to the "laws of thought"—identity, contradiction, and excluded middle—Korzybski characterizes as Aristotelian. In mathematics the Aristotelian logic gives rise to Euclidean systems; and applied in physics both together give us Newtonian science. The Aristotelian-Euclidean-Newtonian system of thinking is semantically infantile. Its use presupposes that the descriptions of things are themselves things and that inferences about descriptions are themselves descriptions. It confuses the things which are the ultimate reference of discourse—(that which is pointed at)—with the words which are used as labels for them. It fails to distinguish between statements of what is the case and statements concerning statements. Our traditional linguistic tools are too crude to facilitate the processes of discrimination and abstraction. The upshot is that even when our scientific techniques are successful, our methods are confused and our explanations are muddled.

What we have knowledge of, Mr. Korzybski insists, is never of things but of the structure of things. If our language reactions are to be adequate to the world in which we live, they must exhibit a structure which is cognate to the structure of that world. The structure of the Aristotelian-Euclidean-Newtonian system is too simplistic and the psychology, sociology, and culture based upon it are necessarily defective. Our only salvation from the intellectual morass in which we wallow today is to elaborate a non-elementalistic semantic system, characterized by Mr. Korzybski as non-Aristotelian, non-Euclidean, and non-Newtonian. Such a system is free from the straitjacket of the law of identity, recognizes the multi-ordinality or functional context of terms, gives an enormous flexibility to language, makes us conscious of our processes of abstraction and discrimination, endows us with wings for creative flight, and by means of a reformed and generalized mathematics, enables us to both test and preserve our sanity.

I believe that Mr. Korzybski's fundamental position is sound and that his *obiter dicta* contain some seminal ideas which undoubtedly will bear fruit in the minds of others. But if he had deliberately set about to obscure his primary insight he could not have proceeded any differently from the way he has—or succeeded so well. First of all, his book of more than eight hundred large, closely printed pages is nothing more than a program and suffers from a painful circumlocution and repetitiousness. He says what he has to say in the fifteen pages of his Supplement III; the rest of the book adds very little illumination to the propositions contained in that Supplement. Secondly, Mr. Korzybski is exceedingly naive in believing that the world waited for him to make his momentous discoveries about language, logic, and natural structure in the year 1925. Mr. Korzybski has restated views, held by many philosophers, some of whom lived long before Aristotle, with the air of a Columbus discovering a new America. I do not in any way wish to detract from the importance of the restatement, especially so because Mr. Korzybski draws most of his illustrative material from the fields of mathematics and physics. Yet the slightest acquaintance with the technical philosophical work of John Dewey, beginning with his *Studies in Logical Theory,* would convince Mr. Korzybski that his fundamental position has been worked out—and not merely stated—in psychology, logic, and metaphysics. And although some of Dewey's work is listed in the Bibliography there is not a single reference to Dewey in the text. More important, Mr. Korzybski's attack on the law of identity is an attack on a straw man—no, on a man of gossamer. He assumes that the law of identity (*A* is *A*) states that "one thing is identical with another in all respects," that it asserts "absolute sameness in all respects." Now the law of identity has been variously interpreted throughout the ages from Aristotle down to Meyerson, the great French scholar and philosopher of science (curiously enough the latter held that the law of identity is the presupposition of all science and sanity but his name is not even mentioned). But I am acquainted with no one, and I challenge Mr. Korzybski to point to anyone, who has held to this interpretation of the law of identity.

Now it is clear that there is a sense in which it is perfectly legitimate to use the principle of identity once we distinguish between things, properties, and classes. Things can never be identical with each other but they can be identical in respect to their inclusion in the same class or in respect to their possession of the same property. Science would be impossible if this were not recognized. If failure to recognize non-identity sometimes leads to insanity, failure to recognize some types of identity is a good working definition of idiocy. Mr. Korzybski, despite his ban upon all identification, constantly uses the concept of identity in his descriptions. He admits the validity of the phrase "sameness in some respect," but in what way is this incompatible with Aristotle's statement that "the same attribute cannot at the same time belong and not belong to the same subject in the same respect." In fact Korzybski himself uses the notion of identity uncritically. He holds that the structure of our language and nervous system must be similar (which means identical in some respect) to the structure of the world. But he does not properly explain the creative activity of man which consists in changing the structure of some aspect of the world to make it conform to our ideals.

Even more questionable is the organic connection which Korzybski assumes to exist between his researches in logic and psychology and his views on sanity and civilization. Social and economic problems have no more to do with the interpretation of the law of identity than "the flowers that bloom in the spring, tra-la." Korzybski assumes that if a semantic system could be developed which enabled human beings to understand the world and each other mankind would have rest from its evils. No evidence is introduced to show that semantics has anything to do with the causes of depression or war and it is not unlikely that if two nations or classes or individuals really understood each other, they might fight each other—more intelligently perhaps—but just as bitterly. To hold, as Korzybski does, that "some trends of history are foregone conclusions because of the structure of the human nervous system" is to reveal an amazing confusion concerning the categories proper to physical science and so-called social science. If space permitted, I would take strong exception to the neuro-psychological corollaries which Korzybski gratuitously draws from his discussion of logical and physical principles. Psychiatry has not developed beyond the stage of classification and anyone can prove anything by selecting his data. The very title of Korzybski's book, **Science and Sanity,** is prejudicial to the best pages in it.

The author would be well advised to develop his views on logic and mathematics and keep out of the fields of economics, history, and culture study in which he is obviously not at home. Here he makes up in dogmatism for what he lacks in detailed knowledge. If any proof were wanted, one need but point to his sympathy with the work of Spengler whose intellectual charlatanries are a byword among competent critics. What appeals to him is Spengler's conception of morphological determinism, the view that every culture is organic through and through, and that to understand anything about a civilization we must understand everything about it. This notion is a mystical vulgarization of Hegel's theory of objective Mind. Korzybski holds to

an even more thorough-going morphological cultural determinism than either Spengler or Hegel, but whereas these latter two were consistent and postulated a spiritualistic metaphysics as the source of the pattern of the culture, Korzybski cannot follow them, for this is precisely what his semantic philosophy forbids.

Korzybski's book ought to be read by all who are interested in problems of communication. It is sure to open fresh vistas on fundamental questions of language and logic to all those who can discount the author's prophetic tone and manner and treat the peripheral fantasia of his social doctrines as so much poetry.

Oliver L. Reiser   (essay date 1936)

SOURCE: "Modern Science and Non-Aristotelian Logic," in *The Monist,* Vol. XLVI, No. 2, July, 1936, pp. 299-317.

[*In the following essay, Reiser discusses Korzybski's formula for replacing Aristotelian reasoning with a system that repudiates the notion of identity common to Western logic.*]

It is generally recognized that we are living in a period of profound reorganization in human culture. There is a demand not only for practical readjustment in the social order, but there is now developing the belief that we need also a fundamental reconstruction of the theoretical foundations of science. A searching investigation would probably reveal that these two developments are not isolated manifestations, but phases of the same unitary phenomenon—the demand for a new mode of orientation.

The statement that we need a new mode of orientation to deal with the practical and theoretical difficulties which confront us is more radical than some might suppose. We are here referring not merely to the *content* of our "thoughts," but to the very *forms* themselves. So thoroughgoing is this proposed reconstruction that it reaches down into a critical examination of the "logical" and linguistic tools we employ in all our orientations. In other words, one of the reformations which is now being advocated as an essential part of the new methodology is that we develop a theory of coherence to take the place of the traditional Aristotelian "logic," which the human race has employed for over two thousand years, and adopt a non-Aristotelian system, thereby rejecting the most fundamental "laws of thought" which have regulated our "reasoning" processes, inductive as well as deductive. If such a proposed reconstruction of our "thinking" technique should succeed in establishing its claims, we would be in for an intellectual revolution which would alter the entire character of our culture. In his recent book, *The Search for Truth,* E. T. Bell states that Euclid hog-tied mathematics and Aristotle hand-cuffed human thought. And just as Lobatchewsky in the nineteenth century emancipated mathematics from the idea of "truth" in geometry, so Bell holds that non-Aristotelian systems free man from slavery to traditional "laws of thought." In the one example of non-Aristotelian systems we shall examine, that of Count Alfred Korzybski, Aristotelian logic, Euclidian geometry, and Newtonian physics are regarded as forming one coherent system, with non-Euclidian geometry, non-

Newtonian (relatively) physics, and non-Aristotelian system forming another coherent system.

The demand for a non-Aristotelian system is not an isolated phenomenon. The several independent sources of the revision are found in physics, organic phenomena, and mathematics. We cannot here examine these several non-Aristotelian "logics," but will confine ourselves to the system of Alfred Korzybski, as presented in his treatise, *Science and Sanity, An Introduction to Non-Aristotelian Systems and General Semantics*. We turn our attention to this system mainly because Korzybski has much to say about biological and psychological phenomena which is of interest to students of human nature. Before passing on, however, it may be pointed out that Kurt Lewin has contrasted what he designates as the Aristotelian and Galileian modes of thought. If Lewin had taken the additional step of establishing a necessary connection between the Aristotelian "mode of thought" and Aristotelian "logic," he might also have arrived at the conclusion that modern scientific findings require a non-Aristotelian system for their organization. That gestalt psychology will eventually have to adopt a non-Aristotelian approach is a point on which there can be little doubt.

Returning to Korzybski, the first observation to make is that the focal point of attack in his system is against "identity." The most fundamental of the three traditional "laws of thought," implicitly assumed in Aristotelian logic, is that a thing is what it is, or is identical with itself in all respects. On the basis of this "law" traditional thought has argued that the human "mind," observing these "identities" in nature, can generalize the observed uniformities and make statements about classes of objects, and these constitute the "laws of nature." Thus science was tied up with a logic developed by ancient Greek thought.

This view, as Korzybski points out, was elaborated long before the theory of relativity. Now the Minkowski-Einstein doctrine teaches us that *a physical thing is a space-time fact,* and that the temporal dimension cannot be separated from the spatial coördinates. For this reason the statement that an electron, or an apple, or any thing, is "identical" with itself is *false to facts,* since there is no such thing as an identical piece of matter at successive times. No object ever occupies the same ("identical") space-time twice. Human beings, by virtue of their power of abstraction, can isolate "things" from their "environments" and label these supposedly self-identical objects with names; but we must not let language mislead us into believing that because we use the same name for an object, it is therefore the same object. Every object is unique, and should have a unique symbol. To avoid the fallacy of false identification, Korzybski states, we should label all our names with subscripts indicating dates, thus—$apple_1$, $apple_2$, etc. Any given object is a complex of submicroscopic events in space-time, which can be treated as an "object" or "substance" when its behavior remains invariant in a given situation; but no two macroscopic objects are alike in "all" respects, and the "same" object is not identical with itself at some previous instant of time. Since it is language which misleads us into making these false identifications, it is necessary to consider in more detail the relation between language and thought.

LANGUAGE AND THOUGHT

It is quite generally known that in primitive thought word-magic is an essential part of the culture-pattern. The conception of an occult connection between "words" and "things" leads to taboos against the use of certain sacred words and to such practices as giving evil names to dolls representing your enemies, on the assumption that the original of the manikin will thereby be injured. But that this verbal magic also crept into the culture of Western Europe, largely through the influence of Greek philosophy, is not so generally recognized. And yet this fact is not difficult to establish. The momentous consequences of this fact will appear as we proceed.

That some of the Greeks regarded words as the revelation of the nature of things is familiar to all students of ancient Greek philosophy. This is true, for example, of Heraclitus. As F. M. Cornford states [in his *From Religion to Philosophy*] of his philosophy: "The Logos is revealed in speech. The structure of man's speech reflects the structure of the world; more, it is an embodiment or representation of it." This Logos doctrine, interpreted in terms of the creative power of sound, entered into Christian theology through the Gospel of St. John, as everyone knows.

This fact itself is of great historical importance in the subsequent history of Western European culture, but when we take into consideration the interplay of thought and language in Aristotelian logic, and the tremendous influence of the Aristotelian tradition, the significance of word-magic in our own civilization becomes far more obvious and important. This is a strong statement, and it becomes all the more impressive if we grant the validity of the contention of Bertrand Russell, who on several occasions has declared that he doubted whether anyone trained in Aristotelian logic could ever free himself sufficiently from that tradition to think clearly. Russell's view that the civilization of Western Europe has been corrupted by its slavishness to Aristotelian habits of thought rests in part on his theory of the tyranny of language. In his book, *The Analysis of Mind,* Russell argues that many philosophers have erred in assuming that the structure of sentences corresponds to the structure of facts. He here refers to the doctrine of Sayce, who maintained that all European philosophy since Aristotle had been dominated by the fact that all philosophers spoke Indo-European languages, and therefore supposed that the world, like the sentences they used, was necessarily divisible into subjects and predicates. This theory of the relation of thought to language is entirely consistent with the statement of Mauthner that "if Aristotle had spoken Chinese or Dacotan, he would have had to adopt an entirely different logic." The fact is, however, that Aristotle *did not* speak these languages, and so we find that, for better or for worse, Greek language and logic have formed the backbone of Western science and philosophy.

To see how this came about it is necessary to make a brief excursion into "theory of knowledge."

THE PROBLEM OF PERMANENCE AND CHANGE

One of the most obvious things about the universe is that it is constantly suffering change but that in the midst of change there are foci of permanence. To explain this problem of change it has been the natural tendency to postulate some underlying substratum as the seat of qualitative changes, which are therefore regarded as transformations of this primal stuff. One of the earliest problems of Greek philosophy was to describe the nature of this original "stuff." The formulation of the view that qualities inhere in a thing-like core, as pins stick in a pin cushion, is generally credited to Aristotle. In favor of this view it may be noted that the categories of "substance" and "quality" first appear explicitly in Aristotle's system, who is therefore held responsible for fixing in human thought the notion of the "thing" as the bearer of the qualities which inhere in this "substantial" substratum.

It is held by some that this metaphysics of matter is a consequence of the Aristotelian logic of classes. The foundation of Aristotelian logic is the doctrine that every proposition must affirm or deny a predicate of a subject. Since Aristotle's definition of a primary substance is that which can be a subject but never a predicate, propositions about subjects must predicate qualities of the substances. In other words, in propositions the subjects are represented by class names, and in a logic of classes the predicates are the ascription to, or denial of, a quality or attribute to the subject terms. One aspect of this logic which is especially noteworthy is the way in which the verb "to be" functions in expressing the various relations between subjects and predicates. The relations of "class inclusion," "identity," and "class membership," are regarded in modern mathematical logic as distinct in nature, and therefore requiring distinct symbolization; but in Aristotelian logic they are lumped together under the common form of "*A is B*." According to Bertrand Russell, the use of "is" to express both predication and identity is a disgrace to the human race!

To be sure, there *is* room for difference of opinion on the matter of just what Aristotle meant by "substance." Among those who take the stand that the faulty Aristotelian conception of substance is intimately connected with the Aristotelian logic of classes is Professor A. N. Whitehead. As Professor Whitehead says [in his *The Concept of Nature*]: "Aristotle asked the fundamental question, What do we mean by 'substance'? Here the reaction between his philosophy and his logic worked very unfortunately. In his logic, the fundamental type of affirmative proposition is the attribution of a predicate to a subject. Accordingly, amid the many current uses of the term 'substance' which he analyses, he emphasises its meaning as 'the ultimate substratum which is no longer predicated of anything else.'

"The unquestioned acceptance of the Aristotelian logic has led to an ingrained tendency to postulate a substratum for whatever is disclosed in sense-awareness, namely, to look below what we are aware of for the substance in the sense of the 'concrete thing.' This is the origin of the modern scientific concept of matter and ether, namely they are the outcome of this insistent habit of postulation." This criticism of the Aristotelian notion of substance as a thing-like core was anticipated by E. G. Spaulding, who also regards it as a consequence of Aristotle's logic [in his *The New Rationalism*, 1918]. In justice to the situation, however, it needs to be kept in mind that there *are* those who hold that this is not an adequate interpretation of Aristotle. Thus, in connection with Professor Whitehead's views, J. D. Mabbott argues [in his article "Substance," *Philosophy*, Vol. X, 1935] that Whitehead has misunderstood Aristotle. Mr. Mabbott holds that while Professor Whitehead claims to be attacking the notion of substance as it comes down to us from Aristotle, he really accepts the Aristotelian conception of substance and is attacking the notion of a permanent independent physical object as it has come to us from the Greek atomists. Somewhat along the same lines, we find that Professor J. A. Leighton [in his *Man and the Cosmos*, 1922] has protested against the misinterpretation of Aristotle as embodied in Professor Spaulding's presentation.

Whatever its origin, this substance-quality view has influenced all subsequent philosophy and science. One needs only to note that it is the metaphysical basis of the religious doctrine of transubstantiation to see its importance in Western thought,—an importance which was not nullified until, as V. F. Lenzen points out [in "World Geometry," *Monist*, Vol. XLI, 1931], relativity physics, through the electrodynamic conception of matter, eliminated the last vestige of Scholasticism from physics. Perhaps, also, the contempt for matter as a principle of evil (*e.g.*, as in Puritanism and Christian Science) is to be sought in the turn which the Greeks gave to the problem of "being" and "becoming." Both in Plato and in Aristotle a dualism appears between the purposive activity of the "idea" or "form" and the resistance of matter. In science this notion of matter as a "retarding" principle reappears in the concept of "inertia." Here the consequence of Aristotelian physics was definitely unfortunate. Aristotle's law of falling bodies, making velocity dependent upon mass, was false, and had to be corrected by Galileo. (It makes no difference to the argument whether Galileo established the new law by experiments from the leaning tower of Pisa, or whether this alleged historical event is only a myth, as Lane Cooper states.) This substantialistic view of matter as a substratum of inertial mass—identified with the "primary qualities" of space-occupancy, impenetrability, etc.—exercised its authority in determining the theory of "space" as the vessel or *container* in which the motions of "matter" occur; of "time" as the history of the transformations of matter in space; of "force" as the active cause of the motions of matter; and of the "ether" as the underlying continuum of the interactions of the "bodies" of nature. It is only recently that we have sufficiently disengaged ourselves from this attitude to permit ourselves to ask whether a *thing-like stuff* represents the foundational reality, or whether *events* and *relational structure* are more fundamental. The subsequent history of physics, guided by the Newtonian conception of "space," "matter," "force," etc., as *absolutes* of nature, and the transformation of Newtonian mechanics into the *additive-particle-picture* of Laplace is the story of the inevitable movement of thought toward the inescapable consequences of the materialistic theory. This story is so well known as to make its retelling here a work of supererogation.

This, in brief, is the story of the alliance between Aristotelian logic and classical physical science. Now modern science must undo the cumulative effects of two thousand years of tradition. Physics is the first of the contemporary sciences to demand a new orientation. Relativity (non-Newtonian) physics is moving toward a new system which requires a non-Aristotelian approach. The attack on the classical system was first directed against the traditional notion of "substance" as an absolute and self-identical underpinning of the phenomenal world. *Events* (space-time facts) are now conceived to be primary in nature. "Particles" must be regarded as nodes of permanence, invariant within their contexts of contemporaneous change. Complex "matter" is an aggregate, a relatively stable equilibrium, of such foci of electrical density. "Substance" is only a kind of resting-place for thought, expressing an unwillingness to analyse further. Einstein's thesis concerning the equivalence of "matter" and "energy" destroys the materialistic philosophy of Newton and Laplace. The old Aristotelian, subject-predicate (substance) logic is gone, never to return.

This is the present situation in physics. But what are the implications of this logical-physical revolution for science in general? Let us here return to Korzybski's views.

NON-ADDITIVE RELATIONS AND ORGANISMIC PROCESSES

We have said that Korzybski has been the most thorough investigator thus far to trace out the consequences of these ideas in biology, psychology, etc. Indeed, one of the most interesting features of this writer's views is the manner in which they link up with other contemporary movements in science. Korzybski has much to say about organism-as-a-whole processes, and by this he seems to mean what others express by *non-summative, gestalt,* or *emergent* properties and behavior. For Korzybski this type of process is an instance of phenomena represented mathematically by *non-linear equations.* Until Korzybski, no one—with the possible exception of W. Köhler—has stressed this connection between organismic processes and non-linearity.

In every instance where we are dealing with organism-as-a-whole processes we are face to face with a situation in which the function of the sum (whole) is not the sum of functions of the part processes. Thus we have two types of equations to represent the two types of processes: *linear* or *additive functions* and *non-linear* or *non-additive functions* (equations). Korzybski suggests that the following equation, based on additivity, be taken as a definition of linearity: $f(x+y)=f(x)+f(y)$. In linear equations of this type a function of the sum is equal to the sum of functions, and has only one solution. Such a relation holds in vector analysis when the addition of vectors is defined by the familiar parallelogram of forces, and in calculus when we deal with linear equations where the "derivative of the sum is the sum of derivatives" and the "integral of the sum is the sum of integrals." But in all cases where the effect of two or more causes working together is *not* the *sum* of their effects working separately, linear equations are inadequate.

Count Korzybski points out that the notion of organism-as-a-whole is central in biology, psychiatry, etc., and terms this general principle *non-elementalism,* meaning by this

that an organism is *not* a mere algebraic *sum* of its parts, but is more than that and must be treated as an integrated whole. Bodily changes are frequently non-additive, as, for example, when the heart, for any reason, slows down the circulation, this may produce an accumulation of carbonic acid in the blood, which again increases the viscosity of the blood and so throws more work on the already weakened heart. In the same way the superposition of new neurological processes on old ones is non-additive, for this may fundamentally alter the whole character of the organism. "Thought" also represents the reaction of the organism-as-a-whole, and like all associative connections may be a non-additive function. Similarly, fears are not an additive or a linear function, but follow some more complex function of a higher degree. In general the typical functioning of the nervous system is connected with what Korzybski calls *time-binding,* which is represented mathematically by an exponential function of time.

It is part of Korzybski's thesis that this same general situation appears in physics, and that the theory of relativity illustrates the principle of non-elementalism. He states that only since Einstein have we come to see that the simplest and easiest-to-solve linear equations are not structurally adequate. These non-linear equations are more complex and difficult to handle, and are often solved by approximations; but it is no one's fault that the world does not happen to be an additive affair. In relativity theory this appears when the ordinary theorem concerning the addition of vectors (or compounding of velocities) is rejected. The corresponding parallel between gestalt theory and relativity was apparently first pointed out by George Humphrey [in "The Theory of Einstein and the *Gestaltpsychologie:* A Parallel," *American Journal of Psychology* Vol. XXXV, 1934], and the writer [in "Gestalt Psychology and the Philosophy of Nature," *Philosophy Review,* Vol. XXXIX, 1930], in commenting on the analogy, expressed doubts as to its value, but in the light of Korzybski's thesis this judgment may have to be reconsidered.

We have stated that Korzybski's claim to the development of a non-Aristotelian system rests upon the fact that his system rejects "identity." It is true that Korzybski also is committed to abandonment of the "law of excluded middle"; thus the *two*-valued "logic" which requires that a proposition be either "true" or "false" is replaced by a *multiple-valued* system. Since Korzybski's notion of what he terms *infinite-valued orientations* has points in common with this more general non-Aristotelian movement, it is unfortunate that lack of space compels us to pass over this phase of his system. Before leaving this matter, however, it needs to be pointed out that this system should *not* be described as a non-Aristotelian "logic." All existent "logics," Korzybski argues, are *elementalistic,* in the sense that they claim to study the activity of "reason," of "thought," independently of "emotion," whereas in reality the separation of "intellect" *and* "emotion" is just as objectionable as the separation of "space" *and* "time," or "mind" *and* "body." The science of the adjustment of man to his environment is a *psycho-logic,* and this is based on a non-Aristotelian *system* rather than a *logic.*

It is because of the broad scope of its principles and applications that the system of Korzybski is of interest to psychiatrists and educators. And this brings us to what might be called the pragmatic sanction of this system. Noting the fact that there is much false to facts "thinking," infantilism, and consequent maladjustment in the world, and noting the fact that certain types of insanity are based upon false identifications, and that there are obvious analogies between the irrational "thinking" of schizophrenics and the magic of primitive peoples (as Dr. Alfred Storch has shown in his study, *The Primitive Archaic Forms of Inner Experience and Thought in Schizophrenia*), Korzybski concludes that if we abandon "identity" we will at one stroke render impossible, not only the type of disorientation we have in *in*sanity (delusion and false identifications), but also the *un*sanity of those who are functioning in accordance with Aristotelian habits of "thought." The practical need for a non-Aristotelian semantics rests upon the fact that human problems grow out of linguistic abuses. Our difficulties of adjustment are *neuro*-semantic and *neuro*-linguistic. Only by retraining in an *extensional* orientation can we undo the evil effects of false identifications. The infinite-valued adjustments of Korzybski's system require a new canalization of energy. This is a laborious process, but the end justifies the means. The results, Korzybski assures us, are automatic, far-reaching, and entirely beneficial.

Having thus presented in thumb-nail sketch some of the important features of Korzybski's system and suggested a few of its applications, it now remains to say something of the criticisms that are made of this interesting scheme.

A CRITIQUE OF NON-ARISTOTELIANISM

In looking over some of the reviews of the book, **Science and Sanity,** and talking with interested parties, I find that some of the main reasons critics give for regarding Korzybski's argument as not convincing are as follows:

(A) It will be argued by some that the very fact of *false* identifications presupposes that there are also *true* identifications. Thus John Doe, a patient in a psychiatric institution, may be there because he suffers from the delusion that he is Napoleon; but this "false identification" would never have occurred had John Doe observed the "law of identity,"—that John Doe is John Doe. Moreover, in order to observe this principle of personal identity we need not be guilty of confusing the name of the man with the man himself.

(B) Again, it will be argued by some critics that Korzybski is forced to employ the very principle he claims to eliminate from his system. This, it may be held, is illustrated in a number of ways: (1) The law of identity is presupposed in observing the principle that in any given "universe of discourse" the meanings of our terms (defined and undefined) are to remain constant. (2) The notion of *isomorphic structures,* which Korzybski cannot get along without, and which is becoming increasingly useful in all natural science, is an instance of "identity" of logical structure. (3) Even though in nature we never discover true instances of "absolute identity in all respects," nevertheless, we need the notion of identity in our thinking. Emile Meyerson, for example, has argued at great length

that the formulation of scientific laws and theories involves the process of "identification." For Meyerson the "irrational" is simply that which defies such "identification."

In connection with Meyerson's thesis concerning "identification," let us be careful to note that if we take a mathematical equation as an example of an "identity," as Meyerson proposes, it turns out that the "equality" asserted between what is on the left and the right sides of the equality sign is by no means an "identity," as has been pointed out by Professor A. N. Whitehead [in his *The Principle of Relativity*]. Moreover, certain non-Aristotelian enthusiasts might argue, even in purely formal logic the meaning of, and necessity for, "identity" still remains to be established. The classical work in the field of mathematical logic is the *Principia Mathematica* of Whitehead and Russell. But no less an authority than F. P. Ramsey [in *The Foundations of Mathematics,* 1932] argues that one serious defect of this monumental work is found in the treatment of "identity." Ramsey holds that the definition "does not define the meaning with which the symbol for identity is actually used." To escape the difficulties he suggests that we adopt the proposal of Wittgenstein and eliminate the sign of identity, replacing it by the convention that different signs must have different meanings.

This argument might be put forth by some non-Aristotelians as final confirmation of the repeal of this famous "law" of traditional logic. But in reply the opposition will argue that this is only another example of fools rushing in where angels fear to tread. To avoid grave mistakes it is necessary to know precisely what is being done in the above instances. The real fact is that Wittgenstein and Ramsey have never criticised the Aristotelian *principle* of identity. They are concerned with the *concept* of identity, and find fault with the Leibniz-Russell *definition* of identity as derived from the principles of the identity of indiscernibles, when interpreted as a convention stipulating unrestricted mutual substitutibility.

It will be recalled that Leibniz's principle of the identity of indiscernibles appeared legitimate to him because of the atomism of his system: the perfect individuality of the monad made it a completely closed entity through all eternity. Without accepting Leibniz's monadology, the modernized version of this principle has found it very useful in the logic of analogies, etc. Thus the identity of an object may be defined in terms of its properties, and *a* and *b* are identical if all the properties of *a* are properties of *b,* and vice versa. In the *Principia Mathematica* a similar use is made of this principle when it is asserted that two classes are identical if the propositional functions from which they are derived are "equivalent." Unfortunately this definition of identity in terms of predicative functions makes it self-contradictory for two things to have all their elementary properties in common. As Max Black points out [in *The Nature of Mathematics*], there is clearly some difficulty here, for, aside from the fact that to say two things are identical is merely a clumsy way of asserting that in reality there is only one thing, there is the additional difficulty due to the fact that it is not permissible in the logistic scheme to speak of *all* the properties which two things have in common. This last difficulty is met in *Principia Mathematica* by the use of the *axiom of reducibility (i.e.,* to any characteristics of a higher order there are equivalent characteristics of a lower order), but this axiom in turn has created more problems than it has solved. Thus, say the opponents of non-Aristotelianism, the difficulties in mathematical logic on this point are a result of treating "identity" as a propositional function of two arguments, and these difficulties are by no means insuperable.

And now what can those who advocate a non-Aristotelian system say in reply to this? Since it happens that the foregoing argument represents the statement of one of the outstanding logical positivists, let us address ourselves to this viewpoint. It is recognized that logical positivism is pretty well committed to the "operational" theory of meaning. On this theory the meaning of a concept is found in its consequences, its implications, and how it functions in its own system. Moreover this view subscribes to the *tautological* theory of implication: deductive reasoning in logic and mathematics consists in the elaboration of strings of tautologies. Since inference is the result of the manipulation of meaningless symbols according to *arbitrarily* selected rules of operation, we can grind out of the symbolic machine only what we put into it. *But on this view the Aristotelian "laws of thought" become mere conventions (or postulates) which validate certain forms of inference, and one could equally well substitute other postulates (rules of operation on symbols).* Either this, or we must deny that other rules are possible, in which case we return to the traditional view and assign the old unique status to the three traditional "laws of thought" of Aristotelian logic. *But this is to abandon the tautological theory!* How can we say that the laws of Aristotelian logic are *no more* and *no less* important than, *e.g.,* the commutative law, admit that this latter principle may be set aside (as in the non-commutative algebra of the new quantum theory), and then turn around and deny the possibility and utility of a non-Aristotelian logic? Professor Herbert Feigl has restated the Peirce-Wittgenstein criterion of meaning thus: *An unverifiable difference is no difference.* I wonder if we may in turn revise this formulation and say: *An unverifiable identity is no identity*? If so, where are we?

So far as the validity of Korzybski's system is concerned, it seems to me that one's views on the question of whether Korzybski has made good his case for the elimination of "identity" will be determined in some measure by one's reaction to his claim that the notion of "levels of abstraction" renders unnecessary Russell's theory of types. This theory, plus the very troublesome "axiom of reducibility," was supposed to provide an escape from the fallacy of "illegitimate totalities" and the vicious circle paradoxes arising out of the use of "all." According to Korzybski, the vicious circle arises from identifying different orders of statements: statements about statements represent the results of new neurological processes, their content varies, so that multi-ordinal terms (like "class") have a unique meaning *only* in a given context, *where the order of abstraction is definitely indicated.* If, therefore, we observe the rule of non-confusion of orders of abstraction, abandon the term class and the "is of identity," and accept the

four-dimensional language of abstractions of *different* orders, with a temporal coördinate, the axiom of reducibility becomes superfluous. Thus says Korzybski.

For my own part, I can only say that physical identity is really a limiting case of analogy, as two things become more and more alike, and this ideal limit is an asymptotic goal which no two things or situations ever attain. And so far as pure logic is concerned, it would be better to term the "law of identity" the *principle of symbolic univalence,* thus avoiding the ambiguity which has always resided in this "law." In justice to Korzybski it should always be remembered that he is little interested in "formal logic." His system is really a psycho-logic, *and is concerned with the harmful effects of identification as an orientation.* However else we may react to Count Korzybski's views, let us not make the mistake of judging the new *system* by the conventions of an alternative *logic.*

George A. Lundberg   (essay date 1937)

SOURCE: "The Diseases of Language," in *Social Forces,* Vol. 16, No. 2, December, 1937, pp. 291-93.

[*In the following review of* Science and Sanity, *Lundberg praises Korzybski's theories, but offers reservations about the repetitive nature of the book.*]

The most that a reviewer of a volume of such scope as [**Science and Sanity**] can legitimately undertake on his own responsibility is to estimate it as far as it touches the fields in which he considers himself qualified to judge critically. For other portions he must rely on the opinions of qualified authorities in the respective fields concerned. On the basis of such consideration it may be said that Korzybski has succeeded to a remarkable degree in satisfying the authorities in the various fields from which he draws his data. I base this statement not mainly on the formidable collection of possibly *ex parte* testimonials on the jacket, but on extended reviews by authorities of unquestioned standing, as well as on private discussion with such authorities. There remains the question of logic and scientific methods in the social sciences, which is the chief concern of the present review.

The main thesis of the volume may be briefly summarized as follows: It is known that primitive languages characteristically consist of a great number of *names for individual things,* i.e. they are "kind" languages with comparatively few relation-words. As a result, higher analysis is practically impossible. As science emerges we are forced to rely increasingly on a "degree" language of which mathematics is the most adequate form yet evolved. Now, while our adjustments (thought, speech, and other actions) to the physical world are dominated almost exclusively by the latter technique, we still attempt absurdly to make our social adjustments with word-tools suited only to a primitive culture. Our institutions are furthermore largely enshrined in and maintained through the prevailing language mechanisms, thus foisting upon us institutional patterns resting upon postulates and logic completely discredited and discarded by science, such as the law of identity and the law of excluded middle. The constant contradiction and conflict between the thinking technique (language) of modern physical science and that of the social sciences results in a schizophrenic civilization affecting both individual and collective behavior. Since culture is largely a language phenomenon and our adjustments to it must be linguistic, the fundamental remedy lies in the adaptation of our language and logical systems so as to make them correspond to the realities which modern science reveals, as contrasted with a primitive view of the world. Space necessitates passing over the interesting and cogent argument, heavily buttressed with data from psychiatry, neurology, and biochemistry, by which the author arrives at the conclusion that the only language adequate to intelligent reaction in the world of 1933 is mathematics. In short, only a statistical view of the world corresponds adequately to the realities of present environment.

> As words are *not* the things we are talking about, the only possible link between the objective world and the verbal world is structural. If the two structures are similar, then the empirical world becomes intelligible to us—we 'understand', we can adjust ourselves. If we carry out verbal experiments and predict, these predictions are verified empirically. If the two structures are not similar, then our predictions are not verified—we do not 'know', we do not 'understand,' the given problems are 'unintelligible' to us, we do not know what to do to adjust ourselves. Psychologically, in the first case we feel security, we are satisfied, hopeful; in the second case we feel insecure, a floating anxiety, fear, worry, disappointment, depression, hopelessness, and other harmful semantic responses appear. . . . We hear everywhere complaints of the stupidity or dishonesty of our rulers . . . without realizing that although our rulers are admittedly very ignorant, and often dishonest, yet the most informed, gifted, and honest among them cannot predict or foresee happenings, if their arguments are performed in a language of a structure dissimilar to the world *and* to our nervous system.

No summary of the length here attempted can, of course, pretend to give an adequate account of the enormous content of this volume. It is likewise impossible to take up all of the more or less serious objections one notes in the course of a careful reading. Chief among these objections is the tremendous repetitiousness of the work. From the standpoint of pure exposition of a position or of a system the work could profitably be reduced to one-fourth its present length. From an evangelistic or pedagogical viewpoint the value of repetition is, of course, well established, and the author makes no secret of his desire to convert the masses of men as quickly as possible. To this end he introduces at times devices for training and drill to which are imputed almost magical properties. Readers who already have formed the habit of thinking of human society in terms of the probability calculus are likely to weary after the first three hundred pages or before. Also, sociologists familiar with the works of Child and Herrick will find the biology and neurology of this work quite familiar. That it leans heavily on these authors is, of course, a matter of praise and not of criticism. The same is true of the frequent references to Whitehead, Russell, Poincare, Bridg-

man, W. M. Wheeler, W. A. White, and others of equal repute.

There remain a number of apparent contradictions and lapses into the type of thinking which the book is calculated to annihilate. Thus, although there is constant warning against "elementalistic" terminology, we nevertheless come upon references to "absolute" individuals. Also, there is the usual infatuation with the phrase "organism-as-a-whole" and "situation-as-a-whole" which results in the implication that wholeness is some intrinsic quality or characteristic instead of merely a term describing the selectivity or scope of human responses in a given case. Thus there is frequent warning against dividing verbally that "which cannot experimentally be so divided." Yet the whole phenomenon of abstraction and conceptual analysis clearly consists of just such division inasmuch as human response mechanism can react to only one or a few aspects of the universe at one time. Elsewhere the author recognizes this point. The same fallacy finds expression in the assumption that an individual constitutes some kind of more objective reality than does a group. Most curious of all are the references to "United States Behaviorism" always without citation of authors or works. Take, for example, this astonishing sentence: "It would be very interesting to see the Behaviorists *deny* that the writing of a mathematical treatise, or of some new theory of quantum mechanics represents a form of *human behavior* which they should study." In view of the fact that the Behaviorists were not only the first but have been the most vigorous defenders of the notion that speech is an important form of behavior, an outburst of this kind without any attempt to cite the source or basis for it, is perhaps itself the best illustration of the kind of semantic response to which Korzybski devotes much space. Watson's name appears in the bibliography as the lone representative of this dreadful school. His works are usually relied on to furnish substantiation for the strange ideas attributed to Behaviorists. Yet it was Watson who said: "Let me make this fundamental point at once: that *saying* is doing—that is *behaving*. Speaking overtly or to ourselves (thinking) is just as objective a type of behavior as baseball." [J. B. Watson, *Behaviorism*, 1924]. One wonders what would remain of the whole polemic literature against Behaviorism if critics first took the trouble to find and cite some defender of the position attacked.

The author admits that the statisticians have in the theory of probability and related approaches arrived at the same general conclusions as does this volume by a different type of analysis. Personally, the reviewer prefers the analysis which the statisticians and mathematicians have contributed. But the chief importance of the book under review probably lies in the fact that it arrives at these conclusions through philosophical and dialectical methods and will therefore be able to reach sociologists and psychiatrists who are linguistically immune to direct attack by statisticians.

It is reasonably clear that the social sciences are at present in an impasse from which only a fairly radical reorientation can liberate them. They are badly in need of the kind of release which Newton and Einstein in their respective ages contributed to physics and which Darwin provided in biology. The attempt to fit our more adequate observations into primitive frames of reference is becoming increasingly difficult and involves a constantly more flagrant violation of the law of parsimony. *Science and Sanity* is a good analysis of this impasse. It contains devastating implications for the social sciences and shows the abysmal gap that separates the technique of social thinking from our technique of thinking about other aspects of the universe. It is also an exposure of the naïveté of the assumption that the human social scene is so unique a phenomenon that social scientists really need not be concerned about developments in the other sciences.

There is no doubt that man-made verbal systems can greatly facilitate or frustrate the functioning of the human nervous system and the adjustments dependent thereon. Sociologists have only recently begun turning their attention to the fundamental importance of verbal behavior as an adjustment technique. Korzybski must be credited with an interesting and important synthetic contribution to this subject.

Max Black   (essay date 1949)

SOURCE: "Korzybski's General Semantics," in *Language and Philosophy: Studies in Method,* Cornell, 1949, pp. 221-46.

[*In the following excerpt, Black considers Korzybski as an innovative and influential thinker whose theories of semantics have the potential to improve the human condition.*]

Ever since men began to reflect critically upon the quality of their thinking, they have been conscious of the imperfections of their language. The ambitious designs of science and philosophy must be executed with no better instruments of expression than the "perfected cries of monkeys and dogs"—to use the vivid phrase of Anatole France. And centuries of effort by distinguished scholars have been devoted to the cause of linguistic improvement.

Yet the results remain disappointing; and never before has so much attention been given to the criticism and reform of symbolism. The popular name for such studies in the science of meaning is *semantics*—a discipline to which Peirce, Mead, Karl Bühler, C. K. Ogden, I. A. Richards, Bertrand Russell, Wittgenstein, and Carnap, among others, have made noteworthy contributions.

None of these writers, however, has had so much popular influence as Count Alfred Korzybski, the remarkable man whose doctrines I wish to examine in this essay. (The label, "*General* Semantics," serves to distinguish his doctrines from those of the other writers who have been mentioned.)

There exists today an Institute of General Semantics, which publishes, researches and offers advanced instruction; popularizations by Stuart Chase and [S. I.] Hayakawa have become national bestsellers; and the proceedings of the Second American Congress on General Semantics (held at Denver in 1941) contain an impressive array of papers by some seventy contributors on applications of semantics to subjects as varied as marital counseling, child guidance, musical appreciation, stuttering, and the prevention of dental decay.

The popular appeal of general semantics can be traced in part to the personality of the movement's founder. Any reader of Korzybski's major work, *Science and Sanity,* must be impressed by the liveliness, vigor, and freshness of the exposition. Korzybski is no plodding, minute thinker, laboriously adding, in a spirit of academic detachment, a few fragments to the coral reef of knowledge: he is a reformer and evangelist. For him, society is riddled with mental disease, induced by linguistic maladjustment—a condition which he is anxious to improve.

One quotation, of many which might be chosen, will serve to establish the tone and temper with which Korzybski approaches the problems of general semantics:

> Our rulers, who rule our symbols, and so rule a symbolic class of life, impose their own infantilism on our institutions, educational methods, and doctrines. This leads to nervous maladjustment of the incoming generations which, being born into, are forced to develop under the unnatural (for man) semantic conditions imposed on them. In turn, they produce leaders afflicted with the old animalistic limitations. The vicious circle is completed; it results in a general state of human un-sanity, reflected again in our institutions.

Insistence upon the "unsanity" of present society is a theme to which Korzybski constantly returns.

Now the man in the street will usually not welcome accusations of "infantilism," "animalism," and pathological "unsanity." But he *will* respond with interest and hope to any promise of a cure for the world's too obvious disorders. This is precisely what Korzybski has to offer—a detailed and practical system for re-education in better mental and linguistic habits, "such as can be grasped and applied by any individual who will spend the time and effort necessary to master this system and acquire the corresponding *s.r.* [semantic reactions]."

The benefits offered are immediate and substantial: "They help any individual to solve his problems by himself, to his own and others' satisfaction. They also build up an *affective* semantic foundation for personal as well as for international agreement and adjustment."

How should these claims be tested? If our concern were mainly practical, we would want to investigate empirically the outcome of the linguistic therapy recommended. Sweeping claims of the beneficial results of semantic treatment have been made; but the data are as yet insufficient for a final evaluation.

There is, however, another and related question which can already be discussed with some profit—the question of the coherence and adequacy of the general principles from which the recommended therapy is derived. Fortunately, Korzybski, for all his urgent concern in practical affairs, is free from that short-sighted "practicalism" which shows itself in contempt for theory. He insists rather, in a most commendable way, upon the necessity of an adequate general theory and ascribes the difficulty of institut-ing semantic reforms to the previous absence of sound theoretical foundations: "The difficulty was that no methodological general theory based on the new developments of life and science had been formulated until general semantics and a general extensional, teachable and communicable, non-aristotelian system was produced."

On Korzybski's showing, then, the program of general semantics depends upon the validity of its theoretical foundations, to which alone this essay will be devoted.

It is worth noting, in parentheses, that Korzybski's theories have important theoretical consequences for a number of controversial and perplexing problems in the philosophy and methodology of science: Here are some representative items:

> In psychiatry it [i.e. the theory of general semantics] indicates on colloidal grounds the solution of the "body-mind" problem. . . . It gives the first definition of "consciousness" in simpler physicochemical terms. . . . It leads to a general theory of psycho-therapy, including all existing medical schools. . . . In biology it gives a semantic and structural solution of the "organism-as-a-whole" problem. . . . It formulates a new and physiological theory of mathematical types of extreme simplicity and very wide application. . . . It offers a non-aristotelian solution of the problem of mathematical "infinity". . . . It offers a new non-aristotelian semantic definition of *mathematics* and *number*. . . . In physics, the enquiry explains some fundamental, but as yet disregarded, semantic aspects of physics in general, and of Einstein's and the new quantum theories in particular. . . . It resolves simply the problem of "indeterminism" of the newer quantum mechanics.

To this striking but still incomplete catalogue of achievements Korzybski adds the disarming comment: "I realize that the thoughtful reader may be staggered by such a partial list. I am in full sympathy with him in this. I also was staggered."

Any theory which can accomplish so much deserves a respectful hearing—whatever the verdict on its practical bearings upon individual and social reforms may prove to be.

I shall try to do just two things: First, to make a little more definite the general method used in Korzybski's investigations; and then to explain in more detail two components of his theory which seem to be of crucial importance. The topics I have selected for more intensive discussion are Korzybski's attacks upon Aristotelian logic and his theory of abstraction.

KORZYBSKI'S GENERAL APPROACH

A distinctive feature of Korzybski's approach to problems of symbolization and meaning is his intention to make general semantics a *scientific* discipline. Repeatedly he insists that general semantics is as empirical as biology or physics.

The program, therefore, is to solve problems of meaning by just those methods of observation, generalization, and experimentation which have proved outstandingly effective in the empirical sciences. Korzybski uses the results of other sciences extensively and wishes his own theses to be submitted to just the kind of test which would be appropriate to the confirmation of a physical or biological hypothesis.

If semantics is to be an empirical science, some operational definition is needed of the central term "meaning": "meaning" must be as accessible to empirical recognition as kinetic energy or electrical charge. The important decision is now made to use physiological criteria of meaning, i.e., to test statements about meanings by observations of what is known or assumed to be happening in the nervous system of a biological organism.

This choice of procedure gives a distinctive slant to Korzybski's investigations, for he is, in his own words, mainly interested in "the neurological attitude toward 'meaning'." It follows that one of the most important and basic notions of general semantics will be that of the nervous response made by an organism to a stimulus consisting of symbols.

We are to understand, accordingly, that the reception by an organism of any spoken word, or other symbol, induces a certain response (and especially so in the nervous system). Such response, determined in part by the nature of the symbol-stimulus, but also in large measure by the previous experiences and present condition of the receiving organism, is called a "*semantic reaction.*" (The term refers to emotive as well as cognitive reactions; a feeling of response of dislike or fear on hearing the word "Hitler" is counted as part of the semantic reaction to that word.) First order responses to symbols can themselves act as stimuli to further semantic reactions; and these in turn to others, induced still more indirectly.

Inasmuch as semantic reactions, whether first-order effects of symbolic stimuli, or responses to other semantic reactions previously induced, are *specific natural events* in the nervous system of the organism, the study of meanings becomes a branch of physiology.

But the study of meanings also falls outside the province of physiology. For general semantics undertakes to examine the *correctness* or adequacy of semantic reactions. This, in turn requires us to determine how far semantic reactions are a faithful reflection of the physical reality outside the organism. There is needed a theory as to what constitutes "physical reality," in the light of which to criticize statements purporting to represent that "reality."

It might be supposed that physics would supply all the information that could be needed about the external environment of the organism in a symbol situation. But a mere *description* of the physical world will not suffice for Korzybski's purposes; he requires criteria for distinguishing the "real" from the unreal or illusory. In the end, this leads him into metaphysics.

Korzybski's reliance upon the empirical sciences is colored by his conception of the character of scientific method. Other thinkers, from Hume to Bertrand Russell, Dewey, and the Logical Positivists, who have hoped to use science as a key to philosophical problems have been anxious to stress the "unity" of the scientific method upon which their hopes were fixed. Just because scientific method is a unified, identifiable system of procedures, one may hope, according to these writers, to apply it to unsolved problems of ethics or other controversial disciplines; conversely, if the character of scientific method varied according to the subject matter of its application, the call to *use* that method in untried fields would be less persuasive.

It is very characteristic of Korzybski's approach, however, to stress the *discontinuity* rather than the uniformity of scientific method. He regards contemporary science as having made a sharp and revolutionary departure from older ways of scientific thought, especially those associated with the names of Aristotle, Euclid, and Newton.

The theories of these three great pioneers, we are told, have by now been discredited. But the breakaway has not been complete; nor have its implications been sufficiently recognized. Einstein freed us from the shackles of the Newtonian cosmology; Lobachevski and the other inventors of non-Euclidean geometries overturned the absolute monarchy of Euclid; but Aristotle, in spite of pioneering modern discoveries in multivalued logics, remains the archenemy of correct thinking and sane behavior.

"Aristotelian" is, accordingly, always a term of reproach for general semanticists; and for parallels to the vigor with which they attack this ancient intellectual idol, we must return to Francis Bacon and his tremendous onslaught against the Aristotelian tradition. Non-Aristotelianism is as integral to general semantics as its neurological approach to meaning and its reliance upon scientific method.

Let us, therefore, begin our more detailed examination of Korzybski's doctrines by determining the basis of his quarrel with Aristotle. What exactly is the ground of complaint?

In part, it seems to be a hostile response (shared by many contemporary logicians) to the restrictive assumptions of Aristotle's theory of the syllogism. It is widely recognized today that the type of proposition discussed by Aristotle and his followers is a very special case; that statements need not be analyzed *only* into the "subject-predicate" form; and that many arguments depend for their validity upon formal properties of relations which cannot be described in the Aristotelian scheme.

It is, therefore, correct to say that Aristotelian logic is inadequate—in exactly the same way as simple arithmetic is inadequate. Arithmetic is a good instrument to use in counting sheep or dollars, but more refined mathematical instruments are needed to determine the time taken for a liquid to cool or a plant to grow. The theory of the syllogism is a good logical instrument to use in the evaluation of certain very simple arguments, but more refined logical theories are needed in order to represent the structure of quantum mechanics or the theory of relativity.

But to denounce syllogistic logic on *this* account would be as absurd as to throw away forks and knives because they cannot cut steel. Korzybski has other and more remarkable reasons for his denunciations of Aristotelian logic.

Aristotle, we are told, inculcated the vicious habit of using the copula, "is," as a sign of *identity*. He it was whose influence promoted this "delusional" and "unsane" procedure; and we are warned repeatedly against using "the pernicious 'is' of identity." What Aristotle is alleged to have believed and taught is that such statements as "Water is wet" and "Dewey is a philosopher" mean that water is *identical* with wetness, and Dewey is *identical* with the characteristic of being a philosopher. In other words, anybody who believes such statements, in the sense in which an adherent of Aristotelian logic would interpret them, is supposed to be committed to the belief that water is the very same thing as wetness, and Dewey (the man) is the very same thing as being a philosopher (the abstract characteristic).

It is worth noting that Korzybski gives no quotation from Aristotle to support this charge. And it should be said, as a matter of historical justice, that there is no evidence that Aristotle or his followers believed anything so absurd. One sufficient reason is that the view with which they are charged would be inconsistent with the standard syllogistic doctrine of the impossibility of converting universal propositions. If the "is" in "Water is wet" were the "is" of identity, as alleged, the truth of that proposition would automatically entail the truth of the converse proposition that all wetness is water. Now it is, of course, a central part of the doctrine of Aristotelian logic that the proposition *All A is B* can*not* be automatically replaced by the converse, *All B is A*. Again, if Aristotle believed the absurd doctrine which is ascribed to him, he would have to believe that Plato and Socrates and Aristotle himself were all the same person. For, if all of them were *identical* with being a philosopher, all of them must be identical with one another. Even a stupid man would hardly believe in these absurd consequences; and Aristotle was very far from being stupid.

I think, therefore, that Korzybski is setting up a mere bogey when he tries to scare us away from what he calls Aristotelian logic.

Yet after all, it may be objected, what difference does it make, except to the historian of ideas, whether Aristotle was responsible for the vice of "identification"? If the mistake is prevalent, might it perhaps be conveniently referred to as "Aristotelianism," no matter who was the error's original parent?

Two replies should be made to this. First, a semanticist should himself live according to the code of accurate thought and clear expression for which he is campaigning. Nothing but confusion can result from inserting into what claims to be a sober scientific account the ghosts of historical traditions that never existed. Semanticists should be the last people to go tilting at fictitious windmills.

A more important comment is this. Korzybski's own lack of understanding of what is asserted in Aristotelian logic leads him into the absurdity of supposing the use of the auxiliary verb "to be" is in itself deplorable. Here is one illustrative quotation: "If we use the 'is' at all, and it is extremely difficult to avoid entirely this auxiliary verb when using languages which, to a large extent, depend on it, we must be particularly careful not to use 'is' as an identity term."

This passage intimates that it would be well to avoid the use of "is" entirely, if it were possible. It would be interesting to know whether the speakers of Chinese and Hebrew, languages which contain no auxiliary verb, are free from the delusional identifications from which the Occidental civilizations suffer.

But Korzybski has a simple device for overcoming "the 'is' of identity." It consists, as the following argument illustrates, in confining oneself to *negative* statements.

> The present non-aristotelian system is based on fundamental *negative* premises; namely, the complete denial of "identity," which denial *cannot be denied* without imposing the burden of proof on the person who denies the denial. If we start, for instance, with a statement that "a word is *not* the object spoken about," and some one tries to deny that, he would have to produce an actual physical object which would *be the word*—impossible, even in asylums for the mentally ill. Hence my security, often "blasphemously cheerful," as one of my friends calls it.

It should be plain that this argument is unsound. If the assertion of negative premises gave "unusual security of conclusion," to use Korzybski's phrase, it would be easy to disprove his own contention that the meaning of a symbol is the semantic reactions it produces. It would be sufficient to say, "The meaning of a word is *not* the semantic reaction it evokes"; and "the burden of proof" would be on Korzybski, who would be denying a denial! It ought to be obvious that a negative statement is *in general* no more "secure" than its logical contradictory, which of the two is true depending entirely upon the nature of the situation to which the statements refer. Korzybski's preference for *negative* statements can only be accounted for by his supposing that *whenever* the word "is" occurs in a statement it stands for identity. If it does not, there is no need to be more suspicious about the positive than about the negative statement.

Korzybski's "general denial of the 'is' of identity" and his consequent misguided preference for negative statements are details, though important ones in his system. More basic in his procedure are the nature of the grounds invoked for this "denial" of identity and the related denial of the traditional laws of thought.

Very often in attacking an "Aristotelian" principle or concept, Korzybski uses the phrase "false to facts"; and he expressly states his objection to the view that logic has no physical content. He believes, in fact, that the correctness of logical principles is established like the correctness of physical principles, by appeal to "the facts." We look at the sky to see if the sun has appeared in the position predicted by astronomers; we look at an electron to see if it is identical with itself, as predicted by logicians.

This position sounds attractively empirical and free from rationalistic nonsense. Yet it seems to me to involve a profoundly mistaken view of the nature and function of logic.

Let us contrast the process of physical verification of an astronomical prediction with the proposed process of verification of the logical law of identity. In order to test a statement about the sun's position in the sky, we must first understand the words used to make the statement; but when such words as "sun," "transit," "meridian," and the others used in the astronomical statements *have* been defined, it remains an open question, to be settled by appropriate observation, whether the prediction is true or not. Contrast this with the case of the logical principle. Here too we must have a well-defined language in which to formulate our statement; but this time the specification of the language *already* determines the logical principles. We have not yet described the language if we have failed to say whether "A is B" is to be understood to mean the same as "B is A"; the so-called "laws of thought" are, therefore, already determined by our choice of a language; and there remains nothing to test.

A simple mathematical analogy will make the point clearer. If we find that one drop of mercury combines with another drop of the same substance to produce a *single* drop of mercury, we do not, if we are wise, say that the equation $1 + 1 = 2$ is wrong and that arithmetic ought to be revised. We say instead drops of mercury "so combined" are not the kinds of things to which the principles of arithmetic apply. If we find that a woman loses weight after studying semantics, we ought similarly to say *not* that identity is an illusion, but rather that the principle "A is A" is not intended to be applicable to that sort of situation. (We may notice, however, that it is perfectly correct to say that the lady in question is still the *same* woman—Korzybski's warnings against identity to the contrary.)

What has here been said about the relation of logic to experience and observation is neither new nor original. The propositions of logic have long been recognized as being "necessary" and so nonempirical; and this view of the nature of logic is held almost without exception by logicians and philosophers. If Korzybski insists on regarding logic as empirical, he must be willing to dispense with the support of expert authority for this part of his doctrine.

I am not quite clear as to the difference which would be made to Korzybski's theories if he were to abandon his crusade against "Aristotelianism." The moderate and defensible position that syllogistic logic is an instrument of limited application, needing supplementation by other types of formal calculi, would hardly generate the heat of his present invectives against "identification." And abandonment of the principle that logic must be "true to fact" would, I am afraid, play havoc with another plank of the platform of general semantics—the principle that scientific knowledge is restricted to reflection of the *structure* of reality. On the other hand, it seems to me that his theory of abstraction would hardly need to be changed; the critical discussion upon which we are now to embark is therefore independent of what has gone before.

KORZYBSKI'S THEORY OF ABSTRACTIONS

The topic of the nature of abstractions is of crucial importance in any systematic semantics. When a person who is philosophically unsophisticated compares a language such as English with the world to which it refers, he is easily impressed by the relative poverty of the language. The world seems full of objects and relationships which cannot be adequately described in words; nor is this merely a deficiency of vocabulary—an absence of enough names to be used. Every name that is already in our possession seems incurably "thin" or "abstract" by contrast with the rich specificity of the real things to which it refers. Such vague and confused feelings of the inadequacy of language provoke the ancient philosophical problem of the reality of abstractions. Inasmuch as semantics sets out to be a critic of ordinary language, it can hardly evade this problem; for whatever decision is made with respect to the reality of abstractions will clearly determine some of the paths which semantic criticism of language will have to follow.

Let us now see what Korzybski has to say about the subject. In view of what I said previously, it will be expected that Korzybski will adopt the neurological standpoint; in the case, therefore, of somebody's perceiving an apple (which is said to be a low-order abstraction) Korzybski is interested in describing the relation between the external physical event and the reactions in the nervous system of the person who perceives that apple. As pointed out earlier, for this description to be complete we need some fairly definite notions about the nature of the physical end of the relation; we must have some notion of what is happening "out there." Korzybski's position on this point is stated forcefully and unequivocally:

> If we use a language of adjectives and subject-predicate forms pertaining to "sense" impressions, we are using a language which deals with entities *inside our skin* and characteristics entirely non-existent in the outside world. Thus the events outside our skin are neither cold nor warm, green nor red, sweet or bitter, but these characteristics are manufactured by our nervous system inside our skins, as responses only to different energy manifestations, physico-chemical processes. When we use such terms, we are dealing with characteristics which are absent in the external world, and build up an anthropomorphic and delusional world non-similar in structure to the world around us.

What Korzybski calls the "scientific object," the real apple "outside our skins," is accordingly

> a mad dance of "electrons," which is different every instant, which never repeats itself, which is known to consist of extremely complex dynamic processes of very fine structure, acted upon by, and reacting upon, the rest of the universe, inextricably connected with everything else and dependent on everything else.

Especially important is it to notice that the scientific object, this inextricable knot of subatomic energy processes, has *infinitely many characteristics:*

> If we inquire *how many characteristics (m.o.)* we should ascribe to such an event [i.e., to the scientific object] the only possible answer is that we should ascribe to an event infinite numbers of characteristics, as it represents a process which never stops in one form or another; neither, to the best of our knowledge, does it repeat itself.

If the scientific object, the real apple outside our skins, has infinitely many characteristics, we can perceive only a selection from these characteristics. This implication accords well with Korzybski's view that abstraction consists essentially in the *omission of details.* "What we see is structurally only a specific *statistical mass-effect* of happenings on a much finer grained level. We *see* what we see because we *miss* all the finer details." And to illustrate what happens, according to this view, during the process of abstraction, Korzybski has "the familiar example of a rotary fan, which is made up of separate radial blades, but which, when rotating with a certain velocity, gives the impression of a *solid disk.* In this case the 'disk' is not 'reality,' but a nervous integration, or abstraction from the rotating blades."

What Korzybski calls the "ordinary object," the apple which is red, cool to the touch, and slightly acid in taste, is to be understood therefore as having the same relation to the external "sub-microscopic physico-chemical processes" as the apparently solid disk to the really separate blades of the rotating fan.

Since the common-sense or "ordinary" apple is obtained by the omission of fine-grained detail, the common-sense apple, (unlike its scientific correlate in the real world) has only a *finite* number of characteristics:

> The object represents in this language [i.e., in the language of everyday affairs] a gross macroscopic abstraction, for our nervous system is not adapted for abstracting directly the infinite numbers of characteristics which the endlessly complex dynamic fine structure of the event represents.

I hope the picture is so far clear. The "scientific" object, the real object outside the skin, is the source of energy radiations which impinge upon the nervous system of the receiving organism. This proceeds to "leave out" details and to "manufacture" the gross macroscopic object, the so-called ordinary object.

So far we have been talking about what Korzybski calls "first abstractions." It is important to notice that when Korzybski uses this term or the equivalent phrase, the "ordinary (non-scientific) object," he intends to refer to something *nonverbal,* something that can be tasted or felt. The apple in my hand is a first abstraction; the *word* "apple" however is something else again: "We see that the object *is not* the event but an abstraction from it, and that the label *is not* the object nor the event, but a still further abstraction."

We therefore have three levels to distinguish: that of the scientific reality outside the skin, where the event E occurs; the first-order abstraction or common-sense object, O; and finally the second-order label, L. But this hierarchy of orders of abstraction can obviously be extended; the label L is used in making statements about the object O; if we find new labels which are in turn used for making statements about L itself we shall have advanced to a higher level of abstraction:

> We know very well that Smith can always say something *about* a statement (*L*), on record.

Neurologically considered, this *next* statement (*LI*) about a statement (*L*) would be the nervous response to the former statement (*L*) which he has seen or heard or even produced by himself inside his skin. So his statement (*LI*) about the former statement (*L*) is a *new abstraction* from the former abstraction. In my language, I call it an abstraction of a higher order.

We see, therefore, that the step from using abstractions of one order to abstractions of the next highest order is taken whenever we *talk about* the lower-order abstraction. But Korzybski also, in a way which puzzles me, considers an increase in order of abstraction to occur whenever we make an *inference*: "Obviously, if we consider a description as of the nth order, then an inference from such a description (or others) should be considered as an abstraction of a higher order (*n + 1*)."

The next point to emphasize is that the hierarchy of orders of abstraction—from scientific event to common-sense object, from common-sense object to verbal description or label, from description to inference, from inference to inferences regarding inferences, and so on indefinitely—constitutes a series containing increasingly more subjective components. The scientific object has highest value—is "the only possible survival concern of the organism"; every other term in the generated series of increasing orders of abstraction "represents only a shadow cast by the scientific object." The various orders of abstraction accordingly constitute a series, as Korzybski puts it, "decreasing in value." We have shadows, and shadows of shadows, and shadows of shadows of shadows, and so on.

This somewhat complicated theoretical analysis has direct and important practical consequences. For ordinary, semantically miseducated people have been systematically encouraged to overlook the difference between the different levels of abstraction. Their thinking, feeling, and behaving is, consequently, vitiated by the tendency to "identification" of the various levels of abstraction. They confuse the "ordinary" or common-sense object (the colored apple) with the infinitely complex scientific object of which it is the mere shadow; they confuse the word apple and its definition with the ordinary object; and they confuse the higher levels of abstraction with one another.

In so doing, the semantically benighted revert to the condition of a child or animal who is unaware of the fact that he is abstracting. Such "infantilism" or "animalism" lead to the construction of a delusional world in which the subjective products of the nervous system are systematically identified with the scientific reality upon which survival depends. This way lies madness—the peculiar madness of the highly verbalized civilization to which we belong.

The way back to mental health is found by inculcating the "consciousness of abstracting." But careful training is needed: differentiation between levels of abstraction cannot be achieved merely by good intentions—it requires careful and prolonged re-education of the nervous system. Perhaps the most interesting aspect of the retraining procedure described by Korzybski is the introduction of what he calls "silence at the objective level." For one great point to be achieved in fighting delusional identification of levels

of abstraction is the conviction that reality is nonverbal: *"The objective level is not words, and cannot be reached by words alone. We must point our finger and be silent, or we shall never reach this level."*

The central aim is to produce a healthy "delay" in nervous reaction; so that in responding to verbal or nonverbal stimuli, we are aware of what it is that we are doing:

> There is no doubt that this "delayed action" has many very beneficial effects upon the whole working of the nervous system. It somehow balances harmful *s.r.* [semantic reactions] and also stimulates the higher nervous centres to more *physiological* control over the lower centres.

At a somewhat more sophisticated level of training, the correction of delusional identification is much assisted by the use of special linguistic devices, notably that of attaching subscripts to any words which are commonly used to refer ambiguously to objects belonging to different levels of abstraction. Many of the central terms of discourse (such as "true," "false," "object," "name," "knowledge," "fact," "reality," etc.) are "multi-ordinal" in this way—ambiguous as to the level of abstraction to which reference is intended. Clarity of theoretical discourse about language requires such multi-ordinal terms to be handled with full awareness of their systematic ambiguity.

So far I have been trying to give a sympathetic account of Korzybski's central theory of abstraction without injecting any comment of my own. Now I turn to criticism.

We have seen that a central doctrine of general semantics is that of the sole reality of the so-called scientific object, that swarm of infinitely complex submicroscopic processes of which the "ordinary object" and all the higher abstractions are mere shadows. And this is where the difficulties of the philosophic critic begin. For surely the terms used in describing this alleged reality are themselves of a very high order of abstraction. The characteristics ascribed to the scientific object, energy, electric and magnetic charge, and so on, are by no means experienced directly at what Korzybski calls the "unspeakable" level. They are, on the contrary, defined in terms of complicated manipulations of scientific instruments and calculated with the help of theoretical physics of a very high degree of abstractness. Now if we should assert, with Korzybski, that all abstractions are "manufactured by the nervous system" we should be compelled to say also that the "mad dance of electrons" constituting the scientific object is likewise manufactured by the nervous system. Korzybski seems close to admitting this when he says that on his view "science becomes an extra-neural extension of the *human* nervous system."

But this line of reasoning leads into hopeless logical circularity. The reason for giving a superior status to the scientific object—for referring to it as a reality and to the series of abstractions emanating from it as shadows—was its alleged independence of what went on "inside our skins"; the swarm of electrons, unlike the abstractions derived from it, was *not* manufactured by the nervous system. If it be granted, however, that the scientific object, also, is a complex of abstract characteristics, the original basis for differentiation between reality and subjective abstractions disappears. We shall have to say, if we are to continue to use the language of Korzybski's account, that the common-sense object is manufactured by the nervous system under the influence of stimuli from the scientific object, which itself, as a complex of abstract characteristics, is *also* manufactured by the nervous system. We are naturally left wondering what this highly productive and creative nervous system is able to use as the raw material for its amazing construction.

And we shall have to go a stage further. For the "nervous system" itself is a physical (or physicochemical) object of a complex sort, whose characteristics are known to us not directly, but rather by complicated inferences from observation and physiological theory. To be consistent, therefore, we shall have to say also that the nervous system itself is manufactured *by* the nervous system. Or, as Adam said in William Blake's poem, "It is all a vain delusion of the all-creative imagination."

Some of Korzybski's popularizers have by-passed these difficulties by supposing that Korzybski was condemning *all* abstraction as such. As we should expect, they themselves made plentiful use of abstractions in their own strictures against abstractions. For a pledge *never* to use abstractions would be tantamount to a vow of silence. The success of language as an instrument of communication depends upon the possibility of using symbols to refer to recognizable and recurring aspects of experience, that is to say, of *abstract* characteristics of experience. As Korzybski himself says, "All speaking is using abstraction of a very high order."

Now Korzybski, unlike some of his popularizers, is aware of this central importance of the use of abstractions and is free from the absurd desire to ban their use in discourse. In many a passage he refers approvingly to the use of abstractions as when he says that "higher abstractions are extremely expedient devices," or again "Happy, structurally high abstractions really have a strong creative character." And in at least one important passage he explicitly makes the point here stressed, viz., that the scientific object itself must be regarded as characterized by high-order abstractions: "If we enquire: What do the characteristics of the event represent? We find that they are given only by science and represent at each date the highest, most verified, most reliable abstractions. . . . "

This brings us back again to the logical circle. Once it is admitted that the characteristics of the scientific object, which was to have been the touchstone of reality, are themselves abstractions, there is no longer any basis for the sharp distinction between the alleged external reality and the supposed subjectively manufactured abstractions.

Korzybski's reference, in the quotation used a little while ago, to the scientific object as being characterized by "the most verified and reliable abstractions" does suggest another and, it seems to me, more hopeful way of criticizing the use of abstractions. Since abstractions are used to make verifiable predictions, their validity can reasonably be tested by the success of the predictions in which they occur. If any abstraction is an indispensable component

of a system of statements whose truth is confirmed by observation and experiment, we can regard it as valid. On the other hand, if the introduction of a term leads to the making of false or meaningless predictions, we may regard that term as improperly used. (If a man claims that electrons are inhabited by devils, we can properly ask him to specify the verifiable consequences which flow from his claim; and we may eventually conclude that he was misusing the terms which occurred in his statement.) But such a pragmatic approach to problems of meaning would certainly provide no grounds for the sweeping assertion that terms such as "red," "warm," and "sweet" refer only to events occurring inside the skin. Or that the objects to which we refer in everyday contexts are "manufactured" by the nervous system. On the contrary, such investigation would very soon show that the central terms of the statements in which Korzybski's theory is presented (such terms as "reality" and "manufactured") are themselves instances of semantic confusion. My conclusion is that Korzybski's epistemological doctrines, on which so much else in his system depends, are confused. And I do not see how this part of his theories can be salvaged.

Another major respect in which Korzybski's account of abstraction needs improvement is his description of what goes on during the *process* of abstraction.

We have seen already that Korzybski holds the view that abstraction consists in "leaving out details." He thinks of the nervous system as a kind of coarse-grained sieve or filter; infinitely complex waves of physical energy distributions strike the filter, lose much of their individual detail in passing through it, and eventually produce the abstraction. The nervous system of the receiving organism has to play a part in this process—for have we not been told that the nervous system "manufactures" the abstraction?—yet its role is passive, like that of a camera, radio, or other mechanical device for recording energy.

This account of the function of the nervous system in abstraction is dangerously oversimplified. Consider a very simple case of abstraction—say that in which a man perceives that a group of geometrical figures are all alike in being isosceles triangles. Not even this simple process could well be described as consisting in mere omission of details. Certainly the man who sees that a number of geometrical figures are all isosceles triangles is deliberately neglecting all kinds of details in which the several figures differ from each other—their size, specific shape, orientation, relative positions to one another, and so on. But he might continue indefinitely neglecting one item after the other, without ever arriving at the positive perception of the general respect in which all the figures are similar. The process of abstraction, as this simple case illustrates, has a positive as well as a negative side. If we abstract a general character from a group of specimens, we must allow ourselves to overlook certain respects in which the specimens differ among themselves; but we must also, on pain of failing to perform a genuine act of abstraction, see clearly the elements of resemblance on which our selection of the particular abstraction is founded.

Korzybski tells us:

We can now define "consciousness of abstracting" as "*awareness* that in our process of abstracting we have *left out* characteristics." Or, consciousness of abstracting can be defined as "*remembering* the '*is not*'" and that some characteristics have been left out.

If I were using this kind of language to describe my point of difference, I should have to say that more useful "consciousness of abstracting" would require awareness that we have left characteristics *in* as well as awareness that we have left characteristics *out*; and the self-critical employment of abstractions would require us to remember *what it is* that we have "left in" as well as *what it is* that we have left out. In other words, criticism of the employment of abstraction should induce lively awareness of the specific processes used in arriving at the particular abstraction in question. And this awareness should include attention to both the positive and negative aspects of the abstractive process.

One reason for regarding this point as important is the fact that the term "abstraction" is highly ambiguous, being used to refer to a number of different processes which sometimes have very little in common with one another. Only detailed attention to what is meant by "abstraction" in the specific context in which the term is used will guard us against the mistakes which might otherwise result.

It is ironical that Korzybski himself, for all his warnings against imputing unwarranted identity to the objects denoted by any general term, should himself have used the central term, "abstraction," so misleadingly. For consider some of the different ways in which he uses that word:

(i) Energy waves strike the organism which then sees something which it recognizes as a red apple. The apple (not its name) is said to be an abstraction from the swarm of electronic processes from which the energy waves radiated.

(ii) Smith *calls* the apple which he sees (the "ordinary" or "commonsense" object) by the name "apple." The name "apple" is said by Korzybski to be an abstraction from the apple.

(iii) Smith talks about the word "apple," as, for instance, when he says " 'apple' is a noun." Each word he now uses, e.g., the word "noun," is said to be an abstraction from the word "apple." We need not proceed to the higher levels of abstraction in Korzybski's scheme.

In these three cases we have three *different* kinds of relations: (i) the relation between a common-sense object and the scientific object which is alleged to generate it; (ii) the relation between an object and the word which is a label for it; (iii) the relation between a word and some other word which can be used in a description of that first word.

The strange thing is that in none of these three cases do we have an instance of what is *commonly* understood by abstraction. For we commonly mean a process in which we notice resemblances and common elements in a group of presented individuals. But nobody *first* perceives the colorless and odorless scientific object and *then* abstracts color from it. (Still more absurd is it to suppose that this unconscious perceiving involves leaving out details and so arriving at a residue of sensible qualities, color, shape, etc., which were not even present in that from which the details were omitted.)

I hope it is sufficiently obvious that the process of naming the apple and that of describing the name of an apple are equally remote from what we have in mind when we commonly talk about "abstraction." Nor can either of *these* processes be regarded as processes of neglecting details. We do not get the *name* "apple" by neglecting to notice the ways in which one apple differs from another; we do not get the word "noun" by omitting details of the word "apple."

It seems to me, in short, that the first three steps in Korzybski's hierarchy of orders of abstraction are based on different relations, and that neither the second or third of the steps could be regarded as involving "abstraction," either on Korzybski's view of that process or on any other which is generally accepted today.

If one takes these difficulties seriously, very little remains of Korzybski's theory of abstractions except some hypothetical neurology fortified with dogmatic metaphysics.

I say "dogmatic metaphysics" advisedly, because I have been unable to find any better ground for the principle of the superior unshadowy reality of the so-called "scientific object." It should be added that Korzybski is an unabashed metaphysician, though he flaunts his metaphysics too seldom for this to be noticed by a casual reader. His system, he explains, "involves full-fledged structural metaphysics . . ." and again, "The real problem before mankind presents itself in the selection of a structural metaphysics." It is a weakness of Korzybski's presentation that his own metaphysics is presented without any explicit considerations in its favor. Repeated invocations of the supposed support of scientific findings is no substitute for reasoning, even in metaphysics.

Enough has been said to make it clear that I regard the theoretical foundations of general semantics as logically incoherent and in need of thoroughgoing revision. This does not necessarily imply a finally adverse judgment on the merits of general semantics; the history of science has provided a number of examples of confused theoretical systems, which were able to produce useful and interesting results. But we must not make the mistake of supposing that lack of clarity and self-consistency is a positive merit in a theoretical system. The little girl who asked her mother whether it was necessary to be married in order to have a baby was told that marriage was a help. It would be a help to logicians, philosophers, and other champions of clarity of thought, if the foundations of general semantics received some house cleaning. And it is in the hope of encouraging such logical renovation that this essay was prepared.

Stuart Chase   (essay date 1953)

SOURCE: "Eminent Semanticists," in *Power of Words,* Harcourt Brace & Company, 1954, pp. 125-50.

[*In the following excerpt, Chase combines a personal de-*

scription of Korzybski with an assessment of his study of language.]

Alfred Korzybski, who died in 1950, was the originator of what he called "General Semantics," a discipline which took the study of language and meaning into some pretty deep mathematical and neurological waters. It is still early to tell whether his contribution was as epoch-making as some starry-eyed followers believe, but it was unquestionably an important addition to the whole subject of communication. . . .

I shall never cease to be grateful for the wholesome shock my nervous system received when I first read Korzybski's magnum opus, *Science and Sanity*. It forced me to realize some of the unconscious assumptions imbedded in the language which I as a writer had been calmly accepting. Nature, he said, does not work the way our language works; and he proceeded to give some suggestions for a closer relationship.

As I knew him in his later years—he was 70 when he died—he had the general aspect of an amiable Buddha, bald as a newel post, with kindly, intelligent eyes behind vast, round spectacles, and with a rich Polish accent. He wore as a kind of uniform a khaki shirt, open at the throat, which sometimes kept him out of hotel dining rooms. He was rude, formidable, over-verbalized and strangely appealing—for all I know, an authentic genius. Poland has produced more than her share of mathematical philosophers.

Piecing together parts of his background, we note that he was a count from a proud and ancient family, with an estate in the country and large properties in Warsaw. Trained as a chemical engineer at the Warsaw Polytechnic Institute, he read widely in law, mathematics, and philosophy. He was also, we are told, handsome and a bit wild, the traditional young nobleman. In World War I he served on the Grand Duke's staff, was three times wounded, and then came to America as an artillery expert for the Czarist Russian Army. He added English to his five Continental languages; and while he never got his phonemes straight, he acquired great fluency and came to prefer it. He wrote his books and articles in English and thought in this language. In 1919 he married a talented American painter.

He published two books and a score of papers, all hard to read. It took me two years of reasonably steady application to bulldoze my way through *Science and Sanity,* and I do not think this sluggish pace was altogether my fault. By a curious paradox, Korzybski, who had dedicated his life to clearing communication lines, had the utmost difficulty in clearing his own—at least in English prose. When he conducted an oral seminar, with a full display of kinesics and his extraordinary accent, the line was far more open. I can see him now, reaching stout, muscular arms into the air and wiggling two fingers of each hand to make the "quote" sign, somewhat the way Churchill made the "V" sign. In semantics the quote sign around a word usually means: "Beware, it's loaded!"

"TIME BINDING"

Korzybski's chief claim to fame will rest, I think, on *Sci-*

ence and Sanity, difficult as it is. His earlier book, *The Manhood of Humanity,* is shorter and easier to read. Its thesis is that man is distinguished from the rest of earth's creatures by his language and the ability to pass down what he learns from one generation to the next. Even the most intelligent elephant has to begin over with each generation. "The proper life of man *as man,* is not life-in-space like that of the animals, but life-in-time. . . . Bound-up time is literally the core and substance of civilization."

This passing-down process, to which Korzybski gives the curious name "time-binding," we described earlier when discussing the culture concept, noting that the invention of writing greatly speeded it. Scientists generally confirm the thesis. Both the anthropologists and such sociologists as W. F. Ogburn anticipated Korzybski. He believed, however, that the theory was new. Once the idea was mastered, he thought, the race would achieve "manhood," become fully mature, and shake off its infantilisms, verbal and otherwise.

> All through history man has been groping to find his place . . . to discover his role in the "nature of things." To this end he must first discover himself and his "essential nature" . . . then perhaps our civilizations will pass by peaceful evolution from their childhood to the manhood of humanity.

Cultural change, unfortunately, can go downhill as well as up, but the opportunity is undeniably there to find our manhood, as knowledge about nature and human nature accumulates. This aspiration Korzybski shares, however, with many earlier writers and idealists—the early Utopians, for instance, and H. G. Wells. I myself used to cherish a private dream which I called "the man on the cliff." He was boldly outlined against the sky—the man we all might be if we put accumulated knowledge really to work.

Following *The Manhood of Humanity,* Korzybski spent ten years of intensive work writing *Science and Sanity*. It was published in 1933 at the bottom of the depression—hardly an auspicious year to bring out a book, especially a costly one. In it Korzybski explored relativity, quantum theory, colloid chemistry, biology, neurology, psychology, psychiatry, mathematical logic, and what was then available by other students of communication and semantics. Later, he urged his classes to read Whorf on linguistics. The question he set himself to answer was how the structure of language could be brought closer to the structure of the space-time world. He cited the new talk of physicists, following the Einstein revolution. If scientists could teach themselves to communicate more clearly, why should not the rest of us do likewise?

DEFINITIONS

Before summarizing what Korzybski discovered, let us glance at some of his forerunners in the field of semantics. The word first appeared in dictionaries about fifty years ago, defined as "studies having to do with signification or meaning." The International Society for General Semantics has issued two short, comprehensive definitions, as follows:

Semantics . . . The systematic study of meaning.

General Semantics . . . The study and improvement of human evaluative processes with special emphasis on the relation to signs and symbols, including language.

Note the accent on "evaluation" in defining General Semantics, and the absence of the word "is" in defining both. Whenever we become conscious about the meaning of a context—"What is the Senator trying to say?" . . . "How can I tell her more clearly?" . . . "What kind of double talk is that?"—we are practicing elementary semantics.

The goals of General Semantics are three:

> 1. To help the individual evaluate his world. As our environment grows more and more complex, greater precision is needed to interpret it.
> 2. To improve communication between A and B, also within and between groups of all sizes.
>
> 3. To aid in clearing up mental illness. . . .

Dictionary definitions are useful, but the semanticists make no obeisances to verbal absolutes. David Guralnik, who supervised a recent drastic revision of Webster, reported that his friends were shocked at his temerity. He was shattering their faith in the infallibility of "the dictionary," and probably, by extension, of the Scriptures and other sacred writs. Dictionaries, like certain brands of cigarettes, he said, are supposed to be untouched by human hands. Another serious difficulty was what he called the "semantic merry-go-round that leads the reader on a wild chase from one entry to another only to bring him back in a mad finish to his starting point." "*Gangrene*: mortification of a part of the body. . . . *Mortification*: gangrene." He had to be careful, too, of his etymologies, avoiding anything that might suggest Mark Twain's famous derivation of *Middletown* from *Moses*—you drop the "oses" and add the "iddletown."

FROM ARISTOTLE TO BERTRAND RUSSELL

Resolved to refute the logic of Aristotle, Korzybski goes so far as to call General Semantics "a non-Aristotelian system," and invents the symbol, $\bar{A}$, to abbreviate "non-Aristotelian." We must give Aristotle his due, however; for along with his creative curiosity about nature, he was also genuinely curious about the power of words. Linguistics, cultural anthropology, and relativity being two thousand years away, he sometimes mistook the peculiar structure of his own Greek for the universal laws of thought, a most natural error.

Aristotle's formal logic . . . was a great achievement for the time, but today it is hardly more useful than the medicine of Galen. Galen has passed respectably into the history of medicine; but Aristotle's logic continues to distort our use of reason. It is still taught in the universities, still in active use by philosophers, lawyers, theologians, and essayists. A standard political speech would be impossible without the aid of its simple two-valued syllogisms.

One of the first students to question the Aristotelian logic was Bishop William of Occam, who insisted that "entities are not to be multiplied beyond what is necessary." This principle was nicknamed in academic circles "Occam's razor," because it sheared off lush verbalisms. The Bishop was troubled by the clouds of entities, essences, classes, and Absolutes released by the Aristotelian laws. The Bacons, both Roger and Francis, were likewise skeptical. It was Galileo, of course, who broke clean away from Aristotle by substituting experiment and observation for *a priori* reasoning. Instead of deriving the number of teeth in a horse's mouth by logic, it is better to go out in the barn and count them.

A fascinating book might be written on the history of the revolt against language. The age of scientific inquiry, following Galileo, saw an increasing number of first-rate minds questioning the validity of verbal processes. In the last hundred years the critics include Jeremy Bentham, William James, Alexander Bryan Johnson, George Herbert Mead, John Dewey, Ludwig Wittgenstein, Bertrand Russell, F. C. S. Schiller, Rudolf Carnap, E. T. Bell.

Allen Upward, a British philologist, pursued the word "idealism" all over Western cultures in an attempt to get at its meaning [in his *The New Word*]. His initial bouts with the dictionary were unsatisfactory, thus:

> *Mind*, defined as thoughts, sentiments, et cetera.
>
> *Thought*, defined as operations of the mind, ideas, images formed in the mind.

Combining the two, Upward gets a kind of recurring decimal: Mind equals thought equals images formed in the images formed in the images . . . the same tautology we observed with gangrene—mortification.

H. G. Wells was a searching questioner of verbal processes. In 1891, just turned thirty, he wrote a monograph called "Scepticism of the Instrument," in which he quoted a geologist on rock classifications: "They pass into one another by insensible gradations"—a phrase not lightly to be dismissed. This is true, said Wells, of most things in nature. "Every species is vague, every term goes cloudy at its edges, and so in my way of thinking, relentless logic is only another phrase for a stupidity—for a sort of intellectual pigheadedness."

Bronislaw Malinowski, the anthropologist, reported that it was impossible for him to learn a native language unless he spent considerable time in hunting, fishing, and living the lives of the people who spoke it. This sequence illustrates again the intimate connection between language and culture. People talk what they do; that is how talking began.

Lady Viola Welby published *What is Meaning?* in 1903, shortly before Einstein announced his first great work on relativity. A serious student of language and communication, she was perhaps the founder of modern semantics. A few years later Bertrand Russell and A. N. Whitehead, in their profound work, *Principia Mathematica*, were forced to deal with language and verbal logic, as well as mathematical symbols. They evolved what they called the Theory of Types, to offset "illegitimate totalities" concealed in language. Here is an example:

> ALL STATEMENTS
>
> IN THIS SQUARE
>
> ARE FALSE

If we suppose the proposition inside the square to be true, we must conclude it is false. But if we begin by supposing it false, we have to end by finding it true. The "illegitimate totality" in this logical run-around is the little word "all." The "all" must be limited so that a statement about that totality must itself fall outside the totality. *Principia Mathematica* is an excellent example of scientists in the throes of trying to remove shackles imposed by their mother tongue.

THE MEANING OF MEANING

A very important landmark in semantic history was the publication in 1921 of *The Meaning of Meaning* by C. K. Ogden and I. A. Richards. The approach was more literary than mathematical, but the conclusions paralleled those of Bridgman, Korzybski, Whorf. It is always exciting when tunnelers from different sides of a mountain manage to meet in the center.

Ogden and Richards present us with the famous triangle where the *event,* or object in nature, is called the "referent"; the brain is the area of "reference"; and the word is the "symbol." The sign comes to us from an object, say a dog; we proceed counterclockwise and refer to memory traces in the brain; presently, we utter the word "dog."

> Reflection or *Reference*
>
> Word or *Symbol*
>
> Object or *Referent*

The lesson . . . is to keep the object in mind as one talks, to *find the referent* of one's discourse. Too much human talk, as Occam noted, razor in hand, is in abstract terms, where the mind manipulates the words, but loses sight of the space-time events to which the words refer. On this high level logic can be vigorously employed, but it is the logic of Zeno proving that the tortoise can outrun Achilles, the logic of the number of angels that can dance on a pin, the logic of the inside of the square, cited by Russell.

Let us imagine a high-level discussion between A and B about dogs. "All dogs are trustworthy," says A, with a dog lover's rapt expression. "Try trusting one of them with a five-dollar steak," says B, with a dog hater's glare. The difference can develop into a stupendous row on this "all dogs" level. But if A and B can come down to an inspection of some actual dogs, they will find, of course, that $Rover_1$ is so savage he must be constantly chained up; that $Rover_2$ is so gentle he is welcome at a cat show; and that $Rover_3$ to $Rover_n$ are at various stations of trustworthiness between these limits. The variations could be plotted to form the standard frequency distribution curve. By finding the referent down below, A and B avoid a meaningless battle up above. Agreement can be reached in ordinary affairs, as well as in science, when both A and B can point to the same dog, pat his head and say, "You see what I mean?" Up on the high level, anything can happen. "The ablest logicians," say Ogden and Richards, "are precisely those who are led to evolve the most fantastic systems by the aid of their verbal technique. . . . "

FIND THE REFERENT

"All dogs" cause trouble enough, but where are the referents for those higher and vaguer terms which form the common coin of discussion in political and economic affairs? Newspapers today in America carry many words like these below. What do they mean? What can A and B both point to so they may come to some agreement?

American Way	Leftist, Rightist
Appeasement	Loyalty,/Security
Balanced Budget	Monopoly
Big Business	New Deal
Bureaucracy	Politicians
Communism	Socialized Medicine
Creeping Socialism	Spending
Democracy	Statism
Fascism	Subversives
Free Enterprise	Totalitarianism
Free World	Wall Street
Government Interference	Welfare State
Labor Agitators	

Two or more Americans can start an argument on any of these terms which may rage for hours without a referent in sight, beyond "Uh, I knew a man whose brother had it straight that—" Yet below and behind these words are events and issues of the first importance which Americans must face.

Every item in the above list belongs in Korzybski's upraised fingers: "Quote—unquote. Beware, it's loaded!" They are in marked contrast to such low-order terms as 100 F., my cat Boots, pure oxygen, the key of C♯ minor, 40 mph. When I was writing *The Tyranny of Words,* everybody was talking, if not shouting loudly, about "Fascism." I asked a hundred persons from various walks of life to tell me what they meant by Fascism. They shared a common dislike for the term, but no two agreed what it meant. There were fifteen distinguishable concepts in the answers submitted. This gave an idea of the chaos involved in high-order terms.

Today Fascism is out of style, and everybody is talking about "Communism." Reporters from the *Capital Times* in Madison, Wisconsin (1953), asked almost 200 persons on the street to answer the question: "What is a Communist?" Here are some of the replies:

> *Farmer*: "They are no good to my notion. I can't figure out what they are."

> *Stenographer*: "If a person didn't have a religion I would be tempted to believe he was a Communist."

Housewife: "I really don't know what a Communist is. I think they should throw them out of the White House."

High-school student: "A Communist is a person who wants war."

Office worker: "Anyone that stands for things that democracy does not."

Not only was there no agreement, but 123 out of 197 persons interviewed frankly admitted *they did not know what a Communist is*. All this came at a time when Congressional investigations were flooding the newspapers with the "Communist Menace" inside America. The danger of drowning we know about; but where shall the wayfaring citizen point to the specific danger of Communism within our borders, in the light of this exhibit? . . . Here we repeat the admonition: "Beware, they're loaded!" Find the referent; keep your eye on that dog.

THE SEMANTICS OF POETRY

In addition to *The Meaning of Meaning,* with its insistence on the referent, Ogden and Richards have each done sound work in communication; Ogden in Basic English, his partner as a writer and lecturer on poetry and criticism. Richards, who has taught at Harvard since 1939, constantly emphasizes the importance of communication and the difficulty of conveying complex meanings. Poetry, of course, tries to convey the most complex meanings expressible in language, and when it succeeds can wield great power.

A measure of its failures appears in Richard's famous study, *Practical Criticism.* He tells how he presented a variety of poems, unsigned, to a large and able class for evaluation. Not only did these readers disagree, sometimes diametrically, about every poem, but they often failed to comprehend either its sense or its intention. (None of the poems was especially obscure. What these readers would make of samples of "modern" poetry is past imagining!)

The poet's intention, says Richards, is the first thing for the reader to consider. What is he trying to say? Richards lists ten difficulties the reader meets; for instance, the tendency to "stock responses . . . whenever a poem seems to, or does, involve views and emotions already fully prepared in the reader's mind, so that . . . the button is pressed." Another difficulty Richards calls "doctrinal adhesions," meaning ideological preconceptions in the reader. The whole study illustrates in a startling way what can happen to messages when they reach the semantic decoder.

Common experience is needed to understand any message. "In difficult cases the vehicle of communication must inevitably be complex. . . . What would be highly ambiguous by itself becomes definite in a suitable context. . . . Even in such shallow communication as . . . merely making out the letters in a handwriting this principle is all-important. . . .

"Difficulty of communication . . . should not be confused with the difficulty of the matter communicated. . . . Some very difficult calculations, for example, can be communicated with ease." "The view that meanings belong to words in their own right," says Richards scornfully [in his

Philosophy of Rhetoric], "is a branch of sorcery, a relic of the magical theory of names." He pretty well demolishes the one-proper-meaning superstition when he says: "What a word means is the missing parts of the contexts from which it draws its delegated efficiency."

Richards and Ogden in their side of the mountain emphasized language and the arts. Korzybski in his emphasized the language of science. The tunnelers met and let in light from both directions. They meet for us who read them, though I believe the two schools were not in the closest harmony.

THE LAST TWENTY YEARS

Science and Sanity made readers slowly, partly because reading rates were slow. Gradually, however, a large circle of interest was built up. My book, *The Tyranny of Words,* published in 1938, was the first attempt to interpret both semantics and Korzybski's General Semantics for the layman. Other interpretations soon appeared. The total influence of **Science and Sanity** must now be very considerable, both in America and abroad. The rancor of some of its critics would indicate this, if nothing else.

S. I. Hayakawa's *Language in Action,* a Book-of-the-Month, appeared in 1941, a clear and readable exposition of semantics. Irving J. Lee of Northwestern University, Wendell Johnson of Iowa State, Anatol Rapoport of the University of Chicago, among others, have contributed important books to the gathering literature.

Two organizations were founded, the Institute of General Semantics, now under the direction of M. Kendig, through which Korzybski conducted his famous seminars; and the International Society for General Semantics, which, among other activities, publishes the quarterly journal *ETC,* well edited by Hayakawa. Many local groups have been formed. By 1953 courses were being given in more than one hundred American universities, especially favored by speech departments, while a number of elementary schools were experimenting with semantic methods to make children better masters of their language.

KORZYBSKI'S CONTRIBUTION

Korzybski often used the simile of the map. A map of the territory, he says, useful as it may be to travelers, is not the territory. Similarly, language is not the world around us, but rather an indispensable guide to that world. The map, however, is worthless if it shows the traveler a structure different from the terrain he sets out upon. Structure in this context means order and relations, what comes after what. If the order of cities on our map does not agree with the order on the territory, we may find ourselves driving to Montreal when we hoped to go to Chicago—in which case it would be better to steer by the sun.

However detailed the map may be, it can never tell *all* about the territory. Similarly, language cannot tell "all" about an event; some characteristics will always be omitted. At the end of every verbal definition, if it is pushed far enough, there are undefined terms; we reach the silent level where we can point, but we cannot say. If there is nothing to point to, the communication line may break.

This is one reason why the modern physicists were driven to devise operational definitions.

APPLE₁ AND APPLE₂

Korzybski places an apple on the table and asks us to describe it. We can say it is round, red, appetizing, with a short stem, and one worm hole. But carefully as we may observe it, in the laboratory or out, we can never tell all the characteristics of the apple, especially as we approach the submicroscopic level. What all the billions of atoms are up to nobody knows except in the most general, statistical way.

Korzybski sets another apple beside the first, of similar shape and color. Is it identical? We are inclined to think so, but looking more closely we see that the stem is shorter, the red color is less vivid, and there are two worm holes instead of one. Apple₂ is not apple₁. By the same token, amoeba₂ is not amoeba₁; Adam₂ is not Adam₁. Nothing in nature is ever identical with anything else if the observations are carried far enough. Beware of false identifications, says Korzybski; you will only confuse yourself and your hearers. Beware of thinking of "Baptists," "Americans," "businessmen," "workers," as identical. Whatever characteristics they may have in common, they have others which are different. Frank Costello and President Eisenhower are both "Americans."

But certainly an object is identical with itself. Or is it? Let us leave the apple on the table for a month. Is it the "same" apple; is apple₍Oct 1₎ the same as apple₍Nov-1₎? Obviously not; the clear skin has turned brown and wrinkled, and the firm flesh, soft and rotten. Apple₁ accordingly is a *process,* changing its characteristics imperceptibly in a minute, slightly in a day, drastically in a month. Nothing in nature is quite what it was a moment ago. Even the Matterhorn wears slowly away, as rock avalanches come down the *couloirs.* Diamonds last longer than apples, but not forever. Some of the new isotopes have a half life of only a few seconds. Be careful of thinking of apples, diamonds, people, or nations as unchanging events. Remember to correct the verbal map which implies that they do not change. Said Korzybski:

> The only possible link between the *objective* world and the verbal world is *structural.* If the two structures are similar, then the empirical world becomes intelligible to us—we "understand," can adjust ourselves. . . . If the two structures are not similar . . . we do not "know," we do not "understand," the given problems are "unintelligible" to us . . . we do not know how to adjust ourselves.

Korzybski, as we have said, was profoundly influenced by the new language of science. Thermodynamics, he observed, could not have been built on such loose terms as "hot" and "cold"; a language showing minute quantitative changes and relations had to be developed. Also science could not have advanced without Arabic numerals and their invaluable zero. "Every child is now more skillful in arithmetic than great experts before the decimal system."

Our languages, continues Korzybski, are full of primitive metaphysical concepts, and the effect is like emery dust in a delicate machine. Whorf, we remember, came to a similar conclusion. General Semantics seeks to substitute a good lubricant for the emery. "We usually have sense enough to fit our shoes to our feet, but not sense enough to revise older methods of orientation to fit the facts."

STOP, LOOK, AND LISTEN

How shall we go about revising older methods? Korzybski suggests five little warning signals in our talking and writing:

> (1) the symbol *etc.* to remind us of characteristics left out;
>
> (2) *index numbers* to break up false identifications;
>
> (3) *dates* to remind us that objects are in process, in a state of constant change;
>
> (4) *hyphens* to show that events are connected and nature is all of a piece;
>
> (5) *quotes* to remind us that the term we are using is high up the abstraction ladder, and so, "Beware, it's loaded!"

When I first collected and listed these warning signals from the pages of *Science and Sanity,* I thought them rather elementary. Yet I have been using them constantly in my thinking for fifteen years. They work, and their very simplicity makes them the easier to employ.

ETC.

By writing, or by thinking, *etc.* after a statement, we remind ourselves that characteristics have been left out; we have not told *all.* The semantic quarterly is called *ETC,* and thereby warns the reader that it is not the sum total of wisdom.

William James once put it this way: "The word 'and' trails along after every sentence." Forgetting this, we become candidates for the know-it-all fraternity. *Etc.* helps us to keep alert in complicated territory, to delay the dogmatic cocksure response.

Advertisers may tell us about a beautiful streamlined television set with polished walnut cabinet which is being practically given away. The natural reaction of an experienced shopper is: "What are they *not* telling us?" He is using the equivalent of *etc.* on the advertising copy, wondering about the characteristics left out.

In employing this warning signal, however, a warning is in order. Never expect to round up *all* the missing characteristics, for, as we have seen, they are unlimited. Look for enough major characteristics to make a reasonable decision. You will need only a few for a commercial television set, more for a conclusion about U.S. policy in China.

INDEX NUMBERS

[These signals] serve to remind us of the diversity of nature, and of the diversities among human beings: Adam₁ is not Adam₂. They are useful to break up stereotypes, fixed ideas, and ideological convictions about "Catholics," "Yankees," "women," "Jews," "Negroes," "Japs," "Wall

Streeters." How often do we say, "Politicians are no good, look at Pendergast," then in the next breath praise the integrity of Senator Douglas? Politician$_1$ is not politician$_2$.

Index numbers keep us out of the pitfalls of formal logic. Here are Aristotle's three famous laws:

> 1. *The law of identity.* A is A.
>
> 2. *The law of the excluded middle.* Everything is either A or not-A.
>
> 3. *The law of contradiction.* Nothing is both A and not-A.

The letter A is the letter A, all right, and the word "Apple" is the word "Apple," with five letters and phonemes all correct. The law of identity works satisfactorily with words in our heads, but for events outside our heads, such as Korzybski's apple, it does not work without extensive qualification. Apple$_1$ is *not* Apple$_2$. An object is not even identical with itself over a period of time. The fresh sweet apple rots away.

Aristotle's second and third laws are full of mantraps. Take, for instance, the distinction between plants and animals—A and not-A. There is a little organism called *euglena,* which becomes green in abundant sunlight and behaves like a "plant," but when the sunlight disappears, it digests carbohydrates like an "animal." Euglena is thus either a "plant" or an "animal," depending on the time of day. Or, perhaps better, it is neither plant nor animal, it falls outside the categories. Medical history shows authentic cases of men being converted into women surgically, and vice versa. In 1953 the newspapers made much of an attractive young woman who was recently a man. The person has been both a "man" and a "woman," thus denying the law of contradiction.

Formal logic starts with language and tries to force nature into its verbal categories. The scientist starts with a wordless observation of nature, and then tells what he observes, constructing new categories as needed. Index numbers help us begin the analysis at the right end.

DATES

Korzybski's time signal is especially useful for events in process, where the change is clearly recognizable. Seeing the date, one stops and reflects that the situation *now* is not what it was a hundred years ago, or a year ago, or ten minutes ago. Britain$_{1066}$ is not Britain$_{1920}$, and Britain$_{1939}$ is not Britain$_{1953}$. America$_{1783}$ is not America$_{1953}$, and to speak of "The American Way" as something fixed and unchangeable is to speak nonsense.

Appending a date helps to break up slogan thinking: "That's the way it's always been and always will be"; "Once a Communist, always a Communist"; "The leopard cannot change its spots" . . . It offers a personal reminder that one is himself a process, and if he feels badly now he may not feel badly tomorrow. It helps deliver one from fixed ideas, and replaces static concepts with dynamic ones.

HYPHENS

Nature is all of a piece, but language divides it. This is, on the whole, a necessary procedure, enabling us to grasp one thing at a time. We must be careful not to mistake the verbal categories, however, for the real thing. Korzybski suggests that hyphens on the page, or in the mind, help us to remember. Instead of "body and mind" it is closer to reality to write *body-mind*; to write *space-time, psycho-logics.*

QUOTES

The [essay] you are reading is full of examples of this warning signal of Korzybski's. I try to put quotation marks around abstract terms which are easy to misunderstand. The quotes bid the reader slow down, remember that the term means different things to different people, look carefully to the context. Words like "free enterprise," "statism," "appeasement," vary for every user, depending on his past experience. . . .

Words like "water," "trees," "houses," "motorcars," are closer to referents, and quotes are seldom needed—except as I set them off in this sentence. For terms like "the flowers in that vase," "my 1954 Chevrolet," the communication line is about as clear as it can get; the referent is being pointed to.

Why use abstractions at all, when they can be so dangerous to understanding? Why not always point to what you are talking about? Well, why use water at all when you can drown in it? Without abstractions we could not think in a human way. The problem is to be aware of them, to remember what level the discourse is on, and the quote signs help that awareness.

ABSTRACTION LADDER

We have spoken repeatedly of levels of abstraction, or abstraction ladders. Here is one ladder, starting with the space-time event.

> That apple there on the table
>
> Apples-in-general
>
> Apples as part of the term "fruit"
>
> Foodstuffs
>
> Living standards
>
> Economic goods
>
> Economic systems

When discussing economic systems, it is a good idea to see that apple from time to time, and other tangible products at the bottom of the ladder. Some economists apparently do not eat.

Here is another ladder, beginning at the top and working downward:

Mountains. What can be said about mountains which applies in all cases? Almost nothing. They are areas raised above other areas on land, under the sea, on the moon. The term is purely relative at this stage; something higher than something, farther from the center.

Snow-capped mountains. Here on a lower rung we can say a little more. The elevations must be considerable, except in polar regions—at least 15,000 feet in the tropics. The snow forms glaciers which wind down the sides. They are cloud factories, producing severe storms, and they require special techniques for climbing.

The Swiss Alps. These are snow-capped mountains about which one can say a good deal. The location can be described, also geology, glacier systems, average elevation, climatic conditions, first ascents, and so on.

The Matterhorn. Here we can be even more specific. It is a snow-capped mountain 14,780 feet above the sea, shaped like a sharp wedge, constantly subject to avalanches of rock and ice. It has four faces, four ridges, three glaciers; was first climbed by the Whymper party in 1865, when four out of seven were killed—and so on. We have dropped down to a specific space-time event.

To the question whether it is "safe" to climb the Matterhorn, Leslie Stephen, one of the greatest of the Alpinists, gave two answers of large semantic importance in 1871, long before the word appeared in the dictionary.

Statement 1. "There is no mountain in the Alps which cannot be climbed by a party of practised mountaineers with guides, in fine weather and under favorable conditions of the snow, with perfect safety."

Statement 2. "There is no mountain in the Alps which may not become excessively dangerous if the climbers are inexperienced, the guides incompetent, the weather bad and the snow unfavorable. . . . There are circumstances under which the Righi is far more dangerous than the Matterhorn under others. Any mountain may pass from the top to the bottom of the scale of danger . . . in a day or sometimes in an hour."

Stephen gives us an unforgettable example of the dangers of generalization. The "Matterhorn" in the morning is not the "Matterhorn" in the afternoon. A is not A. $_{\text{Mattehorn1}}$ is an easy day for a woman climber; $_{\text{Matterhorn2}}$ is certain death for the best climber who ever lived.

"LAZY BOY"

Korzybski shows how language manufactures substantives out of adjectives, often with unfortunate results. Here is a boy who persists in getting up late in the morning. Soon his parents are calling him "a naturally lazy boy," a boy characterized by a thing called "laziness." "Laziness" is akin to "badness" in the American culture, and warrants drastic correction. The parents try hard words, then cuffs and whippings. The boy becomes deranged and unmanageable. Fortunately, a doctor is called in and finds, after an examination, that the patient's glands are seriously out of order. He proceeds to correct the condition, and the boy gets up on time. By identifying their son with "laziness," a substantive, the parents might well have ruined him for life.

People are labeled "troublemaker," "Red," "good guy," "bad girl," and action is taken on that one characteristic, rather than on the many characteristics which every individual possesses. You pass in society not for the person you are, but as a labeled dummy. U.S. congressional committees have been pasting the label "Communist Sympathizer" on many loyal Americans, to the extreme damage of both the citizen and the community. Korzybski would have us tear off the labels and look at the real person.

TWENTY-ONE STATEMENTS IN GENERAL SEMANTICS

To the second edition of **Science and Sanity,** Korzybski contributed an introduction which summarized the main principles of General Semantics. I have cast his list into the following twenty-one propositions or statements, trying to make a fair and objective digest. The reader is urged to consult the volume for himself, in case I have erred.

In any scientific endeavor, we borrow foundations from those who have gone before—a part of the process of "time-binding." All the propositions put forth by Korzybski are built on groundwork laid by earlier scientists. Nobody makes unsupported inventions nowadays. The first twelve statements seem to me to rely heavily on the work of preceding scientists, while the last nine are more Korzybski's own. Certainly he stated them uniquely. The five warning signals were of course his own, and I have added them, along with some personal comments, to some of the statements.

1. *No two events in nature are identical.* This proposition is accepted by modern scientists. It runs counter to the "is of identity" in Indo-European languages and to the "A is A" of formal logic. (As a warning signal, we use *index numbers.*)

2. *Nature works in dynamic processes.* Accepted by modern scientists and by some schools of philosophy. It disagrees with the linear, cause-and-effect structure of our language. (Warning signals: *dates* and *hyphens.*)

3. *Events flow into one another in nature by "insensible gradations."* Nature is all of a piece, though our language tends to separate it into classes. (Korzybski suggests the use of hyphens to join events—such as body-mind.)

4. *Nature is best understood in terms of structure, order, relationships.* Einstein helped to establish this through the principles of relativity. Indo-European languages, with substantives, entities, absolutes, are at odds with the proposition.

5. *Events in nature are four-dimensional.* Modern physicists, as well as the Hopi Indians, think in terms of space-time. Some other languages are structured for three dimensions, and those who speak them have difficulties with the concept of time.

6. *Events have unlimited characteristics.* Our languages leave many of them out and thus may often distort a judgment. (Korzybski suggests *"etc."* as a warning signal.)

7. *There is no simultaneity in nature.* Western languages assume it as a matter of course; modern physicists do not.

8. *There are no abstract qualities outside our heads.* But language may create verbal spooks which seem to be moving out there. Philosophers back to Bishop Occam have been aware of this difficulty. (*Quotes* give a warning.)

9. *Natural "laws" are at best only high probabilities.* Most scientists are now committed to probability theory. The structure of English, among other languages, favors absolute laws and eternal principles.

10. *Multivalued logic is cardinal in understanding and explaining nature.* Indo-European languages tend to force us into two-valued thinking, fortified by formal logic. (Korzybski suggests the use of *indexes* and *etc.* as warning signals.)

11. *A word is not a thing but an artificial symbol.* This has long been known, but the language structure still objectifies words and encourages word magic. (*Quotes* help to offset this danger.)

12. *A fact is not an inference: an inference is not a value judgment.* The distinction is well known to the law, but not to the laity, and vast semantic confusion results. The distinction may be illustrated by three statements:

> (1) This train is going at 20 miles an hour. A *fact.*
>
> (2) At this rate we'll be an hour late. An *inference.*
>
> (3) This lousy railroad is never on time! A *value judgment.*

Asked to define an event, most of us jump to the level of value judgment. A proper identification begins at the other end, with the facts.

Now let us list the nine statements which seem more uniquely Korzybski's.

13. *A map is not the territory.* Our words are not nature, but their structure should correspond to the structure of nature if we are to understand our world.

14. *The language of mathematics contains structures which correspond to the structure of nature.* Korzybski expected a crop of young geniuses in physics as a result of the new talk—and sure enough, they appeared.

15. *"Reality" is apperceived on three levels: macroscopic, microscopic, submicroscopic.* This point is not unique with Korzybski, but his emphasis is unique.

16. *The systems of Aristotle, Euclid, and Newton are now special cases, and outmoded as general systems.* Korzybski does not hold that these three great men were wrong, only that their "laws" cover less territory than was formerly supposed.

17. *Extensional, or objective, thinking is clearer and more accurate than intensional, or thinking inside one's skull.* This is another way of saying "find the referent"—a phrase which Korzybski did not like to use.

18. *At the end of all verbal behavior are undefined terms.* This is the point where the senses must pick up the signs from nature. Korzybski has emphasized this "unspoken level" more forcefully than any other student.

19. *Language is self-reflexive.* It is possible to make statements about a statement about a statement indefinitely. (No apologies to Gertrude Stein.)

20. *Man, alone among earth's creatures, "binds time";* that is, profits by the experience of past generations. This was well known and obvious long before Korzybski, but

uniquely phrased by him. (Not included in his list directly.)

21. *The nervous system can be consciously reoriented to improve evaluation.* Science can restore sanity. Korzybski deeply believed this, titled his book as a result of it, but his proof is not conclusive. If the proposition turns out to be true it may add considerably to his stature. Delayed response, the use of the warning signals, awareness of abstractions, and the rest, do improve evaluation without question. But does the use of General Semantics *retrain the whole nervous system,* so that improved evaluation becomes as automatic as the knee jerk? Psychiatrists are skeptical. Korzybski has been called a "thwarted psychiatrist," perhaps with justice.

A CRITICAL EVALUATION

It seems plain that while General Semantics has made important contributions to the study of communication it has not seized the leadership. Compared with cultural anthropology, with linguistics, cybernetics, the work of Shannon, it is more a point of view than a rigorous scientific discipline.

Korzybski "brought together a useful way of thinking and talking about human thinking and talking," says Irving J. Lee. At his death in 1950, "he had devised and explained the principles; he had not established a training-testing program with equal thoroughness." He inaugurated no clinic for practicing his methods, no controlled experiments to validate them. There are few reliable case studies of effects on individual persons or groups, in the sense that clinical psychologists make case studies.

Korzybski was something of a prima donna, and he had a few unfortunate prejudices. He was overcritical of the work of others in his field. I felt the sting of this criticism from time to time, though I had done my best to make his work more widely known. At one point the whole movement seemed to be heading toward a cult, with disciples who knew the lingo, but little else. This danger I believe has been safely passed.

Sometimes it seemed as if the originator of General Semantics were trying to set up a one-man philosophy in the great tradition, which would supersede the system of Aristotle, Aquinas, or Hegel. Yet the scientific method, upon which he constantly relied, is incompatible with one-man philosophies. Korzybski could not have it both ways. If he had been more of a scientist he would have written a shorter and better structured book and given himself more time to inaugurate the research which Professor Lee calls for. He would thus have allayed a good deal of frustration in persons like myself who were trying to understand him.

Despite the frustration, some of us kept at it, and rich was our reward. Doors which had been closed began to open; the world took on a new dimension. Among the semanticists who have been carrying on since his death are objective scholars, shy of cults and revelations. They will succeed, I believe, in steering General Semantics into the moving front of the social sciences, where it belongs. Korzybski included in his approach both the natural sciences, represented by physics, and the social sciences, represented by psychology. One of his favorite phrases was "organism-as-a-whole." He did not station himself behind any of the verbal partitions.

Twenty years of General Semantics have demonstrated that one's evaluation of men and events can be sharpened by its use, that certain mental blocks can be remedied, that one's speaking and writing can be clarified.

Students of General Semantics report a better ability to listen, a reduction in the terrors of stage fright, help in cases of stuttering. General Semantics can aid in teaching children, and in bringing "backward" scholars up to mark. It has led to a healthy re-examination of verbal proof and exerted some influence on the law. It promotes techniques of agreement, and encourages a new appraisal of philosophies formulated before Einstein. Perhaps best of all, General Semantics helps the student know what he does not know.

This is no small contribution for one person to make. We owe Korzybski good deal, not only for what he discovered or highlighted, but for the furor created by his personality. He lit fires, started controversies, caused people to look to their terms, and so gave a much-needed impetus to the whole subject of communication.

"What is the difference, Count Korzybski, between man and other living creatures?" he was sometimes asked. His eyes would gleam behind the great round spectacles and his deep voice with its rolling accent would reply: "A quar-rter-r- of an inch of cor-rtex."

Martin Gardner (essay date 1957)

SOURCE: "General Semantics, Etc.," in *Fads and Fallacies in the Name of Science*, Dover Publications, 1957, pp. 281-91.

[*In the following excerpt, Gardner dismisses Korzybski's* Science and Sanity *as unoriginal and poorly written.*]

Korzybski was born in 1879 in Warsaw. He had little formal education. During World War I, he served as a major in Russia's Polish Army, was badly wounded, and later sent to the United States as an artillery expert. He remained in the States, and for the next ten years drew on his personal fortune to write *Science and Sanity,* the 800-page Bible of general semantics. The book was published in 1933 by the Count's International Non-Aristotelian Library Publishing Company. It is a poorly organized, verbose, philosophically naive, repetitious mish-mash of sound ideas borrowed from abler scientists and philosophers, mixed with neologisms, confused ideas, unconscious metaphysics, and highly dubious speculations about neurology and psychiatric therapy.

Allen Walker Read, in two scholarly articles on the history and various meanings of the word "semantics" (*Trans/formation*, Vol. 1, Numbers 1 and 2, 1950, 1951), disclosed that the word had not been used in the Count's original draft of *Science and Sanity*. Before the book was published, however, the word had been adopted by several Polish philosophers, and it was from them that Korzybski borrowed it.

Most contemporary philosophers who use the word "semantics," restrict it to the study of the meaning of words and other symbols. In contrast, the Count used the word so broadly that it became almost meaningless. As Read points out, Korzybski considered a plant tropism, such as growing up instead of down, a "semantic reaction." In *Science and Sanity* he discusses a baby who vomited to get a second nursing, and writes, "Vomiting became her semantic way of controlling 'reality.' " Modern followers of the Count tend to equate "semantic" with "evaluative," defining "general semantics" as "the study and improvement of human evaluative processes."

Korzybski never tired of knocking over "Aristotelian" habits of thought, in spite of the fact that what he called Aristotelian was a straw structure which bore almost no resemblance to the Greek philosopher's manner of thinking. Actually, the Count had considerable respect for Aristotle (one of the many thinkers to whom his book is dedicated). But he believed that the Greek philosopher's reasoning was badly distorted by verbal habits which were bound up with the Indo-European language structure, especially the subject-predicate form with its emphasis on the word "is." "Isness," the Count once said, "is insanity," apparently without realizing that such concepts as "isomorphic," which he used constantly, cannot be defined without assuming the identity of mathematical structures.

Another "Aristotelian" habit against which the Count inveighed is that of thinking in terms of a "two-valued logic" in which statements must be either true or false. No one would deny that many errors of reasoning spring from an attempt to apply an "either/or" logic to situations where it is not applicable, as all logicians from Aristotle onward have recognized. But many of the Count's followers have failed to realize that there is a sense in which the two-valued orientation is inescapable. In all the "multi-valued logics" which have been devised, a deduction within the system is still "true" or "false." To give a simple illustration, let us assume that a man owns a mechanical pencil of a type which comes in only three colors—red, blue, and green. If we are told that his pencil is neither blue nor green, we then conclude that it is red. This would be a "true" deduction within a three-valued system. It would be "false" to deduce that the pencil was blue, since this would contradict one of the premises. No one has yet succeeded in creating a logic in which the two-valued orientation of true and false could be dispensed with, though of course the dichotomy can be given other names. There is no reason to be ashamed of this fact, and once it is understood, a great deal of general semantic tilting at two-valued logic is seen to be a tilting at a harmless windmill.

One finds in *Science and Sanity* almost no recognition of the fact that the battle against bad linguistic habits of thought had been waged for centuries by philosophers of many schools. The book makes no mention, for example, of John Dewey (except in bibliographies added to later editions), although few modern philosophers fought harder or longer against most of what the Count calls "Aristotelian." In fact, the book casts sly aspersions on almost every contemporary major philosopher except Bertrand Russell.

Korzybski's strong ego drives were obvious to anyone who knew him or read his works carefully. He believed himself one of the world's greatest living thinkers, and regarded **Science and Sanity** as the third book of an immortal trilogy. The first two were Aristotle's *Organon* and Bacon's *Novum Organum*. . . . [He] was convinced that his therapy would benefit almost every type of neurotic, and was capable of raising the intelligence of most individuals to the level of a genius like himself. He thought that all professions, from law to dentistry, should be placed on a general semantic basis, and that only the spread of his ideas could save the world from destruction. In the preface to the second edition of **Science and Sanity,** he appealed to readers to urge their respective governments to put into practice the principles of general semantics, and in the text proper (unchanged in all editions) expressed his belief that ultimately his society would become part of the League of Nations.

The Count's institute of General Semantics, near the University of Chicago, was established in 1938 with funds provided by a wealthy Chicago manufacturer of bathroom equipment, Cornelius Crane. Its street number, formerly 1232, was changed to 1234 so that when it was followed by "East Fifty-Sixth Street" there would be six numbers in serial order. The Count—a stocky, bald, deep-voiced man who always wore Army-type khaki pants and shirt—conducted his classes in a manner similar to Kay Kyser's TV program. Throughout a lecture, he would pause at dramatic moments and his students would shout in unison, "No!" or "Yes!" or some general semantic term like "Et cetera!" (meaning there are an infinite number of other factors which need not be specified.) Frequently he would remark in his thick Polish accent, "I speak facts," or "Bah—I speak baby stuff." He enjoyed immensely his role of orator and cult leader. So, likewise, did his students. In many ways the spread of general semantics resembled the Count's description, on page 800 of **Science and Sanity,** of "paranoiac-like semantic epidemics" in which followers fall under the spell of a dynamic leader.

According to the Count, people are "unsane" when their mental maps of reality are slightly out of correspondence with the real world. If the inner world is too much askew, they become "insane." A principal cause of all this is the Aristotelian mental orientation, which distorts reality. It assumes, for example, that an object is either a chair or not a chair, when clearly there are all kinds of objects which may or may not be called chairs depending on how you define "chair." But a precise definition is impossible. "Chair" is simply a word we apply to a group of things more or less alike, but which fade off in all directions, along continuums, into other objects which are not called chairs. As H. G. Wells expressed it, in his delightful essay on metaphysics in *First and Last Things*:

> . . . Think of armchairs and reading-chairs and dining-room chairs, and kitchen chairs, chairs that pass into benches, chairs that cross the boundary and become settees, dentist's chairs, thrones, opera stalls, seats of all sorts, those mi-raculous fungoid growths that cumber the floor of the Arts and Crafts Exhibition, and you will perceive what a lax bundle in fact is this simple straightforward term. In cooperation with an intelligent joiner I would undertake to defeat any definition of chair or chairishness that you gave me.

The non-Aristotelian mental attitude is, in essence, a recognition of the above elementary fact. There is no such thing as pure "chairishness." There are only chair 1, chair 2, chair 3, et cetera! This assigning of numbers is a process Korzybski called "indexing." In similar fashion, the same chair changes constantly in time. Because of weathering, use, and so forth, it is not the same chair from one moment to the next. We recognize this by the process of "dating." We speak of chair 1952, chair 1953, et cetera! The Count was convinced that the unsane, and many insane, could be helped back to sanity by teaching them to think in these and similar non-Aristotelian ways. For example, a neurotic may hate all mothers. The reason may be that a childhood situation caused him to hate his own mother. Not having broken free of Aristotelian habits, he thinks all mothers are alike because they are all called by the same word. But the word, as Korzybski was fond of repeating, is not the thing. When a man learns to index mothers— that is, call them mother 1, mother 2, mother 3, et cetera—he then perceives that other mothers are not identical with his own mother. In addition, even *his* mother is not the same mother she was when he was a child. Instead there are mother 1910, mother 1911, mother 1912, et cetera. Understanding all this, the neurotic's hatred for mothers is supposed to diminish greatly.

Of course there is more to the non-Aristotelian orientation than just indexing and dating. To understand levels of abstraction, for example, the Count invented a pedagogical device called the "structural differential." It is a series of small plates with holes punched in them, connected in various ways by strings and pegs. The "Semantic Rosary," as it was called by *Time* magazine, is impressive to anyone encountering epistemology for the first time.

Obviously there is nothing "unsane" about the various general semantic devices for teaching good thinking habits. In psychiatry, they may even be useful to doctors of any school when they try to communicate with, or instruct, a patient. But Korzybski and his followers magnified their therapeutic value out of all sane proportions. At conventions, general semanticists have testified to semantic cures of alcoholism, homosexuality, kleptomania, bad reading habits, stuttering, migraine, nymphomania, impotence, and innumerable varieties of other neurotic and psychosomatic ailments. At one conference a dentist reported that teaching general semantics to his patients had given them more emotional stability, which lessened the amount of acid in their mouths. As a consequence, fillings stayed in their teeth longer.

Korzybski's explanation of why non-Aristotelian thinking has therapeutic body effects was bound up with a theory now discarded by his followers as neurologically unsound. It concerned the cortex and the thalamus. The cortex was supposed to function when rational thought was taking place, and the thalamus when emotional reflexes were involved. Before acting under the impulse of an emotional response, Korzybski recommended a "semantic pause," a kind of counting-to-ten which gave the cortex time to arrive at an integrated, sane decision. For a person who developed these habits of self-control, there was a "neuro-semantic relaxation" of his nervous system, resulting in normal blood pressure, and improved body health.

It is interesting to note in this connection that a special muscular relaxation technique also was developed by the Count after he observed how often he could ease a student's worried tenseness by such gestures as a friendly grasp of the student's arm. The technique involves gripping various muscles of one's body and shaking them in ways prescribed in *The Technique of Semantic Relaxation,* by Charlotte Schuchardt, issued by the institute of General Semantics in 1943.

Modern works of scientific philosophy and psychiatry contain almost no references to the Count's theories. In Russell's technical books, for instance, which deal with topics about which Korzybski considered himself a great authority, you will not find even a passing mention of the Count. This is not because of stubborn prejudice and orthodoxy. The simple reason is that Korzybski made no contributions of significance to any of the fields about which he wrote with such seeming erudition. Most of the Count's followers admit this, but insist that the value of his work lies in the fact that it was the first great synthesis of modern scientific philosophy and psychiatry.

But is it? Few philosophers or professional psychiatrists think so. On matters relating to logic, mathematics, science, and epistemology, *Science and Sanity* is far less successful as a synthesis than scores of modern works. It is more like a haphazard collection of notions drawn from various sources accessible to the Count at the time, and bound together in one volume. Many of the Count's ideas give a false illusion of freshness merely because he invented new terms for them. For example, his earlier book, *The Manhood of Humanity,* 1921, describes plants as "energy binders," animals as "space binders," and men as "time binders." When this is translated, it means that plants use energy in growing; animals, unlike plants, are able to move about spatially to meet their needs; and man makes progress in time by building on past experience. All of which would have been regarded by Aristotle as a set of platitudes.

It is true that Korzybski made a valiant attempt to integrate a philosophy of science with neurology and psychiatry. It is precisely here, however, that his work moves into the realm of cultism and pseudo-science. Teaching a patient general semantics simply does not have, in the opinion of the majority of psychiatrists, the therapeutic value which followers of the Count think it has. Where the Count was sound, he was unoriginal. And where he was original, there are good reasons for thinking him "unsane."

Samuel I. Hayakawa, in many ways a saner and sounder man than the Count, is still waving the banners of general semantics in Chicago, even though he made a break with Korzybski shortly before the Count moved his headquar-

ters to Lakeville, Connecticut, in 1946. Hayakawa continues to edit his lively little magazine, *Etc.,* and work with the International Society of General Semantics, founded in Chicago in 1942 and not connected with the Lakeville group. His *Language in Action,* 1941 (revised in 1949 as *Language in Thought and Action*) remains the best of several popular introductions to Korzybski's views. One night in a Chicago jazz spot—Hayakawa is an authority on hot jazz—he was asked what he and the Count had disagreed about. Hayakawa paused a few moments (perhaps to permit a neurological integration of reason and emotion), then said, "Words."

Since the Count's death in 1950, the cult seems to be diminishing in influence. An increasing number of members, including Hayakawa himself, are discovering that almost everything of value in Korzybski's pretentious work can be found better formulated in the writings of others. Then too, many of its recruits from the ranks of science fiction enthusiasts, especially in California, have deserted general semantics for the more exciting cult of dianetics.

Anatol Rapoport   (essay date 1976)

SOURCE: "What I Think Korzybski Thought—and What I Think about It," in *ETC.: A Review of General Semantics,* December, 1976, Vol. 33, No. 4, pp. 351-65.

[*In the following essay, Rapoport reminisces about his first exposure to Korzybski's principles and remembers the author as an inept instructor and sloppy thinker.*]

I first heard the word "semantics" when a classmate at the University of Chicago recited a satirical poem in a campus coffee shop. In the poem "semantics" rhymed with "antics," and it ended something like this:

> "He could pass, were he but pinker
> As, who knows, perhaps a thinker."

To which someone added, "as it is, he is a stinker." The epigram was aimed at Bertrand Russell, who had just given a lecture and shocked the left-wing students by advocating accommodation to Hitler's demands in preference to war. Aged 26, I was, I think, the oldest freshman at the University and abysmally ignorant.

The second time "semantics" appeared on my intellectual horizon was in 1942 in Montgomery, Alabama, soon after I was commissioned in the U.S. Air Force. People were talking about a book by an author said to be Japanese (Imagine!). I saw the book and the author's picture on the jacket, but didn't get around to reading it.

The third time was decisive. I was then in Nome, Alaska. Work came in feverish spurts. When the skies cleared, swarms of lend-lease P-39's, A-20's and B-25's took off across the Bering Strait, in summer, around the clock. When the base was socked in and during Arctic darkness, there was nothing to do except play chess or billiards with the Russians, or do whispered simultaneous translations for them at the movies, or read. During those two years I read many books sent to me by friends intent on educating me. Among these books was *Science and Sanity*.

My first impulse was to dismiss Korzybski as a crackpot.

I was reading Hegel's *Science of Logic* at the same time, and the "non-Aristotelian system" constructed on a "law of non-identity" looked to me an impertinent and awkward imitation. I could not see how anyone could take Korzybski seriously. But Hayakawa evidently did, as I was told by a Red Cross girl who had read *Language in Action* and talked the G.S. lingo. I recalled what I had heard about that book, borrowed it from her, and was enchanted.

My attitude toward Korzybski changed from contempt to anger. If this is what the man meant, why didn't he say so? What's this about colloids? (I knew very little about colloids, but I was sure Korzybski knew less.) What's this about Cantor's "alephs" being products of pathological semantic reactions? (I understood Cantor's theory of transfinite numbers and was sure that Korzybski didn't.) Korzybski identified sanity with the mode of thinking that evolved in the natural sciences and in mathematics, and so did Bertrand Russell (if "sanity" is taken as a synonym of "rationality-cum-morality"), and so did Hayakawa (if pragmatism is assumed to be the psychological substrate of sanity). But why couldn't Korzybski write lucid prose like Russell's or Hayakawa's? Was he deliberately obfuscating in order to appear erudite like the German "system-building" philosophers? This was hard to believe since Korzybski dismissed philosophical speculations as nonsense, much as Wittgenstein did in his *Tractatus Logico-philosophicus,* which Korzybski cited with approval. But Wittgenstein's *Tractatus,* although abstruse, was logically as tightly knit as Euclid's *Elements* or Whitehead and Russell's *Principia.* Why could not Korzybski be at least logically rigorous? If he was not a crackpot (this previous impression of mine was now vigorously shaken), why was he so repetitive, verbose, pugnacious, redundant and self-congratulatory, manifesting all the symptoms of crackpot delusions? Later I found out why, or thought so, and thereupon my ambivalent attitude toward Korzybski crystallized, persisting to this day.

One afternoon in the summer of 1944, when I was in Chicago on leave, I dropped in at 1234 56th Street and was shown into a room where Korzybski was lecturing to some 20-30 people. There were diagrams on the blackboard, only one of which I recall, a graph showing how the number of links between individuals grows with the number of individuals. Korzybski was demonstrating the law of gravity by dropping a box of matches, the phenomenon of visual fusion by twirling a toy electric fan, exhibiting levels of abstraction on his structural differential gadget, and so on. To the extent that the lecture had a topic, it was that "things are not what they seem," something Longfellow had said in a sentimental poem a century earlier. Bored by the lecture, I scanned the audience and recognized Hayakawa sitting on the extreme left. He was the man I really wanted to meet. After one or two articles of mine were published in *ETC.,* we corresponded. I had not mentioned my bewilderment concerning the discrepancy between his straightforward and engaging presentation of the basic ideas of general semantics and the opaqueness of the source; and I intended to ask him how he was able to distill those ideas from Korzybski's writings.

After the lecture, I introduced myself and was cheerfully greeted. Hayakawa insisted on introducing me to Korzybski, to whom, he said, he had spoken about me. We went to Korzybski's study, where he, too, greeted me with disarming warmth. It was embarrassing. I had formed an unflattering opinion about Korzybski's intellect. Now I sat facing the man who assumed the role of venerable authority, exuding paternal benevolence to a promising aspirant. Korzybski's first remark to me made the situation definitive: "You have read *Science and Sanity* . . . how many times?"

I made some noncommittal remarks about rereading certain portions and started halfhearted attempts to engage him in a substantive discussion about his assumptions, lines of reasoning, and conclusions. It was useless. Korzybski did not listen (I was told later that he was deaf, or said he was). There was nothing to hang the conversation on; so I gave up and assumed the stance of deference expected of me.

During the few hours I spent with Hayakawa on that occasion, I did not bring up my misgivings. We talked about ourselves. He asked me about my plans in civilian life. I told him that my qualifications were in mathematics and that I would settle anywhere I could find a job. He said he hoped it would be in Chicago, and I said I hoped so, too. We parted friends.

After the war, jobs were plentiful, and I did find one in Chicago. Then it was that a long and, to me, immensely fruitful collaboration with Hayakawa (editing *ETC.*) started.

In the beginning I still hesitated to ask Hayakawa point-blank what he really thought of Korzybski. To all appearances, theirs was a master-disciple relationship. Other disciples whom I soon met spoke with enthusiasm of Korzybski's charisma and of their personal attachment to him. I learned also that Korzybski's "seminars" (I never participated in one) were structured like psychotherapeutic sessions and that Korzybski even practised individual psychotherapy. It seemed unlikely that I could engage any "disciple" in a fruitful discussion about the intellectual content of Korzybski's ideas. And so, the conversation that I planned to have with Hayakawa in 1944 (which, I confess, I had rehearsed mentally in Alaska) never took place.

As it turned out, it became unnecessary. A rift between Hayakawa and Korzybski became apparent and was even "formalized" in the split between the Institute of General Semantics and the Society for General Semantics. When the Institute moved to Connecticut, there was no longer any necessity, dictated by decorum, for either Hayakawa or me to maintain personal contact with Korzybski, and we talked about him freely. Our talks were not centered on Korzybski's baffling excursions into neurophysiology (Hayakawa didn't give a damn about the colloidal level and things like that). We talked about the man himself. However, our conversations were not just gossip. They centered around Korzybski's qualities as a teacher. They brought out in my mind another dimension of general semantics and illuminated Korzybski from another angle.

He became, in my estimation, a tragic instead of a somewhat ludicrous figure.

Hayakawa was a superb teacher. He was probably that before he ever heard of general semantics. My guess is that he became attracted to general semantics because in it the method of teaching that he had used all along was spelled out for him—the method of extensional orientation, maintaining eternal vigilance in preserving links between verbal expression and nonverbal experience. To teach this orientation, one must practice it; that is, one must maintain continual contact with the inner world of the student, in order to use *his* experience as the point of departure, above all, to make the teaching situation a two-way traffic of shared experience. To Hayakawa, all this came naturally. He was a teacher of language skills. In the light of general semantics (which he completely identified with extension orientation), the teaching of language skills became for him the job of establishing and firming connections between experience imparted by the senses and communication. He engineered a quiet revolution in the teaching of English. Formal grammar, the parsing of sentences, the classification of figures of speech, the "enrichment" of vocabulary, in short, all the school-marmish aspects of "English" were subjected to good-natured ridicule. He did not espouse or condone illiteracy. Rather, by nurturing the need to communicate, ingrained in every human being, he revealed literacy as an effective tool of communication. The pragmatic philosophy of pedagogy, based on the fulfillment of felt needs, has been spelled out by John Dewey. Hayakawa was a most successful practitioner of that philosophy. He nurtured the need to communicate by rewarding attempts to do so: he listened.

Korzybski was a poor teacher. This judgment will shock his disciples, especially those who came to him in search of a focus of personal integration and found it. This aspect of "teaching," however, is related more to revelation than to enlightenment. It characterizes the "teaching" of gurus, demagogues, revivalists and charlatans. Mao Tse Tung and Maharaj Ji have their hosts of disciples. Spawned by Korzybski's charisma, a general semantics cult came into being, indistinguishable from hundreds of other cults, cemented by jargon and adoration of a domineering personality.

The cult, however, is not the issue here. I doubt very much that in writing **Science and Sanity** Korzybski had in mind the creation of a cult. If he had, he could be put once and for all in a class with Mary Baker Eddy and L. Ron Hubbard. Here is where I part company with those who see Korzybski as an exploiter of gullibility or as a crackpot obscurantist. This revision of my original impression of Korzybski was a consequence of comparing Korzybski to Hayakawa.

Korzybski, as I said, was incompetent as a teacher because he did not share the inner world of his *intended* audience. He saw himself (and said so) as next in line in the succession of synthesizers of the ever-expanding scientific world view: Aristotle, Euclid, Bacon, Newton, Einstein. His intended audience, therefore, must have been the entire community of Western scientific thought. But he did not write in the language of that community. He did not discipline his thought, did not channel it along the paths already beaten by the synthesizers, so as to press it against the next barrier. Had he done so, his "non-Aristotelian system" might have been recognized as an important contribution to modern philosophy. Instead, he gave the impression of preaching rather than of reasoning. And so the academic community rejected him.

The usual accusations against the academic community of having dismissed a thinker ahead of his time are not justified. Korzybski was not ahead of his time; he was most fortunately in tune with his time. As he was writing **Science and Sanity,** the revolution in philosophy instigated by the Vienna Circle was in full swing. Korzybski's ideas overlap strongly with those of the logical positivists. Wittgenstein's *Tractatus* begins with the proposition, *"Die Welt ist alles was der Fall ist"* ("The world is all that is the case," meaning the *specific* case). It ends with "Wovon man nicht sprechen kann, darueber muss man schweigen" ("About what one cannot speak one must remain silent"). A neater formulation of the alpha and omega of general semantics as a philosophy of language and cognition is hard to imagine.

I keep referring to general semantics as a philosophy, knowing that Korzybski categorically rejected this designation. "General semantics," he kept repeating, "is an empirical science." This assertion also served to alienate the academic community from him. An empirical science proceeds from systematized observations to hypotheses to be tested by further observations. Korzybski's reported observations (for instance, on mental patients) were by any accepted standards haphazard, and his discussion of the functioning of the nervous system reads like a factual explanation, not as a formulation of hypotheses. And, of course, there are no traces of subjecting these conjectures to critical tests.

The phrase "academic community" calls to mind vested interests of a tradition-bound cabal. This stereotype hardly fits the American scene. In the U.S., Academe comprises the vast majority of "professional thinkers." This is because there is no prestigious leisure class in the United States. Practically every one works, and the natural work milieu of the "professional thinker" is Academe. This field (sometimes called the "knowledge industry") is the largest in the world, and because of its loose, fluid structure, the most diversified. It has its share of mediocrity, but it is also practically the only social niche for a serious, creative thinker, provided he has equipped himself with a requisite competence in teaching, research, or communication of ideas in a language understood by the academic community. Because neither an established religion nor an officially sanctioned philosophy have ever become rooted in the United States, orthodoxy is by no means a requirement for membership in Academe. On the contrary, nonconformity, if coupled with brilliance or even the appearance of brilliance, is often an asset. Korzybski, however, wrote and spoke of technical matters with which he was only superficially familiar, or not at all, as if he knew more about them than specialists who had spent years of painstaking research.

It was easy to hit back: for neurophysiologists to pooh-

pooh Korzybski's pontifical disquisitions on the brain, for mathematicians and logicians to punch holes in his critique of the foundations of mathematics. The invention of psychiatric doctrines requires less technical knowledge and logical rigor (if any); but without an M.D. degree, Korzybski could not be a psychiatrist in an academic setting.

General semantics did penetrate several colleges and universities as a course or a course topic; but this came about through the energetic efforts of the "popularizers," S. I. Hayakawa, Irving J. Lee, Wendell Johnson, Elwood Murray, Lee Thayer, and several others, all professors in good standing, almost exclusively in departments of language arts, communications, or speech. To Korzybski himself, Academe was closed and with it the opportunity to develop general semantics in its proper setting.

The proper setting of general semantics as a framework of thought (distinguished from its special pedagogical or psychotherapeutic offshoots) is philosophy. In denying vigorously that general semantics is a "philosophy," Korzybski was emphasizing what he thought was its scientific potential. About this he was much too sanguine, as I will try to show below. General semantics was certainly not a science in his day, is still not a science, may not even ever become a science in its own right. But it is an outlook, a framework of thought comprising far more than a pedagogical method or a help to "self-realization," as it has come to be popularly conceived.

The basic tenet of general semantics is that man does not experience his environment; he experiences what he *tells* himself about his environment. To put it in another way, language is a screen between man and his environment. Man looks at the screen, not at reality behind it. This screen is of man's own making. It evolves over generations and develops during an individual's lifetime. There may be more or less correspondence between what is on the screen and what goes on "out there" in reality. But the correspondence is never complete. At best it is a drastic simplification of reality; at worst, a monstrous distortion.

Korzybski called the screen a "map." "The map is not the territory" (the word is not the thing—the principle of non-identity) was a favorite maxim of his. "The map is not all of the territory" (the principle of non-allness) was another. So much is the AB of general semantics, understood by every one who has read and understood any primer on that subject. The "C" ("the map is self-reflexive") touches on much more complex matters. Its implications go far beyond anything that can be explained in a primer.

A striking metaphorical illustration of the third principle was given by the Russian psychologist-philosopher Vladimr Lefebvre in his book *Konfliktuyushchiye Struktury.* In Lefebvre's illustration, the screen is a distorting mirror. And since he is concerned with the social context, he introduces a whole system of mirrors. He writes:

> Imagine a room full of crooked mirrors like those in amusement parks. The mirrors are placed at different angles. Let a pencil be dropped. Its fall will be fantastically reflected in the mirrors, and the reflections will also be re-

flected. Thus, the trajectory, already distorted in the various mirrors, will be further distorted in the avalanche of reflected images. A reflexive system can be thought of as a system of mirrors and the multitude of reflections in them. Each mirror represents a persona characterized by a particular position. The vastly complex flow of reflections represents the reflexive process.

> The example illustrates the difference between a physical process and a social-psychological one. The trajectory of the pencil is a physical process; the entire flow of reflections is a social-psychological one.

> Imagine now an investigator entering this room (he too, is a mirror). The situation has fundamentally changed. Each movement of the investigator is accompanied by a continual change in the multiple reflections.

If Lefebvre's mirrors are interpreted as screens of language, interposed between an individual and reality, his model can serve as an illustration of Korzybski's third axiom, moreover in a social context.

Someone dismissed Korzybski by pointing out that everything that is good in *Science and Sanity* is not new, and everything that is new is not good. On the face of it, the verdict is amply justified. Korzybski's attempts to link the inadequacy of verbal maps with malfunctionings of the human nervous system were amateurish. The heavy emphasis on the distinction between maps and territories was anticipated by Alexander Bryan Johnson, a century earlier [in his *A Treatise on Language*]. A few citations will suffice.

> "To understand the relation which words bear to created existences, we must contemplate creation apart from words."

> "We must discriminate between the extent and variety of creation and the paucity of language."

> "Words are confounded with things."

> "We must subordinate language to what we discover in nature."

> The medical question of contagion is embarrassed by not discriminating the oneness of language from the plurality of nature. The contagiousness of cholera generally is less a unit than the contagiousness of a single case. Even the contagiousness of a single case during its whole continuance is less a unit than its contagiousness on any given moment—hence to investigate the contagiousness of cholera and to proceed by supposing that the contagiousness possesses the oneness which the word contagion imports, is like seeking for magnetism as a unit among the numerous magnetic phenomena. It is seeking in nature for a unit that exists in language only.

> But cholera is not a unit . . . not only is cholera in general not a unit, the particular cholera of Thomas is not a unit . . . I admit the propriety of combining them under one name; but if we would escape delusion, we must construe their

oneness by nature and not by the oneness of their name.

Here are the principles of non-identity and non-allness completely spelled out a hundred years before *Science and Sanity*. Even Thomas appears as the ancestor of Korzybski's Smith!

What then was Korzybski's contribution? I keep asking myself why I go on defending him when he is ridiculed by academics and debunking his extravagant claims when he is venerated by the faithful. Is the Korzybski in my "mirror," half-genius, half-crackpot, the "true" Korzybski? Or is the image in my mirror a reflection of another image, the one that formed when I, allied with Hayakawa against the academic critics, first defended him, which made it necessary to defend the defense, and so on? Clearly, this question leads to infinite regression; so I put it aside. I take my defense of Korzybski, such as it is, at face value and maintain that his contribution was substantial, albeit impaired by unfortunate flaws in his personality. Further, I maintain that the contribution was to philosophy, his own disclaimers on this score notwithstanding.

The reasons for his denial that general semantics was a philosophy are clear. He thought that the most significant facet of the "non-Aristotelian system" was the link between psycholinguistics and physiology. Hence his insistence that general semantics was an "empirical science," by which I strongly suspect he meant a practical or an applied science. Evidence for this conjecture is in Korzybski's repeated allusions to general semantics as a "method for retraining the nervous system," supposedly based on physiological considerations. Actually, Korzybski's vision of the linkage between the psychology of language and the functioning of the nervous system was a chimera. To be sure, speech impairment can be traced to specific areas of the brain, but these connections tell us next to nothing about how the brain actually "works" (in the engineering sense, as Korzybski understood "working") and the way language functions or malfunctions.

To illustrate, I return to that classmate of mine from whom I first heard the word "semantics." That was Jerry Lettvin, who subsequently became a psychiatrist and a prominent experimental neurophysiologist. Jerry did experimental work at the Massachusetts Institute of Technology jointly with Warren S. McCulloch (psychiatrist-neurophysiologist) and Walter H. Pitts (mathematician). In a now classical paper ["A Logical Calculus of the Ideas Immanent in Nervous Activity," *Bulletin of Mathematical Biophysics* (1943),] McCulloch and Pitts presented a model of the brain working like a digital computer. They showed that the basic operator terms of formal logic, namely "and," "or," "not," "implies," etc., can be represented physically as elements of such a computer, thereby possibly as neural elements. Moreover, they showed that any proposition of arbitrary complexity, expressible in terms of formal logic, could be "realized" by a network of such elements. It seemed at the time that this model opened a whole field of investigation centered on discovering functioning structures of the brain responsible for "purposeful" and "rational" mental operations. Here, then, was a possible juncture of mathematics and neuro-

physiology, fervently espoused by Korzybski, who, it will be recalled, regarded mathematics as a language with a structure most closely corresponding to that of reality.

Sixteen years later, Lettvin, jointly with H. R. Maturama, W. S. McCulloch and W. H. Pitts, published a paper entitled "What the Frog's Eye Tells the Frog's Brain" [*Proceedings I. R. E.*, (1959)], in which it was shown how the "information" impinging on the frog's retina is "processed" (or "coded") even before it is transmitted to the brain. Here one could argue that since the retina is ontogenetically and phylogenetically an extension of the brain, it is still in the brain that all information processing takes place. But this argument does not bear on the point I wish to make.

The point is this: Korzybski insisted that "semantic reactions" are imbedded in the intricate structure of our nervous system (this is what he presumably meant by the "colloidal level"). These structures keep changing as we "learn." "Learning," in turn, is mediated by language. Hence language habits modify important structural aspects of the nervous system, directing what we abstract from our experience, how we react to these abstractions, and what we shall learn later. All this is eminently reasonable. But how are these changes "on the colloidal level" to be directed in the "right" direction, that is, toward greater correspondence between the structure of the semantic reactions and the structure of reality, if we know next to nothing about what happens on that deeper level, whether the changes are pathological or therapeutic?

The paper by Lettvin et al., shows how much technical knowledge and intricate work is required to "decode" a *simplest imaginable* semantic reaction (a small dark moving spot means "fly"). *And this is not yet a semantic reaction to verbal stimuli*. Now if we could get hold of the Celebrated Jumping Frog of Calaveras County, trace his semantic reactions to Jim Smiley's command "Flies, Dan'l, flies!" and compare them with the semantic reactions of Lettvin's frog, we could start the program envisaged by Korzybski. But even then we would "extensionalize" a semantic reaction of a nervous system incomparably more primitive than ours. What can we possibly say about the events associated with the internalization in our nervous system of what we "breathe in," so to say, from our semantic environment, that is, the whole baggage of conventional wisdom that governs the semantic reactions of most of us most of the time? Nothing.

This is why Korzybski's discussion of retraining the nervous system appears on critical examination to be irrelevant to his thesis. His detractors can reasonably dismiss this discussion, bristling with neologisms, as window dressing, as recourse to scientism calculated to impress the uninformed and the gullible. I am not among these detractors. I rather see Korzybski as a man completely carried away by his vision, of which the basis is sound. A critical examination of language in the context of human thinking, feeling and acting, and above all, in the context of the human condition and human destiny is imperative. It is from this standpoint that the various offshoots of general semantics as well as the various critiques of the "non-Aristotelian system" should be evaluated.

In my opinion, the pedagogical offshoot, represented by the so-called "popularizers," has been the most salutary and practical application of general semantics, specifically of the "extensional orientation." At times, however, the insistence on concrete referents for every term as the only credential of "meaning" was pushed too far, driving the enthusiasts of the extensional orientation to a sort of nihilistic "barefoot" empiricism. Elsewhere I discussed the pitfalls in Stuart Chase's *Tyranny of Words* and the ill-fated dismissal of "ideology" in mature politics. Oliver Wendell Holmes' famous "operational" definition of law has been repeatedly quoted with approval by general semanticists (including myself): "The prophesies of what the courts will do in fact, and nothing more pretentious are what I mean by law." I withdrew my unqualified approval after reading an article on international law, in which that citation was taken as the motto.

That article can be summarized in a definition just one step removed from Holmes': "The prophesies of what the *litigants* will do in fact, and nothing more pretentious are what we (the proponents of *realpolitik*) mean by international law."

Pragmatism, carried too far, blocks imagination, turns off vision, and strangles hope. In more prosaic terms, the extensional orientation, carried to an extreme, is like an economy without credit. It cannot even be a cash economy, since money is only a "symbol" of goods and services. To be "completely extensional," it must be a barter economy. A completely "extensional" epistemology is that of Stuart Chase's cat Hobie Baker. Fascination with it leads to just what Korzybski condemned: copying animals.

The "extensional orientation" is carried even further in Zen Buddhism. Of course this direction is not an offshoot of general semantics, being much older. I mention it because some see an affinity between it and general semantics. Zen Buddhism, as it appears to me, is an attempt to bypass the screen of language altogether in order to experience reality "directly." The resort to the "silent level" of experience in general semantics training seems to have a similar aim. Whatever effects these exercises may have on individual psyches (about which I am ignorant), I don't think they have any relation to the normative aspects of general semantics, namely, the concern with man as a symbol using class of life, hence as a creature who cannot be torn from a social context defined by verbal communication. Just because air is polluted does not mean that we can live without air. Just because our semantic environment is polluted does not mean that we can survive by shutting it off, hoping to come into direct contact with "ultimate reality." Experiencing the world on the silent level is all right, just as going under water is all right for a while. One can even train oneself to stay under water for I don't know how many minutes; and I understand mystics can stay in contact with "ultimate reality" for very long stretches of time. But if we want to live (in the ordinary earth-bound sense), we must come up for air.

Of the psycho-therapeutic offshoots of general semantics I have little to say, for want of competence. I suspect that practically all psycho-therapeutic methods based on personal interaction are about equally effective or equally in-

effective. People with emotional problems gravitate toward the sort of therapy that "rings a bell," and it is the ringing bell rather than the inherent specifics of the method that helps them, if they are helped. I have known people who were genuinely helped by purest hogwash. No aspersion on general semantics psycho-therapy is intended. I am merely pointing out that in psychotherapy "success" tells us little about the inherent effectiveness of any particular therapy.

Finally, let us turn to the critiques of the "non-Aristotelian system." The inadequacy and irrelevance of Korzybski's neurophysiological doctrine have been discussed. It remains to examine the ABC of the system, namely non-identity, non-allness, and self-reflexiveness, that Korzybski juxtaposed to the three axioms of Aristotelian logic: identity, non-contradiction, and the excluded middle.

Korzybski presented his non-Aristotelian system as a generalization of Aristotelian logic, analogous to non-Euclidean geometry as a generalization of Euclid's system and to relativistic physics as a generalization of the Newtonian system. The analogy sounded grandiose but did not stand up under critical scrutiny. A generalization of a system involves an elimination of one or more of its postulates. Non-Euclidean geometry is indeed a generalization of Euclidean geometry, because it is obtained by dropping the famous postulate of parallels. Similarly non-Newtonian physics (both relativistic and quantum) are generalizations of Newtonian physics, since the latter is revealed as a special case of the more general systems. We have also some genuine non-Aristotelian logics obtained by dropping the axiom of the excluded middle; for example, the multivalued logics developed by the Polish School (to which Korzybski often referred) and the infinite-valued logic of probability, where the truth value of a proposition can assume any value from 0 ("false") to 1 ("true"). Aristotelian logic is a special case with only two values, 0 and 1, admitted.

However, the ABC of the non-Aristotelian system exhibits no such feature. Stretching the point, it might be argued that self-reflexiveness is related to Goedel's Theorem, a proof that in any mathematical system involving transfinite induction there must be propositions that cannot (within the system) be proved to be either true or false. And the principle of non-identity *looks* like dropping the first axiom of Aristotelian logic (the principle of identity: A = A). But the consequences of dropping that principle (or the principle of non-contradiction) means opening the door to contradiction, something that cannot be tolerated in *any* logic. Once contradiction is admitted, *any* proposition can be "proved" to be both true and false, which is very different from saying that *some* propositions *cannot* be proved to be *either* true *or* false. Obliterating the distinction between true and false makes the concept of truth devoid of meaning (rather than just ambivalent) and so spells the demise not only of logic but also of the notion of correspondence between "maps" and "territories."

To be sure, in some philosophical systems contradiction has been raised to the status of a fundamental principle of "logic"; for example, by Hegel, in dialectical materialist polemics, and in Orwellian double-think. But these "logics" have nothing to do with rules of inference. They are rather styles of verbalization, just the sort of excrescences against which Korzybski raised the standards of general semantics. (I mean standards in the heraldic, not normative sense—pun not intentional.)

Korzybski left himself vulnerable to the logicians by denigrating formal logic. (Tarski, whom Korzybski admired, dismissed general semantics with a few sarcastic remarks.) Obsessed by his mission of promoting the "extensional orientation," Korzybski exaggerated the pitfalls of formal logic (especially of two-valued logic), forgetting that the pitfalls are not in the rules of inference themselves but rather in what he himself was most concerned with, namely the failure to distinguish between verbal constructs and the realities they are tacitly assumed to represent. Korzybski's insistence that in the non-Aristotelian system the Aristotelian laws of identity and non-contradiction are supplanted by (or generalized to) the principles of nonidentity and non-allness was a grave mistake. In the sense of *logic,* only the law of the excluded middle can be safely dropped.

Had Korzybski been more careful in drawing a sharp line between formal rules of inference and internalized habits of thought, he could not have been so easily attacked. His specific contribution would have stood out more clearly, namely the identification of the degree of sanity, both individual and collective, with the degree of structural correspondence between semantic reactions engendered by language and objective reality.

This view of language has much wider implications than the formal multivalued logics developed by the Polish School (Tarski, Sierpinski, Lukasiewicz) and the views derived from language analysis pursued by the logical positivists (Wittgenstein, Carnap, Reichenbach). The former were not concerned with the relation of formal logic to reality at all; logic to them was a system of rules for manipulating symbols. For the latter, analysis of language was regarded as the principal task of the philosophy of science. Semantic legitimacy was denied to all other branches of philosophy.

For Korzybski logic was inseparable from the psychology and even the physiology of thought processes. This, as I have already said, was unfortunate because this confusion made it appear that Korzybski was attacking two-valued logic as such, instead of its psychological (or even physiological) correlate embodied in the two-valued orientation. Nevertheless, this very weakness of his approach was at the basis of Korzybski's original contribution. He accepted implicitly the philosophy of science espoused by the logical positivists but emphasized the urgent necessity to extend the associated critique of language to all areas of human life. Finally, he envisaged a spectrum in modes of thinking ranging from the pathological, where the connection between language and reality is completely severed, to that characteristic of science, where these connections are constantly checked, tested, "repaired," or replaced to insure the greatest possible correspondence between the structure of language and the structure of reality.

Man, the symbol user, as a species rather than his symbol

systems themselves, was central in Korzybski's thought. In this way, his "non-Aristotelian system," although in a way a misnomer, was a harbinger of "the proper study of mankind." It differs from formal semantics, from traditional philosophies, and even from logical positivist philosophy (although it shares its ontology and epistemology), to the extent that none of these emphasize sufficiently the vital significance of ontology and epistemology for the human condition.

Nevertheless, general semantics is a philosophy. It is that primarily, because it is not a science. It remains for specialists to trace the neurophysiological components of pragmatics, the branch of semiotics that relates symbols to behavior rather than to other symbols (syntactics) or to referents (semantics proper). Because of Korzybski's failure to give a sober and lucid account of his ideas, it is not likely that psycholinguists, neurophysiologists, and scientifically-oriented psychiatrists will give much credit to him. Not being a science but being a rich source of ideas and of new directions in the study of cultural evolution, psychology, psycho-pathology, above all of socio-pathology, general semantics well deserves to be called a philosophy not in the pejorative sense that this word has acquired for positivists, pragmatists, and even many scientists, but in its original etymological sense.

This is essentially what I said in my first book, *Science and the Goals of Man.* I sent the galleys to Korzybski, but had no reaction from him directly. Instead, one of his associates wrote me that Korzybski was appalled and "deeply hurt" by what I had written. Why he reacted this way I could only guess. Perhaps he was vexed by my failure to send him a draft inviting his criticism or suggestions. Perhaps he was angry because Hayakawa (with whom he had broken off relations) wrote the foreword. Possibly, in Korzybski's estimation, whoever was not with him was against him. If there were more substantial grounds for Korzybski's reaction to my first book, I had no way of examining them. On the very day the book was published (March 1, 1950), Korzybski died.

As I said, Korzybski was not ahead of his time. He was very much with his time. The bloody nightmares of the thirties and forties can be seen as direct results of the manipulation of masses by exploiting signal reactions. The socio-pathology underlying Naziism and Stalinism provides classical examples. The degradation of American policy in the post-war decades was no less severe, even though its genocidal effects were perceived by Americans only on television screens. General semanticists have often pointed out that movies engendered false-to-fact identification because celluloid phantasies were mistaken for reality. In televised newscasts the reverse happened: reality was identified with the tube image. Pictures of massacres in Vietnam were indistinguishable from shoot-'em-ups. The obscene vocabulary of "defense community" with its "first strike capabilities," "second strike capabilities," "nuclear exchanges," "nuclear umbrellas," "deterrence," "limited wars," "counter-insurgency," etc., etc., and the sick humor with which horror weapons are christened ("Bambi," "Infants"), are manifestations of a severely polluted semantic environment, as severely polluted as the physical environment of our ravished globe.

Korzybski's lasting achievement consisted in pointing out the dangers of that pollution at the time when its toxic effects were just becoming manifest.

James D. French (essay date 1989)

SOURCE: "Time-Binding: To Build a Fire," in *ETC.: A Review of General Semantics,* Vol. 46, No. 3, Fall, 1989, pp. 194-96.

[*In the following essay, French analyzes Korzybski's concept of time-binding and its role in the progress of human civilization.*]

Perhaps we knew about fire before we even knew we were human. We were using fire to drive and trap animals and to roast meat 500,000 years ago, during the Pleistocene Era. However, exactly when or how *Homo Erectus* discovered fire is unknown, although there are theories: A woman may have been chipping flakes from a piece of flint, and the sparks that flew from the blows ignited nearby leaves and twigs; then again, there may have been a lightning strike and a forest fire, and our man Grog took a burning branch home to light and warm the cave.

Of course, the generations of humans that came after the great discovery started out life with the knowledge of fire, a knowledge passed to them in childhood by their parents. Because it is in the nature of human beings to pass information from one generation to the next—to build on the achievements of past generations over time—there was no turning back to pre-fire days. Each generation added to the storehouse of knowledge about fire, until by the Neolithic Era, humans could produce fire at will, with such tools as the fire plow, the fire drill, and the bow drill.

In 1669, phosphorus, a volatile, deadly poison, and the starter ingredient of modern matches, was discovered. John Walker, an Englishman, built on that discovery and produced the first practical friction match in 1827. In 1855, the safety match appeared; it could only be lighted when struck against a strip of red phosphorus. Finally, the Diamond Match Co. created a safe, non-poisonous phosphorus formula in 1911 from a French patent, and the modern match came into being.

It may seem strange, but even such a simple task as striking a match is not an independent act; it is the result of the efforts of countless generations over time.

Ten years after the appearance of the Diamond match, Alfred Korzybski formulated a new theory of human existence based on the interdependence of the generations. He saw, as we have seen in the history of fire, the links between the generations that are integral to the development of human culture. In the words of Abraham Lincoln:

> Fishes, birds, beasts, and creeping things are not miners, but feeders and lodgers merely. Beavers build houses; but they build them in no wise differently or better now than they did five thousand years ago. Ants and honey bees provide food for winter; but just in the same way they did

when Solomon referred the sluggard to them as patterns of prudence. Man is not the only animal who labors; but he is the only one who improves his workmanship.

Korzybski, an immigrant to America, called his theory "time-binding." Because time-binding is fully compatible with the great religions and science, it can be the foundation of a new American ethic.

Korzybski said that there are three primary classes of life: plants, animals, and human beings; and each of these classes can be distinguished according to its function.

Plants take in energy from the sun and the atmosphere and convert it into chemical elements and compounds through the process of photosynthesis. The chemicals are released back to the atmosphere or stored and later converted into growth and plant tissue; and thus plants may be called the *chemical-binding* class of life.

Animals take in stored energy from plants and other animals, and from the atmosphere, and use it for mobility. Animals are the *space-binding* class of life, because unlike plants, they can voluntarily move about in terrestrial space—they can roam about over the land or in the sea in search of food (energy).

Human beings use stored chemical energy and the ability to move over the land to discover and develop knowledge and information. Human knowledge is stored in the minds of individuals and in books and other media, and is passed with the aid of language to the next generation. This process creates new sources of energy: for example, the applied knowledge of plant cultivation produces more food energy than would otherwise be available. By storing knowledge and information, the achievements of each generation are passed to the next generation, which in turn adds its own achievements and passes them on to its descendants, and so on, as in the case of fire. Thus, as a species, we have a degree of interdependence that is greater by far than that of any animal. Consider the millions of human beings who would not be alive today were it not for the medical knowledge (of such procedures as vaccination, for example) discovered and passed on by bygone generations. Not only do we depend on those now living, we also depend on the countless individuals of the past; and future generations depend on us. Because we have this special ability, this unique capacity to advance through time, we are the *time-binding class of life*.

Humans, as time-binders, do not differ in kind from animals, but in dimension, just as a square and a cube are the same kind of figure but different in dimension. Through our special ability to utilize the time dimension, we have achieved a level of existence unknown to that of the beasts. Of course, it is possible that animals may also have a limited capacity to bind time; but if so, then it must be at a negligible rate. It is our unique, unmatched rate that sets us apart. If all that we have gained in the course of time—art, industry, language, philosophy, religion, and science—were to be suddenly taken away from us, it would be impossible for an outside observer to distinguish between our behavior and that of the beasts. In large measure, time-binding is what makes human beings *human*.

It seems evident that Korzybski's theory has important social implications. Consider the ethical question of whether egoism comes before altruism. Egoism seems to come first for animals because, as Herbert Spencer said, "A creature must live before it can act"; but does it come first for the time-binding class of life? Korzybski said no. Human beings, because of our time-binding capacity, are not finders but *creators* of food and shelter, which is why we are able to live in such vast numbers. Thus we must act first (by utilizing our time-binding ability) in order to be able to live. Otherwise, said Korzybski, if we were to live in complete accord with the animalistic view of humankind, time-binding production would cease and ninety percent of humankind would perish by starvation. For the human race, it's not inevitably a "dog eat dog world"; we have the capacity and opportunity to act otherwise.

For the society that adopts it, Korzybski's theory could provide a secure, rational foundation for ethical behavior, an ethics based on the verifiable fact of human interdependence in time and space. If taught well in the schools, the theory could transform the whole outlook of our culture. As the mathematician Cassius J. Keyser said, the future depends in large part both upon what we human beings *are* and in equal or greater measure upon what we *think we are.*

We are the time-binding class of life.

FURTHER READING

Criticism

Acklom, George Moreby. "The Cleavage between Science and Human Activities." *The New York Times* (11 February 1934): 4, 14.

Discusses Korzybski's strategy to save civilization through mathematics and psychiatry.

Bois, J. Samuel. "Korzybski's Living Logic." *Etc.* 32, No. 2 (June 1975): 165-68.

Praises Korzybski's philosophy in a discussion of the evolution of human thought away from the subjective and toward the objective.

Boyd, Christopher. "Piaget and Korzybski: Parallels." *Etc.* 43, No. 1 (Spring 1986): 47-51.

Discusses Piaget's theory of child development in relation to Korzybski's principles of probability and identity.

Breitwieser, J. V. A review of *The Manhood of Humanity. Journal of Philosophy* XIX, No. 11 (25 May 1922): 301-3.

Mostly favorable review of *The Manhood of Humanity* that examines the nature of human intelligence and Korzybski's vision of a harmonious human civilization.

Brewer, Joseph. "A Reminiscence of Alfred Korzybski." *Etc.* 33, No. 4 (December 1976): 377-79.

A remembrance of friendship with Korzybski and his wife, Mira, including a description of the author's search for a publisher.

Exton, William Jr. "What 'Is' GS?" *Etc.* 37, No. 4 (Winter 1980): 340-46.

Traces through a series of questions and answers the resources provided by general semantics to improve daily life.

Forsberg, Geraldine E. *Critical Thinking in an Image World: Alfred Korzybski's Theoretical Principles Extended to Critical Television Evaluation.* Lanham, Maryland: University Press of America, 1993, 208 p.

Promotes Korzybski's theories as a method for evaluating electronic images.

Fox, Roy F. "A Conversation with the Hayakawas." *Etc.* 48, No. 3 (Fall 1991): 243-50.

Highlights of Hayakawa's life as a semanticist, U.S. senator, and protégé of Korzybski.

Fritz-Bailey, Susan, and Buckalew, M. W. "Alfred Korzybski and Marcel Duchamp: A Study in Science and Art." *Etc.* 33, No. 4 (December 1976): 380-84.

Examines philosophical similarities between Korzybski and the twentieth-century Dadaist artist Marcel Duchamp with respect to their views on the failure of words to convey meaning and the existence of a fourth dimension.

Gorman, Michael E. "A. J. Korzybski, J. Krishnamurti, and Carlos Castaneda: A Modest Comparison." *Etc.* 35, No. 2 (June 1978): 162-74.

Relates Korzybski's belief that human afflictions are rooted in a misperception of the world to the writings of the philosopher J. Krishnamurti and the author Carlos Castaneda.

Johnson, Kenneth G. "Relevant?" *Etc.* 48, No. 1 (Spring 1991): 59-61.

Comments on the relevance of Korzybski's writings more than 40 years after his death.

Review of *Science and Sanity. Journal of Philosophy* XXXI, No. 3 (1 February 1934): 80-1.

Discusses *Science and Sanity* as a work with some notable insights into mathematics but one that is ultimately undermined by the author's inadequate scholarship.

MacNeal, Edward. "Semantics and Decision Making." *Etc.* 40, No. 2 (Summer 1983): 158-76.

Examines the constraints of imprecise language as they affect the way decisions are made.

Postman, Neil. "The Limits of Language." *Etc.* 43, No. 3 (Fall 1986): 227-33.

Reviews the major themes in Korzybski's work and assesses their impact.

Pula, Robert P. "Alfred Korzybski—*Collected Writings: 1920-1950.* An Appreciation and a Review." *Etc.* 48, No. 2 (Winter 1991-1992): 424-33.

Favorably reviews a selection from Korzybski's papers, transcripts, reviews, and books.

Read, Allen Walker. "The Relation of Semiotics to General Semantics." *Etc.* 44, No. 3 (Fall 1987): 291-92.

Provides explanations for the recurrent terms used by Korzybski to describe his theories.

Temple, G. Review of *Science and Sanity. Philosophy* X, No. 38 (April 1935): 245-47.

Contends that much of *Science and Sanity* is unintelligi-

ble to anyone without a detailed knowledge of all the social sciences.

Winters, Warrington. "Korzybski in the Shadow of War."
Etc. XXXI, No. 4 (December 1974): 425-27.
　　Recollects attendance in a class taught by Korzybski in
　　1941 on the eve of Germany's invasion of Russia.

Additional coverage of Korzybski's life and works is contained in the following source published by Gale Research: *Contemporary Authors*, Vol. 123.

The Rainbow

D. H. Lawrence

The following entry presents criticism of Lawrence's novel *The Rainbow*. For information on Lawrence's complete career, see *TCLC*, Volumes 2 and 9. For discussion of *Sons and Lovers*, see *TCLC*, Volume 16; for discussion of *Women in Love*, see *TCLC*, Volume 33; for discussion of *Lady Chatterley's Lover*, see *TCLC*, Volume 48.

INTRODUCTION

An outstanding figure among twentieth-century modernist writers, Lawrence is known for his novels that explore the nature of self-fulfillment, relationships between men and women, and the conflicts that arise between individuals and society. *The Rainbow* (1915) was one of Lawrence's first novels to examine these themes, and is considered, along with its sequel *Women in Love* (1920), to be one of the writer's greatest works. An amalgamation of symbolic narrative, bildungsroman, and psychoanalytic novel, the work is seen as both Lawrence's prophetic vision of the possibility of renewal in society and a scathing critique of modern civilization.

Plot and Major Characters

The Rainbow opens with a description of the traditional, rural way of life in mid-nineteenth century England on Marsh Farm, the Brangwen family land situated near the Midlands town of Ilkeston. Tom Brangwen, a farmer ruled by his instincts rather than his intellect and marked by an inner emotional turmoil, marries Lydia Lensky, a Polish widow whose "foreignness" he finds particularly attractive. Their marriage, while loving, is characterized by a vague emotional detachment, punctuated by moments of fervent passion. When their child, the proud and somewhat aloof Anna, reaches adulthood she marries her cousin, Will Brangwen, a lace-designer whose frustrated artistic temperament soon becomes the defining aspect of his character. Their intensely sexual relationship mirrors in part that of Anna's parents, and like Tom and Lydia's is dominated by a constant struggle of wills. After a tumultuous first year of marriage their eldest daughter, Ursula, is born. She, like her father, is artistically sensitive and fascinated by the symbolism of Christianity. While still young she enters into a relationship with Anton Skrebensky, a young officer in the corps of engineers, who she learns does not share her ardent spirituality. Their affair temporarily ends when Ursula returns to teaching and Anton leaves to fight in the South African Boer War. In his absence Ursula has an abortive homosexual relationship with Winifred Inger, a fellow teacher, whom Ursula later convinces to marry her uncle, the younger Tom Brangwen, a manager at the colliery at Wiggiston. Accepting a teaching post at the Brinsley Street School, Ursula moves to Ilkeston, but her ordeals there and later at

Nottingham University College leave her disillusioned with modern education. When Anton returns, six years after his departure, he asks Ursula to marry him. The engagement ends in failure primarily because of Ursula's feeling that he lacks a passion to match her own. Soon after, Anton marries another woman and leaves for India. Subsequently learning that she is pregnant, Ursula discovers a renewed love for Anton and writes to him, asking for forgiveness. At the end of the novel she is nearly run down by a drove of galloping horses. Fearful for her safety, she escapes from danger by climbing a nearby tree. The incident causes her to miscarry the child. While ill Ursula receives a cable from Anton declaring that he has married, which serves as tacit proof that the relationship is over. Sitting at her window, Ursula then sees a rainbow that seems to sweep away the corruption of the world around her and afford the hope of regeneration in the future.

Major Themes

While no critical agreement exists as to the precise thematic structure of *The Rainbow*, the forces at work are generally seen as a conflict between masculine and feminine, played out within the contexts of a larger antagonism, that of the individual personality versus modern society. The male Brangwens, Tom and Will, represent the instinctual and spiritual sides of humanity; they contrast with the female Brangwens, who are prone to intellectualization and abstraction. The result of these consistently opposed forces is played out in the sexual relationships of the characters. In broader terms, *The Rainbow* also levels a critique against modern industrial society, which Lawrence dramatizes as destructive and dehumanizing. This commentary is apparent throughout the novel, and personified in the almost soulless characters of Ursula's uncle, the younger Tom Brangwen, and his wife Winifred Inger. Along with these issues is the problem of spiritual and emotional self-fulfillment that Lawrence addresses primarily in the character and actions of Ursula. As the representative of three generations of the Brangwen family, she symbolizes both an overall decline in the success of male/female relationships, and—in her perception of the rainbow at the close of the novel—a hope for reconciliation, harmony, and fullness of being.

Critical Reception

The Rainbow was refused by Lawrence's publisher and appeared only after he had rewritten some passages and excised others that the new publisher considered too sexually explicit. Even in its revised form the novel was suppressed in England as obscene. After publication, the work met with some staunch criticism, especially in reaction to its style. Arnold Kettle has since written that the "intensity [of the writing] leads to an overwrought quality," while other commentators have leveled accusations of "emotional falsity" at the end of the novel, or simply of "bad writing." Likewise, many have observed that the quality of Lawrence's writing deteriorates in the second half of the novel. In more recent years, however, these assessments have been ignored or overturned by critics who emphasize the innovative nature of *The Rainbow*. In his oft-quoted letter to his publisher Edward Garnett, Lawrence wrote, "You mustn't look in my novel for the old stable *ego* of the character"; rather, Lawrence claimed to have been searching for a new way to express emotion. This new form has been hailed as revolutionary, but has also lead many critics to call *The Rainbow* ambiguous or imprecise, and left certain aspects of the novel—particularly Ursula's encounter with the horses and the appearance of the rainbow in later portions of the novel—open to multiple interpretations. The ensuing controversies over interpretation and a new-found approval for modernist experimentation have elevated *The Rainbow* from its initial notoriety to the level of a modern classic.

CRITICISM

Solomon Eagle (review date 1915)

SOURCE: A review of *The Rainbow*, in *New Statesman*, Vol. VI, No. 137, November 20, 1915, p. 161.

[*In the following review, Eagle criticizes* The Rainbow *as "dull and monotonous," but defends the novel against censors.*]

Last Saturday, at Bow Street, Mr. D. H. Lawrence's new novel ***The Rainbow*** was brought before the bench and sentenced to death. Who lodged an information against the book I don't know. It is conceivable, at a time when the patriotism of our criminals must leave our policemen plenty of leisure, that some cultured constable may have got hold of the work and rushed to his superiors with it. But it is likelier that the prosecution was the work of some Society or individual set upon Mr. Lawrence's track by one of the violent attacks upon the book which appeared in the Press. Two of these attacks figured in court, those of Mr. James Douglas and Mr. Clement Shorter. The prosecution attached much importance to them and the magistrate blamed the publishers for not withdrawing the book as a direct result of these gentlemen's criticisms. And both these critics as well as counsel for the prosecution and the magistrate himself talked a good deal of hyperbolical nonsense.

Some qualification must be made with regard to Mr. Douglas and Mr. Shorter. Mr. Douglas is a man with a genius for invective which I myself heartily appreciate when it is aimed at politicians whom I don't like—and who, incidentally, are never impounded and destroyed by the police as the result of his attacks. It is a weakness of Mr. Douglas to turn sometimes his powers of epigrammatic vituperation against books which he considers obscene. The last time that I remember him doing it the book in question was a volume of boring, erotic, old-fashioned verse (all about breasts, purple lips, etc.) which would have attracted no attention at all had he left it alone. On the present occasion he was irritated by seeing a man like Mr. Lawrence wasting his powers, and fairly let himself go about the obscenity of ***The Rainbow***. Mr. Shorter, again, to do him justice, appears to be hostile to censorship, and, in the middle of his abuse, remarked that Mr. Lawrence's book would have "served one good purpose" in that "the next writer of a piece of frank, free literature who is an artist will assuredly run no risk of a police prosecution." All the same both critics carried their language to an indefensible pitch. Mr. Shorter said that "Zola's novels are child's food compared with the strong meat" in the book. He did not personally charge Mr. Lawrence "with a deliberate attempt to provide nastiness for commercial purposes"; but he had unfortunately said quite enough to put the hounds upon the scent. His reservations were little good in court. The prosecuting counsel, Mr. Muskett, referred to the book as "this bawdy volume"; and the magistrate, Sir John Dickinson, described it as "utter filth" and said that he had "never read anything more disgusting than this book."

Mr. Muskett we may pass over. Various kinds of lawyers affect various kinds of language. In the case of the magistrate one can only be astonished. I am quite unacquainted with Sir John Dickinson's antecedents. For all I know he may have been Mother-Superior of a Convent before he was translated to the more lucrative but less secluded position that he now graces. But if he has never seen anything more disgusting than *The Rainbow,* all I can say is that he cannot be familiar with many books that are sold in this country and that he must be abysmally ignorant of the literatures of our two Allies, France and Great White Russia. For the critics the excuse of ignorance cannot be advanced. That influential critics, with the interests of literature—not to speak of the livings of authors—in their charge should let loose as Mr. Shorter did is unpardonable. *The Rainbow,* he says, is "strong meat" compared with Zola. Did he ever read *La Terre?* Of course he did! He must have known that he was talking rubbish. People who dislike censorships should not go miles out of their way to assist censors.

Now, I am not arguing the whole of censorship. Most people will agree that there is a point at which the police must interfere: we can all imagine things, in our heads, which certainly ought not to be written down and exposed for sale. And I am not maintaining that *The Rainbow* is a great work of art. Its author has a strain of genius, but in this novel he is at his worst. It is a dull and monotonous book which broods gloomily over the physical reactions of sex in a way so persistent that one wonders whether the author is under the spell of German psychologists, and so tedious that a perusal of it might send Casanova himself into a monastery, if he did not go to sleep before his revulsion against sex was complete. I think it a bad novel: and it contains opinions unpalatable to me and tendencies that I personally believe to be unhealthy. But in the first place it is very much to be doubted whether, the good faith of the book being evident, censorship in this case was desirable; in the second place if *The Rainbow* is to be interfered with there are scores of other books that demand prior attention; and in the third place it is doing Mr. Lawrence common justice to protest against the way in which his name has been dragged through the mud. How many of those who read the criticisms and gloated over the police court proceedings will realise that he is an uncommercial young writer who, whatever he may write, writes it as he does because of an earnestness which is almost awe-inspiring? It will be no consolation to him that many people, who look on in smug silence whenever a distinguished writer is stigmatized as bawdy, will treasure up his name and rush to buy his next novel when it appears. Critics really should try to keep their sense of proportion.

But on the whole, I suppose, we ought to thank our stars that the censorship in this country is not worse than it is. It is really very seldom that the police act, and when they do they do not act very thoroughly. Once it was Zola; but you can now buy him anywhere. Another time it was Balzac: but the *Contes Drôlatiques* have not, in spite of a horrified bench, disappeared from the booksellers' catalogues. We might be much worse off. If one took the trouble to start prosecutions one could certainly get scores of books condemned each year: there would be not the slightest difficulty about getting judgment, for it is the easiest thing in the world to make a magistrate blush. And the public would be no more excited than it was about the Dramatic Censorship. The larger public gets the kind of literature it wants and is happy. There was a jolly example of it, words and music, in Lord Northcliffe's *Weekly Dispatch* last Sunday. It is a song. It outlines the healing qualities of love. And it has this beautiful, beautiful, beautiful chorus:

> All the time you're living, do a little loving,
>   Just a little loving ev'ry day, all the day!
> You've not started living, till you've started loving,
>   So, just start the loving right away.
>   For life is short;
>   No one ought
>   To throw an opportunity away.
>   Ev'ry day, late or early,
>   Take an armful of girlie;
>   When you've found her,
>   Just cuddle round her,
>   Do a little loving ev'ry daa-a-a-y.

That is how we really like it put.

John Middleton Murry   (essay date 1931)

SOURCE: *"The Rainbow,"* in *Son of Woman: The Story of D. H. Lawrence,* Jonathan Cape & Harrison Smith, 1931, pp. 59-75.

[*In the following essay, Murry focuses on the theme of sexual conflict in* The Rainbow.]

In *The Rainbow* is [an] . . . intimate record of the experience confessed in *Look! We Have Come Through!* The correspondence is exact and unmistakable. The story of Anna Lensky and Will Brangwen is, in essentials, the story of [Lawrence's] poems; but the story is told more richly, and more fearfully. I know nothing more beautiful or more powerful in all Lawrence's writing than the opening of the long chapter ominously entitled "Anna Victrix." It describes their "honeymoon"; the rebirth of the shy and shamefaced man in a long world-forgetful ecstasy of passion with a carefree, beautiful, passionate, unashamedly physical woman.

> *She* didn't care. *She* didn't care in the least. Then why should he? Should he be behind her in recklessness and independence? She was superb in her indifference. He wanted to be like her.

Lawrence's favourite image comes to him to describe his new felicity. "Suddenly, like a chestnut falling out of a burr, he was shed naked and glistening on to a soft, fecund earth, leaving behind him the hard rind of worldly knowledge and experience." He is surrendered to the woman utterly: he gives himself up into her keeping.

> She got up at ten o'clock, and quite blithely went to bed again at three, or at half-past four, stripping him naked in the daylight, and all so gladly and perfectly, oblivious quite of his qualms. He let her do as she liked with him, and shone with strange pleasure. She was to dispose of him as she would. He was translated with gladness to be in her hands. And down went his qualms, his maxims, his rules, his smaller beliefs, she scattered them like an expert skittle-player. He was very much astonished and delighted to see them scatter.

We are, we have learned to be, afraid in Lawrence of that yielding of himself to the woman's leading. It is delightful, it is ecstasy; but it is also, to him, humiliation. We look for the reaction. It comes with sickening speed. "Shame at his own dependence upon her drove him to anger. . . . Driven by fear of her departure into a state of helplessness, almost of imbecility, he wandered about the house." And she is irritated beyond bearing by his helplessness, his clinging.

> These followed two black and ghastly days, when she was set in anguish against him, and he felt as if he were in a black, violent underworld, and his wrists quivered murderously. And she resisted him. He seemed a dark, almost evil thing, pursuing her, hanging on to her, burdening her.

The struggle becomes nightmarish, and ends in a frenzied sexual consummation. It is the story of the poem **"In the Dark,"** re-enacted in large. "He was not interested in the *thought* of himself or of her: oh, and how that irritated her. . . . The verity was his connection with Anna and his connection with the Church, his real being lay in his dark emotional experience of the Infinite, the Absolute." And as in the poem, Anna reacts in horror. "But I am myself, I have nothing to do with these."

> What did she want herself? She answered herself that she wanted to be happy, to be natural, like the sunlight and the busy daytime. And, at the bottom of her soul, she felt he wanted her to be dark, unnatural. Sometimes, when he seemed like the darkness covering and smothering her, she revolted almost in horror, and struck at him. She struck at him, and made him bleed, and he became wicked. Because she dreaded him and held him in horror, he became wicked, he wanted to destroy. And then the fight between them was cruel.

> She began to tremble. He wanted to impose himself on her. And he began to shudder. She wanted to desert him, to leave him a prey to the open, with the unclean dogs of the darkness setting on to devour him. He must beat her, and make her stay with him. Whereas she fought to keep herself free of him.

As in the poems, he does foolish, frantic things. "Frantic is sensual fear," he asserts his rights as master and as male.

> "Fool!" she answered. "Fool! I've known my own father, who could put a dozen of you in his pipe and push them down with his finger-end. Don't I know what a fool you are!"

> He knew himself what a fool he was, and was flayed by the knowledge. Yet he went on trying to steer the ship of their dual life. He asserted his position as captain of the ship. And captain and ship bored her. . . . She jeered at him as master of the house, master of their dual life. And he was black with shame and rage. He knew, with shame, how her father had been a man without arrogating any authority.

Then the story of *The Rainbow* departs from the naked facts of Lawrence's experience. Anna Brangwen is with child; she is fulfilled. But, since that is an imaginary fulfil-

ment, the struggle goes on, ever more fearful, and always the same.

> Then she turned fiercely on him, and fought him. . . . What horrible hold did he want to have over her body? Why did he want to drag her down, and kill her spirit? Why did he want to deny her spirit? Why did he deny her spirituality, hold her for a body only? . . .

> Some vast hideous darkness he seemed to represent to her.

> "What do you do to me?" she cried. "What beastly thing do you do to me? . . . There is something horrible in you, something dark and beastly in your will. What do you want of me? What do you want to do to me? . . . "

> He hated her for what she said. Did he not give her everything, was she not everything to him? And the shame was a bitter fire in him, that she was everything to him, that he had nothing but her. And then that she should taunt him with it, that he could not escape! The fire went black in his veins. For try as he might, he could not escape. She was everything to him, she was his life and his derivation. He depended on her. If she were taken away, he would collapse as a house from which the central pillar is removed.

> And she hated him, because he depended on her so utterly. He was horrible to her. . . . It was horrible that he should cleave to her, so close, so close, like a leopard that had leapt on her, and fastened.

> He went on from day to day in a blackness of rage and shame and frustration. How he tortured himself, to be able to get away from her. But he could not. She was as the rock on which he stood, with deep, heaving water all round, and he was unable to swim. He *must* take his stand on her, he must depend on her.

> What had he in life, save her? Nothing. The rest was a great heaving flood. The terror of the night of heaving, overwhelming flood, which was his vision of life without her, was too much for him. He clung to her fiercely, and abjectly. . . .

> He wanted to leave her, he wanted to be able to leave her. For his soul's sake, for his manhood's sake, he must be able to leave her.

> But for what? . . . The only tangible, secure thing was the woman. He could leave her only for another woman. And where was the other woman, and who was the other woman? Besides, he would be in just the same state. Another woman would be woman, the case would be the same.

"He could leave her only for another woman. . . . Another woman would be woman, the case would be the same." There is the adamantine fact, the grim and fatal destiny. He is ruthless in his self-knowledge. The naked confession goes on.

> The only other way to leave her was to die. The only straight way to leave her was to die. His

dark raging soul knew that. But he had no desire for death. . . .

A woman, he must have a woman. And having a woman, he must be free of her. It would be the same position. For he could not be free of her.

For how can a man stand, unless he have something sure under his feet? . . . And upon what could he stand, save upon a woman? Was he then like the old man of the seas, impotent to move save upon the back of another life? Was he impotent, or a cripple, or a defective, or a fragment?

It was black, mad, shameful torture, the frenzy of fear, the frenzy of desire, and the horrible, grasping back-wash of shame.

The quotation is long; but it cannot be avoided. It takes us, with pitiless intimacy, closer to the core of Lawrence's strange and fearful experience than anything he has yet written.

In the story, Will Brangwen escapes from the horror which, it seems, he cannot escape. Anna, at last, finds the oppressive darkness of his physical contact unbearable. She makes him sleep alone. He is so wretched, that she takes him back; and again it is too much for her. She sends him away again. "He went and lay down alone. And at length, after a grey and livid and ghastly period, he relaxed, something gave way in him."

So he reached a sort of rebirth. It consists in the fact that "he could sleep with her, and let her be." But it is claimed as a veritable rebirth.

He could be alone now. He had just learned what it was to be able to be alone. It was right and peaceful. She had given him a new deeper freedom. The world might be a welter of uncertainty, but he was himself now. He had come into his new existence. He was born for a second time, born at last unto himself, out of the vast body of humanity. Now at last he had a separate identity, he existed alone, even if he were not quite alone. Before he had only existed in so far as he had relations with another being. Now he had an absolute self—as well as a relative one.

But we cannot be deceived. This is the experience of the child who no longer sleeps in his mother's bed, but in a room alone. "To have learned to be alone," for a man, is an incomparably sterner experience; that death, for which "he had no desire." An absolute self is hardly to be had at a lesser price; and even in the story, the dawn is a false dawn. Will Brangwen cannot believe in himself, apart from Anna. In the end, he is as he was. "In the long run he learned to submit to Anna. She forced him to the spirit of her laws, while leaving him the letter of his own." The dark, destructive rage comes on him as before. "Their fights were horrible, murderous. And then the passion between them came just as black and awful." But a certain human wisdom arose between them. She left him alone in his rage, and he struggled to submit to her, "for at last he learned that he would be in hell until he came back to her."

But she has destroyed his belief in himself, and his belief absolutely. She has undermined his own separate creative purpose. He has lost faith in his own ideal, his own vital illusions. In their symbolic visit to Lincoln Cathedral, Anna deliberately shatters her husband's passionate ecstasy in the pure upsurge of the building by insisting upon the gargoyles. The mason, she said, had carved the portrait of his detested wife. "You hate to think he put his wife in your cathedral, don't you?" And, of course Will Brangwen did hate to think it. The symbol of pure spirituality was degraded. "Yet somewhere in himself he responded more deeply to the sly little face that knew better, than he had done before to the perfect surge of his cathedral." The meaning of all this symbolism is patent. Through the woman, through sex, the spiritual ideal is destroyed; and it is good that it should be destroyed. For the spiritual ideal is partial and false. It is based on the negation of sex, of the mighty principle of life itself. But Will Brangwen, in whom the old spirituality has been thus, and rightly destroyed, cannot move forward to create and embody a new harmony. He lapses into the woman, lapses and rebels, and at last is content to lapse altogether.

At this point Lawrence's own destiny is distinct from that of his creation. Will Brangwen, so to speak, is a Lawrence who has given up the effort—the effort to make the spirit and the flesh dwell together into harmony. But Lawrence, who conceived and contained him, has not given up the effort. The effort is to find the rainbow—the bright arch that spans in beauty the conflicting elements. Both Will and Anna come to have a sense of the goal; but it is not they, but their child, Ursula, who will reach it. "The child she might hold up, she might toss the child forward into the furnace, the child might walk there, amid the burning coals and the incandescent roar of heat, as the three witnesses walked with the angel in the fire."

So the story passes to the next generation. Ursula grows, and her sister Gudrun. Their final history is chronicled in *Women in Love*. In the remainder of *The Rainbow*, Gudrun is nothing, simply a small girl. Ursula becomes the chief figure, with her lover, Anton Skrebensky. Once more the sexual struggle between them is a nightmare, a worse nightmare than the sexual struggle between Anna and Will. Anton is also a spiritual man, but of a lower (or later) order of spirituality than Will Brangwen. Will is an artist, with a direct creative purpose; Anton an engineer in the army, with a consciousness of his mission as the servant of the nation. Again, he is like Lawrence: not, indeed, so like him as Will Brangwen, who apart from his paternity and his final submission was Lawrence himself; but like enough. Ursula and he together meet a man and woman who live on a canal boat.

He was envying the lean father of three children for his impudent directness and worship of the woman in Ursula, a worship of body and soul together, the man's body and soul wistful and worshipping the body and spirit of the girl. . . .

Why could not he himself desire a woman so? Why did he never want a woman, not with the whole of him; never loved, never worshipped, only just physically wanted her. But he would

Dust jacket for The Rainbow. *The dust jacket copy was probably written by Lawrence.*

want her with his body, let his soul do as it would.

The struggle begins, in these now familiar conditions. Ursula, unlike her mother, and unlike her essentially in only this, resists from the first. Not with any ordinary resistance, but with the instinctive will to entice and destroy her man. The scene in the moonlight, after the dance, becomes a phantasmagoria. Anton "was afraid of the great moon-conflagration of the corn-stacks rising above him. His heart grew smaller, and began to fuse like a bead. He knew he would die."

> She was afraid of what she was. Looking at him, at his shadowy, unreal, wavering presence a sudden lust seized her, to lay hold of him and tear him and make him into nothing. . . . She tempted him.
>
> And timorously, his hands went over her, over the salt, compact brilliance of her body. If he could but have her, how he would enjoy her! If he could but net her brilliant, cold, salt-burning body in the soft iron of his own hands, net her, capture her, hold her down, how madly he would enjoy her! . . . Obstinately, all his flesh burning and corroding, as if he were invaded by

some consuming, scathing poison, still he persisted, thinking at last he might overcome her. Even, in his frenzy, he sought her mouth with his mouth, though it was like putting his face into some awful death. . . .

> She took him in the kiss, hard her kiss seized upon him, hard and fierce and burning corrosive as the moonlight. She seemed to be destroying him. He was reeling, summoning all his strength to keep his kiss upon her, to keep himself in the kiss.
>
> But hard and fierce she had fastened upon him, cold as the moon and burning as a fierce salt. Till gradually his warm, soft iron yielded, yielded, and she was there fierce, corrosive, seething with his destruction, seething like some cruel, corrosive salt around the last substance of his being, destroying him in the kiss. And her soul crystallised with triumph, and his soul was dissolved with agony and annihilation. So she held him there, the victim, consumed, annihilated. She had triumphed: he was not any more.

The experience, as one might expect, is fatal. Though Ursula is horrified at what she has done or at what has been done through her, and is kind to him thereafter, Anton's "core is gone," it has been irreparably destroyed. "His triumphant, flaming, overweening heart of the intrinsic male would never beat again. . . . She had broken him." Rather strangely, he seems to forget about it, when he has gone off to fight in the Boer war. But we are given to understand that the killing of the intrinsic male in him, and his unhesitating acceptance of service to the state, are complementary. One nullity is corollary to the other.

With Anton's return, six years later, the struggle becomes more intense and ghastly, for now the need for physical union is upon them both. The record is difficult to follow, because it is beyond the range of ordinary experience, and also because it seems to be in itself inconsequent, without the convincing inevitability of the story of Anna and Will. At first, Anton and Ursula seem to be happy as lovers, in spite of her destruction of his "intrinsic male core" six years before. But, Lawrence insists, they are happy like two wild animals, outlaws and enemies of the light of social day. Ursula goes about "in a dark richness, her eyes dilated and shining like the eyes of a wild animal, a curious half-smile which seemed to be gibing at the civic pretence of all the human life about her"; while Anton "watched as a lion or a tiger may lie with narrowed eyes watching the people pass before its cage, the kaleidoscopic unreality of people." Both live "in the sensual sub-consciousness all the time." So for a few weeks they live together in London. Suddenly, Ursula has a desire to leave England. She insists on staying at Rouen.

> For the first time, in Rouen, he had a cold feeling of death; not afraid of any other man, but of her. She did not want him. The old streets, the cathedral, the age and monumental peace of the town took her away from him. She turned to it as if to something she had forgotten. This was now the reality; this great stone cathedral slumbering there in its mass, which knew no transience nor heard any denial. It was majestic in its stability, its splendid absoluteness.

To judge by the symbolic significance of the cathedral in the history of Will and Anna, Lawrence must have meant by this that Ursula at this crucial moment has a recoil from the sensual sub-consciousness to spirituality. From this time onward both have a premonition of "the death towards which they are wandering."

Ursula returns home. And, when she leaves him, a cold horror takes possession of Anton. "He went mad. He had lived with her in a close, living, pulsing world, where everything pulsed with rich being. Now he found himself struggling amid an ashen-dry, cold world of rigidity, dead walls and mechanical traffic, and creeping, spectre-like people." She is his one salvation from "the horror of not-being which possesses him." To marry her, "to be sure of her"—that is all. He writes to her desperately, she answers easily: his agony means nothing to her, really. But she believes she loves him. They are together again for a few days.

> She owned his body and enjoyed it with all the delight and carelessness of a possessor. But he had become gradually afraid of her body. He wanted her, he wanted her endlessly. But there had come a tension into his desire, a constraint which prevented his enjoying the delicious approach and the lovable close of the endless embrace. He was afraid. His will was always tense, fixed.

Suddenly she declares open war upon his "idealism," his democratic humanitarianism. "I'm against you, and all your old, dead things," she cries in fury. He "felt cut off at the knees, a figure made worthless." She does not esteem him. He tries to make her esteem him by flirting with other women. Then, the secret is out.

> In passionate anger she upbraided him because, not being man enough to satisfy one woman, he hung round others.
>
> "Don't I satisfy you?" he asked of her, again going white to the throat.
>
> "No," she said. "You've never satisfied me since the first week in London. You never satisfy me now. What does it mean to me, your having me—"
>
> She lifted her shoulders and turned aside her face in a motion of cold, indifferent worthlessness. He felt he would kill her.
>
> When she had aroused him to a pitch of madness, when she saw his eyes all dark and mad with suffering, then a great suffering overcame her soul, a great, inconquerable suffering. And she loved him. For oh, she wanted to love him. Stronger than life or death was her craving to be able to love him.
>
> And at such moments, when he was mad with her destroying him, when all his complacency was destroyed, all his everyday self was broken, and only the stripped, rudimentary, primal man remained, demented with torture, her passion to love him became love, she took him again, they came together in an overwhelming passion, in which he knew he satisfied her.
>
> But it all contained a developing germ of death. After each contact, her anguished desire for him or for that which she had never had from him was stronger, her love was more hopeless. After each contact his mad dependence on her was deepened, his hope of standing strong and taking her in his own strength was weakened. He felt himself a mere attribute of her.

Gradually, Anton breaks down. Ursula says she does not want to marry him, and he collapses upon himself. Yet although she is afraid of the fearful compulsion of his utter dependence upon her, tacitly she seems to have given in to marrying him. They go away together to a house by the sea as an engaged couple. The physical contact goes on, but she is indifferent. One night, once more in the presence of a great burning moon, beneath which once more Anton "felt himself fusing down into nothingness, like a bead that rapidly disappears in an incandescent flame," they reach their terrible consummation.

> Then there in the great flare of light, she clinched hold of him, hard, as if suddenly she had the strength of destruction, she fastened her arms round him and tightened him in her grip,

whilst her mouth sought his in a hard, rending, ever-increasing kiss, till his body was powerless in her grip, his heart melted in fear from the fierce, beaked, harpy's kiss. The water washed again over their feet, but she took no notice. She seemed unaware, she seemed to be pressing in her beaked mouth till she had the heart of him. Then, at last, she drew away and looked at him—looked at him. He knew what she wanted. He took her by the hand and led her across the foreshore back to the sand-hills. She went silently. He felt as if the ordeal of proof was upon him, for life or death. He led her to a dark hollow.

"No, here," she said, going out to the slope full under the moonshine. She lay motionless, with wide-open eyes looking at the moon. He came direct to her, without preliminaries. She held him pinned down at the chest, awful. The fight, the struggle for consummation was terrible. It lasted till it was agony to his soul, till he succumbed, till he gave way as if dead, and lay with his face buried, partly in her hair, partly in the sand, motionless, as if he would be motionless now for ever, hidden away in the dark, buried, only buried, he only wanted to be buried in the goodly darkness, only that, and no more.

This is the end. Anton has failed at the proof. Ursula lies in a cold agony of un-satisfaction, and he creeps away a broken man.

To discover all that underlies this fearful encounter, we should have to go to *Lady Chatterley's Lover,* to Mellors' account of his sexual experience with Bertha Coutts. That is, in the present state of affairs, unquotable. But in that page and a half the curious will find not only the naked physical foundation—"the blind beakishness"—of this experience of Ursula and Anton, but also Lawrence's final account of the sexual experience from which both the sexual experience of Will and Anna, and of Anton and Ursula is derived. *The Rainbow* is, radically, the history of Lawrence's final sexual failure.

It is much beside that; but that it is. And unless we grasp the fact, the inward meaning of *The Rainbow* and its sequel, *Women in Love,* must be concealed from us. One shrinks from the necessity of thus laying bare the physical secrets of a dead man; but in the case of Lawrence we have no choice. To the last he conceived it as his mission to teach us the way to sexual regeneration, and he claimed to give the world the ultimate truth about sex. If we take him seriously, we must take his message seriously. Continually, in his work we are confronted with sexual experience of a peculiar kind; it is quite impossible to ignore it. The work of a great man, as Lawrence was, is always an organic whole. If we shrink from following the vital thread of experience from which it all derives, then we shrink from him altogether. It is all or nothing, with such a man as Lawrence; and, since it must not be nothing, it must be all.

The Rainbow is the story of Lawrence's sexual failure. The two men, who have succumbed to the woman, are one man—himself. The rainbow, in the symbolic sense of a harmony between spirit and flesh, is as far away as ever at the end of the book. It shines over the first generation,

where man is really man, and does not need to arrogate authority over woman; it begins to be remote in the second, where the woman begins to establish the mastery; in the third, where woman is not only "victrix" but "triumphans," it fades into the dim future. Ursula, the woman, becomes the protagonist; the man is secondary, an attribute of the woman. Nevertheless, Ursula is an unconvincing character in *The Rainbow.* She is a composite figure, made of the hated sexual woman, and of some of Lawrence's own manly experiences. Thus she is made to carry much of his experience as a schoolmaster, and of his own disappointment with the university; and more important, she is made to undergo a sort of physical-mystical experience, an annihilation of the personality. When in the last chapter the horses stampede upon her, she dies, and rises again in a new world: she becomes the mouthpiece of Lawrence's own visions.

The chief vision of which she is the vehicle is the vision of the darkness with which the conscious, personal, deliberate, social life of mankind is surrounded.

> This inner circle of light in which she lived and moved . . . suddenly seemed like the area under an arc-lamp, wherein the moths and the children played in the security of blinding light, not even knowing there was any darkness, because they stayed in the light. . . .

> Nevertheless the darkness wheeled round about, with grey shadow-shapes of wild beasts, and also with dark shadow-shapes of the angels, whom the light fenced out, as it fenced out the more familiar beasts of darkness. And some, having for a moment seen the darkness, saw it bristling with the tufts of the hyæna and the wolf; and some, having given up their vanity of the light, having died in their own conceit, saw the gleam in the eyes of the wolf and hyæna, that it was the flash of the sword of angels, flashing at the door to come in, that the angels in the darkness were lordly and terrible and not to be denied, like the flash of fangs.

It is not easy to be sure what Lawrence means by this. Is the surrounding darkness the darkness of "the sensual sub-consciousness" which Ursula and Anton inhabited like wild animals? Or is it that darkness whose "unclean dogs" Will Brangwen feared would devour him if Anna left him? Or are both these darknesses the same darkness? Is this darkness beneficent, or is it horrible?—creative, or destroying?

It would be hard to say. For this conception of the surrounding "darkness," which will return in many forms in Lawrence's work, is an intensely personal conception. It derives, once more, from his peculiar experience. It is the darkness of pure animality as conceived and experienced by an intensely spiritual man. It is, therefore, essentially a horrible darkness of sin and evil, the enemy and destroyer of the light. To explore it, to surrender to it, is for Lawrence a self-violation, a perversity. Of this deliberate and willed surrender to the horror of darkness, the woman really knows nothing; because the woman is not spiritual. To her, what darkness she knows is warm and natural.

Her darkness is not the same as his, because she is not divided. In the religious phrase, she has no sense of sin.

Therefore, to represent her in Ursula as realising the horror and majesty of the darkness is false. Neither the conception nor the experience belongs to her at all. All that she knows of this darkness comes to her from and through the man. She represents that darkness to him; indeed she *is* that darkness to him: but she is completely unconscious of it. That the man should regard her as the creature and embodiment of *his* darkness horrifies her. She repudiates it utterly. She does not belong to his darkness at all. She recoils instinctively away. The truth of the whole strange situation is in the momentous poem **"In the Dark,"** where she cries:

> *"I am afraid of you, I am afraid, afraid!*
> *There is something in you destroys me—!"*

And it is so. His darkness is necessarily death to her. For she is the real animal, unconscious of evil; but he is a spiritual man, willing himself into animality, into a deadly darkness, which if once she really entered, her innocent integrity would be shattered, and she would be destroyed.

This profound conflict is terrible indeed. The man is trying to compel the woman out of her own innocent darkness into the utterly different darkness of depravity. Neither he nor she knows quite what is happening; but he knows far better than she. She is simply conscious of a horror from which she shrinks. And in creating the character of Ursula in **The Rainbow,** Lawrence has begun an effort of imaginative duplicity which will be decisive. For, in creating Ursula, he makes the woman a denizen of his darkness, not of her own; and he makes her in the final pages consciously submit herself and do homage to the darkness in which she would die. Ursula Brangwen of **The Rainbow,** is, in fact, a completely incredible character. She is the woman who accepts the man's vision of herself; accepts it, believes in it, and obeys it. She therefore, becomes a monster, a chimaera.

Only in **Women in Love** does Ursula Brangwen really come alive; and then she is manifestly her mother, Anna Brangwen, continued from the point at which her imaginary child-bearing began. She becomes the Woman who is constant in Lawrence's books—the Woman whom Lawrence can never really understand, the innocent sensual woman, whom he can only watch and wonder at, love and hate, and cleave to until the end.

Roger Sale (essay date 1959)

SOURCE: "The Narrative Technique of *The Rainbow,*" in *Modern Fiction Studies,* Vol. V, No. 1, Spring, 1959, pp. 29-38.

[*In the following essay, Sale analyzes Lawrence's use of an original narrative technique in* The Rainbow, *while commenting on "the marked inferiority" of the second half of the novel.*]

> You mustn't look in my novel for the old stable ego of the character. There is another ego, according to whose action the individual is unre-

cognisable, and passes through, as it were, allotropic states which it needs a deeper sense than any we've been used to exercise, to discover are states of the same single radically unchanged element.

This passage of a letter from D. H. Lawrence to Edward Garnett is often cited in connection with **The Rainbow,** the novel to which it presumably refers. Yet the task of finding literary means to break down "the old stable ego of character" would seem to be difficult, and it is surprising that no one, at least to the best of my knowledge, has ever attempted to analyze thoroughly the narrative method of **The Rainbow** to see if and how the expression of this "deeper sense" is possible. We may have become so accustomed to interior monologues, objectifications of dream images, and other ways of accomplishing similar tasks that Lawrence's method, which is certainly unique, may have been accepted as accomplished fact before its constituent features have been identified.

The result of this silence might not be of any great importance were the problem a strictly aesthetic one. But despite the considerable attention that has been paid to various features of the novel, **The Rainbow** remains a relatively undefined quantity. Even worse, the reasons for the marked inferiority of the second half, the fact of which is widely enough accepted, have never been stated. This essay is designed not only to identify the narrative method of **The Rainbow** but also to find a measure of this achievement by discussing when and how the novel begins to deteriorate.

"Rhythm" is a critical term used to denote any movement which is not cumbersome, and I use the term in connection with **The Rainbow** only because the usual references to "continuity" and "blood consciousness" give no indication of the basic movements in the novel. There is the same general rhythm in a sentence or a paragraph that there is in the large movements from generation to generation, and it is this essential unity of movement that enables Lawrence to break down the "old stable ego" and to assert the existence of a "deeper sense" beneath.

The simplest declarative sentence is one of the main aids the novelist has in building up a stable ego, an identity. For instance: "Morel found the photograph standing on the chiffonier in the parlor. He came out with it between his thick thumb and finger" (**Sons and Lovers**). This makes no reference to egos at all, yet whatever qualities these sentences give to Morel, they are his and his alone. A series of such statements, especially if they form a pattern, create a "character," a stable ego, however ill-defined this identity may be. In the short conversation that follows between Morel and his wife about the photograph of William's girl, Lawrence builds up a character by virtue of the fact that Morel is separate from his wife, and that he has his own attitudes and ways of speaking. We may infer the Morels' relationship from this conversation, but we do this on the basis of what we know of each person individually.

If we turn to a passage in **The Rainbow,** we can show how Lawrence tries there to break down this natural building-up process: "And she loved the intent, far look of his eyes when they rested on her: intent, yet far, not near, not with her. And she wanted to bring them near. She wanted his eyes to come to hers, to know her. And they would not." This is from "Anna Victrix," the chapter that describes the early months of the marriage of Anna and Will Brangwen in their little cottage. Some differences between this passage and that quoted above from *Sons and Lovers* are clear immediately. It is not enough to be content with saying that one is external and objective and the other internal and subjective. The difficulty we have with the passage from *The Rainbow* is that we know nothing about the time in which it takes place. The verbs seem as though they would be, in a language that provided it, in the imperfect tense. The force of this is achieved by the simple "when," which gains the sense of "whenever" as the action proceeds without being temporally specified.

The issue becomes more complex in the next paragraph:

> Then immediately she began to retaliate on him. She too was a hawk. If she imitated the pathetic plover running plaintive to him, that was part of the game. When he, satisfied, moved with a proud, insolent slough of the body and a half-contemptuous drop of the head, unaware of her, ignoring her very existence, after taking his fill of her and getting his satisfaction of her, her soul roused, its pinions became like steel, and she struck at him. When he sat on his perch glancing sharply round with solitary pride, pride eminent and fierce, she dashed at him and threw him from his station savagely, she goaded him from his keen dignity of a male, she harassed him from his unperturbed pride, till he was mad with rage, his light brown eyes burned with fury, they saw her now, like flames of anger they flared at her and recognized her as the enemy.

Here we have a combination of the imperfect "when," which removes the action from a specific time, and the metaphor of the hawks, which removes the action from its immediate spatial context. In establishing a causal "when he, then she" relationship, Lawrence breaks down the specific time and replaces it with a tight unity of the two figures at a general time. This effect is enforced by the metaphor. Will sits on his perch; he is mounted on his wife. But in making "perch" and the subsequent "station" metaphorical, Lawrence makes the relationship metaphorical. Will is thus perched on Anna not only physically; he is generally in a position from which Anna can "goad him from his keen dignity of a male."

In the next short paragraph all time and space are missing: "Very good, she was the enemy, very good. As he prowled round her, she watched him. As he struck at her, she struck back." It is difficult to imagine another novel in which the complete withdrawal could be justified, and it is justified here only because the barriers between specific and general time and space have been gradually broken down in the preceding paragraphs. Here Will and Anna are only hawks, divorced from everything except themselves. This is followed by: "He was angry because she had carelessly pushed away his tools so that they got rusty. 'Don't leave them littering in my way, then,' she said. 'I shall leave them where I like,' he cried. 'Then I shall throw them where I like!' " This is the same kind of world as that

of *Sons and Lovers*; the time and place are unspecified but fixed. It is impossible to know how we arrived here or how much time has elapsed since the dialogue on the preceding page or since the scene in bed. By the end of the next paragraph, we have returned to general time and space: "They would fight it out." The force of this little dialogue comes in part from the fact that we must, despite its obvious specificity, see this too as a metaphor, part of a larger pattern, an action that may well have been repeated in essence many times.

Thus, in less than a page, we move from an action unspecified in time and space, to one in which time and space are ambivalent, to one in which they do not exist, to one in which they are very much present, and back again to one where they are unspecified. We learn not only about particular events, but also about a world in which there is nothing but Will and Anna. It is not enough to say that the particular here is an analogue for the general, because that is true in almost any novel. Will Brangwen ceases to be, for a time, a single person performing acts in a time sequence, and becomes part of something apart from time and of which Anna is a part. As the events become more generalized, the things that are not integral parts of the relationship gradually disappear. It is for this reason that scenes in *The Rainbow* always seem longer than they are. Time is suspended, we leave a scene only to return to it, we learn with some surprise that morning or evening or Sunday comes because much that takes place seems to be happening outside of time.

This constant movement in time continuums, which is the essential narrative technique of *The Rainbow,* allows Lawrence to describe a large segment of time very quickly, and this, in turn, creates the impression that no time is left undescribed, that the sequence of events and relationships is never broken but is only made either more or less definite temporally. For instance, Lawrence says that when Anna was nine years old, she went to the dames' school in Cossethay. Soon she is "about ten," and two pages later she is a "lofty demoiselle of sixteen." But we feel that no time has been skipped, that Lawrence is able to choose his definite times because the indefinite time is so full. The paragraphs which describe Anna from nine to sixteen begin with such sentences as "For at the Marsh life had indeed a certain freedom and largeness," "So Anna was only easy at home, where the common sense and the supreme relation between her parents produced a freer standard of being than she could find outside," "At school, or in the world, she was usually at fault, she felt usually that she ought to be slinking in disgrace," and "Still she kept an ideal: a free, proud lady absolved from the petty ties, existing beyond petty considerations." The paragraphs are never complete in themselves; the same subject is approached from a number of different angles and, presumably, at a number of different positions in time. The effect is of great movement, yet of a constant thread of "unstable ego" unifying the movement.

It is only after we have noticed this "rhythm" in particular scenes and series of actions that we can see the rhythm of the larger components of the novel, the movements from one generation to another, from an individual towards the larger symbols that exist completely outside of time and space. I will make no effort to cover all of the book, but I should like to show some examples of the way in which the specific movement is expanded into a larger context.

Of the three generations in the novel, Tom Brangwen and Lydia Lensky have the most difficulty in establishing a relationship; yet their success is greater than that of their children or their grandchildren. Their greatest triumph comes when least expected. Tom cannot understand his wife's foreign language and manners and he finds it difficult to communicate with her. One evening he announces that he is going out and Lydia protests that "You do not want to be with me any more." He protests weakly, but she continues to attack him: " 'Why should you want to find a woman who is more to you than me?' she said. The turbulence raged in his breast. 'I don't,' he said. 'Why do you?' she repeated. 'Why do you want to deny me?' Suddenly, in a flash, he saw she might be lonely, isolated, unsure. She had seemed to him the utterly certain, satisfied, absolute, excluding him. Could she need anything?" They proceed from here to a knowledge of their uncertainty and fear: "He did not understand her foreign nature, half German, half Polish, nor her foreign speech. But he knew her, he knew her meaning, without understanding." We believe this because of the constant insistence on the relationship to exclusion of time, space, and stability of ego. They reach out to each other in acknowledgment of their failure, and, in so doing, form a rainbow for their daughter:

> Anna's soul was put at peace between them. She looked from one to the other, and she saw them established to her safety, and she was free. She played between the pillar of fire and the pillar of cloud in confidence, having the assurance on her right hand and the assurance on her left. She was no longer called upon to uphold with her childish might the broken end of the arch. Her father and her mother now met to the span of the heavens, and she, the child, was free to play in the space beneath, between.

Although Tom and Lydia now join heaven and earth like the rainbow for Anna, the novel is, clearly, already focused on the daughter.

It is in terms of the success of Tom and Lydia that we come to Anna and Will in the next chapter. They realize their love in the scene in which they carry the sheaves across the field in the autumn moonlight:

> Then she turned away towards the moon, which seemed glowingly to uncover her bosom every time she faced it. He went to the vague emptiness of the field opposite, dutifully.
>
> They stooped, grasped the wet, soft hair of the corn, lifted the heavy bundles, and returned. She was always first. She set down her sheaves, making a pent house with those others. He was coming shadowy across the stubble, carrying his bundles. She turned away, hearing only the sharp hiss of his mingling corn. She walked between the moon and his shadowy figure.

The failure of Will and Anna is implicit in their first love

scene. The speed with which they come together contrasts with the painful slowness with which Tom courted Lydia. Anna, set afire by the moon, is always first, looking beyond, while Will follows, like a shadow. The motifs of woman in the light of the heavens-man in the shadow are used earlier in connection with Tom and Lydia and later with Ursula and Anton Skrebensky. Even though the time and place are specified completely here, the larger movement, the reassertion of the relationship between men and women, is apparent.

Through this emphasis on the larger action, individual scenes and generalized actions of different sets of characters become organized into a large single movement. As the second generation takes over, we can see how much of what they do is interpreted in the language used in describing Anna's parents. Their marriage, as indicated in the "hawk" passage quoted previously, is frustrating and unhappy. Will turns away, tries to establish himself outside the home, and gradually "his life was shifting its centre, becoming more artificial." His response to marital frustration is to negate relationships whereas Tom's response was to insist on growth by acknowledging frustration. Anna gains control over Will, but this is fatal. Her "triumph" comes when, eight months pregnant, she dances naked to the moon in her room, "like a full ear of corn," and Will "was burned, he could not grasp, he could not understand." Lydia, in the face of similar victory, reached out to Tom, but now Anna taunts her husband, forces him from the room; and "after this day, the door seemed to shut on his mind."

As a result, "Anna was indeed Anna Victrix":

> Soon, she felt sure of her husband. She knew his dark face and the extent of its passion. She knew his slim, vigorous body, she said it was hers. Then there was no denying her. She was a rich woman enjoying her riches. . . . She forgot that the moon had looked through a window of the high, dark night, and nodded like a magic recognition, signalled to her to follow. Sun and moon traveled on, and left her, passed her by, a rich woman enjoying her riches. She should go also. But she could not go, when they called, because she must stay at home now. . . . If she were not the wayfarer to the unknown, if she were arrived now, settled in her builded house, a rich woman, still her doors opened under the arch of the rainbow, her threshold reflected the passing of the sun and moon, the great travelers, her house was full of the echo of journeying.
>
> She was a door and a threshold, she herself. Through her another soul was coming, to stand upon her as upon the threshold, looking out, shading its eyes for the direction to take.

The chapter to which this is the close represents one of the great moments in modern fiction. If the irony of "settled in her builded house, a rich woman" carries anything like the force attributed to it placed as it is against the image of the arch of the rainbow, Anna's failure is a great triumph of Lawrence's method. We back off from a scene in which Anna is crooning to her baby as we back off from so many scenes in the chapter, only to discover that the action is assuming, gracefully and without specific warning, the book's larger symbols; the finality of this moment echoes the finality of the earlier one, and, at the same time, opens the door for the action to come.

In the next two chapters, Ursula comes to the fore as Anna did in Chapters III and IV. As before, the parents' marriage, the terms of which have been made clear, is seen through the child, and both Will and Anna try to defeat the other by establishing the stronger relationship with Ursula. Will, defeated here, grows more and more ineffectual; he fails in his job, he fails in his fumbling attempts with other women, and he fails finally to hurt Anna as he would like.

Then, in "The Marsh and the Flood" the scene shifts back to the home of the elder Brangwens. Tom is caught out in a cloudburst, and we see in his death the final success of his marriage, and, by implication, the final failure of Will and Anna's. But here, for the first time, the forward flow of the novel is checked; the preceding chapter does not lead into it as we have seen was the case in earlier chapters nor does the subsequent chapter lead away from it. At the end of the chapter Lydia describes to Ursula her first marriage, and she insists on the greatness of her love for both her husbands. Ursula cannot understand this, and neither can we see what it is doing here. We are told at the end: "Ursula was frightened, hearing those things. Her heart sank, she felt she had no ground under her feet. She clung to her grandmother. Here was peace and security. Here, from her grandmother's peaceful room, the door opened on to the greater space, the past, which was so big, that all it contained seemed tiny; loves and births and deaths, tiny units and features within a vast horizon." Having stopped the movement of the book, Lawrence also contradicts one of the novel's central symbols. The door here, instead of opening on to the "beyond," the "rainbow," and, always, the future, opens on to the past, the "tiny units and features."

In itself this contradiction might not be important. But it is indicative of more important changes in tone and method that are manifested in subsequent chapters. "The Marsh and the Flood" serves as a watershed; before it Lawrence is in control, forcing our perception of each experience into a larger series of units, and after it, as we will see, he becomes more tentative and less careful. With Ursula we come to the period in the history which corresponds to Lawrence's own youth. Lawrence now begins to introduce small characters, names of people who are mentioned but who never appear, long conversations that are not worked into the fabric of the shifting verb tenses and the continuity of time. The reason, obviously, is that Lawrence is beginning to transcribe almost directly from his own experience. The twelve-page description of Ursula's conception of Sunday in the Brangwen household is clearly a recording of the Sundays of Lawrence's youth. Leavis writes of this [in *D. H. Lawrence: Novelist,* 1956]: "But if it should be necessary to show that there is more to be said about the place of the English Sunday in the history of English civilization, it would be enough to adduce this chapter of *The Rainbow,* so illustrating once again the incomparable wealth of the novel as social and cultural

history." There is no reason, however, why we should demand that *The Rainbow* be a social history at all, and this long passage seems to be placed here as something that Lawrence was interested in—something, indeed, that is interesting—but as nothing that belongs. The very title of the chapter, "The Widening Circle," illustrates how Lawrence has apparently lost interest in his central theme. What is widened here is completely different from what is widened earlier; both the matter and manner have altered.

There is an attempt to return to the novel's original terms in dealing with Ursula and Skrebensky. But even in the scene in which they make love in the stackyard, which echoes the sheaves-gathering scene with Will and Anna, something is out of control:

> And timorously, his hands went over her, over the salt, compact brilliance of her body. If he could but have her, how he would enjoy her! If he could but net her brilliant, cold, salt-burning body in the soft iron of his own hands, net her, capture her, hold her down, how madly he would enjoy her. He strove subtly, but with all his energy, to enclose her, to have her. And always she was burning and brilliant and hard as salt, and deadly. Yet obstinately, all his flesh burning and corroding, as if he were invaded by some consuming, scathing poison, still he persisted, thinking at last he might overcome her. Even, in his frenzy, he sought for her mouth with his mouth, though it was like putting his face into some awful death. She yielded to him, and he pressed himself upon her in extremity, his soul groaning over and over.

We can applaud the use of the light woman-dark man motifs of the earlier portions of the novel, but everything else seems desperately wrong: the strident "If he could have her, how he would enjoy her!," the needless vagueness of "subtly" and "madly," the vulgar flatness of "even in his frenzy, he sought for her mouth with his mouth," leading to the dismal last line. It is a blessing that Lawrence had to cut Anton's subsequent, "Let me come, let me come" from the later editions. All this contrasts sharply with the firmness and assurance of the scene with Will and Anna in the field. The vagueness here is a real vagueness, all the worse because it is offered to us as a great moment, and it is this kind of writing that has led so many to impute all manner of disease to Lawrence from homosexuality to the fascism of the dark gods.

But at the close of this scene, after Ursula tries to bring Anton "back from the dead," we have this: "Looking away, she saw the delicate glint of oats dangling from the side of the stack, in the moonlight something proud and royal, and quite impersonal. She had been proud with them, where they were, she had been also. But in this temporary warm world of the commonplace, she was a kind, good girl. She reached out yearningly for goodness and affection. She wanted to be kind and good." Here we have the old Lawrence. The insistent "kind and good," coming right after Ursula's enormous wilfulness in her subjection of Anton earlier, is perfect. Like her mother, she has won, she is now a woman with riches.

Unlike her mother, however, Ursula hates the victory, realizes that Anton exists for her now "in her desire only." All this is the proper expansion of the theme, the weakness of the shadowy man and the wilfulness of the brilliant woman. But these terms are used less and less as the novel proceeds, to be replaced either by direct transcription from Lawrence's experience, as in the long chapter dealing with Ursula as a school teacher, in which case the ego is all too stable, or by the kind of passage quoted above, in which there is hardly any ego at all—or anything else. Every now and again, as in the scene late in the book in which Ursula and Anton dance on the heath, we have a return to the classic form, and Ursula and her dark lover become, for a moment, the rightful heirs of the two preceding generations of Brangwens. Nevertheless, there is no constant movement of which this episode is a part, and without this the symbols seem pasted on and not, as before, a perfectly legitimate and exciting expansion of the central concerns of the novel.

It is not enough, I think, to say that the shift is justified because Lawrence had reached a period in history when he thought the failure in human relationships was closest to being absolute and that therefore some breakdown was necessary. For one thing Lawrence, if anything, handles the failure of Will and Anna better than he does the success of Tom and Lydia. But the whole vitality and enormous "felt life" of the first half of the novel is the result of placing human relationships in the foreground; the social history is there, perhaps, but only when it can be utilized in the personal drama. In the second half, social history occasionally becomes an excuse for personal failure, and, even if Lawrence did not know better than this, such speculations have no place in this novel. The colliers, the woman's movements, the ennui of the university—these matters are thrust forward, the characters are moved into the background, and even Ursula becomes shadowy. Lawrence becomes a victim of that tentativeness Leavis has described so well in connection with the novels of the early twenties. He writes on and on, looking for a place to stop, almost as though he were mindless of the methods used and terms established in the first half of the novel.

This criticism, however, in no way mars our sense of the achievement of the first eight chapters. As long as Lawrence maintains his position *as a novelist,* as an artist with a new way to describe human experience, it is difficult to say too much for him. To use Leavis' terms, *The Rainbow* adds something as only a work of genius can. The assertion of the supreme importance of human relationships finds its formal counterpart in the flow, the constant motion in time, the dramatic description of eternal movement in human experience as it reaches outward, through the door, towards the rainbow.

S. L. Goldberg　(essay date 1961)

SOURCE: "*The Rainbow*: Fiddle-Bow and Sand," in *Essays in Criticism,* Vol. XI, No. 4, October, 1961, pp. 418-34.

[*In the following essay, Goldberg explores the thematic, sty-*

listic, and symbolic factors that limit the overall success of The Rainbow *as a work of art.*]

> . . . don't look for the development of the novel to follow the lines of certain characters: the characters fall into the form of some other rhythmic form, as when one draws a fiddle-bow across a fine tray delicately sanded, the sand takes lines unknown.

Lawrence to Edward Garnett, 5 June, 1914.

Although Lawrence himself warned us never to trust the artist but to trust the tale, or that 'there may be didactic bits, but they aren't the novel', with his own work it isn't quite so easy to distinguish. The common tactic, of course, is to try to split him into two Lawrences: such a good novelist, before he became a tiresome whiskery prophet. Yet really there was only one Lawrence, and the critic can't avoid dealing with him whole—even, indeed especially, in *The Rainbow* and *Women in Love*: if the Imagination is the whole soul of man in activity, the novelist's intellect partly shapes his work and his will guides it towards conclusions. 'Prophecy,' in these two books particularly, is infused in the 'novel': to assess them we have to assess the total result, 'prophecy' and all—which means, in effect, discriminating the constructive forms of the art itself. For the 'prophecy' is compounded subtly and not always deliberately. It lies, for example, in the very disposition of the chapters, in narrative 'method', in the formal shape of plot, in the symbolic patterns: is more effective there, indeed, than in overt emphases and commentary. And it is these aspects of *The Rainbow,* the effects of the fiddle-bow on the sand, that I want to explore a little, not simply in order to underline their 'prophetic' function, but to weigh their relevance to the work as a whole. For the indisputable greatness of *The Rainbow* (indisputable, that is, since Dr Leavis showed what it is) is also, as Leavis himself suggests, in the end limited; and what limits it, I think, emerges most clearly if we examine the relation of form and idea in the book. It is not the prophetic vision, which inspires it throughout, nor Lawrence's experimental approach, which leads him to transgress against the accepted formalities of the novel, nor his attempt to render experiences that perhaps cannot be rendered at all; not his actual criticisms of modern society, nor even his uncertainty about what, finally, he wants to say. The limiting factor (which underlies some of these things) is rather his developing *over*-certainty about what he wants to say, the rising note of asserted will, his insistence on *putting* lines in the sand, which eventually comes to over-simplify his insight—in short, the drastic results of getting his prophetic vision (as he would say) 'in the head'.

I

Despite its general impression of spontaneous, exploratory freedom, *The Rainbow* is also constructed as an 'argument', solidly and intellectually wrought; but it is easy to overlook the most elementary way in which that argument is built up—the basic unit of the *chapter*. Each chapter of the book crystallizes one of Lawrence's fundamental intuitions about life, and their sequence embodies one kind of relation he sees between those intuitions—a kind of argumentative logic. Of course, the chapters do not crudely illustrate his 'beliefs' one by one, but establish, specify, define his insights in dramatic terms; if he generally adds more explicit commentary than a strictly 'dramatic' novelist in the line of Flaubert or James would, it is only offered *ex post facto*, as an intellectual summation of what is presented to the imagination. His 'philosophic' insights pervade and shape the action, and they do so in such a way that the individual chapters really perform a double function: to trace the unbroken line of natural growth, with its eddies and returns, over the generations of Brangwens, unfolding the stages of human experience; and at the same time, to unfold Lawrence's thematic purpose, to mark the stages in the total argumentative sweep of the novel.

As a 'story', the book is naturally divided by the three generations that form its subject-matter; as an 'argument', it also falls into three main sections; but the two kinds of division overlap. Again, where the over-all pattern of the story is a gradual opening outwards, a widening range, the thematic pattern is a gradual concentrating, a process of clarification and application. From the opening chapter itself the Brangwens' life emerges as the image of a human norm (a dynamic norm, not a static ideal), a richly imagined symbol that assumes, in relation to the rest of the book (and even to Lawrence's whole *œuvre*), the force of an argumentative premise: *here* is human being fulfilling itself within, and in vital connection with, its context of impersonal natural forces and social traditions. The following four chapters develop this image; the 'dark' eternal forces of physical life, selfhood, marriage, the mutual implication of growth and decline, the relevant social traditions, the limited consciousness of this rural generation, are all felt and realised, given a specific, though provisional, definition. The thematic unfolding continues unbroken even through the shift in the story at chapter 4, where Anna's spontaneous development begins to emerge, until it is at last recapitulated in the wedding-scene at the end of chapter 5. From there, however, Lawrence begins the process of analysis he saw as his new direction in this book, seeking now (through Anna and Will) to clarify and define more explicitly terms that have become problematical, have turned into issues. An earlier harmony of forces collapses into a sterile victory for one; the natural and the transcendental, the past and the present, tend to fall apart. Again the thematic 'argument' is carried through the story's gradual shift to Ursula (in chapter 8) until it reaches (in chapter 10) the nature of the vital 'religious' sense she has absorbed from still present traditions—a sense that will develop in her both as the result, and as the touchstone, of her subsequent experience. And at this point—heavily marked by an intruded, rather parsonical rhapsody from Lawrence—the central theme has become clearly manifest within the action. As the opening of chapter 11 openly indicates, this is the first major turn in the *thematic* progress of the book: up to here, Lawrence has been concerned to define modes of a genuinely organic, 'religious' vitality; from here, his subject is its present viability. He has now reached his destination—the critical exploration of the modern world.

This he undertakes through Ursula's experience of it, and particularly through her gradual penetration to the vital meaning of *love*. It is not, as she discovers, any merely sensual awakening (ch. 11); not the perverse, intellectualised, narcissistic indulgence to which our mechanical, collective society tends to corrupt it (ch. 12); not the fruitless idealism of personal relationships (ch. 13); not the stagnant, in-turned warmth of the family (ch. 14); not even a 'dark' sexual ecstasy which, engaging only part of the total self, is also doomed to sterility (ch. 15). And thus she (and the novel) reach a conscious articulation of the issues that guide the whole book. In the last chapter, her almost ritual trial crystallises one of its basic implications—the connection, and the difference, between vital moral consciousness and vital animal energy—and, concluding her *via negativa*, it leaves her at last clarified in herself, in a state of vital receptivity, as it were.

This argumentative drive of **The Rainbow** is of course only one of its various structures, and Lawrence manages it far more subtly, gives it far more life, than I have been able to suggest. But even to note it so briefly is perhaps enough to suggest how central a rôle his 'ideas' play in the work, how pervasive is his intellectual control of his material. The programmatic aspect of certain sections has often been noted; in fact, though it is not always equally obvious, Lawrence's control is continuous all through. (Considering his many rewritings, it would be surprising if it were not.) Even if we don't consciously notice its unremitting presence, nevertheless we feel it, for it is a large part of his characteristic intensity. He strikes straight to the basic realities as he sees them, and never lets go; the book bears a single-minded purposiveness, the concentrated force of a profoundly serious philosophic imagination. Clearly, his well-known remark in **Lady Chatterley's Lover** has a direct relevance to **The Rainbow**: properly handled, the novel can 'inform and lead into new places the flow of our sympathetic consciousness and can lead our sympathy away in recoil from things gone dead . . .' As always, the critical problems Lawrence raises are those of an art deliberately and fully dedicated to *leading*.

II

At its most characteristic, Lawrence's narrative reaches through outward behaviour, and even inner feelings, desires, or values, to the unseen direction in which these things move, the ends they express but also subserve. It is the texture and the flow of vitality, the whole 'man alive', rather than the circumstances and cruces of moral decision, that concern him; so that the Craft of Fiction is less to his purposes than a responsive, plastic, rhythmic *flow* which (as one critic has recently pointed out) constantly shifts and submerges specific time and place in the action, blends scene, narrative, analysis, description, and can give appropriate weight to any manifestation of life in a living universe. Nor is it only the sense of growth (as with Anna and Ursula) that Lawrence can make us feel so subtly by this means; the same flow also serves his more analytical purposes (as in 'Anna Victrix' or 'The Bitterness of Ecstasy'), where he renders not only continuity in length, as it were, but continuity in depth as well. The conventions of situation, climax, dénouement, are largely replaced by a continuous interplay, a counter-pointing, of different 'levels' of experience—of the 'old stable ego' and the impersonal 'carbon', for instance, or the everyday world and the

Sunday world, conventionally social 'realism' and vision-ary depth—for Lawrence's theme is the whole organic complexity of life (the rainbow, the arch), not the supreme importance of any one element. And at his best, the various planes do interfuse: the social realities of institutions and public relationships; the moral realities expressed in traditions, memory, choice; the individual realities of emotion, desire, growing awareness; and the over-arching realities, the vast, impersonal forces of life and death. The natural and the religious vision combine, the one giving the other definition and executive power, the other in turn (to use Forster's excellent term) *irradiating* the details of life with the profoundest significance.

'The novel,' as Lawrence said, 'is the highest example of subtle inter-relatedness that man has discovered'; and the real achievement of *The Rainbow* lies just where that organic view of art is given meaning in the organic view of life it expresses. In the first chapter of all, for instance, the dynamic inter-relations of life are both projected by and embodied in the art itself. The episode of Tom's proposal to Lydia, as Leavis has remarked, only crystallises the meaning of the whole: everything, from the weather and the falling dusk, the details of Tom's preparations, the curious personal suspension of the characters, to the final view of the night sky as Tom leaves, is—and is felt to be—integral to the chapter and the theme alike. Writing of this kind we can only perhaps compare vaguely with 'Myth', or call (in Leavis's sense) 'dramatic poem'.

Yet *The Rainbow* also includes a rather different sort of art. In other places, the action seems dominated by the determination to make some point conceived outside it, seems designed to embody that point and that point only, and therefore appears slightly factitious, manufactured. The landscape through which Ursula and Skrebensky walk just before their discussion of social issues in chapter 11—a passage Leavis praises for its symbolic subtlety—seems to me to reveal a touch of careful stage management such as nowhere appears in, say, the first three chapters. Ursula and Skrebensky's visit to the barge after their discussion is another case. Leavis describes Lawrence's general method perfectly: statement and explicit analysis, as he says, are secondary, and 'owe their force, as they come in the book, to the dramatically and poetically rendered significances they resume. We have here, in fact, one of the characteristic methods (a triumphantly successful one) of *Women in Love*. The statement or analysis relates immediately to what has been said in the discussion of the same themes between the actors, discussion that comes with perfect dramatic naturalness and has its completion and main force in some relevant episode or enactment. We have an instance in the episode of the barge in the chapter, "First Love" '. But these valuations (applied to *The Rainbow*) are perhaps more doubtful than Leavis allows. Leaving aside for the moment the question whether Skrebensky is 'done' fairly as well as dramatically and poetically, the phrase 'some relevant episode or enactment' surely needs qualification. For is it not precisely the *quality* of the relevance that occasionally seems so limited? Such an episode as this barge scene is certainly relevant; it is even rendered 'dramatically'; but it is a relevance that appears with a disconcerting promptness and obviousness. Vivid and sharp

though the scene is, its inter-relations with its context are comparatively simple and clear-cut; we feel the 'drama' as *instrumental,* a function of Lawrence's argumentative intent. We must be careful not to confuse the moral power of the 'argument' too readily with the imaginative power of the art. For the confusion is possible, I think, with many other passages as well—the scenes enacting Will's compensatory use of Ursula, for example, or the values enacted by Winifred Inger, uncle Tom Brangwen, Wiggiston, or Brinsley St. School. The writing here has a clarity, a broad, swingeing effectiveness; the implicit values are pressed sharply home; but whereas the sort of 'enactment' to be found in the first chapter, despite its argumentative direction, seems to exhibit a genuine 'negative capability'—a capacity to let things be themselves and speak in all complexity for themselves—this other seems to rely on a different capacity, more intellectual but narrower—a capacity to generalise by means of relevant particulars. It is a difference that suggests some further distinctions.

III

If we have to call *The Rainbow* a 'dramatic poem', we also have to see it as a novel. For a large part of the book we do not need to bother about how faithful Lawrence is to social or psychological probability; as we can see, he is concerned to achieve a truth, to explore human experience, at a profounder level than that. His vision of life extends beyond any of its particular contingencies—even though, of course, it is realised only by means of them. But the book gradually shifts into another key as he also begins to use that vision as a critical touchstone, and when it does so we *do* have to bother about its accuracy to the social and psychological facts it criticises. Lawrence enters the traditional field of the novel—our familiar, everyday world, where we relate people's values to what they are, and where the novelist has to give people, beliefs, principles, forces, a socially representative significance, and in simple honesty to confront them with the recalcitrant facts, with representative opposing people, beliefs, principles, and forces. Perhaps it is being unduly suspicious of terms like 'dramatic poem' and 'myth' to insist on calling *The Rainbow* a novel; but we do well to remember that the artist has not only to dramatise his themes, but to do so with complete integrity to his chosen material, his 'sand'. In directing *The Rainbow* to the familiar social material of the novel, no doubt Lawrence tried to achieve that integrity; I very much doubt, however, whether he actually did. Beside the taut honesty of *Women in Love* or many of the *Tales,* parts of *The Rainbow*—and a great deal of its second half—seem to me (as they have seemed to others) significantly weak in definition and in dramatic power.

The first signs of this appear just where Lawrence begins to shift key: most particularly, in the treatment of Anna and Will. Brilliant as his presentation of their conflict is, he is hardly precise about one important issue: how far his characters are morally responsible for themselves or their common failure. His attention is directed to the level of experience where we cannot finally distinguish between necessity and freedom, between unconscious forces that cause individual behaviour, and life-values that direct it, values that are in some sense chosen. Hence the peculiar way the characters seem to be both helpless and wilful. Yet there are times when we may wonder if Lawrence isn't perhaps shuttling between the two points of view rather than mediating between them—treating his characters at some points as genuinely 'free' individuals whose behaviour and values are convincing enough to elicit our moral judgment, and at others as symbols embodying irreconcilable forces of existence that we can only accept for what they are. Of course, to present various life-values to us as both necessary and in different contexts right, he must do both; but one result (which he never took much pains to avoid anyway) is that, in his double attitude to character, he may seem to be judging human essences with an arrogant God's-eye simplicity rather than merely urging certain values. In any case, by his very concentration on this level of experience—the level at which most of our ethical and social dilemmas have both their beginning and their end—he also raises an old familiar question, which is a more radical one than he seems always to realise. For if our life-values are somehow fated to us, can our conscious choice among competing life-values be real or effectual? To go on and insist, as Lawrence does, that such choice is not only effectual but urgently necessary, is to raise problems that need subtler thought—thought on what we may call a *political* level—than he offers in *The Rainbow*.

It is unresolved difficulties of this sort, I think, that cause a slight strain, a tremor, in the writing—a sense that his ultimate judgments (for example, that on Will Brangwen) seem rather arbitrary, that he is beginning to force the issues. At various points of the book the same kind of tremor appears as a stylistic flaw. Lawrence's peculiar jargon, his repetitions, his pseudo-Biblical cadences, and what is often called (obscurely, though always angrily) his 'sheer bad writing', have been frequently attacked; but in themselves they are only part of his characteristic idiom. It is where they obtrude very noticeably—and this happens only occasionally—that they indicate a real weakness: a degree of over-pitched insistence, an extravagant verbal energy that is devoted not to rendering the action dramatically, but to forcing a special sense of it. The most striking examples, of course, are some of the sexual encounters, like the kiss of Ursula and Skrebensky in chapter 15, after he returns to Nottingham; here the style, and the style alone, with an almost obsessive insistence, tries to convey the profound, dark, 'fecund' depths to which Ursula is carried, while the dramatic context (not to mention Lawrence's own criticisms of the characters' relationship) leaves no doubt just how unlikely they are to reach such profound levels of vitality at all. But the strain appears on other occasions as well: in the Resurrection sermon at the end of chapter 10, for example, or in the rainbow vision in the last few pages of the book. Obviously, more is involved than Lawrence's view of certain sexual experiences. Whenever he tries to impose a value on a dramatic situation other than the situation itself conveys, or tries to make sure we do not miss a point so important that he feels he can't trust the tale to convey it by itself—that is to say, whenever he relies on language instead of drama—the writing betrays the same over-excitement. His all-embracing vision of life constantly tends to reduce the ac-

tion to a symbolic instrument; while the reduction is actually in process, the writing seems to be urging merely personal attitudes, to achieve only a compulsive, inspirational lyricism.

But if the style of *The Rainbow* suffers only intermittently, the effect on its social implications, deeply embedded as they are in the whole work, is more far-reaching; and in Ursula's vision of the rainbow at the end there culminates a weakness that is obviously more than stylistic and is also more than local. Again it begins to emerge at the point of modulation, in chapter 7 ('The Cathedral'), where the social bearings of the action shift with a rather obscure logic: is it really clear how ecstatic, transcendental 'spirituality', the failure of nineteenth-century manhood to live with its own Industrialism, nineteenth-century Christianity, Christianity in general, and perhaps any universal system or institution, are related to each other? The uncertainty here isn't vital perhaps, but in the light of what follows it is at least symptomatic.

The other end of the process, the emotional falsity of the last few pages, is so glaring that every critic has remarked on it. Leavis, for example, mentions the limiting 'kind of commentary provoked by that ending', though he doesn't himself develop it or think it more than peripheral. He argues (as I understand him) that the 'radical mood' of those pages was left behind by Lawrence long before he reached the end of the book; that it is really only a momentary lapse, a sign of Lawrence's inability to find a suitable note, in the mood he was now in, to conclude what he had actually done; that the passage is so strikingly false, in fact, because its mood is incongruous with the rest of the book. But is it so incongruous or so incidental? Does not the same radical mood pervade and weaken most of the second half? And is it not built into the very structure of the whole?

No one has discussed better than Leavis himself the way Lawrence develops the subtle, complex relationships between each of the three Brangwen generations, the vividly realised values and problems that recur and develop, the meaning of continuity and change, the continuous influence of the past, the widening circle of interest, the growing burden of consciousness—in short, all the rhythms caught up in the book's triple-turning, opening spiral. But of course Lawrence's object is not simply a superior, profounder kind of 'realism' (beating the family-sagas, the Arnold Bennett's, at their own game). He renders the processes of life as truly as he can, but he does so largely in order to support upon that certain judgments about the modern world. The book moves towards its argumentative conclusion in its apparently *natural* turn to the 'modern' experience of Ursula. (After all, what is there about the predicament of Anna and Will that belongs so specifically, so exclusively, to *their* generation and society?) The movement of natural growth is intertwined with the movement of the argument, visibly so, indeed, at the beginning of chapter 11. At the same point, moreover, the focus of attention shifts from the interplay of life-values available to all, to the conflict between the values of society and the deep, but unformulated, religious sense of the individual.

Such a split between the individual and his society is simply one of the facts of our age; nevertheless, a good deal depends on how we define it and how far back we trace it. And Lawrence's critique of modern society in *The Rainbow* develops with a number of expectations, which are really assumptions, implicit in its spiral structure. The tacit intention, if it can be called by so definite a term, is for us naturally to expect the terms of Ursula's problems to be at least similar to those of the earlier Brangwen generations. We are to take her as the embodiment of the vital process so subtly rendered earlier; the very impetus of the action sweeping forward gives her a symbolic authority as the new embodiment of life. We are not to question her basic vitality even while we see it clarified by a series of experimental mistakes; we are to endorse the underlying mood of her response to experience. And we are also led to expect that that experience, the values, forces, attitudes she meets, will be truly representative of the modern world. In short, her basic attitudes are to assume moral authority because they seem natural, inevitable. She is the chosen vessel of 'vitality'.

All this is obvious enough perhaps, and in itself only to say how Lawrence tries to give his social judgments moral force. The moral strategy of *The Rainbow* is not very complicated. Yet to put it so baldly may help, I think, to explain the dissatisfaction I feel with the *art* of the last five chapters of the book, a dissatisfaction that isn't simply an ideological objection to Lawrence's judgments (as it happens, I agree with most of them), or to the length of his treatment. It is rather closer to Leavis's observation that certain issues are proposed in *The Rainbow* that Lawrence was still incapable of dealing with. Certainly one reason why *Women in Love* is the finer book is its greater maturity, but these issues are just as central to *The Rainbow,* and what limits its achievement is surely Lawrence's belief that he was capable of dealing with them. The 'dramatic poem', in which he realises a timeless, universal vision of life, when it narrows down to criticise a particular society, where the specific facts of time and place are of the essence, becomes rather like a social *fable*—an application, an exposition, of values, rather than a dramatic exploration. As a critique of *society,* the second half of *The Rainbow* comes closer to *Hard Times* or *The Secret Agent* than to *Middlemarch* or *The Possessed*. The attitudes it endorses are not rigorously tested in dramatic opposition. Ursula has the world brought to her passively; it never kicks back hard; and of course the real judgment on it is already implicit in that very passivity. Her apparent freedom from the social phenomena she rejects also works to prejudge the issues. Lawrence's 'reverence for life', his sense of the organic complexity of experience and of natural continuity, magnificently realised as they earlier are, do not really validate either his specific judgments of modern society or the implicit assumption that genuine 'vitality' must be radically and totally at odds with all its values and institutions.

The truth is that *The Rainbow* offers not a critique of modern society, as Lawrence seems to have thought, but an explosive, outraged protest against it—with all the disturbing over-simplifications that implies. One is the oversimplification of representative fact. Skrebensky, for example, is little more than an illustrative collection of atti-

tudes; he is certainly not realised fully enough to bear the weight of implication Lawrence tries to erect upon him. And some critics, even while prepared to agree with Lawrence that the values Skrebensky represents are vicious, have properly questioned if this is imaginatively established simply by associating them with a personal nullity as marked as his. But the issue goes even deeper just because that nullity seems so equivocal. For if Skrebensky were more fully realised, would this not involve a more subtle—but perhaps inconvenient—discrimination among his values? Winifred Inger is another case of the same kind: is Feminism or Humanism in itself only a symptom of perversity, to be rejected *in toto*? Could such attitudes not express, in however limited a way, vitality in some people, sterility in others? Does Brinsley St. School represent all that modern society could permit in education? Once again, Lawrence is not entirely wrong, but discriminations that need to be made are not made. To Ursula, he says at one point (with no apparent irony), 'the vote was never a reality. She had within her the strange, passionate knowledge of religion and living far transcending the limits of the automatic system that contained the vote'. The vote won't save us, we can agree; yet does Lawrence show it so totally irrelevant to social life that we have to dismiss it as part of an 'automatic system'? A transcendence that takes so little along with it on so ambitious a flight seems a curious form of 'vitality'.

That vitality *is* imaginatively realised in Ursula's progressive rejections of merely sensual or merely intellectual experience, in her gradual conscious realisation of what she is seeking, and in the two important scenes by moonlight with Skrebensky. Even so, Lawrence tends to give her specific feelings far more authority than they warrant. She sweeps Winifred Inger's liberal humanism aside as she sweeps the vote aside: she cannot desire mere 'love' or mere power; she wants to be like lions and wild horses rather than lambs or doves; yet, although her desires echo Anna's and the story later on endorses them, they don't in themselves focus the critical light very sharply. She comes to feel critical of Nottingham University College: 'the religious virtue of knowledge was become a flunkey to the god of material success'; perhaps so, but nothing we are actually shown supports her feeling, and nothing really qualifies it. This tendency sometimes appears with an almost disarming frankness, as when Ursula ponders her past: 'She did not know what she was. Only she was full of rejection, of refusal. Always, always she was spitting out of her mouth the ash and grit of disillusion, of falsity.' Lawrence, indeed, all too often presents an asserted disillusion in the character for an evident falsity in society.

Of course he continually criticises her mistakes, her *affaires* with inadequate values, her immature, inarticulate thrashings about. On the other hand, however, her underlying attitudes, her 'good heart' as it were, escape criticism altogether. Her characteristic Luddite reaction to industrialism, for instance, ranges from impotent fury to tearful sentiment, but it is never critically placed; nor is the equally sentimental violence that catches, in the surrounding darkness, at the gleam of savage animal eyes, of flashing swords of overpowering 'angels', like fangs, 'not to be denied'. The wholesale destructiveness she unleashes on

Skrebensky is just this radical, apocalyptic mood in action. And what is remarkable is not her adolescence, but Lawrence's readiness to identify himself with her. The 'vitality' this part of the book offers, in fact, seems so opposed to industrial society that it doesn't prompt any fine awareness of its complexities or those of the people who try to live in it. (Poor Skrebensky! it turns out, after all, that *God* had created him that way and you can't make an angel of the lord out of a sow's ear.) Even apart from the question of how far the individual can change his own life-values is the more immediate question of his power to affect the society of which he is a part. Against those who represent their society fully, the Skrebenskys, the Winifred Ingers, the uncle Tom Brangwens, the irrevocably lost, are the Ursulas, alienated and struggling towards full humanity. But what about the horrible Harbys or the people of Wiggiston, those who are shown to be very much of the system and yet, as Lawrence occasionally insists (he certainly doesn't demonstrate), are mainly its victims: 'like creatures with no more hope, but which still live and have passionate being, within some utterly unliving shell'? Is it too much of a parody to sum up his pervasive suggestion as, that the 'unliving shell', the whole 'automatic system that contains the vote', has to be smashed open (somehow); it *will* be (somehow), by human vitality itself; and although (somehow) it has no visible social embodiment, that vitality still lies deep (somewhere) inside (some) people? Applied to modern society, metaphors of eggs and nuts, however 'organic' they are, can involve a grievous fuzziness.

It may seem absurdly irrelevant to press Lawrence in this way when he is only urging questions, not writing a political programme. But we can't avoid the terms in which he puts those questions; and it is precisely these same romantic assumptions, this impatience and vagueness, that reach their culmination in the last pages of the book. The hollow rhetoric there emerges inevitably from the social attitudes of the last five chapters or so; and through them it is also related, I think, to certain aspects of the whole work. If we were to look at the opening pages, for example, as the actual representation of English society, could we deny a significant golden, paradisal haze about it, a touch of nostalgic softening . . . ?

IV

Not all the lines in the sand are equally unknown or equally deep; and we may gauge the depth of Lawrence's imaginative insight by the symbols it creates no less than by the inter-relatedness of the action or its social implications. The broad distinction, I think, lies between programmatic symbolism like that of the rainbow (or arch or doorway), or the Cathedral (church, spire), and other symbols, equally recurrent, but less visibly manipulated, more organic. The first sort seem rather like leitmotifs, which provide a kind of unity only at the expense of a certain artificiality. They are given meaning by the action; they are carefully used; but their power to concentrate and radiate meaning is limited by the air of conscious deliberation that accompanies them. The chapter on 'The Cathedral', for example, partly does as Leavis claims, create and explore its own significance. Yet beneath its subtlety, the writing seems rather too sure about its final destination, rather unresponsive to other possible attitudes (which isn't, of course, incompatible with vagueness elsewhere); so that, despite the fact that the Church, the pointing spire, is part of the Brangwens' life from the beginning, or that it is at Rouen, for instance, with its cathedral 'which knew no transience nor heard any denial', that Ursula begins to break from the sensual bond with Skrebensky, the symbol itself still seems something of a *device*. So, too, with the rainbow-arch-doorway imagery, even though early on it arrives as organic metaphor and then recurs through the whole book; or the wild horses, where early metaphor later becomes rather obvious symbol. The effect here is less of rhythm than of design.

Other symbols, however, do seem to arise spontaneously and to continue to work more flexibly. The imagery of *birds,* for example, which runs all through the Anna-Will section, is never heavily underlined (even in its most explicit use, the episode of the fighting blue-caps), but its effective meaning is established with a delicate strength that maintains it through the book. Again, the three or four major scenes involving the *moon* have a disturbing power characteristic only of Lawrence: the capacity to create symbolism of this order is at the centre (though it is by no means the whole) of his imaginative achievement. He makes no attempt here to comment discursively or even to probe. We could cite his *ex post facto* remarks about the moon in **Fantasia of the Unconscious,** but the novel itself actually weaves together the human sexual rhythms and the corn glistening in the darkness or the movement of the sea, while the moon beats down its signal, its challenge, of 'almost malignant apartness'. If the scene with Anna and Will is less wrought-up than those with Ursula and Skrebensky, all enact quite explicit themes, yet they do so with no contrived or superficial relevance. In the end, we can't explain their meaning in other terms any more than Ursula or even Lawrence could; their power derives from a full, firm grasp of experience, a vision that remains irreducibly poetic.

The related symbolism of *darkness* illustrates how Lawrence can successfully evolve prophetic argument from within prophetic vision so long as his use of the symbol—urgent and insistent as it is sometimes—remains faithful to what is deeply imagined, never committing it to a significance narrower than he has in fact created. That significance emerges from the total action of the early chapters particularly: at the end of chapter 1, Tom's apartness from Lydia and the passion that draws them together to their long, dark, marital embrace, are reflected in the dynamic elements themselves—in the flying darkness of the clouds and the terrible liquid-brilliance of the moon. In the next chapter, darkness is the element of withdrawal, and of birth, fecundity, a sensual vitality in harmony with a deep moral vitality as well; Tom, in the pain of loss, watches Anna and Will embrace by night in the fowl-loft; at night, he is overborne by the flood: the symbol assumes meaning without strain, apparently without conscious intent. Yet it gradually becomes more explicit, deployed more openly, as in 'The Cathedral', or when Ursula and Skrebensky kiss, or in the 'darkness' surrounding present consciousness, or in the constant juxtaposition of 'dark' with 'fecund', 'flame', and the like. Nevertheless, Lawrence's desire to generalise and direct does not here falsify the organic wholeness of his grasp. The symbol expresses complexities that still remain complex; emphatic insistence and repetition do not destroy its felt significance, a poetic rhythm genuinely there.

The actual discriminations to be made in **The Rainbow** are not simple. As I have tried to suggest, Lawrence's 'prophetic' impulse doesn't simply overtake and then wholly dominate his imagination. **The Rainbow** is profoundly original and profoundly meaningful because of, not in spite of, the pervasive presence of intellect; and 'prophecy'—radical insight, judgment, emphasis—is its very condition. Nor is it simply that the art weakens when Lawrence turns, in the second half, from universal to local issues. That is broadly true perhaps, but not entirely, for Lawrence is right to insist on their vital continuity and only provokes criticism when he fails to realise that continuity imaginatively—when, in fact, he falls victim to the very situation he attacks. The elements of the whole 'man alive', alive in his social relations as in his individual, passional consciousness, fall apart; 'blood-relationships' become 'mere spirit or mind'. Sometimes Lawrence seems to know our situation so well that he wants only to refuse it; exploration of it from within lapses into analysis of it from without; and so he comes to over-simplify the subtle interrelatedness even of our life, however sick. The result—an art of serious 'fable'—usually demands both attention and respect (though it only adumbrates the success of **Women in Love**). Occasionally, although we can understand and even endorse his mood, his undifferentiating violence compromises the values it is meant to serve, and the art fails to integrate insight and moral intent on any level. Where Lawrence is most deeply at one, however, **The Rainbow** does possess a magnificent and challenging vitality. In the end, Lawrence's greatness is that he gives us the reality by which we can judge him.

Edward Engelberg   (essay date 1963)

SOURCE: "Escape from the Circles of Experience: D. H. Lawrence's *The Rainbow* as a Modern *Bildungsroman,*" in *PMLA,* Vol. LXXVIII, No. 1, March, 1963, pp. 103-13.

[*In the following essay, Engelberg describes the symbolic narrative of* The Rainbow *as that of a modern interpretation of the novel of maturation.*]

I

Late in his life, in 1933, Yeats read **Sons and Lovers, The Rainbow,** and **Women in Love** "with excitement," and found the love story of **Lady Chatterley's Lover** "noble." In Lawrence he found an ally "directed against modern abstraction"; and he considered that, with Joyce, Lawrence had "almost restored to us the Eastern simplicity." A hatred of Abstraction; a fearless plunge into the mire of human existence; an anti-intellectual stance (which was almost at times a pose); and a mythopoeic conception of art and life; these Yeats and Lawrence shared, whatever their differences—which were considerable. And what they shared accounts in part for their similar response to Goethe's *Wilhelm Meister* and that hero's search for experience: it was, they felt, guided too dominantly by intellec-

tual choices. In 1928 Lawrence wrote to Aldous Huxley that he thought "*Wilhelm Meister . . .* amazing as a book of peculiar immorality, the perversity of intellectualised sex, and the utter incapacity for any *development* of contact with any other human being, which is peculiarly bourgeois and Goethian." Yeats remarked that Goethe, a man "in whom objectivity and subjectivity were intermixed," could "but seek . . . [Unity of Being] as Wilhelm Meister seeks it intellectually, critically, and through a multitude of deliberately chosen experiences." He insisted that "true Unity of Being . . . is found emotionally, instinctively, by the rejection of all experience not of the right quality, and by the limitation of its quantity." But for Yeats, the poet, it was less problematic than for Lawrence, the novelist, to crusade against Abstraction and Intellection: the poem had its gnomic power to snap meaning at you in an instant of time; the novel had somehow to have people and a story—and a world in which both could occur.

The problem for Lawrence, as for most of the novelists of the nineteenth century, was the meaning of experience. For Goethe, who established the prototype of the *Bildungsroman,* the question was simpler. Wilhelm Meister must endure two trials of experience: the first would consist of *Lehrjahre* (apprenticeship), the tilt with experience, high and low, elevating and degrading; the second would then be a reaping of the rewards, for the *Wanderjahre* are the years when the *Lehrjahre* are tested in the large world, and at the end of which the hero emerges as a man of some wisdom who has found his place on the horizontal plane of worldly existence. Such a path through life made it necessary for the hero to adapt his inner self, in some degree, to the outer reality he faced, for the ultimate goal was selfhood within society: to attain it certainly involved the hero in intellectual discriminations and abstract values—though it was also an act of free will. The inability to engage the world on these terms led, in Goethe's conception, to the subjective weakness of a Werther who, unable to endure experience *except* emotionally, can only shoot himself. "It is justly said," Goethe told Eckermann, "that the communal cultivation of all human powers is desirable and excellent. But the individual is not born for this; everyone must form himself as a particular being—seeking, however, to attain that general idea of which all mankind are constituents." Although Lawrence would not have quarreled with the notion of man forming his "particular being," he would hardly have gone so far as to require that being to adjust his identity to the "general idea" of "all mankind."

It is not surprising that nineteenth-century fiction nourished itself on the *Bildungsroman,* particularly in England, though it encountered problems with the form that Fielding and Smollett were spared. After all, the Victorians were *engagé* in a brave new world, and one had much to experience, and to learn from that experience, in order to come to terms with hard times in a hard world. Orphans and waifs, like David Copperfield and Heathcliff, Becky Sharp and Jane Eyre, serve their apprenticeship in countless novels; but the *Wanderjahre* are not always so neatly apportioned to a second volume—in equal balance to the first—as Goethe had been able to manage it (in *David Copperfield* three *Wanderjahre* are compressed into one short chapter.) A novelist like Dickens became increasingly uncertain what the hero ought to *do* at the end of his experience, or perhaps what he, the author, ought to do with his hero's experience. If David Copperfield finally achieves his patriarchal peace by the familiar hearth, in spite of the harrowing experiences from which Dickens spares neither his hero nor us, the case of Pip was harder to solve. We know of the two endings to *Great Expectations,* the happy and the unhappy: and was not Dickens' problem to decide how—or whether—to reward his heroes? In the happy ending Pip reaps his benefits as an exchange of values; suffering and wisdom are educative, and a pitying Pip rescues a pitiable Stella. But the unhappy ending is quite a different matter: Pip's expectations remain as unfulfilled as Stella's, whose face, voice, and touch at their final interview assured Pip that "suffering had been stronger than Miss Havisham's teaching." Experience on either side leaves both wiser, sadder, and—on the level of immediate attainment or "adjustment"—unrewarded. Experience had indeed taught both what the world can be like, but it provided no guarantees that one could, or proscriptions that one ought, to live in it. Pater's notorious remark, "Not the fruit of experience, itself, is the end," seemed a logical conclusion by 1873: *Lehrjahre* and *Wanderjahre* had become merged in the instantaneous time-present; the future could not be relied upon to preserve either the meaning or intensity of experience, and the notion that wisdom was the fruit of experience was becoming as passé as the idea that emotion could be recollected in tranquility. *The Picture of Dorian Gray* is also a *Bildungsroman* in which the "Bild" after all is the central character; but Wilde had stood *Wilhelm Meister* on its head, fictionalizing Pater's doctrine of experience: *Wanderjahre* precede *Lehrjahre*, though time hardly separates them. While Dorian Gray experiences, his portrait learns: true suffering had been (almost) successfully projected onto a canvas in the attic.

Of course the *Bildungsroman* did not die; it merely changed some of its organizing principles, for the novelist still faced his problem: what was the hero to make of his experience? Was it to lead him to know the world in order to reject what was evil in it, or to accept what he found worth saving? And what if that find was, after all, not in the world but in the soul or psyche? Joyce's hero flies his nets, but then he was an artist and the case was therefore special. When Lawrence came of literary age with *Sons and Lovers* and *The Rainbow,* the *Bildungsroman* in English fiction was, if not moribund, in a state of suspension. The hero still learned and he still wandered, but he did less of both; and his education was as likely to lead him to the fate of Wells's Mr. Polly as to have, like Galsworthy's young Jolyon, the door slammed in his face, or to end like Conrad's Heyst in a funeral pyre of his own making. Experience was proving to be a fairly ineffectual method of coping with the world.

Lawrence hated all enclosures, whether Marxian, Darwinian, or Freudian, and he had his quarrels with all three. But in particular, as he wrote in his essay on Franklin, he hated that kind of "barbed wire moral enclosure that Poor Richard rigged up." Barbed wire: the metaphor is aptly commensurate with Lawrence's conception of life as

struggle. To break through enclosures took not only a passionate will but the endurance to drive through all entanglements toward the periphery—and then beyond it. Unlike Daedalus you could not make your escape from the labyrinth merely by making a pair of wings: you had first to "come through" (to use Lawrence's language) on foot and bleed in the process. And that was truly to experience the world before you earned the *right* to reject it for what you found wanting in it.

Lawrence, of course, lived his own *Bildungsroman—Lehrjahre* and *Wanderjahre*: he would go his own ways. Toward his contemporary novelists he had little but contempt, ranging from mere petulance to hatred. One finds scattered in his writings condemnations of almost all the great novelists whom we consider today the giants of modern fiction: Flaubert, Proust, Gide, Mann, Joyce, Conrad (nor did he like Bennett, Galsworthy, Gertrude Stein, or Dorothy Richardson). He wanted no part, either of their subject or form: as innovators from whom he might learn he rejected them absolutely. In what sense, then, is Lawrence really modern, speaking of him as a novelist, not a philosopher or myth-maker? His modernity—like Yeats's—seems to be inherent in his apparent isolation from his contemporaries, an isolation that permitted him to solve (or attempt to solve) his aesthetic problems outside the great revolutionary innovations, from a position where it was still possible—because he ignored the experiments that lay between him and the past—to attach oneself to tradition by dint of one's own originality.

"The free moral and the slave moral," he wrote in an essay on Galsworthy, "the human moral and the social moral: these are the abiding antitheses." And these antitheses he would attempt to resolve in at least three novels—*Sons and Lovers, The Rainbow,* and *Women in Love*. In some fashion all three novels were variations of the *Bildungsroman,* but only in one—*The Rainbow*—did Lawrence fully succeed in achieving the kind of balance leaving him visibly aligned to a tradition and yet marking out a solution that defined what a modern *Bildungsroman* could be like—what the relation of the hero to his experience had become in the twentieth century.

II

Like all of Lawrence's novels, *The Rainbow* has suffered its share of abuse, but even admirers have attacked its ending—as they have that of *Sons and Lovers* and, to a lesser degree, *Women in Love*. This disaffection with the conclusions of novels otherwise highly regarded constitutes a serious charge: it calls in doubt not only the coherence of Lawrence's ideology but, more damaging, Lawrence's capacity as an artist to sustain his work and bring it to a proper end. With respect to *Sons and Lovers* and *The Rainbow* the question raised is the same: does the hero earn the rewards which the novelist bestows at the end? Or are Paul Morel's rather sudden determination to live purposefully and Ursula Brangwen's dramatic vision of the rainbow mere curtain-drops, the impatient gestures of a novelist already hurrying on to his next work? And what of Birkin's final disagreement with Ursula at the end of *Women in Love*—does it not sabotage the "star equilibrium" toward which the novel seems to be shaped? It is difficult to defend the ending of *Sons and Lovers* without reservations; the conclusion to *Women in Love* is more defensible; but with *The Rainbow* the problem seems crucial: to call in doubt that novel's resolution is to question the structure and meaning of the whole book, and to undercut the vision of the rainbow is to undercut all that precedes it. The risks are so high because the structure of the novel and the meaning that it carries forward depend on the validity of the rainbow image. Without the rainbow we would have something radically different from what Lawrence in fact has achieved, and this novel, which occupies the central position between *Sons and Lovers* and *Women in Love,* could not be—as I think it is—a higher achievement than its predecessor or successor.

The major clue to the success of Lawrence's conclusion to *The Rainbow* lies in the criticism of the failure in *Sons and Lovers.* "The trouble" with that novel, complains one critic [Louis Fraiberg, in *Twelve Original Essays on Great English Novels,* edited by Charles Shapiro, 1960], "is that the characterization is too flat and that the contest is over too soon. As a consequence, no changes—either developmental or disintegrative—can take place. . . . This is not a finished book." Such a criticism, of course, assumes certain conventions, about both the novel and this novel in particular. One of them is that a novel like *Sons and Lovers* is intended to show growth of character, growth which leads to change, and precisely to such change, such "resolution of tensions," that makes the final achievement of the hero both believable and earned. It is also assumed that growth and change emerge out of "contest," and that in order to convince the reader that the fruits of such a contest are legitimate the struggle must be worthy of its rewards. If, then, *Sons and Lovers* fails in part because character remains static and contest is too inconclusive, it is precisely on those points that *The Rainbow* succeeds.

Tested against the criteria of character growth and significant struggle *Sons and Lovers* fails as a *Bildungsroman* where, traditionally, the hero meets the experiences of life by trial and error, by suffering and failure, and at the end is rewarded for his trials by faith and for his errors by knowledge. Whatever one says about the ending of *Sons and Lovers,* one fact is abundantly clear: Paul Morel's experience of the world has made him neither wise nor foolish but rather helpless. And the sudden shift in direction at the close betrays confusion and a poor sense of timing more than impatience: Lawrence had not yet solved what his hero was to do with his experience—if, indeed, it had been experience at all. Yet, in spite of the faltering at the end, Lawrence intuitively, I think, meant to have the sudden turn, just as later he fully intended to give us (and his heroine)—at the right moment—the image of the rainbow. Lawrence insisted with vigor that the novel had form: "I tell you it has got form—*form,*" he wrote to Garnett, and one supposes he meant chiefly that *Sons and Lovers* was well constructed (which it was), unaware perhaps that it lacked the sort of form that goes beyond construction to attain a dimension of psychological truth. When Lawrence wrote to Garnett about his intentions in *The Rainbow* he spoke of gaining that dimension in what he considered a new way altogether: "I don't care about physiology of matter—but somehow—that which is phys-

ic—non-human, in humanity, is more interesting to me than the old-fashioned human element—which causes one to conceive a character in a certain moral scheme and make him consistent. . . . You musn't look in my novel for the old stable *ego* of the character. There is another *ego.*"

Since Ursula is after all the heroine of *The Rainbow,* it is to her that we look for the book's texture. And—Lawrence to the contrary—Ursula is really more human than non-human, more a stable ego than a plastic psyche; old-fashioned she may not be, but she is both consistent (to her inner self) and inescapably committed to a "moral scheme," if such commitment implies an honest confrontation of life in the search for truth. The consistent—and human—character within a moral scheme: that has always been the traditional framework of the *Bildungsroman*; and a careful reading of *The Rainbow* reveals not a less traditional novel than *Sons and Lovers* (as Lawrence thought) but a traditional novel which has made its own space in the continuum. What Lawrence could not solve in *Sons and Lovers* he did solve in *The Rainbow.* This is not to imply that the novel is entirely conventional, or that Ursula is wholly a stable ego, for the timely ritual scenes—the moon episodes, the cathedral tableau—do attempt to convey some sense of a plastic psyche being molded beneath the character's secondary ego.

In rejecting the Proustian and Joycean techniques of projecting their characters' inner life, Lawrence substituted a real persona whose psyche would operate as a kind of anti-self. In that way the hero's journey through experience would become a sort of dialogue of self and soul, a dialectic between the character's objective experience and his subjective assimilation of it. This provided the novel with a realism without depriving it of the psychological subtleties that Joyce or Virginia Woolf achieved by different routes. But the ritual scenes occur less frequently in *The Rainbow* than they do in *Women in Love* where, it is fair to say, they from the very choreography of the novel, holding it in place with delicately interlaced continuity. On close inspection, the letter to Garnett more accurately applies to *Women in Love.* In *The Rainbow,* the ritual scenes arrest, at crucial points, the more traditional narrative of the hero's pilgrimage toward knowledge; but, from each of these climactic pictorial dramas, Lawrence moves back to the central motion of his story. So that in the end, the stable ego is somehow made to accommodate the plastic ego. Ursula remains a fully realized character, whose inner life has been almost completely appropriated by her outer. Pared to the bone of her Being as she is at the end, we think of her, as we leave the novel, as character rather than psyche. And we feel, as we do not always feel in Lawrence, that the author has cared for that character: it makes for a unique accomplishment of integration—perhaps correlation is a better term—between the intentional direction of the artist and the demands that his character seems to have made against them. It is a triumph which Lawrence failed to repeat, not because his powers declined but because by the time he wrote *Women in Love,* he had truly achieved another—and radically different—dimension, from which there was no turning back.

III

The Rainbow, as we know, was scheduled at one point in its writing—when *Women in Love* was not yet conceived of as a separate novel—to be entitled *The Wedding Ring;* that title proved to be unsuitable for both novels. Lawrence probably rejected the title for *The Rainbow,* in spite of its apparent aptness to the marriage theme traced through several generations, because the ring image, wrongly conceived, might contradict an essential element of meaning in the novel. For it is Ursula's express triumph over her experience to break through all circles, all encircling hindrances, and among them, particularly, the circle of the wedding ring. Even in *Women in Love* she still rejects the ring, flinging Birkin's gift of three rings into the mud; and she can only accept the rings when they are joined by the flower, which she brings to her reconciliation with Birkin as a symbol of continuing growth. It is growth, indeed, that *The Rainbow* is centrally occupied with: two long chapters in the novel are headed "The Widening Circle," and both circles—the first leading from childhood to adolescence, the second from adolescence to adulthood—as they increase in circumference increase in the threat of enclosing and arresting Ursula's growth. Paradoxically, the widening circles cannot keep pace with the widening of Ursula's aspiring soul, and the larger her world becomes, the more acute is her realization of its limitations. Growth is Ursula's emblem; at times, as in the moon scene, it is a frightening, inhuman vitality, saved only by the humanness of character which Lawrence succeeds in building into her. Experience may be a teacher, but to Ursula it is more than that—it is the very motive of life, something she hunts out as an end in itself (though the rainbow is at the end of it) until, in *Women in Love,* Lawrence, through Birkin, teaches her its limitations. At the beginning of *Women in Love,* when Gudrun and Ursula talk discursively about marriage, Gudrun suggests that the experience of wifehood may, after all, be a necessary treasure in one's life. But Ursula is skeptical that marriage *is* an experience: "More likely," she says, "to be the end of experience."

This voracious appetite for experience is not unique with Ursula: her mother, Anna, possessed it in its barest state, and her grandmother, Lydia, had merely disguised it under her aristocratic pretensions, her "foreignness." One aim in tracing the three generations of women is to demonstrate the progressive shades of meaning in their appetites for experience: in Lydia it is partially subdued by convention, only to stir underneath as melancholia and frustration; in Anna it is wild and undirected and self-consuming. Only in Ursula does this appetite become truly attached to a conscious being, become, ultimately, directed and *civilized.* Therefore, the striving—and the failure of achievement—of the earlier generations prepares us for the vital center of the novel: the education of Ursula, through whom the preceding, and partial, impulses are carried to successful completion.

In the opening pages of *The Rainbow* we are told that the women looked to the "spoken world beyond," to the Word within the World. Facing outward, just as the men face inward, the women seek to fulfill their "range of motion" by searching for "knowledge," "education," and "experience." Only Ursula finds all three—and finds them wanting. Anna is a primitive version of Ursula, and her experiences so often resemble Ursula's that Lawrence at times seems almost to be straining the point. But the differences are more significant than the similarities, for Anna remains unconscious, to the end, of the full meaning of her experiences. Her main defense against the encircling world and the roofed-in arch of the church is multiplication of self: by producing scores of children she erects a kind of shield around herself. But children remain at best unwilling ambassadors and cannot negotiate for her. Ursula realizes this almost from the start as she chooses the opposite way: not padding the self protectively but stripping it to the core.

In the harvest scene between Will and Anna, the latter reveals the doomed nature of her relationship with life which consists in trying to achieve the impossible simultaneity of isolation and relatedness, the repulsion of being within the ring (of marriage) and the passionate necessity to possess its very center. There is no Birkin here who can explain the complex "star equilibrium" in which a man and a woman find separateness in union. Anna is torn between what she fears most and craves most, and it is this scene which clearly presages her future. It is a ritual, very Lawrentian with its moon and mood of incantation. Anna is always first in returning her harvest to the stooks. As Will comes with his bundle Anna leaves: it is a "rhythm" in which she "drift[s] and ebb[s] like a wave." But the rhythm that keeps them together keeps them apart: "As he came, she drew away, as he drew away, she came. Were they never to meet?" Always there remains the "space between them" until at last they meet and make love—until, that is, Anna, with her Brangwen passion, subdues her opposing Will.

Now the point of this scene is, in part, to convey Anna's violation of the rhythm that had kept her apart from intimacy; or, to put it differently, to show how she chooses one way, though committed to another. The intimacy is all too temporary, severed during the fortnight of honeymoon. And the "space between them" is never finally breached. Anna's pursuit of experience is therefore always blinded by the insistent demands of an inner resistance to accept experience, to go through with it to the end in order to test its validity. Ursula commits herself to experience in the full knowledge of risk and is willing to taste—again and again—the ashen fruits of the experiences that fail her—religion, education, knowledge, passion. Anna's incomplete and arrested tilt with experience rewards her with only an incomplete and arrested vision of the rainbow, and Lawrence could not be clearer about his meaning:

> Dawn and sunset were the feet of the rainbow that spanned the day, and she saw the hope, the promise. Why should she travel any further?

> Yet she always asked the question. As the sun went down . . . she faced the blazing close of the affair, in which she *had not played her fullest part,* and she made her demand still: "What are you doing, making this big shining commotion?"

. . . With satisfaction *she relinquished the adventure to the unknown.*

. . . If she were not the wayfarer to the unknown, if she were arrived now, settled in her builded house, a rich woman, still her doors opened under the arch of the rainbow, her threshold reflected the passing of the sun and moon, the great travellers, her house was full of the echo of journeying. [Italics mine]

Were Anna content with the "echo of journeying" as a fit substitute for the journey itself, her attainment of family, house, and children would be well enough for creative life. But she is not content. And since she has no way of working out her discontent other than yearning for that in which she is unwilling, always, to play her full part—the experience of life measured to its ends—she is left with a finite vision after all, a rainbow whose two ends bind her to the rising and setting sun, to the limited existence of an everyday world.

It is a mistake Ursula does not make because she has the courage to face the annihilating, but paradoxically freedom-giving moment of having journeyed fully committed to the end of experience. In the central Cathedral scene, Anna "claimed the right to freedom above her, higher than the roof. She had always a sense of being roofed in"; yet her claim is undercut by her incapacity to approach anything beyond the roof. She turns immediately to the gargoyles which she reduces, defensively, to human shapes, an act of reassurance, not of faith. Ursula's struggle for the beyond is differently shaped. To each new experience she brings the whole of herself. Her encounter with religion is total: she even plays out, against her intuition, the practical results of offering the other cheek, and only rejects the act after her cheeks burn with the slap of her sister's hand. Failing in religious faith she puts next her faith in love, though she enacts it, at first, amidst the ruins of her old faith, in the interior of the church which, with its fallen stones, its ruined plaster, its scaffolding, is all too symbolically under constant repair.

Always, with Ursula, there is yearning followed by enactment: she never retreats, she always chooses. Three quarters through the novel we find her amidst an emblematic landscape, which aptly projects her state of being constantly on the verge of setting foot into another world, of widening her circle:

The blue way of the canal would softly between the autumn hedges, on towards the greenness of a small hill. On the left was the whole black agitation of colliery and railway and the town which rose on its hill, the church tower topping all. The round white dot of the clock of the tower was distinct in the evening light.

That way, Ursula felt, was the way to London, through the grim, alluring seethe of the town. On the other hand was the evening, mellow over the green watermeadows. . . .

Ursula and Anton Skrebensky walked along the ridge of the canal between. . . . The glow of evening and the wheeling of the solitary pee-wit and the faint cry of the birds came to meet the shuffling noise of the pits, the dark, fuming stress of the town opposite, and they two walked the blue strip of water-way, the ribbon of sky between.

The canal divides the two shores which together form the whole of Ursula's potential world and, incidentally, the whole of the world which she experiences in the novel. On the right lie the fields of her birth, the fecund earth on which she and Skrebensky first consummate their love; on the left lie the colliery, the town, the church, and London, each of which is once tested and discarded. She rejects the fecund earth when she renounces the blood-prescient nature of Anthony for the sake of the journey onwards: "But she was a traveller, she was a traveller on the face of the earth, and he was an isolated creature living in the fulfilment of his own senses." The refusal of the church we have already pointed to; with Winifred Inger, Ursula pushes away the colliery of her uncle Tom—"impure abstraction, the mechanisms of matter"—and London as well, the London of Miss Inger, sophisticated perversion. And the town, where Ursula is so brutally initiated into the man's world, is gladly forsaken too: "The stupid, artificial, exaggerated town. . . . What is it?—nothing, just nothing." She will have to walk through the town, not towards it, like Paul Morel, and the transcendence can only occur vertically toward a vision, since on the horizontal plane—where Anna was always condemned to move—the landscape of the world is, at the end of the novel, fully exhausted of possibilities.

To say that Ursula searches for selfhood is descriptive but not very profoundly interpretive, for that fact is of lesser importance by far than the manner of her search. I have already said that the growth of Ursula's world coincides with the diminishing possibilities of her functioning creatively within it. From that point of view the novel is largely negative, consisting of a number of refusals and rejections without any corresponding affirmations. But the search for self, in the fitting image of husk and kernel at the end of the book, is a process of stripping away all layers that disguise and protect self from the truth of self (it resembles Lear's stripping process). So while the circle of the world widens, the circle of the self narrows in inverse proportion: the larger the one, the smaller—and the nearer to the core—the other. Ursula's annihilation of Skrebensky under the moon is no mere repetition of Anna's subjugation of Will under the same moon: it is, indeed, a far more violent and total act, but one with more results as well, and more motive. Ursula has the ability—which Anna lacked—to convert experience into knowledge: she masters the economics of experiencing to perfection. What she discovers is Skrebensky's lack of self and through it she is illumined on the nature of self—her own and in the abstract. She triumphs—not as Anna had, in order to subdue Will, but to create a self of her own. There under the moon she is awakened for the first time to the awful power of self—and its dangers; and it frightens her, enough to prevent her from severing her relationship with Skrebensky. It is true that her lust motivates her to "tear him and make him into nothing," but that impulse itself spells out the nature of a ceaselessly moving self. After she destroys Skrebensky, her soul is, understandably enough, "empty and finished": destruction has not come without its price. When he leaves she feels that emptiness even more acutely. Although she has seen the power of self she has not gained control of it by far, "since she *had* no self." Only after turning with shame and hatred on Winifred Inger and uncle Tom does she get any closer to it, and that double rejection makes way for her final struggles.

The last episodes with Skrebensky have puzzled a good many readers and some, like Hough, have suggested that Lawrence himself was not clear on the subject. Yet if Lawrence was not, Ursula was, for she predicts the failure of her resumed affair before she ever embarks on it: "Passion is only part of love. And it seems so much because it can't last. That is why passion is never happy." Yet, in the tradition of the hero undergoing the education of life, knowledge—of a kind—often precedes the experience that will confirm it. The true hero must always experience before he can truly know: he never substitutes intuitional wisdom for the living through itself. Often, as with Ursula, this is a conscious sacrifice at the alter of life's suffering, and it is consciousness, as I have said, that distinguishes Ursula as the kind of hero she is. "Ursula suffered bitterly at the hands of life": and that is proper for the hero whom life educates in its bitter school. But consciousness makes such suffering even more intense and makes it so precisely because it injects and maintains some ideal toward which all action gravitates with certainty and direction. When she and Anthony face a beautiful sunset, it is Ursula's consciousness of its beauty that gives her the capacity for feeling pain—the pain that comes with recognizing the inevitable disparity between the achieved and the achievable. "All this so beautiful, all this so lovely! He did not see it. He was one with it. But she saw it, and was one with it. Her seeing separated them infinitely." Sight precedes perception; acknowledgment precedes knowledge.

It is this aspect of conscious perception in the pursuit of experience that I have earlier called civilized; but the cost of such awareness is very high and makes for the awful negation that burdens the whole novel. Ursula is hardly unaware of it: the pressure is always there, to seek out life, to encounter it in battle, to discard and to be defeated, and to move on again:

> She had the ash of disillusion gritting under her teeth. Would the next move turn out the same? Always the shining doorway ahead; and then, upon approach, always the shining doorway was a gate into another ugly yard. . . .
>
> No matter! Every hill-top was a little different, every valley was somehow new. . . .
>
> But what did it mean, Ursula Brangwen? She did not know what she was. Only she was full of rejection, of refusal. Always, always she was spitting out of her mouth the ash and grit of disillusion. . . . She could only stiffen in rejection, in rejection. She seemed always negative in her action.

Such is her state as Lawrence moves into the final pages of his story, and to extricate Ursula from her negation, to provide her with an earned vision at the close was, as is apparent, no easy task. At this point Ursula begins to per-

ceive, dimly, a world outside experience, a world outside the "circle lighted by a lamp," a world dark and mysterious where "she saw the eyes of the wild beast gleaming." Towards that world she must move, out of the circle of the lighted lamp, from the illumination of familiarity into the shadows of the unknown, truly the unknown. This constitutes the search beyond the finite self the personal self.

One day, watching the sea roll in, she comes to know that through the self-consciousness of seeking life one is heir to the shocks of recognition which reveal what one has *not* attained, an exercise of the imagination which presupposes fulfillment of things the other side of the present. Touched by the beauty of the rhythmically moving sea— as she was by the sunset—she laughs and weeps from a single impulse. Then she follows "a big wave running unnoticed, to burst in a shock of foam against a rock . . . leaving the rock emerged black and teeming." Her wish for the fate of the wave is symbolic: "Oh, and if, when the wave burst into whiteness, it were only set free!" If, that is, the wave, making its climactic collision with the rock of the opposing world, could only be liberated from its flux of experience, prevented somehow from falling into the sea again, only to become water for another wave. If only Ursula could fly the flux of her experience and bear away her trophy, the fruits of experience, to the safety of some timeless region that would not condemn her to this ceaseless repetition of battle with life. The image of the liberated wave resembles the circle lighted by a lamp, and both resemble the encircling horde of stallions at the end.

Ursula's final experience with the lighted circle of the world is her futile passion with Skrebensky, and it is preceded by the botany classroom scene in which Ursula makes her penultimate leap. She sees the speck under her microscope moving and it appears vitally alive, but Ursula questions its beingness, its teleology, if it has one: "She only knew that it was not limited mechanical energy, nor mere purpose of self-preservation and self assertion. It was a consummation, a being infinite." By being a fully realized self, one could in fact fly the circle into a "oneness with the infinite": "To be oneself was a supreme, gleaming triumph of infinity." To capture the wave out of the sea was to catapult it into the infinite reaches, where it might be preserved with wholeness. Such an insight followed by yet another disillusionment is not meaningless. The affair with Skrebensky, aside from providing proof of what she has perceived, serves also to clarify the contours of the circle which Ursula must flee. Already as a school teacher she had felt increasingly the "prison . . . round her"; and the sense of wishing to break out of the enclosing and binding circles becomes sharply defined in the penultimate chapter in which, on two occasions, the final rainbow image is clearly prefigured. "This inner circle of light in which she lived and moved" has become too much to bear; and finally she would "not love [Skrebensky] in a house any more." She must go to the downs, into the open spaces, where in the darkness of night she experiences the final "bitterness of ecstasy." They await the dawn: "She watched a pale rim on the sky. . . . The darkness became bluer. . . . The light grew stronger, gushing up against the dark . . . night. The light grew stronger, whiter, then over it hovered a flush of rose. A flush of rose, and then yellow . . . poising momentarily over the fountain on the sky's rim." Here the spectrum of colors certainly suggests the rainbow—the rose burns, then turns to red; "great waves of yellow" are flung over the sky, "scattering its spray over the darkness, which became bluer and bluer . . . till soon it would it self be a radiance." And finally the sun breaks through, "too powerful to look at." Some pages earlier appeared another image, also suggestive of the rainbow, and again Ursula and her lover were in the open: "And in the roaring circle under the tree . . . they lay a moment looking at the twinkling lights on the darkness opposite, saw the sweeping brand of a train past the edge of their darkened field." Such deliberate preparation hardly suggests haste and impatience when Lawrence came to the final pages of his novel.

IV

That Ursula's journey through the widening circles of experience, and her ultimate flight beyond those circle into the arches of heaven, may be limited acts after all is a question Lawrence does not raise until *Women in Love.* There, in retrospect, Ursula sees at one point the possibility that even the exhaustion of experience may bring one only to the threshold of death. Socrates was right: the unexamined life was not worth living; but the modern novelist had to ask whether the examined life was worth living: "She had travelled all her life along the line of fulfilment, and it was nearly concluded. She knew all she had to know, she had experienced all she had to experience, she was fulfilled in a kind of bitter ripeness, there remained only to fall from the tree into death."

But in *The Rainbow* it is not the falling into death but the falling away from it which dominates as an image. In the scene with the stallions Ursula finally accomplishes her transcendence of the circles, precisely by letting herself drop from a tree. In doing so she fulfills the wish given us in an earlier image: "She saw herself travelling round a circle, only an arc of which remained to complete. Then, she was in the open, like a bird tossed into mid-air, a bird that had learned in some measure to fly." Repeatedly the horses come to ring her—"Like circles of lightning came the flash of hoofs"; "They had gone by, brandishing themselves thunderously about her, enclosing her." As the circle closes, every horizontal route of escape "to the highroad and the ordered world of man" is cut off. There is only one way she can move—up: "She might climb into the boughs of that oak tree, and so round and drop on the other side of the hedge." So she proceeds; and her symbolic drop liberates her—as such drops often do in literature—into a consciousness of separateness done with temporal and spatial dimensions of world: "time and the flux of change passed away from her, she lay as if unconscious . . . like a stone . . . unchanging . . . whilst everything rolled by in transcience . . . [she was] sunk to the bottom of all change." Now may the kernel shed the enclosing husk and "take itself the bed of a new sky"; only the child remains: "[it] bound her . . . like a bond round her brain, tightened on her brain." But when that bond is loosened she is ready for her rainbow—ready because free at last from the perpetuity of experience which had victimized her for so long. There is no taking the past away, for

it had to be; only the full commitment to the circles of experience allows one to escape them. Ursula has escaped the fate of her father, who had gained "knowledge and skill without vision."

At the end of the novel there is no doubt that the reader has earned a vision of the rainbow, for he, unlike Ursula, has been subjected to the struggle of not one but three generations. But, if we look upon *The Rainbow* as a modern *Bildungsroman,* a trial and error warfare with experience, which allows finally a glimpse of an ideal that rises inevitably out of experience, then there can be little doubt that Ursula too has earned the right to her open, semi-circular rainbow, leaving her free like a bird "that has learned in some measure to fly."

In none of the three major novels—*Sons and Lovers, The Rainbow, Women in Love*—does Lawrence resolve his ending as the logical, inevitable conclusion to a single ruling passion. Had he done so Paul Morel should have committed suicide; Ursula should have died of her heavy losses; and *Women in Love* should have been altogether an impossible book to write. Those who accuse Lawrence of a sleight of hand at the end of novels fail to see the intuition and later the consciousness of his purpose, for he was quite aware that his conclusions were not the neat, conventional climaxes that satisfy a reader's expectations because they are coincident with his prophecies. Such endings he would have considered "immoral":

> Because *no* emotion is supreme, or exclusively worth living for [or dying for, he might have added]. *All* emotions go to the achieving of a living relationship between a human being and the other human being or creature or thing he becomes purely related to. . . . If the novelist puts his thumb in the pan, for love, tenderness, sweetness, peace, then he commits an immoral act: he *prevents* the possibility of a pure relationship, a pure relatedness . . . and he makes inevitable the horrible reaction, when he lets his thumb go, towards hate and brutality, cruelty and destruction.

No one emotion carried to its end tells the whole truth, because it obstructs the basic complexity of the human psyche, its multifarious potential to act, to fulfill, at many levels, its inner needs in balance with the outer demands of the world. "The business of art is to reveal the relation between man and his circumambient universe, at the living moment." Lawrence goes on to call this "living moment" a "fourth dimension," "a revelation of the perfected relation, at a certain moment, between a man" and his object. And that "which exists in the non-dimensional space of pure relationship is deathless, lifeless, and eternal . . . beyond life, and therefore beyond death." So precisely does Ursula exist at the conclusion of *The Rainbow.* Here Lawrence succeeded in capturing the "momentaneous" (it is a favorite word) in the midst of timelessness: this is the essential meaning of the rainbow. Ursula's "living moment" is therefore beyond life or death, in the fourth dimension where neither hope nor despair has any business.

In its demand that the hero experience—indeed, that he seek out experience—and suffer for it, *The Rainbow* remains an entirely conventional *Bildungsroman,* a type of novel naturally suited to a man of Lawrence's passionate pedagogic temperament. But in rejecting, at the end both the hero who is a helpless victim of experience and the hero whom experience transforms into a malcontent, Lawrence achieved a new dimension for the novel of education in the twentieth century: the hero has been "*emotionally* educated [which] is rare as a phoenix." Here lies the true originality of form in *The Rainbow*: at the end of experience the hero has gained the privilege of release from it; and the *Lehrjahre*—post-apprenticeship learning—really lie ahead in the *Wanderjahre,* in the inconclusiveness of *Women in Love,* where experience is not tested against the world but against one's self. The end of experience, in the modern world, is only the beginning of selfhood. Life is no longer just a school nor experience a mere teacher: both have become antagonists to conquer in exchange for freedom. It is a fair war since Lawrence never refuses to exact the price of suffering. The "human moral," having fully tested the "social moral," is at liberty to discriminate. Such a view of experience has influenced a writer like Hemingway (one of the few modern novelists Lawrence admired), whose heroes—despite their hunger for experience—wish finally to become educated "emotionally" and thereby be liberated from the compulsive tests of experience, Hemingway going Lawrence one better by suggesting a "fifth dimension" in which this might be achieved. Certainly the ending of *The Old Man and the Sea* owes something in spirit to that of *The Rainbow*: after the worst that experience can inflict, the old man comes home to dream of the lions on the beach.

"While a man remains a man, a true human individual," Lawrence insisted, "there is at the core of him a certain innocence or naïveté. . . . This does not mean that the human being is nothing but naïve or innocent. He is Mr. Worldly Wiseman also to his own degree. But in his essential core he is naïve." Here surely is an account of Ursula as we find her at the end of the novel: worldly-wise but purged, and at the core innocent. For Goethe the end of experience was also the end of innocence, for in his world the hero's path was still clearly marked so that, in proportion as the hero grew wise, he would choose the right way: the flux of experience gave way to the steadiness of wisdom. For Lawrence—as for others, of course—the modern world offered no such clear topography, and experience had indeed become, in a way, as Pater had said, an end in itself. *Wilhelm Meister,* Goethe told Eckermann, "seems to say nothing more than that man, despite all his follies and errors, being led by a higher hand, reaches some happy goal at last." Love, Lawrence said, "travels heavenwards": "Love is not a goal; it is only a travelling. . . . death is not a goal; it is a travelling. . . . There is a goal . . . absolved from time and space, perfected in the realm of the absolute." For a moment Ursula and the rainbow merge to chart that absolute—vertical, not horizontal; and in that merging they objectify what Lawrence set down as a definition of art: "the relation between man and his circumambient universe." But Ursula reaches no "happy goal" at the end of her experience in *The Rainbow,* and the novelist, like his heroine, had to begin again, from a different perspective, where Goethe could contentedly end.

Richard Wasson   (essay date 1968)

SOURCE: "Comedy and History in *The Rainbow,*" in *Modern Fiction Studies,* Vol. XIII, No. 4, Winter, 1967-68, pp. 465-77.

[*In the following essay, Wasson interprets* The Rainbow *as a comedy wherein marriage and the union of the individual and society are the end goals.*]

Scholarship on D. H. Lawrence reminds one of a guerrilla war; Leavisites, Christians, Marxists, Freudians, Liberals, Utopians, and a few confessed demonics ambush each other and stage coups and counter-coups within their own groups. Yet for all their warfare they disagree less than one might suppose over the substance of any given novel. In discussions of *The Rainbow* critics compulsively return to the same scenes interpreting them with some variation, but generally functioning within a narrow area of agreement. For all the talk about Ursula's encounter with the horses, for example, criticism has not advanced much beyond saying that some repressed passion returns to Ursula's consciousness. For all the debate about Lawrence and tradition, no critic has talked about the structural principles of *The Rainbow,* a result of the unquestioned assumption that Lawrence's novels are poetic dramas or even *symboliste* poems. Nor, for all the discussion of Lawrence's theories of history, society, and personality, are these related to each other and to the form of the work.

Considered in structural terms *The Rainbow* is a comedy whose central metaphor is, as the first title implied, marriage, the traditional comic image for fulfillment in personal, social and sexual terms. Conventionally, in comedy, erotic youth struggles against age seeking to replace a repressive legal, moral and social code with a freer, less distorted style of life. In comedy eros seeks fulfillment and freedom while the society in power seeks to preserve its repressive order.

In most comedy, eros and its enemies are externalized, but in Lawrence's works they are internalized. In most comedies children battle parents, but in *The Rainbow* the child (Anna and Ursula) often prevents adult fulfillment. Putting these two hypotheses together, it follows that the struggle for fulfillment often takes place against the internalized child. Though Lawrence rejected Freud's notion that adult sexuality is always conditioned by the incest motive, he agreed that the erotic motive rarely achieves mature fulfillment in our time. Hence the fulfillment of eros means for both Freud and Lawrence overcoming object relationships dictated by childhood wishes, and hence comedy depends not so much on a struggle against external parent figures, as in overcoming the parent and child hidden in oneself.

But that is comic structure in its broadest mythological and psychological framework; we also want to know about structure in the sense of the novel's organization. Criticism on this level usually treats the novel in three sections based on character relationships; Tom and Lydia, Anna and Will, Ursula and Skrebensky. Yet *The Rainbow* like *Women in Love* has two central chapters, "The Child" and "The Marsh and the Flood," which, though they catch up the central themes of the novel, are analytical and seldom treated by critics bent on reading the novel as symbolic drama.

The job then is to analyze the novel in terms of its comic structure. Such analysis clarifies one central theme revolving around the interaction between the individual personality and society. In its treatment of the development of society (history) the novel shows how unresolved personal conflicts contribute to the dissolution of society which in turn only aggravates personal conflicts. Historical processes become manifestations of psychological ones (or vice versa) and Lawrence's achievement lies in his formal expression of these intricate relationships. The essentially comic struggle of eros to achieve mature fulfillment of desire becomes in Lawrence's hands an immensely effective tool for providing a psycho-analytic view of history.

By now criticism has proven that the opening passages of the novel create two worlds which are somehow to be reconciled—those of the Brangwen men and of their women. The male world is characterized by blood intimacy, the natural cycle, work, animals, the land, by creative darkness, silence and safety. The masculine myth centers in the seasonal cycle of nature and the pulse of animals; hence history is simply repetition and inheritance. The world of the women is social, of the towns, class, knowledge, experience, thought, comprehension, and language. The principle of this world is dominance, while that of the male world is unity. Its myth is the aspiring quest for position: hence history is power and culture. The women wish for experience, the men for a kind of innocence, and the lifelong project of both is to keep the two in balance. Three centers are implied: one in the natural world, the other in the verbal and cultural world, and a third in the stable unity of the two in marriage.

History has made the tenuous balance difficult to maintain. By 1840, in Tom's youth, society has thrust a canal into the farm driving back its boundary; a colliery and railway move in to take up the ground. The natural and social myths are disturbed by "the rhythmic run of the winding engines" and the old social order begins to disintegrate. The Brangwen men "still live on the safe side of civilization" but they become "almost tradesmen." The women's world is no longer rural and aristocratic, but industrial. History jeopardizes the precarious centers of balance and becomes a threat to complete marriage, a blocking figure.

But internal forces are at work as well. Tom Brangwen as the last boy in the family "belonged . . . to the company of his sisters. He was his mother's favorite." "Rooted in his mother and sisters," Tom goes out into the world for an education, but school violates his male nature and he rejects not civilized society but himself. An inward-gazing Brangwen, he cannot relate anything "known in himself" to his learning, "so he had a low opinion of himself." Finally, he returns to the farm, and firmly centered in his own world, attempts to find fulfillment in the traditional way—through marriage. But his wish is blocked by his relation to his mother and sister, for he cannot find a woman who is both sexual and civilized. His first experience with a prostitute leads only to nullity. His object choice is split between loose women and his mother and sister, none of whom can give complete fulfillment. Then in a remarkable

and seldom discussed scene he meets a girl accompanied by an older foreign aristocrat. It is the man who is "most significant" for Tom. "The man was most amazingly a gentleman all the time, an aristocrat." "Brangwen loved the other man for his exquisite graciousness, for his tact and reserve, and for his ageless monkey-like self-surety." The chief quality which Brangwen appreciates in this embodiment of the aristocracy is "the gracious manner, the fine contact." This wise old man, potent enough to win a young girl, wishes Brangwen a "bon voyage" in life and makes him acutely aware of a manner of living different from blood intimacy. Education failed to put him into relation with the social world, but this encounter constitutes an awakening to life's possibilities: "What was there outside his knowledge, how much? Where was life, in that which he knew or all outside him?"

Shortly afterward he meets Lydia Lynsky, eight years older than himself, representative of the aristocratic outer world. In a situation ripe with comic possibilities the rustic plain dealer courts the aristocratic lady; Lawrence arranges a marriage emblematic of the union between the two, though the world represented by Lydia is far different from that the Brangwen women imagine. Lydia is the daughter of a debt ridden, anti-semitic nobleman, who scandalized the neighborhood by riding through the countryside in a railway wagon full of naked girls, and the widow of a cosmopolitan patriot, who like Yeats's political prisoner, becomes a bitter, abstract thing, full of phrases but without sexual passion. Lydia's world is one of waste and deprivation where sexual relations deteriorate, children die and exile is necessary to existence. She stands as a refutation of the dreams of Brangwen women and foreshadows the coming dissolution of English society. Involvement in the social world breeds involvement with history and that breeds abstraction and corruption in personality. But, because Lydia's childhood was spent in the country, and Brangwen remains "rooted in the order of the stars," they manage to marry.

In typical comedy the marriage would signal the new society, but for Lawrence the victory of love over law comes only with perfect sexual union. In typical comedy the blocking figures are usually aging parents, but here the child Anna acts as the frustrating force: "like one bewitched," "like a changeling," she refuses to accept her new father. Tom, in trying to cope with her, comes to recognize childishness as a thing "so utter and so timeless . . . a thing of all ages." Returning to his own childhood he empathizes with Anna's helplessness and is reminded of his mother by a shawl Anna wears. He lives in a world bounded by mother and step-daughter, who block for the moment matrimonial fulfillment. In the barn scene Tom thaws Anna's frozen resistance, but only because he goes "back again in the old irresponsibility and security, becoming a boy." As a result "they were like lovers, father and child."

Such a relationship serves only to increase sexual tensions. Trying to resolve them, Tom decides to make Anna a lady, thus encouraging the aggressive instincts latent in the female view of the world. Seeking a solution to his problems, Tom visits his brother Alfred's mistress to discover the nature of sexual contact in the aristocratic world. His wish to make Anna a lady is clearly sexual. His visit, however, creates a crisis in his relationship with Lydia who quickly spots his erotic motive—at least in relation to his brother's mistress—and shocks Tom by suggesting that he too take another woman. In anger she accuses him of taking her "like your cattle," and holds up her dead husband as a model who treated her "as if [she were] something to him," demanding from Tom the gracious contact he so admired in the aristocratic stranger and his brother's mistress. Lydia then demonstrates her meaning, by embracing him and revealing to him the "mould of his own nakedness" making him "passionately lovely to himself." This "gracious contact" releases Tom from bondage, for he at last finds acceptance by the aristocratic world and need no longer remain in the closed world of "blood intimacy" nor despise himself for his failure in the world of society and culture. Though that world remains a mystery to him, it is no longer a matter of concern and fear; he need no longer consume energy trying to comprehend it. He is able finally to let himself go from both mother and child, "from both past and future" and establish a bond with the present: "What was memory after all, but the recording of a number of possibilities which had never been fulfilled?" Lydia too forgets her old life and finds fulfillment with Tom.

The central obstacles—the historical and personal past—are overcome in comic sexual union. Tom is no longer rooted in mother and child; through passionate contact with the myth of the Brangwen women as it lives in the body of Lydia, he approaches mature fulfillment. In refuting the past foisted upon him by familial females, by getting beyond the "blood-intimacy" of the oedipal situation (according to Lawrence, not Freud), he passes into adult sexuality. With Lydia, freed from her aristocratic past, he establishes a familial society and frees Anna from the bondage imposed by his appeal to her.

However, this integration of self through marriage, the establishment of a small esoteric society, has little effect on the progress of society. Though one can overcome one's own past, one cannot overcome the forces of history. Anna must seek her salvation in a world where confusion and chaos have progressed, and the simple distinctions defining the world of Tom's ancestors no longer obtain. Though Anna begins her quest protected by the pillar of fire and the pillar of cloud, she is caught in social and psychological forces which lead her not to Zion but to the suburbs of the dreadful city. The possibility of fulfillment is made difficult because the outward oriented woman, urged on not only by mother but by father love, can find no land-oriented man.

Will Brangwen, the son of Alfred, whose artistic spirit was cramped by industrialized lace making, functions only in the female world. He seeks a place in cultured society, having lost all contact with nature's intimate rhythms. Anna, rooted in Tom, has the advantage here, and in the harvest scene quickly establishes her dominance over him. The scene recalls the rhythmic work in the barn in which Anna's resistance to Tom was weakened and turned to a kind of love by his movement; but Anna's lover can only

exercise his will in the hope of meeting her movement. He is subjugated to her rhythms.

The masculine and feminine roles are reversed; Will seeks unity of experience in the creation and appreciation of art, specifically art related to churches. The consequences of this role-reversal are made so explicit in the cathedral scene that only symbol hunting critics could ignore it. The debate between Anna and Will is really a debate over the nature of the aesthetic symbol. To Anna the carved gargoyle is a fact, the artist's satirical representation of his wife. To Will the gargoyle is primarily a part of the total religious conception of the church which includes all life. The comedy here is simple. Anna plays eiron to Will's alazon while the gargoyle plays eiron to the spiritual world symbolized by the church's soaring arches. For Will the church represents an absolute and coherent totality in a chaotic world: "a world . . . within a chaos: a reality, an order, an absolute, within a meaningless confusion." Like some symbolists, Hulme, Eliot and the new critics, Will wants the aesthetic symbol to be free from contingency, a perfectly ordered reality operating in its own created world. For Anna such a construction is nothing but dead matter, inferior to the living world which has its own order. The ironic gargoyles "knew quite well, these little imps that retorted on man's own illusion, that the cathedral was not absolute. They winked and leered, giving suggestion of the many things that had been left out of the great concept of the church."

Like them Anna knows the church is only "dead matter lying there," "a shapely heap of dead matter—but dead, dead." It becomes shapely rubbish to Will also: "That which had been his absolute, containing all heaven and earth, was become to him as to her." Yet Will cannot give it up: "Still he loved the Church. As a symbol he loved it." The church, a cultural and aesthetic symbol, once served to define the worlds of Brangwen men and women but no longer exists in living relation with them. It is a dead symbol signalizing the moribund but still controlling past. History becomes neither the reassuring cycles of generation nor the story of progressive dominance, but a stultifying memory, which, like Tom's memory of his childhood, blocks life in the present.

Without the natural cycle, with only dead cultural forms to respond to, Anna and Will turn to their isolated selves. Unlike the typical Brangwen woman, Anna very soon learned to be indifferent to public life and Will finds fulfillment not in his daytime work but in tending the dead body of the local church. The sexual roles are reversed, for Will seeks selfhood in the society, Anna in the reproductive rhythm of her body.

And Ursula suffers the consequences. In the book's central chapter, "The Child," Lawrence details the effects of the parents's perversion on the first born. Will, isolated from work and wife, waits for the child to come to consciousness and "then he took Ursula for his own." But he takes her, as Tom first took Anna, in terms of his childish helplessness: "her cry is his cry of his own vulnerable nakedness"; he is "a child along with her." "Between him and the little Ursula there came into being a strange alliance. . . . His life was based on her, even whilst she was a tiny child, on her support and her accord." As Anna abandons them to bear more children, they draw closer together. "It was then that his child Ursula strove to be with him. She was with him, even as a baby of four. . . ."

But strive as she might, she finds her relationship with him doomed to failure. First, she senses that something is wrong with Will. "Ursula knew that he was wrong. In the outside, upper world, he was wrong." Then comes the sense of her own inferiority: "But there was the dim childish sense of her own smallness, and inadequacy, a fatal sense of worthlessness. She could not do anything. She was not enough. This knowledge deadened her from the first." Awakened by her father's clasping her to his body for love and fulfillment, she finds him unresponsive and herself unable to provide the necessary "love."

The key scene comes when she tries to help Will plant potatoes, an episode which recalls in its emphasis on the rhythms of work, those between Tom and Anna, Anna and Will. While he moves up and down the rows in his characteristic mechanical way, he chastizes her incapacity. She becomes "conscious of the great breach between them. She knew she had no power."

As a consequence, Ursula finds herself "helplessly stranded on his world," a world she considered inherently hostile: "So very soon, she came to believe in the outward malevolence that was against her. And very early, she learned that even her adored father was part of this malevolence. And very early she learned to harden her soul in resistance . . . harden herself upon her own being."

The perfect emblem of Will's death-dealing mechanical nature comes in the scene on the swingboats, for he seeks to reach the "high horizontal" which will dump the two of them out. His misplaced eros, his guilt turns him toward death: "His eyes were full of the blackness of death. It was as if death had cut between their two lives, and separated them." Perceiving the dominance of his death instinct, Ursula's soul turns "dead toward him." She "continued to love him, but ever more coldly."

Of the effect of this family romance on Ursula, more will be suggested later: but Lawrence's analyses of Will's role provides so intricate an insight into the relation of personality and history that it deserves full commentary. Isolated from his wife, guilty in his relationship with Ursula, he seeks an extramarital affair, the consequences of which provide a devastating comment on contemporary marriage and society. In the Empire Theatre he meets a young girl, "small almost like a child, and pretty. Her childishness whetted him keenly. She would be helpless in his hands." Unlike Tom who defined himself in the terms of the aristocracy, Will finds a labor class girl, a product of encroaching industrial society. Further he enters a sadistic, death dominated sexual world: "He was for himself, the absolute, the rest of the world was the object that should contribute to his being." Like the Marquis de Sade and Gerald Crich, he perceives himself as a superior being for whom the rest of the world exists to be subjugated and exploited. He seeks a sexual partner who will fulfill his unresolved love for Ursula, a girl with no identity of her own: "About the girl herself, who or what she was, he cared

nothing, he was quite unaware that she was anybody. She was just the sensual object of his attention." His minute climb in social station, his participation in the town, the creation of a proletariat, the decline of the aristocratic idea contribute to the depersonalization begun by his response to Ursula. Where Tom perceived superiority and otherness, Will perceives inferiority and the sense of himself as an absolute.

As a consequence of his flirtation, Will comes back to Anna, not to find as Tom did, an aristocratic woman who through gracious contact can free him from himself, but a woman ready to answer the challenge of his perverse sensuality. They find not unity, but isolation: "He was the sensual male seeking his pleasure, she was the female ready to take hers: but in her own way." As isolated selves, they abandoned "in one motion the moral position, each was seeking gratification pure and simple." "There was no tenderness, no love . . . only the maddening, sensuous lust for discovery. . . ." Their physical contact becomes "a sensuality violent and as extreme as death. It was all the lust and infinite, maddening intoxication of the sense, a passion of death." They are led, like de Sade's characters, to "unnatural acts of sensual voluptuousness."

Thus Will's love for his child leads not to adult fulfillment but to infantile, immoral sensuality. And this sensual awakening leads Will back to the outside world; he becomes a teacher of woodworking in a night school. But this too is a result of his unresolved love for Ursula. Lawrence could not be clearer, for, in thinking about his new job, Will dimly perceives that Ursula "seemed to be at the back of his new night-school venture." The results of Will's conflict are an allegoric-cultural history, for, as Lawrence explains in *Psychoanalysis and the Unconscious,* "incest is the logical conclusion of our ideals when these ideals have to be carried into passional effect." But the process is circular, for the escape from actual incest leads only to a social life motivated by the same wish. Hence, culture breeds a downward spiral, urging the individual to carry his immoral wish into his work. Here the comedy moves toward irony, for society is a collection of egos held together only by naked dominance and the urge for death; in society Will merely acts out his unresolved feelings for Ursula, his death dominated sensuality.

That death is the chief force at work in social and psychological processes is made even clearer in the chapter "The Marsh and the Flood" which shares with "The Child" the center of the novel. Like the Noah story on which it is modeled, the flood comes at a time in history when civilization has reached a dead end. But where the Hebraic-Christian flood brings a redemptive promise and Noah is seen as the bringer of a new age who rescues mankind from the return to chaos, Lawrence's flood signals the end of the old order. With Tom passes the agricultural myth which no longer can sustain society. The old world has been broken, and Anna and Will live in a society dominated by incest and death, by fruitless and unregenerating work, a new world modeled on hell, on the demonic.

In literary terms we move from esoteric comedy where at least one family can be saved from destruction, to an ironic world ruled by forces of death. From now on the novel presents a world in which fire and water, light and dark, are almost always destructive a world of bondage, beatings, torture places and prisons of hyenas and wolves, of sexual inversion and perversion (the marriage of [Winifred] Inger and Uncle Tom), a world of ghouls, vampires, werewolves, incubi, invisible men driven mad, of dung heaps and cities of dread. "All was grey, dry ash, cold and dead and ugly."

The flood marks a point in history similar to that in Yeats's system when the thread reverses direction on the gyres. Hence Ursula's quest is Blakean: in a demonic world one must seek what others think demonic, for paradoxically that is the God-like. The touchstone of her quest comes from the Noah story for she takes as her slogan the phrase "The Sons of God came into the daughters of men." According to some conventions of Christianity the "Sons of God" are the fallen Angels whose brutal power led to political violence and sexual corruption; it was the intercourse between these fallen angels which produced a degenerate progeny making God's wrath necessary.

To her the angels are not devils, but symbols of man's prelapsarian strength: "And perhaps these children, these sons of God, had known no expulsion, no ignominy of the fall." Yet, they are not pagan Gods: "Not Jove or Pan nor any of those gods, not even Bacchus nor Apollo, could come to her." Thus her quest is conceived in Christian terms and her wish so strong that she "believed more in her desire and its fulfillment than in the obvious facts of life." For her, sexual fulfillment becomes a refutation of the demonic present, for the Sons of God are in Lawrence's word "unhistoried." Essentially, Ursula, like Stephen Dedalus, seeks to escape from the nightmare of history.

Ursula's quest is conditioned, as William Walsh has so perceptively pointed out, by her father's love. Her notion of time, of objects, of the hostility of the external world are all related to her early awakening to her father's needs. Will's love "communicates its distortion to the child's very sensibility so that it sees a disturbed and malicious world from which it must flee into itself. . . . A child can tolerate a malevolent world only by denying its reality, and so like Ursula it becomes convinced of, and tortured by, the illusion and trickery of everything beyond its own identity." Her participation in the women's myth of power and dominance is conditioned by the incest motive; powerless against her father she makes herself cold and hard in order to exercise her power over the world. Though her fights with the Phillips boys, her teaching, her relationship with Miss Inger all reflect her situation, her affair with Skrebensky most fully describes her relationship with her father. Not only does he remind her of Will both physically and in his personality but in the earlier phases of their relationship, she repeats the experience she had with her father. One of the first things they do is go for a ride on the swingboats, an almost too obvious parallel. Ursula sees the invitation to ride as a challenge: "She would have liked to hang back, but she was more ashamed to retreat from him than to expose herself to the crowd or to dare the swingboat." Accepting the dare "she was not afraid. She was thrilled" and finds her blood fanned to fire—not of love

but destruction: "Daring and reckless and dangerous they knew it was, their game, each playing with fire not with love." Their love, like that of Will and Anna, is aggressive sensuality: "It was magnificent self-assertion on the part of both of them, he asserted himself before her, he felt himself infinitely male and infinitely irresistible, she asserted herself before him, she knew herself infinitely desirable, and hence infinitely strong. And after all, what could either of them get from such passion but a sense of his or of her own maximum self, in contradistinction to all the rest of life?" Ursula now a woman, plays for love with the power she lacked in her relationship with her father.

Eros no longer seeks unity of opposites, but sets self against the world and sexual life burns with diseased fever. In this state, Ursula makes her assault on the man's world and in the microcosm of the school room learns again that "power and power alone . . . mattered." It is like de Sade's world, in which there are only the strong and the weak, the punishers and the punished. Dominating it is Mr. Harby, the "evil spirit" who though he has strength, male power and a certain beauty, is a bully knowing only how to inflict his punishing will on his subordinates and students. Just as Will's world has Ursula behind it, hers is dominated by her relationship with him: "In the government, she knew which minister had supreme control over Education, and it seemed to her that, in some way, he was connected with her, as her father was connected with her." Ursula's condition is not some personal disease needing treatment, but the condition of the world. The processes of history have so affected individual personalities that society, made up of isolated and aggressive egos, can only reflect unresolved needs. Further, as they fail to resolve those needs and continue to act, they create a society which confirms and encourages the disease. Though Ursula's quest leads through one gateway after another, each "was a gate into another ugly yard, dirty and active and dead."

The central problem lies in the failure of the world to provide adequate sexual objects. Ursula cannot find restoration with a Brangwen-like man, for she has gone too far into a world which is radically different from the way the Brangwen women imagined it. She rejects Maggie's brother because he is at one with the universe while "she saw it, and was at one with it. Her seeing separated them infinitely."

History has left behind the old solutions and Ursula cannot escape from the internalized relationship with her father. Feeling powerless, she seeks power through aggressive sex. But the old gracious contact of the aristocracy corrupted, driven beyond the possibility of the old precarious Brangwen balance, she seems blocked by the combined forces of history and personality. She toys with the notion of marrying Skrebensky and becoming a submissive woman, but that idea only drives her to further emotional turmoil. Driven by her emotional plight she one day sets out on a walk and encounters a group of horses.

Though critics agree that Ursula faces repressed passion in the scene, they have generally avoided specific comments on its nature. She re-enacts her power struggle with her father, overcomes the childish block, and confirms her quest for the Sons of God. The wood is a phallic prison: "The myriads of tree-trunks . . . thrust like stantions upright between the roaring overhead and the sweeping of the circle underfoot. She glided between the tree-trunks, afraid of them. They might turn and shut her in as she went through their martialled silence." The horses themselves are equally phallic, full of that male power against which Ursula has for so long struggled: "All the hardness and looming power was in the massive body of the horse-group." The looming power of the angry father, the man's world, and Anton Skrebensky are caught up in this symbol, and Ursula feels that fatal inferiority, brought on by her relationship to her father. Freud might see in this scene the menacing power of the desires of the Id united with the angry Super Ego and surely he would be right in reading Ursula's flight as a curative escape from a psychically destructive situation. But Lawrence thought that Freud made the Id only a garbage heap of repressions and that he ignored the deeper level of the unconscious which expressed the laws of nature working in man. "The great laws of the universe are no more than the fixed habits of the living unconscious." On this level the manifestations of the unconscious are, to use Jung's phrase, the dreams of reason. And the reason here is evident, for in Lawrence the horse is a mystic beast. As he puts it in *Apocalypse*:

> Far back in our dark soul the horse prances. . . . and as a symbol he roams the dark underworld meadows of the soul. He stamps and threshes in the dark field of your soul and of mine. *The sons of God who came down and knew the daughters of men and begot great Titans,* they had "the members of the horse," says Enoch. Within the last fifty years man has lost the horse. Now man is lost. (italics mine)

Paradoxically, the horses represent both the power of the father from which Ursula is trying to escape, and the promise of true contact with a male, the prelapsarian sons of God. On one level she escapes from the psychologically oppressive world created by her relationship with Will, and, having escaped from it, confirms her hope for true sexuality, for fulfillment.

Thus unlike the comedy of Tom and Lydia which ends in the temporary establishment of an esoteric society, or Anna and Will, which ends in an ironic society of sensual egos, Ursula's ends with the esoteric insight of a single person who, though she cannot escape from society, is able to maintain herself through a vision of something better. Though the old society is still in power, Ursula's insight enables her to sense a possibility of change.

The rainbow which appears at the end of the novel stands not, as most critics think, for the regeneration of society, but for Ursula's new perception. Freed from the guilt and inferiority she feels imposed upon her by her father's needs, she no longer sees the world as malevolent and hostile, a thing which she must resist with a hard and cold isolation, but as a place of hope and possibility. Lawrence is presenting no Pisgah vision of wholeness, for to him that is not only impossible but destructive. "The moment you attain that sense of Oneness and Wholesomeness, you become cold, dehumanized, mechanical, and monstrous." Ursula's vision confirms not a new society but a new self,

a new perception of the world. Unlike Tom who must isolate his family from society, and Will who returns to society with an oedipally inspired death wish, Ursula returns with a self purged of destructive impulses. Though the old society is unchanged in the comic ending, Ursula has successfully come through a demonic society and self to a new perception of both. She has halted within herself the downward spiral of history, the infection of incest, and has seen the possibility of a less distorted mode of life for herself and perhaps for her society.

David J. Kleinbard   (essay date 1974)

SOURCE: "D. H. Lawrence and Ontological Insecurity," in *PMLA,* Vol. 89, No. 1, January, 1974, pp. 154-63.

[*In the following essay, Kleinbard undertakes a psychological analysis of Will Brangwen.*]

Lawrence's warning to Edward Garnett not to look for "the old stable *ego* of the character" in *The Rainbow* has been a road sign for many commentaries on characterization in that and later novels. In his letter to Garnett he defines his departure from conventional fiction as the portrayal of "another *ego,* according to whose action the individual is unrecognisable, and passes through, as it were, allotropic states which it needs a deeper sense than any we've been used to exercise, to discover are states of the same single radically unchanged element."

It is a mistake to conclude from these remarks that Lawrence has not created recognizable personality configurations in *The Rainbow*. The novel shows a further development of the extraordinary understanding of human psychology that won him the respect of psychoanalysts with the publication of *Sons and Lovers*. In *The Rainbow* Lawrence focuses upon patterns of feeling and thought that have not been adequately interpreted in psychological theory until recently. Will Brangwen most clearly exemplifies Lawrence's intuitive grasp of a mental condition that R. D. Laing analyzes extensively in his study of mental illness, *The Divided Self*. Laing labels this pervasive state of anxiety "ontological insecurity." A person afflicted with "ontological insecurity" has the feeling that he is unreal and the related fantasy that he is almost entirely dependent upon other people for his reality as well as his personal identity. Anyone who is haunted by this fantasy feels "precariously differentiated" from other people. And for this reason "ontological insecurity" often causes a person to imagine that "every relationship threatens [him] with loss of identity" and autonomy.

Such fantasies are apt to seem alien and incomprehensible to persons who have not experienced them and to others who have experienced them without understanding the nature of their own anxieties. But anyone reading *The Divided Self* side by side with the chapters of *The Rainbow* devoted to Will and Anna Brangwen will come away with an ample understanding of ontological insecurity. For Will Brangwen's experience consists very largely of ramifications of this nuclear anxiety.

Lawrence's characterization of Paul Morel in *Sons and Lovers* foreshadows his more extensive development of this state of mind in Will Brangwen and Anton Skrebensky in *The Rainbow,* Hermione Roddice and Gerald Crich in *Women in Love,* and Sir Clifford Chatterley in *Lady Chatterley's Lover.* Will's fantasy that he will "collapse as a house from which the central pillar is removed" if Anna, his wife, is "taken away" from him, closely resembles Paul Morel's belief that his mother is "the only thing that [holds] him up, himself, amid all this." Paul's terror that night and space will annihilate him, at the end of *Sons and Lovers,* after his mother's death, echoes in Will's fear of the "night of heaving, overwhelming flood," which is "his vision of life without" Anna, and in his feeling that he will "drown" in a "flood of unreality" if Anna leaves him:

> She was as the rock on which he stood, with deep, heaving water all round, and he was unable to swim. He must take his stand on her, he must depend on her.
>
> . . . . .
>
> She was the ark, and the rest of the world was the flood.
>
> . . . . .
>
> What had he in life, save her? Nothing. The rest was a great heaving flood. The terror of the night of heaving, overwhelming flood, which was his vision of life without her, was too much for him. He clung to her fiercely and abjectly.

Before considering such fantasies in terms of Laing's analysis of ontological insecurity, I wish to examine briefly Sigmund Freud's theory of anxiety for the sake of comparison. Will's anxiety is analogous to an infant's fear in his mother's absence. In *The Problem of Anxiety* Freud concludes that an infant feels intense anxiety in his mother's absence because he fears that he will be overwhelmed by the tensions arising from needs and impulses that he cannot gratify without his mother's help. According to psychoanalytic theorists the terrifying trauma of birth, involving an unprecedented tidal wave of painful stimuli, lies at the root of all anxiety, as memory traces in the unconscious. The infant lacks the adult's means of delaying gratification and release, as well as the adult's means of obtaining them.

In Will Brangwen the defenses against instinctual drives are insufficiently developed. To some extent he shares the infant's fear that he will be overwhelmed by the wild chaos of his own emotions and impulses and by the tensions that they create. His mind objectifies his fear of massive inundation by internal stimuli in a fantasy that seems very close to hallucination, "the night of heaving, overwhelming flood." This is one of a number of passages in Lawrence's work in which images of drowning and darkness together represent the fearful crumbling of the conscious mind's defenses against unconscious masses of suppressed feelings and drives charged with volcanic energies.

The emphasis upon darkness in Will's fantasy of the flood can be analyzed in very simple terms. For the child as for Will, darkness is fearful largely because it intensifies his sense of his mother's or mother-substitute's absence and of his own isolation.

Another passage in *The Rainbow* supports this comparison of Will's anxiety with the infant's fears. At the beginning of the chapter "The Child" his baby daughter Ursula's crying brings an "answering echo from the unfathomed distances" in her father, terrifying him. "Must he know in himself such distances, perilous and imminent?" The infant's cry seems inhuman to Will, "impersonal, without cause or object." "Yet he echoed to it directly, his soul answered its madness. It filled him with terror, almost with frenzy." He feels that he is not what he conceives himself to be. He experiences the "vulnerable nakedness, the terror of being so utterly delivered over, helpless at every point" that the infant feels. Lawrence explicitly tells us that Will's needs in his dependence on Anna resemble those of a helpless child: "Yet he wanted her still, he always, always wanted her. In his soul, he was desolate as a child, he was so helpless. Like a child on its mother, he depended on her for his living."

Time and again Lawrence dramatizes Will's infantile dependence on Anna and his nearly insane anxiety when he is or thinks he is separated from her. Will's fantasy that he is "clinging like a madman to the edge of reality, and slipping surely, surely into the flood of unreality" that will "drown him" has been anticipated earlier in the novel by a passage describing his sudden dread when he thinks that Anna has left him alone in the house, in the early days of their marriage. His belief that he is alone in the empty house awakens in him a feeling of "horrible emptiness" that makes "his heart ring with insanity."

II

If the psychoanalytic theory of anxiety helps to elucidate Will's fantasy of drowning, Laing's concept of ontological insecurity is equally illuminating. In *The Divided Self* Laing observes that the fantasy of drowning is a fairly universal experience among ontologically insecure persons: "The individual experiences himself as a man who is only saving himself from drowning by the most constant, strenuous, desperate activity." The drowning episode involving Will calls attention to another fantasy pattern typical in persons suffering from severe ontological insecurity. In Will's mind, as in Paul Morel's, the belief that another person supplies him with existence is complemented by the fear that another person will deprive him of his existence and his separate identity. For Will, both these fantasies focus on his wife, Anna: "she was his life and his derivation." "She was as the rock on which he stood, with deep, heaving water all round, and he was unable to swim." At the same time, Anna is the worst threat to his existence. He feels that she is trying to destroy him, "breaking his fingers from their hold on her . . . thrusting him off, into the deep water."

When Anna forces him to sleep alone, Will fears that he will "fall through endless space, into the bottomless pit, always falling, will-less, helpless, non-existent, just dropping to extinction, falling till the fire of friction [has] burned out, like a falling star, then nothing, nothing, complete nothing." After this night of crisis he rises in the morning feeling that he is "unreal."

Will's terror in this passage becomes more comprehensible

in the light of Freud's and Laing's comments on the infant's struggles to master anxiety in his mother's absence. In *Beyond the Pleasure Principle* Freud describes and interprets a baby boy's game with a wooden reel while his mother is away. The boy throws the reel, attached to a string in his hand, out of sight, crying "o-o-o-o" when it disappears. Freud interprets this "o-o-o-o" to mean *"fort"* ("gone"). Then the baby draws the reel back on the string, crying *"da"* ("there") in delight when it reappears. According to Freud, the game helps the child to master his anxiety at his mother's absence. As Freud puts it, the child "compensated himself" for "the renunciation of instinctual satisfaction" that his mother's absence forced upon him, by "staging the disappearance and return of the objects within his reach." In a footnote Freud describes a related game that the child plays with a mirror when his mother is away for a long period of time. This time the child makes *himself* disappear by crouching in front of a full-length mirror. Crouching, he cries, "Baby o-o-o-o!" which means "Baby gone!" And then, of course, he can make himself reappear by standing up again. It is Laing's interpretation of this game that makes it meaningful in terms of Will Brangwen's experience. Laing points out that "the [boy's] fear of being invisible, of disappearing, is closely associated with the fear of his mother disappearing. It seems that the loss of the mother, at a certain stage, threatens the individual with loss of his self." At an early stage the child's sense of himself—of his reality and of his very existence—seems to depend upon his experience of his mother's or a substitute's perception of him as a person, her manifest recognition of and response to his feelings, desires, and "concrete bodily actuality." "The child who cries when [his] mother disappears" feels threatened with his own disappearance into nothingness "since for him also *percipi*=*esse.*" The insecurity in persons like Will Brangwen derives from a similar feeling of dependence. Will's sense of his own reality hinges precariously upon confirmation received from the presence and responses of his mother-substitute wife.

Forced to sleep by himself, Will is afraid to fall completely asleep. In Anna's absence he fears that if "he [relaxes] his will," he will fall to "extinction" and be reduced to "nothing." In the absence of the mother, the baby boy observed by Freud devises a mirror game in which he can fill, by watching himself, the role his mother plays in assuring him of his existence and reality. Similarly, an ontologically insecure person, deprived of the mother or the mothering companion upon whom he feels his existence depends, may substitute unrelaxing self-awareness for the mother figure's attention, as a means of sustaining his sense of his own reality. Such a person is constantly "assuring himself that he exists" by maintaining ceaseless awareness of himself. In this psychological condition falling asleep may be especially fearful, as it is for Will, because it consists "in a loss of one's own awareness of one's being as well as that of the world." "Not to be conscious of oneself . . . may be equated with nonentity." In his fantasy that he must continually exert his will if he is to maintain his existence in Anna's absence, Will resembles one of Laing's patients who fears that her "being" (self and world) is "slipping away" now that her "will power" is "used . . . up." She believes that she can no longer "hold on to herself." Simi-

larly, Will's ontological insecurity is characterized as a "horrible slipping into unreality," which "drove him mad" so that "his soul screamed with fear and agony." "He felt as if he were suspended in space, held there by the grip of his will."

The image of the bottomless pit, which appears in the passage describing Will's crisis when he sleeps alone, recurs in **The Crown,** the group of essays Lawrence wrote after finishing **The Rainbow** in 1915. Will very closely resembles a type of person described in **The Crown** who feels that there is an "abyss" at the core of him, that he has "no being," that he must "stop up his hollowness" continually "by pouring vast quantities of matter down his void," as Will feels he must psychologically devour others' identities, interests, emotional vitality, etc. Laing's characterization of "orality" as a facet of ontological insecurity applies to Will as well as to the type of person delineated by the passage in **The Crown** to which I have referred. In extreme instances of ontological insecurity "orality is such that it can never be satiated by any amount of drinking, feeding, eating, chewing, swallowing. . . . It remains a bottomless pit; a gaping maw that can never be filled up."

Anna recurrently has the fantasy that Will wants to "devour her." In other terms he wants "her to be part of himself, the extension of his will." Will's experience with a girl he picks up in a music hall suggests that Anna's fantasy of his desire to devour her psychologically is accurate. The passage portraying Will's encounter with the girl he picks up emphasizes his wish to "absorb" her, to devour all her "properties" through his senses, "to have her in his power, fully and exhaustively to enjoy her." Will tries to relate to the girl as a usable object rather than as a person. He goes for her because he believes she will "be helpless between his hands." He feels that his own life is "barren" and wishes to fill his emptiness and quicken his deadness with her life. And this is how Will relates not only to the girl but to everyone else, defending himself against all real relationships, in his ontological insecurity, by depersonalizing others: "the rest of the world was the *object that should contribute to his being*" (italics added).

In short, one might say that Will is trying to "fill up his emptiness . . . with others," to use Laing's metaphor. Discussing people with a weak sense of identity in "The Problem of Ego Identity," Erik Erikson indicates that they may wish to achieve an identity by devouring the therapist's, by filling or strengthening their own "weak core" with the therapist's "essence" and "identity": "There is first a sudden intense impulse to completely destroy the therapist, and this, it seems, with an underlying 'cannibalistic' wish to devour his essence and identity. At the same time, or in alternation, there occurs a fear and a wish to be devoured, to gain an identity by being absorbed in the therapist's essence." Will's very similar desire to merge and remain fused ("knitted one rock") with Anna derives from his weak sense of identity.

III

Will is intensely ashamed of his dependence on Anna. Much as he cannot bear the thought of separation from her, he longs to be free from her: "He went on from day to day in a blackness of rage and shame and frustration. How he tortured himself, to be able to get away from her. But he could not. . . . He wanted to leave her, he wanted to be able to leave her. For his soul's sake, for his manhood's sake, he must be able to leave her." The repetition communicates the urgency of Will's need to leave Anna and his desperation, frustration, and shame. But he feels that he is in an impossible trap. To leave her is "to die."

In *The Self and Others* Laing makes the rather obvious point that a person who "lives vicariously . . . through the lives of others" will inevitably come to feel that his own life is unfulfilling and that his development of his potential for creative activity has stopped. Will's relationship with Anna clearly illustrates this argument. Living entirely through Anna, having "nothing but her," Will feels that he will never find satisfactory channels for creative, self-expressive activity. And for this reason he imagines that his latent, potential self will never be realized: "He was aware of some limit to himself, of something unformed in his very being, of some buds which were not ripe in him, some folded centres of darkness which would never develop and unfold whilst he was alive in the body. He was unready for fulfilment. Something undeveloped in him limited him, there was a darkness in him which he could not unfold, which would never unfold in him." "He had failed to become really articulate, failed to find real expression . . . in spirit, he was uncreated." Clinging to Anna for "his very life," Will feels that his life and identity are submerged in hers.

Lawrence himself must have faced this dilemma at one time. In a letter he sent to Katherine Mansfield in December 1918, he says that the man who "casts himself as it were into his woman's womb," when his woman is "the devouring mother" or "Magna Mater" type, finds it "awfully hard, once the sex relation has gone this way, to recover. If we don't recover, we die." In other words, a man must not make his woman "his goal and end" in the hope of finding "his justification in her" alone (*Letters*).

Lawrence formulates the same argument in simpler terms in *Fantasia of the Unconscious*: "When [man] makes woman, or the woman and child the great centre of life and of life-significance, he falls into the beginnings of despair." Will sees that in doing this "he must put out his own light." In the worst moments of his emotional crises he feels that "he must kill her [Anna] or himself." He feels this way because his utter dependence on her makes him proportionately desperate to be freed from her and, at the same time, paradoxically, because she is insisting that he achieve independence from her and thus (in his fantasy) is attempting to deprive him of "his life and his derivation." In terms of his fantasy life, killing Anna would be just as suicidal as killing himself. Ontological insecurity involves a person in webs of paradoxical thought and contradictory impulses.

IV

Now I would like to explore at greater length Lawrence's recurrent suggestions that Anna is a mother-substitute for Will. This aspect of their relationship seems to me to be the nucleus of the difficulties between them. Laing discuss-

es the fear and anger of the "hysteric" who discovers that another person is not "the embodiment of his or her phantasy prototype of the other." Will resists "recognizing his wife as a real person, rather than as an embodiment of his [unconscious] phantom [fantasy image] of his mother." (In this respect his experience recalls Paul Morel's way of perceiving Miriam Leivers in *Sons and Lovers*.)

Even after Will has ceased to depend on Anna "like a child on its mother," Lawrence tells us, "he [serves] his wife and the little matriarchy" that his own family has become under Anna's maternal rule.

On first introducing Will, Lawrence suggests his mother's importance to him. Will describes his feeling for her as "a love that was keenly close to hatred, or to revolt." Like Paul Morel, Will is in league with his mother against his father, who goes after other women and keeps a mistress, "neglecting his indignant bourgeois wife without a qualm." Will's ambivalent feelings for his father are precisely the reverse of his attachment to his mother: "Sometimes, he talked of his father, whom he hated with a hatred that was burningly close to love." His "hot," "half articulate" conversations concerning his parents make the parents such a reality for Anna that she feels they are "two separate people in her life." Will's affection for the church, his one persistent interest apart from his life with Anna, springs primarily out of his intimacy with his mother in league against his father, as we see in the following conversation with his uncle, Tom Brangwen:

> "Oh, you go to church then!" said Brangwen.
>
> "Mother does—father doesn't," replied the youth.
>
> It was the little things, his movement, the funny tones of his voice, that showed up big to Anna.

Finally, Lawrence's association of Will with John Ruskin and his mention of Ruskin's influence on Will in juxtaposition with his mention of Will's attachment to his mother suggest that as Lawrence began his characterization of Will he may have had in mind Ruskin's incestuous attachment. In *Fantasia of the Unconscious* Lawrence refers to a statement by Ruskin's wife that her husband was married to his mother: "When Mrs. Ruskin said that John Ruskin should have married his mother she spoke the truth. He *was* married to his mother." I am encouraged in this interpretation because Lawrence makes it clear that Will's mother and Ruskin together are the principal sources of Will's devotion to a church whose maternal significance becomes apparent in the chapter "The Cathedral."

In that chapter Will's visit to Lincoln Cathedral brings to consciousness his fantasy of entering the womb: "He was to pass within to the perfect womb." "His soul leapt up into the gloom . . . it quivered in the womb. . . ." As he approaches the cathedral he refers to it as "she" rather than "it," and Anna's angry reaction to his use of the feminine pronoun stresses its importance. His feeling that the church is "a world . . . within a chaos: a reality, an order, an absolute, within a meaningless confusion" suggests that it unconsciously represents for Will the sheltering home and the mother of his childhood: in this way too his mother remains closely associated with the church to which she committed him as a child. Will's conception of his ecstasy on this occasion as a "passionate intercourse with the cathedral," and the comparison of his "soul" leaping up into the cathedral vaults, with "seed of procreation in ecstasy," make it clear that this entry into the womb involves a fantasy fulfillment of unconscious incestuous desire.

The kind of unconscious attachment to the mother that we find in Will is the subject of Lawrence's group of three essays, entitled **"Education of the People."** There he argues that the mother who encourages too intimate and symbiotic a relationship with her son when he is a child is damning him to a lifelong emotional dependence: "the whole individual crawls helplessly and parasitically . . . to establish himself in a permanent life-oneness with another being, usually the mother."

V

Laing points out that "one's identity is in the first instance conferred on one" by one's parents and parental figures. Often the identity given a person by his parents or parental figures seems alien to his nature; a person acting consciously or unconsciously according to his parents' conception of him often feels that his actions are not meaningful in terms of his own feelings, impulses, and values; his activities are not self-expressive or self-fulfilling. As a result he may suffer from a feeling of emptiness and a sense of the futility of his life. Like Will, he may feel that he is "impotent," "a cripple," "defective," "a fragment," "uncompleted," and "uncreated." He may experience guilt, anxiety, and anger at his failure to fulfill "the obligation one owes to oneself to be oneself, to actualize oneself"; and these emotions may be intensified by the sense that *he* is responsible for his estrangement "from his own true possibilities."

In his feeling that he is "defective," "a fragment," "impotent to move save upon the back of another life," Will is immersed in "the horrible, grasping back-wash of shame." Laing says, "Shame . . . appears to arise when a person finds himself condemned to an identity, a definition of himself, through being the complement of another, that he would wish to repudiate, but cannot." A "complement" is that other person "in and through a relationship with whom self's identity is actualized" or defined. If we assume that Will's mother, because of her own needs, has involved him in a fantasy of dependence upon her, as Paul Morel's mother does in *Sons and Lovers,* we may conclude that Will lives in fantasy as the "complement" of such a maternal figure, now embodied in Anna. Although Anna herself fights against this fantasy, Will's "hatred" and "revolt" are directed against her now, rather than against his mother, in his desire to repudiate this identity, this definition of himself as a childishly dependent, crippled fragment of a man. He hates her and revolts against her as the embodiment of the unconsciously experienced phantom who condemns him to this hateful identity, constraining him from self-fulfillment. Yet he hates Anna all the more because she fights against his confusing her with his unconscious fantasy image of his mother, and refuses to embody that image for him.

Confusion concerning one's identity and the ontological insecurity that results from such confusion are likely "if the definitions of [oneself] given by others are inconsistent or even simultaneously and mutually exclusive." This insight helps to explain Will's experience, as his wife insists that he define himself in a way that is incompatible with the definition developed in his relationship with his mother. In addition, Laing points out that there may be "intolerable dissonances between those different identities-for-others and a feasible identity-for-self." These may result in what Erik H. Erikson calls "role confusion" or "identity confusion" in his book *Childhood and Society.* Erikson considers role confusion a major factor in the failure to achieve self-delineation or a firm sense of identity during the crucial period when a young person should be making choices with regard to his roles in the community, family, sexual relations, and other important aspects of his life; these choices help to define his identity. At this time he should also be integrating earlier identifications with parents and parental figures in "a new *Gestalt* which is more than the sum of its parts" or repudiating these early identifications (*Identity and Anxiety*). According to Erikson, failure to achieve some sort of self-delineation in this way may "lead to a sense of outer isolation and to an inner vacuum which is wide open for old libidinal objects," such as the unconsciously entertained phantom of his mother which Anna embodies for Will. As a consequence of this failure a person may also suffer a "regressive pull" to "more primitive forms of identification," such as Will's fantasy that he lives through Anna.

Will's role or identity confusion arises partly from the conflict between his desire to be master of his family and his feeling that he is completely dependent on Anna. In his sense of his weakness in the relationship with Anna he realizes that his assertion of his right to the "old position of master of the house" is foolish and arrogant. Nevertheless, he is "black with shame and rage" when Anna harps on his folly and presumption and refuses to acknowledge his right to this position.

Will is also involved in another, closely related role or identity confusion. A lace designer like his father, in his frustration at work he resembles his father, who has done *his* work "stubbornly, with anguish, crushing the bowels within him." While at work in his office, Will keeps himself "suspended." He loses all sense of his own existence, working "automatically." He feels that "the man's world" is "exterior and extraneous to his own real life with Anna." "The great mass of activity" in which most men are engaged means "nothing to him." "By nature" he has "no part in it." Yet he experiences contradictory feelings, longing to "loom important as master of one of the innumerable domestic craft [sic] that make up the great fleet of society." He wants to gain "some form of mastery" through his work and his role in the community.

Not only Will's choice of profession but also his desire to be the strong man in the house may arise at least partly from an unconscious identification with his father. Early in the novel Lawrence tells us that "no-one dared gainsay [Alfred Brangwen, Will's father], for he was a strong-willed, direct man." His wife cannot prevent him from living for part of the time with another woman. The resemblance between father and son is suggested when Will, frustrated in his struggle for mastery at home, goes off in search of other women and tries to seduce the girl whom he meets in the music hall. When he returns from this encounter, with a new sense of himself, Anna decides not to fight for "her old, established supremacy," because the sight of him transformed by his new sense of himself reminds her of his father: "And looking at him, and remembering his father, she was wary."

Here it seems probable that an unconscious identification with his strong-willed father leads Will to demand mastery in the house, while at the same time, the childish dependence that his mother encouraged in him continues to play an equally important part in his experience. If this is the case, these two factors cause identity confusion, setting up "intolerable dissonances in the jarring definitions" of the self. Anna's desire to free herself from the burden of Will's dependence and her desire to maintain her "supremacy" in the "matriarchy" she establishes encourage this confusion in her husband's sense of himself. (I do not mean to hang the blame around Anna's neck. Her feelings and behavior are pervasively affected by Will's insecurity and his identity confusion. The couple are involved in a vicious circle.) Will's unconscious identification with his father recalls Paul Morel's use of his father's dialect when he is making love.

Will's identity confusion in his relationship with his daughter Ursula also deserves attention. He experiences fatherly feelings of tenderness for her. Yet at times he is also motivated by sadistic impulses with sensual undertones, and at such times his feelings and behavior seem more appropriate to a perverted lover than a father. Frequently the demands that he makes for confirmation and support from Ursula are the sorts of demands one would expect a child to make on its parent rather than the other way around. His fatherly tenderness appears in a number of passages: "Ursula became the child of her father's heart. . . . He was patient, energetic, inventive for her. He taught her all the funny little things, he filled her and roused her to her fullest tiny measure." "Once she fell as she came flying to him . . . and when he picked her up, her mouth was bleeding. He could never bear to think of it, he always wanted to cry, even when he was an old man." In a subsequent passage Lawrence portrays Will's unusual and completely uncalled-for cruelty to the child: "He would smash into her sensitive child's world destructively." His baffling cruelty creates in Ursula a general sense of "the outward malevolence . . . against her" and causes her to withdraw into herself. And gradually Lawrence suggests the sensual nature of the father's sadism. We are told that his feeling for Ursula is "red-hot" and "passionate." The "lust for destruction" which frequently dominates Will's feelings for Anna is apparent in his treatment of Ursula as well. In one incident after another destructive and erotic impulses together govern Will's behavior toward his daughter. When Ursula is about seven, she and her father often go swimming and diving together. Lawrence tells us that Will loves "to feel the naked child clinging on to his shoulders." They become involved in a battle of wills, as he leaps again and again from the bridge

over a canal, risking both their lives. Despite the strength of the connection between them, Ursula has begun to harden herself against Will's needs and his demands for emotional support and intimacy. These swimming and diving escapades are her father's attempts to break down her resistance. As Lawrence tells us in ambiguous language, "he still wanted her." After each perilous crash into the water with Ursula clinging to Will's shoulders, they sit on the grass and the child looks "wonderingly" at her father. But she remains "unfathomable" and "impregnable," and Will laughs "almost with a sob," not only because of his desperate and frustrated needs, but also because he is aware of his own mad destructiveness:

> She was used to his nakedness. . . . They were clinging to each other, and making up to each other for the strange blow that had been struck at them. Yet still, on other days, he would leap again with her from the bridge, daringly, almost wickedly. Till at length, as he leapt, once, she dropped forward on to his head, and nearly broke his neck, so that they fell into the water in a heap, and fought for a few moments with death. He saved her, and sat on the bank, quivering. But his eyes were full of the blackness of death. It was as if death had cut between their two lives, and separated them.

Lawrence describes the relationship between father and daughter at this time, when Ursula is a girl of seven, as a "curious taunting intimacy." On one occasion Will takes her up dangerously high in the swingboats at a fair and sends their swingboat sweeping through the air at that fearful altitude so that the jerk at the top of its arc almost shakes them out. As he plays upon her fears and endangers both their lives, his face is "evil and beautiful to her." The saner people in the crowd around them cry shame when he and Ursula leave the swingboat. Afterwards, when Anna hears about this incident, Will's response to her contemptuous anger is "a strange, cruel little smile."

Will's encounter with the girl he meets at the music hall illuminates the unconscious motivation of his behavior toward Ursula. This encounter frees his sadistic sensuality from nearly all constraint. He goes for this girl because she seems to him "almost like a child." "Her childishness whetted him keenly." He feels that she will be "helpless between his hands." Like Ursula, she will be "cruelly vulnerable." He enjoys the girl's attraction to his violence and sensuality and delights in her "terror," as he has relished similar reactions in Ursula.

Will's third role in his relationship with Ursula conflicts with his fatherly tenderness and his sadistic destructiveness. Paradoxically, he wishes his daughter to become a substitute for his mother. Anna, his wife, has refused to play this part. Consequently, even when Ursula is tiny, he feels compelled to demand from her the kind of sympathy and emotional support one might expect a child to ask from its parent:

> When he was disagreeable, the child echoed to the crying of some need in him, and she responded blindly. . . . But her father came too near to her. The clasp of his hands and the power of his breast woke her up almost in pain from the tran-

sient unconsciousness of childhood. Wide-eyed, unseeing, she was awake before she knew how to see. She was wakened too soon. Too soon the call had come to her, when she was a small baby, and her father held her close to his breast, her sleep-living heart was beaten into wakefulness by the striving of his bigger heart, by his clasping her to his body for love and for fulfilment, asking as a magnet must always ask. From her the response had struggled dimly, vaguely into being.

Like a narcissistic child Will is oblivious to Ursula's feelings much of the time. Irresistibly he importunes her for emotional support. But when she struggles to meet this need, he frequently turns on her with an outburst of thoughtless rage that shatters "her sensitive child's world." His demands for help and his swift rejections of her efforts to respond fill her with a feeling of inadequacy: "He took no notice of her, only worked on." " 'You didn't help me much.' " "She stood helplessly stranded on his world. . . . She knew she could not help him."

The harm Will does Ursula exemplifies the disastrous effects of the parasitical relationship between parent and child which Lawrence angrily discusses in *Psychoanalysis and the Unconscious, Fantasia of the Unconscious,* and **"Education of the People."** As Will turns to his child for succor which he can no longer obtain from either his mother or his wife, his behavior dramatizes the pernicious tendency of the parent-child symbiosis to involve the child in a vicious cycle when he becomes a parent, enmeshing his own children, in turn.

VI

In many respects Will Brangwen fails to achieve what Erik Erikson calls a "sense of ego identity." Erikson defines this feeling as "the accrued confidence that the inner sameness and continuity prepared in the past are matched by the sameness and continuity of one's meaning for others." Even after Will has weathered the crisis in which he feels that he is drowning in "unreality," he undergoes experiences of "inchoate rage, when his whole nature [seems] to disintegrate." And long after he frees himself from his subservience to Anna and becomes creatively active in the community, we meet him again in *Women in Love,* seen through Rupert Birkin's eyes as a "strange, inexplicable, almost patternless collection of passions and desires and suppressions and traditions and mechanical ideas, all cast unfused and disunited into this slender, bright-faced man of nearly fifty." Birkin feels that Will is "not a coherent human being," but "a roomful of old echoes." And on this occasion Will still seems tormented by a sense of his own lack of coherence and personal identity: "His face was covered with inarticulate anger and humiliation."

Homer O. Brown　(essay date 1974)

SOURCE: " 'The Passionate Struggle into Conscious Being': D. H. Lawrence's *The Rainbow,*" in *The D. H. Lawrence Review,* Vol. 7, No. 3, Fall, 1974, pp. 275-90.

[*In the following essay, Brown interprets* The Rainbow *in light of Lawrence's writings on human consciousness.*]

At the beginning of **The Rainbow** the experience of the early Brangwen men and the kind of relationship they have with their world are described:

> They felt the rush of the sap in spring, they knew the wave which cannot halt, but every year throws forward young-born on the earth. They knew the intercourse between heaven and earth, sunshine drawn into the breast and bowels, the rain sucked up in the daytime, nakedness that comes under the wind in autumn, showing the birds' nests no longer worth hiding. Their life and interrelations were such; feeling the pulse and body of the soil, that opened to their furrow for the grain, and became smooth and supple after their ploughing, and clung to their feet with a weight that pulled like desire, lying hard and unresponsive when the crops were to be shorn away. The young corn waved and was silken, and the lustre slid along the limbs of the men who saw it. They took the udder of the cows, and the cows yielded milk and pulse against the hands of the men, the pulse of the blood of the teats of the cows beat into the pulse of the hands of the men. They mounted their horses, and held life between the grip of their knees, and they harnessed their horses at the wagon, and, with hand on the bridle-rings, drew the heaving of the horses after their will.

> In autumn. . . . the men sat by the fire in the house where the women moved with surety, and the limbs and the body of the men were impregnated with the day, cattle and earth and vegetation and the sky, the men sat by the fire and their brains were inert, as their blood flowed heavy with the accumulation from the living day.

> The women were different. . . . the women looked out from the heated, blind intercourse of farm-life, to the spoken world beyond. They were aware of the lips and the mind of the world speaking and giving utterance, they heard the sound in the distance, and they strained to listen.

> It was enough for the men, that the earth heaved and opened its furrow to them, that the wind blew to dry the wet wheat, and set the young ears of corn wheeling freshly round about; it was enough that they helped the cow in labour, or ferreted the rats from under the barn, or broke the back of a rabbit with a sharp knock of the hand. So much warmth and generating and pain and death did they know in their blood, earth and sky and beast and green plants, so much exchange and interchange they had with these, that they lived full and surcharged, their senses full fed, their faces always turned to the heat of the blood, staring into the sun, dazed with looking towards the source of generation, unable to turn round.

Perhaps the most obvious thing we can say about this passage, besides the fact that it is a most generalized experience, a group experience, that is being described, is to point to the heavy emphasis on the experience of touch, on tactile and kinesthetic imagery; the passage is hardly visualized at all. If we proceed from this idea to ask ourselves what is the precise nature of this "point of view," the nature of the experience presented to us, we might ask first whether the omniscient narrator is inside the characters or is describing them only from the outside. The question may seem irrelevant, because we are both inside and outside at the same time, or rather, more precisely, there seems to be no *inside* and *outside* in the normal senses of these terms. The language, the point of view, is "impregnated" with the being of the Brangwens in the same way that they are "impregnated with the day, cattle and earth and vegetation and sky." In fact, the normal directions of *inside* and *outside* are explicitly reversed or even overlap. "The Brangwen men faced inwards to the teeming life of creation, . . . their faces always turned to the heat of the blood, . . . so much warmth and generating and pain and death did they know in their blood, earth and sky and beast and green plants." On the other hand, the Brangwen women "looked out" to what is normally inside: the world of thought and utterance and knowledge.

When Lawrence reported to his friend and editor, Edward Garnett (5 June 1914), that he had been reading Marinetti and the Italian Futurists and that **The Rainbow** would be "a bit futuristic—quite unconsciously so," he was undoubtedly referring at least in part to this intermingling of planes of reality. In the early "Technical Manifesto" of Futurist painting, for example, Umberto Boccioni had stressed this interpenetration of surfaces:

> Our bodies penetrate the sofas upon which we sit, and the sofas penetrate our bodies. The motor-bus rushes into the houses which it passes, and in their turn the houses throw themselves upon the motor-bus and are blended with it.

> The construction of pictures has hitherto been foolishly traditional. Painters have shown us the objects and the people placed before us. We shall henceforward put the spectator in the center of the picture.

If we might say the narrator brings us into the center of his picture, we note at once an important difference between him and his characters. Their experience is hardly conscious in the normal sense; it is at best a physical consciousness or awareness, yet the point of view provides us with a verbalized account of their consciousness. We are allowed to understand and participate in an experience that is for them so immediate that they cannot be fully conscious of it: they "knew the intercourse between heaven and earth" but "their brains were inert." What I am suggesting is an apparent contradiction between the conventional view of Lawrence as promoting a return to primitivism, a kind of mindless blood-intimacy with the universe, and the fact that Lawrence as narrator is highly conscious.

Fairly late in the novel, a much later Brangwen, the modern and highly conscious Ursula, confronts again a life like that of her forbears in the form of the animal-like Anthony Scofield, who tempts her with a proposal of marriage, in another Garden of Eden environment. The conventional myth about Lawrence suggests that he would have Ursula jump at the chance of this return to paradise. She considers the proposal wistfully and nostalgically, but something in her will not let her accept it, a something that urges her on to a more complete state of being: "she was a traveller on the face of the earth, and he was an isolated creature lying in the fulfillment of his own senses." Ursula's awareness of the meaning of Scofield parallels the narrator's consciousness of the early Brangwens:

> She turned away, she turned round from him, and saw the east flushed strangely rose, the room coming yellow and lovely upon a rosy sky, above the darkening, bluish snow. All this so beautiful, all this so lovely! He did not see it. He was one with it. But she saw it, and was one with it. Her seeing separated them infinitely.

The inadequacy of Scofield's unconscious participation in nature is already apparent in the lives of the early Brangwens: they are "dazed with looking towards the source of generation, unable to turn round, . . . the teeming life of creation . . . poured unresolved into their veins." They are caught in the flow of blood process, but the Brangwen woman seeks liberation through consciousness:

> Looking out, as she must, from the front of her house towards the activity of man in the world at large, whilst her husband looked out to the back at sky and harvest and beast and land, she strained her eyes to see what man had done in fighting outwards to knowledge . . . her deepest desire hung on the battle that she heard, far off, being waged on the edge of the unknown. She wanted to know, and to be of the fighting host.

The Brangwen men are contrasted to other men "who moved dominant and creative, having turned their back on the pulsing heat of creation, and with this behind them, were set out to discover what was beyond, to enlarge their own scope and range and freedom."

This constant impulse to reach toward what is beyond, to enlarge one's scope and range and freedom by waging battle on the edge of the unknown, carries the seeds of the development of **The Rainbow,** which moves constantly toward a greater range and circle of consciousness: hence, the importance of the word "unknown." In the second paragraph of the novel this sense of the unfulfilled potentiality and the idea of something coming from the "unknown" are emphasized:

> There was a look in the eyes of the Brangwens as if they were expecting something unknown, about which they were eager. They had that air of readiness for what would come to them, a kind of surety, an expectancy, the look of an inheritor.

But this greater consciousness to which the Brangwens are heir is not simply a greater intellectuality, the dominance of mind in the modern world. Again, late in the novel, when Ursula begins to realize the limitations of her own intellectuality, its inadequacies are expressed in the same terms as the limitations of the early Brangwens:

> This world in which she lived was like a circle lighted by a lamp. This lighted area, lit up by man's completest consciousness, she thought was all the world: that here all was disclosed for ever. Yet all the time, within the darkness she had been aware of points of light, like the eyes

of wild beasts, gleaming, penetrating, vanishing, and her soul had acknowledged in a great heave of terror only the outer darkness. This inner circle of light in which she lived and moved, wherein the trains rushed and the factories ground out their machine produce and the plants and animals worked by the light of science and knowledge, suddenly it seemed like the area under an arc-lamp, wherein the moths and children played in the security of blinding light, not even knowing there was any darkness, because they stayed in the light.

But she could see the glimmer of dark movement just out of range, she saw the eyes of the wild beast gleaming from the darkness, watching the vanity of the camp fire and the sleepers: she felt the strange, foolish vanity of the camp, which said "Beyond our light and order there is nothing," turning their faces inward towards the sinking fire of illuminating consciousness, which comprised sun and stars, and the Creator, and the System of Righteousness, ignoring always the vast darkness that wheeled round about, with half-revealed shapes lurking on the edge.

The people of the modern world are confined by a narrow circle of consciousness, a condition that Ursula is already in the process of transcending in this passage, but the people of this world are "turning their faces always inward toward the sinking fire of illuminating consciousness," whereas the early Brangwens always "faced inwards to the teeming life of creation, which poured unresolved into their veins." The curse of modern man. Lawrence later wrote in "Education of the People," was not that we have become too conscious—far from it:

> We have become too fixedly conscious. We have limited our consciousness, tethered it to a few great ideas, like a goat to a post. We insist over and over again on what we know from one mere centre of ourselves, the mental centre. We insist that we are essentially spirit, that we are ideal beings, conscious personalities, mental creatures.

The true movement, for modern man, as well as for the Brangwens and Ursula, is always outward to a fuller consciousness beyond that of the mind, and this movement is the controlling direction of both the action and the point of view of *The Rainbow*.

In the "Foreword" to the American edition of *Women in Love,* the sequel to *The Rainbow* (the two novels originally projected as one), Lawrence wrote:

> The creative, spontaneous soul sends forth its promptings of desire and aspiration in us. These promptings are our true fate, which it is our business to fulfill. A fate dictated from outside, from theory or from circumstance, is a false fate.

> This novel pretends only to be a record of the writer's own desires, aspirations, struggles; in a word, a record of the profoundest experiences in the self . . . man struggles with his unborn needs and fulfillment. New unfoldings struggle up in torment in him, as buds struggle forth from the midst of a plant. Any man of real indi-

viduality tries to know and to understand what is happening, even in himself, as he goes along. This struggle for verbal consciousness should not be left out in art. It is a very great part of life. It is not superimposition of a theory. It is the passionate struggle into conscious being.

While this might be taken as a motto for all of Lawrence's work, it has special value for *The Rainbow,* which, as I shall try to suggest, traces the development of the Brangwen soul from its first primitive "promptings of desire and aspiration," which we have seen in the early Brangwens, to the much higher level of "struggle into conscious being" by Ursula Brangwen in modern times. Lawrence goes on in this "Foreword" to point up the relationship between the style of his novels and this concept of growth:

> In point of style, fault is often found with the continual, slightly modified repetition. The only answer is that it is natural to the author; and that every natural crisis in emotion or understanding comes from this pulsing, frictional to-and-fro which works up to culmination.

An example of this "to-and-fro" rhythmic repetition can be found in that passage quoted earlier from the first few pages of *The Rainbow*. We have first a passage about the Brangwen men and their relationship to their environment, then the Brangwen women's discontent, then the Brangwen men repeated, then the Brangwen women amplified, and back and forth until the passage breaks off into a greater exposition of the Brangwen women's desire for a finer life, a more extended being. Also, the passage quoted above about Ursula and the modern circle of consciousness and the greater part of the novel from which it was taken, moves back and forth in the same way, describing an ever greater circle of understanding with each swing.

There is probably a buried sexual metaphor in this phrase Lawrence uses to characterize his own style: "this pulsing, frictional to-and-fro which works up to culmination." That metaphor and the other metaphor relating the struggle toward consciousness to the idea of organic growth, in the phrase "as buds struggle forth from the midst of a plant," not only characterize Lawrence's style but also are used in *The Rainbow, Women in Love,* and throughout his work in terms of the development of consciousness. Moreover, there is an intimate relationship between this style, this language, adapted to the workings of consciousness and the point of view of the novel. The narrator always stands between us and his characters, or rather he is the medium by which we are allowed entry into an awareness that is not yet verbal. Sensitive somehow to these unspoken, unconscious promptings, basic relationships and interactions of feeling, he must find the means of translating this primordial data into language. The point of view must, at once, adapt itself to the ever-widening consciousness of the characters and stand detached from it. In other words, it must at the same time describe and manifest its subject matter.

The nature and growth of consciousness was so important and fundamental a problem to Lawrence that he continued to return to the subject from *The Rainbow* on throughout his life, amplifying and developing a theory of consciousness in several books and articles. Much of what he later says throws light on *The Rainbow*. As basic as primary consciousness is a physical consciousness that is immediate and direct, and which consists of an interchange between the self and other selves or, as in the case of the early Brangwens, with what Lawrence calls "the contiguous universe." Another example of that consciousness in unconsciousness is born in Tom Brangwen, shortly after he meets his future wife, Lydia:

> A daze had come over his mind; he had another centre of consciousness. In his breast, or in his bowels, somewhere in his body, there had started another activity. It was as if a strong light were burning there, and he was blind within it, unable to know anything, except that this transfiguration burned between him and her, connecting them, like a secret power.

A little later, it is described as "an inner reality, a logic of the soul, which connected her with him." The word "soul" in both this passage and the "Foreword" to *Women in Love* is the key for Lawrence to the organic growth of consciousness toward full individuality. The unconscious *is* the soul, from which all life spins itself out. The evolution of consciousness is the soul's quest for full incarnation. Lawrence defined the unconscious as

> that active spontaneity which rouses in each individual organism at the moment of fusion of the parent nuclei, and which, in polarized connection with the external universe gradually evolves or elaborates its own individual psyche and corpus, bringing both mind and body forth from itself. Thus it would seem that the term unconscious is only another word for life. But life is a general force, whereas the unconscious is essentially single and unique in each individual organism; it is the active, self-evolving soul bringing forth its own incarnation and self-manifestation. Which incarnation and self-manifestation seems to be the whole goal of the *unconscious* soul: the whole goal of life. Thus it is that the unconscious brings forth not only consciousness, but tissue and organs also. And all the time the working of each organ depends on the primary spontaneous conscious centre of which it is the tissue—if you like, the soul-centre. And consciousness is like a web woven finally in the mind from the various silken strands spun forth from the primal centre of the unconscious.

The proper function of the mind, then, is to register the more primary consciousness, to translate its promptings into acts and language as directly as possible, rather than, as with the modern world, to attempt to set itself up as the only center of knowing and the personality, to direct and control. This process of translation of the unconscious into consciousness is necessary to the progress of life, the progress of the soul toward its full incarnation.

This unconscious consciousness takes two forms for Lawrence, two basic modes of knowing which must be in a tense polarized opposition. He calls them variously, subjective-objective or volitional-sympathetic. He takes pains to emphasize that this duality is not the subject-object di-

vision which he considers a fiction of the intellect, the mind divided against itself:

> Let us realize that the subjective and objective of the unconscious are not the same as the subjective and the objective of the *mind*. Here we have no concepts to deal with, no static objects in the shape of ideas. We have none of that tiresome business of establishing the relation between the ideal thing-in-itself and the mind of which it is the content. We are spared that hateful thing-in-itself, the idea, which is at once so all-important and so *nothing*. We are on straightforward solid ground; there is no abstraction.

The thing-in-itself is a concept, an ideal or idea, and therefore a fiction: it doesn't exist. Yet this does not mean a completely subjective or solipsistic view of knowledge. The self has a real knowledge of the other; there is an interpretation of consciousness, at least to a degree. Here perhaps, the pervasive metaphors Lawrence uses are helpful: besides the electric buzzing between the poles of separate selves that Lawrence is so fond of, he talks constantly of knowledge by contact through the use of various physical-sensual metaphors: imbibing, tasting, feeling in both its senses as the feelings that arise inside me and as what I "feel," that is to say, touch. And there is always the sexual metaphor of penetration and the Biblical sense of the word "knowledge."

In the Lawrentian system, there is no thing-in-itself, because there is no thing-*by*-itself; there is only relationship: "But the individual is never purely a thing-by-itself. He cannot exist save in polarized relation to the external universe, a relation both functional and psychic-dynamic." Development for the individual consciousness, Lawrence goes on to say, comes only through such polarity:

> The actual evolution of the individual psyche is a result of the interaction between the individual and the outer universe. Which means that just as the child in the womb grows as a result of the parental blood-stream which nourishes the vital quick of the foetus, so does every man and woman grow and develop as a result of the polarized flux between the spontaneous self and some other self or selves. It is the circuit of vital flux between itself and another being or beings which brings about the development and evolution of every individual *psyche* and physique. This is a law of life and creation, from which we cannot escape.

And the organic growth of the self-evolving soul is linked to a larger movement of life itself. In his **"Study of Thomas Hardy,"** which he began while working on *The Rainbow,* Lawrence describes this movement:

> It seems as though one of the conditions of life is, that life shall continually and progressively differentiate itself, almost as though this differentiation were a *Purpose*. Life starts crude and unspecified, a great mass. And it proceeds to evolve out of that mass ever more distinct and definite particular forms, an ever multiplying number of separate species and orders, as if it were working always to the production of the in-

finite number of perfect individuals, the individual so thorough that he should have nothing in common with any other individual. It is as if all coagulation must be loosened, as if the elements must work themselves free and pure from this compound.

This movement is basic to *The Rainbow*: it begins "crude and unspecified, a great mass" with the general "Brangwens." Then it gradually "evolves out of that mass ever more distinct and definite particular forms"—the Brangwen men and women, then the Brangwen man and woman, then the parents of Tom Brangwen, the lives of Tom and Lydia, then Will and Anna, to the thoroughly individualized Ursula and her liberation. The prose of the novel and its point of view develop along the same pattern, beginning with the vastly generalized group experience and gradually accumulating weight and particularity of detail, accommodating an ever widening range of experience. The phrase "The Widening Circle" appears twice as a chapter title, emphasizing this movement. The fact that more than half of the novel is devoted to Ursula and her groping toward consciousness and selfhood alone testifies to the greater specification given to the treatment of her experience and to the wider range of that experience. By the very end of the novel, the point of view is almost inseparable from her experience.

This same movement recurs time after time on a more individual level in the novel. Tom emerges gradually as a separate person from the description of the early Brangwens. Anna comes into the novel's focus of attention only gradually against the background of her parents' developing relationship. We see her first as the strange little girl with the Polish widow. She becomes a more important figure on the night when the first child is born of Tom's marriage with Lydia. More than half of the chapter entitled "Childhood of Anna Lensky" is devoted to the fluctuating relationship of her parents—when that relationship becomes stable at the end of that chapter, the focus of the novel turns directly to her: "When at last they had joined hands, the house was finished, and the Lord took up his abode" and Anna "was no longer called upon to uphold with her childish might the broken end of the arch. Her father and her mother now met to the span of the heavens, and she, the child, was free to play in the space beneath, between." But Anna is at the beginning a more individualized and conscious person than Tom was as a child, and her experiences are more varied and are treated in greater detail. The same pattern holds true on a higher level and with greatly extended range for Anna's daughter, Ursula.

The larger movement of life is also the movement of the individual. "And the more that I am driven from admixture," Lawrence said in the **"Study of Thomas Hardy,"** "the more this intrinsic me rejoices. For I am as yet a gross impurity, I partake of everything. I am still rudimentary, part of a great, unquickened lump." The goals of a more complete consciousness and a more complete individuality and singleness are closely related, and Lawrence goes on to say, in the same passage, that

> man's consciousness, that is, his mind, his knowledge, is his greater manifestation of individuality. With his consciousness he can perceive and know that which is not himself. The further he goes, the more extended his consciousness, the more he realizes the things that are not himself. Everything he perceives, everything he knows, everything he feels, is something extraneous to him, is not himself and his perception of it is like a cell-wall, or more, a real space separating him.

Ursula reaches self-definition not only through her widening range of experience but also by constant transcending of each experience, a constant rejection of and separation from what is not herself: her family, her affair with her teacher Winifred, the colliery world, the school in which she teaches, Scofield, her own intellectual aspirations, the planned marriage with Skrebensky. But this constant rejection and liberation does not mean a total break in the "living continuum" that connects all things. Individuation and selfhood come from polarized relationships and more toward an ever greater fulfillment of self and soul in relationship. As Lawrence said (in **"Him with His Tail in His Mouth"**), "But what is the soul of man, except *that* in him, which is himself alone, suspended in immediate relationship to the sum of things? Not isolated and cut off " (*Reflections on the Death of a Porcupine and Other Essays*).

The Lawrentian world is a thoroughly intersubjective world. His omniscient point of view reflects a kind of awareness that his characters seek not only for themselves, and achieve to some degree, but also an intuitive awareness, which is almost physical, that they can have of each other. Lawrence's description of Birkin in the unpublished first chapter of *Women in Love* might be used to describe the operation of his own point of view as narrator:

> He knew how to pitch himself into tune with another person. He could adjust his mind, his consciousness, almost perfectly to that of Gerald Crich, lighting up the edge of the other man's limitation with a glimmering light that was the essence of exquisite adventure and liberation to the confined intelligence.

That this attunement of consciousness is a "liberation" is characteristic. Lawrence's characters, when "polarized," that is to say, when they are in an intimate living relationship, seem to exist in some realm where their consciousnesses intermingle. Much of the strangely abstract narration which is not quite discursive exposition takes place on this level. Much of the important action of the novel— those extended moments when souls meet and have intercourse with each other and achieve "entry into another circle of existence"—much of this "action" happens in this curious place. The most precise statement Lawrence gives us of this realm is right after Tom has seen Lydia for the first time and has become aware of some basic connection with her: "He moved within the knowledge of her, in the world that was beyond reality." This knowledge of Lydia that Tom moved *within*, comes from a direct and basic experience of her. Lawrence's characters have experience, and thus knowledge, of each other on many levels, but since it is a knowledge based on direct experience, it is always a knowledge of the other as he exists in relationship to me, never complete, never wholly unambiguous.

It is not a knowledge through mystic merger or union, for the identities remain separate.

The basic model for this knowing relationship is, on one level, sexual intercourse, but on another, the family:

> A family, if you like, is a group of wireless stations, all adjusted to the same, or very much the same vibration. All the time they quiver with the interchange, there is one long endless flow of vitalistic communication between members of one family, a long, strange *rapport,* a sort of life-unison. It is a ripple of life through many bodies as through one body.

It is this "life-unison" that the early Brangwens share at the beginning of the novel and which is also the way the later family groups are described. But this rapport must also offer enough distance for the separate selves to exist simultaneously in singleness and freedom; it must be flexible enough for growth. For this reason, the family is usually an unsatisfactory relationship. For all the time there is this "life-unison," Lawrence said, "there is the jolt, the rupture of individualism, the individual asserting himself beyond all ties or claims. The highest goal for every man is the goal of pure individual being." And the ultimate goal of relationship is that relationship-in-freedom between separate, fully conscious, individual beings that Birkin seeks in *Women in Love.*

In *The Rainbow,* however, as I said earlier the movement is outward, breaking bonds that one has outgrown. The self grows toward consciousness through close relationship with the unknown *other,* but once that relationship becomes stable, once it no longer opens onto the unknown, it seems static and confining to Anna or Ursula of the next generation. For example, Ursula's home, her parents, especially her mother, Anna, who "remained dominant in the house," form a limitation against which Ursula must fight for her very life.

> Brangwen continued in a kind of rich drowse of physical heat, in connection with his wife. They were neither of them quite personal, quite defined as individuals, so much were they pervaded by the physical heat of breeding and rearing their young.

> How Ursula resented it, how she fought against the close, physical, limited life of herded domesticity!

But Anna herself has experienced a similar discontent and need to escape from *her* parents, earlier in the novel, when she was seventeen:

> Often she stood at the window, looking out, as if she wanted to go. Sometimes she went, she mixed with people. But always she came home in anger, as if she were diminished, belittled, almost degraded.

> There was over the house a kind of dark silence and intensity, in which passion worked its inevitable conclusions. There was in the house a sort of richness, a deep, inarticulate interchange which made other places seem thin and unsatisfying. Brangwen would sit silent, smoking in his chair, the mother would move about in her

quiet, insidious way, and the sense of the two presences was powerful, sustaining. The whole intercourse was wordless, intense and close.

> But Anna was uneasy. She wanted to get away.

The figure standing "at the window, looking out, as if she wanted to go" is a constant of the book, closely related to a whole complex of imagery and symbolism: windows and other barriers or semi-barriers, houses or buildings that become prisons that no longer give meaning to the life lived in them, doors and gateways or thresholds, and that pervasive organic image, usually of a seed that must break and cast off its husk for germination, all of which suggest the constant breaking from confinement, the constant transcending in and of relationships by the travelling soul in quest of consciousness and individuation. This complex of imagery and symbolism, along with other associated symbols, too extensive to trace here, provides Lawrence with a symbolic language with which he can picture a level of consciousness too deep to describe in normal language. One small example: on Will's first visit to the Marsh as a young man, something has happened between him and Anna; they have responded to each other in some secret way that will draw him back to the Marsh again. Lawrence tells us that

> without knowing it, Anna was wanting him to come. In him she had escaped. In him the bounds of her experience were transgressed: he was the hole in the wall, beyond which the sunshine blazed on an outside world.

What Lawrence has put into language here is some unspoken, unconscious feeling of Anna's, some new hope and release she has experienced in a deep way. But the terms here of "escape," of "the hole in the wall, beyond which the sunshine blazed on an outside world," go beyond a merely figurative way of describing Anna's feelings. By repetition, through the way in which these terms are amplified and extended, drawing to them similar terms, they become symbolic of the basic experience of the soul in its groping toward an opening into a new, wider circle of being. In the same way, the title symbol of the book—the rainbow—represents the aspirations urging the soul forward. The rainbow does not suggest merely an all-embracing relationship, or a harmonious tension between opposites, as it has been described by many of the book's critics. Unlike the symbol of star-equilibrium of *Women in Love,* which not only stands for such a relationship but is itself a form of that relationship, the rainbow is the promise, always the promise, of greater fulfillment, constantly leading the soul forward in its quest.

Lawrence's description and analyses of such basic experiences of the soul require such a symbolic language, since the real movement of the book lies in the development of a self-evolving soul at a level of which the character's ego is not conscious. Lawrence wrote in his first essays on American literature that

> the art-symbol or art-term stands for a pure experience, emotional and passional, spiritual and perceptual, all at once. The intellectual idea remains implicit, latent and nascent . . . art-speech is a use of symbols which are pulsations

on the blood and seizures upon the nerves, and at the same time pure percepts of the mind and pure terms of spiritual aspiration.

A narrative controlled by "the logic of the soul" must be given in the soul's language—symbolism. In a letter, written at the time he was working on *The Rainbow,* Lawrence said, "The old symbols were each a word in a great attempt at formulating the whole history of the soul of man." The great religious symbols, he added, "mean a moment in the history of my soul."

Lucia Henning Heldt   (essay date 1975)

SOURCE: "Lawrence on Love: The Courtship and Marriage of Tom Brangwen and Lydia Lensky," in *The D. H. Lawrence Review,* Vol. 8, No. 3, Fall, 1975, pp. 358-70.

[*In the following essay, Heldt analyzes the relationship of Tom Brangwen and Lydia Lensky, based on the theories of love propounded by Lawrence in his other writings.*]

Precisely what D. H. Lawrence means by the term "love," as opposed to what other writers mean, has perplexed even his most careful readers. In part, this problem of definition stems from Lawrence's conviction that a spurious "moon-love" predominates in the modern world and from his consequent determination always to emphasize his objections to this corrupt emotion. In both *The Rainbow* and *Women in Love,* for example, the novelist portrays a whole series of unsatisfactory sexual relationships, those between Anna and Will, Ursula and Skrebensky, Hermione and Birkin, Gudrun and Gerald, to demonstrate the devastating effects of the modern "idea" of love that derives from the head. Even in the Ursula-Birkin relationship, which Lawrence presents as something of a model, the writer prefers to discuss their love—and have the lovers describe it to each other—primarily in negative terms. They usually express their emotions by saying what they do not feel as opposed to what they do feel. Moreover, the tentative note on which *Women in Love* ends suggests that the Ursula-Birkin relationship can be taken only as pointing towards Lawrence's definition of love rather than representing a final or full statement of his ideas. However, in these novels the author does make one exception to his general practice of discussing love in negative rather than in positive terms. Although he finds it difficult to conceive of a satisfactory sexual relationship in the modern world, Lawrence can imagine an almost perfect love relationship in an earlier period, as we see in the opening section of *The Rainbow*. The courtship and marriage of Tom Brangwen and Lydia Lensky set the standard by which all of the other sexual involvements in the two novels can be judged and provide the reader with a rare, fully developed example of exactly what Lawrence has in mind when he speaks of love.

Before turning to *The Rainbow* itself, a look at some of Lawrence's statements concerning love relationships may prove useful if we are to appreciate what the author is conveying in his treatment of Tom and Lydia. At this point one of Lawrence's essays, *Psychoanalysis and the Unconscious,* appears particularly helpful. Here, the author proposes that the attainment of "a perfected harmony between the beloved," which is the necessary condition for Lawrence's end goal, "the perfecting of each single individuality," depends upon a double achievement. First, the self on its most basic level, which Lawrence defines as the vital "life-motive" or unconscious, must enter into a relationship with another "life-motive." Then, within this relationship the self develops by participating, simultaneously, in the movements of attraction and repulsion, the movements towards unity and towards separateness. These movements are what Lawrence means by love, the activity through which the self can expand, express itself, and finally achieve wholeness. Quite obviously, relationship and individuality do not prove contradictory according to Lawrence's way of thinking. Instead, relationship provides the necessary means by which the end, individuality, is achieved. As Ursula says in *The Rainbow* and as Birkin repeats in *Women in Love,* sexual love represents a means, not an end; but it is the only means to Lawrence's particular end, and thus the author stresses love, in both of these novels, as *the* activity his characters must pursue.

Furthermore, in Lawrence's opinion genuine as opposed to false love always occurs on the unconscious level; healthy love is necessarily impersonal and non-human because it engages that part of the self that lies beneath the conscious or mental plane of existence, the level of ego or personality. As Lawrence states in *Psychoanalysis,* the unconscious, with its "two synchronizing activities of love," contains "nothing in the least conceptual, and hence nothing in the least personal, since personality, like the ego, belongs to the conscious or mental-subjective self." Real love is based in "the great abdominal centers," and thus is "so impersonal that the so-called *human* relations are not involved."

Clearly, in order to experience love in Lawrence's sense, as Tom and Lydia do, the individual must first be in touch with his unconscious. Yet, how can one be in touch with the unconscious, aware of its existence if, as Lawrence declares, the unconscious is inconceivable, ungraspable by the mind? "We know it," Lawrence answers, "by direct experience. . . . Knowledge is always a matter of whole experience, what St. Paul calls knowing in full, and never a matter of mental conception merely." However, according to Lawrence, men in the modern industrial world rarely participate in this direct experience of "dark knowledge" because they have elevated the mind to a position of supreme importance, rather than regarding it simply as the tool of the unconscious.

But at an earlier stage in history, the mind did not hold such a superior position, and men could experience more easily that "dark knowledge" of the unconscious. In simpler, agricultural societies, where men lived and worked in close harmony with their surroundings and where the needs and activities of the body superseded those of the mind, the natural rhythms of the seasons, which corresponded to the natural rhythms of the unconscious, to the ebb and flow of life, constantly reminded men of the "two synchronizing activities of love" in which they, too, participated. The external as well as the internal guided men towards a recognition of the rhythmic movements of the universe. Moreover, these movements maintained a careful balance: winter lasted for its appointed time and then was followed by spring; summer stretched out for just so long and then inevitably turned to autumn. No one movement ever predominated at the expense of the others; instead, a harmonious relationship existed among the different movements. Patterning their lives after this regular configuration of the seasons, the men, also, lived in harmony and in balance.

Lawrence begins *The Rainbow* with a flowing, almost drowsy description of just such a society. But the novelist immediately dramatizes the fragility of this balanced relationship among all members of the community, between the men and the women, and between the conscious and the unconscious within each man and each woman. A canal is dug, a railroad built, and the mental begins to assume precedence over the non-mental. Although Tom Brangwen's parents can still achieve, with some difficulty, the blessed state of balance between the two of them, the vital connection among all men has been sundered, and the union between male and female also appears endangered. The larger question of the barriers dividing all men is not resolved in this novel, and in fact these barriers grow stronger as the story recounts the increasing encroachment of the industrial world upon this rural community. But the writer still does see hope in the realm of individual sexual relationships, and, with the introduction of Tom and Lydia, Lawrence turns almost exclusively to this realm of experience.

The first task facing Tom and Lydia consists of their regaining a sense of their own unconscious selves. Perhaps because they are only slightly removed from the paradise of harmonious balance pictured in the opening pages, Tom and Lydia experience far less difficulty in achieving this step than Lawrence's later characters. Still, when we first encounter them in the novel, both are suffering the consequences of a divided soul. As one might expect in Lawrence, Tom's problems stem from his relationship with his misguided mother. Mrs. Brangwen makes the mistake of overestimating the worth of the mind and of disassociating it from what she wrongly considers the less valuable body or unconscious; moreover, she seeks to transmit this erroneous sense of values to her four sons. As Tom is her favorite child, she tries especially hard to instill in him this excessive admiration for the intellect; rather than allowing him to grow up on the farm, she insists on sending Tom to school, where he proves "an unwilling failure." Tom's very inability to function successfully in this highly mental environment actually supplies the first hint that he will be saved, particularly since Lawrence juxtaposes this failure with Tom's definite ability to respond emotionally. But at the time this lack of academic success causes Tom to think poorly of himself and thus leads to the failure of his first personal involvement outside the family, a school boy friendship, because Tom feels that he cannot approach the other lad as an equal, a necessary condition in Lawrence's view for any successful relationship.

Because Tom believes that his mother's conception is right and his own being wrong, because he thinks that an inevitable, unbridgeable division exists between the mind and the body, the conscious and the unconscious, the youth also experiences failure in his first adolescent sexual adventures. His sexual initiation, which occurs with a prostitute in a public house, leaves him with "a pang of anger, of disappointment, a first taste of ash and a cold fear," but he cannot, on the other hand, find sexual satisfaction with "nice" girls because he associates them with his mother and sister whom he in turn associates with the spiritual and mental. Again, the fact that Tom does not despise either himself or "loose" girls but only the net result of the experience demonstrates the young man's basic healthiness in Lawrence's eyes, but the agony portrayed in these pages also conveys the author's unmitigated hatred for the modern division of man's being into opposing rather than complementary aspects of mind and body and his conviction that only anguish can come of such an approach to life. Only an experience akin to the religious, a revelation that will shock man back into a realization of the powers and claims of the unconscious, can halt the downward progress towards madness to which the self is doomed once the mind gains ascendency. Tom's first view of Lydia represents just such a revelation: " 'That's her,' he said involuntarily." Lawrence signals to us through the immediacy of the response and its involuntary quality that at this moment Tom's deepest self, his unconscious, is stirred and is once more beginning to assert its importance.

The confrontation on the country road similarly calls forth an involuntary, mysterious response from Lydia's innermost being, which Lawrence, as is his habit when he is trying to convey a sense of the unconscious through the highly conscious medium of language, expresses as a physical reaction: "She had felt Brangwen go by almost as if he had brushed her. She had tingled in body as she had gone on up the road." Like Tom, Lydia has been experiencing not life but a death-like state, occasioned by the predominance of the intellect in her world. As a young girl in Poland, she married Paul Lensky, an intellectual and revolutionary, who quickly gained complete control over her being. She was "carried alone in her husband's emphasis of declaration," overwhelmed by "the vividness of his talk" and thus "obliterated." Paul's death frees Lydia from her literal bondage, but the consequences of having bound her very being to him, spiritually as well as physically, only disappear gradually. But just as Lawrence hints at Tom's eventual salvation during his period of anguish by noting the boy's emotional capacities and his refusal to despise himself and others, so does the writer suggest that Lydia, too, will be saved. Shortly before Paul's death she bears a child and thus maintains one contact with the living world and with the future. Nevertheless, for a time Lydia seems to be following her husband's path: "she walked always in a shadow"; "she walked without passion, like a shade. . . ."

Then slowly and in spite of her conscious wishes, she begins to awaken to life. In *Psychoanalysis* Lawrence remarks that "pain is a living reality, not merely a deathly," and the pages that recount Lydia's rebirth to life are certainly among the most "painfull" in the novel. Her child "torments" her into moments of love; when she moves to Yorkshire, the open country and moors "hurt her brain," "hurt her and hurt her." But these are quite clearly birth rather than death pains, for Lydia is indeed regaining an awareness of her deep, unconscious self: "Her automatic consciousness gave way a little. . . . Her soul roused to attention." Finally, just before she encounters Tom on the road, Lydia takes the last step in liberating herself from her former deadness, and this last movement towards the realization of her nascent self proves an excruciating one for her, one that reminds us of the courage Lawrence declares essential in facing "life pains":

> She was full of trouble almost like anguish. Resistant, she knew she was beaten, and from fear of darkness turned to fear of light. . . . She could not bear to come to, to realise. The first pangs of this new parturition were so acute, she knew she could not bear it. She would rather remain out of life, than be torn, mutilated into this birth, which she could not survive.

Yet she does survive, and although she thinks that this new life is fragile, although she dreads it, she also feels like "a new person, quite glad." Now Lydia is prepared for her meeting with Tom. In vital contact with her own living unconscious self, she represents a force so powerful that it can shock Brangwen back into an awareness of his own unconscious. Indeed, their meeting signifies the fulfillment of the first condition for a successful love affair as outlined in *Psychoanalysis*: having regained a sense of self on its most basic level, both Tom and Lydia are now ready, for the first time, to enter into a genuine relationship between two individual "life-motives."

Whereas earlier writers might have ended their stories with this meeting on the road when Tom and Lydia "fall in love," Lawrence, of course, sees this meeting as only the beginning of Tom and Lydia's relationship. As he states in *Psychoanalysis,* the new lovers must now begin to participate in movements of attraction and repulsion; they must allow themselves to experience both "a wonderful rich communion" and "a continually increasing cleavage"; they must remain aware of themselves and yet at the same time become aware of the "other." As we see in his treatment of the Brangwen marriage, Lawrence refuses to simplify any aspect of the development of such a genuine relationship. And, without some knowledge of the author's definition of love, one can become hopelessly bewildered in trying to analyze such a Lawrentian model relationship. At certain moments, for example, Lawrence portrays Tom and Lydia as feeling rage and hostility towards each other; the relationship at these times appears doomed. Yet at other times the lovers experience moments of intense bliss, and the marriage seems almost perfect. Of course, the emphasis on fluctuation in itself accords with Lawrence's notion of love as movement, as progression towards an end, so it should come as no surprise that from the start Lawrence stresses the ever-changing nature of Tom and Lydia's marriage. Still, unhealthy as well as healthy relationships go through periods of fluctuation, as we see in Ursula and Skrebensky's ill-fated affair. Thus, if he wants us to regard Tom and Lydia's relationship as promising, Lawrence must give additional indications that the Brangwens' marriage conforms to his definition of true love.

From the beginning of their association, Tom and Lydia often respond to one another in an impersonal manner. If we were unfamiliar with Lawrence's insistence upon the impersonality of true love, we might interpret these occasions as indications of an unpromising relationship, for by traditional standards Tom and Lydia often appear curiously detached as they go about their love-making: "They did not take much note of each other, consciously." But, as discussed earlier, Lawrence feels that genuine love must be impersonal since it occurs on the unconscious level and is consequently far removed from the conscious or personal level of experience. The air of detachment displayed by Tom and Lydia actually reveals not that they are detached from one another but that they are oblivious to their own and each other's surface personalities; they are, in other words, in touch with the unconscious. The "strangely impersonal" look in Tom's eyes as he proposes and the impersonal tone in which Lydia responds to his proposal represent Lawrence's way of dramatizing the unconscious aspect of their love and thus suggesting its soundness. Similarly, Lawrence characterizes one of the Brangwens' closest times, the period of her labor in the birth of their first child, as another of these impersonal moments:

> Something made him go and touch her fingers that were still grasped on the sheet. Her brown-grey eyes opened and looked at him. She did not know him as himself. But she knew him as the man. She looked at him as a woman in childbirth looks at the man who begot the child in her: an impersonal look, in the extreme hour, female to male.

As is seen in Tom's feelings after this encounter, Lawrence does not allow us to view this incident, which at first seems so terrifying, as other than a positive experience: "But his heart in torture was at peace, his bowels were glad."

In addition to this emphasis on impersonality, Lawrence also suggests his approval of Tom and Lydia's relationship by depicting their marriage as one that encompasses both the movement towards unity and the movement towards separateness. During the kiss in the proposal scene and during the "elemental embrace" that occurs on their wedding night, Tom and Lydia experience intense feelings of oneness with each other. Such moments, which Lawrence describes as a combination of agony and bliss, leave both of them renewed and awakened, as if for the first time, to the world about them, to its vital "life-motive" with which they now feel their connection. But such moments always pass quickly because, in Lawrence's opinion, for every movement towards the beloved there must be a movement away from the loved one. The self must retain a sense of its own individuality as well as a sense of universal unity. Thus, right after the kiss in the proposal scene, which conveys such a strong sense of oneness, the lovers begin at once to separate, to re-affirm individuality. Lydia leans against Tom but "in her tiredness was a certain negation of him"; after still another embrace, he feels that "she was drifting away from him again."

By stressing both the impersonality of their love and its capacity to include the two different movements, Lawrence successfully conveys his approbation of this marriage. Yet this does not mean that Tom and Lydia have reached complete fulfillment during these first years. Nor will they actually ever reach the limits of their potential within this one relationship, for the novelist believes that the sexual love relationship exemplifies only one among many love relationships that the self can engage in. But even within their own marriage Tom and Lydia have not as yet reached fulfillment. What prevents the Brangwens from taking the final step in love and thus transcending it by entering into a perfectly balanced, harmonious relationship is their initial failure to realize fully, accept fully, the "otherness" of the beloved.

True, they feel this acceptance at certain moments. They can sometimes delight in their different cultural backgrounds—"It was to him a profound satisfaction that she was a foreigner"—and occasionally they can recognize with a sense of reverence the tremendous distinction between the sexes. But frequently they feel only anguish or anger when faced with the "otherness" of the person with whom they live. In Lydia's case, "it irritated her to be made aware of him as a separate power," and in Tom's case, when he listens to her stories of Poland and feels that "he had nothing to do with her. . . . he grew into a raging fury against her." When they do not accept the beloved as an "other," the results prove devastating, for the two activities of love do not then synchronize; the movements of each of the lovers oppose rather than complement the movements of the partner. They fail "to connect," to coordinate their movements, and "when a force flashes and has no response, there is devastation." That Tom and Lydia are not immediately able to co-ordinate their movements can be seen in the battles that mark their courtship and the early part of their marriage. Feeling self-assured and delighting in her new existence, Lydia "unsheathes" herself like a flower and stands "ready, waiting, receptive"; but Tom fails to meet her flash because he is overwhelmed by a sense of her "otherness," and so she closes up again in disappointment. Or, remembering the closeness of the kiss in the vicar's kitchen, Tom will approach Lydia, but encountering only vagueness rather than response because she does not yet completely trust him, he withdraws into his own anger.

Tom and Lydia's initial reluctance to accept the "other" apparently stems from their misunderstanding of the relationship in a love affair between individuality and togetherness. Each is determined to keep hold of a strong sense of his or her own separate being, a determination Lawrence fully sympathizes with, but each fails, as Lawrence does not, to see that, far from destroying this sense of individuality, knowledge of an "other" actually confirms one's own sense of a separate self by defining the limits of that self. Not until their reconciliation scene in "Childhood of Anna Lensky" do the lovers finally consciously realize their mistake and encourage each other, step by step, to approach the mysterious "other" who will ultimately reveal each to himself or herself.

First, they need to recognize that they have tried to deny the "other" and assert only their own existence. "Why do you want to deny me?" Lydia asks Tom; "I want you to know there is somebody there besides yourself." Her accusation immediately causes Tom to perceive her not as an opposing, hostile "other" but as an "other" who also has

needs and emotions: "Suddenly, in a flash, he saw she might be lonely, isolated, unsure." But Lydia, too, has been guilty of false egoism, as Tom now informs her: "You make me feel as if *I* was nothing." These accusations in turn now lead to one of those critical Lawrentian pauses—"They were silent"—until Lydia, though terrified, signals her willingness to move beyond this futile state and meet and embrace Tom on a deeper plane of existence: " 'Come here,' she said unsure."

However, Tom experiences tremendous difficulty in meeting Lydia's challenge: to approach her "required an almost deathly effort of volition, or of acquiescence." Still half convinced that if he goes to her he will lose himself, Tom finds himself torn between his desire to respond to his wife's plea and his lingering fear that to do so will mean his own destruction:

> And it was torture to him, that he must give himself to her actively, participate in her, that he must meet and embrace and know her, who was other than himself. There was that in him which shrank from yielding to her, resisted the relaxing towards her, opposed the mingling with her, even while he most desired it. He was afraid, he wanted to save himself.

But slowly acquiescence in the desires of the unconscious triumphs, and Tom lets go of his false sense of self so that he can meet Lydia and, by actively embracing the unknown, at last know his true self:

> There were a few moments of stillness. Then gradually, the tension, the withholding relaxed in him, and he began to flow towards her. She was beyond him, the unattainable. But he let go his hold on himself, he relinquished himself, and knew the subterranean force of his desire to come to her, to be with her, to mingle with her, losing himself to find her, to find himself in her. He began to approach her, to draw near.

Here we see dramatized in full Lawrence's belief that the individual only finally exists within a relationship. Far from being the destructive experience that the false sense of self would have us fear, this embracing of the "other" in a relationship is an experience of joy to the unconscious: "There is a tremendous great joy in exploring the beloved. For what is the beloved? She is that which I myself am not." Joy certainly predominates at the close of the reconciliation scene, where for the first time the lovers seek actively to encounter that which is outside themselves:

> Their coming together now, after two years of married life, was much more wonderful to them than it had been before. It was the entry into another circle of existence, it was the baptism to another life, it was the complete confirmation. . . . At last they had thrown open the doors, each to the other, and had stood in the doorways facing each other, whilst the light flooded out from behind on to each of their faces, it was the transfiguration, glorification, the admission.

By passing through this particular stage in the relationship, Tom and Lydia have at last passed "beyond love" and entered into the eternally blissful realm of harmony and balance prefigured in the novel's opening pages. They have achieved the "equilibrized," "polarized" state that is the end of love; they have finished travelling and have finally arrived:

> And always the light of the transfiguration burned on in their hearts. He went his way, as before, she went her way, to the rest of the world there seemed no change. But to the two of them, there was the perpetual wonder of the transfiguration.

Tom and Lydia's achievement remains unmatched in the rest of the novel. They alone not only see but also become a part of the novel's prevailing symbol, the rainbow. The next generation, Anna and Will, can only sporadically get in touch with their unconsciousnesses and can never finally embrace the "other"; the church that stands next to their house, rather than the rainbow, dominates their affair, just as their subservience to the conscious rather than an acquiescence in the unconscious determines the development of their relationship. Although, at the end of the novel their daughter Ursula does have a vision of the rainbow, until she meets Birkin in *Women in Love* and even afterwards as the ending of that novel suggests, she must remain content with vision instead of achievement. Thus, the only full dramatization of D. H. Lawrence's notion of love in *The Rainbow* and *Women in Love* is found in the courtship and marriage of Tom Brangwen and Lydia Lensky. In their relationship Lawrence depicts the complete working through of the steps of love as outlined in *Psychoanalysis*; in Tom and Lydia the author has created characters who are capable of reaching his goal, not the state of love but "the realm of perfection" that "encompasses love in a new transcendence."

Evelyn J. Hinz   (essay date 1976)

SOURCE: "*The Rainbow*: Ursula's 'Liberation',' " in *Contemporary Literature,* Vol. 17, No. 1, Winter, 1976, pp. 24-43.

[In the following essay, Hinz explores Ursula's character in terms of her developing perception of reality.]

Why "liberated" women have found D. H. Lawrence so infuriating must puzzle those male, particularly modern, critics of *The Rainbow* who have interpreted Ursula's role in the novel as Lawrence's exploration of the value of self-realization, independence, and individualism. What more could a liberationist want than a positive treatment of "woman becoming individual, self-responsible, taking her own initiative"—as the theme of *The Rainbow* is supposed to be. There is, of course, that problem of the visionary ending of *The Rainbow*—Ursula's final contended surrender of herself to a "vaster power" and her happy willingness to "hail" the man whom it should send to her—but the ending of *The Rainbow* has also been criticized as one which is unprepared for by the development of the novel. Why, then, are the feminists so antagonistic to a man who has made the "maturely joyous independence" of a woman the focus of one of his greatest novels?

The question is mainly rhetorical, for I am directly concerned with the negative attitude of female liberationists toward Lawrence only insofar as it points to the necessity of reconsidering his attitude toward Ursula, the quest for self, and the conclusion of *The Rainbow*. In passing, though, I would like to suggest the ironic possibility that it is not merely the intellectual recognition that Lawrence is *not* sympathetic to the cause which explains the outrage, but rather the emotional recognition on the part of the modern woman of the accuracy of Lawrence's insights into the frustrated needs that motivate liberationist tendencies. If Lawrence were simply a male chauvinist he could be dismissed along with the others; because he is the emotional enemy within the ranks, he must be destroyed.

Now, *The Rainbow* is concerned with "woman becoming individual, self-responsible, taking her own initiative," and Ursula's role in the novel is to be the spokesperson for, and the final product of, this movement. But Ursula, as Lawrence repeatedly reminds us, is also a terribly confused and frustrated young woman: "She was dissatisfied, but not fit as yet to criticise," he cautions us on the eve of her career as a liberated woman; "But her fundamental, organic knowledge had as yet to take form and rise to utterance. . . . and there remained always the want she could put no name to," he explains in the middle of her development; "She could not understand what it all was," he warns just before she enunciates her conclusion that "to be oneself was a supreme, gleaming triumph of infinity." Only at the end of the novel does Lawrence consider her "fit to criticise," and there her "fundamental, organic knowledge" takes the form of her understanding that what she really wants is freedom from the compulsion to strive after liberation, freedom from pursuing the ideals of self-determination, individualism, and independence, the freedom that comes from the recognition that one cannot be other than that which eternity predicts—that one struggles equally foolishly "to be or not to be."

Furthermore, Ursula Brangwen is not presented as a young woman who is liberationist by nature. Indeed, her every move in her quest for independence is presented as a laceration and violation of her innately reticent being: "In coming out and earning her own living she had made a strong, cruel move towards freeing herself." The move is "cruel" not because of the suffering she has experienced at the hands of others but because "she had paid a great price out of her own soul, to do this." To make her way as a teacher in "The Man's World" she is forced to be "cruel" to others; but to be cruel to others is for Ursula to be cruel to herself.

Finally, if it is with a religious solution that Ursula's quest for liberation ultimately ends, it is also with a religious problem that it begins. Ursula becomes an advocate of self-determination and personal infinitude only after she despairs of finding a sanction for her feeling of, and desire for, a direct connection with the "vaster power" of the cosmos. Her turning to "The Man's World" is neither a happy nor a voluntary decision; her liberationist tendencies are consequent upon her religious frustrations and thus they are symptomatic of her religious despair. At the same time, however, Ursula's despair is also the result of the first of her many confusions and her limited point of view. Because the religion in which she has been raised fails in its rainbow role of asserting the perpetual and dynamic relationship between the individual and the cosmos, the finite and the infinite, it does not mean that the relationship has ceased; rather it means that the religion of her culture is a faulty one—and faulty not merely in the sense of decadent, but in terms of the premises from which it is derived. In turn, when at the conclusion of the novel Ursula is given a vision of "the rainbow" and senses the reality of the "vaster power," Lawrence is not advancing a "new" religious consciousness but a return to the kind of religious consciousness which preceded that of our culture, the kind Ursula originally experienced but felt forced to relinquish.

If we explore Ursula's development as a liberated woman by beginning with her religious dilemma and by respecting Lawrence's repeated warnings that she is confused, then not only will we recognize the appropriateness of the conclusion of **The Rainbow** but we will also come to a better understanding of the meaning of that conclusion, of Lawrence's attitude toward religion and the self, and possibly of the factors which really lie behind the liberationist tendencies of the discontented modern woman. Lawrence's explanation of the nature of myth in his review of Carter's *Dragon of the Apocalypse* is a good point of departure, for Ursula's problem originates in the anti-mythic character of her Judaeo-Christian heritage, while the prevailing critical attitude is that the Bible plays a positive role in **The Rainbow**. Myth and allegory, Lawrence begins, have one thing in common: both are "descriptive narrative using, as a rule, images." But in allegory, "each image means something, and is a term in the argument and nearly always for a moral or didactic purpose, for under the narrative of an allegory lies a didactic argument, usually moral"; myth, in contrast, "is never an argument, it never has a didactic nor a moral purpose, you can draw no conclusion from it." What then is myth? "Myth is an attempt to narrate a whole human experience, of which the purpose is too deep, going too deep in the blood and soul, for mental explanation or description." Therefore, though we "*can* expound" myth—historically, scientifically, anthropologically, or morally—"we can only look a little silly," because a myth "lives on beyond explanation, for it describes a profound experience of the human body and soul, an experience which is never exhausted and never will be exhausted, for it is being felt and suffered now, and will be felt and suffered while man remains man." To tamper with mythology is consequently to do ourselves the greatest harm: "You may explain the myths away; but it only means you go on suffering blindly, stupidly, 'in the unconscious,' instead of healthily and with the imaginative comprehension playing upon the suffering." It is precisely because her cultural-religious inheritance is one that has explained the myths away that Ursula suffers so much; and her suffering is blind because unlike Lawrence she does not see that the myths cannot be explained away.

The Judaeo-Christian tradition, as Lawrence explains it in terms of Ursula's frustrated response to the Bible, has demythicized religion in two major ways. Ursula's favorite book of the Bible is Genesis, and her favorite section is the passage describing how "the Sons of God saw the daughters of men that they were fair." The passage, we realize, is one version of the hierogamy myth, the mating of the sky and earth. That she should have this experience herself, that she should move "in the essential days" is Ursula's greatest desire, and as a myth the experience is available to her. What ultimately blocks her, however, are the implications of that crucial phrase "in those days," in the passage in question. Though the phrase is of course the equivalent of the mythological formula, *in illo tempore*, which is designed to establish the event in question as mythic—as something beyond time and eternally potential—the Judaeo-Christian tradition has made the phrase an historical one. Consequently, Ursula is confronted with the related theological questions: "Who were the sons of God? Was not Jesus the only begotten Son? Was not Adam the only man created from God?" The Old Testament, then, has explained the myths away by historicizing them—by presenting them as unique occurrences.

The New Testament, in turn, frustrates Ursula's religious yearnings because it is allegorical. Whereas myth speaks to the emotions and employs natural images which are meaningful in themselves, the New Testament subordinates the physical world to the role of vehicle in a moral and didactic argument. Ursula, for example, responds emotionally to the image of Christ's gathering his beloved to him: "So he must gather her body to his breast, that was strong with a broad bone, and which sounded with the beating of the heart, and which was warm with the life of which she partook, the life of the running blood." But her intellect reminds her that this is not the designed import of the biblical passage: "Vaguely she knew that Christ meant something else. . . . something that had no part in the weekday world, nor seen nor touched with weekday hands and eyes." Thus whereas the Old Testament insists that it is historically remote from the present, the New Testament insists that it is spiritually remote.

"As yet, she was confused, but not denied," Lawrence observes of Ursula in the early stage of her dilemma, for Ursula's first attempt to cope with the problem is to become schizophrenic: "She lived a dual life, one where the facts of daily life encompassed everything, being legion, and the other wherein the facts of daily life were superseded by the eternal truth." Lawrence's "As yet" prepares us for the inadequacy of this solution and thence for the time when Ursula's confusion will result in her feeling that she *has been denied* her desire to be taken by a strong and physical god and her consequent sublimated revenge upon the lovers whom she takes.

Before he moves to this second stage, however, Lawrence suspends his narrative of Ursula's development to place her problem into the kind of perspective which will enable us to recognize its cultural dimensions on the one hand, and his cosmic perspective on the other. Immediately following upon his observation that Ursula was "dissatisfied, but not fit as yet to criticise," Lawrence turns to a description of the Brangwen family as they prepare for Christmas—the coming of the Son of God into this world. After describing the way the natural world prepares for the sacred event—"Winter came, pine branches were torn down in the snow. . . . the wonderful, starry straight track of a pheasant's footsteps. . . . birds made a lacy pattern"— Lawrence turns to the human preparations. First there is the practicing of "the old mystery play of St. George and Beelzebub"—the Christianized version of the ancient ritual of the slaying of the marine serpent or chaos; then, the learning of the "old carols"; but finally, and most importantly, there is the preparation of the church for the occasion: "The time came near, the girls were decorating the church, with cold fingers binding holly and fir and yew about the pillars, till a new spirit was in the church, the stone broke out into dark, rich leaf, the arches put forth their buds, and cold flowers rose to blossom in the dim, mystic atmosphere. Ursula must weave mistletoe over the door, and over the screen, and hang a silver dove from a sprig of yew, till dusk came down, and the church was like a grove."

As Lawrence's diction indicates, the girls have not merely transformed the church into a primitive place of worship, they have also evoked the presence of the pagan deity of incarnation and rebirth; for the "new spirit" which manifests itself in such miraculous bursting of stone into vegetable life is clearly the Dionysian rather than the Christian one. In *Dionysus: Myth and Cult,* Walter F. Otto relates the mythic narrative of the effect of Dionysus upon the ship in which he has been captive: "Vines with swelling grapes wind themselves around the sails, ivy grows around the mast, and wreaths hang down from the tholepins." Otto then goes on, "Miracles of this type also announce the imminence of the god to the daughters of Minyas. The loom on which they are working is suddenly overgrown with ivy and grape vines. . . ."

Lawrence's purpose in describing the Christmas preparations of the Brangwen family, then, is twofold: first, to suggest that Christmas is a pagan ritual in disguise and to evoke the pagan prototype for the Christian Savior; second, to demonstrate that the event which Christians commemorate at Christmas is really a mythic one, a recurring event rather than an historical one. Periodic regeneration, not eschatological redemption, is the reality, or as Lawrence explains in **"The Middle of the World"**:

> This sea will never die, neither will it ever grow
>   old
> nor cease to be blue, nor in the dawn
> cease to lift up its hills
> and let the slim black ship of Dionysos come
>   sailing in
> with grape-vines up the mast, and dolphins leap-
>   ing.

Although we see Christ as having once descended and the Sons of God as having had their day, Lawrence sees

> . . . descending from the ships at dawn
> slim naked men from Cnossos, smiling the ar-
>   chaic smile
> of those that will without fail come back again,
> and kindling little fires upon the shores
> and crouching, and speaking the music of lost
>   languages.

In continuing his description of the Brangwens' preparations for Christmas, Lawrence further distinguishes between the Judaeo-Christian and the pagan concepts of the event: "The star was risen into the sky, the songs, the carols were ready to hail it. . . . The star was the sign in the sky." But then he adds, "Earth too should give a sign." Like the rainbow in the sky, the star *in the sky* is a remote sign, and as a biblical sign, a sign of remoteness of the event: Christmas is a *commemoration* of the *birth* of the Savior. Lawrence demands that it be a *celebration* of the *rebirth* of the god, the cosmos, and man. Heaven and earth must equally attest to the event. And in the *sensations* of the Brangwens the regeneration does take place: "As evening drew on, hearts beat fast with anticipation, hands were full of ready gifts. There were the tremulously expectant words of the church service, the night was past and the morning was come, the gifts were given and received, joy and peace made a flapping of wings in each heart, there was a great burst of carols, the Peace of the World had dawned, strife had passed away, every hand was linked in hand, every heart was singing."

On the one hand, then, Lawrence has demonstrated that the mythic event has occurred—that the rebirth of the cosmos is an "experience which is never exhausted and never will be exhausted." Having done so, however, Lawrence immediately turns to the bitter afternoon consciousness of the Brangwens that Christmas has become a "domestic feast," a tame, civilized "sort of bank holiday," instead of an event with cosmic significance. Why was the world not changed as a result of the rebirth of the god; why did not the everyday world "give way to ecstasy? Where was the ecstasy?" In formulating the discontent of the Brangwens in this manner, Lawrence also implies the reason for it. "Ecstasy" is the definitive feeling which Dionysus, the god of divine madness, inspires and which is now absent: "Where was the fiery heart of joy, now the coming was fulfilled; where was the star, the Magi's transport, the thrill of new being that shook the earth?" The ecstasy, the transport, is gone because Dionysus is gone, or rather because he has been replaced for the Brangwens by Jesus—the helpless infant and the meek man. The thrill of new being is gone because the incarnation of the god has been interpreted as a unique occurrence, because the physical joy has been allegorized into something spiritual, and because the fulfillment has been pushed into a remote and unearthly future. Or as the long polemic on the nature of Easter and the Resurrection which follows Lawrence's dramatization of Christmas indicates, it is the historical and eschatological premises of Judaeo-Christianity which are responsible for the Brangwens' religious despair.

The polemic consists of a series of questions. As direct interrogatives they represent the cry of the soul of mankind in bondage, for each of them expresses a desire to which the biblical answer is no; but as the style of these questions indicates, they are also rhetorical and as such provide a positive and cosmic answer which is designed to demonstrate the limitations of the Christian perspective. Easter is the central feast in the Christian calendar, and Christmas merely a means to this end: "birth at Christmas for death on Good Friday." Nor is the Resurrection a rebirth of soul and body but the resurrection of a "dead body," an event promising not a new life but a spiritual future life: "What was the hope and the fulfilment? Nay, was it all only a useless after-death, a wan, bodiless after-death?" Furthermore, "A small thing was Resurrection compared with the Cross and death, in this cycle." The function of the ritual and rebirth in pagan mythologies is the abolition of historical time and the instigation of the new beginning; Christian liturgy apparently has an opposite function: "But why the memory of the wounds and the death? Surely Christ rose with healed hands and feet, sound and strong and glad? Surely the passage of the cross and the tomb was forgotten? But no—always the memory of the wounds, always the smell of grave-clothes?" It is the Christian concept of the Resurrection, then, that is the answer to the questions "Where was the ecstasy?" and "Where was the fiery heart of joy . . .?": "Did not Christ say, 'Mary!' and when she turned with outstretched hands to him, did he not hasten to add, 'Touch me not; for I am not yet ascended to my father.' Then how could the hands rejoice, or the heart be glad, seeing themselves repulsed."

The point that Lawrence is making, then, is that Judaeo-Christianity has turned the cycle of creation into a linear and incomplete action, into a half-cycle like the bow *in the sky* in the Noah story. The cycle itself has not ceased of course: "Year by year the inner, unknown drama went on in them, their hearts were born and came to fulness, suffered on the cross, gave up the ghost, and rose again to unnumbered days, untired, having at least this rhythm of eternity in a ragged, inconsequential life." Because their religious orientation provides no sanction for this emotional experience, however, instead of imaginatively comprehending the inner drama they experience it "blindly, stupidly, 'in the unconscious.'" Furthermore, because daily life in turn appears directionless and haphazard, there arises the need to establish one's own direction, to make something of one's self.

Thus immediately following the polemical excursus on Judaeo-Christianity, Lawrence returns to Ursula, and specifically to the beginning of her quest for self-realization. His purpose in speaking out at the end of this first chapter concerned with Ursula's development, it would seem, is to locate for us the cause of her dissatisfaction with the type of religious orientation she has inherited and to point to her liberationist tendencies as the direct and logical consequence of that dissatisfaction. At the same time his purpose is to emphasize the misdirected nature of her dissatisfaction—her confusion. Ursula cannot see beyond Jesus and the Sons of God to Dionysus, the physical god whom she so passionately desires; indeed, in true Judaeo-Christian fashion she fights against "any comparison of myths." As a result, when her schizophrenic accommodation of the Bible can no longer be sustained, she will reject "religion" altogether. In emphasizing her confusion in this first chapter, in short, through *his* demonstration that the mythic is neither a thing of the past nor a thing of another world, Lawrence is attempting to ensure that the conclusions which Ursula comes to in the succeeding stages of her development are not mistaken for his, but viewed as symptomatic of her problem.

"She became aware of herself, that she was a separate entity in the midst of an unseparated obscurity, that she must go somewhere, she must become something," we read at the beginning of the second chapter concerned with Ursula's development. Thus self-consciousness, a feeling of isolation, and a sense of the inconsequential and ragged character of life are related attitudes, and that they symptomize blindness rather than insight Lawrence emphasizes by describing them as the "cloud" which has gathered over Ursula. He suggests, furthermore, that this feeling of self-responsibility is something which is alien to Ursula's basic impulses, for he describes it as a painful feeling and as something which has been bequeathed to her: "This was torment, indeed, to inherit the responsibility of one's life." Ursula's quest for self-realization, then, is a burden placed upon her not by Lawrence but by her heritage—by the discontentedness and centrifugal aspirations of her maternal ancestors and by the failure of her culture's religion to connect the temporal with the eternal and to dispel the "cloud" which renders the universe an "obscurity."

Instead of concluding that it is her Judaeo-Christian heritage which is at fault, however, Ursula concludes that she is at fault: "Early in the year, when the lambs came, and shelters were built of straw, and on her uncle's farm the men sat at night with a lantern and a dog, then again there swept over her this passionate confusion between the vision world and the weekday world. Again she felt Jesus in the countryside." This "passionate confusion" makes her ashamed of herself, for she knows that the biblical "lamb" is a metaphor. Or again, when in response to Jesus' words "she craved for the breast of the Son of Man, to lie there. And she was ashamed in her soul, ashamed. For whereas Christ spoke for the Vision to answer, she answered from the weekday fact. It was a betrayal, a transference of meaning, from the vision world, to the matter-of-fact world. So she was ashamed of her religious ecstasy, and dreaded lest any one should see it." Rather than concluding that her "passionate confusion" is the sign of a true and vital religious response, Ursula becomes maddened by what she considers to be her carnality: "She hated herself, she wanted to trample on herself, destroy herself. How could one become free?"

Instead of concluding, as Lawrence rhetorically encourages us to do, that the answer is to liberate oneself from the mentality which is occasioning her confusion, Ursula decides to give up her desire for a passionate love affair with the visionary world and to become a seeker of pure passion: "She wanted to become hard, indifferent, brutally callous to everything but just the immediate need, the immediate satisfaction. To have a yearning towards Jesus, only that she might pander to her own soft sensation, use him as a means of reacting upon herself, maddened her in the end. There was then no Jesus, no sentimentality. With all the bitter hatred of helplessness she hated sentimentality."

It is at this point in her development that Ursula meets Anton Skrebensky, and as the logic of the episodes would suggest, this relationship constitutes her attempt to assert her independence and revenge herself for the helplessness she has experienced in her desire for a godly lover. Ursula is not interested in a sexual relationship with Anton, but rather with using him and sex to establish her separateness and her individuality. "She laid hold of him at once for her dreams," Lawrence observes, and the operative phrase is "laid hold of him." Similarly, it is not Anton but herself with whom Ursula is in love. Earlier Ursula had been in love with a vision of something beyond the temporal; now, "for the first time she was in love with a vision of herself: she saw as it were a fine little reflection of herself in his eyes."

As much as she was maddened earlier by her feeling that she was using Jesus to pander to her own soft sensation, now she is ruthless in her use of Skrebensky to discover the extent of her power. For the purpose for which it was designed—by Ursula—the relationship does succeed: "he asserted himself before her, he felt himself infinitely male and infinitely irresistible, she asserted herself before him, and knew herself infinitely desirable, and hence infinitely strong." The reason it is unsatisfactory is not Skrebensky's fault, as we so often hear, but rather that it is not what Ursula herself really wants: "after all, what could either of them get from such a passion but a sense of his or of her own maximum self, in contradistinction to all the rest of life? Wherein was something finite and sad, for the human soul at its maximum wants a sense of the infinite."

"Nevertheless, it was begun now, this passion," Lawrence explains, "and must go on, the passion of Ursula to know her own maximum self, limited and so defined against him." Under the moon, the night of her uncle's wedding, Ursula does discover her own maximum self, and the process involves her annihilation of her lover as well as the annihilation of the lover in her self. For as Lawrence explains in **Apocalypse,** individuality and love are mutually exclusive: "To yield entirely to love would be to be absorbed, which is the death of the individual: for the individual must hold his own, or he ceases to be 'free' and individual. . . . And the modern man or woman *cannot* conceive of himself, herself, save as an individual. And the individual in man or woman is *bound* to kill, at last, the lover in himself or herself." So as much as Ursula succeeds in defining herself through Skrebensky, so much "she had bruised herself, in annihilating him." The "nothingness" that accompanies her triumph is the chasm which surrounds the individual.

There remains one last connection to be broken, however, and this is effected the morning after her "mad" encounter under the moon, when Ursula for a last time turns her attention to the Bible. The particular biblical passage is the Noah story, and the point of her criticism is suggested in the term used to describe that story: "But Ursula was not moved by the *history* this morning" (emphasis mine). She approaches the story of Noah as history, rather than as myth; she approaches the story, that is, in the way the Judaeo-Christian mentality demands, and in doing so she comes to the conclusion that it is a tale of power politics and material greed.

In the first place, the announcement that " 'the fear of you and the dread of you shall be upon every beast of the earth' " leaves her quite cold, for what is it but "man's stock-breeding lordship over beast and fishes." The Lord's promise that he will never again destroy all flesh by water leads her to wonder, "why 'flesh' in particular? Who was this lord of flesh? And after all, how big was the Flood?" And by way of answering these questions and suggesting that the biblical story indicates a very limited and self-conscious point of view, she imagines how an outsider

would relate the episode: "Some nymphs would relate how they had hung on the side of the ark, peeped in, and heard Noah and Shem and Ham and Japeth [*sic*] sitting in their place under the rain, saying, how they four were the only men on earth now, because the Lord had drowned all the rest, so that they four would have everything to themselves, and be masters of everything, sub-tenants under the great Proprietor." The Bible history then is not the vision world to which she feels a tie, and having looked at it from a larger perspective, Ursula now feels freed from it: "What ever God was, He was, and there was no need for her to trouble about Him. She felt she had now all licence."

License, of course, is not liberty; nor is Ursula's dismissal of the Bible as narrow political history the final answer. She has looked at the Noah story from a broader perspective and has placed it into a larger context, but this broader perspective is not a more positive one. It is instead an indifferent one. The episode, therefore, marks the beginning of the third phase in her questioning of her heritage, the atheistic and scientific phase, which is given explicit expression in the philosophy of religion which she formulates under the influence of her third love affair, her lesbian relationship with the "liberated" Winifred Inger in the chapter "Shame."

Miss Inger "had had a scientific education. She had known many clever people. She wanted to bring Ursula to her own position of thought," which is, that religion is merely the projection of man's aspirations and needs: "Winifred humanised it all." Whereas earlier Ursula had fought against the "comparison of myths," she is now brought around to the comparative approach: "Religions were local and religion was universal. Christianity is a local branch." And what religion consists in, she is taught, is "two great motives of fear and love." Both operate according to a principle of identification: fear makes for submissive identification and takes the form of reverence; love consists in delight in identification and creates the sense of triumph.

Religion, therefore, is not a response to something outside man but an externalization of his desire for power and self-preservation; thus Ursula is "brought to the conclusion that the human desire is the criterion of all truth and all good. Truth does not lie beyond humanity, but is one of the products of the human mind and feeling." And consequently, "there is really nothing to fear" because there is nothing beyond man to be afraid of. Fear, therefore, is the sign of an unenlightened mentality; the reverence it begets, the submission it involves, is "base, and must be left to the ancient worshippers of power, worshippers of Moloch. We do not worship power in our enlightened souls." Again, this attitude is not Lawrence's but the problem he is exploring needs emphasis, and Lawrence provides it by emphasizing that these conclusions are Ursula's *and* that they are conclusions explicitly resulting from her limited experience of limited religions: "Gradually it dawned upon Ursula that all the religion *she knew* was but a particular clothing to a human aspiration" (emphasis mine).

Her new religion, as Ursula subsequently defines it, is at once an anti-Christian and an enlightened one. She cannot help "dreaming of Moloch" but she dreams of him not in the reverential way of the "base" primitives but in the enlightened sense of a projection of her own aspiration; it is the strength, pride, and self sufficiency to which she aspires which will constitute her god. As a result, whereas both the Christian and the primitive religions operate upon the principle of identification, Ursula's will be based upon the principle of separateness; whereas the "base" religions are concerned with man's relationship to the cosmos, Ursula's is concerned with distinguishing herself from it, with the "knowing herself different from and separate from the great, conflicting universe that was not herself." She will, in short, be a god unto herself.

A better expression of an egotistical attitude would be hard to find, and hence it is at this point that one should consider the letter that is invariably introduced into discussions of *The Rainbow*—the famous diamond-carbon letter. In that letter Lawrence announces that he is done with the "old-fashioned human element" in characterization and what he is interested in is what a woman, for example, "*is* as a phenomenon (or as representing some greater, inhuman will), instead of what she feels according to the human conception." He does not care, he writes, about what the woman feels, for "that presumes an *ego* to feel with." Don't, he warns, "look in my novel for the old stable *ego*—of the character." Lawrence is, of course, talking explicitly about technique, but we must either conclude that this technique is innovation for the sake of innovation or that the technique is a consequence of his attitude toward ego-orientation in life itself. But if it is the latter, then Ursula's relegation of religion to the human scheme and her self-conscious concept of identity are, from his point of view, limitations to be explored. Such an interpretation, therefore, would solve the problem which this letter poses for many critics of *The Rainbow*—that it is only during certain ritual scenes and at the conclusion of *The Rainbow* that Ursula's personality is dissolved and that she appears as a non-individualized psyche.

That this is indeed the case, that Ursula's new religion of self is not Lawrence's solution to the limitations of the Judaeo-Christian scheme, is demonstrated negatively in the next three chapters of *The Rainbow* and positively in the last. Whereas the first three chapters devoted to Ursula's education were replete with biblical issues, in the next three there is a conspicuous absence of biblical allusions. In these last three chapters, then, we find Ursula attempting to live without a vision world and in accordance with her own credo.

In "The Man's World," Ursula attempts to put her theory of personality and self-sufficiency into practice. She becomes a teacher, thus financially independent and equal rather than subordinate to man, and in her teaching she tries the "personal" approach. The personal approach is an utter failure, and so to remain "free," ironically, she must follow the demands of the system; she must become an instrument and abnegate her personality. She becomes the type of teacher demanded by the system; she becomes the type of woman demanded by the times, a suffragette. At the same time that Ursula realizes her aspirations, therefore, she gradually begins to realize the meaninglessness of her success and of the need of a different way to

realize one's self. Despite her material success, "She felt that somewhere, in something, she was not free. . . . For once she were free she could get somewhere"—not to some geographical place or some distant future goal—not to *go* to a temporal or spatial somewhere but to "the wonderful, real somewhere that was beyond her, the somewhere that she felt deep, deep inside her." Evocative as this is of Ursula's earlier dilemma of wanting to reject the Sunday world and yet feeling a "residue" of it "within her," this chapter is designed to suggest the rightness of Ursula's old desire and the wrongness of her current attempts to satisfy it. As earlier, when "she was dissatisfied, but not fit as yet to criticise," so now "her fundamental, organic knowledge had as yet to take form and rise to utterance."

It is this intuitive appreciation that the somewhere-something she desires is more than a place or object which is involved in Ursula's "involuntary" refusal of the "Garden of Eden" that Anthony Schofield offers her in the second "Widening Circle." To accept the "proffered licence suggested to her" would not be to find liberty; to turn primitive is not the solution to civilized man's "inconsolable sense of loneliness." Ursula must find a different way to recover Paradise. Right as her intuitions are, however, her idea of how this should be accomplished is wrong. The first half of "The Widening Circle" concerns her relation to Anthony; the second half centers upon the move of the Brangwens to Beldover and "higher" cultural status, and upon Ursula's plans for college. This move, as Ursula sees it, will be the agent of her release: "Come college, and she would have broken from the confines of all the life she had known."

But what she discovers, is that college is merely her former classroom writ large: "It pretended to exist by the religious virtue of knowledge. But the religious virtue of knowledge was become a flunkey to the god of material success." Learning was to have been her new religion, education her redemption; now "she was sick with this long service at the inner commercial shrine. Yet what else was there? Was life all this, and this only? Everywhere, everything was debased to the same service." Self-realization and independence were to have been her god, but instead of realizing herself she has merely been the link between a series of events—in "a history": "In every phase she was so different. Yet always she was Ursula Brangwen. But what did it mean, Ursula Brangwen? She did not know who she was." Instead of positive development, "she seemed always negative in her action." Having "freed" herself from the past and all extra-human frames of reference, she finds herself left with a meaningless present and future.

Disillusioned, then, Ursula comes to realize that the direction she has taken has been the wrong one: "This world in which she lived was like a circle lighted by a lamp. This lighted area, lit up by man's completest consciousness, she *thought* was all the world" but now "she felt the strange, foolish vanity of the camp, which said 'Beyond our light and order there is nothing' . . . ignoring always the vast darkness that *wheeled round* about, with half-revealed shapes lurking on the edge" (emphasis mine). It is in this mood that she becomes "fascinated by the strange laws of the vegetable world. She had here a glimpse of something working entirely apart from the purpose of the human world."

Reminiscent as this is of Lawrence's statement in the letter quoted earlier that his concern is with the nonhuman element, this allusion suggests that in rejecting her earlier restriction of life to humanity in favor of a recognition of an extra-human concept of order, Ursula is on the right track. But that the conclusion she comes to is premature is suggested by Lawrence's warning, "She could not understand what it all was"; and that its inadequacy resides in its ego-orientation is demonstrated by her unsuccessful attempt to put the theory into practice. Her conclusion is that self is "a being infinite. Self was a oneness with the infinite. To be oneself was a supreme, gleaming triumph of infinity." Thus inspired, she leaves her microscope to meet Skrebensky, with and through whom she plans to realize her individual infinitude.

She sees herself before him "no mere Ursula Brangwen. She was Woman, she was the whole of Woman in the human order. All-containing, universal, how should she be limited to individuality?" What she discovers, however, through this second unsuccessful love affair with him, is that as an individual she is limited to her individuality. And this knowledge comes to her in two ways: first, in her experience in Rouen that the cathedral and the monumental peace of the town represent "something she had forgotten and wanted," and second, in her recognition at the seashore that there is something beyond herself, something beyond self-consciousness and humanity, that alone is infinity.

The error in Ursula's penultimate perspective is her conscious grasping after the infinite and her belief that the individual can become commensurate with the cosmos. It is, in short, what Lawrence would call her Whitmanesque error of "The One Identity." In the essay, **"Democracy,"** Lawrence observes that Whitman's concept of a "Great Consciousness" as the principle of "One Identity" in the sense in which the "Whole is inherent in every fragment" is "very nice, theoretically"; but he goes on, "when you have extended your consciousness, even to infinity, what then? Do you really become God? When in your understanding you embrace everything, then surely you are divine? But no! With a nasty bump you have to come down and realize that, in spite of your infinite comprehension, you are not really other than you were before: not a bit more divine or superhuman or enlarged. Your *consciousness* is not *you*: that is the sad lesson you learn in your superhuman flight of infinite understanding." The lesson one must learn then is that one's relation to the cosmos cannot be comprehended consciously and that man is an instrument rather than an agent of cosmic forces. As he observes in the essay **"Life"**: "There is an arrival in us from the unknown, from the primal unknown whence all creation issues. Did we call for this arrival, did we summon the new being, did we command the new creation of ourselves, the new fulfillment? We did not, it is not of us. We are not created of ourselves."

In "The Rainbow," the ultimate chapter of the book, Ur-

sula does come to this knowledge of herself and of her relation to the cosmos. The coming to utterance of her "fundamental, organic" knowledge takes place in three stages. First, in her encounter with the horses in the rain she experiences directly the "wheeling" movements of the cosmos. Further, she feels the weight of these black forces as something not only outside her, but also as something within. Finally, she realizes the power of the horses, she fears them, and is aware of her fear. And from her fear of their power comes her own power to save herself from them: "Then suddenly, in a flame of agony, she darted, seized the rugged knots of the oak tree and began to climb. . . . She knew she was strong. She struggled in a great effort till she hung on the bough. She knew the horses were aware. . . . She was working her way round to the other side of the tree. As they started to canter towards her, she fell in a heap on the other side of the hedge." As the symbolic imagery would suggest, the Crucifixion and the Edenic fall are here made coincident. And the episode therefore is designed to suggest negatively that the "fall" is synonymous with the Judaeo-Christian concept of religion and time, and positively that history is cyclic in the sense that ends and beginnings are coincident. The tree is the bridge between life and death, night and day, the world and the cosmos, and the tree is the oak tree, the emblem of Dionysus.

The second stage in Ursula's perception of the reality at the heart of things occurs significantly when her mind is in abeyance—during her delirious dream, and again using a Dionysian symbol, the "acorns." Preparatory to her dream is her repudiation of her lineage, of her social identity, and of her " 'allocated place in the world of things.' " And thus historically disengaged, "to her feverish brain, came the vivid reality of acorns in February lying on the floor of a wood with their shells burst and discarded and the kernel issued naked to put itself forth." And in this image she finds not only a new identity—"She was the naked, clear kernel"—but also a new perception of the nature and direction of life—"to create a new knowledge of Eternity in the flux of Time." What she discovers, in short, is the dynamic way in which the past is related to the present, the eternal to the ephemeral, the individual to the cosmos. The eternal never changes but it manifests itself differently every time because it manifests itself in time. History is the record of past manifestations; the present is a current manifestation; sterility results from a clinging to the old form; alienation and anxiety result from an inability to recognize the eternal beneath the forms. Each kernel must burst from its husk in order to put forth its new shoot; but in doing so it is at once demonstrating its own originality and an eternal law of nature. It is in this paradoxical rather than egotistic sense that "Self is a oneness with the infinite."

The final prelude to Ursula's vision of the rainbow is precipitated by a message from Anton, from the past, and consists in her recognition of the rightness of her earlier intuition occasioned by her grandmother's unique "Bible" of "the tiny importance of the individual, within the great past." "It was not for her to create, but to recognise a man created by God. The man should come from the Infinite and she should hail him. She was glad she could not create her man. She was glad she had nothing to do with his creation. She was glad that this lay within the scope of that vaster power in which she rested at last. The man would come out of Eternity to which she herself belonged." If next to this perception of Ursula we place an observation by Lawrence from a letter of 1914, a letter written while he was completing *The Rainbow,* exactly how we are to interpret this conclusion to Ursula's liberation will be self-evident: "Then the vision we're after, I don't know what it is—but it is something that contains awe and dread and submission, not pride or sensuous egotism and assertion. . . . Behind in all are the tremendous unknown forces of life, coming unseen and unperceived as out of the desert to the Egyptians, and driving us, forcing us, destroying us if we do not submit to be swept away." Ursula has discovered, in short, not "joyous independence" but the joyousness of dependence.

What the vision of the rainbow finally signifies, therefore, is Ursula's archetypal perception of man's relation to the cosmos and of the ultimate truth embodied within the many attempts to portray this relation. The rainbow she sees is a mythic one—a real rainbow at the same time that it is an echo from the past. Its significance lies in its ability to span time and place. It is a promise—not that something will never happen again but of eternal recurrence.

The best summary of Lawrence's treatment of Ursula in *The Rainbow* is therefore, ironically, the description of the educational procedure against which she set herself because "she believed entirely in her own personality":

> Children will never naturally acquiesce to sitting in a class and submitting to knowledge. They must be compelled by a stronger and wiser will. Against which they must always strive to revolt. So that the first great effort of every teacher of a large class must be to bring the will of the children into accordance with his own will. And this he can only do by an abnegation of his personal self, and an application of a system of laws, for the purpose of achieving a certain calculable result, the imparting of certain knowledge.

Ursula had thought "she was going to become the first wise teacher by making the whole business personal, and using no compulsion." Lawrence's method is to make her see the wiser methods of the impersonal rule, the dignity of surrender to a stronger will, the true meaning of liberation.

R. P. Draper   (essay date 1978)

SOURCE: A review of *The Rainbow,* in *Critical Quarterly,* Vol. 20, No. 3, Autumn, 1978, pp. 49-64.

[*In the following essay, Draper surveys* The Rainbow, *touching on elements of theme, character, style, and plot.*]

The pursuit of self-fulfilment might be said to be the purpose or theme of all Lawrence's work; but the book in which this is most prominently the end, even more than *Women in Love,* is *The Rainbow.* Or to be more precise, the third section of *The Rainbow,* the one which concerns the development into a distinctively modern conscious-

ness of Ursula Brangwen, schoolteacher, university student and mistress.

Tom and Lydia, and Ursula's parents, Will and Anna, are also engaged in the struggle towards fulfilment, and like Ursula are involved in tormenting and bafflingly obscure experiences which seem to wrench their very being apart. The 'old stable ego' (in a famous letter of 5 June 1914 Lawrence wrote, 'you mustn't look in my novel for the old stable ego of the character'), is split as by an earthquake and strata of personality are revealed which the characters themselves scarcely understand. At times they move as sleepwalkers in a dream, or nightmare, world where their actions are controlled by forces outside their conscious grasp and they are not individuals so much as elements in a dimly perceived, but powerfully heaving flux: 'Then he saw her come to him, curiously direct and as if without movement, in a sudden flow'. At crucial moments their cry could be that of Lawrence himself in his poem, **'The Song of a Man Who Has Come Through'**:

> Not I, not I, but the wind that blows through me!
> A fine wind is blowing the new direction of Time.

Such awareness is common to all the leading characters of *The Rainbow,* and when so carried beyond themselves they are like creatures possessed, rapturous or demoniacal, as they share the delights or frustrations of a sexual communion which is akin to a primitively religious ritual. There is even a sense in which their individual experiences are forced into one common experience, repetitive and seemingly undifferentiated; for the differences which lie at the surface level of the psyche are transcended and they share in a corporately human life, an archetypal pattern of birth, death and renewal which is the resonating bass note of all animate existence. Beyond 'the old stable ego' is 'another ego', according to whose action, Lawrence continues in the letter already cited, 'the individual is unrecognisable, and passes through, as it were, allotropic states which it needs a deeper sense than any we've been used to exercise, to discover are states of the same radically unchanged element'.

The surface differences, however, remain important. They are, indeed, what constitute this, or any novel. It is how this contact with the mindless flux of life is translated into conscious behaviour and day-to-day reality that makes the variable substance of the fiction. Continuity and discontinuity are its dual aspects, as are sameliness and difference. The three generations of the Brangwen family whose chronicle is *The Rainbow,* grow and differentiate themselves, but their separate experiences echo and overlap so that the novel seems to move forward in time, from one generation to the next, while yet falling back on itself before surging on again in a repetitive tidal motion.

The forward motion is created by the complementary magnets of fulfilment and consciousness, culminating in the uncompromising eagerness of Ursula Brangwen for a complete realisation of self which will also be a 'oneness with the infinite'. Her heredity is itself symbolic of these complementary urges: the Brangwen blood in her responds with unconscious immediacy to the call of instinct and sensuality, while the Polish blood of the Lenskys, derived from her grandmother, Lydia, makes her demand sensitive awareness and the satisfaction of her intelligence. She must have both, and in harmony. Though she does not fully recognise it for what it is, an elusive, glimmering ideal of human completeness draws her on and endows her with something like a Shelleyan zeal for a perfection which is impossible of attainment, and yet indispensable for her sense of purpose and meaning in life. Without it all seems ashy and mechanical, a sterile pursuit of means without end, a mere functioning, not flowering, of self.

The experience of the previous generations points forward to this acute awareness of the fundamental dilemma of life. In Tom and Lydia, and then more boldly in Will and Anna, the rhythm is initiated and the conflicts broached which reach their climax in the desperate problems of Ursula's struggle for the realisation of her being. She stands apart from her mother and father, grandmother and grandfather, as a distinctively twentieth-century, educated and would-be independent woman—in her the novel takes a stride from the Victorian to the modern—but she belongs to the same stream of aspiration as they, and her conflicts are their conflicts writ large. She represents what Lawrence was later to call, in an essay on **'Indians and an Englishman'** published in February 1923, 'the great devious onward-flowing stream of conscious human blood' which draws its warmth from, and deeply responds to, 'the old tribal fire', but must grow into greater conscious life. Reflecting on the Indians whom he had met in New Mexico Lawrence wrote:

> Our darkest tissues are twisted in this old tribal experience, our warmest blood came out of the old tribal fire. And they vibrate still in answer, our blood, our tissue . . . But I don't want to go back to them, ah, never. I never want to deny them or break with them. But there is no going back. Always onward, still further. The great devious onward-flowing stream of conscious human blood. From them to me, and from me on.

Ursula's parents and grandparents are not tribal ancestors as primitively remote from her as the New Mexican Indians were from Lawrence, but the structure of **The Rainbow** and its poetic matrix create a comparable sense of 'darkest tissues' and 'the old tribal fire' as an inheritance which her forebears hand on to Ursula. They themselves, however, are stages on the journey through the ancestral tunnel to Ursula's contemporary crisis and they foreshadow in their own crises the dilemmas that afflict her in hers.

The novel begins with the words, 'The Brangwens had lived for generations on the Marsh Farm . . . ' The sense of long residence in the same place, of rooted, continuous living in close contact with animals and nature, is the Brangwens' leading characteristic; theirs is 'the look of an inheritor'. And then follows the great prose poem which makes their farming life symbolic of 'the old tribal fire':

> But heaven and earth was teeming around them and how should this cease? They felt the rush of the sap in spring, they knew the wave which cannot halt, but every year throws forward the seed to begetting and, falling back, leaves the young-

born on the earth. They knew the intercourse between heaven and earth, sunshine drawn into the breast and bowels, the rain sucked up in the daytime, nakedness that comes under the wind in autumn, showing the birds' nests no longer worth hiding. Their life and inter-relations were such; feeling the pulse and body of the soil, that opened to their furrow for the grain, and became smooth and supple after their ploughing, and clung to their feet with a weight that pulled like desire, lying hard and unresponsive when the crops were to be shorn away. The young corn waved and was silken, and the lustre slid along the limbs of the men who saw it. They took the udder of the cows, the cows yielded milk and pulse against the hands of the men, the pulse of the blood of the teats of the cows beat into the pulse of the hands of the men. They mounted their horses, and held life between the grip of their knees, they harnessed their horses at the wagon, and, with hand on the bridle-rings, drew the heaving of the horses after their will.

The image of the wave is embedded in the text ('they knew the wave which cannot halt, but every year throws forward the seed to begetting, and, falling back, leaves the young-born on the earth'), and the uncomplex, participially extended sentences which take their energy from the initial, urgent statements ('They felt the rush of the sap . . . They knew the intercourse . . . They took the udder of the cows . . . ') echo this tidal thrust in their own syntactic movement. Luscious sibilants that seem to voice 'the rush of the sap', a vocabulary heavy with sexual overtones ('intercourse . . . breast and bowels . . . nakedness . . . opened to their furrow . . . pulled like desire . . . '), an almost too insistent rhythmic beat echoing the milking of the cows—these aspects of the language of the passage create an impression of the bonding of sensations into a continuous flow from nature and animal to man, and this connectedness is further emphasised in such phrasing as 'The young corn waved and was silken, and the lustre slid along the limbs of the men who saw it', 'They mounted their horses and held life between the grip of their knees', and ' . . . with hand on the bridle-rings, drew the heaving of the horses after their will'. Here oneness with 'great creating nature' is complete; fulfilment, of a kind, is achieved in mindless fusion with the source of fertility and warmth which vitalises both the Brangwens themselves and the world they inhabit.

All this is powerfully and intensely positive. But its conclusion is less so. On returning to their houses these Brangwen men sit by the fire and their brains are 'inert'. Here, it is the women who move 'with surety', and though they, too, feel what is now called 'the *drowse* of blood-intimacy', they look away from 'the heated, blind intercourse of farm-life' and out towards 'the spoken world beyond'. The point of view has shifted from the men to the women, and with this shift comes dissatisfaction with such a limitingly physical and sensuous existence. The literal sense of touch gives way to metaphorical sight and sound as the women look out to the larger world of society and listen for its spoken utterances. 'Blood-intimacy' is not enough for them; they want 'to discover what was beyond, to enlarge their own scope and range and freedom'. If they cannot achieve this in themselves, then they wish it for their children, and the means will be education. The end towards which the women aim is said to be a 'higher form of being'. In some respects this sounds like commonplace social aspiration (for example, 'Mrs Brangwen's imagination was fired by the squire's lady at Shelly Hall . . .'), but the more complex truth is not as banal as that. The appeal lies not in the social position of Mrs Hardy, but in her greater fineness of being. She herself is 'like a winter rose, so fair and delicate. So fair, so fine in mould, so luminous . . .', and she is recognised as representing a more complete development towards the realisation of humanity's potentiality for subtle, delicate flowering of being than anything that the farmers and their wives can show. And likewise with Lord William and the vicar:

> The women of the village might be much fonder of Tom Brangwen, and more at their ease with him, yet if their lives had been robbed of the vicar, and of Lord William, the leading shoot would have been cut away from them, they would have been heavy and uninspired and inclined to hate.

Here again it is not a matter of snobbery, despite the forelock-tugging conservatism which the passage seems to suggest. The crucial meaning is conveyed in the image of 'the leading shoot'. If the blood-intimacy of the male Brangwens is the rich, nourishing soil which the plant of being must have for its growth, the prospect of a wider life reflected in the vicar and Lord William is the equally essential light to which the plant must be drawn for its flowering. The precise reality of the fineness which Mrs Hardy and Lord William represent in the minds of the Brangwen women (it may be, and very probably is, an illusion) is not of great significance in itself. Disillusionment would still leave the women with a yearning for the possibility which the image, albeit a false one, had denoted and which acts as the necessary stimulant to their development. Disillusionment with one image after another, reaching near catastrophic proportions with Ursula in the third generation, does in fact become much of the story of *The Rainbow,* but the illusion and its constant re-creation remains none the less essential. For a fundamentally organic conception governs the idea of fulfilment to which the novel is dedicated. Fulfilment results from a tension between the darkness of the subsoil and the stimulus of the light, urging to growth and blossom. This is the basic polarity on which, in Lawrentian terms, life itself depends; without it there is only dead, sterile matter, at the best mechanically activated.

Accordingly, the novel shows a recurrent pattern of action and reaction between the dark and the light, the known and the unknown, the familiar and the foreign. Tom Brangwen, 'a youth fresh like a plant, rooted in his mother and his sister', is disgusted and disillusioned in his first contact with women in the shape of a prostitute. Mere carnality offers no stimulating balance to his own intensely physical existence. His Matlock adventure, however, brings him 'fine contact' the result of which is that he dreams 'day and night, absorbedly, of a voluptuous woman and of the meeting with a small, withered foreigner of ancient breeding'. Intimacy with 'fine-textured sub-tle-mannered people' blends with 'the satisfaction of a voluptuous woman', and 'He set his teeth at the commonplace, to which he would not submit'. The answer to his need comes in the form of Lydia Lensky, who has the glamour of the foreign and the unknown on her: 'It was to him a profound satisfaction that she was a foreigner'. Lydia for her part previously lived in Poland as the wife of an intellectual; in that now dead life everything had been sacrificed to her husband's revolutionary ideals, and with their collapse he became 'skin and bone and fixed idea'. Tom therefore, despite his limited Marsh Farm background—or, rather, precisely because of it—is the 'unknown' for her in the form of darkness and mindless natural forces. His courtship of her, with daffodils in his hand and a wild booming wind outside, comes to her as an 'invasion from the night', and he himself is a black, dark-clad figure compelling her to a 'will-less lapsing into him, into a common will with him'. The chief crisis after their marriage develops, however, from his relapse into a love that is inertly sensual. ('You only leave me alone,' complains Lydia, 'or take me like your cattle, quickly, to forget me again—so that you can forget me again'.) It is only when this is overcome that they can reach the paradoxically 'blazing kernel of darkness' and receive the light of 'transfiguration'. Then they create an arch, a complementary rainbow meeting 'to the span of the heavens', where Anna, the child, is 'free to play in the space beneath, between'.

Although it is denied a major thematic importance, the subject of relations between parents and children is given rich substance in *The Rainbow*. Lawrence is fully aware of the influence of the father and mother on the possibilities of development in the child, and he was to write intelligently on it in the later didactic work, *Fantasia of the Unconscious*. What is perhaps not given its complete due, either here or in the other great parent-child novel, *Sons and Lovers,* is the significance of the family context as a condition for adult fulfilment. It is implicit in the marvelous scenes of the first section of *The Rainbow* where Tom gradually wins the confidence of his insecure and therefore aggressive step-daughter in their shared trips to Nottingham and Derby markets. But the doctrine which at roughly the same time as the composition of *The Rainbow* Lawrence was hammering out in the **'Study of Thomas Hardy'** limits the scope of his imaginative exploration of these scenes. 'Seed and fruit and produce,' he wrote, 'these are only minor aims; children and good works are a minor aim . . . The final aim is the flower . . . The final aim of every living thing, creature, or being is the full achievement of itself.' That the flower might itself be in part a fine interplay of parent and child and not exclusively the mature individual being held in balance with another mature being of the opposite sex, that marriage, in fact, is a family as well as a personal affair, is, not entirely ignored, but treated as a side-issue. As so often in Lawrence's work, the artist can be seen responding to the pull of certain kinds of material drawn from the actual life to which he was acutely sensitive, while the theoriser in him either does not find the same significance in it, or positively denies it. At such times, turning Lawrence's own dictum against him, we often trust the artist rather than the tale, and perhaps we should do so here. The contribution of children to their parents, as well as the influence of parents on children, is more important in *The Rainbow* than the author seems willing to allow, and that Tom and Lydia seem more successful in creating the rainbow arch of fulfilment than the later generations may be, in part at least, due to their, but especially Tom's, relation with Anna.

As the novel moves into the second generation Tom's experience of being stirred to a source of richer possibilities through contact with foreigners who carry the lure of the unknown is echoed in Anna's feeling that her mother's Polish friend, Baron Skrebensky, is the first 'real living person' she has known. But her relationship with Tom himself counterbalances this, and, especially as it is sealed by the episode in her childhood when he soothes her by taking her out into the night to feed the cows, it forms her standard of a rooted masculine sensuality. It is perhaps for this reason that Will Brangwen's animal strangeness possesses her and draws her to him. She finds his head curious: 'it reminded her she knew not of what: of some animal, some mysterious animal that lived in the darkness under the leaves and never came out, but which lived vividly, swift and intense'. There is an ominous hint in this of a skulking reluctance of face life, and yet Will affects Anna at first in the way Lydia had affected Tom, as a liberating force: 'In him the bounds of her experience were transgressed: he was the hole in the wall, beyond which the sunshine blazed on an outside world'.

The symbol of their love is the newly created Eve which Will begins to carve, 'issuing like a flame towards the hand of God, from the torn side of Adam', and flanked by Angels 'who cover their faces with their wings' and look like trees. This represents a delicate balance of flesh and spirit, suggested in the further detail of 'a bird on a bough overhead, lifting its wings for flight, and a serpent wreathing up to it', the creature of light and air and the creature of darkness and earth in harmony. The carving, however, is unfinished and destined never to become complete, for Will destroys it in his later frustration with Anna. Balance also seems to characterise the stooking scene which follows in that it is a night-scene, drenched in brilliant moonlight (the creative paradox of this is caught in Anna's sense of 'All the moonlight upon her, all the darkness within her! All the night in his arms, darkness and shine . . .') and also that the rhythm of the lovers' work poises the one against the other till they gradually meet in an ecstatic climax. But as the carving remains incomplete, so this balance fails to satisfy entirely. The lovers' movement to and fro echoes the soothing movements of Tom in the cowshed carrying the fretful Anna in his arms (a scene which is jealously remembered by Tom only a page or two before the stooking is described), but its real predecessor, as the hypnotic repetitions and splashing sibilants remind us, is the opening passage on the farm life of the Brangwens, and especially the strong rhythms of the milking of the cows, with all which that implies of a rich sensuality carried to excess.

This underlying imbalance becomes more apparent after Will and Anna's wedding. The tantalising potentiality of their honeymoon relationship is conveyed in the image, used to express Will's strange new awareness, of a 'chest-nut falling out of a burr', and shedding him 'naked and glistening on to a soft fecund earth'. But Will's brave new world is also a retreat to the womb, where time and familiar routine is abrogated in favour of a timeless wonder of intimacy and love. Anna is the first to grow tired of this. It pains Will that she wants to return to the commonplace world of housework and tea-parties, but in doing so she is not, in fact, reverting to the conventionality which he feels they have transcended. She is reacting, as it becomes increasingly clear that it is her nature to do, against his dark, clinging dependence ('He seemed a dark, almost evil thing, pursuing her, hanging on to her, burdening her') and his tendency to diminish the fulness of life to a mysterious, but safer, and secretly sensual, inward replica of it.

This, it seems, (though here Lawrence enters obscure territory where it is difficult to follow him), is the explanation of her violent antagonism towards his feeling for the little Cossethay church and towards his even deeper passion for Lincoln Cathedral. Though far from being a morally orthodox Christian herself, Anna is peculiarly irritated by Will's indifference to the conscious meaning of the church and its doctrines. She takes a sceptical 'modern' line, not because she is an intellectual sceptic herself, but because she wants Will to *think*, not merely *feel*. And his ecstasy over the interior of the cathedral, which echoes his womb-like experience during their honeymoon (his soul 'quivered in the womb, in the hush and the gloom of fecundity, like seed of procreation in ecstasy'), though it can cast a potent spell on her also, arouses an instinctive opposition in her because of its unacknowledged abandonment of the need for further development and fulfilment. In some ways Will's Lincoln Cathedral experience seems to be the perfect consummation of all the novel's opposites:

> Away from time, always outside of time! Between east and west, between dawn and sunset, the church lay like a seed in silence, dark before germination, silenced after death. Containing birth and death, potential with all the noise and transitation of life, the cathedral remained hushed, a great, involved seed, whereof the flower would be radiant life inconceivable, but whose beginning and whose end were the circle of silence. Spanned round with the rainbow, the jewelled gloom folded music upon silence, light upon darkness, fecundity upon death, as a seed folds leaf upon leaf and silence upon the root and the flower, hushing up the secret of all between its parts, the death out of which it fell, the life into which it has dropped, the immortality it involves, and the death it will embrace again.

The symbol of the arch is also part of this experience, recalling the arch denoting fulfilment between Tom and Lydia: 'There his soul remained, at the apex of the arch . . . And there was no time nor life nor death, but only this, this timeless consummation, where the thrust from earth met the thrust from earth and the arch was locked on the keystone of ecstasy'. It differs, however, from the previous occurrence in that it is not a symbol for a polarity achieved between a man and woman complementary to each other, a mutually embracing psychological state creating a free space for a third, the child, to play in, but a symbol for the exclusively inner world of Will himself, and coloured with his characteristically sensual darkness, a 'jewelled gloom'. Anna, therefore, with her inherited sense of a different kind of freedom rejects this magnificent creation which would lock her in: 'But she would never consent to the knitting of all the leaping stone in a great roof that closed her in . . . She claimed the right to freedom above her, higher than the roof'. And in an image which echoes the bird in Will's carving she is seen as lifting herself out of the fixed rhythm of the cathedral's gothic arches to an independent movement, like a bird rising from a sea which would impose an alien motion on it to gain its own freedom of action:

> She wanted to get out of this fixed, leaping, forward-travelling movement, to rise from it as a bird rises with wet, limp feet from the sea, to lift herself as a bird lifts its breast and thrusts its body from the pulse and heave of a sea that bears it forward to an unwilling conclusion, tear herself away like a bird on wings, and in the open space where there is clarity, rise up above the fixed, surcharged motion, a separate speck that hangs suspended, moves this way and that, seeing and answering before it sinks again, having chosen or found the direction in which it shall be carried forward.

Anna's victory (Chapter VI is entitled, 'Anna Victrix') is secured, but it is a Pyrrhic victory. By dominating she loses the polarity necessary to fulfilment, and she, in fact, passes on the struggle to the next generation. 'If her soul had found no utterance, her womb had'. She gives herself up to childbearing, in which form the sensuality that she had resisted seems none the less to take her over. As for Will, 'He was aware of some limit to himself, of something unformed in his very being, of some buds which were not ripe in him, some folded centres of darkness which would never develop and unfold whilst he was alive in the body'. There is a belated renewal of their passion for each other after Will's expedition to Nottingham and his affair with the girl he meets at the Empire; but his is an abandonment to total sensuality which signals the arrest of forward movement. Their flower buds, but never blossoms, and their rainbow is only a broken arch.

Will's episode with the Nottingham girl occurs in Chapter VIII, 'The Child'. This chapter, even while it continues the experience of Will and Anna, is already transferring interest towards Ursula. Will, indeed, now begins to seem almost like a male version of Mrs Morel in *Sons and Lovers*. His frustration with Anna drives him to find response in Ursula, who is not freed as her mother was by Tom and Lydia, but 'wakened too soon' by Will's unsatisfied need. The development of Ursula therefore, like that of Paul Morel, is complicated and compromised from the beginning—though the third section of *The Rainbow* does not, for all that, become the kind of psychological study that *Sons and Lovers* is. Behind her is a sense of tradition which is peculiar to *The Rainbow,* and hardly to be found anywhere else in Lawrence's work. If she has a special intimacy with her father (there is no mention of incest, but the intensity of feeling between them is at times near-incestuous), she also develops a relationship with her grandmother which puts her consciously in touch (the genetic connection is, of course, implicit in the structure of the novel) with her Polish ancestry, rousing her to the glamour of the foreign and the unknown. The theme of education also, which reaches back to the yearning of the Brangwen women towards the larger social world, leading to Tom's baffled attempts at learning and his determination to give Anna a lady-like education, becomes dominant in this section of the novel with Ursula's attendance at the High School and her experiences first as elementary school teacher at Ilkeston and then as student at Nottingham. The fact that the importance of education is something magnified in her rather than made to originate solely with her is worth noting. By being shown in the process of development from earlier generations education is enabled to take its part in that struggle towards greater richness of being which runs throughout the novel. It is organically related to the whole and thus one more instance of the plant reaching towards the light.

At this stage, however, a crisis occurs in the working out of the theme of fulfilment which involves not merely an antithesis between education and instinct, but a threat to the organic process itself on which, in the Lawrentian scheme of things, the very concept of fulfilment depends. The phenomenon of insentient mechanism arises. This is not altogether unrelated to what has gone before, since the curiously amicable, yet sinister figure of Uncle Tom (son, by Lydia, of the Tom Brangwen of the first generation) has flitted in and out of the previous pages of the novel from time to time. He now emerges, however, as manager of the colliery at Wiggiston and is a clearly destructive figure. Wiggiston is a place where human life and relationships are brutally subordinated to the 'hard, mechanical activity, activity mechanical yet inchoate' which characterises the room that Uncle Tom has converted as a laboratory and reading room. The colliery itself represents a reversal of normal ends and means. It is not a means to further human fulfilment, but something which has become an end in itself. The 'red-brick confusion' of the town spreads 'like a skin-disease' and the coal-miners die of consumption contracted in the colliery, reckoning themselves not as individuals with major purposes of their own, but as functions of the dominant mechanical process. Their human and sexual relationships are a mere side-show accepted by them and their wives as such. 'They're all colliers', says Uncle Tom:

> 'What do you mean?' asked Ursula. 'They're all colliers?'
>
> 'It is with the women as with us,' he replied. 'Her husband was John Smith, loader. We reckoned him as a loader, he reckoned himself as a loader, and so she knew he represented his job. Marriage and home is a little side-show. The women know it right enough, and take it for what it's worth. One man or another, it doesn't matter all the world. The pit matters. Round the pit there will always be the side-shows, plenty of 'em.'
>
> He looked round at the red chaos, the rigid, amorphous confusion of Wiggiston.
>
> 'Every man his own little side-show, his home, but the pit owns every man. The women have what is left. What's left of this man, or what is

left of that—it doesn't matter altogether. The pit takes all that really matters.'

In Ursula's personal development ecstatic commitment alternates with anxiety, creating a recurrent pattern of illusion and disillusionment which seems to concentrate into an emotionally turbulent adolescence the more extended tensions of the preceding generations. As a girl of thirteen or fourteen she goes through a religious phase in which an idealised Sunday version of Christianity combines a Jesus 'beautifully remote, shining in the distance' with 'dark clouds' reminiscent of Calvary to create a visionary world where 'the marriage of dark and light was taking place'. But reaction against Christianity's other-worldly preoccupation with the cross and the denial of the flesh produces a reaction towards the previously rejected world of the commonplace and a demand that 'The vision should translate itself into weekday terms'. In the wake of this Skrebensky arrives, once more offering that appeal of the unknown which is part of the recurrent Brangwen experience. He is idealised by Ursula as one of the 'Sons of God', and, to emphasise the continuity, we are told that he walks with her where Tom had walked with his daffodils to woo Lydia and Anna with Will. The inevitable reaction against him slowly takes place, however, as Ursula discovers the shallowness of his military and engineering professional life and the low estimate which he holds of himself as an individual: 'What did a man matter personally? He was just a brick in the whole great social fabric, the nation, the modern humanity'. Following this, the lesbian affair with Miss Inger constitutes further action and reaction leading into the corruption of Wiggiston and the teaching at Brinsley Street School, and the latter converts the Brangwen dream of education as the way to a 'higher form of being' into the total subjection of self to a mechanical impersonal discipline necessary for mere survival. Escape from school to university allows illusion to flourish again for a while, but 'the religious virtue of knowledge' dwindles into 'a flunkey to the god of material success' so that Ursula now sees herself (less critically, however, than might be expected) as prey to an almost routine cycle: 'Always the shining doorway ahead; and then, upon approach, always the shining doorway was a gate into another ugly yard, dirty and active and dead. Always the crest of the hill gleaming ahead under heaven; and then, from the top of the hill only another sordid valley full of amorphous, squalid activity'.

The crisis here is a serious one for Ursula; she is in danger of becoming herself the victim of a psychological mechanism that can only produce cynicism: 'She could only stiffen in rejection, in rejection'. In a sense it is also a crisis for Lawrence in the writing of the novel, since the chronicle of illusion and disillusion which he is recording is in danger of assuming the predictability of a formula. The paragraphs which follow the culmination of Ursula's disillusion with education at Nottingham University may therefore be read as an attempt to break out of this impasse by a sudden and striking change of perspective. They are spoken by a voice which is midway between that of the authorial commentator and that of the created character of Ursula. For Lawrence at this moment (though not, it must be insisted, continuously throughout the third section of *The Rainbow*) is close to identifying himself with his char-

acter. Hence it is that his words take on a dual aspect: they are at once an admonition from author to reader to look beyond the seeming mechanism towards an organic continuity still existing with the Brangwen tradition, and of a sudden realisation by Ursula of a truth, about herself and the world she inhabits, which none the less has always been lurking unrecognised in her mind:

> That which she was, positively, was dark and unrevealed, it could not come forth. It was like a seed buried in dry ash. This world in which she lived was like a circle lighted by a lamp. This lighted area, lit up by man's completest consciousness, she thought was all the world: that here all was disclosed for ever. Yet all the time, within the darkness she had been aware of points of light, like the eyes of wild beasts, gleaming, penetrating, vanishing. And her soul had acknowledged in a great heave of terror only the outer darkness. This inner circle of light in which she lived and moved, wherein the trains rushed and the factories ground out their machine-produce and the plants and the animals worked by the light of science and knowledge, suddenly it seemed like the area under an arc-lamp, wherein the moths and children played in the security of blinding light, not even knowing there was any darkness, because they stayed in the light.

> But she could see the glimmer of dark movement just out of range, she saw the eyes of the wild beast gleaming from the darkness, watching the vanity of the camp fire and sleepers; she felt the strange, foolish vanity of the camp, which said 'Beyond our light and our order there is nothing', turning their faces always inward towards the sinking fire of illuminating consciousness, which comprised sun and stars, and the Creator, and the System of Righteousness, ignoring always the vast darkness that wheeled round about, with half-revealed shapes lurking on the edge . . .

> . . . Nevertheless the darkness wheeled round about, with grey shadow-shapes of wild beasts, and also with dark shadow-shapes of the angels, whom the light fenced out, as it fenced out the more familiar beasts of darkness. And some, having for a moment seen the darkness, saw it bristling with the tufts of the hyena and the wolf; and some, having given up their vanity of the light, having died in their own conceit, saw the gleam in the eyes of the wolf and the hyena, that it was the flash of the sword of angels, flashing at the door to come in, that the angels in the darkness were lordly and terrible and not to be denied, like the flash of fangs.

There is a recognition here that development is arrested, cannot 'come forth', but also that there still exists a vital essence in Ursula which is not exhausted and desiccated into cynicism, but which is lying dormant as 'seed' in the seemingly barren 'dry ash'. In making herself a schoolteacher able to hold her own against Mr Harby Ursula had all but capitulated to the values of his world, so running the risk of reducing herself to ash in a world of ash and of succumbing to the worldly wisdom that sees idealism as mere immaturity and illusion. Now, however, she glimpses the living reality which is the underlying source of that resurgence of illusion which persists in taking place within her. Without simply re-asserting such idealism in the same form which it had taken at the beginning of her teaching experience, or in any of the other forms which it had assumed for her, only to be discarded again, Ursula is nevertheless enabled to have faith in herself once more. Her/Lawrence's analogy of the inner circle of light and the surrounding darkness recalls for the reader the opening of the novel with its stress on the blood-intimacy of the men balanced by the wider mental consciousness demanded by the women. The implication now, however, is that it is mental consciousness, not blood-intimacy, which is in excess. Mental consciousness, with its concomitants of science, knowledge, factories, and machine-produce, has shrunk life to a narrow pool, and the polarity of light and dark is almost destroyed by the over-emphasis on light. At the same time it is an essentially optimistic passage. Hope remains, in the fact of the darkness still existing beyond the fence of civilisation and in the creatures inhabiting it who, from within the light, look grey and bestial, but as seen by those 'having died in their own conceit' are transfigured into angels of darkness.

'Transfiguration' is the religiously charged word which frequently occurs in the text of *The Rainbow* at moments of emotional intensity in relations between the sexes. It occurs soon after this crucial passage when Ursula, having seen the gleaming nucleus under her microscope which confirms her sense of the vitality still present beneath the ashiness of her life, hurries to renew her association with Skrebensky: 'She was in dread of the material world, and in dread of her own transfiguration'. The two 'dreads' in this sentence are not, of course, the same. The one is a fear of nullification, the other a sense of awe before the mystery of organic life carrying with it a deeply religious sense of potential change, or 'transfiguration', and therefore a positive 'dread', that 'fear of the Lord' which is 'the beginning of wisdom'. That the renewal of her love for Skrebensky does not lead to a final restoration of the living polarity shared by her grandparents, and subsequently almost extinguished, is perhaps a puzzling contradiction of the hopes which the circle of light passage has re-lit. In the structure of the third section it might have seemed more fitting if the second part of the Skrebensky affair had developed as a successful counterbalance to the failure of the first, with the renewed awareness of a living darkness as the link between the two. To some extent the novel seems to demand this. But *The Rainbow* does not follow such a neat pattern. On the contrary, the second part seems to become a more disastrous repetition of the first. It gives an interval of consummation between the lovers in which Skrebensky is declared to be his real self ('He had no longer any necessity to take part in the performing tricks of the rest. He had discovered the clue to himself . . .'), and for a while he is able to match the standard that Ursula's inveterate idealism sets for him; but that interval is very brief. Skrebensky is afflicted with the same inability as before to sustain the exacting sexual and spiritual demands of Ursula, and he collapses again into his merely conventional self.

With this collapse the novel again becomes as bafflingly difficult as it is in the obscure conflicts between Anna and Will after their marriage. Ursula seems almost mad, a creature possessed by her neurotic demands for satisfaction, and Skrebensky's manhood is shattered in the attempt to meet her on the Lincoln-shire beach. It is undoubtedly part of the intended meaning of this final section that Skrebensky as a product and servant of the modern world dominated by mental consciousness is thereby incapacitated for fulfilment; but Ursula appears as an impossible creature for whom no man, it seems, would be adequate. Like Ibsen's Hedda Gabler she seems to have turned tragically destructive.

Lawrence's mode of writing here, in passionate identification with Ursula's point of view, makes it difficult to judge whether this destructive excess is seen for what it is, and 'placed'. In the illness that follows the ultimate collapse of her relationship with Skrebensky she feels, and Lawrence seems to want to make us share her feeling, that 'The compression was Anton and Anton's world, not the Anton she possessed, but the Anton she did not possess, that which was owned by some other influence, by the world'. Two pages later, as she is recovering from the miscarriage of the child which she was to have had by Skrebensky, we are justified in thinking of this state of mind as itself the consequence of sickness, for we have the first sign of a serious self-criticism emerging in her:

> Who was she to have a man according to her own desire? It was not for her to create, but to recognize, a man created by God. The man should come from the Infinite and she should hail him. She was glad she could not create her man. She was glad she had nothing to do with his creation. She was glad that this lay within the scope of that vaster power in which she rested at last. The man would come out of Eternity to which she herself belonged.

None the less the language is not in any sense that of remorse. There is no regret for what *she* might have done to Skrebensky, nor criticism of her own conduct, no remorse for intolerable pride.

To make such a criticism as this, of course, is to introduce a criterion of Christian humility and repentance which is inappropriate to the terms of the novel. It is inappropriate to the whole imaginative effort that Lawrence was making, i.e. to reject the Christian ideal of self-abnegation and to urge a new concept of spiritual health based on a return (as so much that is 'new' returns) to a pre-Christian pride in burgeoning self. The offence implicit in the question 'Who was she to have a man according to her own desire?' is an offence against spontaneity rather than humility; it recognises the element of will in the demand that the man should measure up to *her* standard, the refusal to wait for the patient flowering from an uncontrolled root into the light of consciousness which will give him as well as herself. On the basis of this interpretation it is possible to reconcile the circle of light passage as an affirmation of Ursula's underlying vitality with the destruction which nevertheless continues to follow it. The seed is alive but the husk through which it must burst is the will. The seed-in-darkness metaphor gives way to the kernel issuing from its shell (anticipated in Will and Anna's honeymoon period), and a concomitant emphasis on nakedness, clarity and freedom. With this vision, which comes to Ursula at the height of her fever, the grip of the will seems to relax and she is, in fact, able to sleep a real, peaceful and restorative sleep from which she eventually wakens to a sense of fineness and fragility which is completely remote from her clenched harpy-like condition on the Lincolnshire beach. The recognition of her wilful arrogance follows, and then, finally, the vision of a rainbow which promises a new germination for mankind from the husk of its own will-created corruption.

As many readers have observed, however, too much is claimed on these last two pages for the final 'rainbow' to appear altogether satisfactory. The rush from Ursula's convalescence and the gentle image of the acorn on the floor of the wood to an apocalyptic New Jerusalem in Beldover and Lethley is precisely what it should not be—forced, assertive and brittle. What the novel has shown is that growth is slow, tortuous and constantly perilous, and even though the claim made is only that the rainbow is 'arched in the blood' of 'the sordid people who crept hard-scaled and separate on the face of the world's corruption', that a potentiality for renewal still exists, the up-beat rhetorical ending is out of key with what has gone before. It is itself too much an act of the Lawrentian will. The tone of the paragraph on Ursula's flower-like opening after her convalescent sleep seems more truly appropriate. Perhaps this remained, like so much else in *The Rainbow,* a suggestion to be fulfilled in Lawrence's later work and finally matured in his poetry rather than his prose. For the right and appropriate ending comes sixteen or seventeen years afterwards when, in his poem, **'The Ship of Death,'** Lawrence combines the organic imagery of fulfilment with his meditations on his own approaching death. What he then evokes is a renewal that has all the delicate and fragile tenderness implicit in the self-critical awareness which is the culmination of Ursula's, and the Brangwens', long struggle, but none of the strident assertiveness with which *The Rainbow* itself inappropriately ends:

> The flood subsides, and the body, like a worn
>   sea-shell
> emerges strange and lovely.
> And the little ship wings home, faltering and
>   lapsing
> on the pink flood,
> and the frail soul steps out, into her house again
> filling the heart with peace.

Lawrence B. Gamache   (essay date 1978)

SOURCE: "The Making of an Ugly Technocrat: Character and Structure in Lawrence's *The Rainbow*," in *Mosaic: A Journal for the Comparative Study of Literature and Ideas,* Vol. XII, No. 1, Autumn, 1978, pp. 61-78.

[*In the following essay, Gamache argues that the younger Tom Brangwen personifies the negative and dehumanizing forces at work in modern society.*]

In his essay **"Pan in America,"** D. H. Lawrence concluded with a call to his contemporaries to recover the vital sources of genuine human life:

> Yet live we must. And once life has been conquered, it is pretty difficult to live. What are we going to do, with a conquered universe? The Pan relationship, which the world of man once had with all the world, was better than anything man has now. The savage, today, if you give him the chance, will become more mechanical and unliving than any civilized man. But civilized man, having conquered the universe, may as well leave off bossing it. Because, when all is said and done, life itself consists in a live relatedness between man and his universe: sun, moon, stars, earth, trees, flowers, birds, animals, men, everything—and not in a 'conquest' of anything by anything. Even the conquest of the air makes the world smaller, tighter, and more airless.

> And whether we are a store-clerk or a bus-conductor, we can still choose between the living universe of Pan, and the mechanical conquered universe of modern humanity. The machine has windows. But even the most mechanized human being has only got his windows nailed up, or bricked in.

This statement contains, in capsule, a central theme of much of his fiction, including *The Rainbow*. His optimistic affirmation of the human capacity to counter-balance the forces of dissolution underlies the stories of the main Brangwen characters; the role of the second Tom Brangwen subsumes the negative thrust of this theme. It is the younger Tom who represents the evil effects of the deadly growth of nineteenth-century modernism, with those influences and aspirations which have "bricked in" the lives of the other characters. He embodies, in the second half of the novel, the kind of dehumanization which each major character must struggle to overcome.

Young Tom Brangwen has hardly been mentioned in critical commentaries on *The Rainbow*; yet he is the only Brangwen character who appears early, as part of the world of Tom and Lydia, his parents, and continues throughout to perform an important function, revealing the lives of the successive Brangwen generations as they struggle against an infectious contamination: the impulse to accommodate themselves to modern beliefs which, for Lawrence, cause human impotence.

It is possible to summarize young Tom's character as he appears in the adult Ursula's life by simply quoting parts of the final episode in the "Shame" chapter, where he meets Winifred Inger. This is, in fact, what most of the few references to him do. But it is essential for an understanding of his importance to realize how he came to be what Ursula so detests when she brings Winifred to him: to see him as the product of his time, the nineteenth century in England as Lawrence viewed it, and of his parents, whose lives could not but be affected by the changes portrayed in the opening of the novel, epitomized by the descriptions of the growth of the canals and the coming of the railroads:

> About 1840, a canal was constructed across the meadows of the Marsh Farm, connecting the

newly-opened collieries of the Erewash Valley. A high embankment travelled along the fields to carry the canal, which passed close to the homestead, and, reaching the road, went over in a heavy bridge.

So the Marsh was shut off from Ilkeston, and enclosed in the small valley bed, which ended in a bushy hill and the village spire of Cossethay.

The Brangwens received a fair sum of money from this trespass across their land. Then, a short time afterwards, a colliery was sunk on the other side of the canal, and in a while the Midland Railway came down the valley at the foot of the Ilkeston hill, and the invasion was complete. The town grew rapidly, the Brangwens were kept busy producing supplies, they became richer, they were almost tradesmen.

The novel begins with a vision of the past, expansive world of the Brangwen's gradually being enclosed, shut in by growing mechanisms; it ends with the rhetorically embellished vision of Ursula of the future. The novel is framed by Lawrence's interpretation of history and his hope for amelioration of the ills he embodies in the portrait of young Tom.

The nineteenth century was, for Lawrence, a century of betrayal:

> Now though perhaps nobody knew it, it was ugliness which really betrayed the spirit of man, in the nineteenth century. The great crime which the moneyed classes and promoters of industry committed in the palmy Victorian days was the condemning of the workers to ugliness, ugliness: meanness and formless and ugly surroundings, ugly ideals, ugly religion, ugly hope, ugly love, ugly clothes, ugly furniture, ugly houses, ugly relationship between workers and employers. The human soul needs actual beauty even more than bread.

In their own time, the great exponents of progress were usually driven by some form of perfectibilian idealism generated by a confidence in man's power to control all circumstances affecting human existence. For some, dazzled by science and technology, there was confidence in human intellectual potential; for others, there was confidence in the inevitability of the survival and ultimate triumph of the best in man despite the evidences of the persistence of the worst. There were those who cried out against the naiveté of such idealists even to the point of arguing their destructive potential; but few, up to and including the writers of Lawrence's time, argued that their motivation itself was perverse. Lawrence, in his portrayal of the younger Tom Brangwen, exhibits not only the twisted motivation of the apostles of the machine but also their destructive power. As a man, young Tom is a kind of Dorian Grey, without the power to hide completely his ugliness, as it grows, from himself or from Ursula. Behind the mask of health and affluence, his eyes speak his degeneracy. His portrayal represents the degeneration of humanity, escaping through technocracy the need to realize human potential as Lawrence so earnestly interpreted it. His final condition in the novel, coupled with that of Winifred, prefig-

ures the ultimate quality of human life Lawrence saw such people engendering.

It is his early life that suggests most vividly the causes of young Tom's perversion as a man; his relationship to his family, or lack of vital relationship to be more precise, is focussed by the reactions to him of his parents and half-sister, Anna, and by the differences between him and his brother Fred. His early development accomplishes two functions: it illuminates the stories of his parents and of his own generation, and it prepares his role in Ursula's life in the later episodes. The role of young Tom is a unifying thread in the novel, and considerations of the novel's unity will be weaker to the extent that they fail to take into account his function.

The younger Tom Brangwen becomes significant very early in the novel. During Lydia's first pregnancy after her marriage to the older Tom, the strain in her relationship with her husband intensifies. The causes of this strain in the character of her husband are given in the beginning of the novel, in the portrayal of the breakdown of the old Brangwen world with the growth of the technology separating the men from their awareness of the open expanse of land and sky, and in the story of the early life of Tom under the influence of his mother's vision of the town, leading to "the magic land, where secrets were made known and desires fulfilled." The responses of the parents to the infant in the context of the breakdown of the old Brangwen way of life and the strange world, for them, which Lydia represents, become the foundation of the boy's development into tormented manhood.

The marriage of Tom and Lydia is often cited as the model of man-woman fulfillment according to Lawrence. Lucia Henning Heldt stated this view [in *D. H. Lawrence Review* 8 (Fall 1975)]: "The courtship and marriage of Tom Brangwen and Lydia Lensky set the standards by which all of the other sexual involvements in the two novels [i.e., *The Rainbow* and *Women in Love*] can be judged and provide the reader with a rare, fully developed example of exactly what Lawrence has in mind when he speaks of love." This view is valid when related to Lawrence's notions of intimate man-woman fulfillment. But Lawrence conceived of man-woman love as a stage in a man's life which should lead beyond, to "some passionate, purposive activity." That Tom's life does not adequately go beyond the limitations of a circumscribed world on the Marsh farm shows his failure to achieve something his children could grow through as they have to move into the society about them. The measuring of the success of Tom and Lydia cannot ignore the consequences of their limitations in the lives of their children; young Tom embodies these effects in their most extreme and persistent form throughout the novel.

The older Tom married Lydia after a prolonged period of alienation from his community. He failed to adapt to the modern world from the moment in his childhood when his mother, in her aspiration for contact with "the activity of man in the world at large," sent him to school, thereby imposing on him an aspiration always alien to his character. That Lawrence himself was preoccupied with this kind of impact mothers can have on sons is well-known. But his extension of this perception to the society and its development, in that sons of mothers become fathers of sons and thereby perpetuate the evil consequences, is very appropriate to an understanding of the older Tom's influence on his son's life. Lawrence stated the point precisely:

> We are such stuff as our grandmothers' dreams are made on. This terrible truth should never be forgotten. Our grandmothers dreamed of wonderful 'free' womanhood in a 'pure' world, surrounded by 'adoring, humble, high-minded' men. Our mothers started to put the dream into practice. And we are the fulfilment. We are such stuff as our grandmothers' dreams were made on. . . .

The older Tom's mother had dreams for him:

> So Tom went to school, an unwilling failure from the first. He believed his mother was right in decreeing school for him, but he knew she was only right because she would not acknowledge his constitution. He knew, with a child's deep, instinctive foreknowledge of what is going to happen to him, that he would cut a sorry figure at school. But he took the infliction as inevitable, as if he were guilty of his own nature, as if his being were wrong, and his mother's conception right. If he could have been what he liked, he would have been that which his mother fondly but deludedly hoped he was. He would have been clever, and capable of becoming a gentleman. It was her aspiration for him, therefore he knew it as the true aspiration for any boy. But you can't make a silk purse out of a sow's ear, as he told his mother very early, with regard to himself; much to her mortification and chagrin.

The older Tom grew up convinced of his own inadequacy when faced with the society developing around the Marsh farm. His failure to adapt to that world made it the focus for his unfulfilled sense of self; anything which represented the sophisticated world with which his mother's hopes forced him to cope becomes a source of fascination and mystery for him. As a boy his friendship with a frail but intelligent fellow student was rooted in this attitude. Later, the people at Matlock, especially the lady who seduced him, and her friend, the monkey-faced foreign gentleman, attracted him because he could not understand them, yet he felt they were superior because of their sophistication:

> His mind was one big excitement. The girl and the foreigner: he knew neither of their names. Yet they had set fire to the homestead of his nature, and he would be burned out of cover. Of the two experiences, perhaps the meeting with the foreigner was the more significant. But the girl—he had not settled about the girl.

> He did not know. He had to leave it there, as it was. He could not sum up his experiences.

> The result of these encounters was, that he dreamed day and night, absorbedly, of a voluptuous woman and of the meeting with a small, withered foreigner of ancient breeding. No sooner was his mind free, no sooner had he left his own companions, than he began to imagine an intimacy with fine-textured, subtle-mannered

people such as the foreigner at Matlock, and amidst this subtle intimacy was always the satisfaction of a voluptuous woman.

It is the strange separateness of Lydia, her power to create in him a sense "as if he were walking again in a far world, not Cossethay, a far world, the fragile reality" that first attracts him to her. He becomes fascinated by her mysterious connection with a larger, unknown world. After learning about her background, his feeling for her, which at first was "like a mist" that kept out "the common, barren world," yet tormented with doubt "like a sense of infinite space, a nothingness, annihilating," becomes established by knowledge of her foreign origins:

> Brangwen felt that here was the unreality established at last. He felt also a curious certainty about her, as if she were destined to him. It was to him a profound satisfaction that she was a foreigner.

The Matlock experience left him in torment; Lydia, he fears, will reopen that wound:

> The feeling that they had exchanged recognition possessed him like a madness, like a torment. How could he be sure, what confirmation had he? The doubt was like a sense of infinite space, a nothingness, annihilating. He kept within his breast the will to surety. They had exchanged recognition.

> He walked about in this state for the next few days. And then again like a mist it began to break to let through the common, barren world. He was very gentle with man and beast, but he dreaded the starkness of disillusion cropping through again.

Brangwen's state of mind, the effect of his upbringing, is complex: he is unable to feel at ease outside of the farm world of the Brangwen past, yet he needs to join, somehow, the mysterious modern, cosmopolitan world into which he has been made to move in order to fulfil his mother's desire. Lydia Lensky is a connection to the world the monkey-faced foreigner represents, and she meets the need represented by the girl.

The attraction of Brangwen to Lydia is not simply to what she is in herself but, more importantly at this stage, to what she represents. The irony of the situation is central to an understanding of both Brangwen and his first son. That which attracted him to Lydia becomes the focus of his anger and frustration in the early stages of his marriage: her "separateness," her unknowable "otherness." Tom is both attracted by Lydia's strangeness and confused by his inability to comprehend that in her. The resulting torment as he moves toward the woman tends to confirm his negative assessment of himself. At this point in his life he looks to Lydia as the fulfillment for him of what he thinks he needs but lacks: "He was nothing. But with her, he would be real."

In an essay Lawrence describes the difference between two attitudes towards love, the one ending in a death of love and the other leading the lover to a new transcendence:

> . . . love is strictly a traveling. 'It is better to

travel than to arrive,' somebody has said. This is the essence of unbelief. It is a belief in absolute love, when love is by nature relative. It is a belief in the means, but not in the end. . . . We travel in order to arrive. . . . Love is the hastening gravitation of spirit towards spirit, and body towards body, in the joy of creation. But if all be united in one bond of love, then there is no more love. And therefore, for those who are in love with love, to travel is better than to arrive. For in arriving one passes beyond love, or, rather, one encompasses love in a new transcendence.

The love of Tom and Lydia in its early stages is not a "passing beyond" but a "passing away" or a "trespass" in that their love is the end for him. Tom wants to live in her rather than to go out into the world of work as a man; he wants to find his satisfaction in knowing her and cannot rest easy with the distance between them which their different backgrounds cause:

> They were such strangers, they must for ever be such strangers, that his passion was a clanging torment to him. Such intimacy of embrace, and such utter foreignness of contact! It was unbearable. He could not bear to be near her, and know the utter foreignness between them, know how entirely they were strangers to each other. He went out into the wind. Big holes were blown into the sky, the moonlight blew about. Sometimes a high moon, liquid-brilliant, scudded across a hollow space and took over under electric, brown-iridescent cloud-edges. Then there was a blot of cloud, and shadow. Then somewhere in the night a radiance again, like a vapour. And all the sky was teeming and tearing along, a vast disorder of flying shapes and darkness and ragged fumes of light and a great brown circling halo, then the terro of a moon running liquid-brilliant into the open for a moment, hurting the eyes before she plunged under cover of cloud again.

The moon is the symbol of the female principle. The exposure of Tom to the light of the moon hurts his physical eyes as the exposure to the fleeting female in Lydia, the thing in her he wants to know and understand with his mind, comes and goes, and its light hurts him. Until he is able to accept the female for what she is without trying to grasp her in his mind, and until he becomes the male completely in his relationship to her, the hurt will not only remain but grow more severe.

Before meeting Tom, Lydia had retired from active involvement in the outer world. Tom made her tingle in her body from the first moment when they saw each other on the road. Between the times of their early meetings, however, "she lapsed into the old unconsciousness, indifference and there was a will in her to save herself from living anymore." But the impact of Tom was strong, and although her "impulse was strong against him, because he was not of her sort," her "blind instinct" led her to accept him. During their courtship and early marriage Lydia shifts constantly between two attitudes: indifference and being "attentive and instinctively expectant before him, unfolded, ready to receive him." The vascillation drives Tom to despair:

And after a few days, gradually she closed again, away from him, was sheathed over, impervious to him, oblivious. Then a black, bottomless despair became real to him, he knew what he had lost. He felt he had lost it for good. . . . In misery, his heart like a heavy stone, he went about unliving.

Another attitude in Tom which further intensifies the difficulty of the relationship is his suffering "very much from the thought of actual marriage, the intimacy and nakedness of marriage." The same attitude was evident earlier in his reticence regarding the "nice" girls of his home town. The image of his mother and sisters on the farm came between him and any physical contact with them. In connection with Lydia, this attitude is linked to his awareness of her foreignness:

> They were so foreign to each other, they were such strangers. And they could not talk to each other. When she talked, of Poland or of what had been, it was all so foreign, she scarcely communicated anything to him. And when he looked at her, an over-much reverence and fear of the unknown changed the nature of his desire into a sort of worship, holding her aloof from his physical desire, self-thwarting.

The Matlock image, which is in itself the embodiment of the ideal inculcated into Tom by his mother, and the image of woman based on her significance to him on the farm are the two influences which thwart Tom's spontaneous response to the flow of Lydia's female force into his being: "He wanted to drink, to get rid of his forethought and afterthought, to set the moment free. But he could not. The suspense only tightened at his heart." The thought patterns built in Tom's mind out of earlier experiences have the combined effect of hindering an open, natural response to Lydia in the beginning of their marriage and of stopping him from moving beyond the love relationship to a realization of his fullness of being as a man. Lawrence's comments on the proper development of a man in his middle years offer a contrast to the description of Tom:

> When a man approaches the beginning of maturity and the fulfilment of his individuals self, about the age of thirty-five, then is not his time to come to rest. On the contrary. Deeply fulfilled through marriage, and at one with his own soul, he must now undertake the responsibility for the next step into the future. He must now give himself perfectly to some further purpose, some passionate purposive activity. Till a man makes the great resolution of aloneness and singleness of being, till he takes upon himself the silence and central appeasedness of maturity; and *then, after this,* assumes a sacred responsibility for the next purposive step into the future, there is no rest. The great resolution of aloneness and appeasedness, and the further deep assumption of responsibility—this is necessary to every parent, every father, every husband, at a certain point. If the resolution is never made, the responsibility never embraced, then the love-craving will run on into frenzy, and lay waste to the family.

During the wedding of Anna Tom sees that his small, farm

world cannot go unchanged; at that moment his self-perception becomes complete:

> Brangwen was staring away at the burning blue window at the back of the altar, and wondering vaguely, with pain, if he ever should get old, if he ever should feel arrived and established. He was here at Anna's wedding. Well, what right had he to feel responsible, like a father? He was still as unsure and unfixed as when he had married himself. His wife and he! With a pang of anguish he realised what uncertainties they both were. He was a man of forty-five. Forty-five! In five more years fifty. Then sixty—then seventy—then it was finished. My God—and one still was so unestablished!
>
> How did one grow old—how could one become confident? He wished he felt older. Why, what difference was there, as far as he felt matured or completed, between him now and him at his own wedding? He might be getting married over again—he and his wife. He felt himself tiny, a little, upright figure on a plain circled round with the immense, roaring sky: he and his wife, two little, upright figures walking across this plain, whilst the heavens shimmered and roared about them. When did it come to an end? In which direction was it finished? There was no end, no finish, only this roaring vast space. Did one never get old, never die? That was the clue. He exulted strangely, with torture. He would go on with his wife, he and she like two children camping in the plains. What was sure but the endless sky? But that was so sure, so boundless.
>
> Still the royal blue colour burned and blazed and sported itself in the web of darkness before him, unwearingly rich and splendid. How rich and splendid his own life was, red and burning and blazing and sporting itself in the dark meshes of his body: and his wife, how she glowed and burned dark within her meshes! Always it was so unfinished and unformed!

Unestablished, unfinished, and unformed—each term is indicative of a lack of larger purpose, leading into the unknown which he fears. The failure of the father to achieve fullness of being as a man in a larger human community leads to the poverty of Fred and the emptiness of Tom, both of whom must move beyond the small world of the farm, especially with the father's death ending its reality for all the Brangwens. The older Tom never truly "assumes a sacred responsibility for the next purposive step into the future." He is swept away by the modern "deluge." The father's limitations become, in his son and namesake, the source of spiritual death. A chain has been established from generation to generation—young Tom represents its destructive power; Anna and Will and Ursula represent the struggle against that power.

The elder Tom's attitude towards his newborn son is negative; he identifies the child with the mother's foreignness and therefore with the modern world alien to the Marsh farm. The larger process figured in the opening of the novel, of rural England moving into the age of technocracy, is the frame within which Brangwen moves and into which the child is born. The total process has had a cumu-

lative effect on the formation of the father, on the father-son relationship, and therefore on what the son will become.

The father does not love his son except as a confirmation of his own masculinity:

> Tom Brangwen never loved his own son as he loved his stepchild Anna. When they told him it was a boy, he had a thrill of pleasure. He liked the confirmation of fatherhood. It gave him satisfaction to know he had a son. But he felt not very much outgoing to the baby itself. He was its father, that was enough.

Anna has been a surrogate for Lydia during those moments of greatest estrangement which the stepfather has felt. The girl, simple and wanting his affection, becomes an outlet for his frustrated need for a being beyond himself to whom he can uncomplicatedly relate: as Lydia's daughter and as a responsive "other," she helps him cope with his unresolved need to give himself without destroying himself. He identifies his own child with that in his wife with which he cannot cope, her past.

The mother, through the birth of their child, is finally able to break from her past, at least enough to begin to become the wife and mother of the Marsh farm community:

> She was serene, a little bit shadowy, as if she were transplanted. In the birth of the child she seemed to lose connection with her former self. She became now really English, really Mrs. Brangwen. Her vitality, however, seemed lowered.

The break with the past has cost her something; she has lost the memory of her "noble" past, her sacrificial life with the intense Lensky, which gave her a sense of self by which she maintained her will to persist. Until her new husband accepts her as a woman, not as a Matlock substitute, she will be unable to "bear the full light" of her new role. He demands that she be an object for his total fulfillment, but the child divides her from him:

> He wanted to give her all his love, all his passion, all his essential energy. But it could not be. He must find other things than her, other centres of living. She sat close and impregnable with the child. And he was jealous of the child.

Anna relieves him: "Gradually a part of his stream of life was diverted to the child [Anna], relieving the main flood to his wife."

The passages which reveal the father's attitude to his newborn son are crucial for an understanding of the son's role. One of the most revealing is that which relates his and Anna's game involving the infant:

She shared a sort of recklessness with her father, a complete, chosen carelessness that had the laugh of ridicule in it. He loved to make her voice go high and shouting and defiant with laughter. The baby was dark-skinned and dark-haired, like the mother, and had hazel eyes. Brangwen called him the blackbird.

'Hallo,' Brangwen would cry, starting as he heard the wail of the child announcing it wanted to be taken out of the cradle, 'there's the blackbird tuning up.'

'The blackbird's singing,' Anna would shout with delight, 'the blackbird's singing.'

'When the pie was opened,' Brangwen shouted in his bawling bass voice, going over to the cradle, 'the bird began to sing.'

'Wasn't it a dainty dish to set before a king?' cried Anna, her eyes flashing with joy as she uttered the cryptic words, looking at Brangwen for confirmation. He sat down with the baby, saying loudly:

'Sing up, my lad, sing up.'

And the baby cried loudly, and Anna shouted lustily, dancing in wild bliss:

'Sing a song of sixpence
Pocketful of posies,
Ascha! Ascha!. . . . '

Then she stopped suddenly in silence and looked at Brangwen again, her eyes flashing as she shouted loudly and delightedly:

'I've got it wrong, I've got it wrong.'

That the son is called "blackbird" is appropriate since the baby is "dark-skinned and dark-haired, like the mother." Also, the child resembles his Brangwen grandmother:

The Alfred Brangwen of this period had married a woman from Heanor, a daughter of the 'Black Horse.' She was a slim, pretty, dark woman, quaint in her speech, whimsical, so that the sharp things she said did not hurt. She was oddly a thing to herself, rather querulous in her manner, but intrinsically separate and indifferent.

Later, the young Tom's resemblance to his grandmother will become much more apparent. The child symbolically embodies, at this point in his physical appearance, the two strains of heritage that have most hindered the father: his mother's influence and his wife's non-Brangwen strangeness.

The song of Anna also contributes to the portrayal of the infant's early situation. She is acting like a child; after having been almost unnaturally attached to her mother, jealous and defensive, she is released from a burden with the birth of the infant:

The child ceased to have so much anxiety for her mother after the baby came. Seeing the mother with the baby boy, delighted and serene and secure, Anna was at first puzzled then gradually she became indignant, and at last her little life settled on its own swivel, she was no more strained and distorted to support her mother.

She became more childish, not so abnormal, not so charged with cares she could not understand. The charge of the mother, the satisfying of the mother, had developed elsewhere than on her. Gradually the child was freed. She became an independent, forgetful little soul, loving from her own centre.

The baby is, to Anna, like an offering to her father which has released her from bondage; the English folk songs of her stepfather have replaced the "poignant folk-tales she has had from her mother, which always troubled and mystified her soul." Brangwen is Old King Cole. The "laugh of ridicule" in their singing is directed at "the blackbird tuning up." The baby does not sing; it cries—loudly. The scene, which I consider is the seed of young Tom's developing function in the novel, is representative of Lawrence's use of singular scenes which typify recurring patterns of behavior of his characters. The actions of Anna and Brangwen described in the passage are presented as representative rather than as singular. The child's place in the family, especially for his father and step-sister, is to focus for them their relationships with each other; the child is not included in their vital interaction.

The use of "cryptic" to describe Anna's completion of the nursery rhyme the father begins suggests her attitude. The word suggests a sense of the mysterious and baffling in Anna's statement. She "uttered the phrase; she did not sing it. She looked to her stepfather for confirmation." There is a mysterious, ritual quality in the use of the nursery rhyme; the game is more than mere childish play. For Anna, Brangwen is "king" and the baby is "a dainty dish" set before him. She confuses "Sing a song of six-pence" with "Ring-a-ring a Rosie." Each of these nursery rhymes is associated with death: the first song suggests a sacrificial offering and the second the image of death itself. She dances wildly round the child, laughing in the joy of her new-found freedom. The behavior of both father and daughter is suggestive of a kind of Death rite with Dionysian undertones. The irony of this scene, so innocent and playful in appearance, so suggestive of disaster for the child, will be completed by the effect of these attitudes on the future of young Tom.

Given the total development of the characters and the heritage each is influenced by, the situation for young Tom Brangwen is at this point foreboding. He is the avenue of escape from the past for his mother, his father, and his stepsister. He is not accepted by the father because of Brangwen's unresolved relationship with Lydia, because the boy's physical appearance associates him with the world beyond the Marsh farm in which Brangwen feels incapable of living and fulfilling himself. Anna, as will soon be seen, becomes isolated from her stepbrother as he grows older. The mother uses him as a kind of tool to escape her past and, more importantly, to defend herself during the strained period of her developing life with her husband and his English farm world. In a way similar to many of Lawrence's mothers, at least to the end of the chapter called "Childhood of Anna Lensky," Lydia centers herself on her child; yet she loves her baby "with a sort of dimness, a faint absence about her, a shadowiness even in her mother-love." Again the child, as himself, is not vitally connected, not even with his mother. To avoid the fury and intensity of demand made on her by Brangwen which she cannot satisfy, she puts the child between them, further intensifying the isolation of the baby from his father and building his role as the tool of others to whom he cannot relate through genuine human interaction.

Between the episodes centered around the child's birth and the father's death, young Tom appears twice. At the beginning of the chapter "Girlhood of Anna Brangwen" is a brief description of Anna's relationship with her two half-brothers:

> She had two brothers, Tom, dark-haired, small, volatile, whom she was intimately related to but whom she never mingled with, and Fred, fair and responsive, whom she adored but did not consider as a real, separate thing.

Each of the narrator's comments on Anna, Tom and Fred in this passage carries forward the motifs established earlier around these characters and forms a link between the first generation portion of the novel and the third generation story, where Tom's role becomes fulfilled.

Anna's isolation from Tom is absolute: she "never mingled" with him. In contrast, Anna does feel a strong emotional attachment to Fred, as suggested by the word "adored." Her attitude towards each brother shows how each is accepted as part of the family life on the Marsh farm: Tom is isolated; Fred is identified with the world of his father. Tom provided Anna's way of escape from the bondage of her mother's past as a child. Her life is intimately entwined with his, but she does not feel any bond of affection with him as she does with the younger brother. As Tom's role evolves, his isolation from the reality of life centered on the farm will become total. Contrary to custom, the second son, Fred, will inherit the Marsh. He is very much his father's son, in appearance, in attitudes, and in his father's mind. The older son, who should have inherited the farm, will depart entirely from the Brangwen society when, at a relatively early age, he will be sent to London.

The brief description of Tom, contrasting him with Fred, continues what he was seen to be as an infant and prepares for his role as an adult in Ursula's portion of the novel. Being "dark-haired and small," he is the child of his mother's non-Brangwen world and grandson of his father's town born and bred mother. His inner being lacks the Brangwen strength which enabled his father to sustain himself despite the attacks against his sense of self-worth as a child and young man before his meeting with Lydia. These aspects of the youngster's character, which the description of him at this point suggests, will come to fruition as his role expands after his father's death. Their importance now is that they continue and strengthen the portrayal of the roots of his character in his childhood role on the Marsh farm, which, in turn, must modify our conception of the nature of the separate universe created by his parents: their world succeeds only to the extent they can exclude from it signs of things alien to their way of life.

The second direct mention of young Tom during the portion of the novel devoted to Anna is related to her ridiculing, through laughter, Will Brangwen's singing in church. The boy Tom, in the scenes on the way to and in the church, is not present—he sings in the choir. Anna is with Will and Fred when the intensity of Will's singing makes her laugh. When Tom learns about Anna's behavior later at home, his eyes are "bright with joy" over the spectacle his sister created. He takes pleasure in her denigrating the religious feelings so important to Will. Later Tom, along with Winifred, will take pleasure in attacking the value of anything but the machine. His attitude in this episode is indicative of what he will come to represent; his enjoyment of the comedy Anna has made of religious seriousness is a prelude to his desire as an adult to belittle genuine human feeling or human commitment of any kind. The machine will become his god, the factory his church, and technology his religion.

The chapter "The Marsh and the Flood" is pivotal: it marks the passing of the father, the transition from Will and Anna to Ursula as the center of attention, and the movement away from the Marsh farm into the world of the town. The figure of young Tom occupies a dominant position. The chapter begins with the completion of the story of his boyhood and adolescence, and the story of his development into manhood is identified with the change of the way of life of the second and third generations of Brangwens. The resumé of his development into his early twenties is followed by the story of old Tom's death and funeral. The chapter ends with Lydia's telling the story of her first husband, Lensky, to Ursula. The linking of characters through the structuring and emphases of the chapter does much to develop and clarify the purpose of the son's role.

The names of Tom and Fred are linked, but the vast differences between the brothers are stressed. Fred "was a Brangwen, large-boned, blue-eyed, English. He was his father's very son, the two men father and son, were supremely at ease with one another. Fred was succeeding to the farm." Fred is at home on the Marsh farm; he fits totally into his father's world, and the weakness of that world as a basis for living in a modern society will be revealed through Fred's eventual accommodation to the world outside of the Marsh. Tom is described as the opposite of Fred:

> Tom was a rather short, good-looking youth, with crisp black hair and long black eyelashes and soft, dark, possessed eyes. He had a quick intelligence. From the High School he went to London to study. He had an instinct for attracting people of character and energy. He gave place entirely to the other person, and at the same time kept himself independent. He scarcely existed except through other people. When he was alone he was unresolved. When he was with another man, he seemed to add himself to the other, make the other bigger than life size. So that a few people loved him and attained a sort of fulfilment in him. He carefully chose these few.
>
> He had a subtle, quick, critical intelligence, a

mind that was like a scale or balance. There was something of a woman in all this.

This passage adds to the portrait of Tom as it has been developed thus far: it suggests his sophistication through education, making him more like the Matlock people and the Skrebenskys than his own family; it suggests his femininity, making him symbolic of the importance of the modern man; and it suggests his "unresolved" sense of self, making him the inheritor of his father's debility—his grandmother's dream fulfilled.

Young Tom at this point in the novel has developed into an inwardly tormented and isolated human being. Just after high school he left the Marsh farm for further education in London, the one Brangwen to become absorbed into sophisticated society early in life. The description of his life in London clearly emphasizes his inner isolation and suggests his subtle, uncommitted approach to sophisticated people. It begins with the mention of his "master," suggestive of a Lord Henry Wotton type, and ends with the portrait of his attractive external appearance, suggestive of a Dorian Gray type:

> In London he had been the favourite pupil of an engineer, a clever man, who became well-known at the time when Tom Brangwen had just finished his studies. Through this master the youth kept acquaintance with various individual, outstanding characters. He never asserted himself. He seemed to be there to estimate and establish the rest. He was like a presence that makes us aware of our own being. So that he was while still young connected with some of the most energetic scientific and mathematical people in London. They took him as an equal. Quiet and perceptive and impersonal as he was, he kept his place and learned how to value others in just degree. He was there like a judgment. Besides, he was very good-looking, of medium stature, but beautifully proportioned, dark, with fine colouring, always perfectly healthy.

His parents' reality has nothing to do with the modern ways he must accommodate. Having nothing of which he is a part, neither family roots nor community, he "scarcely existed except through other people," yet he "kept himself independent." He is not a man as a person, given Lawrence's sense of manhood; he does not and will not live through a woman as did his father when he was young and unresolved. He lives through others without becoming anything in himself; "There was something of a woman in all this."

What Lawrence says elsewhere of the effects of modern education on young minds offers a commentary on young Tom:

> We talk about education—leading forth the natural intelligence of a child. But ours is just the opposite of leading forth. It is a ramming in of brain facts through the head, and a consequent distortion, suffocation, and starvation of the primary centres of consciousness. A nice day of reckoning we've got in front of us. . . .
>
> The whole of a child's development goes on from the great dynamic centres, and is basically non-

mental. To introduce mental activity is to arrest the dynamic activity, and stultify true dynamic development. By the age of twenty-one our young people are helpless, hopeless, floundering mental entities, with nothing in front of them, because they have been starved from the roots, systematically, for twenty-one years, and fed through the head. They have had all their mental excitements, sex and everything, all through the head, and when it comes to the actual thing, why, there's nothing in it. Blasé. The affective centers have been exhausted from the head.

These comments can be applied to our understanding of the elder Tom and both of his sons, but the "starvation" increases in its extremity as time progresses; Fred is less capable of fulfillment than his father, and Tom, lacking even that measure of vital resource his brother has in the farm, will become incapable of anything but the "sterile substitute of brain knowledge."

The adulthood of young Tom begins with his removal to London where he becomes "the favourite pupil of an engineer, a clever man." It is "this master" who introduces the youngster to "some of the most energetic scientific and mathematical people in London." The insinuation of homosexuality in young Tom's makeup is evident in his "woman" mind and in the "woman's poignant attention and self-less care" with which he "watched over" his younger brother. Whether or not the psychological aberration is homosexuality as such is not the important point. What is important is the fact that the personal relationships of the young man, from the youthful "uneasy friendship between him and one of the Hardys at the Hall" to his association with his "chief," which mysteriously suffers "some breach . . . never explained" when he is twenty-three, are with men, never with a woman.

He meets and then breaks with an older man and begins to travel the world, "always the same good-looking, carefully dressed, attractive young man, in perfect health, yet somehow outside of everything." He is alone: "He belonged to nowhere, to no society." So it is that young Tom comes to represent a reality alien to the Marsh world of Tom and Lydia, and to bring a "change in tone over the Marsh":

> It was young Tom Brangwen, with his dark lashes and beautiful colouring, his soft, inscrutable nature, his strange repose and his informed air, added to his position in London, who seemed to emphasize the superior foreign element in the Marsh. When he appeared, perfectly dressed, as if soft and affable, and yet quite removed from everybody, he created an uneasiness in people, he was reserved in the minds of the Cossethay and Ilkeston acquaintances to a different, remote world.

The linking of young Tom to the alien world outside the farm is associated directly with the foreign heritage of Lydia. The mother's relationship with the son is strange:

> He and his mother had a kind of affinity. The affection between them was of a mute, distant character, but radical. His father was always uneasy and slightly deferential to his eldest son.

Tom also formed the link that kept the Marsh in real connection with the Skrebenskys, now quite important people in their own district.

Also, the mother herself remains separated, except as her husband's wife, from the Brangwen way of life:

> His wife, as ever, had no acquaintances. Her hair was threaded now with grey, her face grew older in form without changing in expression. She seemed the same as when she had come to the Marsh twenty-five years ago, save that her health was more fragile. She seemed always to haunt the Marsh rather than to live there. She was never part of the life. Something she represented was alien there, she remained a stranger within the gates, in some ways fixed and impervious, in some ways curiously refining. She caused the separateness and individuality of all the Marsh inmates, the friability of the household.

She was also little concerned about her sons' behavior, except when they were ignoble or awkward:

> She was furious if the boys hung around the slaughterhouse, she was displeased when the school reports were bad. It did not matter how many sins her boys were accused of, so long as they were not stupid, or inferior. If they seemed to brook insult, she hated them. And it was only a certain gaucherie, a gawkiness on Anna's part that irritated her against the girl. Certain forms of clumsiness, grossness, made the mother's eyes glow with curious rage. Otherwise she was pleased, indifferent.

Her affection for Tom, "of a mute, distant character, but radical," suggests the nature of the mother-son relationship. The etymological sense of "radical" applies as well as the current sense of "extreme": the boy's roots are in the mother's heritage, which has been buried for her except as a memory; the Polishness of Lydia is in him and this gives them their affinity. Yet their relatedness is not immediate and dynamic because she broke with that part of her past at the time of the child's birth. As the father saw the infant as a reminder of Lydia's foreign roots, so the mother situates her son in her affections as a kind of extension of her past self, held vitally, at a distance.

Tom represents this dead Polish past; he "formed the link that kept the Marsh in real connection with the Skrebenskys." It is the nature of the mother-son relationship which explains why the narrator says of Lydia, "She caused the separateness and individuality of all the Marsh inmates, the friability of the household." The Brangwen heritage will crumble under the pressure of a new way of life intruding into the Marsh, and Ursula's Uncle Tom is the leading wave of a deluge which will finally end the old way with the death of the father. In a sense, the isolated farm is a self-made prison, functioning as a shelter, in which Tom and Lydia and the children other than young Tom are "inmates," until the dam bursts and the "Skrebensky world" Ursula will come to despise overwhelms the past.

When Tom, then twenty-three, met Lydia, and Will and Anna met the Skrebensky's and visited Lincoln Cathedral,

these older Brangwen men began a journey toward the resolution of a vital male-female relationship. At the age of twenty-eight each faces a crisis, a challenge which culminates in a kind of resolution of the destructive tensions in their marriages. However one may estimate the relative degrees of success each couple achieves in their marriages, the fact is clear that at about the same age each does reach a higher plateau in their mutual satisfaction. Young Tom, at twenty-three, broke with his "chief" and began to travel alone. The death of his father, given Ursula's age (eight), would have occurred when Tom was in his mid to late twenties. The scenes after that death signal the irrevocable disintegration of the son. The age parallels direct attention to the significance of the son's role, which is not simply to "represent [his] society fully . . . the irrevocably lost," and not simply to provide a gauge against which to measure the success and failure of the other characters, but also to portray the effects on an individual, and on particular human communities like that of the Brangwens, of the process of disintegration figured in the opening chapter. The depth of Tom's failure must heighten appreciation of whatever success the main characters achieve.

For Tom, the funeral of his father is climactic and his function henceforth will be to introduce Ursula, both directly by his acts, and indirectly by his recurring presence, to the world old Tom was frightened and transfixed by, the world represented by the Matlock episode. He brings that world to her, by bringing Anton Skrebensky to her, and he reveals it gradually, first at the funeral and finally with Winifred at Wiggiston, for what it is—destructive of vital human life. His final appearance in the novel, in "The Bitterness of Ecstasy" chapter, is an ominous foreshadowing of the continuation into the future of what he represents. He and Winifred have had a child.

Daniel R. Schwarz   (essay date 1980)

SOURCE: "Lawrence's Quest in *The Rainbow,*" in *Ariel: A Review of International English Literature,* Vol. 11, No. 3, July, 1980, pp. 43-66.

[*In the following essay, Schwarz maintains that* The Rainbow *reveals Lawrence in the act of self-definition.*]

A major subject of much modern literature is the author's quest for self-definition. In particular, the search for moral and aesthetic values is central to the novels of Joyce, Proust, Woolf, Conrad, and Lawrence. Yet we have neglected how novels reveal their authors because much modern criticism has been uncomfortable with the expressive qualities of texts. Certainly, the New Criticism insisted that texts be examined as self-referential ontologies which are distinct from their authors' lives. Unwilling to commit the intentional fallacy, Anglo-American formalism ceded discussion of the author to biographers, psychoanalytic critics, and, more recently, to phenomonologists, structuralists, and their successors. Yet because the quest for values, form, and language is a central subject in much modern fiction, it must be discussed as a formal component within the text, separate and distinct from the narrator or implied author. To neglect the dialogue between the creative process and the subject matter of the story is to ignore a fundamental part of the novel's imagined world. Lawrence's struggle with his subject (his relationship with Frieda) is a major aspect of *The Rainbow,* just as *Sons and Lovers* dramatizes his struggle to come to terms with his relationship with Jessie Chambers and his mother. Moreover, the author's quest for self-understanding is central to other late nineteenth and early twentieth century British novelists: Conrad in the Marlow tales, Joyce in *A Portrait of the Artist* and *Ulysses,* and Woolf in *Mrs. Dalloway* and *To the Lighthouse.*

Lawrence's quest within *The Rainbow* for values and for the appropriate form is as important to the experience of reading the novel as his polemic. Lawrence wanted to write about the passions of men and women in a new way. He also wanted to re-create himself and to urge his readers to re-create themselves. Lawrence felt that the novel is particularly suited in its spaciousness for proposing, testing, and discarding formulations as its author seeks truth. *The Rainbow*'s unfolding process presents a history of his struggle for fulfillment. Each phase of the Brangwens' history dramatizes a crucial episode in Lawrence's development. We must read *The Rainbow* with a pluralistic perspective that takes accounts of its prophetic and polemical impulses, but does not grant them an authority over the text. The reader must be attentive to the novel's oscillation between, on the one hand, its prophetic and mythic impulses and, on the other, its dramatization of Lawrence's own process of discovery. I shall argue that 1) *The Rainbow* dramatizes Lawrence's quest for the kind of fiction that is appropriate both for passionate sexual relationships between men and women and for the struggle within each man between, to use his terms, mind-consciousness and blood-consciousness. 2) *The Rainbow* enacts Lawrence's quest for self-realization. In one sense, each generation represents aspects of his psyche and is a means by which he uses the novel to discover his own individuality.

As with *Sons and Lovers,* the telling of *The Rainbow* is as crucial an agon as the tale. Although the Ursula section was written first and the opening last, the book still roughly mimes the history of Lawrence's self-development. In the traditional novel narrated by an omniscient voice, one expects the voice to embody the values to which the characters evolve. But, in *The Rainbow,* the narrator's values evolve and grow just like his characters, and the standards by which he evaluates behavior become more subtle and more intricate as the novel progresses. What is good for Tom and Lydia would not necessarily be sufficient for Ursula, or even Anna and Will. Each generation must go beyond its predecessor to sustain itself; Lawrence seeks to discover new standards as the family chronicle moves forward toward the time when Lawrence wrote the novel in the second decade of the twentieth century.

Lawrence sought to dramatize the importance of sexuality but he also sought to discover an aesthetic that would embody his ideas. Proposing a Newer Testament to replace the extant one is part of the dialectical struggle that is at the center of life. In life and in art, the best we can do is open up infinite possibilities. The climactic rainbow is not only for Ursula and for England, but represents an *enactment* of the aesthetic success achieved by writing the novel; Lawrence walks through the final arch to create anew in *Women in Love.* Like Ursula, his surrogate, he had to overcome dubiety and anxiety before he could go forward; hadn't he written in January, 1915, "My soul lay in the tomb—not dead, but with a flat stone over it, a corpse, become corpse-cold. . . . I don't feel so hopeless now I am risen. . . . We should all rise again from this grave. . . . I know we shall all come through, rise again and walk healed and whole and new in a big inheritance, here on earth." This pattern—a downward movement followed by an upward one—anticipates the closing scene when Ursula overcomes despair by rediscovering not only her biological self, but her potential to be alive passionately and sensually.

Lawrence wrote his novel to announce a credo to replace the Christian mythology and value system that dominated English life for several centuries. He conceived himself as prophet, seer, visionary, shaman, and Divine Messenger. Reduced to its simplest terms, his message is that mankind must rediscover the lost instinctive, biological passionate self that has become sacrificed to democracy, imperialism, industrialism, and urbanization. Lawrence adopts biblical tales, images, syntax, and diction for the purpose of expounding a doctrine that undermines the traditional reading of the Bible. Yet he uses the biblical material to confer the stature of a Holy Book upon his novel, which argues for the centrality not of God but of the relationship between man and woman.

Given Lawrence's evangelical background, it was essential to his psyche that he come to terms with rather than reject the Bible. For Lawrence, the Bible itself was the prototypical novel because of its prophetic message. It has as its acknowledged purpose to announce God's Law, and to show by its dramatic incidents how man correctly and incorrectly should behave. Influenced undoubtedly by Frazer's *The Golden Bough* and the turn-of-the-century's interest in ethnology, Lawrence understood that the Bible embodied the ethical archetypes of European civilization. As with Hardy, the shape and intensity of Lawrence's unorthodox beliefs are only possible because he had once been a believer. *The Rainbow* reflects the needs of Lawrence's Puritan conscience (which he owed to his mother's fastidious piety) to atone for the sacrilege of allowing his imagination to supplant faith and reason. Lawrence sought to create myths that would be more true to his generation than the ones it inherited.

The Rainbow is Lawrence's quest to rediscover mankind's instinctive, libidinous, biological potential which he believed lay underneath the trappings of the social self that civilization has produced and required to play acceptable roles. While each novel contains its own genesis with its own physical and moral geography, few novels take us into such an extraordinary world as *The Rainbow* does. What Lawrence must do in his early chapters is nothing less than re-educate the reader to a new grammar of motives where the value of a character's behavior is understood according to the degree it is true to its inner essence. Readers of *The Rainbow* are often baffled by what happens because the terms with which Lawrence describes behavior are so strange. Often they read the novel in an undergraduate course after a series of English novels in which manners and morals are stressed. Just as the episodes of Genesis provide us with the standards—the grammar of motives—to measure the rest of the Old Testament, the purpose of *The Rainbow*'s early chapters is to provide a grammar of passions so that in later chapters we will understand and recognize the deeper self beneath the conscious self.

Lawrence argues that passionate sexual relationships are not only beyond man's understanding, but beyond man's conscious control. That in *The Rainbow* Lawrence meant to propose a strikingly different kind of novel is clear from his oft quoted letter about characterization: "I don't so much care about what the woman *feels*—in the ordinary usage of the word. That presumes an *ego* to feel with. I only care about what the woman *is*—what she IS—inhumanely, physiologically, materially . . .". But as he writes the novel, the characterization becomes increasingly complex until he does show us something of Ursula's feelings and ego.

The Rainbow shows how a writer's exploration of the potential of a genre can itself become part of his subject. Writing of an early draft of the then nameless book, he remarked: "It is all crude as yet . . . most cumbersome and foundering . . . so new, so really a stratum deeper than I think anybody has ever gone in a novel". He wished to write about "*the* problem of today, the establishment of a new relation, or the readjustment of the old one, between men and women". Lawrence deliberately tries to reinvent the genre to address the passions of men and women. He writes of the unconscious life that he believed had escaped articulation by his predecessors and eschews, for the most part, the world of manners and morals that had provided the principal subject of the English novel. His prophetic voice displaces the ironic gentility of the traditional omniscient narrator of Victorian fiction. Nor does Lawrence adhere to the linear chronology of the realistic novel; he ignores references to the characters' ages and dates, and moves backwards and forward when he chooses. Highlighting certain episodes and details while overlooking others not only aligns him with the biblical tradition but also with cubism and post-impressionism, both of which had immense influence in England from the time of the major exhibitions in the period 1910-1912.

The structure and aesthetic of *The Rainbow* reflect his evolving relationship with Frieda who, in fact, gave the novel its title. *The Rainbow* is part of his effort to destroy the old within him and to build a new self based on but not limited by his passionate marriage. Writing the novel became inextricably related to loving Frieda: "I am going through a transition stage myself. . . . But I must write to live. . . . It is not so easy for one to be married. In marriage one must become something else. And I am changing, one way or the other". For all the certainty of the prophetic voice, his love for Frieda created new anxiety and uncertainty: "I seem to spend half my days having revulsions and convulsions from myself". The concept of the novel as process and movement derives from Lawrence's personal needs. In the famous letter to Garnett in which he rejected the old concept of character, he commented

scathingly of novelists' using a "moral scheme into which all the characters fit"; he wrote of *The Rainbow* (which, in this letter, he still called by the earlier title *The Wedding Ring*): "Don't look for the development of the novel to follow the lines of certain characters: the characters fall into the form of some other rhythmic form".

Thus *The Rainbow* is a personal novel, even at those moments when it is most prophetic. The novel dramatizes Lawrence's quest for the myth of the passionate Elect. It is also an outlet for his frustrated messianic impulses, impulses that neither his wife nor friends took very seriously. Emile Delavenay speaks of Lawrence's "constant search for disciples, which goes with the sense of a divine mission, of being predestined to make some revelation to mankind." No less than his romantic predecessors—Blake, Shelley, and Wordsworth—Lawrence sought refuge from the stress of life in the comfort of his fictions. The opening pages of *The Rainbow* express his fantasy of men who live purposeful, proud, sexually fulfilled lives and who are not inhibited by artificial social restraints. Each Brangwen generation 1) corresponds to an historical period, 2) to stages of growth in the passionate Elect, 3) to an historical phase of England's development—from rural (Tom and Lydia) to village (Will and Anna) to urban, industrial society (Ursula) and, 4) to important phases of Lawrence's relationship with Frieda. The process of mythmaking, the reaching out for biblical archetypes, is part of Lawrence's effort to cleanse and to refresh himself. Each generation of Brangwens registers a partial recovery of freshness for Lawrence.

In the very first pages, the anonymous pre-verbal Brangwens represent the reaffirmation of the primitive instinctive origins of man. They dominate the space they inhabit as if they were twenty times or fifty times the size of normal men. They are giants of the earth bestriding their land like Colossi. For Lawrence this generation represents mythic forbears whose example still has meaning for modern man. Even as the opening renders the energy within nature and the men who are inseparable from nature, it announces the hyperbole, myth, and process that are central to the novel's aesthetic. After the canal and the railroad are introduced, the familial, agrarian life is no longer possible. Thus within Lawrence's myth of the Giants of the earth, the Nephelim version of the creation myth, he also proposes a fortunate fall. The women are not content to live in "the drowse of blood intimacy". They feel that their world is anachronistic once industrialism touches it. They begin a quest for a richer life, for a life that contains an awareness of oneself and the world beyond the farm.

Lawrence is ambivalent towards the women's quest for knowledge and their turning away from a way of life where language and the life of the mind are secondary. Part of him wishes to return to the innocence of prehistory. But, as the novel evolves, he acknowledges that this existence may obliterate distinctions among men, prevent the growth of the individual, and limit people's possibilities to contribute to the community. On the one hand, a nostalgic Lawrence eulogizes a world that had never really been and longs for what that past represents. On the other hand, Lawrence, the contentious polemicist, wishes to change the world through his fiction and assumes the prophetic mantle to speak for the religion of the body.

Although, interestingly, she bears the first name of Lawrence's mother, Lydia, the experienced foreign woman, is a version of Frieda; Tom, the man aroused to his sexual and instinctual potential, is Lawrence's fantasy version of himself as a deeply passionate, intellectually unsophisticated figure. Their instinctive relationship corresponds to Lawrence's sense of the early stage of his relationship with Frieda. Their climactic consummation is a paradigm for the surrender of ego and rebirth that Lawrence sought. Tom's hesitant steps outward to acknowledge and fulfill his deepest needs, followed by his subsequent immersion in a passionate, sensual embrace, represent the kind of unconscious life flow that man must rediscover. *Sons and Lovers* left Lawrence with some residual effects of his mother-love and the frigid relationship with Jessie Chambers. Tom, I believe, represents another attempt to get things right sexually. (Nor should we forget, if we understand the personal nature of this novel, that variations on Lawrence's own Oedipal problems are central to Anna's relationship with her stepfather and Ursula's with her father.)

Tom and Lydia provide the first principle of Lawrence's grammar of passion. Lawrence uses the relationship between Tom and Lydia to show that *passionate* attraction takes place beneath the conscious level and disarms the intellect and the will. Lydia is roused to life despite her intention to withdraw from passionate attachments after the death of her husband. In Lawrence's Bible, passionate sexual attraction is akin to discovering Christ. On the basis of the most superficial acquaintance, of a few scant words between them, Tom feels her influence upon him: "There was an inner reality, a logic of the soul, which connected her with him." Tom is "nothingness" until he is completed and fulfilled by Lydia's acknowledgment. Stressing the impersonal physiological nature of this attraction, Lawrence uses pronouns which are adrift from their antecedents to describe the scenes of passionate interaction. Thus when Tom comes to announce his intention, she responds to his eyes:

> The expression of his eyes changed, become less impersonal, as if he were looking almost at her, for the truth of her steady and intent and eternal they were, as if they would never change. They seemed to fix and to resolve her. She quivered, feeling herself created, will-less, lapsing into him, into a common will with him.

The scene is a deliberate parody of the traditional Victorian courtship scene where a man asks for the hand of the woman. Not only is the father absent, and the woman a widow with child; not only has the man's announcement preceded any social relationship; but the amenities and conventions of English proper behavior are flouted at every turn. Lawrence's audience would have hardly been accustomed to the following dialogue in a relationship that took place in the 1860s:

"You want me?" she said. . . .

"Yes," he said. . . .

"No," she said, not of herself. "No, I don't know."

Nor did it conform to conventions of 1915. Such a scene could serve as Lawrence's epigraph, if not epitaph, to the novel of manners and morals that continued to be England's dominant genre, despite the recent work of Joyce, an exiled Irishman, and Conrad, a Polish emigré.

As we read *The Rainbow* we experience Lawrence's search for the appropriate language with which to convey unconscious, physiological states. When the voice speaks in biblical diction, he provides a benediction for his characters; echoing Genesis to describe Tom's and Lydia's first passionate kiss, he implies that a new beginning is something that is continually possible for every individual soul. "[Tom] returned gradually, but newly created, as after a gestation, a new birth, in the womb of darkness. . . . And the dawn blazed in them, their new life came to pass, it was beyond all conceiving good, it was so good that it was almost a passing-away, a trespass".

Lawrence goes beyond *Sons and Lovers* in the use of nature imagery to confer value on his characters' sexual responses and to make human sexuality a microcosm of the natural cycle of the cosmos. In a realistic novel, the following sentence, describing Lydia's response to Tom, would not mean much: "But she would wake in the morning one day and feel her blood running, feel herself lying open like a flower unsheathed in the sun, insistent and potent with demand". The gathering sexual energy of such words as "running", "open", "female", "unsheathed", "insistent", "potent", and "demand" charges the sentence with implication and power independent of its syntactical meaning. Furthermore, "blood", "flower", and "sun" place the urgent sexuality in the context of nature's rhythms. The sentence's one metaphor, "open like a flower", suggests that the opening of the woman for sex is akin to the receptiveness of the flower to the fertilizing bee. Beginning with the first use of "feel", moving to "blood", and continuing through "potent" and "demand", the heavily stressed prose (suggestive of Hopkin's poetry) gathers to a crescendo the sentence's power and urgency. As if to mime the arousing of her unconscious self, "running" carries Lydia's awakened instincts through to "potent" and "demand". The onomatopoeia of "running" stands in a phonic tension with the slow, stately power of "potent with demand". Within the sentence the sexual act is encapsulated. Not only does the male sperm "run" to the awaiting female, but the male, who feels incomplete, turns to the eternal female. And this is exactly what happens in the action of the novel. While it might be objected that the sentence describes only Lydia's awakening, the sentence is proleptic of the sexual act which her arousal makes possible. Once Lydia becomes awakened in her instincts and passion, she stands in readiness for the male. Lydia's awakening becomes a standard, albeit not the only one, by which Lawrence measures the more complex psyches of Anna and Ursula. Lydia is representative of immersion in sexuality and family, immersion that becomes increasingly difficult as England moves from agrarian to industrial society. The purity and simplicity of analogies with nature in the above passage disappear from the novel when the sexuality of later generations is described. Yet even

Lydia's life is a quantum jump in complexity from the anonymity of the opening pages. Each of the four phases of Brangwen life takes Lawrence more time to describe because changing external conditions introduce new complexities into man's quest to realize his being.

A major difficulty in Lawrence's quest for form is that he wished to dramatize the continuing flux of passions for what he called an "external stillness that lies under all movement, under all life, like a source, incorruptible and inexhaustible." He found this stillness in myth. *The Rainbow* depends on a tension between the movement of the narrative and the stasis of myth, which by its nature implies iteration of human experience. In the climax of the story of each generation, myth displaces process. The result is more like an elaborate rococo painting than a linear episode.

In the climax of the Tom and Lydia section Lawrence proposes a parallel to the apocalyptic wedding in *Revelation*; Lydia as the Holy City comes down from Heaven as a bride adorned for her husband, Tom, who has heretofore held something of himself back and not fully accepted her otherness. Tom and Lydia surrender their egos and give themselves over to their passionate embrace, but something seems to be missing. Their victory comes at the expense of separateness and individuality. Part of the problem is the religious context: "He relinquished himself . . . losing himself to find her, to find himself in her". The very terms of the victory make us aware of the limitations of the biblical parallel. While the Bible moves toward apocalypse and the suspension of time, the displacement of *chronos* by *kairos,* the regenerate soul never comes to rest. It is always seeking but never finding *kairos* except during the sex act. By definition, apocalypse implies that all become one in the kingdom of heaven, and distinctions will no longer be possible. But Tom and Lydia must return to the everyday temporal world.

Thus while they are born into another life, there is something unsatisfactory about their kind of union. On one hand, it provides a shelter for the children, or, at least Anna, in whom the Brangwen's passionate heritage resides, although she was not born a Brangwen. But, on the other hand, the children of blood-intimacy do not develop their full potential, as if there was something stifling to the growth of the soul in the marriage of Tom and Lydia. Their sexual passion creates a "richness" of physiological energy at the expense of mental activity and awareness of the world. Anna finally lapses into such a condition and Ursula is tempted by it when she is pregnant. While one part of Lawrence longed for this, another knew that such a life placed a constraint upon further development.

Lawrence is ambivalent towards Tom's and Lydia's victory, because their embrace *excludes* that part of him that must take part in the world of community and utterance. He moves on to the next generation in part because once he establishes the quality of Tom's and Lydia's passionate embrace, he is no longer interested in Tom and can no longer identify with him. Tom, who once had the need to explore new and strange experiences, lapses into the blood-intimacy of his forebears. Gradually, almost reluctantly, the voice acknowledges that Tom's achievement comes at the expense of giving up his quest into the unknown. Lawrence needs to extricate himself from his immersion in Tom because he is no longer an appropriate model for his own quest to resolve blood-consciousness and mind-consciousness. Tom has been the means of dramatizing one aspect of Lawrence to the exclusion of others. But Lawrence resists easy answers in defining his grammar of passions, and that resistance, that refusal to allow his myth to triumph over his own insights, is part of the novel's aesthetic, its meaning, and ultimately, its greatness. Competing for Lawrence's attention with the prophetic impulse is the nominalistic impulse which insists on making distinctions and undermining the simplifications of polemics.

Lydia articulates Lawrence's basic premise in the novel: "Between two people, the love itself is the important thing, and that is neither you nor him. It is a third thing you must create." But neither the novel's opening dumb-show nor the story of Tom and Lydia speaks to the problem between Anna and Will. In his impulse to lose himself either in sexuality or religious mystery, Will is trying to go back to a simpler world. His effort to reconcile his aesthetic impulse with passionate embrace mimes Lawrence's. Except when they come together in passion, Anna and Will must inevitably remain separate; nor do they have, like Tom and Lydia, the teeming richness of the farm to sustain them.

The Anna and Will section corresponds to the passionate struggle that raged between Lawrence and Frieda while he wrote the novel. In the Will-Anna relationship, Lawrence explores the second principle of the grammar of passions: each person must bring an independent existence to marriage. The sheaf-gathering scene defines the essential problem between Will and Anna. Like Hardy, who uses the May-dance in *Tess,* he knew that within rural life vestiges of primitive rites survived in England. Lawrence implies that the way forward may be to reach back to man's anthropological origins when man was one with nature. Anna is defined in terms of extended space and of nature ("she called . . . from afar . . . like a bird unseen in the night"), but Will is restricted by something within him that keeps him from fully participating in the pagan sexual dance. Will cannot lapse out of consciousness; his name defines the quality that holds him back: will. By will, Lawrence means an active need to assert one's consciousness upon the world, a need he recognized in himself.

The chapter entitled "Anna Victrix" defines the problem of man and woman after they have awakened to self-consciousness and are no longer in rhythm with nature in a pastoral world. Now that he has introduced new social and economic conditions, Lawrence must redefine the terms with which to describe physiological, passionate needs. Lawrence opens "Anna Victrix" with a passage suggesting that Anna's and Will's marriage resembles both the expulsion from Paradise and the family of Noah after the old world has been destroyed. But since Anna and Will do not fulfill the Brangwen promise, Lawrence discards these parallels and does not perceive them in terms of a consistent biblical pattern. Because their separation from the rest of the world mimes the dislocation caused by his own relationship to Frieda, there are passages in which the language strains to the point of breaking down. We feel Lawrence's excruciating pain embodied in the voice's narration of the difficulties between Anna and Will. Will has the potential either to become alive passionately or to lapse into a kind of passional anomie, when, despite his sexual satisfaction with Anna, he does not fulfill himself and his passionate energy becomes corrupted. Deprived of his male pride and lacking an independent identity, Will's destructive passion is not so dissimilar from Uncle Tom's or from Gerald's in **Women in Love**. For a time the couple succeed in creating a timeless world within the diurnal world. As if to stress the parallel between generations, Lawrence echoes the earlier biblical language ("They were unalterably glad"). But the struggle between them is different and more complex. Will must come to terms with an industrial world that Tom and Lydia can virtually shut out. Will's dark intensity is a function of his need to believe in something more than the relationship between man and woman. He believes in the miracle of Cana and "loved the Church"; in defense, Anna, "almost against herself, clung to the worship of the human knowledge". They never discover an equilibrium in which their separate selves enrich one another to form a union, a third entity stronger than the other. Rather each often becomes the other's emotional antithesis. As the passionate needs of one define contrary impulses in the other, the tension creates a destructive emotional friction that is never quite resolved.

Thus "Anna Victrix" is an ironic title. By winning Anna loses. Anna is indifferent to the outside world, but like Lawrence she needs to find a balance between mind-consciousness and blood-consciousness. Just like Lawrence, Will requires his life in the world beyond; like Frieda, Anna is oblivious to these needs, and thus must share with Will the blame for the couple's problems. She needs to defeat him in body and spirit. She defeats him by despising his job, depriving him of his spiritual life, and taking away his pride. Will may be more the average sensual man than any other male figure, but he also objectifies Lawrence's fear that sexual passion will deprive him of his creativity. By abandoning his wood-carving of Adam and Eve, Will submits to the routine of the everyday world. In an ironic echo of the sheaf-gathering scene, during her pregnancy Anna dances alone in her search for the something that her life lacks: at an unconscious level, she is trying to "annul" him by means of the primitive and atavistic dance. Anna's victory is not only Will's defeat, but ultimately her own.

Corresponding to the medieval period, the period between an agrarian and industrial society, the period in which villages and crafts dominate life in England, the Anna-Will section is the one in which religion is explored in its most personal form. Lawrence's evangelical conscience required that he explore the Church as a putative source of values. At the center of the novel is the very short chapter entitled "Cathedral". The cathedral, like the novel itself, is a man-made artifice that reconciles opposing dualities. But, to use Lawrence's terms, the cathedral, like Raphael's painting, arrests motion while Lawrence's form, like the painting of Botticelli, is in motion. In "Cathedral",

Lawrence shows the constraints that Christianity has placed upon man's efforts to realize fully his potential. Lawrence stresses how the Church denies process and movement and reduces everything to oneness. The Romanesque arch is a false rainbow because it reduces the variety of life to itself, something that Lawrence believed Christianity does by imposing arbitrary shibboleths ("Only the poor will get to heaven"; "The meek shall inherit the earth").

The Cathedral represents a historical phase that man must put behind him if he is to continue the journey to fulfillment. Moreover, its geometric *resolution* is reductive. In Laurentian terms, the arch denies the Two-in-One and represents nullifying fusion, rather than union between two strong, contending souls that are independent in themselves. Like the blood-intimacy of the early Brangwens, it is another form of the dominance of what Lawrence called the Will-to-Inertia. For Anna, as for Lawrence, God is something within and beyond one's self, but not within the Church. We may regard Anna as a Moses figure who has viewed the Promised Land, but will not enter. Before Anna lapses into child-bearing she carries on the Brangwen promise by refusing to submit her individuality to the church. Anna resists submission to "the neutrality, the perfect, swooning consummation, the timeless ecstasy" of the Romanesque arches. When she responds to the separateness of the gargoyles, she is compared to Eve. She seduces Will to a knowledge that he would deny; for him the church can no longer be a "world within a world". Her resistance is described in terms of a bird taking flight, a striking image because it suggests the natural world that, Lawrence felt, was absent from the Cathedral and that has been shut out by the man-made rainbow. Her desire to rise anticipates that of Ursula in the section when she assumes the mantle of Christ; her refusal to be fixed anticipates Ursula's refusal to submit to Skrebensky. The bird has freedom of movement in contrast to the Church's insistence on one direction. Anna's victory over Will's desire to use the Church as a spiritual womb to which they both might return is a significant step towards defining the Brangwens' values and creating Lawrence's consciousness.

Lawrence proposes as the third principle of his grammar of passions that certain elect souls can struggle by themselves to fulfillment, and can reconcile blood-consciousness and mind-consciousness, if they are true to their own impulses and if they avoid submitting to lesser beings and social conventions. Choosing a female as his surrogate enabled Lawrence to achieve distance and objectivity. Like Lawrence, Ursula is torn, on the one hand, between the female "secret riches" of the body and, on the other, the "man's world" of work, duty, and community. When Lawrence's chronicle reaches the turn of the century, the Brangwen quest for symbols becomes more urgent because it mimes his own central concerns. Lawrence's surrogate, Ursula, seeks for the symbols that will make her life whole. Her discovery of the appropriate one in the figure of Christ reborn to the life of the body parallels Lawrence's discovery of biblical archetypes as mythic analogues for his fictive characters. As the vessel of substantive insight, she becomes the central prophetic figure, just as Birkin is in *Women in Love*. Her quest is Lawrence's and that quest is enacted in the rushing, urgent form of the novel as well as in specific episodes such as Ursula's confrontation with the horses. Ursula's crises, defeats, and final victory mime Lawrence's own. Capable of growth and passion, she is Lawrence's ideal. Her role is not unlike that of Christ in the New Testament. She is the paradigmatic figure of Lawrence's secular scripture.

Ursula embodies both Lawrence's quest for a mental knowledge besides the knowledge of passionate embrace and his need to reconcile that quest with his marriage. Lawrence was not satisfied to fulfill himself apart from other men. He oscillated between the hope that he could transform England and the desire to subtract himself and a small number of the Elect into an enclave. Ursula's certainty that the mythical sons of God would have taken her for a wife expresses Lawrence's wish for a passionate Elect. She dramatizes Lawrence's own desire to leave behind the pedestrian life of modern England; she needs to go beyond the village life of her ancestors and existence as a provincial schoolteacher. Like Lawrence, she becomes increasingly iconoclastic about manners, morals, and social pressures. Like Lawrence, Ursula lives in a world of hyperbole. In a sense, "the wave which cannot halt" defines Lawrence's growth; the telling of the Brangwen saga gave the necessary energy, vitality, and confidence to transcend the limited world in which he found himself.

As Ursula imagines Christ speaking for the Law of the Body in the diction of the Bible, Lawrence's voice subsumes Ursula's. In the climax of Lawrence's quest for a new credo, Lawrence insists that Christ's return must be in the body and that man be reborn in the body:

> The Resurrection is to life, not to death. Shall I not see those who have risen again walk here among men perfect in body and spirit, whole and glad in the flesh, living in the flesh, loving in the flesh, begetting children in the flesh arrived at last to wholeness . . . ?

This is the moment when Lawrence, at the center of the novel, ascends his rhetorical Pisgah and looks to the future. As he speaks with urgency and intensity, we realize that the prophetic voice is a major character in the novel, that he is not only the teller but an essential character in the tale. Thus the chapter in which the above passage appears (and the first of two with that title), "The Widening Circle", describes not only Ursula's expanding range of experience, but that of the voice. He has progressed from rendering the impersonal and anonymous life in the opening to creating an individualized life where personal values and attitudes are important. Just as the Brangwens lose their anonymity and their individual quests become important, so Lawrence affirms through his intrusive, prophetic, idiosyncratic voice the value of a self-aware, unique personality. This is a value that was unknown to the early Brangwens, but is crucial to Ursula as she seeks her own identity even while responding to the demands of her body.

That her first love affair with Skrebensky is prolonged, unsatisfactory, and inhibiting reflects Lawrence's own view

of his relationship with Jessie. At twenty-one, Ursula has experienced the kind of philosophical and psychological development Lawrence had achieved in his late twenties when he was creating her. He takes pleasure in Ursula's unconventional attitudes towards Christianity and in her flouting of traditional standards as, for example, when she argues for making love in a Cathedral. Her feelings of superiority and iconoclasm are Lawrence's as he sought to define a new aristocracy of passionate Elect. Election should be understood not only in terms of Evangelical theory that there are men and Men, damned souls and saved souls, but also in terms of Lawrence's snobbery and iconoclasm. The Brangwens, like Lawrence, have a pathological fear of being undifferentiated from the mass of people.

Yet if Lawrence is Ursula, he is also Skrebensky. Skrebensky embodies Lawrence's fear that he will not be able to fulfill Frieda. Skrebensky is unformed and lacks the potential for growth and fulfillment. In their first love-making under the moon, he needs to "enclose" and "overcome her". He lacks the passionate energy that she requires: "What was this nothingness she felt? The nothingness was Skrebensky". Whereas Will has a problem of unconsciously restraining and thus corrupting his passionate potential, Skrebensky is inherently defective. While Will struggles towards a kind of limited fulfillment, Skrebensky becomes a factotum for the social system, a soldier who mindlessly fights for the nation's political goals.

Ursula's oscillation between the demands of the conscious self and the passional self continues in an upward spiral to the novel's final pages as she moves toward the unreachable goal of what Lawrence calls "full achievement" of herself (*Phoenix*). (It is Lawrence's version of Zeno's paradox that this goal recedes as it is approached, for there are always further levels of self-realization beyond the one that has been reached.) We recall in the Cathedral her mother's desire to take flight in order to escape Will's confinement. But Skrebensky holds her back. Because Skrebensky exists "in her own desire only," she did not "live completely"; her first love baptizes her into "shame" (the title of the ensuing chapter), as Lawrence believed Jessie had done to him.

Like her Brangwen forebears, Ursula is at ease in nature and open to experience. But at this point she does not have the independence that she will later have and desperately searches for someone to complete her. Yet her failure with Skrebensky, like Lawrence's own with Jessie Chambers, intensifies her quest. She turns her passion to a beautiful and proud young teacher, Winifred Inger. At first, Winifred seems to Ursula an example of one who has combined the best of female and male: "She was proud and free as man, yet exquisite as a woman". But after a brief affair, lesbian love proves a dead end. (Lawrence, who endorsed Birkin's bisexuality, has a different standard for women.) While Ursula is associated with lions and later horses, Winifred is associated with moist clay and prehistoric lizards: "[Ursula] saw gross, ugly movements in her mistress, she saw a clayey, inert, unquickened flesh, that reminded her of the great prehistoric lizards". Lawrence is not above name-calling to denigrate characters who are unsuitable for his major figures. Winifred and Uncle Tom are arbitrarily aligned with the corruption of Wiggiston, although Lawrence does not *dramatize* why. It is as if Lawrence needed to turn against part of his creation and to expel it from the heightened passionate world he has created for the Elect: "[Uncle Tom's and Winifred's] marshy, bitter-sweet corruption came sick and unwholesome in Ursula's nostrils. Anything to get out of the foetid air. She would leave them both forever, leave forever their strange, soft, half-corrupt element. Anything to get away". Within the Brangwen strain and Lawrence's psyche is a struggle between the living, represented by Ursula, and the dead, represented by Uncle Tom. That the Brangwens have a corrupt line creates within the novel a viable threat to Ursula's and Lawrence's own quest.

At the close Lawrence and Ursula are inseparable. When she agrees to marry Skrebensky, her capitulation to conventions mimes Lawrence's own fear that he lacked the strength to break free. But the horses represent the atavistic energy that he felt he needed to write *The Rainbow*. The painful activity of writing is mirrored by Ursula's terrible confrontation with an unacknowledged energy that must be expressed in spite of her conscious self. Just as Ursula must return from experiencing the "hard, urgent, massive fire" of the horses to "the ordered world of man", so must Lawrence. After she decides not to marry Skrebensky, her declaration prior to the final vision is also Lawrence's:

> I have no father nor mother nor lover, I have no allocated place in the world of things, I do not belong to Beldover nor to Nottingham nor to England nor to this world, they none of them exist. I am trammelled and entangled in them, but they are all unreal. I must break out of it, like a nut from its shell which is an unreality.

Very much like the dark night of the soul in traditional Christianity, this denial is a necessary prologue to her final vision. One must experience the Everlasting No on the road to the Everlasting Yea. Ursula is *enacting* the crucial prophetic passage where Lawrence has assumed the voice of Christ and imagined his own resurrection:

> [Ursula] slept in the confidence of her new reality. She slept breathing with her soul the new air of a new world. . . .
>
> When she woke at last it seemed as if a new day had come on the earth. How long, how long had she fought through the dust and obscurity, for this new dawn?

The "new dawn" and "new day" confirm the novel's insistence that the possibility of transfiguration is always present.

The final vision is not only Ursula's but Lawrence's. It is the moment to which the narrative and the narrator have moved. The novel has redefined God to be something remote, whose presence pervades nature but is indifferent to man's individual quest. (Ursula thinks: "What ever God was, He was, and there was no need to trouble about Him"). Yet God also becomes the name of each individual's fullest potential, the aspect of life that is immune to Dr. Frankstone's mechanism. ("I don't see why we should

attribute some special mystery to life"). Thus Ursula is recognizing the God within her when she understands that "Self was a oneness with the infinite. To be oneself was a supreme, gleaming triumph of infinity". Such an insight is an essential prelude to the ending. Although Genesis is her favorite book, and her grandfather's death in a Flood established him as a Noah figure, she mocks God's command to Noah: "be ye fruitful and multiply". Ursula must discover what Lawrence sees as the meaning of that myth—as a figuration of death followed by rebirth, despair by hope—if she is to carry out the Brangwen promise. Her vision of the rainbow is the fulfillment of God's Covenant that he will never destroy the things of the earth:

> And the rainbow stood on the earth. She knew that the sordid people who crept hard-scaled and separate on the face of the world's corruption were living still, that the rainbow was arched in their blood and would quiver to life in their spirit, that they would cast off their horny covering of disintegration, that new, clean, naked bodies would issue to a new germination, to a new growth, rising to the light and the wind and the clean rain of heaven. She saw n the rainbow the earth's new architecture, the old, brittle corruption of houses and factories swept away, the world built up in a living fabric of Truth, fitting to the over-arching heaven.

Here the narrator and Lawrence are like a suspended series of intersecting circles. Her vision is the fulfillment for Lawrence of the urgent quest that produced both **"Study of Thomas Hardy"** and *The Rainbow*; it signifies the continuing possibility of transfiguration for all men. Lawrence takes the worst case—the men of Wiggiston—and imagines them bursting forth, like the red poppy in **"Study of Thomas Hardy,"** with new life. Lawrence's novel is the equivalent to Ursula's final vision, the rainbow that follows the terrible task of creation. If we recall Lawrence's denial of life after death, we see that heaven means, paradoxically, a transformed life on earth where men will be alive passionately. Each man must discover the God within himself, or in different terms, rewrite the Bible for himself.

However, the ending presents some difficulties. *The Rainbow* announces itself as an alternative to the novel of manners and morals. At the end of *The Rainbow* Ursula has cleaned herself of inhibiting manners and morals, but she has not formed any attachments on which the kind of community Lawrence desired could be based. What precedes belies the final vision. Furthermore, the vision is an epiphany for Lawrence and Ursula of the possibility of transfiguration, but it does not dramatize a future. His novel does not prepare his readers for a new community and offers no more than the vaguest hope that such a community can occur within England. And *Women in Love,* by showing the world in disintegration, takes back the hope of a transfigured community that is offered by the ending of *The Rainbow*.

Like Hardy, Lawrence proposes a cosmology other than the traditional Christian one that dominates the English novel. Lawrence appropriates the Christian myth stretching from Eden to the Apocalypse to define his passionate Bible. But does that myth also appropriate Lawrence's plot? What distinguishes Hardy is the fulfillment of a malevolent pattern. As if Lawrence could not sustain the implication of his insights, he imposes an apocalyptic ending on his material. Lawrence's ending undercuts and discards the novel's dramatization of the pervasive growth of a destructive strand of human life, represented by Skrebensky, Winifred, Uncle Tom, and Dr. Frankstone. His prophecy and his testimony are at odds. One cannot quite believe in the utopian simplification of Ursula's transforming vision because it is contradicted by the cumulative power of Lawrence's dramatic evidence. Within the novel, her triumph is hers alone. Lawrence's myth contradicts the novel's unfolding process. Moreover, by relying on the Judaic-Christian mythology for his epiphanies, Lawrence inadvertently restores some credibility to the very system that he is criticizing as anachronistic.

The movement of *The Rainbow* reflects Lawrence's efforts to clarify his own ideas and feelings, and to search for the appropriate aesthetic. Reading Lawrence, we must be attentive to the authorial presence embodied within the text. Knowing something about Lawrence's life and beliefs is essential. While *The Rainbow* nominally has an omniscient voice, we gradually realize that Lawrence's self-dramatizing voice reveals his values, emotions, idiosyncracies, and conflicts. Straining the convention of omniscient narration to its breaking point, Lawrence desperately tries to create a prophetic form out of his personal needs.

When we read *The Rainbow,* we participate in Lawrence's struggle to define his values and his concept of the novel. Lawrence writes of his own passions and experiences even when he assigns them to invented characters. We respond to the process by which his subject is converted into art. Like Rodin in his sculptures, Lawrence never detaches himself from the medium in which he is working. But the novel is the more exciting for his involvement. This involvement is characteristic of other great innovators in British fiction in the period 1895-1941: Conrad, Joyce, and Woolf. In these authors, the reader experiences a dialogue between the author's avowed subject and his effort to discover an appropriate language and form. These writers, like Lawrence, wrote to define themselves. And, as we know from the work of Picasso, Matisse, Pollock, and Rothko, the process of creation, the struggle to evaluate personal experience, and the quest for values become the characteristic concerns not only of modern literature but of modern painting and sculpture.

Paul Rosenzweig   (essay date 1980)

SOURCE: "A Defense of the Second Half of *The Rainbow:* Its Structure and Characterization," in *The D. H. Lawrence Review,* Vol. 13, No. 2, Summer, 1980, pp. 150-60.

[*In the following essay, Rosenzweig contends that the second half of* The Rainbow *is not aesthetically inferior to the first, but merely reflects developments in the novel's theme through changes in style and characterization.*]

Both the pioneering sense of character in *The Rainbow* and its intricacy of form organic to such characterization are now largely appreciated. The second half of the novel, depicting the development of Ursula Brangwen, has often been singled out for criticism as inferior because it seems to depart from the unique form and vision of the first half. For instance, Marvin Mudrick writes [in *Spectrum* 3, Winter 1959] that "much of the last half of *The Rainbow* seems to have been written with a slackening of Lawrence's attention to proportion and detail." David Daiches [in *The Novel and the Modern World,* 1960] refers to Lawrence's "method of presentation" as "murky and overinsistent"; and even Arnold Kettle, choosing to defend the second half as more complex, "more moving, more courageous, more fully relevant to the twentieth-century," suggests [in *An Introduction to the English Novel,* volume II, 1960] that Ursula's unrealized vision "should be given no coherent, concrete expression. . . . but a misty, vague and unrealized vision which gives us no more than the general sense that Lawrence is, after all, on the side of life."

Other critics contend that the quality of the second half diminishes because Lawrence has drawn his critique of modern society too finely, elaborating his particular annoyances of various institutions without achieving any larger transcendent vision. In this vein, S. L. Goldberg writes [in *"The Rainbow" and "Women in Love": A Casebook,* edited by Colin Clarke, 1969], "The art weakens when Lawrence turns, in the second half, from universal to local issues"; and Roger Sale, also critical of the Ursula section, suggests [in the same volume] that "with Ursula we come to the period which corresponds to Lawrence's own youth. Lawrence now begins to introduce small characters, names of people who are mentioned but never appear. . . . The reason, obviously, is that Lawrence is beginning to transcribe almost directly from his own experience."

Perhaps because of Lawrence's general reputation for insufficient attention to form and detail, such judgements seem to have gained easy currency even among critics generally praising the novel, even though *The Rainbow* is Lawrence's most carefully written and most revised work and the intricate structure of the novel as a whole has been increasingly appreciated. Much of the trouble with this negative assessment arises from measuring the second half too rigidly by the apparent standards of the first part. Although the earlier part has a rhythmic beauty in its characterization and structure which the latter half largely loses, it is misconceiving the larger pattern of the novel to see these formal changes as a diminution of Lawrence's artistry. While I do not wish to engage in the debate over the relative merits of the two halves, I do wish to defend the second half by arguing for the thematic appropriateness of the structural split itself and its placement and the subsequent changes in form and characterization.

At the thematic center of *The Rainbow* lies Lawrence's vision of man's dualistic nature: the inherent tendency toward a split in that duality in each individual, relationship, and society; the increased disjunction between the two halves of the duality in progressive generations and the need in the Western societies of the twentieth century for a reconciliation—an organic coordination—between polarities as symbolized in the title metaphor of the rainbow. While Lawrence himself characterized this duality by various sets of polarities elsewhere in his writings, the split is essentially one between "being" and "knowing," between man's original tendency to live instinctively through the action of his body and his increasing disposition in modern times to live cerebrally and unspontaneously through the abstracting processes of his mind.

Lawrence regards each half ambivalently. While man in the more primitive state is more in touch with his essentially instinctual nature, he has no understanding and thus little control of that nature. He lacks the freedom to shape his future. Modern man has the potential for that freedom through coordinating the two halves of his nature; but his tendency to repress his instincts and falsify his emotions is potentially far more dangerous. Severed from his instincts, his mental processes are themselves then falsified and the two halves of his nature battle self-destructively instead of complementing one another.

Lawrence traces the gradual development of this internal split from the very first pages of the novel. Tom Brangwen's mother initiates it by inculcating in her son a feeling of incompletion and a longing for the power which knowledge promises. Yet it is only in Ursula's generation that mind is almost totally separated from body. Ursula herself struggles against this alienation from self and society; the separation is more fully embodied in those half-formed, rootless ghosts which float about Ursula and to whom she is ominously attracted—foremostly, Tom Brangwen, Jr., Winifred Inger, and Anton Skrebensky, all of whom attempt to live a mechanical life of abstraction and willed control, denying completely their deeper selves.

Within Ursula's own life, the separation is reflected in a myriad of ways. In her childhood, she bemoans the complete separation of her ideal of "the Sunday world" from the mundane "weekday world." Ultimately even that "Sunday world" is secularized and commercialized so that no magical, sacred time remains. Her own separation from the agrarian tradition of her forefathers, with its natural daily rhythms which keep the workers of the land in touch with their own internal rhythms, also reflects this break. While her father's pursuit of the artistic impulse is an earlier manifestation of this movement away from the land and toward urbanization, reflected in his movement to the industrial town of Beldover in order to teach art in the workshops, still his roots are in the soil and he is a transitional figure caught between the two worlds. ("He worked in the garden to propitiate his uncle. He talked churches to propitiate his aunt.") The first image of Ursula and him together foreshadows their and their generations' subsequent differences. While Will sows seeds in his garden, Ursula is symbolically unable to follow in her father's footsteps and sow his seed; instead she inadvertently destroys his careful work.

This break between parent and child in Ursula's generation is not only a symbolic change of direction but an actual break as well. Anna returns repeatedly to her parents' home after her marriage, more attached to her father than

her husband. Her very mode of existence, dedicated solely to the fulfillment of the body at the expense of any higher growth, reflects this dedication to her ancestral past. ("There was always a regular connection between the Yew Cottage [Will's and Anna's abode] and the Marsh [Tom's and Lydia's].") In contrast, Ursula breaks completely with her parents, particularly her father, and their way of life (although the final act of this split occurs in *Women in Love*). Neither reaction to the past is fully satisfactory. In turning solely to her body and the past, Anna sacrifices any further growth and ultimately both her soul and her body atrophy; the last picture we are given of her is of a woman who has remained a child in many ways. Unable or refusing to grow in the direction of the future, she is "hard" and "meaningless," her mind "callous, superficial." Ursula's temporary rejection of the past, on the other hand, also reflects an ignorance of the fact that for either half of one's nature to develop it must be joined to the other. In the end, wiser, she will find that the future can only be gained through the past.

As with parents and offspring, the relationship between man and woman reaches a point of rupture in Ursula's time. While Tom Brangwen's parents were not perfectly united, still they were "vitally connected, knowing nothing of each other, yet living in their separate ways from one root." Will and Anna increasingly live in a marriage of form only, each in his own interior world. By Ursula's time, no marriage at all seems possible; the only ring she accepts from Skrebensky is a mock one and the only child is either imagined or aborted. No actual union is ever achieved, and what semblance of one is fragilely pieced together is ultimately totally and brutally severed. For a time Ursula turns away from all men, seeking union only with her own sex during her affair with Winifred Inger.

Such splits are external manifestations of a basic internal split within Ursula herself which is reflected in the schizoid tendencies she demonstrates in her most extreme moments. In denying her deeper self through romantic abstraction, she denies her essential identity. It is only in her generation that characters have true crises of identity (although there are faint foreshadowings in her father, Will). While the earlier generations never know fully who they are, they never really know that they do not know. Only with the approach toward "knowing" can Ursula look back and see how far she has strayed from "being."

While the gradual evolution of these ruptures can be traced from the first generations of Brangwens, the pivotal break occurs midway through the novel in the chapter, "The Marsh and the Flood," which depicts the death of the patriarch of the Brangwen clan, Tom. After this short, transitional chapter, the second half of the novel—Ursula's story indicative of the modern age—truly begins and so do the controversial changes of structure and characterization in the novel. This congruence is not accidental.

The chapter both serves as a retrospective for the first half of the novel, an epilogue to the physical mode of existence which passes with Tom Brangwen's passing, and at the same time, in its final scene between Lydia and Ursula, it provides a gateway to the future. It is set off, in part detached from both preceding and succeeding chapters, signifying a break between the two halves of the novel and what each symbolizes. Roger Sale notes exactly this in his critique of the novel and yet misunderstands it as a failure of design presaging a loss of control in the second half:

> Here, for the first time, the forward flow of the novel is checked; the preceding chapter does not lead into it as we have seen was the case in earlier chapters nor does the subsequent chapter lead away from it. At the end of the chapter, Lydia describes to Ursula her first marriage, and she insists on the greatness of her love for both her husbands. Ursula cannot understand this, and neither can we see what it is doing here. . . . Having stopped the movement of the book, Lawrence also contradicts one of the novel's central symbols. The door here, instead of opening on to the "beyond," the "rainbow," and, always, the future, opens on to the past. . . .
>
> In itself this contradiction might not be important. But it is indicative of more important changes in tone and method that are manifested in subsequent chapters. "The Marsh and the Flood" serves as a watershed; before it Lawrence is in control, forcing our perception of each experience into a larger series of units, and after it . . . he becomes more tentative and less careful.

Quite to the contrary. The structural isolation of the chapter serves as a formal reinforcement to the thematic focus of the chapter—a break between past and future and a break for the next generation between two halves of man's duality. Not only the fact of Tom's death but the manner of his passing suggests this break. His essentially physical nature from which he has always tried to escape returns with a vengeance. He is swept away not only by an external flood but by the returning flood of his youthful indulgence in liquor and is returned to his element—the earth. "Hay and twigs and dirt were in the beard and hair." In our last picture of him, he is revealed in what has been his essential strength and limitation; he is solely body. "The body was dead. . . . There, it looked still and grand," Lawrence writes.

As Tom is washed back to his essential element, the tenuous balance between Lydia and him is broken, and she retreats to her essential self. For, like the snowdrops Lydia notices in her first months in England, she is "anchored by a thread to the grey-green grass." As Tom dies in actuality, she is left to die in spirit and increasingly turns her back on life, living only in the world of memory and abstraction. It is this world—the world of civilization which Lydia symbolizes to others because of her past life in Poland—which she bequeaths to Ursula at the end of the chapter. Lawrence represents this split between man and wife, body and spirit, by the physical placement of the two in the death scene. Lydia retreats in the face of the flood to an upstairs window, only a viewer on life cut asunder from the earth, while Tom is borne downward by the flood to the road, on the only trip he will ever make toward the horizon he has always dreamed of achieving.

The other break in the chapter—the canal's collapse—is

similarly appropriate. Symbol of the collieries for which it was built, its breaking suggests the gathering tide of industrialization which, no longer controllable, threatens to sweep the old world away. The flood's implicit comparison with the Biblical flood is thus partially ironic, for this flood—a product of the devil of mechanization—destroys an older, truer world.

Lawrence's precise control of his symbols and their effective placement and coordination with structure is suggested by this pivotal chapter's prefigurement in the very first chapter of the novel and its division into two sections—the only chapter so designed. The brief first section, opening the novel, is a pre-historical prologue of sorts which depicts a Garden of Eden where the Brangwen forefathers are totally one with their land and thus with themselves, lacking any self-conscious separation. Yet even in this most ideal of settings, Lawrence's realism plants the seeds for that utopia's undoing in the Brangwen women who function as Eves with their yearning for godlike power which they fancy knowledge and its embodiment in civilization can bring.

With the first sentence of the second section, the Brangwens fall out of Eden and into history through the introduction of the symbol of civilization and industrialization—the canal: "About 1840, a canal was constructed across the meadow of the Marsh Farm, connecting the newly-opened collieries of the Erewash Valley." A sentence later we are told: "A high embankment travelled along the fields to carry the canal. . . . So the Marsh was shut off from Ilkeston," and—it might be added—the new Brangwen generation shut off from their innocent forefathers, each isolated structurally in their own half of the chapter. Thus, this first structural break in the novel is also thematically appropriate. The canal, which will complete its function of separation and isolation midway through the novel, suggests that final break in its first appearance. The date, 1840, signalling the advent of history, stands out not merely because of its sudden introduction as the first words of the section contrasting with the timelessness of the first section but also because of the fact that in this—the most historical of Lawrence's novels—it is practically the only date in the entire novel.

Such tight integration of structure with theme is indicative of the entire pattern of the novel. The central structural break in the middle of the novel, foreshadowed in the very first pages of the novel, prepares for a radical change in the manner of life for Ursula's generation, one that is accompanied by appropriate changes in form as well. The beauty and uniqueness of the first half is principally formed by the rhythms between man and nature and corresponding rhythms between man and woman. It is the disappearance of these rhythms—the separation of man from nature and, concurrently, of men from one another—which is at the heart of Lawrence's wasteland vision of the ugliness and mechanicalness of the modern world. If the second half of the novel is not so immediately pleasing, it should not be.

The change in the mode of characterization toward flatter, seemingly more shallow, personalities also reflects the novel's change of thematic tempo and is a product of this essential split. It is appropriate to Lawrence's conception of identity and the disintegration of character in modern times. Like the aesthetics of the first half, so the characterization there is derived from the natural rhythms within man. For Lawrence, identity is composed of two major aspects: personality or ego—which is responsible for one's individuality—and the deeper, generic self that unites humanity as "man" and "woman" with the larger impersonal forces of nature. This latter, more essential self is progressively lost as each generation moves further into a world of mere "mentality," and without this foundation the remaining personality constitutes no real identity but merely a hollow facade. Thus the very element—the rhythms of the larger self—which produces the richness and depth of Lawrence's unique style of characterization disappears in accordance with, rather than in departure from, Lawrence's larger vision.

Lawrence demonstrates a tendency toward creating flatter characters, usually with an accompanying satirical viewpoint, when he surveys modern, industrial society. This congruence of satire and flat characterization with a vision of modern society occurs in the early chapters of *Women in Love* as well. It is perhaps most pronounced in *The Lost Girl* where the novel, like *Women in Love,* moves in the opposite direction from *The Rainbow,* changing from very sharp satire to a far richer, more realistic mode of writing as soon as the central couple leaves modern England and takes up residence in a primitive village in Italy. In *The Rainbow,* Ursula herself feels the effect of this change in environment on character. She feels the need to "alter one's personality" to accommodate "the man's world" of industrialization and bureaucracy, the pressure to "put away the personal self, become an instrument, an abstraction."

The introduction of "small characters, names of people who are mentioned but never appear" in the second half of the novel reflects this change in character development as well as reflecting the general fragmentation of society and the rootlessness of its members. And for all her isolation, Ursula is not immune to the effects of these conditions. The episodic structure of her section is produced not only by the manner of people she meets but also by her own compulsive movement from place to place in search of meaningful experience; it is not a sign of some lapse in the integrity of Lawrence's vision. Indeed, the psychology of Ursula's point of view is crucial in explaining the form of this part of the novel. While she is not one with society neither is she totally separate from it, and she mirrors its characteristics and problems.

Perhaps her most salient characteristic—one which Lawrence establishes in his depiction of her as a child—is her tendency to externalize her problems and falsely exorcise them by romantically projecting their heroic antithesis upon others. The flatness in character portrayal is also determined, therefore, by her limited, oversimplified viewpoint through which most of the action of the second half is seen. Except for the intermittent intensity of her relationship with Anton, she does not know nor truly interact with the other characters she encounters, but rather reacts to a caricature which both she and they themselves create,

and, when that image inevitably fails her needs, she discards it and moves on, fundamentally unaffected, to the next "hero" and his heroic world.

The split which lies at the heart of the modern condition is reflected in this manner in which Ursula, as Everyman, divides the world into two mutually exclusive antinomies in order to escape herself and her inadequacies. Ursula adopts this strategy of self-denial in her childhood in order to combat her sense of impotence in the face of her father's domination and it results in her attempt to complete herself through the "otherness" of the external world. This personal psychology—which creates a false dichotomy between I and thou—is encouraged by and indicative of the larger Christian outlook of post-Renaissance Europe. In *Twilight in Italy,* written at the same time as *The Rainbow,* Lawrence outlines in more abstract form the Protestant polarization of the world at the time of the Reformation into mutually exclusive antinomies of body and soul—the conflict between the corrupt, material world and the ideal, spiritual world. By means of the apotheosis of science—the supremacy of mind replacing that of spirit—this original Christian prototype of a heavenly "other" is metamorphosed into a version ironically belonging to the world of Mammon. In the industrial age, this reversal leads to the worship of technology and the machine—that external god by which one can hope to gain the illusion of immortality upon Earth. In all these dualistic versions of the cosmos, unlike Lawrence's own version, the mutually exclusive nature of the polarities allows the individual to escape himself and reality by living vicariously in the illusion of the "other." Ursula symbolically travels through all these realms of romantic otherness—religion, science, intellectual scholarship—in an attempt to escape herself and find her identity through another.

Indeed, the tendency to find oneself through another— that ego ideal which one fears missing in oneself and projects externally—is the force not only behind Ursula's choice of lovers both male (Anton) and female (Winifred) but behind both Tom's and Will's earlier choices of wives. In all cases this attempted evasion of reality bears bitter fruit. Although Lydia in fact embodies that "other" life Tom seeks, it is a life she wishes to forget for its memories are fraught with pain. Anna, whom Will sees as his potential muse, becomes the force which destroys both his art and his artistic impulse. And Anton and Winifred, both selected as towers of strength and certainty by Ursula in her weakness, end up turning to her for support.

Thus the predominance of flat characters and continually changing environment in Ursula's section of the novel is doubly appropriate—the thinness of character an attestation both to the loss of the rhythmic foundations of self from which true identity arises and to the distortion of Ursula's vision through which we view the action, a distortion appropriate to the age's tendency to project falsely. The mechanical nature by which Lawrence seems to transport Ursula from chapter to chapter and from one world to the next—the lack of integration and cohesion of episodes—is similarly appropriate, a reflection of the lack of organic connection within society and between it and Ursula. For the most part, the characters move through the final pages like mechanized zombies, not because Lawrence has been unable to bring them to life, but because, detached from themselves and one another, they cannot bring themselves to life. And thinking the answer to life lies outside themselves—that the unifying rainbow indeed lies upon a distant hilltop as Ursula envisions—they discard people and worlds, as Ursula does, since in each effort they inevitably fail to fulfill this unrealistic hope.

Lawrence regarded as anathema this naive attitude toward "experience," as if it were just another case of material accretion building gradually toward a heavenly epiphany. Only late in her experience does Ursula truly begin to look inward and to accept the necessity of coupling a journey toward the horizon with an internal journey. Looking "inward" through a microscope at a speck of life, she understands the purpose of all life is to realize its identity, "to be itself." Although at this point her external movement increases to whirlwind dimensions as she races with Anton across Europe trying to escape him and herself, Ursula has already begun to concentrate unconsciously on her inward journey. Only by travelling inward can one paradoxically reach the horizon. "Self was a oneness with the infinite. To be oneself was a supreme, gleaming triumph of infinity."

Ursula's gradual awakening is reflected in the sudden re-emergence of ritual scenes in the last two chapters of the novel. Ultimately both what depth of character and what resulting beauty appear in the second half appear in these ritual scenes. As elsewhere, such rituals are attempts, largely unconscious, to resolve the tensions—the distances between polarities. In Ursula's generation these tensions and distances are necessarily more violent and "out of control." Rather than the more simple and soothing harmonies of Tom Brangwen's forefathers, the beauty which is wrested here from the complexities of Lawrence's vision is a rich but terrible one. As she makes evident in *Women in Love,* Ursula, like T. S. Eliot in "Little Gidding," does learn in the end, not that she should "cease from exploration" but that ". . . the end of all [her] exploring / Will be to arrive where [she] started / And know the place for the first time."

Ronald Schleifer   (essay date 1980)

SOURCE: "Lawrence's Rhetoric of Vision: The Ending of *The Rainbow*," in *The D. H. Lawrence Review,* Vol. 13, No. 2, Summer, 1980, pp. 161-78.

[*In the following essay, Schleifer investigates the narrative strategies of* The Rainbow, *and argues that the ending of the novel is "continuous with the work as a whole."*]

The last chapter of *The Rainbow* has generated a great deal of critical commentary. Critics who disapprove of the novel's ending usually argue, one way or another, that it has not been sufficiently prepared for earlier in the text, and those who defend the ending usually do so by attempting to demonstrate its continuity with what precedes it. In any case, the ending of the novel is of recognized importance, and Edward Engleberg, one of the defenders of the ending, puts most succinctly the issues which are involved [in *PMLA* 78, 1963]:

To call into doubt the novel's resolution is to question the structure and the meaning of the whole book, and to undercut the vision of the rainbow is to undercut all that precedes it.

Of course, most of the critics of the conclusion do just this, either unconsciously or consciously: they describe the ending as "no real conclusion of the book, only a breaking off," the "emotional falsity of the last few pages," and the "marked inferiority of the second half" of the novel. Thus, in the end, writes Graham Hough [in *The Dark Sun: A Study of D. H. Lawrence,* 1957], it is possible that Lawrence "has mistaken his ultimate: that sexual fulfilment stands to Lawrence for some other more inclusive kind of integration whose nature he does not know; that he has mistaken the part for the whole." Both critics and defenders of the last chapter (or the last half) of the novel are trying to read the ending in terms of the beginning, to have the end resolve or fail to resolve "the structure and the meaning" of the novel. Even Alan Friedman, who [in *The Turn of the Novel,* 1969] admirably accounts for the apparent lack of resolution in *The Rainbow* in terms of the novel's structural "openness," doesn't examine the implications for the vision and the language of *The Rainbow* which are contained in the ending and its central scene, Ursula's encounter with the horses.

In *The Sense of the Ending,* Frank Kermode argues that literature develops out of the dialectic of what he calls "justice" or "paradigms" and "reality". Endings are paradigmatic, fictional impositions on a world without ends which give a sense of significance to the world. Yet while an ending can produce "concordance" in which "the end is in harmony with the beginning, the middle with beginning and end," it should also allow for the contingent: an ideal ending would create a "transfiguration, as it were, of the contingent." "Here is the problem," Kermode writes of novels,

the consulting and ignoring of continuity and especially the successiveness of time. Ignoring it, we fake to achieve the forms absent from the continuous world; we regress toward myth, out of this time into that time. Consulting it, we set the word against the word, and create the need for difficult concords in our fictions.

The novel, in other words, needs to balance concessions to our sense of disorder and "inhumanity"—the endlessness of continuity—and significant critical moments—that is, ends—which fulfill our desire for order and meaning.

In these terms the ending of *The Rainbow* is especially problematic: by and large, the defenders of the ending defend it simply in terms of its thematic consonance with what precedes it while those who criticize it do so in terms of the incongruity of plot and theme. Kermode, in an article primarily concerned with *Women in Love* [in *Critical Quarterly* 10, 1968], accounts for this disparity in the most general terms. Lawrence, he says,

will not make up stories which *explain* how one thing leads to another. There are concessions to contingency, for without them we should fail to recognize the book as a novel, but we move with a minimum of formal continuity from one crux to the next.

It is true that Lawrence depends more than most novelists on cruxes in the creation of his novels. Yet the significant moments in **The Rainbow** have a greater formal continuity than appears at first glance, and they create the difficult concords between continuity and discontinuity which Kermode prescribes for novels. Lawrence's is a difficult language, it is both obscure and willful, yet with that language he addresses himself to just those problems which concern Kermode. I will argue that the structure and the meaning of **The Rainbow** are related to one another in a more complex and problematic way than any of these judgments on the novel imply and that its conclusion—the crucial encounter between Ursula and the horses—is both continuous with the novel as a whole and finally creates a syntax and a symbolic language which sustain a delicate balance between language and vision, continuity and discontinuity and the special problem for **The Rainbow,** the known and the unknown. In other words, the ending of **The Rainbow** concludes by giving us a language with which to read the novel as a whole, so that we can read the beginning in terms of the end.

I

The last chapter of the novel, itself called "The Rainbow," presents four events: Ursula's letter to Skrebensky, her encounter with a herd of horses, her illness and miscarriage, and finally the vision of the rainbow with which the novel ends. Critics have not objected to the transition between the end of Ursula's affair with Skrebensky and her letter: that she should be with child is indeed "contingency" which she hadn't counted on, yet her response to that event, her letter to Skrebensky, has been well prepared for. What remains problematic is the shift to the crucial scene of the chapter, Ursula's encounter with the horses. That encounter is described in a passage that follows without transition the novel's indirect quotation of Ursula's letter to Skrebensky into which she puts "her true self, forever": with her marriage "her history would be concluded forever." Even though while she writes she does not quite acknowledge the conflict between her "unnatural calm" and "a gathering restiveness, a tumult impending within her," in the end she tries "to run away from it" and runs to the horses. The encounter, then, opens with its time and space specified: "One afternoon in early October, feeling the seething rising to madness within her, she slipped out in the rain, to walk abroad, lest the house should suffocate her." Yet the specific time and space are curiously detached from the time of her letter. In this initial sentence already the language is charged with an abstractness—both of its terms (i.e. "*the* seething") and from its context—which seems to bear meanings beyond the specific incident at hand: Ursula's madness is out of proportion to even the "bondaged" peace which precedes it. This pressure of unspecified significance, an almost inarticulate knowledge, is created in and through the difficult transition Lawrence presents, the rhetoric of opposing states of mind, the conflict between conscious and unconscious awareness which the final scene of the novel most clearly depicts.

Alan Friedman in his account of **The Rainbow** in *The Turn of the Novel* puts great emphasis on this crisis in Ursula's life and demonstrates that "**The Rainbow** is planned to provide, inevitably, for the absence of any conclusion." Friedman argues that from the beginning of the novel a clear-cut dichotomy is produced between "open" and "closed" forms of experience and that Ursula's fear of suffocation is one pole in a dialectic existing throughout the novel. From the opening chapter a dichotomy is created between acceptance and outward movement, the "horizontal land" and "the church tower . . . in the empty sky," the known and "something unknown": living on the land, the Brangwens are constantly "aware" of something beyond, are constantly "eager" and expectant. Thus Tom marries a woman who "belonged to somewhere else," and their marriage flowers when he realizes that "she was the awful unknown . . . wonderful, beyond him." So, too, Anna found an escape in Will—"in him the bounds of her experience were transgressed: he was the hole in the wall, beyond which the sunshine blazed on an outside world"— even though unlike Tom she is finally disillusioned about Will so that "with satisfaction she relinquished the adventure to the unknown." Moreover, the visions of the rainbow associated with Tom and Anna are rendered in terms of doorways, leading to "the beyond," "like an archway, a shadow-door with faintly coloured coping above it." "Whither?" the text asks of Tom's relation with his wife, and there is no answer: Lydia was "the awful unknown."

Like her mother and her grandfather, Ursula too feels the pressure outward towards something beyond her life, something unknown. In her last encounter with Skrebensky on the beach, seeing the stars and the darkness, "she wanted to reach and be amongst the flashing skies, she wanted to race with her feet and be beyond the confines of the earth. . . . She must leap from the known to the unknown." In the same way, throughout her life Ursula had been constantly pressing outward in widening circles, creating "illusions" for herself in terms of the Grammar School, religion, her own goodness, teaching, Schofield, college, and Skrebensky, illusions of increasing intensity.

In the light of this continued urge toward boundless or "open" experience, Friedman argues that "the absence of any conclusion" is the only possible conclusion for **The Rainbow** and that Ursula's pen-ultimate reversion to a resignation parallel to her mother's embodied in her letter is only an allusion to the "closed" form of experience which the novel rejects. "The final rainbow," he writes, "is an attempt, managed with some artistry, not to 'conclude,' an attempt to stop without concluding, an anti-conclusion, if you like." The experience portrayed in the novel doesn't conclude, but is always pushing beyond, and the end is in concordance with the novel as a whole.

While Friedman's account of the "anti-conclusion" seems to me to be correct in structural terms, his notion of "open" experience is too abstract to explore adequately the *rhetorical* problem of rendering what is "unknown." Not only does it avoid examining the discontinuities which are integral elements of the novel and its rhetoric; it does so by emphasizing only one aspect of the double movement which characterizes the novel. Rather than an allusion to the "closed" novel, Ursula's penultimate decision to emulate her mother is consistent with the constant check the "weekday" world makes on experience in the novel: the novel creates conflict rather than continued outward movement, and, as one critic has noticed, Ursula's widening circles can also be seen as progressively more confining.

Moreover, this conflict is a struggle of language, the search for an appropriate rhetoric. Following the failure of the Brangwen Christmas and that extraordinary passage at the end of chapter ten, Ursula passes from girlhood towards womanhood and discovers the unreality of religion. She learns that the "old duality" of a "weekday world of people and trains and duties and reports" and "a Sunday world of absolute truth and living mystery" was suddenly "broken apart."

> She turned to the visions, which had spoken far off words . . . , and she demanded only the weekday meaning of the words.

> There *were* words spoken by the vision: and words must have a weekday meaning, since words were weekday stuff. Let them speak now: . . . the vision should translate itself into weekday terms.

Ursula is striving throughout the novel to make this translation, to find an ordinary language which will make her extraordinary experience real in the face of the constant check "weekday" fact makes on "Sunday" experience.

The most striking example of this check on experience comes after Ursula's "leap . . . to the unknown" when she "annihilates" Skrebensky at the dance:

> Gradually a sort of daytime consciousness came back to her. Suddenly the night was struck back into its old, accustomed, mild reality. Gradually she realized that the night was common and ordinary, that the great blistering, transcendental night did not really exist.

After her experience under the moonlight with Skrebensky—which itself repeats her mother's encounter with Will and will be repeated again by Ursula in her last meeting with Skrebensky—Ursula reacts with disbelief and denial. Once again the transition is "sudden" in a way which would lead Kermode to object, yet it is counterpointed with Ursula's "gradual" awakening. It is just such transitions, sudden yet apparently gradual and ordinary to the characters, which characterize the narrative as a whole and prepare for its inconclusive conclusion. As the novel ultimately shows, there is no choice between experiences of this kind: rather, the conflict between them itself produces the progression of the work.

Throughout the novel many characters have this "open" nighttime experience which is outward and boundless and, by virtue of this fact, discontinuous with "daytime" experience and weekday words. The real problem that the characters face, to a greater and lesser degree, is how to deal with this experience. Moreover, this problem is intimately connected to Lawrence's larger novelistic problem of how to render such moments and such dealings. In *The Deed of Life*, Julian Moynahan objects to Lawrence's use

of symbols in terms close to Kermode's objection to the discontinuous nature of the narrative. Remarking on the recurrent and inconsistent use of the rainbow symbol, he says, "each time we encounter the symbol we must in effect forget where we have gotten to in the novel and move onto a sacred ground of quasi-religious contemplation." By and large this criticism is sound, and it raises broader questions concerning Lawrence's use of language and his sense of metaphor in *The Rainbow*—questions concerning the rhetoric of vision—which, as we shall see, are more fully resolved in the final scene of the novel.

In an often-cited and important letter to Garnett in 1914, in which he outlined some of his intentions for his novel, Lawrence himself raises these questions:

> I don't so much care about what the woman *feels*—in the ordinary usage of the word. That presumes an ego to feel with. I only care about what the woman is—what she IS—inhumanly, physiologically, materially—according to the use of the word: but for me, what she is as a phenomenon (or as representing some greater, inhuman will), instead of what she feels according to the human concept. . . . You mustn't look in my novel for the old stable *ego* of character. There is another *ego,* according to whose action the individual is unrecognisable, and passes through, as it were, allotropic states which it needs a deeper sense than any we've been used to exercise, to discover are states of the same radically unchanged element. . . . You must not say my novel is shaky. . . . it is the real thing. . . .

From one point of view, Lawrence's intention for *The Rainbow* is that of the traditional novel, seeking to depict some sort of order and significance amid the welter of experience, to find the reality of the "same radically unchanged element" through the appearance of its "allotropic states." Yet from another vantage Lawrence's intentions destroy the traditional expectations we bring to a novel. Unlike, say, *Don Quixote* in which narrative and significance are generated in the ironic tension between appearance and reality, between novelistic fiction and human and inhuman fact, *The Rainbow* attempts to deal, unironically, with a "new" reality; it tries to render an inhuman vision in a human expression, to deal with the "unknown" in terms of the "known." Even in the letter in which Lawrence announces his intention, the struggle between vision and language has already begun: by means of the "ordinary usages" Lawrence is trying to intimate some "deeper sense." Thus, the same word, *"ego,"* is used to describe opposite attributes of human being according to human and inhuman "concepts," and the passage itself opens up into the metaphoric use of scientific analogy to express itself. At once the analogy asserts the reality of Lawrence's vision and his necessity to find or create a language to express it. The use of the allotrope/element metaphor reveals this double tendency: on the one hand, it asserts a strict, scientifically factual analogy to his vision, and given his interest in the non-human "physic," the "inhuman will, call it . . . physiology of matter," it asserts the physical reality of his vision as well; yet at the same time the ubiquitous "call it . . ." reveals his necessary struggle with his language. The rhetoric Lawrence seeks is one that would reconcile his novelistic and extranovelistic concerns; within the novel, it would reconcile "weekday" and "Sunday" experience, rendering the latter as real as a physical presence.

As we have seen, in *The Rainbow* this problem of articulation is explicitly faced by Ursula:

> How to act, that was the question? Whither to go, how to become oneself? One was not oneself, one was merely a half stated question. How to become oneself, how to know the question and the answer of oneself, when one was merely an unfixed something-nothing, blowing about like the winds of heaven, undefined, unstated.

These questions about speech and action are the questions discontinuous experience and inhuman vision raise in a weekday world. In the face of these questions, for Ursula and ultimately for Lawrence himself, irony pales before desperation and engagement. Irony, we might say, sustains the novel in a tense self-contradictory balance of action and meaning, feeling and thought, narration and significance: the novel must consult, as Kermode says, both continuity and discontinuity. Yet Lawrence creates conflict in his novel between poles of experience which, in terms of "the living fabric of Truth" the novel itself raises, cannot balance. Tom finally responds to this conflict in Anna's wedding with "bewilderment" and rage and *unconscious* anguish, Anna with resignation, and Ursula with the continued outward movement Friedman describes. And Lawrence himself desperately tries to make action meaning, feeling knowledge, and interpretive passages part of the narrative itself. He attempts to create, here in *The Rainbow* and throughout his work, a sense of the physical presence of value, which is why this spacious novel seems so much more interested—and so much more successful—in rendering the physical rhythms of life and death, birth and growth, than it is in creating character. In one sense, Lawrence's intention makes him more distant from his characters than any novelist I know: he puts word against word and uses his characters' experience for some "inhuman" end which is completely detached from their conscious lives. Yet this detachment is far from ironic: Lawrence is seeking the same end as his characters, not love or feeling, "but something impersonal" as Ursula says, and the goal of his art is the same as his characters'. What one is and how to act are the questions with which the novel grapples and which it must settle for itself. And they are settled, both for Lawrence and for Ursula, in the penultimate scene of the novel, with Ursula and the horses.

II

In her letter Ursula enacts the check which daytime reality has put upon her more visionary experiences throughout the novel: she again thinks of her life as virtually "concluded" history just as earlier, after her college disillusionment, she had thought that her life was "already" history only to meet Skrebensky again soon afterwards. So this rainy afternoon she leaves the suffocation of her home. Ursula walks towards Willey Green in the downpour, and again the image of a doorway appears, now in terms of "a bird who has flown in through the window of a hall where vast warriors sit at board . . . till she emerged through the far window and out into the open." Then, "suddenly she knew there was something else," and the horses are felt by Ursula before she looks up.

Like so many scenes in *The Rainbow,* Ursula's encounter with the horses is marked by a great deal of ambiguity; it presents a real event, one from the everyday world, and also presents the "unknown" knowledge of an extraordinary experience. Here, as in Lawrence's letter, ambiguity is created by using the same word to describe different levels of experience, in this case the same verb: "she *knew* there was something else. . . . she did not want *to know* they were there. . . . she *knew* without looking. . . . she was *aware.* . . ." In this way the scene creates a double sense of reality, not so much a reality which is informed by a larger meaning as two distinct realities created by two ways of *knowing.* Lawrence's language attempts to join these realities: Ursula "knows" unconsciously—she is "aware" in an almost physical way of the horses' presence—yet she does not consciously want to acknowledge her awareness. Unlike other modern writers—Forster, say, or Woolf and Joyce—Lawrence is not interested in making the unconscious conscious. Rather, he attempts to render it as *present,* and to this end he continually shifts between an ordinary and extraordinary sense of knowledge, from his character's conscious understanding to her unconscious awareness. These shifts attempt, rhetorically, to overcome the checks the everyday world puts on Sunday experience, to give metaphor a real presence.

We have already seen that Friedman sees the "known" and the "unknown" in terms of closed and open forms of the novel, in terms of rendering completed and incomplete experience. Yet there is another way to examine this dichotomy which points to central issues in this expansive work: the known and the unknown can be seen in terms of the past and the present, in terms of time. In the hotel room where Skrebensky and Ursula went after his breakdown Ursula watches Skrebensky dress:

> He seemed completed now. He aroused no fruitful fecundity in her. He seemed added up, finished. She knew him all round, not on any side did he lead to the unknown.

In the novel, the finished, the complete, the known, as Friedman observes, are "perfected," and "the narrative has taken the greatest pains to establish in its own terms that whatever is perfected or perfectable, 'has been a failure'; and whatever is to be perfect, must lead only into the unknown." Yet Friedman has failed to notice that this is precisely because what is perfected—as Ursula says, what is defined or stated—is past and done with, while what is "unknown" is the present moment, by definition "unfinished." Looking at a "plant-animal" in college and questioning deeply the nature of life, Ursula suddenly realizes that "it intended to be itself. . . . Suddenly she had passed away into an intensely-gleaming light of knowledge. . . . It was a consummation, a being infinite. Self was oneness with the infinite."

In 1920 Lawrence also spoke of living tissue and life in terms very close to those of Ursula:

But there is another kind of poetry: the poetry of that which is at hand: the immediate present. In the immediate present there is no perfection, no consummation, nothing finished. . . . There are no gems of the living plasm. The living plasm vibrates unspeakably, it inhales the future, it exhales the past, it is the quick of both, yet it is neither. There is no plasmic finality, nothing crystal, permanent. . . .

Life, the ever-present, knows no finality, no finished crystalization. The perfect rose is only a running flame, emerging and flowing off, and never in any sense at rest, static, finished. Herein lies its transcendent loveliness. The whole tide of all life and all time suddenly heaves, and appears before us as an apparition, a revelation.

In this passage Lawrence makes his characteristic assertion of the "transcendental loveliness" of the "momentaneous" presence of an object, a revelation contained in a grain of sand. The "business of art," he says elsewhere, is to reveal the relation between man and his universe "at the living moment," the "quick moment of time." With a questionable "therefore," which clothes the discontinuous language of revelation in the ordinary usage of argumentative discourse, he asserts that life itself, "for mankind," is the "pure [momentaneous] relationship" that is "beyond life, and therefore beyond death"—the quick of both the past and the future.

In *The Rainbow* Lawrence depicts Ursula's predicament in just these temporal terms. Ursula's Sunday world, like her "transcendental night," "was not real, or at least, not actual. And one lived by action." The moment excludes action, and to speak it makes it dead, finished, perfected. Yet, as we have seen, there is also what Lawrence calls the "knowledge" of the moment, unspeakable, unreflected upon, and unconscious: simply physical awareness of the moment. The emphasis on sensation in Lawrence—on sexuality and feeling—is thus intimately related to his sense of the "momentaneous" quality of life: if action is characteristic of the "lived" life, then physical awareness is characteristic of "living" life.

This is why the narrator always "knows" more than the characters in *The Rainbow:* he can consciously know and speak the present moment of his characters in his retrospective narrative while the characters themselves are merely present and aware: they are, as Lawrence would say, in the unknown. The problem for the novel is to render the "quick moment of time" in the past tense, shifting constantly between the characters' knowledge and the narrator's knowledge, between present and past, without deadening the present and without losing the articulation that retrospection affords.

This movement can best be seen in Ursula's encounter with the horses. Throughout the novel this duality of narrative is present, yet it is rendered in such a way as to create the obscurity and rhetorical excesses which have so often been noticed in Lawrence's prose. Here in the last scene, however, Lawrence utilizes both time and space to pit knowledge against knowledge, word against word. He recreates in the narration the conflict between actuality and the unknown.

Suddenly, she knew there was something else. Some horses were looming in the rain, not near yet. But they were going to be near. She continued her path, inevitably. There were horses in the lee of a clump of trees beyond, above her. She pursued her way with bent head. She did not want to lift her face to them. She did not want to know they were there. She went on in the wild track.

She knew the heaviness of her heart. It was the weight of the horses.

Ursula's sudden "knowledge" of the horses is a present knowledge, physical and unconscious (she "knows" the heaviness), and throughout this scene she struggles against this knowledge. Consciously, she refuses her knowledge and walks on "inevitably," denies it by the action—the continuity of action—which negates the unknown moment. Ursula's action—"her feet went on and on. . . . on and on"—staves off vital knowledge through mechanical repetition just as, earlier, the mechanism of the Christian year destroyed the Brangwen Christmas. The suddenness with which Ursula is made aware of the momentary physical presence of the horses marks her experience as discontinuous with everyday life, and she mechanically struggles against it: within Ursula, then, is repeated the novel's conflict between Sunday and weekday experience, between her present and past.

Ursula's unconscious struggle, however, is also enacted on another level, between the narrator's understanding and her understanding. Insofar as this event "actually" occurs, it marks the difference between Ursula's awareness and the narrator's conscious, retrospective knowledge. Ursula's awareness of "something else" is unarticulated and unconscious knowledge, while retrospectively the narrator "knows" and can say that "some horses were looming in the rain." Ursula is not in a position to know this (they were "not near yet") just as she cannot know the future event of the next sentence. Rather, by shifting from her awareness to his own, the narrator fills and articulates the unknown; he depicts the physical and temporal "actuality" of the event against Ursula's possible awareness. In this way the narrator distances himself from his character and creates the usual narrative irony: the narrator knows more than his character can possibly know. Yet insofar as Ursula "knows" the horses in a moment which contains the future as well as the present there is no irony at all: the knowledge of the narrator and character coincide. The shifting narrative between past and present, knowledge and awareness, creates a sense of the living moment "beyond life and death" which constitutes the unknown present: the narrator fills the moment with Ursula's own unknown knowledge.

Problems elsewhere in the narrative can be understood in these terms as well. For instance, in the scene in which Schofield proposes to Ursula, she realizes that she was "going inevitably to accept him," yet moments later she "involuntarily" refuses.

She turned away, she turned round from him, and saw the east flushed strangely rose, the moon coming yellow and lovely upon a rosy sky, above the darkening, bluish snow. All this is

> beautiful, all this so lovely! He did not see it. He
> was one with it. But she saw, and was one with
> it. Her seeing separated them infinitely.

The separation of the last sentence is completely unknown and unarticulated in terms of what precedes it in this passage, a discontinuous moment of narrative. Yet by using "but" the narrative creates the illusion of continuity, and the repetition of "was one with it" shifts a large and obscure metaphoric burden onto "saw" which, in terms of this passage, it cannot bear. The passage gives no event against which to read the metaphor in "inhuman" terms: that she saw the rainbow-like sky, after all, might mean almost anything to Ursula. In contrast, in the horse scene the limits of Ursula's possible awareness are determined by her physical placement, and whatever knowledge she has must be unconscious, inhuman—indeed, her knowledge coincides with the narrator's The later scene, then, reveals the syntax of the earlier passage: the narrator shifts from actual to metaphorical meanings of "see." The last sentences are not thought by Ursula at all; they are hers in some vital, unconscious way, and, despite the fact that she immediately acts on her awareness by refusing Schofield, her motives remain unknown to her.

The simultaneous substantiation and breakdown of irony in the last scene renders the "unspeakable" present of the character in the past tense of the narrative and, at the same time, creates the illusion of presence in the past tense. The second achievement is as important as the first: as Lawrence says, the "pure relationship" of the quick moment must give us "the feeling of being beyond life or death." Although this would seem the easier task, in fact it presents the greatest dangers to Lawrence's art. In part, it is his attempt to create the illusion of this presence, I believe, which creates Lawrence's re-current rhetorical excesses, his interpolations of his own voice within his narratives. The most striking example of this is the passage which ends chapter ten. At first glance this passage seems to be the narrator's response to his own narration, an identification of fiction and reality parallel to the identification of metaphor and fact his rhetoric strives to create. As the Christian year "was becoming a mechanical action now" for the whole Brangwen family, the narrator's voice enters the narrative to articulate questions about that failure and to imply answers. In this passage the narrator explicitly assumes the role of Christ in the present tense: "Why shall I not rise with my body whole and perfect, shining with strong life? Why, when Mary says: Rabboni, shall I not take her in my arms and kiss her . . . ?" At the same time, however, the narrator is also assuming the role of the Brangwen children who "lived the year of christianity, the epic of the soul of mankind." This epic creates the "rhythm of eternity in a ragged, inconsequential life," so that the assumption of Christ's role is also the assumption of that of the Brangwens. In this way the narrator uses his only first-person intrusion to articulate the unknown in the lives of the Brangwens and to further his narrative.

This intrusion reveals the discontinuous method of narration which creates the power and effect of the book's ending. Moreover, it reveals a more sobering implication of Lawrence's method. The narrator's response to this extraordinary experience, unlike any of the Brangwen's, yet like Birkin's in *Women in Love,* is to theorize about it. In so doing the novel is not only invested with the authority of a biblical account by means of the recurrent and overall biblical allusiveness of the text; it is also invested with the authority of its "radically unchanged" reality by means of its repeated revelations. When the moment is the quick of life, the narrator not only can articulate the unknown which the characters experience, he can also expand the moment into a revelation of things, a definition and statement, apparently no longer metaphorical, of the "unfixed, something-nothing" of life.

Yet definition is the antithesis of the experience Lawrence is trying to portray. In the final scene he avoids the danger the identification of metaphor and fact creates by continuing the narrative from Ursula's point of view while simultaneously identifying and detaching the narrator from her. While Ursula's experience is not visionary in the sense that she imagines the horses—a sense in which it is possible to read, say, Anna's rainbow or certainly this interpolation—it is visionary in the sense that she knows the vital present moment. In this last scene, Lawrence brings together the ordinary and extraordinary experiences which have been in conflict throughout the novel and balances them to create his narrative.

III

We have seen what Lawrence does with the "open" experience he is dealing with; how Ursula deals with her experience is a matter which is more difficult. Here we have to turn to the significance of the horse scene for Ursula and its significance in the context of the novel. Ursula's meeting with the horses has received virtually every conceivable interpretation: it has been seen as Ursula's triumph over her dark experience, her acceptance of her own dark side, and her failure in both of these cases. Moreover, the use of horses in this crucial scene influences interpretation by virtue of the fact that Lawrence considered the horse a *"significant* dream image" in itself and catalogued its meanings in the *Fantasia* and elsewhere. Nevertheless, I would argue that the significance of the encounter for Ursula is not, as one critic [Julian Moynahan] has said, that she sees "the truth about herself," but rather that she comes to realize and possess the double measure of her experience. Ursula becomes conscious, in a way her forebears could not, of the reality of both weekday and Sunday experience by achieving the "translation" she was seeking, a language for her experience.

After her initial awareness of the horses, Ursula walks on "knowing" the tension of her nerves and that "she must die."

> But the horses had burst before her. In a sort of
> lightning of knowledge their movement travelled through her, the quiver and strain and
> thrust of their powerful flanks, as they burst before her and drew her on, beyond.

Just as her knowledge of the "plant-animal" came to her in a flash, so too the horses flash before her in an array of color. This actual bursting forth of the horses illuminates the metaphorical flash at the college. The "intensely-gleaming light of knowledge" in the earlier scene is a moment of awareness, yet here Ursula sees or feels such a flash in the horses themselves. In other words, because of the ambiguity created between the knowledge of the narrator and character in this scene, the metaphors of the novel take on actual (active) existence for the reader in the horses, while at the same time Ursula can see in them a "metaphoric" correlative for her experience, a possible rhetoric for her visionary, Sunday experience. The horses act, for her, like Lawrence's "perfect rose": "the whole tide of all life and all time suddenly heaves, and appears before [her] as an apparition, a revelation." The horses flash before her, and she sees them "running against the wall of time," she sees the "massive fire that was locked within [their] flanks." After her escape, Ursula even recognizes that the horses possess a kind of knowledge similar to that which she had experienced: "she knew the horses were aware. . . . The horses were loosening their knot, stirring, trying to realize."

Ursula's escape ends with her "sunk to the bottom of all change," and after a "long time" she starts home. Her return home, finally, is put in terms which Ursula has thought earlier about her college experience. There she had seen her life as a succession of "gleaming" hills from which she repeatedly encountered "another sordid valley," and now once again she thinks, "Why must one climb the hill [to Beldover]? . . . Why force one's way up when one is at the bottom? . . . Still, she must get to the top and go home to bed." Here again metaphor is repeated in fact, but now it is the physical fact of the hill before Ursula. Her encounter with the horses allows her consciously to see, as in metaphor, her extraordinary experience, and by continuing on she makes that vision and that experience her own: her return from the horses allows her to transform, as it were, the sordid valleys of her experience.

This can perhaps be better understood if we examine Ursula's activity subsequent to this encounter, her vision of the rainbow. Throughout this essay I have been considering Ursula's encounter with the horses as the final event of the novel because the rainbow scene, I believe, in broad structural terms stands outside the novel as a sort of epilogue in the same way the opening pages of the book create a timeless prologue. The latter creates a sense of the vastness of an immemorial past and the former opens to an "infinite" future. Moreover, as I have already suggested, multi-colored "rainbows" occur throughout the novel at vital, timeless moments; in terms of my argument, they are "unknown" and consciously possessed only by the narrator. The rainbows which end both Tom's and Anna's sections of the book embody, as Moynahan says, moments when the narrative stops, and both are outside of consciousness: Tom forms one end of a metaphoric rainbow and Anna's door opens under the arch of another metaphoric rainbow. Ursula's rainbow is categorically different: hers is a conscious vision of which she, not the narrator, has possession, and it is this fact which realizes the significance of her encounter with the horses and ends and fulfills the novel.

The content of Ursula's rainbow vision has never been defended even by the ending's staunchest defenders, yet it is just here that the full significance of the structure and the meaning of the novel can be seen. As we have seen, the novel consists in its overall structure, in its narrative progression, and ultimately in its meaning as well, of the conflict of continuous and discontinuous experience. Throughout Ursula's life vision has been qualified by fact, Sunday by weekday experience, vital momentary life by a dead past. Yet now after her encounter with the horses, Ursula has a vision in which the known is qualified and transformed by the unknown, a vision in which, to use Kermode's language, the contingent is transfigured:

> And the rainbow stood on the earth. She knew that the sordid people who crept hard-scaled and separate on the face of the world's corruption were living still, that the rainbow was arched in their blood and would quiver to live in their spirit. . . . She saw in the rainbow the earth's new architecture, the old brittle corruption of houses and factories swept away, the world built up in a living fabric of Truth, fitting to the over-arching heavens.

The novel ends with the conflict which has characterized it from the beginning still in operation in the image of the rainbow which is both the moment and a promise, like life itself momentarily vital and ongoing. Yet for Ursula that conflict, though ongoing, is somehow changed. As her vision attests—a vision that sees beyond the sordid world to the rainbow overhead—she can discover truth in metaphor and value in fact, and discover and articulate both in a "fitting" image.

Andrew Kennedy   (essay date 1982)

SOURCE: "After Not So Strange Gods in *The Rainbow*," in *English Studies*, London, Vol. 63, 1982, pp. 220-30.

[*In the following essay, Kennedy explores Lawrence's use of religious language and the attitude he displays toward Christianity in* The Rainbow.]

I

The Rainbow can be seen as a mythic/religious novel, yet it does not seem to have a clear shaping myth at its centre; and the exploration of a changing Christian spirituality is only one of the novel's many aspects. Even so, all the central characters use a certain kind of *religious language* to express a variety of experiences that are profoundly important to them. We know that this novel owes a good deal to the Bible (especially to the Book of Genesis) and, remembering that Lawrence called the Bible a 'great confused novel', we may at times ask whether *The Rainbow,* with its biblical analogues, has not taken a measure of 'confusion' into itself along with the 'greatness'. Or is there a persistent groping towards new insight and illumination, towards a new personal *and* fictional language in *The Rainbow*?

That question can only be answered through detailed inquiry. First, we may distinguish between a writer who uses a myth (sacred or secular) as the controlling structure of the novel and one who uses the language of an established yet challenged religion (like Christianity) as something *given*—something inherited and to be used, unsystematically, like any other language borrowed from the common pool. The first type of writer will produce works like Joyce's *Ulysses,* where the Homeric epic controls much of the narrative and imagery (whether or not the reader is always aware of the analogies); or else a work like Golding's *Lord of the Flies,* where the Fall from Eden controls most of the narrative and imagery in such a way that one can hardly miss it. The second type of writer will produce works like **The Rainbow,** where the biblical-religious language is part of the cultural inheritance of two generations of Brangwen men (Tom and Will), and where even Anna as antagonist and Ursula as doubting seeker, cannot abandon, can only parody, that language.

If we accept this critical distinction, we need not approach the novel with expectations of a grand mythic/religious design; we may expect from the start an exploratory, groping, even improvisatory re-creation of certain types of religious experience and language. (I differ in this initial view from George Ford, who [in *Double Measure, A Study of the Novels and Stories of D. H. Lawrence,* 1965] compares Lawrence's 'ambitious scheme of biblical analogies' to Joyce's Homeric parallels in *Ulysses*). It would follow, further, that instead of a controlling or prefiguring mythology, this or that element of the Judeo-Christian myth will be resorted to by this or that character under the pressure of experience. What kind of experience? Almost any experience felt by the character to be *awe*-some, numinous, or initiating something unknown, testing nothing less than his or her authentic being. (It is almost impossible to avoid such existential terms when the emphasis shifts from the religious system to the person, from structure to texture, from doctrine to experience.) A character will not then be embarking on a specifically religious quest, (something the reader can identify as shadowing or foreshadowing one or the other archetypal patterns for such a quest); a character may be embarking on 'ordinary living', with extraordinary moments seen as moments apart—requiring a different, more strongly value-charged kind of language. In Lawrence such moments include personal encounter, and, inseparably from that, the search for meaning 'incarnated' in relationship. And the religious language used, though it has great variety, may have a certain underlying imagistic and rhythmic kinship—the biblical echoes.

In attempting to account for this aspect of **The Rainbow** critically, I shall attempt to test simultaneously, (through bifocal lenses, so to speak) both the function of religious language in this particular novel, and the quality of Lawrence's post-Christian 'heterodoxy', (which Eliot, in *After Strange Gods,* reduced to a 'sick spirituality'.) For the sake of clarity, I shall largely follow the pattern of the three generations, which provides the novel's narrative backbone. I shall focus on passages that clearly embody a mode of religious experience and language in dramatic episode or authorial comment.

II

Religious language is used most simply and explicitly when Lawrence attempts to find words for marriage as a sacrament: to rescue meaning from cliché, to see a wedding as an entry into the unknown, and consummation as communion. Typologically, Lawrence wants to re-create,

it seems, a living analogy between the miracle of Cana and marriage. (The figure of Cana is used, in the second generational cycle, to point the abyss between Anna's empirical and Will's mythic religion: 'Did he believe the water turned to wine at Cana? . . . In his blood and bones, he wanted the scene, the wedding . . . '.) Psychologically, Lawrence offers a simple key to the nature of Tom Brangwen's 'sublimation': 'The disillusion of his first carnal contact with woman, strengthened by his innate desire *to find in a woman the embodiment of all his inarticulate, powerful religious impulses,* put a bit in his mouth.' And stylistically, the religious images are used broadly, that is, simply borrowed and transferred, for the sake of intensified meaning. Thus, Tom Brangwen, as he stands tormented and unsmiling beside Lydia, (the foreign woman who embodies the unknown), experiences a kind of holy terror immediately after the wedding. 'The time of his trial and his admittance, his Gethsemane and his Triumphal Entry in one, had come now'. Out of context, this has the feel of a forced sacramental image, the analogies with the Passion suggest intensifications that work like an inverted blasphemy. But it is at least in keeping with the sustained sequence on Tom's approach to the 'unknown', his almost desolated sense of momentary separateness from his newly married wife, when 'a certain terror, horror took possession of him'.

The reconciliation after significant estrangement, the fullness of encounter after two years of married life, is seen as a spiritual consummation:

> It was the entry into another circle of existence, it was the baptism to another life, it was the complete confirmation.

> At last they had thrown open the doors, each to the other, and had stood in the doorways facing each other, whilst the light flooded out from behind on to each of their faces, it was the transfiguration, glorification, the admission.

Here the cadences, the biblical parallelism, the images of door, doorway, and light, and the final doxological triad (like the earlier triad: entry, baptism, and confirmation) attempt to do for the narrative, the writing, what the word 'transfiguration' implies. The *données* of the couple's experience—the way Lydia's direct questions force Tom to acknowledge his indirect estrangement from his wife—are embodied in the preceding pages of narrative: there the scene, the transformation of feeling, is re-created in an exact dialogue. What we get in the final sequence is something else: a climax, a deliberate epitome from which all circumstantial and psychological (or 'novelistic') detail has been refined away, until the everyday experience is seen as transfigured by the 'holy language' into a personal epiphany.

III

There is a similarity, but also subtle variation, in Lawrence's portrayal of Will Brangwen's 'holy terror' in the presence of love: when he cannot think of Anna, her person, her ringing confession of love, without instantly invoking the name of God the Almighty. His inner monologue is an attempt to come to terms with an authentic experience of 'fear and trembling':

> The veils had ripped and issued him naked into the endless space, and he shuddered. The walls had thrust him out and given him a vast space to walk in. Whither, through this darkness of infinite space, was he walking blindly? Where, at the end of all the darkness, was God the Almighty still darkly seated, thrusting him on? 'I love you, Will, I love you.' He trembled with fear as the words beat in his heart again. And he dared not think of her face, of her eyes which shone, and of her strange, transfigured face. The hand of the Hidden Almighty, burning bright, had thrust out of the darkness and gripped him. He went on subject and in fear, his heart gripped and burning from the touch.

Will Brangwen can only experience, and can only account for his experience, through that awe, that trembling of the soul in the presence of the unknown, which we find in the traditional language of mysticism. It speaks of love in terms of the *mysterium tremendum,* to recall Rudolf Otto's term: 'the hushed, trembling, and speechless humility of the creature in the presence of—whom or what?' And this numinous experience comes across not only through the explicit naming of God, but also through the rhythms and verbs of inward fear: 'ripped and issued him naked into the endless space, and he shuddered. The walls had thrust him out . . . He trembled with fear as the words beat in his heart again. And he dared not think . . . thrust out of the darkness and gripped him.' The old 'holy' language is given a new authenticity; the archaic-biblical ('whither . . . God the Almighty still darkly seated'), and the inescapably everyday language ('I love you, Will, I love you') are both set in a new key. The context, the rhythm, the interaction of words, lift such phrases away from the hackneyed state which, in an old culture, threatens the explicit language of both religion and love.

We find, on the contrary, a complete fusion of the 'sacred' and the 'profane' in this language. Just as in a certain tradition of mystical writing—sometimes taking its metaphors from *The Song of Songs,* as in St. John of the Cross—erotic language alone can express the wounding approach of divine love, so for Will Brangwen only a language charged with mystical overtones can express the presence of human love.

It is necessary to stress that it is Will's language and not, in this instance, Lawrence's 'authorial voice' that we are attending to, even though Lawrence was probably the last writer in our culture who *could* use this language from his own experience and without brackets and inverted commas, psychological knowingness and critical self-consciousness. (The self-tormenting ironies of erotic/metaphysical fear in the language of *Prufrock*—'And indeed there will be time to wonder, "Do I dare?" and, "Do I dare?" '—may be set against the tradition-bound Brangwen language). Will's 'holy language' is in character: in keeping with all the details of his upbringing and sensibility, portrayed in Chapter VI, with his mole-like, self-absorbed and backward-looking intelligence, with his clinging to the church (neighbouring of his own house)

and to church crafts; with his passion for illuminations in old missals, for the unintelligible German text under a carving of Bamberg cathedral and for the mere sounds of a prayer that need not be intelligible. (One thinks of the lady in the anecdote who thanked the preacher for 'that blessed word Mesopotamia which brings me so much comfort'—a magical language like 'speaking in tongues'.) All this adds up to a circumstantial, fully embodied and tacitly distanced, portrayal of a certain type of religious aestheticism which later finds expression in the rhapsodic, Ruskin-like cadences on Will's response to Lincoln cathedral.

If there is a rough general truth in saying—with Martin Turnell [in *Modern Literature and Christian Faith,* 1961]—that 'Lawrence looked for something absolute in a realm where, in the nature of things, it could not exist', then in Tom and Will Brangwen at least we see this kind of transference (or transfiguration) at work in a precise novelistic art and in the appropriate language.

But that is not all. When Will meets his sceptically laughing antagonist in Anna, the Brangwen men's urge to transcendence becomes merely one pole in a tension, in a dialectic; and the silent monologue of the 'holy language' is turned into a grappling, externalised dialogue. 'Pouf' is the answer of Anna's earth-bound laughter to Will's vision of the Lamb (in the stained glass window of the church, which rouses Will to an ecstasy broken by Anna's disdain):

> 'Whatever it means, it's a *lamb!*' she said. 'And I like lambs too much to treat them as if they had to mean something. As for the Christmas-tree flag—no—'
>
> And again she poufed with mockery.
>
> 'It's because you don't know anything', he said violently, harshly. 'Laugh at what you know, not at what you don't know.'
>
> 'What don't I know?'
>
> 'What things mean.'
>
> 'And what does it mean?'
>
> He was reluctant to answer her. He found it difficult.
>
> '*What* does it mean?' she insisted.
>
> 'It means the triumph of the Resurrection.'
>
> She hesitated, baffled, a fear came upon her. What were these things? Something dark and powerful seemed to extend before her. Was it wonderful after all?
>
> But no—she refused it.
>
> 'Whatever it may pretend to mean, what it *is* is a silly absurd toy-lamb with a Christmas-tree flag ledged on its paw—and if it wants to mean anything else, it must look different from that.'
>
> He was in a state of violent irritation against her. Partly he was ashamed of his love for these things; he hid his passion for them. He was ashamed of the ecstasy into which he could

throw himself with these symbols. And for a few moments he hated the lamb and the mystic pictures of the Eucharist, with a violent, ashy hatred.

The couple's verbal battle is illuminated by the narratorial comment and by the context. In terms of characterisation, the overt dialogue between Will and Anna, seeming polar opposites, is cut across by the inner dialogue with its flicker of uncertainty: an unspoken half-recognition makes Anna momentarily question her denial ('Was it wonderful after all?') and makes Will recoil from his over-intense clinging to 'these symbols'. ('Partly he was ashamed . . .') So the spoken and the unspoken dialogue interact. The polemical cut-and-thrust of the former is balanced by the subtler flicker of responses in the minds of the speakers. The words uttered pull them towards hardened positions, they are limited by the limitation of words as counters for experience; the groping repetition of 'mean', in the dialogue, itself points to a need for verbal formulations likely to prove inadequate. Their experiences are less far apart than their conceptions, their language or naming: Anna's inquisitorial questioning and 'debunking', Will's catechism-dictated affirmations. (There are three other examples in the same episode). In context, Anna is rebelling not only against her husband's intense spirituality, but also against the stock symbols and phrases—in brief, the repetitions—of a religious tradition in danger of becoming fossilised. The pages immediately preceding this passage elucidate her hostility to the *ostensible* church: it can no longer fulfil anything in her, since it talks as if 'by doing this and by not doing that' her soul could be saved; while Anna, a tamer precursor of Ursula, wants to explore the potentialities of being, of her self ('her soul and her self were one and the same in her').

This whole episode foreshadows the Lincoln cathedral chapter, where the clash between Will and Anna feeds on a tension between the 'closed' and the 'open', or the monistic and pluralistic ways of encountering experience and meaning. Since this chapter has been frequently discussed, we need only recall here that Will perceives the cathedral as an all-embracing total world: in 'timeless ecstasy' and 'consummation'; while Anna wishes, as it were, to push the vault open to the sky. For her: 'the altar was barren, its lights gone out. God burned no more in that bush.' Finally, though she herself comes to feel a new reverence, Anna succeeds in changing Will's vision of the cathedral: it is only a 'world within the world' and not, as before, 'a world . . . within a chaos.' To enforce this change (or conversion, *metanoia*) Anna at one point pits the implike, winking and leering 'odd little faces carved in stone' against the supreme architectural structure. To shatter Will's total absorption, but also to loosen up, or prise open, experience from the carapace of a closed system, '*she caught at little things,* which saved her from being swept forward headlong in the tide of passion that leaps on into the Infinite . . .'.

Lawrence is here exploring, through counterpointing types of character and language, one of the great modern shifts of sensibility: the search for lived values or inwardness through catching at 'little things', in the gaps, the breaking points, of the fixed traditional (Christian) sym-

bols. The modern novel has many analogous scenes. To take only two examples from the English novel: Stephen's epiphany on the Dublin shore (in the episode of the wading girl in Joyce's *A Portrait of the Artist*), which marks the transmutation of the priest into the artist, the transference of the sacred into a new holiness of the profane; and the motif of the old woman climbing the stairs in Virginia Woolf's *Mrs. Dalloway* carries with it the significance of 'little things', an implicit revelation through the glimpsed phenomenon, set against the explicit religiousness of a Miss Kilman, who arouses only antagonism in Mrs. Dalloway. Anna's experience, and Ursula's after her, can be seen to connect with such a far-reaching shift, in and beyond the pattern of one novel.

To put it another way, the ostensible church is 'dissolved' into the invisible inner church; the fixed symbol or framed ikon gives way to the self-exploring or existential image. But in Anna this shift is uncertain and incomplete. In terms of character, her post-Christian prophetic urges are tamed by her role as mother or victorious matriarch. In terms of her religious experience, and language, she is parasitical on what is handed down by the tradition: the lamb, the de-symbolised woolly lamb, is seen in relation to, skips in the light of, the Lamb of God: the stone carvings, 'the odd little faces', are still part of the cathedral; the sky seems to be framed by the cathedral roof, which had been mentally torn open. In Chapter VI Anna repeatedly lapses, if that is the word, into religious-biblical imagery: 'Sometimes, when he [Will] stood in the doorway, his face lit up, he seemed like an Annunciation to her . . . She was subject to him as to the Angel of the Presence. She waited upon him and heard his will, and she trembled in his service'. Again, in her pregnancy: 'She walked glorified and the sound of the thrushes, of the trains in the valley, of the far-off, faint noises of the town, were her "Magnificat".' Her famous dance of exultation is a dance 'before the unknown' . . . 'lifting her hand and her body to the Unseen, to the unseen Creator who had chosen her, to whom she belonged'. And in the concluding sequence it is Anna who is given one of the three visions of the rainbow in the book—'from her Pisgah mount'.

The recurrent use of the 'holy language', by a character portrayed as being in revolt against the traditional religion, raises a difficult stylistic question. Are these uses really lapses in Anna in the sense that she has no *other* language to fall back on—only the language of transfiguration, like Tom and Will Brangwen—to mark off and hallow her points of significant experience? Or, since all the examples occur in passages of commentary, are they lapses in the 'authorial voice', in the sense that Lawrence has no other language for symbolising significant experience? If so, Anna's sensibility is not made concrete enough in these places. In either case we seem to be witnessing a parasitical use of the old language: it is to yield some of its stored-up power, in a new context of meaning. It is as if the holy language survived Anna's mockery, and spurts of 'pouf'.

IV

The fluctuations of religious experience become more central, are pushed towards a controlled excess, in the vivid portrayal of Ursula's adolescence (mainly in Chapter X). In Ursula the parental dialogue is at once intensified and internalised: the religious conflict becomes *psychomachia* or inner dialogue once more, for, at this stage, she has no outer antagonist to argue with. The school-girl's daydreams mingle with immortal longings and with the 'mirage of her reading' (Launcelot via *The Idylls of the King*); and the father's absorption in the ultimate is re-lived in a gaily fantastic vein. (It is, among other things, one of the best accounts of girlhood religiosity, comparable to the opening of Chapter 6 in *Madame Bovary*). Ursula shifts from point to point, from 'fancy' to 'imagination', from Preraphaelite reverie to the visionary 're-writing' of the Bible. In revulsion from her mother's down-to-earth, evangelical Christ ('What would Jesus do if he were in my shoes?'), she longs for the non-human, 'the shadowy Jesus with the stigmata'; then shifts (indifferent to logical or theological consistency) to a celebration of the bodily life of the risen Christ. Her romantic-erotic fantasies, her verbal self-dramatisations, are nourished by 'the non-literal application of the scriptures'; she has an intuitive sympathy with the Eastern mind, its alternatives of hyperbole or silence. And it is out of these elements that her 'texts' are woven.

The first of these texts is the playful fantasy on the 'Sons of God', a spontaneous meditation on some verses from Genesis (6: 2-4) heard in the church, which on Sundays still opened a visionary world for Ursula: 'the Voice sounded, re-echoing not from this world, as if the church itself were a shell that still spoke the language of creation'. The quoted biblical passage and Ursula's meditation—a string of racy questions and hypotheses on the time 'when the Sons of God came in unto the daughters of men'—are made to interact: the sombre primitivism of Genesis is turned into a free-wheeling personal myth in which 'the daughter' is taken to wife by one of the sons of God (preferred, in divine courtship, to the figures from lesser mythologies, Jove, Pan, Bacchus or Apollo.) Stylistically, as the biblical citation is allowed to flow into the girl's fantasy or mythic life, the effect is that of light, non-parodic pastiche:

> These came on free feet to the daughters of men, and saw they were fair, and took them to wife, so that the women conceived and brought forth men of renown. This was a genuine fate. She moved about in the essential days, when the sons of God came in unto the daughters of men.

It is a particularly well-controlled sequence, for it both dramatises a stage in Ursula's adolescence and links up with certain key themes in the novel (genesis/generation; the sacred marriage). And in a gay myth it recaptures 'the language of creation' without strain.

The meditation or parable on the risen Christ (concluding Chapter X) is more problematic, its connection with Ursula's character and the structure of the novel more precarious. It is possible to read it as a detachable passage on a key Lawrentian theme—the inversion or transvaluation of the gospel: redemptive love here and now through the life of the resurrected body—anticipating *The Man who Died* (1929). It seems to go beyond the reach of Ursula's experi-

ence and language. The lament for the incomplete resurrection turns, with a crucial pronoun-shift ('But why? Why shall *I* not rise with my body whole and perfect, shining with strong life?') into a sensuously mystical dramatic monologue spoken by the Christ-figure. It seems to burst through the confines of the novel or any of the conventions it has so far used. Although these pages seem to resemble Lawrence's non-fictional writing on religion, the little parable is subtler and more moving than are his articles—**'Resurrection'** (*Phoenix I*) or **'The Risen Lord'** (*Phoenix II*)—with their direct doctrinaire fervour, as if out of Nietzsche's *Zarathustra* crossed by a revivalist preacher. Yet there is a clear context. The **'Resurrection'** passage (less than two pages) issues straight from the celebration of 'the year of Christianity, the epic soul of mankind'. This seems to put the stress on the continued creative power of the cycle of *holy* days in the Christian year, the 'rhythm of eternity in a ragged, inconsequential life'. But there is a flaw in this rhythm, as experienced by the modern consciousness represented by Ursula, in that 'the life-drama' with its store of images was in danger of becoming mere 'mechanical action'; and the Resurrection seemed a 'small thing', overshadowed in the mind by the powerful memory of death on Good Friday. Hence the intensity of the lament and the dramatised parable:

> Alas, that a risen Christ has no place with us! Alas that the memory of the passion of Sorrow and Death and the Grave holds triumph over the pale fact of Resurrection!
>
> But why? Why shall I not rise with my body whole and perfect, shining with strong life? Why, when Mary says: Rabboni, shall I not take her in my arms and kiss her and hold her to my breast? Why is the risen body deadly and abhorrent with wounds?

It is an attempt at re-mythologising, in the language of parable (which 'exceeds' the language of the Authorised Version, though it draws on its rhythms and vocabulary). As a dramatisation of a particular experience it exceeds, but is in tune with, Ursula's experience. And formally, as a way of concluding a chapter, it looks like an extension of the lyrical 'coda' that ends Chapters III and VI (the first two 'rainbow' sequences, the former including the 'transfiguration' passage discussed). It is a dramatised version of the language of transfiguration.

The next chapter quickly establishes a contrary movement. The old religious life, which had been a 'glorious sort of play-world' for Ursula, is further diminished; the old duality of life (Sunday/everyday, sacred/profane) is broken apart. Ursula now experiences a revulsion from the Sunday world, from the numinous vision. And with this goes a kind of fatigue with the words spoken by the vision: 'words must have a weekday meaning, since words were weekday stuff. Let them speak now: let them bespeak themselves in weekday terms. *The vision should translate itself into weekday terms.*' (Ch. XI. We may contrast this with Ursula's earlier craving for the non-literal, for hyperbole.)

From this point on, a good deal in the novel is an attempt at such a 'translation', a transference of meaning and a search for new words. Much of this involves the complex relationship with Anton Skrebensky (who is 'translated' from one of the Sons of God into a sterile, will-directed lover); this relationship is not our present concern, but it should be borne in mind as the full context of Ursula's first explicitly parodic text on 'generation'. Shortly after the central 'wedding feast' ritual (where the lovers are first united and then alienated as Ursula reaches out for some state of pure being, for the sterile white moon) Ursula is again in church, looking at a passage in Genesis, her favourite book. It concerns the divine blessing on Noah and his sons: 'Be fruitful and multiply and replenish the earth' (Gen. 9). But Ursula is bored; her mental dialogue mocks all this fertility as 'merely a vulgar and stock-raising sort of business'. Then she quizzically objects to the word 'flesh' in the verses on the covenant (key symbol of *The Rainbow*) and spins another personal myth, and another 'translation':

> Ursula wished she had been a nymph. She would have laughed through the window of the ark, and flicked drops of the flood at Noah, before she drifted away to people who were less important in their Proprietor and in their Flood.

> What was God, after all? If maggots in a dead dog be but God kissing carrion, what then is not God? She was surfeited of this God. She was weary of the Ursula Brangwen who felt troubled about God. What ever God was, He was, and there was no need for her to trouble about Him. She felt she had now all licence.

The shift from the pert nymph-fantasy to Ursula's own new covenant with God (taking in the 'mad' speculative language of Hamlet on 'God kissing carrion') is characteristic. It also marks a point in the novel where Ursula's re-valuation of her religious experience, in terms of myth and language, is taken to a new turning point: the parody, the serio-comic speculations are part of the 'licence' to convert the traditional religion into a personal experience and language.

v

At this point the quest for new religious values and words seems to fade away from the centre of the book. Or, to be more precise, the symbiotic interaction between the traditional and the new gets disconnected. It gives way, for example, to the exploration of 'darkness' (Ursula's new vision of 'the glimmer of dark movement just out of range'); to the moon-possessed 'yearning for something unknown . . . a passion for something she knew not what'; to the barely conscious encounter with the demonic (Ch. XV). Perhaps the 'strange gods' spring from there; certainly, the language becomes looser, something like a 'symphonic' poem in prose, no longer controlled by the traditional images. But the rest of the book is, as we saw, a more patient religious novel: there is a gradual tilting of Judeo-Christianity, and its old 'language of creation', in a new direction.

In one of the final paragraphs of the novel we find this explicit statement:

> In everything she [Ursula] saw she grasped and

groped to find the creation of the living God, instead of the old, hard barren form of bygone living. Sometimes great terror possessed her. Sometimes she lost touch, she lost her feeling, she could only know the old horror of the husk which bound in her and all mankind.

This seems to point back, from Ursula's fevered search, to the whole cycle of 'groping' across three generations: Tom Brangwen's experience of marriage in terms of the old 'holy language'; Will's further intensities of experience and language, in a more isolated mysticism, questioned and mocked by a dialogue with Anna; and Ursula's spiritual play-world that re-creates the 'holy' figures and words/in bold new frames of parable and parody. This pattern corresponds to what Lawrence later explicitly argued for: the re-living of the religious images and 'the phrases that have haunted us all our lives' in terms of a personal and many-layered meaning. The symbolic figures are to lead, through their 'dramatic movement' to 'a release of the imagination into some new sort of world': and the language is *given*, it has a 'power of echoing and re-echoing in my unconscious mind'. But the pattern in the novel is less 'neat'; it traces a more gradual groping through experiences that precede formulation. All the same, it is a pattern that links up with a general culture shift from 'dogma' to 'experience', from ikon or fixed symbol to image—something central in the modern consciousness and in modern literature.

Mark Kinkead-Weekes   (essay date 1986)

SOURCE: "The Marriage of Opposites in *The Rainbow*," in *D. H. Lawrence: Centenary Essays*, edited by Mara Kalnins, Bristol Classical Press, 1986, pp. 21-39.

[*In the following essay, Kinkead-Weekes examines the thematic movement of opposing forces toward conflict and possible synthesis in* The Rainbow.]

The opening chapter of *The Rainbow* is, rather pointedly, divided into two: a first section beginning with a timeless world; a second section beginning with a date. This suggests two very different ways of looking at the novel. From one angle, the opening pages show us human life and consciousness in basic forms, against a background untroubled by historical process and social chance. We begin, not with individual personalities, but with archetypal Men and Women, in a timeless Nature. If we then ask what it is that is basic in the life and consciousness of the Brangwens, framing their land on the border of Derbyshire and Nottinghamshire, what is eternally and universally so, we find that Lawrence is developing a language we can use to understand all the individual men and women and all the particular relationships in his three generations. From this point of view we can approach the stories of Tom and Lydia, of Anna and Will, of Ursula and Skrebensky, as though they were undated pictures on the same subject, hung side by side for us to compare and contrast, in order to grasp their underlying significance. But, on the other hand, as soon as we move into the second section of the opening chapter, we are confronted with that date, 1840, and a marked change in the social environment which affects the everyday life of the Brangwens, the building of a canal across their land. From this moment *The Rainbow* begins also to be a social history, seriously concerned to trace major changes in English life from 1840 to 1905. From this angle the structure of the novel looks quite different. Now we must consider a progressive development in time, a gradual movement into history, and ask how each generation of the Brangwens is affected by the gathering pace of social change. We become aware of industrialism and urbanisation; of the spread of education after the 1870 Act; of the gradual emancipation of women; of the growth of rational scepticism and the decline of religious faith. From one point of view the three generations of Brangwens reorchestrate the same basic conflicts in human consciousness and relationships, so that we can understand them better. From the other point of view each generation is in a different position because of the history of their society, and we have to measure the effects of change.

Most accounts of the novel concentrate on the archetypal, ahistorical view because that is where Lawrence is most original, and where consequently it has taken longest to learn how to read him, though by following his lead we do discover a basic language which will help to understand and compare the complex individuals and relations that come later. But I want to argue that the historical view is also vitally important—and I'll come back to it.

What we see first, then, is (for Lawrence) true of human beings anywhere and any time. We begin not with individual characters, but with Men and Women in a timeless Nature. There is the flat, rich earth, which the eye moves across, binding it into a unified landscape in which man is at one with nature. There is also however the road, the village, the church tower on the hill, calling the eye up, out, and beyond—what the eighteenth century artist would have called a 'prospect'—a fingerpost pointing to the city, another world of civilisation, intellect and art, the fulfilment of individuality. Between them is the human dwelling, facing both ways. By exploring and opposing the visions of the Men of the Landscape and the Women of the Prospect, we discover two opposite impulses at work below the surface of personality, two kinds of consciousness that we must grasp before we can talk of individual 'character'.

The Brangwen Men do not merely live 'on' the rich earth, they are at one with it, and the charged poetic language tries to realise imaginatively what this involves and means. We are made to experience in these Men what they know in their own emotions, bodies and blood: the variable weather of the skies, the intercourse between the heavens and earth, the seasonal change from Spring to Summer to Autumn to Winter that is the rhythm of the life of all created nature. The life of Man and the life of Nature, seen in this way, are each reflected in the other. It hardly matters from which angle you choose to look; what you see is the same unified existence. In Man, as in Nature, the sap rises, the wave of natural fertility throws the seed forward and leaves the new-born on the earth. The feel of the soil to man at ploughing time and at reaping time is the responsiveness of the lover and the unresponsiveness of the woman awaiting her delivery. We become aware of the

earth enacting a human process and of the human being enacting an earthly process. The body and blood of man is both entered by and participates in the lustre of plants and the pulse and energy of animals. His life is at one with the life of the sky, the earth, the beasts of the field, and its vegetation. He uses the world of nature but he is also surcharged with its living, its rhythms of fertility, of harvest, of accumulation and inertia, 'warmth and generating, pain and death'. As our eyes move across the landscape, peopled with human figures, what we see is unity; a togetherness of man with the whole of created nature, done in us as we read, in concrete and rhythmic language.

Such a life is rich and vital—yet the Brangwen Women make us aware of the opposite impulse towards a radically different kind of human consciousness. To them the intercourse of man and nature is blind, dazed with looking 'towards the source of generation'. The key words for the Women of the Prospect are 'outwards', 'towards' that which lies 'beyond'. The front door of the house opens onto the road, up the hill, beyond the village to the City, to Civilisation, the World of Nations. The Women are 'aware of the lips and the mind of the world speaking and giving utterance, they heard the sound in the distance, and they strained to listen'. What is 'beyond' is the life of the mind, of articulate awareness, which not only reflects being but can reflect on it, sharpen it into definition and differentiation, comprehend and utter it in language. What is 'beyond' is also a new freedom and scope for the individual. The women see (even, half-comically in the Vicar, the Squire's Lady, the Local MP) a range of experience, an education of the mind, enabling it to lay hold of the unknown and store up knowledge. Such people have acquired definition as individuals; their children are already marked out from the farm-children, distinctive. And they have a new kind of power and mastery. They do not merely exist in unity with their environment, but are capable of acting on it, shaping and dominating it. Finally this life of mental discovery and individuality can liberate the imagination and become articulate utterance. The voyage of exploration, man's power to traverse the beyond and unknown, can become epic art like the *Odyssey*. Yet we are made aware too, that if this impulse can raise human existence to new freedom, scope and conquest, it is also without the stability of the natural life and can fall below it. (In the village, the Squire is a drunk with a scandalous brother; in the epic, Odysseus has to reckon with Circe and her crew of men degraded below the animals, as well as with the excitements and discoveries of the beyond.)

The impulse of the Women therefore reveals itself as the polar opposite to the impulse of the Men. Where one is a world of being, the other is a world of knowing and acting upon. Where one is a unity with all Nature, the other is a process of separation and distinction. One is a life of the flesh, the other a life of thought and utterance. In one, man is conscious of himself only in togetherness with Nature; in the other he becomes conscious of himself as individual defining and differentiating himself against what is not-him, other. One is permanent and stable; the other holds in change a threat as well as a promise.

There is of course a danger, talking so, that one will make this basic language seem abstract and theoretic, some kind of skeleton key—whereas it is the strength of the novel's opening that it is done so naturally and concretely. And one must not talk too glibly of 'Men' and 'Women'. It very soon becomes clear that we are not meant to think of male and female in any simply differentiated way—we shall soon find both impulses, or forces, operating in everyone of either sex, though in differing proportions. Nor can there be any question of choice or preference: it seems self-evident that life at either extreme would be life impoverished. Rather we are to see all human beings as subject to the opposite pulls of these impulses or kinds of consciousness, below the surface of particular character or deliberate choice. How the conflict is resolved will depend upon differing personalities and relationships and the pressure of different social situations. But by isolating, at first, his basic vision from the complications of individual character and social history, Lawrence seeks to clarify the nature of the opposition in itself. The opening section thus provides a kind of prelude, a pattern of chords announcing major themes, a basic language which we must apply to the novel as a whole.

When we look, then, at the betrothal of Tom Brangwen and Lydia Lensky in the first story, we are able to see why it is both very matter-of-fact and very strange. When Tom caught slight of the woman in black on the road outside Cossethay, the recognition was instantaneous: 'That's her, he said involuntarily'. Everything else seems to follow as of course: the awareness 'almost without thinking', when the time has come to ask her; the simplicity of ' "What's to do? . . . Bit of courtin', like" '; the straightforward words ' "I came up", he said, speaking curiously matter of fact and level, "to ask if you'd marry me" . . . "No, I don't know" . . . "Yes I want to", she said impersonally . . ." ' But the very simplicity—that is nearly all that is said—pinpoints the strangeness: involuntary, impersonal, without knowledge. They do not respond to each other's personality, about which they know nothing. They are utter strangers, emphasized by the fact that she is a Polish refugee. They seem impelled towards each other by forces well below the level of choice, or even what we would normally understand by sexuality, though that will come. What we seem to be watching is the inevitable, necessary, and therefore matter-of-fact impulse of one 'pole' toward its opposite, because it is opposite; happening at a level which neither the words nor the thoughts of the two people can reach, and that is beyond choice. We have to think in terms of forces impelling men and women to seek the marriage of opposites.

So in the darkness, where storm clouds scud before a great wind and the trees drum and whistle, the black-clad figure confronts the otherworld, lit-up, fire-warmed, beyond the separating glass of the window. Behind him is the unitary world of nature; behind her—the foreign woman, the unintelligible song, the alien child—lie London and Warsaw, politics and revolution, the world beyond the church tower on the hill. But though we are talking of the impersonal attraction of opposites, a kind of natural law, we are now also looking at this man, and that woman, who have individual names and histories. And by this stage we know

enough to see that there are conflicts within them, too, which have left them dissatisfied with themselves and their lives, unfulfilled, displaced. So as we watch the scene, we not only see the man from the darkness, the woman in the light; we see also the fragile yellow flowers in his hand, and the darkness in the eyes of the woman and the child. The marriage will have to resolve oppositions within them, as well as between them. And as the opposites meet, the threshold is crossed, the challenge is issued and accepted, we see that for Lawrence the marriage of opposites involves a kind of death of the self, and a kind of rebirth. As Tom and Lydia kiss, there is a self-obliteration, an oblivion, a sinking into darkness. This is painful, a 'blenched agony'; for it is difficult to let go of the self, to commit it to a kind of extinction at the hands of the 'other'. Yet the darkness turns out to be like a womb, and what is born is blazing light, a world freshly created, a whole newness of life. It is only a kiss, but it contains for the Lawrence of 1915 the essence of marriage and of sexual relationship: the committal of opposites to mutual transformation; the loss of the self in order to find it again more fully than before.

Yet this is a continuous process, which is never finished or accomplished. Indeed, to go on talking merely in the terms I have used is not nearly enough, because what authenticates them is the study of a marriage in everyday and concrete realism, and as a process in time: the difficulties of relationship, the tensions over Lydia's child and at the time of her pregnancy, the credible and continuous fluctuation between conflict and harmony. Lawrence's determination to deal with these, in detail and complexity, saves his story from ever becoming merely symbolic or diagrammatic. I only wish I could go into detail—but we can at least notice the conditions for success. Tom and Lydia always respect the otherness of each other, and of little Anna. There is conflict, but no victory or defeat, dominance or subservience, and because of this the conflict is creative. They are able to abandon themselves to each other, but never to merge or absorb; rather they pass through the crucible of self-extinction like phoenixes, 'dying' to their old selves in order to be reborn more fully. In another set of images we approach the novel's title, and its continual biblical reference. The man and the woman, pillars of fire and cloud, are each firmly grounded on their own base, opposite each other. Each springs both towards and against the other, with its own force. But because neither overbears, the opposite forces pass right through each other, and the result is an arch like a rainbow. They both marry, and fulfil, their separate impulses. But the arch is also a doorway to the unknown and the beyond; the lovers become thresholds for each other, though which each can pass from exile and the wilderness into the undiscovered beyond themselves, the Promised Land. Moreover the marriage of opposites, remaining distinct when they have passed through each other, creates freedom for man, woman, and child, respecting their continuing otherness. The echoing of the Bible by a writer who called himself 'a passionately religious man' insists that we see marriage as a religious mystery: the one way he knows and trusts in which man and woman can participate in the fundamental creative power which men call 'God'; can experience Genesis and Exodus, the Promises of new life, the realities of Death and Resurrection, in their own daily lives; can build, not in stone or ark but in human relationship, a house for the Lord to dwell in.

There is also, however, a limiting judgement to be made: an arch may be like a rainbow, the basic form, but it doesn't marry the height of heaven with the breadth of earth. In some ways Tom and Lydia remain personally unfulfilled despite the success of their marriage; and there are areas of human potential which stay barricaded away from them, as it were, beyond the canal. When that canal bursts, Tom is drowned. It is the reverse of the Flood in the Bible: Noah perishes; yet it is not a wicked world that is inundated, but a beautiful, if limited one. And Tom has laid hold of eternity, albeit in a primitive dispensation.

With the second generation, we embark on a process of comparison, looking on this picture and on that. The scene corresponding to the betrothal of Tom and Lydia is the coming together of Anna and Will in the moonlit cornfield, stacking the sheaves; and we need to ask both what is like Tom and Lydia, and what is different. Once again the two human figures move between a pull toward the darkness and an opposing pull toward the brilliant defining moon. Again they seem to obey forces that operate below personality, choice, or even physical passion. Will out of darkness, Anna drenched in moonlight, set towards each other, and away, with a deep natural rhythm, like tides beneath the moon. The stacking of dewy corntresses, hissing together like water, is rich with associations of fertility, harvest, the creative processes of nature. The human beings are at one with this, feeling its rhythms, tidally flowing towards each other. Yet there is also the opposite and equally natural and tidelike rhythm of separation. But they meet as two 'others', each with its own motion; and they work together to make something out of nature beyond themselves. There is a change from being to doing: a weaving, combining, structuring. It is important to notice how Lawrence's style itself taps what is anterior to 'character' and cannot be articulately conscious in the people concerned. The prose can be seen to be working not only in suggestive symbol (in this wordless relationship) but in *rhythms* which themselves mime, and create, the forces at work. Gradually the beat of separate actions approaching and receding, the short sentences, modulate into longer and cumulative swellings and turning, until the meeting is achieved. And as the two 'others' finally come together, we are very much aware of the wonder and mystery of the marriage of opposites both within and between them:

> All the moonlight upon her, all the darkness within her. All the night in his arms, darkness and shine . . . all the mystery to be entered, all the discovery to be made. Trembling with keen triumph, his heart was white as a star as he drove his kisses nearer.

We reach that moment, incandescence within darkness, when the doorway seems about to open into a mysterious dimension beyond, a kind of death and rebirth.

But though the scene re-enacts Tom and Lydia, the comparison alerts us to a sharp sense of anticlimax and loss. Throughout the coming together there has sounded a note

of strain, on both sides. There is a tendency in Anna to hold back, resisting the natural movement toward her lover, and its consequences. We have seen this resistance from her earliest childhood—the obverse of the qualities that made her a 'little princess': the assured individuality, self-awareness and wary intelligence, so much greater than her mother's. She is reluctant to meet Will, or give up herself to go through him, beyond; she insists on pulling him out of the kiss into awareness. She shortcircuits the process to which Tom and Lydia were able to abandon themselves. And Will's name is also resonant, though this is far removed from allegory. More and more clearly we become aware of 'a low, deep-sounding will in him', vibrating low at first, but beginning, in the prose itself, to drum 'persistently, darkly', till 'it drowned everything else'. When they meet, his voice is 'twanging and insistent'. The conflict of opposites has a new tone, a struggle to withhold the self or dominate the other, which the relationship between Tom and Lydia had not. The cornstacking, then, prepares us for a developing relationship which will partly fail to achieve the marriage of opposites, and in which the woman eventually conquers.

Yet again, looking at the quality of the long chapter 'Anna Victrix', which traces this process, I must emphasise again that I have only pointed to the basic paradigm of the relation of Anna and Will. What Lawrence then does is to authenticate, and develop, and concretise it in convincing detail, in the process of their honeymoon, their marriage, their parenthood. The timeless essence is interfused with the realistic fluctuation of day-to-day. But we now have, also, to reckon with that other dimension: the historical. We can still use the 'Old Testament' terms to show the 'essential' difference between Tom and Lydia, and Anna and Will. Having conquered, Anna builds a house for herself, rich in possession; but she does not open the door of the promised land for her husband, and cannot enter herself. Because of their vital connection she remains in sight of it, on Mount Pisgah; her house opens under the sign of the rainbow and is filled with the sound of journeying; but Anna and Will do not build the arch or explore the space beyond the threshold as fully as Tom and Lydia had done, despite their limitations. And yet . . . though the achievement is less, the potential strikes one as a great deal more. Anna and Will have wider horizons, and a greater zenith, because they are of the second generation. There are whole new dimensions of life in their story, and new tensions: religion and art, faith and scepticism, education and emancipation, the life of the intellect and the life of the spirit. Perhaps we could say that there is more to marry in Anna and Will, though we would have to say also that the new dimensions of life imply new dimensions of conflict, and make coming together more difficult. This is the point of that great scene in Lincoln Cathedral. To try to imagine Tom and Lydia in such a context is to grasp how much more defined and articulate in consciousness Will and Anna have become; and how much more complex our awareness of what is at stake for them now has to be. The Cathedral, for Will's passionate religious sensibility, is already a union of opposites in which the soul can find consummation. For Anna's rational scepticism, there must be greater multiplicity and separateness, more individualism, greater freedom and space. And the conflict has become more aware, beginning to be articulate, issuing in argument. Still there can be no taking sides for Lawrence. Both lovers have half a truth; but their conflict is not creative, for they do not marry their oppositions and go through, beyond. They seek to impose themselves upon each other, destructively. The greater intensity, the wider scope, the richer potential, not only make the marriage of such opposites more difficult, but offer greater possibilities of damage and partiality. And people are now not only seen as themselves and in their personal relations, but as articulations of the growth of consciousness in history. For Will and Anna inherit a new England born of the industrial revolution and the Education Act of 1870. Will works as a lacedesigner in a world of factories, mines and railways. But his inner life, that passion for art and religion, is fuelled by Ruskin and the Gothic revival; and he will go up in the world as the Arts and Crafts movement is taken up by the new Nottinghamshire Education Department. The family move to Beldover is part of the increasing speed of urbanisation. And Anna has had a kind of education and a degree of intellectual emancipation unknown to her mother. As they quarrel in the Cathedral, we are aware of them as people of a new world, as well as variations of an archetypal challenge.

I hope I've suggested something of the kind of reading *The Rainbow* demands. By learning the 'basic' language of the marriage of opposites, one tries to understand Tom and Lydia, and Anna and Will, and to find ways of grasping the nature of their relationships in *essence*. One has also to understand their *personal histories*, as relationships change and settle, through the passage of time. By then bringing to bear the sweep of *social history* into an increasingly complex definition of personality, one sees how what Lawrence meant by marriage becomes both richer in potential, and more difficult to achieve. One could then hope to go on to the most complex story of all, the story of Ursula Brangwen, using all we have learnt, and developing it still further both personally, in her affairs with Anton Skrebensky, and also in relation to the greater multitude of possibilities her world offers her.

But this time I'd like to reverse the angles, and begin with the historical dimension, which I have rather neglected. It is surprising how elaborate and careful the novel's chronology turns out to be, how much social detail there is, and how naturally one finds one has taken in, simply by living through them imaginatively, the major changes in the nineteenth century that would affect a middle-class Midlands family like the Brangwens. Beginning with that timeless rural landscape, and ending with Ursula looking out at the hideous new housing that has spread across it, we can focus the results of industrialism and urbanisation. The sprawling ugliness without communal centre shows both the atrophy of the impulse to togetherness, among men and with nature, and the corresponding hypertrophy of the rational intellect. Lawrence is also appalled by the possibility of work-people losing individuality and giving themselves over to mechanical systems, becoming 'instrumental' like John Smith, Loader—or Tom Brangwen Jr., Mine-Manager. But we also, and crucially, see new prosperity and opportunity for the middle-class. The coming of canals and railways has opened new markets for coal

and new industrial possibilities. Alfred Brangwen and his son are drawn into the lace factory; but the rapid expansion of Ilkeston makes the farming Brangwens so prosperous that Tom becomes squire-like, and buys an education for his children that puts them almost on the social level of the sons of the Hall. *The Rainbow* has a sharp eye for the mobilities and discriminations of a rapidly changing society; we can see exactly how and why Tom's sons are gentlemen but the young Will is not.

It was of course the spread of education after the great Act of 1870 that allowed Bert Lawrence, miner's son, to become the D.H. Lawrence we know. Tom Brangwen was not really educable, and Will is largely self-educated, but Tom Jr. goes to Nottingham High School, an ancient foundation, and then to what must be the Royal School of Mines which became Imperial College under Thomas Huxley. Lydia had a governess, but Anna becomes one of the first pupils of the Nottingham High School for Girls, only the sixth to be founded by the Girls Public Day School Trust—but unfortunately at such an early stage that it is still like a young ladies' seminary. But in Ursula's time it has become an established girls' grammar school leading to London matriculation, qualification as a teacher, and university entrance. (On the other hand, the seamier side of universal education is also visible in Brinsley Street School, where compulsory attendance up to Standard Five and the raising of the school-leaving age have caused desperate overcrowding—hence those three classes of over fifty each, being taught in the same 'great room' with only glass partitions between.)

The 'widening circles' of the new England reveal greater human potential, the liberation of imagination, art and intellect, and a new personal freedom—especially for women. We see great strides in emancipation and the start of the suffragettes. Yet the new dimension of self-awareness may bring new difficulty in human relations. In a sentence, of Ursula: 'She was aware now . . . And so, it was more difficult to come to him.' Education and emancipation do not seem to bring fulfilment to the 'new women' in the novel; not to Winifred Inger who, for all her liberating influence on Ursula, turns out to be a compromised Diana, only half-formed, settling for a domesticity within a system, both of which she had affected to despise; nor for Maggie Schofield, who has had to divide herself in two in order to succeed in the man's world. Increased self-awareness in Anna, and still more in Ursula, makes them less ready to abandon self in relationship, and fosters a destructive self assertion.

In Ursula's 'liberated' experience, moreover, both school and university are like factories, concerned with system, power, commodity. When knowledge becomes material, it goes dead. In reaction against the scientific materialism of her biology teacher, Ursula glimpses the mystery of living things, the strange organic being of the cell under her microscope. Lawrence is deeply concerned, not by the decay of church religion (which we can watch happening) but by the loss of the religious sense itself, and its replacement by scientific rationalism or anthropological 'comparative religion'. *The Rainbow* at its deepest is indeed a kind of bible, recalling its readers to a religious sense of the world against the current of the nineteenth and early twentieth century. This has nothing to do with creeds or churches of course; as we have seen, human relationship becomes the only true church, and Lawrence rejects Christianity insofar as it has become a religion of death, denial of the body, and aspiration toward a heavenly other world. But he reinterprets the Bible so that the central stories of the Old and the New Testament can be seen to recur in every generation. While portraying the historical decline of religion, *The Rainbow* seeks also to recover a new language for 'God' out of the old scriptures.

The Rainbow at its deepest is indeed a kind of bible, recalling its readers to a religious sense of the world against the current of the nineteenth and early twentieth century.

—Mark Kinkead-Weekes

So the more we go into these socio-historical perspectives, the clearer it becomes that we cannot talk merely in terms of the effects of industrialism and urbanisation, education and emancipation, rational scepticism and the decline of religion, upon the lives and consciousness of the 'characters' in the novel. For Lawrence, one can understand neither 'history' nor 'character' truly without a much more deep-structural sense of the forces ultimately at work in the universe, and within the human being. History must be seen as sacred, governed by primal energies whose marriage produces Genesis, the Promised Land, Resurrection; and whose disjunction the destructiveness of the Cities of the Plain, the Exile, and the burning fiery furnace. And a true sense of 'character' required a revolution in the novel, a conception of human consciousness quite different from the picture of man-in-society that we get in nineteenth century fiction—which was why *The Rainbow* was so difficult for Lawrence to write, and so little understood by its first readers. After his third attempt, Lawrence wrote to his then publisher Edward Garnett on 5 June 1914: 'You mustn't look in my novel for the old stable ego of the character. There is another ego, according to whose action the individual is unrecognisable, and passes through, as it were, allotropic states which it needs a deeper sense than any we've been used to exercise, to discover are states of the same single radically-unchanged element. (Like as diamond and coal are the same pure single element of carbon . . .)'. There are two kinds of objection here. First, Lawrence is wishing to transcend the old stable *ego* of the nineteenth century novelist (and historian, and philosopher): the view of man as a coherent personality, analysable in terms of his choices. He wants to pierce beyond motivated behaviour, beyond 'thoughts' or even 'feelings' that a man might be aware of, to get to his elemental being—the part of the iceberg that is hidden below the surface. Hence that basic language of the beginning, the opposite impulses that relate man both to the whole physical

universe and to his being-in-himself. This is the 'carbon' which is anterior to any particular personality or 'character' and which, in its peculiar state of oppositions, is there in all phases of an individual person. So much has become clear in our experience of the first and second generation: how Lawrence has gone deeper below the surface than the novel had done before. But with Ursula particularly, one sees that Lawrence is just as opposed to the old *stable* ego; that he wants to capture a sense of the human being as continually fluctuating and changeful because of the oppositions within itself. This will be clearer when we see how many different forms Ursula, the most complex organism of all, throws herself into without ever ceasing to be Ursula. So the iceberg is not a good metaphor—Lawrence wants not only to go deeper under the surface, but also to capture being in a continuous state of transformation, in and out of the crucible of conflict, crystallising in different forms under different conditions, but always elementally the same. Which in turn means that we should not think of Lawrence as merely trying to tap the *un*conscious; for the constant dialectic and change is always between being and knowing in all his people, and that is the ground of creative growth. Moreover it would be false to describe even the Brangwen Men at the beginning as unconscious, if by that one meant 'having no consciousness'. They could not put their experience into words or become articulately aware of it in thought; but they have a richly real and vital sense of themselves and of their life-in-nature, a kind of consciousness opposed to the defining analysing kind. So there are in Lawrence different kinds of consciousness, which antedate 'character' and for which the author must find the language. He must find it, since it involves a kind of penetration, and a kind of flux, only part of which his characters could put into words. Lawrence is of course also an effective dramatist, and uses drama in *The Rainbow* to authenticate and develop what he has discovered, yet drama depends on what people can *say,* and that is not nearly enough. The risk is that he will analyse his people too abstractly, too conceptually, and above all too insistently, telling us what to think—and alas, he does not always avoid it, though I do not think the fault shows in the scenes I've dealt with. For there he seems to have found ways of using language with an intensely exploratory imagination that embodies the impulses of life, and doesn't merely tell us about them. He uses ordinary experience, but makes it richly suggestive; not in the *symboliste* way which makes the art world separate from life, but in a way which can capture a mysterious inner vitality, seeing deeper into concrete experience. And he has learnt to write rhythmically, so that the movements of the propose itself seem to enact in us, as we read, a process-in-time going on in his people. Moreover he came to think of his art, too, as a marriage of opposites: a continuous process of capturing being, which simply is, and trying to make known what had been captured; a systole and diastole between what is palpably there and what is understood; but always in process, always moving on beyond.

Let me finally try to illustrate all this in an outline—necessarily skeletal I fear—of the Ursula story, but leading up to what I think is the most impressive scene of all, gathering the whole book together: the mysterious, disturbing and challenging final episode, where Ursula is terrified by the horses. What we are made to realise about Ursula from the start is that she embodies all the opposites of her family, at peak intensity, and in greater awareness and self-consciousness. She is intensely visionary and intensely sceptical, spiritual and fleshly, arrogant and unfixed, emancipated and primitive, and it is her fate (because of her world) to be aware of herself in all these aspects. Her world also allows her a new freedom and independence that her mother never had, to choose for herself. We watch her continuously trying to resolve her contradictions by pursuing one element of herself to the exclusion of others, but never finding a way of marrying them: 'always the shining doorway was a gate into another ugly yard, dirty and active and dead'. She fluctuates, 'allotropically', from possibility to possibility: a female, lesbian relationship with Winifred Inger; the 'male' world of power and dominance in Brinsley Street School: the purely physical life of the five senses with Andrew Schofield; the life of pure mind at Nottingham University. But none can satisfy or fulfil her because all are partial, and reductive of her complex being. In the three crises of her love-affair with Anton Skrebensky—so different in fact, that they are more safely thought of as different relationships—we see further re-orchestrations of the betrothal of her grandparents, and the coming together of her parents in the cornfield. We measure the increasing difficulty of the marriage of opposites, and the increasing destructiveness that results from the assertion of only one part of the self. When the young lovers dance at a wedding, between the fires and lanterns and the dark where cornstacks loom under a brilliant moon, the dance becomes a destructive context for dominance in which Ursula, like her mother, is Victrix, in self-assertion. When Skrebensky returns from Africa in 1905, some years after the South African War, Ursula is reacting against the university and the life of mind. This time they both want, and achieve, a physical fulfilment that is also a superb consummation—of a sort, but it is a meeting in pure darkness, a mating of only the dark sides of themselves. Then, in inevitable reaction again, the terrible scene on the beach shows that she cannot be satisfied while her infinitely aspiring, aware, bright side is denied. Under an incandescent moon, beside brilliant water, she tries to force the polar opposite of the dark consummation, a coming-together in intense awareness, and succeeds only in destroying, like a harpy. Finally she tries to settle for simple domesticity, but that is reducing herself still more. She has tried all the reductive ways. Only the inclusive one, the marriage of opposites remains, and Lawrence faces her with it at the end.

The encounter with the huge horses confronts the girl, so ready now to deny the elemental forces in herself, with the powerful presence of those forces and their eternal challenge. The sophisticated, highly educated, self-conscious twentieth century girl of the Prospect and the City, is faced with the unitary landscape of nature: the big wind through which her grandfather walked, the earth with its looming trees, the teeming rain, the power of the animal world that Tom so confidently mastered, the fire from their nostrils. But the summons is not merely to the elemental: it is, as always, to the marriage of opposites. The bird-soul of the aspiring girl comes to the hall of Warriors, attesting the eternity of conflict; but she searches also for

a lost stability, beyond conflict and flux. When she looks at the horses she becomes:

> aware of their breasts gripped, clenched narrow in a hold that never relaxed, she was aware of their red nostrils flaming with long endurance, and of their haunches, so rounded, so massive, pressing, pressing, pressing to burst the grip upon their breasts, pressing forever till they went mad, running against the walls of time and never bursting free. Their great haunches were smoothed and darkened with rain. But the darkness and wetness or rain could not put out the hard, urgent, massive fire that was locked within these flanks, never, never.

What the elemental world reveals, again, is the clash of opposites in all created things. The horses are an intensity of conflicting forces that cannot be denied or reduced and must not be, in Ursula. Always the rain tries to put the fire out. Always the fire must remain unquenched, battling against the rain. It is the opposed energies that make the horses what they are, give them their looming archetypal power. But the horses are also gripped, clenched, unfinished. Their oppositions are trying to get free. And if the fire could pass right through the rain and the rain right through the fire there would be . . . a Rainbow. So the horses re-state, both to Ursula and to us, the whole challenge of the marriage of opposites.

But, like all Lawrence's best scenes, the real significance lies not in symbol but in process, in what happens. If we ask, not merely 'what are the horses?' but 'what happens to Ursula?', we see her confronting the challenge, *and failing to meet it*. The challenge, as ever, is to meet the Other and pass through into the beyond. But we know that this must mean a marriage of opposites in oneself that is like a death, and a rebirth. In the first movement of the scene Ursula does succeed in going through, bursting the barrier of the Other; but only by walking with bent head, refusing to look, refusing to think, refusing to know. She merely follows her feet, blindly and instinctively; and she comes through the crucible where her nerves and veins 'ran hot, ran white hot, they must fuse, and she must die'. This is the condition of Tom and Lydia, the old dispensation, unaware. But Ursula is a modern, twentieth century woman, and in the act of bursting through she is forced to know. (The repetition of the words know, and aware, marks the crucial point.) Continually, in Ursula's story, it is her awareness of her intensities that has made her predicament the hardest of all in the novel. So it proves here. As she and the horses pass and repass she is forced to know them. As they work themselves up for a climactic confrontation she will have, this time, to go through in full awareness. And she cannot do it. She is terrified. Her limbs turn to water. She climbs a tree and collapses on the other side of the hedge. Instead of going through, she lapses into the element of water alone, becomes unconscious, inert, unchanging, unchangeable, like a stone at the bottom of a stream. This is her 'Flood'. She fails, and failing, she nearly dies literally, as well as inwardly.

On the physical and psychological level this is perfectly explicable. She is pregnant, she has been terrified and in shock, and she miscarries. But on a deeper level Lawrence is suggesting that Ursula has failed, not only because of the inadequacies of Skrebensky, but also because she herself has seemed incapable of the marriage of opposites. As she stumbles along the road and up the hill she is a bitterly ironic commentary on the aspirations of the Brangwen women at the beginning. Yet in her illness she is able to diagnose what has gone wrong. All her efforts to attach herself to life, all her relationships, have been unreal entanglements forced by her will. She has to 'die' to her own self-assertion, to burst all the 'rind' of false relations and unrealities within which her egotism has enclosed her, to trust herself to the elemental forces in life as the naked kernel of a nut does when it bursts its hard covering, before a creative self can be born. The world she is then reborn into, as she recovers, is the mysterious work of divine creation, and she lands on its boundary after crossing chaos. It is an 'undiscovered land', where she recognises only 'a fresh glow of light and inscrutable trees going up from the earth like smoke'—as in the Book of Genesis. She is only on the outmost perimeter, but she is there, on the First Day of her new creation. She must no longer try to manipulate herself, or others, or relationships. She must wait for the coming of a Son of God, from the infinite and eternal to which she now belongs, 'within the scope of that vaster power in which she rested at last.' The Rainbow is not achieved in the novel; the story of how Ursula found her Son of God has to wait for **Women in Love**. But as Ursula sees the sign in the sky at the end it remains covenanted, promised despite tragedy and failure, like the one in the Bible. One may perhaps feel that the promise isn't the logical outcome of the story; that it is Lawrence's own revolutionary optimism breaking through in the language of assertion. But the one in the Bible was gratuitous too, and the promise is no more unconditional here than there. The vision is only seen by the reborn soul that has 'died' to its old self, in the Flood.

Consciousness in time, in flux, in history, must always, for Lawrence, be married to, and transfigured by, consciousness of the timeless, the archetypal and eternal—or man will perish from an inadequate conception of his nature and his world.

FURTHER READING

Adam, Ian. "Lawrence's Anti-Symbol: The Ending of *The Rainbow*." *Journal of Narrative Technique* 3, No. 2 (May 1973): 77-84.
    Presents a meta-symbolic reading of the horse scene at the close of *The Rainbow*.

Adelman, Gary. *Snow of Fire: Symbolic Meaning in 'The Rainbow' and 'Women in Love.'* New York: Garland Publishing, Inc., 1991, 140 p.
    Defines a "psychology of industrialism . . . and traces its central position in the symbolic meaning of *The Rainbow* and *Women in Love*."

Aldington, Richard. Introduction to *The Rainbow*, by D. H. Lawrence, pp. vii-xi. London: Heinemann, 1955.

Briefly recaps the composition and early publication history of *The Rainbow*.

Balbert, Peter. *D. H. Lawrence and the Psychology of Rhythm: The Meaning of Form in 'The Rainbow.'* The Hague: Mouton, 1974, 130 p.
    Argues that "the rhythmic arrangement of phrases, character gradations, incidents, expanding and fixed symbols, and interweaving themes unifies and intensifies the meaning of life that Lawrence wishes to convey" in *The Rainbow*.

———. " 'Logic of the Soul': Prothalamic Pattern in *The Rainbow*." In *D. H. Lawrence: A Centenary Consideration*, edited by Peter Balbert and Philip L. Marcus, pp. 45-66. Ithaca, N.Y.: Cornell University Press, 1985.
    Explores the theme of marriage in *The Rainbow*.

Berthoud, Jacques. "*The Rainbow* as Experimental Novel," in *D. H. Lawrence: A Critical Study of the Major Novels and Other Writings,* edited by A. H. Gomme, pp. 53-69. Sussex, England: Harvester Press, 1978.
    Describes *The Rainbow* as an experimental novel that invokes "a new mode of expressing feeling."

Blanchard, Lydia. "Mothers and Daughters in D. H. Lawrence: *The Rainbow* and Selected Shorter Works." In *Lawrence and Women*, edited by Anne Smith, pp. 75-100. London: Vision Press, 1978.
    Outlines the mother and child relationship as a significant thematic corollary in *The Rainbow*.

Daleski, H. M. "Two in One: The Second Period (A) *The Rainbow*." In his *The Forked Flame: A Study of D. H. Lawrence*, pp. 74-125. Evanston, Ill.: Northwestern University Press, 1965.
    In-depth analysis of *The Rainbow* that focuses on the struggle between masculine and feminine forces.

Ford, George H. "*The Rainbow* as Bible" and "*The Rainbow* as Novel." In his *Double Measure: A Study of the Novels and Stories of D. H. Lawrence*, pp. 115-62. New York: W. W. Norton & Company, Inc., 1965.
    Traces Biblical analogies and treats the theme of male/female relationships in *The Rainbow*.

Hill, Ordelle G. and Woodbery, Potter. "Ursula Brangwen of *The Rainbow*: Christian Saint or Pagan Goddess?" *D. H. Lawrence Review* 4, No. 3 (Fall 1971): 274-79.
    Finds evidence for the origins of Ursula Brangwen's character in "the pagan roots of the St. Ursula legend."

Hinz, Evelyn J. "The Paradoxical Fall: Eternal Recurrence in D. H. Lawrence's *The Rainbow*." *English Studies in Canada* 111, No. 4 (Winter 1977): 466-81.
    Contends that "the theme of *The Rainbow* is the Fall from a cosmic to an historical or egocentric point of view and correlatively from a cyclic to a linear and sequential concept of time."

Kay, Wallace G. "Lawrence and *The Rainbow*: Apollo and Dionysus in Conflict." *The Southern Quarterly* X, No. 3 (April 1972): 209-22.
    Analyzes the conflicts in *The Rainbow* in terms of the Nietzschean dichotomy of Apollonian versus Dionysian.

Kinkead-Weekes, Mark. Introduction to *The Rainbow*, by D.

H. Lawrence, pp. xix-lxxvi. Cambridge: Cambridge University Press, 1989.

Comprehensive survey of issues related to the composition, textual history, and critical reception of *The Rainbow*.

Lainoff, Seymour. "*The Rainbow*: The Shaping of Modern Man." *Modern Fiction Studies* 1, No. 4 (November 1955): 23-27.

Defines the evolution of modern man dramatized in *The Rainbow* as one of decline toward a "vacancy of spirit" and a "barrenness of instinct."

Leavis, F. R. "Lawrence and Tradition: *The Rainbow*." In his *D. H. Lawrence: Novelist*, pp. 108-74. New York: Alfred A. Knopf, 1956.

Commentary on *The Rainbow* that outlines several stylistic flaws, but acknowledges the work as a superb study of contemporary civilization.

Moynahan, Julian. "The Discovery of Form: *The Rainbow*." In his *The Deed of Life: The Novels and Tales of D. H. Lawrence*, pp. 42-72. Princeton, N.J.: Princeton University Press, 1963.

Discusses theme, narrative technique, style, and symbolism in *The Rainbow*, as well as investigating five scenes in the novel that celebrate "the relation of the human soul to God" in a manner analogous to religious ritual.

Mudrick, Marvin. "The Originality of *The Rainbow*." In *Twentieth Century Interpretations of 'The Rainbow': A Collection of Critical Essays*, edited by Mark Kinkead-Weekes, pp. 11-32. Englewood Cliffs, N.J.: Prentice-Hall, 1971.

Calls Lawrence revolutionary for the new awareness of character and society he exhibits in *The Rainbow*.

Nicholes, E. L. "The 'Simile of the Sparrow' in *The Rainbow* by D. H. Lawrence." *Modern Language Arts* LXIV, No. 3 (March 1949): 171-74.

Examines Lawrence's symbolic use of animal imagery in *The Rainbow*.

Nixon, Cornelia. "To Procreate Oneself: Ursula's Horses in *The Rainbow*." *ELH* 49, No. 1 (Spring 1982): 123-42.

Treats the subtle birth and rebirth imagery at the end of *The Rainbow*.

Raddatz, Volker. "Lyrical Elements in D. H. Lawrence's *The Rainbow*." *Revue des langues vivantes* XL, No. 3 (1974): 235-42.

Connects the spiritual elements of *The Rainbow* to the lyrical rhythms of Lawrence's prose.

Ross, Charles L. *The Composition of 'The Rainbow' and 'Women in Love': A History*. Charlottesville: University Press of Virginia, 1979, 168 p.

Historical and textual analysis of the manuscripts of Lawrence's Brangwen novels.

Sagar, Keith. "The Perfect Medium 1913-1914: *The Rainbow*." In his *The Art of D. H. Lawrence*, pp. 41-72. Cambridge: Cambridge University Press, 1966.

Study of *The Rainbow* that highlights biographical aspects of the novel and the course of Lawrence's artistic development.

Spano, Joseph. "A Study of Ursula (of *The Rainbow*) and H. M. Daleski's Commentary." *Paunch*, No. 33 (December 1968): 22-31.

Maintains that Ursula is not simply "an exemplary Lawrencian character" as several critics have observed, but rather an individual partly "motivated by destructive, egotistical drives."

Stewart, Jack F. "Expressionism in *The Rainbow*." *Novel* 13, No. 3 (Spring 1980): 296-315.

Investigates affinities between the aesthetic of *The Rainbow* and that of early twentieth-century visual art.

Tobin, Patricia Drechsel. "The Cycle Dance: D. H. Lawrence, *The Rainbow*." In her *Time and the Novel: The Genealogical Imperative*, pp. 81-106. Princeton, N.J.: Princeton University Press, 1978.

Examines cyclic resonances in *The Rainbow*, within the contexts of Tobin's theory of time in the modern novel.

Additional coverage of Lawrence's life and career is contained in the following sources published by Gale Research: *Contemporary Authors,* **Vols. 104, 121;** *Concise Dictionary of British Literary Biography,* **1914-1945;** *DISCovering Authors; Dictionary of Literary Biography,* **Vols. 10, 19, 36, 98;** *Major 20th-Century Writers; Short Story Criticism,* **Vol. 4;** *Twentieth-Century Literary Criticism,* **Vols. 2, 9, 16, 33, 48; and** *World Literature Criticism.*

Of Time and the River

Thomas Wolfe

The following entry presents criticism of Wolfe's novel *Of Time and the River: A Legend of Man's Hunger in His Youth* (1935). For discussion of Wolfe's complete career, see *TCLC*, Volumes 4 and 13; for discussion of his novel *Look Homeward, Angel*, see *TCLC*, Volume 29.

INTRODUCTION

Of Time and the River has in common with Wolfe's other novels several features that have contributed to his reputation as one of America's leading twentieth-century authors: vividly drawn characters; a universal theme—the lonely individual in search of knowledge, experience, and self-sufficiency—given epic scope through its development against an American landscape that is powerfully depicted as at once magisterial and brutal, fascinating and terrifying; and a sensuous, exuberant prose style characterized by lyrical passages that have frequently been compared to the poetry of Walt Whitman. Autobiographical in content, *Of Time and the River* is a continuation of Wolfe's first novel, *Look Homeward, Angel* (1929), in which he portrayed his coming of age through the character of Eugene Gant. In *Of Time and the River*, Gant, now an aspiring writer, leaves his home in a small southern town and embarks on a pilgrimage to find the source of his creative inspiration and the true meaning of American life. Although *Of Time and the River* was published to mixed reviews, it received the attention of major literary critics, and it was also the only one of Wolfe's books to reach the best-seller lists in the United States.

Plot and Major Characters

The narrative of *Of Time and the River* closely follows the events of Wolfe's own life from 1920 to 1925. The novel, which ran to 912 pages in its first edition, is divided into eight books, the titles of which are borrowed from myths and legends that provide insight into the various stages of Eugene's pilgrimage. When the story opens, Eugene is preparing to board a northbound train that will take him from his hometown of Altamont, Catawba (modeled after Wolfe's hometown of Asheville, North Carolina) to Harvard University, where he intends to study writing in a graduate program. Along the way, Eugene stops to visit his dying father in a Baltimore hospital; Wolfe's account of Old Gant's traumatic death from cancer later in the novel is considered one of the work's most powerful scenes. After three years at Harvard, Eugene returns to Altamont for a summer, awaiting news from a Broadway producer to whom he has submitted one of his plays. When the play is rejected, Eugene accepts a position as an English instructor at the downtown branch of New York University in order to support himself until he is discovered as a writer. However, he soon becomes disillusioned

with the city, which he considers impersonal, corrupt, and dirty, and, in his continuing search to find fulfillment as both a man and writer, he journeys to Europe. He first visits England and then travels to Paris, where he encounters his close friend from Harvard, Francis Starwick. Eugene, Starwick, and two female companions travel around Paris and the French countryside for a while, but before long Eugene becomes disgusted with their dissipated lifestyle and breaks away from the group. He then spends some time alone in the southern provinces of France, finding new insight into his vocation as a writer. At the novel's close, as Eugene is embarking on his journey home to America, he sees an unidentified woman who, he tells the reader, is destined to become his lover.

Major Themes

Pilgrimage is the central theme of *Of Time and the River*. According to Wolfe in *The Story of a Novel* (1936), an essay in which he describes his life as a writer and the composition of *Of Time and the River*, the primary object of Eugene's quest is his "search to find a father, not merely the father of his flesh, not merely the lost father of his youth, but the image of a strength and wisdom external to his need and superior to his hunger, to which the belief and power of his own life could be united." Thus, Wolfe's idea of a father has both literal and figurative meaning, and critics have interpreted the concept variously: as the fatherland, America; as the meaning of life; as the means of access to Eugene's buried creativity; as the security of childhood. Another important theme in the novel is time. As Wolfe explained in *The Story of a Novel*, he sought through Eugene's odyssey to work out a three-part vision of time: time present (the actual events of the novel); time past, which refers to all the accumulated experience that conditions and shapes the present (Eugene's memories); and time immutable, the eternal time of rivers, oceans, and forests (Eugene's desire to immortalize his memories through his art). A dominant aspect of Eugene's obsession with time is his fear of loss, which is evoked through both incident and imagery: Eugene's profound sorrow at the death of his father; symbols such as smoke and dreams, which represent the transiency of human life; and recurrent metaphors of death and resurrection. Critics have also pointed out other significant themes in the novel, including Eugene's love of America, his Faustian thirst for knowledge, and the element of flight or escape—from the South to the North, from America to Europe, from one social milieu to another—that attends his pilgrimage.

Critical Reception

In *The Story of a Novel*, Wolfe tells how *Of Time and the River* brimmed forth from him "for almost five years like burning lava from a volcano." By December, 1933, Wolfe had written over a million words, and he and his editor at Scribner's, Maxwell Perkins, began the difficult task of cutting back the manuscript to publishable size. The process was slowed by Wolfe's reluctance to delete any material and by his desire to wait another season before sending the book to press. Typically, Perkins would excise long passages, usually where he felt that Wolfe's language was overly poetic, and Wolfe would respond with revisions that were even longer than the originals. Perkins, working in conjunction with a copy editor, eventually sent the manuscript to the printer in October 1934 without Wolfe's final consent, and the book was published in March 1935. Initial critical reaction to *Of Time and the River*, while lavish, was mixed. A number of reviewers praised the power and beauty of Wolfe's rhapsodic, elegiac style, viewing the novel's raw energy as confirmation of the talent displayed in *Look Homeward, Angel*, but they objected to Wolfe's lack of rhetorical restraint, complaining that he invested even the most trivial details with monumental significance. Many reviewers felt that the long poetic passages were out of place in a novel; the book's lyricism, combined with its episodic nature, caused some critics to question whether *Of Time and the River* could properly be called a novel at all. The most famous contemporary review of *Of Time and the River* was Bernard DeVoto's landmark attack against Wolfe in the Saturday Review of Literature. Entitled "Genius Is Not Enough," DeVoto's indictment of Wolfe was based on the author's record of his working methods and relationship with Perkins in *The Story of a Novel*. DeVoto, while acknowledging that Wolfe possessed genius of the passionate, romantic sort, offered *Of Time and the River* as proof that Wolfe was undisciplined and incapable of restraining his emotions or of organizing his material into a coherent whole. DeVoto's conclusions were widely accepted for several years after the publication of his essay, and to this day the stereotype of Wolfe as a poor craftsman persists. Later critics have continued to be preoccupied with the apparent formlessness of *Of Time and the River* and with the question of Wolfe's editorial dependence, but in general they have judged the novel to be less disconnected than early reviewers, many arguing that *Of Time and the River* has a coherent design that derives from the unifying motif of the pilgrimage and the themes that represent the objects of Eugene's quest. In addition, critics note, the loose structure allowed Wolfe to interrupt the narrative with poetic meditations that developed his ideas on the diversity of the American landscape and population. One aspect of *Of Time and the River* that critics have tended to agree upon over the years is its characterization. Wolfe has been consistently praised for his skill at portraiture, especially for his effective blending of satire and affection and for his attention to the seemingly minor details of speech, habit, and dress that can capture the essence of personality. Popular and critical interest in *Of Time and the River* steadily declined after its much-hyped publication, largely because of increasing enthusiasm for *Look Homeward, Angel*. Today, *Of Time and the River* continues to be overshadowed by *Look Homeward, Angel*—a fact that some critics attribute to the latter's more traditional structure—but fans of *Of Time and the River* predict that the novel only

serves to benefit from the recent resurgence of interest in Wolfe's writings as a whole.

CRITICISM

Clifton Fadiman   (essay date 1935)

SOURCE: "Thomas Wolfe," in *The New Yorker,* Vol. XI, No. 4, March 9, 1935, pp. 68-70.

[*In the following review of* Of Time and the River, *Fadiman discusses the strengths and weaknesses of Wolfe's style and characterization and comments on the novel's themes.*]

If, as a child, you ever clambered out of the thrill-car of a death-defying scenic railway, you may recall the curiously divided state of your emotions. It was a tossup as to whether you felt excited beyond the point of endurance or just enormously tired. Emerging at this instant from the nine-hundred-and-twelfth page of Thomas Wolfe's long-awaited *Of Time and the River,* I have very much that scenic-railway feeling, at once feverish and groggy. Just watching Mr. Wolfe release his magnificent, inexhaustible energy leaves one flushed and punchdrunk. It will be some time before the literary bookkeepers have cast up their accounts and told us just how good a novel he has written. What matters right now to most readers is that he gives you an experience you can't just file away under Miscellaneous.

Of Time and the River is a sequel to *Look Homeward, Angel,* following the fortunes of Eugene Gant, its young hero, through the years 1920 to 1925. Mr. Wolfe has taken five years to write about these five years. He is now nearing thirty-five and his autobiographical hero, when we leave him, is twenty-five, so Mr. Wolfe is keeping about a decade ahead of himself. It is not quite clear, however, whether his book is written from the point of view of Thomas Wolfe, in his mature thirties, or from that of Eugene Gant, in his callow early twenties. This sometimes makes for confusion.

The actual material is familiar to the point of banality; it is what the author does to it that is important. Can one conceive of a more unpromising scenario than this: Eugene Gant, the genius of the family, rebels against small-town narrowness; goes to Harvard, where his mind opens to beauty, art, personalities, et cetera; returns, after the death of his father, to Altamont, where he waits for the postman to bring him good news from the Theatre Guild; finally accepts a position as a teacher of English in New York University (downtown branch) and proceeds to explore the city; gets fed up, collects his savings, and makes the requisite European pilgrimage; finds Oxford full of Englishmen, France full of Frenchmen, and himself full of nostalgia; and catches the boat (where the inevitable Older Woman awaits him) home. Mr. Wolfe does not invite you to stop him if you've heard that one, for he knows that he can't be stopped by you or anyone else, including himself. That his experiences are a set pattern, hugely unoriginal, does not deter him. It is enough for him that he feels them for the first time, and so powerful and overwhelming is his conviction of their novelty that the reader is often bludgeoned into sharing it. Which is certainly a kind of genius.

And he has other kinds. It is open to debate whether he is a master of language or language a master of him; but for decades we have not had eloquence like his in American writing. His declamations and apostrophes, such as the one to America on page 155, are astounding and often beautiful; and even when mere rhetoric, they are mere gorgeous rhetoric. He might with some justice apply to his own style his description of Carlyle's "vast stormrounding cadences, now demented and now strong as light." At their best these tempests of poetic prose, far more exuberant than in ***Look Homeward, Angel,*** are overwhelming, and at their worst they are startlingly bad:

> And against the borders of the East, pure, radiant, for the first time seen in the unbelievable wonder of its new discovery, bringing to all of us, as it had always done, the first life that was ever known on this earth, the golden banner of the day appeared.

There are thousands of these prose Swinburne passages, all marvellous until you ask what they mean. Thus it is impossible to say any one thing of Mr. Wolfe's style. At its best it is wondrous, Elizabethan. At its worst it is hyperthyroid and afflicted with elephantiasis. As Stevenson and Pater well knew, it is the blue pencil that creates the purple patch; but I suppose if Thomas Wolfe could use a blue pencil he would not be Thomas Wolfe. Still, he might be somebody even better.

We would have had a different and to my taste finer book if that same blue pencil had been used on some of the characters. Here again, at his best he is incomparable. The whole gigantically lunatic Gant family, that tirading, panting, poetical clan of grown-up children, escape the bounds of the probable only to establish themselves solidly in the inevitable. Mother Gant is as wonderful as she was in the first book; old Gant in his very dying is terribly alive; and Bascom Pentland, that combination of gargoyle and titan, is an unforgettable addition to the family gallery. They are all oversize and monstrous. They have but to open the sluice gates of their mouths to leap into roaring life; their temperaments are always at the flood; they are excessive; the report of their life is grossly exaggerated. But you can't forget them. And there are minor characters, too, dozens of them, conceived in the same spirit of detailed frenzy: the family of Boston Irish with whom Eugene lives in Cambridge; the students at the drama course, and particularly the professor—don't let anybody tell you it isn't the late George Pierce Baker; the semi-corpses in the dingy lobby of the Leopold Hotel; Morison the synthetic Englishman.

With these people he performs miracles; yet he can at the same time waste his energy on dry sticks, stock characters, like the elegant Francis Starwick, who plays the Steerforth to Eugene's David; on a crowd of Hudson Valley millionaires who could not possibly be animated out of their waxwork existence save by the scorpions of satire; on a wearisome French marquise; on corn-liquor college boys whose shrill sadistic violence no longer kicks the attention to life.

Mr. Wolfe's people are either giants or piddlers, the confusing thing being that he works with the same enthusiasm on both.

However, he could blow a false, momentary breath into dozens of mannikins and still his book would swarm with life. A much more serious fault shows itself in connection with the hero himself. I believe in Thomas Wolfe; but I do not believe in Eugene Gant, who, according to all the laws of probability, is Thomas Wolfe. Eugene is one of those romantic life-engulfers who are so many things so intensely that, in fiction at least, they end by becoming a mere blur of energy. "He loved life so dearly that he was driven mad by the thirst and hunger which he felt for it." I submit that to make such fellows credible you have to show up their madness concretely, which Mr. Wolfe does not do. We may be told a dozen times that they are terrific, extravagant, titanic, but on paper they remain just another super-production.

We have spent a great deal of time and effort carefully working out of our systems the nineteenth-century notion of the amoral, frenzied artist. Now Mr. Wolfe asks us to grow young along with Eugene, whom he describes as "life's hungry man, the glutton of eternity, beauty's miser, glory's slave." With the best will in the world and with the greatest admiration for Mr. Wolfe, I cannot swallow gluttons of eternity, my narrow imagination cringes at the idea of anyone who "simply wanted to know about everything on earth." One goes crazy trying to keep up with Eugene's madness, trying to conceive of this omnivorous human being who can reject nothing, who was filled by everything he saw "with haunting sorrow, hunger, joy, the sense of triumph, glory and delight, or with a limitless exuberance of wild humor." It's enough to send one back to Humanism. As a matter of fact, it is when Eugene is not trying to swallow the universe, when he is merely an imaginative Southern kid who can't hold his liquor and socks his best friend and gets put in jail, that he suddenly leaps to life. As a questing genius, he doesn't wash. The Faustian man, perhaps, is a possibility, but the Faustian college boy is funny.

And yet, when Mr. Wolfe is not running amok amid the cosmos, how surely and sensitively he can touch upon the sweet lunacy of youth: the way the youngster in the upper berth feels when the lady in the lower sighs heavily in her sleep, the whole romance of travel, the agitated discovery of the "thickness" of human life.

If only he didn't try to crowd it all in! If only he would occasionally turn over his doormat reading "Welcome to the Universe"! In the prefatory note to ***Look Homeward, Angel,*** Mr. Wolfe wrote: "Fiction is not fact, but fiction is fact selected and understood, fiction is fact arranged and charged with purpose." Shrewd words, wise words. He would gain by pondering them. He does not select, and he does not reduce. There is too much of everything in his book, and much of it is too large. If he has written a masterpiece, it is a masterpiece of the excessive; hence it tends to the grotesque. He describes a baseball game, with Mathewson in the box, Speaker up, as if it were a struggle of astronomical forces. This is grand; but it is grandly false.

Of Time and the River is a wonderful, flashing, gleaming riot of characters, caricatures, metaphors, apostrophes, declamations, tropes, dreams, but what ideas it has are confused and sparse. It is defiantly, frenziedly anti-intellectual, which is a pity, for Thomas Wolfe's mind is potentially powerful and he will gain nothing by this fanatic reliance upon emotion. In great writers there is no rivalry between the mind and the feelings.

Instead of ideas, there are certain motifs, musical rather than intellectual, which give the book whatever pattern it has. These include the Telemachus theme, Eugene's despairing search for the father of his youth; the conviction that "we are so lost, so naked and so lonely in America," an insight which would have great tragic weight if Mr. Wolfe, instead of merely elegizing, had tried to find out just why Americans are lost and lonely; great bursts of love for his country, an affection that is unanalyzed, grounded on animal faith, and therefore occasionally sentimental, even chauvinistic; and a constant asseveration that life is strange, mysterious, and terrible, which it no doubt is. But one can have too much of "the strange and bitter miracle of life" kind of thing. It is all too easy, this facile adolescent poetry. Mr. Wolfe tells us so many times that men are afraid of "a dark too vast and terrible, an earth too savage in its rudeness, space and emptiness" that our common sense, partly paralyzed by the electricity of his rhetoric, feebly struggles to its feet to inquire whether most men, after all, aren't afraid of the empty larder, the last pay check, the soup line, the lapsed insurance policy. There is too much cosmos in Mr. Wolfe's ego.

Yet there is in him, in addition to his brilliant technical gifts, also so much nobility and generosity of soul, so great and so undefiled a desire to become a great writer, that one can only hope he will submit himself to a Wolfian orgy of self-criticism, that he will lop and prune and refine, that he will learn that the radiant English language gives herself, at last, only to those who distrust her. A single informing vision of life is yet to become his; he will never attain it by rhapsody or self-hypnosis or incantation, but only by the conscience and the intelligence working in harmony together.

Henry Seidel Canby (essay date 1935)

SOURCE: "Estimates of the Living," in *Seven Years' Harvest: Notes on Contemporary Literature,* Farrar & Rinehart, 1936, pp. 133-70.

[*In the following essay, which was first published in 1935, Canby remarks on the dual nature of the style and content in* Of Time and the River.]

There was much laughter when years ago D. H. Lawrence in his *Studies in Classical American Literature* described an Old Indian Devil who was always plaguing the great Americans with sudden flushes of paganism, great resurgences of sex, and obstinate maladjustments between their European souls and their unfenced continent. It is not so funny now, for some devil, Indian, Marxian, or psychoanalytic, has surely been torturing the best American writers of our era. They squirm, they lash, they spit out filth

and imprecations, they whine, they defy. They are not at ease in this Zion of our ancestors.

For Thomas Wolfe in his recent novel, *Of Time and the River,* the curse is impotence. There is for him a brooding loneliness in the American landscape which drives the manmass into a nervous activity of hurrying on trains, motors, subways, airplanes, a restlessness which drives the sensitive writer into an agony of frustration because the towns, the cities, the countryside oppress him with unrealized and inexpressible energy. It is a country that grips the imagination and lets the heart go, a country in which humanity mixed and at the boiling point—black Negro flesh, amber Jewish flesh, dark, light, sanguine—is incited by fierce energies toward no end but movement and frustration, a country where life has sacrificed its mass for its force, and the observer can neither hold on or let go of a rush of experience that always seems to have, yet never quite achieves, a meaning.

The impotence of America is an impotence of expression. When in Wolfe's novel Gene Gant's train shrieks through the night on his first journey northward, he feels the enormous push of continental energy and can rise to it only by drunken hysteria. When in the last chapter he meets the ocean liner sailing from France, he sees that vast organization of speed and change floating above his tender, and knows that it is America again, clutching at his sensitive spirit. In three hundred years the American soul has not made itself a home.

And hence the strange impulse toward autobiography which has carried so many Americans to the verge of incoherence!—Melville in *Moby Dick* wrestling with transcendental interpretations of his restlessness, or Whitman in the "Song of Myself" blatantly proclaiming his identity with the expansiveness of a continent. They cannot write novels, these rebel Americans, there is nothing stable to write of. They can only proclaim their egos, in defiance of the inhumanity of a continent which the energy of their race has exploited but to which they are not yet assimilated. Hence an impotence which prevents complete expression, and books which are, as the eighteenth century would have said, far more nature than art.

Of Time and the River, time being the time of youth, the river that mysterious current of life which flows under the perplexing surface of America, is the epitome, after so many books, of the troublous and disintegrating years of the Twenties when Mr. Wolfe was young. And those who wish to get in fullest and most impassioned form the spiritual record of those years, or who would see as in a newsreel the typical scenes of that period as youth saw them, will find, if they are persistent, what they want in this book, which is neither fiction nor autobiography, but both.

For although the scene of Mr. Wolfe's long-expected narrative changes from North Carolina to the biting realities and warped romance of New England, from New England to the aloofness of Oxford, from Oxford to the loneliness of an American's France, yet it is a wholly American book, one of the most American books of our time. It is in the direct tradition of those earlier anguished spirits and great seekers on our soil, Thoreau, Melville, Whitman. It is in the tradition, but with a momentous difference for which the break-up of the Twenties and Mr. Wolfe's own idiosyncrasies are responsible. Yet if I should wish to know what these Twenties meant to an American youth still asking the questions asked by his spiritual ancestors, "Why are we here?", "What does this continent mean to us?", "What are we becoming?" I should go to this book. If I fail to give a clear account of Mr. Wolfe's thousand-page story of how a passion-driven youth tried to tear all knowledge from the Harvard library, all experience from America, all wisdom from Europe, and to pluck out, in his twenties, the secret of the loneliness and the fascination of America, forgive me. Have you ever tried to review the *Encyclopædia Britannica*?

Mr. Wolfe's odd thousand pages are condensed but not adequately described in the paragraphs above. He calls them fiction, and fiction they are of the kind that he put into **Look Homeward, Angel,** but better organized, more poetical where poetical, more sharply realistic when realistic; and they are to be followed by a million words more or less in which the ego which is the raison d'être of them all is to conclude the story. But fiction in the strict sense they are not, nor story, nor drama, but rather spiritual autobiography in which the thousand incidents, many of them trivial, and the dozens of characters, many of them extraordinary, have as their excuse for being that a youth met them on his way. Plot there is none. Structure in the ordinary narrative sense, there is none. It is a picaresque novel with the distraught mind of a poet of the Twenties as *picaro,* and the incidents adventures in seeking a spiritual home.

To be more precise, this book is a study of American dualism and it is this which gives it poignancy. Leaf through it and you will see as in a moving picture successive moments of prose and poetry. Here are the fleshy people of an intensely actual Carolina, of a literal Boston, and of a photographic France. No reporter could have done them more vividly as news, and indeed Wolfe is a great reporter. No one of them is usual, indeed for such a passionate student of humanity no man or woman could be merely usual; most of them are eccentrics, half mad from pain, or love, or greed, or vanity, or frustration; or wholly lost in what is really fantasy, like Starwick the homosexual, or the pathetic collegiate Weaver, or the gross sensualist Flood who is like some mushroom sprung from, yet alien to, the good earth. And between these flashes of intimate, literal humanity from the man-swarm, the novel leaves the literal entirely and in a poetic prose that owes much to Whitman and a little to Joyce, but has become Wolfe's own, rises into a chorus of anguish, perplexity, and delight, which chants the loneliness and the impotence and the beauty of this America, and struggles to break through to some solution which will satisfy the seeker, who is the youth Gant, the hero, and the excuse for all this profusion of words.

And linking the two worlds is the decaying but still mighty figure of the Father, the old stone cutter who was the center of **Look Homeward, Angel.** Dying (and his death scene is Mr. Wolfe at his best), he still dominates the imagination of the youth, for he in his vast energy and incredible vitality is the old America where man almost became worthy of his continent; and in his cancerous decline, in his frustrated career, and in the immense confusion of his brain, he symbolizes what has happened in a twentieth century in which there seems to be no graspable relation between the prose and the poetry of a continent.

So much for the purpose of this novel. Its achievement is less. With all its richness of detail, its passion, its poetry, and its intense realism of contemporary life, there is an impotence in this book like the impotence Wolfe ascribes to his America.

In America it is an impotence of wandering men at home wherever wheels carry them yet never strong enough to grip the continent and make it serve their happiness. In this America, "so casual and rich and limitless and free," they become arid or lonely or broken, or have got the "new look" of the machine-ridden masses. With Mr. Wolfe the impotence is exactly equivalent. His imagination has provided him with a great theme and his accurate memory flashes infinite exact detail of the life of which he intends to make his book. But he cannot control the theme or reduce his substance to a medium. He will write neither poetry nor prose, but both. He will not be content with the literal autobiographic description of men and events which his journalistic sense supplies so readily but must intersperse with passages of sheer fantasy or poetical uplift. He will stick neither to fiction nor to fact. Hence the reader never enters into that created world of the real novelist which has its own laws, its own atmosphere, its own people, but goes from here to there in Mr. Wolfe's own life, seeing real people as he saw them, and often recognizing them (as with George Pierce Baker in Professor Hatcher, and many others) not as created characters but as literal transcripts from the life. So that the effect is always of being in two worlds at once, fiction and fact, until curiosity takes the place of that ready acceptance of a homogeneous life in the imagination which a fine novel invariably permits. You are forced to read this book as an autobiography with a poetic accompaniment, and for the first five or six hundred pages the personality of the narrator, this passion-driven youth, is too vague, too unimportant to hold suspense, so that it is for the objective realistic incidents that one reads and these change and succeed one another without relation or real consequence, except that one ego experiences them all. Hence a book that is verbose, and which seems much more verbose, much more repetitive than it is. Not until well past its vast middle is the reader caught up and carried on. Before that he reads either a passage of extravagant but vital poetry (drunken poetry in this quotation)—

> *Casey Jones!* Open the throttle, boy, and let her rip! Boys, I'm a belly-busting bastard from the State of old Catawba—a rootin' tootin' shootin' son-of-a-bitch from Saw Toop Gap in Buncombe—why, God help this lovely bastard of a train—it is the best damned train that ever turned a wheel since Casey Jones's father was a pup—why, you sweet bastard, run! Eat up Virginia!

or he reads a complete realistic episode in which the Pentlands snigger "k, k, k, k, k," pull at their cleft chins, smolder with their hidden fires. Or an aggressive Jew boy pulls out the stopper of young Gant's wrath, and makes a friend for life. Or an attempted seduction. Or a satire on silly young Harvard intellectuals poohing and pahing and saying "Ace" for "Yes." Immense power, immense variety, little control, less continuity, and an almost complete failure to make this true epic of longing youth in a lonely, disintegrated America either drama, fiction, poetry, satire, any *one* thing, *one* medium of expression, into which the imagination of the reader can enter and stay, for more than twenty pages, at home.

I think that this novel, like many other fiery and ambitious American books—like Melville's *Pierre,* like many of Whitman's poems, like the now forgotten romantic-philosophic extravaganzas so common in the magazines of a century ago—is an artistic failure. And Mr. Wolfe's books, as wholes, will continue to be artistic failures until he finds and controls a medium in which the ego is sublimated into an imagination less involved in the immediate circumstances of his life. Yet it is an important book, and Mr. Wolfe is an important writer. He has more material, more vitality, more originality, more gusto than any two contemporary British novelists put together, even though they may be real novelists and he is not. He stands to them as Whitman stood to the wearied *Idylls of the King.* And he entirely escapes the sordid, whining defeatism of so many of his American contemporaries. I am not fool enough to try to teach him how to write. No one can do that. He can write like his own angel now, he can make speech that is a new speech in fiction and yet unmistakably authentic, he can strike off flashing pictures.

> In waning light, in faint shadows, far, far away in a great city of the north, the 40,000 small empetaled faces bend forward breathless, waiting—single and strange and beautiful as all life, all living, and man's destiny. There's a man on base, the last flash of the great right arm, the crack of the bat, the streaking white of a clean-hit ball, the wild, sudden, solid roar, a pair of flashing legs have crossed the rubber, and the game is over!

But he has not yet made his book. He has poured out his heart into a mold, over a mold, spilling through a thousand pages. He has tried to be philosopher, poet, journalist-observer, satirist, story-teller, historian, and dreamer, not all at once which is quite possible, but one after the other, which cannot be done in a book, which, like a man, no matter how complex, should be integrated, harmonious, homogeneous, and unmistakably not many but one.

Robert Penn Warren   (essay date 1935)

SOURCE: "The Hamlet of Thomas Wolfe," in *The Enigma of Thomas Wolfe: Biographical and Critical Selections,* edited by Richard Walser, Cambridge, Mass.: Harvard University Press, 1953, pp. 120-32.

[*In the following essay, which was first published in the American Review in 1935, Warren assesses Wolfe's capabilities as a writer, focusing on his presentation of character.*]

Thomas Wolfe owns an enormous talent; and chooses to exercise it on an enormous scale. This talent was recognized promptly enough several years ago when his first novel, *Look Homeward, Angel,* came from the press to overwhelm a high percentage of the critics and, in turn, a high percentage of the cash customers. Nor was this sensational success for a first novel undeserved, even if the book was not, as Hugh Walpole suggested, as "near perfect as a novel can be." Now Mr. Wolfe's second novel, *Of Time and the River,* appears, and the enthusiasm of the reception of the first will probably be repeated; though, I venture to predict, on a scale scarcely so magnificent. That remains to be seen; but it may not be too early to attempt a definition of the special excellence and the special limitations of the enormous talent that has produced two big books and threatens to produce others in the near future.

If Mr. Wolfe's talent is enormous, his energies are more enormous, and fortunately so. A big book is forbidding, but, at the same time, it carries a challenge in its very pretension. It seems to say, "This is a serious project and demands serious attention from serious minds." There is, of course, a snobbery of the threedecker. Mr. Wolfe is prolific. His publishers assure the public that he has written in the neighborhood of two million words. In his scheme of six novels two are now published (*Look Homeward, Angel,* 1884-1920, and *Of Time and the River,* 1920-1925); two more are already written (*The October Fair,* 1925-1928, and *The Hills Beyond Pentland,* 1838-1926); and two more are projected (*The Death of the Enemy,* 1928-1933, and *Pacific End,* 1791-1884). Presumably, the novels unpublished and unwritten will extend forward and backward the ramifications of the fortunes of the Gant and Pentland families.

Look Homeward, Angel and the present volume are essentially two parts of an autobiography; the pretense of fiction is so thin and slovenly that Mr. Wolfe in referring to the hero writes indifferently "Eugene Gant" or "I" and "me." There may be many modifications, omissions, and additions in character and event, but the impulse and material are fundamentally personal. The story begins in *Look Homeward, Angel* in the latter part of the nineteenth century with the arrival of Gant, the father of the hero, in Altamont, in the State of Old Catawba, which is Asheville, North Carolina. It continues with the marriage to Eliza Pentland, the birth of the various children, the debaucheries and repentance of old Gant, the growth of the village into a flourishing resort, the profitable real-estate speculations of Eliza, her boarding house, the education of Eugene Gant in Altamont and at the State University, the collapse of old Gant's health, and the departure of Eugene for Harvard. *Of Time and the River* resumes on the station platform as Eugene leaves for Harvard, sees him through three years there in the drama school under "Professor Hatcher," presents in full horror of detail the death of old Gant from cancer of the prostate, treats the period in New York when Eugene teaches the Jews in a college there, and takes the hero to Europe, where he reads, writes, and dissipates tremendously. He is left at the point of embarking for America. During this time he is serving his apprenticeship as a writer and trying to come to terms with his own spirit and with America. So much for the bare materials of the two books.

The root of Mr. Wolfe's talent is his ability at portraiture. The figures of Eliza Gant and old Gant, of Ben and Helen, in *Look Homeward, Angel,* are permanent properties of the reader's imagination. Mr. Wolfe has managed to convey the great central vitality of the old man, for whom fires would roar up the chimney and plants would grow, who stormed into his house in the evening laden with food, and whose quality is perpetually heroic, mythical, and symbolic. It is the same with Eliza with her flair for business, her almost animal stupidity, her great, but sometimes aimless, energies, her almost sardonic and defensive love for her son, whom she does not understand, her avarice and her sporadic squandering of money. These two figures dominate both books; even after old Gant is dead the force of his personality, or rather the force of the symbol into which that personality has been elevated, is an active agent, and a point of reference for interpretation.

These two characters, and Ben and Helen in a lesser degree, are triumphs of poetic conception. The uncle in *Of Time and the River,* Bascom Pentland, exhibits likewise some of the family lineaments, the family vitality, and something of the symbolic aspect of the other characters; but the method of presentation is more conventional and straightforward, and the result more static and anecdotal.

Mr. Wolfe's method in presenting these characters, and the special quality of symbol he manages to derive from them, is subject to certain special qualifications. Obviously it would not serve as a routine process for the treatment of character, at least not on the scale on which it is here rendered. The reader of a novel demands something more realistic, less lyrical; he demands an interplay of characters on another and more specific level, a method less dependent on the direct intrusion of the novelist's personal sensibility. As I have said, the figures of the Gant family are powerful and overwhelming as symbols, as an emotional focus for the novel, and as a point of reference. But the method collapses completely when applied to Starwick, a character of equal importance in Mr. Wolfe's scheme.

We amass a great fund of information concerning Francis Starwick. He was born in a town in the Middle West and early rebelled against the crudities and ugliness of his background. At Harvard he assists Professor Hatcher in the drama school and leads the life of a mannered and affected aesthete, foppish in dress, artificial in speech, oversensitive and sometimes cruel. He becomes the best friend of Eugene at Harvard. Later he appears in Europe in company with two young women of Boston families, somewhat older than he, who are in love with him and who are willing to pay, with their reputations and their purses, for the pleasure of his conversation. With these three Eugene enters a period of debauchery in Paris. Finally he discovers that Starwick is homosexual, and in his undefinable resentment beats him into unconsciousness.

But this body of information is not all that the writer intends. F. Scott Fitzgerald and Ernest Hemingway have been able to use effectively such characters as Starwick

and to extract their meaning, because as novelists they were willing to work strictly in terms of character. But in *Of Time and the River* the writer is forever straining to convince the reader of some value in Starwick that is not perceptible, that the writer himself cannot define; he tries, since he is writing an autobiography, to make Starwick a symbol, a kind of *alter ego,* for a certain period of his own experience. The strain is tremendous; and without conviction. The writing about Starwick, as the climax of the relationship approaches, sinks into a slush of poetical bathos and juvenility. And here is the scene of parting:

". . . you had a place in my life that no one else has ever had."

"And what was that?" said Starwick.

"I think it was that you were young—my own age—and that you were my friend. Last night after—after that thing happened," he went on, his own face flushing with the pain of the memory, "I thought back over all the time since I have known you. And for the first time I realized that you were the first and only person of my own age that I could call my friend. You were my one true friend—the one I always turned to, believed in with unquestioning devotion. You were the only real friend that I ever had. Now something else has happened. You have taken from me something that I wanted, you have taken it without knowing that you took it, and it will always be like this. You were my brother and my friend—"

"And now?" said Starwick quietly.

"You are my mortal enemy. Good-bye."

"Good-bye, Eugene," said Starwick sadly. "But let me tell you this before I go. Whatever it was I took from you, it was something that I did not want or wish to take. And I would give it back again if I could."

"Oh, fortunate and favored Starwick," the other jeered. "To be so rich—to have such gifts and not to know he has them—to be forever victorious, and to be so meek and mild."

"And I will tell you this as well," Starwick continued. "Whatever anguish and suffering this mad hunger, this impossible desire, has caused you, however fortunate or favored you may think I am, I would give my whole life if I could change places with you for an hour—know for an hour an atom of your anguish and your hunger and your hope. . . . Oh, to feel so, suffer so, and live so!—however mistaken you may be! . . . To have come lusty, young, and living into this world . . . not to have come, like me, still-born from your mother's womb—never to know the dead heart and the passionless passion—the cold brain and the cold hopelessness of hope—to be wild, mad, furious, and tormented—but to have belief, to live in anguish, but to live,—and not to die." . . . He turned and opened the door. "I would give all I have and all you think I have, for just one hour of it. You call me fortunate and happy. *You* are the most fortunate and happy man I ever knew. Good-bye, Eugene."

"Good-bye, Frank. Good-bye, my enemy."

"And good-bye, my friend," said Starwick. He went out, and the door closed behind him.

The dialogue, the very rhythms of the sentences, and the scene itself, scream the unreality.

The potency of the figures from the family and the failure with Starwick may derive from the autobiographical nature of Mr. Wolfe's work. Eliza and old Gant come from a more primary level of experience, figures of motherhood and fatherhood that gradually, as the book progresses, assume a wider significance and become at the same time a reference for the hero's personal experience. And the author, knowing them first on that level, has a way of knowing them more intimately and profoundly as people than he ever knows Starwick. Starwick is more artificial, because he is at the same time a social symbol and a symbol for a purely private confusion the roots of which are never clear.

Most of the other characters are treated directly. Mr. Wolfe has an appetite for people and occasionally a faculty of very acute perception. The portrait of Abe Jones, the Jewish student at the college in New York, and those of the people at the Coulson household in Oxford, are evidence enough of this capacity. But his method, or rather methods, of presentation are various and not unvaryingly successful. There are long stretches of stenographic dialogue that has little focus, or no focus whatsoever, for instance the first part of the conversation of the businessmen in the pullman in Book I, of the residents of the hotel in Book IV, of the artistic hangers-on at the Cambridge tea parties, or even of Eugene and his companions in the Paris cafés. Some of this reporting is very scrupulous, and good as reporting, but in its mass, its aimlessness, and its lack of direction it is frequently dull; the momentary interest of recognition is not enough to sustain it, and it bears no precise relation to the intention of the novel. It is conversation for conversation's sake, a loquacity and documentation that testifies to the author's talent but not to his intelligence as an artist. Generally this type of presentation is imitative of Sinclair Lewis's realistic dialogue, but it lacks the meticulous, cautious, and selective quality of the best of Lewis, the controlled malice; it is too random, and in an incidental sense, too heavily pointed.

Further, there are tremendous masses of description and characters. Mr. Wolfe has the habit of developing his own *clichés* for description of character, and of then exhibiting them at irregular intervals. It is as if he realized the bulk of the novel and the difficulty a reader might experience in recognizing a character on reappearance, and so determined to prevent this, if possible, by repetition and insistence. For instance, Starwick and Ann, one of the young women from Boston who is in love with Starwick, have a complete set of tags and labels that are affixed to them time after time during the novel. Mr. Wolfe underrates the memory of the reader; or this may be but another instance of the lack of control that impairs his work.

Only in the section dealing with the Coulson episode does

Mr. Wolfe seem to have all his resources for character presentation under control. The men who room in the house, the jaunty Captain Nicholl with his blasted arm and the other two young men from the motor-car factory—these with the Coulsons themselves are very precise to the imagination, and are sketched in with an economy usually foreign to Mr. Wolfe. The Coulson girl, accepting the mysterious ruin that presides over the household, is best drawn and dominates the group. Here Mr. Wolfe has managed to convey an atmosphere and to convince the reader of the reality of his characters without any of his habitual exaggerations of method and style. This section, with slight alterations, originally appeared as a short story; it possesses what is rare enough in *Of Time and the River,* a constant focus.

I have remarked that some of Mr. Wolfe's material is not subordinated to the intention of the book. What is his intention? On what is the mass of material focussed? What is to give it form? His novels are obviously autobiographical. This means that the binding factor should be, at least in part, the personality of the narrator, or since Mr. Wolfe adopts a disguise, of the hero, Eugene Gant. The two books are, in short, an account of the development of a sensibility; obviously something more is intended than the looseness and irresponsibility of pure memoirs or observations. The work demands comparison with such things as Joyce's *Portrait of the Artist as a Young Man* or Lawrence's *Sons and Lovers*; it may even demand comparison with proper autobiographies such as Rousseau's *Confessions* or *The Education of Henry Adams*. But the comparison with these books is not to the advantage of Mr. Wolfe's performance. It has not the artistry of the first two, the constant and dramatic relation of incident to a developing consciousness of the world, nor has it the historical importance of the third, or the philosophical and intellectual interest of the last.

The hero of *Look Homeward, Angel,* though a child and adolescent, is essentially more interesting than the Eugene of *Of Time and the River*. He is more comprehensible, because there is a real (and necessarily conventional) pattern to his developing awareness of the world around him. Further, the life of the Gant household, and even of the community, is patterned with a certain amount of strictness in relation to Eugene: the impress of the vast vitality of old Gant, the lack of understanding on the part of the mother and the perpetual emotional drag of resentment and affection she exerts on her son, the quarrels with Steve, the confusion and pathos of the sexual experiences, the profound attachment between Ben and Eugene, and the climatic and daring scene with Ben's spirit. There is a progress toward maturity, a fairly precise psychological interest. The novel contains much pure baggage and much material that is out of tone, usually in the form of an ironic commentary that violates the point of view; but the book is more of a unit, and is, for that reason perhaps, more exciting and forceful.

In *Of Time and the River* as Eugene in his pullman rides at night across Virginia, going "northward, worldward, towards the secret borders of Virginia, towards the great world cities of his hope, the fable of his childhood legendry," the following passage is interpolated:

> Who has seen fury riding in the mountains?
> Who has known fury striding in the storm? Who
> has been mad with fury in his youth, given no
> rest or peace or certitude by fury, driven on
> across the earth by fury, until the great vine of
> his heart was broke, the sinews wrenched, the
> little tenement of bone, blood, marrow, brain,
> and feeling in which great fury raged, was twist-
> ed, wrung, depleted, worn out, and exhausted by
> the fury which it could not lose or put away?
> Who has known fury, how it came?
>
> How have we breathed him, drunk him, eaten
> fury to the core, until we have him in us now and
> cannot lose him anywhere we go? It is a strange
> and subtle worm that will. . . .

Now this furious Eugene is scarcely made so comprehensible. The reader amasses a large body of facts about him,
as about Starwick, but with something of the same result.
He knows that Eugene is big; that he is a creature of enormous appetites of which he is rather proud; that he has the
habit of walking much at night; that he is fascinated by the
health and urbanity of his friend Joel and by the personality of Starwick; that he ceases to like Shelley after spending
an afternoon in a jail cell; that he reads 20,000 books in
ten years; that he is obsessed by the idea of devouring all
of life. Then, the reader knows the facts of Eugene's com-
ings and goings, and knows the people he meets and what
they say. But the Eugene susceptible to such definition is
not the hero of the book, or at least does not function adequately as such. The hero is really that nameless fury that
drives Eugene. The book is an effort to name that fury, and
perhaps by naming it, to tame it. But the fury goes un-
named and untamed. Since the book is formless otherwise,
only a proper emotional reference to such a centre could
give it form. Instead, at the centre there is this chaos that
steams and bubbles in rhetoric and apocalyptic apostrophe, sometimes grand and sometimes febrile and empty;
the centre is a maelstrom, perhaps artificially generated at
times; and the other, tangible items are the flotsam and jet-
sam and dead wood spewed up, iridescent or soggy as the
case may be.

It may be objected that other works of literary art, and
very great ones at that, have heroes who defy definition
and who are merely centres of "fury." For instance, there
is Hamlet, or Lear. But a difference may be observed.
Those characters may defy the attempt at central definition, but the play hangs together in each case as a structure without such definition; that is, there has been no confusion between the sensibility that produced a play, as an
object of art, and the sensibility of a hero in a play. (And
the mere fact that *Hamlet* and *Lear* employ verse as a vehicle adds further to the impression of discipline, focus,
and control.)

There are two other factors in the character of Eugene that
may deserve mention. The hero feels a sense of destiny and
direction, the sense of being "chosen" in the midst of a
world of defeated, aimless, snobbish, vulgar, depleted, or
suicidal people. (This is, apparently, the source of much
of the interpolated irony in both books, an irony almost
regularly derivative and mechanical.) In real life this conviction of a high calling may be enough to make a "hero"

feel that life does have form and meaning; but the mere
fact that a hero in a novel professes the high calling and
is contrasted in his social contacts with an inferior breed
does not, in itself, give the novel form and meaning. The
transference of the matter from the actuality of life to the
actuality of art cannot be accomplished so easily. Second,
at the very end of the novel Eugene, about to embark for
America, sees a woman who, according to the somewhat
extended lyrical epilogue, makes him "lose" self and so be
"found":

> After all the blind, tormented wanderings of
> youth, that woman would become his heart's
> centre and the target for his life, the image of im-
> mortal one-ness that again collected him to one,
> and hurled the whole collected passion, power,
> and might of his one life into the blazing certi-
> tude, the immortal governance and unity, of
> love.

Certainly this is what we call fine writing; it may or may
not be good writing. And probably, falling in love may
make a man "find himself"; but this epilogue scarcely
makes the novel find itself.

It is possible sometimes that a novel possessing no structure in the ordinary sense of the word, or not properly
dominated by its hero's personality or fortunes, may be
given a focus by the concrete incorporation of an idea, or
related ideas. Now, *Of Time and the River* has such a
leading idea, but an idea insufficient in its operation. The
leading symbol of the father, old Gant, gradually assumes
another aspect, not purely personal; he becomes, in other
words, a kind of symbol of the fatherland, the source, the
land of violence, drunkenness, fecundity, beauty, and vig-
our on which the hero occasionally reflects during his
wanderings and to which in the end he returns. But this
symbol is not the total expression of the idea, which is
worked out more explicitly and at length. There are long
series of cinematic flashes of "phases of American life": lo-
comotive drivers, gangsters, pioneers, little towns with the
squares deserted at night, evangelists, housewives, rich
and suicidal young men, whores on subways, drunk college boys. Or there are more lyrical passages, less effective
in pictorial detail, such as the following:

> It was the wild, sweet, casual, savage, and in-
> credibly lovely earth of America, and the wilder-
> ness, and it haunted them like legends, and
> pierced them like a sword, and filled them with
> a wild and swelling prescience of joy that was
> like sorrow and delight.

This kind of material alternates with the more sedate or
realistic progress of the chronicle, a kind of running commentary of patriotic mysticism on the more tangible
events and perceptions. For Mr. Wolfe has the mysticism
of the American idea that we find in Whitman, Sandburg,
Masters, Crane, and Benét, or more recently and frivo-
lously, in Coffin and Paul Engle. He pants for the Word,
the union that will clarify all the disparate and confused
elements which he enumerates and many of which fill him
with revulsion and disgust. He, apparently, has experienced the visionary moment he proclaims, but, like other
mystics, he suffers some difficulty when he attempts to
prepare it for the consumption of ordinary citizens of the

Republic. He must wreak some indignity on the chastity of the vision. This indignity is speech: but he burns, perversely, to speak.

The other promulgators of the American vision have been poets. Mr. Wolfe, in addition to being a poet in instinct, is, as well, the owner on a large scale of many of the gifts of the novelist. He attempts to bolster, or as it were to prove, the mystical and poetic vision by fusing it with a body of everyday experience of which the novelist ordinarily treats. But there is scarcely a fusion or a correlation; rather, an oscillation. On the tangible side, the hero flees from America, where his somewhat quivering sensibilities are frequently tortured, and goes to Europe; in the end, worn out by drinking and late hours, disgusted with his friends, unacquainted with the English or the French, and suffering homesickness, he returns to America. But Mr. Wolfe, more than most novelists, is concerned with the intangible; not so much with the psychological process and interrelation as with the visionary "truth."

The other poets, at least Whitman and Crane, have a certain advantage over the poet in Mr. Wolfe. They overtly consented to be poets; Mr. Wolfe has not consented. Therefore their vision is purer, the illusion of communication (*illusion,* for it is doubtful that they have really communicated with central vision) is more readily palatable, because they never made a serious pretense of proving it autobiographically or otherwise; they were content with the hortatory moment, the fleeting symbol, and the affirmation. (Mr. Benét, of course, did attempt in *John Brown's Body* such a validation, but with a degree of success that does not demand comment here.) It may simply be that the poets were content to be lyric poets, and therefore could more readily attempt the discipline of selection and concentration; in those respects, even Whitman shows more of an instinct for form than does Mr. Wolfe. Mr. Wolfe is astonishingly diffuse, astonishingly loose in his rhetoric—qualities that, for the moment, may provide more praise than blame. That rhetoric is sometimes grand, but probably more often tedious and tinged with hysteria. Because he is officially writing prose and not poetry he has no caution of the *clichés* of phrase or rhythm, and no compunction about pilfering from other poets. His vocabulary itself is worth comment. If the reader will inspect the few passages quoted in the course of this essay he will observe a constant quality of strain, a fancy for the violent word or phrase (but often conventionally poetic as well as violent): "wild, sweet, casual, savage . . . ," "haunted them like legends," "no rest or peace or certitude of fury," "target of his life," "blazing certitude, the immortal governance and unity, of love." Mr. Wolfe often shows very powerfully the poetic instinct, and the praise given by a number of critics to his "sensuousness" and "gusto" is not without justification in the fact; but even more often his prose simply shows the poetic instinct unbuckled on a kind of week-end debauch. He sometimes wants it both ways: the structural irresponsibility of prose and the emotional intensity of poetry. He may overlook the fact that the intensity is rarely to be achieved without a certain rigour in selection and structure.

Further, Mr. Wolfe, we understand from blurbs and re-

viewers, is attempting a kind of prose epic. American literature has produced one, *Moby Dick.* There is much in common between *Moby Dick* and *Of Time and the River,* but there is one major difference. Melville had a powerful fable, a myth of human destiny, which saved his work from the centrifugal impulses of his genius, and which gave it structure and climax. Its dignity is inherent in the fable itself. No such dignity is inherent in Mr. Wolfe's scheme, if it can properly be termed a scheme. The nearest approach to it is in the character of old Gant, but that is scarcely adequate. And Mr. Wolfe has not been able to compensate for the lack of a fable by all his well-directed and misdirected attempts to endow his subject with a proper dignity, by all his rhetorical insistence, all the clarity and justice of his incidental poetic perceptions, all the hysteria or magnificent hypnosis.

Probably all of these defects, or most of them, are inherent in the autobiographical impulse when the writer attempts to make this special application of it. In the first place, all the impurities and baggage in the book must strike the author as of peculiar and necessary value because they were observed or actually occurred. But he is not writing a strict autobiography in which all observations or experiences, however vague, might conceivably find a justification. He is trying, and this in the second place, to erect the autobiographical material into an epical and symbolic importance, to make of it a fable, a "Legend of Man's Hunger in his Youth." This much is definitely declared by the sub-title.

Mr. Wolfe promises to write some historical novels, and they may well be crucial in the definition of his genius, because he may be required to re-order the use of his powers. What, thus far, he has produced are fine fragments, several brilliant pieces of portraiture, and many sharp observations on men and nature. . . . Despite [Mr. Wolfe's] admirable energies and his powerful literary endowments, his work illustrates once more the limitations, perhaps the necessary limitations, of an attempt to exploit directly and naïvely the personal experience and the self-defined personality in art.

And meanwhile it may be well to recollect that Shakespeare merely wrote *Hamlet;* he was *not* Hamlet.

Charles I. Glicksberg   (essay date 1936)

SOURCE: "Thomas Wolfe," in *The Canadian Forum,* Vol. XV, No. 180, January, 1936, pp. 24-5.

[*In the following excerpt from a review of* Of Time and the River, *Glicksberg examines Wolfe's prose style.*]

Of Time and the River is an astonishing book. It towers like a rugged mountain above the contemporary literature landscape. Whatever the critics have said or may still say about it, they seem to agree on one point: it is imbued with an extraordinary vitality and it is instinct with lyricism and splendor. It is the work of a man drunk with the wine of life, intoxicated with the rich multiplicity of sensations, emotions and thoughts. Indeed, it is this almost frenzied vehemence, this unbridled excess of emotion and perception which so definitely stamps his work as individual.

The reaction to the naturalistic novel with its emphasis on psychopathology, was bound to come. Naturalistic fiction lacks exaltation, the tragic intensity of vision which makes man of central importance in the universe. It is bitter and pessimistic in its conclusions. But the tide turned with the advent of *Anthony Adverse*. That dreamlike allegory of adventure and love in a glamorous past, in a world of refined sensuality and wealth and noble striving, paved the way for *Of Time and the River*. The popularity of the latter novel is understandable. It is the saga of youth, superbly told, catching all the glory and hunger of youth. There are the weaknesses, of course, that are inseparable from any ambitious effort. But they are weaknesses that stand nakedly exposed, weaknesses inherent in the scheme and structure of the tale, weaknesses that are consistent with the nature of the experiences described. In many of its passages, the book is sheer poetry; it is mystical and obsessed, profound and naive at the same time.

Thomas Wolfe is young and like many novelists in their early stages, he feels tempted to reveal everything. Everything that he has felt, known, yearned for, is described. He lives and writes at such high pressure that he evidently does not realize that he is frequently irrelevant and diffuse; the plot is retarded by essays on his reading, philosophic dissertations on time, love, death and fame. Despite these choral interludes, which are essentially incompatible with the form of the novel, the book is unified because it revolves around the central character of Eugene Gant. He is individual and universal, an atom and a cosmos, man aching, sensual, drunk, foolish and generic, lifting his fist against the sky of fate in reckless defiance, taking the pilgrimage that all must take to death. Although Wolfe has an enormous lust for new experiences, he is not satisfied with experience alone, and this differentiates him sharply from the novelists of the naturalistic school. He strives manfully to understand, to ask again questions that have never really been answered. It is this faculty of vision, this Faustian metaphysical longing, which makes this book, as well as [*Look Homeward, Angel*], a vast and fruitful allegory of the modern soul. In explaining the central design for his work, Thomas Wolfe said: "I guess the general plan back of these books is the story of a man's looking for his father. Everybody in the world—not only men, but women—are looking for a father. Looking for someone of superior strength. Some person outside of themselves to whom they can attach their belief."

The author's comments on America, like so many of his critical reflections, do not betray deep insight. It is only when he describes and experiences or longs for more life that his prose burns with the fire of truth; when he begins to speculate he falls into loose generalities. Americans, it seems to him, are "so lost, so naked and so lonely." "Immense and cruel skies bend over us, and all of us are driven on forever and we have no home." America is vast, solitary. It is a fabulous country nevertheless, a land to be proud of, the one place "where miracles can not only happen but happen all the time." With remarkable gusto he retails the characteristics and beauties of this land. Many of these descriptions resemble a poem by Whitman but they are more artistically done, with more scrupulous regard for details and words. His account of life at Harvard

and his glimpse of the "passionate enigma of New England" constitute a prose poem, exuberant, overflowing with hyperbolical indiscretions. Yet he has caught the spirit of the place, the genius of Boston, temporarily fallen in love with New England. The best parts of the book, indeed, are those dealing with native material. After Eugene leaves America for England and France, Wolfe's style loses some of its fervour and eloquence; the note becomes forced, the music often literary. He is writing, one suspects, for writing's sake. Avariciously he is cramming all kinds of information into his brain; fastening gestures, faces, conversations, scenes and ideas on paper, lest he forget them and they be lost.

As for himself, Thomas Wolfe has found in the history of his own family "all the substance and energy of the human drama." Art he regards, in short, as fundamentally autobiographical. *Of Time and the River* is unmistakably a confession, a creative revelation of himself and the family from which he sprang. His sisters and brothers and uncles were full of the folly and passions, the ambitions and frustrations of all living creatures; they were "not to be praised nor blamed, but just blood, bone, marrow, passion and feeling—the whole swarming web of life and error in full play and magnificently alive". There speaks the artist. People are not to be judged by moral standards, neither praised nor condemned. They are to be understood for what they are and loved.

His prose may be either considered as a superb achievement or as a memorable failure. It has the stamp of recorded experiences deeply felt, it flows with symphonic amplitude, it is rich and resonant and in the grand tradition. Above all, it is dynamic. His style brings to mind the majestic sweep, although not the simplicity, of the Bible, the contrapuntal music of De Quincey's prose, the sonorous tonalities of Whitman's poetry. But, although the influence of his intensive reading is apparent, it does not result in weak, flabby imitation. He does not ape any writer.

Unfortunately Wolfe has attempted to cover too vast a canvas, to include too much within the framework of his conception. Just as he has endeavoured to experience every variety of sensation, to read all books ever printed, visit all secret places of the earth and absorb their essence, so the book in style, form and treatment is a kaleidoscopic medley of diverse literary influences. He will no doubt grow in restraint and therefore in power; and in time he will learn that the quality of the incommunicable, no matter how obsessive, cannot be suggested by a riotous welter of sensuous and sonorous phrases.

Herbert J. Muller   (essay date 1947)

SOURCE: "The Legend of a Man's Hunger in His Youth," in *Thomas Wolfe,* New Directions Books, 1947, pp. 23-76.

[*In the following excerpt, Muller compares* Of Time and the River *to* Look Homeward, Angel *in order to illustrate Wolfe's development as a writer.*]

Up to a point, *Of Time and the River* may be considered as of a piece with *Look Homeward, Angel*—another huge length sliced off the story that Wolfe apparently will go on writing forever. . . . I should pause to remark that he is indeed taking an unconscionably long time in growing up. *Of Time and the River* still reads like a first novel. Although published six years after *Look Homeward, Angel,* it is full of the same extravagances and is not a more finished technical performance; Wolfe appears to have learned little or nothing about his craft. Offhand, in fact, *Look Homeward, Angel* comes off better in a comparison. It remains the most unified of his novels, lyrically and dramatically, because it naturally falls into a simple pattern. It covers a natural stage in a man's life; it tells with wholehearted intensity the story of growing pains, which to the youth are very complicated but to the grown man an old story. By contrast, *Of Time and the River* is an arbitrary slice of a man's life, with practically no plot unity, no climax, no dramatic beginning, middle and end. It has more breadth and variety because Eugene Gant has got out into the great world; it also seems more formless and muddled because he is lost there, at the end appearing to be just about where he was at the beginning.

Perhaps the best index to the range and the limits of Wolfe's capacities at this stage is the creation of Francis Starwick, the esthete who is Eugene's best friend at Harvard and who turns out to be a homosexual. On the whole, it is an impressive creation. It is the more notable because, though drawn from life, this is a kind of life utterly foreign to the world of *Look Homeward, Angel* and to Wolfe's natural bent. But it was too foreign for him wholly to command. He never convinces us that Starwick was quite so rare and brilliant a spirit as he declares—"one of the most extraordinary figures of his generation." His admiration of Starwick seems rather provincial; the uncouth country boy is envious of the polished gentleman-artist. The country boy is also exasperated by him, however, and becomes tiresome in his mimicry of Starwick's precious accents: "The thing is so *utterly* French . . . really *quite* astonishing. . . *terribly* amusing . . . perfectly *grand.*" In his impassioned moments, on the other hand, Starwick is apt to talk like Wolfe: "My God! to come into this world scarce half made up, to have the spirit of the artist and to lack his hide, to feel the intolerable and unspeakable beauty, mystery, loveliness, and terror of this immortal land—this great America—and a skin too sensitive, a hide too delicate and rare . . . to declare its cruelty, its horror, falseness, hunger, the warped and twisted soul of its frustration." Here Wolfe romanticizes the pathetic story of Starwick's inadequate talent, as if it were the tragic ruin of genius, because he identifies himself with Starwick and conceives the frustration of the artist as the most terrible of life's cruelties. The basic uncertainty of his conception is most apparent in the closing scenes, where Starwick emerges as "his friend, his brother—and his mortal enemy." Wolfe is characteristically attempting to create a symbolic, mythical figure, and by his characteristic method of incongruity; but the only apparent basis for the mortal enmity is that Starwick got the girl for whom Eugene had a fancy. In the scene of their final parting—goodbye, my one true friend, and goodbye, my mortal enemy, and "Oh, to feel so, suffer so, and live so!"—the myth collapses into banality.

Hence when Wolfe died, three years after the appearance of *Of Time and the River,* with his subsequent work not yet published, the more critical obituaries generally expressed the attitude that still persists. It was agreed that he had splendid talent, energy, ambition; but he had no art, no perspective, no humor, no philosophy, no social consciousness—in effect, no mind. He was compared to an automobile "with unlimited horsepower, a tiny steering wheel, and no brakes." Others dated the automobile. "Wolfe belonged to the high-pitched, unreal 1920's . . . " wrote Louis Kronenberger. "When he died, young as he was, he had lived too long. For the soberer life that came after the 20's, when the accent fell not on the individual but on society, was something Wolfe could not understand." Kronenberger added that he "never acquired, of course, any values—either intellectual or moral—that were worth consideration." John Peale Bishop, on the other hand, placed Wolfe in the disenchanted 'thirties. Appreciating his values as a mythmaker, Bishop linked him with Hart Crane, as the two most conspicuous failures in recent American literature. Both Crane and Wolfe sought their subject in the greatness of America, but both found that the America they longed to celebrate did not exist. "Both were led at last, on proud romantic feet, to Brooklyn. And what they found there they abhorred." The depression in particular killed Wolfe's faith, Bishop thought. Hence Wolfe could find no meaning, no structure, for *Of Time and the River.*

Such verdicts were understandable enough at the time. Although they should have been more generally revised after the appearance of *You Can't Go Home Again,* I cite them here chiefly to emphasize the real limits of Wolfe's achievement up to this point. His central meaning was not clear; his critics were confused about his purposes and his values because he was himself confused. Yet *Of Time and the River* does give signs that he was really developing, coming out of confusion. The signs may escape notice because they involve the realization of a few elementary truths that will be no revelation to the reader. They may be apparent chiefly in rereading, in the light of Wolfe's final accomplishment. I may be overemphasizing them here simply because it is the critic's business to make out unity and continuity, to get things into shape. Nevertheless this is the critic's business; and Wolfe does not have to be pounded into shape. He was in fact acquiring both moral and intellectual values, entering on the "soberer life that came after the 20's."

The most obvious sign of this growth is an increasing strain of self-criticism. Although Wolfe is still far from mastering his follies, as man and as artist, at least he now recognizes them. In *Look Homeward, Angel* he is pleased by his romantic image, proud of such discoveries as his dislike for "whatever fits too snugly in a measure"; he is pleased to be Dr. Faustus, at whatever cost of mad hunger, fury and despair, because this is the divine madness of the Artist; and while he admits his human failings, the grievous fault is always in the world around him. Although his romanticism is not shallow—he notes that his quality as a romantic was not "to escape out of life, but into it"—his realism is also youthful. He wants Life, which is a glowing abstraction, necessarily different from all the life he knows; he wants the world, even though the world is his natural enemy. In *Of Time and the River,* however, he becomes aware that his mad hunger may be literally mad, and its futility no sign of divinity. At moments "the hopeless and unprofitable struggle of the Faustian life" become "horribly evident." It is unprofitable, as Starwick points out to Eugene, because it is unnecessary as well as hopeless:

> Do you think that you will really gain in wisdom if you read a million books? Do you think you will find out more about life if you know a million people rather than yourself? Do you think you will get more pleasure from a thousand women than from two or three—see more if you go to a hundred countries instead of six?

Eugene does think so, or for the most part continues to act as if he does; but at least Wolfe no longer does. If he may still rant about the futility of ranting, and his passion may grow madder because he is horrified by the thought that it is mad, he is getting more distance between Eugene and himself, viewing his story with more detachment. Furthermore, his maturer attitudes are coloring the substance and quality of his narrative, not merely punctuating it with reflective passages. An incidental example is the appearance of a quieter, cooler satire, approaching subtlety, as in the skilful portrait of Professor Hatcher. ("He was one of those rare people who really 'chuckle,' and although there was no doubting the spontaneity and naturalness of his chuckle, it is also probably true that Professor Hatcher somewhat fancied himself as a chuckler.") Similarly there appears a quieter kind of drama, as in Eugene's experience with the Coulson household in England: the crisp, competent, self-assured Coulsons who are lost in fog, failure and ruin, always friendly but unapproachable behind "the armor of their hard bright eyes"; while their boarders, who have also lost something precious and irrecoverable, nightly improvise negro jazz, fighting their emptiness with a "deliberate, formidable, and mad intensity of a calculated gaiety, a terrifying mimicry of mirth," as the storm-wind howls through the dark trees around them. In this episode Wolfe handles his typical incongruities with something like the melancholy, ironic detachment of Joseph Conrad; and his tone differs from Conrad's less in its higher pitch than in its more apparent tenderness.

This relative sobriety is most notable in Wolfe's treatment of his family, especially his father and mother. They have not changed, but they appear more admirable and more pitiable in *Of Time and the River* than in *Look Homeward, Angel*; Wolfe is no longer taking out on them his own bitterness. In the death of Gant—another of his unforgettable scenes—he does complete justice to their humanity. There is horror enough, or possibly even too much: the old stone-cutter, long a spectre except for his grotesquely powerful hands, suffers from enough cancer to kill a battalion of ordinary men. There is also a quality of tenderness and pity that has been rare in Wolfe. In the last conversation between Gant and Eliza he makes amends, yet without sacrificing truthfulness:

> "Eliza,"—he said—and at the sound of that unaccustomed word, a name he had spoken only twice in forty years—her white face and her worn brown eyes turned toward him with the quick and startled look of an animal—"Eliza," he said quietly, "you have had a hard life with me, a hard time. I want to tell you that I'm sorry."
>
> And before she could move from her white stillness of shocked surprise, he lifted his great right hand and put it gently down across her own. And for a moment she sat there bolt upright, shaken, frozen, with a look of terror in her eyes, her heart drained of blood, a pale smile trembling uncertainly and foolishly on her lips. Then she tried to withdraw her hand with a clumsy movement, she began to stammer with an air of ludicrous embarrassment, she bridled, saying—"Aw-w, now, Mr. Gant. Well, now, I reckon,"—and suddenly these few simple words of regret and affection did what all the violence, abuse, drunkenness and injury of forty years had failed to do. She wrenched her hand free like a wounded creature, her face was suddenly contorted by that grotesque and pitiable grimace of sorrow that women have had in moments of grief since the beginning of time, and digging her fist into her closed eye quickly with the pathetic gesture of a child, she lowered her head and wept bitterly:
>
> "It was a hard time, Mr. Gant," she whispered, "a hard time, sure enough. . . . "

But presently she is ashamed of her tears, and adds hastily, "Not that I'm blamin' you, Mr. Gant . . . I reckon we were both at fault . . . there was always something strange-like about you that I didn't understand." Then, drying her eyes, she returns to her dauntless self, sublime and ridiculous in her optimism: "Well, now, Mr. Gant, that's all over." Now he must set his mind on getting well. She winks at him briskly. Half our ills are imagination, she adds sententiously. But if he'll just make up his mind to it, he'll get well. They both have years before them, perhaps the best years of their life; they can now profit by their mistakes. "That's just exactly what we'll do!" A few minutes later blood is pouring out of his mouth and nostrils; and Mr. Gant is dead.

The matrix of all these developments in *Of Time and the River* is Wolfe's growing realization of the deep bonds that united him with his fellowmen. With nature the childgiant from the mountains had been one, but in society he had been one apart; he was "called" but had no clearly recognized or generally respected calling; and he had prized his loneliness as a token that his spirit, like Shelley's, was "tameless and swift and proud." But now Wolfe is less proud. After a drunken escapade that lands him in jail, Eugene comes out feeling more than remorse. He is conscious "of a more earthly, common, and familiar union with the lives of other men than he had ever known." Wolfe tells us that Shelley is no longer his favorite poet: the sense of "proud and lonely inviolability" that he had treasured in Shelley has lost its magic.

This consciousness of community is again an elementary discovery, and in part a matter of mood. It has not yet got into Wolfe's habitual feeling—for a long time he had been at home with his feeling of homelessness. Yet his new consciousness was clear and deep enough to be of decisive importance in the myth that he was living as well as writing. It gave him a self-knowledge that his intense self-consciousness had denied him; for only through identification with others can one really know one's self, only through a full recognition of the typical and communal can one fully realize his individuality. Wolfe's romantic individualism had stamped him as a familiar type and impeded the growth of a real individuality, much as the popular worship of personality hinders people from becoming real persons. By the same token, Wolfe now came closer to the sources of myth; for at its broadest and deepest the typical is the mythical. And the realization of the living truth in such truisms is not, perhaps, so elementary a discovery after all. As Thomas Mann has said, the mythical represents an early, primitive stage in the life of humanity, but a late and mature one in the life of the individual. . . .

Look Homeward, Angel remains a very personal legend of a very young man who is literally lost and seeking an actual home. Already Wolfe begins to say that he can't go home again, but by home he means simply Asheville. Even in these terms, to be sure, the legend has universal significance: countless young men have felt lost, homeless, hungry for life, love and fame—and have believed themselves unique. Nevertheless Wolfe was still thinking primarily in personal terms, as the old mythmakers did not. He also differed from them in that where they perceived chiefly likenesses or identities, he perceived incongruities and profound oppositions as well. So must we all today; only in these complex terms can the myth still be valid. In his egocentricity, however, Wolfe magnified the oppositions, or even created them. And it is these that begin to dissolve in *Of Time and the River*. Although Wolfe is still confined to his own experience, incapable of a detached, objective view of the world around him, he now recognizes that his experience is not singular and that he has much in common with the world. Although he is prone to create other men in his own lonely image, he recognizes their community in loneliness, and despite loneliness. In general, his personal legend becomes increasingly typical and symbolical. Specifically, it becomes an American legend.

Thus his highly individualized, even eccentric characters are now presented as characteristic American products or types. His father's life is an American tragedy: the life of "the lost American who has been brought forth naked under immense and lonely skies, to 'shift for himself,' to grope his way blindly through the confusion and brutal chaos of a life as naked and unsure as he, to wander blindly down across the continent, to hunt forever for a goal, a wall, a dwelling place of warmth and certitude, a light, a door." In particular, old Gant is a symbol of the old pioneer America which has been increasingly corrupted by commercialism: thus as a young man he had carved a marble angel, in his dream of becoming a sculptor, and as an old man he sold it to ornament the grave of a whore. American, too, is the "dissonance and frenzied unrest" of Eugene's brother Luke, hurling himself along lonely roads at night, "going furiously from nowhere into nowhere, rushing ahead with starlight shining on his knit brows and his drawn face, with nothing but the lonely, mournful, and desolate red-clay earth about him, the immense, the mer-

ciless emptiness and calm of the imperturbable skies above him." Even the rare, the precious Francis Starwick turns out to be the son of a Mid-Western small-town school superintendent; and his story is at bottom the pitifully common one of a precious devotion to "culture" because of the "rawness" and "crudeness" of American life. So a host of unrelated characters, who had entered Wolfe's novel chiefly because they had entered his life, are now related to a common theme—the magnificent promise and the appalling blight of American life.

Similarly a host of sensuous images of the physical background become related to a more philosophical image. Initially, they owed much more to memory than to reflection; they constituted a panorama of America rather than a vision; and the meaning of the spectacle changed with Eugene's mood. Often Wolfe's image of America is an enchanted one of an immense, exultant, fabulous country "where miracles not only happen, but where they happen all the time." As often it is a disenchanted view of an immense desolation, ugliness, cruelty, savagery; the miracles do not happen. But now he is more earnestly seeking a central meaning, and more clearly perceiving that he must find it in precisely these violent contradictions. Eugene makes the "desperate and soul-sickening discovery" that he must find goodness, truth and beauty, not in radiant, magical images, but in "the mean hearts of common men," in "all the blind and brutal complications" of the destiny of America. There, in ways still darklier and stranger than he had thought, lay his heart's desire: "buried there in the grimy and illimitable jungles of its savage cities—a-prowl and raging in the desert and half-mad with hunger in the barren land, befouled and smutted with the rust and grime of its vast works and factories, warped and scarred and twisted, stunned, bewildered by the huge multitude of all its errors and blind gropings, yet still fierce with life, still savage with its hunger, still broken, slain and devoured by its terrific earth, its savage wilderness—and still, somehow, God knows how, the thing of which he was a part, that beat in every atom of his blood and brain and life, and was indestructible and everlasting, and that was America!"

This whole development, finally, gives *Of Time and the River* a kind of form, which helps to explain the cumulative power of the novel that many readers feel even while they feel troubled by the absence of conventional plot or dramatic unity. As Joseph Warren Beach remarks, it is a musical form, comparable to a tone poem of Richard Strauss or a Wagnerian opera—or in the novel to Gide's *The Counterfeiters*. The central theme is the idea of a pilgrimage; the *leitmotifs* are the recurrent images of loneliness and hunger, the quest of a father, of a gate or door, of a tongue or word by which to articulate and "possess" all life; and the basic incongruities may serve as counterpoint. In terms of episode, the related themes are the pilgrimages of the Southerner to the North, of the country boy to the big city, of the American to Europe—all projected against the background of time and the river, the pilgrimage of man's life on the timeless earth. Such elements of form are clearer when *Of Time and the River* is viewed in relation to Wolfe's whole "book," and in any view are blurred by considerable extraneous material. Unlike Gide, Wolfe did not consciously plan his novel so. Yet his central theme, at least, is clear and explicit; and as the passionate pilgrim becomes more conscious of its implications, the related themes emerge more clearly from the sprawl and dissonance of his experience.

The most significant experience that the North afforded Wolfe was the experience of cosmopolitan New York, the melting pot of rural as well as foreign-born America, and the symbol of the multitudinous life he had a passion to absorb.

—Herbert J. Muller

The least significant of these themes is Wolfe's flight from the "lost and lonely South." He was indeed a selfconscious rebel, who wrote bitterly of the sterile romanticism of the South with its "swarming superstition," its "cheap mythology," its "hostile and murderous intrenchment against all new life." He accordingly angered many Southerners; one critic suggested that perhaps he "should be obliged, in the vast area of his sympathies, to make room for the people who bred him." In fact, however, Wolfe never lost his sympathy for these people. He always wrote with deep feeling of "Old Catawba," and its obscure but magnificent history "full of heroism, endurance, and the immortal silence of the earth"; in his last work he was writing this history. His very pride in it intensified his scorn of the legends of an "aristocratic culture," especially in South Carolina. At any rate, he had not been deeply affected by the romantic mythology of the South, and quickly outgrew his boyish attachment to it. For him the road to the "proud fierce North," the land of his father, was doubtless the road to freedom and life; his flight was a sign of the realistic quality of his own romanticism. Yet the North was not itself the land of freedom; he was no less critical of it, and lost and lonely in it. And though his criticism sometimes betrays the proud Southerner, who is sometimes embarrassed by a feeling of apostasy, this was a more or less incidental complication of his thought and feeling. The chief point is that no merely regional tradition could satisfy his hunger or provide an image large enough for his belief and his power.

Hence the most significant experience that the North afforded Wolfe was the experience of cosmopolitan New York, the melting pot of rural as well as foreign-born America, and the symbol of the multitudinous life he had a passion to absorb. This stage of his pilgrimage reveals his exceptional ability to recapture the marvelous and the mythical in the commonplace. Because the coming of a country boy to the big city is so old a tale, we are apt to forget what a thrilling, magical and meaningful adventure it is; and no other writer has rendered its quality so fully and so glowingly as has Wolfe. But this experience is also fundamental to his whole legend. Inevitably he was disil-

lusioned by New York, unable to digest its multitudes, and his revulsion inspired his blackest, bitterest pages. Necessarily he had to outgrow or transcend this disillusionment if his myth was to accommodate the terms of modern experience. For it New York is not the whole of America, it is the symbol of modern industrial America at its best and its worst. It is the quintessential manifestation of the exuberant energy and the might of a polyglot land; of the fabulous power of "natural knowledge" expressed in the soar of skyscrapers, the sweep of bridges, the blaze of swarming streets; of the grandeur and the glory realized in concrete, steel and glass. It is also the quintessence of the grime and filth, the dreary waste, the raucous vulgarity, the blatant materialism, the brutal violence of industrial America. So must it be accepted, as magnificent monument and as foul blot. So Wolfe did in time accept it. "And that was America!" was the conclusion of his "desperate and soul-sickening discovery." If the discovery seems needlessly desperate, at least he earned his exclamation point.

The turning point in his experience, however, was the pilgrimage to Europe. In Europe he saw a way of life magical in its grace, its form, its assurance; here were people who had found a way, a door; here were actual pleasure and joy, immediately realized and shared, instead of the lonely joys of expectancy and promise that he knew in America. Yet it was an alien life, he could not enter this door or share this joy; he remained a lonely American who could thrill only to the splendid promise. As he wandered, his memories and his desires were extraordinarily intensified by his aching homelessness. And so he discovered America, he tells us, by leaving it. His years abroad made him realize his profound need of it.

This discovery no doubt owed something to the jealous pride of the provincial, and a resentment of the European condescension toward America. But Wolfe was also a sensitive, penetrating observer. While fully appreciating both the superficial charms and the deep satisfactions of the ancient culture of Europe, he saw clearly the vanities, the ancient fears and hatreds, the corruption and decay beneath the charming surface. He thereby got a perspective on the notorious limitations of America. If Americans were provincial and cocky, the British were no less insular and complacent; if they were materialistic, they had no more reverence for the dollar than French peasants and merchants had for the sou; if they were standardized, the very superiority of Europe was supposed to lie in its settled manners or standardized way of life. Although Wolfe did not formulate the generalization, in effect he began to realize that every society must have the defects of its virtues, its over-emphases and under-emphases. The glory of Europe lies in its traditional way of life; but tradition preserves a great deal of junk as well as precious achievement, and a reverence for it can also be a symptom of stagnation. The limitations of America lie in its raw, reckless youth; but youth is also the source of its energy, vitality, humor, faith and hope.

Hence Wolfe was able to end *Of Time and the River* on a triumphant note that does not sound forced or shrill. The wanderer returns from Europe, more enthralled by the homecoming than was Ulysses. Wolfe describes the voyage to America as "the supreme ecstasy of the modern world." "There is no other experience that is remotely comparable to it, in its sense of joy, its exultancy, its drunken and magnificent hope which, against reason and knowledge, soars into a heaven of fabulous conviction, which believes in the miracle and sees it invariably achieved." Here Wolfe is mythicizing, in the heroic manner; and good Americans may be embarrassed. Yet if this grandiloquence is "against reason and knowledge," Wolfe by now does have the reason and knowledge. His view of America is far more realistic, complex and ironic than was, say, Homer's view of Greece. He has not come by his enthrallment easily or cheaply; and once we have modestly admitted that a trip to America is not the supreme ecstasy, we may be grateful for the ecstasy that he has legitimately recaptured. His primary gift as a mythmaker, once more, was this quick feeling for the wonderful strangeness of the familiar, the enchantments of routine modern experience.

Meanwhile Wolfe's growing awareness of the meaning of his legend has not yet brought the peace, strength and wisdom he is seeking. His image of America is very large, and none too clear or steady; his supreme ecstasy at the end of *Of Time and the River* is not a supreme certainty. Moreover, Wolfe's emotion will swell to fit this mighty subject, and swell the more because his America too is created in his own image. In his exultant moods he must now celebrate not only his own youthful hopes but the power and promise of a youthful nation; in his dark, bitter moods he must now agonize over not only his personal frustrations but the loneliness and waste of American life. He still has too few general ideas, and too little interest in such ideas. He has the more need of them because he still has a great deal of unemployed emotion.

Yet the important thing is that Wolfe is finding a meaning for his book. It will become more explicit, it will broaden and deepen; but the design is already apparent. Granted that all Wolfe's discoveries are rather elementary, as well as rather belated, the really effective ideas in human history—the great ideas by which men and nations live—are usually platitudes. His discoveries are at least an adequate groundwork for his myth—myths do not require novel or highly original themes. And so with a still more elementary and more fundamental discovery that is stressed in the closing pages of *Of Time and the River*. In the little towns of France an ancient faith, latent in Wolfe's blood, was quietly but powerfully awakened. His senses, his heart, his mind were filled with rich, drowsy sensations of the unutterable familiarity of this strange world. Life in these towns, he was pleased to rediscover, was the same as life in the little towns of America, and everywhere on earth. "And after all the dark and alien world of night, of Paris, and another continent . . . this re-discovery of the buried life, the fundamental structure of the great family of earth to which all men belong, filled him with a quiet certitude and joy."

More specifically, the sound of a cathedral bell, as Wolfe sat in a cobbled square in the ancient city of Dijon, served him much like the famous *madeleine* that inspired

Proust's *Remembrance of Things Past*. With the sound of the old bell, "everything around him burst into instant life," a life he had always known. His school bell, the distant chimes on a street at night, the lonely sounds of old Catawba—a host of long-forgotten things swarmed back, incredibly alive and near. Then, after a moment of brooding silence, began the sound of men going home for lunch; and Wolfe was closer to the lost America of his childhood than he would ever be when in America:

> They came with solid, lonely, liquid shuffle of their decent leather, going home, the merchants, workers, and good citizens of that old town of Dijon. They streamed across the cobbles of that little square; they passed, and vanished, and were gone forever—leaving silence, the brooding hush and apathy of noon, a suddenly living and intolerable memory, instant and familiar as all this life around him, of a life that he had lost, and that could never die.

> It was the life of twenty years ago in the quiet, leafy streets and little towns of lost America—of an America that had been lost beneath the savage roar of its machinery, the brutal stupefaction of its days, the huge disease of its furious, ever-quickening and incurable unrest. . . . And now, all that lost magic had come to life again here in the little whitened square, here in this old French town, and he was closer to his childhood and his father's life of power and magnificence than he could ever be again in savage new America; and as the knowledge of these strange, these lost yet familiar things returned to him, his heart was filled with all the mystery of time, dark time, the mystery of strange million-visaged time that haunts us with the briefness of our days.

This experience obviously helped Wolfe to amplify the meaning of his legend, by linking the pilgrimage of a lost American with the universal destiny of lonely man. So he had felt at the death of old Gant, that his father was unlike any other man who had ever lived, and that every man who ever lived was like his father. Less obviously, however, this experience also threatened to cut short his pilgrimage or narrow its meaning. Like Proust, Wolfe was seeking to recapture his whole past experience, through his sensory impressions; but like Proust he sometimes sought the remembrance of things past as a refuge, an escape from adult frustrations. He hankered to go home again, to this lost America, the world of his childhood; his quest of a father sometimes looks more like the quest of a mother, a yearning for the womb—we may recall that he was not weaned until he was three and a half years old. Yet Wolfe did not go home again, finally. He returned instead to the actual America. Literally and figuratively, he returned to his senses: the exceptionally alert, acute senses that were the springs of his art. And the abiding value of his experience in the ancient towns of France, even if he did not clearly realize it, was that it deepened and clarified this source of his strength.

Unlike Proust, Wolfe did not attempt a minute analysis of all his sensory impressions, or an elaborate rationalization of his whole method; he did not erect his intuitive practice into a Bergsonian philosophy of intuitionism. The most difficult problem that he wrestled with, he explains in *The Story of a Novel* was the problem of time; but his concept of time was a very simple one, not mystical or metaphysical. He wanted to give at once the sense of the actual present in its continuous flow, the sense of past time as living in the present and at every moment conditioning the lives of his characters, and the sense of time immutable—the timeless time of earth and sea against which would be projected the transience of man's life. He wanted, in other words, to render permanence and change as they are felt in immediate experience, in which both are very real; whereas Proust, like the mystics, aspired to the realm of pure Time, the realm of Essence or Being, where change is mere appearance. And the sensory image, fully apprehended, was the key to Wolfe's time problem, the means of rendering at once the transient and the timeless. It is the carrier of the essential meanings of art, the key to its magical union of the material and the ideal, the passing and the surpassing; for the universal and the eternal are realized only in the particular, and our loftiest, rarest, most "spiritual" ideas are stirred by sensory images, brought home by them, and embodied in them. Through the senses, so commonly despised by philosophers, by theologians, by scientists and even by poets in their Platonic moods, one is led to an intense realization of natural continuities, the rhythms of the universe, the vast enveloping whole; and so one may apprehend the "deeper reality" or "higher reality" that all aspire to.

In short, Wolfe was now realizing more than the face value of his extraordinarily keen senses and retentive memory, which make possible the uncommon perceptions, the deep associations and the complex syntheses that are one way of defining genius.

Irving Halperin　(essay date 1959)

SOURCE: "Wolfe's *Of Time and the River*," in *The Explicator*, Vol. XVIII, No. 2, November, 1959, Item #9.

[*In the following essay, Halperin comments on the artistic unity of the train episode in Book I of* Of Time and the River.]

The train episode in the opening section of *Of Time and the River* appears, at first glance, like a series of disjointed fragments. Now covering some eighty pages, it originally was, according to Wolfe's own admission in *The Story of a Novel,* many times that length. Here I intend to show how this episode is organized into an artistic whole through (1) the use of characters representing certain ideational values, and (2) the pattern of the protagonist's discoveries.

The episode begins aboard a New York-bound train. As he is being carried further away from the hills of Altamont, Eugene Gant ponders on the unreality of things. The faces and voices of friends and kinsmen back home seem "far and strange as dreams." Gradually, the continuous rhythm of the train's movement through space stimulates him to muse on the mystery of time, which is compared to the South of his boyhood. Both are "buried," "silent," "dark." Thus at this point in the episode, the hero, having escaped from home, from the circumstances which

were frustrating his development, feels "lost," lacking in identity and purpose.

Escaping from these disquieting thoughts, Eugene leaves his seat to seek human companionship. In the smoking compartment he finds some Altamont business men; their myopic, greedy temperaments repel him. In the course of conversation, these men evoke the name of Ben Gant. They speak respectfully of him because he had been a hard worker, because he had kept his "nose clean." But for Eugene the memory of his dead brother has more significant associations. For example, in presenting him with a watch on his twelfth birthday, Ben had asked, "Do you know what a watch is for?" "To keep time with," he had answered. Then Ben had warned that he "keep it better than the rest of us. Better than Mama or the old man—better than me! God help you if you don't!" Now the connection between this remembrance and the men in the smoking-car is clarified: first, Eugene avows he will not only keep time better than his family, but also better than the townspeople of Altamont; secondly, he recognizes the narrowness of the latter in contrast to Ben, who was "a flame, a light, a glory."

Eugene's identification with his brother is implicit in his remembrance of Ben as one who "lived here a stranger . . . trying to recall the great forgotten language, the lost faces, the stone, the leaf, the door." The former also thinks of himself as a stranger, a "misunderstood" one in a world of transiency. Until he finds a door (the ordering of flux in the present through the creative process), Eugene will be haunted by the "dream of time"; he will feel unreal, "like a creature held captive by an evil spell." Once having discovered a door, he will achieve the real and permanent (a stone); that is, he will rescue experience from the flow (a leaf) of time and give it lasting meaning.

In the next scene of the episode there is a transition from the smoking-car to the frenzied drinking party staged by Eugene and two young companions. Liquor, like the train (the symbol of enormous man-made energy), gives a "rhyme to madness, a tongue to hunger and desire, a certitude to all the savage, drunken, and exultant fury that keeps mounting, rising, swelling in them all the time!" Compared to the "eternal silent waiting earth" over which the train passes, the young men are "three atoms," "three ciphers," "three nameless grains of life." Yet they have about them a kind of heroic aura, for they have left their roots and are going forth to do battle with the cities of the North. Hence the three youths, like Ben, represent for Eugene the nobility of "little" man adventuring courageously in an impersonal universe.

There remains Part V of the train episode—Eugene's awakening in his pullman berth the morning after the drinking party. The "old brown earth" that he sees through a window is related to the recurring hill image of the novels. The earth, like the hills, symbolizes permanence and purpose. To Eugene, this plot of earth is more familiar than his mother's face with its associations of endurance and "fixity." While looking out of the window and listening to the steady, stroking rhythm of the train, he perceives an image of "eternity forever—in moveless movement, unsilent silence, spaceless flight." In the suspended moment, he feels that there is permanence in change and that he, like the earth, will prevail through the continuing growth of the self.

In sum, it may be seen that the shape of the train episode consists of a three-part pattern: in the first part, Eugene feels "lost," because in escaping from home he loses a sense of identity; in the second he returns to his "roots" in the past by recalling the significance of Ben's life, and in the third, he attempts to adjust to his present circumstances by becoming aware of his peculiar strength—the capacity for growth. Thus the pattern formed by the hero's experiences and recognitions during the train trip both unifies the various sections of the episode and relates to the controlling idea of the novel—the quest of the hero to achieve order and maturity in his life and art through growth.

Francis E. Skipp   (essay date 1970)

SOURCE: "*Of Time and the River*: The Final Editing," in *Critical Essays on Thomas Wolfe,* edited by John S. Phillipson, G. K. Hall & Co., 1985, pp. 57-65.

[*In the following essay, Skipp examines the various deletions Maxwell Perkins made to Wolfe's typescript of* Of Time and the River, *finding that the cuts provide insight into both Perkins's editorial style and Wolfe's characteristics as a writer.*]

Toward the end of December 1933 Thomas Wolfe and his editor at Charles Scribner's Sons, Maxwell Perkins, began to prepare for publication more than a million words of what Wolfe called *Of Time and the River*. Although Wolfe went on writing to the extent of about 500,000 words during the months that followed, by the early fall of 1934 Perkins, cutting *en bloc,* produced a working typescript of about 415,000 words.

The book was in galleys by October, but the typescript had gone to the printer bearing the marks of 142 additional cuts which shortened it by some 33,500 words. Lyrical prose that made the story line go slack came out. So did residual pockets of what Perkins apparently considered to be banal, irrelevant, redundant, or in bad taste. To analyze this cutting-in-detail, the evidence of which survives upon the typescript, is to enlarge our understanding of Perkins as an editor and Wolfe as an author.

On leaves 437-40 Perkins placed characteristic brackets at the corners of a section eighty lines long and cut it all with a swift line running down the center of each page from top to bottom. This long passage, unmistakably lyrical in tone, is concerned with Eugene's penchant for accumulating all sorts of odds and ends, a characteristic he knows he inherited from the string-and-bottle-saving Eliza. It is a catalogue in rhythm, rich in the associations each item draws from the boy's memory. Toward the end of the passage occurs this paragraph:

> And for this reason, all these dreary and worthless accumulations of past time are pitiable mementos of this passion, the lifeless relics of man's bitter hug on life. Is it an old letter, a post-card scrawled with a few commonplace words, a note

written years ago by someone met one time and never seen again? Oh, keep it, keep it! Perhaps someday we will find a use for it, discover in it a rare and priceless value. Perhaps the person who wrote this will then have died, and all that we should have to make him live in memory—to hear him speak again, to see him as he was—will be the few scrawled words of this dull note. It is a jumble of scrawled words upon a thousand scraps of paper made out a thousand times at midnight in our room when we were twenty-one: keep it, keep it—perhaps there is a flash of fire here, a sinew of bright blood and agony, the priceless stuff of proud beginnings. Perhaps from this we shall preserve for other men the way the snow came at a certain time, and the way the sun was shining, the sound of gravel raked outside our window on a path, a boy's shout, or the hoof and wheel upon a morning street long long ago.

This passage would seem to be as good as many which Wolfe published. Like Whitman, Wolfe here becomes more pronounced in his rhythm as his emotion rises. He reaches a peak of intensity in the pulsebeat of the spondee "bright blood" and thereafter descends to the lower key of melancholy recollection in a diminuendo of smooth iambs broken only by another spondee where the sound again conveys the sense in "boy's shout" and ends in the appropriately long vowels of "upon a morning street long long ago." And in addition to whatever poetic qualities the passage may have, it shows one reason why Wolfe wrote in the first place—to give an objective and more permanent existence to his memories.

Perkins cut the passage, however, regardless of its poetic qualities and the insight it provides into its author. He put it in the category he called "dithyramb" and disposed of it. There is an unmistakable odor of scorn about Perkins's choice of the word "dithyramb" to describe Wolfe's lyrical passages, and it is difficult not to conclude that he valued it less than he valued solid story and characterization. It is scarcely surprising, therefore, that when he was faced with an enormous typescript that obviously had to be cut, his hand fell heavily on the lyrical passages.

Wolfe was sometimes willing to retain tentative lines merely because they were "the priceless stuff of proud beginnings." On pages 664-65 of *Of Time and the River* are Eugene's notebook jottings for one December day in Paris—descriptive metaphors and random musings. They give an interesting view of the mind of the literary artist before the shaping process begins, before he evaluates the images, inchoate thoughts, and verbal rhythms that float up into his consciousness. In the typescript there were about twice as many jottings as the book now contains. Before Perkins made his cut there appeared after the lines "The gull swerves seaward like a hope—September full of departing leaves and wings" these additional notebook entries:

> A star I never saw before
> The latticed hearts of whores
> The windy bells across the snow
> The loosened
> Heard windy bells across the sheeting snow
> The sunsets in the blinded eyes

How through my jaundiced heart the conspira-
    torial world
"Burn off my rust"
"Batter against my heart"
By the waters of Babylon
Painter of ghostly woods Olympian
B-long-B-long-B-long-B-long-Snap-Tap

Then after the published lines "He sat alone four thousand miles from home—the lonely death of seas at dawn," the lines cut from the typescript continue:

The debauched swine
His heart danced madly to the jazz
The island of my life
The sin's winter
How muttering life goes up and down
Purge
Our lives last inch
Bronchial horsecough
The sounding gong-notes of a drum
Green lily-depths
The sunken mouth of toothless age
The lake washed wings of dipping birds
Smooth bellied fish that glimmer in a pool
As one looks at a sleeping person and will not
    waken her
              because—because.

Perkins plainly saw what Wolfe was attempting here, for he made no effort to cut selectively, to choose the more striking lines and reject the obvious failures. His only basis for cutting was that of disproportionate development. From an artistic point of view Perkins probably was right, but the intrinsic interest of the lines themselves, transcribed virtually without modification from one of Wolfe's pocket notebooks, is such that his decision in this instance might be regretted. To Wolfe, "priceless stuff" was lost thereby, and, as was the case with all such detailed cutting, there could be no hope of preserving it in manuscript for later publication.

Where Perkins apparently recognized and cut the banal, the trite, the anticlimactic or the false he was on more defensible ground. If these numerous cuts irritated Wolfe it was probably because Wolfe quickly recognized their justice and was chagrined that he himself had written the material in the first place, or having written it, had not cut it on his own initiative. Here is a passage from the section Wolfe called "The River People," that portion of "Proteus: The City" that takes place on the Hudson River estate of Joel Pierce and his family. It is an analytical description of Joel's sister, Rosalind:

Her beauty was wonderfully like that beauty which one sometimes sees in girls in England—a beauty that is at once Madonna-like in its noble purity, and warm and plain and living as earth, at once strong and robust as all natural life is, and equal to all life's natural shocks and burdens, and yet so fresh, fair and delicate that it haunts one like a dream. Nevertheless, no one could have mistaken her for an English girl: she was so unmistakably American that there were no words, no language, to tell the reason for it, yet she was so indubitably, as one saw the moment that he looked at her. It was the real America, the true America, the America we all have

in our hearts, and live and hunger for, and always know that we shall find. It was not the accursed America of the illustration drawings, not the Harrison Fisher America of empty, brainless little faces, sweet rose-leaf lips and pure, sweet eyes and tooth-paste, moving-picture liveliness. It was not the America of the slender painted doll—the America of long, graceful legs, slender hips, pretty little nubs and buds and pippins of bright, infertile breasts, and slender little cups of shallow bellies and little sterile, tender, nervous grisettes of quick-coming———! It was not the little come-on, phony, flash-and-tease America, the horrible little flirt-and-twitch-it, get-your-man-by-baby-talk and roll-your-roguish-eyes America, it was not the horrible, cheap little empty doll with sawdust entrails that they have foisted off on America:—it was the real thing, the real America of the big hips and the melon-heavy breasts, the strong, wide hands with tender palms, the sweet warm mouth as fragrant as a flower, as rich and tender as the earth, and good for love and bold new adventuring and loyalty and courage and hard labor—the grand and sweet and casual America of the plains, the mountains, and the rivers, and it was deep as a well, and wider than a barn door, and as true and rich and fertile as the earth.

There are a number of literary sins here, of course. Eugene's consciousness is at work, comparing Rosalind's beauty to girls in England, but Eugene's basis for such a comparison lies yet in his future. Perkins would pick out this inconsistency unfailingly. Eugene's frothing scorn for the slender painted doll occupies a disproportionate place in the passage in both length and intensity, competing for the central emphasis with Rosalind herself. The last three clauses are ludicrously, though unintentionally, suggestive. But dwarfing these peccadilloes is the cardinal sin of banality.

At the end of a letter to Ernest Hemingway written on 28 March 1934, Perkins had added, "Old Tom has been trying to change his book into a kind of Marxian argument (having written most of it some years before he ever heard of Marx), and I have been trying to express to him . . . that what convictions you hold on economic subjects will be in whatever you write, if they are really deep." Perkins was right in principle, and he was right in cutting those passages where Wolfe violated it. Almost all instances where Wolfe steps before the curtain and comments upon the action are instances where he is trying to make his book speak a vaguely Marxian argument in technically improper passages tacked flimsily to the narrative. When old Gant is dying—actually dying at last—his friends and relatives come to the house and stand in small groups quietly talking, awaiting news of his condition. Among the visitors are both propertied men and laboring men. Helen, his devoted daughter, after trying to persuade herself that Gant had been the proprietor of his own "place" (her euphemism for "shop"), finds that her vision of Gant as a businessman is suddenly displaced by her recollection of his powerful workman's hands as they lay at his sides upon the deathbed. She realizes suddenly that his real friends were working men, and "having joined this group of working men . . . immediately felt an indefinable but powerful sense of comfort and physical well-being which the presence of such men as these always gave her. . . . She not only felt an enormous relief and joy to get back to these working people, it even seemed to her that everything they did . . . gave her a feeling of wonderful joy and happiness." In the typescript at this juncture Wolfe steps in to ask rhetorically:

> Why is this? The reason is not hard to find. The true fellowship of working people is not one of mind and spirit but of blood, unless one comes from people who have worked with their [hands] their lives are jaded, feverish, impotent and sterile, their only dignity a feeble mocking of their own futility, a stale irony of hugging desolation to the bone and while enjoying lavish incomes, of crying "we are lost"—the child of the worker recoils from them with hatred and disgust, they smell bad to him and their whole lives stink, and thereafter his feeling toward them is tinged by the contempt and hatred of one who has known orchards, morning, and the smell of supper; has heard his father's great voice sounding from the darkness of the vineclad porch in summer, and hearing then the sound of great wheels pounding on the rail across the river, the tolling bell, the whistle's wail, has felt joy and glory stirring in his guts; and like a runner straining at the leash has had his vision of new lands, morning, and a shining city, the loves of glorious women, the fortunate and happy life of the enfabled rich!

This passage was manifestly the worst sort of nonsense with a curious *nonsequitur* ending that nullified whatever validity its beginning possessed. In cutting it Perkins did Wolfe's reputation a great service.

On other occasions Perkins's reasons for cutting were more ambiguous. Kenneth Raisbeck (Francis Starwick in the novel) had been a close friend of Wolfe's at Harvard. When on 29 September 1931 Raisbeck came to a violent and mysterious death in a Westport, Connecticut, graveyard, Wolfe, according to Philip Barber, a friend of both men in "47 Workshop" days, was violently shocked. A few days later, dropping in at Yale, where Barber then was assisting George Pierce Baker, Wolfe told an excited story:

> He said that Raisbeck had borrowed a car to drive to New Haven [Barber reported] . . . and had picked up a young man for company. On the way, somewhere near Greenwich where Route One passes a cemetery, Raisbeck overcome by lust (this was Tom's word) had abruptly stopped the car, dragged the young man out of the car and into the cemetery in an attempt to assault him; the young man had fought back but was losing the fight when his hand found a stone with which he hit Raisbeck on the head, killing him. Leaving Raisbeck among the graves the young man had run away.

An autopsy revealed subsequently that Raisbeck had died of acute meningitis, a disease distinguished by its sudden onset and violent termination. The examining physician thought that Raisbeck, in unbearable pain, had stopped his car, staggered into the graveyard, and died in a mortal spasm that produced upon him the marks suggesting violence at another's hands.

Weighing the evidence more soberly as the days passed, however, Wolfe in October wrote to a friend unidentified by the editor of Wolfe's letters:

> Of one thing I feel reasonably convinced now— that Kenneth came to his death by natural causes, that he was not murdered. Of these other facts which you and————have told me, I don't know what to say or think—I have at times a sickening sense of horror and doubt, but I think that these things must now remain forever in mystery, buried in our memory or obliterated by our faith. My final sense about the matter is this: I remember him as he was when we were students together at Harvard, as my friend—the remarkable, fine and brilliant person I believed and I believe him to have been.

And yet Wolfe was unable to leave his sinister construction of the fate of Kenneth Raisbeck buried in his memory and obliterated by his faith. *Of Time and the River* now gives Wolfe's apostrophe to drunkenness in Chapter XXXV, a lyrical passage following upon a speakeasy bacchanal celebrated by Eugene and Francis Starwick. The second paragraph on page 281 ends with the lines "for they were drunken, young, and twenty—immortal confidence and immortal strength possessed them—and they knew that they could never die." The next paragraph commences with the invocation "Immortal drunkenness!" But in the typescript, standing between the two paragraphs, are these lines, cut by Perkins: "And in ten years time, one of them, destroyed by the corruption of his soul, would be found mangled, horribly mutilated, beaten to death by a maniac in a graveyard in New England."

Perkins might have cut these lines because they were libelous or because they anticipated action not within the timescope of the novel or because they showed in their author an immature want of charity. Possibly he eliminated them because they offended his taste, for elsewhere he cut sordid descriptions or passages of horror when they seemed to him excessive. The material Perkins cut from the now-famous scene of Gant on his deathbed shows the editor's sense of decorum opposed to Wolfe's lack of reticence even in matters where his affection and loyalty were strongly involved, his obsession with the need to put everything he remembered into every scene he wrote. Perkins had let stand the stark horror of Gant's moment of death, but when Helen embraced the body he suppressed the most harrowing touches Wolfe had given the scene. As Helen hurled herself upon the dead man, Wolfe had written: " 'Oh, papa, papa'—she caught the body in her arms, and oblivious of the bloody froth and greenish matter that covered it, she hugged it to her, rocking back and forth, showering kisses on the cold, dead face and lips and moaning to it with demented broken phrases."

Perkins cut all but the three spoken words and then let stand six lines which became paragraph three, page 269, of the novel as far as the phrase "with a dead man in her arms." Between that phrase and the clause introducing the lines of dialogue which now end the paragraph, Perkins cut the lines "a corpse already cold and stiff with death, and not yet decently composed or straightened out, a corpse whose head shook stiffly, grotesquely, indecently, as she rocked with it and to which she was oblivious."

Another cut, made primarily on grounds of taste, is of interest if only for the reason that Wolfe thought highly enough of it to rework it a little and use it in *The Web and the Rock*. While the train that is carrying Eugene toward Baltimore is still in the mountains of Old Catawba it toils slowly upward past a mountaineer's shack where a woman "stands in the doorway . . . holding a dirty little baby in her arms." Here the paragraph in the novel ends, but in the typescript the description as Wolfe originally intended it continues with these additional lines: ". . . her ever-pregnant belly, like some foul ripeness fructifying from the dregs of nature, coarsely prepared, bulged outward from her gaunt starved frame beneath the unconcealing hanging of a gingham gown. And around her lop-edged skirts are clustered three or four more little dirty tow-haired children, all gaunt, wide-eyed and starting with slow stunned wonder at the train."

It is possible that this cut was made to prevent the overdevelopment of a passage which, after all, described a thing seen from a train, slowly moving though it was. When Wolfe reworked this description for the later novel the slattern was placed amidst the poor whites of Libya Hill, and the good phrase was inapplicable.

Finally there is this passage with which Wolfe intended to complete the paragraph now ending on line two, page 422 of the novel, and thus to round out his impressions of a group of persons he had come to know in the city:

> Already he had seen from repeated and damning evidences how their envenomed souls fed on any rumor of corruption, how they shrank back in terror or shame before the proofs of life and richness: he saw with what a slimy thirst they lapped up every scandal of whoredom, cuckoldry, and treachery, baring their teeth in rat-like snickers at every sterile abomination of lesbic and pederastic loves, how even the barren and exhausted humor of their theaters was tricked out with the slimy garbage of a filthy and brutal innuendo, and how their souls shrank back resentfully, full of hate and shame if one spoke the words and gave the proof of love and faith and mercy.

Eugene's judgments here bear unmistakably the stamp of Wolfe's approval and show us something frightening and ugly in the author. We wonder how Perkins justified this cut to Wolfe, who only could have seen the editor's action as pusillanimous.

Maxwell Perkins had made his most drastic cuts in the typescript by eliminating more than seven hundred lines of Thomas Wolfe's lyrical prose. It was there that Wolfe had expressed his most deeply felt insights and certainties, and in giving up these passages, he lost what was closest to his heart. The most extensive cutting Perkins did after eliminating the lyrical passages was in disposing of banality, falseness, irrelevancy, digression, disproportional development, and related faults. These were cuts which Wolfe ought to have made for himself, for they represented plain bad writing or at the very least an inadequate sense of what was to the point and what was not.

Louis D. Rubin, Jr.   (essay date 1980)

SOURCE: "In Search of the Country of Art: Thomas Wolfe's *Of Time and the River*," in *A Gallery of Southerners*, Louisiana State University Press, 1982, pp. 85-106.

[*In the following essay, Rubin discusses Eugene Gant's artistic inspiration in terms of his experience of various social milieus in* Of Time and the River.]

Thomas Wolfe's long second novel has never been mistaken for a harmoniously shaped, unitary work of fiction. Sprawling, episodic, uneven, often greatly overwritten, *Of Time and the River* contains, as is often said, some of Wolfe's best and some of his worst writing.

With the notion that it is indeed an up-and-down affair, sometimes very much overburdened, I have no quarrel. What I would contend is that, whatever its artistic sins, it is not merely the impressionistic anthology of a volatile artistic sensibility, an unshaped narrative achieving such coherence as it possesses only through the force of the author's personality. It is concerned with something of notably more specificity than a young artist's *wanderjahre* on two continents; nor is that something merely the protagonist's discovery of his love for America, as is so frequently asserted. What it involves is a young American writer's flight from a very detailed and palpable social milieu—his involvement in a middle-class southern community—and his subsequent effort to discover a better place in which to live and write, and it culminates not in the finding of such a Good Place, but of a perspective from which, as an artist, he can write about his experience.

In other words, *Of Time and the River* is the story of its protagonist's search for a way into his art. As such it details the process whereby as man and writer he first rejects his community, then finally learns the terms on which he can accept its meaning. It is my contention that this is worked out in considerably more definite and concrete terms than are usually recognized. I want to focus upon some details, especially in the opening section, that generally go unremarked, and to try to interpret what they signify.

We know that in *Look Homeward, Angel* Eugene Gant, born into a middle-class family in the city of Altamont in the mountains of Old Catawba, grows up, attends college at Pulpit Hill, then prepares to leave for a literary career in the northeastern United States. When *Of Time and the River* opens he is waiting with some members of his family at the railroad station for the train that will take him to Boston, where he will study playwriting at Harvard. His sister and mother gossip about others who await the train, and occasionally someone comes over to say hello. One such is George Pentland, the son of Will Pentland, Eugene's uncle. As we know from *Look Homeward, Angel*, Will Pentland has become very wealthy, and his son George detaches himself from "a group of young men and women who wore the sporting look and costume of 'the country club crowd' " to walk over and talk with the Gants. Eugene's mother has already made a remark about how George's mother considered the Pentland family "common." George Pentland tells Eugene that " 'you'll be gettin' so educated an' high-brow here before long that you won't be able to talk to the rest of us at all.' " And the narrator tells us that "his speech had become almost deliberately illiterate, as if trying to emphasize the superior virtue of the rough, hearty, home-grown fellow in comparison with the bookish scholar."

Next another young man turns up. We are told that he is wearing "a fine brown coat" and that he sports a Delta Kappa Epsilon fraternity key. This is Robert Weaver, the son of a judge. Eugene's mother declares that " 'He's all right. . . . He's got good manners. . . . He looks and acts like a gentleman. . . . You can see he's had a good bringing up. . . . I like him!' " His sister advises him to " 'stick to people like that. . . . He looks like a nice boy and—' with an impressed look over toward Robert's friends, she concluded, 'he goes with a nice crowd. . . . You stick to that kind of people. I'm all for him.' "

The train arrives and the trip gets under way. That evening Eugene enters the smoker of the pullman car, where a group of Altamont businessmen are talking. One of them, the publisher of the local newspaper, recognizes Eugene. " 'You're one of those Gant boys, ain't you?' " he asks. There is talk of Eugene's brothers. What is Steve doing? someone asks. Is he in business? "For a moment the boy was going to say, 'No, he runs a pool room and lives over it with his wife and children,' but feeling ashamed to say this, he said, 'I think he runs some kind of cigar store out there.' "

Then they talk about Luke Gant, and someone tells a story about Luke's youthful persistence as a magazine salesman in the streets of Altamont. After that there is talk of Eugene's brother Ben, who died several years earlier. The newspaper publisher recalls him admiringly as a former employee. Eugene remembers an occasion when Ben presented him with a gold watch, to keep time with: " 'And I hope to God you keep it better than the rest of us! Better than Mama or the old man—better than me! God help you if you don't.' "

One of the men, a politician, then mentions Eugene's father, and specifically an occasion when W. O. Gant was supervising the unloading of some blocks of marble and granite and some tombstones for his stonecutting shop. What impressed him, he says, was how well the elder Gant was dressed. " 'He always wore his good clothes when he worked—I'd never seen a man who did hard labor with his hands who dressed that way. . . . Of course, he had his coat off, and his cuffs rolled back, and he was wearing one of those big striped aprons that go the whole way up over the shoulders—but you could see his clothes was good,' said Mr. Candler. 'Looked like black broadcloth that had been made by a tailor, and wearing a *boiled* shirt, mind you, and one of those wing collars with a black silk neck-tie—and not afraid to work, either.' "

A little later Robert Weaver shows up, along with two others, one of them a man named John Hugh William McPherson Marriott, who is "the younger son of an ancient family of the English nobility and just a year or two before he had married the great heiress, Virginia Willets." We are informed that the Altamont businessmen and others in the smoker are very much in awe of Marriott, for the Willets

are immensely wealthy and live at a 90,000-acre estate near town, in "a huge stone structure modelled on one of the great châteaux of France," inside which few of the local folk had ever been invited. "To be a part of that life, to be admitted there, to know the people who belonged to it would have been the highest success, the greatest triumph that most of the people in the town could imagine. They could not admit it, but it was the truth.' "

After everyone else except Eugene, Robert Weaver, and another youth, has left the smoker, Robert, we are told once again, "thrust one hand quickly and impatiently into the trousers' pocket of his well-cut clothes in such a way that his Delta Kappa Epsilon key was for a moment visible." He begins teasing Eugene. "Do you know what they're saying about you at home. . . . Do you know what these people think of you?" Eugene becomes quite upset, especially when told that one local woman has been praying for him because of the way he has supposedly been "going to the devil" since entering the state university. The three of them begin drinking, and they get very drunk. Later on, Eugene insists upon telling Robert something. I quote several portions of his conversation. " 'You made a remark t'night I didn' like—Prayin' for me, are they, Robert? . . . Prayin' for me, are you?—Pray for yourself, y'bloody little Deke!' "

It turns out, however, that what Eugene, his inhibitions removed by whiskey, really wants to chastise Robert Weaver for is not that remark, but something that had happened some years previously, when both had been students at a private school. Weaver, it seems, had been in the company of a number of other young people, and had remarked, upon encountering Eugene, " 'Here's Mr. Gant the tomb-stone cutter's son.' " Weaver claims not to remember any such incident, but Eugene says, " 'Yes, you do, you cheap Deke son-of-a-bitch—Too good to talk to us on the street when you were sucking around after Bruce Martin or Steve Patton or Jack Marriott—but a life-long brother—oh! couldn't see enough of us, could you, when you were alone?' "

He informs Robert Weaver that " 'my people were better people than your crowd ever hoped to be—we've been here longer and we're better people—and as for the tombstone cutter's son, my father was the best damned stonecutter that ever lived—he's dying of cancer and all the doctors in the world can't kill him—he's a better man than any little ex-police court magistrate who calls himself a judge will ever be—and that goes for you too—you—.' "

The presence, and I think the significance, of the episode with Robert Weaver in Eugene's voyage northward to Harvard has not been properly noticed. The train trip from Altamont to the Northeast has generally been viewed, appropriately for the most part, as that of the outward-bound artist in quest of his destiny. Wolfe certainly saw it that way, as indicated by the narrator's remarks about its being the first occasion on which Eugene experienced an access of so-called Fury. He speculates on how the fury must have been present earlier in his life, but until then it had not been apprehended: "He never knew if fury had lain dormant all those years, had worked secret, silent, like a madness in his blood. But later it would seem to him that fury had first filled his life, exploded, conquered, and possessed him, that he first felt it, saw it, knew the dark illimitable madness of its power, one night years later on a train across Virginia."

By *Fury* is obviously meant the impassioned, emotion-filled apprehension of his experience, which finds its literary expression in the kind of rhetorical evocation that characterizes the narrative method of much of *Of Time and the River*. The technique throughout is for the youthful Eugene to feel the "fury" and for the approving narrator to interpret how he felt. That the narrator, the authorial personality who tells us Eugene's story, is the somewhat older, remembering Eugene, is obvious.

Leaving Altamont for the Northeast, therefore, is the act which had first brought out into open consciousness his intense hunger for experience, for emotional fulfillment: and with this the intensity of the creative urge that ultimately led him to articulate and give form and meaning to its apprehension. In this sense the episode is similar to Stephen Dedalus' realization, while strolling along the shore, that instead of becoming a Jesuit father, he wishes to be a priest of the imagination of man and thus eventually write *A Portrait of the Artist as a Young Man*; or to the speaker's response to the bird in Whitman's "Out of the Cradle Endlessly Rocking":

> Never more the cries of unsatisfied love be absent from me,
> Never again leave me to be the peaceful child I was before
>   what there in the night,
> By the sea under the yellow and sagging moon,
> The messenger there arous'd, the fire, the sweet hell within,
> The unknown want, the destiny of me.

What seems clear is that the apprehension and enunciation of the impulse toward artistic fulfillment, and the celebration of such fulfillment, are directly linked with the Robert Weaver episode and what it represents. For they happen almost simultaneously, in alternating and interwoven sequence. The drunkenness that enables Eugene Gant to express his long-cherished grudge against Robert Weaver is also what triggers the access of "Fury," as he calls it. In both instances, we must assume, the impulse had been present for some time; the whiskey merely released it into open consciousness and uninhibited assertion.

Thus if we place the outburst against Robert Weaver within the context of social detail of which it is the culmination, it seems obvious that the urge for artistic fulfillment is directly tied in with the prospect of liberation from the social snobbery and sense of caste and class, and his own position vis-á-vis them, within his home community. Eugene—the Eugene of that time, and the remembering narrator—resents the social hierarchy of Altamont. He resents being thought of merely as one of the Gant boys. He does not want to live in a community in which he is labeled as a stonecutter's son, even if that stonecutter does wear collar, tie, and protective apron when working with his hands. He resents the fact that his mother operates a boardinghouse—in *Look Homeward, Angel* she embarrassed him when she came to visit him at college by seeking to drum up trade among his friends. He resents the fact that Robert Weaver, unlike him, is a member of what Andrew Turnbull referred to as "the Asheville clique which qualified automatically for the old-line fraternities . . . the snobs who stared superciliously from the porches of fraternity row." He resents his sister's penchant for social climbing. Later in the novel, when Gant is dying, Helen is made to gravitate instinctively toward the more socially distinguished of the townsfolk who come to pay their respects, and to tell herself that her father was not a working man but a businessman, a property owner. But then she realizes that W. O. Gant was indeed one who worked with his hands, and that his true friends were other working men who were also there, stonecutters, jewelers, plasterers, plumbers, building contractors, "men who had all their lives done stern labor with their hands, and who were really the men who had known the stone-cutter best, [and who] stood apart from the group of prominent and wealthy men who were talking so earnestly to Eliza."

It seems to me that, particularly in the opening episodes of *Of Time and the River,* an unusually strong emphasis is being placed upon Eugene's awareness of considerations of caste and class; thus the admonition he remembers Ben having given him upon presentation of the watch, to make better use of his time than the others in the family have done, would appear to be a way of saying that Eugene must not allow himself to be entrapped within the materialism and petty social striving of the town. His furious wish to pursue an artistic career, therefore, is a way of fleeing from confinement within the values of that community.

The prospect of escape, of being an artist and achieving fame, fortune, and status upon his own, is tremendously exciting. Now that he is departing from Altamont he can begin by telling off Robert Weaver, just as later, in his writing, he can also begin paying off old scores with the community. In *Look Homeward, Angel* we are told that "finally, it occurred to him that these people had given him nothing, that neither their love nor their hatred could injure him, that he owed them nothing, and he determined that he would say so, and repay their insolence with a curse. And he did."

Yet if this is so, it would seem an anomaly that some of the best writing in *Of Time and the River,* as well as almost the entirety of *Look Homeward, Angel,* is set in and among those people, and however caustic the portraiture becomes at times, it is by no means without much affection for and joy in that town from which Eugene is so desperately escaping. For we must remember that not only are both *Look Homeward, Angel* and *Of Time and the River* inescapably autobiographical in form, involving the narrator's recall of the protagonist's life as a basic dimension of the telling, but also that in a real sense the second novel is a book about learning how to write the first. Clearly the Eugene who is riding the train north from Altamont is in no condition to begin writing anything resembling *Look Homeward, Angel.* He is looking for fulfillment as an artist, all right; but he is also fleeing from involvement in a social situation that is so strident in its claims that the only thing he wants to do with it, the only response he wants to make, is to tell it off and put it behind him. Something will have to happen before he can begin to deal with it for the purposes of literary art. And what happens is the story related in *Of Time and the River*.

The drama workshop at Harvard is Eugene's first experience with Fashionable Culture—with life and work in a group supposedly dedicated to artistic activity. He is free at last of the provincial world of philistinism and social caste. But he finds his fellow *litterateurs* precious, mannered, effeminate. He feels ill at ease among the sophisticates of the drama at Harvard. He is unfamiliar with their ways of talking about literature and the arts. He considers them overrefined, ignorant of real life.

He does, however, form one close friendship, with Frank Starwick, who though of plebeian origins like his own has adapted very well to the Harvard style of Culture. Starwick's sophistication, his offhand manner, his fashionable enthusiasms and even affectations are acceptable to Eugene, not because he would emulate them, but because they seem to go along with a considerable admiration for his own genius. Though living and flourishing among the aesthetes and pretenders, Starwick supposedly can recognize the genuine article when he sees it. Thus Eugene can entertain the hope that once he succeeds as a playwright he too will be honored, admired, valued in a world of devotees of art. He will find the Good Place, where he can know true literary and social fulfillment.

That place, however will not be Cambridge, with its ultrarefinement, its artificiality, its pseudoartistic fashionableness. Nor does he find the nonartistic inhabitants of Cambridge and Boston, the working-class Irish of a northern industrial city, any more compatible than the devotees of Culture. They are brutal, barren, ugly. He compares the Boston Irish with the Irish he had known back in Altamont; the Boston variety has "none of the richness, wildness, extravagance, and humor of such people as Mike Fogarty, Tom Donovan, or the MacReadys—the Irish he had known at home."

Eugene's next stop, in order to earn his living by teaching while living close to the place where plays are produced and books published, is the city of American cities, New York. Here at the night school classes of the School for Utility Cultures he encounters another kind of people: urban Jews. Unlike the Boston Irish they are not sterile or brutal; they are filled with passion, and like him many of them are eager for literature, culture. But their ways are not his own; as a southern Protestant from the provinces he finds them alien and ugly. His xenophobia, his hatred and fear of the foreign, the strange, the different, comes to the forefront. Moreover, the Jews are very much at home in the city, whereas the massive impersonality of the metropolis, his sense of insignificance among its huge buildings and swarms of urban dwellers, brings him only frustration and futility. The Shining City of his youthful dreams of glory and fulfillment has become a place of spiritual and physical imprisonment, a charnel house: "Already he had come to see the poisonous images of death and hatred at work in the lives of a million people—he saw with what corrupt and venomous joy they seized on every story of man's dishonor, defeat, or sorrow, with what vi-

cious jibe and jeer they greeted any evidence of mercy, honesty, or love."

The compacted impersonality, ugliness, and unfamiliarity of the city, as he now experiences it, is profoundly disturbing. Wherever the Good Place is, it is not New York City as he now knows it while working as an instructor in the School for Utility Cultures.

In the midst of his sojourn in the metropolis there comes an interlude in which he moves briefly from one social extreme to the other. He leaves the city for a visit to the Hudson River estate of his friend Joel Pierce's family. It is as if he had been abruptly transported to the fabulous Willets estate back in Altamont. He has never before known the life of the ultra-rich. The magnificence of the place, the extensive and costly library, the pantry stocked with the finest foods in lavish profusion, astonish him. From his bedroom he looks out upon the landscape by night, "a landscape such as one might see in dreams," and he is overwhelmed: "It seemed that all his life he had dreamed of one day finding such a life as this, and now that he had found it, it seemed to him that all he had dreamed was but a poor and shabby counterfeit of this reality—all he had imaged as a boy in his unceasing visions of the shining city, and of the glamorous men and women, the fortunate, good and happy life that he would find there, seemed nothing but a shadowy and dim prefiguration of the radiant miracle of this actuality." That night he reads the play he has been writing to Joel Pierce and his sister, who listen intently and admiringly. Ultimately Joel invites him to stay in the gatekeeper's lodge of the estate and do his writing: " 'It's no use to anyone the way it stands, and we'd all be delighted if you'd come and live in it.' "

At once Eugene declines the invitation. For despite his admiration for his friend and his enthrallment with the beauty of the setting and the comfort of their home and surroundings, he would be out of place there. He has the sense of a basic futility and triviality among those who are so rich that they need not work for a living, which, together with his awareness of the social injustice involved in the privilege attendant upon great wealth, makes him feel that a life among the very rich would not be sufficiently *real* for him: "It was a bitter pill to know that what had seemed so grand, so strong, so right and so inevitable at the moment of discovery was now lost to him—that some blind chemistry of man's common earth, and of his father's clay, and of genial nature, had taken from him what he seemed to possess, and that he could never make this enchanted life his own again, or ever believe in its reality."

Moreover, despite his friends' admiration for his play, he knows that in such a place of enormous wealth and privilege, the talents of an artist, even a successful one, would count for comparatively little. Only wealth and family would confer status among the Hudson River aristocracy; such interest in art as he has seen there is that of the dilettante, the collector. The immense library of the house is crowded with fine books, in costly leather bindings and paper "white and soft and velvet to the touch," but in that great house, amid "that proud power of wealth and the impregnable security of its position," books count for little: "All of the great poets of the earth were there, unread, unopened, and forgotten, and were somehow, terribly, the mute small symbols of a rich man's power." So he gets aboard the New York City-bound train, listens to the banality of the chattering Jews and the foul anger of a drunken Irishman, and he returns to his hotel room in the metropolis.

Thus far we have seen the protagonist depart from the community in which he was born and grew up, wishing desperately to put behind him everything it seemed to symbolize in the way of materialism, caste and class, limitation. Intent upon becoming a writer he has gone first to Harvard and then to New York City. He has rejected the affectation and pose of the Fashionable Culture of the university, and found urban life as a teacher in the metropolis ugly and alien. His visit to a palatial estate on the river has convinced him of his inability and unwillingness to fulfill himself as man and artist among the very rich. So now he travels across the ocean to Europe.

First he visits England, where the poets and dramatists he has studied and loved once walked the earth; at Oxford "was the whole structure of an enchanted life—a life hauntingly familiar and just the way he had always known it would be." But it too proves unreal, alien to him, "another door Eugene could not enter." He lives in an English home, but cannot enter the lives of those who live there. He visits a group of Americans who are Rhodes scholars, and who profess to be rapturously at home at the English university—all except one man, a Jew from the Northeast, who much to Eugene's approval declares bluntly that *he* isn't at home at Oxford, that none of the others has been, and that " 'you can stay here for three years and none of [the English] . . . will ever give a tumble to you! You can eat your heart out for all they care, and when you leave here you'll know no more about them than when you came. . . . W'at t' hell do you get out of it that's so wonderful?' "

So the Old Home, as the New England writers used to call it, the country of poets and literature, will not serve as the Good Place, and Eugene goes on to Paris. There is a period spent wandering about looking at pictures and places, sampling the coasts of Bohemia, and thinking about Literature and being a Literary Man. The report is in the form of journal entries—excerpts from a Diary of the Artist as a Young American, as it were—and is full of a painful self-consciousness.

A diary is the least coherent of literary forms; its only order and progression are chronological. James Joyce, in *A Portrait of the Artist as a Young Man,* has Stephen Dedalus keep a diary, and gives it the effect of randomness while actually developing his story page by page. Eugene Gant's diary *is* random. Yet the randomness does serve a formal purpose, I think. Eugene Gant, the apprentice artist, has traveled all the way from the boardinghouse in Altamont to the City of Light, the place where Artists hold forth, where one can live in Montparnasse, the Latin Quarter, visit the Louvre, sip drinks at sidewalk cafés, go strolling along the Seine. The diary displays him trying to comport himself like a Man of Letters, have creative and critical opinions, compose literary anecdotes, meditate upon the nature of Art and Time, absorb the artistic atmo-

sphere. His performance reeks of contrivance and artificiality. He is very much out of place, and absolutely without direction.

Then he encounters Frank Starwick, who is in Paris with two American women, and all changes. Eugene is very happy now, not only because he is among friends, but also because his companions know how to play the role of Americans in Paris: "The whole world became an enormous oyster ready to be opened, Paris an enormous treasure hoard of unceasing pleasure and delight." But soon this too passes. Starwick, the brilliant man of sensibility and culture, of "rare and solitary distinction," turns out to be a homosexual. Eugene for his part falls in love with one of the women, who will have none of him; both women are infatuated with Starwick. There are quarrels, ugly scenes, until finally Eugene, enraged at Starwick's petulant behavior and his selfishness, hurls him against a building. The next day there is an attempt at reconciliation, and in perhaps the most overwritten and embarrassing episode in the novel, Eugene bids his former friend farewell.

> "You were my one true friend—the one I always turned to, believed in with unquestioning devotion. You were the only real friend that I ever had. Now something else has happened. You have taken from me something that I wanted, you have taken it without knowing that you took it, and it will always be like this. You were my brother and my friend—"
>
> "And now?" said Starwick quietly.
>
> "You are my mortal enemy. Good-bye."

Robert Penn Warren declares that "the dialogue, the very rhythms of the sentences, and the scene itself, scream the unreality"; Starwick, he says, "is at the same time a social symbol and a symbol for a purely private confusion of which the roots are never clear." John Peale Bishop comments that "what we have been told about Starwick from his first appearance in the book is that, despite a certain affection and oddness of manner, he is, as Eugene is not, a person capable of loving and being loved. What is suddenly revealed in Paris is that for him, too, love is a thing the world has forbidden. In Starwick's face Eugene sees his own fate." The narrator's own explanation of Eugene's difficulties with Starwick, in the novel itself, is that "the feeling that Starwick would always beat him, always take from him the thing he wanted most, that by no means could he ever match the other youth in any way, was now overpowering in its horror."

To these hypotheses I would add a fourth, which is that, as is pointed out several times, Starwick, like Eugene, has made his escape from an undistinguished middle-class provincial social situation, and has exemplified for Eugene the young man of taste and ambition who has won through to a cultural and social distinction that can replace those provided by wealth or social standing. To have him revealed as a homosexual and a shameless sponger off his friends seems to tell Eugene that—just as the middle-class citizenry of Altamont would assume—the only way to earn the friendship and admiration of those who are successful in the world of Culture that Starwick represents is at the cost of one's masculinity and personal integrity. Only a feminine sensibility like Starwick's, in other words, can exemplify the attitude toward the value and importance of artistic experience that Eugene finds so admirable; one cannot be a middle-class American male and a genuine artist at the same time. As George Pentland had warned, " 'You'll be gettin' so educated an' high-brow here before long that you won't be able to talk to the rest of us at all.' " *That* is what Eugene fears; it is what Starwick's emergence as a homosexual seems to confirm, which is why he rages. (One might add that if this hypothesis is valid, then it only places Eugene Gant and his creator in the same social and cultural situation as Faulkner and Hemingway, in both of whom very much the same equation was at work.)

Why is Starwick Eugene's "mortal enemy"? The answer is that if Eugene Gant is ever to become the writer he intends to be, it will have to be by rejecting everything that Starwick seems to represent: which is to say, an art that seeks to escape from the terms, conditions, subject matter, and meanings of general American experience through avoiding them. For Starwick exemplifies, in Eugene's mind, the Man of Culture—a preference for George Moore's *Confessions of a Young Man* rather than the *Saturday Evening Post* and Booth Tarkington—and Starwick's homosexuality symbolizes what Eugene fears that Fashionable Culture, and a secure place within it, means: an art, and an existence as an artist, devoid of passion, vitality, reality. Thus when Eugene asserts his horror at the apparent fact that "by no means could he ever match the other youth in any way," what he means is that the approach to life that Starwick represents is what the literary world to which Eugene also aspires honors and rewards. The fact that the two women with whom he and Starwick have been touring France love Starwick and are not attracted to Eugene symbolizes for Eugene what he most dreads: that Starwick's aestheticism, his preciousness, his lack of masculine passion are what are expected of an artist. And the knowledge that he could never, either as writer or as member of fashionable literary society, fulfill that requirement, or want to, is what prompts him to hurl his erstwhile friend against the building and resume his wandering.

From what had become the nightmare of Paris Eugene departs for the French provinces. At Orléans he encounters an absurd little countess, who had traveled to America during the recently ended First World War to promote the war effort. To Eugene's astonishment she not only knows that Altamont exists; she has visited there, and her acquaintances include persons known to Eugene. She passes Eugene off as a correspondent for the New York *Times* in order to gain an invitation to the great château of the Marquis de Mornaye. " 'Think what it means to me,' " she begs Eugene when he balks at the deception. " 'I am so poor, so miserable—for years I have waited for an opportunity to see this woman—it means so much to me, so little to you.' "

At the château the marquise showers Eugene with attention, feeds him a sumptuous meal, and proposes that he write—for a percentage of the profits—an article for the *Times* that will raise a large sum of money for a veteran's hospital. She also reveals herself as a monarchist, an implacable foe of democracy: " 'Zere vill never be a France until ze kink is restored to his rightful office and zese creeminals and traitors 'ave been sent to ze guillotine vere zey belonk.' " Mornaye too has a fine library, with fine bindings and costly editions, but the marquise does not read, and she has no more use for the modern French authors than for the political leaders of the Third Republic.

It is a comic episode—but in terms of what has happened thus far in *Of Time and the River* it is considerably more than random comedy. For the visit to Mornaye is also a parody of the visit to the Pierce estate on the Hudson River, even down to the splendid table fare and the magnificent but unread library. More than that, the château at Mornaye is precisely the kind of place upon which the Willets estate outside Altamont is modeled, and the little countess' burning desire to gain admission to it is on a par with that of the citizens of Altamont to be admitted to the Willets estate. And if Eugene Gant is at Mornaye on false pretenses, he had felt equally out of place at the Pierce estate, and would presumably feel so at the Willets' mansion as well.

In short, the episode at Mornaye is a vivid demonstration for Eugene of the absurdity of just those notions of caste and class that had helped make his situation at home seem so unpalatable. Here in a foreign province he encounters the real aristocracy, of which the Willets and the Pierces can only be pale copies; Mornaye is no imitation château made possible by great wealth earned in industrial America, but the genuine thing, the seat of centuries of aristocratic privilege. And what Eugene finds is the same materialism, social injustice, literary insensitivity, and snobbery that had impelled him northward from Altamont.

It is the final, comic perspective on what he has experienced. On the one hand, Eugene has learned to discount the falsely materialistic values of wealth and social status within his society. On the other he has discovered the incompatibility of his integrity as an artist with the life of a Fashionable Culture that eschews or sidesteps everyday American life; Paris has shown him that. In effect Eugene Gant's European apprenticeship is now all but complete; in England, in Paris with Starwick, and now at Orléans and Mornaye he has learned to identify what he does not want or need, either as man or as artist.

The cycle of withdrawal and return has almost run its course. Now "he had come at last to a place of quietness and pause; and suddenly he was like a desperate man who has come in from the furious street of life to seek sanctuary and repose in the numb stillness of a tomb." In the old city of Tours he is filled with thoughts of home; he knows "the impossible, hopeless, incurable and unutterable homesickness of the American, who is maddened by a longing for return, and does not know to what he can return." What he now sees and hears in the French provinces, following all he has experienced in Europe and in America, can provide him with the key to the door, the access to the texture of the life he had known at home.

In good Proustian fashion he now receives a series of signs.

He hears a church bell ringing, and is reminded of the bell that rang for classes at college in Pulpit Hill. Inhabitants of the town walk by the café where he is seated, "and suddenly he was a child, and it was noon, and he was waiting in his father's house to hear the slam of the iron gate, the great body stride up the high porch steps, knowing his father had come home again." An automobile speeds through the town square; he thinks of the gay blades of Altamont, boasting of their sexual prowess as they lounge outside a drugstore: "Then, for a moment there was a brooding silence in the square again, and presently there began the most lonely, lost and unforgettable of all sounds on earth—the solid, liquid, leather-shuffle of footsteps going home one way, as men had done when they came home to lunch at noon twenty years ago, in the green-gold and summer magic of full June, before he had seen his father's land, and when the kingdoms of this earth and the enchanted city still blazed there in the legendary magic of his boyhood vision." It is only then that he begins to write his book.

If the "fury" passage in the train sequence at the outset of *Of Time and the River* is in effect the assumption of the artistic vocation, then this sequence, near the close, announces the discovery, there in the town of Dijon in southern France, of the true substance of what that art must be. It will be his memory: *his* America, the experience of *his* childhood in Old Catawba. That older time is gone now, and, he say, "drowned beneath the brutal flood-tide, the fierce stupefaction" of modern industrial urban society. What remains is "a suddenly living and intolerable memory, instant and familiar as all this life around him, of a life that he had lost, and that could never die."

In other words, he will write about the stuff of his childhood: Altamont, his family, his early years. But it should be noted that what is "drowned" beneath the "flood-tide" and "brutal stupefaction" of modern America is not the town itself, or even the ways of the town; rather, it is *his* experience of it. He is the one who has gone out into the urban life of the Northeast; what has been lost is what that life had been for him as a child. Thus what he recalls and will be writing about is not merely that early experience as such, but also and crucially the experience of growing up and therefore away from it. His book will be structured by the passage of time, and imbued with the dimension of change. His art will be its recovery; he will find his fulfillment as an artist through the recapture, in language, of what he has known and been.

At last he has escaped from the domination of that experience *as life*—as that which had compelled him as a child and as a young adult to respond to it in certain compulsive ways, act out a certain role, attempt to deny important aspects of his own identity. He can begin to recreate it on his own terms, which is to say, to discover its meaning as art. But it will not be the art of nostalgia, for the perspective from which he can now view his early experience is through, and *as,* change. To recreate it will be to show it as structured by time, and his experience of time.

To be a writer, then, is not to search for escape from the life he has known into a Good Place where Being an Artist is possible for the protagonist. What happens at the close of *Of Time and the River,* with the protagonist alone and beginning to write, in the southern provinces of a foreign land and in so many ways reminiscent of his origins and yet inescapably alien, is that he realizes that he will find his true milieu and ambiance as a writer not in playing a role as Sensitive Artist in an appropriate social setting, but in recreation of his own middle-class experience, the life he has known, in language. He has learned that the pretense of trying to find the Good Place was "always to seek the magic skies, the golden clime, the wise and lovely people who would transform him. . . . always to seek in the enchanted distances, in the dreamy perspectives of a fool's delusions, the power and certitude he could not draw out of himself." It was within himself that his art was to be found. " 'The place to write' was Brooklyn, Boston, Hammersmith, or Kansas—anywhere on earth, so long as the heart, the power, the faith, the desperation, the bitter and unendurable necessity, and the naked courage were there inside him all the time."

On the one hand *Of Time and the River* is a novel that describes, in detail and often with considerable wisdom, Eugene Gant's discovery of the perspective for creating his art. On the other hand, it is a novel in which the narrator's relation to his autobiographical protagonist is all too often without proper artistic distance, so that it develops into hyperbolic self-celebration and self-justification.

—Louis D. Rubin, Jr.

So, just as Stephen Dedalus can think himself into being an Artist but must learn how to view his relationship to his own human experiences in order to become a writer, so Eugene Gant is ready now to go back home to America. As he boards the ship that will take him there, he sees for the first time a woman, who, he tells us, is to become his lover, and that "from that moment on he never was again to lose her utterly, never to wholly re-possess unto himself the lonely, wild integrity of youth which had been his."

This is what "happens" in *Of Time and the River*. I have sought to show that, rather than being merely an overwritten rhetorical evocation of the alienated American artist who discovers his love for his homeland while in a foreign country, it has a quite specific and articulated social context, and develops a very definite pattern involving the discovery of a perspective from which to view his experience so that he can use it as a writer rather than merely being used by it as a man. In Aristotelian terms, this is its "plot," its structure.

But there is more to *Of Time and the River* than this. As noted, it is related to us by a remembering author, who not only describes what Eugene Gant is doing and thinking, but often addresses himself directly to the reader. And here we get into trouble. For a great deal of what that older narrator has to say about the meaning of Eugene Gant's experience is less than entirely convincing as an interpretation of that experience. Indeed, many of the most overwritten, least credible sections of *Of Time and the River* are not those in which Eugene's experience is being described, but those in which that remembering narrator is directly speaking to us. The truth is that the authority with which the story is told to us is, if anything, diminished by that narrator's direct utterance, and is strongest when he is recreating the social texture rather than pronouncing the imaginative meaning of Eugene's actual experience. We feel quite often that the narrator is attempting to force upon the remembered experience a significance in excess of what it actually embodies. And in the worst-written episode in the novel, that involving Eugene's break with Starwick, the perspectives merge so that the youthful Eugene and the somewhat older remembering narrator are as one: action and interpretation, dialogue and rhetoric are fused into histrionics. All distance between the naïve youth and the supposedly more mature narrator disappears.

Consider, then, what we have. On the one hand *Of Time and the River* is a novel that describes, in detail and often with considerable wisdom, Eugene Gant's discovery of the perspective for creating his art. To write the literature he wants to write, he must divest himself of the social and cultural compulsions of his middle-class American background, without also losing his passionate commitment to the texture and meaning of his own experience. We observe the stages of this process of discovery, which will permit the recapture of the past as an aesthetic act. On the other hand, it is a novel in which the narrator's relation to his autobiographical protagonist is all too often without proper artistic distance, so that it develops into hyperbolic self-celebration and self-justification. How can these conflicting dimensions—the move toward artistic maturity, the assertive denial of it—exist within the same work?

For coexist they do, and without destroying the work containing them. The explanation I would propose is that in this story about a young man searching for a way to tell his own story, the intensity of his attempt at self-definition and self-discovery is such that we will accept him, warts and all, even when he seems absurdly and histrionically confused about what his own experience means. For the best sections of this novel are so very good, so beautifully and honestly rendered, that very early on we become convinced of the basic integrity of this young man's talent, and thereafter, no matter how vexed at his clumsiness and recurrent failure at self-understanding we may become, we do not doubt either the sincerity of his quest or the rightful importance that he places upon learning how to use what he knows. When he fails it is because he is unable to give the young Eugene Gant's experience the significance that as remembering author he feels it should have, and not because he is pretending to a significance and importance that he does not himself really believe is there.

In the hands of a more disciplined writer, Eugene Gant's discovery of the true perspective for his vocation as an American writer might have been related with considera-

bly less fustian and loose rhapsodizing. But a more disciplined, more restrained writer might never have told this story in the first place. A less egocentric and romantic author would have trained upon the Sturm und Drang of the youthful Eugene a mocking irony that would doubtless have made it impossible for us to view Eugene Gant's particular quest in other than satiric terms. And that, no matter how literarily more acceptable, would be to falsify it. For it seems to me that Thomas Wolfe, more so than any other American writer I have read, was engaged totally and wholeheartedly in writing *about* the intensity with which an incipient young author such as himself apprehended his experience. And it was not only his authorial stance; it was his actual subject matter. It may well be, as Robert Penn Warren said, that his performance demonstrates "the limitation, perhaps the necessary limitations, of an attempt to exploit directly and naively the personal experience and the self-defined personality in art." But has anyone else ever tried just that with anything like the degree of Wolfe's success?

It seems to me of more than merely descriptive interest that Eugene Gant is a young American from the provinces. For in terms of what happens in the novel he is engaged in doing what many American authors have done, but no others have written about in just that way. He is not only moving toward a point at which he can attain an aesthetic perspective upon his experience, but engaged in the discovery of a cultural and social perspective for an American writer who would understand his place within American life; and this is his *theme*. To aid him in this attempt he has available to his imagination no such richly delineated religious tradition as was James Joyce's by right of birth, no lucidly defined intellectual and literary heritage such as the young Marcel Proust found around him, against which to measure the intensity and authority of his imagination. He had to do it all for himself.

Needless to say, this has been a problem for the American author from the early nineteenth century onward. Melville's invocation to the muse in *Moby-Dick*—"if then to meanest mariners, and renegades and castaways, I shall hereafter ascribe high qualities, though dark; weave round them tragic graves"—is a statement of the issue, as is Hawthorne's preface to *The House of the Seven Gables,* and James's discourse upon Hawthorne and upon the "complex fat" of the American. The lines that open "Song of Myself,"

> I celebrate myself, and sing myself,
> And what I shall assume you shall assume,
> For every atom belonging to me as good belongs
>   to you,

are a succinct enunciation of where the transaction must take place. Mark Twain, for whom the problem was a life-long artistic preoccupation, humorously suggests its implications in *Huckleberry Finn* when the Duke and the Dauphin put together their Shakespearean monologue. John Crowe Ransom confronts it in his remarks in "Philomela" upon the literary nightingale:

> Not to these shores she came! this other Thrace,
> Environs barbarous to the royal Attic;
> How could her delicate dirge run democratic,

Delivered in a cloudless boundless public place
To an inordinate race?

And so on. But with Thomas Wolfe, precisely because of the egocentric intensity of his talent, the problem becomes an overt theme, the shaping experience of plot and characterization. What is remarkable may not be that much of it is overwritten and full of imprecision and exaggeration, but that so much of it *is* apprehended. That Wolfe could, however awkwardly and unevenly, invest Eugene Gant's experience with so much form and passion is really quite astonishing. By all the truths of aesthetic distancing and necessary authorial detachment, no one, working with Wolfe's assumptions and attitudes, should have been able to make literary sense of such experience; yet Wolfe does it again and again. And it is that success, however flawed, that gives an authority to the autobiographical protagonist's search that finally validates it, when all the remembering narrator's efforts to do so through emotive rhetorical assertion cannot do so.

There is a problem of fictional form here that the terms one normally uses seem unable to encompass. This is, that the contrast between the powerfully rendered account of the young Eugene Gant's experience, and the attempts of the narrator intermittently to force inappropriate or excessive meanings upon that experience, seems to set up a kind of autobiographical tension within the fiction, an artistic crisis, the resolution of which makes the best episodes in *Of Time and the River* extraordinarily authentic and helps validate the overall shapping as well. Maybe this is what Wright Morris meant when he remarked that "if one desires what one cannot have, if one must do what one cannot do, the agony in the garden is one of self-induced impotence. It is Wolfe's tragic distinction to have suffered his agony for us all." Yet it must also be obvious that the romantic agony was, however imperfectly, made into art, since otherwise it would not be available to us as readers. It succeeds as language, as fiction; which is why one would not willingly part with *Of Time and the River*.

John Hagan   (essay date 1982)

SOURCE: "Thomas Wolfe's *Of Time and the River*: The Quest for Transcendence," in *Thomas Wolfe: A Harvard Perspective*, edited by Richard S. Kennedy, Croissant & Company, 1983, pp. 3-20.

[*In the following essay, Hagan addresses the issue of the novel's structure, concentrating on Eugene's obsession with time and his quest to transcend the limits of mortality.*]

> "In a system where things forever pass and decay, what is there fixed, real, eternal? I search for an answer . . . "
>
> —Letter to Horace Williams, September 9, 1921

Criticism today has left *Of Time and the River* largely ignored, Thomas Wolfe's reputation—such as it is—resting almost exclusively on *Look Homeward, Angel*. There are several reasons for this unfortunate situation. In part, of course, it is simply the result of current taste and academic fashion. But paramount among its deeper causes is the fact that ever since its publication in 1935 Wolfe's second novel has been almost unanimously assailed for its "formlessness." Some critics have even gone so far as to deny that it is a novel at all. The latter view is obviously arbitrary and extreme, but the first is so plausible that any attempt to question it might seem to be perverse revisionism. Nevertheless, it may be that our detailed knowledge of the extremely disorderly way in which the book was written and of the facts of Wolfe's life on which it is heavily based has predisposed us to read *Of Time and the River* in an inadequate way—to see it too much as raw, undisciplined autobiography rather than as self-contained fiction. Because it is a mixture of radically different rhetorical modes, we must be careful not to assume that it lacks unity of theme or action. Above all, because it is not a tightly constructed Flaubertian or Jamesian novel, we must not jump to the conclusion that it is therefore chaotic. Between chaos and strict order there is a very broad spectrum of possibilities, ranging from those "loose, baggy monsters" like Thackeray's *The Newcomes* and Tolstoy's *War and Peace* that James stigmatized but that have turned out on subsequent analysis to be more satisfactorily structured than he realized, to novels like some by Scott and Cooper in which the coherent design is less perfectly achieved, but is nonetheless discernible and significant. It is in the latter category, I believe, that *Of Time and the River* belongs, and it is an outline of that kind of design that I should like to sketch in the present paper. Flawed Wolfe's book certainly is, but it can still offer the sympathetic reader a uniquely compelling, deeply moving experience. Essential to its appreciation, as I hope my discussion will suggest, is a recognition that although it is undeniably "realistic" in its overall method, there runs very deep in it a strain of the mythical, the parabolic, and the visionary.

I

As many commentators have noted, a basic constituent of *Of Time and the River* (as of all Wolfe's novels, for that matter) is the Quest. On whatever level we examine the work—its language, its action, its authorial commentary, or the psychology of its protagonist, Eugene Gant—the motif of questing is everywhere. But what are the objects of Eugene's quests? What is he looking for? The answer to this question lies in his obsession with time. In few major American novels of this century is time a more pervasive presence than in *Of Time and the River*; dramatic evocations of it appear on almost every page. Eugene's preoccupation with time, however, has little in common with the technical, abstract, and specialized interest of the professional metaphysicians. His concern is emotional rather than intellectual, and pertains to those familiar aspects of time that each of us immediately experiences in his ordinary, everyday life—in particular, loss of various kinds and especially the dreadful reality of death. Time is a source of some of Eugene's deepest anguish, because, having been profoundly affected by the unforgettably poignant deaths of his brother Ben and his father, he habitually regards it as a threat, an enemy, which destroys not only everything we value, but ultimately our very existence itself. Innumerable passages record his horror of extinction, his vision of "the bitter briefness of our days," of all things being swept up by time into the huge graveyard of the past. The theme of transiency is also richly developed by several recurring metaphors and symbols, such as smoke, dreams, the river, the sea, trains, a face glimpsed for a moment in passing and never seen again, and various places, especially Dixieland, Mrs. Gant's old boardinghouse, which for Eugene is almost literally haunted by the ghosts of all "the lost, the vanished people," including himself as a child, who have ever lived there. In fact, it is just at Eugene's age, Wolfe asserts, that "the knowledge of man's brevity first comes to us" and that "we first understand . . . that the moment of beauty carries in it the seeds of its own instant death, that love is gone almost before we have it, that youth is gone before we know it, and that, like every other man, we must grow old and die."

In the light of this theme, the incentives and objects of Eugene's quests become clear. For time, Eugene's preoccupation with it, and the profound anxiety it instills in him are not merely incidental features of the main action of the novel; they are its essential impetus. Between Eugene's sense of time and his quests there is a vital causal connection, in that the core of all his longing is his desire to transcend the limits of mortality, his tireless will to believe that "he could never die," after all, or, as Wolfe succinctly put it in one of his notebooks, his yearning to "escape into life . . . that has no death in it." The epigraph of the novel (from *Ecclesiastes*, 3:21) points both to "the spirit of the beast that goeth downward to the earth," which in this context is a metaphor of various kinds of death, and to "the spirit of man that goeth upward," which serves as a metaphor of resurrection. Death and resurrection are also juxtaposed in the prose poem that precedes Chapter 1: after "wandering forever," there comes "the earth again"—that is, the grave; but from the grave emerge "the big flowers, the rich flowers, the strange unknown flowers" of "immortal love," to which "we cried" and which will rescue us "from our loneliness." Moreover, the river and the sea, which, as I have just remarked, symbolize on one level the ephemerality of all things, can inspire the traveler with hope too, as in the magnificent passage at the end of the novel where the ship that Eugene boards both connotes man's tragic journey toward death, and is "alive with the supreme ecstasy of the modern world, which is the voyage to America." Another, more traditional way in which Wolfe depicts death and resurrection is by the cycle of the seasons. The month of October, in particular, is a microcosm of this cycle, because it is the season of both endings and beginnings, departures and returns, "sorrow and delight," "huge prophecies of death and life," the "sense of something lost and vanished, gone forever," and the "still impending prescience of something grand and wild to come." If his trip in October, 1920, takes Eugene to the dying Gant in Baltimore, it also takes him to what he believes will be a thrilling new life in the North; and if, after his return to Altamont in October, 1923, he laments the death of his father and the rejection of his play by a Broadway producer, he also hears the voice of a spirit that is both "a demon and a friend" assuring him that Ben and all the other dead young men will "walk and move again tonight . . . speaking to you their messages of flight, of triumph, and the all-exultant darkness, telling you that all will be again as it was once."

Such thematic patterns indicate that, although Eugene has no formal religion or even any discernible belief in God, his quests for some kind of deliverance from death spring essentially—albeit unconsciously and in a broad, elementary sense—from a powerful religious instinct, a desperate craving for a secular equivalent of transcendent religious faith. What Wolfe said in a letter about one of these quests definitively illuminates them all: "it comes, I think, from the deepest need in life, and all religiousness is in it." Eugene is an image of "modern man caught in the Faustian serpent-toils of modern life," who is always searching for a way back to Eden, a return to the lost Earthly Paradise, a "door" (one of the novel's key terms) through which he can pass from the harsh reality of pain and death into an idyllic realm of beatitude like that celebrated by Mignon's famous lyric in *Wilhelm Meister*, "Kennst du das Land," which prefaces **Of Time and the River**, Book I. He is seeking a "shining," "elfin," "glorious," and "fabulous" region of "enchantment" and "magic," where he can find "strength" and "love," "triumph" and "splendor," "exultancy" and "ecstasy." He is looking, in short, for a fusion of Actuality and Romance in a world so intense, vital, and magnificent that it is larger than life, ideal, "more true than truth, more real than . . . reality." The imagery of the novel is consistently polarized between this kind of paradisaical vision, on the one hand, and various kinds of Wasteland or Hell, on the other.

Above all, the "religious" or "mythic" character of Eugene's quest for an Earthly Paradise is apparent in his hunger for permanence. Eugene is very much like one of Wolfe's favorite poets, Keats, in that, although he takes a lusty delight in all the pleasures of the senses, he also yearns for the changeless and eternal, as in the following typical passage, which describes the earliest and best phase of his relationship with Starwick:

> Now, with Starwick, and for the first time, he felt this magic constantly—this realization of a life forever good, forever warm and beautiful, forever flashing with the fires of passion, poetry, and joy, forever filled with the swelling and triumphant confidence of youth, its belief in new lands, morning, and a shining city, its hope of voyages, its conviction of a fortunate, good, and happy life—an imperishable happiness and joy—that was impending, that would be here at any moment.

Both contributing to and reflecting this insatiable desire for an immutable Earthly Paradise, and setting up an insistent counter-current to his sense of flux, are numerous important occasions scattered throughout the book when Eugene experiences a certain radiant and visionary sensation of timelessness suggestive of "the calm and silence of eternity." These experiences are of several kinds. Again and again, he is aware, for example, that time, although it is the enemy that brings change and death, is itself changeless and deathless, in the sense that it is a feature of reality inherent in Being itself. Similarly, he repeatedly perceives the earth and the cosmos as a whole as "everlasting" and "eternal," in contrast to the fleeting lives of individual men. But Eugene's most significant experiences of timelessness are those that result from his recurring sense that the "lost" past is not really lost at all—that it survives somehow, somewhere, in defiance of death, and can be recaptured, made to "blaze instantly with all the warmth and radiance of life again." Such Proustian moments or Wordsworthian "spots of time" appear everywhere in the novel, especially in connection with Eugene's experiences of *déjà vu*—that strange, dream-like sensation that something which has happened before, or seems to have happened before, is repeating itself. Thus, as Eugene makes his first visit to the estate of his friend, Joel Pierce, in Rhinekill on the Hudson, the whole scene seems "hauntingly familiar" to him, and he encounters it "without surprise, as one who for the first time comes into his father's country, finding it the same as he had always known it would be, and knowing always that it would be there." Other equally memorable experiences occur, as we might expect, on trains, which, when used as a symbol of time, powerfully heighten the *déjà vu* effect by contrast, as in the marvelously luminous passage on the town of Troy in up-state New York, which Eugene's train passes through in the middle of the night, and which, as he glimpses it through the window, seems to him "as familiar as a dream" and "like something he had known forever."

The most important means by which Eugene experiences the illusion of recapturing the past, however, is his phenomenal memory—a "memory that will not die"—which enables him to recall with extraordinary intensity not only major happenings and persons, but "the 'little' things of life—a face seen one time at a window, a voice that passed in darkness and was gone, the twisting of a leaf upon a bough. . . ." This power of almost total recall, this enormous retentiveness, is both a liability and an asset: a liability, because it makes Eugene agonizingly aware of time and death in the first place; but an asset too, because it permits him to transcend those limits by restoring the lost world to life again—making it "living, whole, and magic"—and thereby imparting to it a kind of immortality.

All these various, quasi-mystical experiences, then, help to develop in Eugene an unusually strong sense of timelessness, which in turn nourishes and mirrors his "religious" longing for an Earthly Paradise. But the principal roots of that longing pre-date all of these experiences and lie deep in Eugene's childhood. It was then that he heard "the sound of something lost and elfin and half-dreamed," and glimpsed a "half-captured vision of some magic country he has known . . . which haunts his days with strangeness and the sense of imminent, glorious re-discovery"— wonderful phrases that suggest those recollections of a Platonic and Wordsworthian pre-natal "heaven" that played an even more conspicuous part in *Look Homeward, Angel*. Furthermore, partly because of these recollections, partly because of the reading of fairy-tales and romantic literature that stimulated his boyhood's imagination, and partly because of the rich, colorful life once provided him by the great life-force figure of his father, Eugene now, looking nostalgically back, sees his childhood itself as a Paradise, the loss of which as a result of both his father's death and the disappearance of small-town America in general, he always regards "with an intolerable sense of pain." Paradoxically, therefore, his quests to

transcend the limits of mortality, no matter how far and wide they lead him, are always at the deepest level expressive of a desire to recapture what he perceives as the lost pastoral idyll of his childhood by discovering an equivalent Paradise in the present.

II

These quests for transcendence are mainly of four overlapping kinds. One is a quest for *adventure*—for plenitude of experience—which is motivated by a "Faustian" desire to race against death, a voracious passion to conquer time by seeing and doing as much as possible in the brief span of days that life allows: Eugene "was driven by a hunger so literal, cruel and physical that it wanted to devour the earth and all the things and people in it."

A second kind of quest on which he embarks is for *knowledge*, especially that "recorded knowledge" that is to be obtained by " 'reading all the books that were ever printed'." Through such knowledge Eugene hopes to reach beyond time and death by discovering ultimate meaning— by plumbing "the source, the well, the spring from which all men and words and actions, and every design upon this earth proceeds"; by finding some definitive "answer to the riddle of this vast and swarming earth"; by acquiring " 'an everlasting and triumphal wisdom'."

A third quest is for *security*—or, as Wolfe designated it in *The Story of a Novel*, for "a father . . . the image of a strength and wisdom external to . . . [a man's] need and superior to his hunger, to which the belief and power of his own life could be united." In his horror of oblivion, Eugene is yearning for that simple, elemental kind of physical and emotional stability and happiness that the words "father" and "home" connote literally, and that he identifies with the "silence, peace, and certitude" he enjoyed in that lost paradise of his childhood where the foundations of all his other quests were laid as well. The very first episode in the novel—Eugene's journey to Harvard— results not only from his desire for adventure and knowledge, but from his desire to travel to the North, which, because W. O. Gant had been born and raised in Pennsylvania, he envisages as "his heart's hope and his father's country, the lost but unforgotten half of his own soul." After Gant's death, his search intensifies, and reaches a brilliant climax in one of the novel's most moving passages, the eloquent prayer that constitutes the penultimate paragraph of Chapter 39:

> Come to us, Father, in the watches of the night, come to us as you always came, bringing to us the invincible sustenance of your strength, the limitless treasure of your bounty, the tremendous structure of your life that will shape all lost and broken things on earth again into a golden pattern of exultancy and joy . . . For we are ruined, lost, and broken if you do not come, and our lives, like rotten chips, are whirled about us onward in darkness to the sea.

Finally, and most important, there is a fourth way by which Eugene attempts to transcend time and death: this is his quest for *art*, his desire to become a writer. For he not only dreams of art as a means of winning fame and fortune, but, lacking the religious faith he unconsciously craves but cannot attain, ultimately comes to believe that art alone can triumph over flux, and, acting on that belief, begins the process of transforming his life itself into the Earthly Paradise by recapturing the otherwise irretrievable past in memory and rendering it immortal in artistic form. Although he certainly does not think of it in such terms, art becomes, in effect, his surrogate religion.

Before Eugene can appreciate the full significance of art or begin authentically creating it, however, he must first learn that the ideal life he is seeking is unattainable in any other way; he must discover the vanity of all his other quests. The stages of this discovery add up to most of the novel's main action, and are deeply ironic. The basic structural pattern of Eugene's experiences is a series of cycles, each of which (almost like the mood swings of a manic-depressive) consists of some great expectation followed by frustration and disillusionment, some youthful dream shattered by its denial. No matter how often his hopes fail to materialize, they revive, but only inevitably to be dashed again. Nothing ever turns out as he has imagined it would; fantasy and reality always collide; the satisfactions for which he struggles prove unattainable. As in the cycles of futile striving and eternal recurrence described in one of Wolfe's favorite texts, *Ecclesiastes,* each of the attempts Eugene makes to escape some kind of death only brings him back to death in another form. The pattern of Book I, in which the euphoria that he enjoys while traveling northward on the train gives way to "a feeling of horror" when he stops in Baltimore to see his dying father, thus encapsulates the plot of the novel as a whole: five major cycles are climaxed by his disenchantments with Professor Hatcher's play-writing course at Harvard in Book II; with the Broadway producer who rejects his play in Book III; with New York City, his teaching job, and the Pierce family in Book IV; with Starwick in Book V; and with Europe in Books VI and VII. Within these main cycles there are also several smaller ones. In short, although Eugene's hunger is like that of Faustus, his fate is like that of Tantalus, the victim of "a thousand shapes of impossible desire."

Reinforcing the irony produced by this cyclical pattern is Wolfe's use of another device: the alter ego. Eugene's experiences of hope and disillusionment are paralleled throughout the novel by those of various other characters who have also sought and failed. The most important of these characters fall into two groups. One consists of the young, like Eugene's brothers Ben and Luke, his sister Helen, and his friends, Robert Weaver and Frank Starwick—characters of or close to Eugene's own age, whose hopes and disillusionments are more or less contemporaneous with his own (or, in the case of Ben, would have been contemporaneous, if Ben had lived). The other group consists of the old, like Uncle Bascom Pentland, Dr. Hugh McGuire, and, most important of all, W. O. Gant, Eugene's father—characters much farther along in life than Eugene, whose hopes and disillusionments have for the most part taken place a long time in the past or have extended over a great many years, and who now have nothing left to confront but despair and death. Both of these groups of characters function not only to exemplify the kinds of "death-in-life" from which Eugene is confident he

can escape, but to comment ironically, as a kind of chorus, on the naivete of that confidence by foreshadowing or playing variations on his inevitable frustrations and defeats. Each is a *memento mori*—a death's head at the feast of life—whose presence in the novel is a constant reminder of that vanity of human wishes that Eugene is trying so hard not to face, but that his own disappointments sooner or later force him to acknowledge. The unromantic reality his alter egos experience and symbolize is very different from his romantic conceptions, but one that he must eventually confront.

Yet the final effect of *Of Time and the River* is far from despairing or cynical. On the contrary, like that of all Wolfe's books, it is profoundly affirmative, for not all of Eugene's quests for an Earthly Paradise that is immune to death end ironically in defeat; his solitary and painful pilgrimage through the darkness leads him ultimately to the light. What distinguishes Eugene from his alter egos and makes possible his transcendence of the trap of mortality and futility in which they are caught is his possession of artistic talent. If *Of Time and the River* is a specimen of the *Bildungsroman,* it is also an example of its subgenre, the *Künstlerroman,* because, as I have noted, along with the bitter story of the disillusionments and frustrations resulting from Eugene's quests for adventure, knowledge, and security, and in counterpoint to that story, there has been running throughout the novel another one, less conspicuous, perhaps, but essential to the denouement— namely, that of his successful growth as a writer. This development consists of several clearly marked stages, results in three vital discoveries about the nature of art and the artistic process, and culminates in a feverish act of authentic and redemptive creation.

III

In Book I, which begins where *Look Homeward, Angel* left off, Eugene sets out for graduate study at Harvard, dreaming naively "that he would write a book or play every year or so, which would be a great success, and yield him fifteen or twenty thousand dollars at a crack." He soon discovers, however, that the creation of art is not so easy. For, although in Book II he enrolls in Professor Hatcher's "celebrated course for dramatists" and there writes a play that we later learn he submits to a Broadway producer, he is plagued by self-doubts that are only too emphatically confirmed in Book III when his work is rejected. His next effort, a play called *Mannerhouse,* which he writes in Book IV while teaching in New York City, is presumably somewhat better; at any rate, the praise he receives from his friend Joel Pierce and Joel's sister, Rosalind, to whom he reads it does much to restore his confidence. But again self-doubts emerge when he contemplates the great Pierce library, and reflects on the power of wealth to reduce "all the glory, genius, and magic of a poet's life . . . [to] six rich bindings, forgotten, purchased and unread." Seeking to regain his inspiration, he travels in Book V to Europe, where he manages to fill "a great stack of . . . ledgers," and at last begins to recognize that the artist's life consists of "the sweat and anguish of hard labor. . . ." Two crises, however, soon develop. The first results from his lack of any coherent artistic purpose: driven by an insane, "Faustian" desire to cram all human experience into "one final, perfect, all-inclusive work," he succeeds only in filling his notebooks with a "mad mélange" of "splintered jottings." The second crisis arises when his old friend from Harvard, Starwick, suddenly appears in Paris with two women from Boston who are in love with him. Eugene becomes infected for a time with Starwick's growing apathy, and consequently falls into a life of idleness and dissipation that brings his writing to a halt and nearly overwhelms him with feelings of shame and guilt. Even after he has broken off with Starwick and the women, he continues in Book VI merely to drift from place to place, accomplishing little or nothing. Nevertheless, he finally recovers and begins writing again, more earnestly than ever before, after his arrival in Tours in the opening two chapters of Book VII. Indeed, not only are these chapters among Wolfe's finest lyrical passages, but they carry Eugene's development as an artist as far as the novel will take it, and thus bring *Of Time and the River* as a whole to its true climax and resolution.

To understand what happens in these key chapters and makes them possible we first have to examine three crucial discoveries about art that Eugene has made earlier. One of these concerns is the process of creation itself and where it can be performed. Influenced by his desire for an Earthly Paradise in general, Eugene has long hoped to find a place where he can write under the most ideal and romantic conditions. In Orleans, however, he realizes the folly of such a dream; making a giant leap from romanticism to realism, he concludes that, as a condition for the creation of art, an Earthly Paradise of any literal, physical, geographical sort is wholly unnecessary: ". . . he knew now . . . 'the place to write' was Brooklyn, Boston, Hammersmith, or Kansas—anywhere on earth, so long as the heart, the power, the faith, the desperation . . . were there inside him all the time."

A second major discovery, analogous to this, concerns the subject-matter of art: just as the artist must look for some never-never land of fantasy and romance in which to create, so he must not try to depict such a place in his work itself, but, drawing heavily upon memory, must faithfully represent the reality of life as he has come to know it. Eugene begins to make this discovery in Book III, after he and some companions are arrested and jailed in Blackstone, South Carolina, for drunken driving. The extreme humiliation he suffers on this occasion leads Eugene to feel "a more earthly, common, and familiar union with the lives of other men than he had ever known," and thus ultimately results in his rejecting Shelley's poetry "of aerial flight and escape into some magic and unvisited domain" in favor of Homer, the poets of the Bible, Chaucer, the Elizabethans, and others, "who wrote not of the air but of . . . the golden glory of the earth, which is the only earth that is . . . the only one that will never die." Another step toward realism and an art based on memory occurs when Eugene writes the play that he reads to Joel and Rosalind Pierce at their estate in Rhinekill. Although this work is uneven in quality, and, as was his earlier one, is still in many respects imitative of stale theatrical conventions, he has begun to use in it "some of the materials of his own life and experience," and to depict "some of the

real grandeur, beauty, terror, and unuttered loneliness of America." Finally, to complete his realization that his art is now moving in the right direction there is the town of Rhinekill itself. For this privileged, sheltered world of the Hudson Valley rich is merely the counterpart of the dream worlds created by the Harvard esthetes and Shelley. However painful it is, therefore, to return to the ugliness of New York City, Eugene now knows that upon doing so depends his artistic salvation.

The third and last discovery that leads to the climax of his development as an artist and to the resolution of the novel as a whole occurs during the reading of his play to Joel and Rosalind, when he suddenly realizes, "in one blaze of light," that, of all man's works, art and art alone can achieve timelessness. The passage that describes this epiphany is, in fact, the fullest and most memorable statement of the theme in all Wolfe:

> This is the reason that the artist lives and works and has his being: that . . . he may distill the beauty of an everlasting form . . . cast his spell across the generations, beat death down upon his knees, kill death utterly, and fix eternity with the grappling-hooks of his own art. His life is soul-hydroptic with . . . the intolerable desire to fix eternally in the patterns of an indestructible form a single moment of man's living, a single moment of life's beauty, passion, and unutterable eloquence, that passes, flames, and goes, slipping forever through our fingers with time's sanded drop, flowing forever from our desperate grasp even as a river flows and never can be held.

In these three major discoveries about art, then, lies the key to Eugene's coming-of-age as a writer and hence to the achievement of his quests for transcendence and the resolution of the entire novel. The Earthly Paradise immune to death that he has so futilely sought in his quests for adventure, knowledge, and security, will turn out to be his life as he has already lived it (including, presumably, his quests themselves, with all their cycles of hope and disappointment) when that life has been recaptured by memory and embodied in art. He will be able to confer transcendence upon his own earlier self and experiences by means of the immortalizing and apotheosizing power of the creative process itself. All that remains to complete the design of *Of Time and the River,* therefore, is for such a process to begin, and this is precisely what happens in the two great opening chapters (96-97) of Book VII. The catalyst is an unbearable feeling of homesickness that has been building up in Eugene for months and now becomes profounder and more intense than ever before.

Arriving by chance in the old French town of Tours, and there finding peace and quiet for the first time after months of hectic travel, Eugene falls almost immediately into a rapt, mesmeric, trance-like state that lasts for several weeks, during which he feels himself transported into the very realm of timelessness that he has apprehended so often before. His surroundings virtually disappear from his conscious awareness, and are replaced by preternaturally vivid memories of "home" and teeming impressions of America that from the beginning of the novel have been embedding themselves "in every atom of his flesh and tissue. . . . " He knows now that, although he has been "wandering forever," he must return to "the earth [i.e., America] again."

The consequence of all this is not only his literal return a few chapters later, but, far more crucially, his return by means of art. For in Tours all his memories bred of homesickness finally trigger a furious burst of creativity, the object of which is to get every scrap of his remembered experience down on paper, to disgorge all of his life into language:

> . . . he began to write now like a madman . . . all ordered plans, designs, coherent projects for the work he had set out to do went by the board, were burned up in the flame of a quenchless passion, like a handful of dry straw . . . he wrote ceaselessly from dawn to dark, sometimes from darkness on to dawn again . . .
>
> And in those words was packed the whole image of his bitter homelessness, his intolerable desire, his maddened longing for return . . .
>
> They were all there—without coherence, scheme, or reason—flung down upon paper like figures blasted by the spirit's lightning stroke, and in them was the huge chronicle of the billion forms, the million names, the huge, single, and incomparable substance of America.

This episode is the point toward which Eugene's development as an artist has been implicitly tending from the beginning, and, as such, it constitutes the novel's climax and resolution. If only in a half-conscious way, Eugene has now begun the process of dealing more compulsively and completely than ever before with what must henceforth be the central subject of his art—America and the life he has already lived there. It is true that his frenzied burst of creativity is very brief; it is both the first and the last of its kind in the novel. But we are not allowed to imagine that such a crucial event will have no long-range consequences, for Eugene's memory, now more powerfully and purposefully activated than ever before, continues to operate strongly even after he leaves Tours, and thus provides a source of inspiration to which his creative impulse will surely return many times in the future. In short, Eugene has embarked upon the task of producing an authentic autobiographical art that will rescue his past from the maw of time, confer upon it "the beauty of an everlasting form," and thereby impart to it a radiant immortality. In doing so, he is at least on the verge of attaining the goal of all his quests—the transcendence of death.

This account of the novel's closure is, of course, incomplete. After Chapters 96-97, for instance, Eugene's futile, romantic quests for transcendent adventure, knowledge, and security continue anticlimactically for five more chapters, which culminate in his shipboard meeting with the woman who, in *The Web and the Rock* and *You Can't Go Home Again,* is to be known as Esther Jack, and to become the mistress of Wolfe's next protagonist, George Webber. Distracted, perhaps, by the mere "chronicle" aspect of what he was writing, Wolfe clearly did not know when to stop, and for this, as well as other reasons, *Of Time and the River* is far from being a perfect book. So

much I conceded at the outset. Nevertheless, it is also far from being "formless." Considered in its broadest outline, indeed, the form turns out to be nothing less than a late avatar of that age-old, fundamentally religious one so brilliantly described by M. H. Abrams in his distinguished study of Romanticism, *Natural Supernaturalism.* This is the design (originating in pagan and Christian Neo-Platonism, modified by the nineteenth-century Romantics, and passed on to a number of moderns) of the "circuitous journey" or "the great circle," which expresses a vision, in Abrams's words, of "the course of all things" as "a circuit whose end is its beginning, of which the movement is from unity out to the increasingly many and back to unity, and in which this movement into and out of division is identified with the falling away from good to evil and a return to good.' In the terms implicitly proposed by *Of Time and the River,* this circle consists of four phases related to the key concepts of "home" or "paradise": paradise itself, paradise lost, paradise sought, and paradise regained. Paradise corresponds to the recollections of pre-existence and the romantic dreams that Eugene enjoyed in childhood and even to his childhood itself when in later years he nostalgically recalls it; paradise lost corresponds to the anguished awareness of time and death that comes to him in his youth; paradise sought corresponds to his many (also cyclical) quests for adventure, knowledge, and security; and paradise regained corresponds to the beginning of authentic artistic creation whereby he will finally be able to transcend time and death by making of all the transitory and tormented moments of his life itself a thing of timeless beauty.

Richard S. Kennedy (essay date 1985)

SOURCE: "What the Galley Proofs of Wolfe's *Of Time and the River* Tell Us," in *The Thomas Wolfe Review,* Vol. 9, No. 2, Fall, 1985, pp. 1-8.

[*In the following excerpt, Kennedy examines the galley proofs of* Of Time and the River *for the light they shed on the final version of the novel, Wolfe's relationship with his editors, his work habits, and his talents as a writer.*]

The story is well known how Maxwell Perkins, senior editor at Scribner's, helped Thomas Wolfe put together his second novel, *Of Time and the River,* and how Wolfe, ever ready to add more material to this excessively long book, was reluctant to let his manuscript go to the printers. As time goes on and more evidence turns up, it becomes possible to see in more detail the situation that prevailed in the bringing forth of this remarkable book. Both Wolfe and Perkins have recorded statements that blurred or distorted the picture. Wolfe asserted dramatically in *The Story of a Novel* that Perkins had suddenly sent his book to the printers while Wolfe was away on a two-week vacation in October 1934. When he returned, galley proof was beginning to come in. Perkins has provided information about Wolfe's unwillingness to see his book go into print. He wrote that Wolfe sat in the Scribner library day after day brooding over the galley proofs but not doing anything with them and that the proofs were read by another Scribner editor, John Hall Wheelock, and then sent to the printer.

With the publication of *The Letters of Thomas Wolfe* [edited by Elizabeth Nowell] and *Editor to Author: The Letters of Maxwell E. Perkins* and, above all, Elizabeth Nowell's biography of Wolfe, a less dramatic story began to emerge. In July 1934, Wolfe wrote to Robert Raynolds, "It seems unbelievable, but Perkins and I finished getting the manuscript ready for the printer last night," and he went on to add that there were still some scenes to be written. A few days later he wrote to his brother Fred, "Believe it or not, Perkins sent the manuscript of my book to the press three days ago. There is a great deal I want to do and must do yet, but it must be done within the next two and a half months—because after that, it will be too late. We will start getting proofs back in two or three weeks, and from then on I have got to keep feeding it to the printers. I have been at work on it so long that it was hard to give it up. He almost had to take it away from me; but he is the best judge. . . . There are many, many more things that I would like to do. It has cost me many a wrench to see the tremendous chunks and pieces we have had to cut out of it. There is much more that I would like to put in."

Additional evidence has recently emerged that brings us even closer to the situation. In 1983, the first forty sheets of galley proof for *Of Time and the River* appeared in the literary market and were purchased by the University of North Carolina Library. They correspond to Books I and II of the novel, the first 133 pages—that is, they include Eugene's long train ride to the North, his early experiences at Harvard, and his coming to know Uncle Bascom in Boston. These galley proofs are part of the set John Hall Wheelock corrected. At the top of galley 1, he has written "Tom: you have galley 82," which indicates that by that time at least one-fourth of the book had come back from the printer. Wolfe's own set of these forty galleys, now in the Houghton Library at Harvard, are completely unmarked. The University of North Carolina galleys, however, show the hands of both Wheelock and Wolfe, and in examining them, we can see the two of them at work together.

What kind of marks and changes had Wheelock made? What we find are only corrections of errors and some minor copy editing. The substantive changes are of this sort: "if" in place of "whether"; "complacent," rather than "complaisant"; "smoking wheat cakes," rather than "country wheat cakes." Wheelock makes an adverb more appropriate when " 'yes, thank God,' someone murmured softly but devoutly" becomes "softly but fervently." Mr. Flood's movement of his arm with a painful grunt was referred to in the galley as a "delicate movement"; Wheelock made it a "delicate operation." Luke Gant is assessed by one of the men in the parlor car as one who could "sell Palm Beach suits at the North Pole"; Wheelock changed it to "sell Palm Beach suits to the Esquimaux." Wheelock also supplied an explanation at the point Wolfe introduced Starwick as being in "Professor Hatcher's class"; he expanded it to "Professor Hatcher's celebrated course for dramatists, of which he was himself a member." But Wheelock's chief contribution was to insert space between portions of the text when a jump in time took place or when the narrator began one of his meditations on time

or the American landscape or when Eugene's mind flashed back to the past.

Wheelock's contribution then had been merely functional and we can dispense with the myth that he had to go through the galleys changing all the "I"s to "he"s. As a matter of fact, a look at the final typescript, now in the Houghton Library, shows that all the material for these 40 galleys had been written in the third person with the exception of one portion of Book II about Eugene's reading in the Harvard Library, which had to be changed in typescript from first-person narration. One other exception is part of the material about Uncle Bascom that had been pasted on pages clipped from the *Scribner's Magazine* story, **"A Portrait of Bascom Hawke."** All those paste-ups from the magazine pages had been in the first-person but the evidence of other typewritten pages shows that even the Uncle Bascom material had been written originally in the third person.

What the forty galley sheets show without question is that the predominant number of changes and additions were made by Wolfe. In the first place he had been very careless about the typescript that was sent to the printer. He had not made all the necessary changes from an early version of the drunken conversation on the train, and corrections were needed in the galleys: the name "John" instead of "Eugene" appears three times. This is something Wheelock could not have recognized, because the drunken dialogue among the three young fellows does not indicate clearly who is speaking to whom. Again, Eugene's brother Steve is called "Gil" in galleys seven times, and only Wolfe knew to correct it. Also typographical errors in the typescript were not always evident to Wheelock, so some still remained in the galleys when he passed them on to Wolfe. Only the author would know, for example, that a reference to "that Cleveland guy" should have been "that Cleveland gang," or that "the thinning noises" should have been "thrumming noises."

Wolfe also made many changes in the names of characters—the names of Altamont men in the smoking car and of Altamont boys mentioned when Eugene was arguing with Robert Weaver. It appears that some real-life names of Asheville citizens had remained in the story right up to the galley-proof stage.

As Wolfe went through the galleys, he occasionally made small stylistic improvements in both narration and dialogue: "long stride" becomes "lunging stride"; Warren G. Harding's service "to the public" becomes service "to his country"; Eugene's father's "huge form" becomes "long form"; Robert Weaver's "look of restlessness" becomes an "expression of restlessness." There are a large number of these revisions on the galley sheets.

The change in point-of-view that Wolfe had made from some early versions of this material also affected one of the meditations on the American earth, a passage that occurs when Eugene wakes on the train and looks out the window. One can see why Wheelock made no change in it because it refers to "men's hearts" responding to the appearance of the earth at dawn's first light. In the galleys, it appears in the first-person plural:

The earth emerged with all its ancient and eternal quality: stately and solemn and lonely-looking in that first light, it filled men's hearts with all its ancient wonder. It seemed to have been there forever, and though we had never seen it before, to be more familiar to us than our mother's face. And at the same time, it seemed we had discovered it once more, and if we had been the first men who ever saw the earth the solemn joy of this discovery could not have seemed more strange or more familiar. Seeing it, we felt nothing but silence and wonder in our hearts, and were naked and alone and stripped down to our bare selves, as near to truth as men can ever come.

On the passage goes. Wolfe altered it all to third-person plural: "Seeing it, they felt nothing but silence and wonder in their hearts," and so on.

But the principal kind of alteration that Wolfe made was to add material. In the very second paragraph he inserted a long clause. The people waiting on the railroad platform are said to have been drawn there by a common experience, an event of the first importance to all Americans, the arrival of a train—then comes the clause that Wolfe added: "because in it has been compacted the legend of dark time—our thousand weathers and our billion lives, all of our vast and unrecorded history, the awful stillness of the wilderness, all of the hope, the hunger and the waiting that lay buried in our father's heart and of the whole huge memory of the old swarm-haunted mind of man."

You will note that Wolfe does not hesitate to use the first-person plural here when he as narrator is referring to Americans in general. Nor need he have worried about the long passage that I was describing a moment ago. Wolfe as narrator does not trouble a normal reader when he speaks with a communal voice.

But here is a surprise: this lengthy clause does not appear in the printed copy of *Of Time and the River*. Nor do two other insertions of substantial length. One is a two-page digressive description of an odd-looking interne at the hospital. Another is a fascinating elaboration about Eugene's paranoiac response to life. In the dialogue with Robert Weaver, Eugene learned that a certain local matron had been praying for him as if he were well on the way to perdition. He became furious about town gossip and he feels attacked by "them." Wolfe wanted to add the following sentence. "And like a man faced fiercely and alone against the blind brute mass and hatred of a senseless world, he now told himself bitterly that he did not care what 'they' might say about him, without knowing who 'they' were, without understanding whence 'they' came, or why 'they' were arrayed against him—hating, fearing only 'they,' immortal and phantasmal 'they,' the scourge of youth, and life's great bane of deathling men, that goads us on forever with its scorpion-whip of scorn and fury, and that will not let us rest."

But other small additions do get inserted, as well as one major passage that comes at the conclusion of the drunken revelry as Eugene goes to bed in the Pullman car: the imagined riders Pale Pity and Lean Death on their horses, whose hooves pound to the rhythm of a line from Virgil, "Quadrupedante putrem sonitu quatit ungula campum."

Some time in August, Wolfe returned the first eleven galleys to Wheelock with a note. He said, "I found little to do here although I am not wholly satisfied with the way it *flows*—I put some question marks in margins of galleys 10 and 11 for this reason: the tense changes from past to present—present when describing the look of the little town from the train window. Do you find this change of tense jumpy and confusing—and if you do will you change it to past tense?" (*Letters*). The question he asks is characteristic of the way he sought advice of editors, and of his literary agent, all though his career.

In mid-September, Wheelock wrote Wolfe: "When are you going to let me have back the first thirty-eight galleys which you and I went over together and which are, as I recall it, ready for the printer?"

At this point, we can ask what does all this tell us about Wolfe's situation with respect to his editors? The indications are that at first he was working hard but slowly over the galleys, yet was so full of misgivings and uncertainties that he was delaying to return the galleys and have them go into pages. But it further appears that when he and Wheelock went over the first thirty-eight galleys together, Wheelock (and perhaps Perkins) found most of Wolfe's changes and additions valuable but rejected four of the additions as unworthy of his text. Thus, Wolfe found that some of the sentences he had wished to add, whatever their appropriateness or lack thereof, he was unable to get into his book. Earlier he had submitted to Perkins's judgment about his manuscript; now he was losing control of his galley proofs to someone, either Wheelock or Perkins. His reaction, it seems, was to retreat from the scene entirely. He took a trip to the Chicago Fair and made a leisurely return home, stopping off in Ohio and in Pittsburgh. When he returned in October after a two-weeks' absence, he found that Perkins and Wheelock had waited for him no longer. They had sent a huge batch of galleys back to the press to be put into page proof. This is the situation Wolfe was referring to in *The Story of a Novel* when he said he returned from Chicago to discover that Perkins had sent his book to the printer.

The remainder of the Wheelock-Wolfe galleys, now in the Houghton Library, tell the rest of the story. Wolfe had ceased cooperating with Wheelock, after galley 40, or perhaps 52. On galleys 52 through 213, Wheelock's routine corrections appear, including his improvement of Wolfe's French grammar. Occasionally, he had scribbled "Revise" at the tops of the galley sheets, but Wolfe had done nothing with them during the weeks he had them in hand. Suddenly on galley 214, Wolfe's marks appear again as he changes "Eugene" to "he" or "Eugene's" to "his" thirteen times in the next few galleys. The novel by this time had reached Eugene's sojourn in Paris. There are no more Wolfe corrections until one change for page 823, Eugene's conversation with the Countess.

The galleys have reached almost to the end of the book now and Wolfe has done almost nothing since galley 40 or 52. It would appear that he was so discouraged by the fact that not all of his insertions in the first forty galleys were accepted that he sank into inaction. Perhaps his misgivings so unsettled his resolve that he could not keep up to the schedule for the printer. Or perhaps he was even frozen into indecision by the fact that he could not make revisions without adding substantially to his text. In any case, this was not the way he was used to working. He was used to a lot of give-and-take with an editor and was frequently doubtful enough about his own purposes that he would ask an editor's opinion. When he had published stories in magazines, he was accustomed to making changes and additions right up to the last stage of publication. For example, he left a note with the revised typescript of his story, **"Dark in the Forest, Strange as Time,"** saying to Alfred Dashiell, the editor of *Scribner's Magazine,* "Here's the story, with such corrections as I could now make. I think I've succeeded in changing it to *past* tense everywhere—and will you please look at the insertion which I have written in on page 9 to see if it is clear—and if I have succeeded in doing what you suggested there. . . . As to the title, will you consider this one tentatively—**"Dark in the Forest, Strange as Time"** (or "Dark in the Forest, Dark as Time" as a variant). Don't ask me what the title means, I don't know, but think it may capture the feeling of the story, which is what I want to do. This is all for the present—and please let me go over it again when you get proofs. P.S. I did not make the *cuts* on page 5 and 6 as you suggested. . . . If you think there's too much of this dialogue, go ahead and cut it out, but I wish you'd look it over again to make sure" (*Letters*).

In the progress on *Of Time and the River* there was suddenly now a major addition to the book that does not appear in the galley proofs. This apparently came about in December 1934 when Perkins finally was convinced by Wolfe's argument that a greater sense of conclusion was needed for the book. In this way, Wolfe created Book VII, "Kronos and Rhea." He took some material from the end of Book VI and the beginning of the next book, "Faustus and Helen" and wove into it two thematic fugues about time. Then he added another scene to the end of Book VIII (now entitled "Faust and Helen"), in which Eugene and Esther see each other from a distance on board ship and Eugene feels "impaled upon the knife of love." This concludes the novel and provides a link with the volume that was to follow.

What else do the galleys tell us about Wolfe as a writer and about his working relationship with his editors at Scribner's?

First of all, it is clear that Wolfe's creative talent was for proliferation and that he lacked that kind of secondary creativity which involves cutting, revising, or restructuring. His idea of clarifying a passage was to add a clause, a sentence, a paragraph, or a page. If Wheelock wrote "Revise" at the top of a galley, Wolfe did nothing, or he changed a character's name to a pronoun. What he really wanted to do was to write several pages, such as he was able to supply in creating "Kronos and Rhea."

The weeks of delay in getting the galleys back to Wheelock certainly reflect Wolfe's reluctance to let the book go, but this worry, he tells us in *The Story of a Novel,* attended

all his approaches to publication: ". . . it is literally true that with everything I have ever written or had printed, not only my two books but also all the long and short stories that *Scribner's Magazine* and other magazines have published, I have felt at the last moment when the hour of naked print drew nigh a kind of desperation and have even entreated my publisher not only to defer the publication of my book until another season, but have asked the editors of magazines to put off the publication of a story for another month or two until I had a chance to look at it again, work on it some more, do something to it, I was not sure what."

The publication of *Of Time and the River* was further complicated, however, by the help that Perkins and Wheelock had contributed. To his own doubts Wolfe now added his uncertainty as to whether the judgment of his editors was right. Yet the situation he found himself in was of his own making. Although his statement in *The Story of a Novel* seems to convey a charge that his editors had taken his book away from him, this is really his paranoiac personality speaking. The case was quite the reverse.

In December 1933, Wolfe felt hopeless about the state of his book. He had been working for four years and his novel was still only an accumulation of fragments. When Perkins offered to look over what he had on hand, Wolfe welcomed the editorial rescue. He gave Perkins a mountain of manuscript made up of several disjunctive narrative strands and lyrical celebrations of the American experience, saying, ". . . in spite of all the rhythms, chants—what you call my dithyrambs—which are all through the manuscript, I think you will find when I get through that there is plenty of narrative—or should I say when *you* get through, because I must shamefacedly confess that I need your help now more than I ever did" (*Letters*). He had been trying to write a work that was not just another autobiographical novel, but he was unable to create any kind of lengthy narrative that was not based closely on his own life. When Perkins found that Wolfe's manuscript was a series of autobiographical episodes in an intermittent chronological order, he urged him to revive the persona of Eugene Gant again and pick up his story where *Look Homeward, Angel* had ended. This simple suggestion solved Wolfe's narrative problem. Thereafter he and Perkins worked together recasting the episodes and Wolfe wrote necessary material to fill in the gaps.

By submitting himself to Perkins's supervision in this way, Wolfe soon found himself caught in the exigencies of the publishing world. First, the publication of a book is announced, catalogues are prepared, advertising is planned, salesmen are advised. Second, manuscripts must go to printers if a schedule is to be met; once manuscripts are in galley proof, they cannot be delayed without increased costs; the same is true for page proofs. The publication of *Of Time and the River,* planned for publication in fall 1934, had already been postponed once and held over until spring 1935. The pressure on Wolfe was overwhelming.

Temperamentally he was not made for a world like this. Thus arose his resentment over being forced by circumstances to see his book go into the finality of print. Yet it seems irrefutably clear that if it had not been for Perkins and Wheelock, the book would never have been published at all, and American literature would have been deprived of one of its unique monuments.

Some critics, unfamiliar with Wolfe's working methods and not fully aware of the peculiarities of his creativity, have accused Perkins of harming Wolfe's work. I hope this examination of the evidence will have shown that, on the contrary, Perkins's advice, prodding, and insistence (plus Wheelock's patient contribution of his time) helped get into print the book that established Wolfe's reputation as the American writer who best carried on the tradition of Whitman and Melville in the twentieth century. . . .

Carol Johnston   (essay date 1987)

SOURCE: "The Critical Reception of *Of Time and the River*," in *The Thomas Wolfe Review,* Vol. 11, No. 1, Spring, 1987, pp. 45-54.

[*In the following excerpt, Johnston discusses Bernard De-Voto's assessment of* Of Time and the River *in relation to Scribner's marketing campaign for the novel.*]

Bernard DeVoto's "Genius Is Not Enough" [*The Saturday Review of Literature,* April 25, 1936], a review of [*Of Time and the River* usually referred to hereafter as *T/R*] thinly disguised as a review of *The Story of a Novel,* focused on seven points: (1) the rawness or "placental" nature of the work, (2) Wolfe's contempt for the medium, (3) giantism, (4) infantilism, (5) editorial collaboration, (6) abdication of authorial responsibility in the revision process, and (7) the fact that Wolfe had been presented to the reading public as a genius. The review was illustrated with a portrait of a grinning, shirtsleeved DeVoto, pistol-in-hand, supposedly taking aim at the young Wolfe. DeVoto later wrote that he regretted and had not approved the use of the photograph, which had been sent to the offices of *The Saturday Review of Literature* [SRL] by an ill-advised publicity man at Little, Brown [see *The Letters of Bernard DeVoto,* edited by Wallae Stegner].

Most of the charges were not unique. The few readers who chose to participate in an *SRL* poll, voting on the best and worst novels of 1935, honored *T/R* with both distinctions. Robert Penn Warren commented on the "slovenly" autobiographical pretense of the novel, the writer's tendency to slip from the third person into the first person [*The American Review* 5 (May 1935)]. Burton Rascoe, in the book review section of *The New York* Herald Tribune [March 10, 1935], commented on Wolfe's magnificent malady, his "gigantism of the soul," and Isobel Patterson wrote of Wolfe's tendency toward exaggeration: "All his principal characters are highly exaggerated . . . seven feet tall with megaphone voices" [*New York Herald Tribune Books,* February 24, 1935]. Even Clifton Fadiman whose review was liberally quoted in Scribner's advertisements, made some negative comments. Fadiman wrote of Wolfe's style that "At its best it is wonderous Elizabethan. At its worst it is hyperthyroid and afflicted with elephantiasis" [*The New Yorker* 11 (March 9, 1935)].

Still, most of the reviewers tempered criticism of the novel with praise for the power of the young novelist, perceiving

in the raw energy of the work the promise of genius. De-Voto, a superb selfeditor was, however, more concerned with craftsmanship than with inspiration—with the work as a final product than with the potential of the author. His assessment of *T/R,* for this reason, differs most significantly from that of his contemporaries not in substance, but in focus. Henry Seidel Canby in the *SRL* [March 9, 1935] called the book an "artistic failure," but, he admitted, it was an "artistic failure" like many other fiery and ambitious books, like the failures of Melville and Whitman. Wolfe, he concludes, "has more material, more vitality, more originality, more gusto than any two contemporary British novelists put together, even though they may be real novelists and he is not. He stands to them as Whitman stood to the wearied *Idylls of the King.*" And V. F. Calverton in *The Modern Monthly* [June, 1935] spoke of Wolfe's weaknesses, but not as the weaknesses of a weak writer. "They are," he writes, "the weaknesses of a strong writer, a powerful writer, who when he overcomes them will be stronger and more powerful still."

This article (based on a study of the pre-publication history of *T/R* and of the corrections made in the first six printings of that book, of the Scribner records at Princeton, of the advertisements for [*Look Homeward, Angel* (*LHA*)] and *T/R* run in *The New York Times Book Review,* and of DeVoto's annotated copy of the second printing of *T/R*) focuses on the second and seventh of DeVoto's charges: his charge that the errors in the text of *T/R* indicated Wolfe's disrespect for the medium and his charge that Wolfe had been, inaccurately, presented by Scribner's to the reading public as a genius. The first of these, was largely a response to the happenstance that dropped the second printing of *T/R* into DeVoto's hands, and the second was a response to the advertising strategy Scribner's believed would make Wolfe most marketable.

There is, of course, no accurate means of gauging the impact of any promotional campaign on an author's career, either in terms of sale or reputation; the elements contributing to each are simply too complex and ill-defined to be dealt with in terms of one-to-one relationships. However, an examination of Scribner's promotion of Wolfe suggests how that firm regarded him as a marketable commodity and the nature of the public image it felt would make him saleable. The whole question of advertising, Roger Burlingame notes in his study of Scribner's, *Of Making Many Books,* is seen in proportion to sales. If the sale of a book does not justify what the publisher spends promoting it, then the publisher loses money. Since much of a promotional campaign is planned before publication, much of the advertising strategy is a matter of guesswork, an expression of the publisher's confidence in the ultimate success of a work. Before the publication of *LHA* in 1929, few at Scribner's could have anticipated its success. The earliest *New York Times Book Review* advertisement is an unframed 2-inch-square blurb quoting from a review by Thomas Beer. "Mr. Wolfe," it reads, "seems to me to be the most interesting writer of fiction to appear in America since Glenway Westcott" (Nov. 3, 1929). This note appeared near the bottom of a full-page, 140-square-inch collective advertisement, dwarfed by framed advertisements for Hemingway's *A Farewell to Arms,* Galsworthy's *A*

Modern Comedy, Edwin Franden Dakin's *Mrs. Eddy,* Theodore and Kermit Roosevelt's *Trailing the Giant Panda,* and Will James's *Smoky,* each of which was five-times the size of the Wolfe note.

On Oct. 18, 1929, Scribner's invested in a first printing of 5,540 copies of *LHA,* some 3,000 more copies than they had invested in the first novel of another young author, F. Scott Fitzgerald, only nine years earlier, but some 15,000 fewer copies than they printed of that established author's third novel, *The Great Gatsby,* in 1925. By Nov. 6, 1929, *LHA* had entered a second printing of 3,000 copies. Scribner's had increased its investment by over 50%, and, subsequently stepped up its promotional campaign, tripling the size of the advertisement for the book in the November 24 issue of *The New York Times Book Review,* framing it, and positioning it at the top center of the page, next to the advertisement announcing the fifth printing of *A Farewell to Arms.* By December 1 *LHA* had entered its third printing. Advertisements appearing in the next two issues of *The New York Times Book Review* measured 9 square inches and 25 square inches, respectively (December 1 and December 8, 1929). The latter of these, for the first time, focused attention on Wolfe as well as on the book, featuring a drawing of the author in profile.

The change in size and prominence of these advertisements reflects the change in the publicity department's perception of the saleability of *LHA* over a two-month period, but there was also a change in the nature of these advertisements. These changes suggest the nature of the public image that Scribner's felt would make Wolfe most marketable. By the time *LHA* reached its second printing, the bland assertion of interest evident in the Thomas Beer blurb had been replaced by quotes from reviewers focusing on the vitality, raw energy, and unconventionality of the book. According to these blurbs, the book "breathe[d]" the spirit of youth and was "vigorous and striking" with the "buoyant health of the roaring Elizabethan tales of Nashe and Greene." The writer, the advertisement continued, had dodged "neither life's vulgarity, bestiality, profanity, and horror nor its fine strivings, its hopes and its invincible optimism" (Dec. 8, 1929).

LHA sold 125,000 copies in Scribner printings within the first fifteen years and an additional 103,000 copies in Modern Library printings within its first twenty-five years. By 1935, it had matriculated through at least eight Scribners and two Modern Library printings, making Wolfe a major Scribner author, but one whose name had not appeared on a book in six years.

Over a period of three months in 1929, the promotion of *LHA* accelerated into a high energy campaign. The advertising strategy for a novel by an established author necessarily differed significantly from that planned for the first novel of an unknown author. From its inception, the advertising campaign for *Of Time and the River* was more enthusiastic and energetic than the campaign for *Look Homeward, Angel* had ever been. Of even greater interest to Wolfe scholars and in a way that would make Wolfe more vulnerable to the "enemies" he feared, it developed into a campaign that focused as much on the novelist as it did on the novel—suggesting in ways that were far more blatant than in any of the promotional campaigns for Fitzgerald, Hemingway, or Faulkner, appearing at about the same time, that Wolfe had become a writer of international prominence, the recorder of the American epic, the "genius" who would fulfill the search for the Great American Novelist.

The first printing of *T/R,* 10,000 copies, took place in February 1935, although Scribner's did not officially publish it (put the book on sale to the general public) until March 8. Advertisements in *The New York Times Book Review* indicate that the book entered a fifth printing within three weeks. By the time the novel had entered its sixth printing in April, one month after its publication, two months after its first printing, and only three months after page proofs had been set, Scribner's had printed 30,000 copies. Advertisements in *The New York Times Book Review* heralded the advent of each new printing, much as they had in the campaign for Hemingway's *A Farewell to Arms* in 1929 [See "Marketing, Ernest Hemingway," by John J. Fenstermaker, in *Fitzgerald/Hemingway Annual 1978,* edited by Matthew J. Bruccoli and Richard Layman], creating a "steamroller" effect, the sense of a book so much in demand that new printings were required on a weekly basis.

Considering the rapid succession of the first six printings of *T/R,* few corrections might be expected. In fact, nearly one-hundred corrections were made in the first six printings. Many are substantives. Heinemann's, setting from galleys sent them in January, was provided in February and April with corrections lists and caught most of the errors prior to setting type in August 1935. John Hall Wheelock chose to send Wolfe's German publishers, Rowohlt-Verlag, stitched gatherings of the sixth printing of *Of Time and the River* in March 1935, specifically because that printing incorporated all of the corrections made to that date. Wolfe first indicated his awareness of the problems in the early printings of *T/R* on Mar. 31, 1935 in a fourpart letter to Maxwell Perkins (Nowell). He sent a list of corrections, but 75% of the errors had already been corrected by the time his letter was received.

Wheelock explained the problem in a letter to Frere-Reeves of Heinemann's dated Apr. 19, 1935 (Scribner records). The manuscript of *T/R* had been given to a typist, in Wolfe's hand, to copy. The typist had difficulty decoding the handwriting, and, as a result, the typescript which came into the printers' hands had a number of words which, although they made sense, were not the words that Wolfe had written. Where Wolfe wrote "transmuted," the typist read "transmitted"; where Wolfe wrote "loveliness," the typist read "loneliness"; where Wolfe wrote "clay," the typist read "day." Most of the corrections made by Scribner's in the first six printings were of this nature; others, errors in pronoun usage, resulted from the failure of the Scribner staff to translate the first-person story published as **"A Portrait of Bascom Hawke"** in the April 1932 issue of *Scribner's Magazine* into the third person when that story was incorporated into the novel.

Wheelock's letter to Frere-Reeves admitted, in good, businesslike fashion, an embarrassing situation. Wolfe's letter to Maxwell Perkins, on the other hand, was frenzied and anxiety-ridden. Wolfe blamed himself for not having read proof carefully and Scribner's for rushing the book into print. "Max, Max," he wrote, "I cannot go on, but am sick at heart—we should have waited six months longer—the book, like Caesar, was from its mother's womb untimely ripped—like King Richard, brought into the world 'scarce half made up' " (Nowell). Wolfe spoke of his enemies, more numerous he imagined than Perkins suspected. "I fear," he wrote, "we have played directly into their hands by our carelessness and by our frenzied haste" (Nowell).

Wolfe's fears were prophetic, though possibly not for the reasons he suspected. The nature of the advertising campaign for *T/R,* a campaign that finally focused on Wolfe as the Great American Novelist, made him vulnerable, if not to his "enemies," at least to those whose creative philosophies differed from his own. In addition, more by chance than by choice, the copy of *T/R* that fell into De-Voto's hands was of a second printing, in which fewer than a third of the errors had been caught.

The Scribner campaign for *T/R* differs most significantly from the campaign for *LHA* in its focus. Although its advertising blurbs continued to stress the vitality of Wolfe's novels, Scribner's began to market the author as well as the product. On Mar. 10, 1935, *The New York Times Book Review* contained a full-page advertisement promoting eleven Scribner books. Of the 140-square inches of space in that advertisement, nearly 85-square inches were devoted to *T/R*. The section devoted to this book contained two illustrations, each measuring 9-square inches: a portrait of Wolfe and a facsimile of the dust jacket for the book. The 14-line blurb for the novel, printed in 16-point type with 18-point leading, heralded a second printing and quoted from Sinclair Lewis's Nobel Prize Speech describing Wolfe as, potentially, one of the world's greatest writers. Two weeks later, as the book entered its fifth printing, Scribner's devoted over 90-square inches of a *New York Times Book Review* advertisement to *T/R,* dramatically reproducing the front pages of issues of *The New York Times Book Review,* the *New York Herald Tribune,* and the *Saturday Review of Literature.* All that is legible in these facsimiles are banners reading: "The River of Youth"; "Mr. Wolfe's Pilgrim Progresses: *Of Time and the River* Carries on *Look Homeward, Angel*"; and "The Ecstasy, Fury, Pain and Beauty of Life: Thomas Wolfe Sings and Shouts in His Gargantuan New Novel." Wolfe's portrait appears in *The New York Times Book Review* and in the *New York Herald Tribune Book Review* facsimiles. In addition, the advertisement quotes from reviews by Peter Munro Jack, Mary Colum, Herschell Brickell, Lewis Gannett, and Clifton Fadiman. Of these five review blurbs, three refer to the book and two to the author. Peter Munro Jack called the novel a "triumphant demonstration that Thomas Wolfe has the stamina to produce a magnificent epic of American life." Clifton Fadiman wrote that "For decades American writing had not had eloquence like Wolfe's" (24 March 1935).

On Apr. 7, 1935, half of the 112-square inch Scribner advertisement in *The New York Times Book Review* was devoted to the new book, labeled "A New National Best-Seller Enthusiastically Acclaimed by Leading Critics from Coast to Coast." Wolfe's portrait, paraded in a single col-

umn along the left-hand margin of the advertisement, appears six times. Of the nine reviewers and reviews quoted, more than half focus on Wolfe and not on the novel. Peter Munro Jack speaks of Wolfe's stamina; Mary Colum likens Wolfe to Joyce and Proust; James Gray calls Wolfe "a genius . . . a terrific elemental force"; Sterling North comments that "never before in a book by an American has there been such a raw and rich profusion of Life"; and Paul Jordan Smith remarks that "no man has ever told the story of youth's tragi-comedy in such golden words."

Two weeks later, in a 33-square-inch advertisement, Scribner's quoted Harry Hansen, who referred to *T/R* simply as "Wolfe's great book," and John Chamberlain, who suggested that "Wolfe may supply the motive power to change our literature" (Apr. 31, 1935). Later advertisements refer to *T/R* as the "Greatest novel of the year" (Apr. 28, 1935), "the most remarkable novel since *Moby Dick*" (May 5, 1935), and liken Wolfe to Dickens and Rabelais (May 12, 1935). Wolfe, one reads, towers "head and shoulders above anyone now writing" (May 19, 1935).

Wolfe and Bernard DeVoto never met—they could scarcely have been considered enemies; yet, they stood at opposite poles in their perception of the writing process. When DeVoto wrote "Genius Is Not Enough" he had only recently assumed the Editor's Easy Chair at the *Saturday Review of Literature* and was fresh from what he perceived to be a resounding defeat at Harvard, where the temporary position he held had not been made permanent. The political process that denied him continuity at Harvard, inadvertently, had impugned DeVoto's integrity—as a result of some confusion as to whether he had actually been offered the position at the *Saturday Review of Literature* or had used the offer merely to bolster his candidacy at Harvard [See Wallace Stegner, *The Uneasy Chair*].

A study of DeVoto's annotated copy of *T/R* reveals two things: (1) that he was a careful reader, copiously marking the text, and (2) that the response to the book described in "Genius Is Not Enough" was an honest one. DeVoto did find much in *T/R* to value, although far more of the criticism than the praise found its way into his review article. Brought up in Ogden, Utah, the grandson of pioneer Mormon farmers, inevitably a cultural outsider at Harvard, DeVoto approved of Wolfe's initial description of Francis Starwick, "the youngest of a middle-western family of nine children, small business and farming people in modest circumstances [who] gave the impression of wealth because . . . [he had been] endowed with wealth by nature." DeVoto drew a vertical line next to the entire passage and wrote, "Good stuff. He catches it here." He found Wolfe's depiction of the Boston Irish "damn good," "Much better . . . than O'Neill's." He thought the scene in which Eugene visited the Simpsons on pages 208-209, a "good scene," writing beneath it with an arrow directed to several lines and without apparent sarcasm, "This is how you write the Great American Novel." He labeled Wolfe's characterization of Dr. McGuire "great" and noted that the chapter in which McGuire collapses in a drunken stupor, simultaneously the object of Luke Gant's appeals for miracles and nurse Creasman's contempt was "A hell of a good scene." It seemed of great importance to him that Eugene's notebook jottings came "closer to inspiring respect . . . than [anything] else," and he marked it with a star. But he does not mention it in his review.

It would be misleading to imply that DeVoto's annotations are uncritical; more often his responses were negative—notes on what he perceived to be technical problems—incredulous, occasionally coarsely phrased, epithets in the face of what seemed to him to be prose that exaggerated simple human acts. He catches nearly every error in pronoun reference in the book, noting the failure to translate **"A Portrait of Bascom Hawke"** into the third person, but interpreting it as evidence of Wolfe's inability to disguise the autobiographical substrata of the novel. In addition, he pinpointed a chronological inconsistency (corrected prior to the fifth printing) on page 886, when Eugene, who has earlier claimed to have seen the last of Ann, comes across her in a Marseilles cafe. Commenting on Eugene's escape from the scene, DeVoto characterized it "Another casual orgasm of violent feeling with no reason."

He commented in other places that the "Dialogue [was] lousy," that much of the book was "Romantic nonsense" that the novel "creaked like an O'Neill play," was "worse than Lewis's worst," and more "heavy handed" than Dreiser. "Infantile voyeurism," he added, "marks his whole book." "Somehow," he wrote on page 609 next to a burlesque of Queen Victoria, "naivete is not enough." This was, in all likelihood, the seed for the title of his review article—a title that might have remained untransformed had the Scribner campaign not so successfully focused on Wolfe's genius.

DeVoto's own, well-disciplined novels, patterned after his writing philosophy, achieved little critical success. Somewhere in this fact lies a clue to his perplexity in handling Wolfe as a novelist. For throughout his copy of *T/R* there are points of confusion, a confusion seemingly based on an inability to understand why a novel "intolerably bad" in so many places, should also be "intolerably good." He writes, for instance, on page 769 beneath the scene in which Eugene takes leave of Ann and returns to Paris with Starwick: "An utterly senseless scene, unaccounted for, without motive or meaning. And yet a truly dramatic situation handled with much force." It would have been difficult for Milton to have justified the ways of Thomas Wolfe to Bernard DeVoto, difficult to explain the raw, frenzied, and often undisciplined phrases of the young writer to the seasoned editor who valued discipline and craftsmanship. DeVoto defined his predicament best in an anonymously written article printed in *Harper's Monthly Magazine* some four months after the publication of "Genius Is Not Enough." "Age," he wrote of the mature novelist, "may have given you confidence in your material and skill, so that you know you will avoid many of the pitfalls and most of the torment that are your professional risks; but also it has taught you your limitations, deprived you of a young novelist's fine carelessness, given you obstinacy and vigorousness and a respect for your job that have their satisfaction but also take their toll."

FURTHER READING

Biography

Donald, David Herbert. *Look Homeward: A Life of Thomas Wolfe.* Boston: Little, Brown and Co., 1987, 579 p.

A study of Wolfe's life and career that Donald claims is more complete than any previous biography because he had access to all of Wolfe's papers and correspondence with Aline Bernstein and because he was at liberty to speak frankly about Wolfe's close relatives, all of whom had died by the time this book was written.

Nowell, Elizabeth. *Thomas Wolfe: A Biography.* Garden City, N.Y.: Doubleday & Co., 1960, 456 p.

Important biography by Wolfe's agent and the editor of the 1956 collection *The Letters of Thomas Wolfe.* Nowell's chapter on *Of Time and the River* discusses contemporary critical reaction to the novel and its effect on Wolfe.

Criticism

Field, Leslie A., ed. *Thomas Wolfe: Three Decades of Criticism.* New York: New York University Press, 1968, 304 p.

A collection of twenty-three essays on Wolfe, along with a bibliography of criticism on his works. The volume contains two essays specifically devoted to *Of Time and the River,* and commentary on the novel can also be found in more general essays that address Wolfe's themes and style.

Gurko, Leo. "*Of Time and the River,*" in his *Thomas Wolfe: Beyond the Romantic Ego* pp. 79-107. New York: Thomas Y. Crowell, 1975.

Argues that Wolfe departs from standard fictional techniques in *Of Time and the River* by subordinating plot and character to observation and representation.

Idol, John Lane, Jr. *A Thomas Wolfe Companion.* Westport, Conn.: Greenwood Press, 1987, 205 p.

A reference book that contains a primary and secondary bibliography; a glossary of characters and places in Wolfe's writings; general essays on Wolfe's life, his ideas and attitudes, his relationships with his editors and critics, and his major themes; and specific commentary on each of his works. The section devoted to *Of Time and the River* contains information on its themes, structure, style, characters, and critical reception.

Jones, Howard Mumford. "Social Notes on the South." *Virginia Quarterly Review* 11, No. 3 (July 1935): 452-57.

A review of southern fiction in which Jones praises *Of Time and the River* for its exactness of detail but censures the novel for its lack of structure and overblown prose.

Rascoe, Burton. "The Ecstasy, Fury, Pain, and Beauty of Life: Thomas Wolfe Sings and Shouts in His Gargantuan New Novel." *New York Herald Tribune Books* 11, No. 27 (March 10, 1935): 1-2.

A sympathetic early review that is frequently quoted.

Reeves, Paschal, ed. *Thomas Wolfe: The Critical Reception.* New York: David Lewis, 1974, 256 p.

A comprehensive collection of the earliest reviews of each of Wolfe's books. The section devoted to *Of Time and the River* reprints twenty-six contemporary essays on the novel.

Wade, John Donald. "Prodigal." *Southern Review* 1, No. 1 (July 1935): 192-98.

A mixed review of *Of Time and the River* commending Wolfe's energy, erudition, and command of language but faulting a variety of stylistic flaws in the novel as well as Wolfe's self-absorption, failure to treat the topic of religion, and denial of his southern roots.

Additional coverage of Wolfe's life and career is contained in the following sources published by Gale Research: *Contemporary Authors*, **Vols. 104, 132;** *Concise Dictionary of American Literary Biography*, **1929-1941;** *DISCovering Authors*; *Dictionary of Literary Biography*, **Vols. 9, 102;** *Dictionary of Literary Biography Documentary Series*, **Vol. 2;** *Dictionary of Literary Biography Yearbook*, **1985;** *Major 20th-Century Writers*; *Twentieth-Century Literary Criticism*, **Vols. 4, 13, 29; and** *World Literature Criticism*.

Twentieth-Century Literary Criticism

Cumulative Indexes
Volumes 1-61

How to Use This Index

The main references

> Calvino, Italo
> 1923-1985.....CLC 5, 8, 11, 22, 33, 39,
> 73; SSC 3

list all author entries in the following Gale Literary Criticism series:

BLC = *Black Literature Criticism*
CLC = *Contemporary Literary Criticism*
CLR = *Children's Literature Review*
CMLC = *Classical and Medieval Literature Criticism*
DA = *DISCovering Authors*
DC = *Drama Criticism*
HLC = *Hispanic Literature Criticism*
LC = *Literature Criticism from 1400 to 1800*
NCLC = *Nineteenth-Century Literature Criticism*
PC = *Poetry Criticism*
SSC = *Short Story Criticism*
TCLC = *Twentieth-Century Literary Criticism*
WLC = *World Literature Criticism, 1500 to the Present*

The cross-references

> See also CANR 23; CA 85-88;
> obituary CA 116

list all author entries in the following Gale biographical and literary sources:

AAYA = *Authors & Artists for Young Adults*
AITN = *Authors in the News*
BEST = *Bestsellers*
BW = *Black Writers*
CA = *Contemporary Authors*
CAAS = *Contemporary Authors Autobiography Series*
CABS = *Contemporary Authors Bibliographical Series*
CANR = *Contemporary Authors New Revision Series*
CAP = *Contemporary Authors Permanent Series*
CDALB = *Concise Dictionary of American Literary Biography*
CDBLB = *Concise Dictionary of British Literary Biography*
DLB = *Dictionary of Literary Biography*
DLBD = *Dictionary of Literary Biography Documentary Series*
DLBY = *Dictionary of Literary Biography Yearbook*
HW = *Hispanic Writers*
JRDA = *Junior DISCovering Authors*
MAICYA = *Major Authors and Illustrators for Children and Young Adults*
MTCW = *Major 20th-Century Writers*
NNAL = *Native North American Literature*
SAAS = *Something about the Author Autobiography Series*
SATA = *Something about the Author*
YABC = *Yesterday's Authors of Books for Children*

Literary Criticism Series
Cumulative Author Index

Anouilh, Jean (Marie Lucien Pierre)
1910-1987 . . . . . . **CLC 1, 3, 8, 13, 40, 50**
See also CA 17-20R; 123; CANR 32;
MTCW

Anthony, Florence
See Ai

Anthony, John
See Ciardi, John (Anthony)

Anthony, Peter
See Shaffer, Anthony (Joshua); Shaffer,
Peter (Levin)

Anthony, Piers 1934- . . . . **CLC 35**
See also AAYA 11; CA 21-24R; CANR 28;
DLB 8; MTCW

Antoine, Marc
See Proust, (Valentin-Louis-George-Eugene-)
Marcel

Antoninus, Brother
See Everson, William (Oliver)

Antonioni, Michelangelo 1912- . . . . . **CLC 20**
See also CA 73-76; CANR 45

Antschel, Paul 1920-1970
See Celan, Paul
See also CA 85-88; CANR 33; MTCW

Anwar, Chairil 1922-1949 . . . . **TCLC 22**
See also CA 121

Apollinaire, Guillaume . . **TCLC 3, 8, 51; PC 7**
See also Kostrowitzki, Wilhelm Apollinaris
de

Appelfeld, Aharon 1932- . . . . **CLC 23, 47**
See also CA 112; 133

Apple, Max (Isaac) 1941- . . . . **CLC 9, 33**
See also CA 81-84; CANR 19; DLB 130

Appleman, Philip (Dean) 1926- . . . . . **CLC 51**
See also CA 13-16R; CAAS 18; CANR 6,
29

Appleton, Lawrence
See Lovecraft, H(oward) P(hillips)

Apteryx
See Eliot, T(homas) S(tearns)

Apuleius, (Lucius Madaurensis)
125(?)-175(?) . . . . **CMLC 1**

Aquin, Hubert 1929-1977 . . . . **CLC 15**
See also CA 105; DLB 53

Aragon, Louis 1897-1982 . . . . **CLC 3, 22**
See also CA 69-72; 108; CANR 28;
DLB 72; MTCW

Arany, Janos 1817-1882 . . . . **NCLC 34**

Arbuthnot, John 1667-1735 . . . . **LC 1**
See also DLB 101

Archer, Herbert Winslow
See Mencken, H(enry) L(ouis)

Archer, Jeffrey (Howard) 1940- . . . . **CLC 28**
See also BEST 89:3; CA 77-80; CANR 22

Archer, Jules 1915- . . . . **CLC 12**
See also CA 9-12R; CANR 6; SAAS 5;
SATA 4

Archer, Lee
See Ellison, Harlan (Jay)

Arden, John 1930- . . . . **CLC 6, 13, 15**
See also CA 13-16R; CAAS 4; CANR 31;
DLB 13; MTCW

Arenas, Reinaldo
1943-1990 . . . . **CLC 41; HLC**
See also CA 124; 128; 133; DLB 145; HW

Arendt, Hannah 1906-1975 . . . . **CLC 66**
See also CA 17-20R; 61-64; CANR 26;
MTCW

Aretino, Pietro 1492-1556 . . . . **LC 12**

Arghezi, Tudor . . . . **CLC 80**
See also Theodorescu, Ion N.

Arguedas, Jose Maria
1911-1969 . . . . **CLC 10, 18**
See also CA 89-92; DLB 113; HW

Argueta, Manlio 1936- . . . . **CLC 31**
See also CA 131; DLB 145; HW

Ariosto, Ludovico 1474-1533 . . . . **LC 6**

Aristides
See Epstein, Joseph

Aristophanes
450B.C.-385B.C. . . . . **CMLC 4; DA;
DAB; DC 2**

Arlt, Roberto (Godofredo Christophersen)
1900-1942 . . . . **TCLC 29; HLC**
See also CA 123; 131; HW

Armah, Ayi Kwei 1939- . . . . **CLC 5, 33; BLC**
See also BW 1; CA 61-64; CANR 21;
DLB 117; MTCW

Armatrading, Joan 1950- . . . . **CLC 17**
See also CA 114

Arnette, Robert
See Silverberg, Robert

**Arnim, Achim von (Ludwig Joachim von
Arnim)** 1781-1831 . . . . **NCLC 5**
See also DLB 90

Arnim, Bettina von 1785-1859 . . . . **NCLC 38**
See also DLB 90

Arnold, Matthew
1822-1888 . . . . . **NCLC 6, 29; DA; DAB;
PC 5; WLC**
See also CDBLB 1832-1890; DLB 32, 57

Arnold, Thomas 1795-1842 . . . . . . **NCLC 18**
See also DLB 55

Arnow, Harriette (Louisa) Simpson
1908-1986 . . . . **CLC 2, 7, 18**
See also CA 9-12R; 118; CANR 14; DLB 6;
MTCW; SATA 42; SATA-Obit 47

Arp, Hans
See Arp, Jean

Arp, Jean 1887-1966 . . . . **CLC 5**
See also CA 81-84; 25-28R; CANR 42

Arrabal
See Arrabal, Fernando

Arrabal, Fernando 1932- . . . **CLC 2, 9, 18, 58**
See also CA 9-12R; CANR 15

Arrick, Fran . . . . **CLC 30**
See also Gaberman, Judie Angell

Artaud, Antonin 1896-1948 . . . . . **TCLC 3, 36**
See also CA 104

Arthur, Ruth M(abel) 1905-1979 . . . . **CLC 12**
See also CA 9-12R; 85-88; CANR 4;
SATA 7, 26

Artsybashev, Mikhail (Petrovich)
1878-1927 . . . . **TCLC 31**

Arundel, Honor (Morfydd)
1919-1973 . . . . **CLC 17**
See also CA 21-22; 41-44R; CAP 2;
CLR 35; SATA 4; SATA-Obit 24

Asch, Sholem 1880-1957 . . . . **TCLC 3**
See also CA 105

Ash, Shalom
See Asch, Sholem

Ashbery, John (Lawrence)
1927- . . . . . . **CLC 2, 3, 4, 6, 9, 13, 15, 25,
41, 77**
See also CA 5-8R; CANR 9, 37; DLB 5;
DLBY 81; MTCW

Ashdown, Clifford
See Freeman, R(ichard) Austin

Ashe, Gordon
See Creasey, John

Ashton-Warner, Sylvia (Constance)
1908-1984 . . . . **CLC 19**
See also CA 69-72; 112; CANR 29; MTCW

Asimov, Isaac
1920-1992 . . . . . . **CLC 1, 3, 9, 19, 26, 76**
See also AAYA 13; BEST 90:2; CA 1-4R;
137; CANR 2, 19, 36; CLR 12; DLB 8;
DLBY 92; JRDA; MAICYA; MTCW;
SATA 1, 26, 74

Astley, Thea (Beatrice May)
1925- . . . . **CLC 41**
See also CA 65-68; CANR 11, 43

Aston, James
See White, T(erence) H(anbury)

Asturias, Miguel Angel
1899-1974 . . . . **CLC 3, 8, 13; HLC**
See also CA 25-28; 49-52; CANR 32;
CAP 2; DLB 113; HW; MTCW

Atares, Carlos Saura
See Saura (Atares), Carlos

Atheling, William
See Pound, Ezra (Weston Loomis)

Atheling, William, Jr.
See Blish, James (Benjamin)

Atherton, Gertrude (Franklin Horn)
1857-1948 . . . . **TCLC 2**
See also CA 104; DLB 9, 78

Atherton, Lucius
See Masters, Edgar Lee

Atkins, Jack
See Harris, Mark

Atticus
See Fleming, Ian (Lancaster)

Atwood, Margaret (Eleanor)
1939- . . . . . **CLC 2, 3, 4, 8, 13, 15, 25, 44,
84; DA; DAB; PC 8; SSC 2; WLC**
See also AAYA 12; BEST 89:2; CA 49-52;
CANR 3, 24, 33; DLB 53; MTCW;
SATA 50

Aubigny, Pierre d'
See Mencken, H(enry) L(ouis)

Aubin, Penelope 1685-1731(?) . . . . **LC 9**
See also DLB 39

Auchincloss, Louis (Stanton)
1917- . . . . **CLC 4, 6, 9, 18, 45**
See also CA 1-4R; CANR 6, 29; DLB 2;
DLBY 80; MTCW

Auden, W(ystan) H(ugh)
1907-1973 ..... **CLC 1, 2, 3, 4, 6, 9, 11,**
14, 43; DA; DAB; PC 1; WLC
See also CA 9-12R; 45-48; CANR 5;
CDBLB 1914-1945; DLB 10, 20; MTCW

Audiberti, Jacques 1900-1965 ...... **CLC 38**
See also CA 25-28R

Audubon, John James
1785-1851 .... **NCLC 47**

Auel, Jean M(arie) 1936- .... **CLC 31**
See also AAYA 7; BEST 90:4; CA 103;
CANR 21

Auerbach, Erich 1892-1957 ...... **TCLC 43**
See also CA 118

Augier, Emile 1820-1889 .... **NCLC 31**

August, John
See De Voto, Bernard (Augustine)

Augustine, St. 354-430 ..... **CMLC 6; DAB**

Aurelius
See Bourne, Randolph S(illiman)

Austen, Jane
1775-1817 ..... **NCLC 1, 13, 19, 33, 51;**
DA; DAB; WLC
See also CDBLB 1789-1832; DLB 116

Auster, Paul 1947- .... **CLC 47**
See also CA 69-72; CANR 23

Austin, Frank
See Faust, Frederick (Schiller)

Austin, Mary (Hunter)
1868-1934 .... **TCLC 25**
See also CA 109; DLB 9, 78

Autran Dourado, Waldomiro
See Dourado, (Waldomiro Freitas) Autran

Averroes 1126-1198 .... **CMLC 7**
See also DLB 115

Avicenna 980-1037 .... **CMLC 16**
See also DLB 115

Avison, Margaret 1918- .... **CLC 2, 4**
See also CA 17-20R; DLB 53; MTCW

Axton, David
See Koontz, Dean R(ay)

Ayckbourn, Alan
1939- .... **CLC 5, 8, 18, 33, 74; DAB**
See also CA 21-24R; CANR 31; DLB 13;
MTCW

Aydy, Catherine
See Tennant, Emma (Christina)

Ayme, Marcel (Andre) 1902-1967 ... **CLC 11**
See also CA 89-92; CLR 25; DLB 72

Ayrton, Michael 1921-1975 .... **CLC 7**
See also CA 5-8R; 61-64; CANR 9, 21

Azorin .... **CLC 11**
See also Martinez Ruiz, Jose

Azuela, Mariano
1873-1952 .... **TCLC 3; HLC**
See also CA 104; 131; HW; MTCW

Baastad, Babbis Friis
See Friis-Baastad, Babbis Ellinor

Bab
See Gilbert, W(illiam) S(chwenck)

Babbis, Eleanor
See Friis-Baastad, Babbis Ellinor

Babel, Isaak (Emmanuilovich)
1894-1941(?) ...... **TCLC 2, 13; SSC 16**
See also CA 104

Babits, Mihaly 1883-1941 .... **TCLC 14**
See also CA 114

Babur 1483-1530 .... **LC 18**

Bacchelli, Riccardo 1891-1985 ..... **CLC 19**
See also CA 29-32R; 117

Bach, Richard (David) 1936- ...... **CLC 14**
See also AITN 1; BEST 89:2; CA 9-12R;
CANR 18; MTCW; SATA 13

Bachman, Richard
See King, Stephen (Edwin)

Bachmann, Ingeborg 1926-1973 ..... **CLC 69**
See also CA 93-96; 45-48; DLB 85

Bacon, Francis 1561-1626 .... **LC 18**
See also CDBLB Before 1660; DLB 151

Bacon, Roger 1214(?)-1292 ...... **CMLC 14**
See also DLB 115

Bacovia, George .... **TCLC 24**
See also Vasiliu, Gheorghe

Badanes, Jerome 1937- .... **CLC 59**

Bagehot, Walter 1826-1877 ...... **NCLC 10**
See also DLB 55

Bagnold, Enid 1889-1981 .... **CLC 25**
See also CA 5-8R; 103; CANR 5, 40;
DLB 13; MAICYA; SATA 1, 25

Bagritsky, Eduard 1895-1934 ..... **TCLC 60**

Bagrjana, Elisaveta
See Belcheva, Elisaveta

Bagryana, Elisaveta .... **CLC 10**
See also Belcheva, Elisaveta
See also DLB 147

Bailey, Paul 1937- .... **CLC 45**
See also CA 21-24R; CANR 16; DLB 14

Baillie, Joanna 1762-1851 .... **NCLC 2**
See also DLB 93

Bainbridge, Beryl (Margaret)
1933- .... **CLC 4, 5, 8, 10, 14, 18, 22, 62**
See also CA 21-24R; CANR 24; DLB 14;
MTCW

Baker, Elliott 1922- .... **CLC 8**
See also CA 45-48; CANR 2

Baker, Nicholson 1957- .... **CLC 61**
See also CA 135

Baker, Ray Stannard 1870-1946 ... **TCLC 47**
See also CA 118

Baker, Russell (Wayne) 1925- ...... **CLC 31**
See also BEST 89:4; CA 57-60; CANR 11,
41; MTCW

Bakhtin, M.
See Bakhtin, Mikhail Mikhailovich

Bakhtin, M. M.
See Bakhtin, Mikhail Mikhailovich

Bakhtin, Mikhail
See Bakhtin, Mikhail Mikhailovich

Bakhtin, Mikhail Mikhailovich
1895-1975 .... **CLC 83**
See also CA 128; 113

Bakshi, Ralph 1938(?)- .... **CLC 26**
See also CA 112; 138

Bakunin, Mikhail (Alexandrovich)
1814-1876 .... **NCLC 25**

Baldwin, James (Arthur)
1924-1987 ...... **CLC 1, 2, 3, 4, 5, 8, 13,**
15, 17, 42, 50, 67, 90; BLC; DA; DAB;
DC 1; SSC 10; WLC
See also AAYA 4; BW 1; CA 1-4R; 124;
CABS 1; CANR 3, 24;
CDALB 1941-1968; DLB 2, 7, 33;
DLBY 87; MTCW; SATA 9;
SATA-Obit 54

Ballard, J(ames) G(raham)
1930- .... **CLC 3, 6, 14, 36; SSC 1**
See also AAYA 3; CA 5-8R; CANR 15, 39;
DLB 14; MTCW

Balmont, Konstantin (Dmitriyevich)
1867-1943 .... **TCLC 11**
See also CA 109

Balzac, Honore de
1799-1850 ..... **NCLC 5, 35; DA; DAB;**
SSC 5; WLC
See also DLB 119

Bambara, Toni Cade
1939- .... **CLC 19, 88; BLC; DA**
See also AAYA 5; BW 2; CA 29-32R;
CANR 24, 49; DLB 38; MTCW

Bamdad, A.
See Shamlu, Ahmad

Banat, D. R.
See Bradbury, Ray (Douglas)

Bancroft, Laura
See Baum, L(yman) Frank

Banim, John 1798-1842 .... **NCLC 13**
See also DLB 116

Banim, Michael 1796-1874 ...... **NCLC 13**

Banks, Iain
See Banks, Iain M(enzies)

Banks, Iain M(enzies) 1954- .... **CLC 34**
See also CA 123; 128

Banks, Lynne Reid .... **CLC 23**
See also Reid Banks, Lynne
See also AAYA 6

Banks, Russell 1940- .... **CLC 37, 72**
See also CA 65-68; CAAS 15; CANR 19;
DLB 130

Banville, John 1945- .... **CLC 46**
See also CA 117; 128; DLB 14

Banville, Theodore (Faullain) de
1832-1891 .... **NCLC 9**

Baraka, Amiri
1934- .... **CLC 1, 2, 3, 5, 10, 14, 33;**
BLC; DA; PC 4
See also Jones, LeRoi
See also BW 2; CA 21-24R; CABS 3;
CANR 27, 38; CDALB 1941-1968;
DLB 5, 7, 16, 38; DLBD 8; MTCW

Barbauld, Anna Laetitia
1743-1825 .... **NCLC 50**
See also DLB 107, 109, 142

Barbellion, W. N. P. .... **TCLC 24**
See also Cummings, Bruce F(rederick)

Barbera, Jack (Vincent) 1945- ...... **CLC 44**
See also CA 110; CANR 45

Barbey d'Aurevilly, Jules Amedee
1808-1889 .... **NCLC 1; SSC 17**
See also DLB 119

Barbusse, Henri 1873-1935 . . . . **TCLC 5**
　See also CA 105; DLB 65

Barclay, Bill
　See Moorcock, Michael (John)

Barclay, William Ewert
　See Moorcock, Michael (John)

Barea, Arturo 1897-1957 . . . . **TCLC 14**
　See also CA 111

Barfoot, Joan 1946- . . . . **CLC 18**
　See also CA 105

Baring, Maurice 1874-1945 . . . . **TCLC 8**
　See also CA 105; DLB 34

Barker, Clive 1952- . . . . **CLC 52**
　See also AAYA 10; BEST 90:3; CA 121;
　129; MTCW

Barker, George Granville
　1913-1991 . . . . **CLC 8, 48**
　See also CA 9-12R; 135; CANR 7, 38;
　DLB 20; MTCW

Barker, Harley Granville
　See Granville-Barker, Harley
　See also DLB 10

Barker, Howard 1946- . . . . **CLC 37**
　See also CA 102; DLB 13

Barker, Pat 1943- . . . . **CLC 32**
　See also CA 117; 122

Barlow, Joel 1754-1812 . . . . **NCLC 23**
　See also DLB 37

Barnard, Mary (Ethel) 1909- . . . . **CLC 48**
　See also CA 21-22; CAP 2

Barnes, Djuna
　1892-1982 . . . **CLC 3, 4, 8, 11, 29; SSC 3**
　See also CA 9-12R; 107; CANR 16; DLB 4,
　9, 45; MTCW

Barnes, Julian 1946- . . . . **CLC 42; DAB**
　See also CA 102; CANR 19; DLBY 93

Barnes, Peter 1931- . . . . **CLC 5, 56**
　See also CA 65-68; CAAS 12; CANR 33,
　34; DLB 13; MTCW

Baroja (y Nessi), Pio
　1872-1956 . . . . **TCLC 8; HLC**
　See also CA 104

Baron, David
　See Pinter, Harold

Baron Corvo
　See Rolfe, Frederick (William Serafino
　Austin Lewis Mary)

Barondess, Sue K(aufman)
　1926-1977 . . . . **CLC 8**
　See also Kaufman, Sue
　See also CA 1-4R; 69-72; CANR 1

Baron de Teive
　See Pessoa, Fernando (Antonio Nogueira)

Barres, Maurice 1862-1923 . . . . **TCLC 47**
　See also DLB 123

Barreto, Afonso Henrique de Lima
　See Lima Barreto, Afonso Henrique de

Barrett, (Roger) Syd 1946- . . . . **CLC 35**

Barrett, William (Christopher)
　1913-1992 . . . . **CLC 27**
　See also CA 13-16R; 139; CANR 11

Barrie, J(ames) M(atthew)
　1860-1937 . . . . **TCLC 2; DAB**
　See also CA 104; 136; CDBLB 1890-1914;
　CLR 16; DLB 10, 141, 156; MAICYA;
　YABC 1

Barrington, Michael
　See Moorcock, Michael (John)

Barrol, Grady
　See Bograd, Larry

Barry, Mike
　See Malzberg, Barry N(athaniel)

Barry, Philip 1896-1949 . . . . **TCLC 11**
　See also CA 109; DLB 7

Bart, Andre Schwarz
　See Schwarz-Bart, Andre

Barth, John (Simmons)
　1930- . . . . . . **CLC 1, 2, 3, 5, 7, 9, 10, 14,**
　　　　　　　　　　　27, 51, 89; SSC 10
　See also AITN 1, 2; CA 1-4R; CABS 1;
　CANR 5, 23, 49; DLB 2; MTCW

Barthelme, Donald
　1931-1989 . . . . . . **CLC 1, 2, 3, 5, 6, 8, 13,**
　　　　　　　　　　　23, 46, 59; SSC 2
　See also CA 21-24R; 129; CANR 20;
　DLB 2; DLBY 80, 89; MTCW; SATA 7;
　SATA-Obit 62

Barthelme, Frederick 1943- . . . . **CLC 36**
　See also CA 114; 122; DLBY 85

Barthes, Roland (Gerard)
　1915-1980 . . . . **CLC 24, 83**
　See also CA 130; 97-100; MTCW

Barzun, Jacques (Martin) 1907- . . . . **CLC 51**
　See also CA 61-64; CANR 22

Bashevis, Isaac
　See Singer, Isaac Bashevis

Bashkirtseff, Marie 1859-1884 . . . **NCLC 27**

Basho
　See Matsuo Basho

Bass, Kingsley B., Jr.
　See Bullins, Ed

Bass, Rick 1958- . . . . **CLC 79**
　See also CA 126

Bassani, Giorgio 1916- . . . . **CLC 9**
　See also CA 65-68; CANR 33; DLB 128;
　MTCW

Bastos, Augusto (Antonio) Roa
　See Roa Bastos, Augusto (Antonio)

Bataille, Georges 1897-1962 . . . . **CLC 29**
　See also CA 101; 89-92

Bates, H(erbert) E(rnest)
　1905-1974 . . . . . . **CLC 46; DAB; SSC 10**
　See also CA 93-96; 45-48; CANR 34;
　MTCW

Bauchart
　See Camus, Albert

Baudelaire, Charles
　1821-1867 . . . . . **NCLC 6, 29; DA; DAB;**
　　　　　　　　　　　PC 1; SSC 18; WLC

Baudrillard, Jean 1929- . . . . **CLC 60**

Baum, L(yman) Frank 1856-1919 . . . **TCLC 7**
　See also CA 108; 133; CLR 15; DLB 22;
　JRDA; MAICYA; MTCW; SATA 18

Baum, Louis F.
　See Baum, L(yman) Frank

Baumbach, Jonathan 1933- . . . . . . **CLC 6, 23**
　See also CA 13-16R; CAAS 5; CANR 12;
　DLBY 80; MTCW

Bausch, Richard (Carl) 1945- . . . . . . **CLC 51**
　See also CA 101; CAAS 14; CANR 43;
　DLB 130

Baxter, Charles 1947- . . . . **CLC 45, 78**
　See also CA 57-60; CANR 40; DLB 130

Baxter, George Owen
　See Faust, Frederick (Schiller)

Baxter, James K(eir) 1926-1972 . . . . **CLC 14**
　See also CA 77-80

Baxter, John
　See Hunt, E(verette) Howard, (Jr.)

Bayer, Sylvia
　See Glassco, John

Baynton, Barbara 1857-1929 . . . . . . **TCLC 57**

Beagle, Peter S(oyer) 1939- . . . . **CLC 7**
　See also CA 9-12R; CANR 4; DLBY 80;
　SATA 60

Bean, Normal
　See Burroughs, Edgar Rice

Beard, Charles A(ustin)
　1874-1948 . . . . **TCLC 15**
　See also CA 115; DLB 17; SATA 18

Beardsley, Aubrey 1872-1898 . . . . . **NCLC 6**

Beattie, Ann
　1947- . . . . **CLC 8, 13, 18, 40, 63; SSC 11**
　See also BEST 90:2; CA 81-84; DLBY 82;
　MTCW

Beattie, James 1735-1803 . . . . **NCLC 25**
　See also DLB 109

Beauchamp, Kathleen Mansfield 1888-1923
　See Mansfield, Katherine
　See also CA 104; 134; DA

Beaumarchais, Pierre-Augustin Caron de
　1732-1799 . . . . **DC 4**

Beauvoir, Simone (Lucie Ernestine Marie
　Bertrand) de
　1908-1986 . . . . . **CLC 1, 2, 4, 8, 14, 31, 44,**
　　　　　　　　　　　50, 71; DA; DAB; WLC
　See also CA 9-12R; 118; CANR 28;
　DLB 72; DLBY 86; MTCW

Becker, Jurek 1937- . . . . **CLC 7, 19**
　See also CA 85-88; DLB 75

Becker, Walter 1950- . . . . **CLC 26**

Beckett, Samuel (Barclay)
　1906-1989 . . . . . . **CLC 1, 2, 3, 4, 6, 9, 10,**
　　　　　　　　11, 14, 18, 29, 57, 59, 83; DA; DAB;
　　　　　　　　　　　　　SSC 16; WLC
　See also CA 5-8R; 130; CANR 33;
　CDBLB 1945-1960; DLB 13, 15;
　DLBY 90; MTCW

Beckford, William 1760-1844 . . . . **NCLC 16**
　See also DLB 39

Beckman, Gunnel 1910- . . . . **CLC 26**
　See also CA 33-36R; CANR 15; CLR 25;
　MAICYA; SAAS 9; SATA 6

Becque, Henri 1837-1899 . . . . **NCLC 3**

Beddoes, Thomas Lovell
　1803-1849 . . . . **NCLC 3**
　See also DLB 96

Bedford, Donald F.
　See Fearing, Kenneth (Flexner)

Berne, Victoria
　See Fisher, M(ary) F(rances) K(ennedy)

Bernhard, Thomas
　1931-1989 . . . . CLC **3, 32, 61**
　See also CA 85-88; 127; CANR 32;
　　DLB 85, 124; MTCW

Berriault, Gina　1926- . . . . CLC **54**
　See also CA 116; 129; DLB 130

Berrigan, Daniel　1921- . . . . CLC **4**
　See also CA 33-36R; CAAS 1; CANR 11,
　　43; DLB 5

Berrigan, Edmund Joseph Michael, Jr.
　1934-1983
　See Berrigan, Ted
　See also CA 61-64; 110; CANR 14

Berrigan, Ted . . . . CLC **37**
　See also Berrigan, Edmund Joseph Michael,
　　Jr.
　See also DLB 5

Berry, Charles Edward Anderson　1931-
　See Berry, Chuck
　See also CA 115

Berry, Chuck . . . . CLC **17**
　See also Berry, Charles Edward Anderson

Berry, Jonas
　See Ashbery, John (Lawrence)

Berry, Wendell (Erdman)
　1934- . . . . CLC **4, 6, 8, 27, 46**
　See also AITN 1; CA 73-76; DLB 5, 6

Berryman, John
　1914-1972 . . . . . . CLC **1, 2, 3, 4, 6, 8, 10,
　　　　　　　　　　　　　　13, 25, 62**
　See also CA 13-16; 33-36R; CABS 2;
　　CANR 35; CAP 1; CDALB 1941-1968;
　　DLB 48; MTCW

Bertolucci, Bernardo　1940- . . . . CLC **16**
　See also CA 106

Bertrand, Aloysius　1807-1841 . . . . NCLC **31**

Bertran de Born　c. 1140-1215 . . . . . CMLC **5**

Besant, Annie (Wood)　1847-1933 . . . TCLC **9**
　See also CA 105

Bessie, Alvah　1904-1985 . . . . CLC **23**
　See also CA 5-8R; 116; CANR 2; DLB 26

Bethlen, T. D.
　See Silverberg, Robert

Beti, Mongo . . . . CLC **27; BLC**
　See also Biyidi, Alexandre

Betjeman, John
　1906-1984 . . . CLC **2, 6, 10, 34, 43; DAB**
　See also CA 9-12R; 112; CANR 33;
　　CDBLB 1945-1960; DLB 20; DLBY 84;
　　MTCW

Bettelheim, Bruno　1903-1990 . . . . . . CLC **79**
　See also CA 81-84; 131; CANR 23; MTCW

Betti, Ugo　1892-1953 . . . . TCLC **5**
　See also CA 104

Betts, Doris (Waugh)　1932- . . . . CLC **3, 6, 28**
　See also CA 13-16R; CANR 9; DLBY 82

Bevan, Alistair
　See Roberts, Keith (John Kingston)

Bialik, Chaim Nachman
　1873-1934 . . . . TCLC **25**

Bickerstaff, Isaac
　See Swift, Jonathan

Bidart, Frank　1939- . . . . CLC **33**
　See also CA 140

Bienek, Horst　1930- . . . . CLC **7, 11**
　See also CA 73-76; DLB 75

Bierce, Ambrose (Gwinett)
　1842-1914(?) . . . . TCLC **1, 7, 44; DA;
　　　　　　　　　　　　　　SSC 9; WLC**
　See also CA 104; 139; CDALB 1865-1917;
　　DLB 11, 12, 23, 71, 74

Billings, Josh
　See Shaw, Henry Wheeler

Billington, (Lady) Rachel (Mary)
　1942- . . . . CLC **43**
　See also AITN 2; CA 33-36R; CANR 44

Binyon, T(imothy) J(ohn)　1936- . . . . CLC **34**
　See also CA 111; CANR 28

Bioy Casares, Adolfo
　1914- . . . CLC **4, 8, 13, 88; HLC; SSC 17**
　See also CA 29-32R; CANR 19, 43;
　　DLB 113; HW; MTCW

Bird, Cordwainer
　See Ellison, Harlan (Jay)

Bird, Robert Montgomery
　1806-1854 . . . . NCLC **1**

Birney, (Alfred) Earle
　1904- . . . . CLC **1, 4, 6, 11**
　See also CA 1-4R; CANR 5, 20; DLB 88;
　　MTCW

Bishop, Elizabeth
　1911-1979 . . . . . . CLC **1, 4, 9, 13, 15, 32;
　　　　　　　　　　　　　　DA; PC 3**
　See also CA 5-8R; 89-92; CABS 2;
　　CANR 26; CDALB 1968-1988; DLB 5;
　　MTCW; SATA-Obit 24

Bishop, John　1935- . . . . CLC **10**
　See also CA 105

Bissett, Bill　1939- . . . . CLC **18**
　See also CA 69-72; CAAS 19; CANR 15;
　　DLB 53; MTCW

Bitov, Andrei (Georgievich)　1937- . . . CLC **57**
　See also CA 142

Biyidi, Alexandre　1932-
　See Beti, Mongo
　See also BW 1; CA 114; 124; MTCW

Bjarme, Brynjolf
　See Ibsen, Henrik (Johan)

Bjornson, Bjornstjerne (Martinius)
　1832-1910 . . . . TCLC **7, 37**
　See also CA 104

Black, Robert
　See Holdstock, Robert P.

Blackburn, Paul　1926-1971 . . . . . . CLC **9, 43**
　See also CA 81-84; 33-36R; CANR 34;
　　DLB 16; DLBY 81

Black Elk　1863-1950 . . . . TCLC **33**
　See also CA 144; NNAL

Black Hobart
　See Sanders, (James) Ed(ward)

Blacklin, Malcolm
　See Chambers, Aidan

Blackmore, R(ichard) D(oddridge)
　1825-1900 . . . . TCLC **27**
　See also CA 120; DLB 18

Blackmur, R(ichard) P(almer)
　1904-1965 . . . . CLC **2, 24**
　See also CA 11-12; 25-28R; CAP 1; DLB 63

Black Tarantula, The
　See Acker, Kathy

Blackwood, Algernon (Henry)
　1869-1951 . . . . TCLC **5**
　See also CA 105; DLB 153, 156

Blackwood, Caroline　1931- . . . . CLC **6, 9**
　See also CA 85-88; CANR 32; DLB 14;
　　MTCW

Blade, Alexander
　See Hamilton, Edmond; Silverberg, Robert

Blaga, Lucian　1895-1961 . . . . CLC **75**

Blair, Eric (Arthur)　1903-1950
　See Orwell, George
　See also CA 104; 132; DA; DAB; MTCW;
　　SATA 29

Blais, Marie-Claire
　1939- . . . . CLC **2, 4, 6, 13, 22**
　See also CA 21-24R; CAAS 4; CANR 38;
　　DLB 53; MTCW

Blaise, Clark　1940- . . . . CLC **29**
　See also AITN 2; CA 53-56; CAAS 3;
　　CANR 5; DLB 53

Blake, Nicholas
　See Day Lewis, C(ecil)
　See also DLB 77

Blake, William
　1757-1827 . . . . NCLC **13, 37; DA; DAB;
　　　　　　　　　　　　　PC 12; WLC**
　See also CDBLB 1789-1832; DLB 93;
　　MAICYA; SATA 30

Blake, William J(ames)　1894-1969 . . . PC **12**
　See also CA 5-8R; 25-28R

Blasco Ibanez, Vicente
　1867-1928 . . . . TCLC **12**
　See also CA 110; 131; HW; MTCW

Blatty, William Peter　1928- . . . . CLC **2**
　See also CA 5-8R; CANR 9

Bleeck, Oliver
　See Thomas, Ross (Elmore)

Blessing, Lee　1949- . . . . CLC **54**

Blish, James (Benjamin)
　1921-1975 . . . . CLC **14**
　See also CA 1-4R; 57-60; CANR 3; DLB 8;
　　MTCW; SATA 66

Bliss, Reginald
　See Wells, H(erbert) G(eorge)

Blixen, Karen (Christentze Dinesen)
　1885-1962
　See Dinesen, Isak
　See also CA 25-28; CANR 22; CAP 2;
　　MTCW; SATA 44

Bloch, Robert (Albert)　1917-1994 . . . CLC **33**
　See also CA 5-8R; 146; CAAS 20; CANR 5;
　　DLB 44; SATA 12; SATA-Obit 82

Blok, Alexander (Alexandrovich)
　1880-1921 . . . . TCLC **5**
　See also CA 104

Blom, Jan
　See Breytenbach, Breyten

Bloom, Harold　1930- . . . . CLC **24**
　See also CA 13-16R; CANR 39; DLB 67

Bloomfield, Aurelius
See Bourne, Randolph S(illiman)

Blount, Roy (Alton), Jr. 1941- . . . . . **CLC 38**
See also CA 53-56; CANR 10, 28; MTCW

Bloy, Leon 1846-1917. . . . . **TCLC 22**
See also CA 121; DLB 123

Blume, Judy (Sussman) 1938- . . . **CLC 12, 30**
See also AAYA 3; CA 29-32R; CANR 13,
37; CLR 2, 15; DLB 52; JRDA;
MAICYA; MTCW; SATA 2, 31, 79

Blunden, Edmund (Charles)
1896-1974 . . . . **CLC 2, 56**
See also CA 17-18; 45-48; CAP 2; DLB 20,
100, 155; MTCW

Bly, Robert (Elwood)
1926- . . . . **CLC 1, 2, 5, 10, 15, 38**
See also CA 5-8R; CANR 41; DLB 5;
MTCW

Boas, Franz 1858-1942. . . . . **TCLC 56**
See also CA 115

Bobette
See Simenon, Georges (Jacques Christian)

Boccaccio, Giovanni
1313-1375 . . . . **CMLC 13; SSC 10**

Bochco, Steven 1943- . . . . **CLC 35**
See also AAYA 11; CA 124; 138

Bodenheim, Maxwell 1892-1954 . . . **TCLC 44**
See also CA 110; DLB 9, 45

Bodker, Cecil 1927- . . . . **CLC 21**
See also CA 73-76; CANR 13, 44; CLR 23;
MAICYA; SATA 14

Boell, Heinrich (Theodor)
1917-1985 . . . . **CLC 2, 3, 6, 9, 11, 15, 27,
32, 72; DA; DAB; WLC**
See also CA 21-24R; 116; CANR 24;
DLB 69; DLBY 85; MTCW

Boerne, Alfred
See Doeblin, Alfred

Boethius 480(?)-524(?) . . . . **CMLC 15**
See also DLB 115

Bogan, Louise
1897-1970 . . . . **CLC 4, 39, 46; PC 12**
See also CA 73-76; 25-28R; CANR 33;
DLB 45; MTCW

Bogarde, Dirk . . . . **CLC 19**
See also Van Den Bogarde, Derek Jules
Gaspard Ulric Niven
See also DLB 14

Bogosian, Eric 1953- . . . . **CLC 45**
See also CA 138

Bograd, Larry 1953- . . . . **CLC 35**
See also CA 93-96; SATA 33

Boiardo, Matteo Maria 1441-1494 . . . . **LC 6**

Boileau-Despreaux, Nicolas
1636-1711 . . . . **LC 3**

Boland, Eavan (Aisling) 1944- . . . **CLC 40, 67**
See also CA 143; DLB 40

Bolt, Lee
See Faust, Frederick (Schiller)

Bolt, Robert (Oxton) 1924-1995 . . . . **CLC 14**
See also CA 17-20R; 147; CANR 35;
DLB 13; MTCW

Bombet, Louis-Alexandre-Cesar
See Stendhal

Bomkauf
See Kaufman, Bob (Garnell)

Bonaventura . . . . **NCLC 35**
See also DLB 90

Bond, Edward 1934- . . . . . . **CLC 4, 6, 13, 23**
See also CA 25-28R; CANR 38; DLB 13;
MTCW

Bonham, Frank 1914-1989 . . . . **CLC 12**
See also AAYA 1; CA 9-12R; CANR 4, 36;
JRDA; MAICYA; SAAS 3; SATA 1, 49;
SATA-Obit 62

Bonnefoy, Yves 1923- . . . . **CLC 9, 15, 58**
See also CA 85-88; CANR 33; MTCW

Bontemps, Arna(ud Wendell)
1902-1973 . . . . **CLC 1, 18; BLC**
See also BW 1; CA 1-4R; 41-44R; CANR 4,
35; CLR 6; DLB 48, 51; JRDA;
MAICYA; MTCW; SATA 2, 44;
SATA-Obit 24

Booth, Martin 1944- . . . . **CLC 13**
See also CA 93-96; CAAS 2

Booth, Philip 1925- . . . . **CLC 23**
See also CA 5-8R; CANR 5; DLBY 82

Booth, Wayne C(layson) 1921- . . . . . **CLC 24**
See also CA 1-4R; CAAS 5; CANR 3, 43;
DLB 67

Borchert, Wolfgang 1921-1947 . . . . . **TCLC 5**
See also CA 104; DLB 69, 124

Borel, Petrus 1809-1859. . . . . **NCLC 41**

Borges, Jorge Luis
1899-1986 . . . **CLC 1, 2, 3, 4, 6, 8, 9, 10,
13, 19, 44, 48, 83; DA; DAB; HLC;
SSC 4; WLC**
See also CA 21-24R; CANR 19, 33;
DLB 113; DLBY 86; HW; MTCW

Borowski, Tadeusz 1922-1951 . . . . . . **TCLC 9**
See also CA 106

Borrow, George (Henry)
1803-1881 . . . . **NCLC 9**
See also DLB 21, 55

Bosman, Herman Charles
1905-1951 . . . . **TCLC 49**

Bosschere, Jean de 1878(?)-1953 . . . **TCLC 19**
See also CA 115

Boswell, James
1740-1795 . . . . . . **LC 4; DA; DAB; WLC**
See also CDBLB 1660-1789; DLB 104, 142

Bottoms, David 1949- . . . . **CLC 53**
See also CA 105; CANR 22; DLB 120;
DLBY 83

Boucicault, Dion 1820-1890 . . . . . . **NCLC 41**

Boucolon, Maryse 1937-
See Conde, Maryse
See also CA 110; CANR 30

Bourget, Paul (Charles Joseph)
1852-1935 . . . . **TCLC 12**
See also CA 107; DLB 123

Bourjaily, Vance (Nye) 1922- . . . . **CLC 8, 62**
See also CA 1-4R; CAAS 1; CANR 2;
DLB 2, 143

Bourne, Randolph S(illiman)
1886-1918 . . . . **TCLC 16**
See also CA 117; DLB 63

Bova, Ben(jamin William) 1932- . . . . **CLC 45**
See also CA 5-8R; CAAS 18; CANR 11;
CLR 3; DLBY 81; MAICYA; MTCW;
SATA 6, 68

Bowen, Elizabeth (Dorothea Cole)
1899-1973 . . . . . . **CLC 1, 3, 6, 11, 15, 22;
SSC 3**
See also CA 17-18; 41-44R; CANR 35;
CAP 2; CDBLB 1945-1960; DLB 15;
MTCW

Bowering, George 1935- . . . . **CLC 15, 47**
See also CA 21-24R; CAAS 16; CANR 10;
DLB 53

Bowering, Marilyn R(uthe) 1949- . . . **CLC 32**
See also CA 101; CANR 49

Bowers, Edgar 1924- . . . . **CLC 9**
See also CA 5-8R; CANR 24; DLB 5

Bowie, David . . . . **CLC 17**
See also Jones, David Robert

Bowles, Jane (Sydney)
1917-1973 . . . . **CLC 3, 68**
See also CA 19-20; 41-44R; CAP 2

Bowles, Paul (Frederick)
1910- . . . . **CLC 1, 2, 19, 53; SSC 3**
See also CA 1-4R; CAAS 1; CANR 1, 19;
DLB 5, 6; MTCW

Box, Edgar
See Vidal, Gore

Boyd, Nancy
See Millay, Edna St. Vincent

Boyd, William 1952- . . . . **CLC 28, 53, 70**
See also CA 114; 120

Boyle, Kay
1902-1992 . . . . . **CLC 1, 5, 19, 58; SSC 5**
See also CA 13-16R; 140; CAAS 1;
CANR 29; DLB 4, 9, 48, 86; DLBY 93;
MTCW

Boyle, Mark
See Kienzle, William X(avier)

Boyle, Patrick 1905-1982. . . . . **CLC 19**
See also CA 127

Boyle, T. C. 1948-
See Boyle, T(homas) Coraghessan

Boyle, T(homas) Coraghessan
1948- . . . . **CLC 36, 55, 90; SSC 16**
See also BEST 90:4; CA 120; CANR 44;
DLBY 86

Boz
See Dickens, Charles (John Huffam)

Brackenridge, Hugh Henry
1748-1816 . . . . **NCLC 7**
See also DLB 11, 37

Bradbury, Edward P.
See Moorcock, Michael (John)

Bradbury, Malcolm (Stanley)
1932- . . . . **CLC 32, 61**
See also CA 1-4R; CANR 1, 33; DLB 14;
MTCW

Bradbury, Ray (Douglas)
1920- . . . . **CLC 1, 3, 10, 15, 42; DA;
DAB; WLC**
See also AAYA 15; AITN 1, 2; CA 1-4R;
CANR 2, 30; CDALB 1968-1988; DLB 2,
8; MTCW; SATA 11, 64

Bradford, Gamaliel 1863-1932..... TCLC 36
See also DLB 17

Bradley, David (Henry, Jr.)
1950-.................. CLC 23; BLC
See also BW 1; CA 104; CANR 26; DLB 33

Bradley, John Ed(mund, Jr.)
1958-...................... CLC 55
See also CA 139

Bradley, Marion Zimmer 1930-..... CLC 30
See also AAYA 9; CA 57-60; CAAS 10;
CANR 7, 31; DLB 8; MTCW

Bradstreet, Anne
1612(?)-1672...... LC 4, 30; DA; PC 10
See also CDALB 1640-1865; DLB 24

Brady, Joan 1939-............... CLC 86
See also CA 141

Bragg, Melvyn 1939-.............. CLC 10
See also BEST 89:3; CA 57-60; CANR 10,
48; DLB 14

Braine, John (Gerard)
1922-1986............... CLC 1, 3, 41
See also CA 1-4R; 120; CANR 1, 33;
CDBLB 1945-1960; DLB 15; DLBY 86;
MTCW

Brammer, William 1930(?)-1978.... CLC 31
See also CA 77-80

Brancati, Vitaliano 1907-1954..... TCLC 12
See also CA 109

Brancato, Robin F(idler) 1936-..... CLC 35
See also AAYA 9; CA 69-72; CANR 11,
45; CLR 32; JRDA; SAAS 9; SATA 23

Brand, Max
See Faust, Frederick (Schiller)

Brand, Millen 1906-1980.......... CLC 7
See also CA 21-24R; 97-100

Branden, Barbara .... CLC 44
See also CA 148

Brandes, Georg (Morris Cohen)
1842-1927.................. TCLC 10
See also CA 105

Brandys, Kazimierz 1916-........ CLC 62

Branley, Franklyn M(ansfield)
1915-...................... CLC 21
See also CA 33-36R; CANR 14, 39;
CLR 13; MAICYA; SAAS 16; SATA 4,
68

Brathwaite, Edward Kamau 1930-... CLC 11
See also BW 2; CA 25-28R; CANR 11, 26,
47; DLB 125

Brautigan, Richard (Gary)
1935-1984.... CLC 1, 3, 5, 9, 12, 34, 42
See also CA 53-56; 113; CANR 34; DLB 2,
5; DLBY 80, 84; MTCW; SATA 56

Braverman, Kate 1950-........... CLC 67
See also CA 89-92

Brecht, Bertolt
1898-1956...... TCLC 1, 6, 13, 35; DA;
DAB; DC 3; WLC
See also CA 104; 133; DLB 56, 124; MTCW

Brecht, Eugen Berthold Friedrich
See Brecht, Bertolt

Bremer, Fredrika 1801-1865..... NCLC 11

Brennan, Christopher John
1870-1932.................. TCLC 17
See also CA 117

Brennan, Maeve 1917-............ CLC 5
See also CA 81-84

Brentano, Clemens (Maria)
1778-1842.................. NCLC 1
See also DLB 90

Brent of Bin Bin
See Franklin, (Stella Maraia Sarah) Miles

Brenton, Howard 1942-........... CLC 31
See also CA 69-72; CANR 33; DLB 13;
MTCW

Breslin, James 1930-
See Breslin, Jimmy
See also CA 73-76; CANR 31; MTCW

Breslin, Jimmy .... CLC 4, 43
See also Breslin, James
See also AITN 1

Bresson, Robert 1901-............ CLC 16
See also CA 110; CANR 49

Breton, Andre 1896-1966... CLC 2, 9, 15, 54
See also CA 19-20; 25-28R; CANR 40;
CAP 2; DLB 65; MTCW

Breytenbach, Breyten 1939(?)- .. CLC 23, 37
See also CA 113; 129

Bridgers, Sue Ellen 1942-......... CLC 26
See also AAYA 8; CA 65-68; CANR 11,
36; CLR 18; DLB 52; JRDA; MAICYA;
SAAS 1; SATA 22

Bridges, Robert (Seymour)
1844-1930.................. TCLC 1
See also CA 104; CDBLB 1890-1914;
DLB 19, 98

Bridie, James.................. TCLC 3
See also Mavor, Osborne Henry
See also DLB 10

Brin, David 1950-................ CLC 34
See also CA 102; CANR 24; SATA 65

Brink, Andre (Philippus)
1935-.................... CLC 18, 36
See also CA 104; CANR 39; MTCW

Brinsmead, H(esba) F(ay) 1922-.... CLC 21
See also CA 21-24R; CANR 10; MAICYA;
SAAS 5; SATA 18, 78

Brittain, Vera (Mary)
1893(?)-1970................. CLC 23
See also CA 13-16; 25-28R; CAP 1; MTCW

Broch, Hermann 1886-1951....... TCLC 20
See also CA 117; DLB 85, 124

Brock, Rose
See Hansen, Joseph

Brodkey, Harold 1930-............ CLC 56
See also CA 111; DLB 130

Brodsky, Iosif Alexandrovich 1940-
See Brodsky, Joseph
See also AITN 1; CA 41-44R; CANR 37;
MTCW

Brodsky, Joseph .. CLC 4, 6, 13, 36, 50; PC 9
See also Brodsky, Iosif Alexandrovich

Brodsky, Michael Mark 1948- ..... CLC 19
See also CA 102; CANR 18, 41

Bromell, Henry 1947-............. CLC 5
See also CA 53-56; CANR 9

Bromfield, Louis (Brucker)
1896-1956.................. TCLC 11
See also CA 107; DLB 4, 9, 86

Broner, E(sther) M(asserman)
1930-...................... CLC 19
See also CA 17-20R; CANR 8, 25; DLB 28

Bronk, William 1918-............. CLC 10
See also CA 89-92; CANR 23

Bronstein, Lev Davidovich
See Trotsky, Leon

Bronte, Anne 1820-1849.......... NCLC 4
See also DLB 21

Bronte, Charlotte
1816-1855......... NCLC 3, 8, 33; DA;
DAB; WLC
See also CDBLB 1832-1890; DLB 21

Bronte, Emily (Jane)
1818-1848 .... NCLC 16, 35; DA; DAB;
PC 8; WLC
See also CDBLB 1832-1890; DLB 21, 32

Brooke, Frances 1724-1789......... LC 6
See also DLB 39, 99

Brooke, Henry 1703(?)-1783........ LC 1
See also DLB 39

Brooke, Rupert (Chawner)
1887-1915....... TCLC 2, 7; DA; DAB;
WLC
See also CA 104; 132; CDBLB 1914-1945;
DLB 19; MTCW

Brooke-Haven, P.
See Wodehouse, P(elham) G(renville)

Brooke-Rose, Christine 1926-...... CLC 40
See also CA 13-16R; DLB 14

Brookner, Anita
1928-........... CLC 32, 34, 51; DAB
See also CA 114; 120; CANR 37; DLBY 87;
MTCW

Brooks, Cleanth 1906-1994 ..... CLC 24, 86
See also CA 17-20R; 145; CANR 33, 35;
DLB 63; DLBY 94; MTCW

Brooks, George
See Baum, L(yman) Frank

Brooks, Gwendolyn
1917- ...... CLC 1, 2, 4, 5, 15, 49; BLC;
DA; PC 7; WLC
See also AITN 1; BW 2; CA 1-4R;
CANR 1, 27; CDALB 1941-1968;
CLR 27; DLB 5, 76; MTCW; SATA 6

Brooks, Mel..................... CLC 12
See also Kaminsky, Melvin
See also AAYA 13; DLB 26

Brooks, Peter 1938-.............. CLC 34
See also CA 45-48; CANR 1

Brooks, Van Wyck 1886-1963...... CLC 29
See also CA 1-4R; CANR 6; DLB 45, 63,
103

Brophy, Brigid (Antonia)
1929-................... CLC 6, 11, 29
See also CA 5-8R; CAAS 4; CANR 25;
DLB 14; MTCW

Brosman, Catharine Savage 1934-.... CLC 9
See also CA 61-64; CANR 21, 46

Brother Antoninus
See Everson, William (Oliver)

Broughton, T(homas) Alan 1936- ... CLC 19
See also CA 45-48; CANR 2, 23, 48

Broumas, Olga 1949-.......... CLC 10, 73
See also CA 85-88; CANR 20

Brown, Charles Brockden
1771-1810 . . . . **NCLC 22**
See also CDALB 1640-1865; DLB 37, 59, 73

Brown, Christy 1932-1981 . . . . **CLC 63**
See also CA 105; 104; DLB 14

Brown, Claude 1937- . . . . **CLC 30; BLC**
See also AAYA 7; BW 1; CA 73-76

Brown, Dee (Alexander) 1908- . . **CLC 18, 47**
See also CA 13-16R; CAAS 6; CANR 11, 45; DLBY 80; MTCW; SATA 5

Brown, George
See Wertmueller, Lina

Brown, George Douglas
1869-1902 . . . . **TCLC 28**

Brown, George Mackay 1921- . . . . **CLC 5, 48**
See also CA 21-24R; CAAS 6; CANR 12, 37; DLB 14, 27, 139; MTCW; SATA 35

Brown, (William) Larry 1951- . . . . . . **CLC 73**
See also CA 130; 134

Brown, Moses
See Barrett, William (Christopher)

Brown, Rita Mae 1944- . . . . . **CLC 18, 43, 79**
See also CA 45-48; CANR 2, 11, 35; MTCW

Brown, Roderick (Langmere) Haig-
See Haig-Brown, Roderick (Langmere)

Brown, Rosellen 1939- . . . . **CLC 32**
See also CA 77-80; CAAS 10; CANR 14, 44

Brown, Sterling Allen
1901-1989 . . . . **CLC 1, 23, 59; BLC**
See also BW 1; CA 85-88; 127; CANR 26; DLB 48, 51, 63; MTCW

Brown, Will
See Ainsworth, William Harrison

Brown, William Wells
1813-1884 . . . . **NCLC 2; BLC; DC 1**
See also DLB 3, 50

Browne, (Clyde) Jackson 1948(?)- . . . **CLC 21**
See also CA 120

Browning, Elizabeth Barrett
1806-1861 . . . . . **NCLC 1, 16; DA; DAB; PC 6; WLC**
See also CDBLB 1832-1890; DLB 32

Browning, Robert
1812-1889 . . **NCLC 19; DA; DAB; PC 2**
See also CDBLB 1832-1890; DLB 32; YABC 1

Browning, Tod 1882-1962 . . . . **CLC 16**
See also CA 141; 117

Brownson, Orestes (Augustus)
1803-1876 . . . . **NCLC 50**

Bruccoli, Matthew J(oseph) 1931- . . **CLC 34**
See also CA 9-12R; CANR 7; DLB 103

Bruce, Lenny . . . . **CLC 21**
See also Schneider, Leonard Alfred

Bruin, John
See Brutus, Dennis

Brulard, Henri
See Stendhal

Brulls, Christian
See Simenon, Georges (Jacques Christian)

Brunner, John (Kilian Houston)
1934- . . . . **CLC 8, 10**
See also CA 1-4R; CAAS 8; CANR 2, 37; MTCW

Bruno, Giordano 1548-1600 . . . . **LC 27**

Brutus, Dennis 1924- . . . . **CLC 43; BLC**
See also BW 2; CA 49-52; CAAS 14; CANR 2, 27, 42; DLB 117

Bryan, C(ourtlandt) D(ixon) B(arnes)
1936- . . . . **CLC 29**
See also CA 73-76; CANR 13

Bryan, Michael
See Moore, Brian

Bryant, William Cullen
1794-1878 . . . . . . **NCLC 6, 46; DA; DAB**
See also CDALB 1640-1865; DLB 3, 43, 59

Bryusov, Valery Yakovlevich
1873-1924 . . . . **TCLC 10**
See also CA 107

Buchan, John 1875-1940 . . . **TCLC 41; DAB**
See also CA 108; 145; DLB 34, 70, 156; YABC 2

Buchanan, George 1506-1582 . . . . **LC 4**

Buchheim, Lothar-Guenther 1918- . . . **CLC 6**
See also CA 85-88

Buchner, (Karl) Georg
1813-1837 . . . . **NCLC 26**

Buchwald, Art(hur) 1925- . . . . **CLC 33**
See also AITN 1; CA 5-8R; CANR 21; MTCW; SATA 10

Buck, Pearl S(ydenstricker)
1892-1973 . . . . **CLC 7, 11, 18; DA; DAB**
See also AITN 1; CA 1-4R; 41-44R; CANR 1, 34; DLB 9, 102; MTCW; SATA 1, 25

Buckler, Ernest 1908-1984 . . . . **CLC 13**
See also CA 11-12; 114; CAP 1; DLB 68; SATA 47

Buckley, Vincent (Thomas)
1925-1988 . . . . **CLC 57**
See also CA 101

Buckley, William F(rank), Jr.
1925- . . . . **CLC 7, 18, 37**
See also AITN 1; CA 1-4R; CANR 1, 24; DLB 137; DLBY 80; MTCW

Buechner, (Carl) Frederick
1926- . . . . **CLC 2, 4, 6, 9**
See also CA 13-16R; CANR 11, 39; DLBY 80; MTCW

Buell, John (Edward) 1927- . . . . **CLC 10**
See also CA 1-4R; DLB 53

Buero Vallejo, Antonio 1916- . . . **CLC 15, 46**
See also CA 106; CANR 24, 49; HW; MTCW

Bufalino, Gesualdo 1920(?)- . . . . **CLC 74**

Bugayev, Boris Nikolayevich 1880-1934
See Bely, Andrey
See also CA 104

Bukowski, Charles
1920-1994 . . . . **CLC 2, 5, 9, 41, 82**
See also CA 17-20R; 144; CANR 40; DLB 5, 130; MTCW

Bulgakov, Mikhail (Afanas'evich)
1891-1940 . . . . **TCLC 2, 16; SSC 18**
See also CA 105

Bulgya, Alexander Alexandrovich
1901-1956 . . . . **TCLC 53**
See also Fadeyev, Alexander
See also CA 117

Bullins, Ed 1935- . . . . **CLC 1, 5, 7; BLC**
See also BW 2; CA 49-52; CAAS 16; CANR 24, 46; DLB 7, 38; MTCW

Bulwer-Lytton, Edward (George Earle Lytton)
1803-1873 . . . . **NCLC 1, 45**
See also DLB 21

Bunin, Ivan Alexeyevich
1870-1953 . . . . **TCLC 6; SSC 5**
See also CA 104

Bunting, Basil 1900-1985 . . . . **CLC 10, 39, 47**
See also CA 53-56; 115; CANR 7; DLB 20

Bunuel, Luis 1900-1983 . . **CLC 16, 80; HLC**
See also CA 101; 110; CANR 32; HW

Bunyan, John
1628-1688 . . . . . . **LC 4; DA; DAB; WLC**
See also CDBLB 1660-1789; DLB 39

Burckhardt, Jacob (Christoph)
1818-1897 . . . . **NCLC 49**

Burford, Eleanor
See Hibbert, Eleanor Alice Burford

Burgess, Anthony
. **CLC 1, 2, 4, 5, 8, 10, 13, 15, 22, 40, 62, 81; DAB**
See also Wilson, John (Anthony) Burgess
See also AITN 1; CDBLB 1960 to Present; DLB 14

Burke, Edmund
1729(?)-1797 . . . . **LC 7; DA; DAB; WLC**
See also DLB 104

Burke, Kenneth (Duva)
1897-1993 . . . . **CLC 2, 24**
See also CA 5-8R; 143; CANR 39; DLB 45, 63; MTCW

Burke, Leda
See Garnett, David

Burke, Ralph
See Silverberg, Robert

Burney, Fanny 1752-1840 . . . . **NCLC 12**
See also DLB 39

Burns, Robert 1759-1796 . . . . **PC 6**
See also CDBLB 1789-1832; DA; DAB; DLB 109; WLC

Burns, Tex
See L'Amour, Louis (Dearborn)

Burnshaw, Stanley 1906- . . . . . **CLC 3, 13, 44**
See also CA 9-12R; DLB 48

Burr, Anne 1937- . . . . **CLC 6**
See also CA 25-28R

Burroughs, Edgar Rice
1875-1950 . . . . **TCLC 2, 32**
See also AAYA 11; CA 104; 132; DLB 8; MTCW; SATA 41

Burroughs, William S(eward)
1914- . . . . **CLC 1, 2, 5, 15, 22, 42, 75; DA; DAB; WLC**
See also AITN 2; CA 9-12R; CANR 20; DLB 2, 8, 16, 152; DLBY 81; MTCW

Burton, Richard F. 1821-1890 . . . . **NCLC 42**
See also DLB 55

Busch, Frederick 1941- ... **CLC 7, 10, 18, 47**
See also CA 33-36R; CAAS 1; CANR 45;
DLB 6

Bush, Ronald 1946- .... **CLC 34**
See also CA 136

Bustos, F(rancisco)
See Borges, Jorge Luis

Bustos Domecq, H(onorio)
See Bioy Casares, Adolfo; Borges, Jorge
Luis

Butler, Octavia E(stelle) 1947- ..... **CLC 38**
See also BW 2; CA 73-76; CANR 12, 24,
38; DLB 33; MTCW

Butler, Robert Olen (Jr.) 1945-..... **CLC 81**
See also CA 112

Butler, Samuel 1612-1680 .... **LC 16**
See also DLB 101, 126

Butler, Samuel
1835-1902 ...... **TCLC 1, 33; DA; DAB;**
WLC
See also CA 143; CDBLB 1890-1914;
DLB 18, 57

Butler, Walter C.
See Faust, Frederick (Schiller)

Butor, Michel (Marie Francois)
1926- .... **CLC 1, 3, 8, 11, 15**
See also CA 9-12R; CANR 33; DLB 83;
MTCW

Buzo, Alexander (John) 1944-...... **CLC 61**
See also CA 97-100; CANR 17, 39

Buzzati, Dino 1906-1972 .... **CLC 36**
See also CA 33-36R

Byars, Betsy (Cromer) 1928-....... **CLC 35**
See also CA 33-36R; CANR 18, 36; CLR 1,
16; DLB 52; JRDA; MAICYA; MTCW;
SAAS 1; SATA 4, 46, 80

Byatt, A(ntonia) S(usan Drabble)
1936- .... **CLC 19, 65**
See also CA 13-16R; CANR 13, 33;
DLB 14; MTCW

Byrne, David 1952-............... **CLC 26**
See also CA 127

Byrne, John Keyes 1926-
See Leonard, Hugh
See also CA 102

Byron, George Gordon (Noel)
1788-1824 ..... **NCLC 2, 12; DA; DAB;**
WLC
See also CDBLB 1789-1832; DLB 96, 110

C. 3. 3.
See Wilde, Oscar (Fingal O'Flahertie Wills)

Caballero, Fernan 1796-1877..... **NCLC 10**

Cabell, James Branch 1879-1958 ... **TCLC 6**
See also CA 105; DLB 9, 78

Cable, George Washington
1844-1925 .... **TCLC 4; SSC 4**
See also CA 104; DLB 12, 74

Cabral de Melo Neto, Joao 1920-... **CLC 76**

Cabrera Infante, G(uillermo)
1929- .... **CLC 5, 25, 45; HLC**
See also CA 85-88; CANR 29; DLB 113;
HW; MTCW

Cade, Toni
See Bambara, Toni Cade

Cadmus and Harmonia
See Buchan, John

Caedmon fl. 658-680............. **CMLC 7**
See also DLB 146

Caeiro, Alberto
See Pessoa, Fernando (Antonio Nogueira)

Cage, John (Milton, Jr.) 1912-..... **CLC 41**
See also CA 13-16R; CANR 9

Cain, G.
See Cabrera Infante, G(uillermo)

Cain, Guillermo
See Cabrera Infante, G(uillermo)

Cain, James M(allahan)
1892-1977 .... **CLC 3, 11, 28**
See also AITN 1; CA 17-20R; 73-76;
CANR 8, 34; MTCW

Caine, Mark
See Raphael, Frederic (Michael)

Calasso, Roberto 1941- .... **CLC 81**
See also CA 143

Calderon de la Barca, Pedro
1600-1681 .... **LC 23; DC 3**

Caldwell, Erskine (Preston)
1903-1987 .... **CLC 1, 8, 14, 50, 60;**
SSC 19
See also AITN 1; CA 1-4R; 121; CAAS 1;
CANR 2, 33; DLB 9, 86

Caldwell, (Janet Miriam) Taylor (Holland)
1900-1985 .... **CLC 2, 28, 39**
See also CA 5-8R; 116; CANR 5

Calhoun, John Caldwell
1782-1850 .... **NCLC 15**
See also DLB 3

Calisher, Hortense
1911- .... **CLC 2, 4, 8, 38; SSC 15**
See also CA 1-4R; CANR 1, 22; DLB 2;
MTCW

Callaghan, Morley Edward
1903-1990 .... **CLC 3, 14, 41, 65**
See also CA 9-12R; 132; CANR 33;
DLB 68; MTCW

Calvino, Italo
1923-1985 ..... **CLC 5, 8, 11, 22, 33, 39,**
73; SSC 3
See also CA 85-88; 116; CANR 23; MTCW

Cameron, Carey 1952-............ **CLC 59**
See also CA 135

Cameron, Peter 1959-............. **CLC 44**
See also CA 125

Campana, Dino 1885-1932........ **TCLC 20**
See also CA 117; DLB 114

Campbell, John W(ood, Jr.)
1910-1971 .... **CLC 32**
See also CA 21-22; 29-32R; CANR 34;
CAP 2; DLB 8; MTCW

Campbell, Joseph 1904-1987 .... **CLC 69**
See also AAYA 3; BEST 89:2; CA 1-4R;
124; CANR 3, 28; MTCW

Campbell, Maria 1940-............ **CLC 85**
See also CA 102; NNAL

Campbell, (John) Ramsey
1946- .... **CLC 42; SSC 19**
See also CA 57-60; CANR 7

Campbell, (Ignatius) Roy (Dunnachie)
1901-1957 .... **TCLC 5**
See also CA 104; DLB 20

Campbell, Thomas 1777-1844 .... **NCLC 19**
See also DLB 93; 144

Campbell, Wilfred .... **TCLC 9**
See also Campbell, William

Campbell, William 1858(?)-1918
See Campbell, Wilfred
See also CA 106; DLB 92

Campos, Alvaro de
See Pessoa, Fernando (Antonio Nogueira)

Camus, Albert
1913-1960 .... **CLC 1, 2, 4, 9, 11, 14, 32,**
63, 69; DA; DAB; DC 2; SSC 9; WLC
See also CA 89-92; DLB 72; MTCW

Canby, Vincent 1924-............. **CLC 13**
See also CA 81-84

Cancale
See Desnos, Robert

Canetti, Elias
1905-1994 .... **CLC 3, 14, 25, 75, 86**
See also CA 21-24R; 146; CANR 23;
DLB 85, 124; MTCW

Canin, Ethan 1960-............... **CLC 55**
See also CA 131; 135

Cannon, Curt
See Hunter, Evan

Cape, Judith
See Page, P(atricia) K(athleen)

Capek, Karel
1890-1938 ...... **TCLC 6, 37; DA; DAB;**
DC 1; WLC
See also CA 104; 140

Capote, Truman
1924-1984 ...... **CLC 1, 3, 8, 13, 19, 34,**
38, 58; DA; DAB; SSC 2; WLC
See also CA 5-8R; 113; CANR 18;
CDALB 1941-1968; DLB 2; DLBY 80,
84; MTCW

Capra, Frank 1897-1991........... **CLC 16**
See also CA 61-64; 135

Caputo, Philip 1941-.............. **CLC 32**
See also CA 73-76; CANR 40

Card, Orson Scott 1951- .... **CLC 44, 47, 50**
See also AAYA 11; CA 102; CANR 27, 47;
MTCW; SATA 83

Cardenal (Martinez), Ernesto
1925- .... **CLC 31; HLC**
See also CA 49-52; CANR 2, 32; HW;
MTCW

Carducci, Giosue 1835-1907....... **TCLC 32**

Carew, Thomas 1595(?)-1640........ **LC 13**
See also DLB 126

Carey, Ernestine Gilbreth 1908-.... **CLC 17**
See also CA 5-8R; SATA 2

Carey, Peter 1943-............. **CLC 40, 55**
See also CA 123; 127; MTCW

Carleton, William 1794-1869...... **NCLC 3**

Carlisle, Henry (Coffin) 1926-...... **CLC 33**
See also CA 13-16R; CANR 15

Carlsen, Chris
See Holdstock, Robert P.

Chandler, Raymond (Thornton)
1888-1959 .... **TCLC 1, 7**
See also CA 104; 129; CDALB 1929-1941;
DLBD 6; MTCW

Chang, Jung 1952- .... **CLC 71**
See also CA 142

Channing, William Ellery
1780-1842 .... **NCLC 17**
See also DLB 1, 59

Chaplin, Charles Spencer
1889-1977 .... **CLC 16**
See also Chaplin, Charlie
See also CA 81-84; 73-76

Chaplin, Charlie
See Chaplin, Charles Spencer
See also DLB 44

Chapman, George 1559(?)-1634...... **LC 22**
See also DLB 62, 121

Chapman, Graham 1941-1989 ...... **CLC 21**
See also Monty Python
See also CA 116; 129; CANR 35

Chapman, John Jay 1862-1933 ..... **TCLC 7**
See also CA 104

Chapman, Walker
See Silverberg, Robert

Chappell, Fred (Davis) 1936-.... **CLC 40, 78**
See also CA 5-8R; CAAS 4; CANR 8, 33;
DLB 6, 105

Char, Rene(-Emile)
1907-1988 .... **CLC 9, 11, 14, 55**
See also CA 13-16R; 124; CANR 32;
MTCW

Charby, Jay
See Ellison, Harlan (Jay)

Chardin, Pierre Teilhard de
See Teilhard de Chardin, (Marie Joseph)
Pierre

Charles I 1600-1649 .... **LC 13**

Charyn, Jerome 1937- .... **CLC 5, 8, 18**
See also CA 5-8R; CAAS 1; CANR 7;
DLBY 83; MTCW

Chase, Mary (Coyle) 1907-1981 ...... **DC 1**
See also CA 77-80; 105; SATA 17;
SATA-Obit 29

Chase, Mary Ellen 1887-1973....... **CLC 2**
See also CA 13-16; 41-44R; CAP 1;
SATA 10

Chase, Nicholas
See Hyde, Anthony

Chateaubriand, Francois Rene de
1768-1848 .... **NCLC 3**
See also DLB 119

Chatterje, Sarat Chandra 1876-1936(?)
See Chatterji, Saratchandra
See also CA 109

Chatterji, Bankim Chandra
1838-1894 .... **NCLC 19**

Chatterji, Saratchandra .... **TCLC 13**
See also Chatterje, Sarat Chandra

Chatterton, Thomas 1752-1770 .... **LC 3**
See also DLB 109

Chatwin, (Charles) Bruce
1940-1989 .... **CLC 28, 57, 59**
See also AAYA 4; BEST 90:1; CA 85-88;
127

Chaucer, Daniel
See Ford, Ford Madox

Chaucer, Geoffrey
1340(?)-1400 .... **LC 17; DA; DAB**
See also CDBLB Before 1660; DLB 146

Chaviaras, Strates 1935-
See Haviaras, Stratis
See also CA 105

Chayefsky, Paddy .... **CLC 23**
See also Chayefsky, Sidney
See also DLB 7, 44; DLBY 81

Chayefsky, Sidney 1923-1981
See Chayefsky, Paddy
See also CA 9-12R; 104; CANR 18

Chedid, Andree 1920-............. **CLC 47**
See also CA 145

Cheever, John
1912-1982 ...... **CLC 3, 7, 8, 11, 15, 25,**
64; DA; DAB; SSC 1; WLC
See also CA 5-8R; 106; CABS 1; CANR 5,
27; CDALB 1941-1968; DLB 2, 102;
DLBY 80, 82; MTCW

Cheever, Susan 1943-.......... **CLC 18, 48**
See also CA 103; CANR 27; DLBY 82

Chekhonte, Antosha
See Chekhov, Anton (Pavlovich)

Chekhov, Anton (Pavlovich)
1860-1904 ..... **TCLC 3, 10, 31, 55; DA;**
DAB; SSC 2; WLC
See also CA 104; 124

Chernyshevsky, Nikolay Gavrilovich
1828-1889 .... **NCLC 1**

Cherry, Carolyn Janice 1942-
See Cherryh, C. J.
See also CA 65-68; CANR 10

Cherryh, C. J. .... **CLC 35**
See also Cherry, Carolyn Janice
See also DLBY 80

Chesnutt, Charles W(addell)
1858-1932 .... **TCLC 5, 39; BLC; SSC 7**
See also BW 1; CA 106; 125; DLB 12, 50,
78; MTCW

Chester, Alfred 1929(?)-1971....... **CLC 49**
See also CA 33-36R; DLB 130

Chesterton, G(ilbert) K(eith)
1874-1936 .... **TCLC 1, 6; SSC 1**
See also CA 104; 132; CDBLB 1914-1945;
DLB 10, 19, 34, 70, 98, 149; MTCW;
SATA 27

Chiang Pin-chin 1904-1986
See Ding Ling
See also CA 118

Ch'ien Chung-shu 1910-............ **CLC 22**
See also CA 130; MTCW

Child, L. Maria
See Child, Lydia Maria

Child, Lydia Maria 1802-1880 .... **NCLC 6**
See also DLB 1, 74; SATA 67

Child, Mrs.
See Child, Lydia Maria

Child, Philip 1898-1978 .... **CLC 19, 68**
See also CA 13-14; CAP 1; SATA 47

Childress, Alice
1920-1994 .. **CLC 12, 15, 86; BLC; DC 4**
See also AAYA 8; BW 2; CA 45-48; 146;
CANR 3, 27; CLR 14; DLB 7, 38; JRDA;
MAICYA; MTCW; SATA 7, 48, 81

Chislett, (Margaret) Anne 1943-.... **CLC 34**

Chitty, Thomas Willes 1926-....... **CLC 11**
See also Hinde, Thomas
See also CA 5-8R

Chivers, Thomas Holley
1809-1858 .... **NCLC 49**
See also DLB 3

Chomette, Rene Lucien 1898-1981
See Clair, Rene
See also CA 103

Chopin, Kate
.... **TCLC 5, 14; DA; DAB; SSC 8**
See also Chopin, Katherine
See also CDALB 1865-1917; DLB 12, 78

Chopin, Katherine 1851-1904
See Chopin, Kate
See also CA 104; 122

Chretien de Troyes
c. 12th cent. - .... **CMLC 10**

Christie
See Ichikawa, Kon

Christie, Agatha (Mary Clarissa)
1890-1976 ...... **CLC 1, 6, 8, 12, 39, 48;**
DAB
See also AAYA 9; AITN 1, 2; CA 17-20R;
61-64; CANR 10, 37; CDBLB 1914-1945;
DLB 13, 77; MTCW; SATA 36

Christie, (Ann) Philippa
See Pearce, Philippa
See also CA 5-8R; CANR 4

Christine de Pizan 1365(?)-1431(?) .... **LC 9**

Chubb, Elmer
See Masters, Edgar Lee

Chulkov, Mikhail Dmitrievich
1743-1792 .... **LC 2**
See also DLB 150

Churchill, Caryl 1938-... **CLC 31, 55; DC 5**
See also CA 102; CANR 22, 46; DLB 13;
MTCW

Churchill, Charles 1731-1764........ **LC 3**
See also DLB 109

Chute, Carolyn 1947-............. **CLC 39**
See also CA 123

Ciardi, John (Anthony)
1916-1986 ....**CLC 10, 40, 44**
See also CA 5-8R; 118; CAAS 2; CANR 5,
33; CLR 19; DLB 5; DLBY 86;
MAICYA; MTCW; SATA 1, 65;
SATA-Obit 46

Cicero, Marcus Tullius
106B.C.-43B.C. .... **CMLC 3**

Cimino, Michael 1943-............. **CLC 16**
See also CA 105

Cioran, E(mil) M. 1911-........... **CLC 64**
See also CA 25-28R

Cisneros, Sandra 1954-...... **CLC 69; HLC**
See also AAYA 9; CA 131; DLB 122, 152;
HW

Clair, Rene..................... **CLC 20**
See also Chomette, Rene Lucien

Colwin, Laurie (E.)
1944-1992 . . . . **CLC 5, 13, 23, 84**
See also CA 89-92; 139; CANR 20, 46;
DLBY 80; MTCW

Comfort, Alex(ander) 1920- . . . . **CLC 7**
See also CA 1-4R; CANR 1, 45

Comfort, Montgomery
See Campbell, (John) Ramsey

Compton-Burnett, I(vy)
1884(?)-1969 . . . . . . **CLC 1, 3, 10, 15, 34**
See also CA 1-4R; 25-28R; CANR 4;
DLB 36; MTCW

Comstock, Anthony 1844-1915 . . . . **TCLC 13**
See also CA 110

Conan Doyle, Arthur
See Doyle, Arthur Conan

Conde, Maryse 1937- . . . . **CLC 52**
See also Boucolon, Maryse
See also BW 2

Condillac, Etienne Bonnot de
1714-1780 . . . . **LC 26**

Condon, Richard (Thomas)
1915- . . . . **CLC 4, 6, 8, 10, 45**
See also BEST 90:3; CA 1-4R; CAAS 1;
CANR 2, 23; MTCW

Congreve, William
1670-1729 . . . . **LC 5, 21; DA; DAB;
DC 2; WLC**
See also CDBLB 1660-1789; DLB 39, 84

Connell, Evan S(helby), Jr.
1924- . . . . **CLC 4, 6, 45**
See also AAYA 7; CA 1-4R; CAAS 2;
CANR 2, 39; DLB 2; DLBY 81; MTCW

Connelly, Marc(us Cook)
1890-1980 . . . . **CLC 7**
See also CA 85-88; 102; CANR 30; DLB 7;
DLBY 80; SATA-Obit 25

Connor, Ralph . . . . **TCLC 31**
See also Gordon, Charles William
See also DLB 92

Conrad, Joseph
1857-1924 . . . . **TCLC 1, 6, 13, 25, 43, 57;
DA; DAB; SSC 9; WLC**
See also CA 104; 131; CDBLB 1890-1914;
DLB 10, 34, 98, 156; MTCW; SATA 27

Conrad, Robert Arnold
See Hart, Moss

Conroy, Pat 1945- . . . . **CLC 30, 74**
See also AAYA 8; AITN 1; CA 85-88;
CANR 24; DLB 6; MTCW

Constant (de Rebecque), (Henri) Benjamin
1767-1830 . . . . **NCLC 6**
See also DLB 119

Conybeare, Charles Augustus
See Eliot, T(homas) S(tearns)

Cook, Michael 1933- . . . . **CLC 58**
See also CA 93-96; DLB 53

Cook, Robin 1940- . . . . **CLC 14**
See also BEST 90:2; CA 108; 111;
CANR 41

Cook, Roy
See Silverberg, Robert

Cooke, Elizabeth 1948- . . . . **CLC 55**
See also CA 129

Cooke, John Esten 1830-1886 . . . . . **NCLC 5**
See also DLB 3

Cooke, John Estes
See Baum, L(yman) Frank

Cooke, M. E.
See Creasey, John

Cooke, Margaret
See Creasey, John

Cooney, Ray . . . . **CLC 62**

Cooper, Douglas 1960- . . . . **CLC 86**

Cooper, Henry St. John
See Creasey, John

Cooper, J. California . . . . **CLC 56**
See also AAYA 12; BW 1; CA 125

Cooper, James Fenimore
1789-1851 . . . . **NCLC 1, 27**
See also CDALB 1640-1865; DLB 3;
SATA 19

Coover, Robert (Lowell)
1932- . . **CLC 3, 7, 15, 32, 46, 87; SSC 15**
See also CA 45-48; CANR 3, 37; DLB 2;
DLBY 81; MTCW

Copeland, Stewart (Armstrong)
1952- . . . . **CLC 26**

Coppard, A(lfred) E(dgar)
1878-1957 . . . . **TCLC 5; SSC 21**
See also CA 114; YABC 1

Coppee, Francois 1842-1908 . . . . . . **TCLC 25**

Coppola, Francis Ford 1939- . . . . **CLC 16**
See also CA 77-80; CANR 40; DLB 44

Corbiere, Tristan 1845-1875 . . . . . **NCLC 43**

Corcoran, Barbara 1911- . . . . **CLC 17**
See also AAYA 14; CA 21-24R; CAAS 2;
CANR 11, 28, 48; DLB 52; JRDA;
SAAS 20; SATA 3, 77

Cordelier, Maurice
See Giraudoux, (Hippolyte) Jean

Corelli, Marie 1855-1924 . . . . **TCLC 51**
See also Mackay, Mary
See also DLB 34, 156

Corman, Cid . . . . **CLC 9**
See also Corman, Sidney
See also CAAS 2; DLB 5

Corman, Sidney 1924-
See Corman, Cid
See also CA 85-88; CANR 44

Cormier, Robert (Edmund)
1925- . . . . **CLC 12, 30; DA; DAB**
See also AAYA 3; CA 1-4R; CANR 5, 23;
CDALB 1968-1988; CLR 12; DLB 52;
JRDA; MAICYA; MTCW; SATA 10, 45,
83

Corn, Alfred (DeWitt III) 1943- . . . . **CLC 33**
See also CA 104; CANR 44; DLB 120;
DLBY 80

Corneille, Pierre 1606-1684 . . . . **LC 28; DAB**

Cornwell, David (John Moore)
1931- . . . . **CLC 9, 15**
See also le Carre, John
See also CA 5-8R; CANR 13, 33; MTCW

Corso, (Nunzio) Gregory 1930- . . . **CLC 1, 11**
See also CA 5-8R; CANR 41; DLB 5, 16;
MTCW

Cortazar, Julio
1914-1984 . . . . . . **CLC 2, 3, 5, 10, 13, 15,
33, 34; HLC; SSC 7**
See also CA 21-24R; CANR 12, 32;
DLB 113; HW; MTCW

CORTES, HERNAN 1484-1547 . . . . . **LC 31**

Corwin, Cecil
See Kornbluth, C(yril) M.

Cosic, Dobrica 1921- . . . . **CLC 14**
See also CA 122; 138

Costain, Thomas B(ertram)
1885-1965 . . . . **CLC 30**
See also CA 5-8R; 25-28R; DLB 9

Costantini, Humberto
1924(?)-1987 . . . . **CLC 49**
See also CA 131; 122; HW

Costello, Elvis 1955- . . . . **CLC 21**

Cotter, Joseph Seamon Sr.
1861-1949 . . . . **TCLC 28; BLC**
See also BW 1; CA 124; DLB 50

Couch, Arthur Thomas Quiller
See Quiller-Couch, Arthur Thomas

Coulton, James
See Hansen, Joseph

Couperus, Louis (Marie Anne)
1863-1923 . . . . **TCLC 15**
See also CA 115

Coupland, Douglas 1961- . . . . **CLC 85**
See also CA 142

Court, Wesli
See Turco, Lewis (Putnam)

Courtenay, Bryce 1933- . . . . **CLC 59**
See also CA 138

Courtney, Robert
See Ellison, Harlan (Jay)

Cousteau, Jacques-Yves 1910- . . . . . . **CLC 30**
See also CA 65-68; CANR 15; MTCW;
SATA 38

Coward, Noel (Peirce)
1899-1973 . . . . **CLC 1, 9, 29, 51**
See also AITN 1; CA 17-18; 41-44R;
CANR 35; CAP 2; CDBLB 1914-1945;
DLB 10; MTCW

Cowley, Malcolm 1898-1989 . . . . **CLC 39**
See also CA 5-8R; 128; CANR 3; DLB 4,
48; DLBY 81, 89; MTCW

Cowper, William 1731-1800 . . . . **NCLC 8**
See also DLB 104, 109

Cox, William Trevor 1928- . . . **CLC 9, 14, 71**
See also Trevor, William
See also CA 9-12R; CANR 4, 37; DLB 14;
MTCW

Coyne, P. J.
See Masters, Hilary

Cozzens, James Gould
1903-1978 . . . . **CLC 1, 4, 11**
See also CA 9-12R; 81-84; CANR 19;
CDALB 1941-1968; DLB 9; DLBD 2;
DLBY 84; MTCW

Crabbe, George 1754-1832 . . . . **NCLC 26**
See also DLB 93

Craig, A. A.
See Anderson, Poul (William)

Craik, Dinah Maria (Mulock)
1826-1887 . . . . NCLC **38**
See also DLB 35; MAICYA; SATA 34

Cram, Ralph Adams 1863-1942 . . . . TCLC **45**

Crane, (Harold) Hart
1899-1932 . . . . TCLC **2, 5**; DA; DAB;
PC **3**; WLC
See also CA 104; 127; CDALB 1917-1929;
DLB 4, 48; MTCW

Crane, R(onald) S(almon)
1886-1967 . . . . CLC **27**
See also CA 85-88; DLB 63

Crane, Stephen (Townley)
1871-1900 . . . . TCLC **11, 17, 32**; DA;
DAB; SSC **7**; WLC
See also CA 109; 140; CDALB 1865-1917;
DLB 12, 54, 78; YABC 2

Crase, Douglas 1944- . . . . CLC **58**
See also CA 106

Crashaw, Richard 1612(?)-1649 . . . . . . LC **24**
See also DLB 126

Craven, Margaret 1901-1980 . . . . CLC **17**
See also CA 103

Crawford, F(rancis) Marion
1854-1909 . . . . TCLC **10**
See also CA 107; DLB 71

Crawford, Isabella Valancy
1850-1887 . . . . NCLC **12**
See also DLB 92

Crayon, Geoffrey
See Irving, Washington

Creasey, John 1908-1973 . . . . CLC **11**
See also CA 5-8R; 41-44R; CANR 8;
DLB 77; MTCW

Crebillon, Claude Prosper Jolyot de (fils)
1707-1777 . . . . LC **28**

Credo
See Creasey, John

Creeley, Robert (White)
1926- . . . . . CLC **1, 2, 4, 8, 11, 15, 36, 78**
See also CA 1-4R; CAAS 10; CANR 23, 43;
DLB 5, 16; MTCW

Crews, Harry (Eugene)
1935- . . . . CLC **6, 23, 49**
See also AITN 1; CA 25-28R; CANR 20;
DLB 6, 143; MTCW

Crichton, (John) Michael
1942- . . . . CLC **2, 6, 54, 90**
See also AAYA 10; AITN 2; CA 25-28R;
CANR 13, 40; DLBY 81; JRDA;
MTCW; SATA 9

Crispin, Edmund . . . . CLC **22**
See also Montgomery, (Robert) Bruce
See also DLB 87

Cristofer, Michael 1945(?)- . . . . CLC **28**
See also CA 110; DLB 7

Croce, Benedetto 1866-1952 . . . . . . TCLC **37**
See also CA 120

Crockett, David 1786-1836 . . . . NCLC **8**
See also DLB 3, 11

Crockett, Davy
See Crockett, David

Crofts, Freeman Wills
1879-1957 . . . . TCLC **55**
See also CA 115; DLB 77

Croker, John Wilson 1780-1857 . . NCLC **10**
See also DLB 110

Crommelynck, Fernand 1885-1970 . . CLC **75**
See also CA 89-92

Cronin, A(rchibald) J(oseph)
1896-1981 . . . . CLC **32**
See also CA 1-4R; 102; CANR 5; SATA 47;
SATA-Obit 25

Cross, Amanda
See Heilbrun, Carolyn G(old)

Crothers, Rachel 1878(?)-1958 . . . . . TCLC **19**
See also CA 113; DLB 7

Croves, Hal
See Traven, B.

Crowfield, Christopher
See Stowe, Harriet (Elizabeth) Beecher

Crowley, Aleister . . . . TCLC **7**
See also Crowley, Edward Alexander

Crowley, Edward Alexander 1875-1947
See Crowley, Aleister
See also CA 104

Crowley, John 1942- . . . . CLC **57**
See also CA 61-64; CANR 43; DLBY 82;
SATA 65

Crud
See Crumb, R(obert)

Crumarums
See Crumb, R(obert)

Crumb, R(obert) 1943- . . . . CLC **17**
See also CA 106

Crumbum
See Crumb, R(obert)

Crumski
See Crumb, R(obert)

Crum the Bum
See Crumb, R(obert)

Crunk
See Crumb, R(obert)

Crustt
See Crumb, R(obert)

Cryer, Gretchen (Kiger) 1935- . . . . . . CLC **21**
See also CA 114; 123

Csath, Geza 1887-1919 . . . . TCLC **13**
See also CA 111

Cudlip, David 1933- . . . . CLC **34**

Cullen, Countee
1903-1946 . . . . . . TCLC **4, 37**; BLC; DA
See also BW 1; CA 108; 124;
CDALB 1917-1929; DLB 4, 48, 51;
MTCW; SATA 18

Cum, R.
See Crumb, R(obert)

Cummings, Bruce F(rederick) 1889-1919
See Barbellion, W. N. P.
See also CA 123

Cummings, E(dward) E(stlin)
1894-1962 . . . . . . CLC **1, 3, 8, 12, 15, 68**;
DA; DAB; PC **5**; WLC **2**
See also CA 73-76; CANR 31;
CDALB 1929-1941; DLB 4, 48; MTCW

Cunha, Euclides (Rodrigues Pimenta) da
1866-1909 . . . . TCLC **24**
See also CA 123

Cunningham, E. V.
See Fast, Howard (Melvin)

Cunningham, J(ames) V(incent)
1911-1985 . . . . CLC **3, 31**
See also CA 1-4R; 115; CANR 1; DLB 5

Cunningham, Julia (Woolfolk)
1916- . . . . CLC **12**
See also CA 9-12R; CANR 4, 19, 36;
JRDA; MAICYA; SAAS 2; SATA 1, 26

Cunningham, Michael 1952- . . . . CLC **34**
See also CA 136

Cunninghame Graham, R(obert) B(ontine)
1852-1936 . . . . TCLC **19**
See also Graham, R(obert) B(ontine)
Cunninghame
See also CA 119; DLB 98

Currie, Ellen 19(?)- . . . . CLC **44**

Curtin, Philip
See Lowndes, Marie Adelaide (Belloc)

Curtis, Price
See Ellison, Harlan (Jay)

Cutrate, Joe
See Spiegelman, Art

Czaczkes, Shmuel Yosef
See Agnon, S(hmuel) Y(osef Halevi)

Dabrowska, Maria (Szumska)
1889-1965 . . . . CLC **15**
See also CA 106

Dabydeen, David 1955- . . . . CLC **34**
See also BW 1; CA 125

Dacey, Philip 1939- . . . . CLC **51**
See also CA 37-40R; CAAS 17; CANR 14,
32; DLB 105

Dagerman, Stig (Halvard)
1923-1954 . . . . TCLC **17**
See also CA 117

Dahl, Roald
1916-1990 . . . . . . CLC **1, 6, 18, 79**; DAB
See also AAYA 15; CA 1-4R; 133;
CANR 6, 32, 37; CLR 1, 7; DLB 139;
JRDA; MAICYA; MTCW; SATA 1, 26,
73; SATA-Obit 65

Dahlberg, Edward 1900-1977 . . . CLC **1, 7, 14**
See also CA 9-12R; 69-72; CANR 31;
DLB 48; MTCW

Dale, Colin . . . . TCLC **18**
See also Lawrence, T(homas) E(dward)

Dale, George E.
See Asimov, Isaac

Daly, Elizabeth 1878-1967 . . . . CLC **52**
See also CA 23-24; 25-28R; CAP 2

Daly, Maureen 1921- . . . . CLC **17**
See also AAYA 5; CANR 37; JRDA;
MAICYA; SAAS 1; SATA 2

Damas, Leon-Gontran 1912-1978 . . . CLC **84**
See also BW 1; CA 125; 73-76

Daniel, Samuel 1562(?)-1619 . . . . LC **24**
See also DLB 62

Daniels, Brett
See Adler, Renata

Dannay, Frederic 1905-1982 . . . . CLC **11**
See also Queen, Ellery
See also CA 1-4R; 107; CANR 1, 39;
DLB 137; MTCW

Deloria, Vine (Victor), Jr. 1933-.... **CLC 21**
See also CA 53-56; CANR 5, 20, 48;
MTCW; NNAL; SATA 21

Del Vecchio, John M(ichael)
1947-...................... **CLC 29**
See also CA 110; DLBD 9

de Man, Paul (Adolph Michel)
1919-1983 .... **CLC 55**
See also CA 128; 111; DLB 67; MTCW

De Marinis, Rick 1934-........... **CLC 54**
See also CA 57-60; CANR 9, 25

Demby, William 1922-....... **CLC 53; BLC**
See also BW 1; CA 81-84; DLB 33

Demijohn, Thom
See Disch, Thomas M(ichael)

de Montherlant, Henry (Milon)
See Montherlant, Henry (Milon) de

Demosthenes 384B.C.-322B.C. ... **CMLC 13**

de Natale, Francine
See Malzberg, Barry N(athaniel)

Denby, Edwin (Orr) 1903-1983..... **CLC 48**
See also CA 138; 110

Denis, Julio
See Cortazar, Julio

Denmark, Harrison
See Zelazny, Roger (Joseph)

Dennis, John 1658-1734........... **LC 11**
See also DLB 101

Dennis, Nigel (Forbes) 1912-1989.... **CLC 8**
See also CA 25-28R; 129; DLB 13, 15;
MTCW

De Palma, Brian (Russell) 1940-.... **CLC 20**
See also CA 109

De Quincey, Thomas 1785-1859 ... **NCLC 4**
See also CDBLB 1789-1832; DLB 110; 144

Deren, Eleanora 1908(?)-1961
See Deren, Maya
See also CA 111

Deren, Maya .... **CLC 16**
See also Deren, Eleanora

Derleth, August (William)
1909-1971 .... **CLC 31**
See also CA 1-4R; 29-32R; CANR 4;
DLB 9; SATA 5

Der Nister 1884-1950............ **TCLC 56**

de Routisie, Albert
See Aragon, Louis

Derrida, Jacques 1930-......... **CLC 24, 87**
See also CA 124; 127

Derry Down Derry
See Lear, Edward

Dersonnes, Jacques
See Simenon, Georges (Jacques Christian)

Desai, Anita 1937-...... **CLC 19, 37; DAB**
See also CA 81-84; CANR 33; MTCW;
SATA 63

de Saint-Luc, Jean
See Glassco, John

de Saint Roman, Arnaud
See Aragon, Louis

Descartes, Rene 1596-1650 .... **LC 20**

De Sica, Vittorio 1901(?)-1974 ..... **CLC 20**
See also CA 117

Desnos, Robert 1900-1945....... **TCLC 22**
See also CA 121

Destouches, Louis-Ferdinand
1894-1961 .... **CLC 9, 15**
See also Celine, Louis-Ferdinand
See also CA 85-88; CANR 28; MTCW

Deutsch, Babette 1895-1982 .... **CLC 18**
See also CA 1-4R; 108; CANR 4; DLB 45;
SATA 1; SATA-Obit 33

Devenant, William 1606-1649 ...... **LC 13**

Devkota, Laxmiprasad
1909-1959 .... **TCLC 23**
See also CA 123

De Voto, Bernard (Augustine)
1897-1955 .... **TCLC 29**
See also CA 113; DLB 9

De Vries, Peter
1910-1993 .... **CLC 1, 2, 3, 7, 10, 28, 46**
See also CA 17-20R; 142; CANR 41;
DLB 6; DLBY 82; MTCW

Dexter, Martin
See Faust, Frederick (Schiller)

Dexter, Pete 1943-............ **CLC 34, 55**
See also BEST 89:2; CA 127; 131; MTCW

Diamano, Silmang
See Senghor, Leopold Sedar

Diamond, Neil 1941- .... **CLC 30**
See also CA 108

Diaz del Castillo, Bernal 1496-1584 .. **LC 31**

di Bassetto, Corno
See Shaw, George Bernard

Dick, Philip K(indred)
1928-1982 .... **CLC 10, 30, 72**
See also CA 49-52; 106; CANR 2, 16;
DLB 8; MTCW

Dickens, Charles (John Huffam)
1812-1870 ...... **NCLC 3, 8, 18, 26, 37,
50; DA; DAB; SSC 17; WLC**
See also CDBLB 1832-1890; DLB 21, 55,
70; JRDA; MAICYA; SATA 15

Dickey, James (Lafayette)
1923- .... **CLC 1, 2, 4, 7, 10, 15, 47**
See also AITN 1, 2; CA 9-12R; CABS 2;
CANR 10, 48; CDALB 1968-1988;
DLB 5; DLBD 7; DLBY 82, 93; MTCW

Dickey, William 1928-1994 ...... **CLC 3, 28**
See also CA 9-12R; 145; CANR 24; DLB 5

Dickinson, Charles 1951-.......... **CLC 49**
See also CA 128

Dickinson, Emily (Elizabeth)
1830-1886 .... **NCLC 21; DA; DAB;
PC 1; WLC**
See also CDALB 1865-1917; DLB 1;
SATA 29

Dickinson, Peter (Malcolm)
1927-................... **CLC 12, 35**
See also AAYA 9; CA 41-44R; CANR 31;
CLR 29; DLB 87; JRDA; MAICYA;
SATA 5, 62

Dickson, Carr
See Carr, John Dickson

Dickson, Carter
See Carr, John Dickson

Diderot, Denis 1713-1784 .... **LC 26**

Didion, Joan 1934-..... **CLC 1, 3, 8, 14, 32**
See also AITN 1; CA 5-8R; CANR 14;
CDALB 1968-1988; DLB 2; DLBY 81,
86; MTCW

Dietrich, Robert
See Hunt, E(verette) Howard, (Jr.)

Dillard, Annie 1945-............ **CLC 9, 60**
See also AAYA 6; CA 49-52; CANR 3, 43;
DLBY 80; MTCW; SATA 10

Dillard, R(ichard) H(enry) W(ilde)
1937-...................... **CLC 5**
See also CA 21-24R; CAAS 7; CANR 10;
DLB 5

Dillon, Eilis 1920-1994............ **CLC 17**
See also CA 9-12R; 147; CAAS 3; CANR 4,
38; CLR 26; MAICYA; SATA 2, 74;
SATA-Obit 83

Dimont, Penelope
See Mortimer, Penelope (Ruth)

Dinesen, Isak.......... **CLC 10, 29; SSC 7**
See also Blixen, Karen (Christentze
Dinesen)

Ding Ling...................... **CLC 68**
See also Chiang Pin-chin

Disch, Thomas M(ichael) 1940-... **CLC 7, 36**
See also CA 21-24R; CAAS 4; CANR 17,
36; CLR 18; DLB 8; MAICYA; MTCW;
SAAS 15; SATA 54

Disch, Tom
See Disch, Thomas M(ichael)

d'Isly, Georges
See Simenon, Georges (Jacques Christian)

Disraeli, Benjamin 1804-1881 .. **NCLC 2, 39**
See also DLB 21, 55

Ditcum, Steve
See Crumb, R(obert)

Dixon, Paige
See Corcoran, Barbara

Dixon, Stephen 1936-..... **CLC 52; SSC 16**
See also CA 89-92; CANR 17, 40; DLB 130

Dobell, Sydney Thompson
1824-1874 .... **NCLC 43**
See also DLB 32

Doblin, Alfred .... **TCLC 13**
See also Doeblin, Alfred

Dobrolyubov, Nikolai Alexandrovich
1836-1861 .... **NCLC 5**

Dobyns, Stephen 1941-............ **CLC 37**
See also CA 45-48; CANR 2, 18

Doctorow, E(dgar) L(aurence)
1931- ..... **CLC 6, 11, 15, 18, 37, 44, 65**
See also AITN 2; BEST 89:3; CA 45-48;
CANR 2, 33; CDALB 1968-1988; DLB 2,
28; DLBY 80; MTCW

Dodgson, Charles Lutwidge 1832-1898
See Carroll, Lewis
See also CLR 2; DA; DAB; MAICYA;
YABC 2

Dodson, Owen (Vincent)
1914-1983 .... **CLC 79; BLC**
See also BW 1; CA 65-68; 110; CANR 24;
DLB 76

Doeblin, Alfred 1878-1957........ **TCLC 13**
See also Doblin, Alfred
See also CA 110; 141; DLB 66

Doerr, Harriet 1910- . . . . **CLC 34**
See also CA 117; 122; CANR 47

Domecq, H(onorio) Bustos
See Bioy Casares, Adolfo; Borges, Jorge
Luis

Domini, Rey
See Lorde, Audre (Geraldine)

Dominique
See Proust, (Valentin-Louis-George-Eugene-)
Marcel

Don, A
See Stephen, Leslie

Donaldson, Stephen R. 1947- . . . . **CLC 46**
See also CA 89-92; CANR 13

Donleavy, J(ames) P(atrick)
1926- . . . . **CLC 1, 4, 6, 10, 45**
See also AITN 2; CA 9-12R; CANR 24, 49;
DLB 6; MTCW

Donne, John
1572-1631 . . **LC 10, 24; DA; DAB; PC 1**
See also CDBLB Before 1660; DLB 121,
151

Donnell, David 1939(?)- . . . . **CLC 34**

Donoghue, P. S.
See Hunt, E(verette) Howard, (Jr.)

Donoso (Yanez), Jose
1924- . . . . **CLC 4, 8, 11, 32; HLC**
See also CA 81-84; CANR 32; DLB 113;
HW; MTCW

Donovan, John 1928-1992 . . . . **CLC 35**
See also CA 97-100; 137; CLR 3;
MAICYA; SATA 72; SATA-Brief 29

Don Roberto
See Cunninghame Graham, R(obert)
B(ontine)

Doolittle, Hilda
1886-1961 . . . . . **CLC 3, 8, 14, 31, 34, 73;
DA; PC 5; WLC**
See also H. D.
See also CA 97-100; CANR 35; DLB 4, 45;
MTCW

Dorfman, Ariel 1942- . . . . **CLC 48, 77; HLC**
See also CA 124; 130; HW

Dorn, Edward (Merton) 1929- . . . **CLC 10, 18**
See also CA 93-96; CANR 42; DLB 5

Dorsan, Luc
See Simenon, Georges (Jacques Christian)

Dorsange, Jean
See Simenon, Georges (Jacques Christian)

Dos Passos, John (Roderigo)
1896-1970 . . . . . . **CLC 1, 4, 8, 11, 15, 25,
34, 82; DA; DAB; WLC**
See also CA 1-4R; 29-32R; CANR 3;
CDALB 1929-1941; DLB 4, 9; DLBD 1;
MTCW

Dossage, Jean
See Simenon, Georges (Jacques Christian)

Dostoevsky, Fedor Mikhailovich
1821-1881 . . . . . . **NCLC 2, 7, 21, 33, 43;
DA; DAB; SSC 2; WLC**

Doughty, Charles M(ontagu)
1843-1926 . . . . **TCLC 27**
See also CA 115; DLB 19, 57

Douglas, Ellen . . . . **CLC 73**
See also Haxton, Josephine Ayres;
Williamson, Ellen Douglas

Douglas, Gavin 1475(?)-1522 . . . . **LC 20**

Douglas, Keith 1920-1944 . . . . **TCLC 40**
See also DLB 27

Douglas, Leonard
See Bradbury, Ray (Douglas)

Douglas, Michael
See Crichton, (John) Michael

Douglass, Frederick
1817(?)-1895 . . . . **NCLC 7; BLC; DA;
WLC**
See also CDALB 1640-1865; DLB 1, 43, 50,
79; SATA 29

Dourado, (Waldomiro Freitas) Autran
1926- . . . . **CLC 23, 60**
See also CA 25-28R; CANR 34

Dourado, Waldomiro Autran
See Dourado, (Waldomiro Freitas) Autran

Dove, Rita (Frances)
1952- . . . . **CLC 50, 81; PC 6**
See also BW 2; CA 109; CAAS 19;
CANR 27, 42; DLB 120

Dowell, Coleman 1925-1985 . . . . **CLC 60**
See also CA 25-28R; 117; CANR 10;
DLB 130

Dowson, Ernest Christopher
1867-1900 . . . . **TCLC 4**
See also CA 105; DLB 19, 135

Doyle, A. Conan
See Doyle, Arthur Conan

Doyle, Arthur Conan
1859-1930 . . . . **TCLC 7; DA; DAB;
SSC 12; WLC**
See also AAYA 14; CA 104; 122;
CDBLB 1890-1914; DLB 18, 70, 156;
MTCW; SATA 24

Doyle, Conan
See Doyle, Arthur Conan

Doyle, John
See Graves, Robert (von Ranke)

Doyle, Roddy 1958(?)- . . . . **CLC 81**
See also AAYA 14; CA 143

Doyle, Sir A. Conan
See Doyle, Arthur Conan

Doyle, Sir Arthur Conan
See Doyle, Arthur Conan

Dr. A
See Asimov, Isaac; Silverstein, Alvin

Drabble, Margaret
1939- . . **CLC 2, 3, 5, 8, 10, 22, 53; DAB**
See also CA 13-16R; CANR 18, 35;
CDBLB 1960 to Present; DLB 14, 155;
MTCW; SATA 48

Drapier, M. B.
See Swift, Jonathan

Drayham, James
See Mencken, H(enry) L(ouis)

Drayton, Michael 1563-1631 . . . . **LC 8**

Dreadstone, Carl
See Campbell, (John) Ramsey

Dreiser, Theodore (Herman Albert)
1871-1945 . . . . . . **TCLC 10, 18, 35; DA;
WLC**
See also CA 106; 132; CDALB 1865-1917;
DLB 9, 12, 102, 137; DLBD 1; MTCW

Drexler, Rosalyn 1926- . . . . **CLC 2, 6**
See also CA 81-84

Dreyer, Carl Theodor 1889-1968 . . . . **CLC 16**
See also CA 116

Drieu la Rochelle, Pierre(-Eugene)
1893-1945 . . . . **TCLC 21**
See also CA 117; DLB 72

Drinkwater, John 1882-1937 . . . . . . **TCLC 57**
See also CA 109; DLB 10, 19, 149

Drop Shot
See Cable, George Washington

Droste-Hulshoff, Annette Freiin von
1797-1848 . . . . **NCLC 3**
See also DLB 133

Drummond, Walter
See Silverberg, Robert

Drummond, William Henry
1854-1907 . . . . **TCLC 25**
See also DLB 92

Drummond de Andrade, Carlos
1902-1987 . . . . **CLC 18**
See also Andrade, Carlos Drummond de
See also CA 132; 123

Drury, Allen (Stuart) 1918- . . . . **CLC 37**
See also CA 57-60; CANR 18

Dryden, John
1631-1700 . . . . **LC 3, 21; DA; DAB;
DC 3; WLC**
See also CDBLB 1660-1789; DLB 80, 101,
131

Duberman, Martin 1930- . . . . **CLC 8**
See also CA 1-4R; CANR 2

Dubie, Norman (Evans) 1945- . . . . . . **CLC 36**
See also CA 69-72; CANR 12; DLB 120

Du Bois, W(illiam) E(dward) B(urghardt)
1868-1963 . . . . . . **CLC 1, 2, 13, 64; BLC;
DA; WLC**
See also BW 1; CA 85-88; CANR 34;
CDALB 1865-1917; DLB 47, 50, 91;
MTCW; SATA 42

Dubus, Andre 1936- . . . **CLC 13, 36; SSC 15**
See also CA 21-24R; CANR 17; DLB 130

Duca Minimo
See D'Annunzio, Gabriele

Ducharme, Rejean 1941- . . . . **CLC 74**
See also DLB 60

Duclos, Charles Pinot 1704-1772 . . . . . **LC 1**

Dudek, Louis 1918- . . . . **CLC 11, 19**
See also CA 45-48; CAAS 14; CANR 1;
DLB 88

Duerrenmatt, Friedrich
1921-1990 . . . . . . **CLC 1, 4, 8, 11, 15, 43**
See also CA 17-20R; CANR 33; DLB 69,
124; MTCW

Duffy, Bruce (?)- . . . . **CLC 50**

Duffy, Maureen 1933- . . . . **CLC 37**
See also CA 25-28R; CANR 33; DLB 14;
MTCW

Dugan, Alan 1923- . . . . **CLC 2, 6**
See also CA 81-84; DLB 5

Eiseley, Loren Corey 1907-1977 . . . . . **CLC 7**
See also AAYA 5; CA 1-4R; 73-76;
CANR 6

Eisenstadt, Jill 1963- . . . . **CLC 50**
See also CA 140

Eisenstein, Sergei (Mikhailovich)
1898-1948 . . . . **TCLC 57**
See also CA 114

Eisner, Simon
See Kornbluth, C(yril) M.

Ekeloef, (Bengt) Gunnar
1907-1968 . . . . **CLC 27**
See also CA 123; 25-28R

Ekelof, (Bengt) Gunnar
See Ekeloef, (Bengt) Gunnar

Ekwensi, C. O. D.
See Ekwensi, Cyprian (Odiatu Duaka)

Ekwensi, Cyprian (Odiatu Duaka)
1921- . . . . **CLC 4; BLC**
See also BW 2; CA 29-32R; CANR 18, 42;
DLB 117; MTCW; SATA 66

Elaine . . . . **TCLC 18**
See also Leverson, Ada

El Crummo
See Crumb, R(obert)

Elia
See Lamb, Charles

Eliade, Mircea 1907-1986 . . . . **CLC 19**
See also CA 65-68; 119; CANR 30; MTCW

Eliot, A. D.
See Jewett, (Theodora) Sarah Orne

Eliot, Alice
See Jewett, (Theodora) Sarah Orne

Eliot, Dan
See Silverberg, Robert

Eliot, George
1819-1880 . . . . . **NCLC 4, 13, 23, 41, 49;
DA; DAB; WLC**
See also CDBLB 1832-1890; DLB 21, 35, 55

Eliot, John 1604-1690 . . . . **LC 5**
See also DLB 24

Eliot, T(homas) S(tearns)
1888-1965 . . . . . **CLC 1, 2, 3, 6, 9, 10, 13,
15, 24, 34, 41, 55, 57; DA; DAB; PC 5;
WLC 2**
See also CA 5-8R; 25-28R; CANR 41;
CDALB 1929-1941; DLB 7, 10, 45, 63;
DLBY 88; MTCW

Elizabeth 1866-1941 . . . . **TCLC 41**

Elkin, Stanley L(awrence)
1930-1995 . . . . . . **CLC 4, 6, 9, 14, 27, 51;
SSC 12**
See also CA 9-12R; 148; CANR 8, 46;
DLB 2, 28; DLBY 80; MTCW

Elledge, Scott . . . . **CLC 34**

Elliott, Don
See Silverberg, Robert

Elliott, George P(aul) 1918-1980 . . . . . **CLC 2**
See also CA 1-4R; 97-100; CANR 2

Elliott, Janice 1931- . . . . **CLC 47**
See also CA 13-16R; CANR 8, 29; DLB 14

Elliott, Sumner Locke 1917-1991 . . . **CLC 38**
See also CA 5-8R; 134; CANR 2, 21

Elliott, William
See Bradbury, Ray (Douglas)

Ellis, A. E. . . . . **CLC 7**

Ellis, Alice Thomas . . . . **CLC 40**
See also Haycraft, Anna

Ellis, Bret Easton 1964- . . . . **CLC 39, 71**
See also AAYA 2; CA 118; 123

Ellis, (Henry) Havelock
1859-1939 . . . . **TCLC 14**
See also CA 109

Ellis, Landon
See Ellison, Harlan (Jay)

Ellis, Trey 1962- . . . . **CLC 55**
See also CA 146

Ellison, Harlan (Jay)
1934- . . . . **CLC 1, 13, 42; SSC 14**
See also CA 5-8R; CANR 5, 46; DLB 8;
MTCW

Ellison, Ralph (Waldo)
1914-1994 . . . . **CLC 1, 3, 11, 54, 86;
BLC; DA; DAB; WLC**
See also BW 1; CA 9-12R; 145; CANR 24;
CDALB 1941-1968; DLB 2, 76;
DLBY 94; MTCW

Ellmann, Lucy (Elizabeth) 1956- . . . . **CLC 61**
See also CA 128

Ellmann, Richard (David)
1918-1987 . . . . **CLC 50**
See also BEST 89:2; CA 1-4R; 122;
CANR 2, 28; DLB 103; DLBY 87;
MTCW

Elman, Richard 1934- . . . . **CLC 19**
See also CA 17-20R; CAAS 3; CANR 47

Elron
See Hubbard, L(afayette) Ron(ald)

Eluard, Paul . . . . **TCLC 7, 41**
See also Grindel, Eugene

Elyot, Sir Thomas 1490(?)-1546 . . . . . **LC 11**

Elytis, Odysseus 1911- . . . . **CLC 15, 49**
See also CA 102; MTCW

Emecheta, (Florence Onye) Buchi
1944- . . . . **CLC 14, 48; BLC**
See also BW 2; CA 81-84; CANR 27;
DLB 117; MTCW; SATA 66

Emerson, Ralph Waldo
1803-1882 . . . . . **NCLC 1, 38; DA; DAB;
WLC**
See also CDALB 1640-1865; DLB 1, 59, 73

Eminescu, Mihail 1850-1889 . . . . . **NCLC 33**

Empson, William
1906-1984 . . . . **CLC 3, 8, 19, 33, 34**
See also CA 17-20R; 112; CANR 31;
DLB 20; MTCW

Enchi Fumiko (Ueda) 1905-1986 . . . . **CLC 31**
See also CA 129; 121

Ende, Michael (Andreas Helmuth)
1929- . . . . **CLC 31**
See also CA 118; 124; CANR 36; CLR 14;
DLB 75; MAICYA; SATA 61;
SATA-Brief 42

Endo, Shusaku 1923- . . . . . **CLC 7, 14, 19, 54**
See also CA 29-32R; CANR 21; MTCW

Engel, Marian 1933-1985 . . . . **CLC 36**
See also CA 25-28R; CANR 12; DLB 53

Engelhardt, Frederick
See Hubbard, L(afayette) Ron(ald)

Enright, D(ennis) J(oseph)
1920- . . . . **CLC 4, 8, 31**
See also CA 1-4R; CANR 1, 42; DLB 27;
SATA 25

Enzensberger, Hans Magnus
1929- . . . . **CLC 43**
See also CA 116; 119

Ephron, Nora 1941- . . . . **CLC 17, 31**
See also AITN 2; CA 65-68; CANR 12, 39

Epsilon
See Betjeman, John

Epstein, Daniel Mark 1948- . . . . **CLC 7**
See also CA 49-52; CANR 2

Epstein, Jacob 1956- . . . . **CLC 19**
See also CA 114

Epstein, Joseph 1937- . . . . **CLC 39**
See also CA 112; 119

Epstein, Leslie 1938- . . . . **CLC 27**
See also CA 73-76; CAAS 12; CANR 23

Equiano, Olaudah
1745(?)-1797 . . . . **LC 16; BLC**
See also DLB 37, 50

Erasmus, Desiderius 1469(?)-1536. . . . **LC 16**

Erdman, Paul E(mil) 1932- . . . . **CLC 25**
See also AITN 1; CA 61-64; CANR 13, 43

Erdrich, Louise 1954- . . . . **CLC 39, 54**
See also AAYA 10; BEST 89:1; CA 114;
CANR 41; DLB 152; MTCW; NNAL

Erenburg, Ilya (Grigoryevich)
See Ehrenburg, Ilya (Grigoryevich)

Erickson, Stephen Michael 1950-
See Erickson, Steve
See also CA 129

Erickson, Steve . . . . **CLC 64**
See also Erickson, Stephen Michael

Ericson, Walter
See Fast, Howard (Melvin)

Eriksson, Buntel
See Bergman, (Ernst) Ingmar

Ernaux, Annie 1940- . . . . **CLC 88**
See also CA 147

Eschenbach, Wolfram von
See Wolfram von Eschenbach

Eseki, Bruno
See Mphahlele, Ezekiel

Esenin, Sergei (Alexandrovich)
1895-1925 . . . . **TCLC 4**
See also CA 104

Eshleman, Clayton 1935- . . . . **CLC 7**
See also CA 33-36R; CAAS 6; DLB 5

Espriella, Don Manuel Alvarez
See Southey, Robert

Espriu, Salvador 1913-1985 . . . . **CLC 9**
See also CA 115; DLB 134

Espronceda, Jose de 1808-1842 . . . **NCLC 39**

Esse, James
See Stephens, James

Esterbrook, Tom
See Hubbard, L(afayette) Ron(ald)

Estleman, Loren D. 1952- . . . . **CLC 48**
See also CA 85-88; CANR 27; MTCW

Feydeau, Georges (Leon Jules Marie)
 1862-1921 . . . . TCLC 22
See also CA 113

Ficino, Marsilio 1433-1499 . . . . LC 12

Fiedeler, Hans
See Doeblin, Alfred

Fiedler, Leslie A(aron)
 1917- . . . . CLC 4, 13, 24
See also CA 9-12R; CANR 7; DLB 28, 67;
 MTCW

Field, Andrew 1938- . . . . CLC 44
See also CA 97-100; CANR 25

Field, Eugene 1850-1895 . . . . NCLC 3
See also DLB 23, 42, 140; MAICYA;
 SATA 16

Field, Gans T.
See Wellman, Manly Wade

Field, Michael . . . . TCLC 43

Field, Peter
See Hobson, Laura Z(ametkin)

Fielding, Henry
 1707-1754 . . . . . . LC 1; DA; DAB; WLC
See also CDBLB 1660-1789; DLB 39, 84,
 101

Fielding, Sarah 1710-1768 . . . . LC 1
See also DLB 39

Fierstein, Harvey (Forbes) 1954- . . . CLC 33
See also CA 123; 129

Figes, Eva 1932- . . . . CLC 31
See also CA 53-56; CANR 4, 44; DLB 14

Finch, Robert (Duer Claydon)
 1900- . . . . CLC 18
See also CA 57-60; CANR 9, 24, 49;
 DLB 88

Findley, Timothy 1930- . . . . CLC 27
See also CA 25-28R; CANR 12, 42;
 DLB 53

Fink, William
See Mencken, H(enry) L(ouis)

Firbank, Louis 1942-
See Reed, Lou
See also CA 117

Firbank, (Arthur Annesley) Ronald
 1886-1926 . . . . TCLC 1
See also CA 104; DLB 36

Fisher, M(ary) F(rances) K(ennedy)
 1908-1992 . . . . CLC 76, 87
See also CA 77-80; 138; CANR 44

Fisher, Roy 1930- . . . . CLC 25
See also CA 81-84; CAAS 10; CANR 16;
 DLB 40

Fisher, Rudolph
 1897-1934 . . . . TCLC 11; BLC
See also BW 1; CA 107; 124; DLB 51, 102

Fisher, Vardis (Alvero) 1895-1968. . . . CLC 7
See also CA 5-8R; 25-28R; DLB 9

Fiske, Tarleton
See Bloch, Robert (Albert)

Fitch, Clarke
See Sinclair, Upton (Beall)

Fitch, John IV
See Cormier, Robert (Edmund)

Fitzgerald, Captain Hugh
See Baum, L(yman) Frank

FitzGerald, Edward 1809-1883 . . . . NCLC 9
See also DLB 32

Fitzgerald, F(rancis) Scott (Key)
 1896-1940 . . . . TCLC 1, 6, 14, 28, 55;
                         DA; DAB; SSC 6; WLC
See also AITN 1; CA 110; 123;
 CDALB 1917-1929; DLB 4, 9, 86;
 DLBD 1; DLBY 81; MTCW

Fitzgerald, Penelope 1916-. . . CLC 19, 51, 61
See also CA 85-88; CAAS 10; DLB 14

Fitzgerald, Robert (Stuart)
 1910-1985 . . . . CLC 39
See also CA 1-4R; 114; CANR 1; DLBY 80

FitzGerald, Robert D(avid)
 1902-1987 . . . . CLC 19
See also CA 17-20R

Fitzgerald, Zelda (Sayre)
 1900-1948 . . . . TCLC 52
See also CA 117; 126; DLBY 84

Flanagan, Thomas (James Bonner)
 1923- . . . . CLC 25, 52
See also CA 108; DLBY 80; MTCW

Flaubert, Gustave
 1821-1880 . . . . NCLC 2, 10, 19; DA;
                         DAB; SSC 11; WLC
See also DLB 119

Flecker, (Herman) James Elroy
 1884-1915 . . . . TCLC 43
See also CA 109; DLB 10, 19

Fleming, Ian (Lancaster)
 1908-1964 . . . . CLC 3, 30
See also CA 5-8R; CDBLB 1945-1960;
 DLB 87; MTCW; SATA 9

Fleming, Thomas (James) 1927- . . . . CLC 37
See also CA 5-8R; CANR 10; SATA 8

Fletcher, John Gould 1886-1950 . . . TCLC 35
See also CA 107; DLB 4, 45

Fleur, Paul
See Pohl, Frederik

Flooglebuckle, Al
See Spiegelman, Art

Flying Officer X
See Bates, H(erbert) E(rnest)

Fo, Dario 1926-. . . . . CLC 32
See also CA 116; 128; MTCW

Fogarty, Jonathan Titulescu Esq.
See Farrell, James T(homas)

Folke, Will
See Bloch, Robert (Albert)

Follett, Ken(neth Martin) 1949- . . . . CLC 18
See also AAYA 6; BEST 89:4; CA 81-84;
 CANR 13, 33; DLB 87; DLBY 81;
 MTCW

Fontane, Theodor 1819-1898 . . . . . NCLC 26
See also DLB 129

Foote, Horton 1916- . . . . CLC 51
See also CA 73-76; CANR 34; DLB 26

Foote, Shelby 1916- . . . . CLC 75
See also CA 5-8R; CANR 3, 45; DLB 2, 17

Forbes, Esther 1891-1967. . . . . CLC 12
See also CA 13-14; 25-28R; CAP 1;
 CLR 27; DLB 22; JRDA; MAICYA;
 SATA 2

Forche, Carolyn (Louise)
 1950- . . . . CLC 25, 83, 86; PC 10
See also CA 109; 117; DLB 5

Ford, Elbur
See Hibbert, Eleanor Alice Burford

Ford, Ford Madox
 1873-1939 . . . . TCLC 1, 15, 39, 57
See also CA 104; 132; CDBLB 1914-1945;
 DLB 34, 98; MTCW

Ford, John 1895-1973. . . . . CLC 16
See also CA 45-48

Ford, Richard 1944- . . . . CLC 46
See also CA 69-72; CANR 11, 47

Ford, Webster
See Masters, Edgar Lee

Foreman, Richard 1937-. . . . . CLC 50
See also CA 65-68; CANR 32

Forester, C(ecil) S(cott)
 1899-1966 . . . . CLC 35
See also CA 73-76; 25-28R; SATA 13

Forez
See Mauriac, Francois (Charles)

Forman, James Douglas 1932-. . . . . . CLC 21
See also CA 9-12R; CANR 4, 19, 42;
 JRDA; MAICYA; SATA 8, 70

Fornes, Maria Irene 1930-. . . . . . . CLC 39, 61
See also CA 25-28R; CANR 28; DLB 7;
 HW; MTCW

Forrest, Leon 1937- . . . . CLC 4
See also BW 2; CA 89-92; CAAS 7;
 CANR 25; DLB 33

Forster, E(dward) M(organ)
 1879-1970 . . . . . CLC 1, 2, 3, 4, 9, 10, 13,
                    15, 22, 45, 77; DA; DAB; WLC
See also AAYA 2; CA 13-14; 25-28R;
 CANR 45; CAP 1; CDBLB 1914-1945;
 DLB 34, 98; DLBD 10; MTCW;
 SATA 57

Forster, John 1812-1876 . . . . NCLC 11
See also DLB 144

Forsyth, Frederick 1938-. . . . . . . CLC 2, 5, 36
See also BEST 89:4; CA 85-88; CANR 38;
 DLB 87; MTCW

Forten, Charlotte L. . . . . TCLC 16; BLC
See also Grimke, Charlotte L(ottie) Forten
See also DLB 50

Foscolo, Ugo 1778-1827. . . . . NCLC 8

Fosse, Bob . . . . CLC 20
See also Fosse, Robert Louis

Fosse, Robert Louis 1927-1987
See Fosse, Bob
See also CA 110; 123

Foster, Stephen Collins
 1826-1864 . . . . NCLC 26

Foucault, Michel
 1926-1984 . . . . CLC 31, 34, 69
See also CA 105; 113; CANR 34; MTCW

Fouque, Friedrich (Heinrich Karl) de la Motte
 1777-1843 . . . . NCLC 2
See also DLB 90

Fourier, Charles 1772-1837 . . . . . . NCLC 51

Fournier, Henri Alban 1886-1914
See Alain-Fournier
See also CA 104

Fournier, Pierre 1916-. . . . . **CLC 11**
　　See also Gascar, Pierre
　　See also CA 89-92; CANR 16, 40

Fowles, John
　　1926- . . . . . . **CLC 1, 2, 3, 4, 6, 9, 10, 15,**
　　　　　　　　　　　　　　　　33, 87; DAB
　　See also CA 5-8R; CANR 25; CDBLB 1960
　　to Present; DLB 14, 139; MTCW;
　　SATA 22

Fox, Paula 1923-. . . . . **CLC 2, 8**
　　See also AAYA 3; CA 73-76; CANR 20,
　　36; CLR 1; DLB 52; JRDA; MAICYA;
　　MTCW; SATA 17, 60

Fox, William Price (Jr.) 1926- . . . . . **CLC 22**
　　See also CA 17-20R; CAAS 19; CANR 11;
　　DLB 2; DLBY 81

Foxe, John 1516(?)-1587 . . . . **LC 14**

Frame, Janet . . . . **CLC 2, 3, 6, 22, 66**
　　See also Clutha, Janet Paterson Frame

France, Anatole. . . . . **TCLC 9**
　　See also Thibault, Jacques Anatole Francois
　　See also DLB 123

Francis, Claude 19(?)- . . . . **CLC 50**

Francis, Dick 1920- . . . . **CLC 2, 22, 42**
　　See also AAYA 5; BEST 89:3; CA 5-8R;
　　CANR 9, 42; CDBLB 1960 to Present;
　　DLB 87; MTCW

Francis, Robert (Churchill)
　　1901-1987 . . . . **CLC 15**
　　See also CA 1-4R; 123; CANR 1

Frank, Anne(lies Marie)
　　1929-1945 . . **TCLC 17; DA; DAB; WLC**
　　See also AAYA 12; CA 113; 133; MTCW;
　　SATA-Brief 42

Frank, Elizabeth 1945-. . . . . **CLC 39**
　　See also CA 121; 126

Franklin, Benjamin
　　See Hasek, Jaroslav (Matej Frantisek)

Franklin, Benjamin
　　1706-1790 . . . . **LC 25; DA; DAB**
　　See also CDALB 1640-1865; DLB 24, 43,
　　73

Franklin, (Stella Maraia Sarah) Miles
　　1879-1954 . . . . **TCLC 7**
　　See also CA 104

Fraser, (Lady) Antonia (Pakenham)
　　1932- . . . . **CLC 32**
　　See also CA 85-88; CANR 44; MTCW;
　　SATA-Brief 32

Fraser, George MacDonald 1925-. . . . **CLC 7**
　　See also CA 45-48; CANR 2, 48

Fraser, Sylvia 1935-. . . . . **CLC 64**
　　See also CA 45-48; CANR 1, 16

Frayn, Michael 1933-. . . . . . **CLC 3, 7, 31, 47**
　　See also CA 5-8R; CANR 30; DLB 13, 14;
　　MTCW

Fraze, Candida (Merrill) 1945- . . . . . **CLC 50**
　　See also CA 126

Frazer, J(ames) G(eorge)
　　1854-1941 . . . . **TCLC 32**
　　See also CA 118

Frazer, Robert Caine
　　See Creasey, John

Frazer, Sir James George
　　See Frazer, J(ames) G(eorge)

Frazier, Ian 1951-. . . . . **CLC 46**
　　See also CA 130

Frederic, Harold 1856-1898. . . . . . **NCLC 10**
　　See also DLB 12, 23

Frederick, John
　　See Faust, Frederick (Schiller)

Frederick the Great 1712-1786 . . . . . . **LC 14**

Fredro, Aleksander 1793-1876. . . . . **NCLC 8**

Freeling, Nicolas 1927- . . . . **CLC 38**
　　See also CA 49-52; CAAS 12; CANR 1, 17;
　　DLB 87

Freeman, Douglas Southall
　　1886-1953 . . . . **TCLC 11**
　　See also CA 109; DLB 17

Freeman, Judith 1946-. . . . . **CLC 55**
　　See also CA 148

Freeman, Mary Eleanor Wilkins
　　1852-1930 . . . . **TCLC 9; SSC 1**
　　See also CA 106; DLB 12, 78

Freeman, R(ichard) Austin
　　1862-1943 . . . . **TCLC 21**
　　See also CA 113; DLB 70

French, Albert 1943- . . . . **CLC 86**

French, Marilyn 1929-. . . . . . **CLC 10, 18, 60**
　　See also CA 69-72; CANR 3, 31; MTCW

French, Paul
　　See Asimov, Isaac

Freneau, Philip Morin 1752-1832 . . **NCLC 1**
　　See also DLB 37, 43

Freud, Sigmund 1856-1939 . . . . **TCLC 52**
　　See also CA 115; 133; MTCW

Friedan, Betty (Naomi) 1921-. . . . . . **CLC 74**
　　See also CA 65-68; CANR 18, 45; MTCW

Friedlaender, Saul 1932- . . . . **CLC 90**
　　See also CA 117; 130

Friedman, B(ernard) H(arper)
　　1926- . . . . **CLC 7**
　　See also CA 1-4R; CANR 3, 48

Friedman, Bruce Jay 1930-. . . . **CLC 3, 5, 56**
　　See also CA 9-12R; CANR 25; DLB 2, 28

Friel, Brian 1929-. . . . . **CLC 5, 42, 59**
　　See also CA 21-24R; CANR 33; DLB 13;
　　MTCW

Friis-Baastad, Babbis Ellinor
　　1921-1970 . . . . **CLC 12**
　　See also CA 17-20R; 134; SATA 7

Frisch, Max (Rudolf)
　　1911-1991 . . . . . **CLC 3, 9, 14, 18, 32, 44**
　　See also CA 85-88; 134; CANR 32;
　　DLB 69, 124; MTCW

Fromentin, Eugene (Samuel Auguste)
　　1820-1876 . . . . **NCLC 10**
　　See also DLB 123

Frost, Frederick
　　See Faust, Frederick (Schiller)

Frost, Robert (Lee)
　　1874-1963 . . . . **CLC 1, 3, 4, 9, 10, 13, 15,**
　　　　　　　　　　26, 34, 44; DA; DAB; PC 1; WLC
　　See also CA 89-92; CANR 33;
　　CDALB 1917-1929; DLB 54; DLBD 7;
　　MTCW; SATA 14

Froude, James Anthony
　　1818-1894 . . . . **NCLC 43**
　　See also DLB 18, 57, 144

Froy, Herald
　　See Waterhouse, Keith (Spencer)

Fry, Christopher 1907-. . . . . . . **CLC 2, 10, 14**
　　See also CA 17-20R; CANR 9, 30; DLB 13;
　　MTCW; SATA 66

Frye, (Herman) Northrop
　　1912-1991 . . . . **CLC 24, 70**
　　See also CA 5-8R; 133; CANR 8, 37;
　　DLB 67, 68; MTCW

Fuchs, Daniel 1909-1993 . . . . **CLC 8, 22**
　　See also CA 81-84; 142; CAAS 5;
　　CANR 40; DLB 9, 26, 28; DLBY 93

Fuchs, Daniel 1934-. . . . . **CLC 34**
　　See also CA 37-40R; CANR 14, 48

Fuentes, Carlos
　　1928- . . . . . . **CLC 3, 8, 10, 13, 22, 41, 60;**
　　　　　　　　　　　　　　DA; DAB; HLC; WLC
　　See also AAYA 4; AITN 2; CA 69-72;
　　CANR 10, 32; DLB 113; HW; MTCW

Fuentes, Gregorio Lopez y
　　See Lopez y Fuentes, Gregorio

Fugard, (Harold) Athol
　　1932- . . . . **CLC 5, 9, 14, 25, 40, 80; DC 3**
　　See also CA 85-88; CANR 32; MTCW

Fugard, Sheila 1932- . . . . **CLC 48**
　　See also CA 125

Fuller, Charles (H., Jr.)
　　1939-. . . . . **CLC 25; BLC; DC 1**
　　See also BW 2; CA 108; 112; DLB 38;
　　MTCW

Fuller, John (Leopold) 1937-. . . . . . . **CLC 62**
　　See also CA 21-24R; CANR 9, 44; DLB 40

Fuller, Margaret . . . . **NCLC 5, 50**
　　See also Ossoli, Sarah Margaret (Fuller
　　marchesa d')

Fuller, Roy (Broadbent)
　　1912-1991 . . . . **CLC 4, 28**
　　See also CA 5-8R; 135; CAAS 10; DLB 15,
　　20

Fulton, Alice 1952-. . . . . **CLC 52**
　　See also CA 116

Furphy, Joseph 1843-1912. . . . . . . **TCLC 25**

Fussell, Paul 1924-. . . . . **CLC 74**
　　See also BEST 90:1; CA 17-20R; CANR 8,
　　21, 35; MTCW

Futabatei, Shimei 1864-1909 . . . . . **TCLC 44**

Futrelle, Jacques 1875-1912 . . . . . . **TCLC 19**
　　See also CA 113

Gaboriau, Emile 1835-1873 . . . . . . **NCLC 14**

Gadda, Carlo Emilio 1893-1973 . . . . **CLC 11**
　　See also CA 89-92

Gaddis, William
　　1922- . . . . . **CLC 1, 3, 6, 8, 10, 19, 43, 86**
　　See also CA 17-20R; CANR 21, 48; DLB 2;
　　MTCW

Gaines, Ernest J(ames)
　　1933- . . . . **CLC 3, 11, 18, 86; BLC**
　　See also AITN 1; BW 2; CA 9-12R;
　　CANR 6, 24, 42; CDALB 1968-1988;
　　DLB 2, 33, 152; DLBY 80; MTCW

Gaitskill, Mary 1954-. . . . . **CLC 69**
　　See also CA 128

Galdos, Benito Perez
　　See Perez Galdos, Benito

Gale, Zona 1874-1938 . . . . **TCLC 7**
See also CA 105; DLB 9, 78

Galeano, Eduardo (Hughes) 1940- . . . **CLC 72**
See also CA 29-32R; CANR 13, 32; HW

Galiano, Juan Valera y Alcala
See Valera y Alcala-Galiano, Juan

Gallagher, Tess 1943- . . . . **CLC 18, 63; PC 9**
See also CA 106; DLB 120

Gallant, Mavis
1922- . . . . **CLC 7, 18, 38; SSC 5**
See also CA 69-72; CANR 29; DLB 53;
MTCW

Gallant, Roy A(rthur) 1924- . . . . **CLC 17**
See also CA 5-8R; CANR 4, 29; CLR 30;
MAICYA; SATA 4, 68

Gallico, Paul (William) 1897-1976 . . . **CLC 2**
See also AITN 1; CA 5-8R; 69-72;
CANR 23; DLB 9; MAICYA; SATA 13

Gallup, Ralph
See Whitemore, Hugh (John)

Galsworthy, John
1867-1933 . . . . . . **TCLC 1, 45; DA; DAB;
WLC 2**
See also CA 104; 141; CDBLB 1890-1914;
DLB 10, 34, 98

Galt, John 1779-1839 . . . . **NCLC 1**
See also DLB 99, 116

Galvin, James 1951- . . . . **CLC 38**
See also CA 108; CANR 26

Gamboa, Federico 1864-1939 . . . . . . **TCLC 36**

Gandhi, M. K.
See Gandhi, Mohandas Karamchand

Gandhi, Mahatma
See Gandhi, Mohandas Karamchand

Gandhi, Mohandas Karamchand
1869-1948 . . . . **TCLC 59**
See also CA 121; 132; MTCW

Gann, Ernest Kellogg 1910-1991 . . . . **CLC 23**
See also AITN 1; CA 1-4R; 136; CANR 1

Garcia, Cristina 1958- . . . . **CLC 76**
See also CA 141

Garcia Lorca, Federico
1898-1936 . . . **TCLC 1, 7, 49; DA; DAB;
DC 2; HLC; PC 3; WLC**
See also CA 104; 131; DLB 108; HW;
MTCW

Garcia Marquez, Gabriel (Jose)
1928- . . . . **CLC 2, 3, 8, 10, 15, 27, 47, 55,
68; DA; DAB; HLC; SSC 8; WLC**
See also AAYA 3; BEST 89:1, 90:4;
CA 33-36R; CANR 10, 28; DLB 113;
HW; MTCW

Gard, Janice
See Latham, Jean Lee

Gard, Roger Martin du
See Martin du Gard, Roger

Gardam, Jane 1928- . . . . **CLC 43**
See also CA 49-52; CANR 2, 18, 33;
CLR 12; DLB 14; MAICYA; MTCW;
SAAS 9; SATA 39, 76; SATA-Brief 28

Gardner, Herb . . . . **CLC 44**

Gardner, John (Champlin), Jr.
1933-1982 . . . . . **CLC 2, 3, 5, 7, 8, 10, 18,
28, 34; SSC 7**
See also AITN 1; CA 65-68; 107;
CANR 33; DLB 2; DLBY 82; MTCW;
SATA 40; SATA-Obit 31

Gardner, John (Edmund) 1926- . . . . . **CLC 30**
See also CA 103; CANR 15; MTCW

Gardner, Noel
See Kuttner, Henry

Gardons, S. S.
See Snodgrass, W(illiam) D(e Witt)

Garfield, Leon 1921- . . . . **CLC 12**
See also AAYA 8; CA 17-20R; CANR 38,
41; CLR 21; JRDA; MAICYA; SATA 1,
32, 76

Garland, (Hannibal) Hamlin
1860-1940 . . . . **TCLC 3; SSC 18**
See also CA 104; DLB 12, 71, 78

Garneau, (Hector de) Saint-Denys
1912-1943 . . . . **TCLC 13**
See also CA 111; DLB 88

Garner, Alan 1934- . . . . **CLC 17; DAB**
See also CA 73-76; CANR 15; CLR 20;
MAICYA; MTCW; SATA 18, 69

Garner, Hugh 1913-1979 . . . . **CLC 13**
See also CA 69-72; CANR 31; DLB 68

Garnett, David 1892-1981 . . . . **CLC 3**
See also CA 5-8R; 103; CANR 17; DLB 34

Garos, Stephanie
See Katz, Steve

Garrett, George (Palmer)
1929- . . . . **CLC 3, 11, 51**
See also CA 1-4R; CAAS 5; CANR 1, 42;
DLB 2, 5, 130, 152; DLBY 83

Garrick, David 1717-1779 . . . . **LC 15**
See also DLB 84

Garrigue, Jean 1914-1972 . . . . **CLC 2, 8**
See also CA 5-8R; 37-40R; CANR 20

Garrison, Frederick
See Sinclair, Upton (Beall)

Garth, Will
See Hamilton, Edmond; Kuttner, Henry

Garvey, Marcus (Moziah, Jr.)
1887-1940 . . . . **TCLC 41; BLC**
See also BW 1; CA 120; 124

Gary, Romain . . . . **CLC 25**
See also Kacew, Romain
See also DLB 83

Gascar, Pierre . . . . **CLC 11**
See also Fournier, Pierre

Gascoyne, David (Emery) 1916- . . . . **CLC 45**
See also CA 65-68; CANR 10, 28; DLB 20;
MTCW

Gaskell, Elizabeth Cleghorn
1810-1865 . . . . **NCLC 5; DAB**
See also CDBLB 1832-1890; DLB 21, 144

Gass, William H(oward)
1924- . . . **CLC 1, 2, 8, 11, 15, 39; SSC 12**
See also CA 17-20R; CANR 30; DLB 2;
MTCW

Gasset, Jose Ortega y
See Ortega y Gasset, Jose

Gates, Henry Louis, Jr. 1950- . . . . . . **CLC 65**
See also BW 2; CA 109; CANR 25; DLB 67

Gautier, Theophile
1811-1872 . . . . **NCLC 1; SSC 20**
See also DLB 119

Gawsworth, John
See Bates, H(erbert) E(rnest)

Gaye, Marvin (Penze) 1939-1984 . . . **CLC 26**
See also CA 112

Gebler, Carlo (Ernest) 1954- . . . . **CLC 39**
See also CA 119; 133

Gee, Maggie (Mary) 1948- . . . . **CLC 57**
See also CA 130

Gee, Maurice (Gough) 1931- . . . . **CLC 29**
See also CA 97-100; SATA 46

Gelbart, Larry (Simon) 1923- . . . **CLC 21, 61**
See also CA 73-76; CANR 45

Gelber, Jack 1932- . . . . **CLC 1, 6, 14, 79**
See also CA 1-4R; CANR 2; DLB 7

Gellhorn, Martha (Ellis) 1908- . . **CLC 14, 60**
See also CA 77-80; CANR 44; DLBY 82

Genet, Jean
1910-1986 . . . **CLC 1, 2, 5, 10, 14, 44, 46**
See also CA 13-16R; CANR 18; DLB 72;
DLBY 86; MTCW

Gent, Peter 1942- . . . . **CLC 29**
See also AITN 1; CA 89-92; DLBY 82

Gentlewoman in New England, A
See Bradstreet, Anne

Gentlewoman in Those Parts, A
See Bradstreet, Anne

George, Jean Craighead 1919- . . . . . . **CLC 35**
See also AAYA 8; CA 5-8R; CANR 25;
CLR 1; DLB 52; JRDA; MAICYA;
SATA 2, 68

George, Stefan (Anton)
1868-1933 . . . . **TCLC 2, 14**
See also CA 104

Georges, Georges Martin
See Simenon, Georges (Jacques Christian)

Gerhardi, William Alexander
See Gerhardie, William Alexander

Gerhardie, William Alexander
1895-1977 . . . . **CLC 5**
See also CA 25-28R; 73-76; CANR 18;
DLB 36

Gerstler, Amy 1956- . . . . **CLC 70**
See also CA 146

Gertler, T. . . . . **CLC 34**
See also CA 116; 121

Ghalib 1797-1869 . . . . **NCLC 39**

Ghelderode, Michel de
1898-1962 . . . . **CLC 6, 11**
See also CA 85-88; CANR 40

Ghiselin, Brewster 1903- . . . . **CLC 23**
See also CA 13-16R; CAAS 10; CANR 13

Ghose, Zulfikar 1935- . . . . **CLC 42**
See also CA 65-68

Ghosh, Amitav 1956- . . . . **CLC 44**
See also CA 147

Giacosa, Giuseppe 1847-1906 . . . . . . **TCLC 7**
See also CA 104

Gibb, Lee
See Waterhouse, Keith (Spencer)

Gibbon, Lewis Grassic . . . . TCLC 4
See also Mitchell, James Leslie

Gibbons, Kaye   1960- . . . . CLC 50, 88

Gibran, Kahlil
1883-1931 . . . . TCLC 1, 9; PC 9
See also CA 104

Gibson, William   1914- . . CLC 23; DA; DAB
See also CA 9-12R; CANR 9, 42; DLB 7;
SATA 66

Gibson, William (Ford)   1948- . . . CLC 39, 63
See also AAYA 12; CA 126; 133

Gide, Andre (Paul Guillaume)
1869-1951 . . . . TCLC 5, 12, 36; DA;
DAB; SSC 13; WLC
See also CA 104; 124; DLB 65; MTCW

Gifford, Barry (Colby)   1946- . . . . CLC 34
See also CA 65-68; CANR 9, 30, 40

Gilbert, W(illiam) S(chwenck)
1836-1911 . . . . TCLC 3
See also CA 104; SATA 36

Gilbreth, Frank B., Jr.   1911- . . . . CLC 17
See also CA 9-12R; SATA 2

Gilchrist, Ellen   1935- . . CLC 34, 48; SSC 14
See also CA 113; 116; CANR 41; DLB 130;
MTCW

Giles, Molly   1942- . . . . CLC 39
See also CA 126

Gill, Patrick
See Creasey, John

Gilliam, Terry (Vance)   1940- . . . . CLC 21
See also Monty Python
See also CA 108; 113; CANR 35

Gillian, Jerry
See Gilliam, Terry (Vance)

Gilliatt, Penelope (Ann Douglass)
1932-1993 . . . . CLC 2, 10, 13, 53
See also AITN 2; CA 13-16R; 141;
CANR 49; DLB 14

Gilman, Charlotte (Anna) Perkins (Stetson)
1860-1935 . . . . TCLC 9, 37; SSC 13
See also CA 106

Gilmour, David   1949- . . . . CLC 35
See also CA 138, 147

Gilpin, William   1724-1804 . . . . NCLC 30

Gilray, J. D.
See Mencken, H(enry) L(ouis)

Gilroy, Frank D(aniel)   1925- . . . . CLC 2
See also CA 81-84; CANR 32; DLB 7

Ginsberg, Allen
1926- . . . . . . CLC 1, 2, 3, 4, 6, 13, 36, 69;
DA; DAB; PC 4; WLC 3
See also AITN 1; CA 1-4R; CANR 2, 41;
CDALB 1941-1968; DLB 5, 16; MTCW

Ginzburg, Natalia
1916-1991 . . . . CLC 5, 11, 54, 70
See also CA 85-88; 135; CANR 33; MTCW

Giono, Jean   1895-1970 . . . . CLC 4, 11
See also CA 45-48; 29-32R; CANR 2, 35;
DLB 72; MTCW

Giovanni, Nikki
1943- . . . . . . CLC 2, 4, 19, 64; BLC; DA;
DAB
See also AITN 1; BW 2; CA 29-32R;
CAAS 6; CANR 18, 41; CLR 6; DLB 5,
41; MAICYA; MTCW; SATA 24

Giovene, Andrea   1904- . . . . CLC 7
See also CA 85-88

Gippius, Zinaida (Nikolayevna)   1869-1945
See Hippius, Zinaida
See also CA 106

Giraudoux, (Hippolyte) Jean
1882-1944 . . . . TCLC 2, 7
See also CA 104; DLB 65

Gironella, Jose Maria   1917- . . . . CLC 11
See also CA 101

Gissing, George (Robert)
1857-1903 . . . . TCLC 3, 24, 47
See also CA 105; DLB 18, 135

Giurlani, Aldo
See Palazzeschi, Aldo

Gladkov, Fyodor (Vasilyevich)
1883-1958 . . . . TCLC 27

Glanville, Brian (Lester)   1931- . . . . . . CLC 6
See also CA 5-8R; CAAS 9; CANR 3;
DLB 15, 139; SATA 42

Glasgow, Ellen (Anderson Gholson)
1873(?)-1945 . . . . TCLC 2, 7
See also CA 104; DLB 9, 12

Glaspell, Susan (Keating)
1882(?)-1948 . . . . TCLC 55
See also CA 110; DLB 7, 9, 78; YABC 2

Glassco, John   1909-1981 . . . . CLC 9
See also CA 13-16R; 102; CANR 15;
DLB 68

Glasscock, Amnesia
See Steinbeck, John (Ernst)

Glasser, Ronald J.   1940(?)- . . . . CLC 37

Glassman, Joyce
See Johnson, Joyce

Glendinning, Victoria   1937- . . . . CLC 50
See also CA 120; 127; DLB 155

Glissant, Edouard   1928- . . . . CLC 10, 68

Gloag, Julian   1930- . . . . CLC 40
See also AITN 1; CA 65-68; CANR 10

Glowacki, Aleksander
See Prus, Boleslaw

Glueck, Louise (Elisabeth)
1943- . . . . CLC 7, 22, 44, 81
See also CA 33-36R; CANR 40; DLB 5

Gobineau, Joseph Arthur (Comte) de
1816-1882 . . . . NCLC 17
See also DLB 123

Godard, Jean-Luc   1930- . . . . CLC 20
See also CA 93-96

Godden, (Margaret) Rumer   1907- . . . CLC 53
See also AAYA 6; CA 5-8R; CANR 4, 27,
36; CLR 20; MAICYA; SAAS 12;
SATA 3, 36

Godoy Alcayaga, Lucila   1889-1957
See Mistral, Gabriela
See also BW 2; CA 104; 131; HW; MTCW

Godwin, Gail (Kathleen)
1937- . . . . CLC 5, 8, 22, 31, 69
See also CA 29-32R; CANR 15, 43; DLB 6;
MTCW

Godwin, William   1756-1836 . . . . . . NCLC 14
See also CDBLB 1789-1832; DLB 39, 104,
142

Goethe, Johann Wolfgang von
1749-1832 . . . . NCLC 4, 22, 34; DA;
DAB; PC 5; WLC 3
See also DLB 94

Gogarty, Oliver St. John
1878-1957 . . . . TCLC 15
See also CA 109; DLB 15, 19

Gogol, Nikolai (Vasilyevich)
1809-1852 . . . . NCLC 5, 15, 31; DA;
DAB; DC 1; SSC 4; WLC
See also AITN 1; BW 1; CA 124; 114;
DLB 33

Goines, Donald
1937(?)-1974 . . . . CLC 80; BLC
See also AITN 1; BW 1; CA 124; 114;
DLB 33

Gold, Herbert   1924- . . . . CLC 4, 7, 14, 42
See also CA 9-12R; CANR 17, 45; DLB 2;
DLBY 81

Goldbarth, Albert   1948- . . . . CLC 5, 38
See also CA 53-56; CANR 6, 40; DLB 120

Goldberg, Anatol   1910-1982 . . . . CLC 34
See also CA 131; 117

Goldemberg, Isaac   1945- . . . . CLC 52
See also CA 69-72; CAAS 12; CANR 11,
32; HW

Golding, William (Gerald)
1911-1993 . . . . CLC 1, 2, 3, 8, 10, 17, 27,
58, 81; DA; DAB; WLC
See also AAYA 5; CA 5-8R; 141;
CANR 13, 33; CDBLB 1945-1960;
DLB 15, 100; MTCW

Goldman, Emma   1869-1940 . . . . . . TCLC 13
See also CA 110

Goldman, Francisco   1955- . . . . CLC 76

Goldman, William (W.)   1931- . . . . CLC 1, 48
See also CA 9-12R; CANR 29; DLB 44

Goldmann, Lucien   1913-1970 . . . . . . CLC 24
See also CA 25-28; CAP 2

Goldoni, Carlo   1707-1793 . . . . LC 4

Goldsberry, Steven   1949- . . . . CLC 34
See also CA 131

Goldsmith, Oliver
1728-1774 . . . . . . LC 2; DA; DAB; WLC
See also CDBLB 1660-1789; DLB 39, 89,
104, 109, 142; SATA 26

Goldsmith, Peter
See Priestley, J(ohn) B(oynton)

Gombrowicz, Witold
1904-1969 . . . . CLC 4, 7, 11, 49
See also CA 19-20; 25-28R; CAP 2

Gomez de la Serna, Ramon
1888-1963 . . . . CLC 9
See also CA 116; HW

Goncharov, Ivan Alexandrovich
1812-1891 . . . . NCLC 1

Goncourt, Edmond (Louis Antoine Huot) de
1822-1896 . . . . NCLC 7
See also DLB 123

Goncourt, Jules (Alfred Huot) de
1830-1870 . . . . NCLC 7
See also DLB 123

Gontier, Fernande   19(?)- . . . . CLC 50

Goodman, Paul   1911-1972 . . . . CLC 1, 2, 4, 7
See also CA 19-20; 37-40R; CANR 34;
CAP 2; DLB 130; MTCW

Gordimer, Nadine
1923- .... CLC **3, 5, 7, 10, 18, 33, 51, 70;**
DA; DAB; SSC 17
See also CA 5-8R; CANR 3, 28; MTCW

Gordon, Adam Lindsay
1833-1870 .... **NCLC 21**

Gordon, Caroline
1895-1981 ... CLC **6, 13, 29, 83; SSC 15**
See also CA 11-12; 103; CANR 36; CAP 1;
DLB 4, 9, 102; DLBY 81; MTCW

Gordon, Charles William 1860-1937
See Connor, Ralph
See also CA 109

Gordon, Mary (Catherine)
1949- .... CLC **13, 22**
See also CA 102; CANR 44; DLB 6;
DLBY 81; MTCW

Gordon, Sol 1923-................. CLC **26**
See also CA 53-56; CANR 4; SATA 11

Gordone, Charles 1925-.......... CLC **1, 4**
See also BW 1; CA 93-96; DLB 7; MTCW

Gorenko, Anna Andreevna
See Akhmatova, Anna

Gorky, Maxim........ TCLC **8; DAB; WLC**
See also Peshkov, Alexei Maximovich

Goryan, Sirak
See Saroyan, William

Gosse, Edmund (William)
1849-1928 .... TCLC **28**
See also CA 117; DLB 57, 144

Gotlieb, Phyllis Fay (Bloom)
1926- .... CLC **18**
See also CA 13-16R; CANR 7; DLB 88

Gottesman, S. D.
See Kornbluth, C(yril) M.; Pohl, Frederik

Gottfried von Strassburg
fl. c. 1210-................. CMLC **10**
See also DLB 138

Gould, Lois .... CLC **4, 10**
See also CA 77-80; CANR 29; MTCW

Gourmont, Remy de 1858-1915.... TCLC **17**
See also CA 109

Govier, Katherine 1948-.......... CLC **51**
See also CA 101; CANR 18, 40

Goyen, (Charles) William
1915-1983 .... CLC **5, 8, 14, 40**
See also AITN 2; CA 5-8R; 110; CANR 6;
DLB 2; DLBY 83

Goytisolo, Juan
1931- .... CLC **5, 10, 23; HLC**
See also CA 85-88; CANR 32; HW; MTCW

Gozzano, Guido 1883-1916 .... PC **10**
See also DLB 114

Gozzi, (Conte) Carlo 1720-1806 .. NCLC **23**

Grabbe, Christian Dietrich
1801-1836 .... NCLC **2**
See also DLB 133

Grace, Patricia 1937-............. CLC **56**

Gracian y Morales, Baltasar
1601-1658 .... LC **15**

Gracq, Julien................. CLC **11, 48**
See also Poirier, Louis
See also DLB 83

Grade, Chaim 1910-1982 .... CLC **10**
See also CA 93-96; 107

Graduate of Oxford, A
See Ruskin, John

Graham, John
See Phillips, David Graham

Graham, Jorie 1951-.............. CLC **48**
See also CA 111; DLB 120

Graham, R(obert) B(ontine) Cunninghame
See Cunninghame Graham, R(obert)
B(ontine)
See also DLB 98, 135

Graham, Robert
See Haldeman, Joe (William)

Graham, Tom
See Lewis, (Harry) Sinclair

Graham, W(illiam) S(ydney)
1918-1986 .... CLC **29**
See also CA 73-76; 118; DLB 20

Graham, Winston (Mawdsley)
1910- .... CLC **23**
See also CA 49-52; CANR 2, 22, 45;
DLB 77

Grant, Skeeter
See Spiegelman, Art

Granville-Barker, Harley
1877-1946 .... TCLC **2**
See also Barker, Harley Granville
See also CA 104

Grass, Guenter (Wilhelm)
1927- ..... CLC **1, 2, 4, 6, 11, 15, 22, 32,**
49, 88; DA; DAB; WLC
See also CA 13-16R; CANR 20; DLB 75,
124; MTCW

Gratton, Thomas
See Hulme, T(homas) E(rnest)

Grau, Shirley Ann
1929- .... CLC **4, 9; SSC 15**
See also CA 89-92; CANR 22; DLB 2;
MTCW

Gravel, Fern
See Hall, James Norman

Graver, Elizabeth 1964-.......... CLC **70**
See also CA 135

Graves, Richard Perceval 1945- .... CLC **44**
See also CA 65-68; CANR 9, 26

Graves, Robert (von Ranke)
1895-1985 ...... CLC **1, 2, 6, 11, 39, 44,**
45; DAB; PC 6
See also CA 5-8R; 117; CANR 5, 36;
CDBLB 1914-1945; DLB 20, 100;
DLBY 85; MTCW; SATA 45

Gray, Alasdair (James) 1934- ...... CLC **41**
See also CA 126; CANR 47; MTCW

Gray, Amlin 1946- .... CLC **29**
See also CA 138

Gray, Francine du Plessix 1930-.... CLC **22**
See also BEST 90:3; CA 61-64; CAAS 2;
CANR 11, 33; MTCW

Gray, John (Henry) 1866-1934 .... TCLC **19**
See also CA 119

Gray, Simon (James Holliday)
1936- .... CLC **9, 14, 36**
See also AITN 1; CA 21-24R; CAAS 3;
CANR 32; DLB 13; MTCW

Gray, Spalding 1941-............. CLC **49**
See also CA 128

Gray, Thomas
1716-1771 ...... LC **4; DA; DAB; PC 2;**
WLC
See also CDBLB 1660-1789; DLB 109

Grayson, David
See Baker, Ray Stannard

Grayson, Richard (A.) 1951-....... CLC **38**
See also CA 85-88; CANR 14, 31

Greeley, Andrew M(oran) 1928-.... CLC **28**
See also CA 5-8R; CAAS 7; CANR 7, 43;
MTCW

Green, Brian
See Card, Orson Scott

Green, Hannah
See Greenberg, Joanne (Goldenberg)

Green, Hannah .... CLC **3**
See also CA 73-76

Green, Henry.................... CLC **2, 13**
See also Yorke, Henry Vincent
See also DLB 15

Green, Julian (Hartridge) 1900-
See Green, Julien
See also CA 21-24R; CANR 33; DLB 4, 72;
MTCW

Green, Julien................. CLC **3, 11, 77**
See also Green, Julian (Hartridge)

Green, Paul (Eliot) 1894-1981...... CLC **25**
See also AITN 1; CA 5-8R; 103; CANR 3;
DLB 7, 9; DLBY 81

Greenberg, Ivan 1908-1973
See Rahv, Philip
See also CA 85-88

Greenberg, Joanne (Goldenberg)
1932- .... CLC **7, 30**
See also AAYA 12; CA 5-8R; CANR 14,
32; SATA 25

Greenberg, Richard 1959(?)-....... CLC **57**
See also CA 138

Greene, Bette 1934- .... CLC **30**
See also AAYA 7; CA 53-56; CANR 4;
CLR 2; JRDA; MAICYA; SAAS 16;
SATA 8

Greene, Gael .... CLC **8**
See also CA 13-16R; CANR 10

Greene, Graham
1904-1991 .... CLC **1, 3, 6, 9, 14, 18, 27,**
37, 70, 72; DA; DAB; WLC
See also AITN 2; CA 13-16R; 133;
CANR 35; CDBLB 1945-1960; DLB 13,
15, 77, 100; DLBY 91; MTCW; SATA 20

Greer, Richard
See Silverberg, Robert

Gregor, Arthur 1923-............. CLC **9**
See also CA 25-28R; CAAS 10; CANR 11;
SATA 36

Gregor, Lee
See Pohl, Frederik

Gregory, Isabella Augusta (Persse)
1852-1932 .... TCLC **1**
See also CA 104; DLB 10

Gregory, J. Dennis
See Williams, John A(lfred)

Haley, Alex(ander Murray Palmer)
　　1921-1992 .... **CLC 8, 12, 76; BLC; DA;**
　　　　　　　　　　　　　　　　　　DAB
　　See also BW 2; CA 77-80; 136; DLB 38;
　　MTCW

Haliburton, Thomas Chandler
　　1796-1865 .... **NCLC 15**
　　See also DLB 11, 99

Hall, Donald (Andrew, Jr.)
　　1928- .... **CLC 1, 13, 37, 59**
　　See also CA 5-8R; CAAS 7; CANR 2, 44;
　　DLB 5; SATA 23

Hall, Frederic Sauser
　　See Sauser-Hall, Frederic

Hall, James
　　See Kuttner, Henry

Hall, James Norman　1887-1951 ... **TCLC 23**
　　See also CA 123; SATA 21

Hall, (Marguerite) Radclyffe
　　1886(?)-1943 .... **TCLC 12**
　　See also CA 110

Hall, Rodney　1935- .... **CLC 51**
　　See also CA 109

Halleck, Fitz-Greene　1790-1867 .. **NCLC 47**
　　See also DLB 3

Halliday, Michael
　　See Creasey, John

Halpern, Daniel　1945- .... **CLC 14**
　　See also CA 33-36R

Hamburger, Michael (Peter Leopold)
　　1924- .... **CLC 5, 14**
　　See also CA 5-8R; CAAS 4; CANR 2, 47;
　　DLB 27

Hamill, Pete　1935- .... **CLC 10**
　　See also CA 25-28R; CANR 18

Hamilton, Alexander
　　1755(?)-1804 .... **NCLC 49**
　　See also DLB 37

Hamilton, Clive
　　See Lewis, C(live) S(taples)

Hamilton, Edmond　1904-1977 .... **CLC 1**
　　See also CA 1-4R; CANR 3; DLB 8

Hamilton, Eugene (Jacob) Lee
　　See Lee-Hamilton, Eugene (Jacob)

Hamilton, Franklin
　　See Silverberg, Robert

Hamilton, Gail
　　See Corcoran, Barbara

Hamilton, Mollie
　　See Kaye, M(ary) M(argaret)

Hamilton, (Anthony Walter) Patrick
　　1904-1962 .... **CLC 51**
　　See also CA 113; DLB 10

Hamilton, Virginia　1936- .... **CLC 26**
　　See also AAYA 2; BW 2; CA 25-28R;
　　CANR 20, 37; CLR 1, 11; DLB 33, 52;
　　JRDA; MAICYA; MTCW; SATA 4, 56,
　　79

Hammett, (Samuel) Dashiell
　　1894-1961 .... **CLC 3, 5, 10, 19, 47;**
　　　　　　　　　　　　　　　　　　SSC 17
　　See also AITN 1; CA 81-84; CANR 42;
　　CDALB 1929-1941; DLBD 6; MTCW

Hammon, Jupiter
　　1711(?)-1800(?) .... **NCLC 5; BLC**
　　See also DLB 31, 50

Hammond, Keith
　　See Kuttner, Henry

Hamner, Earl (Henry), Jr.　1923- ... **CLC 12**
　　See also AITN 2; CA 73-76; DLB 6

Hampton, Christopher (James)
　　1946- .... **CLC 4**
　　See also CA 25-28R; DLB 13; MTCW

Hamsun, Knut .... **TCLC 2, 14, 49**
　　See also Pedersen, Knut

Handke, Peter　1942- .. **CLC 5, 8, 10, 15, 38**
　　See also CA 77-80; CANR 33; DLB 85,
　　124; MTCW

Hanley, James　1901-1985 ... **CLC 3, 5, 8, 13**
　　See also CA 73-76; 117; CANR 36; MTCW

Hannah, Barry　1942- .... **CLC 23, 38, 90**
　　See also CA 108; 110; CANR 43; DLB 6;
　　MTCW

Hannon, Ezra
　　See Hunter, Evan

Hansberry, Lorraine (Vivian)
　　1930-1965 ...... **CLC 17, 62; BLC; DA;**
　　　　　　　　　　　　　　　DAB; DC 2
　　See also BW 1; CA 109; 25-28R; CABS 3;
　　CDALB 1941-1968; DLB 7, 38; MTCW

Hansen, Joseph　1923- .... **CLC 38**
　　See also CA 29-32R; CAAS 17; CANR 16,
　　44

Hansen, Martin A.　1909-1955 ..... **TCLC 32**

Hanson, Kenneth O(stlin)　1922- .... **CLC 13**
　　See also CA 53-56; CANR 7

Hardwick, Elizabeth　1916- .... **CLC 13**
　　See also CA 5-8R; CANR 3, 32; DLB 6;
　　MTCW

Hardy, Thomas
　　1840-1928 ...... **TCLC 4, 10, 18, 32, 48,**
　　　　　　　　53; DA; DAB; PC 8; SSC 2; WLC
　　See also CA 104; 123; CDBLB 1890-1914;
　　DLB 18, 19, 135; MTCW

Hare, David　1947- .... **CLC 29, 58**
　　See also CA 97-100; CANR 39; DLB 13;
　　MTCW

Harford, Henry
　　See Hudson, W(illiam) H(enry)

Hargrave, Leonie
　　See Disch, Thomas M(ichael)

Harjo, Joy　1951- .... **CLC 83**
　　See also CA 114; CANR 35; DLB 120;
　　NNAL

Harlan, Louis R(udolph)　1922- ..... **CLC 34**
　　See also CA 21-24R; CANR 25

Harling, Robert　1951(?)- .... **CLC 53**
　　See also CA 147

Harmon, William (Ruth)　1938- ..... **CLC 38**
　　See also CA 33-36R; CANR 14, 32, 35;
　　SATA 65

Harper, F. E. W.
　　See Harper, Frances Ellen Watkins

Harper, Frances E. W.
　　See Harper, Frances Ellen Watkins

Harper, Frances E. Watkins
　　See Harper, Frances Ellen Watkins

Harper, Frances Ellen
　　See Harper, Frances Ellen Watkins

Harper, Frances Ellen Watkins
　　1825-1911 .... **TCLC 14; BLC**
　　See also BW 1; CA 111; 125; DLB 50

Harper, Michael S(teven)　1938- .. **CLC 7, 22**
　　See also BW 1; CA 33-36R; CANR 24;
　　DLB 41

Harper, Mrs. F. E. W.
　　See Harper, Frances Ellen Watkins

Harris, Christie (Lucy) Irwin
　　1907- .... **CLC 12**
　　See also CA 5-8R; CANR 6; DLB 88;
　　JRDA; MAICYA; SAAS 10; SATA 6, 74

Harris, Frank　1856(?)-1931 .... **TCLC 24**
　　See also CA 109; DLB 156

Harris, George Washington
　　1814-1869 .... **NCLC 23**
　　See also DLB 3, 11

Harris, Joel Chandler
　　1848-1908 .... **TCLC 2; SSC 19**
　　See also CA 104; 137; DLB 11, 23, 42, 78,
　　91; MAICYA; YABC 1

Harris, John (Wyndham Parkes Lucas)
　　Beynon　1903-1969
　　See Wyndham, John
　　See also CA 102; 89-92

Harris, MacDonald .... **CLC 9**
　　See also Heiney, Donald (William)

Harris, Mark　1922- .... **CLC 19**
　　See also CA 5-8R; CAAS 3; CANR 2;
　　DLB 2; DLBY 80

Harris, (Theodore) Wilson　1921-.... **CLC 25**
　　See also BW 2; CA 65-68; CAAS 16;
　　CANR 11, 27; DLB 117; MTCW

Harrison, Elizabeth Cavanna　1909-
　　See Cavanna, Betty
　　See also CA 9-12R; CANR 6, 27

Harrison, Harry (Max)　1925- ...... **CLC 42**
　　See also CA 1-4R; CANR 5, 21; DLB 8;
　　SATA 4

Harrison, James (Thomas)
　　1937- .... **CLC 6, 14, 33, 66; SSC 19**
　　See also CA 13-16R; CANR 8; DLBY 82

Harrison, Jim
　　See Harrison, James (Thomas)

Harrison, Kathryn　1961- .... **CLC 70**
　　See also CA 144

Harrison, Tony　1937- .... **CLC 43**
　　See also CA 65-68; CANR 44; DLB 40;
　　MTCW

Harriss, Will(ard Irvin)　1922- ...... **CLC 34**
　　See also CA 111

Harson, Sley
　　See Ellison, Harlan (Jay)

Hart, Ellis
　　See Ellison, Harlan (Jay)

Hart, Josephine　1942(?)- .... **CLC 70**
　　See also CA 138

Hart, Moss　1904-1961 .... **CLC 66**
　　See also CA 109; 89-92; DLB 7

Harte, (Francis) Bret(t)
   1836(?)-1902 . . . . **TCLC 1, 25; DA;
                                          SSC 8; WLC**
   See also CA 104; 140; CDALB 1865-1917;
   DLB 12, 64, 74, 79; SATA 26

Hartley, L(eslie) P(oles)
   1895-1972 . . . . **CLC 2, 22**
   See also CA 45-48; 37-40R; CANR 33;
   DLB 15, 139; MTCW

Hartman, Geoffrey H.   1929- . . . . **CLC 27**
   See also CA 117; 125; DLB 67

Hartmann von Aue
   c. 1160-c. 1205 . . . . **CMLC 15**
   See also DLB 138

Haruf, Kent   19(?)- . . . . **CLC 34**

Harwood, Ronald   1934- . . . . **CLC 32**
   See also CA 1-4R; CANR 4; DLB 13

Hasek, Jaroslav (Matej Frantisek)
   1883-1923 . . . . **TCLC 4**
   See also CA 104; 129; MTCW

Hass, Robert   1941- . . . . **CLC 18, 39**
   See also CA 111; CANR 30; DLB 105

Hastings, Hudson
   See Kuttner, Henry

Hastings, Selina . . . . **CLC 44**

Hatteras, Amelia
   See Mencken, H(enry) L(ouis)

Hatteras, Owen . . . . **TCLC 18**
   See also Mencken, H(enry) L(ouis); Nathan,
   George Jean

Hauptmann, Gerhart (Johann Robert)
   1862-1946 . . . . **TCLC 4**
   See also CA 104; DLB 66, 118

Havel, Vaclav   1936- . . . . **CLC 25, 58, 65**
   See also CA 104; CANR 36; MTCW

Haviaras, Stratis . . . . **CLC 33**
   See also Chaviaras, Strates

Hawes, Stephen   1475(?)-1523(?) . . . . . **LC 17**

Hawkes, John (Clendennin Burne, Jr.)
   1925- . . . . . . **CLC 1, 2, 3, 4, 7, 9, 14, 15,
                                          27, 49**
   See also CA 1-4R; CANR 2, 47; DLB 2, 7;
   DLBY 80; MTCW

Hawking, S. W.
   See Hawking, Stephen W(illiam)

Hawking, Stephen W(illiam)
   1942- . . . . **CLC 63**
   See also AAYA 13; BEST 89:1; CA 126;
   129; CANR 48

Hawthorne, Julian   1846-1934 . . . . . **TCLC 25**

Hawthorne, Nathaniel
   1804-1864 . . . . **NCLC 39; DA; DAB;
                                          SSC 3; WLC**
   See also CDALB 1640-1865; DLB 1, 74;
   YABC 2

Haxton, Josephine Ayres   1921-
   See Douglas, Ellen
   See also CA 115; CANR 41

Hayaseca y Eizaguirre, Jorge
   See Echegaray (y Eizaguirre), Jose (Maria
   Waldo)

Hayashi Fumiko   1904-1951 . . . . . . **TCLC 27**

Haycraft, Anna
   See Ellis, Alice Thomas
   See also CA 122

Hayden, Robert E(arl)
   1913-1980 . . . . . . **CLC 5, 9, 14, 37; BLC;
                                          DA; PC 6**
   See also BW 1; CA 69-72; 97-100; CABS 2;
   CANR 24; CDALB 1941-1968; DLB 5,
   76; MTCW; SATA 19; SATA-Obit 26

Hayford, J(oseph) E(phraim) Casely
   See Casely-Hayford, J(oseph) E(phraim)

Hayman, Ronald   1932- . . . . **CLC 44**
   See also CA 25-28R; CANR 18; DLB 155

Haywood, Eliza (Fowler)
   1693(?)-1756 . . . . **LC 1**

Hazlitt, William   1778-1830 . . . . . . **NCLC 29**
   See also DLB 110

Hazzard, Shirley   1931- . . . . **CLC 18**
   See also CA 9-12R; CANR 4; DLBY 82;
   MTCW

Head, Bessie   1937-1986 . . . **CLC 25, 67; BLC**
   See also BW 2; CA 29-32R; 119; CANR 25;
   DLB 117; MTCW

Headon, (Nicky) Topper   1956(?)- . . . **CLC 30**

Heaney, Seamus (Justin)
   1939- . . . . **CLC 5, 7, 14, 25, 37, 74; DAB**
   See also CA 85-88; CANR 25, 48;
   CDBLB 1960 to Present; DLB 40;
   MTCW

Hearn, (Patricio) Lafcadio (Tessima Carlos)
   1850-1904 . . . . **TCLC 9**
   See also CA 105; DLB 12, 78

Hearne, Vicki   1946- . . . . **CLC 56**
   See also CA 139

Hearon, Shelby   1931- . . . . **CLC 63**
   See also AITN 2; CA 25-28R; CANR 18,
   48

Heat-Moon, William Least . . . . **CLC 29**
   See also Trogdon, William (Lewis)
   See also AAYA 9

Hebbel, Friedrich   1813-1863 . . . . . **NCLC 43**
   See also DLB 129

Hebert, Anne   1916- . . . . **CLC 4, 13, 29**
   See also CA 85-88; DLB 68; MTCW

Hecht, Anthony (Evan)
   1923- . . . . **CLC 8, 13, 19**
   See also CA 9-12R; CANR 6; DLB 5

Hecht, Ben   1894-1964 . . . . **CLC 8**
   See also CA 85-88; DLB 7, 9, 25, 26, 28, 86

Hedayat, Sadeq   1903-1951 . . . . **TCLC 21**
   See also CA 120

Hegel, Georg Wilhelm Friedrich
   1770-1831 . . . . **NCLC 46**
   See also DLB 90

Heidegger, Martin   1889-1976 . . . . . . **CLC 24**
   See also CA 81-84; 65-68; CANR 34;
   MTCW

Heidenstam, (Carl Gustaf) Verner von
   1859-1940 . . . . **TCLC 5**
   See also CA 104

Heifner, Jack   1946- . . . . **CLC 11**
   See also CA 105; CANR 47

Heijermans, Herman   1864-1924 . . . **TCLC 24**
   See also CA 123

Heilbrun, Carolyn G(old)   1926- . . . . . **CLC 25**
   See also CA 45-48; CANR 1, 28

Heine, Heinrich   1797-1856 . . . . **NCLC 4**
   See also DLB 90

Heinemann, Larry (Curtiss)   1944- . . **CLC 50**
   See also CA 110; CAAS 21; CANR 31;
   DLBD 9

Heiney, Donald (William)   1921-1993
   See Harris, MacDonald
   See also CA 1-4R; 142; CANR 3

Heinlein, Robert A(nson)
   1907-1988 . . . . . . **CLC 1, 3, 8, 14, 26, 55**
   See also CA 1-4R; 125; CANR 1, 20;
   DLB 8; JRDA; MAICYA; MTCW;
   SATA 9, 69; SATA-Obit 56

Helforth, John
   See Doolittle, Hilda

Hellenhofferu, Vojtech Kapristian z
   See Hasek, Jaroslav (Matej Frantisek)

Heller, Joseph
   1923- . . . . **CLC 1, 3, 5, 8, 11, 36, 63; DA;
                                          DAB; WLC**
   See also AITN 1; CA 5-8R; CABS 1;
   CANR 8, 42; DLB 2, 28; DLBY 80;
   MTCW

Hellman, Lillian (Florence)
   1906-1984 . . . . . . **CLC 2, 4, 8, 14, 18, 34,
                                          44, 52; DC 1**
   See also AITN 1, 2; CA 13-16R; 112;
   CANR 33; DLB 7; DLBY 84; MTCW

Helprin, Mark   1947- . . . . . **CLC 7, 10, 22, 32**
   See also CA 81-84; CANR 47; DLBY 85;
   MTCW

Helvetius, Claude-Adrien
   1715-1771 . . . . **LC 26**

Helyar, Jane Penelope Josephine   1933-
   See Poole, Josephine
   See also CA 21-24R; CANR 10, 26;
   SATA 82

Hemans, Felicia   1793-1835 . . . . . . **NCLC 29**
   See also DLB 96

Hemingway, Ernest (Miller)
   1899-1961 . . . . **CLC 1, 3, 6, 8, 10, 13, 19,
       30, 34, 39, 41, 44, 50, 61, 80; DA; DAB;
                                          SSC 1; WLC**
   See also CA 77-80; CANR 34;
   CDALB 1917-1929; DLB 4, 9, 102;
   DLBD 1; DLBY 81, 87; MTCW

Hempel, Amy   1951- . . . . **CLC 39**
   See also CA 118; 137

Henderson, F. C.
   See Mencken, H(enry) L(ouis)

Henderson, Sylvia
   See Ashton-Warner, Sylvia (Constance)

Henley, Beth . . . . **CLC 23**
   See also Henley, Elizabeth Becker
   See also CABS 3; DLBY 86

Henley, Elizabeth Becker   1952-
   See Henley, Beth
   See also CA 107; CANR 32; MTCW

Henley, William Ernest
   1849-1903 . . . . **TCLC 8**
   See also CA 105; DLB 19

Hennissart, Martha
   See Lathen, Emma
   See also CA 85-88

Henry, O......... **TCLC 1, 19; SSC 5; WLC**
See also Porter, William Sydney

Henry, Patrick 1736-1799 .... **LC 25**

Henryson, Robert 1430(?)-1506(?).... **LC 20**
See also DLB 146

Henry VIII 1491-1547............ **LC 10**

Henschke, Alfred
See Klabund

Hentoff, Nat(han Irving) 1925-..... **CLC 26**
See also AAYA 4; CA 1-4R; CAAS 6;
CANR 5, 25; CLR 1; JRDA; MAICYA;
SATA 42, 69; SATA-Brief 27

Heppenstall, (John) Rayner
1911-1981 .... **CLC 10**
See also CA 1-4R; 103; CANR 29

Herbert, Frank (Patrick)
1920-1986 ...... **CLC 12, 23, 35, 44, 85**
See also CA 53-56; 118; CANR 5, 43;
DLB 8; MTCW; SATA 9, 37;
SATA-Obit 47

Herbert, George
1593-1633 .... **LC 24; DAB; PC 4**
See also CDBLB Before 1660; DLB 126

Herbert, Zbigniew 1924-........ **CLC 9, 43**
See also CA 89-92; CANR 36; MTCW

Herbst, Josephine (Frey)
1897-1969 .... **CLC 34**
See also CA 5-8R; 25-28R; DLB 9

Hergesheimer, Joseph
1880-1954 .... **TCLC 11**
See also CA 109; DLB 102, 9

Herlihy, James Leo 1927-1993 ...... **CLC 6**
See also CA 1-4R; 143; CANR 2

Hermogenes fl. c. 175-.......... **CMLC 6**

Hernandez, Jose 1834-1886...... **NCLC 17**

Herrick, Robert
1591-1674 ..... **LC 13; DA; DAB; PC 9**
See also DLB 126

Herring, Guilles
See Somerville, Edith

Herriot, James 1916-1995 .... **CLC 12**
See also Wight, James Alfred
See also AAYA 1; CA 148; CANR 40

Herrmann, Dorothy 1941-........ **CLC 44**
See also CA 107

Herrmann, Taffy
See Herrmann, Dorothy

Hersey, John (Richard)
1914-1993 .... **CLC 1, 2, 7, 9, 40, 81**
See also CA 17-20R; 140; CANR 33;
DLB 6; MTCW; SATA 25;
SATA-Obit 76

Herzen, Aleksandr Ivanovich
1812-1870 .... **NCLC 10**

Herzl, Theodor 1860-1904....... **TCLC 36**

Herzog, Werner 1942-........... **CLC 16**
See also CA 89-92

Hesiod c. 8th cent. B.C.-......... **CMLC 5**

Hesse, Hermann
1877-1962 .... **CLC 1, 2, 3, 6, 11, 17, 25,
69; DA; DAB; SSC 9; WLC**
See also CA 17-18; CAP 2; DLB 66;
MTCW; SATA 50

Hewes, Cady
See De Voto, Bernard (Augustine)

Heyen, William 1940- .... **CLC 13, 18**
See also CA 33-36R; CAAS 9; DLB 5

Heyerdahl, Thor 1914-........... **CLC 26**
See also CA 5-8R; CANR 5, 22; MTCW;
SATA 2, 52

Heym, Georg (Theodor Franz Arthur)
1887-1912 .... **TCLC 9**
See also CA 106

Heym, Stefan 1913-............. **CLC 41**
See also CA 9-12R; CANR 4; DLB 69

Heyse, Paul (Johann Ludwig von)
1830-1914 .... **TCLC 8**
See also CA 104; DLB 129

Heyward, (Edwin) DuBose
1885-1940 .... **TCLC 59**
See also CA 108; DLB 7, 9, 45; SATA 21

Hibbert, Eleanor Alice Burford
1906-1993 .... **CLC 7**
See also BEST 90:4; CA 17-20R; 140;
CANR 9, 28; SATA 2; SATA-Obit 74

Higgins, George V(incent)
1939-................. **CLC 4, 7, 10, 18**
See also CA 77-80; CAAS 5; CANR 17;
DLB 2; DLBY 81; MTCW

Higginson, Thomas Wentworth
1823-1911 .... **TCLC 36**
See also DLB 1, 64

Highet, Helen
See MacInnes, Helen (Clark)

Highsmith, (Mary) Patricia
1921-1995 .... **CLC 2, 4, 14, 42**
See also CA 1-4R; 147; CANR 1, 20, 48;
MTCW

Highwater, Jamake (Mamake)
1942(?)-..................... **CLC 12**
See also AAYA 7; CA 65-68; CAAS 7;
CANR 10, 34; CLR 17; DLB 52;
DLBY 85; JRDA; MAICYA; SATA 32,
69; SATA-Brief 30

Higuchi, Ichiyo 1872-1896....... **NCLC 49**

Hijuelos, Oscar 1951- ...... **CLC 65; HLC**
See also BEST 90:1; CA 123; DLB 145; HW

Hikmet, Nazim 1902(?)-1963....... **CLC 40**
See also CA 141; 93-96

Hildesheimer, Wolfgang
1916-1991 .... **CLC 49**
See also CA 101; 135; DLB 69, 124

Hill, Geoffrey (William)
1932-................. **CLC 5, 8, 18, 45**
See also CA 81-84; CANR 21;
CDBLB 1960 to Present; DLB 40;
MTCW

Hill, George Roy 1921-......... **CLC 26**
See also CA 110; 122

Hill, John
See Koontz, Dean R(ay)

Hill, Susan (Elizabeth)
1942-..................... **CLC 4; DAB**
See also CA 33-36R; CANR 29; DLB 14,
139; MTCW

Hillerman, Tony 1925-........... **CLC 62**
See also AAYA 6; BEST 89:1; CA 29-32R;
CANR 21, 42; SATA 6

Hillesum, Etty 1914-1943 .... **TCLC 49**
See also CA 137

Hilliard, Noel (Harvey) 1929-...... **CLC 15**
See also CA 9-12R; CANR 7

Hillis, Rick 1956-............... **CLC 66**
See also CA 134

Hilton, James 1900-1954........ **TCLC 21**
See also CA 108; DLB 34, 77; SATA 34

Himes, Chester (Bomar)
1909-1984 .... **CLC 2, 4, 7, 18, 58; BLC**
See also BW 2; CA 25-28R; 114; CANR 22;
DLB 2, 76, 143; MTCW

Hinde, Thomas .... **CLC 6, 11**
See also Chitty, Thomas Willes

Hindin, Nathan
See Bloch, Robert (Albert)

Hine, (William) Daryl 1936-....... **CLC 15**
See also CA 1-4R; CAAS 15; CANR 1, 20;
DLB 60

Hinkson, Katharine Tynan
See Tynan, Katharine

Hinton, S(usan) E(loise)
1950-............. **CLC 30; DA; DAB**
See also AAYA 2; CA 81-84; CANR 32;
CLR 3, 23; JRDA; MAICYA; MTCW;
SATA 19, 58

Hippius, Zinaida .... **TCLC 9**
See also Gippius, Zinaida (Nikolayevna)

Hiraoka, Kimitake 1925-1970
See Mishima, Yukio
See also CA 97-100; 29-32R; MTCW

Hirsch, E(ric) D(onald), Jr. 1928-... **CLC 79**
See also CA 25-28R; CANR 27; DLB 67;
MTCW

Hirsch, Edward 1950- .... **CLC 31, 50**
See also CA 104; CANR 20, 42; DLB 120

Hitchcock, Alfred (Joseph)
1899-1980 .... **CLC 16**
See also CA 97-100; SATA 27;
SATA-Obit 24

Hitler, Adolf 1889-1945.......... **TCLC 53**
See also CA 117; 147

Hoagland, Edward 1932-.......... **CLC 28**
See also CA 1-4R; CANR 2, 31; DLB 6;
SATA 51

Hoban, Russell (Conwell) 1925-.. **CLC 7, 25**
See also CA 5-8R; CANR 23, 37; CLR 3;
DLB 52; MAICYA; MTCW; SATA 1,
40, 78

Hobbs, Perry
See Blackmur, R(ichard) P(almer)

Hobson, Laura Z(ametkin)
1900-1986 .... **CLC 7, 25**
See also CA 17-20R; 118; DLB 28;
SATA 52

Hochhuth, Rolf 1931-........ **CLC 4, 11, 18**
See also CA 5-8R; CANR 33; DLB 124;
MTCW

Hochman, Sandra 1936-.......... **CLC 3, 8**
See also CA 5-8R; DLB 5

Hochwaelder, Fritz 1911-1986...... **CLC 36**
See also CA 29-32R; 120; CANR 42;
MTCW

Hochwalder, Fritz
See Hochwaelder, Fritz

Khlebnikov, Viktor Vladimirovich   1885-1922
   See Khlebnikov, Velimir
   See also CA 117

Khodasevich, Vladislav (Felitsianovich)
   1886-1939 . . . . **TCLC 15**
   See also CA 115

Kielland, Alexander Lange
   1849-1906 . . . . **TCLC 5**
   See also CA 104

Kiely, Benedict   1919- . . . . **CLC 23, 43**
   See also CA 1-4R; CANR 2; DLB 15

Kienzle, William X(avier)   1928- . . . . **CLC 25**
   See also CA 93-96; CAAS 1; CANR 9, 31;
   MTCW

Kierkegaard, Soren   1813-1855. . . . **NCLC 34**

Killens, John Oliver   1916-1987. . . . . **CLC 10**
   See also BW 2; CA 77-80; 123; CAAS 2;
   CANR 26; DLB 33

Killigrew, Anne   1660-1685. . . . . **LC 4**
   See also DLB 131

Kim
   See Simenon, Georges (Jacques Christian)

Kincaid, Jamaica   1949- . . . **CLC 43, 68; BLC**
   See also AAYA 13; BW 2; CA 125;
   CANR 47

King, Francis (Henry)   1923- . . . . . **CLC 8, 53**
   See also CA 1-4R; CANR 1, 33; DLB 15,
   139; MTCW

King, Martin Luther, Jr.
   1929-1968 . . . . **CLC 83; BLC; DA; DAB**
   See also BW 2; CA 25-28; CANR 27, 44;
   CAP 2; MTCW; SATA 14

King, Stephen (Edwin)
   1947- . . . . . . **CLC 12, 26, 37, 61; SSC 17**
   See also AAYA 1; BEST 90:1; CA 61-64;
   CANR 1, 30; DLB 143; DLBY 80;
   JRDA; MTCW; SATA 9, 55

King, Steve
   See King, Stephen (Edwin)

King, Thomas   1943- . . . . **CLC 89**
   See also CA 144; NNAL

Kingman, Lee. . . . . **CLC 17**
   See also Natti, (Mary) Lee
   See also SAAS 3; SATA 1, 67

Kingsley, Charles   1819-1875 . . . . . **NCLC 35**
   See also DLB 21, 32; YABC 2

Kingsley, Sidney   1906-1995. . . . . . . **CLC 44**
   See also CA 85-88; 147; DLB 7

Kingsolver, Barbara   1955- . . . . . . **CLC 55, 81**
   See also AAYA 15; CA 129; 134

Kingston, Maxine (Ting Ting) Hong
   1940- . . . . **CLC 12, 19, 58**
   See also AAYA 8; CA 69-72; CANR 13,
   38; DLBY 80; MTCW; SATA 53

Kinnell, Galway
   1927- . . . . **CLC 1, 2, 3, 5, 13, 29**
   See also CA 9-12R; CANR 10, 34; DLB 5;
   DLBY 87; MTCW

Kinsella, Thomas   1928- . . . . **CLC 4, 19**
   See also CA 17-20R; CANR 15; DLB 27;
   MTCW

Kinsella, W(illiam) P(atrick)
   1935- . . . . **CLC 27, 43**
   See also AAYA 7; CA 97-100; CAAS 7;
   CANR 21, 35; MTCW

Kipling, (Joseph) Rudyard
   1865-1936 . . . . . . **TCLC 8, 17; DA; DAB;
                        PC 3; SSC 5; WLC**
   See also CA 105; 120; CANR 33;
   CDBLB 1890-1914; CLR 39; DLB 19, 34,
   141, 156; MAICYA; MTCW; YABC 2

Kirkup, James   1918- . . . . **CLC 1**
   See also CA 1-4R; CAAS 4; CANR 2;
   DLB 27; SATA 12

Kirkwood, James   1930(?)-1989 . . . . . . **CLC 9**
   See also AITN 2; CA 1-4R; 128; CANR 6,
   40

Kirshner, Sidney
   See Kingsley, Sidney

Kis, Danilo   1935-1989 . . . . **CLC 57**
   See also CA 109; 118; 129; MTCW

Kivi, Aleksis   1834-1872 . . . . **NCLC 30**

Kizer, Carolyn (Ashley)
   1925- . . . . **CLC 15, 39, 80**
   See also CA 65-68; CAAS 5; CANR 24;
   DLB 5

Klabund   1890-1928 . . . . **TCLC 44**
   See also DLB 66

Klappert, Peter   1942- . . . . **CLC 57**
   See also CA 33-36R; DLB 5

Klein, A(braham) M(oses)
   1909-1972 . . . . **CLC 19; DAB**
   See also CA 101; 37-40R; DLB 68

Klein, Norma   1938-1989 . . . . **CLC 30**
   See also AAYA 2; CA 41-44R; 128;
   CANR 15, 37; CLR 2, 19; JRDA;
   MAICYA; SAAS 1; SATA 7, 57

Klein, T(heodore) E(ibon) D(onald)
   1947- . . . . **CLC 34**
   See also CA 119; CANR 44

Kleist, Heinrich von
   1777-1811 . . . . **NCLC 2, 37**
   See also DLB 90

Klima, Ivan   1931- . . . . **CLC 56**
   See also CA 25-28R; CANR 17

Klimentov, Andrei Platonovich   1899-1951
   See Platonov, Andrei
   See also CA 108

Klinger, Friedrich Maximilian von
   1752-1831 . . . . **NCLC 1**
   See also DLB 94

Klopstock, Friedrich Gottlieb
   1724-1803 . . . . **NCLC 11**
   See also DLB 97

Knebel, Fletcher   1911-1993 . . . . **CLC 14**
   See also AITN 1; CA 1-4R; 140; CAAS 3;
   CANR 1, 36; SATA 36; SATA-Obit 75

Knickerbocker, Diedrich
   See Irving, Washington

Knight, Etheridge
   1931-1991 . . . . **CLC 40; BLC**
   See also BW 1; CA 21-24R; 133; CANR 23;
   DLB 41

Knight, Sarah Kemble   1666-1727 . . . . . **LC 7**
   See also DLB 24

Knister, Raymond   1899-1932 . . . . . . **TCLC 56**
   See also DLB 68

Knowles, John
   1926- . . . . **CLC 1, 4, 10, 26; DA**
   See also AAYA 10; CA 17-20R; CANR 40;
   CDALB 1968-1988; DLB 6; MTCW;
   SATA 8

Knox, Calvin M.
   See Silverberg, Robert

Knye, Cassandra
   See Disch, Thomas M(ichael)

Koch, C(hristopher) J(ohn)   1932- . . . **CLC 42**
   See also CA 127

Koch, Christopher
   See Koch, C(hristopher) J(ohn)

Koch, Kenneth   1925- . . . . **CLC 5, 8, 44**
   See also CA 1-4R; CANR 6, 36; DLB 5;
   SATA 65

Kochanowski, Jan   1530-1584 . . . . **LC 10**

Kock, Charles Paul de
   1794-1871 . . . . **NCLC 16**

Koda Shigeyuki   1867-1947
   See Rohan, Koda
   See also CA 121

Koestler, Arthur
   1905-1983 . . . . **CLC 1, 3, 6, 8, 15, 33**
   See also CA 1-4R; 109; CANR 1, 33;
   CDBLB 1945-1960; DLBY 83; MTCW

Kogawa, Joy Nozomi   1935- . . . . **CLC 78**
   See also CA 101; CANR 19

Kohout, Pavel   1928- . . . . **CLC 13**
   See also CA 45-48; CANR 3

Koizumi, Yakumo
   See Hearn, (Patricio) Lafcadio (Tessima
   Carlos)

Kolmar, Gertrud   1894-1943 . . . . . . **TCLC 40**

Komunyakaa, Yusef   1947- . . . . **CLC 86**
   See also CA 147; DLB 120

Konrad, George
   See Konrad, Gyoergy

Konrad, Gyoergy   1933- . . . . . . **CLC 4, 10, 73**
   See also CA 85-88

Konwicki, Tadeusz   1926- . . . . **CLC 8, 28, 54**
   See also CA 101; CAAS 9; CANR 39;
   MTCW

Koontz, Dean R(ay)   1945- . . . . **CLC 78**
   See also AAYA 9; BEST 89:3, 90:2;
   CA 108; CANR 19, 36; MTCW

Kopit, Arthur (Lee)   1937- . . . . . **CLC 1, 18, 33**
   See also AITN 1; CA 81-84; CABS 3;
   DLB 7; MTCW

Kops, Bernard   1926- . . . . **CLC 4**
   See also CA 5-8R; DLB 13

Kornbluth, C(yril) M.   1923-1958. . . . **TCLC 8**
   See also CA 105; DLB 8

Korolenko, V. G.
   See Korolenko, Vladimir Galaktionovich

Korolenko, Vladimir
   See Korolenko, Vladimir Galaktionovich

Korolenko, Vladimir G.
   See Korolenko, Vladimir Galaktionovich

Korolenko, Vladimir Galaktionovich
   1853-1921 . . . . **TCLC 22**
   See also CA 121

Landwirth, Heinz 1927-
See Lind, Jakov
See also CA 9-12R; CANR 7

Lane, Patrick 1939- . . . . **CLC 25**
See also CA 97-100; DLB 53

Lang, Andrew 1844-1912 . . . . **TCLC 16**
See also CA 114; 137; DLB 98, 141;
MAICYA; SATA 16

Lang, Fritz 1890-1976 . . . . **CLC 20**
See also CA 77-80; 69-72; CANR 30

Lange, John
See Crichton, (John) Michael

Langer, Elinor 1939- . . . . **CLC 34**
See also CA 121

Langland, William
1330(?)-1400(?) . . . . **LC 19; DA; DAB**
See also DLB 146

Langstaff, Launcelot
See Irving, Washington

Lanier, Sidney 1842-1881 . . . . **NCLC 6**
See also DLB 64; MAICYA; SATA 18

Lanyer, Aemilia 1569-1645 . . . . . **LC 10, 30**
See also DLB 121

Lao Tzu . . . . **CMLC 7**

Lapine, James (Elliot) 1949- . . . . **CLC 39**
See also CA 123; 130

Larbaud, Valery (Nicolas)
1881-1957 . . . . **TCLC 9**
See also CA 106

Lardner, Ring
See Lardner, Ring(gold) W(ilmer)

Lardner, Ring W., Jr.
See Lardner, Ring(gold) W(ilmer)

Lardner, Ring(gold) W(ilmer)
1885-1933 . . . . **TCLC 2, 14**
See also CA 104; 131; CDALB 1917-1929;
DLB 11, 25, 86; MTCW

Laredo, Betty
See Codrescu, Andrei

Larkin, Maia
See Wojciechowska, Maia (Teresa)

Larkin, Philip (Arthur)
1922-1985 . . . . . **CLC 3, 5, 8, 9, 13, 18, 33,**
39, 64; DAB
See also CA 5-8R; 117; CANR 24;
CDBLB 1960 to Present; DLB 27;
MTCW

Larra (y Sanchez de Castro), Mariano Jose de
1809-1837 . . . . **NCLC 17**

Larsen, Eric 1941- . . . . **CLC 55**
See also CA 132

Larsen, Nella 1891-1964 . . . . . **CLC 37; BLC**
See also BW 1; CA 125; DLB 51

Larson, Charles R(aymond) 1938- . . . **CLC 31**
See also CA 53-56; CANR 4

Las Casas, Bartolome de 1474-1566 . . **LC 31**

Lasker-Schueler, Else 1869-1945 . . **TCLC 57**
See also DLB 66, 124

Latham, Jean Lee 1902- . . . . **CLC 12**
See also AITN 1; CA 5-8R; CANR 7;
MAICYA; SATA 2, 68

Latham, Mavis
See Clark, Mavis Thorpe

Lathen, Emma . . . . **CLC 2**
See also Hennissart, Martha; Latsis, Mary
J(ane)

Lathrop, Francis
See Leiber, Fritz (Reuter, Jr.)

Latsis, Mary J(ane)
See Lathen, Emma
See also CA 85-88

Lattimore, Richmond (Alexander)
1906-1984 . . . . **CLC 3**
See also CA 1-4R; 112; CANR 1

Laughlin, James 1914- . . . . **CLC 49**
See also CA 21-24R; CAAS 22; CANR 9,
47; DLB 48

Laurence, (Jean) Margaret (Wemyss)
1926-1987 . . **CLC 3, 6, 13, 50, 62; SSC 7**
See also CA 5-8R; 121; CANR 33; DLB 53;
MTCW; SATA-Obit 50

Laurent, Antoine 1952- . . . . **CLC 50**

Lauscher, Hermann
See Hesse, Hermann

Lautreamont, Comte de
1846-1870 . . . . **NCLC 12; SSC 14**

Laverty, Donald
See Blish, James (Benjamin)

Lavin, Mary 1912- . . . . . . **CLC 4, 18; SSC 4**
See also CA 9-12R; CANR 33; DLB 15;
MTCW

Lavond, Paul Dennis
See Kornbluth, C(yril) M.; Pohl, Frederik

Lawler, Raymond Evenor 1922- . . . . **CLC 58**
See also CA 103

Lawrence, D(avid) H(erbert Richards)
1885-1930 . . . . **TCLC 2, 9, 16, 33, 48, 61;**
DA; DAB; SSC 4, 19; WLC
See also CA 104; 121; CDBLB 1914-1945;
DLB 10, 19, 36, 98; MTCW

Lawrence, T(homas) E(dward)
1888-1935 . . . . **TCLC 18**
See also Dale, Colin
See also CA 115

Lawrence of Arabia
See Lawrence, T(homas) E(dward)

Lawson, Henry (Archibald Hertzberg)
1867-1922 . . . . **TCLC 27; SSC 18**
See also CA 120

Lawton, Dennis
See Faust, Frederick (Schiller)

Laxness, Halldor . . . . **CLC 25**
See also Gudjonsson, Halldor Kiljan

Layamon fl. c. 1200- . . . . **CMLC 10**
See also DLB 146

Laye, Camara 1928-1980 . . . **CLC 4, 38; BLC**
See also BW 1; CA 85-88; 97-100;
CANR 25; MTCW

Layton, Irving (Peter) 1912- . . . . . **CLC 2, 15**
See also CA 1-4R; CANR 2, 33, 43;
DLB 88; MTCW

Lazarus, Emma 1849-1887 . . . . **NCLC 8**

Lazarus, Felix
See Cable, George Washington

Lazarus, Henry
See Slavitt, David R(ytman)

Lea, Joan
See Neufeld, John (Arthur)

Leacock, Stephen (Butler)
1869-1944 . . . . **TCLC 2**
See also CA 104; 141; DLB 92

Lear, Edward 1812-1888 . . . . **NCLC 3**
See also CLR 1; DLB 32; MAICYA;
SATA 18

Lear, Norman (Milton) 1922- . . . . . . **CLC 12**
See also CA 73-76

Leavis, F(rank) R(aymond)
1895-1978 . . . . **CLC 24**
See also CA 21-24R; 77-80; CANR 44;
MTCW

Leavitt, David 1961- . . . . **CLC 34**
See also CA 116; 122; DLB 130

Leblanc, Maurice (Marie Emile)
1864-1941 . . . . **TCLC 49**
See also CA 110

Lebowitz, Fran(ces Ann)
1951(?)- . . . . **CLC 11, 36**
See also CA 81-84; CANR 14; MTCW

Lebrecht, Peter
See Tieck, (Johann) Ludwig

le Carre, John . . . . **CLC 3, 5, 9, 15, 28**
See also Cornwell, David (John Moore)
See also BEST 89:4; CDBLB 1960 to
Present; DLB 87

Le Clezio, J(ean) M(arie) G(ustave)
1940- . . . . **CLC 31**
See also CA 116; 128; DLB 83

Leconte de Lisle, Charles-Marie-Rene
1818-1894 . . . . **NCLC 29**

Le Coq, Monsieur
See Simenon, Georges (Jacques Christian)

Leduc, Violette 1907-1972 . . . . **CLC 22**
See also CA 13-14; 33-36R; CAP 1

Ledwidge, Francis 1887(?)-1917 . . . **TCLC 23**
See also CA 123; DLB 20

Lee, Andrea 1953- . . . . **CLC 36; BLC**
See also BW 1; CA 125

Lee, Andrew
See Auchincloss, Louis (Stanton)

Lee, Don L. . . . . **CLC 2**
See also Madhubuti, Haki R.

Lee, George W(ashington)
1894-1976 . . . . **CLC 52; BLC**
See also BW 1; CA 125; DLB 51

Lee, (Nelle) Harper
1926- . . . . . **CLC 12, 60; DA; DAB; WLC**
See also AAYA 13; CA 13-16R;
CDALB 1941-1968; DLB 6; MTCW;
SATA 11

Lee, Helen Elaine 1959(?)- . . . . **CLC 86**
See also CA 148

Lee, Julian
See Latham, Jean Lee

Lee, Larry
See Lee, Lawrence

Lee, Laurie 1914- . . . . **CLC 90; DAB**
See also CA 77-80; CANR 33; DLB 27;
MTCW

Lee, Lawrence 1941-1990 . . . . **CLC 34**
See also CA 131; CANR 43

Lewisohn, Ludwig 1883-1955...... **TCLC 19**
See also CA 107; DLB 4, 9, 28, 102

Lezama Lima, Jose 1910-1976 ... **CLC 4, 10**
See also CA 77-80; DLB 113; HW

L'Heureux, John (Clarke) 1934-.... **CLC 52**
See also CA 13-16R; CANR 23, 45

Liddell, C. H.
See Kuttner, Henry

Lie, Jonas (Lauritz Idemil)
1833-1908(?) .... **TCLC 5**
See also CA 115

Lieber, Joel 1937-1971............. **CLC 6**
See also CA 73-76; 29-32R

Lieber, Stanley Martin
See Lee, Stan

Lieberman, Laurence (James)
1935-.................... **CLC 4, 36**
See also CA 17-20R; CANR 8, 36

Lieksman, Anders
See Haavikko, Paavo Juhani

Li Fei-kan 1904-
See Pa Chin
See also CA 105

Lifton, Robert Jay 1926-.......... **CLC 67**
See also CA 17-20R; CANR 27; SATA 66

Lightfoot, Gordon 1938-.......... **CLC 26**
See also CA 109

Lightman, Alan P. 1948-.......... **CLC 81**
See also CA 141

Ligotti, Thomas (Robert)
1953-.............. **CLC 44; SSC 16**
See also CA 123; CANR 49

Li Ho 791-817.................... **PC 13**

Liliencron, (Friedrich Adolf Axel) Detlev von
1844-1909 .... **TCLC 18**
See also CA 117

Lilly, William 1602-1681.......... **LC 27**

Lima, Jose Lezama
See Lezama Lima, Jose

Lima Barreto, Afonso Henrique de
1881-1922 .... **TCLC 23**
See also CA 117

Limonov, Edward 1944-.......... **CLC 67**
See also CA 137

Lin, Frank
See Atherton, Gertrude (Franklin Horn)

Lincoln, Abraham 1809-1865..... **NCLC 18**

Lind, Jakov .... **CLC 1, 2, 4, 27, 82**
See also Landwirth, Heinz
See also CAAS 4

Lindbergh, Anne (Spencer) Morrow
1906-.................... **CLC 82**
See also CA 17-20R; CANR 16; MTCW;
SATA 33

Lindsay, David 1878-1945 .... **TCLC 15**
See also CA 113

Lindsay, (Nicholas) Vachel
1879-1931 .... **TCLC 17; DA; WLC**
See also CA 114; 135; CDALB 1865-1917;
DLB 54; SATA 40

Linke-Poot
See Doeblin, Alfred

Linney, Romulus 1930- .... **CLC 51**
See also CA 1-4R; CANR 40, 44

Linton, Eliza Lynn 1822-1898.... **NCLC 41**
See also DLB 18

Li Po 701-763................... **CMLC 2**

Lipsius, Justus 1547-1606 .... **LC 16**

Lipsyte, Robert (Michael)
1938-.................... **CLC 21; DA**
See also AAYA 7; CA 17-20R; CANR 8;
CLR 23; JRDA; MAICYA; SATA 5, 68

Lish, Gordon (Jay) 1934-.. **CLC 45; SSC 18**
See also CA 113; 117; DLB 130

Lispector, Clarice 1925-1977...... **CLC 43**
See also CA 139; 116; DLB 113

Littell, Robert 1935(?)- .... **CLC 42**
See also CA 109; 112

Little, Malcolm 1925-1965
See Malcolm X
See also BW 1; CA 125; 111; DA; DAB;
MTCW

Littlewit, Humphrey Gent.
See Lovecraft, H(oward) P(hillips)

Litwos
See Sienkiewicz, Henryk (Adam Alexander
Pius)

Liu E 1857-1909................. **TCLC 15**
See also CA 115

Lively, Penelope (Margaret)
1933-.................... **CLC 32, 50**
See also CA 41-44R; CANR 29; CLR 7;
DLB 14; JRDA; MAICYA; MTCW;
SATA 7, 60

Livesay, Dorothy (Kathleen)
1909-.................. **CLC 4, 15, 79**
See also AITN 2; CA 25-28R; CAAS 8;
CANR 36; DLB 68; MTCW

Livy c. 59B.C.-c. 17 .... **CMLC 11**

Lizardi, Jose Joaquin Fernandez de
1776-1827 .... **NCLC 30**

Llewellyn, Richard
See Llewellyn Lloyd, Richard Dafydd
Vivian
See also DLB 15

Llewellyn Lloyd, Richard Dafydd Vivian
1906-1983 .... **CLC 7, 80**
See also Llewellyn, Richard
See also CA 53-56; 111; CANR 7;
SATA 11; SATA-Obit 37

Llosa, (Jorge) Mario (Pedro) Vargas
See Vargas Llosa, (Jorge) Mario (Pedro)

Lloyd Webber, Andrew 1948-
See Webber, Andrew Lloyd
See also AAYA 1; CA 116; SATA 56

Llull, Ramon c. 1235-c. 1316..... **CMLC 12**

Locke, Alain (Le Roy)
1886-1954 .... **TCLC 43**
See also BW 1; CA 106; 124; DLB 51

Locke, John 1632-1704 .... **LC 7**
See also DLB 101

Locke-Elliott, Sumner
See Elliott, Sumner Locke

Lockhart, John Gibson
1794-1854 .... **NCLC 6**
See also DLB 110, 116, 144

Lodge, David (John) 1935-........ **CLC 36**
See also BEST 90:1; CA 17-20R; CANR 19;
DLB 14; MTCW

Loennbohm, Armas Eino Leopold 1878-1926
See Leino, Eino
See also CA 123

Loewinsohn, Ron(ald William)
1937-.................... **CLC 52**
See also CA 25-28R

Logan, Jake
See Smith, Martin Cruz

Logan, John (Burton) 1923-1987..... **CLC 5**
See also CA 77-80; 124; CANR 45; DLB 5

Lo Kuan-chung 1330(?)-1400(?)...... **LC 12**

Lombard, Nap
See Johnson, Pamela Hansford

London, Jack.. **TCLC 9, 15, 39; SSC 4; WLC**
See also London, John Griffith
See also AAYA 13; AITN 2;
CDALB 1865-1917; DLB 8, 12, 78;
SATA 18

London, John Griffith 1876-1916
See London, Jack
See also CA 110; 119; DA; DAB; JRDA;
MAICYA; MTCW

Long, Emmett
See Leonard, Elmore (John, Jr.)

Longbaugh, Harry
See Goldman, William (W.)

Longfellow, Henry Wadsworth
1807-1882 ...... **NCLC 2, 45; DA; DAB**
See also CDALB 1640-1865; DLB 1, 59;
SATA 19

Longley, Michael 1939-........... **CLC 29**
See also CA 102; DLB 40

Longus fl. c. 2nd cent. - .... **CMLC 7**

Longway, A. Hugh
See Lang, Andrew

Lopate, Phillip 1943- .... **CLC 29**
See also CA 97-100; DLBY 80

Lopez Portillo (y Pacheco), Jose
1920-.................... **CLC 46**
See also CA 129; HW

Lopez y Fuentes, Gregorio
1897(?)-1966 .... **CLC 32**
See also CA 131; HW

Lorca, Federico Garcia
See Garcia Lorca, Federico

Lord, Bette Bao 1938-............. **CLC 23**
See also BEST 90:3; CA 107; CANR 41;
SATA 58

Lord Auch
See Bataille, Georges

Lord Byron
See Byron, George Gordon (Noel)

Lorde, Audre (Geraldine)
1934-1992 .... **CLC 18, 71; BLC; PC 12**
See also BW 1; CA 25-28R; 142; CANR 16,
26, 46; DLB 41; MTCW

Lord Jeffrey
See Jeffrey, Francis

Lorenzo, Heberto Padilla
See Padilla (Lorenzo), Heberto

Maclean, Norman (Fitzroy)
1902-1990 . . . . **CLC 78; SSC 13**
See also CA 102; 132; CANR 49

MacLeish, Archibald
1892-1982 . . . . **CLC 3, 8, 14, 68**
See also CA 9-12R; 106; CANR 33; DLB 4,
7, 45; DLBY 82; MTCW

MacLennan, (John) Hugh
1907-1990 . . . . **CLC 2, 14**
See also CA 5-8R; 142; CANR 33; DLB 68;
MTCW

MacLeod, Alistair　1936- . . . . **CLC 56**
See also CA 123; DLB 60

MacNeice, (Frederick) Louis
1907-1963 . . . . . . **CLC 1, 4, 10, 53; DAB**
See also CA 85-88; DLB 10, 20; MTCW

MacNeill, Dand
See Fraser, George MacDonald

Macpherson, James　1736-1796 . . . . . . **LC 29**
See also DLB 109

Macpherson, (Jean) Jay　1931- . . . . . . **CLC 14**
See also CA 5-8R; DLB 53

MacShane, Frank　1927- . . . . **CLC 39**
See also CA 9-12R; CANR 3, 33; DLB 111

Macumber, Mari
See Sandoz, Mari(e Susette)

Madach, Imre　1823-1864 . . . . **NCLC 19**

Madden, (Jerry) David　1933- . . . . **CLC 5, 15**
See also CA 1-4R; CAAS 3; CANR 4, 45;
DLB 6; MTCW

Maddern, Al(an)
See Ellison, Harlan (Jay)

Madhubuti, Haki R.
1942- . . . . **CLC 6, 73; BLC; PC 5**
See also Lee, Don L.
See also BW 2; CA 73-76; CANR 24;
DLB 5, 41; DLBD 8

Maepenn, Hugh
See Kuttner, Henry

Maepenn, K. H.
See Kuttner, Henry

Maeterlinck, Maurice　1862-1949 . . . **TCLC 3**
See also CA 104; 136; SATA 66

Maginn, William　1794-1842 . . . . **NCLC 8**
See also DLB 110

Mahapatra, Jayanta　1928- . . . . **CLC 33**
See also CA 73-76; CAAS 9; CANR 15, 33

Mahfouz, Naguib (Abdel Aziz Al-Sabilgi)
1911(?)-
See Mahfuz, Najib
See also BEST 89:2; CA 128; MTCW

Mahfuz, Najib . . . . **CLC 52, 55**
See also Mahfouz, Naguib (Abdel Aziz
Al-Sabilgi)
See also DLBY 88

Mahon, Derek　1941- . . . . **CLC 27**
See also CA 113; 128; DLB 40

Mailer, Norman
1923- . . . . . . **CLC 1, 2, 3, 4, 5, 8, 11, 14,
28, 39, 74; DA; DAB**
See also AITN 2; CA 9-12R; CABS 1;
CANR 28; CDALB 1968-1988; DLB 2,
16, 28; DLBD 3; DLBY 80, 83; MTCW

Maillet, Antonine　1929- . . . . **CLC 54**
See also CA 115; 120; CANR 46; DLB 60

Mais, Roger　1905-1955 . . . . **TCLC 8**
See also BW 1; CA 105; 124; DLB 125;
MTCW

Maistre, Joseph de　1753-1821 . . . . **NCLC 37**

Maitland, Sara (Louise)　1950- . . . . . . **CLC 49**
See also CA 69-72; CANR 13

Major, Clarence
1936- . . . . **CLC 3, 19, 48; BLC**
See also BW 2; CA 21-24R; CAAS 6;
CANR 13, 25; DLB 33

Major, Kevin (Gerald)　1949- . . . . **CLC 26**
See also CA 97-100; CANR 21, 38;
CLR 11; DLB 60; JRDA; MAICYA;
SATA 32, 82

Maki, James
See Ozu, Yasujiro

Malabaila, Damiano
See Levi, Primo

Malamud, Bernard
1914-1986 . . . . . . **CLC 1, 2, 3, 5, 8, 9, 11,
18, 27, 44, 78, 85; DA; DAB; SSC 15;
WLC**
See also CA 5-8R; 118; CABS 1; CANR 28;
CDALB 1941-1968; DLB 2, 28, 152;
DLBY 80, 86; MTCW

Malaparte, Curzio　1898-1957 . . . . . **TCLC 52**

Malcolm, Dan
See Silverberg, Robert

Malcolm X . . . . **CLC 82; BLC**
See also Little, Malcolm

Malherbe, Francois de　1555-1628 . . . . . **LC 5**

Mallarme, Stephane
1842-1898 . . . . **NCLC 4, 41; PC 4**

Mallet-Joris, Francoise　1930- . . . . . . **CLC 11**
See also CA 65-68; CANR 17; DLB 83

Malley, Ern
See McAuley, James Phillip

Mallowan, Agatha Christie
See Christie, Agatha (Mary Clarissa)

Maloff, Saul　1922- . . . . **CLC 5**
See also CA 33-36R

Malone, Louis
See MacNeice, (Frederick) Louis

Malone, Michael (Christopher)
1942- . . . . **CLC 43**
See also CA 77-80; CANR 14, 32

Malory, (Sir) Thomas
1410(?)-1471(?) . . . . **LC 11; DA; DAB**
See also CDBLB Before 1660; DLB 146;
SATA 59; SATA-Brief 33

Malouf, (George Joseph) David
1934- . . . . **CLC 28, 86**
See also CA 124

Malraux, (Georges-)Andre
1901-1976 . . . . . . **CLC 1, 4, 9, 13, 15, 57**
See also CA 21-22; 69-72; CANR 34;
CAP 2; DLB 72; MTCW

Malzberg, Barry N(athaniel)　1939- . . . **CLC 7**
See also CA 61-64; CAAS 4; CANR 16;
DLB 8

Mamet, David (Alan)
1947- . . . . **CLC 9, 15, 34, 46; DC 4**
See also AAYA 3; CA 81-84; CABS 3;
CANR 15, 41; DLB 7; MTCW

Mamoulian, Rouben (Zachary)
1897-1987 . . . . **CLC 16**
See also CA 25-28R; 124

Mandelstam, Osip (Emilievich)
1891(?)-1938(?) . . . . **TCLC 2, 6**
See also CA 104

Mander, (Mary) Jane　1877-1949 . . . **TCLC 31**

Mandiargues, Andre Pieyre de . . . . . . **CLC 41**
See also Pieyre de Mandiargues, Andre
See also DLB 83

Mandrake, Ethel Belle
See Thurman, Wallace (Henry)

Mangan, James Clarence
1803-1849 . . . . **NCLC 27**

Maniere, J.-E.
See Giraudoux, (Hippolyte) Jean

Manley, (Mary) Delariviere
1672(?)-1724 . . . . **LC 1**
See also DLB 39, 80

Mann, Abel
See Creasey, John

Mann, (Luiz) Heinrich　1871-1950 . . . **TCLC 9**
See also CA 106; DLB 66

Mann, (Paul) Thomas
1875-1955 . . . . **TCLC 2, 8, 14, 21, 35, 44,
60; DA; DAB; SSC 5; WLC**
See also CA 104; 128; DLB 66; MTCW

Manning, David
See Faust, Frederick (Schiller)

Manning, Frederic　1887(?)-1935 . . . **TCLC 25**
See also CA 124

Manning, Olivia　1915-1980 . . . . . . **CLC 5, 19**
See also CA 5-8R; 101; CANR 29; MTCW

Mano, D. Keith　1942- . . . . **CLC 2, 10**
See also CA 25-28R; CAAS 6; CANR 26;
DLB 6

Mansfield, Katherine
. . . . . **TCLC 2, 8, 39; DAB; SSC 9; WLC**
See also Beauchamp, Kathleen Mansfield

Manso, Peter　1940- . . . . **CLC 39**
See also CA 29-32R; CANR 44

Mantecon, Juan Jimenez
See Jimenez (Mantecon), Juan Ramon

Manton, Peter
See Creasey, John

Man Without a Spleen, A
See Chekhov, Anton (Pavlovich)

Manzoni, Alessandro　1785-1873 . . **NCLC 29**

Mapu, Abraham (ben Jekutiel)
1808-1867 . . . . **NCLC 18**

Mara, Sally
See Queneau, Raymond

Marat, Jean Paul　1743-1793 . . . . **LC 10**

Marcel, Gabriel Honore
1889-1973 . . . . **CLC 15**
See also CA 102; 45-48; MTCW

Marchbanks, Samuel
See Davies, (William) Robertson

Marchi, Giacomo
See Bassani, Giorgio

Margulies, Donald . . . . **CLC 76**

Marie de France　c. 12th cent. - . . . . **CMLC 8**

Marie de l'Incarnation　1599-1672 . . . . **LC 10**

Mauriac, Claude 1914-............. **CLC 9**
See also CA 89-92; DLB 83

Mauriac, Francois (Charles)
1885-1970 .... **CLC 4, 9, 56**
See also CA 25-28; CAP 2; DLB 65;
MTCW

Mavor, Osborne Henry 1888-1951
See Bridie, James
See also CA 104

Maxwell, William (Keepers, Jr.)
1908- .... **CLC 19**
See also CA 93-96; DLBY 80

May, Elaine 1932- .... **CLC 16**
See also CA 124; 142; DLB 44

Mayakovski, Vladimir (Vladimirovich)
1893-1930 .... **TCLC 4, 18**
See also CA 104

Mayhew, Henry 1812-1887 ...... **NCLC 31**
See also DLB 18, 55

Mayle, Peter 1939(?)-............. **CLC 89**
See also CA 139

Maynard, Joyce 1953- .... **CLC 23**
See also CA 111; 129

Mayne, William (James Carter)
1928- .... **CLC 12**
See also CA 9-12R; CANR 37; CLR 25;
JRDA; MAICYA; SAAS 11; SATA 6, 68

Mayo, Jim
See L'Amour, Louis (Dearborn)

Maysles, Albert 1926- .... **CLC 16**
See also CA 29-32R

Maysles, David 1932-............. **CLC 16**

Mazer, Norma Fox 1931- .... **CLC 26**
See also AAYA 5; CA 69-72; CANR 12,
32; CLR 23; JRDA; MAICYA; SAAS 1;
SATA 24, 67

Mazzini, Guiseppe 1805-1872 .... **NCLC 34**

McAuley, James Phillip
1917-1976 .... **CLC 45**
See also CA 97-100

McBain, Ed
See Hunter, Evan

McBrien, William Augustine
1930- .... **CLC 44**
See also CA 107

McCaffrey, Anne (Inez) 1926-...... **CLC 17**
See also AAYA 6; AITN 2; BEST 89:2;
CA 25-28R; CANR 15, 35; DLB 8;
JRDA; MAICYA; MTCW; SAAS 11;
SATA 8, 70

McCall, Nathan 1955(?)- .... **CLC 86**
See also CA 146

McCann, Arthur
See Campbell, John W(ood, Jr.)

McCann, Edson
See Pohl, Frederik

McCarthy, Charles, Jr. 1933-
See McCarthy, Cormac
See also CANR 42

McCarthy, Cormac 1933-..... **CLC 4, 57, 59**
See also McCarthy, Charles, Jr.
See also DLB 6, 143

McCarthy, Mary (Therese)
1912-1989 ... **CLC 1, 3, 5, 14, 24, 39, 59**
See also CA 5-8R; 129; CANR 16; DLB 2;
DLBY 81; MTCW

McCartney, (James) Paul
1942- .... **CLC 12, 35**
See also CA 146

McCauley, Stephen (D.) 1955- ..... **CLC 50**
See also CA 141

McClure, Michael (Thomas)
1932- .... **CLC 6, 10**
See also CA 21-24R; CANR 17, 46;
DLB 16

McCorkle, Jill (Collins) 1958-...... **CLC 51**
See also CA 121; DLBY 87

McCourt, James 1941-............. **CLC 5**
See also CA 57-60

McCoy, Horace (Stanley)
1897-1955 .... **TCLC 28**
See also CA 108; DLB 9

McCrae, John 1872-1918........ **TCLC 12**
See also CA 109; DLB 92

McCreigh, James
See Pohl, Frederik

McCullers, (Lula) Carson (Smith)
1917-1967 .... **CLC 1, 4, 10, 12, 48; DA;**
DAB; SSC 9; WLC
See also CA 5-8R; 25-28R; CABS 1, 3;
CANR 18; CDALB 1941-1968; DLB 2, 7;
MTCW; SATA 27

McCulloch, John Tyler
See Burroughs, Edgar Rice

McCullough, Colleen 1938(?)-...... **CLC 27**
See also CA 81-84; CANR 17, 46; MTCW

McDermott, Alice 1953- .... **CLC 90**
See also CA 109; CANR 40

McElroy, Joseph 1930- .... **CLC 5, 47**
See also CA 17-20R

McEwan, Ian (Russell) 1948- ... **CLC 13, 66**
See also BEST 90:4; CA 61-64; CANR 14,
41; DLB 14; MTCW

McFadden, David 1940-........... **CLC 48**
See also CA 104; DLB 60

McFarland, Dennis 1950- .... **CLC 65**

McGahern, John
1934- .... **CLC 5, 9, 48; SSC 17**
See also CA 17-20R; CANR 29; DLB 14;
MTCW

McGinley, Patrick (Anthony)
1937- .... **CLC 41**
See also CA 120; 127

McGinley, Phyllis 1905-1978 ...... **CLC 14**
See also CA 9-12R; 77-80; CANR 19;
DLB 11, 48; SATA 2, 44; SATA-Obit 24

McGinniss, Joe 1942-............. **CLC 32**
See also AITN 2; BEST 89:2; CA 25-28R;
CANR 26

McGivern, Maureen Daly
See Daly, Maureen

McGrath, Patrick 1950-........... **CLC 55**
See also CA 136

McGrath, Thomas (Matthew)
1916-1990 .... **CLC 28, 59**
See also CA 9-12R; 132; CANR 6, 33;
MTCW; SATA 41; SATA-Obit 66

McGuane, Thomas (Francis III)
1939- .... **CLC 3, 7, 18, 45**
See also AITN 2; CA 49-52; CANR 5, 24,
49; DLB 2; DLBY 80; MTCW

McGuckian, Medbh 1950-........ **CLC 48**
See also CA 143; DLB 40

McHale, Tom 1942(?)-1982....... **CLC 3, 5**
See also AITN 1; CA 77-80; 106

McIlvanney, William 1936-........ **CLC 42**
See also CA 25-28R; DLB 14

McIlwraith, Maureen Mollie Hunter
See Hunter, Mollie
See also SATA 2

McInerney, Jay 1955- .... **CLC 34**
See also CA 116; 123; CANR 45

McIntyre, Vonda N(eel) 1948- ..... **CLC 18**
See also CA 81-84; CANR 17, 34; MTCW

McKay, Claude
.... **TCLC 7, 41; BLC; DAB; PC 2**
See McKay, Festus Claudius
See also DLB 4, 45, 51, 117

McKay, Festus Claudius 1889-1948
See McKay, Claude
See also BW 1; CA 104; 124; DA; MTCW;
WLC

McKuen, Rod 1933-............. **CLC 1, 3**
See also AITN 1; CA 41-44R; CANR 40

McLoughlin, R. B.
See Mencken, H(enry) L(ouis)

McLuhan, (Herbert) Marshall
1911-1980 .... **CLC 37, 83**
See also CA 9-12R; 102; CANR 12, 34;
DLB 88; MTCW

McMillan, Terry (L.) 1951-..... **CLC 50, 61**
See also BW 2; CA 140

McMurtry, Larry (Jeff)
1936- .... **CLC 2, 3, 7, 11, 27, 44**
See also AAYA 15; AITN 2; BEST 89:2;
CA 5-8R; CANR 19, 43;
CDALB 1968-1988; DLB 2, 143;
DLBY 80, 87; MTCW

McNally, T. M. 1961- .... **CLC 82**

McNally, Terrence 1939-...... **CLC 4, 7, 41**
See also CA 45-48; CANR 2; DLB 7

McNamer, Deirdre 1950-......... **CLC 70**

McNeile, Herman Cyril 1888-1937
See Sapper
See also DLB 77

McNickle, (William) D'Arcy
1904-1977 .... **CLC 89**
See also CA 9-12R; 85-88; CANR 5, 45;
NNAL; SATA-Obit 22

McPhee, John (Angus) 1931- ...... **CLC 36**
See also BEST 90:1; CA 65-68; CANR 20,
46; MTCW

McPherson, James Alan
1943- .... **CLC 19, 77**
See also BW 1; CA 25-28R; CAAS 17;
CANR 24; DLB 38; MTCW

McPherson, William (Alexander)
1933- .... **CLC 34**
See also CA 69-72; CANR 28

Mead, Margaret 1901-1978........ **CLC 37**
See also AITN 1; CA 1-4R; 81-84;
CANR 4; MTCW; SATA-Obit 20

Norton, Caroline 1808-1877...... **NCLC 47**
See also DLB 21

Norway, Nevil Shute 1899-1960
See Shute, Nevil
See also CA 102; 93-96

Norwid, Cyprian Kamil
1821-1883 .... **NCLC 17**

Nosille, Nabrah
See Ellison, Harlan (Jay)

Nossack, Hans Erich 1901-1978..... **CLC 6**
See also CA 93-96; 85-88; DLB 69

Nostradamus 1503-1566........... **LC 27**

Nosu, Chuji
See Ozu, Yasujiro

Notenburg, Eleanora (Genrikhovna) von
See Guro, Elena

Nova, Craig 1945-.............. **CLC 7, 31**
See also CA 45-48; CANR 2

Novak, Joseph
See Kosinski, Jerzy (Nikodem)

Novalis 1772-1801 .... **NCLC 13**
See also DLB 90

Nowlan, Alden (Albert) 1933-1983.. **CLC 15**
See also CA 9-12R; CANR 5; DLB 53

Noyes, Alfred 1880-1958.......... **TCLC 7**
See also CA 104; DLB 20

Nunn, Kem 19(?)-................. **CLC 34**

Nye, Robert 1939-............. **CLC 13, 42**
See also CA 33-36R; CANR 29; DLB 14;
MTCW; SATA 6

Nyro, Laura 1947-................ **CLC 17**

Oates, Joyce Carol
1938-......**CLC 1, 2, 3, 6, 9, 11, 15, 19,
33, 52; DA; DAB; SSC 6; WLC**
See also AAYA 15; AITN 1; BEST 89:2;
CA 5-8R; CANR 25, 45;
CDALB 1968-1988; DLB 2, 5, 130;
DLBY 81; MTCW

O'Brien, Darcy 1939-............. **CLC 11**
See also CA 21-24R; CANR 8

O'Brien, E. G.
See Clarke, Arthur C(harles)

O'Brien, Edna
1936-... **CLC 3, 5, 8, 13, 36, 65; SSC 10**
See also CA 1-4R; CANR 6, 41;
CDBLB 1960 to Present; DLB 14;
MTCW

O'Brien, Fitz-James 1828-1862... **NCLC 21**
See also DLB 74

O'Brien, Flann........ CLC 1, 4, 5, 7, 10, 47
See also O Nuallain, Brian

O'Brien, Richard 1942-........... **CLC 17**
See also CA 124

O'Brien, Tim 1946-.......... **CLC 7, 19, 40**
See also CA 85-88; CANR 40; DLB 152;
DLBD 9; DLBY 80

Obstfelder, Sigbjoern 1866-1900... **TCLC 23**
See also CA 123

O'Casey, Sean
1880-1964...... **CLC 1, 5, 9, 11, 15, 88;
DAB**
See also CA 89-92; CDBLB 1914-1945;
DLB 10; MTCW

O'Cathasaigh, Sean
See O'Casey, Sean

Ochs, Phil 1940-1976............. **CLC 17**
See also CA 65-68

O'Connor, Edwin (Greene)
1918-1968 .... **CLC 14**
See also CA 93-96; 25-28R

O'Connor, (Mary) Flannery
1925-1964 .... **CLC 1, 2, 3, 6, 10, 13, 15,
21, 66; DA; DAB; SSC 1; WLC**
See also AAYA 7; CA 1-4R; CANR 3, 41;
CDALB 1941-1968; DLB 2, 152;
DLBD 12; DLBY 80; MTCW

O'Connor, Frank........... CLC 23; SSC 5
See also O'Donovan, Michael John

O'Dell, Scott 1898-1989........... **CLC 30**
See also AAYA 3; CA 61-64; 129;
CANR 12, 30; CLR 1, 16; DLB 52;
JRDA; MAICYA; SATA 12, 60

Odets, Clifford 1906-1963....... **CLC 2, 28**
See also CA 85-88; DLB 7, 26; MTCW

O'Doherty, Brian 1934-........... **CLC 76**
See also CA 105

O'Donnell, K. M.
See Malzberg, Barry N(athaniel)

O'Donnell, Lawrence
See Kuttner, Henry

O'Donovan, Michael John
1903-1966 .... **CLC 14**
See also O'Connor, Frank
See also CA 93-96

Oe, Kenzaburo
1935-......... **CLC 10, 36, 86; SSC 20**
See also CA 97-100; CANR 36; DLBY 94;
MTCW

O'Faolain, Julia 1932-....... **CLC 6, 19, 47**
See also CA 81-84; CAAS 2; CANR 12;
DLB 14; MTCW

O'Faolain, Sean
1900-1991........ **CLC 1, 7, 14, 32, 70;
SSC 13**
See also CA 61-64; 134; CANR 12;
DLB 15; MTCW

O'Flaherty, Liam
1896-1984.......... **CLC 5, 34; SSC 6**
See also CA 101; 113; CANR 35; DLB 36;
DLBY 84; MTCW

Ogilvy, Gavin
See Barrie, J(ames) M(atthew)

O'Grady, Standish James
1846-1928 .... **TCLC 5**
See also CA 104

O'Grady, Timothy 1951-.......... **CLC 59**
See also CA 138

O'Hara, Frank
1926-1966 .... **CLC 2, 5, 13, 78**
See also CA 9-12R; 25-28R; CANR 33;
DLB 5, 16; MTCW

O'Hara, John (Henry)
1905-1970 .... **CLC 1, 2, 3, 6, 11, 42;
SSC 15**
See also CA 5-8R; 25-28R; CANR 31;
CDALB 1929-1941; DLB 9, 86; DLBD 2;
MTCW

O Hehir, Diana 1922-............ **CLC 41**
See also CA 93-96

Okigbo, Christopher (Ifenayichukwu)
1932-1967 ..... **CLC 25, 84; BLC; PC 7**
See also BW 1; CA 77-80; DLB 125;
MTCW

Okri, Ben 1959-................. **CLC 87**
See also BW 2; CA 130; 138

Olds, Sharon 1942-........ **CLC 32, 39, 85**
See also CA 101; CANR 18, 41; DLB 120

Oldstyle, Jonathan
See Irving, Washington

Olesha, Yuri (Karlovich)
1899-1960 .... **CLC 8**
See also CA 85-88

Oliphant, Laurence
1829(?)-1888 .... **NCLC 47**
See also DLB 18

Oliphant, Margaret (Oliphant Wilson)
1828-1897 .... **NCLC 11**
See also DLB 18

Oliver, Mary 1935-............ **CLC 19, 34**
See also CA 21-24R; CANR 9, 43; DLB 5

Olivier, Laurence (Kerr)
1907-1989 .... **CLC 20**
See also CA 111; 129

Olsen, Tillie
1913-.... **CLC 4, 13; DA; DAB; SSC 11**
See also CA 1-4R; CANR 1, 43; DLB 28;
DLBY 80; MTCW

Olson, Charles (John)
1910-1970 ..... **CLC 1, 2, 5, 6, 9, 11, 29**
See also CA 13-16; 25-28R; CABS 2;
CANR 35; CAP 1; DLB 5, 16; MTCW

Olson, Toby 1937-............... **CLC 28**
See also CA 65-68; CANR 9, 31

Olyesha, Yuri
See Olesha, Yuri (Karlovich)

Ondaatje, (Philip) Michael
1943-........ **CLC 14, 29, 51, 76; DAB**
See also CA 77-80; CANR 42; DLB 60

Oneal, Elizabeth 1934-
See Oneal, Zibby
See also CA 106; CANR 28; MAICYA;
SATA 30, 82

Oneal, Zibby .... **CLC 30**
See also Oneal, Elizabeth
See also AAYA 5; CLR 13; JRDA

O'Neill, Eugene (Gladstone)
1888-1953 ...... **TCLC 1, 6, 27, 49; DA;
DAB; WLC**
See also AITN 1; CA 110; 132;
CDALB 1929-1941; DLB 7; MTCW

Onetti, Juan Carlos 1909-1994... **CLC 7, 10**
See also CA 85-88; 145; CANR 32;
DLB 113; HW; MTCW

O Nuallain, Brian 1911-1966
See O'Brien, Flann
See also CA 21-22; 25-28R; CAP 2

Oppen, George 1908-1984.... **CLC 7, 13, 34**
See also CA 13-16R; 113; CANR 8; DLB 5

Oppenheim, E(dward) Phillips
1866-1946 .... **TCLC 45**
See also CA 111; DLB 70

Orlovitz, Gil 1918-1973........... **CLC 22**
See also CA 77-80; 45-48; DLB 2, 5

Orris
See Ingelow, Jean

Ortega y Gasset, Jose
1883-1955 . . . . TCLC 9; HLC
See also CA 106; 130; HW; MTCW

Ortese, Anna Maria   1914- . . . . CLC 89

Ortiz, Simon J(oseph)   1941- . . . . CLC 45
See also CA 134; DLB 120; NNAL

Orton, Joe . . . . CLC 4, 13, 43; DC 3
See also Orton, John Kingsley
See also CDBLB 1960 to Present; DLB 13

Orton, John Kingsley   1933-1967
See Orton, Joe
See also CA 85-88; CANR 35; MTCW

Orwell, George
. . . . . TCLC 2, 6, 15, 31, 51; DAB; WLC
See also Blair, Eric (Arthur)
See also CDBLB 1945-1960; DLB 15, 98

Osborne, David
See Silverberg, Robert

Osborne, George
See Silverberg, Robert

Osborne, John (James)
1929-1994 . . . . . CLC 1, 2, 5, 11, 45; DA;
DAB; WLC
See also CA 13-16R; 147; CANR 21;
CDBLB 1945-1960; DLB 13; MTCW

Osborne, Lawrence   1958- . . . . CLC 50

Oshima, Nagisa   1932- . . . . CLC 20
See also CA 116; 121

Oskison, John Milton
1874-1947 . . . . TCLC 35
See also CA 144; NNAL

Ossoli, Sarah Margaret (Fuller marchesa d')
1810-1850
See Fuller, Margaret
See also SATA 25

Ostrovsky, Alexander
1823-1886 . . . . NCLC 30

Otero, Blas de   1916-1979 . . . . CLC 11
See also CA 89-92; DLB 134

Otto, Whitney   1955- . . . . CLC 70
See also CA 140

Ouida . . . . TCLC 43
See also De La Ramee, (Marie) Louise
See also DLB 18, 156

Ousmane, Sembene   1923- . . . . CLC 66; BLC
See also BW 1; CA 117; 125; MTCW

Ovid   43B.C.-18(?) . . . . CMLC 7; PC 2

Owen, Hugh
See Faust, Frederick (Schiller)

Owen, Wilfred (Edward Salter)
1893-1918 . . . . . . TCLC 5, 27; DA; DAB;
WLC
See also CA 104; 141; CDBLB 1914-1945;
DLB 20

Owens, Rochelle   1936- . . . . CLC 8
See also CA 17-20R; CAAS 2; CANR 39

Oz, Amos   1939- . . . CLC 5, 8, 11, 27, 33, 54
See also CA 53-56; CANR 27, 47; MTCW

Ozick, Cynthia
1928- . . . . CLC 3, 7, 28, 62; SSC 15
See also BEST 90:1; CA 17-20R; CANR 23;
DLB 28, 152; DLBY 82; MTCW

Ozu, Yasujiro   1903-1963 . . . . CLC 16
See also CA 112

Pacheco, C.
See Pessoa, Fernando (Antonio Nogueira)

Pa Chin . . . . CLC 18
See also Li Fei-kan

Pack, Robert   1929- . . . . CLC 13
See also CA 1-4R; CANR 3, 44; DLB 5

Padgett, Lewis
See Kuttner, Henry

Padilla (Lorenzo), Heberto   1932- . . . CLC 38
See also AITN 1; CA 123; 131; HW

Page, Jimmy   1944- . . . . CLC 12

Page, Louise   1955- . . . . CLC 40
See also CA 140

Page, P(atricia) K(athleen)
1916- . . . . CLC 7, 18; PC 12
See also CA 53-56; CANR 4, 22; DLB 68;
MTCW

Paget, Violet   1856-1935
See Lee, Vernon
See also CA 104

Paget-Lowe, Henry
See Lovecraft, H(oward) P(hillips)

Paglia, Camille (Anna)   1947- . . . . CLC 68
See also CA 140

Paige, Richard
See Koontz, Dean R(ay)

Pakenham, Antonia
See Fraser, (Lady) Antonia (Pakenham)

Palamas, Kostes   1859-1943 . . . . TCLC 5
See also CA 105

Palazzeschi, Aldo   1885-1974 . . . . CLC 11
See also CA 89-92; 53-56; DLB 114

Paley, Grace   1922- . . . . CLC 4, 6, 37; SSC 8
See also CA 25-28R; CANR 13, 46;
DLB 28; MTCW

Palin, Michael (Edward)   1943- . . . . . CLC 21
See also Monty Python
See also CA 107; CANR 35; SATA 67

Palliser, Charles   1947- . . . . CLC 65
See also CA 136

Palma, Ricardo   1833-1919 . . . . TCLC 29

Pancake, Breece Dexter   1952-1979
See Pancake, Breece D'J
See also CA 123; 109

Pancake, Breece D'J . . . . CLC 29
See also Pancake, Breece Dexter
See also DLB 130

Panko, Rudy
See Gogol, Nikolai (Vasilyevich)

Papadiamantis, Alexandros
1851-1911 . . . . TCLC 29

Papadiamantopoulos, Johannes   1856-1910
See Moreas, Jean
See also CA 117

Papini, Giovanni   1881-1956 . . . . TCLC 22
See also CA 121

Paracelsus   1493-1541 . . . . LC 14

Parasol, Peter
See Stevens, Wallace

Parfenie, Maria
See Codrescu, Andrei

Parini, Jay (Lee)   1948- . . . . CLC 54
See also CA 97-100; CAAS 16; CANR 32

Park, Jordan
See Kornbluth, C(yril) M.; Pohl, Frederik

Parker, Bert
See Ellison, Harlan (Jay)

Parker, Dorothy (Rothschild)
1893-1967 . . . . CLC 15, 68; SSC 2
See also CA 19-20; 25-28R; CAP 2;
DLB 11, 45, 86; MTCW

Parker, Robert B(rown)   1932- . . . . . . CLC 27
See also BEST 89:4; CA 49-52; CANR 1,
26; MTCW

Parkin, Frank   1940- . . . . CLC 43
See also CA 147

Parkman, Francis, Jr.
1823-1893 . . . . NCLC 12
See also DLB 1, 30

Parks, Gordon (Alexander Buchanan)
1912- . . . . CLC 1, 16; BLC
See also AITN 2; BW 2; CA 41-44R;
CANR 26; DLB 33; SATA 8

Parnell, Thomas   1679-1718 . . . . LC 3
See also DLB 94

Parra, Nicanor   1914- . . . . CLC 2; HLC
See also CA 85-88; CANR 32; HW; MTCW

Parrish, Mary Frances
See Fisher, M(ary) F(rances) K(ennedy)

Parson
See Coleridge, Samuel Taylor

Parson Lot
See Kingsley, Charles

Partridge, Anthony
See Oppenheim, E(dward) Phillips

Pascoli, Giovanni   1855-1912 . . . . . . TCLC 45

Pasolini, Pier Paolo
1922-1975 . . . . CLC 20, 37
See also CA 93-96; 61-64; DLB 128;
MTCW

Pasquini
See Silone, Ignazio

Pastan, Linda (Olenik)   1932- . . . . . . CLC 27
See also CA 61-64; CANR 18, 40; DLB 5

Pasternak, Boris (Leonidovich)
1890-1960 . . . . . . CLC 7, 10, 18, 63; DA;
DAB; PC 6; WLC
See also CA 127; 116; MTCW

Patchen, Kenneth   1911-1972 . . . CLC 1, 2, 18
See also CA 1-4R; 33-36R; CANR 3, 35;
DLB 16, 48; MTCW

Pater, Walter (Horatio)
1839-1894 . . . . NCLC 7
See also CDBLB 1832-1890; DLB 57, 156

Paterson, A(ndrew) B(arton)
1864-1941 . . . . TCLC 32

Paterson, Katherine (Womeldorf)
1932- . . . . CLC 12, 30
See also AAYA 1; CA 21-24R; CANR 28;
CLR 7; DLB 52; JRDA; MAICYA;
MTCW; SATA 13, 53

Patmore, Coventry Kersey Dighton
1823-1896 . . . . NCLC 9
See also DLB 35, 98

Pinero, Arthur Wing 1855-1934 . . . **TCLC 32**
See also CA 110; DLB 10

Pinero, Miguel (Antonio Gomez)
1946-1988 . . . . **CLC 4, 55**
See also CA 61-64; 125; CANR 29; HW

Pinget, Robert 1919- . . . . **CLC 7, 13, 37**
See also CA 85-88; DLB 83

Pink Floyd
See Barrett, (Roger) Syd; Gilmour, David;
Mason, Nick; Waters, Roger; Wright,
Rick

Pinkney, Edward 1802-1828 . . . . . **NCLC 31**

Pinkwater, Daniel Manus 1941- . . . . **CLC 35**
See also Pinkwater, Manus
See also AAYA 1; CA 29-32R; CANR 12,
38; CLR 4; JRDA; MAICYA; SAAS 3;
SATA 46, 76

Pinkwater, Manus
See Pinkwater, Daniel Manus
See also SATA 8

Pinsky, Robert 1940- . . . . **CLC 9, 19, 38**
See also CA 29-32R; CAAS 4; DLBY 82

Pinta, Harold
See Pinter, Harold

Pinter, Harold
1930- . . . . . **CLC 1, 3, 6, 9, 11, 15, 27, 58,**
73; DA; DAB; WLC
See also CA 5-8R; CANR 33; CDBLB 1960
to Present; DLB 13; MTCW

Pirandello, Luigi
1867-1936 . . . . . . **TCLC 4, 29; DA; DAB;**
DC 5; WLC
See also CA 104

Pirsig, Robert M(aynard)
1928- . . . . **CLC 4, 6, 73**
See also CA 53-56; CANR 42; MTCW;
SATA 39

Pisarev, Dmitry Ivanovich
1840-1868 . . . . **NCLC 25**

Pix, Mary (Griffith) 1666-1709 . . . . . . **LC 8**
See also DLB 80

Pixerecourt, Guilbert de
1773-1844 . . . . **NCLC 39**

Plaidy, Jean
See Hibbert, Eleanor Alice Burford

Planche, James Robinson
1796-1880 . . . . **NCLC 42**

Plant, Robert 1948- . . . . **CLC 12**

Plante, David (Robert)
1940- . . . . **CLC 7, 23, 38**
See also CA 37-40R; CANR 12, 36;
DLBY 83; MTCW

Plath, Sylvia
1932-1963 . . . . . **CLC 1, 2, 3, 5, 9, 11, 14,**
17, 50, 51, 62; DA; DAB; PC 1; WLC
See also AAYA 13; CA 19-20; CANR 34;
CAP 2; CDALB 1941-1968; DLB 5, 6,
152; MTCW

Plato
428(?)B.C.-348(?)B.C. . . . . . **CMLC 8; DA;**
DAB

Platonov, Andrei . . . . **TCLC 14**
See also Klimentov, Andrei Platonovich

Platt, Kin 1911- . . . . **CLC 26**
See also AAYA 11; CA 17-20R; CANR 11;
JRDA; SAAS 17; SATA 21

Plick et Plock
See Simenon, Georges (Jacques Christian)

Plimpton, George (Ames) 1927- . . . . . **CLC 36**
See also AITN 1; CA 21-24R; CANR 32;
MTCW; SATA 10

Plomer, William Charles Franklin
1903-1973 . . . . **CLC 4, 8**
See also CA 21-22; CANR 34; CAP 2;
DLB 20; MTCW; SATA 24

Plowman, Piers
See Kavanagh, Patrick (Joseph)

Plum, J.
See Wodehouse, P(elham) G(renville)

Plumly, Stanley (Ross) 1939- . . . . . . **CLC 33**
See also CA 108; 110; DLB 5

Plumpe, Friedrich Wilhelm
1888-1931 . . . . **TCLC 53**
See also CA 112

Poe, Edgar Allan
1809-1849 . . . . . **NCLC 1, 16; DA; DAB;**
PC 1; SSC 1; WLC
See also AAYA 14; CDALB 1640-1865;
DLB 3, 59, 73, 74; SATA 23

Poet of Titchfield Street, The
See Pound, Ezra (Weston Loomis)

Pohl, Frederik 1919- . . . . **CLC 18**
See also CA 61-64; CAAS 1; CANR 11, 37;
DLB 8; MTCW; SATA 24

Poirier, Louis 1910-
See Gracq, Julien
See also CA 122; 126

Poitier, Sidney 1927- . . . . **CLC 26**
See also BW 1; CA 117

Polanski, Roman 1933- . . . . **CLC 16**
See also CA 77-80

Poliakoff, Stephen 1952- . . . . **CLC 38**
See also CA 106; DLB 13

Police, The
See Copeland, Stewart (Armstrong);
Summers, Andrew James; Sumner,
Gordon Matthew

Polidori, John William
1795-1821 . . . . **NCLC 51**
See also DLB 116

Pollitt, Katha 1949- . . . . **CLC 28**
See also CA 120; 122; MTCW

Pollock, (Mary) Sharon 1936- . . . . . . **CLC 50**
See also CA 141; DLB 60

Polo, Marco 1254-1324 . . . . **CMLC 15**

Pomerance, Bernard 1940- . . . . **CLC 13**
See also CA 101; CANR 49

Ponge, Francis (Jean Gaston Alfred)
1899-1988 . . . . **CLC 6, 18**
See also CA 85-88; 126; CANR 40

Pontoppidan, Henrik 1857-1943 . . . **TCLC 29**

Poole, Josephine . . . . **CLC 17**
See also Helyar, Jane Penelope Josephine
See also SAAS 2; SATA 5

Popa, Vasko 1922-1991 . . . . **CLC 19**
See also CA 112; 148

Pope, Alexander
1688-1744 . . . . . . **LC 3; DA; DAB; WLC**
See also CDBLB 1660-1789; DLB 95, 101

Porter, Connie (Rose) 1959(?)- . . . . . **CLC 70**
See also BW 2; CA 142; SATA 81

Porter, Gene(va Grace) Stratton
1863(?)-1924 . . . . **TCLC 21**
See also CA 112

Porter, Katherine Anne
1890-1980 . . . . . . **CLC 1, 3, 7, 10, 13, 15,**
27; DA; DAB; SSC 4
See also AITN 2; CA 1-4R; CANR 1;
DLB 4, 9, 102; DLBD 12; DLBY 80;
MTCW; SATA 39; SATA-Obit 23

Porter, Peter (Neville Frederick)
1929- . . . . **CLC 5, 13, 33**
See also CA 85-88; DLB 40

Porter, William Sydney 1862-1910
See Henry, O.
See also CA 104; 131; CDALB 1865-1917;
DA; DAB; DLB 12, 78, 79; MTCW;
YABC 2

Portillo (y Pacheco), Jose Lopez
See Lopez Portillo (y Pacheco), Jose

Post, Melville Davisson
1869-1930 . . . . **TCLC 39**
See also CA 110

Potok, Chaim 1929- . . . . **CLC 2, 7, 14, 26**
See also AAYA 15; AITN 1, 2; CA 17-20R;
CANR 19, 35; DLB 28, 152; MTCW;
SATA 33

Potter, Beatrice
See Webb, (Martha) Beatrice (Potter)
See also MAICYA

Potter, Dennis (Christopher George)
1935-1994 . . . . **CLC 58, 86**
See also CA 107; 145; CANR 33; MTCW

Pound, Ezra (Weston Loomis)
1885-1972 . . . . . . **CLC 1, 2, 3, 4, 5, 7, 10,**
13, 18, 34, 48, 50; DA; DAB; PC 4; WLC
See also CA 5-8R; 37-40R; CANR 40;
CDALB 1917-1929; DLB 4, 45, 63;
MTCW

Povod, Reinaldo 1959-1994 . . . . **CLC 44**
See also CA 136; 146

Powell, Adam Clayton, Jr.
1908-1972 . . . . **CLC 89; BLC**
See also BW 1; CA 102; 33-36R

Powell, Anthony (Dymoke)
1905- . . . . **CLC 1, 3, 7, 9, 10, 31**
See also CA 1-4R; CANR 1, 32;
CDBLB 1945-1960; DLB 15; MTCW

Powell, Dawn 1897-1965 . . . . **CLC 66**
See also CA 5-8R

Powell, Padgett 1952- . . . . **CLC 34**
See also CA 126

Powers, J(ames) F(arl)
1917- . . . . **CLC 1, 4, 8, 57; SSC 4**
See also CA 1-4R; CANR 2; DLB 130;
MTCW

Powers, John J(ames) 1945-
See Powers, John R.
See also CA 69-72

Powers, John R. . . . . **CLC 66**
See also Powers, John J(ames)

Raleigh, Richard
    See Lovecraft, H(oward) P(hillips)

Raleigh, Sir Walter   1554(?)-1618 .... **LC 31**
    See also CDBLB Before 1660

Rallentando, H. P.
    See Sayers, Dorothy L(eigh)

Ramal, Walter
    See de la Mare, Walter (John)

Ramon, Juan
    See Jimenez (Mantecon), Juan Ramon

Ramos, Graciliano   1892-1953 ..... **TCLC 32**

Rampersad, Arnold   1941-......... **CLC 44**
    See also BW 2; CA 127; 133; DLB 111

Rampling, Anne
    See Rice, Anne

Ramsay, Allan   1684(?)-1758 .... **LC 29**
    See also DLB 95

Ramuz, Charles-Ferdinand
    1878-1947 .... **TCLC 33**

Rand, Ayn
    1905-1982 ...... **CLC 3, 30, 44, 79; DA; WLC**
    See also AAYA 10; CA 13-16R; 105; CANR 27; MTCW

Randall, Dudley (Felker)
    1914- .... **CLC 1; BLC**
    See also BW 1; CA 25-28R; CANR 23; DLB 41

Randall, Robert
    See Silverberg, Robert

Ranger, Ken
    See Creasey, John

Ransom, John Crowe
    1888-1974 .... **CLC 2, 4, 5, 11, 24**
    See also CA 5-8R; 49-52; CANR 6, 34; DLB 45, 63; MTCW

Rao, Raja   1909- .... **CLC 25, 56**
    See also CA 73-76; MTCW

Raphael, Frederic (Michael)
    1931- .... **CLC 2, 14**
    See also CA 1-4R; CANR 1; DLB 14

Ratcliffe, James P.
    See Mencken, H(enry) L(ouis)

Rathbone, Julian   1935- .... **CLC 41**
    See also CA 101; CANR 34

Rattigan, Terence (Mervyn)
    1911-1977 .... **CLC 7**
    See also CA 85-88; 73-76; CDBLB 1945-1960; DLB 13; MTCW

Ratushinskaya, Irina   1954- .... **CLC 54**
    See also CA 129

Raven, Simon (Arthur Noel)
    1927- .... **CLC 14**
    See also CA 81-84

Rawley, Callman   1903-
    See Rakosi, Carl
    See also CA 21-24R; CANR 12, 32

Rawlings, Marjorie Kinnan
    1896-1953 .... **TCLC 4**
    See also CA 104; 137; DLB 9, 22, 102; JRDA; MAICYA; YABC 1

Ray, Satyajit   1921-1992........ **CLC 16, 76**
    See also CA 114; 137

Read, Herbert Edward   1893-1968.... **CLC 4**
    See also CA 85-88; 25-28R; DLB 20, 149

Read, Piers Paul   1941- ...... **CLC 4, 10, 25**
    See also CA 21-24R; CANR 38; DLB 14; SATA 21

Reade, Charles   1814-1884 .... **NCLC 2**
    See also DLB 21

Reade, Hamish
    See Gray, Simon (James Holliday)

Reading, Peter   1946- .... **CLC 47**
    See also CA 103; CANR 46; DLB 40

Reaney, James   1926- .... **CLC 13**
    See also CA 41-44R; CAAS 15; CANR 42; DLB 68; SATA 43

Rebreanu, Liviu   1885-1944 .... **TCLC 28**

Rechy, John (Francisco)
    1934- .... **CLC 1, 7, 14, 18; HLC**
    See also CA 5-8R; CAAS 4; CANR 6, 32; DLB 122; DLBY 82; HW

Redcam, Tom   1870-1933 .... **TCLC 25**

Reddin, Keith.................... **CLC 67**

Redgrove, Peter (William)
    1932- .... **CLC 6, 41**
    See also CA 1-4R; CANR 3, 39; DLB 40

Redmon, Anne.................... **CLC 22**
    See also Nightingale, Anne Redmon
    See also DLBY 86

Reed, Eliot
    See Ambler, Eric

Reed, Ishmael
    1938-.... **CLC 2, 3, 5, 6, 13, 32, 60; BLC**
    See also BW 2; CA 21-24R; CANR 25, 48; DLB 2, 5, 33; DLBD 8; MTCW

Reed, John (Silas)   1887-1920 ...... **TCLC 9**
    See also CA 106

Reed, Lou........................ **CLC 21**
    See also Firbank, Louis

Reeve, Clara   1729-1807......... **NCLC 19**
    See also DLB 39

Reich, Wilhelm   1897-1957........ **TCLC 57**

Reid, Christopher (John)   1949-..... **CLC 33**
    See also CA 140; DLB 40

Reid, Desmond
    See Moorcock, Michael (John)

Reid Banks, Lynne   1929-
    See Banks, Lynne Reid
    See also CA 1-4R; CANR 6, 22, 38; CLR 24; JRDA; MAICYA; SATA 22, 75

Reilly, William K.
    See Creasey, John

Reiner, Max
    See Caldwell, (Janet Miriam) Taylor (Holland)

Reis, Ricardo
    See Pessoa, Fernando (Antonio Nogueira)

Remarque, Erich Maria
    1898-1970 .... **CLC 21; DA; DAB**
    See also CA 77-80; 29-32R; DLB 56; MTCW

Remizov, A.
    See Remizov, Aleksei (Mikhailovich)

Remizov, A. M.
    See Remizov, Aleksei (Mikhailovich)

Remizov, Aleksei (Mikhailovich)
    1877-1957 .... **TCLC 27**
    See also CA 125; 133

Renan, Joseph Ernest
    1823-1892 .... **NCLC 26**

Renard, Jules   1864-1910 .... **TCLC 17**
    See also CA 117

Renault, Mary............... **CLC 3, 11, 17**
    See also Challans, Mary
    See also DLBY 83

Rendell, Ruth (Barbara)   1930- .. **CLC 28, 48**
    See also Vine, Barbara
    See also CA 109; CANR 32; DLB 87; MTCW

Renoir, Jean   1894-1979 .... **CLC 20**
    See also CA 129; 85-88

Resnais, Alain   1922-............. **CLC 16**

Reverdy, Pierre   1889-1960 .... **CLC 53**
    See also CA 97-100; 89-92

Rexroth, Kenneth
    1905-1982 .... **CLC 1, 2, 6, 11, 22, 49**
    See also CA 5-8R; 107; CANR 14, 34; CDALB 1941-1968; DLB 16, 48; DLBY 82; MTCW

Reyes, Alfonso   1889-1959 .... **TCLC 33**
    See also CA 131; HW

Reyes y Basoalto, Ricardo Eliecer Neftali
    See Neruda, Pablo

Reymont, Wladyslaw (Stanislaw)
    1868(?)-1925 .... **TCLC 5**
    See also CA 104

Reynolds, Jonathan   1942-....... **CLC 6, 38**
    See also CA 65-68; CANR 28

Reynolds, Joshua   1723-1792........ **LC 15**
    See also DLB 104

Reynolds, Michael Shane   1937- .... **CLC 44**
    See also CA 65-68; CANR 9

Reznikoff, Charles   1894-1976 .... **CLC 9**
    See also CA 33-36; 61-64; CAP 2; DLB 28, 45

Rezzori (d'Arezzo), Gregor von
    1914- .... **CLC 25**
    See also CA 122; 136

Rhine, Richard
    See Silverstein, Alvin

Rhodes, Eugene Manlove
    1869-1934 .... **TCLC 53**

R'hoone
    See Balzac, Honore de

Rhys, Jean
    1890(?)-1979 .... **CLC 2, 4, 6, 14, 19, 51; SSC 21**
    See also CA 25-28R; 85-88; CANR 35; CDBLB 1945-1960; DLB 36, 117; MTCW

Ribeiro, Darcy   1922- .... **CLC 34**
    See also CA 33-36R

Ribeiro, Joao Ubaldo (Osorio Pimentel)
    1941- .... **CLC 10, 67**
    See also CA 81-84

Ribman, Ronald (Burt)   1932- .... **CLC 7**
    See also CA 21-24R; CANR 46

Ricci, Nino   1959-................. **CLC 70**
    See also CA 137

Rogers, Will(iam Penn Adair)
        1879-1935 . . . . **TCLC 8**
    See also CA 105; 144; DLB 11; NNAL

Rogin, Gilbert   1929- . . . . **CLC 18**
    See also CA 65-68; CANR 15

Rohan, Koda . . . . **TCLC 22**
    See also Koda Shigeyuki

Rohmer, Eric . . . . **CLC 16**
    See also Scherer, Jean-Marie Maurice

Rohmer, Sax . . . . **TCLC 28**
    See also Ward, Arthur Henry Sarsfield
    See also DLB 70

Roiphe, Anne (Richardson)
        1935- . . . . **CLC 3, 9**
    See also CA 89-92; CANR 45; DLBY 80

Rojas, Fernando de   1465-1541 . . . . . . **LC 23**

Rolfe, Frederick (William Serafino Austin
        Lewis Mary)   1860-1913 . . . . . **TCLC 12**
    See also CA 107; DLB 34, 156

Rolland, Romain   1866-1944 . . . . **TCLC 23**
    See also CA 118; DLB 65

Rolvaag, O(le) E(dvart)
    See Roelvaag, O(le) E(dvart)

Romain Arnaud, Saint
    See Aragon, Louis

Romains, Jules   1885-1972 . . . . **CLC 7**
    See also CA 85-88; CANR 34; DLB 65;
    MTCW

Romero, Jose Ruben   1890-1952 . . . **TCLC 14**
    See also CA 114; 131; HW

Ronsard, Pierre de
        1524-1585 . . . . **LC 6; PC 11**

Rooke, Leon   1934- . . . . **CLC 25, 34**
    See also CA 25-28R; CANR 23

Roper, William   1498-1578 . . . . **LC 10**

Roquelaure, A. N.
    See Rice, Anne

Rosa, Joao Guimaraes   1908-1967 . . . **CLC 23**
    See also CA 89-92; DLB 113

Rose, Wendy   1948- . . . . **CLC 85; PC 13**
    See also CA 53-56; CANR 5; NNAL;
    SATA 12

Rosen, Richard (Dean)   1949- . . . . . . **CLC 39**
    See also CA 77-80

Rosenberg, Isaac   1890-1918 . . . . . . **TCLC 12**
    See also CA 107; DLB 20

Rosenblatt, Joe . . . . **CLC 15**
    See also Rosenblatt, Joseph

Rosenblatt, Joseph   1933-
    See Rosenblatt, Joe
    See also CA 89-92

Rosenfeld, Samuel   1896-1963
    See Tzara, Tristan
    See also CA 89-92

Rosenthal, M(acha) L(ouis)   1917- . . . **CLC 28**
    See also CA 1-4R; CAAS 6; CANR 4;
    DLB 5; SATA 59

Ross, Barnaby
    See Dannay, Frederic

Ross, Bernard L.
    See Follett, Ken(neth Martin)

Ross, J. H.
    See Lawrence, T(homas) E(dward)

Ross, Martin
    See Martin, Violet Florence
    See also DLB 135

Ross, (James) Sinclair   1908- . . . . **CLC 13**
    See also CA 73-76; DLB 88

Rossetti, Christina (Georgina)
        1830-1894 . . . . . **NCLC 2, 50; DA; DAB;
                                            PC 7; WLC**
    See also DLB 35; MAICYA; SATA 20

Rossetti, Dante Gabriel
        1828-1882 . . . **NCLC 4; DA; DAB; WLC**
    See also CDBLB 1832-1890; DLB 35

Rossner, Judith (Perelman)
        1935- . . . . **CLC 6, 9, 29**
    See also AITN 2; BEST 90:3; CA 17-20R;
    CANR 18; DLB 6; MTCW

Rostand, Edmond (Eugene Alexis)
        1868-1918 . . . . . . **TCLC 6, 37; DA; DAB**
    See also CA 104; 126; MTCW

Roth, Henry   1906- . . . . **CLC 2, 6, 11**
    See also CA 11-12; CANR 38; CAP 1;
    DLB 28; MTCW

Roth, Joseph   1894-1939 . . . . **TCLC 33**
    See also DLB 85

Roth, Philip (Milton)
        1933- . . . . . . **CLC 1, 2, 3, 4, 6, 9, 15, 22,
                            31, 47, 66, 86; DA; DAB; WLC**
    See also BEST 90:3; CA 1-4R; CANR 1, 22,
    36; CDALB 1968-1988; DLB 2, 28;
    DLBY 82; MTCW

Rothenberg, Jerome   1931- . . . . **CLC 6, 57**
    See also CA 45-48; CANR 1; DLB 5

Roumain, Jacques (Jean Baptiste)
        1907-1944 . . . . **TCLC 19; BLC**
    See also BW 1; CA 117; 125

Rourke, Constance (Mayfield)
        1885-1941 . . . . **TCLC 12**
    See also CA 107; YABC 1

Rousseau, Jean-Baptiste   1671-1741 . . . **LC 9**

Rousseau, Jean-Jacques
        1712-1778 . . . . . **LC 14; DA; DAB; WLC**

Roussel, Raymond   1877-1933 . . . . . **TCLC 20**
    See also CA 117

Rovit, Earl (Herbert)   1927- . . . . **CLC 7**
    See also CA 5-8R; CANR 12

Rowe, Nicholas   1674-1718 . . . . **LC 8**
    See also DLB 84

Rowley, Ames Dorrance
    See Lovecraft, H(oward) P(hillips)

Rowson, Susanna Haswell
        1762(?)-1824 . . . . **NCLC 5**
    See also DLB 37

Roy, Gabrielle
        1909-1983 . . . . **CLC 10, 14; DAB**
    See also CA 53-56; 110; CANR 5; DLB 68;
    MTCW

Rozewicz, Tadeusz   1921- . . . . **CLC 9, 23**
    See also CA 108; CANR 36; MTCW

Ruark, Gibbons   1941- . . . . **CLC 3**
    See also CA 33-36R; CANR 14, 31;
    DLB 120

Rubens, Bernice (Ruth)   1923- . . . **CLC 19, 31**
    See also CA 25-28R; CANR 33; DLB 14;
    MTCW

Rudkin, (James) David   1936- . . . . . . **CLC 14**
    See also CA 89-92; DLB 13

Rudnik, Raphael   1933- . . . . **CLC 7**
    See also CA 29-32R

Ruffian, M.
    See Hasek, Jaroslav (Matej Frantisek)

Ruiz, Jose Martinez . . . . **CLC 11**
    See also Martinez Ruiz, Jose

Rukeyser, Muriel
        1913-1980 . . . . **CLC 6, 10, 15, 27; PC 12**
    See also CA 5-8R; 93-96; CANR 26;
    DLB 48; MTCW; SATA-Obit 22

Rule, Jane (Vance)   1931- . . . . **CLC 27**
    See also CA 25-28R; CAAS 18; CANR 12;
    DLB 60

Rulfo, Juan   1918-1986 . . . . **CLC 8, 80; HLC**
    See also CA 85-88; 118; CANR 26;
    DLB 113; HW; MTCW

Runeberg, Johan   1804-1877 . . . . . . **NCLC 41**

Runyon, (Alfred) Damon
        1884(?)-1946 . . . . **TCLC 10**
    See also CA 107; DLB 11, 86

Rush, Norman   1933- . . . . **CLC 44**
    See also CA 121; 126

Rushdie, (Ahmed) Salman
        1947- . . . . **CLC 23, 31, 55; DAB**
    See also BEST 89:3; CA 108; 111;
    CANR 33; MTCW

Rushforth, Peter (Scott)   1945- . . . . . **CLC 19**
    See also CA 101

Ruskin, John   1819-1900 . . . . **TCLC 20**
    See also CA 114; 129; CDBLB 1832-1890;
    DLB 55; SATA 24

Russ, Joanna   1937- . . . . **CLC 15**
    See also CA 25-28R; CANR 11, 31; DLB 8;
    MTCW

Russell, George William   1867-1935
    See A. E.
    See also CA 104; CDBLB 1890-1914

Russell, (Henry) Ken(neth Alfred)
        1927- . . . . **CLC 16**
    See also CA 105

Russell, Willy   1947- . . . . **CLC 60**

Rutherford, Mark . . . . **TCLC 25**
    See also White, William Hale
    See also DLB 18

Ruyslinck, Ward   1929- . . . . **CLC 14**
    See also Belser, Reimond Karel Maria de

Ryan, Cornelius (John)   1920-1974 . . . **CLC 7**
    See also CA 69-72; 53-56; CANR 38

Ryan, Michael   1946- . . . . **CLC 65**
    See also CA 49-52; DLBY 82

Rybakov, Anatoli (Naumovich)
        1911- . . . . **CLC 23, 53**
    See also CA 126; 135; SATA 79

Ryder, Jonathan
    See Ludlum, Robert

Ryga, George   1932-1987 . . . . **CLC 14**
    See also CA 101; 124; CANR 43; DLB 60

S. S.
    See Sassoon, Siegfried (Lorraine)

Saba, Umberto   1883-1957 . . . . **TCLC 33**
    See also CA 144; DLB 114

Sabatini, Rafael   1875-1950 . . . . **TCLC 47**

Sabato, Ernesto (R.)
1911- . . . . CLC 10, 23; HLC
See also CA 97-100; CANR 32; DLB 145;
HW; MTCW

Sacastru, Martin
See Bioy Casares, Adolfo

Sacher-Masoch, Leopold von
1836(?)-1895 . . . . NCLC 31

Sachs, Marilyn (Stickle) 1927- . . . . . CLC 35
See also AAYA 2; CA 17-20R; CANR 13,
47; CLR 2; JRDA; MAICYA; SAAS 2;
SATA 3, 68

Sachs, Nelly 1891-1970 . . . . CLC 14
See also CA 17-18; 25-28R; CAP 2

Sackler, Howard (Oliver)
1929-1982 . . . . CLC 14
See also CA 61-64; 108; CANR 30; DLB 7

Sacks, Oliver (Wolf) 1933- . . . . CLC 67
See also CA 53-56; CANR 28; MTCW

Sade, Donatien Alphonse Francois Comte
1740-1814 . . . . NCLC 47

Sadoff, Ira 1945- . . . . CLC 9
See also CA 53-56; CANR 5, 21; DLB 120

Saetone
See Camus, Albert

Safire, William 1929- . . . . CLC 10
See also CA 17-20R; CANR 31

Sagan, Carl (Edward) 1934- . . . . CLC 30
See also AAYA 2; CA 25-28R; CANR 11,
36; MTCW; SATA 58

Sagan, Francoise . . . . CLC 3, 6, 9, 17, 36
See also Quoirez, Francoise
See also DLB 83

Sahgal, Nayantara (Pandit) 1927- . . . CLC 41
See also CA 9-12R; CANR 11

Saint, H(arry) F. 1941- . . . . CLC 50
See also CA 127

St. Aubin de Teran, Lisa 1953-
See Teran, Lisa St. Aubin de
See also CA 118; 126

Sainte-Beuve, Charles Augustin
1804-1869 . . . . NCLC 5

Saint-Exupery, Antoine (Jean Baptiste Marie
Roger) de
1900-1944 . . . . TCLC 2, 56; WLC
See also CA 108; 132; CLR 10; DLB 72;
MAICYA; MTCW; SATA 20

St. John, David
See Hunt, E(verette) Howard, (Jr.)

Saint-John Perse
See Leger, (Marie-Rene Auguste) Alexis
Saint-Leger

Saintsbury, George (Edward Bateman)
1845-1933 . . . . TCLC 31
See also DLB 57, 149

Sait Faik . . . . TCLC 23
See also Abasiyanik, Sait Faik

Saki . . . . TCLC 3; SSC 12
See also Munro, H(ector) H(ugh)

Sala, George Augustus . . . . NCLC 46

Salama, Hannu 1936- . . . . CLC 18

Salamanca, J(ack) R(ichard)
1922- . . . . CLC 4, 15
See also CA 25-28R

Sale, J. Kirkpatrick
See Sale, Kirkpatrick

Sale, Kirkpatrick 1937- . . . . CLC 68
See also CA 13-16R; CANR 10

Salinas, Luis Omar 1937- . . . CLC 90; HLC
See also CA 131; DLB 82; HW

Salinas (y Serrano), Pedro
1891(?)-1951 . . . . TCLC 17
See also CA 117; DLB 134

Salinger, J(erome) D(avid)
1919- . . . . . . CLC 1, 3, 8, 12, 55, 56; DA;
DAB; SSC 2; WLC
See also AAYA 2; CA 5-8R; CANR 39;
CDALB 1941-1968; CLR 18; DLB 2, 102;
MAICYA; MTCW; SATA 67

Salisbury, John
See Caute, David

Salter, James 1925- . . . . CLC 7, 52, 59
See also CA 73-76; DLB 130

Saltus, Edgar (Everton)
1855-1921 . . . . TCLC 8
See also CA 105

Saltykov, Mikhail Evgrafovich
1826-1889 . . . . NCLC 16

Samarakis, Antonis 1919- . . . . CLC 5
See also CA 25-28R; CAAS 16; CANR 36

Sanchez, Florencio 1875-1910 . . . . . TCLC 37
See also HW

Sanchez, Luis Rafael 1936- . . . . CLC 23
See also CA 128; DLB 145; HW

Sanchez, Sonia 1934- . . . CLC 5; BLC; PC 9
See also BW 2; CA 33-36R; CANR 24, 49;
CLR 18; DLB 41; DLBD 8; MAICYA;
MTCW; SATA 22

Sand, George
1804-1876 . . . . . NCLC 2, 42; DA; DAB;
WLC
See also DLB 119

Sandburg, Carl (August)
1878-1967 . . . . CLC 1, 4, 10, 15, 35; DA;
DAB; PC 2; WLC
See also CA 5-8R; 25-28R; CANR 35;
CDALB 1865-1917; DLB 17, 54;
MAICYA; MTCW; SATA 8

Sandburg, Charles
See Sandburg, Carl (August)

Sandburg, Charles A.
See Sandburg, Carl (August)

Sanders, (James) Ed(ward) 1939- . . . CLC 53
See also CA 13-16R; CAAS 21; CANR 13,
44; DLB 16

Sanders, Lawrence 1920- . . . . CLC 41
See also BEST 89:4; CA 81-84; CANR 33;
MTCW

Sanders, Noah
See Blount, Roy (Alton), Jr.

Sanders, Winston P.
See Anderson, Poul (William)

Sandoz, Mari(e Susette)
1896-1966 . . . . CLC 28
See also CA 1-4R; 25-28R; CANR 17;
DLB 9; MTCW; SATA 5

Saner, Reg(inald Anthony) 1931- . . . . CLC 9
See also CA 65-68

Sannazaro, Jacopo 1456(?)-1530 . . . . . . LC 8

Sansom, William
1912-1976 . . . . CLC 2, 6; SSC 21
See also CA 5-8R; 65-68; CANR 42;
DLB 139; MTCW

Santayana, George 1863-1952 . . . . . TCLC 40
See also CA 115; DLB 54, 71

Santiago, Danny . . . . CLC 33
See also James, Daniel (Lewis)
See also DLB 122

Santmyer, Helen Hoover
1895-1986 . . . . CLC 33
See also CA 1-4R; 118; CANR 15, 33;
DLBY 84; MTCW

Santos, Bienvenido N(uqui) 1911- . . . CLC 22
See also CA 101; CANR 19, 46

Sapper . . . . TCLC 44
See also McNeile, Herman Cyril

Sappho fl. 6th cent. B.C.- . . . . CMLC 3; PC 5

Sarduy, Severo 1937-1993 . . . . CLC 6
See also CA 89-92; 142; DLB 113; HW

Sargeson, Frank 1903-1982 . . . . CLC 31
See also CA 25-28R; 106; CANR 38

Sarmiento, Felix Ruben Garcia
See Dario, Ruben

Saroyan, William
1908-1981 . . . . . CLC 1, 8, 10, 29, 34, 56;
DA; DAB; SSC 21; WLC
See also CA 5-8R; 103; CANR 30; DLB 7,
9, 86; DLBY 81; MTCW; SATA 23;
SATA-Obit 24

Sarraute, Nathalie
1900- . . . . CLC 1, 2, 4, 8, 10, 31, 80
See also CA 9-12R; CANR 23; DLB 83;
MTCW

Sarton, (Eleanor) May
1912- . . . . CLC 4, 14, 49
See also CA 1-4R; CANR 1, 34; DLB 48;
DLBY 81; MTCW; SATA 36

Sartre, Jean-Paul
1905-1980 . . . CLC 1, 4, 7, 9, 13, 18, 24,
44, 50, 52; DA; DAB; DC 3; WLC
See also CA 9-12R; 97-100; CANR 21;
DLB 72; MTCW

Sassoon, Siegfried (Lorraine)
1886-1967 . . . . CLC 36; DAB; PC 12
See also CA 104; 25-28R; CANR 36;
DLB 20; MTCW

Satterfield, Charles
See Pohl, Frederik

Saul, John (W. III) 1942- . . . . CLC 46
See also AAYA 10; BEST 90:4; CA 81-84;
CANR 16, 40

Saunders, Caleb
See Heinlein, Robert A(nson)

Saura (Atares), Carlos 1932- . . . . CLC 20
See also CA 114; 131; HW

Sauser-Hall, Frederic 1887-1961 . . . . CLC 18
See also Cendrars, Blaise
See also CA 102; 93-96; CANR 36; MTCW

Saussure, Ferdinand de
1857-1913 . . . . TCLC 49

Savage, Catharine
See Brosman, Catharine Savage

Savage, Thomas 1915- . . . . CLC 40
See also CA 126; 132; CAAS 15

Savan, Glenn   19(?)- . . . . **CLC 50**

Sayers, Dorothy L(eigh)
　1893-1957 . . . . **TCLC 2, 15**
　See also CA 104; 119; CDBLB 1914-1945;
　DLB 10, 36, 77, 100; MTCW

Sayers, Valerie   1952- . . . . **CLC 50**
　See also CA 134

Sayles, John (Thomas)
　1950- . . . . **CLC 7, 10, 14**
　See also CA 57-60; CANR 41; DLB 44

Scammell, Michael . . . . **CLC 34**

Scannell, Vernon   1922- . . . . **CLC 49**
　See also CA 5-8R; CANR 8, 24; DLB 27;
　SATA 59

Scarlett, Susan
　See Streatfeild, (Mary) Noel

Schaeffer, Susan Fromberg
　1941- . . . . **CLC 6, 11, 22**
　See also CA 49-52; CANR 18; DLB 28;
　MTCW; SATA 22

Schary, Jill
　See Robinson, Jill

Schell, Jonathan   1943- . . . . **CLC 35**
　See also CA 73-76; CANR 12

Schelling, Friedrich Wilhelm Joseph von
　1775-1854 . . . . **NCLC 30**
　See also DLB 90

Schendel, Arthur van   1874-1946 . . . **TCLC 56**

Scherer, Jean-Marie Maurice   1920-
　See Rohmer, Eric
　See also CA 110

Schevill, James (Erwin)   1920- . . . . **CLC 7**
　See also CA 5-8R; CAAS 12

Schiller, Friedrich   1759-1805 . . . . **NCLC 39**
　See also DLB 94

Schisgal, Murray (Joseph)   1926- . . . . . **CLC 6**
　See also CA 21-24R; CANR 48

Schlee, Ann   1934- . . . . **CLC 35**
　See also CA 101; CANR 29; SATA 44;
　SATA-Brief 36

Schlegel, August Wilhelm von
　1767-1845 . . . . **NCLC 15**
　See also DLB 94

Schlegel, Friedrich   1772-1829 . . . . **NCLC 45**
　See also DLB 90

Schlegel, Johann Elias (von)
　1719(?)-1749 . . . . **LC 5**

Schlesinger, Arthur M(eier), Jr.
　1917- . . . . **CLC 84**
　See also AITN 1; CA 1-4R; CANR 1, 28;
　DLB 17; MTCW; SATA 61

Schmidt, Arno (Otto)   1914-1979 . . . . **CLC 56**
　See also CA 128; 109; DLB 69

Schmitz, Aron Hector   1861-1928
　See Svevo, Italo
　See also CA 104; 122; MTCW

Schnackenberg, Gjertrud   1953- . . . . . **CLC 40**
　See also CA 116; DLB 120

Schneider, Leonard Alfred   1925-1966
　See Bruce, Lenny
　See also CA 89-92

Schnitzler, Arthur
　1862-1931 . . . . **TCLC 4; SSC 15**
　See also CA 104; DLB 81, 118

Schopenhauer, Arthur
　1788-1860 . . . . **NCLC 51**
　See also DLB 90

Schor, Sandra (M.)   1932(?)-1990 . . . **CLC 65**
　See also CA 132

Schorer, Mark   1908-1977 . . . . **CLC 9**
　See also CA 5-8R; 73-76; CANR 7;
　DLB 103

Schrader, Paul (Joseph)   1946- . . . . . **CLC 26**
　See also CA 37-40R; CANR 41; DLB 44

Schreiner, Olive (Emilie Albertina)
　1855-1920 . . . . **TCLC 9**
　See also CA 105; DLB 18, 156

Schulberg, Budd (Wilson)
　1914- . . . . **CLC 7, 48**
　See also CA 25-28R; CANR 19; DLB 6, 26,
　28; DLBY 81

Schulz, Bruno
　1892-1942 . . . . **TCLC 5, 51; SSC 13**
　See also CA 115; 123

Schulz, Charles M(onroe)   1922- . . . . **CLC 12**
　See also CA 9-12R; CANR 6; SATA 10

Schumacher, E(rnst) F(riedrich)
　1911-1977 . . . . **CLC 80**
　See also CA 81-84; 73-76; CANR 34

Schuyler, James Marcus
　1923-1991 . . . . **CLC 5, 23**
　See also CA 101; 134; DLB 5

Schwartz, Delmore (David)
　1913-1966 . . . **CLC 2, 4, 10, 45, 87; PC 8**
　See also CA 17-18; 25-28R; CANR 35;
　CAP 2; DLB 28, 48; MTCW

Schwartz, Ernst
　See Ozu, Yasujiro

Schwartz, John Burnham   1965- . . . . **CLC 59**
　See also CA 132

Schwartz, Lynne Sharon   1939- . . . . . **CLC 31**
　See also CA 103; CANR 44

Schwartz, Muriel A.
　See Eliot, T(homas) S(tearns)

Schwarz-Bart, Andre   1928- . . . . **CLC 2, 4**
　See also CA 89-92

Schwarz-Bart, Simone   1938- . . . . **CLC 7**
　See also BW 2; CA 97-100

Schwob, (Mayer Andre) Marcel
　1867-1905 . . . . **TCLC 20**
　See also CA 117; DLB 123

Sciascia, Leonardo
　1921-1989 . . . . **CLC 8, 9, 41**
　See also CA 85-88; 130; CANR 35; MTCW

Scoppettone, Sandra   1936- . . . . **CLC 26**
　See also AAYA 11; CA 5-8R; CANR 41;
　SATA 9

Scorsese, Martin   1942- . . . . **CLC 20, 89**
　See also CA 110; 114; CANR 46

Scotland, Jay
　See Jakes, John (William)

Scott, Duncan Campbell
　1862-1947 . . . . **TCLC 6**
　See also CA 104; DLB 92

Scott, Evelyn   1893-1963 . . . . **CLC 43**
　See also CA 104; 112; DLB 9, 48

Scott, F(rancis) R(eginald)
　1899-1985 . . . . **CLC 22**
　See also CA 101; 114; DLB 88

Scott, Frank
　See Scott, F(rancis) R(eginald)

Scott, Joanna   1960- . . . . **CLC 50**
　See also CA 126

Scott, Paul (Mark)   1920-1978 . . . . **CLC 9, 60**
　See also CA 81-84; 77-80; CANR 33;
　DLB 14; MTCW

Scott, Walter
　1771-1832 . . . . **NCLC 15; DA; DAB;
　　　　　　　　　　　　　　 PC 13; WLC**
　See also CDBLB 1789-1832; DLB 93, 107,
　116, 144; YABC 2

Scribe, (Augustin) Eugene
　1791-1861 . . . . **NCLC 16; DC 5**

Scrum, R.
　See Crumb, R(obert)

Scudery, Madeleine de   1607-1701 . . . . . **LC 2**

Scum
　See Crumb, R(obert)

Scumbag, Little Bobby
　See Crumb, R(obert)

Seabrook, John
　See Hubbard, L(afayette) Ron(ald)

Sealy, I. Allan   1951- . . . . **CLC 55**

Search, Alexander
　See Pessoa, Fernando (Antonio Nogueira)

Sebastian, Lee
　See Silverberg, Robert

Sebastian Owl
　See Thompson, Hunter S(tockton)

Sebestyen, Ouida   1924- . . . . **CLC 30**
　See also AAYA 8; CA 107; CANR 40;
　CLR 17; JRDA; MAICYA; SAAS 10;
　SATA 39

Secundus, H. Scriblerus
　See Fielding, Henry

Sedges, John
　See Buck, Pearl S(ydenstricker)

Sedgwick, Catharine Maria
　1789-1867 . . . . **NCLC 19**
　See also DLB 1, 74

Seelye, John   1931- . . . . **CLC 7**

Seferiades, Giorgos Stylianou   1900-1971
　See Seferis, George
　See also CA 5-8R; 33-36R; CANR 5, 36;
　MTCW

Seferis, George . . . . **CLC 5, 11**
　See also Seferiades, Giorgos Stylianou

Segal, Erich (Wolf)   1937- . . . . **CLC 3, 10**
　See also BEST 89:1; CA 25-28R; CANR 20,
　36; DLBY 86; MTCW

Seger, Bob   1945- . . . . **CLC 35**

Seghers, Anna . . . . **CLC 7**
　See also Radvanyi, Netty
　See also DLB 69

Seidel, Frederick (Lewis)   1936- . . . . . **CLC 18**
　See also CA 13-16R; CANR 8; DLBY 84

Seifert, Jaroslav   1901-1986 . . . . . **CLC 34, 44**
　See also CA 127; MTCW

Sei Shonagon   c. 966-1017(?) . . . . . . **CMLC 6**

Slaughter, Frank G(ill) 1908- ...... **CLC 29**
See also AITN 2; CA 5-8R; CANR 5

Slavitt, David R(ytman) 1935-.... **CLC 5, 14**
See also CA 21-24R; CAAS 3; CANR 41;
DLB 5, 6

Slesinger, Tess 1905-1945 .... **TCLC 10**
See also CA 107; DLB 102

Slessor, Kenneth 1901-1971........ **CLC 14**
See also CA 102; 89-92

Slowacki, Juliusz 1809-1849 ..... **NCLC 15**

Smart, Christopher
1722-1771 .... **LC 3; PC 13**
See also DLB 109

Smart, Elizabeth 1913-1986........ **CLC 54**
See also CA 81-84; 118; DLB 88

Smiley, Jane (Graves) 1949- .... **CLC 53, 76**
See also CA 104; CANR 30

Smith, A(rthur) J(ames) M(arshall)
1902-1980 .... **CLC 15**
See also CA 1-4R; 102; CANR 4; DLB 88

Smith, Anna Deavere 1950-........ **CLC 86**
See also CA 133

Smith, Betty (Wehner) 1896-1972... **CLC 19**
See also CA 5-8R; 33-36R; DLBY 82;
SATA 6

Smith, Charlotte (Turner)
1749-1806 .... **NCLC 23**
See also DLB 39, 109

Smith, Clark Ashton 1893-1961 .... **CLC 43**
See also CA 143

Smith, Dave.................. **CLC 22, 42**
See also Smith, David (Jeddie)
See also CAAS 7; DLB 5

Smith, David (Jeddie) 1942-
See Smith, Dave
See also CA 49-52; CANR 1

Smith, Florence Margaret 1902-1971
See Smith, Stevie
See also CA 17-18; 29-32R; CANR 35;
CAP 2; MTCW

Smith, Iain Crichton 1928- .... **CLC 64**
See also CA 21-24R; DLB 40, 139

Smith, John 1580(?)-1631 .... **LC 9**

Smith, Johnston
See Crane, Stephen (Townley)

Smith, Lee 1944-.............. **CLC 25, 73**
See also CA 114; 119; CANR 46; DLB 143;
DLBY 83

Smith, Martin
See Smith, Martin Cruz

Smith, Martin Cruz 1942-......... **CLC 25**
See also BEST 89:4; CA 85-88; CANR 6,
23, 43; NNAL

Smith, Mary-Ann Tirone 1944-..... **CLC 39**
See also CA 118; 136

Smith, Patti 1946- .... **CLC 12**
See also CA 93-96

Smith, Pauline (Urmson)
1882-1959 .... **TCLC 25**

Smith, Rosamond
See Oates, Joyce Carol

Smith, Sheila Kaye
See Kaye-Smith, Sheila

Smith, Stevie .... **CLC 3, 8, 25, 44; PC 12**
See also Smith, Florence Margaret
See also DLB 20

Smith, Wilbur (Addison) 1933-..... **CLC 33**
See also CA 13-16R; CANR 7, 46; MTCW

Smith, William Jay 1918- .... **CLC 6**
See also CA 5-8R; CANR 44; DLB 5;
MAICYA; SATA 2, 68

Smith, Woodrow Wilson
See Kuttner, Henry

Smolenskin, Peretz 1842-1885.... **NCLC 30**

Smollett, Tobias (George) 1721-1771 .. **LC 2**
See also CDBLB 1660-1789; DLB 39, 104

Snodgrass, W(illiam) D(e Witt)
1926- .... **CLC 2, 6, 10, 18, 68**
See also CA 1-4R; CANR 6, 36; DLB 5;
MTCW

Snow, C(harles) P(ercy)
1905-1980 .... **CLC 1, 4, 6, 9, 13, 19**
See also CA 5-8R; 101; CANR 28;
CDBLB 1945-1960; DLB 15, 77; MTCW

Snow, Frances Compton
See Adams, Henry (Brooks)

Snyder, Gary (Sherman)
1930- .... **CLC 1, 2, 5, 9, 32**
See also CA 17-20R; CANR 30; DLB 5, 16

Snyder, Zilpha Keatley 1927-...... **CLC 17**
See also AAYA 15; CA 9-12R; CANR 38;
CLR 31; JRDA; MAICYA; SAAS 2;
SATA 1, 28, 75

Soares, Bernardo
See Pessoa, Fernando (Antonio Nogueira)

Sobh, A.
See Shamlu, Ahmad

Sobol, Joshua..................... **CLC 60**

Soderberg, Hjalmar 1869-1941 .... **TCLC 39**

Sodergran, Edith (Irene)
See Soedergran, Edith (Irene)

Soedergran, Edith (Irene)
1892-1923 .... **TCLC 31**

Softly, Edgar
See Lovecraft, H(oward) P(hillips)

Softly, Edward
See Lovecraft, H(oward) P(hillips)

Sokolov, Raymond 1941-........... **CLC 7**
See also CA 85-88

Solo, Jay
See Ellison, Harlan (Jay)

Sologub, Fyodor .... **TCLC 9**
See also Teternikov, Fyodor Kuzmich

Solomons, Ikey Esquir
See Thackeray, William Makepeace

Solomos, Dionysios 1798-1857 ... **NCLC 15**

Solwoska, Mara
See French, Marilyn

Solzhenitsyn, Aleksandr I(sayevich)
1918- ...... **CLC 1, 2, 4, 7, 9, 10, 18, 26,
34, 78; DA; DAB; WLC**
See also AITN 1; CA 69-72; CANR 40;
MTCW

Somers, Jane
See Lessing, Doris (May)

Somerville, Edith 1858-1949 ..... **TCLC 51**
See also DLB 135

Somerville & Ross
See Martin, Violet Florence; Somerville,
Edith

Sommer, Scott 1951- .... **CLC 25**
See also CA 106

Sondheim, Stephen (Joshua)
1930- .... **CLC 30, 39**
See also AAYA 11; CA 103; CANR 47

Sontag, Susan 1933-... **CLC 1, 2, 10, 13, 31**
See also CA 17-20R; CANR 25; DLB 2, 67;
MTCW

Sophocles
496(?)B.C.-406(?)B.C..... **CMLC 2; DA;
DAB; DC 1**

Sordello 1189-1269............. **CMLC 15**

Sorel, Julia
See Drexler, Rosalyn

Sorrentino, Gilbert
1929- .... **CLC 3, 7, 14, 22, 40**
See also CA 77-80; CANR 14, 33; DLB 5;
DLBY 80

Soto, Gary 1952-........ **CLC 32, 80; HLC**
See also AAYA 10; CA 119; 125; CLR 38;
DLB 82; HW; JRDA; SATA 80

Soupault, Philippe 1897-1990 ...... **CLC 68**
See also CA 116; 147; 131

Souster, (Holmes) Raymond
1921- .... **CLC 5, 14**
See also CA 13-16R; CAAS 14; CANR 13,
29; DLB 88; SATA 63

Southern, Terry 1926- .... **CLC 7**
See also CA 1-4R; CANR 1; DLB 2

Southey, Robert 1774-1843 .... **NCLC 8**
See also DLB 93, 107, 142; SATA 54

Southworth, Emma Dorothy Eliza Nevitte
1819-1899 .... **NCLC 26**

Souza, Ernest
See Scott, Evelyn

Soyinka, Wole
1934- ...... **CLC 3, 5, 14, 36, 44; BLC;
DA; DAB; DC 2; WLC**
See also BW 2; CA 13-16R; CANR 27, 39;
DLB 125; MTCW

Spackman, W(illiam) M(ode)
1905-1990 .... **CLC 46**
See also CA 81-84; 132

Spacks, Barry 1931-.............. **CLC 14**
See also CA 29-32R; CANR 33; DLB 105

Spanidou, Irini 1946-............. **CLC 44**

Spark, Muriel (Sarah)
1918- .... **CLC 2, 3, 5, 8, 13, 18, 40;
DAB; SSC 10**
See also CA 5-8R; CANR 12, 36;
CDBLB 1945-1960; DLB 15, 139; MTCW

Spaulding, Douglas
See Bradbury, Ray (Douglas)

Spaulding, Leonard
See Bradbury, Ray (Douglas)

Spence, J. A. D.
See Eliot, T(homas) S(tearns)

Spencer, Elizabeth 1921- . . . . **CLC 22**
See also CA 13-16R; CANR 32; DLB 6;
MTCW; SATA 14

Spencer, Leonard G.
See Silverberg, Robert

Spencer, Scott 1945- . . . . **CLC 30**
See also CA 113; DLBY 86

Spender, Stephen (Harold)
1909- . . . . **CLC 1, 2, 5, 10, 41**
See also CA 9-12R; CANR 31;
CDBLB 1945-1960; DLB 20; MTCW

Spengler, Oswald (Arnold Gottfried)
1880-1936 . . . . **TCLC 25**
See also CA 118

Spenser, Edmund
1552(?)-1599 . . . . **LC 5; DA; DAB; PC 8;**
WLC
See also CDBLB Before 1660

Spicer, Jack 1925-1965 . . . . . . **CLC 8, 18, 72**
See also CA 85-88; DLB 5, 16

Spiegelman, Art 1948- . . . . **CLC 76**
See also AAYA 10; CA 125; CANR 41

Spielberg, Peter 1929- . . . . **CLC 6**
See also CA 5-8R; CANR 4, 48; DLBY 81

Spielberg, Steven 1947- . . . . **CLC 20**
See also AAYA 8; CA 77-80; CANR 32;
SATA 32

Spillane, Frank Morrison 1918-
See Spillane, Mickey
See also CA 25-28R; CANR 28; MTCW;
SATA 66

Spillane, Mickey . . . . **CLC 3, 13**
See also Spillane, Frank Morrison

Spinoza, Benedictus de 1632-1677 . . . . **LC 9**

Spinrad, Norman (Richard) 1940- . . . **CLC 46**
See also CA 37-40R; CAAS 19; CANR 20;
DLB 8

Spitteler, Carl (Friedrich Georg)
1845-1924 . . . . **TCLC 12**
See also CA 109; DLB 129

Spivack, Kathleen (Romola Drucker)
1938- . . . . **CLC 6**
See also CA 49-52

Spoto, Donald 1941- . . . . **CLC 39**
See also CA 65-68; CANR 11

Springsteen, Bruce (F.) 1949- . . . . . . **CLC 17**
See also CA 111

Spurling, Hilary 1940- . . . . **CLC 34**
See also CA 104; CANR 25

Spyker, John Howland
See Elman, Richard

Squires, (James) Radcliffe
1917-1993 . . . . **CLC 51**
See also CA 1-4R; 140; CANR 6, 21

Srivastava, Dhanpat Rai 1880(?)-1936
See Premchand
See also CA 118

Stacy, Donald
See Pohl, Frederik

Stael, Germaine de
See Stael-Holstein, Anne Louise Germaine
Necker Baronn
See also DLB 119

Stael-Holstein, Anne Louise Germaine Necker
Baronn 1766-1817 . . . . **NCLC 3**
See also Stael, Germaine de

Stafford, Jean 1915-1979 . . . **CLC 4, 7, 19, 68**
See also CA 1-4R; 85-88; CANR 3; DLB 2;
MTCW; SATA-Obit 22

Stafford, William (Edgar)
1914-1993 . . . . **CLC 4, 7, 29**
See also CA 5-8R; 142; CAAS 3; CANR 5,
22; DLB 5

Staines, Trevor
See Brunner, John (Kilian Houston)

Stairs, Gordon
See Austin, Mary (Hunter)

Stannard, Martin 1947- . . . . **CLC 44**
See also CA 142; DLB 155

Stanton, Maura 1946- . . . . **CLC 9**
See also CA 89-92; CANR 15; DLB 120

Stanton, Schuyler
See Baum, L(yman) Frank

Stapledon, (William) Olaf
1886-1950 . . . . **TCLC 22**
See also CA 111; DLB 15

Starbuck, George (Edwin) 1931- . . . . **CLC 53**
See also CA 21-24R; CANR 23

Stark, Richard
See Westlake, Donald E(dwin)

Staunton, Schuyler
See Baum, L(yman) Frank

Stead, Christina (Ellen)
1902-1983 . . . . **CLC 2, 5, 8, 32, 80**
See also CA 13-16R; 109; CANR 33, 40;
MTCW

Stead, William Thomas
1849-1912 . . . . **TCLC 48**

Steele, Richard 1672-1729 . . . . **LC 18**
See also CDBLB 1660-1789; DLB 84, 101

Steele, Timothy (Reid) 1948- . . . . **CLC 45**
See also CA 93-96; CANR 16; DLB 120

Steffens, (Joseph) Lincoln
1866-1936 . . . . **TCLC 20**
See also CA 117

Stegner, Wallace (Earle)
1909-1993 . . . . **CLC 9, 49, 81**
See also AITN 1; BEST 90:3; CA 1-4R;
141; CAAS 9; CANR 1, 21, 46; DLB 9;
DLBY 93; MTCW

Stein, Gertrude
1874-1946 . . . . . . **TCLC 1, 6, 28, 48; DA;**
DAB; WLC
See also CA 104; 132; CDALB 1917-1929;
DLB 4, 54, 86; MTCW

Steinbeck, John (Ernst)
1902-1968 . . . . . . **CLC 1, 5, 9, 13, 21, 34,**
45, 75; DA; DAB; SSC 11; WLC
See also AAYA 12; CA 1-4R; 25-28R;
CANR 1, 35; CDALB 1929-1941; DLB 7,
9; DLBD 2; MTCW; SATA 9

Steinem, Gloria 1934- . . . . **CLC 63**
See also CA 53-56; CANR 28; MTCW

Steiner, George 1929- . . . . **CLC 24**
See also CA 73-76; CANR 31; DLB 67;
MTCW; SATA 62

Steiner, K. Leslie
See Delany, Samuel R(ay, Jr.)

Steiner, Rudolf 1861-1925 . . . . **TCLC 13**
See also CA 107

Stendhal
1783-1842 . . . . **NCLC 23, 46; DA; DAB;**
WLC
See also DLB 119

Stephen, Leslie 1832-1904 . . . . **TCLC 23**
See also CA 123; DLB 57, 144

Stephen, Sir Leslie
See Stephen, Leslie

Stephen, Virginia
See Woolf, (Adeline) Virginia

Stephens, James 1882(?)-1950 . . . . . . **TCLC 4**
See also CA 104; DLB 19, 153

Stephens, Reed
See Donaldson, Stephen R.

Steptoe, Lydia
See Barnes, Djuna

Sterchi, Beat 1949- . . . . **CLC 65**

Sterling, Brett
See Bradbury, Ray (Douglas); Hamilton,
Edmond

Sterling, Bruce 1954- . . . . **CLC 72**
See also CA 119; CANR 44

Sterling, George 1869-1926 . . . . **TCLC 20**
See also CA 117; DLB 54

Stern, Gerald 1925- . . . . **CLC 40**
See also CA 81-84; CANR 28; DLB 105

Stern, Richard (Gustave) 1928- . . . **CLC 4, 39**
See also CA 1-4R; CANR 1, 25; DLBY 87

Sternberg, Josef von 1894-1969 . . . . . **CLC 20**
See also CA 81-84

Sterne, Laurence
1713-1768 . . . . . . **LC 2; DA; DAB; WLC**
See also CDBLB 1660-1789; DLB 39

Sternheim, (William Adolf) Carl
1878-1942 . . . . **TCLC 8**
See also CA 105; DLB 56, 118

Stevens, Mark 1951- . . . . **CLC 34**
See also CA 122

Stevens, Wallace
1879-1955 . . . . **TCLC 3, 12, 45; DA;**
DAB; PC 6; WLC
See also CA 104; 124; CDALB 1929-1941;
DLB 54; MTCW

Stevenson, Anne (Katharine)
1933- . . . . **CLC 7, 33**
See also CA 17-20R; CAAS 9; CANR 9, 33;
DLB 40; MTCW

Stevenson, Robert Louis (Balfour)
1850-1894 . . . . . **NCLC 5, 14; DA; DAB;**
SSC 11; WLC
See also CDBLB 1890-1914; CLR 10, 11;
DLB 18, 57, 141, 156; JRDA; MAICYA;
YABC 2

Stewart, J(ohn) I(nnes) M(ackintosh)
1906-1994 . . . . **CLC 7, 14, 32**
See also CA 85-88; 147; CAAS 3;
CANR 47; MTCW

Stewart, Mary (Florence Elinor)
1916- . . . . **CLC 7, 35; DAB**
See also CA 1-4R; CANR 1; SATA 12

Stewart, Mary Rainbow
See Stewart, Mary (Florence Elinor)

Swenson, May
1919-1989 .... **CLC 4, 14, 61; DA; DAB**
See also CA 5-8R; 130; CANR 36; DLB 5;
MTCW; SATA 15

Swift, Augustus
See Lovecraft, H(oward) P(hillips)

Swift, Graham (Colin) 1949- .... **CLC 41, 88**
See also CA 117; 122; CANR 46

Swift, Jonathan
1667-1745 ...... **LC 1; DA; DAB; PC 9;
WLC**
See also CDBLB 1660-1789; DLB 39, 95,
101; SATA 19

Swinburne, Algernon Charles
1837-1909 ...... **TCLC 8, 36; DA; DAB;
WLC**
See also CA 105; 140; CDBLB 1832-1890;
DLB 35, 57

Swinfen, Ann .... **CLC 34**

Swinnerton, Frank Arthur
1884-1982 .... **CLC 31**
See also CA 108; DLB 34

Swithen, John
See King, Stephen (Edwin)

Sylvia
See Ashton-Warner, Sylvia (Constance)

Symmes, Robert Edward
See Duncan, Robert (Edward)

Symonds, John Addington
1840-1893 .... **NCLC 34**
See also DLB 57, 144

Symons, Arthur 1865-1945 .... **TCLC 11**
See also CA 107; DLB 19, 57, 149

Symons, Julian (Gustave)
1912-1994 .... **CLC 2, 14, 32**
See also CA 49-52; 147; CAAS 3; CANR 3,
33; DLB 87, 155; DLBY 92; MTCW

Synge, (Edmund) J(ohn) M(illington)
1871-1909 .... **TCLC 6, 37; DC 2**
See also CA 104; 141; CDBLB 1890-1914;
DLB 10, 19

Syruc, J.
See Milosz, Czeslaw

Szirtes, George 1948- .... **CLC 46**
See also CA 109; CANR 27

Tabori, George 1914- .... **CLC 19**
See also CA 49-52; CANR 4

Tagore, Rabindranath
1861-1941 .... **TCLC 3, 53; PC 8**
See also CA 104; 120; MTCW

Taine, Hippolyte Adolphe
1828-1893 .... **NCLC 15**

Talese, Gay 1932- .... **CLC 37**
See also AITN 1; CA 1-4R; CANR 9;
MTCW

Tallent, Elizabeth (Ann) 1954- ..... **CLC 45**
See also CA 117; DLB 130

Tally, Ted 1952- .... **CLC 42**
See also CA 120; 124

Tamayo y Baus, Manuel
1829-1898 .... **NCLC 1**

Tammsaare, A(nton) H(ansen)
1878-1940 .... **TCLC 27**

Tan, Amy 1952- .... **CLC 59**
See also AAYA 9; BEST 89:3; CA 136;
SATA 75

Tandem, Felix
See Spitteler, Carl (Friedrich Georg)

Tanizaki, Jun'ichiro
1886-1965 ...... **CLC 8, 14, 28; SSC 21**
See also CA 93-96; 25-28R

Tanner, William
See Amis, Kingsley (William)

Tao Lao
See Storni, Alfonsina

Tarassoff, Lev
See Troyat, Henri

Tarbell, Ida M(inerva)
1857-1944 .... **TCLC 40**
See also CA 122; DLB 47

Tarkington, (Newton) Booth
1869-1946 .... **TCLC 9**
See also CA 110; 143; DLB 9, 102;
SATA 17

Tarkovsky, Andrei (Arsenyevich)
1932-1986 .... **CLC 75**
See also CA 127

Tartt, Donna 1964(?)- .... **CLC 76**
See also CA 142

Tasso, Torquato 1544-1595 .... **LC 5**

Tate, (John Orley) Allen
1899-1979 .... **CLC 2, 4, 6, 9, 11, 14, 24**
See also CA 5-8R; 85-88; CANR 32;
DLB 4, 45, 63; MTCW

Tate, Ellalice
See Hibbert, Eleanor Alice Burford

Tate, James (Vincent) 1943- ... **CLC 2, 6, 25**
See also CA 21-24R; CANR 29; DLB 5

Tavel, Ronald 1940- .... **CLC 6**
See also CA 21-24R; CANR 33

Taylor, C(ecil) P(hilip) 1929-1981... **CLC 27**
See also CA 25-28R; 105; CANR 47

Taylor, Edward
1642(?)-1729 .... **LC 11; DA; DAB**
See also DLB 24

Taylor, Eleanor Ross 1920- .... **CLC 5**
See also CA 81-84

Taylor, Elizabeth 1912-1975 ... **CLC 2, 4, 29**
See also CA 13-16R; CANR 9; DLB 139;
MTCW; SATA 13

Taylor, Henry (Splawn) 1942- ...... **CLC 44**
See also CA 33-36R; CAAS 7; CANR 31;
DLB 5

Taylor, Kamala (Purnaiya) 1924-
See Markandaya, Kamala
See also CA 77-80

Taylor, Mildred D. .... **CLC 21**
See also AAYA 10; BW 1; CA 85-88;
CANR 25; CLR 9; DLB 52; JRDA;
MAICYA; SAAS 5; SATA 15, 70

Taylor, Peter (Hillsman)
1917-1994 ..... **CLC 1, 4, 18, 37, 44, 50,
71; SSC 10**
See also CA 13-16R; 147; CANR 9;
DLBY 81, 94; MTCW

Taylor, Robert Lewis 1912- .... **CLC 14**
See also CA 1-4R; CANR 3; SATA 10

Tchekhov, Anton
See Chekhov, Anton (Pavlovich)

Teasdale, Sara 1884-1933 .... **TCLC 4**
See also CA 104; DLB 45; SATA 32

Tegner, Esaias 1782-1846 .... **NCLC 2**

Teilhard de Chardin, (Marie Joseph) Pierre
1881-1955 .... **TCLC 9**
See also CA 105

Temple, Ann
See Mortimer, Penelope (Ruth)

Tennant, Emma (Christina)
1937- .... **CLC 13, 52**
See also CA 65-68; CAAS 9; CANR 10, 38;
DLB 14

Tenneshaw, S. M.
See Silverberg, Robert

Tennyson, Alfred
1809-1892 .... **NCLC 30; DA; DAB;
PC 6; WLC**
See also CDBLB 1832-1890; DLB 32

Teran, Lisa St. Aubin de .... **CLC 36**
See also St. Aubin de Teran, Lisa

Terence 195(?)B.C.-159B.C....... **CMLC 14**

Teresa de Jesus, St. 1515-1582 ...... **LC 18**

Terkel, Louis 1912-
See Terkel, Studs
See also CA 57-60; CANR 18, 45; MTCW

Terkel, Studs .... **CLC 38**
See also Terkel, Louis
See also AITN 1

Terry, C. V.
See Slaughter, Frank G(ill)

Terry, Megan 1932- .... **CLC 19**
See also CA 77-80; CABS 3; CANR 43;
DLB 7

Tertz, Abram
See Sinyavsky, Andrei (Donatevich)

Tesich, Steve 1943(?)-.......... **CLC 40, 69**
See also CA 105; DLBY 83

Teternikov, Fyodor Kuzmich 1863-1927
See Sologub, Fyodor
See also CA 104

Tevis, Walter 1928-1984 .... **CLC 42**
See also CA 113

Tey, Josephine.................. **TCLC 14**
See also Mackintosh, Elizabeth
See also DLB 77

Thackeray, William Makepeace
1811-1863 .... **NCLC 5, 14, 22, 43; DA;
DAB; WLC**
See also CDBLB 1832-1890; DLB 21, 55;
SATA 23

Thakura, Ravindranatha
See Tagore, Rabindranath

Tharoor, Shashi 1956- .... **CLC 70**
See also CA 141

Thelwell, Michael Miles 1939- ..... **CLC 22**
See also BW 2; CA 101

Theobald, Lewis, Jr.
See Lovecraft, H(oward) P(hillips)

Theodorescu, Ion N. 1880-1967
See Arghezi, Tudor
See also CA 116

Vaculik, Ludvik 1926- . . . . CLC 7
See also CA 53-56

Valdez, Luis (Miguel)
1940- . . . . CLC 84; HLC
See also CA 101; CANR 32; DLB 122; HW

Valenzuela, Luisa 1938-. . . CLC 31; SSC 14
See also CA 101; CANR 32; DLB 113; HW

Valera y Alcala-Galiano, Juan
1824-1905 . . . . TCLC 10
See also CA 106

Valery, (Ambroise) Paul (Toussaint Jules)
1871-1945 . . . . TCLC 4, 15; PC 9
See also CA 104; 122; MTCW

Valle-Inclan, Ramon (Maria) del
1866-1936 . . . . TCLC 5; HLC
See also CA 106; DLB 134

Vallejo, Antonio Buero
See Buero Vallejo, Antonio

Vallejo, Cesar (Abraham)
1892-1938 . . . . TCLC 3, 56; HLC
See also CA 105; HW

Valle Y Pena, Ramon del
See Valle-Inclan, Ramon (Maria) del

Van Ash, Cay 1918- . . . . CLC 34

Vanbrugh, Sir John 1664-1726 . . . . . . LC 21
See also DLB 80

Van Campen, Karl
See Campbell, John W(ood, Jr.)

Vance, Gerald
See Silverberg, Robert

Vance, Jack . . . . CLC 35
See also Vance, John Holbrook
See also DLB 8

Vance, John Holbrook 1916-
See Queen, Ellery; Vance, Jack
See also CA 29-32R; CANR 17; MTCW

Van Den Bogarde, Derek Jules Gaspard Ulric
Niven 1921-
See Bogarde, Dirk
See also CA 77-80

Vandenburgh, Jane . . . . CLC 59

Vanderhaeghe, Guy 1951- . . . . CLC 41
See also CA 113

van der Post, Laurens (Jan) 1906- . . . CLC 5
See also CA 5-8R; CANR 35

van de Wetering, Janwillem 1931- . . CLC 47
See also CA 49-52; CANR 4

Van Dine, S. S. . . . . TCLC 23
See also Wright, Willard Huntington

Van Doren, Carl (Clinton)
1885-1950 . . . . TCLC 18
See also CA 111

Van Doren, Mark 1894-1972. . . . . CLC 6, 10
See also CA 1-4R; 37-40R; CANR 3;
DLB 45; MTCW

Van Druten, John (William)
1901-1957 . . . . TCLC 2
See also CA 104; DLB 10

Van Duyn, Mona (Jane)
1921- . . . . CLC 3, 7, 63
See also CA 9-12R; CANR 7, 38; DLB 5

Van Dyne, Edith
See Baum, L(yman) Frank

van Itallie, Jean-Claude 1936-. . . . . . CLC 3
See also CA 45-48; CAAS 2; CANR 1, 48;
DLB 7

van Ostaijen, Paul 1896-1928 . . . . . TCLC 33

Van Peebles, Melvin 1932- . . . . CLC 2, 20
See also BW 2; CA 85-88; CANR 27

Vansittart, Peter 1920-. . . . . CLC 42
See also CA 1-4R; CANR 3, 49

Van Vechten, Carl 1880-1964 . . . . . . CLC 33
See also CA 89-92; DLB 4, 9, 51

Van Vogt, A(lfred) E(lton) 1912-. . . . . CLC 1
See also CA 21-24R; CANR 28; DLB 8;
SATA 14

Varda, Agnes 1928- . . . . CLC 16
See also CA 116; 122

Vargas Llosa, (Jorge) Mario (Pedro)
1936- . . . . CLC 3, 6, 9, 10, 15, 31, 42, 85;
DA; DAB; HLC
See also CA 73-76; CANR 18, 32, 42;
DLB 145; HW; MTCW

Vasiliu, Gheorghe 1881-1957
See Bacovia, George
See also CA 123

Vassa, Gustavus
See Equiano, Olaudah

Vassilikos, Vassilis 1933-. . . . . CLC 4, 8
See also CA 81-84

Vaughan, Henry 1621-1695 . . . . LC 27
See also DLB 131

Vaughn, Stephanie. . . . . CLC 62

Vazov, Ivan (Minchov)
1850-1921 . . . . TCLC 25
See also CA 121; DLB 147

Veblen, Thorstein (Bunde)
1857-1929 . . . . TCLC 31
See also CA 115

Vega, Lope de 1562-1635. . . . . LC 23

Venison, Alfred
See Pound, Ezra (Weston Loomis)

Verdi, Marie de
See Mencken, H(enry) L(ouis)

Verdu, Matilde
See Cela, Camilo Jose

Verga, Giovanni (Carmelo)
1840-1922 . . . . TCLC 3; SSC 21
See also CA 104; 123

Vergil
70B.C.-19B.C.. . . . . . CMLC 9; DA; DAB;
PC 12

Verhaeren, Emile (Adolphe Gustave)
1855-1916 . . . . TCLC 12
See also CA 109

Verlaine, Paul (Marie)
1844-1896 . . . . NCLC 2, 51; PC 2

Verne, Jules (Gabriel)
1828-1905 . . . . TCLC 6, 52
See also CA 110; 131; DLB 123; JRDA;
MAICYA; SATA 21

Very, Jones 1813-1880. . . . . NCLC 9
See also DLB 1

Vesaas, Tarjei 1897-1970. . . . . CLC 48
See also CA 29-32R

Vialis, Gaston
See Simenon, Georges (Jacques Christian)

Vian, Boris 1920-1959 . . . . TCLC 9
See also CA 106; DLB 72

Viaud, (Louis Marie) Julien 1850-1923
See Loti, Pierre
See also CA 107

Vicar, Henry
See Felsen, Henry Gregor

Vicker, Angus
See Felsen, Henry Gregor

Vidal, Gore
1925- . . . . . CLC 2, 4, 6, 8, 10, 22, 33, 72
See also AITN 1; BEST 90:2; CA 5-8R;
CANR 13, 45; DLB 6, 152; MTCW

Viereck, Peter (Robert Edwin)
1916- . . . . CLC 4
See also CA 1-4R; CANR 1, 47; DLB 5

Vigny, Alfred (Victor) de
1797-1863 . . . . NCLC 7
See also DLB 119

Vilakazi, Benedict Wallet
1906-1947 . . . . TCLC 37

Villiers de l'Isle Adam, Jean Marie Mathias
Philippe Auguste Comte
1838-1889 . . . . NCLC 3; SSC 14
See also DLB 123

Villon, Francois 1431-1463(?) . . . . PC 13

Vinci, Leonardo da 1452-1519. . . . . . LC 12

Vine, Barbara . . . . CLC 50
See also Rendell, Ruth (Barbara)
See also BEST 90:4

Vinge, Joan D(ennison) 1948-. . . . . . CLC 30
See also CA 93-96; SATA 36

Violis, G.
See Simenon, Georges (Jacques Christian)

Visconti, Luchino 1906-1976. . . . . . . CLC 16
See also CA 81-84; 65-68; CANR 39

Vittorini, Elio 1908-1966. . . . . . CLC 6, 9, 14
See also CA 133; 25-28R

Vizinczey, Stephen 1933-. . . . . CLC 40
See also CA 128

Vliet, R(ussell) G(ordon)
1929-1984 . . . . CLC 22
See also CA 37-40R; 112; CANR 18

Vogau, Boris Andreyevich 1894-1937(?)
See Pilnyak, Boris
See also CA 123

Vogel, Paula A(nne) 1951-. . . . . CLC 76
See also CA 108

Voight, Ellen Bryant 1943- . . . . CLC 54
See also CA 69-72; CANR 11, 29; DLB 120

Voigt, Cynthia 1942- . . . . CLC 30
See also AAYA 3; CA 106; CANR 18, 37,
40; CLR 13; JRDA; MAICYA;
SATA 48, 79; SATA-Brief 33

Voinovich, Vladimir (Nikolaevich)
1932-. . . . . CLC 10, 49
See also CA 81-84; CAAS 12; CANR 33;
MTCW

Vollmann, William T. 1959-. . . . . CLC 89
See also CA 134

Voloshinov, V. N.
See Bakhtin, Mikhail Mikhailovich

Voltaire
  1694-1778 . . . . LC 14; DA; DAB;
                              SSC 12; WLC

von Aue, Hartmann   1170-1210 . . . CMLC 15

von Daeniken, Erich   1935- . . . . CLC 30
  See also AITN 1; CA 37-40R; CANR 17,
  44

von Daniken, Erich
  See von Daeniken, Erich

von Heidenstam, (Carl Gustaf) Verner
  See Heidenstam, (Carl Gustaf) Verner von

von Heyse, Paul (Johann Ludwig)
  See Heyse, Paul (Johann Ludwig von)

von Hofmannsthal, Hugo
  See Hofmannsthal, Hugo von

von Horvath, Odon
  See Horvath, Oedoen von

von Horvath, Oedoen
  See Horvath, Oedoen von

von Liliencron, (Friedrich Adolf Axel) Detlev
  See Liliencron, (Friedrich Adolf Axel)
  Detlev von

Vonnegut, Kurt, Jr.
  1922- . . . . . . CLC 1, 2, 3, 4, 5, 8, 12, 22,
          40, 60; DA; DAB; SSC 8; WLC
  See also AAYA 6; AITN 1; BEST 90:4;
  CA 1-4R; CANR 1, 25, 49;
  CDALB 1968-1988; DLB 2, 8, 152;
  DLBD 3; DLBY 80; MTCW

Von Rachen, Kurt
  See Hubbard, L(afayette) Ron(ald)

von Rezzori (d'Arezzo), Gregor
  See Rezzori (d'Arezzo), Gregor von

von Sternberg, Josef
  See Sternberg, Josef von

Vorster, Gordon   1924- . . . . CLC 34
  See also CA 133

Vosce, Trudie
  See Ozick, Cynthia

Voznesensky, Andrei (Andreievich)
  1933- . . . . CLC 1, 15, 57
  See also CA 89-92; CANR 37; MTCW

Waddington, Miriam   1917- . . . . CLC 28
  See also CA 21-24R; CANR 12, 30;
  DLB 68

Wagman, Fredrica   1937- . . . . CLC 7
  See also CA 97-100

Wagner, Richard   1813-1883 . . . . NCLC 9
  See also DLB 129

Wagner-Martin, Linda   1936- . . . . CLC 50

Wagoner, David (Russell)
  1926- . . . . CLC 3, 5, 15
  See also CA 1-4R; CAAS 3; CANR 2;
  DLB 5; SATA 14

Wah, Fred(erick James)   1939- . . . . . . CLC 44
  See also CA 107; 141; DLB 60

Wahloo, Per   1926-1975 . . . . CLC 7
  See also CA 61-64

Wahloo, Peter
  See Wahloo, Per

Wain, John (Barrington)
  1925-1994 . . . . CLC 2, 11, 15, 46
  See also CA 5-8R; 145; CAAS 4; CANR 23;
  CDBLB 1960 to Present; DLB 15, 27,
  139, 155; MTCW

Wajda, Andrzej   1926- . . . . CLC 16
  See also CA 102

Wakefield, Dan   1932- . . . . CLC 7
  See also CA 21-24R; CAAS 7

Wakoski, Diane
  1937- . . . . CLC 2, 4, 7, 9, 11, 40
  See also CA 13-16R; CAAS 1; CANR 9;
  DLB 5

Wakoski-Sherbell, Diane
  See Wakoski, Diane

Walcott, Derek (Alton)
  1930- . . . . CLC 2, 4, 9, 14, 25, 42, 67, 76;
                          BLC; DAB
  See also BW 2; CA 89-92; CANR 26, 47;
  DLB 117; DLBY 81; MTCW

Waldman, Anne   1945- . . . . CLC 7
  See also CA 37-40R; CAAS 17; CANR 34;
  DLB 16

Waldo, E. Hunter
  See Sturgeon, Theodore (Hamilton)

Waldo, Edward Hamilton
  See Sturgeon, Theodore (Hamilton)

Walker, Alice (Malsenior)
  1944- . . . . CLC 5, 6, 9, 19, 27, 46, 58;
                          BLC; DA; DAB; SSC 5
  See also AAYA 3; BEST 89:4; BW 2;
  CA 37-40R; CANR 9, 27, 49;
  CDALB 1968-1988; DLB 6, 33, 143;
  MTCW; SATA 31

Walker, David Harry   1911-1992 . . . . CLC 14
  See also CA 1-4R; 137; CANR 1; SATA 8;
  SATA-Obit 71

Walker, Edward Joseph   1934-
  See Walker, Ted
  See also CA 21-24R; CANR 12, 28

Walker, George F.
  1947- . . . . CLC 44, 61; DAB
  See also CA 103; CANR 21, 43; DLB 60

Walker, Joseph A.   1935- . . . . CLC 19
  See also BW 1; CA 89-92; CANR 26;
  DLB 38

Walker, Margaret (Abigail)
  1915- . . . . CLC 1, 6; BLC
  See also BW 2; CA 73-76; CANR 26;
  DLB 76, 152; MTCW

Walker, Ted . . . . CLC 13
  See also Walker, Edward Joseph
  See also DLB 40

Wallace, David Foster   1962- . . . . CLC 50
  See also CA 132

Wallace, Dexter
  See Masters, Edgar Lee

Wallace, (Richard Horatio) Edgar
  1875-1932 . . . . TCLC 57
  See also CA 115; DLB 70

Wallace, Irving   1916-1990 . . . . CLC 7, 13
  See also AITN 1; CA 1-4R; 132; CAAS 1;
  CANR 1, 27; MTCW

Wallant, Edward Lewis
  1926-1962 . . . . CLC 5, 10
  See also CA 1-4R; CANR 22; DLB 2, 28,
  143; MTCW

Walley, Byron
  See Card, Orson Scott

Walpole, Horace   1717-1797 . . . . LC 2
  See also DLB 39, 104

Walpole, Hugh (Seymour)
  1884-1941 . . . . TCLC 5
  See also CA 104; DLB 34

Walser, Martin   1927- . . . . CLC 27
  See also CA 57-60; CANR 8, 46; DLB 75,
  124

Walser, Robert
  1878-1956 . . . . TCLC 18; SSC 20
  See also CA 118; DLB 66

Walsh, Jill Paton . . . . CLC 35
  See also Paton Walsh, Gillian
  See also AAYA 11; CLR 2; SAAS 3

Walter, Villiam Christian
  See Andersen, Hans Christian

Wambaugh, Joseph (Aloysius, Jr.)
  1937- . . . . CLC 3, 18
  See also AITN 1; BEST 89:3; CA 33-36R;
  CANR 42; DLB 6; DLBY 83; MTCW

Ward, Arthur Henry Sarsfield   1883-1959
  See Rohmer, Sax
  See also CA 108

Ward, Douglas Turner   1930- . . . . CLC 19
  See also BW 1; CA 81-84; CANR 27;
  DLB 7, 38

Ward, Mary Augusta
  See Ward, Mrs. Humphry

Ward, Mrs. Humphry
  1851-1920 . . . . TCLC 55
  See also DLB 18

Ward, Peter
  See Faust, Frederick (Schiller)

Warhol, Andy   1928(?)-1987 . . . . CLC 20
  See also AAYA 12; BEST 89:4; CA 89-92;
  121; CANR 34

Warner, Francis (Robert le Plastrier)
  1937- . . . . CLC 14
  See also CA 53-56; CANR 11

Warner, Marina   1946- . . . . CLC 59
  See also CA 65-68; CANR 21

Warner, Rex (Ernest)   1905-1986 . . . . CLC 45
  See also CA 89-92; 119; DLB 15

Warner, Susan (Bogert)
  1819-1885 . . . . NCLC 31
  See also DLB 3, 42

Warner, Sylvia (Constance) Ashton
  See Ashton-Warner, Sylvia (Constance)

Warner, Sylvia Townsend
  1893-1978 . . . . CLC 7, 19
  See also CA 61-64; 77-80; CANR 16;
  DLB 34, 139; MTCW

Warren, Mercy Otis   1728-1814 . . . NCLC 13
  See also DLB 31

West, (Mary) Jessamyn
1902-1984 . . . . CLC 7, 17
See also CA 9-12R; 112; CANR 27; DLB 6;
DLBY 84; MTCW; SATA-Obit 37

West, Morris L(anglo) 1916- . . . . . CLC 6, 33
See also CA 5-8R; CANR 24, 49; MTCW

West, Nathanael
1903-1940 . . . . . TCLC 1, 14, 44; SSC 16
See also CA 104; 125; CDALB 1929-1941;
DLB 4, 9, 28; MTCW

West, Owen
See Koontz, Dean R(ay)

West, Paul 1930- . . . . CLC 7, 14
See also CA 13-16R; CAAS 7; CANR 22;
DLB 14

West, Rebecca 1892-1983 . . CLC 7, 9, 31, 50
See also CA 5-8R; 109; CANR 19; DLB 36;
DLBY 83; MTCW

Westall, Robert (Atkinson)
1929-1993 . . . . CLC 17
See also AAYA 12; CA 69-72; 141;
CANR 18; CLR 13; JRDA; MAICYA;
SAAS 2; SATA 23, 69; SATA-Obit 75

Westlake, Donald E(dwin)
1933- . . . . CLC 7, 33
See also CA 17-20R; CAAS 13; CANR 16,
44

Westmacott, Mary
See Christie, Agatha (Mary Clarissa)

Weston, Allen
See Norton, Andre

Wetcheek, J. L.
See Feuchtwanger, Lion

Wetering, Janwillem van de
See van de Wetering, Janwillem

Wetherell, Elizabeth
See Warner, Susan (Bogert)

Whalen, Philip 1923- . . . . CLC 6, 29
See also CA 9-12R; CANR 5, 39; DLB 16

Wharton, Edith (Newbold Jones)
1862-1937 . . . . . . TCLC 3, 9, 27, 53; DA;
DAB; SSC 6; WLC
See also CA 104; 132; CDALB 1865-1917;
DLB 4, 9, 12, 78; MTCW

Wharton, James
See Mencken, H(enry) L(ouis)

Wharton, William (a pseudonym)
. . . . CLC 18, 37
See also CA 93-96; DLBY 80

Wheatley (Peters), Phillis
1754(?)-1784 . . . . LC 3; BLC; DA; PC 3;
WLC
See also CDALB 1640-1865; DLB 31, 50

Wheelock, John Hall 1886-1978 . . . . CLC 14
See also CA 13-16R; 77-80; CANR 14;
DLB 45

White, E(lwyn) B(rooks)
1899-1985 . . . . CLC 10, 34, 39
See also AITN 2; CA 13-16R; 116;
CANR 16, 37; CLR 1, 21; DLB 11, 22;
MAICYA; MTCW; SATA 2, 29;
SATA-Obit 44

White, Edmund (Valentine III)
1940- . . . . CLC 27
See also AAYA 7; CA 45-48; CANR 3, 19,
36; MTCW

White, Patrick (Victor Martindale)
1912-1990 . . CLC 3, 4, 5, 7, 9, 18, 65, 69
See also CA 81-84; 132; CANR 43; MTCW

White, Phyllis Dorothy James 1920-
See James, P. D.
See also CA 21-24R; CANR 17, 43; MTCW

White, T(erence) H(anbury)
1906-1964 . . . . CLC 30
See also CA 73-76; CANR 37; JRDA;
MAICYA; SATA 12

White, Terence de Vere
1912-1994 . . . . CLC 49
See also CA 49-52; 145; CANR 3

White, Walter F(rancis)
1893-1955 . . . . TCLC 15
See also White, Walter
See also BW 1; CA 115; 124; DLB 51

White, William Hale 1831-1913
See Rutherford, Mark
See also CA 121

Whitehead, E(dward) A(nthony)
1933- . . . . CLC 5
See also CA 65-68

Whitemore, Hugh (John) 1936- . . . . . CLC 37
See also CA 132

Whitman, Sarah Helen (Power)
1803-1878 . . . . NCLC 19
See also DLB 1

Whitman, Walt(er)
1819-1892 . . . . . NCLC 4, 31; DA; DAB;
PC 3; WLC
See also CDALB 1640-1865; DLB 3, 64;
SATA 20

Whitney, Phyllis A(yame) 1903- . . . . CLC 42
See also AITN 2; BEST 90:3; CA 1-4R;
CANR 3, 25, 38; JRDA; MAICYA;
SATA 1, 30

Whittemore, (Edward) Reed (Jr.)
1919- . . . . CLC 4
See also CA 9-12R; CAAS 8; CANR 4;
DLB 5

Whittier, John Greenleaf
1807-1892 . . . . NCLC 8
See also CDALB 1640-1865; DLB 1

Whittlebot, Hernia
See Coward, Noel (Peirce)

Wicker, Thomas Grey 1926-
See Wicker, Tom
See also CA 65-68; CANR 21, 46

Wicker, Tom . . . . CLC 7
See also Wicker, Thomas Grey

Wideman, John Edgar
1941- . . . . CLC 5, 34, 36, 67; BLC
See also BW 2; CA 85-88; CANR 14, 42;
DLB 33, 143

Wiebe, Rudy (Henry) 1934- . . . CLC 6, 11, 14
See also CA 37-40R; CANR 42; DLB 60

Wieland, Christoph Martin
1733-1813 . . . . NCLC 17
See also DLB 97

Wiene, Robert 1881-1938 . . . . TCLC 56

Wieners, John 1934- . . . . CLC 7
See also CA 13-16R; DLB 16

Wiesel, Elie(zer)
1928- . . . . . . CLC 3, 5, 11, 37; DA; DAB
See also AAYA 7; AITN 1; CA 5-8R;
CAAS 4; CANR 8, 40; DLB 83;
DLBY 87; MTCW; SATA 56

Wiggins, Marianne 1947- . . . . CLC 57
See also BEST 89:3; CA 130

Wight, James Alfred 1916-
See Herriot, James
See also CA 77-80; SATA 55;
SATA-Brief 44

Wilbur, Richard (Purdy)
1921- . . . . CLC 3, 6, 9, 14, 53; DA; DAB
See also CA 1-4R; CABS 2; CANR 2, 29;
DLB 5; MTCW; SATA 9

Wild, Peter 1940- . . . . CLC 14
See also CA 37-40R; DLB 5

Wilde, Oscar (Fingal O'Flahertie Wills)
1854(?)-1900 . . . . TCLC 1, 8, 23, 41; DA;
DAB; SSC 11; WLC
See also CA 104; 119; CDBLB 1890-1914;
DLB 10, 19, 34, 57, 141, 156; SATA 24

Wilder, Billy . . . . CLC 20
See also Wilder, Samuel
See also DLB 26

Wilder, Samuel 1906-
See Wilder, Billy
See also CA 89-92

Wilder, Thornton (Niven)
1897-1975 . . . . . . CLC 1, 5, 6, 10, 15, 35,
82; DA; DAB; DC 1; WLC
See also AITN 2; CA 13-16R; 61-64;
CANR 40; DLB 4, 7, 9; MTCW

Wilding, Michael 1942- . . . . CLC 73
See also CA 104; CANR 24, 49

Wiley, Richard 1944- . . . . CLC 44
See also CA 121; 129

Wilhelm, Kate . . . . CLC 7
See also Wilhelm, Katie Gertrude
See also CAAS 5; DLB 8

Wilhelm, Katie Gertrude 1928-
See Wilhelm, Kate
See also CA 37-40R; CANR 17, 36; MTCW

Wilkins, Mary
See Freeman, Mary Eleanor Wilkins

Willard, Nancy 1936- . . . . CLC 7, 37
See also CA 89-92; CANR 10, 39; CLR 5;
DLB 5, 52; MAICYA; MTCW;
SATA 37, 71; SATA-Brief 30

Williams, C(harles) K(enneth)
1936- . . . . CLC 33, 56
See also CA 37-40R; DLB 5

Williams, Charles
See Collier, James L(incoln)

Williams, Charles (Walter Stansby)
1886-1945 . . . . TCLC 1, 11
See also CA 104; DLB 100, 153

Williams, (George) Emlyn
1905-1987 . . . . CLC 15
See also CA 104; 123; CANR 36; DLB 10,
77; MTCW

Williams, Hugo 1942- . . . . CLC 42
See also CA 17-20R; CANR 45; DLB 40

Williams, J. Walker
See Wodehouse, P(elham) G(renville)

Williams, John A(lfred)
1925- . . . . CLC 5, 13; BLC
See also BW 2; CA 53-56; CAAS 3;
CANR 6, 26; DLB 2, 33

Williams, Jonathan (Chamberlain)
1929- . . . . CLC 13
See also CA 9-12R; CAAS 12; CANR 8;
DLB 5

Williams, Joy 1944- . . . . CLC 31
See also CA 41-44R; CANR 22, 48

Williams, Norman 1952- . . . . CLC 39
See also CA 118

Williams, Sherley Anne
1944- . . . . CLC 89; BLC
See also BW 2; CA 73-76; CANR 25;
DLB 41; SATA 78

Williams, Shirley
See Williams, Sherley Anne

Williams, Tennessee
1911-1983 . . . . . CLC 1, 2, 5, 7, 8, 11, 15,
19, 30, 39, 45, 71; DA; DAB; DC 4; WLC
See also AITN 1, 2; CA 5-8R; 108;
CABS 3; CANR 31; CDALB 1941-1968;
DLB 7; DLBD 4; DLBY 83; MTCW

Williams, Thomas (Alonzo)
1926-1990 . . . . CLC 14
See also CA 1-4R; 132; CANR 2

Williams, William C.
See Williams, William Carlos

Williams, William Carlos
1883-1963 . . . . CLC 1, 2, 5, 9, 13, 22, 42,
67; DA; DAB; PC 7
See also CA 89-92; CANR 34;
CDALB 1917-1929; DLB 4, 16, 54, 86;
MTCW

Williamson, David (Keith) 1942- . . . . CLC 56
See also CA 103; CANR 41

Williamson, Ellen Douglas 1905-1984
See Douglas, Ellen
See also CA 17-20R; 114; CANR 39

Williamson, Jack. . . . . CLC 29
See also Williamson, John Stewart
See also CAAS 8; DLB 8

Williamson, John Stewart 1908-
See Williamson, Jack
See also CA 17-20R; CANR 23

Willie, Frederick
See Lovecraft, H(oward) P(hillips)

Willingham, Calder (Baynard, Jr.)
1922-1995 . . . . CLC 5, 51
See also CA 5-8R; 147; CANR 3; DLB 2,
44; MTCW

Willis, Charles
See Clarke, Arthur C(harles)

Willy
See Colette, (Sidonie-Gabrielle)

Willy, Colette
See Colette, (Sidonie-Gabrielle)

Wilson, A(ndrew) N(orman) 1950- . . CLC 33
See also CA 112; 122; DLB 14, 155

Wilson, Angus (Frank Johnstone)
1913-1991 . . CLC 2, 3, 5, 25, 34; SSC 21
See also CA 5-8R; 134; CANR 21; DLB 15,
139, 155; MTCW

Wilson, August
1945- . . . . . . CLC 39, 50, 63; BLC; DA;
DAB; DC 2
See also BW 2; CA 115; 122; CANR 42;
MTCW

Wilson, Brian 1942- . . . . CLC 12

Wilson, Colin 1931- . . . . CLC 3, 14
See also CA 1-4R; CAAS 5; CANR 1, 22,
33; DLB 14; MTCW

Wilson, Dirk
See Pohl, Frederik

Wilson, Edmund
1895-1972 . . . . CLC 1, 2, 3, 8, 24
See also CA 1-4R; 37-40R; CANR 1, 46;
DLB 63; MTCW

Wilson, Ethel Davis (Bryant)
1888(?)-1980 . . . . CLC 13
See also CA 102; DLB 68; MTCW

Wilson, John 1785-1854 . . . . NCLC 5

Wilson, John (Anthony) Burgess 1917-1993
See Burgess, Anthony
See also CA 1-4R; 143; CANR 2, 46;
MTCW

Wilson, Lanford 1937- . . . . CLC 7, 14, 36
See also CA 17-20R; CABS 3; CANR 45;
DLB 7

Wilson, Robert M. 1944- . . . . CLC 7, 9
See also CA 49-52; CANR 2, 41; MTCW

Wilson, Robert McLiam 1964- . . . . . CLC 59
See also CA 132

Wilson, Sloan 1920- . . . . CLC 32
See also CA 1-4R; CANR 1, 44

Wilson, Snoo 1948- . . . . CLC 33
See also CA 69-72

Wilson, William S(mith) 1932- . . . . . CLC 49
See also CA 81-84

Winchilsea, Anne (Kingsmill) Finch Counte
1661-1720 . . . . LC 3

Windham, Basil
See Wodehouse, P(elham) G(renville)

Wingrove, David (John) 1954- . . . . . . CLC 68
See also CA 133

Winters, Janet Lewis . . . . CLC 41
See also Lewis, Janet
See also DLBY 87

Winters, (Arthur) Yvor
1900-1968 . . . . CLC 4, 8, 32
See also CA 11-12; 25-28R; CAP 1;
DLB 48; MTCW

Winterson, Jeanette 1959- . . . . CLC 64
See also CA 136

Winthrop, John 1588-1649 . . . . LC 31
See also DLB 24, 30

Wiseman, Frederick 1930- . . . . CLC 20

Wister, Owen 1860-1938 . . . . TCLC 21
See also CA 108; DLB 9, 78; SATA 62

Witkacy
See Witkiewicz, Stanislaw Ignacy

Witkiewicz, Stanislaw Ignacy
1885-1939 . . . . TCLC 8
See also CA 105

Wittgenstein, Ludwig (Josef Johann)
1889-1951 . . . . TCLC 59
See also CA 113

Wittig, Monique 1935(?)- . . . . CLC 22
See also CA 116; 135; DLB 83

Wittlin, Jozef 1896-1976 . . . . CLC 25
See also CA 49-52; 65-68; CANR 3

Wodehouse, P(elham) G(renville)
1881-1975 . . . CLC 1, 2, 5, 10, 22; DAB;
SSC 2
See also AITN 2; CA 45-48; 57-60;
CANR 3, 33; CDBLB 1914-1945;
DLB 34; MTCW; SATA 22

Woiwode, L.
See Woiwode, Larry (Alfred)

Woiwode, Larry (Alfred) 1941- . . CLC 6, 10
See also CA 73-76; CANR 16; DLB 6

Wojciechowska, Maia (Teresa)
1927- . . . . CLC 26
See also AAYA 8; CA 9-12R; CANR 4, 41;
CLR 1; JRDA; MAICYA; SAAS 1;
SATA 1, 28, 83

Wolf, Christa 1929- . . . . CLC 14, 29, 58
See also CA 85-88; CANR 45; DLB 75;
MTCW

Wolfe, Gene (Rodman) 1931- . . . . . . CLC 25
See also CA 57-60; CAAS 9; CANR 6, 32;
DLB 8

Wolfe, George C. 1954- . . . . CLC 49

Wolfe, Thomas (Clayton)
1900-1938 . . . . . TCLC 4, 13, 29, 61; DA;
DAB; WLC
See also CA 104; 132; CDALB 1929-1941;
DLB 9, 102; DLBD 2; DLBY 85; MTCW

Wolfe, Thomas Kennerly, Jr. 1931-
See Wolfe, Tom
See also CA 13-16R; CANR 9, 33; MTCW

Wolfe, Tom . . . . CLC 1, 2, 9, 15, 35, 51
See also Wolfe, Thomas Kennerly, Jr.
See also AAYA 8; AITN 2; BEST 89:1;
DLB 152

Wolff, Geoffrey (Ansell) 1937- . . . . . CLC 41
See also CA 29-32R; CANR 29, 43

Wolff, Sonia
See Levitin, Sonia (Wolff)

Wolff, Tobias (Jonathan Ansell)
1945- . . . . CLC 39, 64
See also BEST 90:2; CA 114; 117;
CAAS 22; DLB 130

Wolfram von Eschenbach
c. 1170-c. 1220 . . . . CMLC 5
See also DLB 138

Wolitzer, Hilma 1930- . . . . CLC 17
See also CA 65-68; CANR 18, 40; SATA 31

Wollstonecraft, Mary 1759-1797 . . . . . . LC 5
See also CDBLB 1789-1832; DLB 39, 104

Wonder, Stevie . . . . CLC 12
See also Morris, Steveland Judkins

Wong, Jade Snow 1922- . . . . CLC 17
See also CA 109

Woodcott, Keith
See Brunner, John (Kilian Houston)

Woodruff, Robert W.
See Mencken, H(enry) L(ouis)

Woolf, (Adeline) Virginia
    1882-1941 . . . . **TCLC 1, 5, 20, 43, 56;**
                        DA; DAB; SSC 7; WLC
    See also CA 104; 130; CDBLB 1914-1945;
        DLB 36, 100; DLBD 10; MTCW

Woollcott, Alexander (Humphreys)
    1887-1943 . . . . **TCLC 5**
    See also CA 105; DLB 29

Woolrich, Cornell 1903-1968 . . . . . . **CLC 77**
    See also Hopley-Woolrich, Cornell George

Wordsworth, Dorothy
    1771-1855 . . . . **NCLC 25**
    See also DLB 107

Wordsworth, William
    1770-1850 . . . . **NCLC 12, 38; DA; DAB;**
                        PC 4; WLC
    See also CDBLB 1789-1832; DLB 93, 107

Wouk, Herman 1915- . . . . **CLC 1, 9, 38**
    See also CA 5-8R; CANR 6, 33; DLBY 82;
        MTCW

Wright, Charles (Penzel, Jr.)
    1935- . . . . **CLC 6, 13, 28**
    See also CA 29-32R; CAAS 7; CANR 23,
        36; DLBY 82; MTCW

Wright, Charles Stevenson
    1932- . . . . **CLC 49; BLC 3**
    See also BW 1; CA 9-12R; CANR 26;
        DLB 33

Wright, Jack R.
    See Harris, Mark

Wright, James (Arlington)
    1927-1980 . . . . **CLC 3, 5, 10, 28**
    See also AITN 2; CA 49-52; 97-100;
        CANR 4, 34; DLB 5; MTCW

Wright, Judith (Arandell)
    1915- . . . . **CLC 11, 53**
    See also CA 13-16R; CANR 31; MTCW;
        SATA 14

Wright, L(aurali) R. 1939- . . . . **CLC 44**
    See also CA 138

Wright, Richard (Nathaniel)
    1908-1960 . . . . **CLC 1, 3, 4, 9, 14, 21, 48,**
                74; BLC; DA; DAB; SSC 2; WLC
    See also AAYA 5; BW 1; CA 108;
        CDALB 1929-1941; DLB 76, 102;
        DLBD 2; MTCW

Wright, Richard B(ruce) 1937- . . . . . . **CLC 6**
    See also CA 85-88; DLB 53

Wright, Rick 1945- . . . . **CLC 35**

Wright, Rowland
    See Wells, Carolyn

Wright, Stephen Caldwell 1946- . . . **CLC 33**
    See also BW 2

Wright, Willard Huntington 1888-1939
    See Van Dine, S. S.
    See also CA 115

Wright, William 1930- . . . . **CLC 44**
    See also CA 53-56; CANR 7, 23

Wroth, LadyMary 1587-1653(?) . . . . . **LC 30**
    See also DLB 121

Wu Ch'eng-en 1500(?)-1582(?) . . . . **LC 7**

Wu Ching-tzu 1701-1754 . . . . **LC 2**

Wurlitzer, Rudolph 1938(?)- . . . **CLC 2, 4, 15**
    See also CA 85-88

Wycherley, William 1641-1715 . . . . **LC 8, 21**
    See also CDBLB 1660-1789; DLB 80

Wylie, Elinor (Morton Hoyt)
    1885-1928 . . . . **TCLC 8**
    See also CA 105; DLB 9, 45

Wylie, Philip (Gordon) 1902-1971 . . . **CLC 43**
    See also CA 21-22; 33-36R; CAP 2; DLB 9

Wyndham, John . . . . **CLC 19**
    See also Harris, John (Wyndham Parkes
        Lucas) Beynon

Wyss, Johann David Von
    1743-1818 . . . . **NCLC 10**
    See also JRDA; MAICYA; SATA 29;
        SATA-Brief 27

Yakumo Koizumi
    See Hearn, (Patricio) Lafcadio (Tessima
        Carlos)

Yanez, Jose Donoso
    See Donoso (Yanez), Jose

Yanovsky, Basile S.
    See Yanovsky, V(assily) S(emenovich)

Yanovsky, V(assily) S(emenovich)
    1906-1989 . . . . **CLC 2, 18**
    See also CA 97-100; 129

Yates, Richard 1926-1992 . . . . . **CLC 7, 8, 23**
    See also CA 5-8R; 139; CANR 10, 43;
        DLB 2; DLBY 81, 92

Yeats, W. B.
    See Yeats, William Butler

Yeats, William Butler
    1865-1939 . . . . . **TCLC 1, 11, 18, 31; DA;**
                                        DAB; WLC
    See also CA 104; 127; CANR 45;
        CDBLB 1890-1914; DLB 10, 19, 98, 156;
        MTCW

Yehoshua, A(braham) B.
    1936- . . . . **CLC 13, 31**
    See also CA 33-36R; CANR 43

Yep, Laurence Michael 1948- . . . . . . **CLC 35**
    See also AAYA 5; CA 49-52; CANR 1, 46;
        CLR 3, 17; DLB 52; JRDA; MAICYA;
        SATA 7, 69

Yerby, Frank G(arvin)
    1916-1991 . . . . **CLC 1, 7, 22; BLC**
    See also BW 1; CA 9-12R; 136; CANR 16;
        DLB 76; MTCW

Yesenin, Sergei Alexandrovich
    See Esenin, Sergei (Alexandrovich)

Yevtushenko, Yevgeny (Alexandrovich)
    1933- . . . . **CLC 1, 3, 13, 26, 51**
    See also CA 81-84; CANR 33; MTCW

Yezierska, Anzia 1885(?)-1970 . . . . . **CLC 46**
    See also CA 126; 89-92; DLB 28; MTCW

Yglesias, Helen 1915- . . . . **CLC 7, 22**
    See also CA 37-40R; CAAS 20; CANR 15;
        MTCW

Yokomitsu Riichi 1898-1947 . . . . . . **TCLC 47**

Yonge, Charlotte (Mary)
    1823-1901 . . . . **TCLC 48**
    See also CA 109; DLB 18; SATA 17

York, Jeremy
    See Creasey, John

York, Simon
    See Heinlein, Robert A(nson)

Yorke, Henry Vincent 1905-1974 . . . **CLC 13**
    See also Green, Henry
    See also CA 85-88; 49-52

Yosano Akiko 1878-1942 . . **TCLC 59; PC 11**

Yoshimoto, Banana . . . . **CLC 84**
    See also Yoshimoto, Mahoko

Yoshimoto, Mahoko 1964-
    See Yoshimoto, Banana
    See also CA 144

Young, Al(bert James)
    1939- . . . . **CLC 19; BLC**
    See also BW 2; CA 29-32R; CANR 26;
        DLB 33

Young, Andrew (John) 1885-1971 . . . . **CLC 5**
    See also CA 5-8R; CANR 7, 29

Young, Collier
    See Bloch, Robert (Albert)

Young, Edward 1683-1765 . . . . **LC 3**
    See also DLB 95

Young, Marguerite 1909- . . . . **CLC 82**
    See also CA 13-16; CAP 1

Young, Neil 1945- . . . . **CLC 17**
    See also CA 110

Yourcenar, Marguerite
    1903-1987 . . . . **CLC 19, 38, 50, 87**
    See also CA 69-72; CANR 23; DLB 72;
        DLBY 88; MTCW

Yurick, Sol 1925- . . . . **CLC 6**
    See also CA 13-16R; CANR 25

Zabolotskii, Nikolai Alekseevich
    1903-1958 . . . . **TCLC 52**
    See also CA 116

Zamiatin, Yevgenii
    See Zamyatin, Evgeny Ivanovich

Zamora, Bernice (B. Ortiz)
    1938- . . . . **CLC 89; HLC**
    See also DLB 82; HW

Zamyatin, Evgeny Ivanovich
    1884-1937 . . . . **TCLC 8, 37**
    See also CA 105

Zangwill, Israel 1864-1926 . . . . **TCLC 16**
    See also CA 109; DLB 10, 135

Zappa, Francis Vincent, Jr. 1940-1993
    See Zappa, Frank
    See also CA 108; 143

Zappa, Frank . . . . **CLC 17**
    See also Zappa, Francis Vincent, Jr.

Zaturenska, Marya 1902-1982 . . . . **CLC 6, 11**
    See also CA 13-16R; 105; CANR 22

Zelazny, Roger (Joseph)
    1937-1995 . . . . **CLC 21**
    See also AAYA 7; CA 21-24R; 148;
        CANR 26; DLB 8; MTCW; SATA 57;
        SATA-Brief 39

Zhdanov, Andrei A(lexandrovich)
    1896-1948 . . . . **TCLC 18**
    See also CA 117

Zhukovsky, Vasily 1783-1852 . . . . **NCLC 35**

Ziegenhagen, Eric . . . . **CLC 55**

Zimmer, Jill Schary
    See Robinson, Jill

Zimmerman, Robert
    See Dylan, Bob

Literary Criticism Series
Cumulative Topic Index

This index lists all topic entries in Gale's *Classical and Medieval Literature Criticism, Contemporary Literary Criticism, Literature Criticism from 1400 to 1800, Nineteenth-Century Literature Criticism,* and *Twentieth-Century Literary Criticism.*

TCLC Cumulative Nationality Index

AMERICAN

Adams, Andy **56**
Adams, Henry (Brooks) **4, 52**
Agee, James (Rufus) **1, 19**
Anderson, Maxwell **2**
Anderson, Sherwood **1, 10, 24**
Atherton, Gertrude (Franklin Horn) **2**
Austin, Mary (Hunter) **25**
Baker, Ray Stannard **47**
Barry, Philip **11**
Baum, L(yman) Frank **7**
Beard, Charles A(ustin) **15**
Belasco, David **3**
Bell, James Madison **43**
Benchley, Robert (Charles) **1, 55**
Benedict, Ruth **60**
Benet, Stephen Vincent **7**
Benet, William Rose **28**
Bierce, Ambrose (Gwinett) **1, 7, 44**
Black Elk **33**
Boas, Franz **56**
Bodenheim, Maxwell **44**
Bourne, Randolph S(illiman) **16**
Bradford, Gamaliel **36**
Brennan, Christopher John **17**
Bromfield, Louis (Brucker) **11**
Burroughs, Edgar Rice **2, 32**
Cabell, James Branch **6**
Cable, George Washington **4**
Carnegie, Dale **53**
Cather, Willa Sibert **1, 11, 31**
Chambers, Robert W. **41**
Chandler, Raymond (Thornton) **1, 7**
Chapman, John Jay **7**
Chesnutt, Charles W(addell) **5, 39**
Chopin, Kate **5, 14**
Cohan, George M. **60**
Comstock, Anthony **13**
Cotter, Joseph Seamon Sr. **28**

Cram, Ralph Adams **45**
Crane, (Harold) Hart **2, 5**
Crane, Stephen (Townley) **11, 17, 32**
Crawford, F(rancis) Marion **10**
Crothers, Rachel **19**
Cullen, Countee **4, 37**
Davis, Rebecca (Blaine) Harding **6**
Davis, Richard Harding **24**
Day, Clarence (Shepard Jr.) **25**
De Voto, Bernard (Augustine) **29**
Dreiser, Theodore (Herman Albert) **10, 18, 35**
Dunbar, Paul Laurence **2, 12**
Dunne, Finley Peter **28**
Eastman, Charles A(lexander) **55**
Faust, Frederick (Schiller) **49**
Fisher, Rudolph **11**
Fitzgerald, F(rancis) Scott (Key) **1, 6, 14, 28, 55**
Fitzgerald, Zelda (Sayre) **52**
Flecker, (Herman) James Elroy **43**
Fletcher, John Gould **35**
Forten, Charlotte L. **16**
Freeman, Douglas Southall **11**
Freeman, Mary Eleanor Wilkins **9**
Futrelle, Jacques **19**
Gale, Zona **7**
Garland, (Hannibal) Hamlin **3**
Gilman, Charlotte (Anna) Perkins (Stetson) **9, 37**
Glasgow, Ellen (Anderson Gholson) **2, 7**
Glaspell, Susan (Keating) **55**
Goldman, Emma **13**
Grey, Zane **6**
Guiney, Louise Imogen **41**
Hall, James Norman **23**
Harper, Frances Ellen Watkins **14**
Harris, Joel Chandler **2**
Harte, (Francis) Bret(t) **1, 25**

Hatteras, Owen **18**
Hawthorne, Julian **25**
Hearn, (Patricio) Lafcadio (Tessima Carlos) **9**
Henry, O. **1, 19**
Hergesheimer, Joseph **11**
Higginson, Thomas Wentworth **36**
Hopkins, Pauline Elizabeth **28**
Howard, Robert Ervin **8**
Howe, Julia Ward **21**
Howells, William Dean **7, 17, 41**
James, Henry **2, 11, 24, 40, 47**
James, William **15, 32**
Jewett, (Theodora) Sarah Orne **1, 22**
Johnson, James Weldon **3, 19**
Kornbluth, C(yril) M. **8**
Korzybski, Alfred (Habdank Skarbek) **61**
Kuttner, Henry **10**
Lardner, Ring(gold) W(ilmer) **2, 14**
Lewis, (Harry) Sinclair **4, 13, 23, 39**
Lewisohn, Ludwig **19**
Lindsay, (Nicholas) Vachel **17**
Locke, Alain (Le Roy) **43**
London, Jack **9, 15, 39**
Lovecraft, H(oward) P(hillips) **4, 22**
Lowell, Amy **1, 8**
Markham, Edwin **47**
Marquis, Don(ald Robert Perry) **7**
Masters, Edgar Lee **2, 25**
McCoy, Horace (Stanley) **28**
McKay, Claude **7, 41**
Mencken, H(enry) L(ouis) **13**
Millay, Edna St. Vincent **4, 49**
Mitchell, Margaret (Munnerlyn) **11**
Mitchell, S(ilas) Weir **36**
Monroe, Harriet **12**
Muir, John **28**
Nathan, George Jean **18**
Nordhoff, Charles (Bernard) **23**

Norris, Benjamin Franklin Jr.   24
O'Neill, Eugene (Gladstone)   **1, 6, 27, 49**
Oskison, John Milton   **35**
Phillips, David Graham   **44**
Porter, Gene(va Grace) Stratton   **21**
Post, Melville Davisson   **39**
Rawlings, Marjorie Kinnan   **4**
Reed, John (Silas)   **9**
Reich, Wilhelm   **57**
Rhodes, Eugene Manlove   **53**
Riggs, (Rolla) Lynn   **56**
Riley, James Whitcomb   **51**
Rinehart, Mary Roberts   **52**
Roberts, Kenneth (Lewis)   **23**
Robinson, Edwin Arlington   **5**
Roelvaag, O(le) E(dvart)   **17**
Rogers, Will(iam Penn Adair)   **8**
Rourke, Constance (Mayfield)   **12**
Runyon, (Alfred) Damon   **10**
Saltus, Edgar (Everton)   **8**
Santayana, George   **40**
Sherwood, Robert E(mmet)   **3**
Slesinger, Tess   **10**
Steffens, (Joseph) Lincoln   **20**
Stein, Gertrude   **1, 6, 28, 48**
Sterling, George   **20**
Stevens, Wallace   **3, 12, 45**
Stockton, Frank R.   **47**
Sturges, Preston   **48**
Tarbell, Ida M(inerva)   **40**
Tarkington, (Newton) Booth   **9**
Teasdale, Sara   **4**
Thurman, Wallace (Henry)   **6**
Twain, Mark   **6, 12, 19, 36, 48, 59**
Van Dine, S. S.   **23**
Van Doren, Carl (Clinton)   **18**
Veblen, Thorstein (Bunde)   **31**
Washington, Booker T(aliaferro)   **10**
Wells, Carolyn   **35**
West, Nathanael   **1, 14, 44**
Wharton, Edith (Newbold Jones)   **3, 9, 27, 53**
White, Walter F(rancis)   **15**
Wister, Owen   **21**
Wolfe, Thomas (Clayton)   **4, 13, 29, 61**
Woollcott, Alexander (Humphreys)   **5**
Wylie, Elinor (Morton Hoyt)   **8**

ARGENTINIAN
Arlt, Roberto (Godofredo Christophersen)   **29**
Guiraldes, Ricardo (Guillermo)   **39**
Lugones, Leopoldo   **15**
Storni, Alfonsina   **5**

AUSTRALIAN
Baynton, Barbara   **57**
Franklin, (Stella Maraia Sarah) Miles   **7**
Furphy, Joseph   **25**
Ingamells, Rex   **35**
Lawson, Henry (Archibald Hertzberg)   **27**
Paterson, A(ndrew) B(arton)   **32**
Richardson, Henry Handel   **4**
Warung, Price   **45**

AUSTRIAN
Beer-Hofmann, Richard   **60**
Broch, Hermann   **20**
Freud, Sigmund   **52**
Hofmannsthal, Hugo von   **11**
Kafka, Franz   **2, 6, 13, 29, 47, 53**
Kraus, Karl   **5**

Kubin, Alfred   **23**
Meyrink, Gustav   **21**
Musil, Robert (Edler von)   **12**
Perutz, Leo   **60**
Roth, Joseph   **33**
Schnitzler, Arthur   **4**
Steiner, Rudolf   **13**
Trakl, Georg   **5**
Werfel, Franz (V.)   **8**
Zweig, Stefan   **17**

BELGIAN
Bosschere, Jean de   **19**
Lemonnier, (Antoine Louis) Camille   **22**
Maeterlinck, Maurice   **3**
van Ostaijen, Paul   **33**
Verhaeren, Emile (Adolphe Gustave)   **12**

BRAZILIAN
Andrade, Mario de   **43**
Cunha, Euclides (Rodrigues Pimenta) da   **24**
Lima Barreto, Afonso Henrique de   **23**
Machado de Assis, Joaquim Maria   **10**
Ramos, Graciliano   **32**

BULGARIAN
Vazov, Ivan (Minchov)   **25**

CANADIAN
Campbell, Wilfred   **9**
Carman, (William) Bliss   **7**
Carr, Emily   **32**
Connor, Ralph   **31**
Drummond, William Henry   **25**
Duncan, Sara Jeannette   **60**
Garneau, (Hector de) Saint-Denys   **13**
Grove, Frederick Philip   **4**
Knister, Raymond   **56**
Leacock, Stephen (Butler)   **2**
McCrae, John   **12**
Montgomery, L(ucy) M(aud)   **51**
Nelligan, Emile   **14**
Pickthall, Marjorie L(owry) C(hristie)   **21**
Roberts, Charles G(eorge) D(ouglas)   **8**
Scott, Duncan Campbell   **6**
Service, Robert W(illiam)   **15**
Seton, Ernest (Evan) Thompson   **31**
Stringer, Arthur   **37**

CHILEAN
Huidobro Fernandez, Vicente Garcia   **31**
Mistral, Gabriela   **2**

CHINESE
Liu E   **15**
Lu Hsun   **3**
Su Man-shu   **24**
Wen I-to   **28**

COLOMBIAN
Rivera, Jose Eustasio   **35**

CZECH
Capek, Karel   **6, 37**
Freud, Sigmund   **52**
Hasek, Jaroslav (Matej Frantisek)   **4**
Kafka, Franz   **2, 6, 13, 29, 47, 53**
Nezval, Vitezslav   **44**

DANISH
Brandes, Georg (Morris Cohen)   **10**

Hansen, Martin A.   **32**
Jensen, Johannes V.   **41**
Nexo, Martin Andersen   **43**
Pontoppidan, Henrik   **29**

DUTCH
Couperus, Louis (Marie Anne)   **15**
Frank, Anne(lies Marie)   **17**
Heijermans, Herman   **24**
Hillesum, Etty   **49**
Schendel, Arthur van   **56**

ENGLISH
Barbellion, W. N. P.   **24**
Baring, Maurice   **8**
Beerbohm, Henry Maximilian   **1, 24**
Belloc, (Joseph) Hilaire (Pierre)   **7, 18**
Bennett, (Enoch) Arnold   **5, 20**
Benson, E(dward) F(rederic)   **27**
Benson, Stella   **17**
Bentley, E(dmund) C(lerihew)   **12**
Besant, Annie (Wood)   **9**
Blackmore, R(ichard) D(oddridge)   **27**
Blackwood, Algernon (Henry)   **5**
Bridges, Robert (Seymour)   **1**
Brooke, Rupert (Chawner)   **2, 7**
Butler, Samuel   **1, 33**
Chesterton, G(ilbert) K(eith)   **1, 6**
Conrad, Joseph   **1, 6, 13, 25, 43, 57**
Coppard, A(lfred) E(dgar)   **5**
Corelli, Marie   **51**
Crofts, Freeman Wills   **55**
Crowley, Aleister   **7**
Dale, Colin   **18**
de la Mare, Walter (John)   **4, 53**
Delafield, E. M.   **61**
Doughty, Charles M(ontagu)   **27**
Douglas, Keith   **40**
Dowson, Ernest Christopher   **4**
Doyle, Arthur Conan   **7**
Drinkwater, John   **57**
Eddison, E(ric) R(ucker)   **15**
Elaine   **18**
Elizabeth   **41**
Ellis, (Henry) Havelock   **14**
Field, Michael   **43**
Firbank, (Arthur Annesley) Ronald   **1**
Ford, Ford Madox   **1, 15, 39, 57**
Freeman, R(ichard) Austin   **21**
Galsworthy, John   **1, 45**
Gilbert, W(illiam) S(chwenck)   **3**
Gissing, George (Robert)   **3, 24, 47**
Gosse, Edmund (William)   **28**
Granville-Barker, Harley   **2**
Gray, John (Henry)   **19**
Gurney, Ivor (Bertie)   **33**
Haggard, H(enry) Rider   **11**
Hall, (Marguerite) Radclyffe   **12**
Hardy, Thomas   **4, 10, 18, 32, 48, 53**
Henley, William Ernest   **8**
Hilton, James   **21**
Hodgson, William Hope   **13**
Housman, A(lfred) E(dward)   **1, 10**
Housman, Laurence   **7**
Hudson, W(illiam) H(enry)   **29**
Hulme, T(homas) E(rnest)   **21**
Hunt, Violet   **53**
Jacobs, W(illiam) W(ymark)   **22**
James, Montague (Rhodes)   **6**
Jerome, Jerome K(lapka)   **23**
Johnson, Lionel (Pigot)   **19**
Kaye-Smith, Sheila   **20**

Nationality Index

Nationality Index